JAPANESE CERAMICS

of the
LAST 100 YEARS

JAPANESE

CERAMICS
of the
LAST 100 YEARS

by Irene Stitt

CROWN PUBLISHERS, INC., NEW YORK

To my late father
Percy H. Dannatt

I would like to thank the many people who have been so kind and patient with me over my innumerable questions: Dr. Jan Fonteyn of the Museum of Fine Arts, Boston; Louise Cort of the Fogg Art Museum, Cambridge, Massachusetts; Mrs. W. H. Shreve of the Peabody Museum, Salem; Robert Moes and Mrs. Amy Poster of the Brooklyn Museum; Julia Meech of the Metropolitan Museum of Art, New York; J. L. Ayers of the Victoria and Albert Museum, London; Mrs. J. Semal of Japan House, New York; and August Lux, of Lux-Denise Antiques, whose help has been invaluable to me.

My thanks, too, to all those who lent me their treasures to photograph, especially to Mrs. Dae Bade of Lavender and Old Lace, Otto Bade of Remember When, R. Manning and M. Rudin of Orphans of the Attic, Mrs. Lu Walkowski of Mere Pittance, and Jules Wiegel of Wiegel's Nest of Antiques. Also to Mrs. Kathryn Pinney, without whose help and encouragement this book would have never come into being. Finally, to Veronica Kiley and Cindy Stone for their help with the manuscript, and to Daniel Stone, who has done such a magnificent job of the photography.

Library of Congress Catalog Card Number: 74–80304
Printed in the United States of America
Published simultaneously in Canada by General Publishing Company Limited

Design by Nedda Balter

Contents

Preface

My original intention in writing this book was to try to direct attention to the export ceramic wares Japan produced during the last hundred years, but—once started on this project—it seemed better to include all classes of Japanese ceramic wares of the period.

In my opinion the export wares produced since 1868 have been unjustly maligned in many cases, and the better pieces totally ignored. Although it is true that a lot of worthless junk was produced during this period, and even the best pieces do not measure up to the beauty and fineness of the old wares, there are many good pieces to be found.

The Japanese have long been an art-oriented society, with a deep love of and respect for nature, as illustrated by these quotations from two Japanese who lived twelve hundred years apart. Said the eighth-century Empress Komio, in a poem in which she speaks of offering flowers to the Buddha at Nara:

If I pluck them, the touch of my hand will defile; therefore standing in the meadows as they are I offer these wind-blown flowers to the Buddhas of the past, present, and the future. Translation by Okakura Kakuzō.

And Dr. Yanagi Sōetsu (1889–1961) said:

To me the greatest thing is to live beauty in our daily life and to crowd every moment with things of beauty.

Craftsmen practiced their skills from generation to generation, and whole areas produced a similar kind of art. Theirs is the true way of learning an art, absorbing it from all sides as children, observing their elders working in a centuries-old tradition, trial and error having been the great teacher. In this way art runs in the blood. It cannot be learned and assimilated in a few short years of schooling, as we so often vainly think.

In this last statement we also have the source of the Japanese disasters in their adventures with Western art styles. They could not learn and absorb teachings from the West in just a few years. It took us hundreds of years to evolve our styles, the good and the bad, and to learn to differentiate between the two.

In their enthusiasm for the new, the Japanese took everything Western and threw it back at us in ways that they thought were pleasing to our taste; they did not like the results and neither did we. However, when the Japanese took our methods and used them to please themselves, then they produced works of art in a new style. Perhaps it was not always great art, but it was produced with an artist's individuality.

Osbert Sitwell described Japanese gardens as being the great works of little masters, and the description could be applied to so much that was produced by the Japanese. In this book I have tried to show the great works of the little masters, and to help others see the difference between the good and the bad.

The Japanese approach to ceramics is artistic. Each part is allowed to develop its own character and grow together to form a pleasing whole, which no more needs to be perfect than does anything else in nature. The clays become what they are; if they are gray and coarse, so they will develop and be used as they are—to their best advantage. Nothing will be made to masquerade as what it is not.

The Japanese do not prize whiteness and translucency in porcelain as we do in the West, and, of course, an off-white or gray sets off the enamel colors far more kindly than does a brilliant white. In any case the Japanese prefer pottery to porcelain, and this preference has been influenced by the interior of their homes. Pottery with its softer appearance is much more compatible with the natural woods used in their houses. Herein, too, lies the explanation for the difference in coloring between Japanese and Chinese wares. The Chinese favor dark polished woods, and the colors they use on their ceramics are those that look well against such a background. In the West we lay a dazzling white cloth on the table for formal dining, and our tablewares must show to their best advantage in this setting. White porcelain and bright enamels sparkle in the light and gleam compatibly with the shining silverware. But as we slip away from formality these days, pottery with its quieter tones seems more in keeping with the times—so, fashions and tastes change.

The snob often pretends to good taste, being terrified of being accused of having bad taste or of being old-fashioned. In actual fact to have so-called good taste one must admire the fashions of the moment, and, of course, fashions change from year to year. This stems from two main causes—because manufacturers want to sell their wares and because conditions, economic and otherwise, constantly change. That which is good, however, will survive. Good art will always survive; it may be pushed aside for a time, but it will be there to return again.

The Japanese have changed their feelings for Western things several times. After the opening of Japan in the second half of the nineteenth century there was a great surge of feeling for all things Western. Their own things were forgotten for a time, but in the early part of this century their taste swung back again, and although they produced mountains of cheap goods for the foreign market, they wished for none of it for themselves. It was during this era that the words "Made in Japan" became practically synonymous with "junk."

The more one thinks about it, the more extraordinary it seems that a country which could produce articles of such exquisite workmanship, a country where craftsmen could take such infinite pains over details, would produce such cheap, shoddy stuff for the foreign market.

After World War II, during the Occupation, once again Western ways were held to be good, but now, twenty-five years later, the pendulum has swung back again. As far as modern pottery is concerned, Japan is an acknowledged leader.

The better export wares of the post-1868 years are neglected mainly because they are not in the traditional style of Japanese wares, and although made in European style, not European either. When I first began to be interested in them I found that practically no information was available. What distressed me even more was that people who held European porcelain in high regard would pass up a similar piece if they knew it was made for export in post-1868 Japan. As so many of the Japanese porcelains were made far more artistically than the corresponding European pieces, this seemed rather unfortunate. Consequently, I determined to search out what information I could find, and write a book to help other people evaluate these wares and form their own judgments.

As far as my brief survey of older wares is concerned, I have tried to steer a middle course as to dates and other controversial matters. I do not pretend to be an authority on those wares, but as this book is directed primarily at the less advanced collector, I wished to provide a brief historical background of Japan and her tradition of ceramics. For this reason the illustrations in this book are exclusively of pieces either in the United States or in England, so that readers can go and see these wares. Pictures of famous pieces in Japan can be seen in other books.

I have made particular mention of the two Morse collections of Japanese pottery, one in the Museum of Fine Arts, Boston, and the other at the Peabody Museum, Salem, Massachusetts, as it seems a pity that they are not more widely known and visited. Although the pieces in the collections may not be of such fine quality as those in Japan, at least they are available in this country. In London there is a collection of the same period at the Victoria and Albert Museum; it consists of the wares sent from Japan to the Centennial Exposition in Philadelphia in 1876.

On a recent visit to England I realized that a book about Japanese ceramics exported to the United States would also be of great help to British collectors. The import regulations were far more stringent here than in England, and this resulted in more precise markings, which changed from time to time. These markings are a great help when it comes to giving approximate dates for pieces, dates being one of the many problems with Japanese ceramics. The post-1868 export pieces I have seen in England were either unmarked or had Japanese characters inscribed on them (these inscriptions generally give no useful information), so if British collectors can compare their pieces with those in the United States, they will be at least a little better off.

Throughout the book I have used the Japanese order for names—the family name first, then the given or art name afterward. Japanese potters were always known by their art names, and generally are still so known today in Japan. However, present-day potters are usually known abroad by their family names, except in the few cases when they have succeeded to a renowned family art name.

The spelling of Japanese names is another problem, and again I have tried to steer a middle course. Vowels are pronounced much as in Italian, and if one follows another, each is pronounced separately. For example, Kakiemon: Kaki-yemon. The line over a vowel (ō or ū) gives it a long sound.

Certain of the better known symbols stamped on the backs of export wares are included in an appendix at the end of the book. As explained in Chapter 15, these backstamps have little bearing on the relative quality of the wares, and so a complete list has not been attempted.

Introduction

1

Japan and Her Ceramic Wares before 1868

Japan is a beautiful country with rugged coastlines, mountains, lakes, and forests, with an infinite variety of color in its spectacular sunsets, mists, and rain. It is also a poor country, with no gemstones and very little gold or marble. Because of the lack of such resources, perhaps, the art of Japan closely imitates nature, and her craftsmen display a heightened sense of color and balance in their work.

To the Japanese art is an integral part of life, and the potter has always been considered an artist with no distinction being made between the "fine" arts, the "industrial" arts, or the "decorative" arts. Japan may be a poor country from the point of view of its natural resources, but it is a country of untold wealth as far as its art is concerned. In the art of a country lies a concrete record of its past. The ceramic art of a country in particular provides a most comprehensive record, for it covers the tastes and needs of all the people, rich and poor alike. We can touch these things and begin to understand the people of a bygone age and how they lived.

Jōmon Period: The neolithic age in Japan is called the Jōmon Period, the name being derived from the pottery made during this time. "Jōmon" means rope pattern; the decorations were made by winding ropes around the body of the vessels (Ill. 1). It is interesting that the name of this early period

1. Jōmon urn, c. 2000 B.C. H. 15½". D. 13". These terra-cotta wares were fired at a relatively low temperature. "Urn" is the correct term for a large vessel of this nature, but on account of its association with funerary wares it can be misleading when used for wares of an early period. The Jōmon vessels were essentially for use by living people for cooking and storage purposes. The tapered base enabled the vessel to be placed in a hole in the ground, which was early man's method of keeping his pots steady on an irregular surface. Cleveland Museum of Art, Purchase, John L. Severance Fund

2. *Jōmon vessel, late Jōmon Period.* Private Collection

should come from the type of pottery used, in contrast to the term Stone Age in Europe, which is derived from the primitive tools and weapons used there in that period.

The Jōmon culture was based on a hunting and fishing economy, and, although it extended throughout the whole land, most of the Jōmon remains have been found in eastern Japan. Jōmon pottery is a dull gray, the vessels being made by the coil method. Mainly these vessels were used for boiling game and fish; many were of the type that tapered almost to a point at the bottom so that they could be sunk into the ground in the embers of the fire. It is generally accepted that the earliest Jōmon wares were made about 5000 B.C. and that the period extended to about 200 B.C., when the Yayoi Period began.

Yayoi Period: The Yayoi culture came from Korea and spread from the western part of Japan, bringing agriculture with it. A little kingdom and government were established on the Yamato plains. The emperors of Japan are direct descendants of the Yamato kings, who were priests as well as rulers. The imperial line claimed descent from the Sun Goddess and, among other things, this later gave the emperors a suitably impressive background for communications with China. The three symbols of imperial authority—they are still so today—came to Japan by way of Korea: a semiprecious stone curved like a huge comma, which is a common archaeological find in Korea; the

iron sword from continental Asia; and the bronze mirror, which is a symbol of the sun, from China. Seen from a Western point of view, these three items seem at first to form a somewhat bizarre collection for an imperial regalia. However, as Japan was still in the Stone Age when they were introduced into that country, the iron sword and bronze mirror must have seemed truly wondrous objects to the Japanese and deserving to become imperial possessions.

Pottery of the Yayoi Period (200 B.C.– A.D. 250) was of a warm russet color, and with the emergence of the rice-based economy, storage jars were needed. Bottles, pitchers, and footed jars were common forms. Both Jōmon and Yayoi pottery were low-fired wares. No remains of special kilns for firing pottery from these periods have been found.

Kofun Period: The Kofun, or Grave Mound, Period (A.D. 250–552) saw the development of Hajiki wares, which were very similar to Yayoi wares, but shaping techniques had advanced and new forms appeared. Haniwa figures were made to be placed around royal tombs. Up to this time, as in China, when an emperor or prince died most of his attendants and followers were buried alive with him, a rather distressing custom. However, according to tradition, the Emperor Suinin changed this practice, and clay figures of people and animals standing on circular bases were substituted for the real thing (Ills. 3 and 4). Descendants of the

3. *Haniwa horse. H. 23½". L. 26". Kofun Period*
A.D. *250–552. Royal tombs were encircled with terra-*
cotta figures of all kinds—warriors, ladies, animals,
birds, models of houses, and so on. They were origi-
nally made as substitutes for live members of the royal
entourage. Cleveland Museum of Art, Norweb
Collection

4. *Haniwa head, female, showing headdress. 5th–7th*
century A.D. Metropolitan Museum of Art, New
York, Rogers Fund

haniwa makers, who settled at Toki-mura, near Osaka, are still making pottery there to this day.

Around A.D. 400 Sueki pottery, or Sue ware, a high-grade stoneware, made its appearance. It was a gray brown color, and because of the new methods of firing, was very hard and strong. The technique for making this type of ware came to Japan from Korea. Special sloping kilns were constructed for the purpose—either a tunnel built into a hillside or a ditch roofed over. They could achieve a temperature of about 1825° F. The potter's wheel was also introduced during this period.

With these new methods the type of clay employed was of great importance: It had to be able to withstand the high temperatures without melting into a puddle. The increased heat was responsible for another new development—the natural glaze. When ashes from the fire fell on the wares in the

5. *Terra-cotta jar. Sue ware, Kofun Period, c. A.D. 500. Thickly potted in a rare shape, this piece has a natural glaze resulting from the high temperature in the kiln. There are several small jars on the shoulder, although unfortunately some are fragmentary.* Courtesy of the Brooklyn Museum, Gift of Mrs. Albert H. Clayburgh

kiln, a natural glaze resulted; this might vary from green to brown (Ill. 5).

Asuka Period: Although the *sueki* wares were the products of a superior technique, *hajiki* wares still continued to be made throughout the Asuka Period (A.D. 552–646). It is a characteristic of Japanese ceramics that a new style does not necessarily supersede an older one; the older style continues to be produced side by side with the new. However, *hajiki* wares clung to the traditional style, and were used by the ordinary people; *sueki* wares, with their foreign background, found favor with the court and aristocracy (Ill. 6).

Through the ages Japan has undergone periods of great influence from other lands, when she has taken as much as she wished from other countries and civilizations she admires, then has retreated to the fastness of her islands, absorbed what she has learned, and adapted it to suit her own character and needs. From A.D. 600 to 800, for example, Japan learned as much as she could from China. Students and scholars were sent there, and Buddhist missionaries went from China to Japan. As well as Buddhism, the Chinese written language was brought to Japan, as was Chinese money.

6. *Arc-shaped tile. Asuka Period (A.D. 552–646). Made of light gray clay, it was probably whitewashed on the outer surface. Tiles of this type were used under the eaves.* Courtesy of the Brooklyn Museum, Carll H. De Silver Fund and Others

Buddhism was originally an Indian religion. It traveled by way of China and Korea to Japan, where it was adapted to fit in with their own native Shinto religion, a simple nature worship—each aspect of nature was believed to have its own god: the sun, wind, rocks, trees, flowers, and so on. Shrines were built in beautiful and awe-inspiring places, and the Torii, or gate, purified the visitor. Buddhist deities were accepted as being the same as the Shinto ones, under different names, and as Buddhism was an ethical religion and Shinto a nature worship, there was no conflict between the two.

Appreciation of nature has always played a great part in Japanese life, particularly the principle that in nature there is balance but not symmetry. Simplicity and understatement are other principles generally basic to all their art. Given a choice, they prefer to be obscure rather than over-explicit.

By the eighth century Chinese civilization was declining; the last official Japanese mission was sent there in 838. The Japanese adapted what they had learned from the Chinese to fit their own needs. Nara, the first Japanese capital, laid out in 710, was copied from the Chinese capital of Ch'ang-an.

During the Nara Period (646–794) both the *hajiki* and *sueki* styles of pottery continued to flourish (Ill. 7), and, in addition, a new kind of pottery appeared. This was Nara *sansai*, or "three color." These wares are softly curved and have dappled glazes of greens and browns on a white ground (Ill.8). They were the first Japanese wares to be deliberately glazed, and they were made in a great variety of forms. Cups, jars, bowls, dishes, vases, and incense burners were decorated either with the three colors or else with a green glaze patterned with green spots.

The court did not stay long at Nara, but moved to Kyoto in 794. Kyoto, which means "capital," is about thirty miles north of Nara. It also was laid out like Ch'ang-an. At that time it was called Heian, meaning "peace and tranquillity."

The Heian age is looked on as a kind of Utopian age. Literature, art, and handicrafts flourished; magnificent temples, pagodas, and monasteries were built around the city. The Chinese system of administration and taxation, adopted by the Japanese, provided great wealth for the nobles and extreme poverty and toil for the peasants. In China government was by men of ability; in Japan

7. Jar. Sue ware, Nara Period (646–794). Natural glaze has run onto the shoulder. The shape of the piece appears to have been inspired by a piece of Chinese bronze. Private Collection

8. Jar. Nara sansai *(three-color glaze). Eighth century.* Private Collection

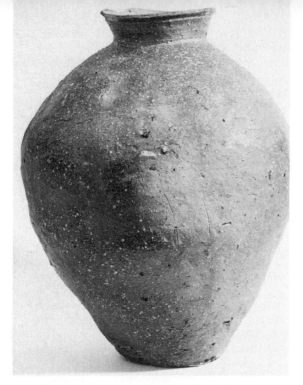

9. *Large grain storage jar. Stoneware, Shigaraki ware, fourteenth century. Shigaraki is one of the Six Ancient Kilns. The local clay is heavy, coarse, and full of fine quartz particles, which come to the surface when the pot is fired. This piece, which is a particularly fine one, has a natural ash glaze with amber-colored scorch marks.* Courtesy of the Brooklyn Museum, Frank L. Babbott Fund

administrative posts became hereditary, and consequently the administration deteriorated. Men were more interested in the niceties of life, as long as the money came from somewhere.

The Heian age was the great age of poetry—every refined person was expected to be able to write a poem at any given moment about anything. This requirement was one of the great dividing lines between the courtiers and the rising class of knights in the provinces; the knights were fighting men on horseback, not poets. The court ladies were the novelists. These ladies had an incredible amount of spare time on their hands—they sat around in the half dark, hardly seeing anyone. Their main preoccupation was what to do with their leisure time, and what some of them did was to write novels and diaries. The men learned to speak and write Chinese, and the Chinese language carried great prestige, but the ladies did not learn it. They wrote their novels in Japanese.

Green glazed wares were still produced during the Heian Period (794–1185). Sueki wares underwent a change in the middle of the tenth century with the introduction of a new firing technique. Oxidizing flames

10. *Jar. Tamba ware. Muromachi Period (1333–1568). This piece is a dark red brown with a natural ash glaze.* Private Collection

could now be produced, and this resulted in bright off-white wares, instead of the coarse iron gray pottery produced by the reduction process.

These elegant and refined whiter wares, often decorated with a pale green transparent glaze, are called Heian *shiki*. Reflecting the aesthetic taste of the Heian aristocracy, they were made in a wide variety of forms: dishes, bowls, pouring vessels with attached handles, ink stones, and so on. As the Heian Period declined, the emperor no longer did the actual ruling; it was done by the Fujiwara family in the shadows behind the emperor. The military deteriorated into a kind of ceremonial color-guard.

Kamakura Period: The nonpoetic knights in the provinces gained more power and became virtually independent of any control from Kyoto. In the mid-twelfth century two factions, the Taira and the Minamoto, fought with each other, and when the Taira faction had been completely crushed, Yoritomo Minamoto had himself proclaimed shogun, or generalissimo. He became military dictator and settled in Kamakura, where the provincial warriors, the samurai, became the dominant class. The Kamakura Period (1185–1333) saw a great change in the most favored pottery style. The court aristocracy were no longer the prevailing arbiters of taste; now it was the turn of the provincial landowners and the military class. The new type of ware was a rough sort of *sueki* teabowl, the *yama-jawan*. The clay used was of a very course nature, and the bowls were turned on a wheel at high speed. The foot was often attached afterward by hand to save time.

This period also saw the development of the Six Ancient Kilns, with wares ranging from the thickly glazed utensils of old Seto to the unglazed strictly utilitarian wares of Bizen, Shigaraki, and Tamba (Ills. 9 and 10).

Muromachi Period: The Kamakura shogunate was overthrown in 1334 by the defecting general Ashikaga, who set up his own shogunate in Kyoto. This shogunate was not as strong as the Kamakura had been, and for two hundred years there were civil wars. Emperors reigned, shoguns ruled, and independent petty domains warred against each other. This was the age of the so-called Japanese pirates, who were not pirates in the modern sense of the word, but were owners of large fleets of boats that roamed the seas even as far away as Siam. Trading ships came and went from the fast-growing port of Osaka. This period is called the Muromachi Period (1333–1568), after the street in Kyoto where Ashikaga's palace stood.

Tea drinking had been popular with the aristocracy and the clergy since the thirteenth century, but during the Muromachi Period it spread to the provinces, where the samurai and other well-situated persons enjoyed it.

Murata Jukō, "father of the tea ceremony" (1423–1502), laid down the rules for it, and the tea master Takeno Jō-ō (1502–1555) helped spread the fashion of secular tea drinking. Middle-class citizens and merchants in the cities, as well as the smaller landowners in the provinces, took up the custom, and so the demand for suitable utensils increased.

The Six Ancient Kilns continued their production, but a new type of ware emerged in the Mino area. This was yellow Seto, a light-toned yellowware made from the fine white clay of that area.

By now Europeans were exploring the East, and in 1543 a Portuguese ship was wrecked off Japan. The strange-looking sailors were welcomed by the Japanese, who, among other things, were fascinated by their guns and learned to make some for themselves. When the Portuguese eventually returned home by way of Korea and China, where European trade was already established, they told about the strange new land. Soon Portugal sent trading ships, complete with missionaries, as missionaries were always part of these expeditions, and trading was begun. The missionaries made converts. Within a short time the Dutch and English also started to trade with Japan, but they were different in that they did not take missionaries along.

The end of the civil war period was

brought about by Oda Nobunaga, who was a powerful daimyo, or lord, in the provinces. After he had gained enough strength by conquering his neighbors, he invaded Kyoto in 1568 and overthrew the shogunate, but although he became undisputed ruler of central Japan, he never succeeded in unifying the whole country. This was known as the Momoyama Period.

Oda Nobunaga, a devotee of the tea ceremony, owned a large collection of tea utensils, a fact mentioned in a letter from the Jesuit father Luis Frois, who visited Japan in the sixteenth century.

When Nobunaga was assassinated in 1582, Toyotomi Hideyoshi, his ablest general, took charge. After building a strongly fortified castle at Osaka, he established his government there. The castle was enormous, with an outer courtyard eight miles in circumference; tens of thousands of workmen were employed in its construction.

Hideyoshi was a man of humble birth, the only one of such origin to achieve greatness in those times. Doubtless this accounted for his love of lavish display and splendor. He was also a very small man, scarcely five feet tall, with a face said to resemble that of a wizened ape.

The name of this period, Momoyama, or "Peach Hill" (1568–1615), is derived from the site of a new fortified palace Hideyoshi built in 1594 on a hill on the southern edge of Kyoto. The palace was dismantled after Hideyoshi's death, and about a century later the whole hillside site was planted with peach trees. Hideyoshi managed to unify Japan within eight years. He decreed that all missionaries must leave because he was afraid they would be followed by soldiers, as had happened in other countries. By this time tea drinking had become a firmly established custom among the whole population, and Hideyoshi, an inveterate tea drinker, ordered the tea master Sen-no-Rikyū to revise and put into writing the rules of the tea ceremony. Rikyū favored a simple and rather monasterial concept of the ceremony. The first independent tearoom, built apart from the house, was his creation. This room was similar to a simple fisherman's hut, with a door so low that guests must enter it kneeling (Ill. 11). The tea ceremony was of such importance to Hideyoshi and his officers that they took teabowls and tea jars on campaign so that they could drink tea on the battlefield. Tea masters even accompanied the military on their campaigns.

Hideyoshi was famous for his huge tea parties, the most well known of which was held in 1587 at the Kitano pine grove near Kyoto. Everyone was invited—all the tea

11. Interior of the Tea House Ceremonial Room at the Philadelphia Museum of Art. Philadelphia Museum of Art; Photograph by A. J. Wyatt

masters of Japan and all the people regardless of class or social distinctions. More than 550 tea masters attended, bringing all their treasures and displaying their art and famous utensils for the admiration of the huge crowds. Hideyoshi conducted his own tea ceremony for a few chosen guests, then went to taste the tea made by the various masters. One hopes that he only had a small sip of each; otherwise he must have drunk an incredible amount of tea. Unfortunately, a rebellion broke out in Higo. Hideyoshi had to leave immediately to quell it, thereby breaking up the great tea party, which had to be terminated after only one day instead of lasting the planned ten days. But the spectacular affair has remained a historical highlight to this day.

Hideyoshi died in 1598 and Tokugawa Ieyasu became shogun in 1603, the same year

Christianity was suppressed, although it was not finally crushed until 1637. This action was not taken because of its religious point of view, but because Christians held a vague kind of allegiance to a foreign pope, which was not desirable.

Trade with Portugal was also stopped, but the Dutch were allowed to use one port, Nagasaki. Their merchants lived on an island in the bay, virtually imprisoned, and could not go to the mainland. No Japanese living abroad could return to Japan, and if he did he was executed; and no Japanese could go abroad. Only small ships were allowed to be built, those that could go no farther than between the four main islands. And any foreigner arriving in Japan, shipwrecked or otherwise, was to be executed.

Japan was now a closed country—peaceful, unified—and so it remained for

12. *Bowl, Seto ware, seventeenth century. The decoration is a Christian cross.* Philadelphia Museum of Art, John T. Morris Fund; Photograph by A. J. Wyatt

that Queen Elizabeth I of England died. Ieyasu established his capital at Edo, which was only a small village at the time. Edo became Tokyo in modern times.

Ieyasu built up a stable society and an efficient government. The people were divided into four rigid classes of society: the samurai, who could hold office and carry swords; farmers, who were rice growers and therefore essential to the well-being of the population; artisans, who produced goods; and finally, merchants and tradesmen, who formed the lowest class, being nonproductive.

two hundred years. Even the population did not increase.

During the Momoyama Period several new kinds of wares were made in the Seto-Mino area. White Shino wares, named for the tea master Shino Sōshin, who died in the early sixteenth century, are covered with a thick white feldspathic glaze; they were popular with contemporary persons of consequence (Ill. 13). The yellow Seto wares made in the Momoyama Period were of a deeper yellow than those produced in the Muromachi Period. Black Seto made its appearance at this time, the color being a much

13. *Stoneware dish, Shino ware; Momoyama or early Edo Period—late sixteenth or early seventeenth century. This is gray Shino, or* nezumi *(mouse gray) Shino. The leaf pattern is dark gray on a light gray ground.* Courtesy of the Brooklyn Museum, Gift of the Mary Griggs Burke Foundation

richer and purer black than anything yet made. Oribe wares, with their rich green glaze and new shapes, were the next type of ware to appear in the Mino area.

Furuta Oribe (1544–1615) was a tea master who served under all three lords—Nobunaga, Hideyoshi, and Ieyasu. He had been a pupil of Sen-no-Rikyū. His taste in tea ceremony wares has exerted a tremendous influence on Japanese ceramics down to the present time. The shapes he preferred were a complete break with the traditional styles, many pieces being in free-form designs.

Oribe became the tea teacher of Hidetada, son of Ieyasu, who succeeded his father as shogun . During the battle between Hidetada and Hideyori, Oribe visited different leaders to perform the tea ceremony for them. One day he needed a piece of bamboo to make a teaspoon, and while he was absorbed in his search for a suitable piece in the bamboo barricades, he was seen by the enemy and wounded, but fortunately was not killed.

14. *Sake bottle, Karatsu ware, seventeenth century. Karatsu wares bear a strong resemblance to Korean wares of the Yi Dynasty, which is not surprising as Korean potters made the Karatsu wares. Pieces with underglaze iron decoration, such as this one, are known as* E-garatsu, *or decorated Karatsu.* Philadelphia Museum of Art, given by S. E. Vanderslice; Photograph by A. J. Wyatt

Kobori Enshū (1579–1674) succeeded Oribe as tea master under the Tokugawa, and did much to encourage the production of tea ceremony wares.

Korean potters were brought to Japan at this time, and they settled in Kyushu and on the western tip of Honshu. Notable among the places where they settled are Karatsu and Satsuma, where they began to produce wares in Korean style (Ill. 14).

In the middle of the Momoyama Period an entirely new type of ware appeared in Kyoto. This was Raku, a light-bodied soft ware molded entirely by hand, and eminently suitable for the tea ceremony. Kyoto itself had no ceramic tradition, and these wares were first made by Chōjirō, a tile maker. Raku ware and tiles are baked in the same type of low temperature kiln and the bodies of both are similar.

Edo Period: With the opening of the Edo Period (1615–1868) came the discovery in 1616 of porcelain clay near Arita, in the province of Hizen, by Ri Sampei, a Korean potter. Some blue and white porcelain had already been made in Japan by Gorodaiyu Shonsui, who had visited China at the beginning of the sixteenth century and had worked for five years in the Ching-tê-Chên factories. When he returned to Japan he took a supply of the necessary materials with him, and made porcelain wares until his material ran out.

After the discovery of suitable local clays for porcelain making, kilns in the Arita area gradually turned from producing Ko-rean-type wares as made at Karatsu to finer porcelain. These new wares were very popular, as the porcelain was much harder and more durable than pottery, and the white background showed off to advantage the underglaze blue decoration.

These blue and white wares were produced exclusively for about thirty years, and then an Imari ceramic dealer named Tojima Tokuzaemon learned the technique of overglaze enameling from a Chinese potter at Nagasaki. Tokuzaemon passed on the secret to Kakiemon, and after the two had worked and experimented together for a time, Kakiemon succeeded in applying overglaze enamels to his porcelain wares. This was around 1644 (the various sources do not agree on the exact date). Kakiemon decorated his wares sparingly, with rarely more than a third of the surface covered, so that the brilliant enamels enhanced and contrasted with the sparkling cream-colored glaze (Ill. 15). In time, the secret of enameling spread, and polychrome enamel porcelain wares were soon being produced by other Arita potters.

The first Japanese ceramics in Europe were probably taken there by the Portuguese at the end of the sixteenth century. By the mid-seventeenth century there was a flourishing export trade in Arita porcelains, which were sent to Europe by way of the Dutch colony at Nagasaki.

Chinese porcelains had been imported into Europe in large quantities, but because of the internal struggles in China the source

15. Bowl, Kakiemon ware, Arita Province. Early eighteenth century. This fine white porcelain bowl has overglaze enamel decoration in green, red, and blue. Courtesy of the Brooklyn Museum, Gift of Carll H. De Silver

16. A. *Imari dish, porcelain, eighteenth century. Decorated with overglaze enamels, with the character* JU, *symbol of longevity, in the center.* B. *Dish turned over to show details of the overglaze enamel decoration on the underside.* Courtesy, Museum of Fine Arts, Boston

had dried up and the Dutch East India Company jumped in to fill the void with the new Japanese porcelains from Arita. Blue and white ware in the Chinese tradition was shipped to Amsterdam, where the Dutch ceramists at Delft began to imitate it, since it was very popular and brought high prices.

Meanwhile, the Japanese began to make pieces especially for the European market, in European style, as described to them by the Dutch traders at Nagasaki. These were called Imari ware because they were exported from that port, although they were actually made in Arita (Ill. 16). These pieces, too, were in great demand, with the result

that during the eighteenth century many leading European factories began making pieces in the same style. The imitations were so well done that it is often hard to tell if a piece was made in Japan or not.

Kilns in other areas in Japan began to produce porcelain, notably the Nabeshima, Hirado, and Kutani kilns (Ill. 17).

Almost at the same time as Kakiemon discovered the secret of enameling porcelain, Ninsei in Kyoto succeeded in enameling his pottery wares. Ninsei was an extraordinarily skillful potter, and his tea jars are held in particularly high regard (Ill. 18). They were formed on the wheel with an impeccable technique, and each had its own pictorial design covering most of the surface.

Ogata Kenzan (1663–1743), a pupil of Ninsei, and brother of Kōrin, the celebrated painter, made pottery wares with simple enamel decoration in a free and bold style. The Kenzan line of potters continues down to this day, making wares in their traditional style.

Other Kyoto potters followed Ninsei and Kenzan, notably Eisen, Mokubei, Dōhachi, and Hozen, all master potters who produced highly original wares.

Besides all this progress, the old styles of wares were still being produced in much the same way as they had always been made, as, for example, at Tamba.

With the Meiji Period (1868–1912) came commercialism and the eclipse of the artist-craftsman.

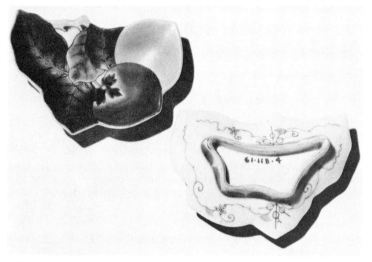

17. *Porcelain sauce dishes with overglaze enamel decoration. L. 4". H. ¾". Nabeshima ware, Genroku Period, c. 1680–1720.* Philadelphia Museum of Art, given by Mrs. Herbert C. Morris; Photograph by A. J. Wyatt

18. *Teabowl by Ninsei (mid-seventeenth century). Pottery with overglaze enamels in blue, red, and green, outlined in gold. This piece bears a strong resemblance to lacquer ware.* Metropolitan Museum of Art, Gift of Charles Stewart Smith

2

Tea, Tea Masters, and the Tea Ceremony

Tea

The tea ceremony has probably had more influence on Japanese taste than any other single factor in Japanese civilization. Besides creating the need for suitable wares for the ceremony itself, it has influenced all forms of Japanese art, as well as the costume, manners, and taste of all classes of Japanese. It has been variously described as an exercise in style in which the host seeks to create the most beautiful effects from the simplest possible means, or the art of concealing beauty that it may be discovered, or suggesting what you dare not reveal. Because of the simplicity and lack of ostentation of the tea ceremony, a poor man can put on as fine a one as a rich man.

Tea was first a medicine before it was a beverage. The plant is a native of southern China, and the early Chinese drank tea to relieve fatigue and to help their eyesight. They also made it into a paste and applied it externally for rheumatic pains. The Taoists believed that drinking tea was essential to the achievement of immortality. By the fourth and fifth centuries tea had become the favorite beverage of the inhabitants of the Yangtse-Kiang valley. They used it in cake form, the leaves being steamed, crushed, and made into a cake, which was then boiled with rice, ginger, orange peel, salt, spices, and milk. A remnant of this an-cient method remains today in the Russian practice of using lemon slices in tea. The modern Chinese ideograph "cha" for tea was coined at about this time, and in England the slang expression for tea is still "char."

In the eighth century Luwuh, the Chinese poet, formulated the Code of Tea in his *Chaking,* a work consisting of ten chapters divided into three volumes. It described the nature of the tea plant, the implements for gathering the leaves, and the selection of the leaves; the necessary tea-making utensils, the desirable methods of making cake tea, and the vulgarity of the ordinary methods in use; a historical summary of illustrious tea drinkers, famous Chinese tea plantations, and possible variations of the tea service, with illustrations of the tea utensils. The final chapter is lost. Although cake tea was still in use, Luwuh eliminated all the other ingredients except salt.

During the Sung Dynasty (960–1280) whipped tea came into fashion. The leaves were ground to a fine powder, and the beverage was made by whipping the powder in hot water with a bamboo whisk; no salt was added. The Zen Buddhist monks originated a ritual that consisted of a formal gathering in front of a statue of the Bodhi-Dharma, where tea was drunk in solemnity from a single bowl.

After the Mongol invasions and the subsequent internal struggles in China, powdered tea was no longer used and finally became altogether forgotten. In the Ming Dynasty tea was made by steeping the leaves in hot water. Tea drinking was introduced into Europe at this time from China, the Europeans learning to make their tea by steeping it.

Tea was first introduced into Japan during the eighth century. It is recorded that in 729 the Emperor Shomu gave tea to one hundred monks at his palace in Nara, and Okakura says in *The Book of Tea* that the leaves were probably imported by Japanese ambassadors to the Tang court in China, and were prepared in the way then in fashion, which would be in the way described by Luwuh. In 801 the monk Saicho brought some seeds from China, which he planted in Yeisan. Cake tea was made from the tea leaves.

The Sung practice of grinding the leaves reached Japan in 1191, along with the tea ritual using the powdered whipped tea. By the thirteenth century the tea ceremony practiced by the Buddhist monks had spread throughout Japan, and in the next two hundred years it became an independent secular performance.

Tea Masters

The patronage of the Shogun Ashikaga Yoshimasa was largely responsible for the general adoption of the ceremony, but the tea masters were also influential. These tea masters were not potters themselves, but through their understanding of the aesthetics of tea and their perception of the simple beauty of unpretentious utensils, they set the standards of the tea ceremony and, as a direct result, of aristocratic taste. The utensils they preferred were simple everyday vessels that originally were not made for the ceremony at all—Korean rice bowls, for instance. The Japanese call such simple objects *shibui*—literally translated, "tastefully astringent."

The beauty that the tea masters discovered is often not readily apparent to the uninitiated, but they took great pride in their sensitivity to this kind of beauty. One day the tea master Kobori Enshū (1579–1647)

was being complimented by his disciples on the taste he had displayed in the choice of his collection. "Each piece is such that no one can help admiring it," they told him. "It shows that you had better taste than had Rikyū, for his collection could only be appreciated by one beholder in a thousand." Enshū replied, "This merely proves how commonplace I am. The great Rikyū dared to love only those objects which personally appealed to him, whereas I unconsciously cater to the taste of the majority. Verily, Rikyū was one in a thousand among tea masters."

It was Murata Jukō, a priest, who introduced the tea ceremony to the Shogun Ashikaga Yoshimasa. Jukō formalized the rules for the ritual, which became popular with the aristocracy. He was the friend of all the aesthetes of his day. One of his contemporaries, Sō-ami, or Nōami (1397–1471), became a famous tea master and is credited with being among the first to create a demand for suitable wares for the tea ceremony. Sō-ami was also a famous gardener and landscape painter in ink monochrome. During the next century, under the influence of the tea master Takeno Jō-ō, a skillful verse writer, the tea ceremony spread to the cities and city merchants began the practice of formal tea drinking.

All these tea masters created and shaped the basic forms of the tea ceremony—the gathering together of a few friends, the ritual of preparing and drinking the tea, eating the frugal meal, the type of utensils to be used, and so on. However, it was Sen-no-Rikyū (1521–1591) who introduced the concept of the small separate tearoom (Ill. 19).

Sen-no-Rikyū was the son of Tanaka Yohei, a wholesale fish dealer. He took the name Sen from his grandfather, an artist and friend of the Shogun Ashikaga Yoshimasa. The name Rikyū, given him by his Zen teacher, was confirmed by Imperial edict. He enjoyed the friendship of the Shogun Hideyoshi, who ordered him to revise and put into writing the rules of the tea ceremony. These rules covered every aspect of the ceremony: the ideal dimensions of the tearoom, the number of guests, the preparation of the tea, the selection of the food and

19. *Ceremonial Tea House, waiting room, and garden at the Philadelphia Museum of Art. The guests assemble in the waiting room at the right, then pass through the garden by the "dewy path," or roji, to the tearoom at the left.* Philadelphia Museum of Art; Photograph by A. J. Wyatt

the order in which the dishes should be presented, as well as the correct gestures of the host and guests.

At the age of seventy Rikyū was obliged to commit suicide on the order of his former friend, the Shogun Hideyoshi, who, some sources say, accused him of living in a style above his station in life. Others say that enemies of Rikyū told Hideyoshi that Rikyū was planning to administer a fatal dose of poison in a bowl of tea.

Two tea masters leave their names perpetuated in special types of tea ceremony wares. They are Shino Sōshin and Furuta Oribe.

Shino Sōshin is associated with a type of pottery made at the Seto kilns (Ill. 20). Shino-*yaki* is still being made, wares with a thick soft cream-colored crackle glaze over designs sketchily drawn in iron pigment on the biscuit. Shino Sōshin is said to have originated incense guessing contests.

Furuta Oribe-no-Shō was born near Seto, the son of a former priest. He served

20. *Dish with design of three wild geese in flight.* Nezumi, or gray Shino ware, c. 1600. Cleveland Museum of Art, Mrs. A. Dean Perry Collection

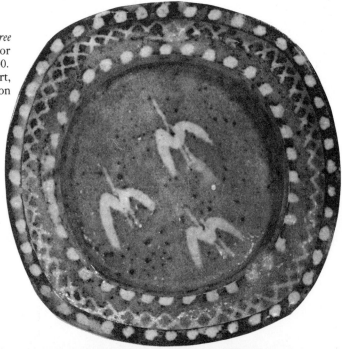

as samurai under Oda Nobunaga until the latter's death in 1582. In 1585 he was created a daimyo, lord, by Hideyoshi and put in charge of a castle near Kyoto, where he met Rikyū and became his pupil. Oribe was present at the famous tea party Hideyoshi held in 1585, which many great tea masters attended, but at that time he was little known.

After Hideyoshi's death Oribe had Ieyasu's son Hidetada as pupil. When Hidetada became the second Tokugawa shogun, Oribe's position as tea master was established, and daimyos competed to become his pupils. His taste became the predominant one of the period, and potters created wares to please his highly developed artistic sensibilities. Oribe had direct contact with foreign goods being imported in his time and these influenced his taste. He preferred wares in free-form shapes, which seem quite modernistic to our eyes; they are known as Oribe-*gonomi*, or Oribe-style wares.

Unfortunately, like Rikyū, Oribe was obliged to commit suicide at an advanced age. In 1614 a battle was fought between Hidetada, Oribe's pupil, and Hideyori, son of Oribe's former master and pupil, Hideyoshi. Oribe fought on the side of Hidetada. When the battle ended in a truce, a group of dissenters led by some of Oribe's retainers tried to set fire to the streets of Kyoto so that they could attack the Tokugawa forces, but this failed and the conspirators were discovered and taken prisoner. Oribe was held responsible for the acts of his retainers, although they had acted without his knowledge, and he had to commit *seppuku*, or hara-kiri. *Seppuku* is the term generally used in Japan; hara-kiri, although used by westerners, is considered a vulgar term in Japanese.

Kobori Enshū served under Ieyasu, and was a landscape designer, poet, painter, and calligraphist as well as tea master. He succeeded Oribe, but was a follower of the style of Sen-no-Rikyū, whose concept of the tea ceremony was monastic as opposed to the more social concept of Oribe. His name is associated with a type of pottery made at a number of kilns throughout Japan. These, known as Enshū's Seven Favorite Kilns, are Shidoro, Zeze, Kosobe, Agano, Takatori, Asahi, and Akahada. All of them, with the exception of Kosobe, are still in production today.

Tea Ceremony

The tea ceremony may be held at any time between 4:00 A.M. and 6:00 P.M., although evening tea is seldom held in the summer because of the mosquitoes, nor dawn tea in winter because of the cold.

The tea is made from green tea leaves ground to a fine powder, which is whipped in boiling water in the bowl with a handmade bamboo whisk to make a frothy jade green beverage. The foods must be a delight to behold, the colors harmonizing with the dishes in which they are served. A delicate fragrance of incense should pervade the room. The success of the tea ceremony lies in its simplicity and subtlety.

Sen-no-Rikyū modeled his tearoom, the *sukiya*, on the thatched huts of Buddhist recluses. He said that the room should not be larger than four and a half mats (8 square feet), and was to accommodate at the most five persons. The entrance should be small, like the entrance to a fisherman's hut. Rikyū's standard entrance was 23 by 27 inches, although a slightly larger entrance was permitted to allow the entry of Hideyoshi's generals wearing armor. The fittings of the room should be of the simplest, plaster and woodwork of the most ordinary kind; rare or precious things should not be used (Ill. 11). The room should suggest an atmosphere of refined poverty, with—ideally— only a simple wall scroll and flower arrangement in the *tokonama*, or alcove, as decoration. The utensils should be of the plainest, and the meal quite frugal, served by the host himself (Ill. 21).

Rikyū emphasized the simplicity of the ceremony, with no rich or out-of-season foods, and no bones or fins for the guests to crunch or spit out. The flowers should be of no more than two colors, arranged in a plain bamboo vase, with no smell to disturb the tranquillity. The scroll should preferably be the writing of a Zen priest or an old Japanese poet or, if a painting, be in ink with little or no color.

The garden through which the tearoom

21. Tray, Oribe ware. Private Collection

22. Kitchen of Ceremonial Tea House at the Philadelphia Museum of Art, showing utensils for the ceremony arranged on shelves. Philadelphia Museum of Art; Photograph by A. J. Wyatt

is approached is as important as the tearoom itself. Rikyū said that the path, or *roji*, should be of "thick green moss, all fair and sunny warm," suggesting a simple mountain path. Only common and naturally planted things are acceptable in the garden—evergreens are desirable, but flowers are out of place. The *roji* is intended to break connection with the outside world and prepare the guest for the full enjoyment of the aesthetic experience to come (Ill. 19).

The host makes his preparations for the tea on the day before the ceremony, getting up early to sweep and prepare the tearoom and garden. He puts fresh water, often from some special source, in the water basin, and arranges the flowers and utensils, which are to be of the simplest and roughest, but selected with great care to avoid any repetition. For instance, if the bowl has a black glaze, the tea caddy should not be of black lacquer.

Many utensils were given names that have since become famous; if the utensils were broken, they were mended with gold lacquer; broken ones that have been mended are highly desirable, and the decoration thus naturally formed is preferable to an elaborate decoration executed by the potter when

he made the piece. Such a piece is called a tribute piece, as no one would presume to make an unnoticeable repair, thereby passing off his own work as the master's. (See Ill. 23 for the teabowl by Kenzan, which not only has been repaired with long lacquer lines, but has a large triangular portion of gold lacquer showing on the front.) Teabowls vary according to season. A deep one is used in winter to conserve the heat, and a wide shallow one is used in summer. In Ill. 23 the teabowl by Kenzan is for summer, and the one by Raku Seisai is for winter.

On the day of the tea ceremony the host again rises early, perhaps at dawn if he wishes to pluck mushrooms and fresh herbs with the dew still on them, and select the fish at the fish market. He sees that all is in readiness in the tearoom and garden, and sprinkles water on the stepping-stones and spreads a few leaves in the garden to present a natural appearance.

The guests assemble in the *yoritsuke*, or waiting place, where there must be no talking or whispering (Ills. 24 and 25). The chief guest, selected in advance, acts as spokesman for the others. He leads the other guests through the garden to the tearoom, which he enters first. His place is near the

23. Part of ceremonial tea set given by Okakura to Mrs. Jack Gardner of Boston. Top left, *iron teakettle, early nineteenth century;* top right, *charcoal basket, mid-nineteenth century, and twig charcoal;* center, *pottery slop jar, Takatori ware, late nineteenth century;* bottom left, *pottery teabowl, "Cormorant Boat" by Kenzan (1663–1743), which has been extensively mended with gold lacquer;* bottom right, *pottery teabowl, "Black Peony" by Raku Seisai (early nineteenth century);* below, *two feather brushes, early twentieth century.* Isabella Stewart Gardner Museum, Boston

24. *Tea House waiting room, from the garden side.* Philadelphia Museum of Art; Photograph by A. J. Wyatt

tokonama, to the left of the host and facing him; he takes the lead at all times in the conversation, with intelligent questions and appropriate comments.

When the guests are seated on the floor the host brings in the necessary utensils with the exception of the brazier and kettle, which are already in place. According to a strict ritual, he prepares tea in the bowl for each guest in turn, who drinks the entire contents appreciatively, and returns the bowl to the host. The host then carefully wipes the bowl and prepares some for the next guest.

The meal, according to Rikyū, should be of the simplest, consisting of no more than two courses. The food served should be as appealing to the eye as to the taste, and, although simple in nature, requires considerable forethought on the part of the host. Tea diaries describing meals served by famous tea masters are still in existence; in one such diary the menu of a meal prepared by Jō-ō in 1554 is described and it included a bowl of minced sparrow broiled in bean paste. This is quite interesting, as sparrows were also eaten in England in Elizabethan times, but seem to have fallen out of favor since, except with cats.

After the meal the utensils are handed to the guests to be admired. Although the teabowls often seem crude and rough, they can cost as much as a hundred dollars. The guests then take their departure, refreshed by the aesthetic experience; the tea ceremony may take from forty minutes to four hours, depending on how elaborate it is.

At the present time there are at least twenty-four major schools of "tea" in Japan, the ceremony having become symbolic of a way of life. In fact, it has been described as being the flower of Japanese civilization.

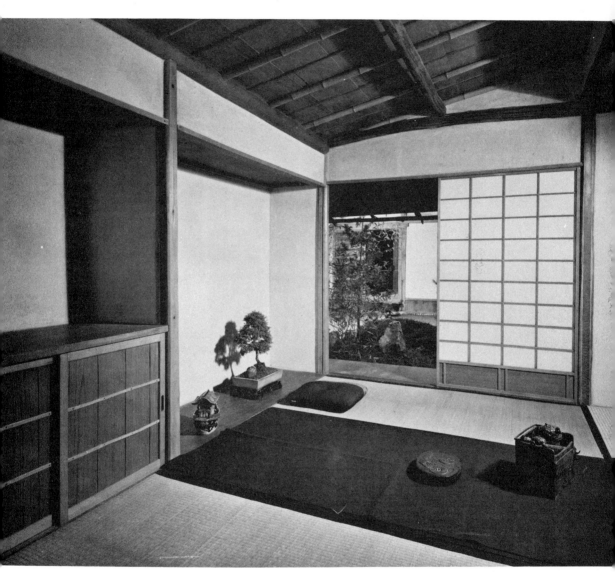

25. Tea House waiting room from the back, looking across the garden to the Ceremonial Tea House. Philadelphia Museum of Art; Photograph by A. J. Wyatt

3

Traditional Japanese Ceramic Techniques

Ceramics are made from clay and baked in a kiln. The different kinds of ceramics, ranging from coarse earthenware to fine porcelain, depend on both the type of clay used and the heat and duration of the baking.

Ceramic clay has to have three properties: first, sufficient plasticity to be molded easily; second, the ability to hold its shape during firing; and third, a rocklike hardness after it has been fired at a suitable temperature. The main source of such clay is feldspar, which is the most common rock on this earth. Clay is weathered, or decomposed, feldspar, ground into particles, with the soluble elements removed. It falls into two categories: primary clay and secondary clay.

Primary, or residual, clay is found in the place where it was formed. It is a very pure clay, but its particles are rather coarse and uneven and it is relatively nonplastic. Secondary clay is formed when the rock is broken up by weathering and the pieces carried away by wind or running water, and finally deposited as silt to form a clay bed. This is the commonest type of clay. Its particles are uniform, fine-grained, and plastic, but contain many impurities.

The Chinese called the residual clay they found near Ching-tê-Chên "Kao-ling," which means "the high hills." Kaolin is a pure white clay but not plastic enough to be used alone, and it is difficult to fire satisfactorily. The Chinese also discovered petuntse (*pai-tun-tzū*), which is a less decomposed

feldspar that fuses into a kind of natural glass under heat. Together with the kaolin, water, and certain mineral salts, they found it made a pliable fine clay that fired at a high temperature to a pure white porcelain.

The Chinese called kaolin the "bones" and petuntse the "flesh." Père d'Entrecolles tells how the workers laughed when some Europeans stole petuntse briquettes and tried to make porcelain out of them. They said it was like trying to make a body without bones.

In Japan clays of all kinds have been used to make ceramics since very early times. Pottery has always been a craft practiced by a large segment of the population. Farmers in many areas, such as Tamba, spend hours every day making wares and tending their clay. Whole villages made pottery from local clays in this way as a secondary occupation.

The kind of clay used is one of the principal indications of where the piece was made. Arita clays are fine and white; Kutani clays are the roughest and very gray. Kyoto wares generally have a gray clay body, but this varies from potter to potter, as the local clays have long been used up and clays are now brought in and blended individually by each potter.

About three hundred years ago a form of semidecomposed feldspar was discovered in Kyushu that would make porcelain without the addition of anything else. This soft stone, called Amakusa stone, has to be well ground to make porcelain. Before its discovery as a potential porcelain clay, it had been used as a sword-sharpening stone. It is still used throughout Japan to make porcelain bodies.

Ceramics divide up roughly into the following categories, with various shades in between. Each category needs its own type of clay and length and temperature of firing.

Earthenware is usually made from natural clay and fired at a low temperature. It is nonvitreous—that is, it does not become transparent. It is usually dark in color, fairly soft and porous, and will not hold liquids unless glazed. Raku ware meets this description.

Faience is a French term loosely applied to glazed earthenware in general. Satsuma export wares are generally referred to as being faience.

Terra-cotta is made from natural clay, fired, and left unglazed. Jōmon, Yayoi, and Hajiki wares fall into this category, as well as the *haniwa* figures. As terra-cotta wares are porous, they do not make satisfactory vessels for holding liquids.

Stoneware can be made either from certain natural clays or from prepared mixed clays. It is fired at a much higher temperature than earthenware, which is why not all natural clays are suitable for stoneware. The red clays in particular could not be fired at stoneware temperature—their melting point is too low, and they would simply melt. Stoneware is hard, vitreous, and able to hold water even when unglazed. The fired color ranges from a light gray to a darker gray or brown. Stoneware first appeared in Japan around A.D. 400, with the Sueki wares.

China is made from a mixture of kaolin, certain other clays, flint, and a flux to lower the melting point. China undergoes two firings, the first at a very high temperature, after which the ware is said to be in the biscuit stage, and the second at a lower temperature for the glaze. China bodies are generally white. The term *china* is commonly used quite loosely to describe all tablewares and/or dishes.

Porcelain is fired at a still higher temperature than china. It is made from a mixture of kaolin and other clays, with the exception of the Amakusa stone mentioned above which can be used alone and makes such a tough porcelain clay that it can even be turned on the wheel. Porcelain is made in one firing, in contrast to china, the body and glaze maturing together. It is the hardest and most vitreous of all ceramics. Porcelain is generally cast in molds. It has been made in Japan since 1616.

Glazes

Glaze is applied to most forms of ceramics. The early glazes were accidental, the result of wood ashes from the kiln fire falling on wares in the kiln and reacting chemically with the clay body.

A glaze produces a glasslike surface on ceramic wares. The glaze materials become vitreous, or glasslike, at a lower temperature than the ceramic body. The difference between a glaze and glass is that a glaze is a coating that becomes vitreous and fuses with the clay body during firing, whereas glass is melted first of all into a liquid and then made into objects. A glaze must not liquefy in the way that glass does or it would run off the ware during firing. Glazes are either produced directly by the action of heat on the body or they are applied before firing as a coating by painting, dipping, pouring, or spraying. Glazing compounds are many and varied.

Salt glazing is effected by throwing salt into the kiln when the temperature has reached its highest point; the vapors from the salt settle on the wares and produce a very hard glaze. The glaze on terra-cotta water pipes is produced by this method. In modern times Rosanjin has produced many fine pieces with salt glazing.

Lead sulfide, ground to a fine white powder and dusted or painted on the clay body, fuses with the surface to produce a smooth shiny glaze at a low temperature. This is a very old glaze. Raku wares have a lead and borax glaze.

Feldspar, when powdered and used alone, will give a milky glaze, and when limestone is added it will fuse at a lower temperature.

Ash glaze, composed of ashes, feldspar, and clay, requires a higher temperature, but is very durable.

Luster glaze is a modern commercial development in Japan. It consists of a thin metallic film on the basic glaze, either added directly to it for an overall effect or put on over a fired glaze surface in the same way as an overglaze enamel.

Crackle glaze has crazed and developed minute cracks. This effect can be created in more than one way. It can be caused by the composition of the glaze itself or it can be the result of a sudden cooling. Raku ware is taken straight from the hot kiln and put into cold water, the sudden shock causing the glaze to crack in all directions. As Raku is a soft porous ware, the cracks in the glaze allow water to penetrate the body, which thus is not waterproof. However, after much use the pores gradually close, and in the course of time the piece no longer leaves a damp mark where it has stood. Edward Morse, in his *Japanese Homes and Their Surroundings,* says that old tiles were considered far superior for roofing a house, and second-hand tiles were in great demand since they were waterproof because the pores had filled with dust and dirt. Raku ware and roofing tiles have much in common.

A crackle glaze can also be rendered waterproof by refiring the piece. Before it is returned to the kiln, underglaze color is rubbed into the crackle so that when the cracks close on the completion of the firing the crackle pattern will be visible in color. Satsuma ware made for export frequently has color rubbed into the crackle, but it is not generally returned to the kiln for sealing (Color Plate 4).

Various decorative effects can be obtained from using two or more glazes of different colors on the same piece. If several colors are added to the glaze, they create a beautiful effect where they run together.

Unless stilts are used in the kiln, the foot of the piece to be fired must be free from glaze or it will stick to the kiln shelf. On large pieces of porcelain a double foot is often found, the second one being a ring toward the center of the piece; this served as additional support during firing. Limoges and Nippon pieces both have the same double foot. Sometimes a bar or star at the center serves the same purpose.

Kilns and firing: The early Jōmon and Yayoi wares had been fired either in the open or in trenches, where the temperature did not rise above 1,350° or 1,475° F. Not until the Kofun Period were more efficient kilns constructed.

The *ana-gama,* or Korean-style cave kiln, was introduced about A.D. 400. The heat in these kilns could rise to as much as 2,200° or 2,375° F. As their name implies, these were semisubterranean kilns, constructed either by roofing over a ditch running up a hillside or by digging a tunnel parallel to the upward slope of the hill. The lower end was used as a firebox, and the smoke escaped out of the upper end. This type of wood-burning kiln is still used by individual studio potters.

In the sixteenth century the *nobori-gama,* or Korean climbing kiln, made its appearance. This type of kiln was really a series of *ana-gama* set one above the other on a hillside and connected to one another. The lowest chamber was fired first of all, and when the wares were done, that chamber was sealed; then the next one, which was already hot from the fire in the lower one, was fired. This process was continued all the way along the kiln, some kilns having as many as fifty chambers.

In the Meiji era European-style kilns and firing methods using coal, oil, or electricity were introduced. These are the commercial methods used today.

The first step after a piece is formed, whether by throwing, molding, pressing, or jiggering, is to let it dry out. In this process the piece shrinks, the fine-grained clays shrinking the most because they hold more water. The drying has to be carefully and evenly done or the piece will crack or warp. When all the water between the clay particles has evaporated, the piece is said to be in the leather-hard state; it is called greenware. The clay particles themselves will still be damp; the piece will not be truly dry until it is in the kiln with the temperature at the boiling point of water, 212° F.

The final drying in the kiln must take place quite slowly or the steam formed inside the pieces will cause them to burst. Footed pieces like the pre-Nippon vase (Color Plate 6) and the Satsuma *koro* (Ill. 162) have holes drilled in the hollow feet to allow the steam to escape without causing damage.

By the time the kiln temperature

reaches about 925° F., the piece has become dehydrated and an irreversible chemical change has taken place. The clay cannot be reclaimed and reused; it has lost its plasticity and it will not disintegrate in water. But it is now highly fragile.

The next state is reached when the temperature has risen to about 1,650° F. and the oxidation is complete, all the carbon having been burned up. When pieces are too close together in a kiln, carbon is trapped and appears on them as black marks. This is a feature of Raku ware. No doubt it was originally accidental when two pieces touched and a shadow appeared on the ware as a result, but such shadows subsequently were created purposely.

The next major change occurs when vitrification, or glassification, begins; the temperature has then passed the red-heat mark. At this temperature the clay begins to harden and tighten, and this causes some shrinkage. Some of the components melt into beads of glass, soak into the surrounding area, and act like glue. The higher the temperature and the better the quality of the clay, the harder and the more transparent it becomes. When a certain critical temperature is reached clay will melt into a kind of glass; therefore, the temperature has to be carefully regulated so that the clay achieves its rocklike quality but does not go into the melting stage. However, tea masters have always deeply appreciated certain wares that have become deformed in the firing, notably the crouching flower vases of Tamba ware.

Glazes, on the other hand, have to melt; that is why they are made up of substances that will melt at a lower temperature than the clay body.

Domestic Wares and Export Wares in Traditional Styles

Famous Old Kilns

Six Ancient Kilns: The term Six Ancient Kilns is the general name for the Seto, Echizen, Tokoname, Bizen, Tamba, and Shigaraki kilns, all of which have been making ceramic wares since very early days. Seto, Echizen, Tokoname, and Bizen all claim to go back to Heian days, descending from Sue kilns in those places. Tamba dates from the early Kamakura Period, and Shigaraki from the middle Muromachi Period, with a branch kiln established later at Iga.

The potters working at these kilns were farmers as well. They worked with a plentiful local supply of clay in a long tradition of craftsmanship, which had developed over the years; the pieces they produced were strictly utilitarian. It was this unpretentious quality that, among other things, was recognized and appreciated by the tea masters. With the natural glaze brought forth by the firing, and with no artificial decoration, such a piece is a natural aesthetic expression of the clay itself and the human labor needed to shape it. Wares from the different kilns bear a strong resemblance to one another, as both the local clays and the techniques used were similar.

Seto: The ancient village of Seto is situated in Owari Province, ten miles northeast of the modern town of Nagoya, the capital of the region. The old kilns stood in a horseshoe around the village, and there were many of them. They continued making pot-

26. Large heavily potted dish, Seto ware, with "Horse Eye" design. This type of ware was intended for peasant use, and is made of heavy gray pottery, covered with pitted and crackled buff glaze. C. 1840. Courtesy of the Brooklyn Museum

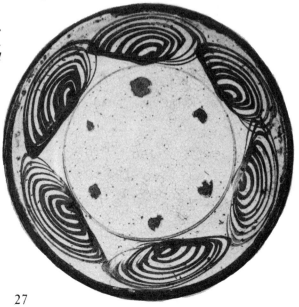

tery down to recent times, when they were either shut down or turned over to making porcelain (Ill. 26). Today Seto is the largest industrial porcelain-making area in the whole world, kilns standing side by side throughout the area. By day the sky is black with their smoke; by night flames shoot upward through the darkness, and day and night the rivers run white from the clay.

Ko-Seto (old Seto) wares. Fine quality clay of great plasticity and of high fire resistance was found in large quantities in the neighborhood of Seto, and stonewares covered with a thick glaze were made from it. Large pieces, like huge water jugs and storage jars, were built by the coil method, but smaller pieces were thrown on the wheel. The wood ash glazes varied from amber to dark brown and yellowish green. Some pieces were decorated with incised designs of plants, Flower Seto, or arabesques, some with a simple stamped device, and others with a raised applied decoration.

There are similar pieces in existence with the designs more deeply incised and a darker green or yellow brown glaze. These for a long time were believed to have been made at about the same date as the Flower Seto, and many were considered in Japan to be pieces of national importance. It now appears, however, that the Japanese authorities were victims of a deception, as two members of the Kato family, both living in Seto, have owned up to making them. The British Museum vase (Ill. 27), according to Soame Jenyns, seems to belong to this family.

During the civil wars in the fifteenth and sixteenth centuries the area around Seto was devastated time after time, and in the mid-sixteenth century the potters moved from there to Mino. Here totally different styles came into being—Ki-Seto (yellow Seto), Setoguro (black Seto), as well as Shino and Oribe wares.

Ki-Seto (yellow Seto). These wares are usually small dishes, flat bowls, incense burners, or boxes. They are decorated with a yellow glaze splashed with green, often over simple incised designs of a plant or vegetable. It has been suggested that the potters were trying to produce glazed wares similar to the celadons of Sung China, but their kilns were inadequate for the purpose. Ki-Seto wares date from the end of the sixteenth century.

Setoguro, black Seto wares, are a small group, consisting mostly of teabowls. This was the first appearance in Japan of a rich true black glaze, called *temmoku* in Japanese.

Shino wares. These wares were made under the direction of the tea master Shino Sōshin, and are almost exclusively tea ceremony pieces. They are heavy, with thick walls and deep cracks in the body. The most important categories are the white or plain Shino, the decorated Shino, and the gray Shino. The white Shino pieces are covered with a thick white feldspathic glaze, the first

28. *Footed cake dish, E-Shino ware (decorated Shino). Early nineteenth century.* Philadelphia Museum of Art, given by Theodore T. Newbold; Photograph by A. J. Wyatt

Japanese ceramics to have a white glaze. The *E*-Shino, or painted Shino wares, have a few graceful brushstrokes of cobalt blue or iron brown, representing grasses or birds (Ill. 28). Nezumi Shino (mouse gray) was first covered with iron slip, through which the designs were scratched; then a thick feldspathic glaze was applied and the piece fired. The iron slip turned a warm gray and the designs appeared white (Ills. 13 and 20).

Oribe wares. These wares reflect the taste of Furuta Oribe. Instead of the tradi-

tional styles, Oribe wares adopted new shapes, sometimes using distortion and imbalance in artistic ways. Square deep dishes, fan-shaped dishes, and linked rectangular dishes are typical shapes, with very simple designs. However, there were also plates, bowls of all kinds, lidded vessels, sake bottles, water jars, incense burners, incense boxes, sweetmeat jars, and jars for powdered tea, as well as teabowls (Ill. 29).

Besides the wide variety of forms, there was also great variety in the decoration.

29. *Sweetmeat jar, Oribe ware. Momoyama Period, sixteenth–seventeenth century. This is a rare piece. It has a tan glaze with overglaze decoration of white slip and green and brownish black glazes.* Courtesy of the Brooklyn Museum, Gift of Robert B. Woodward

Fig. 1. Map showing the principal Japanese kilns.

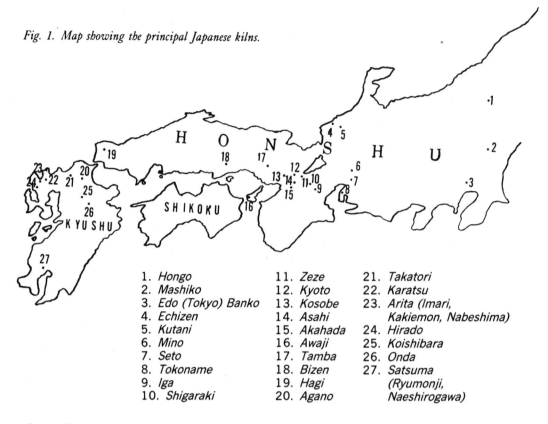

1. Hongo
2. Mashiko
3. Edo (Tokyo) Banko
4. Echizen
5. Kutani
6. Mino
7. Seto
8. Tokoname
9. Iga
10. Shigaraki
11. Zeze
12. Kyoto
13. Kosobe
14. Asahi
15. Akahada
16. Awaji
17. Tamba
18. Bizen
19. Hagi
20. Agano
21. Takatori
22. Karatsu
23. Arita (Imari, Kakiemon, Nabeshima)
24. Hirado
25. Koishibara
26. Onda
27. Satsuma (Ryumonji, Naeshirogawa)

Green Oribe is covered with a copper green glaze, some pieces having underglaze designs in brown iron oxide. Narumi Oribe has green glazes on a white slip and black Oribe wares have black glazes instead of the usual green. There are many more varieties of Oribe wares.

Echizen: The Echizen kiln sites are located in the northwest part of Japan, not far from Kutani. They date from late Heian days, but most of the kilns had ceased production by the mid-sixteenth century. However, the Taira kiln has continued production down to the present day, and the potters working there are descendants of the old families.

The production of these kilns was small, mostly kitchen utensils, which included some huge water jars. These wares have a green natural ash glaze, which drips richly over a dark brown body.

Tokoname: Traces of more than three hundred Tokoname kiln sites have been discovered in an area about twenty miles south of Nagoya. Jars and vases produced by these kilns were much favored by the tea masters

of the Muromachi Period. The high-fired unglazed stonewares, which are similar to the Echizen wares, have a rich warm brown body with a natural green glaze on the upper portions.

The kilns fell into decline in the seventeenth century, although wares were still produced in small quantities. Pieces made during the Meiji era have a yellow glaze over a red brown body. Today bricks and tiles are produced at Tokoname.

Bizen: Bizen stoneware was made in the vicinity of Imbe, in the province of Bizen. The *ko*-Bizen (old Bizen) wares are also known as Imbe-*yaki* (Imbe wares).

During the early Kamakura Period seed storage jars of dark clay were made. The density and high shrinkage of the clay necessitated an unusually long firing period, and this resulted in the wares becoming a dark reddish black with a heavy ash glaze deposit. These old wares were collected by the tea masters and used in the tea ceremony as water pots, often fitted with lacquer lids.

From the mid-fifteenth century models of birds and animals were produced. The

30. *A group of seventeenth-century tea ceremony pieces.* Left: *incense burner in the form of Hotei, god of contentment; Bizen ware. H. 3½".* Center: *tea jar with ivory lid for powdered tea; Tamba ware. H. 2¾".* Right: *flower vase, Iga ware. H. 10".* Victoria and Albert Museum

bodies were made of a fine clay and covered with a dark brown glaze, the finished pieces resembling bronze.

In the Momoyama Period tea ceremony wares such as flower vases, tea jars, water containers, and incense burners (Ill. 30) were made, but the clay was not considered suitable for teabowls.

Today the Bizen kilns produce bricks and drainpipes.

Bizen wares generally carry a mark; the most familiar modern mark is a cherry blossom.

Tamba: Tamba pottery was made in the villages of Oji, Muramori, Inahata, Kamaya, Onobara, and Tachikui, in Tamba Province, to the northwest of Kyoto.

The old wares were limited to a few shapes; large storage jars and sake bottles are the most common forms. The local clay, which has long since been used up, was coarse, and when fired became a dark red brown or gray brown color (Ill. 10). The clay was used much as it was dug from the ground, just wet down and kneaded into coils for use on a slowly revolving wheel. The wares were not glazed before firing, and the natural ash glaze, *bidoro,* was often very thick on account of the long firing necessitated by the type of kiln then in use. This was the *ana-gama,* the cave kiln.

About 1600 Korean-style "split bamboo" kilns were built. They were made of brick, in a shape resembling a split bamboo pole. The long tube was partially buried in the slope of a hill, with about one third of it above the level of the ground. These kilns were more efficient and the firing was accomplished in a much shorter time. Three different types of glazes were used—black, red brown, and amber. Production of the older forms continued, the wares becoming more regular and symmetrical, but new shapes were also introduced, notably the tea jar for storing tea leaves with its four ears for tying on the lid. Kobori Enshū visited Tamba and ordered tea jars to be made for his use. Tea jars to hold powdered tea were also made (Ill. 30).

In the early part of the nineteenth century slip-decorated ware was made at Tamba, but this production was short-lived and died out before the Meiji Period. At the beginning of this century sake bottles were also made at Tamba in large quantities.

In the early 1930s the jigger wheel made its appearance. However, the old hand methods continued to be used side by side with the new.

Modern Tamba wares have a chocolate, mahogany-colored, or blue black glaze, often splashed with yellow, over a red brown body. Another type of modern ware is decorated with simple designs in colored enamels on an unglazed gray body. Clays are brought from elsewhere, as the local clays are exhausted. The Tamba potters use the coil-and-throw method for all larger shapes, starting with a clay disk or slab for the base.

There are over twenty kilns in use at Tachikui at the present time, and although all are of the same type, they are different from any others now in use in Japan. They appear to be survivals and adaptations of the old climbing kilns.

Shigaraki: The Shigaraki kiln sites lie in an area between Kyoto and Seto, a little to the south. There is a legend that Korean potters settled there in the twelfth century.

The wares have a rough, unsophisticated appearance (Ill. 31). The clays, with their high sand and gravel content, cannot be thrown on the wheel, and the coil method has been used down to this day. The typical

31. Shigaraki ware grain storage jar. Muromachi Period (1333–1568). Private Collection

Shigaraki body, gray with coarse granules of partially fired quartz protruding from it, is covered with a natural glaze. The early wares were strictly utilitarian; seed jars, water vats, and grating mortars are the most common types of vessels. In the sixteenth

and seventeenth centuries the tea masters patronized the kilns, using the smaller wares as flower vases or water jars, and also ordering wares made to their own taste.

Today the same type of ware is still being produced, but artificial glazes are used.

Iga: The Iga and Shigaraki kilns are situated on the same mountain range, the Shigaraki kilns on the northern slopes and the Iga kilns on the southern. Up to the sixteenth century the wares of the two areas were very similar, but in later times a viscous, white-bodied clay was used at the Iga kilns.

Furuta Oribe visited Iga at the beginning of the seventeenth century and under his influence Iga began to make tea ceremony wares.

The typical Iga wares have a cracked or split gray body, which is usually distorted (Ill. 30). The natural glaze of brown, gray, and green on the old wares came to the surface when the clay was fired, but today artificial glazes are used here too. The older wares were admired for their roughness and natural flaws, but as time went on the potters learned to contrive these effects, with the consequent self-conscious artificiality.

Enshū's Seven Favorite Kilns

Kobori Enshū, whose real name was Kobori Totomi-no-Kami Masakuzu, was a tea master who served under Ieyasu. A follower of the style of Sen-no-Rikyū, he preferred a polished and tranquil type of ware that was made at a number of kilns in Japan. These kilns, known as Enshū's Seven Favorite Kilns, are Shidoro, Zeze, Kosobe, Agano, Takatori, Asahi, and Akahada. With the exception of Kosobe, all the kilns are still in production today, and there is a movement to rebuild the Kosobe.

Shidoro wares are undecorated; the glaze on the stoneware body is of a rich brown, similar to the Ko-Seto glazes. The kiln was established in 1575 by Kato Shoyemon Kagetada.

Kosobe wares were unknown until 1625, when they were popularized by Enshū. They have a fine hard body, and the

32. Top, at left: *teacup, Asahi, 1880.* Center: *wine cup, Sakurai, 1875.* Right: *bowl, Kosobe, 1875.* Peabody Museum of Salem Morse Collection; Photograph by Y. W. Sexton. Top, right: *tea jar, Zeze ware; early eighteenth century.* Private Collection. Left: *Teabowl, Akahada ware, Yamato Province.* Courtesy Museum of Fine Arts, Boston; Morse Collection

glazes range from white to a dark gray. They are often decorated with a few brushstrokes in brown (Ill. 32).

Zeze wares have a golden or red brown and purple glaze over a dark gray fine-grained biscuit. The kiln was established in 1630 under the direction of Enshū (Ill. 32).

Agano wares were at first Korean in style, but later became more like Takatori wares. The later wares have a bluish green glaze. The kiln was started in 1602.

Takatori wares have either a black brown glaze or combinations of white and dark glazes. The kilns were established by Koreans at the foot of the Takatori mountain about 1600.

The Asahi kiln was founded in 1600, and in 1645 Okumura Tosaku, under Enshū's supervision, made teabowls of light brown or light blue glaze on a coarse biscuit. The name Asahi, which means "morning sun," is said to be derived from the color of the ware. Between 1830 and 1873 modern

wares were produced by a potter named Chobei Matsubayashi.

Akahada wares made for the tea ceremony under Enshū's direction resemble Takatori ware, with a grayish white glaze (Ill. 32). The kiln was started in 1580, but then ceased operation until it was revived in 1645 by Nonomura Ninsei. It closed again and was reopened later, the best wares of its later period being made by Mokuhaku (1799–1870). Many of Mokuhaku's pieces are copies of Ninsei's wares, but he also made teabowls with designs showing Horai, the Taoist land of the immortals, and water jars with pictures in the style of Buddhist scrolls of the Nara Period.

Karatsu

Wares made in the Karatsu area during the first half of the sixteenth century were the first true ceramic wares to be made in

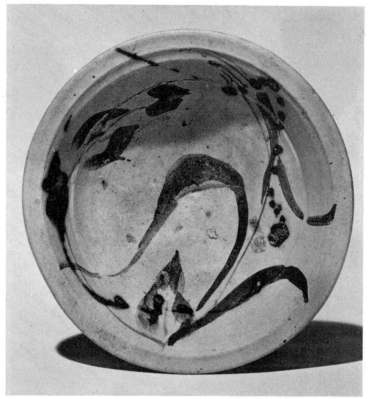

33. Kiln waster, Karatsu ware. Nineteenth century. Philadelphia Museum of Art, given by Theodore T. Newbold; Photograph by A. J. Wyatt

Kyushu. The name Karatsu means literally "China port"; the port of Karatsu lies just across the Tsushima Strait from Korea. Korean potters at Karatsu built Korean-type sloping kilns, and the wares they made were almost identical to those made at the same time in southern Korea. These wares were made by the coiling method, beaten into shape with paddles, and decorated with a dark brown iron glaze.

The Karatsu kilns made both utility and tea ceremony wares. Many pieces originally intended for everyday use by the peasants were taken by the tea masters for use in the tea ceremony.

Karatsu were made in a number of different types. Those covered with a plain ash slip glaze are called Muji-*garatsu*, or undecorated Karatsu; wares with painted designs in underglaze iron are called *E-garatsu* (decorated Karatsu), and the designs depict trees, plants, floral patterns, and birds (Ills. 14 and 33). *Temmoku* Karatsu has a black glaze; *Madara-garatsu* (spotted, or mottled, Karatsu) has a devitrified white glaze over the feldspar-clay ground, whereas *Korai-garatsu*, or Korean Karatsu, is glazed partly in white and partly in an amber color. Wares were also made in Oribe style.

Hagi

The kilns at Hagi in the province of Nagate were also begun by naturalized Korean potters. The kilns were built about 1600 and produced tea ceremony wares during the first part of the seventeenth century. These wares have a crackled grayish white glaze.

Banko

In the middle of the nineteenth century a Karatsu-type ware was made at the Banko kiln in the province of Isé. We are told by Augustus Franks that in 1850 Yusetsu, a native of the village of Obuke, near Kuwana, in Isé, founded a factory at Kuwana.

During the seventeenth century Banko Kichibei had established a kiln on the outskirts of Edo, but the existence of this kiln was quite short-lived. Mori Yusetsu had discovered Banko Kichibei's receipts for glazes and enamels among his father's stock—his father was a dealer in waste paper—and after studying these, decided to become a potter. He bought the Banko seal from a grandson of the original potter, took the name of Banko for himself, and started work at Kuwana (Ill. 34).

The Banko factory is still in existence; it is well known for small teapots of reddish brown stoneware. The lids usually have decorative small knobs in the shape of animals.

34. *Two Banko ware pieces:* Left, *flower vase, 1875.* Victoria and Albert Museum, London. Right, *jar, 1870.* Metropolitan Museum of Art, New York

5

Arita and Imari

The village of Arita is about fifty miles north of Nagasaki. Ri-Sampei, a Korean, first founded a porcelain factory there in the early seventeenth century, and ever since that time other porcelain makers have gathered there, making it a great center of the industry. Ri-Sampei discovered good materials at Idsumi-yama, a hill near the valley in which Arita is situated, in the county of Matsuara. The official catalog of the Japanese section of the Centennial Exposition of 1876 in Philadelphia states:

Within a very limited circuit (of Arita), not half a mile in diameter, there are found imbedded in the rock at different places, all the materials necessary for the glaze, for the "craquelé" etc., the best being of such good quality, that after being powdered and decanted, it is used without any further mixture for the finest ware, the so-called egg-shell porcelain.

The Lord Nabeshima, who governed the district until the revolution, appointed an official to act as overseer of the quarrying, and this man set up a gate on the road to prevent unathorized persons from entering and removing materials from the quarries. After 1868, this system of control was abolished and the clay was needlessly wasted. The first porcelain wares to be produced were in underglaze blue and white *(sometsuke)*, with decoration in a great variety of patterns and motifs: landscapes, flowers, birds, fish, animals, human figures, and geometrical designs.

Kakiemon

Kakiemon I (1596–1666) is generally credited with being the first Japanese potter to apply overglaze enamels successfully to porcelain (Ills. 15 and 35).

Born Sakaida Kizaiemon, the first Kakiemon was the son of Sakaida Ensai, a native of Kakaida in Fujioka Prefecture. Ensai is reputed to have been a man of some social standing who wrote poetry. The family moved to Shiraishi in Hizen, there becoming tile makers. Then they moved to Nangawara, near Arita, where Ensai and his son learned from a Chinese potter how to make blue and white porcelain.

Although Kakiemon's name and reputation are based entirely on his enameled porcelain, he probably did not begin to produce these wares until he was about fifty, and another ten years elapsed before he found the secret of applying gold. According to tradition, he came into contact in Arita with a pottery merchant named Tokuyemon, who had learned the art of overglaze enameling from a Chinese potter in Nagasaki. Tokuyemon in turn taught Kakiemon, and together they experimented to perfect the art. An old document in the Kakiemon family says that in the following year, "the year of the galleon" (i.e., the year the Dutch galleon came (1646), Tokuyemon took the

35. *Dish, Kakiemon ware, Arita. Seventeenth century. Kakiemon I was the first Japanese potter to use overglaze enamels successfully on porcelain. As he and his two sons worked side by side making these decorated wares, the work of the three is very similar.* Metropolitan Museum of Art, Rogers Fund

enameled pieces to Nagasaki, where he sold them to the Dutch and Chinese as well as to the agent of Maeda Toshitune, lord of Kaga. Another traditional version says that Maeda Toshitune founded the kiln at Kutani, and sent Goto Saijiro to learn the secrets of enameling porcelain from Kakiemon in Arita.

Brinkley's well-known version, in his *Japan, Its History, Arts and Literature,* is that Tokuyemon and Kakiemon set out in 1646 to visit China to learn the secrets of overglaze enamel decoration on porcelain. However, in Nagasaki, they made the acquaintance of the master of a Chinese junk, who was able to supply them with the necessary information, and so instead of continuing their journey to China, they returned to Arita. In view of the dire penalties meted out to anyone who went abroad, or even took shorter excursions, as exemplified in the fate of Goto Saijiro in Kutani (see Chapter 7), this story seems most unlikely.

There are two traditional versions of how Kakiemon acquired his art name. The family kiln at Nangawara was in the domain of the lords of Nabeshima, and one version is that when Sakaida Kizaiemon made a *tokonama* decoration *(okimono)* in the form of two red persimmons *(kaki)* and presented it to Nabeshima Katsushigi, the daimyo was so pleased with it that he gave its maker the name of Kakiemon. The other version is that the name was derived from the persimmon red color of the overglaze he used.

Kakiemon was the first potter to produce designs in the Japanese style of simplicity and blank spaces, known as *yamato-e,* in contrast to the crowded Chinese style of decoration that covered the entire surface. His patterns rarely covered more than one third to one half the surface to be decorated, thereby contrasting with and enchancing the beauty of the cream white body and glaze. The patterns, very light and delicate in nature, often with no apparent outline, are generally of flowers, birds, or butterflies, naturalistically painted. A characteristic of the wares is a line of iron red glazing around the edge called *kuchi-beni* (mouth rouge).

The colors used are mainly a soft orange red, the color of a ripe persimmon, and an azure blue, along with a pale yellow, lavender blue, purple, grass green, and black, all sparingly applied. Some pieces have gold highlights, but gold is never used for lavish display as on Imari wares.

The designs are outlined in black or red (for the red and yellow sections). The black is a fine brushstroke of cobalt, but as it was applied on the glaze after the firing, it failed to turn blue. Nabeshima designs were also outlined in cobalt, but since they were drawn directly on the unglazed biscuit, the subsequent high temperature firing brought out the blue.

Kakiemon porcelain wares were always of the best quality and made by expert craftsmen, in contrast to Imari porcelains, which were produced for export and for everyday use. The clay used for the body was far superior to that used for Imari, and the pieces underwent two bakings before enameling, the first firing for the underglazed milk white porcelain bodies, called *nigoshi-de*, and the second for the very thin glaze.

Kakiemon wares were exported to Europe by way of the Dutch settlement at Nagasaki during the second half of the seventeenth century. Along with the so-called old Imari wares, they exerted a tremendous influence on European taste and resulting porcelain production in Europe.

Vestiges of huge European collections of old Japanese wares can still be seen in many countries. In England Queen Mary II collected Japanese porcelain. Although born an English princess, she lived for some years in Holland with her consort William of Orange (who became William III of England) before they were called to England in 1686 to take up the succession, and so she was in Holland during the time when the importation of Japanese wares was at its height. It is interesting to note that her collection includes many fine pieces of Kakiemon, some of which may still be seen at Hampton Court. The first mention of Kak-

iemon ware in the Dutch East India Company inventory was in 1684, and therefore Queen Mary must have been among the first to collect this ware.

Kakiemon porcelain imported at that time is also to be found in English country houses of the same period. Whether Queen Mary's collection had anything to do with the appreciation of these wares in England is a matter for speculation, but her collection was much admired; John Evelyn remarked on it in his diary more than once.

The largest collection of Japanese porcelains was at Dresden, accumulated by Augustus the Strong and installed in the "Japanese Palace." It is a later collection than Queen Mary's, much of it having been bought in 1715 and 1717. The collection was moved to the Johanneum in 1875 and opened to the public the following year, but through subsequent sales, as well as disastrous losses during the Second World War, just a small proportion remains, including only about twenty pieces of Kakiemon.

In France the Prince of Condé assembled a collection of Kakiemon wares between 1735 and 1740, and other collections may be found throughout Europe. The Baroque palaces of Germany, Austria, Hungary, and Sweden, St. James's Palace and Windsor Castle in England, as well as country houses in those countries, all have their share, although the origin of the Japanese pieces was not always recognized. In a Dresden inventory of 1721 there is a note saying that Augustus the Strong was in the habit of calling Kakiemon ware "Old Indian Ware," and old inventories of English country houses speak of "China ware" or even "Old East Indian ware."

Kakiemon porcelain was so well liked that soon copies were being made everywhere. The first were the Japanese copies, starting about 1672, when the secrets of overglaze enameling began to be generally known. They were made at kilns around Arita and at Kutani, many of them being almost impossible to distinguish from wares made at the Kakiemon kiln, although none of them have the fine milk white body of the originals.

Fast on the heels of these came the Chinese copies, made soon after 1700. The Chi-

36. *Three pieces made at Bow, England, c. 1755. Quail design, showing Kakiemon influence.* Private Collection; Photograph by V. R. Pepper

nese pieces usually have underglaze blue in place of the overglaze blue enamel of the originals. They were probably made for export to Europe to compete with the Japanese pieces. But copies were soon being made in Europe too. Since Kakiemon is fairly simple and naturalistic in decoration, it was much easier to copy than the more complicated Chinese designs.

The earliest European copies were made at the Meissen factory near Dresden, the first being produced about 1728. France followed suit shortly afterward in the 1730s. Dutch enamelers were also soon busily decorating porcelain blanks imported "in the white" from Japan and China.

English decorators copied from the Meissen versions, rather than from the original Kakiemon pieces. Chelsea produced some pieces between 1749 and 1752 bearing the raised anchor mark, but many more are to be found with the red anchor mark (1752–1756). Bow made copies during the 1750s (Ill. 36), and Worcester followed closely thereafter.

The Kakiemon family has continued to make fine porcelain wares down to the present day. It is now in its thirteenth generation.

The wares of the first three Kakiemon are very similar, the father and sons working together side by side. Kakiemon IV and Kakiemon V both died young, and the wares they produced were not as fine as those of their predecessors. A revival took place in the time of Kakiemon VI, under his uncle's direction, and wares produced during this period are considered by the Japanese to be among the finest. Kakiemon VII, who marked his wares with the *fuku* (good fortune) mark in a double square, continued to make wares in the same tradition, but they are not regarded as particularly notable. Kakiemon VIII used the *saki-kaki* mark (the wine persimmon mark). Kakiemon IX (1776–1836) and Kakiemon X (1805–1860) produced mostly blue and white wares.

Kakiemon XI, called Shibonsuke (1845–1917), worked in the traditional style and generally used the *fuku* mark in a double square. However, during the Meiji era, when the traditional arts were pushed aside and forgotten in the wild pursuit of Western ideas, the family became very poor and had to sell their mark. Kakiemon XII (born 1879) continued the traditional art, as does his son Kakiemon XIII, who assumed his title in March 1963.

The porcelains being produced by the present members of the family are still of the highest quality, and are relatively expensive when compared to the modern Imari wares. The body is made from a blend of three types of porcelain stone from the mountains in the Arita area. This stone is carefully selected. After being crushed, screened, and mixed, only about 30 percent of it is considered good enough to be used. The resulting wares are very fine copies of the old ones, hard to distinguish from the originals.

Imari Wares

The name Imari ware covers porcelain made at a number of different kilns and exported from the port of Imari. The kilns

37. *Blue and white porcelain bottle, Imari ware, Arita. Seventeenth century.* Courtesy of the Brooklyn Museum, Carll H. De Silver Fund

were at Arita (with six branch kilns at Ichinose, Hirose, Nagawara, Ou-he, Hokao, Kuromuta), and at Okawaji, Shira-ishi, Shida, Koshida, Yoshia, and Matsugaya. Although Imari ware was exported in large quantities to Europe, where it exerted great influence on porcelain manufacture there, it was never solely an export ware. It has always been popular in Japan, but less so than Kutani ware, and the pieces are of a more common nature.

The first pieces were in blue and white (Ill. 37). Although Kakiemon was the first Japanese potter to work successfully in overglaze enamels, the secret soon spread to other potters in the Arita area, and they also began to decorate with overglaze enamels. These wares were first called *aka-e*, or red painted wares, in contrast to *gosu*, or blue and white, even though they included blue and white decoration.

38. *Dishes, Arita. Nineteenth century.* Metropolitan Museum of Art, Gift of Charles Stewart Smith

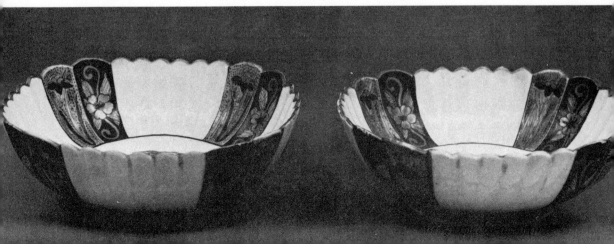

39. *Armorial dish, Arita ware. Eighteenth century. A similar piece, from the British Museum, is shown in Soame Jenyns's* Japanese Porcelain. *He identifies the coat of arms as that of the Portuguese family of Brandao, quartered with the arms of the Carvalhais and Vasconcelos families.* Philadelphia Museum of Art; Photograph by A. J. Wyatt

Old documents of the year 1662 mention the *aka-e machi* ("red picture street," or street of enamelers), which was part of the main street in Arita. There were eleven houses of porcelain decorators on the street; these artists added enamel overglaze colors to the blue and white wares brought to them. The style of decoration they used was developed to please the Dutch market.

The first overglaze enamel wares were in three colors, but other colors were soon added (Ills. 38 and 39). For the period we are surveying here, the following categories will suffice:

1. *sometsuke:* underglaze blue and white
2. *sansai:* three color or Old Japan
3. *nishikide:* brocade Imari
4. *kinrande:* gold designs on a red enamel ground

Sometsuke wares can be found in a great variety of patterns and motifs, although flowers, birds, fish, and animals were the most popular in the later period.

Imari *sansai,* or old Japan wares, are decorated in underglaze blue with overglaze red on a white ground, the designs being highlighted in gold. Most of the surface is covered with decoration, both inside and out. A basket of flowers is a very popular central motif on these wares (Ill. 40).

Imari *nishikide,* or brocade Imari, uses more colors. Originally it was copied from the five color wares of the late Ming and early Ching dynasties of China. The Japanese call any mass of brilliant colors a "brocade," the name being derived from this practice rather than from any resemblance to actual brocades. The designs cover almost all the surface, with hardly any ground glaze left visible. The colors chiefly used are underglaze blue and overglaze enamels in brick red, gold, turquoise green, lemon yellow, and purple.

Imari *kinrande,* or gold-on-red Imari, employs gold Chinese-style designs on the typical Imari red background (Ill. 44). Kutani wares also have gold decoration on a red ground, but the Imari and Kutani reds

40. *Late nineteenth century Imari* sansai, *or old Japan ware. Blue underglaze with red overglaze enamel, highlighted in gold. The basket of flowers in the center is a transfer. The poor quality blotchy decoration must have been made at high speed for the flourishing export market. Beware of Imari wares of this period; some pieces leave much to be desired.*

41. *Imari* nishikide, *or brocade Imari, plate. Late nineteenth or early twentieth century. D. 9".*

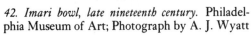

42. *Imari bowl, late nineteenth century.* Philadelphia Museum of Art; Photograph by A. J. Wyatt

43. *Imari* nishikide. *D. 12". Underglaze blue with red, green, and yellow decoration. Early twentieth century.*

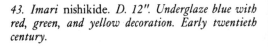

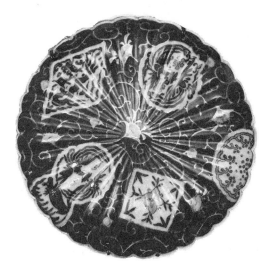

44. *Plate, Imari* kinrande, *or gold-on-red Imari. Chinese-style gold designs (Chinese grass) with green flowers on red background. Five variously shaped reserves with underglaze blue patterns, highlighted in gold. Twentieth century.* Pinney Collection

are quite different (see Color Plates 8 and 11).

A decorative pattern of symbols in underglaze blue is usually found around the rim on the underside of Imari plates and platters. Those most frequently used are the symbols of the eight Chinese Treasures, which are called *happo,* or *hachi ho,* in Japanese. They consist of a gold coin, two books, stone chimes, artemisia leaf, dragon pearl, lozenge, mirror, and rhinoceros horns (Fig. 2).

Imari wares have been made in the same tradition for the last two hundred years, but the general age of a piece is usually fairly

decoration intended to please the barbarian taste of foreigners. Morse's remarks in *Japan Day by Day,* quoted in Chapter 8, could have applied just as well to Imari. The haste and "sickening profusion" of the splashed-on decoration is as evident here as on Awata wares. Not all Imari wares of this period were badly done, however, and the collector has to exercise his own judgment when making a purchase.

In this century all kinds of Imari wares have been exported—good, bad, and indifferent. The good has some very fine deco-

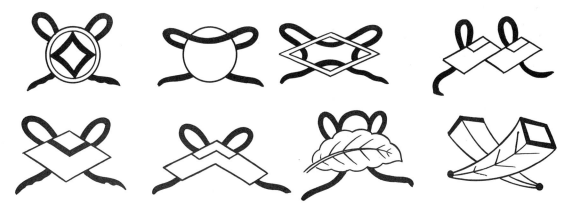

Fig. 2. The eight Chinese Treasures, often used as decoration on the underside of modern Imari wares (left to right, from top): *gold coin, dragon pearl, lozenge, two books, mirror, stone chimes, artemisia leaf, and rhinoceros horns.*

evident. As is true of all the other types of Japanese ceramics, the workmanship was finer and more painstaking before the Meiji era. Imari ware suffered more than any other at the outset of the Meiji era, probably because the brilliant colors readily lent themselves to making dreadful daubs of

ration, and the biscuit is also of good quality. The bad is of the cheap dime-store variety. The Imari wares produced since World War II are of good quality, but in my opinion the type of decoration lends itself too much to mechanical reproduction, so that the charm of the older wares is lost. Unfortunately, the

45. Imari plate, twentieth century, probably made in the 1930s. Poor quality decoration.

perfection of the machine is the antithesis of art, and no matter how beautiful a design may be, unless there is a touch of human imperfection, there is no art. Late nineteenth-century Imari wares have a warmth that, even in their badness, seems preferable to the coldness of perfection.

As a broad indication of dates, the following may be useful. If the foot rim of a piece is worn smooth through much use, the piece is old. If a piece carries a potter's mark, it was almost certainly made after 1868. If the underglaze blue is in cobalt oxide, the piece was made after 1869, the year that imported oxidized cobalt was first used at Arita. Oxidized cobalt is a brighter blue than the native cobalt and is characterized by a much more even application (see Color Plates 6 and 8).

Very bad blotchy decoration would seem to indicate that a piece was made in the first half of the Meiji era. If made on a jigger, the piece probably dates after 1915, and if the piece is very large, it was most likely made after the mid-twenties (Ill. 46). A description of the jigger and how to detect clues indicating its use are given in Chapter 13.

46. Large trencher, D. 18". Imari nishikide. Twentieth century. Well made, with several colors; delicately painted.

Nabeshima Wares

Nabeshima ware was originally made exclusively for Lord Nabeshima, feudal lord of the Arita region, after whom it was named. It was made either for his own use or for him to give to his friends. Since these wares were not made for the commercial market, little was known about them outside Japan until 1867, when some pieces were sent to the International Exposition in Paris.

The Imaizumi family, who still practice their traditional art, were the decorators of this fine porcelain. The older Nabeshima ware is generally considered to be the best porcelain ever made in Japan, the body being a pure white, with a slight bluish tinge. The only other wares that approach the perfection of the Nabeshima are the Hirado, but they were not made in the same styles.

A very high standard of production has always prevailed. In the early days only about 10 percent of the pieces were considered perfect enough for use, the poorest being discarded; even now, about half are still discarded. Clay molds were used so that the pieces would be uniform in shape.

There is a considerable difference of opinion about the date of the founding of the Nabeshima factory with imported Korean potters; dates vary from 1624 to 1672. It is generally believed that the factory was moved in 1675 to its site at Okawachi, which lies in the mountains about eight miles north of Arita. In the eighteenth century the pieces were made and biscuit fired at Okawachi. Then they were brought by retainers of the Nabeshima clan to the Imaizumi family, who lived on the *aka-e machi* in Arita, for decoration. During the decorating and subsequent firing the house was guarded by Nabeshima samurai, who marched back with the completed wares to the clan castle in the mountains.

The original Nabeshima ware was blue and white; then some celadons were made, and in the early eighteenth century *Iro-Nabeshima*, or colored Nabeshima, came into being. The colors used, which resemble watercolors, were underglaze blue, a bright soft red, a soft green, a pale yellow, and a thin purple (Ills. 47 and 48).

What is truly remarkable and unique about Nabeshima ware in comparison with all other ceramic wares produced in Japan at

47. Plate, Nabeshima ware; nineteenth century. Courtesy of the Museum of Fine Arts, Boston, Bigelow Collection

48. *Plate, Nabeshima ware; nineteenth century.* Metropolitan Museum of Art, Gift of Mrs. V. Everit Macy

that time is that the decoration on each piece of a set is exactly the same, as if it had been printed. The method the Nabeshima potters used to transfer the pattern was as follows: First, they drew the design on a piece of tissue paper with gourd charcoal; then they put the paper on the inside of the dish to be decorated, and rubbed it to transfer the pattern onto the biscuit. The process was repeated on all the pieces of the set. The outlines of the pattern were then drawn in *gosu* (cobalt), and the biscuit firing developed the pattern outlines in blue and white, ready for the overglaze enamels.

The age of Nabeshima ware is generally determined by the exactness of the application of the overglaze enamels to the underglaze outlines; the later pieces are not as carefully done. The patterns became much more crowded on nineteenth-century pieces, but the traditional designs have continued to be used by the family down through the

years; new pieces bear the same patterns. The most characteristic pieces are the plates or dishes on a high base, called *takadaizara* (Ill. 49) decorated with a comb-tooth pattern in blue and white. On the early wares the comb-tooth design was perfectly regular, but nineteenth- and twentieth-century pieces lack this regularity.

On the underside of the dishes is a "treasures" pattern in three places, transferred by the same tissue paper method. This placing of patterns on the underside is copied from the traditional style of Chinese porcelain from the Ming and later periods.

The Imaizumi family were the only enamel workers in Arita who had clan protection; all the other decorators worked commercially. In 1871 the clan system was abolished, and the Imaizumi started to work on their own. They began to make their own clay bodies and fired them in a cooperative kiln. About 1890 they built their own

49. *Nabeshima dish, nineteenth century, show-ing the high base called* takadaizara, *with comb-tooth design.* Captain and Mrs. Roger Gerry

50. *Nabeshima dish, Meiji Period (1868–1912), made by Imaizumi Imaemon in Arita.* Philadelphia Museum of Art, given by Mrs. Herbert C. Morris. Photograph by A. J. Wyatt

51. Footed dishes, Hirado ware; nineteenth century. Philadelphia Museum of Art, given by Mrs. Edgar Stone; Photograph by A. J. Wyatt

kiln, but this proved unsuccessful and they lost money and had to sell their house in 1897.

The twelfth generation, Imaizumi Imaemon, however, studied ceramics at the industrial school in Arita, and spent four years studying kiln construction and firing. After completing his studies he was able to construct a small one-chamber kiln, which enabled the family to produce Nabeshima wares successfully once again (Ill. 50).

The wares now being produced are of fine quality in refined taste—technically, almost equal to the old specimens.

Hirado Wares

Like Imari, Hirado wares derive their name from the place of export, not from the site of the kilns. The Mikawachi factory, situated in the village of Use, about six miles south of Arita, was a private factory of the prince of Hirado from 1751 to 1843. Only after the middle of the nineteenth century were the wares on the open market and exported from the port of Hirado (Ill. 51).

Under the patronage of the Matsuura family, princes of Hirado, the Mikawachi kilns produced some very fine porcelain. These pieces were unmarked. After 1843, when a lower grade of wares was produced, the pieces carried a mark.

Hirado wares are famous for their fine milk white porcelain bodies, intricate modeling, and the delicacy of the decoration on the blue and white pieces. Brinkley tells us that the stone for the body was brought from Amakusa, and that not more than five or six feet in every hundred were used; the stone was laboriously pulverized and strained. Satsuma ash was imported at great expense and mixed with the Amakusa stone, the resulting paste being milk white and as fine as pipe clay. The glaze was equally pure and smooth, with a velvety luster.

In the *sometsuke* the underglaze decoration is in a pale delicate blue of a distinctive soft quality, the cobalt being imported from China (Ill. 52). The exquisitely painted designs include landscapes, flowers, and trees, as well as the popular motif of Chinese boys playing under a pine tree. The number of boys depicted depended on the quality of the ware—the best had seven boys, the next had five, and the ordinary ware had only three.

This type of ware is still being produced today. The body is of the finest quality, and the decorations are very carefully done.

Another type of Mikawachi porcelain ware was ornamented with designs in relief. This decoration was produced by painting with a brush dipped in slip.

52. Jar, Hirado ware, c. 1870. Metropolitan Museum of Art, Macy Collection, Gift of Mrs. V. Everit Macy

Eggshell porcelain, a paper-thin glossy translucent porcelain enameled in various colors, was used to make small pieces for export from the mid-nineteenth century onward. Augustus Franks tells us in his *Japanese Pottery* that the pieces were turned on the potter's wheel, and the material used, which came from the island of Amakusa, or Goto, was softer and tougher than that from Idsumi-yama.

The Japanese collection at the Philadelphia Centennial Exposition in 1876 included a teacup with handle and a saucer, both of European form, in eggshell porcelain. They were painted in red with gilding, and had six oblong white panels, each of which contained a figure of a poet. These pieces were made expressly for the Philadelphia Exposition. (See Ill. 78 for a similar decoration on Kutani pieces.)

Hirado wares also include small ornamental objects such as charming models of children, animals, swans, or branches of flowering shrubs.

6

Kyoto

Kyoto was the western capital, the city of the emperor and his court for almost eleven hundred years. From the eighth century, when it was founded by the Emperor Kammu and called Heian, through the civil wars, when it was almost razed, through the splendor of the Momoyama Period of the sixteenth century, to the Meiji Restoration in 1868, it remained a city of culture and refinement.

Beauty and good taste were to be found everywhere; artists of all kinds considered the quiet dreamy atmosphere of the old capital stimulating. It inspired the soft refined beauty of their ceramic wares, so the Japanese tell us. Kenzan's friend and patron, Prince Rinnoji-no-miya, said that even the nightingales sang more sweetly in Kyoto than in Edo.

A Kyoto accent was considered to be the indication of a cultivated person, because of its association with the court and literature. After the shogunate had been established in Edo at the beginning of the seventeenth century and the emperor had no more political authority, the court devoted its attention to poetry, music, and the fine arts, with the result that Kyoto became the cultural center of the country.

Craftsmen had been producing exquisite articles for the court since the city was first built, using as their inspiration all the beautiful things imported by the aristocracy from China and other parts of Asia. Even after the government had passed to Edo, Kyoto still remained the center of production for luxury articles.

In the sixteenth century Kyoto was the chief mercantile city of Japan, although it was not a seaport. Kyoto-owned ships sailed all over the eastern Pacific, going even as far as Siam, and the goods they carried were transported between Kyoto and the ports of Sai and Osaka by way of the Yodo River. After the country was closed to foreign trade in the seventeenth century, memories remained and influenced the arts produced there.

Kyoto's narrow streets could be covered by drawing canvas blinds across from one side to the other, keeping off the hot summer sun and providing welcome shade in the humid heat. Some streets had arcades to shelter shoppers from the sun and rain; bamboo curtains hung from the arcades protected the shops from dust. Each shop also had a curtain (*noren*) in front of its door, the curtain being decorated with an animal, symbol, or a number to identify the shop. Traditional potters, whose families run into many generations, are called *noren* potters, a name derived from this curtain with the family crest on it.

Shutters on the street side of a shop could be raised or slid aside to reveal the shopkeeper and his assistants sitting amid their goods on a raised area covered with *tatami* (a pressed rice-straw mat overlaid with woven rushes). The customer did not enter the *tatami* area, but did his shopping from the edge of the street.

Some type of handicraft was carried on in nearly every house in the city, and members of the same trade lived side by side on certain streets. Where the Tokaido, the old road from Edo (Tokyo), entered the city at Awataguchi, there were kilns for baking pottery. Other potters settled in various areas around the capital, and to this day there is a street of potters (Teapot Lane) on the hillside near Kiyomizu.

Kyoto wares hold the distinction of having been marked with the potter's name or seal from early days, in contrast to wares from other kilns, which are known by their kiln name. The Kyoto potter was an individual artist operating his private kiln; and an artist was a man to be respected. Not only did he have his own style of decoration, but the blend of clays he used was individual as well. Unlike the Arita area, where there were large deposits of clay in a state ready to be used, in Kyoto potters had to use clays brought from other places, and these clays had to be blended together to be workable. Each potter created his own particular blend. Individual Kyoto potters have a long history of working each in his own style, a tradition that continues unbroken today.

Kyoto wares fall into three main types: Raku ware, Awata ware, and Kiyomizu ware, the two last together called Ninsei ware.

Raku Wares

Raku wares have been made in Kyoto since 1580. Today there are two distinct branches of potters making Raku-*yaki*. The *hon-gama* (principal kiln) is the legitimate line of successors to the Raku seal; the family name of these potters is Tanaka, and they are now in their fourteenth generation. The *wake-gama*, or branch kilns, are operated by potters working in the Raku style in a number of areas.

The first maker of these wares was called Chōjirō (1516–1595); he was the son of a Korean potter who settled in Kyoto and made roof tiles. The making of roof tiles was

an important industry in Kyoto. Houses were constructed of wood, and in consequence there were frequent disastrous fires. During the seventeenth century edicts were issued that all the houses in town had to be built with tile roofs.

Chōjirō and his brother Jokei made roof tiles for the Shogun Hideyoshi's pleasure pavilion, the *ju-raku-tei*, and Rikyū, Hideyoshi's favorite tea master, had them make some utensils for the tea ceremony. As a great honor Rikyū gave Chōjirō his own old family name of Tanaka, having himself been given the new family name of Sen by Hideyoshi. Chōjirō is considered the first generation of the Raku line of potters, although Hideyoshi gave the seal with the character "raku" to Chōjirō's brother Jokei, who is known as the second generation. Jokei adopted Raku as a family name.

The legitimate successor to a line of potters is the one to whom the present holder of the title entrusts the secrets of his art. These are never written down, but bequeathed orally either to a son, if there is one capable of holding the succession, or to a promising pupil. This practice can create considerable confusion for the historian, as some families appear to have had an amazing number of generations in a few short years.

Raku ware is a soft, light, thickly glazed type of pottery, essentially the product of small family kilns. When Edward Morse visited the twelfth Raku, he noted that the oven used for the teabowls was so small it could hold only one bowl at a time. The bowls are baked at a low temperature, the firing being similar to that used in tile making.

The wares are formed in two different ways. One is by coiling, thin ropes of clay being coiled around and built up into the shape of the bowl. The foot rim is a separate coil placed at the base, the whole being smoothed with the fingers, but the coils always being apparent. The other way is to form the bowl with the fingers from a lump of clay, and to shape and refine it with the aid of a bamboo spatula.

The irregularities that make each piece individual are the prized qualities in Raku ware. The marks of the bamboo cutting

53. *Two Raku ware pottery teabowls, with bamboo tea whisk. Meiji Period.* Philadelphia Museum of Art, teabowls given by Mrs. John Reilly through Mrs. William Henry Fox; tea whisk given by Y. Hattori of Kyoto; Photograph by A. J. Wyatt

knife are deeply appreciated; the uneven surface, unsymmetrical shape, and varied color are other distinctive qualities.

The teabowl had to have walls thick enough not to conduct the heat so that the bowl could be held comfortably in the hands, but it also had to keep the tea hot at the same time. The thick soft walls of Raku ware perform this task admirably. The bowl must also fit the hands comfortably—it is never a perfect round, and the rim must not be straight, lest it feel unyielding to the mouth.

A portion near the base of a teabowl is always left unglazed so that the material forming the body may be seen and appreciated; the clays used are mostly the iron-bearing clays of Kyoto. There are a number of points to be considered when judging teabowls. Among them is the shape of the pool of tea in the bowl, which should be interesting, but in good taste. There are also various points concerning the base: It should have a pleasant roughness for the hands, but it must not be so uneven that the bowl will not stand steadily on the floor.

Two different glazes are used on Raku teabowls: one black and the other red, both thick and lustrous. These colors are considered to make the best contrast to the bright green of the powdered tea. The black Raku ranges in color from deep shiny black to a red brown; the red Raku is of a soft salmon red, sometimes with a little green or white in it. Both are low-fired lead glazes that are allowed to flow down the bowl unevenly.

In the tea set given to Mrs. Jack Gardner of Boston by Okakura Kakuzō (who was curator at the Museum of Fine Arts, Boston) there is a pottery badger incense case by Raku Kichibei (late eighteenth century), an ash dish by Raku Ryonyu IX, 1800, and a pottery teabowl "Black Peony" (Ill. 23) by Raku Seisai (early nineteenth century). (Famous teabowls were given names.) The teabowl in Ill. 54, made by the twelfth generation Raku Kichizaemon, was made with gray clay, with a brilliant black glaze having three large splashes of dull red. The maker of this bowl was mentioned by Edward Morse in his *Japan Day by Day*, as Morse visited him at his Kyoto home.

The present (fourteenth) Raku uses the same kilns that have been used since the time of the eleventh Raku. There are two of them, one for the black Raku and one for the red, the red being fired at a lower temperature than the black. Both kilns are in the backyard of the same house in Kyoto where the family has lived and worked since the time of the third Raku.

Teabowls can be found in various sizes and shapes. Large bowls were intended for thick pasty tea and smaller ones for thin foamy tea, and different teabowls have always been made for winter and summer use. Those made for winter are higher, with smaller openings, in order to conserve the heat of the tea; summer ones are wider so that there is more surface, to increase the cooling. The teabowl in Ill. 54 is a shallow summer one; in Mrs. Gardner's tea set (Ill. 23) both a summer and a winter one are shown.

54. *Raku teabowl, made by Kichizaemon, twelfth generation, c. 1880. This teabowl* (cha-wan) *is shallow and curved to a small foot. It is of dark gray clay with brilliant black glaze having three large splashes of dull red.* Metropolitan Museum of Art, Gift of Howard Mansfield

55. Vase (shakutate) *of red Raku ware, Kyoto; twentieth century. This is the type used in the tea ceremony to hold the water ladle and the fire tongs.* Metropolitan Museum of Art, Macy Collection, Gift of Mrs. V. Everit Macy

56. Raku ornament in the form of an old woman. Tokyo, 1875. Victoria and Albert Museum

Since Raku wares have a crackled glaze and a soft porous body, they permit liquid to seep into the body of the ware. In the course of time, however, with much use, the pores close and the wares no longer leave a damp ring where they have stood. Many ornaments are made in Raku ware (Ill. 56).

Ninsei

Nonomura Seibei, known by the artist name of Ninsei, was a Kyoto potter. There seems to be considerable doubt about his exact birth date, but it is generally said that he was born and raised in Tamba and learned his potter's craft both there and in Seto. He moved to Kyoto during the first half of the seventeenth century, after the Tokugawa regime had become established at Edo, and founded a kiln on the western edge of the city. There he came under the patronage of the prince-abbot of the Ninna-ji, a large temple at Saga close by, and began to produce decorated wares with overglaze enamel designs.

Kakiemon, in Arita, had discovered the secret of decorating porcelain with overglaze enamels only a short while before, but the two artists favored entirely different styles. Ninsei's decoration was in the traditional style, covering the whole surface, but Kakiemon rarely covered more than one third to one half of the area, contrasting his decoration with the beauty of the glazed surface. Ninsei's work was greatly influenced by the lacquer wares, many of his pieces having a black glaze as background to the enameled designs (Ill. 18).

Ninsei established and worked at kilns in many parts of Japan, and in consequence a wide variety of wares are referred to as Ninsei-*yaki*, some being in faience and some in semiporcelain. His wares are famous for the closeness and lightness of the body, and for the regular closely crackled glazes that enabled the enamels to adhere.

His influence has been far reaching, imitations being made by master potters as well as by those less adept. Mokubei, Ninami, Dōhachi, Eiraku Hozen, and Eiraku Wazen all copied his works, but put their own seals on their wares.

Kenzan

Ogata Shinsei, known by the artist name of Kenzan, was a pupil and follower of Ninsei. Unlike Ninsei, who came from a humble family, Kenzan came from a family that had been wealthy and aristocratic for a long time; they had served the Ashikagas for seven generations. His father, a rich dry-goods merchant, was also a good painter and calligrapher, and Kenzan himself was a poet before he became a potter, and was famous for his calligraphy. Ninsei gave Kenzan a copy of his notes, now in the possession of the Yamato Bunkakan Museum, and Kenzan made a notation inside that he had rewritten them, as they were in the language of a country workman, full of slang and dialect.

Kenzan's brother Kōrin was a celebrated painter. Together the brothers produced a number of ceramic pieces (Ill. 57).

In contrast to Ninsei, Kenzan was essentially a great decorator and not a particularly skillful thrower; many of the pieces he decorated had been thrown by assistants. His wares are in a soft low-fired faience, similar to Raku, and he favored simple shapes that lent themselves well to his painting and calligraphy. His square dishes are famous. His decoration was free and bold, painted in outline or flat designs, with a gift for understatement.

As Kenzan had no son to succeed him, he adopted one of Ninsei's natural sons (Ihachi), who took the title of Kenzan II. In fact, the Kenzan title was transmitted from one potter to another in recognition of style and not through any blood relationship. The third and fourth Kenzans were self-appointed successors to the title. Miura Kenya made wares in the Kenzan style, but renounced the title, transmitting it to Ogata Shigekicki, who became Kenzan VI.

Miura Kenya (1821–1889) was born in Kyoto. He had his first kiln at Fukagawa, and later moved to Mukojima. About 1860 he settled at Asakusa, in the northern part of

57. Square dish, buff pottery, potted by Kenzan, painted by Kōrin, and signed by both. Design of Jurojin, God of Longevity, reading a scroll. Courtesy of the Brooklyn Museum, A. Augustus Healy Fund

58. Bowl made by Miura Kenya. Raku ware, covered with a dark green glaze decorated with large white flowers with yellow centers. Victoria and Albert Museum

Tokyo, where his kiln was so small that it could be used in his house.

Miura Kenya's pottery beads were very popular, and he was famous for his copies of wares made by Haritsu, a potter who lived at the end of the seventeenth century. Haritsu had learned pottery from Kenzan and decorative lacquer work from Korin. He combined both arts, inlaying pottery in lacquer pieces, and using lacquer work on Raku ware, ornamenting the latter with shapes of flowers, grass, insects, and so on (Ill. 58).

Ogata Shigekicki (Kenzan VI) is famous for being the teacher of Bernard Leach, an English potter, and Tomimoto Kenkichi, who together held the title of Kenzan VII.

At the time when Leach sought him out, Kenzan VI was an old man whose art and works had been pushed aside by the new commercialism. He lived in poverty in a little house in the northern slums of Tokyo. No one wanted to buy the traditional-style wares that he made, and like many others trained in the earlier age, he could not adapt his style to the new ways. However, Leach tells us, many pieces now in Western collections said to have been made by Kenzan I were in actual fact made by Kenzan VI, or his predecessor Miura Kenya.

Bernard Leach, like so many before him, went to Japan to teach Western methods and stayed to learn Eastern ways. Trained as an artist, he went to Japan in 1909 as a young man with the intention of giving art lessons. About two years after his arrival, he attended a sort of garden party in Tokyo, given at an artist friend's house, where the guests were invited to write or paint on unglazed pots provided for that purpose. The pots were subsequently fired in a portable kiln set up in the garden. Each guest was able to see his pot come out of the kiln and be set on tiles where the crackle began to form and the true colors of the decoration emerge. This kind of party has been considered a gentlemanly entertainment for a very long time.

As a direct result of this experience, Leach looked for a teacher to instruct him in the art, and found Ogata Kenzan, who agreed to build him a kiln and teach him the traditional recipes. Leach spent nine consecutive years in Japan, learning all that he could of the potter's art (Ill. 59). He also persuaded Tomimoto Kenkichi to study with him under the guidance of Kenzan VI. Leach and Tomimoto together held the rightful title of Kenzan VII, being the only pupils of Kenzan who legally mastered the art. Both Leach and Tomimoto began their careers as potters making Raku ware. Leach then turned his attention to making stoneware and found much inspiration in Korean pottery. On his return to England he began to make English slipware in the tradition of the seventeenth century. Tomimoto's work is discussed in Chapter 9.

59. *Four pieces by Bernard Leach: Stoneware jug, gray body; off-white stoneware glaze inside and out, then outside dipped again in rusty brown iron glaze. The porcelain bowl has a creamy glaze with blue gray underglaze around the rim and iron brushstrokes over the glaze. Porcelain bottle with green tea dust glaze; iron brushwork turns tea dust to rusty* kaki. *Mug has* black temmoku *glaze breaking to rust where it is thin.* Frank Stoke

Awata Wares

Of the two kinds of Kyoto wares known as Ninsei-*yaki,* those made in faience are called Awata ware and those made in porcelain are Kiyomizu ware (Ill. 60).

The Awata wares have a soft appearance, with a pale yellow finely crackled glaze. The body is a light yellowish gray. During the Meiji era flowers, birds, and landscapes were popular motifs, and lavish amounts of gold were used. The main enamel colors were emerald green, lavender, and blue, with red, white, and silver used sparingly.

In the 1880s there were twelve families of potters working at the Awata kilns, each having a kiln and employing workmen. The best known of these potters were Kinkozan Sobei, Taizan Yohei, and Bunzo Hozan (who were all descendants of the original potters), and Tanzan Seikai.

kuemon) began work at Awata in 1693. On the other hand, Kato Tokuro says that the first potter was called Genemon Kobashi (the family calling themselves Kagi-ya) and that he established a kiln at Awataguchi between 1644 and 1647. However, both agree that the potter of the third generation, Kagiya Mohei (Brinkley) or Kibei (Kato), was appointed to the Tokugawa court and took the name of Kinkozan. The Kobayashi family called themselves Kinkozan from this time onward, and, fortunately, thereafter we have less confusion over their names.

Sobei made some porcelain as well as the faience for which he is better known. Assisted by a large staff of potters, he produced a vast amount of export wares, which are signed with the painted Kinkozan mark in red. The family continued until the eighth generation (Ill. 61).

60. Water jug, kiyomizu ware, eighteenth century. Philadelphia Museum of Art, given by Marion E. Potts; Photograph by A. J. Wyatt

KINKOZAN

Kinkozan Sobei, who was active during the latter part of the nineteenth century and early in the twentieth, was the sixth generation of the Kagiya family. According to Brinkley, the first potter (called Kagiya To-

TAIZAN

According to some authorities, the Taizan mark was first used during the seventeenth century, but others state that it does not appear until the early part of the eighteenth century.

The first generation was a potter named Tokuro, whose son Yohei succeeded him. He called himself Taizan Yohei, and the oldest son of each subsequent generation was

61. Bottle with cloisonné, Kinkozan, 1895. The mark reads Nihon Kyoto Kin-kō-zan zo. *Pair of Satsuma tea caddies.* Fogg Art Museum, Gift of William H. Fogg

62. *Incense burner* (koro) *is Satsuma-style ware, made at Awata by Taizan, 1850–1860.* Philadelphia Museum of Art, given by Mrs. William Morrow Roosevelt; Photograph by A. J. Wyatt

named Taizan Yohei. The family continued as far as the ninth generation; the kiln was closed in 1894. The wares are skilfully decorated, and the body is of a good quality (Ill. 62).

HOZAN

The first Bunzo Hozan came to Awata from Omi early in the seventeenth century, and his descendants continued there as potters for several generations. Morse commented on the originality, diversity, and beauty of the wares bearing the Hozan mark, and said that in those respects they exceeded all other Awata pottery (Ill. 63).

TANZAN

Tanzan Seikai was originally educated for the medical profession. He settled in Awata during the early 1850s, but did not assume his art name until 1869. Kato Tokuro says that when Prince Shoreiin established a pottery exchange in 1853, he ordered Tanzan to produce Awata pottery.

Tanzan had two sons, Yoshitaro and Matsuro, both of whom succeeded him at the kiln. Tanzan made porcelain as well as pottery, and produced many showy pieces for the export trade (Ill. 64).

Kiyomizu Wares

We are told in Augustus Franks's *Japanese Pottery* (1880) that the Kiyomizu factory was started by Otowaya Kurobei and others who came from Seikanji-mura, in the Horeki Period (1751–1763). Franks says:

In the beginning of the present (18th) century, Takahashi Dōhachi, Waké Kitei, and Midsukoshi Yosobei commenced to make Sometsuké, or porcelain decorated with cobalt underneath the glaze, in imitation of Arita ware, from clay imported from Idsumi-yama, in Arita, in the province of Hizen. Most of the productions were shaped by hand, and in such good taste that they have grown into favour with drinkers of tea or saké. The factories have since de-

63. Fire bowl, marked Hozan; nineteenth-century Awata ware, Kyoto. Metropolitan Museum of Art, gift of Mr. and Mrs. Samuel Colman

64. Pair of vases by Tanzan, Kyoto; nineteenth century. Metropolitan Museum of Art, Gift of Charles Stewart Smith

veloped and increased in number, and there are now eleven families of porcelain makers, of whom the more prominent are— *Kanzan Denshichi, Muruya Sahei,* and *Kameya Bunpei;* and twenty-one families of faience, notably *Takahashi Dōhachi (second generation), Waké Kitei (second generation), Kiyomidzu Kichibei, Kiyomidzu Rokubei, Seifū Yohei,* and *Mashimidsu Zoruku. Each family has its own factory independent of others, but rarely in common. The total number of factories in this district is twenty-one. Each is formed of six or seven kilns ranged side by side. The produce consists chiefly of tea and saké utensils, and occasionally of ornamental objects, such as flower vases or incense burners. They mostly belong to the Sometsuké class, but recently different coloured enamels have been used for their decoration. The latter, however, is not equal to the former, with the exception of the work of Kanzan Denshichi, who decorated with gold on red ground, in imitation of Yeiraku; and has also invented a manner of representing, in porcelain, iron inlaid with gold.*

DŌHACHI

The first Dōhachi (1737–1804) was the second son of Hachiro Takahasi, a samurai from Isé. He came to Kyoto as a young man and opened a chinaware shop. Later, he studied with Eisen and established a kiln at Awata. Ninami Dōhachi, the second of the line, the son of the first Dōhachi, also studied with Eisen. He was celebrated for porcelains decorated in Chinese-style blue and white and for pottery in the Ninsei and Kenzan style. He died about 1856.

Franks speaks of the Dōhachi at Kiyomizu in the 1880s as being the second generation, but in this he is not correct. No doubt the confusion arose because the third and fourth generations used the same marks as the second, and, as with other dynasties of potters, the works of one generation are often hard to distinguish from those of another, especially when the same seals are used.

Dōhachi III, the son of Ninami, worked at Momoyama but moved to Satsuma about 1850; he went later to Arita. His blue and white pieces are famous, particularly those

65. Bowl by Dōhachi, Kyoto; nineteenth-century Kiyomizu ware. Metropolitan Museum of Art, Gift of Mr. and Mrs. Samuel Colman

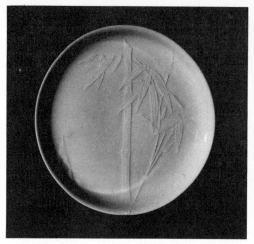

66. Dish and vase, made by Seifu III (1851–1914), Kyoto; nineteenth century. Courtesy, Museum of Fine Arts, Boston; Hoyt Collection

decorated with clouds and crows. He died in 1879, and his son, Dōhachi IV, died in 1897. Dōhachi V became president of the Kyoto Potters Association; he died in 1915. Dōhachi VI is still living.

SEIFŪ

The first potter of this line was called Seifū Yohei (1806–1863); his art name was Baihei. The son of a bookseller in Kanajawa, he went to Kyoto in 1844 and studied ceramics under Ninami Dōhachi. His kiln, where he made porcelain and some faience, was at Goyobashi.

Seifū II, called Gohei, made only porcelain. Seifū III (1851–1914) adopted all the new methods of the day, and is particularly famous for his white pieces decorated in low relief with flower and plant designs (Ill. 66). He also made celadon wares and pieces decorated with underglaze red. Wares made by the three Seifūs are so similar that it is often difficult to differentiate between them.

KITEI

This family made blue and white porcelain wares for seven generations at Gojosake, as well as pottery in the Dōhachi style. The third generation is said to have worked with Rokubei.

ROKUBEI

Rokubei I made finely decorated faience, blue and white wares, and also black Raku, for which he received the art name of Rokubei from Prince Myoin. He was the son of a farmer in Setsu Province who came

to Kyoto and built a kiln at Gojozaka with Waké Kitei in the second half of the eighteenth century. Seisai, the son of Rokubei I, became Rokubei II, and besides making similar wares to those produced by his father, was noted for his blue and white porcelain in the Chinese style and his wares with monochrome glazes. He died in 1847, according to Morse, or 1860, according to Brinkley. Rokubei III, known as Shoun, was famous for his earthenware teapots with enameled decorations of crabs. He also made a large garden lamp in blue and white porcelain, which has been in the grounds of the

67. Porcelain wine pot with polychrome enamel decoration, by Kitei, Kyoto. Late nineteenth century. Metropolitan Museum of Art, Gift of Mrs. V. Everit Macy

68. Late nineteenth-century pottery dish, probably Kyoto, has imprinted blue underglaze design with red brown edge. Greenish glaze, Japanese character fuku *(good fortune) on underside.*

Imperial Palace since 1853. Rokubei IV, Shorin, died in 1920; Rokubei V is still working in Awata. The wares of the different generations are hard to tell apart as they are similar and bear the same seals.

RENGETSU

A Kyoto potter famous for her individual style was the nun Otagaki Rengetsu. Her father was a nobleman of Isé, and she married at an early age. Unfortunately, both her husband and her only child died, and so she went into a monastery in 1823 at the age of thirty-two. There she made unglazed pots, mostly little teapots, without enamels. She modeled leaves and lotus flowers in relief on these wares, and decorated them with her poems.

A wide variety of anonymous pottery and porcelain wares made in Kyoto since the Meiji Restoration (1868) is generally referred to as Kiyomizu ware. Some pieces are decorated with a monochrome glaze, some have a polychrome enamel decoration, and others have blue and white designs on them (Ill. 68). Anonymous wares made in Kyoto prior to 1868 are generally called Kyō-*yaki*, or Kyō ware. If a piece appears to have had its enamel decoration applied by a printing or stamping device, it was almost certainly made after 1868.

Eiraku

The Zengoro family is another line of potters associated with Kyoto. The family

69. *Pottery washer for wine cups, by Zengoro Hozen, Kyoto; nineteenth-century.* Metropolitan Museum of Art, Gift of Charles Stewart Smith

name is Nishimura but Zengoro is the familiar name of these potters.

The first Zengoro was a native of Nara, where he died in 1558; his birth date is unknown. He made articles of unglazed earthenware, and is specially known for his earthenware *furo*, which are braziers used in the tea ceremony for holding charcoal fire. These particular braziers are known as Nara *furo*.

The second and third Zengoros continued to make these *furo*. The third Zengoro moved to Kyoto, where he received recognition from the tea master Kobori Enshū, who gave him a copper seal, which has also been used by the succeeding generations on their *furo*.

The family continued generation by generation to make *furo* in Kyoto. The tenth generation, called Zengoro Ryozen, received a seal from the tea master Sen-no-Ryosai as a mark of approval for his *furo*. He made other pottery wares for the tea ceremony too, as well as copies of Cochin chinaware, or *kochi yaki*, which is a type of pottery decorated in green, yellow, and aubergine glazes, applied in broad washes of color separated by fine lines of molding. He died in 1841; his son, Zengoro Hozen, carried on the making of *furo*.

Hozen (1795–1854), the eleventh generation of the Zengoro family, made a wide variety of wares, both pottery and porcelain, besides the *furo*. Like his father he made copies of Kōchi-*yaki* (Ill. 69), and he also made *sometsuke*, celadons, and wares in the Korean tradition. However, he is best known for his *kinrande* porcelain (with scarlet and gold decoration in brocade style) and his *akaji-kinga* (gold designs on a red background).

Hozen was given two seals, one gold and one silver, by Lord Harutomi of Kishu.

70. *Porcelain bottle for sweets, by Zengoro Hozen, Kyoto; nineteenth century.* Metropolitan Museum of Art, Gift of Charles Stewart Smith

71. *Pottery teabowl made by Zengoro Wazen.* Metropolitan Museum of Art, Gift of Mr. and Mrs. Samuel Colman

One seal had the name Eiraku on it; the other, Kahei Shirui. Eiraku is the Japanese pronunciation of the Chinese ideographs forming the name of the Ming Emperor Yung Lo (1403–1424), in whose reign this red and gold type of ware was first produced. The name Eiraku has been used by succeeding generations in addition to their individual artist names.

The next two generations of the Zengoro line were both sons of Hozen. The elder, Wazen, was the twelfth generation; the younger, Zenshiro, became Zengoro XIII.

In his early years Wazen (1823–1896) helped his father. They made Koto ware at Hakone, Omi, on the shores of Lake Biwa, Koto meaning "east of the lake." Koto ware is a hard porcelain decorated in underglaze blue and overglaze enamels in Chinese *wu ts'ai* style. The kiln closed in 1860.

Like his father and Dōhachi, Wazen also made bowls with designs of maple leaves and cherry blossoms, the tree trunks on the outside of the bowl and the blossoms inside.

After leaving Hakone, Wazen built a kiln in the garden of the Ninna Temple in Kyoto. While there he made tea ceremony wares for the Princess Kazu when she was married to the shogun.

Wazen's most important work was done in Kaga, where his influence still remains. He went there in 1866 on the invitation of the Lord Maeda and stayed for five years. The porcelain wares he made there are known as Kaga Eiraku; they combine underglaze blue and white (*sometsuke*) with gold designs on a red background (*akajikinga*). He also perfected the Kaga *aka-e* style, or red decorations on a white ground.

After leaving Kaga, Wazen went to Okazaki in Mikawa, where he stayed for three years. About 1875 he moved to Higashi-yama, but he was in poor health and

finally, in 1897, he died. He had no children, although he adopted a son called Sozaburo, who made very little ceramics and did not succeed to the title.

Kyokuzen and Toho were two different artist names used by Hozen's younger son Zenshiro. Apart from this, however, not much is known about him. Another potter is also often called the thirteenth Eiraku. This was Yasuke, who had been a pupil of Hozen and worked in a style very similar to his master's.

Tokuzen (1854–1910) was the fourteenth of the Zengoro line, but this generation is considered to extend to 1928, as Tokuzen's widow, Myozen, continued the work. Tokuzen worked in the family tradition and made some fine pieces. Two examples of his wares were shown in the 1876 Philadelphia Centennial Exposition. One was a pair of porcelain flower vases, decorated in gold on a red ground, with phoenixes among formal scrolls on the body and geometrical designs on the neck and foot. The other was a pair of porcelain sake cups with a celadon glaze on the outside and a gilt border.

Myozen, Tokuzen's widow, was an excellent potter. She was given a seal by Takamune Mitsui in 1912, and at the end of her life she used her name, Myozen, to mark her wares.

Shozen, a nephew of Tokuzen, became the fifteenth Zengoro. His succession to the family title was short-lived as he died in 1933.

Hozan, the sixteenth of the line, is at present living and working in Kyoto. He is variously known as Eiraku, Nishimura Zengoro, or Hozan. Besides following the traditional styles of his family, he also makes wares in his own individual style. His workmanship is excellent. The wares are made of a very thin hard porcelain, and the beautiful decoration reflects a modern trend.

7

Kutani

The small village of Kutani lies in the mountains of Kaga Province, near the northwest coast of Japan. It is a lonely place, cut off by mountains on one side from Kyoto and on the other side from the coast. The old way to Kutani was up the Daishoji River by boat. The name Kutani means nine valleys, and is descriptive of this mountain village. The feudal lords of Kaga were members of the Maeda family, which at the beginning of the seventeenth century was among the wealthiest clans in the country, its lands producing vast quantities of rice.

The history of the kiln at Kutani is wrapped in mystery. Records are lacking, and there is much disagreement about dates and even the kiln sites. One version is that in 1639 Maeda Toshiharu, whose mother was the daughter of the Shogun Hidetada, was given the rich rice-producing clan lands of Daishoji by his father. When porcelain stone was discovered at Kutani soon after this, a kiln was built by Tamura Gonzayemon, a retainer of Maeda Toshiharu, by his order. According to tradition, the kiln first produced tea ceremony wares, then blue and white wares.

It is generally believed that Maeda Toshiaki, Toshiharu's son, sent Goto Saijiro to learn the secrets of porcelain making and enameling from Kakiemon in Arita, as mentioned earlier. Goto Saijiro had previously been connected with a gold mine near Kutani. It was no easy task to gain the confidence of Kakiemon, so first he entered the kiln as a servant. Eventually he married Kakiemon's daughter, whom he deserted when he returned to Kutani in 1661.

Some accounts say that, before returning to Kutani, Goto Saijiro went to Nagasaki, where he met Chinese potters whom he took back with him; other accounts say that he visited China and brought Chinese potters back with him. Because of the lack of records, what really happened is a matter for conjecture.

The Kutani kiln closed down around the end of the century, the exact date being disputed. Why it closed is also a mystery, but it is believed to have been because of pressure from the shogunate.

The Maeda family was one of the "outside clans," not deeply attached to the shogunate, and since it was enormously wealthy, it was thus always a potential danger to the shogunate. Any traffic with China was an infringement of the laws of the shogunate, and if Goto Saijiro had gone to China, or brought Chinese potters to Kutani, this would have been enough to warrant his execution. Even a visit to Arita would have been a forbidden excursion.

At some time in the early 1690s the kiln was shut down and all the records destroyed. Goto Saijiro was summarily arrested and led away in chains to be executed. He swore to avenge himself after his death on the house of Maeda. This threat of ghostly vengeance must have had the desired effect on Toshiaki, as a substitute was found to be executed in Saijiro's place. (There is an old Japanese belief that if a man's mind is set

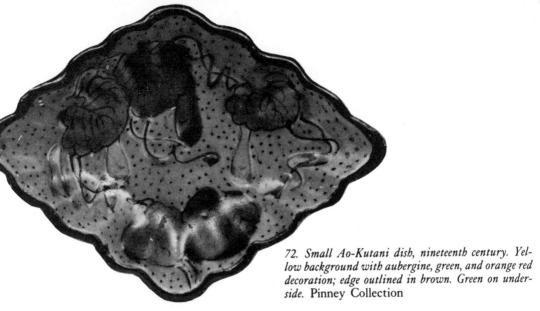

on vengeance at the moment of his death, his spirit will be able to carry it out.) One wonders about the feelings of the substitute, but history has nothing to say on the subject. Saijiro retired to the Jitsusein Temple in Daishoji and died there at the age of seventy in 1704.

Enameled wares of this period are called Ko-Kutani, or old Kutani. Some of them are so similar to Imari wares of the same period that it is purely a matter of opinion where they originated.

Ko-Kutani wares have more variety in the composition of the paste for the body than wares from any other kiln in Japan. The body is generally grayish white, coarse in quality, ranging from stoneware to porcelain. This variety would seem to indicate products from a number of kilns, and it has been suggested that the ships taking rice from Kaga to Hizen returned with undecorated porcelain from Arita as ballast, and that this porcelain was then decorated in Kutani.

The decoration of Ko-Kutani wares has a vigor unequaled by other kilns; it appears to have been originated by artists rather than craftsmen. The enamels are a vivid green, aubergine, Prussian blue, yellow, and a red ranging from cherry to brown; these colors, as well as the brushes used for the decoration, are thought to have come from China. Birds, flowers, and landscapes, as well as decorations of medallions and diapers, are painted in a bold free style. These pieces are either unmarked or have the Chinese ideograph *fuku* in a square.

In the Kutani group is a smaller one called Ao-Kutani, or green Kutani, much of which is made of stoneware. The enamels on these pieces are mainly green, yellow, aubergine, and Prussian blue, applied in broad washes and decorated with strong black lines (Ill. 72).

Nineteenth-Century Kutani Revivals

There were a number of Kutani revivals during the nineteenth century, some

73. *Figure of a girl playing the samisen (one of a group of four). Porecelain, 1870, Kaga.* Metropolitan Museum of Art, Macy Collection, Gift of Mrs. V. Everit Macy

74. Left: *covered jar, red Kaga ware.* Center: *Ao-Kutani flower vase with landscape; mark* fuku *(painted black on green).* Right: *Kutani teapot.* Peabody Museum of Salem; Photograph by M. W. Sexton

quite short-lived. The kilns were at various sites, mostly a short distance from the village of Kutani itself. We need not concern ourselves with most of them; they did not continue production beyond the middle of the century (Ill. 73).

Near the beginning of the nineteenth century (the exact date is uncertain), the Yoshidaya revival took place on the site of the old Kutani kilns under Yoshidaya Denyemon, a rich Daishoji merchant. The kiln was transferred to Yamashiro in 1814 under the supervision of Miyamoto Uyemon. The wares produced—called Saiko Kutani or revived Kutani—are credited with being the first to be stamped with a seal "Kutani."

Miyamoto Uyemon's son, Riyemon, succeeded his father in 1840, and about that time also Iida Hachiroyemon came to the kiln. Hachiroyemon was responsible for introducing a new style of red and gold porcelain ware. The richly decorated pieces with elaborate gold designs painted on a red enamel background are known as *akaji-kinga;* they are called red Kutani by foreigners (Ill. 74).

After Hachiroyemon's death in 1849, two sons of Hozen came to the kiln, and one of them, Zengoro Wazen, stayed for six years. Wazen was the twelfth generation of the family of potters known as Eiraku (see Chapter 6).

Wazen worked in the *akaji-kinga* style, and also brought to perfection the Kaga *aka-e* style, or red designs on a white ground. Many of his pieces have a red ground with gold designs on the outside and a white ground with red designs on the inside. Other pieces have red and gold on the outside and underglaze blue and white on the inside. Both these combinations are known as *hachiroye-yaki.*

These wares became so popular in Europe that kilns to make them sprang up throughout Kaga Province. Many bore the Kutani mark, and some pieces have the potter's signature incised in the biscuit.

The kilns went into a decline at the beginning of the Meiji era, but within ten years production increased, and since that time the kilns have been working steadily. All kinds of pieces are made: bowls, plates, dishes,

75. Porcelain censer, Kutani, 1870. Metropolitan Museum of Art, Macy Collection, Gift of Mrs. V. Everit Macy

76. Modern wheel-turned sake bottle, with Kutani mark. Gray body has shrimp and pine branch design. Pinney Collection. *Two sake cups, with Kutani mark.*

77. *Covered box has Kutani mark in gold on a red brushstroke. The porcelain is of good quality with considerable decorative detail; the European-style enamel decoration is not symmetrical but shows Japanese-style irregularity*

78. *This cup, saucer, and bowl bear the Kutani seal mark and "Made in Japan." Each of the six poets (five men and one woman) is portrayed with one of his poems. The painting of the tenth-century poet Ki no Tsurayuki suggests a source for the decoration on the Kutani pieces. His poem reads: "The breeze is not chilly beneath the cherry tree whose blossoms are flying; yet behold, from the sky falls a strange snow"* (Museum of Fine Arts Bulletin, *February 1921*). Courtesy, Museum of Fine Arts, Boston, William Sturgis Ross Fund

79. *Modern tea set with Kutani mark and "Made in Japan." The design of cranes with outstretched wings appears against a beige background spotted with gold. Red border is decorated with gold lines. Good quality heavy white porcelain. The close-up of the cup shows the Kutani mark in gold on a red circle.*

vases, incense burners, small ornamental objects, chocolate sets, coffee sets, tea sets, and so on (Ills. 75, 76, 77, and 78). Some have only the mark Kutani (Ill. 79); others have the potter's name as well, generally in gold on a red brushstroke. Seals are also used.

Many pieces have a ground enamel color over the glaze, the whole surface being decorated (Ill. 80). The brushwork is generally very good on elaborate designs. The characteristic red and gold is much in evidence, the red ranging from an Indian red through a red brown, differing from the Imari red, which is more orange.

Kaga Redwares (Kaga aka-e). These wares have red designs on a white ground, with touches of gold, mostly Chinese figures and landscapes, which cover the entire surface. They sometimes have a comb design on the foot rim similar to that on Nabeshima wares, but otherwise they are hard to distinguish from Kutani wares. Kaga redwares are usually of a very poor quality porcelain, soft and gray. Quantities of these wares were sent "in the white" from other parts of Japan to Kaga for decoration.

80. *All these Kutani pieces are late nineteenth century. The cup and saucer have Satsuma-style decoration.* Pinney Collection. *On the teapot, sugar, and creamer the ladies in red appear against a pale green enamel background.*

8

Satsuma and Satsuma-Style Wares

Satsuma is the general term for wares made at the Chosa, Ryumonji, Tateno, and Naeshirogawa kilns in Kagoshima Prefecture, Kyushu. These kilns were all in the domain of the feudal lord of Satsuma. However, in the period we are studying, the designation Satsuma covers wares made in the village of Naeshirogawa in the province of Satsuma (Ill. 81), and Satsuma-style wares made in Kyoto (Ill. 82), on the island of Awaji, in Yokohama, and in Tokyo.

At the end of the sixteenth century Shimazu Yoshidiro, lord of Satsuma, returned from an attempted conquest of Korea, and brought with him twenty-two Korean potters and their families. These families settled in Kagoshima and Kushikino, but in 1601 they moved to Naeshirogawa, where there were good white clay materials. Here, after many experiments, they succeeded in producing the ware now known as Satsuma.

81. Jar and wine pot with cover—faience, Satsuma ware, c. 1870. Metropolitan Museum of Art, Macy Collection, Gift of Mrs. V. Everit Macy

82. *Pottery jar (Satsuma type), by Okumura, Kyoto; late nineteenth century.* Metropolitan Museum of Art, Gift of Charles Stewart Smith

In Franks's *Japanese Pottery*, which was published by the Victoria and Albert Museum, London, in 1880 in connection with the Japanese ceramic collection displayed first at the Philadelphia Exposition of 1876 and sent to London the following year, is this description of the kiln:

The kiln is built on the slope of a hill, after the Corean system, and is of peculiar construction, differing from that in Arita and other places. It is built single, and not in a line as in other factories. It has a length of 150 feet to 200 feet, and a height of 5 feet in the centre, of a vault-like form. At the lower end of the kiln is the furnace, or rather the place to commence the firing. The fuel, consisting of dried wood, is thrown directly into the kiln, the inside of which communicates with the outer air by means of an opening in the side wall. Saggars are not used, and in consequence of this and of the irregular distribution of heat throughout the kiln, great damage occurs to the ware. Of the many places to which the art of pottery making was introduced from Corea, this is the only one at which the true Corean kiln exists.

The report goes on to explain that up to the time of the Meiji Restoration the families were kept entirely separate from the Japanese population, and intermarriage was prohibited. This preserved to a considerable extent their language and customs. At the time of the report there were about 1,450 of these people, all engaged in pottery making.

In our parlance (in contrast with old Satsuma and what the Japanese call Satsuma), Satsuma ware is a light porous semiporcelain with a soft cream-colored crackle glaze showing ivory brown undertints. The glaze is a compound of feldspathic materials and wood ash, the crackle being formed naturally when the piece is fired. The biscuit and the glaze do not "fit" exactly; the glaze shrinks more than the biscuit, and this causes fine cracks to appear in it.

This cream-colored crackled ware has two most desirable qualities. One is that

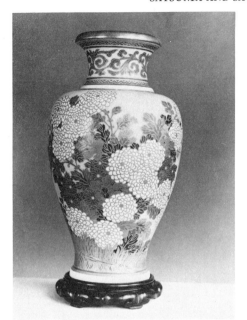

83. Satsuma vase (faience), decorated with poly-chrome enamels and gilded. Mark: a cherry blossom, impressed, and "Isoyaki" in black. Early twentieth century. Victoria and Albert Museum

84. Satsuma vase, late nineteenth century. Excellent quality porcelain and decoration, with fine creamy crackled glaze. The overglaze enamels are in red, blue, turquoise, white, gold, yellow, and pink, with blue and red enamel dots. Color is rubbed into the glaze in places to accentuate the crackle.

white enamels may be used for decoration; the other is that, on account of the crackle, the decorative enamels sink into the cracks, and no matter how heavily they are applied, they adhere closely to the glaze and will not flake off or peel (Color Plate 13). Very often on this type of Satsuma ware the crackle has had color rubbed into it to increase the decorative effect (Color Plate 4).

The decoration is often floral and elaborate, and the brushwork meticulously executed (Ill. 83). Raised enameling was a popular feature (Ill. 84). This type of ware had great appeal for people of the Victorian age, for the heavy ornate decoration was in keeping with the styles of that era. Many pieces were of enormous size. Huge vases were placed at the foot of a staircase or on either side of a fireplace, as they generally came in pairs. Since the disappearance of cheap household help and, in consequence, of large houses, the modern home provides few places to display such pieces properly. Very small objects, such as buttons, hatpins, and buckles, were also made. They are still being made today.

At the turn of the century a blue and white Satsuma ware was made for export.

85. Satsuma vase, c. 1930. Faience, with the neck roughly ornamented with a knife. Mr. and Mrs. Herbert Cohn

86. Satsuma plate. Excellent quality; the brushwork is very fine. Mark on underside reads "Satsuma" in hiragana. Pinney Collection

87. Satsuma pitcher. This is an interesting piece, with Japanese ladies instead of the usual Chinese figures in this type of design. The shape has an oriental appearance. Probably late nineteenth century. The mark on the underside reads "Satsuma" in katakana.

The underglaze designs are mostly of Chinese landscapes and large peony blossoms, and the gray glaze has a fine crackle. These wares, again usually large, are generally incense burners or ornamental bowls.

Another type of ware, also for export only, had human figures in raised designs: warriors, saints, geisha, as well as writhing dragons or hō-ō (phoenix). The body of this kind of ware is almost completely covered with decoration; hardly any of the crackled glaze is visible (Ills. 88 and 89). No figures were ever painted on old Satsuma; the Japanese preferred simple flower decorations and landscapes, sparingly applied.

Almost all these export wares, although

88. *Satsuma bowl with warriors. The Satsuma crest (a cross in a circle) occurs twice on the border.*

89. *Small Satsuma vase. The color is similar to that of the vase in Color Plate 13.*

known to foreigners as Satsuma ware, were manufactured in Kyoto, Awaji, Yokohama, Awata, and Tokyo. They are known under those names to the Japanese.

In *Japan Day by Day*, Morse described a visit to the potteries at Awata and of the conditions that prevailed there around 1880.

> *The entrance to the potteries was reserved and modest; and within we were greeted by the head of the family and tea and cakes were immediately offered us. It seems that members of the family alone are engaged on this work; from the little boy or girl to the old grandfather, whose feeble strength is utilized in some simple process of the work. The output is small, except in those potteries given up to making stuff for the foreign trade, known to the Japanese as Yokohama muke; that is for export, a contemptuous expression. In many cases outsiders are employed; boys often ten years old splashing on the decoration of flowers and butterflies, and the like; motives derived from their mythology, but in sickening profusion, so contrary to the exquisite reserve of the Japanese in the decoration of objects for their own use. Pre-*
>
> *vious to the demands of the foreigner the members of the immediate family were leisurely engaged in producing pottery reserved in form and decoration. Now the whole compound is given over to feverish activity of work, with every Tom, Dick and Harry and their children slapping it out by the gross.*
>
> *An order is given by the agent for a hundred thousand cups and saucers. "Put in all the red and green you can" is the order as told me by the agent, and the haste and roughness of the work confirms the Japanese that they are dealing with a people whose tastes are barbaric.*

Awaji

In 1831 Kashiu Mimpei, a native of the island, erected a kiln in the village of Iganomura on the island of Awaji, after he had found suitable clay materials there.

Mimpei and his son Sampei produced wares that were very acceptable to the export trade. These were of a delicate yellow tint, similar to Awata ware, the glaze being covered with a fine crackle. The decoration was carefully painted with more or less transparent enamels (Ill. 90). However, be-

90. *Flower vase, made by Kashiu Sampei, Awaji.*
Victoria and Albert Museum

sides this type of ware, Mimpei also made
wares with single-color glazes—yellow,
green, or brown red in Chinese style. These
wares are sometimes known as Mimpei-*yaki*.
For them he often used the mark of a Chinese period.

It is of interest to note that at the Philadelphia Exposition of 1876 a tea service by
Sampei was exhibited. This consisted of a
gourd-shaped teapot, sucrier and cover, milk
jug, and two cups and saucers, all European
shapes.

Yokohama

In 1869 two Yokohama merchants established a kiln at Munami Otamachi (Ōta)
near Yokohama for the purpose of manufacturing an imitation of Satsuma ware for export. The materials were to be brought from
the province of Satsuma. The Yokohama habor had just been opened to foreign trade,
and wares in Satsuma style were proving
very popular in the West.

A Kiyomizu porcelain maker,
Miyakawa Kozan, living at Makuzu, was
producing Awata-style Satsuma ware in
Kyoto, and he and his son were brought to
the Ōta kiln. Kozan's chance of success
abroad came with the Philadelphia Exposition of 1876. He applied for permission to
show his work there, and as he was still
young and poor, money was advanced to
him. With this help he produced some very
creditable specimens for the exhibition (Ill.
91). In 1893 he sent a collection of one hundred pieces to the Columbian Exposition at

Chicago. Particularly notable were his
peach-bloom vases with dragon designs.

Kozan was made a member of the Imperial Academy of Tokyo in 1896. He continued to exhibit successfully at foreign
exhibitions, and sent a small group to the
Panama-Pacific International Exposition in
San Francisco in 1915. The catalog mentions
four of his vases: two with landscape designs,
one with dragon design, and one with peonies. Two incense burners are also mentioned, one decorated with a phoenix and
one with a pheasant design.

Tokyo

Much Satsuma-style ware was decorated in the immediate area of Tokyo when
that city had become a center of foreign
trade after 1868. These pieces were brought
from kilns in other districts "in the white"
and decorated and fired in muffle kilns in
Tokyo.

Muffle kilns were also set up for this
purpose near other centers of foreign trade
—for example, Yokohama, Osaka, Nagasaki
—and it is practically impossible to distinguish whether this type of export ware was
decorated in one place or another. Much of
it is unmarked, and the pieces that do carry
a mark give the name of a decorator or kiln
that is not traceable. There were a great
number of such kilns, and many of them
were in operation for only a short time.

91. *Vase and cover, Satsuma style, made at Ōta, by
Kozan, 1869.* Victoria and Albert Museum

92. *Three late nineteenth-century Makuzu porcelains: a vase, a covered jar, and a second vase more bulbous in shape, which is marked "Kozan."* Vase at top: Courtesy of The Brooklyn Muesum; *other pieces,* Metropolitan Museum of Art, Gift of Charles Stewart Smith

93. Pair of blue vases with Satsuma-style decoration.

9

Meiji Classical, Traditional, and Neo-Traditional Potters

Although the advent of the Meiji era, with its onrush of Western ideas, was a disaster to the potters working in the old traditions, there shortly emerged a new generation of potters born into the now-established Western influence. Overall, potters from the late nineteenth century up to the present day fall roughly into the following groups: those who looked back toward China and aimed for the classical perfection of those wares; those who worked in the traditional forms and neo-traditional forms; those who turned to the folk arts for inspiration; the Nitten group; and, last, the avant-garde group. However, the potters in all these groups were influenced to some extent by Western ideas and methods.

In the first group Itaya Hazan and Ishiguro Munemaro are considered the leaders of their generation of potters who worked in the classical style of the Chinese tradition.

Hazan, born in Tokyo in 1872, made wares combining oriental tradition and Western design in a highly compatible manner, creating a form of neoclassical style. He displayed a high degree of technical competence in all his work. Especially worthy of mention are his white porcelains; also his celadons, which are usually decorated with flowers or leaves in shallow relief. Hazan studied European enameling techniques also and succeeded in creating new colors.

He instructed a large number of students, many of whom in their turn became able potters, and many more were influenced by his work, directly or indirectly. He formed a group of potters called Tōtō-kai (Eastern group) who looked to him for leadership.

Although Ishiguro Munemaro was born in Kyoto in 1893, some twenty years after Hazan, his work is more in the pure tradition of the Chinese potters than Hazan's, and it shows little perceptible Western influence. A noted collector of Chinese pottery and stoneware of the Han and Sung dynasties, Munemaro adopted a style derived entirely from Sung Dynasty wares, and the perfection his pieces display is almost that of the originals. His pieces are masterpieces in their own right, however, dignified and elegant in both form and decoration. His teabowls and larger bowls, both with *temmoku* glazes, display a high degree of skill; the glazes are richer and finer than any used by other potters of recent times.

Kato Hajime (1900–1968) born in Yokohama, belonged essentially to the group of potters working in the oriental style and combining with it modern styles and designs from the West. He was a versatile decorator who used many different styles. He made pieces decorated with both the Sung-style decorations called *uki-botan* and *shizumi-botan*. *Uki-botan*, "floating peony," is a technique whereby the background of a decoration is beveled with a knife, so that when glazed with celadon glaze, the decoration (flower, bird, or other

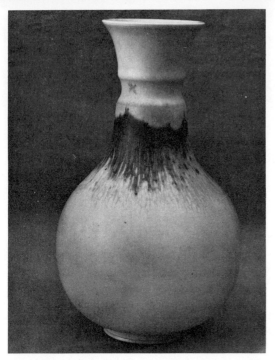

94. *Late nineteenth-century porcelain flower vase by Takemoto of Tokyo. White, faintly green body with flambé collar, in Chinese style.* Metropolitan Museum of Art, Gift of Charles Stewart Smith

celadons, and is outstanding for his mastery in this field. His wares with underglaze red decoration are executed with consummate artistry. He also makes Chinese-style wares, but with a modern interpretation.

Takemoto Hayata, of Tokyo (1848–1892), must be included in this group, although he was born earlier than the others discussed in this section. He was a young man when the trend toward Westernism began, and received the full brunt of the new ideas during his most impressionable years. However, he was one of those who felt it was wrong to replace the ancient arts of Japan with worthless copies of Western fashions, and he determined to demonstrate the value of the old ways to the Western world (Ill. 94). He exhibited some of his wares at the Paris Exposition in 1878, but prepared a much larger collection for the Columbian Exposition in Chicago in 1893, where one hundred of his porcelains in solid colors were shown. Unfortunately, he did not live to see his success at that exhibition. The exhibition catalog reads:

These pieces are the fruit of ten years study and labor in the effort to revive the lost arts of China and Japan. These works are the last results of the artist's untiring and numberless experiments. They were made especially for the exhibition at the World's Columbian Exposition. The artist's over-exertion led to his untimely death. He died shortly after the last of these pieces were taken from the oven.

The group of potters working in traditional and neo-traditional Japanese styles is a large one. The traditional group reproduce as faithfully as possible the traditional wares, but the neo-traditional potters work in a modern adaptation of the old forms, giving the traditional styles a fresh approach.

Sakaida Kakiemon of Arita (born 1906), the thirteenth generation of his family, works in the family tradition. His wares stand comparison with the best wares made by his ancestors.

Imaizumi Imaemon (born 1897), also of Arita and the thirteenth generation of his family, produces excellent quality wares using the old family designs. The Imaizumi family originally decorated the Nabeshima wares, but since the Meiji era they have

motif) appears to float on the surface of the piece. *Shizumi-botan,* "sinking peony," is the opposite technique, with the pattern incised at a lower level than the background, so that when glazed with celadon glaze the motif appears to sink into the body of the piece.

Another form of decoration that Kato Hajime used is in the sprigged-on technique. To make this type, plastic clay is pressed into a mold and then stuck onto the surface of a leather-hard piece with slip.

Kato Hajime also produced fine pieces through his modern adaptation of the carved biscuit mold. This mold has the form of the inside of the bowl, and the decoration is incised in it. A slice of clay is pressed onto the mold and trimmed, and a foot is attached. When the piece is finished, the pattern—now, of course, raised—appears on the inside of the bowl.

Besides these techniques, he also was master of overglaze enamel decoration, and his gold designs on a pale green background are particularly beautiful. He did extensive research into the various glazes used on the old wares of Japan and China, and as professor of ceramics at the Tokyo University of Arts, exerted considerable influence on the younger generation of potters.

Uno Sataro, born in Kyoto in 1888, devoted much of his life to the ancient art of

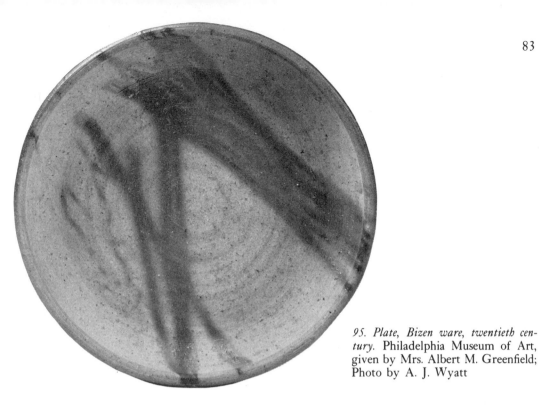

95. *Plate, Bizen ware, twentieth century.* Philadelphia Museum of Art, given by Mrs. Albert M. Greenfield; Photo by A. J. Wyatt

made the biscuit as well. At the present time their wares are technically almost equal to the old wares. Imaizumi Yoshinori (born 1926) also works in the family tradition.

Both Sakaida Kakiemon and Imaizumi Imaemon have been designated *ningen kokuho*, "living national treasure."

Arkawa Toyozo, born in 1894, is a native of Tajime in Gifu Prefecture, the site of the Seto-Mino wares of the Momoyama Period, where Shino and Oribe wares were made. He studied pottery under Miyanaga Tozan of Kyoto, and assisted in the excavation of the old Shino kilns at Okaya. In 1957 he published an authoritative work on old Shino.

Famous for his Shino, Seto-guro, and Ki-Seto wares, Arakawa Toyozo is especially well known for a teabowl in the Shino style. Through careful experimentation he has produced some very successful pieces that are consciously distorted to a high degree. His wares are excellent in quality and almost impossible to tell from the old ones, although certain connoisseurs insist that they do not have the rugged strength of the originals. He uses a semiunderground type of *ana-gama* kiln, which he built himself in 1933; it is the only one of its kind in Japan today. He too is designated a "living national treasure."

A number of potters work in the tradition of the Six Ancient Kilns (Seto, Echizen, Tokoname, Bizen, Tamba, and Shigaraki), as well as other old kilns (Karatsu, Hagi, and so on).

Kaneshige Toyo, born in 1896, of Imbe, Okayama Prefecture, is noted for the faithfulness with which he produces his Bizen ware. He represents the seventy-eighth generation of Bizen potters who have been making pottery continuously for over a thousand years.

The quality of Bizen wares deteriorated greatly during the Meiji era, when the kilns were no longer under the protection of the daimyo. Western methods and ideas had been imported with disastrous results, and Kaneshige determined to improve the quality of this ware that had carried on over such a long period. He revived the traditional methods after considerable experimentation, as the old methods had been allowed to die out; it was only after much trial and error that he rediscovered the secrets of making the fine old ware. Armed with this knowledge, he encouraged the local potters to work again in the old trusted ways (Ill. 95).

The wares he produces are of comparable quality to the Ko-Bizen wares, but despite the time-honored approach, he manages to impart to them a modern touch, like a breath of fresh mountain air.

Kaneshige (modern Japanese potters are generally known by their family name) uses a clay that is not screened—only the large pieces of rock are removed. Many small pieces remain, and during the firing these pieces explode, producing "bumps" on the clay walls, surrounded by cracks radiating from the high spots. As the method of packing the kiln for firing is to stack long-necked pieces on their sides, the pieces are often distorted, a characteristic very attractive to the tea masters, as any natural deformation or change caused by the firing has always been.

Bizen wares are never artificially glazed, the only glaze, called *goma*, being the natural result of ash falling on the ware during firing. Kaneshige's Bizen tea ceremonial pieces with cross-flame effect are highly prized in Japan. His work has been seen by a wide public in the United States in the years immediately following World War II. He was one of the well-known Japanese potters who came to this country for lecture demonstrations and exhibitions of modern Japanese ceramic techniques.

Fujiwara Kei (born 1899) is another native of the district who produces Bizen ware; his is made in a similar style to that of Kaneshige Toyo. The subtle coloring of his glazes and his decorations, which are modern although in the traditional style, makes his wares most pleasing and acceptable. He has achieved some beautiful effects through his use of the traditional Bizen decoration called *hidasuki*. This ancient form of decoration is made by using straw rope that has been soaked in salt water, and wrapping it around the ware; during the firing, the straw is burned up and the ash causes streaks of bright red glaze to form on the otherwise unglazed ware. Fujiwara Ken (born 1924) and Fujiwara Yu (born 1932) also work in the Bizen style.

Asai Rakuzen works in the Tokoname tradition. Tokoname wares are famous for their Chinese-style red, unglazed burnished surfaces. Asai Rakuzen has experimented with the Bizen-style decoration *hidasuki*, but uses seaweed instead of rope to wrap around his leather-hard pots. The resulting red streaks of glaze are very effective on his beige-colored wares.

Kikuyama Taneo began his research into the ancient methods of the Iga tradition in 1937, when he built himself a three-chamber *nobori-gama* kiln. He fires his wares from ten to thirteen times each, and although his kiln holds about three hundred pieces, he may consider only five or ten of the finished pieces to be acceptable. This is on a good firing; on a poor firing there will be fewer.

The Nakazato family of Karatsu has a 360-year tradition as potters, and Toroemon (born 1923), the present head of the family, works in traditional style. Nakano Suemasa is another Karatsu potter.

A descendant of another old potter family, Miwa Kyuwa makes Hagi wares. He is the tenth generation of the Miwa family, the first, Miwa Kyusetsu, having settled at Hagi in the seventeenth century.

Miwa Kyuwa produces tea ceremony wares that show combined Korean and Japanese influences. He uses the local light soft clay, which, when mixed with some darker clay from Mishima and sand, acquires a faintly pinkish color. Although in earlier days he used creamy white glazes as well as pinkish ones, he now confines himself to a variety of white crackled glazes, composed of a mixture of feldspar, wood ash, and rice husk ash. The glaze is applied by dipping the wares in it—he never uses a brush—and the sole decoration consists of drips or runs of glaze. He uses a hundred-year-old climbing kiln, which he fires once or twice a year; the firing lasts forty hours, and the wares are left in the closed kiln for three days to cool.

Ito Tozan, Tozan III, is the last of the traditional Awata ware potters. Although the Kyoto clay used for this ware is no longer available, Tozan has managed to mix a blend of clays that, when fired, has a comparable appearance to the original clay, and the fine mesh crackle glaze also has the good qualities of the original glaze. The creamy body is tastefully decorated in overglaze enamels.

The Kato family has been making pottery in the Seto area ever since the thirteenth century. Because the family is so old and large, there is considerable confusion about the names and dates of its various members, especially as several potters had the same name.

In the beginning of the nineteenth cen-

tury Kato Tamikichi spent four years studying porcelain making at Arita, where he married the daughter of a porcelain manufacturer established there. On his return to Seto he made *sometsuke* porcelain, using the local *gosu.* He died in 1824, and was succeeded by his nephew Tamikichi II, who continued to make fine porcelain. Kato Gusuke also made fine porcelain and sent a collection to the Philadelphia Centennial Exposition of 1876 and to the Paris Exposition in 1878 (Ill. 96).

Kato Tokuro (born in 1898) is well known for his wares in Shino, Oribe, and Ki-Seto styles. Although they are highly traditional in spirit, they show some of the

Western influence he was subject to in his early years.

His son, Kato Mineo, besides working in traditional style, has experimented with modern methods and ideas and has produced some interesting work in a new style. He has made distinctive pieces with rope-impressed designs, in Jōmon style, stark and strong. To make these pieces he forms them first by coiling, then beats them with a paddle wrapped with rope until they have an angular appearance of extraordinary antiquity.

Kitade Tojiro was born in Kanazawa, the district noted for its Kutani ware. He received his early training in the Kutani technique, and to this he has brought a fresh outlook. His mature wares are noted for new designs enhanced by a master's touch of color and brush.

Kyoto potters of the new school who make wares in the Kyō-*yaki* tradition are Kusube Yaichi, Yamada Tetsu, Kiyomizu Rokubei, and Kondo Yuzo. The products of these four potters all retain the characteristics of the older ware, but all have a flavor of the new age.

Kusube Yaichi (born in 1897) is well known for a carved style of decoration, with graceful motifs closely copied from nature. He first outlines the decoration with a sharp knife, then carefully carves and models the details in low relief.

Yamada Tetsu (born in 1898) began to study pottery seriously at the age of thirty-four. At that time he was a Buddhist priest and had been master of a temple since he was twenty-two; he was also a skilled calligrapher. When he became established as a potter, he left the priesthood, and since then he has striven to create a new Japanese style of pottery. Famous in Japan for his teabowls, he decorates his wares with a combination of wax resist and superimposed glazes.

Kiyomizu Rokubei, the fifth generation of the Kyoto family of potters of that name, was born in 1901. His wares have a traditional rustic quality, rich in the strength and vigor of peasant wares. However, the rugged vitality of the structure of the wares looks toward the twentieth century rather than backward to preceding centuries.

Kondo Yuzo (born 1902) has made some very fine blue and white pieces, with the bold designs at once modern yet traditional in style. He also combines other colors under the glaze, in particular a red from a copper mineral. These pieces with their blue and red underglaze decoration on a white background are most effective. Another technique he has mastered with great success is inlaying two clays of different colors on the same piece (zōgan). He has made some beautiful floral decorations in this style, the flowers in one color, the leaves in another, against a natural clay background.

Here we must stop and look at the giant, the master of all the traditional styles, Kitaoji Rosanjin (1883–1959). He was born in Kitaoji, Kyoto, and given the name of Kitaoji Fusajiro. After a very unhappy early childhood in several foster homes, he was adopted by a wood-carver and seal engraver, Fukuda Takeizo, and his wife, and he remained with them and learned to use his adopted father's tools.

His first artistic ambition was to become a calligrapher, and at thirteen he applied for entrance to the Kyoto Municipal Art School, which rejected him. He then entered three examples of his calligraphy in a contest and won first, second, and third prizes, which provided him with enough money to support himself. Thereafter he continued to enter, and to win, contests. However, he wished to study under someone, and he applied to two great calligraphers, asking to become a pupil, but both rejected him. In Japan it is very hard to accomplish anything without a correct introduction, and as Rosanjin had no one to help him, he was rejected for this reason rather than for any lack of talent on his part. Nevertheless, he still persevered, and he called himself *"Doppo"* ("lone wolf").

In spite of the discouragement and difficulties he had suffered, he made a name for himself as calligrapher, signboard carver, and engraver of seals, all of which require considerable artistic ability in Japan. At the age of twenty-seven he took the art name of Fukuda Taikan (Fukuda was the name of his adopted father). Ten years later, around 1920, he changed his art name to Rokyo ("foolish lord"). He altered his name once more, and by 1925 he was calling himself Rosanjin ("foolish mountain person").

Rosanjin had two passions, one for collecting antiques and the other for food. When his antique collection became too large to be comfortably housed in his dwelling, he opened an antique store in Kyobashi, Tokyo. At times he served his customers with choice foods, and as his visitors returned time and again for more of his delicacies, in due course he opened the Bishoku Club on the second floor of his store, a gourmet paradise. Eventually Rosanjin felt it was necessary to have more suitable and specialized dishes on which to serve the food, commenting that dishes are the kimonos of good food.

This wish led him to open the Hoshigaoka kilns at Kita Kamakura, near his large farmhouse residence, and he brought together a number of the best potters to work there. Both Arakawa Toyozo and Kaneshige Toyo were closely associated with him. He was insistent that the right

97. Teabowl with decoration of grasses is stoneware of the Bizen type. Kitaoji Rosanjin. Seattle Art Museum, Gift of Alice Boney

98. Teabowl, Shino ware. Kitaoji Rosanjin. Courtesy of the Brooklyn Museum; Gift of Dr. and Mrs. Robert Dickes

99. *Stoneware dish in the shape of a lotus leaf, brown glaze. Kitaoji Rosanjin.* Philadelphia Museum of Art; Purchased: The Far Eastern Revolving Fund; Photograph by A. J. Wyatt

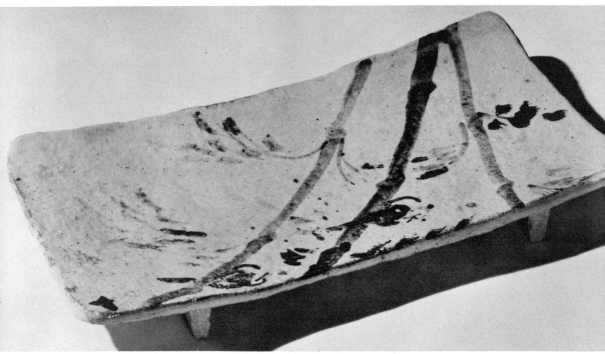

100. *Chopping board* (manaita). *Kitaoji Rosanjin.* Philadelphia Museum of Art; Purchased: The Edgar V. Seeler Fund; Photograph by A. J. Wyatt

101. *Square platter with decoration of birds and grasses in underglaze iron; lower third of the surface is covered in copper green iron glaze; signed with incised* katakana *"ro." 12". Kitaoji Rosanjin.* Mr. and Mrs. Joseph Gordon; Photograph by O. E. Nelson

102. *Vase with pinched ears and decorative marks in iron brown; signed with incised characters.* Kitaoji Rosanjin. Anonymous loan; Photograph by O. E. Nelson

103. *Widemouth soy sauce pitcher with lid, spout, and loop handle attached at side, and overall translucent copper green glaze; signed with incised* katakana *"ro."* Kitaoji Rosanjin. Sidney Cardozo; Photograph by O. E. Nelson

104. *Small dish with design of crab in blue and brown underglaze, stylized star and ovoids, and red enamel rim on white porcelain body; signed with character "ro" in underglaze blue. D. 4 ⅞".* Kitaoji Rosanjin. Robert Ellsworth; Photograph by O. E. Nelson

105. *Bowl with decoration of grapes, vines, and leaves in underglaze iron brown of varying thicknesses as an opaque grayish overglaze, scorched light orange where thin; signed on the side with incised* katakana *"ro."* Kitaoji Rosanjin. Sidney B. Cardozo

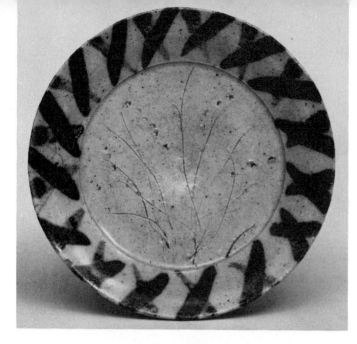

106. Plate D. 7". Delicate incised lines in the center portray tall grasses, heavy with grain, swaying in the wind. Kitaoji Rosanjin. Captain and Mrs. Roger Gerry

clays be used, and he sent for whatever was needed from its original source, no matter how far away, even to Korea.

Rosanjin was always searching for new forms and ideas. When he found something that pleased him he would have it copied, and he was the first contemporary potter to have molds made for his use. He rarely made a piece entirely on his own; instead, he would supervise the making of the basic shape, and when it was finally formed to his satisfaction he would take it in his own hands to finish. It was from this point, however, that the piece took on individuality, as he subtly changed its form, squeezing it here, pulling it there, decorating it with a few brushstrokes, an incised design, or with various glazes. No matter in what style he worked, the finished piece was never a mere copy; it was always a Rosanjin, original in design and rich in aesthetic taste.

Although we have become used to the idea of an individual potter going through the whole process of making his wares on his own, forming them, then decorating them, this is a quite recent development in Japan. Such a task as throwing a piece on the wheel was considered menial work, suitable only for an artisan and completely unworthy of a potter's attention. It was only through the efforts of Bernard Leach and Tomimoto Kenkichi that this idea changed, and an artist-potter came to feel that every aspect of making a pot was part of his artistic creativity. Thus, when Rosanjin personally supervised the making of the basic form of his

wares, he was—according to normally accepted methods—actually paying a remarkable amount of attention to all stages of the process.

Perhaps the most remarkable facet of Rosanjin's genius was that he was able to work in so many styles: *sometsuke,* Chinese porcelains, Kutani, tea wares of the Momoyama Period (Shino, Oribe, yellow Seto, black Seto), Bizen, Shigaraki, Kenzan-style decoration, and so on. He also did a considerable amount of experimental potting, some of it in low-fired wares using various techniques of underglaze and overglaze decoration.

Rosanjin said that, although he had derived inspiration from the classic examples of the potter's art of both East and West, he always looked to the beauties of nature as his sole instructor, and always pursued the study of beauty. His pieces are essentially for use; a delight on their own, they are infinitely more beautiful when they are being used.

Although it was offered to him, Rosanjin never accepted the designation of "national living treasure." He had the self-sufficiency of a true artist who knew he stood apart, and so cared little for the opinion of his fellowman.

Tomimoto Kenkichi (1886–1963), the Kyoto potter, was born in Yamato Province (Nara Prefecture), and although he became Japan's first individual potter, he was originally trained in architecture and did not turn to pottery until he was nearly thirty.

When he was twenty-two he went to England to study architecture, and learned to speak English well. On his return to Japan three years later he met Bernard Leach, who had already spent a year there. Leach had come into contact with Japanese pottery and was anxious to study it himself, so Tomimoto, acting as interpreter, made arrangements for Leach to study under the guidance of Kenzan VI.

Leach tried to persuade Tomimoto to study pottery also, but Tomimoto returned instead to Yamato Province and continued his studies in architecture. However, he remained in almost daily contact with Leach, who wrote to ask for translations of terms that he did not understand. Leach finally managed to interest Tomimoto in studying pottery, and in 1915 Tomimoto built a small kiln for himself in Yamato, where he started to make Raku wares. He and Leach continued to exchange notes in their correspondence, and after a while they both came to the same conclusion: They should learn to throw wares on the wheel. This brought them derision and scorn from all sides, but they persisted and both learned to throw.

Tomimoto's early work was deeply influenced by Korean pottery, but although he worked in Raku and Awata style, he was not a *mingei* (folk art) potter and must be ranked as an important potter of the neoclassical school. He turned to Chinese-style porcelains after he abandoned the folk-art style, and decorated these pure white wares with elegant designs in cobalt. The refined original designs and sharp modeling are two important characteristics of his work. He was also an accomplished calligrapher and decorated his wares with beautiful calligraphic brushwork.

No doubt his greatest contribution to the art of pottery was his discovery of a satisfactory method to combine gold and silver in decorative designs (Ill. 108). Silver melts at a lower temperature than gold, and the old method was to fire first the gold, then the silver. Silver also tarnishes after a time, which is not desirable. After considerable experimentation Tomimoto discovered that if he mixed silver with platinum, it raised the melting point of silver, and permitted both the gold and silver decoration to be fired at the same time. The silver and

107. Shallow dish, stoneware with a gray glaze and lotus painted in iron brown. Tomimoto Kenkichi. 1930–1935. Victoria and Albert Museum

platinum combination did not tarnish, and the addition of platinum did not alter the color of the silver.

His enameled porcelains with decorations in red, green, gold, silver, and other colors are masterpieces of design, either when he adapts an overall pattern to fit the curved surface of one of his covered boxes or brushes a light airy pattern on a colored ground. A type of decoration in which he excelled was the combination of underglaze *gosu* with overglaze enamels. Pieces of this description are rarely made, since blue and white specialists do not generally work with overglaze colors.

Tomimoto worked hard to free Japanese pottery from the overpowering tradition of the *noren* family potters. As an individual potter, he realized to the full the difficulties of the young and struggling individual potter working outside a family tradition. In 1934 he instituted the ceramic section of the Nitten Academy, hoping that potters studying in this atmosphere would be able to realize their own individuality. However, after World War II he felt that the young potter at the Nitten Academy suffered too many restrictions to be able to develop satisfactorily into an individual artist, so he resigned from the academy and formed the Shinshō Craft Association (Shin-shō-kai, New Craftsmen's Group) to help young potters and give them opportunities to exhibit their work. In 1949 he was asked by the government to found a ceramic department at the Kyoto Municipal College of Fine Arts; this was the first ceramic department established in any college in Japan.

108. Porcelain box with gold and silver designs. Tomimoto Kenkichi. Embassy of Japan, London

10

Folk Pottery and the Folk Art Movement

Japanese folk pottery is strictly utilitarian and crude, made of earthenware or stoneware in traditional shapes. It is a rugged ware intended for daily use, but it has a plain and functional beauty that is never ostentatious. The decoration, often in white slip, in simple and abstract designs, is usually combined with a poured or running glaze in a somber color—black, white, gray, dark brown, dark blue, or dark green.

The old oil dishes deserve special mention because—on account of their utilitarian, thick, heavy form—they had never been thought of as objects of aesthetic interest. But, with the awakening interest in the folk arts, their simple beauty became deeply appreciated, and their decoration has had considerable influence on craftsmen working in the movement.

Oil dishes (*aburazara* or *andonzara*) were made at Seto during the late Edo Period and the beginning of the Meiji Period (Ill. 109). They are flat dishes with a projecting rim, usually about seven inches in diameter; they were placed inside the lamp to catch oil dripping from the burning wick. The decorations are of remarkable beauty; usually they consist of just a few bold brushstrokes.

Very similar to these are the larger

109. *Oil dish* (aburazara or andonzara), *Seto*. Metropolitan Museum of Art, Howard Mansfield Collection

110. *Porcelain plate, twentieth century.* Courtesy of the Brooklyn Museum, Gift of David Jones

thicker plates (from ten to fifteen inches) that were also made at Seto of heavy stoneware. Used by peasants in their kitchens, they are known as *ishizara*. The decoration is similar to that on the oil dishes, free and bold with a minimum of strokes, and was either in iron black or the local cobalt found near Seto. Production of these wares ceased when cheaper mass-produced wares became generally available in the early Meiji era. Both these plates and the oil dishes are known as *getomono*, or ordinary wares.

Today folk pottery is made in many places throughout Japan. It ranges from traditional wares produced in the same places where they have been made for centuries to modern versions inspired by the traditional styles (Ill. 110). Traditional folk pottery has continued to be produced mostly in isolated and backward areas, where cheap porcelain is not easily obtainable. Kyushu, in the south, produces fine contemporary folk pottery, and there are several other areas that make these wares.

The kilns at both Ryumonji and Nae-

shirogawa in Kyushu were founded by Koreans, and they continue to work in that tradition. At Ryumonji wares are decorated in a distinctive manner by swinging a dripping brush filled with slip over the ware; this produces a freely controlled pattern of lines and dots. Yanagi Sōetsu considered the wares decorated in this way with white slip over the dark Ryumonji clay body to be one of the distinctive *mingei* products of Japan. Similar effects are also produced with colored glazes over a white engobe. Another method of decoration unique to Ryumonji is *donko*, or superimposed glaze mottling, carried out in white and black glazes.

The Naeshirogawa kiln was originally founded for the purpose of making tea ceremony wares for the Lord Shimazu of Satsuma, who brought back Korean potters for this purpose on his return from Hideyoshi's Korean invasion. At first the kiln produced refined whitewares, but later turned to making black *temmoku* vessels for everyday use by the peasants of the area. The potters are still making wares with this beautiful black

111. Bottle, black Satsuma ware, made at Nae-shirogawa. Courtsey of the Brooklyn Museum, Gift of Frank L. Babbott

Satsuma glaze, which needs no decoration (Ill. 111).

The mountain villages of Koishibara and nearby Onda, also in Kyushu, have kilns operated by the local farmers, who combine pottery with their farmwork. In both villages the potters spend time morning and night, every day, on the preparation of their clay. In Koishibara, which was originally the parent kiln of Onda, there are twenty-five families in all, and nine of these are potter families who share two kilns. Each family owns two clay crushers, which work continuously day and night. The crusher is a pine log with a hammer on one end and a hollowed-out area on the other. Water is diverted from the local stream, and as it fills the hollowed-out portion of the log, it raises the hammer end; then, as the log is tipped up and the water empties out, the hammer falls onto the clay and crushes it. When the clay has been crushed well enough to satisfy the potter, it passes through a series of settling tanks; it is permitted to set in the last tank, and as the water evaporates, the clay is left in the form of a thick smooth mud. It is then put into drying bowls until it is of the right consistency to be placed in storage. The potters of Onda prepare their clay in the same way.

Onda potters had been making their wares for three centuries when Yanagi Sō-etsu discovered the village and brought it out of its obscurity. Again, it too was a small settlement of a few farming families who fired their pots in the community kiln.

Wares made at Koishibara and Onda bear a great deal of similarity. Both are made by the old Korean method of first roughly coil-building large pieces on the wheel, then shaping them by throwing. They are decorated with *nagashi-gusuri,* "glaze that is made to flow," or superimposed glaze dripping; this is a process by which a contrasting glaze is allowed to drip from the top of a piece down the sides. Two contrasting glazes are frequently used.

A unique type of decoration is made by slip patting, and this technique has now spread to Mashiko, where the potters working in the folk art tradition use it with artistic effect. To make this decoration, the potter first centers the piece on the wheel. Then, while it turns slowly, he pats with a wide brush the liquid slip he has put in the center of the bowl. This forms a raised decoration of lines of slip radiating from the center of the bowl to the rim.

Kilns at both places use a sprigged-on decoration consisting of a raised motif stuck to the surface of the ware. This decoration has been used as a means of identification for a long time. The plum flower is the seal of Koishibara and the chrysanthemum the seal of Onda.

A very old traditional technique used at Koishibara is glaze throwing. The glaze is thrown either with a large brush, a small cup, or even by the handful. When a colored glaze is thrown on a white engobe, the result can be of unexpected beauty.

An interesting decoration used at Onda is called *tobi-kanna* or *kasuri-mon*, "chatter marks." This method originated in China during the Sung Dynasty, and although its use had died out in the country of origin, potters at Onda, in their isolation, have continued to use it. The name "chatter marks" is derived from the sound made by the flexible trimming tool as it jumps, or "chatters" on the surface of the ware. The dark body is first coated with a white slip; then it is put back again on the wheel, and the bouncing *kanna* held against the surface digs out small gouges, which show the brown body through the slip and result in a meshlike linear pattern that covers the whole body of the ware. This decoration is frequently used on lidded jars.

Wares made at Onda with a greenish blue glaze are particularly lovely, the beautiful cool color enhancing the quiet dignity of the simple shapes.

Other Kyushu folk kilns still in production are Futugawa, which has suffered a decline over recent years, Shiraishi, and Kuromuta.

In the main island of Honshu, the kiln at Tachikui in the Tamba district continues work in the traditional style of the area. Like Onda and Koishibara, Tamba in northern

Hyogo Prefecture owes its survival as a folk art producing center to its location in an isolated mountain region, although it is actually not situated at a great distance from the large cities. The local potters spend time morning and night preparing their clay, as at Onda and Koishibara; for them life has changed very little over the centuries. The wares they make are still in the simple straightforward shapes, and the usual decoration is a drip glaze over a contrasting color, white on black or brown, or vice versa.

Mashiko, fifty miles north of Tokyo, is a modern folk art producing center. Since Hamada settled there, at least thirty other potters have also arrived, and this village that has made folk pottery since early times has become the center of the modern folk art movement as far as pottery is concerned.

During the last century, wares made at Mashiko consisted mainly of water jars and salt pots with brown and persimmon glazes, as well as teapots with a "window picture" representing Lake Kasumi and Mount Tsukuba. This type of teapot is still being made. Wares known simply as Mashiko wares are made anonymously by the potters living there, and these utilitarian pieces show great taste and beauty, whether in the form of plates, cups, jars, or vases. They combine all that is good in the old tradition with an understanding of present-day needs, but nevertheless are not true folk art.

In northern Honshu the kiln at Naroaka in Akita Prefecture made use of a beautiful think bluish white iron glaze decoration. This glaze is called *namako-gusuri*, and when it is allowed to drip down over the glazed rough brown body the effect calls to mind an old Chinese poem by the Sung poet Lu Yu: "Fresh snow gleams on distant crags/Bathed in first glow of morning light." Unfortunately, this kiln ceased production after World War II.

Interesting folk wares still being produced in northern Japan are made at Hongo in Fukushima Prefecture. These traditional coarse peasant wares have been made for a very long time. The rough thick biscuit of a down-to-earth, unpretentious quality is

112. Cup, Hongo ware, a course peasant ware with thick rough biscuit. Private Collection

decorated with glazes in gray blue, dark brown, and deep green, highlighted with a bluish white *namako-gusuri* glaze (Ill. 112). The effect of these glazes on the dark pitted biscuit is of an exquisite lavender background to the free strokes of the contrasting glaze decoration.

The group of individual potters inspired by *mingei*, or folk art, and the awakened perception of the hidden beauty of those wares were mainly the result of the labors of Dr. Yanagi Sōetsu, considered by many to be a latter-day tea master in the tradition of the great ones of earlier centuries. Yanagi Sōetsu (1889–1961) deplored the passing of the traditional crafts of Japan and the way that they were being replaced by a worthless misunderstood copy of Western ways. Villages that in former times had produced beautiful pottery were now merely farming communities, the potters having returned to the land for their livelihood because their craft was no longer wanted. Up until the beginning of the Meiji era there had always been a ready market for their wares in their own villages or in markets in the area, but when cheap porcelain, mass-produced by European methods, became available throughout the land, the coarse peasant wares were cast aside. Up to this time porcelain had been expensive, and only fairly affluent people had been able to afford it; the peasants had always used pottery or lacquer wares. With the new methods employed at Seto, Kyoto, and Arita, however, porcelain could be produced at a price that made it possible for even the peasants to buy it. Unfortunately, the people did not realize that they were replacing a priceless artistic heritage with cheap inferior products.

Yanagi Sōetsu was deeply distressed over the disappearance of the "unknown craftsman," steeped in a long tradition of hard repetitive work using methods evolved over centuries of trial and error by a patient humble people. Sōetsu's contention was that greater art has been produced by a people working together in such a way over a long period, in an abandonment of egocentricity and pride, than ever could be produced by one solitary artist, no matter how great.

Above all else, Yanagi Sōetsu prized the combination of beauty and usefulness: A pottery vessel should not only possess an abstract or aesthetic beauty, but also be of practical use. He felt that mere ownership of objects of value or those made by famous artists was no indication of a person's aesthetic taste. Rather, one's general surroundings and the objects used daily were the true criteria of taste.

Sōetsu gathered about him others who thought in the same way, notable among them Hamada Shōji and Kawai Kanjiro, and traveled throughout the country to visit potters in all areas and encourage them to take up their craft again. In 1931 Sōetsu, Hamada, and Kawai founded the Japan Folk Art Society (Nihon Mingei Kyokai), with the view of promoting interest throughout the country in the fast-vanishing folk arts.

In 1936 Sōetsu founded and became director of the National Folk Art Museum (Mingei Kwan) in Kokaba, Tokyo. This museum has a magnificent collection of crafts, and although it is primarily concerned with the crafts of Japan and Korea, it also includes those from China and other places abroad. However, besides the folkcrafts, it has work by the leading artist-craftsmen. In addition to the central museum there are now three provincial museums.

Yanagi Sōetsu also founded a magazine devoted to folkcrafts *(kogei)* and spent much of his time writing and making speeches. He awakened interest in Japanese folkcrafts in other countries; Bernard Leach in England and Langdon Warner in the United States have been active in promoting appreciation of Japanese folkcrafts in their countries.

The Japanese folk art movement now has over two thousand active and supporting members. About thirty groups of craftsmen are involved, and their wares are sent to the craft shops. The main folkcraft shops (Takumi and Izumi) are in Tokyo, but there are about fifteen others in other areas. Wares are gathered from all over Japan, and this helps to keep local handcrafts alive, encouraging them so that they do not vanish as mass production steadily grows. In fact, the movement has become a kind of substitute for the pre-Meiji protection of potters by their daimyos, which—although it tended to freeze the wares in traditional styles—also ensured the continued production of the wares.

Besides Japanese folk art, another source of inspiration for potters working in the folk art movement is Korean pottery of the Yi Dynasty. During this dynasty (1392–1912), Korea was invaded first by the Chinese under the Ming emperors and then by the Japanese under Hideyoshi in the sixteenth century. The resulting poverty and depression exerted a strong influence on the tastes and needs of the Korean people.

The ceramics of the period have a rather crude and primitive appearance. Nearly all the pieces were made of white clay with a glaze containing a small amount of iron, which produced a pale green on the white body. The wares seem to have been made quickly and almost carelessly, the glazes and slips being applied in a casual way; bowls are warped and have various other imperfections acquired during firing. The decorative brushwork seems free and spontaneous, whether it is in *hakeme* ("brush grain"), a decoration of swirling slip, or a painted design in underglaze red. These pieces have a simple beauty that has been unmatched in any other country or era.

Artist-potters working in the folk movement inspired by both the old Japanese folk wares and the pottery of the Yi Dynasty have originated a new type of ware, rich in simple beauty. These pieces are marked by their unpretentious style, which, although new, has an ageless quality and timeless appeal.

Hamada Shōji (born in Tokyo in 1894) originally trained as an engineer at the Tokyo Institute of Technology. Only after he began work at the prefectural ceramic research institute in Kyoto did he become interested in pottery. In 1920, curious about a teapot he had used as a child, he visited the pottery village of Mashiko, about fifty miles north of Tokyo, in Tochigi Prefecture, and saw potters working in the traditional ways. In the same year he became a student of Bernard Leach, went with him to England, and helped him start work at St. Ives. He stayed there for four years, and his style has been strongly influenced by the English slipware he saw while in that country. During this time in England he exhibited his wares in London in 1923.

On his return to Japan in 1924 Hamada Shōji settled in Mashiko, where he has re-

113. Stoneware teabowl. Hamada Shōji. Philadelphia Museum of Art, given by Mr. and Mrs. John F. Lewis; Photograph by A. J. Wyatt

115. Stoneware jar, glazed in iron brown. Hamada Shōji. Embassy of Japan, London

114. Teabowl. Hamada Shōji. Museum of Fine Arts, Boston, Hoyt Collection

*116. Dish of Karatsu-type ware. 12½" square.
Hamada Shōji.* Philadelphia Museum of Art,
given by Mrs. Albert M. Greenfield; Photograph
by A. J. Wyatt

*117. Stoneware bottle, Hamada Shōji. H. 9". Rich
warm brown covered with a semitransparent off-white
glaze.* William P. Semon, Jr.

118. Three pieces by Hamada Shōji. Plate, 9": *rough
gray body with celadon glaze showing darker green
where brushed (perhaps with ocher) within the rim.*
Pitcher: *rough reddish buff body with milky off-white
feldspathic glaze with green brushwork (copper pigment) under the glaze.* Shallow dish: *rough gray
body,* black temmoku *glaze with trailed feldspar decoration.* Frank Stoke

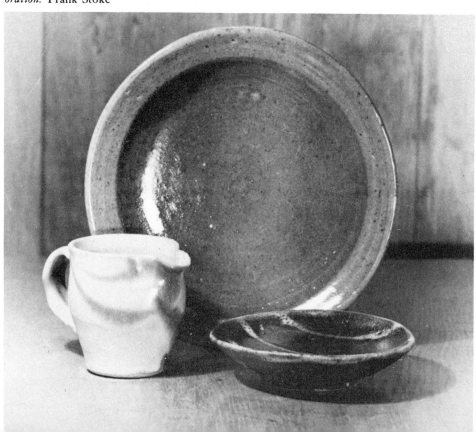

mained ever since, steadily producing fine wares over the years. These wares have had a strong effect on contemporary studio pottery, not only in Japan but in the United States and Europe. In 1929 he held a one-man exhibition in the United States, and in the years following World War II he and other well-known Japanese potters came to the United States for lecture demonstrations and exhibitions.

Hamada works in high-fired stoneware, and prefers to make wares for ordinary use rather than for the tea ceremony. These wares include dishes, plates, bowls, teapots, teabowls, cups, bottles, jars, and flower vases. He works with freedom and ease in a relaxed manner, and throws boldly and fast. The resulting forms are strong, simple, and full of vitality, like peasant wares. His pots are rarely perfectly centered; he is satisfied if the piece is aesthetically pleasing and functions well.

He has a special technique for making large vessels. First, he throws the lower part normally; then, when this has become half hardened, he finishes the upper portion by coiling. This is the opposite of the old Korean method still in use at Koishibara and Ondo, where the lower portion is coil built. In contrast to the smooth curves of the Grecian style, his wares seem almost jointed, and we can sense Hamada's honest workmanship in the vigor of their construction. He makes use of molds to hand-press slabs of stoneware into square bottle forms. All his work is marked by a frank acceptance of the effects produced by a simple and direct approach. The clay he favors is soft and sandy with a high proportion of siliceous grit, which, when fired, gives a broken beady texture to the body of the ware.

Hamada's style is a combination of Japanese folk pottery, Korean pottery of the Yi Dynasty, and English slipware, used in an essentially practical way, modern and traditional at the same time. Like the traditional potter, he appreciates the characteristics of his materials, and uses one to enhance the other. The rough texture of the stoneware body provides an excellent contrast to both the heavy wood-ash glazes and the milky semiopaque feldspar glazes he uses; both body and glaze are shown off to their advantage by decoration in the soft warm colors he likes. His work illustrates in an intensely practical way the ideals set forth by Yanagi Sōetsu, how the ancient traditions may be applied to a modern world in a most acceptable form. Besides being an artist, Hamada is also a great craftsman.

The colors Hamada prefers are a rich brown, olive green, iron red, gray, and black. His designs are restrained and subtle. He makes frequent use of drip painting, letting the glaze drip from his brush apparently at random. He has also achieved new textures and color tones by his salt-glazing technique.

His effects are never contrived; a characteristic of Hamada's work is that he recognizes a spontaneous effect in each of his pieces and brings it out. This may be either in the form itself, a natural irregularity in the glaze, or perhaps a mood suggested by the decoration.

Hamada never signs his wares, although he signs the lids of the boxes collectors keep their pieces in. He feels that a piece should stand on its own merits and not need a signature. He once remarked: "Someday, the best pieces will be attributed to me, and those less good to my students." In 1955 Hamada was honored by the Japanese government with the Order of Living National Treasure, but far more important than that is the worldwide influence his work has exerted on contemporary pottery and will continue to exert during the years to come.

Sakuma Totaro has been a friend of Hamada for many years. He was never one of Hamada's students, but through a close association he has been influenced by Hamada's work. He has done many interesting things with glazes. Besides designs employing heavy applications of glazes (Ill. 119), he uses his own individual methods for dripping, trailing, and throwing them. Glaze throwing is a difficult technique but Sakuma has mastered it, and pieces with this form of decoration present a rich effect.

Sakuma frequently makes a type of inlaylike decoration called *mishima*, which is actually an impressed pattern with the raised areas standing out in a contrasting colored slip. This should not be confused with *zōgan* ("inlay"), which is a decoration made by strips of contrasting slip inlaid in a carved surface. Sakuma uses a clay roller stamp,

119. Stoneware bottle, Sakuma Totaro. Persimmon design in heavy glaze against neutral beige background; leaves of burnt umber. H. 9". William P. Semon, Jr.

120. Vase with mishima *(inlay) decoration by Shimaoka Tatsuzō. The piece has been flattened on four sides with wooden paddles; the glazes are earth tones. H. 9½". William P. Semon, Jr.*

which he carves into complex patterns, for his *mishima*. To counteract too much regularity, after the raised area has been decorated and the piece fired, he splashes a glaze over the entire object so that irregular trails of glaze drip down over the design.

Shimaoka Tatsuzō of Mashiko is one of the leading contemporary Japanese potters who works in Jōmon style using rope decoration. In his early days he studied with Hamada and, under his direction, made copies of Jōmon wares, which were being excavated at that time in the vicinity of Mashiko.

He also makes a *mishima* decoration, but unlike Sakuma's, it is the impressed area of the decoration that is in the contrasting color (Ill. 120). He has two different ways of making the pattern. One way is by rolling short lengths of wet heavy cord over the leather-hard surface to impress the design. The other way is with short lengths of bamboo around which cord has been wrapped and tied in various patterns; the bamboo is used in the same way as the wet cord. When the impressed pattern is completed, he paints over the patterned surface with contrasting slip, and when this is partly dry he scrapes it off the raised areas, leaving the impressed

areas in a contrasting color to the rest.

Another type of *mishima* decoration he uses consists of a stamped impressed design (Ill. 121), and is often combined with free carved lines. Both the stamped and carved designs are filled with a contrasting colored slip, making the pattern stand out in two-color relief.

Some of Shimaoka's wares feature *goma*, "sesame seed," iron spot decoration. These black or brown iron spots look like sesame seeds in the clay; they make their appearance when the piece is being fired and the glaze dissolves the iron in the clay. This decoration occurs naturally with the local clay of Mashiko, which is rich in iron, and Shimaoka uses only a few decorative brushstrokes to highlight a piece of this nature.

He has also made some fine pieces using simple patterns of contrasting glazes. These warm and harmonious glazes in gray tones are particularly beautiful, ranging from an olive gray through a pale blue gray.

Shimaoka uses the wheel, and his wares are mostly symmetrical and sturdily formed. He also uses molds, like Hamada, to hand-press his bottle forms, but he finishes them by the old Korean method of paddling them

121. *Dish by Shimaoka Tatsuzo in a checkerboard pattern in muted browns. D. 9".
Signed storage box.* Captain and Mrs. Roger Gerry

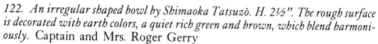

122. *An irregular shaped bowl by Shimaoka Tatsuzō. H. 2½". The rough surface
is decorated with earth colors, a quiet rich green and brown, which blend harmoniously.* Captain and Mrs. Roger Gerry

into an oval form. The wooden paddles used
for this process are carved with a variety of
patterns, some of them very complex.

Funaki Michitada operates his family
kiln near Matsu in the Fujina area of Shimane Prefecture. The Fujina district on the
western end of Honshu is well known for its
tradition of lead glazes; apart from kilns
making Raku ware, there is only one other
area in Japan that has this tradition. Funaki
and other potters of the district have been
deeply influenced by the work of Hamada
and Leach in the English slipware and Korean traditions, and they have adapted their
lead glazes to produce wares with a bright

yellow or creamy white glaze. Funaki has
made many beautiful pieces in the shape and
colors of English slipware.

His son, Funaki Kenji (born 1927), also
works at the family kiln, but his wares show
a more modern trend. One of his methods of
decoration is with a wooden stamping
wheel, and he has made some very effective
designs with it. He also decorates his wares
with simple drawings of fish, birds, horses,
and so on.

The Kyoto potter Kawai Kanjiro was
born in 1890 in Yasugi, Shimane Prefecture.
Like Hamada, he was trained as an engineer
at the Tokyo Institute of Technology, and

123. Two covered pots. Left: *8" pot by Hamada Shōji.* Right: *pot with* temmoku *glaze and wax resist decoration by Kawai Kanjiro. D. 4¾".* Fogg Art Museum

124. Square tray on four feet. Kawai Kanjiro. Courtesy, Museum of Fine Arts, Boston, Morse Memorial Fund

125. Bowl by Kawai Kanjiro is white pottery covered with cream and brown glaze; motifs in brown. Courtesy of the Brooklyn Museum, Anonymous Gift

he was twenty-seven when he decided in 1917 to become an artist-potter in Kyoto.

A bold experimenter, he made technically excellent wares in a wide variety of styles. His pieces range from traditional Chinese-style *temmoku* (Ill. 123) and celadon, through wares inspired by the *mingei* movement in the 1930s, to semicubist shapes decorated with modern abstract designs in relief and splashed with harsh-colored glazes. He is particularly noted for his colors, and those of his middle period in the late 1930s are in soft lovely shades. The wares of his folk art period were inspired by Korean wares of the Yi Dynasty. He made pieces with beautiful simple shapes at this time and they are decorated in tasteful abstract designs with a light touch, usually against a soft gray, brown, or blue background (Ill. 124). He also made many tea ceremony pieces (Ill. 125).

He was a master of the style of superimposed glaze painting, in which the glaze colors of the decoration sink into the overall glaze coating and form one smooth coat of glaze. He also made frequent use of wax resist as a means of decoration (Ill. 123). Like Hamada, he used molds to hand-press earthenware and stoneware slabs into bottle forms.

After his folk art period, Kawai experimented with monochrome wares decorated with abstract designs in flat relief. His glazes at this time were marked by a deepening of the colors; the designs stand out in whitish contrast to the overall color. Later, he exaggerated this technique so that his designs covered the whole surface in a kind of relief sculpture.

At the end of his life (he died on November 18, 1966), Kawai was making pieces in semicubist shapes (Ill. 126) and using harsh-colored glazes in shades of orange, green, and brown. Besides the large quantity of wares he produced, Kawai wrote a number of books as well as many articles on the art of pottery. He also taught students.

In studying Kawai's work one can sense the restless spirit always in quest of further development, never satisfied, feeling that there is always more to discover. It seems to me that if we criticize some of his pieces he probably would have agreed with us—it must have been his critical appraisal of his own work that led him onward through a lifetime of experiment.

Kawai Hirotsugu (born in 1919), Kawai Kanjiro's son-in-law, is the successor to the family tradition. He is a member of the Crafts Department of the Kokugakai Association. Kawai Takeichi, nephew of Kawai Kanjiro, also works in folkcraft style (Ill. 127). Kawai Seitoku (born in 1927) is a mem-

126. Ewer, Kawai Kanjiro. The design, in tones of beige and brown, gives the illusion of a cockscomb. Captain and Mrs. Roger Gerry

ber of both the Nitten Exhibition and the Japan Decorative Arts Association.

Arao Tsunezo, one of Kawai Kanjiro's students, is a Kyoto potter and member of the Mingei Association. He has made Jōmon-style wares decorated with cord patterns, but unlike Shimaoka and Kato Mineo he does not glaze or inlay the pattern with slip, and in consequence his wares are more in the original style. Both Arao Tsunezo and Ueda Tsuneji, another of Kawai Kanjiro's students, have done interesting work in *neriage*, or clay mosaic. This method of pressing clays of different colors into a mold results in the same pattern appearing on both inside and outside of the piece. Kimura Ichiro of Mashiko has used the *neriage* process to make bottle forms.

127. Left: *Square covered box with black and brown* temmoku; *Kawai Hirotsugu. H. 5½".* Right: *Square molded dish by Kawai Takeichi.* Fogg Art Museum

11

Contemporary Styles

The Nitten school made its appearance in 1927, when a group of ceramics was shown in the handicraft section of the Teiten Exhibition, and several master craftsmen were chosen as members of the government-organized Teikoko Bijutsuin. Potters in this group work in many styles; their work has had a great influence on new trends in Japanese ceramics. In 1935 the Ministry of Education sponsored the Buntei Exhibition to show these new-style ceramics, and subsequently organized a Nitten Exhibition. The Nitten Kogei-bu (the Craft Department of Nitten) was founded in 1958.

Since World War II, many different craft associations have been formed and most potters in Japan are members of one or other trend is toward abandoning the con- more of these associations. Tomimoto formed the Shinshō-kai (New Craftsmen's Group) in 1947. The Sōdei-sha was founded in 1948, the Nippon Kogei-kai (Japan Art Crafts Association) in 1955, and the Gendai Kogei Bijutsu-ka-kyokai (Japan Decorative Arts Association) in 1961. There is also an association for women potters.

There are two trends of thought among potters working in the various associations. The trend of one group is to create wares intended for daily use, and these wares are in contemporary styles that have been evolved from the traditional styles. As the potters come from such diverse backgrounds, the styles are consequently very varied. The

128. *Figure of a cormorant, by Kawashima Tennozan. Twentieth century. Black lustrous glaze, with white neck. L. 16¼".* Metropolitan Museum of Art, Rogers Fund

129. *Teapot with cover. Stoneware, with brown iron glaze over pale yellow gray celadon. C. 1930–1935.* Victoria and Albert Museum

cept of wares for practical use and experimenting with free and pure forms, but again generally in the framework of one of the traditional styles.

Kano Mitsue (born in Kyoto in 1903) won a Nitten Exhibition prize in 1949 for a white glazed jar with carved design. Asami Ryuzo (born in Kyoto in 1904) has a white porcelain jar on permanent exhibition in the Düsseldorf Museum. Kusube Yaichi of Kyoto (born 1897), a "national living treasure" and trustee of the Nitten Exhibition, carves and models his wares in low relief. The designs are generally of leaves or flowers, but he also makes use of abstract motifs. Imai Masayuki of Kyoto (born 1930) has decorated wares with designs reminiscent of those used by American Indians. (At this juncture I would like to say that I have seen "Indian pottery" for sale in the Badlands of South Dakota marked "made in Japan." Perhaps during their brief sojourn in Japan these ersatz Indian wares left a slight influence on Japanese pottery!)

Interesting methods of glaze and biscuit decoration are used by many potters who are searching for new means of expression but have not broken radically with the old ways. Uchida Kunio has developed a new *neriage* process, which he uses with artistic effect. His method is to press slices of contrasting colored clay into the surface of a partly shaped piece; the decoration thus

130. *Stoneware water jar. Twentieth century. H. 20¾".* Philadelphia Museum of Art, given by Mr. and Mrs. John F. Lewis; Photograph by A. J. Wyatt

131. *Stoneware jar by Ishakawa Kinya, a Japanese potter working in Bucherville, Quebec. Modern.* Collection of Cindy Stone

formed appears on only one surface of the ware, instead of going right through the biscuit. Ito Suiko has made some remarkably beautiful porcelains with glaze inlay, a very difficult process, and his graceful designs are carried out in delicate colors. Another potter who has developed a high degree of skill in glaze decoration is Tokuriki Magosaburo, who has produced striking effects with his superimposed glaze painting.

Other forms of decoration are produced in the body of the ware. Fujihira Shin coil-builds angular pots decorated with a form of appliqué. The motif, cut from a thin slice of clay, is attached to the pot; it makes a decoration in low relief, generally of human figures, birds, or animals, which are angular like the pots. Tsuji Shindoku makes use of an extended coil of wire to make interesting surface patterns on the body of his wares; he also creates patterns with a comb. Both Shinkai Kanzan and Taniguchi Ryozo use stamps to make impressed decorations on their wares.

Asao Gen, Sozen II, makes unglazed wares with a glossy surface produced by burnishing. His wares have *unka* decoration ("cloud flower"), which is caused by carbon impregnation during the firing. In 1944 he was appointed by the Japanese government as technical expert and preserver of the art of *unka* ware.

Since World War II young potters have been experimenting with totally new concepts and expression in ceramics. Abstract designs, free-form shapes, as well as forms apparently inspired by the machine age and the robot, all vie for our attention. Only time will tell which of these will pass the test of acceptance by future generations and which will quietly sink into oblivion. However, I would like to point out that inventiveness in creating new forms does not necessarily produce a work of art; a piece must possess certain aesthetic qualities, not merely the ability to shock.

Notable among the avant-garde are four Kyoto potters, all members of the Sōdei-sha group, and all working with free-form or abstract shapes. They are Kumakura Junkichi (born 1920), Yamada Hikaru (born 1924), Hayashi Yasuo (born

132. A ceramic exhibition held in a gallery at a department store in Japan. Embassy of Japan, London

1928), and Hayashi Hideyuki (born 1937). Kumakura is well known for his ceramic sculpture. Susuki Osamu, also of Kyoto (born 1926), Satonaka Hideto of Tokyo (born 1932), and Miwa Ryusaku of Hagi, Yamaguchi Prefecture (born 1940), also belong to the Sōdei-sha group, but work in a less radical style.

Araki Takako of Nishinomiya, Hyogo Prefecture (born 1921), and Tsuboi Asuka of Kyoto (born 1932) are members of the Women's Association of Ceramic Art. Their work has received very favorable comment in the press. In 1971 both submitted works that were accepted competitively for exhibition in the Japan Ceramic Art Exhibition organized by the Mainichi newspapers. In the exhibition of contemporary ceramic art of Japan held in 1972 in several cities in the United States and Canada, Araki Takako was represented by four silk-screen printed bowls, and Tsuboi Asuka by "Sleeve Series A" and "Sleeve Series B" decorated in overglaze enamels.

Kato Seiji of Shigaraki, Shiga Prefecture (born 1926), Mishima Kimiko of Osaka (born 1932), Yanagihara Mutsuo of Kyoto (born 1934), Koie Ryoji of Tokoname (born 1938), and Kuze Kenji of Seto (born 1945) are all independent potters working in freeform style.

Exhibitions by contemporary potters are held frequently in Japan and they are always well attended by an interested public. The Kyoto Art Museum held a large exhibition of this nature in 1968 that received considerable attention in the press.

Many department stores have large exhibition halls, and ceramic exhibitions are frequently held in these (Ill. 132). Generally the wares exhibited are by artists belonging to one group or another, but in 1971 the Mainichi newspapers celebrated their centenary by organizing the Japan Ceramic Art Exhibition, which showed wares made by contemporary potters working in all styles. This exhibition was shown in eight cities in Japan, and in 1972 seventy pieces were selected from the exhibition and were shown in the United States and Canada.

For Export Only

12

Japan in the Meiji Era (1868-1912)

Commodore Matthew C. Perry steamed along the coast of Japan on the morning of July 8, 1853. He had two steamers and two sloops under his command, and the people of Shimoda, seeing the black smoke, thought that the foreign ships on the horizon were on fire. They ran up the mountain behind the town for a better look, and as the early morning haze lifted, saw that the smoke was pouring from smokestacks rising up above the decks and that, marvelously, the ships were moving against the wind. Steamships were a new invention, and these were the first that the Japanese had ever seen. However, even more frightening to the Japanese than the strangeness of the ships were the many guns they carried, and these were pointing at the shore. Messengers were sent along the beach to Edo—mountains lay behind Shimoda, and the way to Edo was along the beach.

Although the Dutch at Nagasaki had told the Japanese that an American expedition to their country had been discussed in American and European newspapers, no one in Japan had believed the barbarians would really come. Confusion reigned in Edo. Some officials said the barbarians must be driven away, but others, who had seen the guns, knew that this would not be possible.

Orders were given for shore batteries to be manned, and black and white cloth screens were strung along the shore in front of the forts to hide the defenses. As there had been no wars for two hundred years, weapons were not in readiness for this sudden emergency. The townspeople ran in all directions, taking their valuables for safekeeping to friends who lived farther off.

On his flagship, the *Susquehanna*, Commodore Perry carried a letter from President Millard Fillmore to high officials in Japan. The letter asked the Japanese to break their long seclusion and enter into friendly relations with the United States. It also asked that shipwrecked American seamen be treated with kindness, and ports opened to supply coal and provisions to the whalers on the North Pacific and to steamers going between California and China. Trade was suggested, as well.

Commodore Perry relished the idea of the Japanese visit, for he felt it was highly appropriate that Americans should effect the opening of Japan to the world. Columbus had been on his way to Japan, inspired by the maps of Marco Polo, when he discovered America—it was fitting for the American people to finish what he had begun. Commodore Perry also had a sense of the dramatic.

On the way to Japan Perry paid a visit to Okinawa as a rehearsal; he landed there with bands playing, and even had himself carried to the palace in a sedan chair constructed by the ship's carpenter. But his visit had not been welcomed. The islanders sent messengers saying that the Queen Dowager was sick. The commodore did not believe this, however, and informed them that the music and pageantry would do her good. After considerable negotiation the regent

133. Two gifts from the emperor of Japan to Commodore Matthew C. Perry: a lacquer clothing box and a lacquer writing box (opened to show the inside). Peabody Museum of Salem; Photograph by M. W. Sexton

agreed to receive Perry at the palace, but the Queen Dowager did not appear. This was not really surprising, as—although the excuse had been that she was indisposed after receiving a British naval officer who had behaved in a rude and rambunctious manner —it was said that, in actual fact, she had died five years before.

As they steamed up the Japanese coast to Edo Bay, Commodore Perry looked through his glass at the shore batteries—the cloth screens did not hide much from his telescope. The clans had hoisted flags emblazoned with the crests of the noble houses, but what cannons there were were short-ranged and antiquated. The noise was nonetheless nerve-racking. When the foreign ships had neared the coast the Japanese on the shore had begun to beat their war gongs; the Americans had never heard the like.

After the ships anchored in Edo Bay, negotiations began for the delivery of the letter. Perry refused to see any minor official, saying that he could meet only with someone of equal rank to himself—he had given himself the title of Lord of the Forbidden Interior. It took several days to convince the Japanese that Perry would not be trifled with. Finally it was agreed that the commodore would deliver the letter to Prince Toda, as representative of the emperor.

On the designated day the Lord of the Forbidden Interior stepped from his ship onto his barge and was rowed ashore. Accompanied by martial music played by the brass band on the flagship, an imposing procession marched between the honor guard composed of the ships' crews. The marines led the way, then the sailors, followed by the commodore, who walked between two tall Negroes (most Japanese had never seen a Negro). The commodore also had a bodyguard of the ten biggest men in the fleet. They marched to the reception hall, and the letter, which had been carried from the ship in an ornate rosewood box by two midshipmen, was delivered in solemn silence. In return, the commodore was presented with a scroll in Japanese saying that, since President Fillmore's letter had now been delivered, the Americans should take their departure.

After the commodore had returned to his ship, the vessels did not depart immediately; instead, they remained nearby at anchor for another eight days, and conducted a survey of the coast. When that was completed, the commodore sailed away with his fleet. He planned to return the following spring for an answer.

The shogun (the title meant "barbarian-subduing generalissimo") did not know what to do, so he did something that no shogun

134. Bowl showing Yokohama in Kanagawa Prefecture, decorated by Kogetsu of Tokyo about 1860. Eight large foreign ships are in the harbor, towering over the small Japanese boats. Peabody Museum of Salem

had done in six hundred years. He sent to Kyoto to ask the advice of the emperor. Of course the emperor and his court had not seen the ships and the guns, and they sent back the message: "Expel the barbarians."

When Perry returned in February 1854 with his full complement of ten ships, the shogunate had no choice but to start negotiations. This they did with much feasting on their part (the commodore did not care too much for their food) and with entertainment provided by both sides. Whenever Perry felt that the negotiations were not proceeding to his liking, he threatened to sail up to Edo with his ships and his guns, whereupon the difficulties would vanish.

Shimoda and Hakodate were to be opened as ports, and Perry sailed to Shimoda to inspect that small town. The harbor was good, and they were struck by the beauty of the place. They did not realize immediately, however, that Shimoda had been offered because the mountains behind the town almost shut it off from the rest of Japan.

In June Perry sailed away again, and Japan started on the tremendous leap forward that was to transform her within a hundred years from a backward isolated country into a great modern power. She was

no longer the country at the very end of the world: unreachable, unapproachable, and self-sufficient. The Suez Canal had just been opened, and European ships bound for Japan were now able to make the voyage in a much shorter time than when they had been obliged to go around the Cape of Good Hope. And, of course, Japan lay on the way of American ships going west.

Within two years of Perry's departure, England, Russia, and Holland negotiated similar treaties with Japan, and steady trade developed between those countries and Japan. Foreigners were allowed to live in and trade at five ports, as well as at Osaka and Edo, and the fishing village of Yokohama grew rapidly as foreign merchants began to set up business there (Ill. 134).

For the next decade Japan suffered internal struggles between those who wanted to expel the foreigners and those who knew it was impossible. In 1867, however, after some short sharp battles, the Tokugawa was defeated and the shogun resigned. In 1868 the name Edo was changed to Tokyo, meaning "eastern capital," and the fifteen-year-old emperor, his court, and government moved to the Tokugawa Palace there the next year.

135. Koda wares, 1870, from the Morse Collection. Edward S. Morse said, in his Catalogue of the Morse Collection of Japanese Pottery, *that these wares bear the impressed mark* Gen *(Minamoto) and represent the work of the best potter of Koda in the 1870s.* Courtesy, Museum of Fine Arts, Boston, Morse Collection, Gift by Contribution

The new era was given the name Meiji; the emperor was given the title posthumously, after he died in 1912.

The new leaders realized that Japan was far behind the West and would have to modernize as fast as possible. Groups of students were sent to various Western countries to study the methods used there, and foreign teachers and technicians were brought to Japan. This period of learning was comparable, but on a much larger scale, to the time when Chinese civilization was taken to Japan a thousand years earlier.

After modern Western methods had been adopted, Japanese industry held a unique position in the world. The combination of cheap oriental labor harnessed to Western science produced low-priced goods of excellent quality, although a great many articles of poor quality were also made. The revival abroad of interest in Japanese ways created an almost insatiable market for her exports.

With the opening of Japan, tours of the Far Eastern countries became very popular with both Americans and Europeans of comfortable means. Japan owes the survival of her great artistic heritage to these first foreign visitors, who recognized her art treasures as such. In the mad rush for Western ideas these masterpieces would have been entirely lost without the efforts of such people as Edward Morse, William Sturgis Bigelow, and Ernest Fenollosa.

In the United States there are two important collections of Japanese pottery assembled by Edward Morse. The larger one is at the Museum of Fine Arts, Boston (Ill. 135); the smaller at the Peabody Museum in Salem, Massachusetts. Morse visited kilns throughout Japan, and his collections represent all types of Japanese pottery.

Edward Sylvester Morse, born on June 18, 1838, in Portland, Maine, was a natural collector. He started as a boy with a collection of land shells, which was so comprehensive by the time he was fifteen that other collectors came to see it from as far as Boston and even England.

As a young man, Morse studied zoology under Louis Agassiz at Harvard. He was one of the young student assistants at Harvard's newly built Museum of Comparative Zoology, one of his duties being cataloging and arranging specimens. At Agassiz's suggestion he began a study of brachiopods, tracing their development from fossil to living species, and it was this study that eventually took him to Japan. However, before this —and soon after Harvard—he was appointed a member of the staff of the newly established museum in Salem, Massachusetts. George Peabody had given $140,000 "for the promotion of science and useful knowledge in the county of Essex," and this provided for the purchase of the East India Marine Hall in Salem, owned by the East

India Marine Society, and the establishment of a museum there. (Later, Morse was curator of the museum from 1868 to 1871, director from 1880 to 1914, and director emeritus from 1914 to 1925.)

Morse was a highly succesful lecturer who toured the country speaking on natural history. During one of his tours, late in the spring of 1874 in San Francisco, he heard of Japan's many varieties of brachiopods, but three years passed before he could arrange a three months' visit there to collect specimens.

Morse arrived at Yokohama in June 1877, and at once took a train on the newly constructed railroad to Tokyo to present a letter of introduction to Dr. David Murray, superintendent of the Mombusho (Department of Education). On the way he noticed some fossilized shells lying beside the tracks, and at once recognized that the construction of the railroad bed had unearthed a prehistoric kitchen midden. In Tokyo he told members of the university faculty about the shells and aroused their interest. Archaeology was unknown in Japan at that time, and it was this discovery by Morse that initiated the study.

Dr. Murray took Morse to meet Professor Toyama, a Cornell graduate, and Vice-Minister Tanaka, and both were impressed with Morse's knowledge and personality. When Dr. Murray and Morse returned from a brief trip to Nikko, Japanese authorities asked Morse to remain in Japan and organize a department of zoology at the university and to found a museum of natural history. He accepted a two-year contract at the Imperial University in Tokyo, and was also given the staff to found a marine biological laboratory at Enoshima, the first in the Pacific regions. The laboratory was a rented fisherman's hut!

Morse's interest in Japanese pottery began—this, too, happened by chance—a year later. He was having trouble with his nerves and digestion, and his doctor prescribed a daily five-mile walk. When Morse objected to such a regimen, the doctor suggested that he find a hobby to pursue on his walks, and a few days later Morse discovered Japanese pottery. The first pieces were saucers made in the form of certain shells, which Morse found in the various Japanese shops he passed on his walks. When he showed the saucers to Japanese friends, they told him the pieces were neither old nor from famous potteries, and their attitude made him aware that the Japanese appreciated only the best in pottery.

His friends took him to gatherings of connoisseurs, who amused themselves by guessing the origin of various pieces of pottery handed from one guest to the other. Each guest wrote down the origin, date, and potter's name, and at the end of the game there was a prize for the winner. Morse soon realized that this game was built on exact knowledge—the connoisseurs had to be able to recognize the clays used, the kiln, the techniques, and the style. Resolving to learn all these things, he became the pupil of Noritane Ninagawa, who had written an unpublished book on the subject. Every Sunday afternoon for the next year, until Ninagawa died, Morse took a pottery lesson.

During this period the Japanese were avidly learning from the West, and ignoring or forgetting their ancient arts and customs; the tea ceremony was forgotten for a quarter of a century. Collections in the hands of old families were being dispersed to help their owners out of financial straits. In time, when the Japanese came again to value their ancient heritage, they found that many of their treasures had vanished from their land, never to be recovered. That some remained —and the recognition of their artistic value —were in great part due to Morse, as we shall see later.

Morse came to know Japan very well, traveling to places that no other foreigner had seen. He served as a scientific adviser to the government, and in that capacity had the freedom to travel anywhere he wished. His journal, published later under the title of *Japan Day by Day,* related adventures of all kinds: nearly being caught in a bear trap that held a poisoned arrow, eating raw marine worms for supper, searching for ancient pottery while up to his waist in water in a dark cave under an avalanche of huge poisonous centipedes. His descriptions of these adventures delighted his lecture audiences during the three years he spent in America after his return in 1879.

Those years (1879–1882) were busy ones for Morse. Not only did he give his highly successful lectures; he was appointed director of the Peabody Museum in Salem. However, he missed Japan, and with the ostensible purpose of forming an ethnological collection for the Peabody Museum, as well as adding to his pottery collection, he returned there in 1882, traveling with Dr. William Sturgis Bigelow, whom he had persuaded to visit that country.

Dr. Bigelow was the son of the well-known physician Henry Jacob Bigelow, a founder of the Museum of Fine Arts in Boston. In Japan the younger Dr. Bigelow became interested in Japanese art and assembled a large collection of lacquer, swords, and sword guards, which later was given to the Museum of Fine Arts in Boston.

In Tokyo, joined by Ernest Fenollosa and Okakura Kakuzō, Morse and Bigelow undertook a journey to the great art centers of Japan. The railroad had not yet been extended very far, so they went by jinrikisha and boat through the southern provinces. Morse wrote:

We shall see a little of the life of old Japan. I shall add a great many specimens to my collection of pottery. Dr. Bigelow will secure many forms of swords, guards and lacquers, and Mr. Fenollosa will increase his remarkable collection of pictures, so that we will have in the vicinity of Boston by far the greatest collection of Japanese art in the world.

Okakura Kakuzō, the only Japanese in the party, acted as interpreter. He had learned English as a child. His father, a samurai who had been obliged to open a silk-thread store after the collapse of the feudal system, recognized the importance of learning English for his business, and wanted his sons to learn it also. Okakura Kakuzō proved to be an apt pupil. In due course he entered the Tokyo Institute of Foreign Languages, which became Tokyo University in 1877. Okakura attended the class in Western

philosophy taught by Fenollosa, and because of his fluency in English often acted as class interpreter.

When Fenollosa became interested in Japanese art, he had Okakura translate old books on art and artists for him, and later when he lectured on art at gatherings in Tokyo, Okakura interpreted for him. At these gatherings Fenollosa praised the simplicity of Japanese paintings, and pointed out that the effect created by this artistic simplicity was superior to the masses of color in Western oil paintings. He reproached the Japanese for ignoring their own art in their rush to learn about Western art, which they were accepting without question as being better than their own.

Through the efforts of Fenollosa, Okakura, and others of the same opinion, an Imperial Commission of Fine Arts was established to record, catalog, and study the existing art collections in Japan, many of which were in temples. Fenollosa and Okakura were both named commissioners of fine arts, and traveled together to various parts of Japan in their official capacity. (One of their greatest discoveries was the standing Buddha at Nara, ascribed to the days of Suiko [A.D. 593–629], which had not been seen for centuries.)

In 1882, when they had joined Morse and Bigelow for the trip to the great art centers, a chance remark made by Morse had a far-reaching influence on Okakura. Morse remarked that it was sad so much fine Japanese art was now on the market—it was as if the lifeblood of Japan were seeping from a hidden wound. The words had a profound effect. When Okakura returned to Tokyo he tried to make the authorities and people with influence do something about the unfortunate situation. Two years later, in 1884, through his efforts the law of Koku-Ho (national treasures) was enacted. All the remaining treasures of ancient art were registered and were restricted from export, most of them becoming in due course part of the collections in the Tokyo, Nara, and Kyoto museums.

During his time as professor at Tokyo University, Morse's forthright manner earned him the trust of the university president, Baron Kato. Many bombastic foreigners came to the university, ready to accept well-paid posts that they were not academically qualified to hold. In his usual outspoken way Morse told the president of the situation, and was asked to name suitable candidates for the vacant posts. This he did, either nominating competent people he knew personally or getting recommendations from those whose judgment he trusted.

Many of the people recommended by Morse, once in Japan, became interested in oriental art in one form or another, and made collections of their own. Most of these collections were eventually deposited in the Museum of Fine Arts, Boston, making that museum host to the largest single collection of oriental art in the world. This collection, in turn, has had its influence on other collections, and so Morse can be thanked for contributing in some way to the collections of oriental art in this country and around the world. This is particularly interesting in view of the fact that Morse is so often reproached for a lack of aesthetic taste and judgment.

The two Japanese pottery collections made by Edward Morse are the largest collections of their kind in the world outside Japan. An Englishman, J. L. Bowes, made a similar collection, but it was not as extensive and has since been dispersed.

Morse spent twenty years making his first pottery collection. He traveled all over Japan, visited pottery kilns throughout the country, and collected examples of their products. In 1890 he sold this collection to the Museum of Fine Arts in Boston for the sum of $76,000; the collection is still there in the cases the way he arranged it.

When he became director of the Peabody Museum in Salem, Morse set about making a duplicate collection (Ill. 136). This too is a large collection, but it is not as complete as the one in Boston.

The Museum of Fine Arts in Boston and the Peabody Museum in Salem were intended as sister museums as far as their oriental collections were concerned, with the Peabody Museum as host for the ethnic (arts and crafts) collections. However, nowadays, certain items are considered to belong more rightfully in the Fine Arts section, although at the time of acquisition they were considered ethnic. Anyone interested in Japanese pottery should try to visit one of these collections, which are not widely enough known. The Edward Sylvester Morse Collection in Boston's Museum of Fine Arts is, however, housed in a part of the museum's third floor that is not open to the public. Visitors are requested to make an appointment with the Department of Asiatic Art to see the collection; a letter or phone call is necessary before a visit.

At the Peabody Museum in Salem, a

136. Three pieces from the Morse Collection. Left: dish, Tanzan, 1870; raised floral decoration is pink, blue, yellow, and green. Center: jar with heavy drip glaze; Iga, 1870. Right: bottle with blue and brown decoration on beige background; Iga, 1880. Peabody Museum of Salem; Photo by M. W. Sexton

PLATE 1.   *Pre-Nippon wares: Dish with lace decoration in raised slip has white enamel edging and beading and herbaceous peonies,* shakuyaku. *The glaze is heavy. Inscribed* Shigeki Imanari *in Japanese characters. The covered vegetable dish with Chinese-style design at first glance looks Chinese, but besides the Japanese inscription underneath that reads* Shunkō, *the colors are brighter and the men are wearing Japanese clothing,* kariginu, *and hats,* eboshi.

PLATE 2.   *Nippon bowl, Chinese-style design, with vivid Japanese colors.*

PLATE 4. *Detail of decoration on the Satsuma vase showing color rubbed into the crackle on one petal of the peony and on the bamboo trunk above it.*

PLATE 3. *Satsuma vase, h. 25". Rim is ornamented with knife cuts.*

PLATE 5. *Satsuma temple jar. H. 33".*

PLATE 6. *Pre-Nippon vase. Intricate coralene beading is decorated with gold. There is excellent brushwork on both the floral decoration and the shaded background. Underglaze blue is imported cobalt oxide.*

PLATE 7. *Chocolate pot, pre-Nippon ware. Although there is considerable fluting on the body, the handle is very plain.*

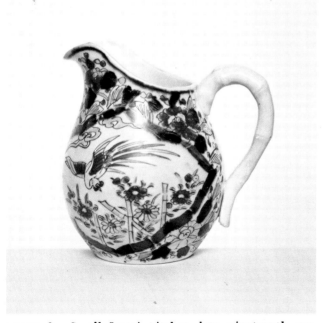

PLATE 8. *Small Imari pitcher, late nineteenth century, Chinese pheasant design. The underglaze blue is the native cobalt,* gosu.

PLATE 9. *Nippon M-in-Wreath vase with beautifully painted sunset landscape scene. A characteristic of these fine wares is that although the principal motif (in this case a landscape) is painted with infinite care and attention to detail, the border decoration is often somewhat irregular.*

PLATE 10. *Left, footed cup and saucer with Satsuma-style decoration of Chinese scenes; saucer inscribed* Haruta *in Japanese characters. Center, condensed milk jar, with hole underneath, and oriental-looking handles. Inscribed* Shimamura *in Japanese characters. Right, cup and saucer with delicately painted design of lady and child.*

PLATE 11. *Chocolate set with Nippon Maple Leaf mark. Chocolate sets had five cups until World War I, when sets with six cups began to be made. This set has handles of unusual shape.* Mrs. Anne Burley

PLATE 12. *Kutani chocolate set decorated with five scenes in reserves shaped like a folding fan, lantern, flat (Chinese) fan, ancient mirror, and cherry blossom. Each scene depicts a season: the landscape view with cherry blossoms is for spring; an old lady seated on the floor by the open* shōji *represents summer (her eyebrows are painted in the shape of a* V, *which was the conventional means used in old prints to show age in a woman); a scene with red maples represents autumn; the other two scenes with pine trees depict winter.*

PLATE 13. *Four pieces of pre-Nippon, all unmarked. Plate,* Mr. and Mrs. D. Stone. *Vase and cup,* Mr. and Mrs. T. M. Lotito

PLATE 14. *Two Nippon pieces with European-style decoration. Vase at left has completely symmetrical decoration. Both back and front are exactly the same, an unusual characteristic. The mark is Kinjo Nippon. The footed dish with bluebirds carries the Rising Sun mark; usually Rising Sun pieces have pastel floral decoration.*

PLATE 15. *Two Satsuma-style vases. In contrast to the Nippon pieces, which portray human figures as types (man, woman, child), the people on Satsuma wares look like individuals.*

PLATE 16. *Pair of Nippon M-in-Wreath vases, front and back views. The overglaze enamel decoration resembles cloisonné.*

PLATE 17. *Four Nippon M-in-Wreath pieces, c. World War I. All are imitative of European wares, but their oriental origin is apparent. The porcelain of the sugar and creamer is of excellent quality.*

PLATE 18. *Nippon Maple Leaf wares: The small bowl must have been shaped by hand after it was taken from the mold—one can feel how the potter pressed the rim between his thumb and fingers to make a fluted edge. Vase in European style*—Veronica Kiley

PLATE 19. *Nippon vases. The gray porcelain has been deepened and shaded to make a beautiful soft background for the floral decoration. Left (anemones), Imperial mark. Center (poppies), t"t" mark. Right (mixed blossoms), Imperial mark.* Mr. and Mrs. J. Schrody

PLATE 20. *This set carries the Nippon Hō-ō bird mark; it is made of good quality porcelain. Although the cups appear to be teacups, the pot is the size of a chocolate pot.* Mrs. Robert Seekamp

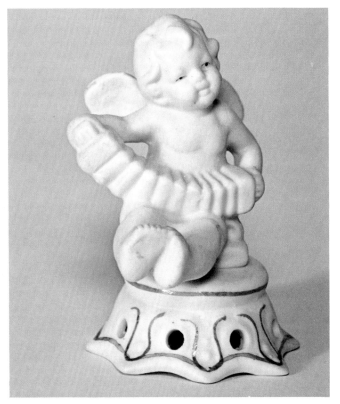

PLATE 21. *A bisque figurine of winged cherub playing the concertina is marked "Made in Occupied Japan."* Pinney Collection

PLATE 22. *The cups in this set are good quality porcelain. The extensive multicolored molded decoration is obviously designed to appeal to the Western market. Note the elaborate gold handles and the overabundance of gold decoration inside the cups. Mark: Occupied Japan.* Mr. and Mrs. T. M. Lotito

137. *Blue and white bowl, Meiji Period (c. 1880).* Collection of Jiromaru-no-Toyohashi. *Garden seat, Kyushu; also Meiji Period. The hexagonal sides are alternating blue and white and celadon.* Captain and Mrs. Roger Gerry

much smaller museum, the limited space makes it impossible to show more than a selection of the specimens from the Morse collection in the public galleries, but the exhibits are changed at frequent intervals. This collection is an extraordinarily interesting one, well worth traveling some distance to see.

During his years in Japan, Morse had a great influence on Japanese education. In the scientific field, his lectures at Tokyo University were so successful that much of Japan's progress in medicine, in biological, botanical, and agricultural research, and in physics and archaeology is said to have stemmed from a group of ninety of his students.

Between his visits to Japan, Morse spend much of his time at home in the United States on lecture tours. His enthusiastic lectures, illustrated by ambidextrous drawings on a blackboard, fired his listeners to go to Japan and see the country for themselves. One such person was Mrs. Jack Gardner.

Isabella Stewart Gardner was the wife of Jack Gardner, whose family had owned sailing ships in Salem, and had moved to Boston when the merchant ships transferred to that port instead of Salem. His mother was a Peabody of Salem.

When Mrs. Gardner and her husband undertook an oriental tour in 1882, they had already heard a great deal about Japan while still in Boston. Besides the Morse lectures, they had a closer source of information: Mrs. Gardner's personal physician, Dr. Henry J. Bigelow, the father of William Sturgis Bigelow.

Isabella Gardner—or Mrs. Jack, as she was called—was a vivacious lady not in the least afraid to shock the staid matrons of Boston society. When William Sturgis Bige-

low met the Gardners in Japan in 1883, he described Mrs. Gardner as "gloom-dispeller, corpse reviver and general chirker-up." Her great interest, especially after her husband died, was her art collection, and in her later years she had a Venetian palace built on the Fenway in Boston, near the Museum of Fine Arts, to house the collection and later to become a museum. Her friends and protégés included artists of all kinds. Okakura gave her advice on oriental additions to her collection, and sent her a tea set (Ill. 23).

Okakura spent most of the last ten years of his life in Boston. In 1903 he became adviser to the Chinese and Japanese Department of the Museum of Fine Arts, and was appointed curator there in 1910, a post he held until his death in 1913.

Japanese and oriental influences in art were everywhere. Whistler, one of Mrs. Gardner's friends, who made a pastel portrait of her, which he called *A Little Note in Yellow,* had painted a picture of a Japanese room. John Singer Sargent, another of her friends, who painted more than one portrait of her, used two huge oriental vases as background in one of his famous portraits.

Japanese art had come into vogue in the

United States with the Centennial Exposition in Philadelphia in 1876. For this exposition the Japanese government sent a large collection of ceramics, the major part being devoted to showing the history and development of the art. However, I am told on good authority that many of the fine old pieces exhibited were not old pieces at all, but very skillfully made copies of the originals. A great many new-style pieces had been specially made for the exhibition, using the new processes the Japanese were fast learning from the West. The ceramic wares in the exhibition were subsequently shipped to London, where they can now be seen in the Victoria and Albert Museum.

By 1883 there was an exhibition of foreign wares in Boston for which a number of Japanese factories had sent examples of their ceramic work. The exhibition catalog mentioned—among others—Kiriu Kosho Kuarsha of Tokyo and Koransha of Arita.

138. *Painting weights, twentieth century, to be hung on the lower corners of a painting (scroll) so that it does not curl up when on display.* Philadelphia Museum of Art, given by Mrs. Edgar Stone; Photograph by A. J. Wyatt

13

Ceramic Methods since 1868

There is a vast difference between wares made in traditional Japanese style and those made since 1868 in Western style for export. Imari wares, described more fully in the earlier part of this book, continued to be decorated in the traditional style, but on account of the mass-production techniques introduced after 1868 the method of applying the decoration underwent various changes. In the 1880s some very poor pieces were made because the hand-painted decoration had to be done at high speed to fill the agent's orders. Later, the type of design used lent itself to machine-made perfection, resulting in perfect but artistically cold pieces. Satsuma-style wares, on the other hand, had an abundance of decoration, which even when meticulously executed is so heavy that it is often unattractive. This type of decoration, intended to please the taste of the foreigner, was completely misunderstood by the Japanese, and in many instances the resulting pieces pleased nobody's taste. An artist can make something of true beauty only when he works to satisfy his own standards.

After 1868 the Japanese also created a new style based on European methods, and turned out some very attractive pieces. This style lies somewhere between the Oriental and the Western. The colors and designs are European, but the workmanship is Japanese. Unfortunately, the period when the best of this work was done was very short, and by the time of the First World War it was over. That does not mean that afterward nothing

good was made for the export market. On the contrary, very good pieces were made, but the period of good work at nominal prices was over.

The finer wares of this period (1868–1918) have never been generally recognized as such. There are two reasons for this situation: the wares are not in the Japanese tradition; and, at the time they were being made, they sold for very little abroad. Of course, the low value was not based on poor quality, but rather that the people who made the wares were not paid in accordance with the time they spent or the quality of their work. Before 1868 Japanese craftsmen were supported by their local daimyos and could spend as long as necessary to make a beautiful article; time was of no importance. This tradition of meticulous work lingered for a while, but when craftsmen were paid only for what they produced, they could no longer afford to spend unlimited time on one object. The pressure, also, was intense from the agents who handled the selling abroad—articles had to be made as fast as possible.

The change from good careful handwork to the frenzy of mass production was accomplished in remarkably few years. Dr. Gottfried Wagner, a German chemist, went to Arita on 1870 to advise on European-style methods of ceramic production. Modern factory equipment was installed, and coal-burning kilns put in instead of wood-burning ones. Plaster molds were introduced, clay molds having been in use up to this

139. Powder box, unmarked, is good quality porcelain with pink roses, green border, and gold star decoration in the center. Pinney Collection. Nippon M-in-Wreath sugar and creamer with interesting oriental-looking shape are decorated in dull gold.

time. European enamel colors were also introduced, with their infinite possibilities of color shading, and European methods of glazing were demonstrated.

Foreign-style wares were in great demand by the Japanese; the traditional was pushed aside as worthless. After the emperor and his court moved to Edo in 1868, and the city was renamed Tokyo, the area became a center of foreign trade. Foreign diplomats and traders bought houses and demanded Western-style comforts and living conditions. The Japanese people, especially those around Tokyo and other centers of foreign trade, fell under this influence, and a craze for Western-style wares swept the country.

Prior to this time the Japanese had abhorred symmetry; tablewares had to be different, each piece contrasting with and enhancing the others. Now matched sets were bought and pairs of vases made—these had not existed for the Japanese people before the coming of foreign trade.

Kilns were set up in and around Tokyo expressly for the purpose of making Western-style wares. The new kilns were of two kinds: either kilns of individual potters producing their own particular style, potting, firing, and decorating each piece themselves; or decorator kilns, which were muffle kilns capable of sufficient heat only to fix the decoration. Wares made elsewhere were

140. Celery dish set; Nippon, M-in-Wreath. The large dish was made in a solid casting mold; the salt dishes in flopover molds. The decoration seems at first glance to be perfectly regular, but on closer inspection the Japanese love for irregularity becomes apparent—the roses are surrounded by leaves, some blue and some green, and no two sets are exactly alike. Gold is freely used.

brought "in the white" to Tokyo to be decorated for the foreign trade. Huge quantities of this type of ware were produced, as mass-production methods improved. Some pieces were marked with the name of the kiln, but the kilns were too numerous and small to be traced or classified, and many lasted for only a short period. Other marks, particularly for the American market, were import-export marks, and were either the symbol of the export company that gathered the pieces together for shipment or that of the importer.

To start with, the wares were fairly individual, but when plaster molds came into common use identical wares could be produced in large quantity.

Molds

Four main types of molds were used. Drain molds, which utilized a liquid slip (clay mixed with enough liquid so that it could be poured), were the most common, and were used for vases, teapots, chocolate pots, cups, and the like. Solid casting molds were also used with liquid slip, and these were for dishes, bowls, and so on (Ill. 140). Flopover molds called for a pancake of clay over the mold; they were used for shallow articles. Press molds, used for cup handles, required lumps of soft clay.

With whatever method used, the dry plaster of the mold absorbed sufficient liquid from the clay so that the molded piece became firm enough to be removed from the mold. The piece was then leather-hard, in the right state for other parts like spouts or handles to be attached to it with slip. All the

parts attached together had to be in the same state of hardness so that they would dry out at the same rate.

Drain Molds: This type of mold was made in the shape of the outside of the piece to be molded; liquid slip was poured into it and, after a few minutes, when a wall of the required thickness was formed on the inside of the mold, the excess slip was poured off. One piece—for instance, a teapot—might require a number of separate molds, depending on what had to be attached: a spout, handle, feet, stem, or finial. The disadvantage of this method is that it is not easy to make two pieces with walls of equal thickness, and the inside of the finished pieces is never as smooth as with other methods. For this reason cups intended for use are not made in this way anymore, but they were made in Japan by this method until the jigger came into general use in the early days of this century. A characteristic of pieces made in a drain mold is that, when a foot or stem is part of the mold and not attached separately afterward, the slip is pulled down into it and forms a hollow on the inside. Better pieces always have the stem molded separately and attached with slip when both parts are leather-hard. Good Meiji pieces were finished with great care, and it is usually hard to find the exact spot where two parts were joined together. The process of smoothing out the leather-hard pieces, or greenware, by hand is called fettling.

Drain molds were made in one piece or several, depending on the shape of the ware. A one-piece mold had to be shaped so that the molded piece would slip out once it was

141. *Chocolate set; Nippon, E-Oh mark. The chocolate pot, cups, and sugar bowl were made in drain molds, with the handles made in press molds and joined with slip. The saucers were made in solid casting molds. These pieces were made toward the end of the Nippon period (probably at the end of World War I), and the brushwork of the decoration was not done with the care used on the older pieces.*

dry. As this placed considerable restriction on the design of a piece, most drain molds were made in two or more pieces, divided at the thickest points, either horizontally or laterally. A two-piece mold can be used only to shape something that has a flat, or almost flat, bottom; a three-piece mold must be used if there is to be an indentation at the foot.

Chocolate pots were made with the lateral division. In the older pieces it is very hard to find any trace of a ridge, or "fettle," where the mold divided. The joint was generally concealed in an indentation in the design, if there was one handy. One has to search very carefully to find the joint in the better pieces; the best way to do so is to tilt the object in all directions in bright sunlight until some clue finally becomes visible. This usually takes the form of a slight line or depression in the biscuit or an irregularity in the glaze, although on poorly made pieces there may be evidence of a ridge. Tilting in bright sunlight is useful for finding many things. One can often read a mark that has been rubbed off in the course of time, as the light picks up the dullness of the glaze where the original mark was located.

I have dealt at length with the construction of drain molds and explained fettling, as an understanding of methods and techniques is necessary for anyone who wants to try to date the later export wares. After the turn of the century, corners were cut in order to turn goods out faster, and wares produced in the 1920s were often made very roughly. Finials were included in the drain mold of a lid, as were handles in the mold of the body, and the result was clumsy.

Solid casting: When a piece is made in a solid cast mold, it is shaped on both sides by the mold. This method has many advantages over drain casting, in that the inside does not have to conform to the outside. Cups and bowls do not have to be of the same thickness throughout; they can have a thicker base with tapering sides. The inside can be perfectly smooth, with no ring inside the foot, as in drain casting. In drain casting two pieces made in the same mold may be of a different thickness, but pieces that are solid cast are identical in form. Plates, cups, and bowls were solid cast.

The molds for solid casting are made in two parts, top and bottom. The slip used must be thicker than that used in drain molds, as excessive shrinkage is not desirable. The slip used for drain molds is about half clay and half water, and it undergoes great shrinkage as it dries out, an advantage in getting the piece out of the mold.

Flopover molds, or drape molds, are the simplest form of mold. They are used to make flat shapes. Only a one-piece mold is necessary, shaped like the inside of the piece,

142. *Bouillon set; Noritake, red M-in-Wreath mark. These wares were made with a jigger. The design is of the Noritake stylized type.*

but in reverse, convex instead of concave. A pancake of clay is rolled out and pressed over the mold. This produces flat-bottomed pieces, and the bottom is left unglazed, having no foot to stand on in the kiln. This type of mold was used for trays (Ills. 164, 209, and 217) and for small pieces like salt dishes (Ills. 220, 230, and many others).

Press Molds: These are mainly used for making handles, although sometimes for figurines. A press mold is made in two pieces, a front and a back. For a cup handle, a cylinder of soft clay is pressed between the two halves, and the excess squeezed out into a trough around the edge. When dry, the handle had to be fettled to remove the ridge where the two halves of the mold joined.

Jiggering: The commercial way of making plates and bowls is with the jigger, which consists of a plaster bat placed on a wheel and a template held by an arm. To make a plate or saucer, a convex bat is used to form the inside of the piece, the template being in the shape of the outside. A flat pancake of clay is placed on the bat, pressed down firmly, and the upper surface wet with a sponge. After the wheel is started, the jigger arm holding the template is lowered —it takes only a few seconds to form the outside of the plate (Fig. 3).

A bowl is made in the opposite way. The plaster bat is concave and forms the

Fig. 3. *The jigger.* Left: *A bat shaped like the inside of a plate is placed on the wheel. A pancake of clay is put on the bat; then the jigger arm with template attached to it is lowered. As the wheel spins, the outside of the plate is formed in a matter of seconds. The bat is then lifted off the wheel and the plate left to dry.* Right: *A bowl, or any deep piece, has to be done in the opposite way. The bat is shaped like the outside of the bowl; then a lump of clay is put in it and roughly pressed against the sides. The template is in the shape of the inside of the bowl, and as the wheel turns it forms the inside. The bowl is left in the bat to dry, and as it shrinks it pulls away from the side of the bat. Were it made in the same way as the plate, it would crack as it shrank in drying.*

outside of the bowl. (If it were done the other way, the bowl would crack open when it shrank in the drying process). A ball of clay is pressed onto the bottom of the plaster bat, and the potter works the clay up the sides with his fingers to make a rough bowl shape. Then he dampens the surface with a sponge and lowers the jigger arm holding the template. The template is, of course, in the shape of the inside of the bowl. Finally the bat is lifted off the wheel and the bowl left in it to dry.

These varying processes of molding the biscuit naturally make for variations in the type of body produced. The most beautiful effects resulted when a liquid slip was used, as the glazed surface had a smooth, slightly undulating appearance that caused it to gleam in the light. Pieces made from a pancake or ball of clay pressed against a mold have a duller, less smooth look, and are often somewhat grainy in appearance.

Decoration

Ceramics can be decorated in two different ways: either with clay, so that the decoration becomes part of the body, or with color. Clay decoration of the post-1868 export porcelains was mainly done through slip-trailing and coralene beading.

Slip-trailing results in a raised ridge of slip; the slip is trailed on when the ware is either leather-hard or in the biscuit state. When applied to leather-hard ware, it generally serves as a raised outline or decorative border for an enameled decoration, and is usually painted gold. Slip can also be applied after the glaze, and in this case the slip used is in one or more contrasting colors (Ill. 143). Slip-trailing was originally done with a bamboo tube, but a rubber syringe is often used now. More elaborate slip decoration was formed by hand and painstakingly applied to the surface of the ware. The Japanese call all these types of raised clay or enamel decoration *moriage*.

Coralene beading is done by a similar process. It consists of a series of dots instead of a continuous ridge, and is always enameled over, again generally in gold. The older pieces have extensive coralene beading, often in patterns using a variety of sizes of dots (Color Plate 6). Later inferior pieces have an

143. Nippon vase, M-in-Wreath mark. The dragon decoration was made by slip-trailing; the dragon is in pale gray slip, and the Chinese-style flames are in turquoise slip. The piece has an interesting mottled gray and green background, the whole design being dominated by the brilliant turquoise blue enamel eyes of the dragon. Note the three claws on this Japanese dragon's visible foot (compare with Ill. 161, for a Chinese dragon).

imitation coralene beading done with dots of enamel.

Colored decoration may be in the form of either colored glazes or underglaze or overglaze enamel designs. Sometimes several different colors are applied to the glaze to make an attractive variegated effect.

Underglaze Designs: Normally, the only color used for underglaze designs is blue; underglaze blue and white decoration is called *sometsuke* in Japanese. Cobalt blue is the only color that does not vary in shade according to the temperature of the firing. Other colors tend to run when used as underglaze colors.

Up to the latter part of the nineteenth century, the native *gosu* was used for blue. This is a pebble found in oriental riverbeds, which contains a mixture of cobalt, manganese, and iron. However, these days, imported cobalt oxide is generally used; it was first used at the Arita kilns in 1869.

Native Japanese *gosu* is very hard to find nowadays, and is much more difficult to apply than imported cobalt oxide. The ground *gosu* has to be mixed with a thick

144. *Dish with raised handle; Nippon, M-in-Wreath. The blue cobalt oxide border has heavy gold decoration.*
Mr. and Mrs. T. M. Lotito

solution of green tea before it is used, as the tannin in the tea fixes the decoration so that it does not spread when the glaze is applied. Imported cobalt oxide is more reliable, cheaper, and stronger than native *gosu*, but has a much harsher and more brilliant color. *Gosu* is of a more gray blue color.

On post-1868 export wares cobalt oxide was used very often as a blue border, and the wares were then sent out "in the white" for decoration. The blue border was customarily decorated with a gold design (Ill. 144). This type of decoration was also used extensively on spouts and handles.

Overglaze Enamel Decoration: A similar type of border decoration, called *kinrande*, in red and gold, was used for Kutani and Kutani-style wares, and also on spouts and handles. The red background, however, was in overglaze enamels.

In the Meiji era, a cheap and efficient method was found for applying the red ground, and this was used for export wares. It consisted of painting the glaze surface with lacquer, and when this was partly dry, dusting on red enamel powder from a cloth bag. In this way an even coating was obtained without brush marks. The red enamel was then fired at a low temperature along with the rest of the overglaze enamel decoration, and after the firing the gold decoration was applied and the piece fired once again at a still lower temperature (Ill. 145). Gold has to be fired at a lower temperature than that used for enamel decoration; otherwise the gold will sink into the enamel and disappear.

As mass production increased and time and costs were cut, yellow enamel was used as a cheap substitute for gold. It could be painted on the red background as soon as that was dry, and they could both be fired together. A method of cutting costs without eliminating the use of gold was to apply the gold directly to the glaze, making sure that none of the gold touched or was on top of the enamel decoration. In this way the gold could be fired at the same time as the rest of the decoration, with no danger of its disappearing under the other colors (Ill. 146).

Gold was used lavishly on export wares of the Meiji Period. On older unmarked

145. *Modern Kutani-style teapot. Gold chrysanthemum pattern on red ground decorates the spout.* Mr. and Mrs. Elliott H. Fischer

146. *Berry bowl set, c. 1925. Although gold was used in this Kaga-style decoration, it was applied directly to the glaze, and nowhere over the enamels. The red rim is decorated with yellow enamel brushstrokes. This method eliminated an extra firing for the gold. The name of a small company appears on the underside in Japanese characters.*

148. *Detail from a Nippon M-in-Wreath vase, showing a finely painted landscape.*

147. *Vase, h. 9"; Nippon, Maple Leaf. This fine piece is beautifully painted, with much goldwork. The coralene beading is in two different sizes, which is a mark of good quality Nippon. This vase also illustrates the Japanese fondness for showing a scene as from some particular vantage point; here the landscape seems to be glimpsed through an ornate window.*

pieces it appears mainly over coralene bead- ing or as a decoration on underglaze blue borders and handles. Kutani pieces have gold decoration on a red ground as well as consid- erable fine gold brushwork in the pictorial designs. Nippon wares have gold on cora- lene beading, which is generally not as or- nate as on the older pieces; the beading is usually in one size or style, in contrast to the varied kinds used on the older wares. Nip- pon Maple Leaf pieces make heavy use of gold (Ill. 147), but Torii pieces have very little.

The styles and skills used in enamel dec- oration vary a great deal. In the transition period toward the end of the nineteenth cen- tury, the decorations range from blobs and daubs to very fine painting (Ill. 148). When judging the age of a piece, it is helpful to remember that there is a feeling of honesty about the porcelains made in the last part of the nineteenth century—even up to, say, 1915. If the work was good, it was very good, and anything missing could be at- tributed to lack of time. On the other hand, if the work was poor, it was the result of haste, and no pretense was made about it. This is the principal difference between wares made during this period and those made a short time later in the twenties. Dur- ing this later period corners were cut to save time and costs; at first glance the wares ap- pear to be of a much better quality than they actually are. Fine brushwork was re- placed by a smear of paint outlined or high- lighted with a few strokes of enamel. In the older pieces the enamel decoration was con- sistent throughout; if, for example, the flow- ers were very well done, then the leaves were equally well done. In the later versions, which are now unmarked, having been shipped with a paper sticker showing the country of origin, often the flowers were painted with care but the leaves were merely dabs of color with an outline to show the shape. In Ill. 149 the leaves on the coffeepot are outlined in gold and deep green, but the middle of the leaves consists only of dabs of green. On the vase in Ill. 150 the leaves have a few lines representing veins. Another tell-

tale indication of age is the lack of symme- try in the enamel decoration: On the older pieces this came as a natural result of the artist's work; in the later imitations it appears contrived.

Another characteristic of the older pieces is that very often something is missing from the design, no doubt through haste at the last moment, for generally the rest of the decoration has been done with great care. On the unmarked vase in Color Plate 6, there is a rosebud in the reserve on the front of the neck, but on the back the picture was never completed.

Symmetrical designs have the appear- ance of being symmetrical, but in actual fact are not (Ill. 151). This lack of symmetry gives the design a warmth and beauty that are the antithesis of the coldness of machine- made perfection. This human inperfection, however, should not be confused with delib- erate deformation, which always appears false and contrived. Dr. Yanagi, in Bernard Leach's translation of various articles pub- lished in *The Unknown Craftsman* by Yanagi Sōetsu, speaks at length on the beauty of irregularity and on other aspects of beauty that we are fast losing sight of in our love affair with the machine.

As mass production increased, hand painting was superseded, or at least aug- mented, by decals. Many pieces are marked "hand painted" but in actual fact have a very small amount of hand painting on them. For example, on the Noritake dish in Ill. 152, only the colored line below the flower bor- der is hand painted; the rest of the decora- tion was made with a decal. This was the method used for many of the cheap pre- World War II wares.

The decal was transferred to the glazed piece and any hand-painted work then added to the printed design, so that both could be fired at the same time. This was a very economical method of producing wares that could truthfully bear the legend "hand painted"; the company was not obliged to say exactly what was painted by hand.

Sometimes it is not easy to see what was

149. *This close-up of the teapot in Ill. 215 shows the method of outlining petals and leaves with a few hasty strokes, in contrast to the painstaking work shown in Ill. 147 and 148.*

150. *Ewer-vase (c. 1930) in the style of late nineteenth-century wares (see Color Plate 6). The brushwork is not as fine on this vase, and the handle was formed in the same mold as the rest of the piece, instead of being made separately and attached with slip.*

151. *Sugar and creamer (M-in-Wreath) are very well made of white porcelain, with small landscapes and gold border decoration. The landscapes are delicately painted with considerable detail in their miniature size, but the gold border is somewhat irregular, with an apparent intent to avoid constricting symmetry.*

152. Celery dish (Noritake, red M-in-Wreath mark) has stylized flowers, a gold edge, and openings at both ends to simulate handles. Although the backstamp reads "Hand painted," the only hand painting is the line around the center of the dish; the rest of the decoration was done with a decalcomania.

hand painted and what was not. In such a case it is best to examine two similar parts of the design and see whether the color misses the outline in both in exactly the same way. If it does, then the decoration is a decal.

Motifs:

Flowers and landscapes were the most popular decorations on the export wares of this period. Certain mythological creatures, human figures, and simple decorative patterns were also widely used.

Flowers: All kinds of flowers were portrayed: the rose, chrysanthemum, violet, iris, orchid, lotus, azalea, poppy, cornflower, plum blossom, cherry blossom, and so on (Ill. 154). On the older pieces, the shading of the background was as important as the actual motif; for instance, a soft gray was often used as a background for flowers in pastel shades.

Anyone wishing to make a collection of this type of Japanese export ware should study the Japanese way of painting roses on pieces of this date; familiarity with the style of the work can be of great help when deciding if an unmarked piece is of Japanese origin or not. The Japanese generally painted a rose with less petal detail than did the English or Germans of the same period. Look carefully at the Nippon Pagoda vase in Ill. 155, the unmarked teapot in Ill. 170, and the Pointed Crown chocolate pot in Ill. 176. I have purposely included this last piece because, although the brushwork is not of the same quality as that on the other two

mentioned, it is still in the same style. Roses were frequently portrayed in combination —a light pink one with a dark pink one.

The way in which flower sprays are arranged is another indication of Japanese origin. For an example of rose spray treatment, study the Maple Leaf celery dish in Ill. 156. In a piece of this nature, a long spray of roses on one side is balanced by a small nosegay of roses on the other side that is not centrally placed. The roses are in several colors, and the leaves in several shades of green; the whole design is artistically balanced both in form and color; to change one color in the roses would be to spoil the whole effect.

The Japanese concept that in nature there is balance but not symmetry is also illustrated in the design on the cover of the Kutani box in Ill. 76. No two nosegays are the same, and—even more interesting—the two with chrysanthemums are next to each other, instead of opposite, as they would have been had the piece been European instead of Japanese.

Certain flowers are symbols of the seasons. Daffodils and the crocuslike *Adonis amurensis* are for spring. The lily and the *shakuyaku*, or herbaceous peony (shown on the lace dish, Color Plate 1), represent summer. The lotus (water lily) is for autumn and the crimson plum for winter. The deer with maple leaves is another symbol for autumn. (See the Kutani chocolate set in Color Plate 11 for a description of this type of decoration.)

Chrysanthemums are said to promote good health and longevity; the Imperial

153. The three Kutani-style pieces are decorated with human figures. The small bowl at left with attached saucer carries a green T-in-Plum-Blossom mark and "Japan." The sugar bowl, which has Mt. Fuji on the other side, bears the green Pagoda Nippon mark, and the jar is marked with Japanese characters reading Kutani on a red brushstroke. These three pieces are similar in coloring, the figures being dressed in red, lilac, and blue. The two Nippon plates with similar decoration have considerable white enamel beading and gold. The one at left, with roses in two shades of pink, bears the M-in-Wreath mark. The one at right, decorated with violets, carries the Maple Leaf mark.

154. *Examples of Nippon floral decoration. The dish with handles has purple and yellow chrysanthemums, not centered. The sugar bowl and creamer are embellished with pink roses; the friendship cup and saucer, with violets. On the three-footed dish are cornflowers outlined in gold against a green band. All are well made, and all are marked M-in-Wreath except the footed dish, which bears the t"t" symbol.*

155. *Nippon vase, H. 10", has Pagoda mark in blue. The brushwork on this piece is not of such good quality as, for example, that on the chocolate cups (green Pagoda mark) in Ill. 180.*

156. Celery dish (Nippon, Maple Leaf mark) with tasteful decoration.

chrysanthemum, emblem of the Imperial family, has sixteen petals. The blue bell-flower *(kikyo)*, an autumn flower, is often used as a contrasting color in a floral spray, particularly by Noritake. Various kinds of nuts are used for decoration, the browns giving much warmth to the design (Ill. 157).

Birds of all kinds are used, either alone or as part of a scene. Certain birds and flowers are often used together. The sparrow and bamboo are shown together on the cup and saucer in Ill. 158, and a dove and plum combination is portrayed on the coffee set in Ill. 159. These associations, along with the quail and millet, the swallow and willow, all probably stem from Chinese sources. The orange and cuckoo, the plum and nightingale, however, are from native Japanese sources.

Mythological Creatures: The Hō-ō bird is another popular decoration that has been used for centuries on ceramic wares (Ill. 160). The Hō-ō is something between a bird of paradise and a phoenix. The word is often translated as "phoenix," but this is not really correct, as the creature does not have the attributes of the phoenix.

Dragons were also frequently used as a

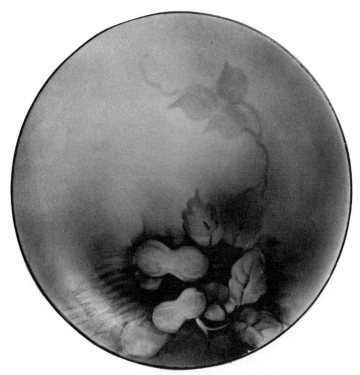

157. Plate with Noritake M-in-Wreath, green mark. The motifs are in autumn shades ranging from red brown through golden brown. Mr. and Mrs. T. M. Lotito

158. Small cup and saucer with "sparrow and bamboo" decoration. Both pieces bear Japanese characters reading "Imura Company at Yokohama, Japan." They are very well made, probably late nineteenth century.

159. Coffeepot, sugar, and creamer have colorful dove and plum decoration. Probably c. 1930, but unmarked. The raised star under each piece, unglazed, served as support during firing.

160. Cups and saucers with Hō-ō bird design in gold and a yellow border. The cherry blossom has a red center, which gives an attractive touch of color. Noritake, red M-in-Wreath. Mr. and Mrs. T. M. Lotito

161. Dish, Occupied Japan, has Chinese-style decoration with a dragon (five-clawed, Chinese style) and the Hō-ō bird.

162. Satsuma-style incense burner (koro), c. 1920, with three shishi dogs; the one on the top holds a ball (tama), the jewel of omniscience. Unmarked.

decorative device on ceramics. They were supposed to inhabit the sky, and the Hō-ō bird the earth (Ill. 161). The Chinese dragon is depicted with five claws, and the Japanese with three.

The *shishi* dog is something between a lion and a dog. Portrayed in pairs, *shishi* keep evil away; when shown singly the *shishi* is pictured with a ball *(tama)*, the jewel of omniscience. Note the Satsuma-style incense burner in Ill. 162. The *shishi* dog is shown on the cover with the ball; the two on the sides are a pair. In pairs, one dog often has its mouth open and the other has it closed. The openmouthed dog is female; the one with the mouth closed is the male.

Landscapes: All kinds of landscapes, and especially lake scenes, are found on all classes of post-1868 export wares. These are not the Chinese-style landscapes with craggy mountains, but true pictures of the Japanese countryside. In my personal opinion, the pieces with landscape scenes are the finest of these wares. They were doubtless inspired by European pieces of a similar nature, but there is a marked difference between the two. On European pieces generally the scenery is a background for figures, animals, or birds, but on the Japanese pieces the scenery is the all-important thing. On a good piece the painting is very fine— the decorator must have taken infinite pains with his picture (Ill. 163). Unfortunately, the

163. At left is a detail photograph of the Nippon M-in-Wreath vase from Color Plate 10. The detail photograph at right shows another Nippon M-in-Wreath vase with good brushwork. Cows drinking in the stream are the central theme, but a peasant in his straw raincoat watches them in the fading light.

fine pieces were produced during a very short period, and the quality of the work deteriorated rapidly when decorators became unable to spend the requisite amount of time on a single piece. Collectors should take good care of the fine pieces they have; they are not likely to be made again.

Sunsets were frequently depicted. Japan has a moist climate, and in consequence has spectacular sunsets. But the Japanese appreciate a rainy day, and prefer natural beauty in rain or mist. This may seem strange to us, who prefer to go out in the sunshine rather than getting wet in the rain, but to the Japanese a landscape can be infinitely more beautiful in the rain than in the sunshine. Bright sunshine dazzles the eyes, and forms and colors become indistinct, whereas a light rain or mist brings out the contours of the land, and shapes and colors are apparent that would otherwise blend into a flat background on a bright sunny day. The Japanese call a rainy day a masculine day and a sunny one a feminine day.

Landscapes are pictured in different ways (Ill. 164). Some sets have parts of a single landscape on each piece so that, placed side by side, they form one whole picture. Generally a landscape on a vase goes all the way around, with no start or finish, although there is always much less detail on the back. The Japanese like to picture scenes as though glimpsed from some special vantage point, again their love of obscurity rather than the obvious. On the small pitcher in Ill. 165, we seem to be standing in a grape arbor and looking through the vines at a scene of Japanese ladies in the distance. On the vase in Ill. 155, we appear to be looking from behind a rosebush toward the mountains.

Figures: Generally the figures por-

164. On the Noritake dresser set (Tree Crest mark), the landscape is depicted in a different way on each piece. This is not one of the better Noritake sets, as the colors are too strong and garish —the hills are deep purple, the roofs too red, and the yellow bridge does not blend well. The brushwork is also poor. The pieces in the other group are all Nippon with quite restrained gold decoration.

165. The four pieces grouped together all have Kaga-style decoration featuring scenes with ladies. The creamer at the right of the group has an underglaze blue border; the other three pieces, red overglaze enamel. The small covered box is unmarked, but the others are Nippon with the Torii mark. The pitcher (left) shown by itself, also Kaga style, shows the figures as if glimpsed through a grape arbor. The sugar and creamer set in the third photograph ("Made in Japan" with the Torii mark) has underglaze blue borders and a scene with a boy carrying baskets.

trayed on these export porcelains represent a type of person (lady, man, child), rather than individuals (Ill. 165). The exception is on Satsuma wares, where the figures look like real people rather than types (Ill. 89 and Color Plate 15). The impersonal figures are usually part of a landscape instead of being the central theme, as on European pieces. Even the peasant in his straw raincoat (see Ill. 163) is part of the scenery, far less important than his cows. This is an interesting concept and a true one: One individual man is insignificant compared to the wonders of nature.

Figures used in other ways are shown in a set on which the Immortal Poets are portrayed (Ill. 78). Chinese men are depicted on the Satsuma-style plate in Ill. 86 and one of the cups in Color Plate 9. A sugar bowl and creamer in Ill. 165 have a boy carrying a basket. Pieces marked Occupied Japan sometimes also have portraits on them.

Some wares have Chinese-style decoration. The vase in Ill. 169 has a Chinese-style landscape with birds. In Color Plate 1 a covered vegetable dish with decoration is reminiscent of Chinese rose medallion, and in Color Plate 2 a Nippon bowl has a Chinese-style bird and blossom decoration. The latter type of decoration can also be found in later wares—Ill. 222 shows a Made in Japan piece, and in Ill. 229 a similar design is marked Occupied Japan.

Decorative Patterns: Such patterns are carried out in colored enamels or in heavy gold (Ills. 164 & 166). They are never perfectly symmetrical, although they may appear to be so at first glance. Cloisonné effects are freely used, either as border decorations (Ill. 167) or as the principal motif (Color Plate 16).

Of course, many other types of decora-

166. The close-up of a cup shows a decorative enamel border design that appears to be symmetrical, but is not. Mark is Nippon, M-in-Wreath. Mr. and Mrs. H. Edward Anderson. The syrup pot shown in close-up is the same one that appears in Color Plate 17.

167. On the Nippon M-in-Wreath vase is depicted a Middle East scene with camels, palm trees, and mountains, and a cloisonné-effect border. The small Nippon mustard pot (Rising Sun mark) appears to present a palm tree growing out of pyramids.

tion were used as well. Middle East scenes were popular, and they are the most amusing to study, as quite often the decorator relied largely on his imagination. The M-in-Wreath vase in Ill. 167 has a credible picture on it, but on the Rising Sun mustard pot in Ill. 167 a palm tree appears to be growing in the middle of a pyramid!

Oddments of decoration turn up all the time. For example, on the vase in Ill. 168 is the picture of an ancient carriage with a lady's sleeves hanging out, and the cookie jar in Ill. 168 shows a tearoom. This type of decoration is generally later than Nippon; most of it dates between the two world wars.

168. Two pieces from the 1921–1939 period. The vase shows an ancient carriage with the lady occupant's sleeves hanging through the doors in front. The cookie jar bears a scene featuring a tearoom. Both are unmarked pieces.

14

Pre-Nippon Porcelain Wares (1868-1890)

169. *Octagonal vase, h. 12", has Chinese-style decoration in overglaze blue. Late nineteenth century. Unmarked.*

This chapter will discuss the pieces that are the forerunners of the Nippon wares. They either have no mark at all or bear a potter's name. They are export wares of a transition period, influenced by the West in form and decoration, but still retaining much of their oriental heritage.

These pieces are generally characterized by artistic merit and good workmanship. They are the most individual of all the ceramic export wares of the entire period, being the potter's own adaptation of the new style. Each piece has something striking about it, either in form or color.

The body is made of good quality porcelain. The earliest of these wares were made in Arita, but Seto soon followed the lead, and by the mid-seventies both areas were producing large quantities of the new type of wares. Decoration was done locally to start with, but within a few years wares were sent to Tokyo for decoration.

In this period the vast impersonality of mass production had not yet been reached, and we can still sense the potter's hand and thoughts in his work, although at times there is evidence of a rush to finish. No doubt the agent was due to arrive shortly to collect the completed pieces. Throughout this period the wares were made by families or small groups of potters, and as most kilns produced porcelain at one time or another, a great deal of porcelain was made.

170. *The unmarked late nineteenth-century tea set has underglaze blue borders and handles decorated with an intricate gold pattern. The roses are in two shades of pink. On this set the lids fit over the openings, in contrast to the lid on the separate teapot pictured in close-up, which sets down into the opening. This teapot, also unmarked and late nineteenth century, is an example of the Japanese predilection for odd numbers: it has five feet (three in front, two in back), five gold flowers on the front, three on the back; the gold flowers on the lid are in two sets of three. There is a great deal of coralene beading in intricate gold tracery over the light and dark pink roses. Lid and body are unglazed where they meet, probably so that both could be fired together. Note the stubby spout and Q-shaped handle.*

The body of pre-Nippon pieces is generally very well made, with no trace of where the mold joined. Handles, spouts, and other parts were attached with great care and smoothed to make a neat join. The shapes have a distinct oriental feeling inter-mixed with their new occidental form, especially in the handles and spouts. In most pieces the Eastern heritage is stronger than the Western influence, as is evidenced by the irregularity the Japanese love in shape and design (see the lace dish, Color Plate 1), and the use of odd numbers like three, five, and seven in the decoration on the teapot in Ill. 170.

The decoration is not generally placed exactly in the center. This is an important point to remember when examining a piece for country of origin. But remember that this is a general rule; it must be considered in conjunction with other things, as there are exceptions all around.

Fluting is much in evidence on all kinds of pieces, and it is another mark of this transition period. Cups and saucers are paper-thin (a speciality of Seto) and very often fluted. These pieces were all made before the introduction of the jigger, and drain molds and solid casting molds lent themselves well to fluting. Even the base of a chocolate pot could be elaborately fluted (see Color Plate 7).

Pieces of this period with a cover or lid were often left unglazed on both cover and body where the two meet. These unglazed areas are important to look for when trying to decide if a piece is of this period or a later imitation. Later pieces are likely to be glazed on these spots.

Lids for teapots, sugar bowls, and the like were made in two styles: so that they fit either over the opening of the pot or down into it (Ill. 170). Lids of the latter type always seem rather small for the openings they cover. This type was also used for Kutani wares (Ill. 80) and for some Nippon.

Finials, mostly very elaborate, were usually made separately from the lid. They were attached when leather-hard, as were the knobs.

The handles on these pre-Nippon pieces retained much of their Japanese style, and

Fig. 4. The main types of handles used on pre-Nippon porcelain wares. Top, left to right: *Plain round handle, generally used on teapots, sugar bowls, and creamers; the same type of substantial handle but used for taller pieces (e.g., chocolate pots); a simple pointed handle used for teapots, sugar bowls, creamers, and other pieces, and—in a finer form—on Kutani wares of the same period. The first two types were often in underglaze blue and had elaborate gold designs painted on them. Bottom, left to right: Q-shaped pointed handle; plain cup handle; the very popular bamboo-style handle, used on all types of pieces and also on later wares.*

Fig. 5. Pre-Nippon spouts and feet. Spouts were generally rather short and pointed, and often did not pour well. A great many pieces were footed. The usual kind of foot was curved, either solid (bottom right) *for smaller pieces—e.g., tea sets—or made in a drain mold* (bottom left) *for larger pieces—e.g., vases. Those made in a drain mold had a small hole on the inside, which allowed the steam to escape while the piece was being fired, so that the foot would not explode.*

were generally substantial and strong. Fig. 4 shows the main types of handles used. Those on teapots and chocolate pots were often in underglaze blue with elaborate designs painted on them. There was plenty of room on these broad handles for even a chrysanthemum design. The plainness of the style was often counteracted by more intricate work where the handle and body joined, as on the vase in Color Plate 6, which has oriental-looking supports at the top, and on the chocolate pot (Color Plate 7) with a ribbon applied handle. Handles of this type are quite indicative of the age of a piece, as later imitations tended to become overelaborate and clumsy.

The spouts were also very characteristic of the period, being generally rather short and pointed (Fig. 5). Very often they do not pour too well. Many of the teapots made between the 1870s and 1900 make far better ornaments for the china cabinet than vehicles for tea making. The potters do not seem to have understood the Western teapot very well; Japanese teapots are of another type.

A great many pieces were footed. The usual kind of foot was curved, solid for smaller pieces and hollow for larger ones (Fig. 5). In both cases the feet were attached to the body with slip after both parts were leather-hard.

Vases are in a class of their own, unique in their mixed heritage of East and West,

and very attractive. Ornamental vases had no place in the Japanese home—that type was made entirely for export. A vase for the Japanese home is intended to hold flowers and to be unobtrusive so that the flowers show to their best advantage. Export vases, on the other hand, were not intended to hold flowers; indeed, putting flowers in them is a mistake, as it spoils the line. The white flared opening at the top is a necessary part of the design. It provides both balance in form and color contrast to the enameled decoration on the body. When flowers are placed in such a vase, this is all lost (Ill. 171).

Characteristic of this period was the large amount of painstaking handwork used. Not only was the decoration painted very delicately with great attention to detail, but the biscuit was given considerable attention after coming out of the mold. Generally there is no trace at all of where the mold joined. As many of these pieces were made in one place, in contrast to pieces later sent away for decoration, the biscuit and enamel decoration are much more homogeneous than in most later pieces. The coralene beading was applied with the painted design in mind; it was an integral part of the decoration, rather than a decorative border as on the later Nippon pieces.

On pre-Nippon wares, often there were as many as four different kinds of coralene beading and patterns on a single piece, and generally that on the front was different from that on the back. On some pieces coralene beading was the major part of the decoration, overshadowing the enamel design, as on the teapot in Ill. 170.

Coralene beading is an important help when estimating the age of a piece. Generally speaking, if a piece has an assortment of coralene beading varying both in the size of the dots and the complexity of the pattern, it can be assumed to be from this period and not a later imitation. Shortcuts that were supposed to give the impression of complex work are a sure indication of a later era.

Coralene beading on a small piece like a cup is a strong indication that the piece belongs to the pre-Nippon era (Ill. 171).

There was much more use of solid colors on pre-Nippon pieces than on later Nippon, particularly the various shades of turquoise, ranging from almost blue to almost green. One wonders if they liked it the best of the new European-style enamels; it does show off most other colors to their greatest advantage. A deep red was also used frequently.

The enamel decoration was painstakingly done all over a piece, everything done equally well, the leaves as well as the flowers. Blobs of color with an outline to show the shape are the mark of a later period (again, a method of cutting corners and eliminating costs and work).

A smaller range of flower varieties was used on these pieces than on the later Nippon. Roses and chrysanthemums were the most frequently used flowers, although flowers native to Japan were also depicted at times. The *shakuyaku*, or pink herbaceous peony, symbol of summer, was used as decoration on the lace dish in Color Plate 1, the blue *kikyo*, or bellflower (an autumn flower), appears on the covered vegetable dish in the same color plate.

Usually the floral designs on the front and back of a piece were different, the one on the back having fewer flowers and the colors being arranged differently. On some pieces the enamel background of the floral design was painted in a different color on the back. On the chocolate pot in Color Plate 7 the background on the front was done in gold, but on the back a light turquoise was used. However, the background of the flowers on the footed vase in Color Plate 6 was painted in the same color front and back, but the pattern of the surrounding coralene beading decoration was simplified on the back.

Gold was freely used on these wares, and elaborate gold designs were painted on the underglaze blue. This blue was done with imported cobalt oxide.

Cobalt oxide, as already explained, is much easier to use than the native cobalt, and can be applied in a perfectly uniform manner, but unfortunately art and perfection are incompatible. The artist strives for perfection, but it is the minute imperfections that give warmth and beauty. This is why meticulous handwork has a beauty that no machine-made article can have. In these pre-Nippon wares, as well as in some Nippon wares, there is still much of this kind of beauty that was lost when the machine took over.

Many cups had the more important pattern painted on the inside, and when this was done the inside of the cup was smoothed very carefully. This decoration is seen frequently on older wares, but it can also be found on later wares, especially those marked Occupied Japan.

Unusual pieces can be found throughout the post-1868 period, and many require study to ascertain if they are Japanese or not. The covered vegetable dish in Color Plate 1 is a good example, for on cursory inspection it looks Chinese. However, besides having a Japanese potter's name on the underside, it is decorated with men wearing Japanese clothing, and there are also many Japanese-style irregularities in the decoration, as well as a difference in the coloring. The Japanese use more vivid shades, and the brightness of the pink is particularly obvious. There are also unglazed portions where cover and body meet.

Condensed milk jars were made in this period as well as later (Color Plate 9). The finger hole at the bottom was put there so that the empty can could be pushed up, but there was no hole in the lid for a spoon—each person was expected to use his own. A jam or jelly pot had no hole in the bottom, but there was one in the lid for a spoon.

171. Two late nineteenth-century pieces with a considerable amount of coralene beading. Mr. and Mrs. T. M. Lotito

15

Nippon Wares (1891-1921)

The name Nippon began to appear on Japanese wares in 1891, after the McKinley Tariff Act was passed in October 1890. This act stated, among other things, that articles imported into the United States from abroad must be marked with the name of the country of origin written in English. The Japanese used their own name for their country, "Nippon," and wares from Japan imported into this country bore that name for thirty years. However, in 1921 the United States Treasury decreed that "Japan" must be used instead of "Nippon," as the latter was a Japanese word.

These wares bear a wide range of other marks, but unfortunately, except as a general form of classification, the marks are of very little use to the collector. For the most part they were either the identification marks of agents in Japan or the marks of importers abroad. The agents made arrangements for pieces to be sent "in the white" from the factories where they were made to decorators in various places, and then returned to the agents for export. This is why the marks have very little meaning, except as a means of dating the pieces. An agent might get blanks from a number of different factories and ship them to a group of decorators; since there were whole communities of decorators, each piece in a batch of identical wares from one factory might pass through the hands of a different decorator. Conversely, the same decorator might work on wares from a number of different factories,

or from different agents, and he might get them mixed up (Ill. 172).

Symbols were used as identification marks because they were the easiest thing. Japanese potters could not read English, and the foreign agents and importers did not read Japanese, but everyone could understand a symbol.

Of course, the marks do provide some information for the collector, although it is of a limited nature. For example, the various agents and importers naturally had their own preferences, so there is some similarity of style and quality in the wares each one dealt with. Location was another factor. Porcelain, for instance, made in the Seto area and decorated in the vicinity was much whiter than that made in factories in the Kaga area and decorated in that style (Ill. 173).

Great changes took place during this period (1891–1921) as mass production increased; wares produced from 1915 to 1921 were generally very different from those made in the early Nippon days around the turn of the century. In 1900 production was still mainly by small groups or families, but by 1920 numerous companies had been formed, some quite small and some much larger. The early Nippon wares were almost as individual as those in the preceding period, but by about 1915 the same shapes were repeated again and again, although with different decoration and often bearing different marks (Ill. 174).

149

172. *Although these Nippon plates with pink roses were obviously decorated as a set, the Nippon marks on the backs are not the same. The top center one has the cherry-blossom Nippon mark, but the others are marked T-in-Wreath.*

173. *Kaga-style Nippon ware chocolate set; Torii mark. Decoration of this type was done mainly by decalcomania, with a few added dabs of overglaze enamel color. Any gold was applied directly over the glaze, never over the enamel decoration. Gray porcelain.*

174. Nippon mayonnaise set. Although this set carries the Square Crown mark, identically shaped pieces with similar decoration can be found in all the Nippon marks. Mayonnaise sets marked Noritake are slightly smaller.

When studying these wares, both the quality of the porcelain and the decoration have to be taken into account. Good quality bodies did not necessarily get correspondingly good decoration, and some poor quality bodies got better decoration than it would seem they deserved. The decoration ranged from fine work, as on the M-in-Wreath vase in Ill. 163, to the blobs and dabs of the Torii pieces (Ill. 173). Pieces made toward the end of the period usually did not have the fine brushwork of the earlier pieces, and later copies of the earlier pieces are interesting to compare (Ill. 175).

When it comes to trying to date a piece of this period, even though we know the general trend of increased mass production, dating is often a difficult task. As a general rule one may assume that if a piece has a look of mixed East and West heritage, it is from the early Nippon period. Coralene beading similar to that on pre-Nippon pieces is also characteristic of the early days of Nippon, and the use of groups of daisylike chrysanthemums, another popular decoration, may indicate an early piece of Nippon.

As the Nippon period progressed, the same type of molds was used again and

175. The plate at the top (Nippon Maple Leaf mark) must have been a copy of the set below (Nippon M-in-Wreath mark). The coloring is similar, but there is much less detail on the plate—for example, the boat on the plate is outlined with a few strokes, but on the dish it is painted with considerable detail. Pyramids have been added to the picture on the plate.

176. The chocolate set bears the Rising Sun mark. Miss Veronica Kiley. *The separate chocolate pot has the Pointed Crown mark. The Rising Sun set is of far better quality than the Pointed Crown pot—the porcelain is sparkling white; the floral decoration is well painted, as is the delicate cross-hatching in gold on the border. The Rising Sun pot is much better made also; the finial was molded separately, in contrast to the Pointed Crown pot, which had the finial included in the mold for the lid. The finial and handle of the Pointed Crown pot have a blurred, clumsy appearance. Most Nippon chocolate sets were made with five cups and saucers only, in Japanese style. Later sets had six.*

again, but the most commercial development was in the use of the jigger. This took over gradually during the middle of the Nippon period; by the end of that period the jigger was in general use for making plates, saucers, cups, bowls, and the like. The manufacture of the ten-inch plate presented the greatest problem, and plates of this size made on a jigger date from the late Nippon period. During the early Nippon period large plates were made in solid casting molds.

The use of the jigger was a great boon to ceramics manufacturers because they could make their wares much faster, but it was very unfortunate for the collector. A piece made on a jigger has perfection but less beauty than a similar piece made by pouring.

The shapes of Nippon period pieces are generally Western, although they have an oriental touch. Good pieces have a lighter and more graceful form than comparable English or German pieces, both of which have more of a sturdy good-sense approach. Pieces made in the Nippon period usually had the handles, finials, or knobs made separately and, when hard, attached to the body with slip. Late in the period the molds began to include handles and similar attachments, although this did not become a general practice until the 1920s.

The most characteristic wares of the Nippon period are the chocolate sets, which carry many different Nippon marks. The molds used were almost identical—only the handles and finials varied slightly—but the quality of the porcelain was variable. It ranged from a very fine white, as in pieces with the Rising Sun mark, to a poor-quality gray. The two chocolate pots in Ill. 176 also show how the ornaments on the handle originally served as strategically placed supports, but after much repetition the original purpose was lost and the ornaments served no purpose.

Handles eventually became mostly Westernized, although there was still a touch of the Orient on many of them. Feet very often were merely a small ball of clay (Ill. 177).

The important characteristics of the pre-Nippon group were their general shape, the use of solid color, and the extensive use of coralene beading. Nippon wares are remarkable for fine painting, particularly of landscape scenes that go entirely around the pieces, and of a vast array of floral decoration. These wares are often not only real works of art, but a labor of love—the time spent painting them must have been out of all proportion to the monetary recompense.

Elaborate coralene beading of the type

177. Mayonnaise bowl and ladle; M-in-Wreath. Mr. and Mrs. H. Edward Anderson.

178. Two plates, c. 1920. The plate on the left, with the swan, carries a mark saying both "Nippon" and "Made in Japan." The one on the right reads "Made in Nippon." The coralene beading on the swan plate was made with very fine dots of slip, but the rose-decorated plate has beading made with drops of white enamel.

used on pre-Nippon wares is rare; a cheaper form superseded it on Nippon wares. Instead of being made with dots of slip, a fine beading was made with dots of enamel painted over in gold. On some older pieces of Nippon it is possible to find both kinds on a single piece. An even cheaper method of producing a beaded line was to make it with enameled dots in a contrasting color (Ill. 178). However, the disappearance of dots of slip for coralene beading was not caused altogether by reasons of economy, but rather on account of mass production. A piece would have to be designed and completed in

one place if the coralene beading was to form part of, and complement, the enamel decoration. If the piece was to be shipped out as a blank to be decorated elsewhere, the coralene beading could be applied only as a border decoration, for example, in conjunction with underglaze blue, which was applied before the biscuit firing. (Incidentally, coralene beading decorated in gold makes a very neat edge to an underglaze blue border.) If the decorator wished to use coralene beading as part of his design, he was obliged to apply it as raised dots of enamel, then paint it with gold (Ill. 179). This last coat of gold, of course, had to have a separate firing at a lower temperature after the other enamels were fired, so if the decorator did not cover the enamel dots with gold, a firing was saved.

As already mentioned, the quality of the porcelain varied considerably. The finest and whitest can be found on pieces bearing the Rising Sun symbol—in fact, Rising Sun pieces are notable for their consistently excellent-quality bodies. Pieces with the Maple Leaf mark are usually of good quality, as are those with the M-in-Wreath. Wares marked with the Pagoda are variable, from excellent to mediocre; the mark was applied in more than one color, according to quality—in

179. Ornamental vase, M-in-Wreath, h. 11", is embellished with flesh-colored roses framed in basketweave motif. The beading on this piece was first made with dots of enamel, then painted with gold.

180. *The chocolate cups and saucers and nut dish (green Pagoda mark) show fine decorative work. The underglaze blue is patterned with gold; the roses are in two shades of pink.*

green, blue, and magenta, in that order (Ill. 180). The Imperial, Torii, and both Crown marks generally appear on grayer bodies (Ill. 181).

It should be pointed out that, as far as decoration was concerned, the decorators often made the most of a gray body by using it as a soft background for a pastel design; in fact, very often more gray was added to create a beautiful shaded background. White is not the best background for colors, since it creates too much contrast. On the other hand, Rising Sun wares glory in their pure white body and glaze, and use floral decoration of a restrained pastel shade as a foil to the sparkling whiteness (Ill. 182).

In speaking of the different Nippon marks, it should be explained that the M-in-Wreath pieces are included here, rather than in the Noritake chapter where they rightfully belong, for several reasons. One reason is that many people do not know M-in-Wreath pieces were made by the Noritake Company, and so they will look for them in this chapter. I feel that they should be included with the rest of the Nippon wares rather than with the Noritake, as they possess so many characteristics of the other Nippon pieces. Unfortunately, the Noritake Company records were destroyed during the war, and as there is very little informa-

tion available about the company, I have not been able to discover a satisfying explanation as to why the name Noritake was omitted from these wares. The "M" in the wreath decoration stands, of course, for the Morimura Brothers in New York, the sole importers of Noritake.

Frankly, I am puzzled at the difference between the bodies of the pieces bearing the Noritake mark and of those with only the M-in-Wreath. The Noritake pieces are of a consistent good quality; their dimensions are slightly different from those of the other Nippon wares, but, on the other hand, the bodies of the M-in-Wreath pieces are of variable quality, and they are of the same dimensions as the other Nippon wares. Since the decoration is always of high quality, I surmise that, in order to fulfill their large export quota, the Noritake Company decorated blanks from other companies and exported them under the M-in-Wreath mark, but without the Noritake name. This is only a suggestion, and to counter it I must point out that Noritake made blanks to be sent out for decoration and exported under other marks. Blanks bearing the M-in-Wreath mark were also exported for decoration elsewhere (Ill. 183).

Two other Noritake marks were used on Nippon wares without the Noritake

181. *The small dish with handles has the Square Crown mark. This is an unusual and attractive piece, but the porcelain body is rather gray. The round bowl, which has the Pointed Crown mark, is a poor quality piece with a heavy gray body and inferior brushwork.*

182. *An assortment of wares with the Rising Sun mark. These pieces are characterized by a sparkling white body and restrained tasteful decoration.*

183. Jam pot marked M-in-Wreath. This must have been exported to a studio abroad for decoration—the signature "W. Rose" appears below the smaller rose. The decoration is not in Japanese style, neither in brushwork nor colors.

184. Octagonal dish, R. C. Nippon mark. An elegant piece in restrained muted colors.

name. They were the R. C. mark (Ill. 184) and the Tree Crest mark (see Chapter 16). The R. C. mark was used on good quality pieces that usually had a restrained style of decoration. Wares bearing the Tree Crest mark were usually decorated with a heavy gold border.

In the Nippon period gold was used plentifully, especially on wares with the Maple Leaf symbol (Color Plate 11 and Ill. 185). Pieces bearing this mark were the most flamboyant of all the Nippon wares, the shapes often quite unusual, although many apparently were made in the same molds as pieces

bearing other marks. These wares, like the M-in-Wreath wares, came from the Nagoya area, and there is a close relationship between the two.

There are many different Nippon marks, probably more than sixty. They can be found on a wide variety of pieces, ranging from fine ornamental ones to some very mediocre wares. However, among these there are many fine pieces for everyday use (Ill. 186). I feel that in their way they correspond to the *getomono* Dr. Yanagi talked about. Although he was speaking of unassuming and sturdy pottery wares made for

185. *The vase, h. 9", bears the Maple Leaf mark. The flowers, leaves, and stems are all outlined in gold. The base is attached with a screw. The sugar and creamer, with t"t" mark, have finely detailed gold decoration highlighted with turquoise blue enamel. The bowl on stand (two pieces) has the M-in-Wreath mark. The black border is heavily decorated with gold; there is a landscape inside the bowl. Notice the interesting handles and feet.* Mr. and Mrs. Henry J. Holst

186. *Three attractive Nippon pieces for everyday use. The celery dish bears azaleas with a border of intertwined leaves. Rising Sun mark. The octagonal dish, Imperial mark; the plate, M-in-Wreath mark. The decoration on the Rising Sun dish is set off by the sparkling whiteness of the body and glaze; on the other two pieces the backgrounds are in delicate shades of green and gray, which blend harmoniously with the floral decorations.*

hard usage, whose beauty lay in their combination of aesthetic appeal and practicality, it seems to me that the same quality exists in some of these export wares. They are in decorated porcelain, but they were intended for Westerners who used decorated porcelains as everyday wares. In these pieces there is the same anonymity of craftsmen who were unconcerned with fame, but who decorated the blanks they were given in very beautiful ways. The blanks were often made very tastefully, with elegant fluting and molding, and the decorator added to it, for example, a beautifully arranged sprig of flowers in delicate colors. Pieces of this nature are essentially ones to be enjoyed while they are being used.

Pieces bearing the Torii mark were direct descendants of Kaga *aka-e*, the red Kaga wares (see Chapter 7). The bodies were made from a course gray porcelain, and the decoration consisted mainly of a decalcomania of a landscape with figures, with added dabs of red, green, blue, and yellow enamel (Ill. 187). Generally a little gold was applied, and as it was always on a glazed area and never over enamel, it could be fired at the same time as the enamels. At times yellow enamel was substituted for gold, and this could be applied over the other enamels

and fired with them, instead of needing a separate firing as would have been necessary with gold. These wares were produced very fast and the decoration done on an assembly-line basis—one decorator painted the red, another the green, and so on. Their technique seems to have been hit or miss, and as often as not it was miss. However, inaccurate as these dashes of color were, the pieces still have a certain charm and warmth to them.

Not all Torii pieces were decorated with decalcomanias, although the majority of pieces were. Some pieces had their enamel decoration painted entirely by hand (Ill. 188). Collectors of moderate means can find plenty of variety and interest in Nippon wares (Ill. 189). The landscape vases are the more expensive items, although, of course, the ones made around 1920 were generally not as good as the earlier ones. The Egyptian scenes are very amusing and can be found on all kinds of pieces (Ill. 190). I have included an illustration of three different views of Mt. Fuji (Ill. 191), and for a modest financial outlay a very interesting collection of this nature could be formed. Nippon dolls may also be found, as well as wall plaques (Ill. 192). Among late Nippon wares are quite a good many copies of popular European styles—of

187. A popular Torii design. Like many other Torii designs, this one can be found on both Nippon and Made in Japan wares.

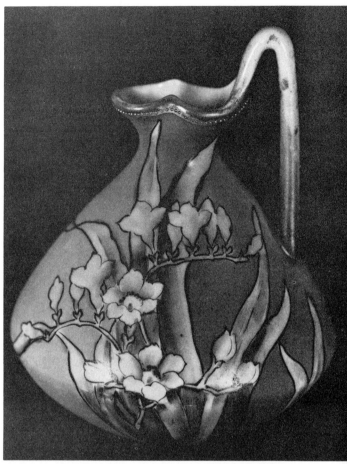

188. *A less usual type of Torii decoration. It is entirely hand painted, in contrast to the frequent use of decalcomania and dabs of paint.*

189. *Two M-in-Wreath pieces: A well-made pitcher of unusual shape with coralene beading decorated in gold; and a small bowl with white flowers.* Mr. and Mrs. T. M. Lotito

190. *Three M-in-Wreath pieces decorated with land-scapes. Plate at left, d. 10", shows a Japanese landscape in black and gold.* Pinney Collection. *Coaster, d. 3½", has a Dutch scene with windmill.* Catharine Lotito. *Plate at right has an Egyptian scene.*

191. *Views of Mt. Fuji. This type of decoration can be found on pieces marked with the Torii symbol and "Nippon" or "Japan," as well as "Made in Japan."*

192. Collectible pieces found on the market today range from this appealing doll (incised "Nippon") to the rather grotesque wall plaque marked M-in-Wreath, which has holes on the back for hanging.

the Royal Bayreuth Rose Tapestry line and of Royal Doulton pieces, to name only two.

Many Nippon pieces were not marked. For example, certain pieces of a set might be marked and the rest unmarked, and so once the set is broken up, the unmarked pieces become unknown quantities. Often only one of a pair of vases would be marked. This situation creates problems in both dating and establishing country of origin. Wares of the Japanese export period are usually not too hard to place, however, if the overall feel of the porcelain is taken into account, as well as the combination of colors and general irregularity.

On Nippon ware, as has been pointed out, decorations that appear symmetrical are never quite that way, although sometimes this is hard to detect. A decoration can be symmetrically designed but unevenly spaced, and not symmetrical at all although it has that appearance (Ill. 193). In my opinion this lack of regularity is the most important thing to look for, and it is always there —perhaps only in the form of two colors reversed or some other slight change.

The question of date is a little more difficult. A piece may be an older one or it may be a copy. In general, more shortcuts were taken as time went by, and these became particularly noticeable as the Nippon period progressed.

193. *M-in-Wreath pieces: The two plates have pink and white roses in reserves and a gold border with coralene beading. Although these plates are part of a set, the central designs are not identical—the one on the right is much larger. In the group of three dishes the shamrock design on the celery dish appears symmetrical, but actually it is not. The covered creamer has a naturalistic floral border. Mr. and Mrs. T. M. Lotito. On the single plate, d. 10½", the rose design has been repeated with attention to regularity, but the border is quite uneven. On the Maple Leaf celery dish with gold border and pink roses, the alternating groups of roses are not the same on both sides—the larger groups are opposite the smaller groups. Mr. and Mrs. T. M. Lotito*

16

Noritake Wares

The Noritake Company, Ltd., was founded in Japan for the exclusive purpose of manufacturing chinawares for export. The company began in a small way early in the Meiji era, when the Morimura brothers established an office in New York in 1876, and a short time later another one in Nagoya. These offices handled the import-export formalities for chinawares made by several small factories in Japan and sold in the United States.

In 1904 the Noritake factory was established in Nagoya; in Japan it was called Nippon Toki Kabushiki Kaisha. The factory housed everything necessary for the making of chinaware: a gypsum shop produced plaster of Paris for the molds; the latest equipment was installed for preparing the clay and making the bodies; facilities for the decoration of the wares were designed on Western models; the kilns were economical and easy to operate. Dinnerwares and fancy items, designed with an understanding of

194. The Noritake mustard pot, green M-in-Wreath mark, has a well-painted landscape and gold decoration on the cobalt blue underglaze border. Interesting lid and handles. The set of nut dishes bears the M-in-Wreath mark.

195. Demitasse cup and saucer and salt dish, bearing Tree Crest mark (green). Blue border, orange flowers, luster.

Western taste and needs, were manufactured there for export to the United States and Europe.

The Noritake Company was the first in Japan to manufacture dinnerwares for export, and was the leader in the field. Other small companies copied its products, but the only company of any size that produced dinnerwares was the Meito Company, which went out of business during World War II.

A variety of other goods was also produced by the Noritake Company: sanitary ware, insulators, and spark plugs, as well as gypsum; in time separate companies were formed for these products. In 1917 a factory for the exclusive production of sanitary wares was established—it is now known as Toto Ltd.; the insulator division became independent in 1919 and split into two companies in 1936, one for porcelain insulators and the other for spark plugs and chemical porcelain; in 1936, also, the gypsum division became a separate company under the name of Nitto Sekko Kaisha Ltd.

Noritake was the only company allowed to continue production of commercial dinnerware during World War II. The government did not want this skill lost, so every effort was made to continue in spite of all difficulties. The company suffered badly during the bombing, and equipment and records were lost.

For a short period after the war, wares made by the Noritake Company were exported under the R.C., or Rose China, mark, as it was felt that the quality was not worthy of the name Noritake. However, wares can be found with the Noritake mark and "Occupied Japan." At present there are eight Noritake factories in Japan that manufacture dinnerware.

A branch of the Noritake Company, the Okura China factory, produces expensive wares that are processed entirely by hand. This factory was begun as the hobby of Baron Okura. Wares (particularly vases) imported into the United States are marked O.A.C. Noritake (Okura Art China).

The "M" in the famous M-in-Wreath mark stands for the name Morimura; it was used until the Morimura office in New York was closed in 1941. After that, the wreath encircled an "N" for Noritake. Another well-known Noritake mark also associated with the Morimura family is the Tree Crest mark (Ill. 195); the symbol, which is sometimes mistakenly called a wheel, or spoke, is the Japanese character for "tree," and is the crest of the Morimura family.

Noritake wares are of a consistent high quality and have their own style and individuality. Unlike the decoration on much of the Nippon ware of the same period, the motifs on Noritake ware were mostly used in the European fashion of decoration.

As the company did both body and

196. *The syrup pot and its underplate are richly decorated in gold; porcelain is of excellent quality. The small covered box on pedestal has gold beading with pink rosebuds on a turquoise background. H. 2½". All have R. C. Noritake mark.*

decoration, the quality of the two on a single piece are comparable. Nippon, on the other hand, can have fine decoration on a poor body, and vice versa. Noritake decoration often echoed the shape, as it did in the lemon-shaped dish in Ill. 198, and the shapes of the pieces were also individual to the company. Even if a corresponding piece is found with a Nippon mark, the dimensions will be different. This is important to remember when looking at an unmarked piece that might be part of a set; if the dimensions are not the same as those of a corresponding piece marked Nippon, the piece in question is very likely Noritake.

Although all Noritake wares are made from high quality paste and the bodies are well finished, the finest pieces are those bearing the old R.C. mark—these wares date from about 1911, and at that time the R.C. stood for Royal Ceramic. They were intended to be worthy to compete with the best European porcelain. The molds used were of distinctive shapes, and very often,

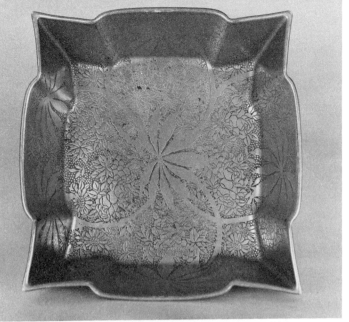

197. Gold Noritake dish with green M-in-Wreath mark. The stamp used to decorate this piece must have had its design etched with acid to produce a surface of this kind. Mrs. Robert Seekamp

198. The spoon holder at left in the group photograph is decorated with pink roses. The two center dishes, both decorated with luster, have a handle formed out of the body; the smaller of the two is not only lemon-shaped but decorated with a lemon. The larger one has a floral motif and a black and gold border. The condiment set at right with azalea decoration and the larger dish are both Noritake green M-in-Wreath; others are red M-in-Wreath. The bowl shown separately, also green M-in-Wreath, has two handles pierced from the body.

199. Although this footed dish carries the green Noritake M-in-Wreath mark, it was probably a blank sent elsewhere for decoration. The floral spray is signed A. Haruno.

after a piece was taken from the mold, it was further shaped by hand. The saucer under the gold-decorated syrup pot in Ill. 196 received this treatment. When a piece like this is held one can feel exactly how the potter manipulated it between his fingers and thumb.

Wares with the old R.C. mark are finely decorated, often with considerable gold-work in excellent taste. The extreme white-ness of the porcelain and the intricate gold decoration combine to give an appearance of great refinement.

In Nippon ware the main interest was in the enameled decoration, but in Noritake the individual shape of the body is often the predominant feature. Frequently a handle is formed out of the body, or openings are made to give a handlelike effect (Ill. 198).

During the first two decades of the twentieth century, the production of blanks to be exported "in the white" for amateur decoration overseas was an important part of the Noritake Company's trade (Ill. 199). The hand painting of china was then a popular way of making a personal gift to a friend, and even complete sets were so decorated and often accompanied by an embroidered matching tray cloth or tablecloth. A semicircular mark with the words "Noritake Nippon" generally was used on these blanks when they were exported to the United States, and pieces with this mark are quite common, with a variety of styles of decoration on them. Some pieces with this mark were sent to other parts of Japan for decoration. On these the Noritake Nippon mark is often seen together with a Nippon symbol, or Japanese characters reading "Kutani" on the same piece (Ill. 200). As the Noritake Company made use of the jigger very early in the history of the company, the manufacture and export of large quantities of blanks was easy.

The Noritake pictorial style of decoration falls roughly into two categories: the

200. The cup and saucer decorated in Kutani style are marked with a semicircular "Noritake Nippon" as well as Japanese characters reading "Kutani" on a red brushstroke. The syrup pitcher has the same semicircular mark, along with the Nippon Maple Leaf mark; it is decorated in gold with turquiose "jewels."

beautifully painted, naturalistic kind, and the stylized (Ill. 201). One type of decoration in the naturalistic style consists of landscapes (Ill. 202); very often a sunset is included, and if it is painted on a set, each piece has a different portion of it, so that if all the pieces are put side by side, the complete scene is encompassed.

In contrast to Nippon ware, which with few exceptions used asymmetrical decoration, Noritake prefers the European symmetrical style. Even when bouquets are painted as natural flowers, they are still used in a rigid pattern and repeated exactly as on European pieces (Ill. 198). A characteristic feature of these bouquet patterns is the use of a kind of shadow painting of a circle of leaves around the bouquet. Another feature is the use, for contrast in bouquets, of one blue *kikyo* flower (bellflower).

The stylized form of decoration, a very distinctive feature of Noritake ware, is generally used on the more commercial lines of

wares. Flowers, fruit, birds, fish, and the like are all portrayed in this style (Ill. 203). Very often they form part of a decalcomania used in conjunction with hand-painted work. The forms are more or less geometric, the flower petals being circles, for example. However, these stylized forms can also be found on superior wares (Ill. 204).

Luster is used a great deal, either for the whole decoration or some part of it. As luster is found mostly on wares bearing the red M-in-Wreath mark, and comparatively rarely on those with the green mark, it would seem as if the process were introduced at about the time the color of the mark was changed (Ill. 206). The Noritake Company says that no record exists of the date of this color change, but as the luster process was introduced after the end of the Nippon period (1921), this would place the transition from green mark to red in the mid-twenties, making the green mark the earlier of the two.

201. *The gold-handled basket has beautifully painted floral decoration; Noritake green M-in-Wreath mark. The dresser set, which carries the Tree Crest mark in green, has stylized floral decorations: pink double cherry blossoms, red and blue plum blossoms, gold leaves, and a blue luster border.*

202. *Scalloped-edge dish has three small landscapes, all different. Mark is Nori-take Tree Crest in a circle. There is lavish use of gold and green, and a magenta border.* Pinney Collection

203. *Examples of Noritake stylized decoration, all with the red M-in-Wreath mark: plate with fruit and flowers; sugar and creamer with flowers and luster; berry set decorated with bowls of fruit.* Mr. and Mrs. T. J. Lotito

204. *Noritake vase, green M-in-Wreath mark, has stylized gold grape decoration on a black ground. The vine even has a stylized root. Note the symmetrical bunches of grapes.*

205. *Sugar and creamer with allover luster; red M-in-Wreath mark.*

206. *The bowl with stylized decoration of fish and birds bears the green M-in-Wreath mark. The identically sized bowl with luster decoration has the same green M-in-Wreath mark, but the third bowl (with luster decoration) bears a red M-in-Wreath mark. The coloring on the second and third bowls is very similar.*

17

Made in Japan (1921-1940)

The mark "Made in Japan" covers wares made in all parts of Japan. These pieces were produced after 1921, when the word "Nippon" was no longer acceptable to the United States government for country of origin. After that time wares were variously marked "Japan" or "Made in Japan," either stamped on the piece or on a paper sticker attached to it.

Many of these export pieces were made in the Seto (Ill. 207) and Nagoya areas, but there was also considerable production in Arita. Pieces made in these areas were sent to decorating studios elsewhere to be finished; Tokyo was a large center for this kind of work. Kaga was another district that specialized in decoration, although kilns there also made the biscuit (Ill. 208).

The "Made in Japan" group presents the largest variety of styles and quality of workmanship, the pieces ranging from excellent to very poor. However, I would like to caution against saying "bad" too quickly. There was a lot of hasty work, but that does not always make a piece totally unacceptable. Quite often such a piece has a certain charm or individuality about it. Of course, there was a tremendous quantity of unquestionably poor quality work, but one should not pass judgment too blindly.

Many pieces carry no mark at all; either they came as part of a set in which only

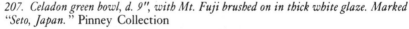

207. Celadon green bowl, d. 9", with Mt. Fuji brushed on in thick white glaze. Marked "Seto, Japan." Pinney Collection

208. *The three cups and saucers with Kaga-style decoration have red brown borders. The six-cup chocolate set is decorated mostly with decalcomania, but the added enamel work is well done. Dots of raised enamel represent the blossoms on the trees. This set is better quality than many of its type. Marked "Made in Japan."* Mr. and Mrs. T. J. Lotito

209. *The demitasse set with tray is marked "Kokura, Japan." It has pink, orange, and blue flowers, with green leaves; a black and white border. Good quality porcelain.* Mr. and Mrs. Frank Petta. *The condiment set with an Egyptian scene is marked "Camel China." The decoration on this set is not of such good quality as on the demitasse set; it looks hastily done, and on one piece the head of the rider is missing. However, the set is attractive, and the metal stand, which looks like a kind of silver, has an impressed mark on it that, on cursory inspection, might be taken as an English hallmark, but is not.*

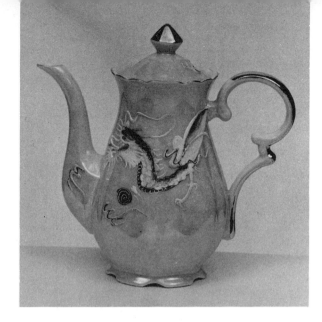

210. Coffeepot, unmarked, has a luster surface with a slip-trailed dragon; gold on handle and lid.

some of the pieces were marked, or they had paper stickers that were soon lost. We have to form our own opinion as to the country of origin. Sometimes this is an easy decision to make, but at other times it is almost impossible to be sure. The problem is further complicated when we have to contend with pieces that were sent out "in the white" for decoration.

In the early part of this century, not only was china painting a popular pastime; there were also any number of small studios specializing in selling hand-painted china. The United States imported blanks from many countries—Japan, France, and Bavaria, to name only a few. Of course, these blanks had to be marked with the country of origin; but blanks from other countries were also sent to Japan for decoration, and those blanks were not always marked, since Japan had no import regulations requiring such marking (Ill. 211).

Certain wares bear other marks besides "Japan." These fall into two categories: either Japanese characters giving the name of the kiln, company, or potter, or symbols that are descendants of the Nippon marks. The latter, like the Nippon symbols, were mainly export marks, the wares being collected by an agent and shipped abroad, mostly to the United States. Again, like the Nippon symbols, they are of little use to the collector, one symbol being affixed to a wide variety of wares. During the transition period of

211. Although the decoration on this dish (13") appears to be Japanese, quite possibly the body was made elsewhere. It is a very light piece, and the frilled edge suggests the appearance of an Austrian blank. Unmarked.

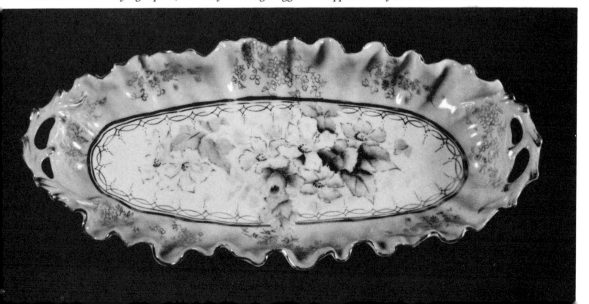

212. *This demitasse set is of excellent quality.*
Mrs. Diane Needleman. *The tiny bowl with
cream-colored crackled glaze in Satsuma style is
marked, in Japanese characters, with the name of
the small company that made it.* Pinney Collection

213. *Kaga pieces with very blotchy decoration.*

change from "Nippon" to "Japan," some wares carry both names.

As a rough-and-ready rule, one might say that if there is some mark besides the word "Japan," this implies a better quality, the makers not hiding under the anonymity of "Japan." Pieces bearing Japanese characters are usually of good quality (Ill. 212). However, this does not mean that pieces marked "Made in Japan" are necessarily of poor quality; after all, Japanese potters traditionally do not sign their wares, so a piece imported into the Unites States would be marked only "Made in Japan." The cormorant (Ill. 128) in the Metropolitan Museum of Art is stamped "Made in Japan" on its base. On the other hand, Kaga pieces usually carry a symbol or the name of the small factory in Japanese characters, and much poor quality ware has come from there (Ill. 213).

In the 1920s many imitations of the earlier Nippon and pre-Nippon pieces were made (Ill. 214). As a copy generally lacks the artistic vision of the piece as a whole, the effect is less artistic than on the original, and the piece is lifeless.

The teapot in Ill. 215 is a good example of pre-Nippon style that has lost much of the original fineness. At first it appears to be a very pretty piece, with pink roses on a green enamel background and gold border decoration on underglaze blue. The finial, however, is clumsy and entirely covered with gold, instead of having a gold pattern painted on the underglaze blue; the finial shows blue underneath where the gold has worn off, so no doubt the original intention was to have a gold pattern on the blue, but this was not carried out. The handle is too heavy and ornate, obviously a copy of a handle from some other piece, as it simply does not go artistically with the rest of the teapot. The roses do not have the shaded detail of the earlier pre-Nippon period (1868–1890); white enamel outlines are relied on to mark the petals and shape the flowers. The leaves are done in the same style, with gold outlines on dabs of green paint. Nevertheless, it is still a colorful piece even if it is not up to the standard of the original style.

The tray in Ill. 217 relies rather heavily on its coloring, which unfortunately cannot be seen in a black and white illustration. It

214. This piece in the shape of a ship's decanter is obviously a copy of a much older piece. On the original the elaborate decoration would have been slip-trailed, but here it was done with thick enamel. The detail photograph shows that the brushwork is not of the fine quality of turn-of-the-century wares. Unmarked.

215. *Teapot made in the 1920s imitating pre-Nippon wares. See Ill. 149 for detail.*

216. *Scalloped bowl with three feet, 1920s. The brushwork on this piece is similar to that on the teapot in Ill. 215, but as this bowl is of an unpretentious nature, the decoration blends well with the style of potting. "Made in Japan."*

217. *Another unpretentious "Made in Japan" piece. Decoration is violets and green leaves.*

looks as if a child might have painted it, and indeed a child could have, as children have always helped with the decorating in Japan.

Some Nippon marks were retained on "Made in Japan" pieces with very little change. The best example of this is the Torii mark. It remained exactly the same; "Nippon" was simply changed to "Made in Japan." The pieces are often identical too, and one has to turn a piece upside down to see which mark it bears (see Ills. 187 and 191).

Kaga wares retain much of their separate identity. Torii wares were derived from the red Kaga wares of the late nineteenth century, and the same style of decoration was used with the "Made in Japan" marking (Ill. 218).

Another Kaga mark is the T-in-Cherry-Blossom, which, like the Nippon marks, was an export mark. The cherry blossom is the crest of the Maeda family, lords of Kaga. As wares were shipped "in the white" to Kaga

218. *The set with Kaga-style decoration showing a man on horseback crossing a bridge is of only medium quality. The other set, featuring a landscape with Mt. Fuji, is good quality porcelain and decoration. Both are unmarked.* Mr. and Mrs. T. J. Lotito

219. *The handleless cup of wheel-turned gray porcelain has a landscape in underglaze blue applied by transfer. Mark: T-in-Cherry-Blossom, Japan. The decalcomania decoration on the small dish must have been applied before the body was very hard, as the edges were not folded over until after it had been put on. Unmarked.* Pinney Collection

Province for decoration, often acting as ballast on returning ships that had carried rice on their outward journey, a wide variety of wares carry this mark. Some pieces are of good quality porcelain, often decorated in Kutani style (Ill. 153) and probably sent from Arita to Kaga for decoration. Some are in the coarse gray porcelain associated with Kaga wares, and can be found with blue underglaze transfer decoration in Kaga style (Ill. 219).

Probably the most important development of the period was luster decoration. This came in after the Nippon period (1891–1921), and Noritake has used it extensively. These pieces rely on their sheen and coloring for decorative effect. In many cases the brushwork is rather hastily done, but the general effect of the colors is pleasing. The shapes are usually quite commercial and unpretentious (Ill. 220).

One very obvious way in which pro-

220. *These salt dishes with landscapes in the center have on orange luster border with gold cherry blossoms. Mark: "Made in Japan," with paulownia leaves.*

221. *"Made in Japan" chocolate set of mediocre quality. The handles are poorly molded and clumsy, and the enamel decoration poorly done.*

222. *Three types of Chinese-style decoration: The plate, d. 10", has a yellow border, pink peonies, and black background. "Made in Japan." The teapot, h. 5½", has red, black, blue, and green panels, a red border on the shoulder, and a black spout. Handle is bamboo. "Made in Japan." The pair of vases, h. 6½ ", have green background. Decoration is mainly a transfer in blue, yellow, and red; clouds are green and black enamel. There is a hand-painted gold line around the base, and neck decoration in red, black, and gold—all careful work, but not much of it. Mark: "Made in Japan" with paulownia leaves.*

223. *Underglaze blue decoration. On the cup and saucer is a dragon design with Chinese-style flames. The dish is decorated with a Hō-ō bird (phoenix) and chrysanthemum and paulownia design; decoration of this kind is popularly called "Flying Turkey." All are marked "Made in Japan."*

224. *Nippon-style vase, h. 9", has Plum Blossom mark and "Hand Painted, Japan." The landscape, which continues around the back, does not have much detail but relies on a few bold brushstrokes. The raised gold decoration is on a shaded brown background; dark green on neck, light green handles.*

225. *Satsuma-style incense burner (h. 8") and bowl, with separate photograph showing the inside of the bowl. Decoration was done with polychrome enamels and a good deal of gold against a black background. The inside of the bowl is an interesting mixture of bas-relief and enamel decoration. Unmarked.*

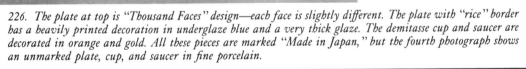

226. The plate at top is "Thousand Faces" design—each face is slightly different. The plate with "rice" border has a heavily printed decoration in underglaze blue and a very thick glaze. The demitasse cup and saucer are decorated in orange and gold. All these pieces are marked "Made in Japan," but the fourth photograph shows an unmarked plate, cup, and saucer in fine porcelain.

227. *The set shown here, with slip-trailed dragons and airbrush design, is unmarked, but an attached paper sticker reads: "Betson, Japan." Mr. and Mrs. T. M. Lotito. The Satsuma-style dark brown vase is also unmarked, but the Imari-style plate is marked "Made in Japan."*

duction costs were cut to the detriment of the finished product was including the handles in the mold instead of making them separately and attaching them to the body with slip. Handles made in this way are much heavier and not so clean-cut. The method of manufacture is immediately apparent if one looks inside a piece. If handle and body were molded in the same mold, porcelain was drawn up into the handle, making a hollow at this point inside the body. If the handle was attached with slip, the body is smooth inside.

A vast quantity of various types of ceramics bears the words "Made in Japan," ranging from pottery to faience to porcelain. Some are good, some are bad. The collector must rely on his own judgment and taste, and have the courage of his convictions.

Form your own opinions rather than listen to the next person, unless you have a particular reason to respect his judgment. In this way your own taste will grow, and if it is not the same as your neighbor's, who is to say that his taste is better than yours? At least you will have your own reasons for liking what you like, and you will not be a poor copy of what you imagine you should be.

Figurines were manufactured by the thousands in the 1921–1940 period, and many were made after Austrian and German models. Usually they are distinguishable from the European ones because they have a brighter gold. The china is of a different quality as well—it is softer, and the wares do not feel as sharp as the Austrian ones.

Satsuma-style and Imari wares have been dealt with elsewhere, and pieces with slip-trailed dragons are mentioned in the discussion of Nippon. All these wares became widely mass-produced and are generally less pleasing than the earlier examples (Ill. 227).

228. *The small vases and cherub figurine (h. 4") are marked "Made in Japan." The Toby mug and the dish are both marked "Japan." The Toby has a decided oriental slant to the eyes.* Mr. and Mrs. T. J. Lotito

18

Occupied Japan (1945-1952) and Later

The Occupation of Japan lasted for six and a half years. It was the first time in her long history that Japan had come under the control of foreign conquerors.

The war left behind a tremendous amount of devastation. Most factories had either been destroyed or else were closed for lack of materials. Japan's foreign markets were gone and her merchant marine, necessary to transport goods for foreign trade, was nonexistent. With the aid of the Americans, however, the Japanese worked hard at clearing the devastation and reviving their economic life.

A great variety of ceramic wares was produced during the Occupation period, especially chinaware, both for sale to GIs stationed there and for export. Some is of fine quality, some rather crude, and some, to say the least, peculiar.

Cups and saucers rank high in the better class of wares. Some were made from a good fine porcelain and have tasteful decoration. Cups can be found in a wide array of shapes: the small friendship variety for gift giving, demitasse cups, coffee cups, teacups, cups in English, French, and German styles, cups with various Japanese styles of decoration,

229. *Occupied Japan pieces: The cup and saucer on opposite page have a black background and are marked "Made in Occupied Japan" and with C-in-Wreath. The creamer at top left is not well done, but the work on the other two pieces is good; creamer and cup are marked "Made in Occupied Japan"; the plate has "Ironstone Ware" added as well. At top right, the little friendship cup and saucer, marked "Ohashi China, Occupied Japan," have pink and orange flowers alternating with gold medallions against a dark green background.* Pinney Collection. *In the group of three demitasse cups and saucers, at center right, the one at the left is marked "Hand Painted" and "Gold China, Occupied Japan"; the center one decorated by decalcomania is marked "Fuji China, Occupied Japan"; the one at right, hand painted, reads "Made in Occupied Japan." At bottom right, the German-style cup and saucer are marked "Gold Castle, Occupied Japan"; the demitasse beside it, simply "Made in Occupied Japan."*

230. *"Occupied Japan" pieces of very good quality: The plate, d. 9½", is in the Chinese style, with cobalt blue background, yellow tree, pink and white plum blossoms, red, pink, and white peonies. The cup and saucer are decorated in black and brown. The miniature coffee set on a 3½" tray has fine decoration consisting of gold flowers and enamel beading on a green background; the flower basket is blue. All are marked "Made in Occupied Japan," but on the cup and saucer the word "Hokutacha" is added also.*

231. Figurines in European style: The two at top left, h. 7½", have green and brown costumes in muted tones. Mrs. C. Howell. The two above, h. 6", are dressed in green and have gold highlights. The couple at lower left, an unusually tall piece (12"), were probably inspired by a European print. All are marked "Made in Occupied Japan."

232. The figurine (h. 5½") of a boy playing a violin may well have been inspired by the popular Hummel figures. Decoration is in warm browns and orange; black hat and umbrella. Marked "Made in Japan." Mr. and Mrs. T. J. Lotito. The figurines in the large group, perhaps also Hummel-inspired, are 4½" high and marked "Made in Occupied Japan."

233. Group of four imitation "German" beer mugs with incised German words are all marked "Made in Japan." Mrs. C. Howell. The other two mugs, with less detail and fuzzy decoration, are very light ware marked "Made in Occupied Japan."

cups decorated mainly on the outside, and cups decorated mainly on the inside. All these, of course, have corresponding saucers (Ill. 229).

By far the largest group of "Occupied Japan" articles is the figurines. They were made in every imaginable shape: figures in European period costume (Ill. 231); in Chinese or Japanese costume; figures playing oriental and European instruments; dancing figures, sailor boys, Dutch girls, mermaids, elves, babies, cherubs, and so on (Ill. 232). There were also animals of all kinds, frogs, swans, and all sorts of birds, as well as baby booties, horse-drawn carriages, and other objects (Ill. 234). In my personal opinion, the figurines of groups of oriental dancers and instrumentalists are the most colorful and interesting.

It seems to me that the better wares usually followed a form of traditional Japanese or Chinese style. Many of the souvenir type of wares appear to have been modeled on the inferior export wares of the twenties and thirties. There are also extraordinary oddities that no doubt were intended to please the resident GI but did not quite come off.

As far as marks are concerned, a great many different ones are in existence, although, of course, many pieces are just stamped "Made in Occupied Japan." I do not know how many different marks there are, but I would hazard a guess at around seventy-five or more, and this may be a conservative estimate. I have even seen a mark saying that the piece was made in Occupied Japan and designed somewhere in Florida. This struck me as exceedingly strange—al-

234. *The pianist and her piano are marked "Made in Occupied Japan." The assortment of doll furniture, quite poorly made, is marked either "Japan" or "Made in Japan."*

though the Japanese may have needed help financially, or with materials; surely they had no problem in designing chinaware. Perhaps the Japanese decorator merely wished to carry out an American design in order to make his wares acceptable for the American market. Interestingly enough, the piece was decorated with a very ordinary landscape of the kind that was done much better on Nippon pieces.

Recently, fake pieces of "Occupied Japan" have come on the market. These are much lighter in weight than the originals, and have a thin soft body that is hollow inside. They carry a mark written in script, either in orange or black on those I have seen so far. However, as they do not have the feel of the originals, no serious collector should have trouble differentiating between the two wares.

Since the end of the Occupation the export of Japanese ceramics has again become a flourishing industry. Excellent quality dinnerwares are in plentiful supply and fancy porcelains are available, as well as peasant-type wares.

Besides the traditional Imari, Kutani, and Satsuma wares, other wares in traditional styles are being produced and exported. In the Arita area the Fukagawa Porcelain Manufacturing Company makes very fine porcelain with decoration in beautiful colors (Ill. 236). Happu folk wares are made in the Isé district and exported abroad in large quantities (Ill. 237). They are made in the local tradition from regional clays.

In conclusion, I hope that this book will have stimulated interest in the enormous variety of wares available to collectors of Japanese ceramics, and the basic information provided will enable readers to move on to more detailed books on the subject.

Because of the scarcity of Japanese written records much controversy exists over dates, kilns, and potters. However, rather than deterring collectors, this should give them an added incentive to form their own collections, and draw their own conclusions as to the correctness of available information. With this in mind, study collections of imperfect wares can be made, and a great deal of firsthand knowledge can be obtained at a very moderate cost.

235. Satsuma-style cup and saucer with Satsuma crest (cross in circle); inside of cup is gold luster. "Made in Occupied Japan."

236. Covered bowl made by the Fukagawa Porcelain Manufacturing Company (established 1689) is excellent quality porcelain with delicate hand-painted gold decoration on cobalt blue background.

Appendix of Marks and Periods

Jōmon Period: c. 4500 B.C.–c. 200 B.C.
Yayoi Period: c. 200 B.C.–A.D. 250
Kofun Period: 250–552
Asuka Period: 552–646
Nara Period: 646–794
Heian Period: 794–1185
Kamakura Period: 1185–1333
Muromachi Period: 1333–1568
Momoyama Period: 1568–1615
Edo Period: 1615–1868
Meiji Period: 1868–1912
Taisho Period: 1912–1926
Showa Period: 1926–present day

大日本道八製

Dōhachi

大日本清風造

Seifû

大日本帯山製

Tanzan

日本万古 太田造

Banko

日本京都錦光山造

Kinkozan

fuku, *good luck*

R.C. Nippon

M-in-Wreath

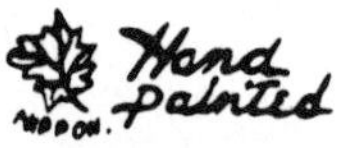

Maple Leaf

Imperial

S.N.B. Nagoya

Pointed Crown

Pagoda

Royal Satsuma

Torii

O.A.C. Nippon

Square Crown

S & K Nippon

R.C. Noritake

T-in-Wreath

M-in-Wreath Noritake

The Yamato Nippon

Tree-Crest Noritake

Cherry Blossom

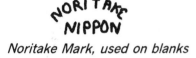

Noritake Mark, used on blanks

T.S. Nippon

Tree-Crest Nippon

HAND PAINTED NIPPON

CHINA
E-OH
HAND PAINTED
NIPPON

Paulownia Blossom

KINJO NIPPON

Rising Sun   Plum Blossom   Cherry Blossom   Hand Painted

NORITAKE CHINA JAPAN

Hand Painted NIPPON

502
NO·70018·
NIPPON

Hand Painted NIPPON

KOKURA JAPAN

Glossary

aburazara: oil dish

aka-: red

aka-e: "red painted" (red pictures). Japanese term for overglaze or polychrome enamels

aka-e machi: "street of enamelers." Arita street, founded in seventeenth century, where Imari ware was decorated and sold

akaji-kinga: gold designs on red

Amakusa stone: a form of semidecomposed feldspar found in Kyushu

ana-gama: "cellar kiln." A single-chamber sloping kiln, first used by the Chinese and introduced into Japan by Korean potters

ao-: "green"; e.g., Ao-Kutani, Ao-Oribe

arabesque: a florid style of ornament developed by Arabian art workers; usually composed of scrolls and floral tracery

Arita ware: porcelain ware produced in Arita; includes Imari, Kakiemon, Nabeshima, and Hirado wares

ash glaze: glaze produced from wood ash falling on the ware in the kiln during firing

aubergine: a deep purple color like the skin of the eggplant

Awata ware: earthenware, or faience, decorated with overglaze enamel

bail handle: a hoop-shaped handle extending over the top from one side to the other

ball clay: a plastic secondary clay that fires white and withstands high temperatures in the kiln

bank kiln: a sloping kiln, the slope taking the place of a chimney

bento-bako: tiered lunch boxes

biscuit: pottery or porcelain that has been fired once but has not been glazed

blue and white ware: white porcelain with decoration in underglaze blue

body: the clay of which a pot is made

bone china: English soft porcelain composed of approximately one part ox-bone ash, one part china clay (kaolin), and one part Cornish stone (petuntse). The addition of bone ash causes vitrification to take place at a relatively low temperature.

brocade: Any mass of bright colors is called a brocade by the Japanese. See *nishikide*

casting: making shapes by pouring liquid clay into plaster molds

celadon: *seiji* in Japanese. The French name for a large family of oriental porcelain and stonewares with soft green crackled glaze. The general explanation for the word was the similarity of the color of the ware to the green ribbons worn by Céladon, the hero of the novel *L'Astrée*, by Honoré d'Urfé. Another explanation is that it was derived from the name of Sultan Sālāh-ed-din (Saledin), who made a gift of forty pieces of celadon to the Sultan of Damascus in 1171.

cha: tea

chajin: tea master

cha-no-yu: Japanese tea ceremony

cha-wan: teabowl

china: a term used for soft-paste porcelains in general

china clay: a form of kaolin, less plastic than that found in China and Japan

Ching-tê-chên: site of imperial Chinese porcelain factories

Chōsen: Korea

clay: semidecomposed feldspar, ground into particles, with the soluble elements removed

cloisonné: enamel decoration set in hollows formed by thin strips of wire welded to a metal plate

cobalt oxide: the coloring agent for almost all blues

Cochin chinaware: see Kōchi-*yaki*

coil building: forming the walls of pots with ropes of clay

Cornish stone: a semidecomposed feldspar, similar but not identical to petuntse

cover finial: a protuberance on the top of the lid or cover of a tureen, sugar bowl, teapot, vase, or the like, by which the cover may be lifted

crackle: intentional network of fine cracks on the surface of a glaze

crazing: an unintentional and faulty crackling of a glaze, caused by the thermal expansion and contraction of the glaze being different from that of the clay body

daimyo: lord

dampers: adjustable shutters used to control the draft in a kiln *dobin:* a ceramic teapot or hot-water kettle with bail handle

doki: "earthen vessel." Japanese term for low-fired pottery

drape mold (or flopover mold): a mold in the shape of the interior contour of the ware

drying: removal of water from the clay. The water added to clay in the formation of the ware is eliminated by the time the firing has reached 212°F.; the chemically combined water that is part of the composition of the clay is driven off at temperatures between about 675° and 1,300°F. After this the clay cannot be reclaimed, as it has undergone a chemical change.

e-: painted; e.g., *E*-Shino, "painted Shino"

earthenware: all glazed wares with a porous body

Edo: old name for Tokyo

eggshell porcelain: a name given to very thin translucent Japanese or Chinese export porcelain

egote: stick used to shape the inside of tall pieces on the wheel

enamels: low temperature colored glazes applied over harder glazes. These are fired at a lower temperature than the harder glaze, and adhere to the glaze without mixing with it.

engobe: slip used to coat the entire surface of a piece, changing its color

faience: a French name loosely applied to glazed earthenware in general

Famille verte, noire, and rose: French names given by the French historian of pottery, Albert Jacquemart (1808–1875), to three classes of Chinese porcelain

feldspar: an opaque white crystal found in granite, which melts between about 2,200° and 2,375°F. It is extensively used for ceramic bodies and glazes.

fettling: the process of smoothing the surface of leather-hard clay

finial: see cover finial

firing: the burning or stoking of a kiln

foot: the expansion at the base (generally circular) of the stem of a vessel, which it stands on

frits: a finely ground glassy substance widely used in the manufacture of commercial glazes

fude: Japanese painting and writing brush; *dami-fude,* large brush used for large washes of color

fuku: Japanese character meaning good fortune or blessing

fusible clays: clays that vitrify and lose their shape at or below 2,200°F.; used in the Orient for stoneware glazes

glost firing: glaze firing

goma: glaze caused by ash falling on the ware during firing; the "sesame seed" effect of Bizen ash glaze

gosu: natural cobalt found in pebble form in oriental creek beds. The term *gosu* is used to distinguish Japanese porcelains decorated in Chinese Ming style from *sometsuke,* the ordinary blue and white wares

gosu-aka-e: overglaze red and green decoration, sometimes with underglaze blue

grain-de-riz: French term for wares decorated with carving in shape of rice grains, filled in with transparent glaze

greenware: unfired pottery

grog: powdered burnt fireclay

hachi-ho: symbols of the Chinese Eight Treasures: the coin, books, stone chime, artemisia leaf, pearl, lozenge, mirror, and rhinoceros horns

hake: wide flat brush with short bristles

hakeme: broomlike brush made from tips of rice stalks or similar material; "brush-grain" decoration

hakudei ware: "white clay." Unglazed burnished ware of Tokoname

hanakago-de: flower basket pattern, showing a wicker basket, usually with a high loop handle, filled with flowers; popular on Imari wares

haniwa: "clay circles." Kofun Period (552 B.C.–A.D. 250) pottery figures and cylindrical forms, which were placed around burial mounds

happo: same as *hachi-ho*

hard paste porcelain: porcelain made from a mixture of china clay, feldspar, and other natural materials, which is fired at over 2,375°F.

hari-awase: "pasting together"; building with clay slabs

hari-tsuke: "sticking on"; a type of appliqué

Heian: old name for Kyoto. Heian Period (794–1185)

hera: bamboo knife or spatula

herame: spatula marks (on tea ceremony wares)

hidasuki: "fire-cord" effect. This was traditional decoration on Bizen ware, made by wrapping the wares with cords made of straw soaked in salt water, before firing. During the firing the straw burns away, depositing the sodium from the salt on the surface of the ware. The sodium combines with the red clay and causes bright red streaks of glaze to appear on the otherwise unglazed surface.

himo-tsukuri: "coil-building"

hiragana: see *kana*

Hō-ō bird: variously translated as phoenix or bird of paradise; the design originally came from China. The Hō-ō motif is associated with the empress of Japan, and is usually pictured with the empress's crest, the leaves of the paulownia tree *(kiri-no-mon).*

hori-dashi: "carving-out" a form from a single clay block

Imari ware: Arita porcelain wares for domestic and export use (excluding Kakiemon, Nabeshima, and Hirado wares) shipped from the port of Imari

impermeable: waterproof; bodies that have become nonporous through vitrification

iro-: "color"; e.g., Iro-Nabeshima

iro-gawari: Ryumonji transparent glaze

iron: a most useful coloring agent for clay, pigments, and glazes, as it withstands high temperatures. In the lower temperatures it gives yellows, browns, reds, and blacks; with higher temperatures, greens, blues, browns, and blacks.

ironstone china: a fine hard earthenware

jigger: a modern mechanical device for forming dinnerware commercially at high speed. It consists of an adjustable arm, which holds a profile that presses soft clay either into or onto a revolving plaster mold.

jiu, also *ju:* the Chinese symbol for longevity

Jōmon: "rope pattern," the oldest prehistoric Japanese earthenware. The name is derived from the impressed rope and cord decoration.

ju: see *jiu*

kachō: flower and bird design

Kaga Province: modern Ishikawa Prefecture

Kaga ware: a general term for ceramics made in Kaga Province

kaki: "persimmon"

kama: kiln

kana: the Japanese syllabary, derived from certain Chinese characters, greatly abbreviated, used as phonetic symbols. Each symbol represents one monosyllabic word or syllable, in contrast to the alphabet, which represents single sounds. These symbols are written in two different ways: *hiragana* and *katakana. Hiragana:* the whole character is written in stylized or cursive form. *Katakana:* an element of the character stands for the phonetic value of the whole.

kanna: "planes"

kaolin: anglicized form of the Chinese word for china clay, Kao-ling, "the high hills." It was named after the hills near Ching-te-Chen, where it was excavated.

Kara: china

karakō: "Chinese children" decoration

Karatsu: "China port"

kasasa: feldspar

kasuri-mon: chatter-mark decoration

katakana: see *kana*

ke-rokuro: "kick wheel"

kezuri: "trimming"

kezuri no dōgu: "trimming tools"

ki-: yellow

kikai rokuro: jigger wheel

Kiyomizu-*yaki:* wares decorated with overglaze enamels, produced in the vicinity of the Kiyomizu temple, Kyoto. The modern (post-1868) term for Kyoto wares, as opposed to the Edo Period term Kyō-*yaki*

ki-zeto: yellow Seto ware

kinrande: porcelain decoration in red and gold, based on Chinese prototypes

ko-: old. *Ko-zeto,* old Seto

Kōchi-*yaki* (Chinese Cochin ware): wares decorated in green and other colored glazes separated by low relief decoration. Originally produced in South China

koge: "scorch marks," found on Iga and Oribe wares

Koku-Ho, Law of: "national treasures." Okakura was responsible for the enactment of this law in 1884; it required all remaining objects of ancient Japanese art to be registered and restricted from export.

kuchi-beni: "mouth rouge"; the line of iron red glazing around Kakiemon wares

kuro-: black. Kuro-Raku, black Raku

kushi: "comb"

kushi-de: the "comb-mark" decoration found on the foot of Nabeshima wares.

After the Meiji Restoration the design was also used by other kilns.

kushime: "comb-grain" decoration

Kutani ware: wares named after the remote village in Kaga Province where it was originally produced. Later wares bearing the Kutani mark were made throughout Kaga Province.

Kyoto: "western capital"

Kyō-*yaki:* "capital ware." Monochrome, underglaze, and overglaze decorated wares, following the tradition of Ninsei and Kenzan, produced in the vicinity of Kyoto during the Edo Period

leather-hard: also called "cheese-hard." The stage in the drying process when the ware is no longer plastic, but not yet dry, and cuts like leather or cheese

luster: a form of decoration made by applying a thin skin of certain metals, in liquid form, to the surface of a glaze. This is subsequently fired in a low reducing atmosphere and imparts an iridescent surface to the glaze.

luting: joining together leather-hard surfaces of clay with slip

Maeda family: rulers of Kaga Province in feudal times, who established a kiln believed to be the original Kutani ware kiln

majolica: a corruption of the name Majorca, given to Italian tin-enameled pottery

maku-gusuri: "wavy-welt glaze"; the wavy surface patterns on Raku ware caused by the thick application of the glaze

matcha: "rubbed tea"; finely powdered tea used for the tea ceremony

matt glaze: glaze with dull surface after firing

mingei: "folk art"

mishima: inlaylike decoration, producing designs of contrasting colors

mizusashi: water jar used in the tea ceremony

mukōzuki: small dishes

nagashi-gusuri: "glaze that is made to flow"; superimposed glaze dripping

naze-kawa: chamois-skin swab for dampening clay

neriage: mosaic pattern developed by pressing clays of different colors into a mold; the pattern is the same inside and outside. This process dates from the Sung Dynasty in China.

neutral atmosphere: atmosphere in the kiln halfway between oxidation and reduction

nezumi-: gray. Nezumi Shino, gray Shino

nigoshi-de: milk white porcelain associated with Kakiemon wares

ningen kokuho: "living national treasure"

nishikide: "brocade-style" type of decoration, which covers the whole surface. Associated with the overglaze enamel decoration of the Imari wares of the eighteenth and nineteenth centuries

nobori-gama: "climbing kiln"; a kiln with stepped chambers, introduced into Japan by Korean potters

Old East Indian ware: old English name for Kakiemon ware

open clays: sandy-textured porous clays

oxidation firing: firing the kiln in such a manner that combustion is complete and the burning gases amply supplied with oxygen. This causes the metals in the clay and glaze to give their oxide colors.

petuntse (pai-tun-tzū): semidecomposed feldspar found in China; it is less decomposed than kaolin.

pilgrim bottle: a canteen-shaped vase, flattened on the two opposite sides

porcelain: pottery that is white, vitrified, and translucent, and has been fired at a high temperature (about 2,375°F.)

pottery: wares made of clay and water that have been fired at a heat of about 1,100°F. or more, and have undergone the resulting chemical changes

press molds: molds into which slabs of clay are pressed to form wares

pyrometers: instruments used in kilns for measuring the temperature

Raku-*yaki:* "pleasure wares," a type of light porous ware with crackled lead glaze, much favored for tea ceremony pieces. The name Raku is derived from a seal presented to Jōkei by Hideyoshi.

raw glazes: glazes that can be applied to greenware

reduction firing: firing a kiln in such a way that combustion is incomplete or smoky, and the carbon present reduces the oxides to their respective metals

redwares, or red-painted wares: seventeenth-century Dutch term for Japanese porcelain with blue underglaze and red overglaze enamels (with or without gold), in contrast to "blue" for blue and white wares

refractory materials: materials able to withstand the high temperatures needed to make hard porcelain

rice-grain decoration: see *grain-de-riz*

rokuro: original oriental potter's wheel: *Ke-rokuro*, kick wheel (always turned counterclockwise). *Te-rokuro*, hand wheel (always turned clockwise)

saggars: fireclay boxes used in the kiln; wares were packed in these to protect them from the direct action of the flames

sake bottle: a pottery bottle, often square, for holding sake (rice liquor)

sansai: "three colors." Wares in imitation of the Chinese three-colored glazed pottery of the Tang Dynasty, produced in Japan during the eighth century for the court at Nara. Also called Nara *sansai*

seiji: see celadon

sgraffito: decoration made by scratching through a covering of slip on leather-hard pots to expose the color of the clay below

shibui: "tastefully astringent." An aesthetic term meaning sober, quiet, or unostentatious

shio-gusuri: "salt glaze"

shiro: white

shizumi-botan: "sinking peony"; an incised decoration covered with celadon glaze

slip: clay diluted with water

slip-trailing: a method of decorating leather-hard wares with lines of raised slip. In Japan a bamboo tube was originally used for this, but nowadays the slip is squeezed out of a rubber syringe.

some-nishiki-de: a characteristic Imari ware technique in which the ware is first decorated in underglaze blue and then in overglaze enamel colors

sometsuke: decoration in underglaze blue on white porcelain

split bamboo kiln: a sloping kiln, so-called because it resembles a split stalk of bamboo. Introduced by Korean potters

spurs: triangular clay supports used in saggars for glazed wares

stilts: clay supports used for firing glazed wares

stoneware: an opaque, vitrified, hard substance between pottery and porcelain

tebineri: "hand pinching"

temmoku: a lustrous black iron glaze. The term is derived from the Tien Mu Mountain in Chekiang, where Zen monks first used Chien ware bowls for the tea ceremony. These bowls were later imitated at the Seto kilns.

terra-cotta: low-fired unglazed pottery

throwing: the process of forming wares on the potter's wheel

tombo: "dragonfly"; bamboo tool used to gauge diameter of cups and bowls

tomoe: commalike symbols

trailing: see slip-trailing

treading: the process of kneading clay by the pressure of the bare human heel, still preferred in Japan

turning: shaving leather-hard clay from the walls of pots on a potter's wheel or lathe

uki-botan: "floating peony"; low-relief decoration adopted by Seto potters from Chinese Northern-Sung celadons, covered with a celadon glaze

underglaze decoration: decoration painted directly on the biscuit, then covered with a translucent glaze and fired

unka ware: "cloud flower"; a burnished unglazed ware decorated with carbon impregnation

vitrification: the change into a glasslike substance resulting from fusion due to heat

wax resist: a decorating technique carried out by first covering a piece with a coat of glaze in the desired color for the decoration; then, when this is dry, painting the decoration in wax. Finally, when the wax has hardened, the piece receives a coating of glaze in the color for the background. As the wax prevents the second coat of glaze from sticking to the first coat in the decorated area, when the piece is fired the wax is burnt off and leaves the decoration in the first color.

-yaki: "ware"

yakimono: ceramic ware

yamato-e: Japanese-style decoration of simplicity and blank spaces

zōgan: "inlay" made with strips of contrasting slip set into a carved surface

Bibliography

ADACHI, BARBARA. *The Living Treasures of Japan*. Tokyo, Japan: Kodansha International Ltd., 1973.

BEASLEY, W. G. *Modern History of Japan*. New York and Washington, D.C.: Frederick A. Praeger, 1963.

BENEDICT, RUTH. *The Chrysanthemum and the Sword*. Boston: Houghton Mifflin Co., 1946.

BEURDELEY, MICHEL. *Chinese Trade Porcelain*. Rutland, Vermont: Charles E. Tuttle Co., 1962.

BRINKLEY, CAPTAIN S. *Japan, Its History, Arts and Literature*. Vol. 8, Keramic Art. London, 1904.

BROOKS, VAN WYCK. *Fenollosa and His Circle*. New York: E. P. Dutton & Co., Inc., 1962.

BUHOT, JEAN. *Chinese and Japanese Art*. Garden City, New York: Doubleday & Co., Inc., 1961.

CARDOZA, SIDNEY. *Rosanjin*. New York: Japan Society, Inc., 1972.

CHAFFERS, WILLIAM. *Marks and Monograms on European and Oriental Pottery and Porcelain*. Borden.

Contemporary Ceramic Art of Japan. Japan: Ministry of Foreign Affairs, 1972.

FRANKS, SIR AUGUSTUS W. *Japanese Pottery, Being a Native Report with an Introduction and Catalogue*. London: Wyman & Sons, 1906.

FUJIOKA, RYOICHI. *Tea Ceremony Utensils*. Tokyo, Japan: Weatherhill/Shibundō, 1973.

GARNER, SIR HARRY. *Oriental Blue and White*. New York and London: Pitman, n.d.

GORHAM, HAZEL. *Japanese and Oriental Ceramics*. Rutland, Vermont: Charles E. Tuttle Co., 1971.

HANNOVER, EMIL. *Pottery and Porcelain of the Far East*. Trans. by Bernard Rackham. London, 1925.

HOBSON, R. L. *Handbook of the Pottery and Porcelain of the Far East in the British Museum*. London, 1924.

HONEY, W. B. *The Ceramic Art of China and Other Countries of the Far East*. London, 1945.

HORIOKA, YASUKO. *The Life of Kakuzō*. Tokyo, Japan: The Hokuseido Press, 1963.

Japan Interpreter, The. Vol. 8, No. 1. Tokyo, Japan: The Japan Center for International Exchange, November 1973.

JENYNS, SOAME. *Japanese Porcelain*. New York and Washington, D.C.: Frederick A. Praeger, 1965.

———. *Japanese Pottery*. New York and Washington, D.C.: Frederick A. Praeger, 1971.

JOLY, HENRI L. *Legend in Japanese Art*. Rutland, Vermont: Charles E. Tuttle Co., 1967.

LEACH, BERNARD. *A Potter in Japan*. New York: Transatlantic Arts, Inc., 1967.

———. *A Potter's Book*. New York: Transatlantic Arts, Inc., 1972.

MIKAMI, TSUGIO. *The Art of Japanese Ceramics*. Tokyo, Japan: Weatherhill/Heibonsha, 1972.

MILLER, ROY ANDREW. *Japanese Ceramics*. Tokyo, Japan: Toto Shuppan Co. Ltd., distributed by Charles E. Tuttle Co., Rutland, Vermont, 1960.

MITSUOKA, TADANARI. *Ceramic Art of Japan*. Tokyo, Japan: Japan Travel Bureau, 1956.

MORISON, SAMUEL E. *"Old Bruin," Commodore Matthew Calbraith Perry*. Boston: Little, Brown & Co., 1967.

MORRIS, IVAN. *The World of the Shining Prince*. New York: Alfred A. Knopf, Inc., 1964.

MORSE, EDWARD SYLVESTER. *Catalogue of the Morse Collection of Japanese Pottery*. Boston, 1901.

———. *Japan Day by Day*. Boston: Houghton Mifflin Co., 1916.

———. *Japanese Homes and Their Surroundings*. New York: Dover Publications, Inc., 1961.

MUNSTERBERG, HUGO. *The Ceramic Art of Japan*. Rutland, Vermont: Charles E. Tuttle Co., 1964.

————. *The Folk Arts of Japan*. Rutland, Vermont: Charles E. Tuttle Co., 1958.

OKAKURA, KAKUZO. *The Book of Tea*. Rutland, Vermont: Charles E. Tuttle Co., 1956.

————. *The Ideals of the East, with Special Reference to the Art of Japan*. Rutland, Vermont: Charles E. Tuttle Co., 1970.

Philadelphia, Official Catalogue of the Japanese Section at the International Exhibition. Philadelphia, 1876.

REISCHAUER, EDWIN O. *Japan: The Story of a Nation*. New York: Alfred A. Knopf, Inc., 1970.

RHODES, DANIEL. *Clay and Glazes for the Potter*. Philadelphia: Chilton Book Co., 1957.

————. *Stoneware and Porcelain*. Philadelphia: Chilton Book Co., 1959.

————. *Tamba Pottery*. Tokyo, Japan: Kodansha International Ltd., 1970.

St. Louis, Official Catalogue of the Louisiana Purchase Exhibition. St. Louis, 1904.

San Francisco, Official Catalogue to the Department of Fine Arts at the Panama-Pacific Exposition. San Francisco, 1915.

SANDERS, HERBERT. *The World of Japanese Ceramics*. Tokyo, Japan: Kodansha International Ltd., 1967.

SATO, MASAHIKO. *Kyoto Ceramics*. Tokyo, Japan: Weatherhill/Shibundō, 1973.

Seattle Art Museum. *International Symposium on Japanese Ceramics*. Seattle, 1972.

SITWELL, SACHEVERELL. *The Bridge of the Brocade Sash*. Cleveland and New York: World Publishing Co., 1959.

STATLER, OLIVER. *The Black Ships Scroll*. Rutland, Vermont: Charles E. Tuttle Co., 1963.

STEINBERG, RAFAEL. *Japan*. New York: Macmillan, 1969.

SWANN, PETER. *Art of China, Korea and Japan*. New York and Washington, D.C.: Frederick A. Praeger, 1963.

TURK, FRANK A. *Japanese Objets d'Art*. New York: Sterling Publishing Co., 1962.

WAYMAN, DOROTHY G. *Edward Sylvester Morse*. Cambridge, Massachusetts: Harvard University Press, 1942.

YANAGI, SŌETSU. *The Unknown Craftsman*. Tokyo, Japan: Kodansha International Ltd., 1972.

Index

Deutsch: Na klar!

FIFTH EDITION

Deutsch: Na klar!

An Introductory German Course

Robert Di Donato
Miami University
Oxford, Ohio

Monica D. Clyde
St. Mary's College of California
Moraga, California

Jacqueline Vansant
University of Michigan, Dearborn

Contributing Writer
Lida Daves-Schneider

Contributing Writer, Instructor Annotations
Michael Conner
Texas State University

Boston   Burr Ridge, IL   Dubuque, IA   Madison, WI   New York   San Francisco   St Louis
Bangkok   Bogotá   Caracas   Kuala Lupur   Lisbon   London   Madrid   Mexico City
Milan   Montreal   New Delhi   Santiago   Seoul   Singapore   Sydney   Taipei   Toronto

 This is an book.

Deutsch: Na klar! An Introductory German Course

Published by McGraw-Hill, an imprint of The McGraw-Hill Companies, Inc., 1221 Avenue of the Americas, New York, NY 10020. Copyright © 2008. All rights reserved. No part of this publication may be reproduced or distributed in any form or by any means, or stored in a database or retrieval system, without the prior written consent of The McGraw-Hill Companies, Inc., including, but not limited to, in any network or other electronic storage or transmission, or broadcast for distance learning.

This book is printed on acid-free paper.

1 2 3 4 5 6 7 8 9 0 DOW / DOW 0 9 8 7

ISBN-13:   978-0-07-353532-6
MHID: 0-07-353532-x (Student Edition)

ISBN-13:   978-0-07-327804-9
MHID: 0-07-327804-1 (Instructor's Edition)

Editor in Chief: *Emily G. Barrosse*
Publisher: *William R. Glass*
Sponsoring Editor: *Christa Harris*
Director of Development: *Scott Tinetti*
Developmental Editor: *Paul Listen*
Marketing Manager: *Nick Agnew*
Media Producer: *Allison Hawco*
Production Editor: *Brett Coker*
Designers: *Violeta Díaz and Anne Flanagan*
Cover Designer: *Susan Breitbard*
Art Editor: *Ayelet Arbel*
Illustrator: *Wolfgang Horsch*
Photo Research: *David Tietz and Sonia Brown*
Supplements Coordinator: *Louis Swaim*
Production Supervisor: *Richard DeVitto*
Composition: *10/12 Melior by Techbooks*
Printing: *45# Publishers Matte Plus by R.R. Donnelley & Sons*

Cover: *© Robert Fishman/dpa/Corbis.*

Credits: The credits section for this book begins on page A-76 and is considered an extension of the copyright page.

Library of Congress Cataloging-in-Publication Data
Di Donato, Robert.
    Deutsch, na klar! : an introductory German course / Robert Di Donato, Monica D. Clyde, Jacqueline Vansant; contributing writer, Lida Daves-Schneider.—5th ed.
    p. cm.
Includes index.
ISBN-13:   978-0-07-353532-6
MHID: 0-07-353532-x (Student Edition)
ISBN-13:   978-0-07-327804-9
MHID: 0-07-327804-1 (Instructor's Edition)
    1. German language—Grammar. 2. German language—Textbooks for foreign speakers—English. I. Clyde, Monica. II. Vansant, Jacqueline, 1954- III. Title.

PF3112.D48 2007
838.2'421—dc22

2006048130

The Internet addresses listed in the text were accurate at the time of publication. The inclusion of a Web site does not indicate an endorsement by the authors or McGraw-Hill, and McGraw-Hill does not guarantee the accuracy of the information presented at these sites.

www.mhhe.com

Contents

	Wörter im Kontext	**Grammatik im Kontext**

	Wörter im Kontext	**Grammatik im Kontext**

| Wörter im Kontext | Grammatik im Kontext |

Preface

Welcome to the Fifth Edition of *Deutsch: Na klar!* Those familiar with this textbook know that *Deutsch: Na klar!* offers a versatile, comprehensive, and colorful program for introductory German courses. The Fifth Edition provides an exciting, innovative package designed to suit a wide variety of approaches, methodologies, and classrooms, while still preserving many standard pedagogical features that instructors have come to trust since the publication of the first edition. Among the trusted and proven features of *Deutsch: Na klar!,* you will recognize the following:

- a rich array of authentic visual and textual materials with accompanying activities and exercises

- succinct grammar explanations

- a commitment to the balanced development of both receptive skills (listening and reading) and productive skills (speaking and writing)

- abundant communicative activities, as well as many form-focused activities and exercises

- the promotion of meaningful acquisition of vocabulary and structures with considerable regard to accuracy

As noted above, one of the trusted hallmarks of *Deutsch: Na klar!* is its unique approach to the use of authentic materials. Authentic materials motivate and interest students and allow them to see the immediate application of their newly acquired skills in authentic contexts. Thus, in *Deutsch: Na klar!,* authentic materials are used to illustrate vocabulary in context, communicative functions of grammatical structures, and cultural points. Moreover, realia-based activities are extremely effective in helping students develop receptive skills.

Vocabulary and grammar are presented in a functional framework so that students begin to associate forms with functions. Vocabulary is introduced in context through the use of visuals, dialogues, short narratives, or "built-in" activities to stimulate meaningful language. **Neue Wörter** boxes help students verify the meaning of words after they have encountered them in an initial presentation. Wherever useful, grammatical structures are contrasted with parallel structures in English. Vocabulary and grammar activities progress from controlled and form-focused to open-ended and interactive, and from receptive to productive.

A Textbook Audio Program is tied to several activities in every chapter. Indicated in the student text with a headphone icon, some of these listening comprehension activities are designed for global comprehension, while others have been designed to give students practice in noting specific details. In a similar fashion, students learn to skim for general information and scan for specific details when reading. In both listening and reading, students are encouraged to use background knowledge and context to aid comprehension.

The Fifth Edition integrates an enhanced interview-based video **(Videoclips)** and computer-based realia into the program. Taped on location in Berlin, these interviews with native speakers of German provide authentic input directly related to the chapter theme and functions. New footage from Bonn and Cologne has been added as visual support for the interviewees' statements. The comprehensible yet natural speech of the interviews, combined with the new images, provides students with a window into the lives and habits of today's German citizens, thus promoting both the development of communicative skills and cultural awareness. The Fifth Edition video also contains cultural snippets that complement and elaborate on the topics of the interviews.

The five Cs of the National Standards—Communication, Connections, Culture, Comparisons, and Communities—developed by ACTFL in collaboration with AATG, AATF, and AATSP (*Standards for Foreign Language Learning: Preparing for the 21st Century*) permeate the activities, exercises, readings, cultural and language tips, and video of *Deutsch: Na klar!* Each chapter provides opportunities for students to communicate in German in real-life situations for real purposes. Authentic materials and the new video, as well as the exercises based on them, stimulate students' thinking about their own language and culture in order to draw cross-cultural comparisons and connect their study of German language and culture with other disciplines. And finally, opportunities for students to reach out to German-speaking communities locally and globally are provided through Internet activities.

In summary, through its authentic materials, cultural features, readings, listening passages, activities, and innovative technology, **Deutsch: Na klar!** teaches skills that will help students to communicate successfully in the German-speaking world.

Organization of the Text

Deutsch: Na klar! consists of a preliminary chapter **(Einführung)**, fourteen regular chapters, and a closing chapter **(Übergang).** Each of the fourteen regular chapters is developed around a major theme and has the following organization:

- Alles klar?
- Wörter im Kontext

  Themen 1, 2, (3)

- Grammatik im Kontext
- Sprache im Kontext

  Videoclips

  Lesen

  Zu guter Letzt

- Wortschatz
- Das kann ich nun!

Cultural collages **(Zwischenspiele),** containing visuals and activities, appear after **Kapitel 3, 6, 9,** and **12** and give students the opportunity to review, consolidate, and apply what they have learned in previous chapters to cultural topics of German-speaking countries in new contexts.

A Guided Tour through Deutsch: Na klar!

Alles klar?

The chapter opener introduces students to the theme of the chapter through a guided two-part activity that involves a visual or an authentic text and a thematically related, global listening comprehension passage.

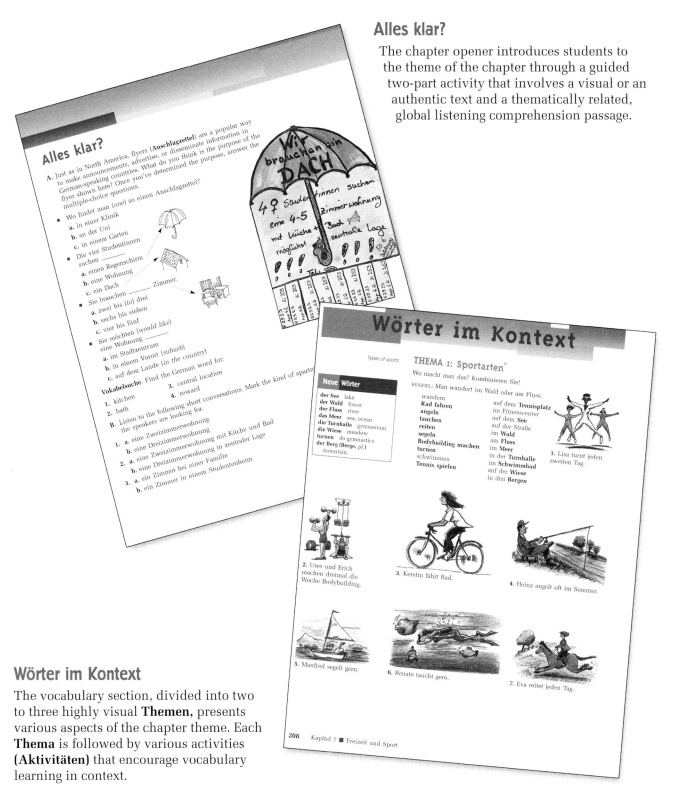

Alles klar?

A. Just as in North America, flyers (**Anschlagzettel**) are a popular way to make announcements, advertise, or disseminate information in German-speaking countries. What do you think is the purpose of the flyer shown here? Once you've determined the purpose, answer the multiple-choice questions.

- Wo findet man (*one*) so einen Anschlagzettel?
  - **a.** in einer Klinik
  - **b.** an der Uni
  - **c.** in einem Garten
- Die vier Studentinnen suchen _____.
  - **a.** einen Regenschirm
  - **b.** eine Wohnung
  - **c.** ein Dach
- Sie brauchen _____ Zimmer.
  - **a.** zwei bis (*to*) drei
  - **b.** sechs bis sieben
  - **c.** vier bis fünf
- Sie möchten (*would like*) eine Wohnung _____.
  - **a.** im Stadtzentrum
  - **b.** in einem Vorort (*suburb*)
  - **c.** auf dem Lande (*in the country*)

Vokabelsuche. Find the German word for:

1. kitchen
2. bath
3. central location
4. reward

B. Listen to the following short conversations. Mark the kind of apartment the speakers are looking for.

1. **a.** eine Zweizimmerwohnung
   b. eine Dreizimmerwohnung mit Küche und Bad
2. **a.** eine Zweizimmerwohnung in zentraler Lage
   b. eine Dreizimmerwohnung bei einer Familie
3. **a.** ein Zimmer in einem Studentenheim
   b. ein Zimmer bei einer Familie

Wörter im Kontext

Types of sports

THEMA 1: Sportarten°

Wo macht man das? Kombinieren Sie!

BEISPIEL: Man wandert im Wald oder am Fluss.

Neue Wörter

der See	lake
der Wald	forest
der Fluss	river
das Meer	sea, ocean
die Turnhalle	gymnasium
die Wiese	meadow
turnen	do gymnastics
der Berg (Berge, *pl.***)**	mountain

wandern
Rad fahren
angeln
tauchen
reiten
segeln
Bodybuilding machen
turnen
schwimmen
Tennis spielen

auf dem **Tennisplatz**
im **Fitnesscenter**
auf dem **See**
auf der **Straße**
im **Wald**
am **Fluss**
im **Meer**
in der **Turnhalle**
im **Schwimmbad**
auf der **Wiese**
in den **Bergen**

1. Lisa turnt jeden zweiten Tag.

2. Uwe und Erich machen dreimal die Woche Bodybuilding.

3. Kerstin fährt Rad.

4. Heinz angelt oft im Sommer.

5. Manfred segelt gern.

6. Renate taucht gern.

7. Eva reitet jeden Tag.

208   Kapitel 7 ■ Freizeit und Sport

Wörter im Kontext

The vocabulary section, divided into two to three highly visual **Themen,** presents various aspects of the chapter theme. Each **Thema** is followed by various activities (**Aktivitäten**) that encourage vocabulary learning in context.

Grammatik im Kontext

Grammar is presented in succinct explanations with abundant charts and examples and, whenever possible, via authentic materials. Some grammar explanations expand on points that are previewed in **Sprachtipps**.

Sprache im Kontext

This culminating four-skills section is divided into three parts: **Videoclips,** featuring interviews with German speakers on topics presented in each chapter and reflecting the vocabulary and grammar presented; **Lesen,** an authentic reading passage with pre- and post-reading activities; and **Zu guter Letzt,** interactive, task-oriented culminating activities that provide open-ended oral and written practice on the chapter theme.

The Deutsch: Na klar! vocabulary system

Vocabulary is presented by means of authentic materials, illustrations, descriptive texts, dialogues, and built-in activities. Students must first "discover" the meaning of the new vocabulary, which is highlighted in the presentation, through contextual guessing. Less transparent new vocabulary is then reflected in the **Neue Wörter** lists, which students should use to verify their contextual guessing.

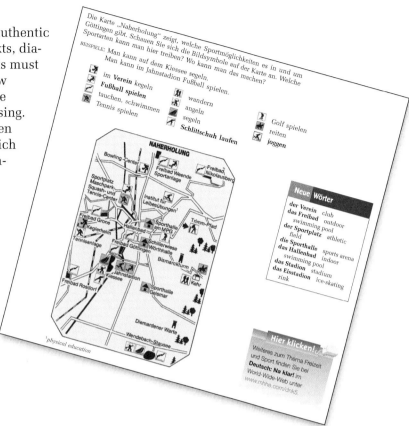

Analyse

Before doing **Aktivitäten** or **Übungen,** students develop receptive skills by examining authentic texts for specific vocabulary or grammatical structures.

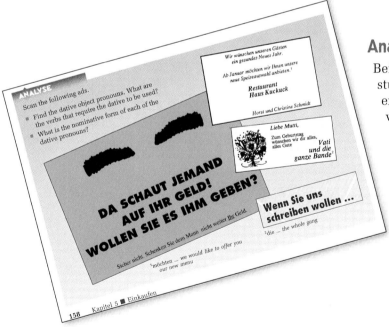

Aktivitäten und Übungen

A broad range of activities and exercises allows for structured communicative practice of vocabulary and grammatical structures. Whereas some activities and exercises are tied to the audio program and provide receptive vocabulary and grammar practice, others develop productive skills.

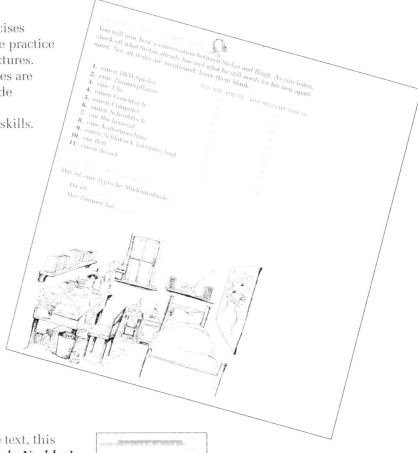

Hier klicken!

At relevant locations throughout the text, this feature directs students to the ***Deutsch: Na klar!*** Online Learning Center (www. mhhe.com/dnk5), which contains additional vocabulary, grammar, and cultural activities.

You'll find more about housing in German-speaking countries in **Deutsch: Na klar!** on the World Wide Web at

Icons

Icons identify pair or small-group activities, video activities, writing activities, information gap, listening comprehension, and activities requiring an extra sheet of paper.

Sprachtipp

Expressions and "grammar for communication" are provided to assist students in carrying out a given activity. These grammar points may be elaborated on in the same or a later chapter.

Das ist **ein** Balkon. Das ist **eine** Küche. Das ist **ein** Badezimmer.

When a masculine noun is used as a direct object, **ein** changes to **einen**; however, feminine **eine** and neuter **ein** do not change:

Mein Haus hat **einen** Balkon, **eine** Küche und **ein** Badezimmer.

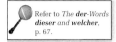

Refer to *The **der**-Words **dieser** and **welcher**,* p. 67.

Closer Look

At relevant locations throughout the **Wörter im Kontext** section, a magnifying glass alerts students where to find supporting grammar explanations that will enable them to complete the communicative activities with substantial attention to structural accuracy.

Kulturtipp

Often enhanced with photos or other visuals, this feature expands on the cultural information presented in the **Themen,** activities and exercises, and readings.

KULTURTIPP

In ihrer Freizeit treiben viele Deutsche gern Sport; besonders beliebt sind Fußball, Rad fahren, Schwimmen und Tennis. Andere bleiben lieber zu Hause und machen Gartenarbeit, pflegen (*take care of*) ihren Wagen, spielen mit ihren Haustieren, sammeln Briefmarken, lesen oder sehen fern. Viele Deutsche haben ein Hobby, das sie in einem Verein ausüben. In vielen Städten gibt es Gesangs- und Heimatvereine sowie (*as well as*) Vereine für Schützen (*marksmen*), Amateurfunker (*ham radio operators*) und Kegler.

Radfahrer auf der Landstraße

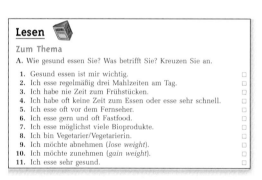

Lesen

Zum Thema

A. Wie gesund essen Sie? Was betrifft Sie? Kreuzen Sie an.

1. Gesund essen ist mir wichtig. ☐
2. Ich esse regelmäßig drei Mahlzeiten am Tag. ☐
3. Ich habe nie Zeit zum Frühstücken. ☐
4. Ich habe oft keine Zeit zum Essen oder esse sehr schnell. ☐
5. Ich esse oft vor dem Fernseher. ☐
6. Ich esse gern und oft Fastfood. ☐
7. Ich esse möglichst viele Bioprodukte. ☐
8. Ich bin Vegetarier/Vegetarierin. ☐
9. Ich möchte abnehmen (*lose weight*). ☐
10. Ich möchte zunehmen (*gain weight*). ☐
11. Ich esse sehr gesund. ☐

Zum Thema

This section contains activities that prepare students to read the text. Students use their background knowledge or brainstorm about the topic to predict what will happen in the reading passage.

Auf den ersten Blick

In this activity, students skim the reading to get the gist or scan it for specific pieces of information in order to achieve a global understanding.

Auf den ersten Blick

A. Skim over the short texts below. Who are the respondents? What are their ages? What is the general topic?

B. Now scan the texts more closely, looking for words of the following types.

- words relating to family
- words related to places where a celebration is held
- compound nouns: locate five compound nouns in the texts, and determine their components and their English equivalents

C. The two most frequently used words in the texts are the verb **feiern** and the noun **Geburtstag.** How do they relate to the expression "**deinen großen Tag**" in the title? What is implied?

Zum Text

Here students read intensively, focusing on content, vocabulary, structures, and finally, implications and interpretation.

Zu guter Letzt

A new task-based culminating project toward the end of each chapter integrates skills and competencies learned in multimodal group or class activities.

Das kann ich nun!

Students check that they've learned the basic material presented by completing a short series of concise exercises at the close of each chapter.

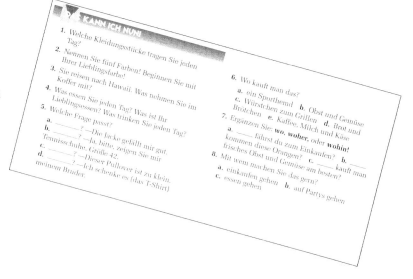

WHAT'S NEW IN THE FIFTH EDITION?

Retaining the aspects that reviewers have praised and that have set *Deutsch: Na klar!* apart from other texts, while at the same time adding new features to keep it lively, contemporary, and up to date, has been our major goal during the revision process. Instructors have given us feedback on the previous edition and we have responded. We have revised many of the dialogues, optimized the grammar explanations for more balance across chapters, added more features to the vocabulary program, included new readings, and improved the video program. Major features appear in the visual *Guided Tour Through Deutsch: Na klar!*

The Fifth Edition has been improved in numerous ways:

- Expanded and improved **Neue Wörter** boxes make it easier for students to learn and use key chapter vocabulary.

- New and updated authentic materials keep the textbook current and interesting for students.

- New and exciting authentic readings in chapters 3, 6, 8, 10, 11, and 13 provide students with high-interest input that reinforces chapter themes and vocabulary.

- Revised and rebalanced grammar presentations streamline and clarify the grammatical points.

- New cross-references in the vocabulary sections provide quick links between communicative activities and supporting grammar explanations.

- A new task-based culminating activity in each chapter, called **Zu guter Letzt,** integrates skills and competencies learned in multimodal group or class projects.

- A new end-of-chapter skill-check called **Das kann ich nun!** uses a series of concise exercises to help students verify that they've learned the basic material in the chapter.

- Video interviews with native speakers have been enhanced with the addition of footage that visually supports the interviewees' statements.

- The **Übergang** chapter has been revised and updated to reflect recent developments in Germany and Europe.

SUPPLEMENTS

The following components of *Deutsch: Na klar!* Fifth Edition are designed to complement your instruction and to enhance your students' learning experience. Please contact your local McGraw-Hill sales representative for details concerning policies, prices, and availability of the supplementary materials, as some restrictions may apply. Available to students and instructors:

- The *Student Text* includes a grammar appendix and German-English/English-German end vocabularies.

- The *Textbook Audio Program* contains material tied to the listening activities in the main text. This audio material is available free of charge at the *Deutsch: Na klar!* Online Learning Center (www.mhhe.com/dnk5).

- The *Workbook,* by Jeanine Briggs, includes additional form-focused vocabulary and grammar exercises as well as abundant guided writing practice.

- The Quia™ online *Workbook* offers all the content of the print *Workbook* plus immediate feedback and a robust instructor gradebook feature.

- The *Laboratory Manual,* by Lida Daves-Schneider and Michael Büsges, contains engaging listening comprehension activities and pronunciation practice. Available on audio CD and free of charge at the *Online Learning Center* (www.mhhe.com/dnk5), the *Laboratory Audio Program* includes an audioscript for instructors.

- The Quia™ online *Laboratory Manual* offers all the content of the print *Laboratory Manual,* integrated audio, plus immediate feedback and a robust instructor gradebook feature.

- New to the Fifth Edition of *Deutsch: Na klar!* is the online *ActivityPak.* The *ActivityPak* replaces the previous editions' *Interactive CD-ROM* and offers students a variety of fun and engaging interactive activities and media. The online *ActivityPak* includes Flash™-based activities that provide interactive review and practice of vocabulary and grammar, as well as the complete video program. This unified language learning experience is practical and convenient and eliminates the need for multiple components. The online *ActivityPak* is contained within and accessed via the *Deutsch: Na klar! Online Learning Center.* Please note that the *ActivityPak* content is a saleable supplement and is not provided free of charge.

- The *Deutsch: Na klar! Online Learning Center* (www.mhhe.com/dnk5) provides a variety of vocabulary and grammar self-quizzes as well as cultural activities and the complete *Laboratory Audio Program.* These quizzes, activities and the *Laboratory Audio Program* are available to students free of charge.

Available to instructors only:

- The *Annotated Instructor's Edition* of the main text includes marginal notes, answers, and an audioscript to the in-text listening comprehension activities.

- The combined *Instructor's Manual and Testing Program* provides theoretical background, practical guidance, and ideas for using **Deutsch: Na Klar!** It also contains tests and exams written by Jennifer Redmann (Kalamazoo College) and Pennylyn Dykstra-Pruim (Calvin College).

- The *Audioscript* found on the Online Learning Center, contains the material found on the *Laboratory Audio Program.*

- The *Video to accompany* **Deutsch: Na Klar!** contains a wide variety of interviews with native speakers of German, newly enhanced with images that support the content and make it more accessible to students.

ACKNOWLEDGMENTS

The publisher would like to thank these instructors who participated in surveys and reviews that were indispensable in the development of **Deutsch: Na klar!** Fifth Edition. The appearance of their names does not necessarily constitute their endorsement of the text or its methodology.

Scott Baker, University of Missouri, Kansas City
John Blair, University of West Georgia
Madelyn Burchill, Concordia College, Moorhead
Troy Byler, Indiana University, Bloomington
Muriel Cormican, University of West Georgia
Katy Fraser, Indiana University, Bloomington
Steve Grollman, Concordia College, Moorhead
Derek Hillard, Kansas State University
Ruth Kath, Luther College
Jurgen Koppensteiner, University of Northern Iowa
Douglas Lightfoot, University of Alabama, Tuscaloosa
Denise Meuser, Northwestern University
Susanne Rott, University of Illinois, Chicago
Frangina Spandau, Santa Barbara City College
Rudi Strahl, College of Dupage
Cynthia Trocchio, Kent State University, Kent
Meike Wernick-Heinrichs, Capilano College

We also wish to thank the instructors who participated in our Introductory German survey. Their input on trends in German language learning today significantly enriched this edition, and we are very grateful.

Zsuzsanna I. Abrams, University of Texas, Austin
Thomas Hendrik Aulbach, University of Florida
Ingetraut R. Baird, Anderson University
Karen Bell, Delta State University
Peter Böhm, Canisius College
Nancy Marie Borosch, Butler University
Kirsten M. Christensen, Pacific Lutheran University
Siegfried Christoph, University of Wisconsin, Parkside
T. Craig Christy, University of North Alabama
Irene B. Compton, Xavier University
Matthew Michael Conner, Texas State University
Michael Davidson-Schmich, University of Miami
Sharon Marie DiFino, University of Florida, Gainesville
Peter Ecke, University of Arizona
Anke Finger, University of Connecticut
Lidia Frazier, American River College
Helen Frink, Keene State College
Gordon Gamlin, Loyola Marymount University
Valentina Glajar, Texas State University, San Marcos
Lawrence F. Glatz, Metropolitan State College of Denver
Amelia J. Harris, The University of Virginia's College at Wise
Ursula Horstmann-Nash, Southern Oregon University
Constance E. Hubbard, Black Hills State University
Dorothea Kaufmann, Oberlin College
Jennifer Kelley-Thierman, University of Cincinnati
Martin Klebes, University of New Mexico
Richard Langston, The University of North Carolina at Chapel Hill
Edward T. Larkin
Caralinda Lee, St. Mary's College of California
Randall Lund, Brigham Young University
Alan D. Lytle, University of Arkansas at Little Rock
Marion Picker, Dickinson College
Hartmut Rastalsky, University of Michigan
Michael H. Rice, Mississippi State University
Claudette Roper, Mineral Area College
Eva-Marie Russo, Washington State University in St. Louis
Ebba W. Schoonover, University of Louisiana, Lafayette
David I. Smith, Calvin College
Elfriede Smith, Drew University
Sabine H. Smith, Kennesaw State University
Lorna Sopcak, Ripon College
Christian P. Stehr, Oregon State University
William E. Stuermann, North Greenville University
John Sundquist, Purdue University
John R. te Velde, Oklahoma State University
Finley M. Taylor, University of Central Florida
Walter G. Tschacher, Chapman University
Mary Upman, McDaniel College
Walter von Reinhart, University of Rhode Island
Jerry T. Wood, Glendale Community College
Amy D. Young, Fort Hays State University
Paul A. Youngman, The University of North Carolina, Charlotte

We would also like to thank the many people who worked on this book behind the scenes: Arden

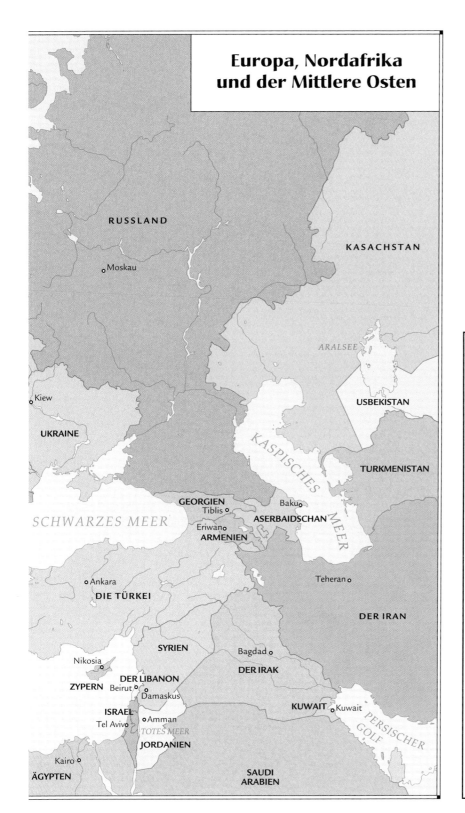

Europa, Nordafrika und der Mittlere Osten

RUSSLAND

KASACHSTAN

o Moskau

ARALSEE

o Kiew

USBEKISTAN

UKRAINE

KASPISCHES MEER

TURKMENISTAN

GEORGIEN
Tiblis o   Baku o
                  ASERBAIDSCHAN
SCHWARZES MEER   Eriwan o
                  ARMENIEN

o Ankara   Teheran o
DIE TÜRKEI

DER IRAN

SYRIEN   Bagdad o
Nikosia
o   DER IRAK
ZYPERN Beirut o
DER LIBANON
        Damaskus
ISRAEL   KUWAIT o Kuwait
Tel Aviv o o Amman   PERSISCHER
TOTES MEER   GOLF
JORDANIEN

Kairo o
ÄGYPTEN   SAUDI
                  ARABIEN

EU-LÄNDER (2006)	EINWOHNER (2006)
	Millionen
Belgien	10,4
Dänemark	5,4
Deutschland	82,5
Estland	1,4
Finnland	5,2
Frankreich	59,9
Griechenland	11,0
Großbritannien	59,7
Irland	4,0
Italien	57,9
Lettland	2,3
Litauen	3,4
Luxemburg	0,5
Malta	0,4
die Niederlande	16,3
Österreich	8,1
Polen	38,2
Portugal	10,5
Schweden	9,0
die Slowakei	5,4
Slowenien	2,0
Spanien	42,3
Tschechien	10,2
Ungarn	10,1
Zypern	0,7
GESAMT	456,8

Deutschland und Luxemburg
Einwohner
Deutschland (2006): 82,5 Mio
Luxemburg (2006): 474 000

Österreich

Einwohner (2006): 8,1 Mio

0 25 50 Meilen
0 25 50 Kilometer

DEUTSCHLAND

TSCHECHIEN

• Gmünd

• Horn

Krems

Donau

WIEN

• Linz

Melk • Sankt Pölten

Wien ★

OBERÖSTERREICH

• Amstetten

Baden •

Neusiedler See

Gmunden •

NIEDERÖSTERREICH

Eisenstadt ★

★ Salzburg

Wiener Neustadt •

Bad Ischl •

Mariazell •

Hallstatt •

Liezen •

Enns

BURGENLAND

Bodensee

★ Bregenz

Kufstein •

Sankt Johann in Tirol

Bischofshofen •

STEIERMARK

Bruck an der Mur •

Oberwart •

VORARLBERG

Reutte •

• Wörgl

Zell am See •

Radstadt •

ARLBERG

Innsbruck ★

Kitzbühel •

Sankt Georgen •

Feldkirch •

Arlberg

• Landeck

Bruck •

SALZBURG

Mauterndorf •

Graz ★

Güssing •

TIROL

Mur

DIE
SCHWEIZ

SÜDTIROL

Osttirol
(zu Tirol)

Lienz •

Spittal an der Drau •

Feldkirchen •

UNGARN

• Meran

Drau

KÄRNTEN

Klagenfurt •

• Bozen

Villach •

Wörther See

ITALIEN

SLOWENIEN

0 25 50 Meilen
0 25 50 Kilometer

Rhein

SCHAFFHAUSEN

Schaffhausen •

DEUTSCHLAND

BASEL
(STADT)

THURGAU

• Kreuzlingen

Basel •

Liestal •

Rhein

Baden •

Winterthur •

Frauenfeld •

Thur

Bodensee

FRANKREICH

BASEL
(LAND)

AARGAU

ZÜRICH

St. Gallen •

St. Margrethen •

Delemont ★

Aarau •

Zürich •

Herisau •

AUSSER-RHODEN

JURA

SOLOTHURN

APPENZELL

Appenzell •

Reuss

INNER-RHODEN

ÖSTERREICH

Solothurn ★

Zürichsee

Vaduz ★

Biel •

LUZERN

Zug •

Einsiedeln •

SANKT GALLEN

LIECHTENSTEIN

Aare

ZUG

Neuchâtel •

BERN

Vierwaldstätter See

SCHWYZ

Glarus •

NEUENBURG

Luzern ★

Schwyz •

GLARUS

Chur •

BERNER

Sarnen •

Stans •

Braunwald •

Klosters •

Neuenburger See

OBERLAND

NIDW.

Altdorf •

Davos •

Bern •

UNTERWALDEN

OBW.

Engelberg •

★ Fribourg

Brienz •

URI

Rhein

Thun •

Andermatt •

Disentis •

GRAUBÜNDEN

Thuner See

Brienzer See

FREIBURG

Interlaken •

WAADT

Jungfrau ▲

Grindelwald •

St. Moritz •

Lausanne •

Jungfraujoch •

Inn

Montreux •

Gstaad •

Brig •

Tessin

Sion •

TESSIN

Bellinzona •

GENF

Genfer See

Rhône

Locarno •

Genf ★

WALLIS

Rotten

Matterhorn ▲

Zermatt •

Lugano •

ITALIEN

Langensee

Die Schweiz
und Liechtenstein

Einwohner

Schweiz (2006): 7,5 Mio
Liechtenstein (2006): 34 000

NIDW = NIDWALDEN
OBW = OBWALDEN

Einführung

Einführung. Note: The **Einführung** aims to familiarize students with the range of activities in the book. Students will use German in simple communicative situations that focus mainly on sharing basic personal information. They will also see authentic texts throughout the book. In some cases the texts and pictures illustrate a particular point; in others they provide the reading and listening material.

Photo. Description: These students are at the Johann Wolfgang Goethe Universität in Frankfurt am Main. With around 35,000 students (over 10% from abroad) it offers some 140 degree programs. Philosophers Max Horkheimer and Theodor Adorno were among the faculty there. **Point out:** It is customary even among young people to shake hands when greeting each other.

—Grüß dich! Geht's gut?
—Na klar!

In diesem Kapitel

- **Themen:** Greetings and farewells, getting acquainted, spelling in German, numbers, useful classroom expressions
- **Kultur:** Forms of address, inquiring about someone's well-being, postal codes and country abbreviations, German-speaking countries and their neighbors

Videoclips
Wer ist das?

Hallo! Guten Tag! Herzlich willkommen!*

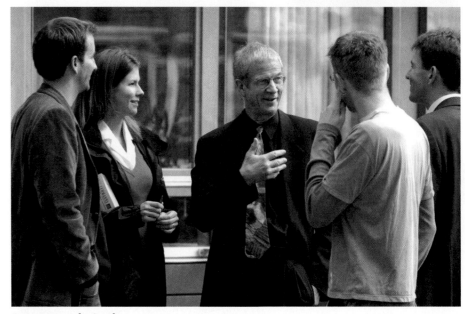

Internationale Studenten

PROFESSOR: **Guten Tag! Herzlich willkommen! Mein Name ist** Pohle, Norbert Pohle. Und **wie ist Ihr Name?**

SABINE: Sabine Zimmermann.

PROFESSOR: Und Sie? **Wie heißen Sie?**

ANTONIO: **Ich heiße** Antonio Coletti.

ARI: Und **ich bin** Ari Pappas.

Auf einer Party

PETER: **Grüß dich.** Ich heiße Peter Sedlmeier.

KATARINA: Mein Name ist Katarina Steinmetz.

PETER: **Woher kommst du?**

KATARINA: **Aus** Dresden. Und du?

PETER: Aus Rosenheim.

---

*New, active vocabulary is shown in bold print.

HERR GROTE: **Frau** Kühne, **das ist Herr** Michels aus Berlin. Frau Kühne kommt aus Potsdam.

HERR MICHELS: **Freut mich.**

FRAU KÜHNE: **Gleichfalls.**

Ein Treffen (meeting) *in Berlin*

Dialog 3. Suggestion: In combination with the **Kulturtipp,** this dialogue can be used to illustrate the uses of *Sie* versus *du* in German-speaking countries. Model the dialogue for students or play the recording, then have students take roles to practice. After practicing the dialogue, ask students what is different from the previous dialogue about how these people address each other. Many students will likely be able to tell what *Herr* and *Frau* mean from context, even if they have not heard these terms before. You may also wish to mention that the term *Fräulein* ("Miss") to address unmarried women has generally become outdated. *Frau* is typically used regardless of a woman's marital status.

KULTURTIPP

German speakers address one another as **Sie** or **du.** The formal **Sie** (*You*) is used with strangers and even co-workers and acquaintances. Family members and friends address one another with **du** (*you*), as do children and, generally, students. Close personal friends address one another with **du** and first names. Most adults address one another as **Herr** or **Frau** and use **Sie** although some might use first names with **Sie. Frau** is the standard title for all women, regardless of marital status.

Kulturtipp. Note: This recurring feature introduces cultural information that relates to the topics of activities or readings in the chapter. In the early chapters they are in English to ensure that the students understand them. In later chapters they are in German.

Aktivität 1 Wie ist der Name?

Introduce yourself to several people in your class.

s1: Mein Name ist _____.

s2: Ich heiße _____.

s1: Woher kommst du?

s2: Aus _____. Und du?

s1: Aus _____.

Aktivität 1. Suggestion: Before beginning the activity, write the necessary phrases on the board so that students can work without their books. Students should stand up and walk around the room and talk to as many different people as possible within the time limit you have set. Make sure that you monitor the students' interactions.

Aktivität 2 Darf ich vorstellen?°

Introduce a classmate to another.

BEISPIEL: GINA: Paul, das ist Chris.
PAUL: Tag, Chris.
CHRIS: Hallo, Paul.

May I introduce?

Aktivität 2. Point Out: University students in German-speaking countries generally use *du* and first names with one another.
Suggestion: Model the interaction by introducing a couple of students to each other. To make the activity as authentic as possible, remind students to introduce people to others whom they might not yet have met.

Wie schreibt man das?°

When you introduce yourself or give information about yourself, you may have to spell out words for clarification. In contrast to English, German follows fairly predictable spelling and pronunciation rules. You will gradually learn these rules throughout the course.

How is that spelled?

Wie schreibt man das? Point Out: Native speakers of German are learning new spelling rules, too, since a spelling reform was instituted in 1998. Model these sounds carefully.

The German alphabet has the same twenty-six letters as the English alphabet, plus four other letters of its own. The four special German letters are written as follows. Note that the letter **ß** has no capital; **SS** is used instead.

Ä	ä	a-Umlaut: **Bär, Käse**
Ö	ö	o-Umlaut: **böse, hören**
Ü	ü	u-Umlaut: **müde, Süden**
	ß	sz („ess tsett"): **süß, Straße**

A pair of dots above a German vowel is called an "umlaut." Although this book refers to these vowels as **a-, o-,** or **u-umlaut,** they are actually distinct letters. When spelling words, speakers of German refer to them as they are pronounced. Listen carefully to these vowels on the laboratory audio recordings and in your instructor's pronunciation of them.

The alphabet house (**Buchstabenhaus**) below shows how German schoolchildren learn to write the letters of the alphabet. In addition to displaying individual letters, the **Buchstabenhaus** also practices such frequently used combinations as **ch, sch,** and the diphthongs.

Buchstabenhaus. Suggestion: Have students discover which letters look different from the letter styles they learned to write in school.

Have students look at the children's handwriting in the letters to President Hoover in the **Übergang** chapter at the end of the book.

Aktivität 3   Das ABC

Repeat the letters of the German alphabet after your instructor.

Aktivität 4   B-E-R-L-I-N: So schreibt man das!°

Listen as your instructor spells some common German words. Write the words as you hear them.

Aktivität 5   Wie bitte?°

Introduce yourself to another student and spell your name.

BEISPIEL: s1: Mein Name ist _____.
             s2: Wie bitte?
             s1: (*repeat your name; then spell it in German*)
             s2: Ah, so!

Aktivität 6   Buchstabieren Sie!°

Think of three German words, names, products, or company names you already know or choose three items from the list below. Then close your book. Without saying the word, spell it in German (**auf Deutsch**) for a class-mate, who writes it down and says the word back to you.

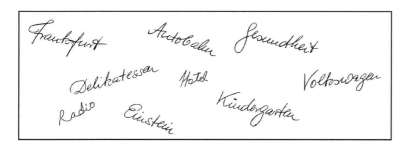

Hallo! – Mach's gut!°

Take care!

How do people in German-speaking countries greet one another and say good-bye? Look at the following expressions and illustrations (pp. 5–6), and see whether you can guess which ones are greetings and which ones are good-byes.

German speakers use various formal and informal hellos and good-byes, depending on the situation and the person with whom they are speaking.

Saying hello:

FORMAL	CASUAL	USE
guten Morgen	Morgen	*until about 10:00 A.M.*
guten Tag	Tag	*generally between 10:00 A.M. and early evening*
guten Abend	'n Abend*	*from about 5:00 P.M. on*
grüß Gott†	grüß Gott	*southern German and Austrian for* **guten Tag**
grüß dich hallo hi		*greetings among young people any time*

Saying good-bye and good night:

FORMAL	CASUAL	USE
auf Wiedersehen	Wiederseh'n	*any time*
	mach's gut	*among young people, friends, and family*
	tschüss	*among young people, family*
gute Nacht	Nacht	*only when someone is going to bed at night*

---

*The **'n** before **Abend** is short for **guten**.
†*Lit.* Greetings in the name of God.

Aktivität 7 Was sagt man?°

What do you say?

What would people say in the following circumstances?

1. __e, g__ your German instructor entering the classroom
2. __c, d, f__ two students saying good-bye
3. __h__ a person from Vienna greeting an acquaintance
4. __b, h, i__ two students meeting at a café
5. __a__ a mother as she turns off the lights in her child's room at night
6. __f__ a student leaving a professor's office
7. __g__ family members greeting one another in the morning

a. Gute Nacht!
b. Grüß dich!
c. Tschüss!
d. Mach's gut!
e. Guten Tag!
f. (Auf) Wiedersehen!
g. (Guten) Morgen!
h. Grüß Gott!
i. Hallo!/Hi!
j. Guten Abend!

Aktivität 7. Suggestion: Have students look over the possible responses before answering the questions. Remind them to think about the intonation and tone of voice that they would use in each situation.

Aktivität 8 Minidialoge

Aktivität 8. Some blanks have more than one correct answer. The focus should be to choose an expression that not only makes sense but is also appropriate for the level of formality or casualness reflected by the way the speakers address one another. Students may need guidance to recognize these clues.

Complete the following short dialogues with an appropriate greeting or leave-taking.

1. A: _____ _____! Ich heiße Stefan. Wie heißt du?
   B: Ich heiße Fusün.
2. C: _____ _____. Mein Name ist Eva Schrittmeier.
   D: Und mein Name ist Georg Stillweg. Woher kommen Sie?
   C: Aus Stuttgart.
3. E: Wiederseh'n und gute _____, Markus.
   F: _____, Johannes, mach's _____!

Na, wie geht's?°

So, how's it going?

German has several ways of asking *How are you?*

Wie geht es dir?
Wie geht's? } *a family member or friend*

Wie geht es Ihnen, Herr Lindemann? *an acquaintance*

You can respond in a number of different ways.

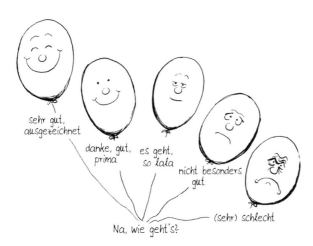

sehr gut, ausgezeichnet

danke, gut, prima

es geht, so lala

nicht besonders gut

(sehr) schlecht

Na, wie geht's?

German speakers will ask someone **Na, wie geht's?**, **Geht's gut?**, or **Wie geht es Ihnen?** only if they already know the person well. When you ask a native German speaker, be prepared for a detailed answer, particularly if the person is not feeling well. **Hi** or **Hallo, wie geht's?** is sometimes used as a general greeting among young people even if they don't know each other.

[1]Ich ... *I don't know! I feel so beat this morning!*

Aktivität 9   Wie geht's?

Listen as three pairs of people greet each other and conduct brief conversations. Indicate whether the statements below match what you hear.

	JA	NEIN
DIALOG 1		
a. The conversation takes place in the morning.	☐	☒
b. The greetings are informal.	☒	☐
c. The man and the woman are both doing fine.	☐	☒
DIALOG 2		
a. The two speakers must be from southern Germany or Austria.	☒	☐
b. The speakers are close friends.	☐	☒
c. Both of them are doing fine.	☒	☐
DIALOG 3		
a. The two speakers know each other.	☒	☐
b. The man is feeling great.	☒	☐
c. They use a formal expression to say good-bye.	☐	☒

Aktivität 10   Und wie geht es dir?

Start a conversation chain by asking one classmate how he/she is.

BEISPIEL: s1: Na, Peter, wie geht's?
    s2: So lala. Wie geht es dir, Kathy?
    s3: Ausgezeichnet! Und wie geht's dir, ...?

This is how you count in German.

So zählt man auf Deutsch.°

Eins, zwei, drei...

0 null	9 neun	18 achtzehn	90 neunzig
1 eins	10 zehn	19 neunzehn	100 (ein)hundert
2 zwei	11 elf	20 zwanzig	200 zweihundert
3 drei	12 zwölf	30 dreißig	300 dreihundert
4 vier	13 dreizehn	40 vierzig	1 000 (ein)tausend
5 fünf	14 vierzehn	50 fünfzig	2 000 zweitausend
6 sechs	15 fünfzehn	60 sechzig	3 000 dreitausend
7 sieben	16 sechzehn	70 siebzig	
8 acht	17 siebzehn	80 achtzig	

The numbers 21 through 99 are formed by combining the numbers 1–9 with 20–90.

21 einundzwanzig	24 vierundzwanzig	27 siebenundzwanzig
22 zweiundzwanzig	25 fünfundzwanzig	28 achtundzwanzig
23 dreiundzwanzig	26 sechsundzwanzig	29 neunundzwanzig

The numbers *one* and *seven* are written as follows:

$$1 \qquad 7$$

German uses a period or a space where English uses a comma.

$$1.000 \qquad 7\ 000$$

In German-speaking countries, telephone numbers generally have a varying number of digits and may be spoken as follows:

24 36 71

↓

zwei vier, drei sechs, sieben eins

[*or*]

vierundzwanzig, sechsunddreißig, einundsiebzig

Zwei,
Fünf,
Neun,
Eins,
Sechs,
Eins:

Telefonische
Anzeigenannahme[1]

BERLINER MORGENPOST
Berlins größte Abonnementzeitung

[1]Telefonische ... *Submit your ad by phone*

Hier klicken!

You'll find more about telephone numbers in **Deutsch: Na klar!** on the World Wide Web at www.mhhe.com/dnk5.

Follow-up: Pass out flash cards with numbers on them. Say numbers at random; the student with the number holds up the card.

Point Out: You might want to mention to students the two different German terms for "number." *Zahl* refers to numbers used by themselves, whereas *Nummer* refers to numbers in context. For example: *Sieben und elf sind Zahlen,* but *Heikes Nummer ist 0651-0001.*

Follow-up: Play bingo. Students draw up own cards of nine numbers between 0 and 20, or 0 and 30, and cross off numbers as you call them. The first person to cross out all numbers calls "bingo" and must then call out the crossed-out numbers so you can verify them. Have a small prize for the first three or four winners.

Point Out: In spoken German, especially on the phone, people often say *zwo* for *zwei* to avoid confusion with *drei.*

So zählt man auf Deutsch. **9**

Aktivität 11 Wichtige Telefonnummern°

You need the phone numbers for the following items and services. Write the phone numbers you hear in the appropriate space.

Telefon-Ansagen	☎		Theater und Konzerte	1 15 17
Polizei	1 10		Feuerwehr/ Rettungsleitstelle	1 12
Kinoprogramme	1 15 11		Wetter	38 53
Küchenrezepte	11 67		Zahlenlotto	11 62
Sport	11 63		Zeit	19 94

ANALYSE

Look over the examples of addresses (**Adressen**) from German-speaking countries. How do they differ from the way addresses are written in your country?

- Locate the name of the street (**Straße**) and the town (**Stadt**).

- Where is the house number (**Hausnummer**) placed? Where is the postal code (**Postleitzahl**) placed?

- Can you guess what the **A** before **9020 Klagenfurt** and the **CH** before **8050 Zürich-Oerlikon** represent?

- Now say each address out loud.

UNIVERSITÄT FÜR BILDUNGSWISSENSCHAFTEN KLAGENFURT

Universitätsstraße 65–67
A-9020 Klagenfurt

Point Out: *CH* stands for Confoederatio Helvetica (= Switzerland) and *A* for Austria.

VERKEHRSMUSEUM DRESDEN
Augustusstraße 1, 01067 Dresden · Tel. 0351/ 86440 · Fax 0351/ 864 41 10
http://www.verkehrsmuseum.sachsen.de
e-mail: verkehrsmuseum@verkehrsmuseum.sachsen.de

Gebecke
Buchhandlung & Antiquariat
Bücher · Musikalien · Graphik
seit 1881
Pölkenstraße 3 · 06484 Quedlinburg 2698 www.antiquariat-gebecke.de

As in the United States, postal codes in Germany consist of five digits. Postal codes in Austria, Liechtenstein, and Switzerland have four digits.

Ferienträume ?
Wir erfüllen sie !

TRAVELLER REISEN
Filiale Oerlikon
CH-8050 Zürich-Oerlikon, Ohmstrasse 14

Telefon 01- 312 10 14
Telex 823 221
Telegramm: Travellerag Zürich

Aktivität 12　Die Adresse und Telefonnummer, bitte!

You will hear three brief requests for addresses and telephone numbers. As you listen, mark the correct street numbers and jot down the postal codes and telephone numbers.

1. Professor Hausers Adresse ist …

   Gartenstraße　9　12　<u>19</u>

   <u>82067</u>　Ebenhausen/Isartal

   Die Telefonnummer ist <u>41 34 76</u>.

2. Die Adresse von Margas Fitnessstudio ist …

   Bautzner Straße　5　<u>15</u>　14

   <u>01093</u>　Dresden

   Die Telefonnummer ist <u>20 86 73</u>.

3. Die Adresse von Autohaus Becker ist …

   Landstuhler Straße　<u>54</u>　44　45

   <u>66482</u>　Zweibrücken-Ixheim

   Die Telefonnummer ist <u>1 88 42</u>.

Hier klicken!

You'll find more about the postal and country codes in **Deutsch: Na klar!** on the World Wide Web at www.mhhe.com/dnk5.

KULTURTIPP

When mail is sent between countries in Europe, international abbreviations are used for the country names. Refer to the map and provide the missing country names and country codes.

Belgien	B	**Rumänien**	(RO)	
Dänemark	(DK)	**Russland**	(RUS)	
Deutschland	D	die Schweiz	CH	
Frankreich	(F)	**die Slowakei**	(SK)	
Griechenland	(GR)	Spanien	E	
Großbritannien	(GB)	**Tschechien**	(CZ)	
Irland	(IRL)	**Ungarn**	(H)	
Italien	(I)			
Liechtenstein	FL			
Luxemburg	L			
die Niederlande	(NL)			
Österreich	A			
Polen	(PL)			
Portugal	(P)			

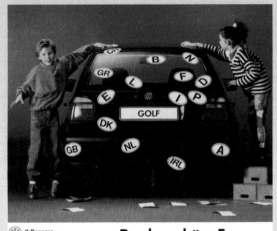

Danke schön, Europa.

Volkswagen – da weiß man, was man hat.

Suggestion: As an introduction to the **Kulturtipp**, you may wish to ask students if they have seen any of the *Nationalitätszeichen* depicted in the Volkswagen ad on vehicles in North America and if they know what they mean. The oval-shaped emblems are no longer mandatory inside the European Union. They have been replaced with an *EU-Kennzeichen* on the license plate of newly registered cars, with the country code for member nations to the immediate left of the registration number. However, the older ones are still required for travel in non-EU nations (except Switzerland, Liechtenstein, Norway, and Croatia, which officially recognize the *EU-Kennzeichen*).

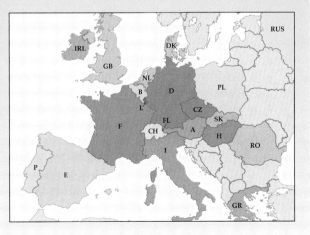

Aktivität 13. This is the first of many information-gap activities designed to create a genuine exchange of information in a controlled context. Each student has only half the information in the chart and must ask his/her partner questions to fill in the gaps. Since this is the first information-gap activity, be sure students understand how the activity works by demonstrating the model with one student and then having the class observe two paired students performing an exchange.

Note: Point out to students that the international country abbreviations are treated as part of the postal code when mail is sent between countries.

Note: Point out to students that the German postal service (*Deutsche Post*) mandates that mail going outside Germany should have the country name written in all capital letters immediately below the *Postleitzahl* and city name, while *Inlandpost* simply has the *Postleitzahl* and city name as the last line (but not the name of the *Bundesland*).

Aktivität 14. Suggestion: Review with students the information sought.

Note: Some students may be reluctant to share personal information with their classmates. Be sure to let them know that they may make up fictional personal information about themselves.

Realia: Explain that *Quelle* is a well-known mail-order company in Germany.

1. Ich ... *I don't know what a* (**ne = eine**)

Aktivität 13   Hin und her°: Wie ist die Postleitzahl?

This is the first of many activities in which you will exchange information with a partner. Here, one of you uses the chart below; the other turns to the corresponding chart in Appendix A. Take turns asking each other for the postal codes missing from your charts.

BEISPIEL: s1: Wie ist die Postleitzahl von Bitburg?
s2: D-54634. Wie ist die Postleitzahl von Salzburg?
s1: A-5020.

D-54634	Bitburg
A-5020	Salzburg
CH-3800	Interlaken
D-94315	Straubing
D-06217	Merseburg
D-21614	Buxtehude
FL-9490	Vaduz
D-99817	Eisenach

Aktivität 14   Ein Interview

Schritt 1: Jot down answers to the following questions.

Wie heißt du?

Woher kommst du?

Wie ist deine Telefonnummer?

Wie ist die Postleitzahl?

Wie ist deine Adresse?

Schritt 2: Use the questions in **Schritt 1** to interview a partner and fill in the information in the grid below.

Name	
Stadt	
Straße und Hausnummer	
Postleitzahl	
Telefonnummer	

Schritt 3: Now tell the class about the person you interviewed.

BEISPIEL: Das ist Kerstin aus Chicago. Die Adresse ist 678 Maple Street. Die Postleitzahl ist 54880. Die Telefonnummer ist 555-4797.

Nützliche Ausdrücke im Sprachkurs°

Useful expressions for the language course

IHR DEUTSCH**LEHRER** / IHRE DEUTSCH**LEHRERIN** SAGT:

Bitte ...	*Please . . .*
Hören Sie zu.	*Listen.*
Schreiben Sie.	*Write.*
Machen Sie die Bücher auf Seite _____ auf.	*Open your books to page _____.*
Lesen Sie.	*Read.*
Machen Sie die Bücher zu.	*Close your books.*
Setzen Sie sich.	*Be seated.*
Wiederholen Sie.	*Repeat.*
Haben Sie Fragen?	*Do you have any questions?*
[Ist] Alles klar?	*Is everything clear?*
Noch einmal, bitte!	*Once more, please; could you say that again, please?*

SIE SAGEN:

Langsamer, bitte!	*Slower, please.*
Wie bitte?	*Pardon? What did you say?*
Wie schreibt man _____?	*How do you write _____?*
Ich habe eine Frage.	*I have a question.*
Wie sagt man _____ auf Deutsch?	*How do you say _____ in German?*
Was bedeutet _____?	*What does _____ mean?*
Das weiß ich nicht.	*I don't know.*
Ich verstehe das nicht.	*I don't understand.*
Alles klar.	*I get it.*
Ja.	*Yes.*
Nein.	*No.*
Danke [schön].	*Thank you.*

Nützliche Ausdrücke im Sprachkurs. Suggestion: Go over the teacher's expressions using mime and demonstration where possible. Have students respond to your commands, so that it is clear they understand them. Make sure that students can say the students' expressions (printed in boldface) properly.

Aktivität 15 Wie sagt man das auf Deutsch?

Match the English expressions to their German equivalents.

1. __j__ I have a question.
2. __f__ I don't understand.
3. __a__ Is everything clear?
4. __e__ Be seated.
5. __h__ How do you write _____?
6. __b__ Open your books.
7. __c__ What does _____ mean?
8. __i__ Pardon, what did you say?
9. __d__ Open your books to page _____.
10. __g__ Once more, please. / Could you say that again, please?

a. Alles klar?

b. Machen Sie die Bücher auf.

c. Was bedeutet _____?

d. Machen Sie die Bücher auf Seite _____ auf.

e. Setzen Sie sich.

f. Ich verstehe das nicht.

g. Noch einmal, bitte.

h. Wie schreibt man _____?

i. Wie bitte?

j. Ich habe eine Frage.

Sie können schon etwas Deutsch!°

Even if you have never studied German before, you will soon find that you know more German than you think. For example, look at the ad below taken from a German phone book's yellow pages (**gelbe Seiten**).

- What is this ad for?
- Which words are *identical* in English?
- Which words in the ad look *similar* to words you use in English?

Zum Dorfkrug

Inh.: Hans Bode
Hannoversche Straße 29
31275 Lehrte
Ruf (0 51 32) 71 31
Empf. ADAC-Hotel-Restaurant

Restaurant
Hotel - Motel

Sauna-Centrum
Hallenbad
Konferenzraum
Biergarten m. offenem
Kamin und Spring-
brunnen im Freien

Words such as **Motel, Hotel, Restaurant,** and **Sauna** are borrowed from other languages: **Motel** from American English, **Restaurant** and **Hotel** from French, and **Sauna** from Finnish. These words are used internationally.

Some words in the ad look similar to English words, for example **Biergarten.** You may already have seen the word **Biergarten** in English-language text. This word has been borrowed from German, along with some other German words commonly used in English, such as **Kindergarten** and **Delikatessen.** You recognize the words *beer* and *garden* in **Biergarten. Bier** and *beer,* **Garten** and *garden* have the same meaning in both languages. These words are cognates. Cognates are descended from the same word or form. Since English and German are both Germanic languages, they share many cognates. This common linguistic ancestry will help you a great deal in understanding German. Recognizing cognates is an important skill stressed throughout this textbook.

Cognates such as **Bier** and **Garten** are easy to recognize. Understanding other words takes more imaginative guessing: for instance, what do you think **Hallenbad** means? Other words in the ad probably look completely unfamiliar. The word **Ruf,** for instance, is not easily guessed. The meaning can be guessed from the context, however, and you already know a synonym for this word. What is it?

Now summarize what you have found out about "Zum Dorfkrug." Add any additional information you were able to extract from the ad by guessing.

Aktivität 16 Sie verstehen schon etwas Deutsch!°

You have learned that you can use visual and verbal cues to understand a considerable amount of written German. Now you will hear some short radio announcements and news headlines. Listen for cognates and other verbal clues as you try to understand the gist of what is being said. As you hear each item, write its number in front of the topic(s) to which it corresponds. Not all the following topics will be mentioned.

_1_ Automobil	_____ Musik	_3_ Sport
_____ Bank	_____ Politik	_____ Tanz
_____ Film	_4_ Restaurant	_2_ Theater
_5_ Kinder		

Aktivität 17   Informationen finden

An important first step in reading is identifying the type of text you have in front of you. Look for verbal as well as visual clues. Look at the texts below. Write the letter of each text in front of the appropriate category in the list below (some categories will remain empty).

1. _e_ ticket for an event
2. _____ short news item about crime
3. _b_ concert announcement
4. _d_ newspaper headline
5. _____ recipe
6. _c_ section from a TV guide
7. _a_ ad for a restaurant

a.

b.

c.

d.

e.

Wo spricht man Deutsch? (*Where is German spoken?*)   Naturally, German is spoken in Germany, but it is also spoken in many other countries. Which of the following countries have relatively large German-speaking populations?

☒ Argentinien	☐ Korea	☒ Rumänien
☒ Belgien	☒ Liechtenstein	☒ Russland
☒ Bosnien	☒ Luxemburg	☒ die Schweiz
☒ Brasilien	☐ die Mongolei	☒ die Slowakei
☒ Italien	☒ Österreich	☒ Tschechien
☐ Jamaika	☒ Polen	☒ Ungarn

German is the official language of Germany (**Deutschland**), Austria (**Österreich**), and Liechtenstein. It is one of four official languages of Switzerland (**die Schweiz**) and one of three official languages of Luxembourg and Belgium. German is also spoken in regions of France, Denmark, Italy, the Czech Republic, Poland, Rumania, Bosnia and Herzegovina, Hungary, Latvia, Lithuania, Estonia, Russia, Slovakia, and Ukraine. Altogether, between 120 and 140 million Europeans speak German as their first language—more than the number of people in Europe who speak English as their first language.

German is also spoken by many people as a first language in other countries such as Brazil, Argentina, Canada, and the United States (Pennsylvania Dutch). In Namibia, German is spoken by a sizable minority. It is estimated that outside Europe, an additional 20 million people speak German as their first language. Another 50 million speak German as a foreign language.

According to U.S. census figures from 2000, over 40 million U.S. citizens claim German descent. In Canada, the figure is approximately 2.7 million.

At present, approximately 20 million people worldwide are learning German in formal courses. Most of these people live in eastern Europe.

Note: For more detail on Europe and the principal German-speaking countries, refer students to the maps in the front of this book.

Point out: In earlier times, the word "Dutch" was sometimes used to refer not only to people from the Netherlands but also to German speakers from many regions of present-day Germany as well.

Note: Namibia is a former German colony.

Note: To counter the stereotype that all German speakers living there are descendants of escaped Nazi war criminals, you may wish to mention that German immigration to Central and South America began well before World War II.

Videoclips
Video

A. Michael, our moderator for the interviews throughout ***Deutsch: Na klar!***, asks people their names in two different ways. Watch the video segment and complete the following questions.

1. Using the informal form, he asks Dennis: "_____ _____ du?"
2. Using the formal form, he asks Herr Borowsky: "_____ _____ Sie?"

B. Several people respond to the preceding questions in one of two ways. Watch and complete the following.

1. „Hallo! _____ Name _____ Dennis".
2. „Ich _____ Beatrice. Guten Morgen!"
3. „_____ _____ ist Kurt Borowsky".

C. Now concentrate on the segments with Peter, Jasmin, and Frau Simon. Complete their profiles.

Suggestion: As a previewing activity, review with students the various ways German speakers greet one another and introduce themselves.

Peter	„Guten Tag! ___ ___ ist Peter Junkel." „Ich ___ ___ Berlin-Spandau." „Die ___ ist Bechsteinweg Numero (*number*) 10 in ___ Berlin." „Meine Telefonnummer ist ___."
Jasmin	„___ Tag! Mein ___ ist Jasmin Walter. ___ komme ___ Berlin. ___ ___ ist die Lietzenburgerstraße Numero 20 in ___ Berlin. Meine Telefonnummer ist ___."
Frau Simon	„Guten Tag, ___ ___ Malle Simon und wohne in ___ auf der Schönhauser Allee." „Meine Telefonnummer ist 030/___."

D. Watch all the interviews again and listen for the following information. Select the correct response.

1. Oliver geht es …
   a. glänzend. **b.** sehr gut. **c.** so lala.

2. Jan wohnt …
   a. in Berlin. **b.** in Hamburg. **c.** in Hannover.

3. Harald kommt ursprünglich (*originally*) …
   a. aus Hannover. **b.** aus Berlin. **c.** aus Leipzig.

4. Nicolettas Adresse ist …
   a. Lietzenburgerstraße 13. **b.** Pappelallee 35. **c.** Schönhauser Allee 41.

5. Saras Postleitzahl ist …
   a. 10557 Berlin. **b.** 12203 Berlin. **c.** 10437 Berlin.

6. Herr Borowsky kommt …
   a. aus Hamburg. **b.** aus Düsseldorf. **c.** aus Berlin.

7. Michael fragt: „Wie heißt du?" Ali sagt: …
   a. „Mein Name ist Ali." **b.** „Ich bin der Ali." **c.** „Ich heiße Ali."

Wortschatz: Vocabulary lists are organized into conceptual groups, where possible, or into grammatical categories. Students should use these lists as a study checklist.

Wortschatz

Zur Begrüßung
grüß dich

guten Abend
(guten) Morgen
(guten) Tag
hallo

herzlich willkommen
hi

Greetings
hello, hi (*among friends and family*)

good evening
good morning
hello, good day
hello (*among friends and family*)
welcome
hi

Beim Abschied
(auf) Wiedersehen
gute Nacht
Mach's gut.

tschüss

Bekannt werden
Frau; die Frau
Herr; der Herr

Saying Good-bye
good-bye
good night
Take care, so long. (*informal*)
so long, 'bye (*informal*)

Getting Acquainted
Mrs., Ms.; woman
Mr.; gentleman

Wortschatz **17**

der **Lehrer**/die **Lehrerin** — teacher
Das ist … — This is . . .
Wie heißt du? — What's your name? (*informal*)
Wie ist dein Name? — What's your name? (*informal*)
Wie heißen Sie? — What's your name? (*formal*)
Wie ist Ihr Name? — What's your name? (*formal*)
Woher kommst du? — Where are you from? (*informal*)
Woher kommen Sie? — Where are you from? (*formal*)
Ich bin … — I'm . . .
Ich heiße … — My name is . . .
Ich komme aus … — I'm from . . .
Mein Name ist … — My name is . . .
bitte — please; you're welcome
danke — thanks
  danke schön — thank you very much
Freut mich. — Pleased to meet you.
gleichfalls — likewise
und — and

Auskunft erfragen
Asking for Information

ja — yes
na klar — absolutely, of course
nein — no
Wie heißt …
  die Stadt? — What is the name of . . . the town; city?
  die Straße? — the street?
Wie ist …
  deine/Ihre Telefonnummer? — What is . . . your (*informal/formal*) telephone number?
die Adresse? — the address?
die Hausnummer? — the street address?
die Postleitzahl? — the postal code?

Nach dem Befinden fragen
Asking About Someone's Well-being

Geht's gut? — Are you doing well? (*informal*)
Na, wie geht's? — How are you? (*casual*)
Wie geht's? — How are you? (*informal*)
Wie geht's dir? — How are you? (*informal*)
Wie geht es Ihnen? — How are you? (*formal*)
  ausgezeichnet — excellent
  danke, gut — fine, thanks
  nicht besonders gut — not particularly well
  prima — great, super
  schlecht — bad(ly), poor(ly)

sehr gut — very well; fine; good
so lala — OK, so-so

Im Deutschunterricht
In German Class

Alles klar. — I get it.
Das weiß ich nicht. — I don't know.
Ich habe eine Frage. — I have a question.
Ich verstehe das nicht. — I don't understand.
Langsamer, bitte. — Slower, please.
Was bedeutet _____? — What does _____ mean?
Wie bitte? — Pardon? What did you say?
Wie sagt man _____ **auf Deutsch?** — How do you say _____ in German?
Wie schreibt man _____? — How do you write _____?

Zahlen
Numbers

0 **null** — 17 **siebzehn**
1 **eins** — 18 **achtzehn**
2 **zwei** — 19 **neunzehn**
3 **drei** — 20 **zwanzig**
4 **vier** — 30 **dreißig**
5 **fünf** — 40 **vierzig**
6 **sechs** — 50 **fünfzig**
7 **sieben** — 60 **sechzig**
8 **acht** — 70 **siebzig**
9 **neun** — 80 **achtzig**
10 **zehn** — 90 **neunzig**
11 **elf** — 100 **(ein)hundert**
12 **zwölf** — 200 **zweihundert**
13 **dreizehn** — 300 **dreihundert**
14 **vierzehn** — 1 000 **(ein)tausend**
15 **fünfzehn** — 2 000 **zweitausend**
16 **sechzehn** — 3 000 **dreitausend**

Deutschsprachige Länder und ihre Nachbarn
German-speaking Countries and Their Neighbors

Belgien — Belgium
Dänemark — Denmark
Deutschland — Germany
Frankreich — France
Italien — Italy
Liechtenstein — Liechtenstein
Luxemburg — Luxembourg
die **Niederlande** (*pl.*) — Netherlands
Österreich — Austria
Polen — Poland
die **Schweiz** — Switzerland
die **Slowakei** — Slovakia
Slowenien — Slovenia
Tschechien — Czech Republic
Ungarn — Hungary

Now that you have completed the **Einführung**, do the following in German to check what you have learned.

1. Formulate appropriate expressions to:
   a. Introduce yourself to a stranger.
   b. Introduce someone to another person.
   c. Greet a friend.
   d. Greet a stranger.
   e. Say good-bye to a friend.

2. Say the alphabet and spell your full name.

3. Ask a friend how he/she is doing and tell him/her how you are doing.

4. a. Give your phone number.
   b. Count from 1 to 100.

5. Formulate an appropriate statement or question for when . . .
   a. you don't understand something.
   b. you don't hear what someone has said.
   c. you want to know what something means.
   d. you want to know how to say something in German.

6. State five countries where German is spoken and give their official abbreviations.

Das bin ich

Kapitel 1. Suggestion: You may preview the theme of this chapter by describing yourself and sharing some personal information (where you are from, where you live, etc.). Some of this will be review from the **Einführung.** Other information can be introduced using mime and pictures.

KAPITEL

1

Photo. Description: These students are chatting in front of a building at the *Franz Liszt Hochschule für Musik* in Weimar in Thüringen. The institution was originally founded in 1872 as an *Orchesterschule* by a pupil of Franz Liszt named Carl Müllerhartung. Today the school has some 850 students—many from other countries—studying a wide range of musical genres ranging from classical and jazz to modern music. **Suggestion:** Write *Wie heißen Sie?* and *Wie heißt du?* on the board or OHP. Ask students

Was macht ihr hier?

Was sagen die Personen hier? Sagen sie „Wie heißen Sie?" oder „Wie heißt du?" As a follow-up question, ask students *Ist das formell oder informell?* in order to reinforce the differences in German between casual and formal contexts.

Videoclips
Beruf, Studium und
Hobbys

20

In diesem Kapitel

- **Themen:** Personal information, characteristics, inquiring about others, hobbies and interests
- **Grammatik:** Nouns, gender, and definite articles; personal pronouns; infinitives and present tense; the verb **sein;** word order; asking questions; interrogatives; **denn**
- **Kultur: Einwohnermeldeamt,** foreigners in Germany
- **Lesen:** "Dialog" (Nasrin Siege)

Alles klar?

Alles klar? Beginning with this chapter, the **Alles klar?** section introduces the major chapter topic through illustrations and other visuals that set the tone for the chapter. Students will be asked to react to them and to express their own opinions.

If this activity is done in class, give students time to scan the information requested as well as the documents. Then call on individuals for responses. Or have them work in pairs, allowing three to four minutes to complete the activity. Otherwise, have students do the activity as homework.

A. One of the things you will learn to do in German is to give information about people in different contexts and situations. People give information about themselves in personal documents—documents they use in everyday life—as, for example, in personal IDs. Let's take a close look at one such ID.

Try to find the following information in the personal ID:

- What is the full name of the ID holder? Niels Emslander
- When was he born? 24.05.85
- What is his nationality? German
- Where does he live? Oldenburg
- What information is provided after the word **Größe**? height (183 cm)
- What color are his eyes? brown
- What does the word **Unterschrift** refer to? signature

Vokabelsuche (*word search*). Find the German word for:

1. birthdate Geburtstag
2. nationality Staatsangehörigkeit
3. color of eyes Augenfarbe
4. height Größe

Gegenwärtige Anschrift

Adresse:
Oldenburg
Am Teich 42

Größe:
183 cm

Augenfarbe:
braun

PERSONALAUSWEIS

Nachname:
Emslander

Vorname:
Niels

Geburtstag:
24.05.85

Staatsangehörigkeit:
Deutsch

Gültig bis:
30.08.2010

Unterschrift:

Niels Emslander

B. You will now hear five speakers introduce themselves. As you listen, see whether you can hear what cities they are from.

1. Berlin Leipzig <u>München</u>
2. Rostock <u>Köln</u> Luzern
3. <u>Wien</u> Jena Mainz
4. Düsseldorf Graz <u>Leipzig</u>
5. Erfurt <u>Zürich</u> Frankfurt

Alles klar! Part B.
Suggestion: As your students listen, you may wish to have them look at the color maps of Germany, Austria, and Switzerland at the front of the book.

Wörter im Kontext

information

THEMA 1: Persönliche Angaben°

Wer sind diese Leute? Scan the information, then create a profile of each person.

1. Mein Name ist Harald Lohmann. Ich **bin** am 23. Mai 1965 in Dessau **geboren** und **wohne jetzt** in Magdeburg. **Ich bin Hochschullehrer von Beruf.** Meine Adresse ist Bahnhofstraße 20. Ich bin 1,82 Meter **groß**.

2. Mein **Nachname** ist Lercher und mein **Vorname** Daniela. Ich bin am 7. Januar 1984 in Graz in Österreich geboren und wohne jetzt in Wien. Meine Adresse ist Mozartstraße 36. Ich bin 1,65 groß und bin Studentin.

3. Anton ist mein Vorname und Rütli mein Nachname. Ich komme aus der Schweiz. Ich bin am 14. September 1960 in Luzern geboren und wohne und **arbeite** in Luzern. Meine Adresse ist Schulstrasse 8. Ich bin Architekt von Beruf. Ich bin 1,79 groß.

Schreiben Sie Steckbriefe (*profiles*) von diesen Personen:

1. Vorname: Harald
   Nachname: Lohmann
   Geburtstag: 23.5.1965
   Geburtsort: Dessau
   Größe: 1,82
   Beruf: Hochschullehrer
   Wohnort: Magdeburg
   Straße und Hausnummer: Bahnhofstraße 20
   Land: Deutschland

2. Vorname: Daniela
   Nachname: Lercher
   Geburtstag: 7.1.1984
   Geburtsort: Graz
   Größe: 1,65
   Beruf: Studentin
   Wohnort: Wien
   Straße und Hausnummer: Mozartstraße 36
   Land: Österreich

Neue Wörter

bin ... geboren was born . . .
wohne (wohnen) live
ich bin ... von Beruf my profession is . . .
der Hochschullehrer university instructor
groß tall
arbeite (arbeiten) work

Wörter im Kontext. Each chapter is divided into three sections:

Wörter im Kontext, Grammatik im Kontext, and **Sprache im Kontext.** The first section provides opportunities to acquire new vocabulary and expressions by exploring authentic materials, dialogues, and visuals. Students are asked to analyze the materials and figure out the meaning of words on their own. The activities of this section practice and recycle the vocabulary. Some grammar is previewed in short notes titled.

3. Vorname: Anton
Nachname: ˙Rütli
Geburtstag: 14.9.1960
Geburtsort: Luzern
Größe: 1,79
Beruf: Architekt
Wohnort: Luzern
Straße und Hausnummer: Schulstrasse 8
Land: die Schweiz

Sprachtipp. This recurring feature focuses on an item of idiomatic usage of the language, or it briefly previews a grammar point that is explained in detail in the grammar section of the same or of a later chapter. Activities are targeted at getting students to interact.

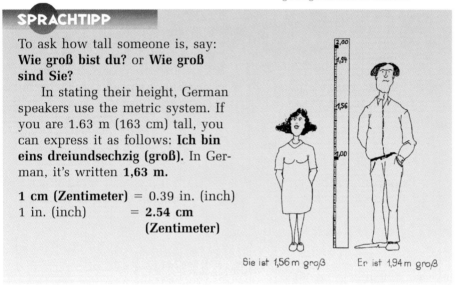

SPRACHTIPP

To ask how tall someone is, say: **Wie groß bist du?** or **Wie groß sind Sie?**

In stating their height, German speakers use the metric system. If you are 1.63 m (163 cm) tall, you can express it as follows: **Ich bin eins dreiundsechzig (groß).** In German, it's written **1,63 m.**

1 cm (Zentimeter) = 0.39 in. (inch)
1 in. (inch) = **2.54 cm (Zentimeter)**

Sie ist 1,56 m groß   Er ist 1,94 m groß

Aktivität ı   Interessante Personen

Listen to the following statements about the people in the profiles and say whether they are true (**das stimmt**) or false (**das stimmt nicht**).

	DAS STIMMT	DAS STIMMT NICHT
1. a.	☒	☐
b.	☐	☒
c.	☒	☐
d.	☐	☒
e.	☒	☐
f.	☒	☐
2. a.	☒	☐
b.	☐	☒
c.	☒	☐
d.	☒	☐
e.	☐	☒
3. a.	☒	☐
b.	☒	☐
c.	☒	☐
d.	☐	☒
e.	☐	☒

Aktivität 1. Play each section of the activity separately. Once students have filled in the answers, ask them to turn to a partner to verify their answers. When going over the information in class, pay particular attention to incorrect information. For instance, *Herr Lohmann ist (nicht) Journalist. Er ist Hochschullehrer.*

Jetzt sind Sie dran! (Now it's your turn!)

Mein Nachname ist _____.

Mein Vorname ist _____.

Ich komme aus _____.

Ich wohne in _____.

Meine Adresse ist _____.

Ich bin ___,_____ groß.

Hier klicken!

You'll find more about the **Einwohnermeldeamt** in **Deutsch: Na klar!** on the World Wide Web at www.mhhe.com/dnk5.

KULTURTIPP

Everyone who lives in Germany must register with the **Einwohnermeldeamt** (residents' registration office) within two weeks of moving to a new community. This applies to everyone, even students living in a community only temporarily. The **Einwohnermeldeamt** must also be notified when one moves from one place to another.

Aktivität 2   Eine neue Studentin

Julie, who recently arrived in Berlin, is registering at the **Einwohnermeldeamt.** Listen to the interview between the official and Julie. What information does the official ask her for? Check **ja** if the information is asked for, **nein** if it is not.

	JA	NEIN
BEISPIEL: Vor- und Nachname	☒	☐
1. Wohnort in den USA	☒	☐
2. Beruf	☒	☐
3. Geburtsort	☐	☒
4. Geburtstag	☒	☐
5. Telefonnummer	☐	☒
6. Straße und Hausnummer	☒	☐
7. Postleitzahl	☐	☒

Aktivität 3   Fragen Sie!°

Ask!

A. Unscramble the following to form questions for a short interview.

1. dein / wie / Name / ist /, bitte / ?

2. Adresse / ist / deine / wie / ?

3. deine / Telefonnummer / wie / ist / ?

4. Geburtsort / was / dein / ist / ?

5. groß / bist / wie / du / ?

B. Now use the questions to interview two people in your class.

C. Tell the class what you've found out.

- Das ist _____.
- (Tims/Elizabeths) Adresse ist _____.
- Seine/Ihre Telefonnummer ist _____.
- Er/Sie ist in _____ geboren.
- Er/Sie ist ___,_____ groß.

Aktivität 4 Wie groß bist du? Wie alt bist du?

Figure out your height in meters with the help of the conversion chart. Then exchange this information with one or two people in the class.

BEISPIEL: s1: Wie groß bist du?
s2: Ich bin 1,64 (eins vierundsechzig) groß.
s1: Wie alt bist du?
s2: Ich bin dreiundzwanzig.

THEMA 2: Sich erkundigen°

„Glücksrad Fortuna": eine Quizshow

Inquiring

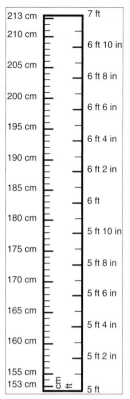

213 cm	7 ft
210 cm	
	6 ft 10 in
205 cm	
	6 ft 8 in
200 cm	
	6 ft 6 in
195 cm	
	6 ft 4 in
190 cm	
	6 ft 2 in
185 cm	
	6 ft
180 cm	
	5 ft 10 in
175 cm	
	5 ft 8 in
170 cm	
	5 ft 6 in
165 cm	
	5 ft 4 in
160 cm	
	5 ft 2 in
155 cm	
153 cm	5 ft

Thema 2. To introduce the new vocabulary, play or read the dialogues to the class. Remind students that they do not need to understand every word at first; rather they should use the context to arrive at the meaning of words they do not know. The **Analyse** that follows will also aid comprehension.

ANSAGER:	Guten Abend, meine Damen und Herren. Willkommen **heute** im Studio bei Glücksrad Fortuna. Und hier kommt Quizmaster Dieter Sielinsky.
HERR SIELINSKY:	Guten Abend und herzlich willkommen. Und **wer** ist unsere Kandidatin? Wie ist Ihr Name, bitte?
FRAU LENTZ:	Lentz, Gabi Lentz.
HERR SIELINSKY:	Woher kommen Sie, Frau Lentz?
FRAU LENTZ:	Aus München.
HERR SIELINSKY:	Und **was machen** Sie denn in Berlin?
FRAU LENTZ:	Ich **besuche Freunde** hier.
HERR SIELINSKY:	Na, und **wie finden Sie** Berlin denn?
FRAU LENTZ:	**Ganz toll,** faszinierend.
HERR SIELINSKY:	Und was sind Sie von Beruf, Frau Lentz?
FRAU LENTZ:	Ich bin Web-Designerin.
HERR SIELINSKY:	Und haben Sie Hobbys?
FRAU LENTZ:	**Aber natürlich! Lesen, Reisen, Wandern, Kochen,** und ich mache **Kreuzworträtsel.**
HERR SIELINSKY:	So, na dann **viel Glück heute Abend.**
FRAU LENTZ:	**Danke sehr.**

Neue Wörter

heute today
wer who
was what
machen are doing
besuche (besuchen) am visiting
Freunde friends
wie finden Sie …? how do you like … ?
ganz toll really great
aber but
natürlich of course
das Lesen reading
das Reisen traveling
das Wandern hiking
das Kochen cooking
das Kreuzworträtsel crossword puzzle
viel Glück good luck
heute Abend this evening
danke sehr thanks a lot

Wörter im Kontext **25**

sag mal   tell me
jetzt   now
hier   here
lerne (lernen)   am learning
das Deutsch   German
studiere (studieren)   am
    studying; am majoring in
echt (*coll.*)   really
die Universität   university
bleibst (bleiben)   are staying
nächstes Jahr   next year

Ein Gespräch an der Uni

HELMUT: Grüß Gott! Helmut Sachs.

JULIE: Guten Tag! Ich heiße Julie Harrison.

HELMUT: Woher kommst du, Julie?

JULIE: Ich komme aus Cincinnati.

HELMUT: Ah, aus den USA! Cincinnati? Ist das im Mittelwesten?

JULIE: Ja, im Bundesstaat Ohio.

HELMUT: **Sag mal**, was machst du **jetzt hier**?

JULIE: Ich **lerne Deutsch** am Sprachinstitut. Und du?

HELMUT: Ich **studiere** Physik an der T.U.

JULIE: **Echt?** Was ist die T.U. denn?

HELMUT: Die Technische **Universität**. Und wie lange **bleibst** du hier in München?

JULIE: Zwei Semester. **Nächstes Jahr** bin ich wieder in Ohio.

HELMUT: Ach so.

To convey strong curiosity or surprise, add the particle **denn** to your question.

> Wo ist **denn** das?
> *Where is that?*
> (strong curiosity)

> Arbeitest du **denn** heute?
> *Are you working today?* (surprise)

Refer to *Personal Pronouns*, p. 34.

ANALYSE

Look at the dialogues again and locate the following information.

Glücksrad Fortuna

▪ How does the quizmaster ask his guest what her name is?

▪ What phrase does the quizmaster use to ask Frau Lentz where she is from?

▪ What does the quizmaster ask to find out Frau Lentz's profession?

▪ What question does he ask to find out about her hobbies?

▪ What question does he ask to find out if Frau Lentz likes Berlin?

▪ What pronoun does the quizmaster use to address Frau Lentz?

Ein Gespräch an der Uni

▪ How do Helmut and Julie greet each other?

▪ How does Helmut ask Julie where she is from? How does this differ from the same question asked by the quizmaster?

▪ What phrase does Helmut use to ask Julie what she is doing in Munich?

▪ Helmut doesn't know where Cincinnati is. What does he ask Julie to get that information?

▪ What pronoun do Julie and Helmut use to address each other?

To say that you are studying at a university or to state your major, use the verb **studieren.**

Ich **studiere** in München.
Ich **studiere** Physik.

To say you are studying specific material, such as for a test, use **arbeiten** or **lernen.**

Ich **lerne** heute Abend für eine Chemieprüfung.
Ich **arbeite** auch für die Matheprüfung.

To say that you are learning or taking a language, use the verb **lernen.**

Ich **lerne** Deutsch.

Aktivität 5   Steht das im Dialog?

Mark whether the statements below are correct or incorrect, based on the information found in the dialogues in **Thema 2.**

	DAS STIMMT	DAS STIMMT NICHT
1. Der Quizmaster heißt Dieter Sielinsky.	☒	☐
2. Gabi Lentz kommt aus Augsburg.	☐	☒
3. Frau Lentz ist Professorin von Beruf.	☐	☒
4. Tanzen ist ein Hobby von Frau Lentz.	☐	☒
5. Frau Lentz findet Berlin zu groß.	☐	☒
6. Julie kommt aus Cincinnati.	☒	☐
7. Julie lernt Deutsch in München.	☒	☐
8. Helmut studiert Mathematik.	☐	☒
9. Julie bleibt zwei Jahre in München.	☐	☒

Aktivität 6   Was sagen diese Leute zueinander?°

Determine whether the following phrases and questions would be used by two students addressing each other, by a professor and a student, or by both pairs of speakers.

	ZWEI STUDENTEN	PROFESSOR UND STUDENT
1. Was studierst du?	☒	☐
2. Grüß dich!	☒	☐
3. Auf Wiedersehen.	☒	☒
4. Wie heißt du?	☒	☐
5. Guten Tag!	☒	☒
6. Wie heißen Sie?	☐	☒
7. Was machst du hier?	☒	☐
8. Was studieren Sie?	☐	☒
9. Tschüss!	☒	☐
10. Mach's gut!	☒	☐

What are these people saying to each other?

Aktivität 6. Suggestion: Have students work in pairs, taking turns saying a sentence and marking an X in the appropriate column. Check responses to several items or to all, keeping in mind that some of the expressions might fall into both categories.

Wörter im Kontext   **27**

Aktivität 7 Fragen und Antworten

Match each question in the left-hand column with a possible answer from the right-hand column. More than one answer is possible for some.

1. _____ Wie heißen Sie?
2. _____ Woher kommst du?
3. _____ Was machen Sie hier?
4. _____ Wo ist das?
5. _____ Wer ist das?

a. Ich studiere hier.

b. Das ist im Mittelwesten.

c. Mein Name ist Meier.

d. Ich heiße Keller.

e. Ich lerne Deutsch.

f. Ich komme aus Deutschland.

g. Das ist Peter.

h. Ich bin aus Kalifornien.

Aktivität 8 Kurzdialoge

Listen to the brief conversational exchanges and indicate in each case whether the response to the first question or statement is logical (**logisch**) or illogical (**unlogisch**).

	LOGISCH	UNLOGISCH
1.	☐	☐
2.	☐	☐
3.	☐	☐
4.	☐	☐
5.	☐	☐
6.	☐	☐
7.	☐	☐
8.	☐	☐
9.	☐	☐
10.	☐	☐

Aktivität 9 Eine Konversation

Number the following sentences in order to form a short conversation between Herr Brinkmann and Frau Garcia, who are just getting acquainted. Then perform it with a partner.

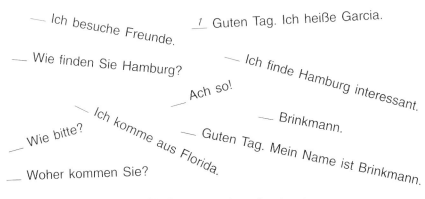

— Ich besuche Freunde.

1 Guten Tag. Ich heiße Garcia.

— Wie finden Sie Hamburg?

— Ich finde Hamburg interessant.

— Ach so!

— Brinkmann.

— Wie bitte?

— Ich komme aus Florida.

— Guten Tag. Mein Name ist Brinkmann.

— Woher kommen Sie?

— Und was machen Sie hier?

Aktivität 10   Was studierst du?

Schritt 1: Find your major in the following list. Then, by asking questions, try to find at least one other classmate who has the same major as you.

Note: Provide students with majors not listed if the need arises. Note also the list in Appendix B.

BEISPIEL: s1: Was studierst du?
  s2: Ich studiere Geschichte. Und du?
  s1: Ich studiere Informatik.

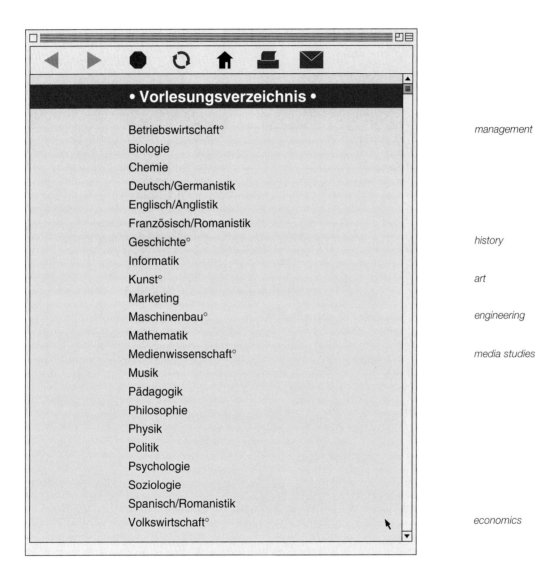

• **Vorlesungsverzeichnis** •

Betriebswirtschaft°	*management*
Biologie	
Chemie	
Deutsch/Germanistik	
Englisch/Anglistik	
Französisch/Romanistik	
Geschichte°	*history*
Informatik	
Kunst°	*art*
Marketing	
Maschinenbau°	*engineering*
Mathematik	
Medienwissenschaft°	*media studies*
Musik	
Pädagogik	
Philosophie	
Physik	
Politik	
Psychologie	
Soziologie	
Spanisch/Romanistik	
Volkswirtschaft°	*economics*

Schritt 2: Now report back to the class. Does anyone have the same major as you?

BEISPIEL: Ich studiere Informatik. Candice und Ben studieren auch Informatik.

THEMA 3: Eigenschaften und Interessen°

Hm ... Wie ist er? **Exzentrisch? Bestimmt nie langweilig.** Und **was macht ihm Spaß? Diskutieren vielleicht?**

Heißt er Rolf oder Florian? Ist er **immer** so **ernst** und **ruhig?** Und **Interessen?** Vielleicht Lesen und **Musik hören.**

Ist sie **freundlich?** Tolerant? Sie ist **wirklich sympathisch.** Und Hobbys? Na, vielleicht Kochen? **Oft** im Internet surfen?

Sie ist bestimmt **sportlich. Was macht ihr Spaß?** Wandern? Bestimmt **nicht Zeitung** lesen.

So bin ich! (*That's me!*) Check the characteristics that apply to you.

- chaotisch
- dynamisch
- ernst
- exzentrisch
- **faul**
- **fleißig**
- freundlich
- interessant
- konservativ
- langweilig

- liberal
- **lustig**
- **nett**
- **praktisch**
- progressiv
- **romantisch**
- ruhig
- sympathisch
- tolerant
- **treu**

Das macht mir Spaß! Check off your interests and hobbies.

- **Bücher** lesen
- ins Café **gehen**
- **Computerspiele spielen**
- **Essen**
- **Fahrrad fahren**
- Fotografieren
- im Internet **surfen**
- **Karten spielen**
- Kochen

- Musik
- Reisen
- **SMS schicken**
- Sport
- **Tanzen**
- Telefonieren
- Wandern
- Zeitung lesen

Aktivität 11 Gegenteile

Refer to the list of characteristics in **Thema 3** and provide the opposite of the following adjectives.

1. lustig ≠ _____ernst_____
2. faul ≠ _____fleißig_____
3. konservativ ≠ _____liberal, progressiv_____
4. langweilig ≠ _____interessant_____
5. dynamisch ≠ _____ruhig_____

Aktivität 12 Interessen und Hobbys

Provide the name of the activity represented by each drawing.

1. _____Zeitung lesen_____

2. _____im Internet surfen_____

3. _____Musik hören_____

4. _____SMS schicken_____

5. _____Fahrrad fahren_____

6. _____Wandern_____

One way to say that you like (doing) something is by using the following expression.

Fotografieren **macht mir Spaß.**   *I like photography.*
Was macht dir Spaß?   *What do you like (to do)?*

Aktivität 13   Ratespiel: Wie bin ich? Was macht mir Spaß?

Write down two adjectives that describe you and one of your interests. Do not write your name. Your instructor will collect and distribute everyone's list. Then each class member will read a description out loud, while the others try to guess who the writer is.

BEISPIEL: Ich bin dynamisch und exzentrisch. Im Internet surfen macht mir Spaß.

Important   **Aktivität 14   Wichtig° oder nicht?**

1. Make a list of three characteristics and three interests that you consider important in a friend.
2. Tally the results on the board.

     Which characteristic is most important for the class?

     Which interest is most frequently mentioned?

Grammatik im Kontext

Nomen, Genus und bestimmte Artikel   ## Nouns, Gender, and Definite Articles°

Nouns in German can be easily recognized in print or writing because they are capitalized.

     German nouns are classified by grammatical gender as either masculine, feminine, or neuter. The definite articles **der, die,** and **das** (all meaning *the* in German) signal the gender of nouns.

MASCULINE: der	FEMININE: die	NEUTER: das
der Mann	die Frau	das Haus
der Beruf	die Adresse	das Buch
der Name	die Straße	das Semester

The grammatical gender of a noun that refers to a human being generally matches biological gender; that is, most words for males are masculine, and words for females are feminine. Aside from this, though, the grammatical gender of German nouns is largely unpredictable.

Even words borrowed from other languages have a grammatical gender in German, as you can see from the following newspaper headline.

Fußball ist der Hit

Since the gender of nouns is generally unpredictable, you should make it a habit to learn the definite article with each noun.

Sometimes gender is signaled by the ending of the noun. The suffix **-in,** for instance, signals a feminine noun.

der Amerikaner, die Amerikaner**in**

der Freund, die Freund**in**

der Professor, die Professor**in**

der Student, die Student**in**

Compound nouns (**Komposita**) are very common in German. They always take the gender of the final noun in the compound.

der Biergarten   = das Bier   + **der** Garten

das Telefonbuch   = das Telefon + **das** Buch

die Telefonnummer = das Telefon + **die** Nummer

Übung 1   Was hören Sie?

Circle the definite article you hear in each of the following questions and statements.

1. <u>der</u> die das   5. <u>der</u> die das
2. der <u>die</u> das   6. der <u>die</u> das
3. der die <u>das</u>   7. der die <u>das</u>
4. der <u>die</u> das   8. <u>der</u> die das

Übung 2   Hier fehlen die Artikel.

Complete each sentence with the missing article—**der, die,** or **das.**

1. <u>Die</u> Studentin aus Cincinnati lernt Deutsch am Sprachinstitut.
2. <u>Der</u> Student studiert Physik an der T.U.
3. <u>Die</u> Frau aus München findet Berlin ganz toll.
4. Was ist <u>das</u> Hobby von Frau Lentz?
5. <u>Die</u> Adresse vom Hotel ist bestimmt im Telefonbuch.
6. Wie heißt <u>das</u> Land südlich von Österreich?
7. Fußballtrainer? <u>Der</u> Beruf ist interessant, aber oft stressig.
8. <u>Das</u> Kreuzworträtsel ist sehr kompliziert.
9. <u>Der</u> Freund von Ute studiert Informatik.
10. <u>Die</u> Zeitung aus München heißt *Süddeutsche Zeitung*.

Übung 3   Wörter bilden°

Create compound nouns using the words supplied.

BEISPIEL: der Garten + das Haus = das Gartenhaus

das Bier	die Frau	das Haus	die Nummer
das Buch	der Garten	der Mann	das Telefon

Personal Pronouns°

A personal pronoun stands for a person or a noun.

Mein Name ist **Ebert. Ich** bin Architekt.
*My name is **Ebert. I** am an architect.*

Du bist immer so praktisch, **Gabi.**
You** are always so practical, **Gabi.

Der Wagen ist toll. Ist **er** neu?
***The car** is fabulous. Is **it** new?*

Ich bin rundum Spitze [1]

[1] Ich ... I am really sharp.
(I am great in every way.)

	SINGULAR	**PLURAL**
1st person	ich *I*	wir *we*
2nd person	du *you (informal)* Sie *you (formal)*	ihr *you (informal)* Sie *you (formal)*
3rd person	er *he; it* sie *she; it* es *it*	sie *they*

Note:

- The pronoun **ich** is not capitalized unless it is the first word in a sentence.

- German has three words to express *you:* **du, ihr,** and **Sie.** Use the familiar singular form **du** for a family member, close friend, fellow student, child, animal, or deity. If speaking to two or more of these, use the familiar plural form **ihr.** Use the formal form **Sie** (always capitalized) for one or more casual acquaintances, strangers, or anyone with whom you would use **Herr** or **Frau.**

- The third-person pronouns **er, sie** (*she*), and **es** reflect the grammatical gender of the noun or person for which they stand (the antecedent).

Mark und Anja sind Studenten.
Mark and Anja are students.

Er kommt aus Bonn und **sie** kommt aus Wien.
He comes from Bonn, and she comes from Vienna.

—Wie ist **der Film?**
—**Er** ist wirklich lustig.
How is the film?
It is really funny.

—Wo ist **die Zeitung?**
—**Sie** ist hier.
Where is the newspaper?
It is here.

—Wo ist **das Buch?**
—**Es** ist nicht hier.
Where is the book?
It is not here.

Übung 4 Du, ihr oder Sie?

Would you address the following people with **du, ihr,** or **Sie**?

1. Frau Lentz aus München
2. Ute und Felix, zwei gute Freunde
3. Sebastian, ein guter Freund
4. Herr Professor Rauschenbach
5. Herr und Frau Zwiebel aus Stuttgart
6. eine Studentin in der Mensa
7. ein Tourist aus Kanada
8. ein Vampir
9. Max, 10 Jahre alt

Übung 5 Herr und Frau Lentz

Working with a partner, take turns asking and answering questions, using a pronoun in each answer.

BEISPIEL: s1: Wie ist Frau Lentz?
  s2: <u>Sie</u> ist nett und freundlich.

1. Wo wohnen Herr und Frau Lentz?   <u>Sie</u> wohnen in München.
2. Was ist Frau Lentz von Beruf?   <u>Sie</u> ist Web-Designerin.
3. Was ist Herr Lentz von Beruf?   <u>Er</u> ist Koch im Hofbräuhaus.
4. Wie groß ist Frau Lentz?   <u>Sie</u> ist 1,63 m groß.
5. Und wie groß ist Herr Lentz?   <u>Er</u> ist 1,90 m groß.
6. Wie heißt Frau Lentz mit Vornamen? <u>Sie</u> heißt Gabi.

Übung 6 Was meinst du?°

What do you think?

Ask a partner for his/her opinion. Create questions and answers with the words and phrases in the two columns, completing each blank with information of your choice. Follow the model.

BEISPIEL: s1: Wie ist der Film „Casablanca"?
  s2: Er ist ausgezeichnet.

FRAGE	ANTWORT
Wie ist der Film [*Titel*]?	freundlich / unfreundlich
… das Buch [*Titel*]?	ausgezeichnet
… das Wetter (*weather*) in [*Stadt*]?	gut / schlecht
… die Studentenzeitung hier?	interessant / uninteressant
… das Essen im Studentenwohnheim?	kompliziert
… das Kreuzworträtsel in der *New York Times*?	langweilig
… die Freundin von [*Name*]?	ernst / lustig
… der Freund von [*Name*]?	nicht besonders gut
… der ____kurs?* (z.B. Deutschkurs)	sympathisch / unsympathisch

---

*Refer to the list of subjects in **Aktivität 10, Was studierst du?,** earlier in this chapter.

The Verb: Infinitive and Present Tense°

In German, the basic form of the verb, the infinitive, consists of the verb stem plus the ending **-en** or, sometimes, just **-n.**

INFINITIVE	VERB STEM	ENDING
kommen	komm	**-en**
wandern	wander	**-n**

The present tense is formed by adding different endings to the verb stem. These endings vary according to the subject of the sentence.

Here are the present-tense forms of three common verbs.

	kommen	**finden**	**heißen**
ich	komm**e**	find**e**	heiß**e**
du	komm**st**	find**est**	heiß**t**
er sie es	komm**t**	find**et**	heiß**t**
wir	komm**en**	find**en**	heiß**en**
ihr	komm**t**	find**et**	heiß**t**
sie/Sie	komm**en**	find**en**	heiß**en**

Note:

■ German has four different endings to form the present tense: **-e, -(e)st, -(e)t,** and **-en.** English, in contrast, has only one ending, -(e)s, for the third-person singular (*comes, goes*).

■ Verbs with stems ending in **-d** or **-t (finden, arbeiten)** add an **-e-** before the **-st** or **-t** ending (**du findest, er arbeitet**).

■ Verbs with stems ending in **-ß, -s,** or **-z (heißen, reisen, tanzen)** add only a **-t** in the **du** form (**du heißt, reist, tanzt**).

Use of the Present Tense

The present tense in German may express either something happening at the moment or a recurring or habitual action.

Wolfgang spielt Karten.   *Wolfgang is playing cards.*

Antje arbeitet viel.   *Antje works a lot.*

It can also express a future action or occurrence, particularly with an expression of time.

Nächstes Jahr lerne ich   *Next year I'm going to learn*
   Spanisch.   *Spanish.*

German has only one form of the present tense, whereas English has three.

Hans **tanzt** wirklich gut.   {   *Hans **dances** really well.*
                    *Hans **is dancing** really well.*
                    *Hans **does dance** really well.*

- Identify the different verb endings in the illustrations.
- What is the subject in each sentence?
  Is it in the singular or in the plural?
- What is the infinitive form of each verb?

Analyse. Note: The purpose of this type of exercise is to take a closer look at the grammatical structure or usage of a grammar point just introduced.

Ich lese das Journal, weil ...

MARS – WIR KOMMEN!

Hat den Flamenco in Berlin mitgeprägt: Amparo de Triana – heute zu erleben auf dem Pfefferberg

Berlin tanzt Flamenco

Foto: Randy Kühn

Ob¹ fünf oder zehn Jahre alt: „Schule macht Spaß"

Fußgänger² findet
10 000 Euro
auf der Straße

Nr. 1234560 Gewinnsparlos

Nr. 1234561 Gewinnsparlos

Gewinnsparverein e.V., Köln

Hier **kommt**
Ihr **Glück!**³

Informationen zum Gewinnsparen

¹Whether ²pedestrian ³happiness

An infinitive can be used as a noun.

Mein Hobby ist **Kochen.**	*My hobby is **cooking.***
Wandern macht Spaß.	***Hiking** is fun.*
Ich finde **Kochen** interessant.	*I find **cooking** interesting.*

conversation Übung 7 Im Gespräch mit Wolfgang und Gisela

Supply the missing verb endings.

„Ich heiß_____ [1] Wolfgang Ebert und studier_____ [2] Mathematik in Zürich." Wolfgang komm_____ [3] aus Deutschland, aber er studier_____ [4] in der Schweiz. Er arbeit_____ [5] viel. Wolfgangs Freundin heiß_____ [6] Gisela. Sie studier_____ [7] auch Mathematik. Nächstes Jahr mach_____ [8] sie (Wolfgang und Gisela) ein Praktikum in Berlin.

Und Hobbys? Sport mach_____ [9] Gisela Spaß. Wolfgang find_____ [10] Kochen interessant. Wolfgang und Gisela geh_____ [11] oft ins Café und diskutier_____ [12] über Politik. Gisela sag_____ [13]: „Wir mach_____ [14] auch oft Musik mit Freunden. Ich spiel_____ [15] Gitarre, und Wolfgang spiel_____ [16] Xylophon." Und heute Abend? „Heute Abend tanz_____ [17] wir Tango!"

Übung 8 Sabine und Michael in Österreich

Working with a partner, complete the following questions and answers by supplying the missing verb endings.

1. s1: Wie heiß_____ du?
   s2: Ich heiß_____ Sabine Keller.

2. s1: Woher komm_____ du?
   s2: Ich komm_____ aus den USA.

3. s1: Was mach_____ du im Internetcafé?
   s2: Na, ich surf_____ im Internet und spiel_____ Videogames.

4. s1: Wie find_____ du das Essen in der Mensa?
   s2: Ich find_____ das Essen da gut.

5. s1: Woher komm_____ Michael?
   s2: Er komm_____ aus Kanada.

6. s1: Was mach_____ ihr in Graz?
   s2: Wir lern_____ Deutsch und wir studier_____ hier.

7. s1: Wie find_____ ihr die Professoren hier?
   s2: Wir find_____ die Professoren sehr gut.

8. s1: Wie lange bleib_____ ihr in Graz?
   s2: Ich bleib_____ zwei Semester hier. Michael bleib_____ ein Semester.

Übung 9   Kombinieren Sie.

Combine elements from the two columns to create as many different sentences as you can.

BEISPIEL: Wolfgang studiert Mathematik.

1. ich	heißt Gisela
2. Wolfgang	studieren in Zürich
3. Wolfgang und Gisela	tanzt wirklich gut
4. Wolfgangs Freundin	machen oft Musik
5. mein Freund und ich	findest Mathematik sehr interessant
6. ihr	machst ein Praktikum
7. wir	studiert Mathematik
8. du	wohne in Zürich

Übung 10   Kleine Szenen

Supply the missing verb endings and then role-play each scene.

Szene 1 (drei Personen)

A: Das ist Herr Witschewatsch. Er komm___t___ aus Rosenheim.

B: Ah, guten Tag, Herr Wischewas.

C: Nein, nein, ich heiß___e___ Witschewatsch.

B: Ach so, Sie heiß___en___ Wischewasch?

C: Nein, Wit-sche-wat-sch.

B: Oh, Entschuldigung (*excuse me*), ich hör___e___ nicht gut.

Szene 2 (zwei Personen)

A: Ich hör___e___, Sie komm___en___ aus Rosenheim?

B: Nein, nein, ich komm___e___ nicht aus Rosenheim. Ich komm___e___ aus Rüdesheim, Rüdesheim am Rhein.

A: Ach, meine Freundin Antje komm___t___ auch aus Rüdesheim.

Szene 3 (drei Personen)

A: Wie find___et___ ihr Andreas?

B: Ich find___e___ Andreas echt langweilig.

C: Ich auch.

A: Sabine find___et___ Andreas super.

C: Na, und er find___et___ Sabine total langweilig.

Szene 4 (zwei Personen)

A: Guten Morgen, meine Damen und Herren. Willkommen in Dresden. Heute besuch___en___ wir das Verkehrsmuseum (*transport museum*).

B: Das Verkehrsmuseum? Ich bleib___e___ im Hotel!

The Verb **sein**

The irregular verb **sein** is used to describe or identify someone or something.

> Marion **ist** Studentin.
>
> Sie **ist** sehr sympathisch.

eagle

sein			
ich	**bin**	wir	**sind**
du	**bist**	ihr	**seid**
er sie es	**ist**	sie	**sind**
Sie	**sind**		

That's the way he is.

Übung 11 So ist er.

Everyone is picking on Thomas. Complete the sentences with the appropriate form of **sein.**

1. Die Freundin von Thomas sagt: „Du _____ so konservativ, Thomas."
2. Thomas sagt: „Wie bitte? Das stimmt nicht. Ich _____ sehr progressiv."
3. Der Vater von Thomas sagt: „Thomas _____ so unpraktisch."
4. Die Mutter von Thomas sagt: „Wir _____ zu kritisch. Thomas _____ sehr intelligent und sensibel."
5. Der Chef von Thomas sagt zu Thomas: „Herr Berger, Sie _____ nicht sehr fleißig."
6. Thomas denkt: „Ihr _____ alle unfair. Ich _____ ein Genie (*genius*)!"

Wortstellung

Word Order° in Sentences

One of the most important rules of German word order is the fixed position of the conjugated verb (the verb with the personal ending).

First Element (Subject, Adverb, etc.)	Second Element (Verb)	Other Elements
Ich	studiere	Informatik in Deutschland.
Nächstes Jahr	mache	ich ein Praktikum.
Heute	besuchen	wir das Verkehrsmuseum.

Note:

- The conjugated verb is always the second element in a sentence.
- The subject of the sentence can either precede or follow the verb.

Übung 12 Leas Freund

Restate the information in each sentence by starting with the boldfaced word or words.

BEISPIEL: Leas Freund heißt **Stefan.**
          Stefan heißt Leas Freund.

1. Stefan ist Musiker **von Beruf.**
2. Er wohnt **jetzt** in Berlin.
3. Er findet **Berlin** ganz fantastisch.
4. Er spielt **oft** im Jazzclub.
5. Stefans Hobby ist **Fahrrad fahren.**
6. Er arbeitet **nächstes Jahr** in Wien.

Übung 12. Answers: *1. Von Beruf ist Stefan Musiker. 2. Jetzt wohnt er in Berlin. 3. Berlin findet er ganz fantastisch. 4. Oft spielt er im Jazzclub. 5. Fahrrad fahren ist Stefans Hobby. 6. Nächstes Jahr arbeitet er in Wien.*

Übung 13 Wer macht was und wann?

Create two sentences for each group of words.

BEISPIEL: besuchen / das Museum / heute / wir →
          Wir besuchen heute das Museum. [*or*]
          Heute besuchen wir das Museum.

1. Karten / wir / spielen / heute Abend
2. bei McDonald's / Peter / arbeitet / jetzt
3. ich / oft / mache / Kreuzworträtsel
4. spielen / wir / vielleicht / Tennis mit Boris
5. ein Praktikum / Peter / nächstes Jahr / macht / in Dresden

Übung 13. Alternate exercise: This exercise can also be done as pair work: one student creates a sentence with subject-first word order, while the other student creates one with inverted word order. Have students switch roles after each sentence.

Übung 14 Meine Pläne°

plans

Tell a partner two things you may do today and tomorrow (**morgen**). Tell the class about your partner's plans.

BEISPIEL: Heute spiele ich Karten. Morgen spiele ich Tennis. →
          Heute spielt Bob Karten. Morgen spielt er Tennis.

Asking Questions°

Fragen stellen

There are two types of questions. We refer to them as *word questions* and *yes/no questions.*

Word Questions

Wann kommst du? | *When* are you coming?
Was machst du? | *What* are you doing?
Wer ist das? | *Who* is that?
Wie findest du Berlin? | *How* do you like Berlin?
Wo wohnst du? | *Where* do you live?
Woher sind Sie? | *Where* are you from?

¹*am ... on the weekend*

Note:

- Word questions begin with an interrogative pronoun. They require specific information in the answer.
- The conjugated verb is the second element in a word question.

Kommst Du?

Ich heiße Petra, bin 28 Jahre alt, 168 cm groß und arbeite in einem Ingenieurbüro.

Jürgen ist 25 Jahre alt, 185 cm groß, blond, sportlich-schlank, gut aussehend und sympathisch.

- German uses only one verb form to formulate a question, in contrast to English.

Wo **wohnst** du? {
*Where **do** you **live**?*
*Where **are** you **living**?*
}

Yes/No Questions

Kommst du?   *Are you coming?*

Studiert Lea in Berlin?   *Is Lea studying in Berlin?*

Heißt der Professor Kuhn?   *Is the professor's name Kuhn?*

Note:

- A yes/no question begins with the conjugated verb and can be answered with either **ja** or **nein.**
- The verb is immediately followed by the subject.

Übung 15   Zwei Menschen

Read the two personal ads and answer the questions.

1. Wie heißt der Mann?
2. Wie heißt die Frau?
3. Wie alt ist die Frau?
4. Wie alt ist der Mann?
5. Wie groß ist der Mann?
6. Wie groß ist die Frau?
7. Wie ist Jürgen? (drei Adjektive)
8. Was macht Petra?

Übung 16   Ergänzen Sie.

Complete each question with an appropriate interrogative pronoun: **wann, was, wer, wie, woher,** or **wo.**

1. _____ heißt du?
2. _____ kommst du?
3. _____ studierst du denn?
4. _____ findest du Heidelberg?
5. _____ wohnst du denn?
6. _____ studiert Mathematik in Zürich?
7. _____ machst du denn hier?
8. _____ besuchst du das Verkehrsmuseum?

Übung 17   Formulieren Sie passende Fragen.

Formulate a word question for each answer.

BEISPIEL: _____Woher kommst du_____? Ich komme aus Kanada.

1. _____? Ich heiße Peter.
2. _____? Ich wohne in Essen.
3. _____? Ich studiere da Medizin.

4. <u>Woher kommst du</u>? Ich komme aus Süddeutschland.

5. <u>Was machst du nächstes Jahr</u>? Nächstes Jahr mache ich ein Praktikum.

6. <u>Wo wohnt deine Familie</u>? Meine Familie wohnt in Nürnberg.

7. <u>Wie findest du Hamburg</u>? Ich finde Hamburg sehr schön.

Übung 18 Ja und nein

What questions could trigger the following answers?

BEISPIEL: _Kommen Sie aus Hamburg_? Ja, ich komme aus Hamburg.

1. _____? Nein, ich bin nicht Frau Schlegel; ich bin Frau Weber.

2. _____? Ja, wir wohnen in Köln.

3. _____? Ja, ich finde Köln sehr interessant.

4. _____? Nein, ich arbeite nicht bei der Telekom.

5. _____? Ja, Köln ist sehr groß.

6. _____? Ja, wir spielen oft Karten.

Übung 19 Zur information

Take a survey and then share some of the results in class.

Schritt 1: Write down five yes/no questions using verbs and other words from the lists below or others if you like. Use the pronoun **du** in each question.

BEISPIELE: Wohnst du im Studentenwohnheim?
　　　　　Surfst du oft im Internet?

spielen	oft	Karten, Fußball
surfen	nie	im Internet
telefonieren	manchmal (*sometimes*)	Kreuzworträtsel
sein	heute Abend	chaotisch, fleißig, praktisch, exzentrisch
studieren	immer	Informatik, Biologie
tanzen	jetzt	in der Disko
wohnen	heute	im Studentenwohnheim
arbeiten		im Café
kochen		Musik
hören		

Schritt 2: Now move around the classroom asking and answering these questions to find classmates who do those things. Your responses to one another need not be complete sentences.

BEISPIEL: s1: Wohnst du im Studentenwohnheim?
　　　　　s2: Ja. / Aber natürlich! / Na klar! / Nein.

Schritt 3: Now report back to the class on who does what.

BEISPIEL: Matt wohnt im Studentenwohnheim. Trudi surft oft im Internet. ...

Schritt 1: Invent a fictitious person and fill in the blanks as if you were that person.

1. Ich heiße _____.

2. Ich komme aus _____.

3. Das ist in _____.

4. Ich studiere _____.

5. _____ macht Spaß.

6. Nächstes Jahr studiere ich in _____.

Schritt 2: Now take turns reading the statements to each other. Imagine you do not entirely understand what the other is saying and ask him or her to repeat it. Follow the model.

BEISPIEL: s1: Ich heiße Karl-Heinz Rüschenbaum.
s2: Wie bitte? Wie heißt du?
s1: Karl-Heinz Rüschenbaum.
s2: Ach so!
s1: Ich komme aus …
s2: Wie bitte? Woher kommst du?

Student life   Übung 21   Das Studentenleben

Schritt 1: You will hear some information about a German university student. Compare what you hear with the statements below. If a statement is incorrect, find the correct answer from among the choices in parentheses.

	DAS STIMMT	DAS STIMMT NICHT
1. Die Studentin heißt Claudia. (____ Katrin, ____ Karin)	☐	☐
2. Sie kommt aus Göttingen. (____ Dresden, ____ Bremen)	☐	☐
3. Der Familienname ist Renner. (____ Reuter, ____ Reiser)	☐	☐
4. Sie studiert jetzt in Tübingen. (____ Göttingen, ____ Dresden)	☐	☐
5. Sie studiert Mathematik. (____ Jura, ____ Informatik)	☐	☐
6. Sie wohnt bei einer Familie. (____ im Studentenwohnheim, ____ allein)	☐	☐
7. Sie geht oft schwimmen. (____ wandern, ____ Tennis spielen)	☐	☐
8. Sie geht oft ins Café. (____ in die Disko, ____ ins Museum)	☐	☐

Schritt 2: Now formulate yes/no questions based on the statements given in **Schritt 1.** Ask another student in your class to verify the information.

BEISPIEL: s1: Heißt die Studentin Claudia?
s2: Nein, sie heißt Karin.

Sprache im Kontext

Videoclips

A. Watch the interviews with Sara and Ali as they talk about what they are studying, their hobbies, and how their friends would describe them. Write **S** if the phrase or word applies to **Sara** or **A** if it applies to **Ali.**

_____ Medienwissenschaft	_____ Schwimmen
_____ Mathematik	_____ spontan
_____ Joggen	_____ zurückhaltend (*reserved*)
_____ Gitarre spielen	_____ lustig
_____ Zeichnen	_____ fröhlich
_____ Tanzen	_____ sehr aktiv
_____ Fahrrad fahren	

Sprache im Kontext. The goal of this section is to activate the four skills through a variety of activities. The section opens with a video activity, includes a reading with accompanying exercises, and culminates in writing and speaking assignments. In the video and reading sections, students are not expected to understand everything. Particularly in the initial chapters, global comprehension is the goal.

B. Who does what? Watch the interviews and match each person with a profession or job.

1. _____ Peter   **a.** ist Grafikdesigner
2. _____ Oliver   **b.** ist Pilot
3. _____ Alex   **c.** ist Bankkauffrau
4. _____ Jasmin   **d.** arbeitet bei KDW im Silbershop
5. _____ Frau Simon   **e.** ist Web-Designer

Lesen. These sections focus on developing effective reading strategies. Here, basic techniques such as skimming, scanning, and reading for specific information are introduced. You should stress recognizing cognates and guessing from context. Although the texts are not meant to be read aloud in class, it may be useful to deal with certain parts of the readings as a class activity, especially at the beginning of the course. Prereading activities, called

C. Watch the interviews again and jot down notes about things you have in common with the interviewees. If you have anything in common, then write a few sentences that describe the commonalities. Follow the model.

BEISPIEL: Ali studiert Mathematik. Ich studiere auch Mathematik. Saras Hobby ist Tanzen. Mein Hobby ist auch Tanzen …

Auf den ersten Blick, require students to brainstorm and speculate about the text. We recommend doing **Auf den ersten Blick** in class the day before the reading is assigned. Such an approach will provide you with an opportunity to clear up any potential misunderstandings or false assumptions about the main topic of the text. In the section titled **Zum Text,** students work with the text to acquire vocabulary and gather more detailed information.

Lesen

Zum Thema°

Where do the students in your German class come from? Were all students in the class born in the same country? What nationalities and ethnic groups are represented? How many students can speak more than one language? How many students have bilingual parents?

Auf den ersten Blick°

1. Look at the title and the text itself. What type of text is this? What led you to your conclusions?

2. Label the exchanges in the dialogue with *S1 (Speaker 1)* and *S2 (Speaker 2)*.

Zum Thema. Note: In order to contextualize this text, it may be useful for students to know that obtaining German citizenship was, until 2000,

About the topic

fairly difficult for foreign-born residents, with a minimum 15-year residency before being allowed to apply. The amended law (in line with European Union standards) mandates an 8-year residence in Germany and

At first glance

certain other conditions being met (such as basic proficiency in German) before applying for citizenship. Children of foreign-born residents are granted automatic German citizenship

at birth if one of the parents has resided in Germany for 8 years or if one parent has held permanent residency for at least 3 years. Thus Nasrin Siege's "Dialog" highlights the prejudice often encountered that those of foreign descent are not "real" Germans. For further information, see: www.germany.info/relaunch/info/archives/background/citizenship.html.

3. Skim the text for references to geographical locations and references to a person's appearance.

4. From the context, what do you think **reden** and **aussehen** (**siehst … aus, sehe aus**) mean?

SPRACHTIPP

In spoken German, the question word **woher** is often split into two, with the **her** coming at the end of the sentence.

Woher kommst du? ⎫
Wo kommst du **her**? ⎭   *Where do you come from?*

DIALOG

von Nasrin Siege

„Du redest so gut deutsch. Wo kommst du denn her?"

„Aus Hamburg."

„Wieso? Du siehst aber nicht so aus!"

„Wie sehe ich denn aus?"

5 „Na ja, so schwarzhaarig und dunkel …"

„Na und?"

„Wo bist du denn geboren?"

„In Hamburg."

„Und dein Vater?"

10 „In Hamburg."

„Deine Mutter?"

„Im Iran."

„Da haben wir's!"

„Was denn?"

15 „Dass du keine° Deutsche bist!"   *not a*

„Wer sagt das?"

„Na ich!"

„Warum?"

Reading. *"Dialog"* by Nasrin Siege appeared in *Texte dagegen*, a volume of fiction against xenophobia and racism. Note the use of colloquialisms such as splitting the interrogative *woher*.

Even if students don't know the exact meaning of a word, they may be able to categorize it. This is a skill that will help them to use a dictionary judiciously. Depending on one's purpose in reading, knowing the general category of something may be sufficient for a general understanding of a text.

About the text

Zum Text

1. What does the text tell you about the birthplace, place of residence, citizenship of Speaker 2? What else can you determine about him or her?

2. Consider what you've learned about different forms of "you" in German. Speculate: How old are the two speakers? How well do they know each other? Where might this dialogue take place? How do you think it started?

3. Why is the nationality of Speaker 2 an issue for Speaker 1?

You'll find information about the topic of foreigners in Germany in **Deutsch: Na klar!** on the World Wide Web at

More than seven million foreigners make up roughly 9% of Germany's population and contribute to the country's economic growth. Most Germans and foreigners live in peaceful coexistence; however, incidents of discrimination and even violence against foreigners have occurred, especially following the economic difficulties in the wake of the unification of Germany in 1990. The German government strives to promote tolerance toward foreigners through media campaigns, and the governments of the German states try to integrate children of foreigners into the German school system.

> Dein Christus ein Jude
> Dein Auto ein Japaner
> Deine Pizza italienisch
> Deine Demokratie griechisch
> Dein Kaffee brasilianisch
> Dein Urlaub türkisch
> Deine Zahlen arabisch
> Deine Schrift Lateinisch
> Und Dein Nachbar nur ein Ausländer?

Plakat gegen Rassismus und Ausländerfeindlichkeit (antiforeigner sentiments), *gesehen in einer Hamburger U-Bahn Station*

Zu guter Letzt

Einander kennen lernen

You are going to be working with other students in the class on various speaking and writing tasks in German. Some students you already know, others you don't. In this activity, you will interview three students you have not already met, tell someone else about one of them, and write a short profile of each of them.

Schritt 1: Before you ask the questions below, formulate them in German. Ask:

- his/her name _____
- where he/she comes from _____
- where he/she was born _____
- what he/she likes to do _____
- what he/she is studying _____
- how he/she likes the university here _____

Schritt 2: Now interview the three students and jot down their responses.

Schritt 3: Using your notes, tell another student about one of the persons you interviewed.

Schritt 4: Write a short profile of each student you interviewed, using complete sentences. Use the model below.

BEISPIEL: Eine Studentin heißt Stacey. Sie kommt aus …

Wortschatz

Eigenschaften	Characteristics
alt	old
ernst	serious
exzentrisch	eccentric
fantastisch	fantastic
faul	lazy
fleißig	hardworking, diligent
freundlich/unfreundlich	friendly/unfriendly
groß	tall
gut	good, well
Er tanzt gut.	He dances well.
interessant	interesting
kompliziert	complicated
konservativ	conservative
langweilig	boring
lustig	cheerful; fun-loving
nett	nice
praktisch/unpraktisch	practical/impractical
romantisch	romantic
ruhig	quiet
sportlich	athletic
stressig	stressful
sympathisch/ unsympathisch	likable/unlikable
toll! (coll.)	super!
ganz toll!	super! great!
treu	loyal

Substantive	Nouns
der Amerikaner / die Amerikanerin	American
der Beruf	profession, occupation
Was sind Sie von Beruf?	What do you do for a living?
das Buch	book
(das) Deutsch	German (language)
das Essen	food; eating
der Freund / die Freundin	friend
der Geburtsort	birthplace
der Geburtstag	birthday, date of birth
das Hobby	hobby
der Hochschullehrer / die Hochschullehrerin	university instructor
das Interesse	interest
das Jahr	year
nächstes Jahr	next year
der Journalist / die Journalistin	journalist

der Mann	man
die Mensa	student cafeteria
die Musik	music
der Name	name
der Nachname	family name, surname
der Vorname	first name, given name
das Praktikum	internship
ein Praktikum machen	to do an internship
der Professor / die Professorin	professor
das Semester	semester
der Spaß	fun
der Student / die Studentin	student
die Universität	university
der Wohnort	place of residence
die Zeitung	newspaper

Verben	Verbs
arbeiten	to work
besuchen	to visit
bleiben	to stay, remain
diskutieren	to discuss
essen	to eat
fahren	to drive, ride
Fahrrad fahren	to ride a bicycle
finden	to find
Wie findest du ...?	How do you like ... ?; What do you think of ... ?
gehen	to go
heißen	to be called, be named
hören	to listen, hear
kochen	to cook
kommen	to come
lernen	to learn, study
lesen	to read
machen	to do; to make
Kreuzworträtsel machen	to do crossword puzzles
reisen	to travel
sagen	to say, tell
sag mal	tell me
schicken	to send
sein	to be
spielen	to play
Computerspiele spielen	to play computer games
Karten spielen	to play cards
studieren	to study

surfen	to surf
tanzen	to dance
telefonieren	to talk on the phone
wandern	to hike
wohnen	to reside, live

Personalpronomen / Personal Pronouns

ich	I
du	you (*informal sing.*)
er	he; it
sie	she; it; they
es	it
wir	we
ihr	you (*informal pl.*)
Sie	you (*formal sing./pl.*)

Interrogativpronomen / Interrogative Pronouns

wann	when
was	what
wer	who
wie	how
wo	where
woher	from where

Sonstiges / Other

aber	but
auch	also
ich auch	me too
bestimmt	no doubt; definitely
danke sehr	thanks a lot
Das macht Spaß.	That's fun.
echt (*coll.*)	really
ganz	quite, very, really
heute	today
heute Abend	this evening
hier	here
ich bin geboren	I was born
immer	always
jetzt	now
natürlich	of course, natural(ly)
nicht	not
nie	never
oft	often
sehr	very
viel	a lot, much
viel Glück!	good luck!
viel Spaß!	have fun!
vielleicht	maybe, perhaps
wirklich	really

DAS KANN ICH NUN!

1. Sagen Sie, wie Sie heißen und wo Sie wohnen. Sagen Sie auch Ihre Telefonnummer, wie groß Sie sind, und wo Sie geboren sind.

2. Was studieren/lernen Sie an der Universität? Nennen Sie zwei Fächer.

3. Beschreiben Sie einen Freund / eine Freundin. Drei Adjektive bitte.

   Mein Freund heißt … Er ist …

   Meine Freundin heißt … Sie ist …

4. Haben Sie Hobbys? Nennen Sie zwei.

5. Ergänzen Sie diese Sätze:

   a. Der Film _____ interessant. **b.** Ich _____ Berlin toll. **c.** Woher _____ Sie? **d.** Fotografieren _____ mir Spaß.

6. Was sind die Artikel?

   a. _____ Semester **b.** _____ Name **c.** _____ Zeitung

7. Sagen Sie „Sie", „du", oder „ihr"?

   a. ein Freund: _____ **b.** Herr und Frau Lentz: _____ **c.** dein Bruder und deine Schwester: _____

8. Wie fragt man auf Deutsch?

   a. *When are you coming?* **b.** *Where do you live?* **c.** *Is Susan studying in Munich?* **d.** *Who is visiting Berlin next year?*

Wie ich wohne

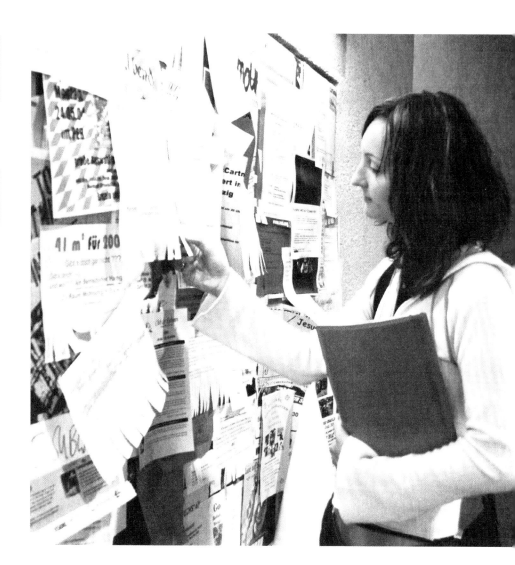

Wie hoch ist die Miete? Hmm, ein Zimmer in einer WG?

In diesem Kapitel

- **Themen:** Types of housing, furnishings, favorite activities
- **Grammatik:** Noun plurals; nominative and accusative case of definite and indefinite articles, nouns, and interrogative pronouns; **haben**; negation with **nicht** and **kein**; **dieser** and **welcher** verbs with stem-vowel changes; demonstrative pronouns; the adverb **gern**
- **Kultur:** Living arrangements, the euro
- **Lesen:** „So wohne ich"

Videoclips
So wohnen sie.

Alles klar?

Alles klar? A. Suggestion: Give students several minutes to scan both the questions and the flyer from a university bulletin board, *das Schwarze Brett,* before responding.

A. Just as in North America, flyers (**Anschlagzettel**) are a popular way to make announcements, advertise, or disseminate information in German-speaking countries. What do you think is the purpose of the flyer shown here? Once you've determined the purpose, answer the multiple-choice questions.

- Wo findet man (*one*) so einen Anschlagzettel?
  - **a.** in einer Klinik
  - **b.** an der Uni
  - **c.** in einem Garten
- Die vier Studentinnen suchen _____.
  - **a.** einen Regenschirm
  - **b.** eine Wohnung
  - **c.** ein Dach
- Sie brauchen _____ Zimmer.
  - **a.** zwei bis (*to*) drei
  - **b.** sechs bis sieben
  - **c.** vier bis fünf
- Sie möchten (*would like*) eine Wohnung _____.
  - **a.** im Stadtzentrum
  - **b.** in einem Vorort (*suburb*)
  - **c.** auf dem Lande (*in the country*)

Vokabelsuche. Find the German word for:

1. kitchen   Küche
2. bath   Bad
3. central location   zentrale Lage
4. reward   Belohnung

B. Listen to the following short conversations. Mark the kind of apartment the speakers are looking for.

1. **a.** eine Zweizimmerwohnung
   b. eine Dreizimmerwohnung
2. **a.** eine Zweizimmerwohnung mit Küche und Bad
   b. eine Dreizimmerwohnung in zentraler Lage
3. **a.** ein Zimmer bei einer Familie
   b. ein Zimmer in einem Studentenheim

Follow-up: You may "narrate" the flyer to the students. Or, with the help of the questions, individual students can explain sections of the flyer.

Realia. This flyer was distributed at the university in Göttingen and demonstrates the imagination required to obtain student housing. The reward reflects how keen competition for housing is.

In German-speaking countries, the kitchen and bathroom are not counted as "rooms" when describing the number of rooms in an apartment. Thus, a **Zweizimmerwohnung** has one bedroom and a living room, while a **Dreizimmerwohnung** has two bedrooms and a living room. An **Appartement** is a studio, or efficiency apartment.

Apartments are expensive in German-speaking countries. Students either live in a **Studentenwohnheim**, a residence hall, or share living accommodations such as an apartment to cut expenses. Many students prefer living in a **Wohngemeinschaft (WG),** a co-op in which each student has a private room while kitchen and bath facilities are shared.

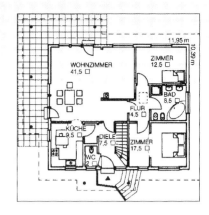

Wörter im Kontext

Was ist denn los? What's the matter?

suche (suchen) am looking for

dringend desperately

die Wohnung apartment

das Zimmer room

so teuer very expensive

nichts nothing

frei free, available

etwas something

da here; there

schönes (schön) beautiful

möbliertes (möbliert) furnished

der Nichtraucher (Nichtraucher, *pl.)* nonsmoker

hoch high

die Miete rent

nur only

recht quite

preiswert reasonable

das Geld money

weit von der Uni far from the university

Da hast du Recht. You're right.

gerade just, exactly

zentral gelegen centrally located

frage (fragen) ask

genau exactly

THEMA 1: Auf Wohnungssuche

Ulla und Stefan treffen sich (meet) *vor der Mensa der Uni Freiburg. Ulla hat ein großes* **Problem.**

STEFAN: Tag, Ulla! Wie geht's?

ULLA: Ach, nicht besonders.

STEFAN: **Was ist denn los?**

ULLA: Ich **suche dringend** eine **Wohnung** oder ein **Zimmer.** Wohnungen sind aber alle **so teuer.**

STEFAN: Ist denn **nichts frei** im **Studentenwohnheim?**

ULLA: Hier in Freiburg? Bestimmt nicht!

STEFAN: Hier ist die Zeitung von heute. Ah, hier ist **etwas. Da,** schau mal: **schönes, möbliertes** Zimmer für **Nichtraucher.**

ULLA: Wie **hoch** ist die **Miete?**

STEFAN: **Nur** 250 Euro.

ULLA: Das ist **recht preiswert.** Ich habe nicht viel **Geld** für Miete. Wo ist das Zimmer?

STEFAN: In Gundelfingen.

ULLA: In Gundelfingen?! Das ist aber **weit von der Uni.**

STEFAN: Na, **da hast du Recht.** Preiswert ist es, aber Gundelfingen ist nicht **gerade zentral gelegen.**

ULLA: Naja, ich brauche dringend ein Zimmer. Ich **frage** mal, **genau** wie weit das bis zur Innenstadt ist.

Mark whether the following statements are correct (**das stimmt**) or incorrect (**das stimmt nicht**) based on the information in the dialogue.

	DAS STIMMT	DAS STIMMT NICHT
1. Stefan sucht ein Zimmer.	☐	☒
2. Im Studentenwohnheim ist nichts frei.	☒	☐
3. Stefan findet ein Zimmer für Nichtraucher.	☒	☐
4. Das Zimmer ist nicht möbliert.	☐	☒
5. Die Miete ist nicht sehr hoch.	☒	☐
6. Gundelfingen ist nicht zentral gelegen.	☒	☐

Wie wohnen Sie? Expressions using the dative case should be treated as lexical items. Dative prepositions will be covered in **Kapitel 5,** prepositions that take either the dative or accusative in **Kapitel 6. Suggestion:** Remind students that *sie* is used to refer to *die Wohnung* and *es* to *das Zimmer* or *das Haus.* Ask them what word would then refer to *Balkon (er).* It may be useful to write *der, die,* and *das* on the board or OHP and then write *er, sie,* and *es* next to them so that students see the correspondence between word gender and pronoun.

Wie wohnen Sie? Kreuzen Sie an.

☐ Appartement
☐ Haus
☐ Studentenwohnheim

☐ **Wohngemeinschaft (WG)**
☐ Wohnung
☐ Zimmer

Ich wohne …

☐ allein (*alone*)
☐ bei den Eltern (*with my parents*)

☐ bei einer Familie

Ich habe …

☐ einen **Mitbewohner** / eine **Mitbewohnerin**
☐ einen Hund (*dog*)
☐ eine Katze

☐ einen Goldfisch
☐ ein **Handy**
☐ ein Telefon

Beschreiben Sie Ihre Wohnung / Ihr Zimmer / Ihr Haus!

Sie/Es hat …

☐ ein **Arbeitszimmer**
☐ eine schöne Aussicht (*view*)
☐ ein **Badezimmer** / **Bad**
☐ einen **Balkon**
☐ ein **Esszimmer**
☐ ein (zwei/drei) **Fenster**
☐ eine **Garage**
☐ einen **Garten**
☐ eine **Küche**
☐ ein (zwei/drei) **Schlafzimmer**
☐ ein **Wohnzimmer**
☐ **Computeranschluss**
☐ eine **Terrasse**

Sie/Es ist …

☐ **groß**
☐ **klein**
☐ **dunkel**
☐ **hell**
☐ möbliert
☐ **unmöbliert**
☐ preiswert
☐ teuer
☐ schön
☐ **hässlich**
☐ zentral gelegen
☐ weit von der Uni

Die Miete ist …

☐ hoch

☐ **niedrig**

Neue Wörter

der Mitbewohner / die Mitbewohnerin roommate, housemate
das Handy cell phone
das Arbeitszimmer study
das Badezimmer/Bad bathroom
das Esszimmer dining room
das Fenster window
die Küche kitchen
das Schlafzimmer bedroom
das Wohnzimmer living room
der Computeranschluss computer connection
die Terrasse patio
groß big
klein small
dunkel dark
hell bright
unmöbliert unfurnished
hässlich ugly
niedrig low

SPRACHTIPP

Das ist **ein** Balkon. Das ist **eine** Küche. Das ist **ein** Badezimmer.

When a masculine noun is used as a direct object, **ein** changes to **einen;** however, feminine **eine** and neuter **ein** do not change:

Mein Haus hat **einen** Balkon, **eine** Küche und **ein** Badezimmer.

Aktivität 1 Welches Zimmer ist das?

With which room do you associate the following?

1. wohnen: _Wohnzimmer_
2. kochen: _Küche_
3. baden: _Bad/Badezimmer_
4. Auto: _Garage_

5. lernen: _Arbeitszimmer_
6. essen: _Esszimmer_
7. schlafen: _Schlafzimmer_

Refer to *The Indefinite Article: Nominative and Accusative,* p. 68.

Scan the five ads from people looking for housing. Label the ads from 1 to 5 in the order in which you hear them.

Freundl. junger 37-jähriger Englischlehrer su. 1 Zi. in WG um mit euch Deutsch zu sprechen und es besser zu lernen.
☎ 570 56 39
_____

Freundlicher Schauspieler[4] aus Hamburg sucht Zi in WG vom 1. Mai bis 1. August in München.
☎ 637 88 78, ♂ Manfred
_____

Musiker (24) sucht Zimmer oder Raum in WG zum 1.6. oder etwas früher. ☎ 040/439 84 20 Markus (rufe zurück[1]) PS.: Zahle[2] bis 250 Euro incl.[3]
_____

Fotodesignerin, 22, sucht preiswertes Zimmer in junger WG, möglichst zentral zum 1.7.07.
☎ 0170 123 45 678, Nichtraucherin.
_____

Architekturstudentin (25) sucht zum 1. od. 15.5. ruhiges Zim. bis 200 Euro incl. in WG ☎ 857 63 90 (oder 50 72 58)
_____

[1]rufe … *call back* [2]*pay*
[3]incl. = inclusive *including utilities* [4]*actor*

KULTURTIPP

The euro (€) is used in the countries of the European Union, including Germany. The currency has seven denominations of bills and eight different coins. The front side of each coin is the same in all countries, but for the reverse side each nation can choose motifs particular to that country.

Short History of the Euro

- January 1, 1999. The euro is born. The euro's exchange rate is established relative to other world currencies; however, people in Germany still used the **Deutsche Mark (D-Mark)** for everyday transactions.

- December 17, 2001. Starter kits are provided to banks for distribution to 53 million homes. The kits contain 20 marks worth of euros.

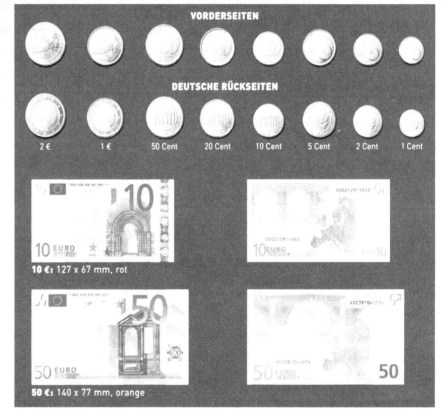

- January 1, 2002. The euro coins and bills make their debut. The euro replaces the **D-Mark** as legal tender in Germany.

- March 1, 2002. In January and February of 2002, people can still exchange D-Marks for euros at any bank. After March 1, only the **Bundesbank** will exchange the D-Mark.

- June 30, 2002. While the new euro postage stamps make their appearance on January 1, 2002, stamps in **D-Mark** and **Pfennig** remain in circulation until June 30, 2002.

Sprachtipp. Point out: Let students know that they are not expected to produce correct adjective endings at this stage. This **Sprachtipp** merely explains that attribute adjectives take endings, so that students are not distracted when they encounter them in realia and texts in early chapters.

Aktivität 3   Wer braucht eine Wohnung?

Schritt 1: Look over the five ads from **Aktivität 2** and complete the following:

1. Der junge Englischlehrer sucht …
   a. eine Wohnung
   b. ein Zimmer in einer WG
   c. ein Appartement

2. Der Musiker braucht ein Zimmer …
   a. zum 1. Juli
   b. zum 1. Juni
   c. zum 1. August

3. Der Schauspieler sucht ein Zimmer …
   a. in München
   b. in Hamburg
   c. in Zürich

4. Die Fotodesignerin sucht …
   a. ein Zimmer
   b. eine Wohnung
   c. eine Nichtraucherin

5. Für das Zimmer zahlt die Architekturstudentin …
   a. bis 250 Euro
   b. bis 200 Euro
   c. bis 300 Euro

Schritt 2: Now look over the ads again and say as much as you can about each, giving more detailed information.

BEISPIEL: Ein Englischlehrer sucht ein Zimmer in einer WG.
   Er ist 37.
   Er ist freundlich und nett.

Aktivität 4   Eine Anzeige° schreiben   *ad*

Using the newspaper ads on the previous page as models, create a simple ad in the following format. Trade ads with another person, who will read yours to the class.

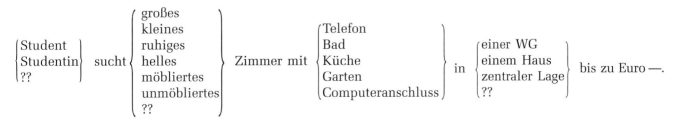

$$\begin{Bmatrix} \text{Student} \\ \text{Studentin} \\ \text{??} \end{Bmatrix} \text{sucht} \begin{Bmatrix} \text{großes} \\ \text{kleines} \\ \text{ruhiges} \\ \text{helles} \\ \text{möbliertes} \\ \text{unmöbliertes} \\ \text{??} \end{Bmatrix} \text{Zimmer mit} \begin{Bmatrix} \text{Telefon} \\ \text{Bad} \\ \text{Küche} \\ \text{Garten} \\ \text{Computeranschluss} \end{Bmatrix} \text{in} \begin{Bmatrix} \text{einer WG} \\ \text{einem Haus} \\ \text{zentraler Lage} \\ \text{??} \end{Bmatrix} \text{bis zu Euro —.}$$

das Bett

das Foto

der Kleiderschrank
€ 2000

€ 600

die Lampe

€ 20

der Wecker

€ 1500

€ 325

die Kommode

der Nachttisch

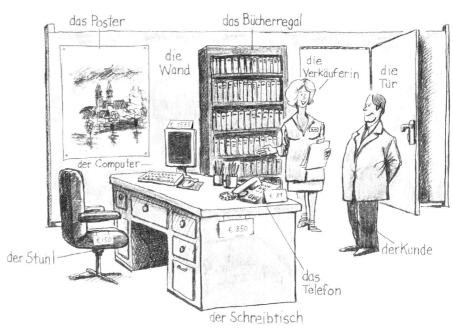

das Poster

das Bücherregal

die Wand

die Verkäuferin

die Tür

€ 1575

der Computer

€ 89

der Stuhl

€ 150

€ 850

der Kunde

das Telefon

der Schreibtisch

das Regal

der Fernseher

€ 1400

der Sessel

die Zimmerpflanze

die Stereoanlage

das Radio

die Uhr

€ 70

das Sofa

der CD-Spieler

der Videorecorder

€ 350

€ 200

der DVD-Spieler

die Lampe

der Couchtisch

der Teppich

Welche Möbel haben Sie **schon** in Ihrem Zimmer / in Ihrer Wohnung?

Ich habe …

☐ einen **Fernseher**　　☐ ein **Radio**　　☐ einen **CD-Spieler**
☐ eine **Lampe**　　☐ einen Computer　　☐ ??

Ich brauche noch …

☐ einen **DVD-Spieler**　　☐ einen **Tisch**
☐ ein **Bücherregal**　　☐ ??

Was **kostet** das?

☐ **Dieser** DVD-Spieler kostet 200 Euro.
☐ **Diese** Lampe kostet 70 Euro
☐ **Dieses** Bett kostet 1500 Euro.
☐ ??

Aktivität 5　Ulla hat jetzt endlich° ein Zimmer.

Listen as Ulla tells her friend Karin about the room she has just found. As you listen, check off the items that Ulla already has.

☒ ein Bett　　　　　☒ einen Sessel
☐ ein Bücherregal　　☒ einen Stuhl
☐ eine Lampe　　　　☐ ein Telefon
☒ einen Schreibtisch　☒ einen Tisch

SPRACHTIPP

When a masculine noun is used as a direct object, **der** changes to **den.** The articles **das** and **die** remain unchanged.

　　Wie findest du **den** Computer?
　　Wie findest du **das** Bett und **die** Lampe?

Aktivität 6　Einkäufe°

Schritt 1: Look at the department store displays at the beginning of **Thema 2** and give your opinion of the furniture and other items shown.

BEISPIEL: s1: Wie findest du den Computer?
　　　　　　　　das Bett?
　　　　　　　　die Lampe?
　　　　　s2: Sehr schön. Und wie findest du _____?

REAKTIONEN

zu (too) …	teuer	praktisch
sehr …	hässlich	(un)bequem
nicht …	schön	billig
	preiswert	toll

Schritt 2: Bring in several photos of pieces of furniture you have in your room, apartment, or house, or bring in several from magazines. Show them to a partner and, using the following model ask them to react.

BEISPIEL: s1: Wie findest du diesen Fernseher?
　　　　　　　　dieses Radio?
　　　　　　　　diese Lampe?
　　　　　s2: Nicht sehr preiswert. Und wie findest du _____?

Refer to *The der-Words
dieser* and *welcher*,
p. 67.

Refer to *The Definite
Article: Nominative
and Accusative*, p. 65.

Neue Wörter

das **Kaufhaus**　department
　store
welche　which
die **Möbel** (*pl.*)　furniture
schon　already
der **Tisch**　table
dieser, diese, dieses　this

finally

Aktivität 5. Follow-up: Ask *Was hat Ulla schon? Was braucht sie noch?* Expect complete sentence answers.

Purchases

Neue Wörter

bequem　comfortable
billig　inexpensive, cheap

Aktivität 6. This activity practices use of several adjectives in a meaningful context. **Schritt 1** reinforces definite articles in the accusative case. **Schritt 2** reinforces **dies-** in the accusative.

You'll find more about home furnishings in German-speaking countries in **Deutsch: Na klar!** on the World Wide Web at

Listen as Ulla talks with a salesperson. Then answer the true/false questions and correct any false statements.

	DAS STIMMT	DAS STIMMT NICHT
1. Ulla braucht nur eine Lampe.	☐	☐
2. Ulla findet die italienische Lampe schön.	☐	☐
3. Die Lampe aus Italien ist nicht teuer.	☐	☐
4. Ulla kauft eine Lampe für 25 Euro.	☐	☐
5. Das Kaufhaus führt (*carries*) keine (*no*) Bücherregale.	☐	☐

THEMA 3: Was wir gern machen

Was machen diese **Leute** gern? Match each caption with the corresponding drawing.

1. _____ Dieser Herr **liest** gern.
2. _____ Diese Frau **isst** gern.
3. _____ Dieser **Mensch schläft** gern.
4. _____ Diese Frau **fährt** gern **Motorrad.**
5. _____ Dieser **Junge sieht** gern Videos.
6. _____ Dieser Mensch **läuft** gern.

SPRACHTIPP

In some German verbs, the stem vowel changes from **e** to **i**, **e** to **ie**, or **a** to **ä** in certain verb forms. Do you recognize these verbs?

 Refer to *Verbs with Stem-Vowel Changes*, p. 73.

a. Ernst Immermüd

b. Herr Wurm

c. Frau Renner

d. Frau Schlemmer

e. Uschi Schnell

f. Gerhard Glotze

Was machen Sie gern?

	JA	NEIN
Hören Sie gern Musik?	☐	☐
Essen Sie gern Sushi?	☐	☐
Fahren Sie gern **Auto**?	☐	☐
Kochen Sie gern?	☐	☐
Schreiben Sie gern E-Mails?	☐	☐
Schwimmen Sie gern?	☐	☐
Laufen Sie gern?	☐	☐
Sprechen Sie gern Deutsch?	☐	☐
Trinken Sie gern Cappuccino?	☐	☐
Schicken Sie gern SMS?	☐	☐

Was machen Sie gern?
Suggestion: Have students check off two or three things they like to do and then have them state what they enjoy doing.

Additional activity: After students have learned about verbs with stem vowel changes, have them work in pairs and ask each other the same questions in the *du*-form. Then have individual students report to the class what their partners like to do.

Neue Wörter

liest (lesen) reads
isst (essen) eats
der Mensch person
schläft (schlafen) sleeps
fährt (fahren) rides
der Junge boy
sieht (sehen) sees, watches
läuft (laufen) runs
schreiben write

SPRACHTIPP

In **Kapitel 1** you learned to express what you like to do, using the expression **Das macht mir Spaß.** Another common way to say you like to do something is to use the adverb **gern** with a conjugated verb.

Ich schwimme **gern.**	*I like to swim.*
Ich esse **gern** Fisch.	*I like to eat fish.*

Sprachtipp. Note: Some students may be tempted to equate **gern** with English "like" and use it as a verb. If so, remind them that it is not a verb. In other words, you cannot "**gern** something" but rather you "do something **gern.**"

If you want to say you dislike doing something, use **nicht gern.**

Ich schwimme **nicht gern.**	*I don't like to swim.*
Ich esse **nicht gern** Fisch.	*I don't like to eat fish.*

Note that **(nicht) gern** usually precedes direct objects.

Ich spiele **gern** Tennis.	*I like to play tennis.*
Frau Spitz hört **nicht gern** laute Musik.	*Ms. Spitz does not like to listen to loud music.*
Frau Heil nimmt **nicht gern** Medikamente.	*Mrs. Heil doesn't like to take medicine.*

Aktivität 8   Hin und her: Machen sie das gern?

Find out what the following people like to do or don't like to do by asking your partner.

BEISPIEL: s1: Was macht Denise gern?
s2: Sie reist gern. Was macht Thomas nicht gern?
s1: Er fährt nicht gern Auto.

Aktivität 8. Note: The chart for s2 is located in the Appendix.

Point out: Some students may tend to repeat *machen* in their answers to all questions of the form *Was macht X gern?* If so, point out that *machen* is not repeated in the answer unless the activity itself uses the verb *machen*, e.g., *Hausaufgaben machen: Was macht X gern?→ X arbeitet gern.; Was macht Y gern? → Y macht Hausaufgaben gern.*

	GERN	**NICHT GERN**
Thomas	arbeiten	Auto fahren
Denise	reisen	kochen
Niko	Eis essen	Karten spielen
Anja	laufen	Bier trinken
Sie		
Ihr Partner / Ihre Partnerin		

What activities are described in the ad and headline?

Can you rephrase the following sentences using **(nicht) gern?**

1. Wandern macht mir Spaß.

2. Arbeiten macht mir keinen (*no*) Spaß.

Warum ich so gern in Hamburg arbeite

Von WOLFGANG JOOP, Hamburg

Ich lebe und arbeite in Hamburg.

Two people from Berlin

Read the following questions and then scan the profiles of the two people from Berlin to find the answers to the questions.

1. Was trinkt Jasmin gern? Und Mehmet?

2. Was essen die beiden gern?

3. Was für (*what kind of*) Musik hören sie gern?

4. Was liest Mehmet gern?

5. Wer kocht gern?

6. Wer fährt gern einen Twingo?

Name: *Jasmin*

Alter: *23*

Lieblingsgetränk: *Rotwein*

Lieblingsessen: *Nudelgerichte*

Lieblingskleidung: *Jeans, Röcke*

Lieblingsmusik: *Klassische Musik, Jazz*

Lieblingsauto: *Renault Twingo*

Hobbys: *im Internet surfen, lesen, kochen, Sport*

Name: *Mehmet*

Alter: *30*

Lieblingsgetränk: *Tee*

Lieblingsessen: *Hackbraten*

Lieblingskleidung: *Jeans, Pullover*

Lieblingsmusik: *die Wise Guys*

Lieblingsauto: *BMW*

Hobbys: *Zeitung lesen, ins Kino gehen, wandern*

Aktivität 10 Wer macht was gern?

Schritt 1: Find out who likes to do the following things by asking different classmates the questions below. If they answer *yes*, have them sign their name in the blank to the right (or keep track by jotting down the people's names on a separate sheet).

BEISPIEL: s1: Siehst du gern Filme?
s2: Ja, ich sehe gern Filme.

1. Wanderst du gern? _____
2. Hörst du gern laute Musik? _____
3. Liest du gern? _____
4. Surfst du gern im Internet? _____
5. Isst du gern Brokkoli? _____
6. Fährst du gern Motorrad? _____

Schritt 2: Now ask three people in your class: **"Was machst du gern und was machst du nicht gern?"** Jot down their responses and report them to the class.

BEISPIEL: Jeff reist gern, aber er tanzt nicht gern.
Sharon spielt gern Karten, aber sie kocht nicht gern.
Dave hört gern Musik, aber er arbeitet nicht gern.

SPRACHTIPP

In order to turn down an invitation, you could offer the following excuses.

s1: Wir gehen ins Konzert.   *We're going to the concert.*
   Kommst du mit?   *Will you come along?*

s2: Nein, ich habe keine Zeit.   *No, I don't have the time.*
   or

s2: Nein, ich habe keine Lust.   *No, I don't feel like it.*
   or

s2: Nein, ich habe kein Geld.   *No, I don't have any money.*

Aktivität 11 Interaktion

You receive invitations from several people. Do you want to accept or reject the invitations?

BEISPIEL: s1: Wir gehen heute tanzen. Kommst du mit?
s2: Schön. Ich komme mit. Ich tanze sehr gern.
   or
s2: Ich habe keine Lust.

EINLADUNG	REAKTION
Ich gehe / Wir gehen heute …	Ja, schön.
in ein Rockkonzert.	Gut.
ins Kino (*to a movie*).	Tut mir leid (*I'm sorry*).
ins Theater.	Ich habe …
schwimmen.	keine Zeit.
Tennis/Fußball spielen.	keine Lust.
	kein Geld.

Grammatik im Kontext

Substantive im Plural

The Plural of Nouns°

German forms the plural of nouns in several different ways. The following chart shows the most common plural patterns and the notation of those patterns in the vocabulary lists of this book.

SINGULAR	PLURAL	TYPE OF CHANGE	NOTATION
das Zimmer die Mutter	die Zimmer die Mütter	*no change* *stem vowel is umlauted*	- ¨
der Tag der Stuhl	die Tage die Stühle	*ending* -e *is added* *ending* -e *is added and stem vowel is umlauted*	-e ¨e
das Buch	die Bücher	*ending* -er *is added and stem vowel is umlauted*	¨er
die Lampe die Frau die Studentin	die Lampen die Frauen die Studentinnen	*ending* -n *is added* *ending* -en *is added* *ending* -nen *is added*	-n -en -nen
das Radio	die Radios	*ending* -s *is added*	-s

Note:

- The definite article (*the*) in the plural is **die** for all nouns, regardless of gender.
- Nouns ending in **-er** or **-el** do not, with a few exceptions, change this ending in the plural.

SINGULAR	PLURAL
der Amerikan**er**	die Amerikan**er**
das Zimm**er**	die Zimm**er**
der Sess**el**	die Sess**el**

However, the stem vowel may change, as follows:

die M**u**tter	die M**ü**tter
der V**a**ter	die V**ä**ter

- Most feminine nouns (over 90%) form the plural by adding **-n** or **-en** to the singular.

SINGULAR	PLURAL
die Küche	die Küche**n**
die Arbeit	die Arbeit**en**

- Feminine nouns ending in **-in** form the plural by adding **-nen** to the singular.

SINGULAR	PLURAL
die Amerikaner**in**	die Amerikaner**innen**
die Mitbewohner**in**	die Mitbewohner**innen**

- Many masculine nouns form the plural by adding **-e.**

SINGULAR	PLURAL
der Tisch	die Tisch**e**
der Teppich	die Teppich**e**

- Nouns ending in vowel sounds and vowels other than **-e** usually form the plural by adding **-s.**

SINGULAR	PLURAL
das Handy	die Handy**s**
das Kino	die Kino**s**
das Sofa	die Sofa**s**

Although most nouns follow a predictable pattern in forming the plural, many do not. Make it a habit to learn the plural formation with each new noun you learn.

Übung 1   Zimmer zu vermieten

Supply the plural forms.

1. Mathias und Susanne suchen zwei <u>Mitbewohnerinnen</u> oder <u>Mitbewohner</u> für eine WG im Zentrum von Leipzig. (Mitbewohnerin, Mitbewohner)

2. Die schöne, große Wohnung hat vier <u>Zimmer</u>. (Zimmer)

3. Sie hat auch eine Küche, zwei <u>Bäder</u> und einen Balkon. (Bad).

4. Preiswerte <u>Wohnungen</u> in zentraler Lage sind rar. (Wohnung)

5. Die <u>Mieten</u> sind sehr hoch. (Miete)

6. Sie sind viel zu hoch für viele <u>Studentinnen</u> und <u>Studenten</u> wie Mathias und Susanne. (Studentin, Student)

7. Mathias und Susanne suchen zwei <u>Nichtraucherinnen</u> oder <u>Nichtraucher</u>. (Nichtraucherin, Nichtraucher)

8. Ein Zimmer in der Wohnung ist sehr groß und hat zwei <u>Fenster</u> zum Garten. (Fenster)

9. Da hört man die <u>Autos</u> auf der Straße nicht so. (Auto)

Übung 2 Wie viele?

List items in your classroom and students in your class.

BEISPIEL: Das Klassenzimmer hat 27 Stühle.

Das Klassenzimmer hat ...	Fenster (-)	Student (-en)
	Tür (-en)	Studentin (-nen)
	Stuhl (¨e)	Buch (¨er)
	Tisch (-e)	??

Übung 3 Im Studentenwohnheim

Choose suitable nouns from the box below to complete Kerstin's e-mail to Lea, making sure to put them in the plural.

das Bett
der Kleiderschrank
das Café
die Lampe
das Buch
die Mitbewohnerin
der Student
das Foto
das Gästezimmer
die Studentin
das Zimmer

Kerstin hat jetzt ein Zimmer im Studentenwohnheim in Berlin. Das Wohnheim ist ganz neu und modern. Hier ist Kerstins E-Mail an eine Freundin.

> Hallo, Lea! Na wie geht's? Ich hab' jetzt endlich ein Zimmer im Wohnheim. Gottseidank! Das Wohnheim hat 100 __________.[a] Es gibt einen Computerraum, einen Fitnessraum, einen Musikraum und zwei Bierkeller. Und wir haben auch fünf __________[b] für Besucher. Ich liebe die vielen __________[c] in der Stadt. Man sieht dort immer viele __________[d] und __________.[e] Sie trinken Kaffee und diskutieren über alles und nichts. Ich habe übrigens eine __________[f] auf meinem Zimmer. Sie kommt aus Stuttgart und ist sehr sympathisch. Das Zimmer hat zwei __________,[g] zwei __________,[h] und zwei __________,[i] aber nur *einen* Schreibtisch und *einen* Stuhl! Und wir haben nur ein Regal für die __________.[j] Ich schicke dir drei __________[k] mit dieser E-Mail als Anhang (*attachment*). Du siehst, es geht mir ausgezeichnet. Tschüss,
> Kerstin

Kasus: der Nominativ und der Akkusativ

The Nominative and Accusative Cases°

In English, the subject and the direct object in a sentence are distinguished by their placement. The subject usually precedes the verb, whereas the direct object usually follows the verb.

In German, however, the subject and the object are not distinguished by their placement in the sentence. Instead, subjects and objects are indicated by grammatical cases. In this chapter you will learn about the nominative case (**der Nominativ**) for the subject of the sentence (as well as the predicate noun) and the accusative case (**der Akkusativ**) for the direct object and the object of certain prepositions.

German typically signals the case and the grammatical gender of a noun through different forms of the definite and indefinite articles that precede a noun.

The Definite Article°: Nominative and Accusative

Der bestimmte Artikel

You are already familiar with the nominative case. Those are the forms you used in **Kapitel 1.** Here are the nominative and the accusative case forms of the definite article (*the*).

NOMINATIVE

Der Stuhl kostet 70 Euro.
The chair costs 70 Euro.

Wo ist **die** Zeitung?
Where is the newspaper?

Wie ist **das** Zimmer?
How is the room?

ACCUSATIVE

Ich kaufe **den** Stuhl.
I am going to buy the chair.

Ich brauche **die** Zeitung.
I need the paper.

Ich miete **das** Zimmer.
I am going to rent the room.

	SINGULAR			PLURAL
	Masculine	*Feminine*	*Neuter*	*All Genders*
Nominative	der Stuhl	die Zeitung	das Zimmer	die Stühle
Accusative	**den** Stuhl	die Zeitung	das Zimmer	die Stühle

Note:

- Only the masculine definite article has a distinct accusative form: **den.**
- The plural has only one article for all three genders: **die.**

Weak Masculine Nouns°

Schwache Maskulina

A few common masculine nouns have a special accusative singular form. Five nouns of this type are shown in the following table.

NOMINATIVE	ACCUSATIVE
der **Mensch**	den Mensch**en**
der **Student**	den Student**en**
der **Herr**	den Her**rn**
der **Name**	den Name**n**
der **Kunde**	den Kunde**n**

Note:

- Weak masculine nouns, as they are called, are indicated in the vocabulary lists of this book by the notation (**-en** *masc.*) or (**-n** *masc.*).

In einer Studentenbude

Student room

Übung 4   Die Studentenbude

What do you think of the things you see in this room?

BEISPIEL: Ich finde den Stuhl praktisch.

Ich finde …

das Zimmer	nicht	praktisch
das Bücherregal	zu (*too*)	unpraktisch
der Stuhl	sehr	hässlich
die Schuhe		klein
der Sessel		modern
der Schreibtisch		unmodern
der Teppich		schön
der Student		bequem
die Bilder		unbequem
die Möbel		groß
der Nachttisch		sympathisch
		unsympathisch

Some adjectives can combine with the prefix **un-** to indicate the opposite meaning.

praktisch	**un**praktisch
practical	*impractical*
sympathisch	**un**sympathisch
likeable	*unlikeable*

Übung 5 Was kaufen Sie?

Sie haben 500 Euro. Was kaufen Sie?

BEISPIEL: Ich kaufe den Tisch für _____ Euro und … .

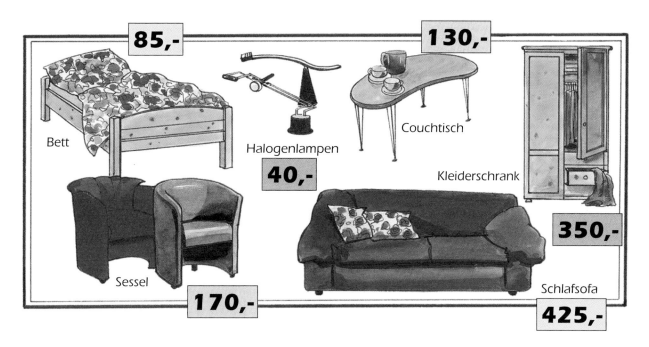

85,- Bett

130,- Couchtisch

Halogenlampen **40,-**

Kleiderschrank

350,-

Sessel **170,-**

Schlafsofa **425,-**

The **der**-Words **dieser** and **welcher**

The word **dieser** (*this*) and the interrogative **welcher** (*which*) have the same endings as the definite article. For this reason they are frequently referred to as **der**-words.

Diese Wohnung ist zentral gelegen	*This apartment is centrally located.*
Dieser Schreibtisch kostet 400 Euro.	*This desk costs 400 Euros.*
Welchen Schreibtisch kaufst du?	*Which desk are you going to buy?*
Dieses Sofa ist nicht sehr bequem.	*This sofa is not very comfortable.*

All **der**-words follow the same pattern as the definite articles.

	MASCULINE	FEMININE	NEUTER	PLURAL
Nominative	dieser	diese	dieses	diese
	welcher	welche	welches	welche
Accusative	diesen	diese	dieses	diese
	welchen	welche	welches	welche

Note:

- Just as with the definite article, only the accusative masculine has an ending different from the nominative.

Übung 5. Suggestion: Give students several minutes to scan the ad in order to think of several items. Have students compare lists. One student can report what another has on his or her list. This activity also works well in pairs, with each student taking a turn asking *Was kaufst du?* If the activity is done in pairs, encourage students to comment on the items to be bought by adding such information as *Das finde ich praktisch.*

Insert the appropriate form of **dieser** or **welcher** in the following sentences.

1. Was kostet _____ Schreibtisch?
2. Ich finde _____ Schreibtisch zu groß.
3. _____ Schreibtisch ist zu groß?
4. _____ Sofa ist bequem?
5. _____ Lampe kostet 250 Euro.
6. _____ Studentin hat nicht viel Geld.
7. _____ Zimmer hat Computeranschluss?
8. _____ Zimmer sind möbliert?
9. _____ Studenten suchen eine Wohnung.

Der unbestimmte Artikel

The Indefinite Article°: Nominative and Accusative

Here are the nominative and accusative forms of the indefinite article (*a/an*).

NOMINATIVE	ACCUSATIVE
Das ist **ein** Stuhl.	Ich brauche **einen** Stuhl.
That is a chair.	*I need a chair.*
Das ist **eine** Zeitung.	Wo finde ich hier **eine** Zeitung?
That is a newspaper.	*Where do I find a newspaper here?*
Das ist **ein** Zimmer.	Ich brauche **ein** Zimmer.
That is a room.	*I need a room.*

SINGULAR		
	Masculine	*Feminine*	*Neuter*
Nominative	ein Stuhl	eine Zeitung	ein Zimmer
Accusative	**einen** Stuhl	eine Zeitung	ein Zimmer

Note:

■ Only the masculine indefinite article has a distinct accusative form: **einen.**

■ There is no plural indefinite article.

Was ist das?

ein Fußballspieler

Nominative and Accusative Interrogative Pronouns°

Interrogativpronomen im Nominativ und Akkusativ

To ask about the subject of a sentence, use **wer** (*who*) or **was** (*what*). To ask about the direct object, use **wen** (*whom*) or **was** (*what*).

Wer braucht Geld?	*Who needs money?*
Was ist ein Praktikum?	*What is an internship?*
Wen besucht Frau Martin?	*Whom is Mrs. Martin visiting?*
Was braucht der Mensch?	*What does a person need?*

Übung 7   Neu in Göttingen

You will now hear a conversation between Stefan and Birgit. As you listen, check off what Stefan already has and what he still needs for his new apartment. Not all items are mentioned; leave them blank.

	DAS HAT STEFAN	DAS BRAUCHT STEFAN
1. einen DVD-Spieler	☐	☐
2. eine Zimmerpflanze	☐	☐
3. eine Uhr	☐	☐
4. einen Couchtisch	☐	☐
5. einen Computer	☐	☐
6. einen Schreibtisch	☐	☒
7. ein Bücherregal	☐	☒
8. eine Kaffeemaschine	☐	☒
9. einen Schlafsack (*sleeping bag*)	☒	☐
10. ein Bett	☐	☒
11. einen Sessel	☐	☐

Übung 8   Was sehen Sie?

Das ist eine typische Studentenbude.

Da ist _____.

Das Zimmer hat _____.

Nominative and Accusative Interrogative Pronouns. Suggestion: This explanation can be elaborated with reference to case of subject and object as well. The nominative case names the subject and answers the questions *wer* or *was: Wer ist diese Studentin?* —*Sie ist Anjas Mitbewohnerin Elke.; Was ist ein PDA?* —*Ein PDA ist ein persönlicher digitaler Assistent.* The accusative case states the direct object and answers the questions *wen* or *was: Wen besucht Petra?* —*Sie besucht ihren Freund.; Was kauft Frau Martin?* —*Sie kauft ein Auto.*

Note: Students may not be sure of the proper use of "who" versus "whom" in English. Tell them that whereas the distinction between "who" and "whom" in casual English is becoming ever more blurred, the distinction between *wer* and *wen* is strictly adhered to in German.

Übung 7. Suggestion: You may wish to elicit complete sentences when reviewing answers: *Was hat Stefan?* —*Er hat einen Schlafsack. Was braucht er noch?* —*Er braucht …*

Übung 8. Point out that **da ist** requires the nominative but **hat** the accusative.

Suggestion: Have students furnish a fantasy room with a certain number of objects. Each draws a picture of the room and furnishings. Then, in pairs, each person tries to find out what is in the partner's room.

You are shopping for several items. Referring to the items and prices under **Thema 2: Auf Möbelsuche im Kaufhaus** in this chapter, create short conversational exchanges with a partner.

BEISPIEL: s1: Ich brauche eine Lampe.
  s2: Hier haben wir Lampen.
  s1: Was kostet die Lampe hier?
  s2: 130 Euro.
  s1: Das ist zu teuer. [*oder:*]
    Das ist preiswert.

The Verb **haben**

The irregular verb **haben** (*to have*), like many other verbs, needs an accusative object (a direct object) to form a complete sentence.

Wir haben **eine Vorlesung** um zwei Uhr.   *We have a lecture at two o'clock.*

Anja hat **einen Schreibtisch.**   *Anja has a desk.*

haben			
ich	habe	wir	haben
du	**hast**	ihr	habt
er sie es	**hat**	sie	haben
Sie haben			

ANALYSE

Lesen Sie den Dialog.

> *Ein Gespräch zwischen zwei Studenten. Es ist 12 Uhr mittags.*

JÜRGEN: Grüß dich, Petra. Hast du Hunger?

PETRA: Warum fragst du?

JÜRGEN: Ich geh' jetzt essen. Ich hab' Hunger. Kommst du mit?

PETRA: Na, gut. Da kommt übrigens Hans. Der hat bestimmt auch Hunger.

HANS: Habt ihr zwei vielleicht Hunger?

PETRA: Ja, und wie! Aber ich hab' nicht viel Zeit. Um zwei haben wir nämlich eine Vorlesung.

- Which forms of the verb **haben** can you find in the dialogue?

- The **ich**-form of **haben** appears without the ending **-e.** What could be the reason for this?

Übung 10 Hast du Hunger?

Complete the sentences with **haben** or **sein.**

Jürgen, Petra und Hans _sind_ᵃ Studenten. Es _ist_ᵇ gerade
Mittagszeit. Jürgen _hat_ᶜ Hunger. Er fragt Petra: „_Hast_ᵈ du Hunger?"
Hans _ist_ᵉ Petras Freund. Hans und Petra _haben_ᶠ um zwei eine
Vorlesung. Sie _haben_ᵍ nicht viel Zeit. Und Jürgen _hat_ʰ nicht viel
Geld (*money*). Er fragt Hans „_Hast_ⁱ du etwas Geld?"

Übung 11 Was ich habe und was ich brauche

Schritt 1: Identify three items from **Übung 7** that you already have and
at least one item that you need. Tell your partner about these things in
German.

Schritt 2: Report to the class what your partner has and needs.

BEISPIEL: John hat einen Computer, einen Schreibtisch, und ein Bett. Er
braucht einen Sessel.

Negation° with **nicht** and the Negative Article **kein**

Verneinung

In **Kapitel 1** you learned to negate a simple statement by adding the word
nicht (*not*) before a predicate adjective.

Die Lampe ist **nicht** billig.   *The lamp is not cheap.*

You can also use **nicht** to negate an entire statement, or just an adverb.

Karin kauft die Lampe **nicht.**   *Karin is not buying the lamp.*

Ralf schreibt **nicht** besonders gut.   *Ralf doesn't write particularly well.*

One other important way to express negation is by using the negative article **kein** (*no, not a, not any*), which parallels the forms of **ein.**

—Ist das **eine** Zeitung?   *Is that a newspaper?*
—Das ist **keine** Zeitung!   *That isn't a newspaper!*

—Hast du **einen** Computer?   *Do you have a computer?*
—Nein, ich habe **keinen** Computer.   *No, I don't have a computer.*

—Hast du Geld?   *Do you have any money?*
—Nein, ich habe **kein** Geld.   *No, I do not have any money.*

—Sind das Studenten?   *Are those students?*
—Nein, das sind **keine** Studenten   *No, those are not students.*

Note:

- Use **kein** to negate a noun that is preceded by an indefinite article or
  no article at all.

- Unlike **ein,** the negative article **kein** has plural forms.

Negation with *nicht* and the Nega-tive Article *kein*. Suggestion: Another way to think about the difference between use of *nicht* and *kein* is that *kein* negates nouns with indefinite articles or no articles (*ein Computer, Geld*), whereas *nicht* negates anything else.

	SINGULAR			PLURAL
	Masculine	*Feminine*	*Neuter*	*All Genders*
Nominative	kein Sessel	keine Lampe	kein Sofa	keine Stühle
Accusative	keinen Sessel	keine Lampe	kein Sofa	keine Stühle

**Zwei Störche
und ein Frosch**

¹Die ... *That line never fails.*

Everyone has a different excuse for turning down an invitation. Listen and check off the excuse given by each person.

1. Reinhard ...
   - ☐ hat keine Zeit.
   - ☐ hat keine Lust.
   - ☐ hat kein Geld.

2. Erika ...
   - ☐ hat keinen Freund.
   - ☐ hat keine Zeit.
   - ☐ hat keine Lust.

3. Frau Becker ...
   - ☐ trinkt keinen Kaffee.
   - ☐ hat keine Lust.
   - ☐ hat keine Zeit.

4. Jens und Ulla ...
   - ☐ haben kein Examen.
   - ☐ haben keine Zeit.
   - ☐ haben keinen Hunger.

5. Peter ...
   - ☐ hat keine Lust.
   - ☐ hat kein Geld.
   - ☐ hat kein Auto.

Breakfast

Was ist hier komisch (*funny*)? In Grimm's fairy tale "The Frog Prince," a prince turned into a frog is transformed back into a prince by a beautiful princess. The cartoon on the left draws on this story for its comical effect. Circle the correct option in each statement.

1. Die zwei Störche (*storks*) suchen ein/kein Frühstück.

2. Der Frosch hat ein/kein Problem.

3. Störche essen gern / nicht gern Frösche zum Frühstück.

4. Der Frosch ist ein/kein Prinz.

5. Der Frosch ist sehr / nicht sehr intelligent.

6. Die Störche essen heute ein/kein Frühstück.

7. Ich finde den Cartoon komisch / nicht komisch.

Complete each sentence with the appropriate form of **kein.**

BEISPIEL: Susanne sucht ___*kein*___ Zimmer, sie sucht eine Wohnung.

1. Ein Zimmer suchen? Das macht _____ Spaß.

2. Haben Sie eine Wohnung frei? —Nein, hier ist _____ Wohnung frei.

3. Brauchst du Geld? —Nein, ich brauche _____ Geld.

4. Ulla hat _____ Zimmer im Studentenwohnheim. Sie wohnt in einer WG.

5. Stefan wohnt bei seiner Familie. Da zahlt er _____ Miete.

6. Ist das Zimmer möbliert? —Es hat ein Bett, aber _____ Schreibtisch.

7. Fährst du einen BMW? —Nein, ich habe _____ Auto.

Find out what your fellow students do not have.

BEISPIEL: s1: Wer hat kein Handy?
s2: Sieben Studenten haben kein Handy.

Wer hat kein- …?

Computer	Bett	Stühle
Stereoanlage	Zimmerpflanzen	Wecker
Schreibtisch	Radio	Nachttisch
Lampe	Auto	Videorecorder
Telefon	Motorrad	Handy
Sessel	Kommode	Poster (*pl.*)
Fernseher	Teppich	DVD-Spieler
Sofa	Regal	

Verbs with Stem-Vowel Changes°

Verben mit Wechsel des Stammvokals

A number of common verbs have vowel changes in some of the present tense forms.

	fahren	schlafen	laufen	essen	sehen	lesen	nehmen
ich	fahre	schlafe	laufe	esse	sehe	lese	nehme
du	**fährst**	**schläfst**	**läufst**	**isst**	**siehst**	**liest**	**nimmst**
er sie es	**fährt**	**schläft**	**läuft**	**isst**	**sieht**	**liest**	**nimmt**
wir	fahren	schlafen	laufen	essen	sehen	lesen	nehmen
ihr	fahrt	schlaft	lauft	esst	seht	lest	nehmt
sie/Sie	fahren	schlafen	laufen	essen	sehen	lesen	nehmen

Note:

- The vowel changes are in the second-person singular (**du**) and the third-person singular (**er, sie, es**).
- The verb **nehmen** (*to take*) has additional consonant changes: **du nimmst; er, sie, es nimmt.**

Verbs with vowel changes in the present tense will be indicated in the vocabulary sections of this book as follows: **schlafen (schläft).**

Übung 16 Kontraste

Mr. and Mrs. Wunderlich don't have a lot in common. Create a profile of each of them using the phrases provided.

BEISPIEL: Frau Wunderlich fährt gern Motorrad.
Herr Wunderlich fährt gern Auto.

fährt gern Motorrad/Auto

sieht gern Horrorfilme/Komödien

isst gern Sauerkraut/Fisch

liest jeden Tag Zeitung/nur das Horoskop

läuft jeden Tag im Park/macht keinen Sport

1. Ich ____ gern italienisch, Karin ____ gern chinesisch. (essen)
2. Klaus und Petra ____ heute im Restaurant. (essen) Petra ____ Fisch und Klaus ____ ein Wiener Schnitzel. (nehmen)
3. Hans braucht eine Lampe. Er ____ eine supermoderne Lampe im Kaufhaus. (sehen)
4. Ilse ____ gern Auto. Morgen ____ wir nach Berlin. (fahren)
5. Herr Renner ____ jeden Tag im Park. Dort ____ viele Jogger. (laufen)
6. —Was ____ du gern? —Ich ____ gern Zeitung. (lesen)

Tell a partner several things you do or don't like to do and how often: **gern, manchmal** (*sometimes*), **nie** (*never*), **oft.** Report to the class what you've learned.

BEISPIEL: s1: Ich esse gern, ich tanze manchmal, ich laufe nie.
       s2: John isst gern, tanzt manchmal und läuft nie.

arbeiten   reisen   schwimmen

Auto/Motorrad fahren   tanzen

laufen

einen Hamburger/Sushi essen   Zeitung lesen

wandern   SMS schicken

schlafen   Spanisch sprechen

Karten/Tennis/Fußball spielen   telefonieren

Demonstrative Pronouns°

Demonstrativpronomen

ROBERT: Hat ⌐Thomas⌐ Hunger?

KARIN: **Der** hat immer Hunger. [*Instead of*: Er hat immer Hunger.]

HERR HOLZ: Was kostet ⌐der Sessel⌐ hier?

VERKÄUFER: **Der** kostet nur 150 Euro.

FRAU HOLZ: Gut, **den** nehmen wir.

ULLA: Wie findest du ⌐die Lampe⌐?

ROBERT: **Die** finde ich prima.

In conversational German, demonstrative pronouns, identical to the definite articles, may be used instead of personal pronouns. Since demonstratives are more emphatic than personal pronouns, they are usually placed at the beginning of a sentence.

Übung 19 Fragen und Antworten

Answer, replacing the nouns or names with demonstrative pronouns.

BEISPIEL: Was macht Frau Schlemmer schon wieder? →
Die isst schon wieder.

1. Was macht Ernst Immermüd schon wieder?
   ____Der____ schläft schon wieder.

2. Was macht Uschi Schnell schon wieder?
   ____Die____ fährt schon wieder Motorrad.

3. Was kostet die Zeitung?
   ____Die____ kostet zwei Euro.

4. Was kostet der Stuhl?
   ____Der____ kostet 35 Euro.

5. Nimmst du den Stuhl?
   Ja, ____den____ nehme ich.

6. Liest du das Horoskop?
   Nein, ____das____ lese ich nie.

7. Wie findest du das Poster?
   ____Das____ ist sehr schön.

8. Siehst du Thomas?
   Nein, ____den____ sehe ich nicht.

9. Wo studiert Lena?
   ____Die____ studiert in Zürich.

Sprache im Kontext

Videoclips

A. Listen to what the following people say about where they live and complete the information.

1. Sabine hat eine _____. Sie hat vier _____, eine _____ und ein _____. Die Wohnung hat ungefähr _____ Quadratmeter. Wiebke und ihr Mann _____ gern.

2. Nicoletta wohnt in Berlin-Kreuzberg in einer _____. Es ist eine _____. Man kann eine Wohnung über die Mitwohnzentrale, über die _____, über _____ oder am Schwarzen Brett finden.

3. Claudia hat eine helle _____ im vierten Stock. Das Wohnzimmer hat eine _____, einen _____ Schreibtisch mit einem _____, verschiedene _____, einen _____ und Regale mit CDs. Die Wohnung war nicht _____.

4. Harald _____ in Berlin-Kreuzberg in einer alten Fabrik. Die Wohnung hat eine große Küche, zwei _____ und ein _____. Harald _____ gern vegetarisch und auch Fisch.

B. Watch the interviews with Sabina and Claudia. Listen as they say what they still need for their apartments. Who needs what?

C. Now describe your house, apartment, or room.

Videoclips. Suggestion: As a warm-up, review with students the kinds of information someone looking for a new apartment would want to find. Write the word _wohnen_ on the board. Beneath _wohnen_, create columns with the categories _WO?_, _WIE?_, and _WAS BRAUCHE ICH?_ Have students come to the board and write vocabulary items that are logically associated with them.

Part C. Follow-up: As a follow-up activity, have students work in groups of two or three and interview each other based on the information they wrote for Part C. Interview questions might include: _Wo wohnst du? Wie ist dein Haus / deine Wohnung / dein Zimmer im Studentenwohnheim? Was brauchst du noch für dein(e) ...?_ Have students report their findings to the class.

Lesen

Wie und wo wohnen junge Leute in Deutschland? In this section you will look at texts in which young people in Germany tell how they live.

Zum Thema

Wie wohnen Sie?

A. Take a few moments to complete the questionnaire; then interview a partner to see how he/she answered the questions.

Wo wohne ich?

1. Ich wohne _____.
   a. in einem Studentenwohnheim
   b. in einer Wohnung
   c. bei meinen Eltern
   d. in meinem eigenen (*own*) Haus
   e. privat in einem Zimmer
   f. ??

2. Ich teile (*share*) mein Zimmer / meine Wohnung / mein Haus mit _____.
   a. einer anderen Person
   b. zwei, drei, vier, ... Personen
   c. niemand anderem. Ich wohne allein.

3. Ich habe _____.
   a. eine Katze (*cat*)
   b. einen Hund (*dog*)
   c. einen Goldfisch
   d. andere Haustiere (eine Kobra, einen Hamster, ...)
   e. keine Haustiere

4. Ich wohne gern/nicht gern _____.
   a. in einer Großstadt
   b. in einer Kleinstadt
   c. auf dem Land

5. Als Student hat man hier _____ Probleme, eine Wohnung zu finden.
   a. keine
   b. manchmal
   c. große

6. Die Mieten sind hier _____.
   a. niedrig
   b. hoch

B. Report to the class what you found out about your partner.

Auf den ersten Blick

In the following passages students in Bonn, the former capital of the Federal Republic of Germany, and Rostock, a city in northeastern Germany, tell about their living arrangements. Skim through the texts, and for each one organize the vocabulary you recognize into the following categories.

PERSON	HOUSING	OBJECTS FOUND IN ROOM
BEISPIEL: Katja	Studentenwohnheim	Betten, Schreibtisch, Esstisch, Regale ...

Name: *Katja Meierhans*
Wohnort: *Rostock*
Hauptfächer: *Mathematik, Chemie*

Während des Studiums wohne ich im Studentenwohnheim mit noch einer[1] Studentin auf einem
Zimmer; Gemeinschaftswaschräume[2] und WCs[3]
für den ganzen Flur[4] (22 Zimmer); im Raum
sind Betten, Schreibtisch, Esstisch, viele Regale,
viele Schränke. Ich bin zufrieden[5]. Zu Hause
(300 km von Rostock) wohne ich bei meinen
Eltern. Wir haben mein Zimmer zusammen aus-
gebaut[6], deshalb[7] ist es natürlich mehr nach
meinen Wünschen. Ich fahre gern nach Hause,
aber in Rostock bin ich unabhängiger[8].

Name: *Christina Stiegen*
Wohnort: *Niederkassel (Rheidt)*
Hauptfächer: *Politologie, Italienisch*

Ich wohne in einer Wohnung etwas außerhalb
von[9] Bonn. Die Wohnung hat 52m², zwei
Zimmer, Küche, Diele[10], Bad. Ich teile mir[11] die
Wohnung mit meinem Freund, der auch in
Bonn studiert. Es handelt sich um[12] eine
Dachwohnung[13].

Name: *Jennifer Wolcott*
Wohnort: *Mönchengladbach*
Hauptfächer: *Englisch, Politische
Wissenschaften*

Ich wohne in einem Zimmer (12m²) in einem
Studentenwohnheim. In dem Zimmer sind ein
Schreibtisch mit einer Schublade[14], ein Bett, ein
Regal, ein Kleiderschrank und ein Waschbecken[15] mit Spiegel[16]. Ich habe einen Teppich[17]
hingelegt, Pflanzen auf die große Fensterbank[18]
gestellt, noch ein Regal (für meine vielen Bücher
und meine Stereoanlage). Außerdem habe ich
Bilder, Poster und Erinnerungen[19] an die weißen
Wände gehängt. Ich teile Bad/Toiletten und eine
große Küche mit zwanzig Studenten.

Name: *Peter Kesternich*
Wohnort: *Euskirchen*
Hauptfächer: *Englisch, Geschichte*

Ich wohne in einem Zimmer bei meinen Eltern.
Ich fahre jeden Morgen mit dem Zug[20] zur Uni
(ca. 50 Min.). Das ist für mich praktischer (und
billiger), als in Bonn ein Zimmer zu suchen.

---

[1]*noch ... one other* [2]*common washrooms* [3]*toilets* [4]*floor* [5]*content, satisfied* [6]*renovated* [7]*for that reason* [8]*more independent*
[9]*etwas ... just outside of* [10]*front hall* [11]*teile ... share* [12]*Es ... It is* [13]*attic apartment* [14]*drawer* [15]*sink* [16]*mirror* [17]*carpet*
[18]*windowsill* [19]*mementos, souvenirs* [20]*train*

Zum Text

A. Read the texts more thoroughly and look at the drawings here and on
the following page. Which description most closely matches which
drawing?

1.

2.

3.   4.

B. Look at the chart below and then scan the texts for specific information in order to complete it. If there is no information given for a particular category, leave that space blank.

NAME	WOHNORT	WIE ER/SIE WOHNT	WAS IM ZIMMER IST	WEITERE INFORMATIONEN

1. Using the information in the chart, construct sentences about the students. Have the rest of the class guess which person you are describing.
2. Using the information in the chart, describe one of the people by creating true and false statements. The rest of the class has to say whether your statements are true or false.

Zu guter Letzt

Wir suchen einen Mitbewohner / eine Mitbewohnerin.

In this chapter you have learned how to talk about student living situations and furnishings. In this project you will join others to interview a prospective roommate, choose a roommate, explain your choice, and report to the class.

Schritt 1: Work in groups of three or four. Imagine that you all live in a large apartment, house, or WG as roommates and that one of you is moving out. You are seeking a replacement for him/her. Create a flyer, in German, in which you describe what you have to offer. Feel free to consult and utilize the housing ads and flyers found in **Kapitel 2** as you create your own. You might start as follows:

> Wir, drei Studentinnen, suchen eine Mitbewohnerin für unsere Wohnung. ...

Distribute your housing flyer to classmates and find at least two people who want to interview for the room.

Schritt 2: Interview each applicant. Use German to ask the questions. You will want to ask the applicant several questions, such as whether . . .

- he/she is a student
- he/she is also working
- he/she is a (non)smoker
- he/she has a pet (**einen Hund, eine Katze, einen Hamster**)
- owns a car, motorcycle, bicycle
- telephones frequently
- plays loud music (**laute Musik**)
- has a lot of visitors (**viel Besuch haben**)
- has a computer and will need a high-speed connection (**Computeranschluss**)
- he/she considers herself/himself chaotic and eccentric or quiet and serious

The applicant might have questions, as well, such as . . .

- how large the room is
- whether the room is furnished
- how much the rent is
- whether there is a telephone, a garage, a yard
- how many people live in the apartment

Schritt 3: After you have interviewed prospective roommates, compare notes about the different people you interviewed, and decide whom to invite to become your roommate.

Schritt 4: Report back to the class on whom you have chosen and why.

BEISPIEL: Wir vermieten (*rent*) das Zimmer an Jeanine. Sie ist sehr nett und sympathisch. Sie studiert Informatik. Sie ist Nichtraucherin und spielt keine laute Musik. ...

Wortschatz

Im Kaufhaus — At the Department Store

das **Bett, -en**	bed
der **CD-Spieler, -**	CD player
der **Computer, -**	computer
der **Computeranschluss, ⸚e**	computer connection
der **DVD-Spieler, -**	DVD player
der **Fernseher, -**	TV set
das **Foto, -s**	photograph
das **Handy, -s**	cell phone
der **Kleiderschrank, ⸚e**	clothes closet
die **Kommode, -n**	dresser
die **Lampe, -n**	lamp
die **Möbel** (*pl.*)	furniture
das **Poster, -**	poster
das **Radio, -s**	radio
das **Regal, -e**	shelf
das **Bücherregal, -e**	bookcase, bookshelf
der **Sessel, -**	armchair
das **Sofa, -s**	sofa
die **Stereoanlage, -n**	stereo
der **Stuhl, ⸚e**	chair
das **Telefon, -e**	telephone
der **Teppich, -e**	rug, carpet

der **Tisch**, -e	table
der **Couchtisch**, -e	coffee table
der **Nachttisch**, -e	nightstand
der **Schreibtisch**, -e	desk
die **Uhr**, -en	clock
der **Videorecorder**, -	video recorder, VCR
der **Wecker**, -	alarm clock

Das Haus — The House

das **Bad**, ̈er	bathroom
der **Balkon**, -e	balcony
das **Fenster**, -	window
die **Garage**, -n	garage
der **Garten**, ̈	garden; yard
das **Haus**, ̈er	house
die **Küche**, -n	kitchen
die **Terrasse**, -n	terrace, patio
die **Tür**, -en	door
die **Wand**, ̈e	wall
das **Zimmer**, -	room
das **Arbeitszimmer**, -	workroom, study
das **Badezimmer**, -	bathroom
das **Esszimmer**, -	dining room
das **Schlafzimmer**, -	bedroom
das **Wohnzimmer**, -	living room

Sonstige Substantive — Other Nouns

das **Auto**, -s	car
der **Euro**, -s	euro
das **Geld**	money
der **Junge** (-n *masc.*), -n	boy
das **Kaufhaus**, ̈er	department store
der **Kunde** (-n *masc.*), -n / die **Kundin**, -nen	customer
die **Leute** (*pl.*)	people
der **Mensch** (-en *masc.*), -en	person, human being
die **Miete**	rent
der **Mitbewohner**, - / die **Mitbewohnerin**, -nen	roommate, housemate
das **Motorrad**, ̈er	motorcycle
der **Nichtraucher**, - / die **Nichtraucherin**, -nen	nonsmoker
das **Problem**, -e	problem
das **Studenten-wohnheim**, -e	dormitory
der **Tag**, -e	day
der **Verkäufer**, - / die **Verkäuferin**, -nen	salesperson
das **Video**, -s	video(tape)
die **Wohngemeinschaft**, -en (WG)	shared housing

die **Wohnung**, -en	apartment
die **Zeit**, -en	time
die **Zimmerpflanze**, -n	houseplant

Verben — Verbs

brauchen	to need
essen (isst)	to eat
fahren (fährt)	to drive, ride
fragen	to ask
haben (hat)	to have
Durst haben	to be thirsty
gern haben	to like (*a person or thing*)
Hunger haben	to be hungry
Lust haben	to feel like (*doing something*)
Recht haben	to be correct
Zeit haben	to have time
kaufen	to buy
kosten	to cost
laufen (läuft)	to run, jog
lesen (liest)	to read
nehmen (nimmt)	to take
schlafen (schläft)	to sleep
schreiben	to write
schwimmen	to swim
sehen (sieht)	to see
sprechen (spricht)	to speak
suchen	to look for
trinken	to drink

Adjektive und Adverbien — Adjectives and Adverbs

bequem	comfortable, comfortably
billig	inexpensive(ly), cheap(ly)
da	there
dringend	desperate(ly)
dunkel	dark
frei	free(ly)
genau	exact(ly)
gerade	just, exactly
gern	gladly
gern + *verb*	to like to do something
groß	big, large
hässlich	ugly
hell	bright(ly), light
hoch	high(ly)
klein	small
möbliert	furnished
unmöbliert	unfurnished
niedrig	low
noch	still; yet

nur	only	**Sonstiges**	**Other**
preiswert	a bargain, inexpensive(ly)	**dieser**	this
		etwas	something; somewhat, a little (*adverb*)
recht	quite, rather		
recht preiswert	quite inexpensive, reasonable	**kein**	no, none, not any
		nichts	nothing
schon	already	**warum**	why
schön	nice(ly), beautiful(ly)	**Was ist denn los?**	What's the matter?
selten	rare(ly)	**weit (weg) von ...**	far (away) from . . .
so	so	**welcher**	which
teuer	expensive(ly)	**zentral gelegen**	centrally located
viel/viele	much/many		
wieder	again		

DAS KANN ICH NUN!

1. Sagen Sie:

   a. Wo und wie wohnen Sie? **b.** Wie hoch ist die Miete? **c.** Haben Sie Computeranschluss und ein Handy?

2. Nennen Sie vier Zimmer in einer Wohnung.

3. Nennen Sie fünf Möbelstücke in Ihrem Zimmer. Was haben Sie nicht? (Zwei Möbelstücke) Ich habe ...

4. Was machen Sie gern? Nennen Sie drei Aktivitäten.

5. Nennen Sie die Artikel und Pluralformen von ...

   a. Zimmer **b.** Buch **c.** Handy **d.** Küche **e.** Stuhl **f.** Mitbewohnerin **g.** Kunde

6. Wie sagt man das auf Deutsch?

   a. A salesperson offers you a desk at a price that she considers reasonable, but you find it too expensive. Express your opinion.
   b. You are telling someone who has invited you for coffee that you have no time.
   c. You are telling someone that Frau Renner likes to ride a motorcycle.

Familie und Freunde

Ein oder zwei gegrillte
Würstchen?

In diesem Kapitel

- **Themen:** Family members, days of the week, months, holidays, celebrations, ordinal numbers
- **Grammatik:** Possessive adjectives; personal pronouns in accusative case; prepositions with accusative; **werden, wissen,** and **kennen**
- **Kultur:** German holidays and celebrations
- **Lesen:** „Wie feierst du deinen großen Tag?"

Videoclips
Familien und Feste

Alles klar?

Alles klar. Alternate activity: Having students look at the photograph of Bernd's family (if the classroom has a document camera, project an image of the picture on the screen), point to him and say *Das ist Bernd*. Point to Bettina and say *Das ist Bettina. Sie ist Bernds Frau*. Ask the class as a group *Wer ist Helene?* (*Sie ist Bernds Mutter*) and so forth. At this point, have students work together in pairs to ask each other about Bernd's other family members and how they are related to him. Ask pairs of students about specific people as a follow-up.

Families are important in every culture. We often define ourselves in terms of our family background. Even with the fast pace of modern life, family members take time to come together for important celebrations such as weddings, birthdays, and holidays.

A. Below you see a picture of Bernd Thalhofer's family with his relatives labeled. Your knowledge of cognates and contextual guessing will help you understand what these words mean. Look at the picture and identify the words for mother, father, sister, brother-in-law, and niece. Now, can you guess at what family celebration the picture was taken?

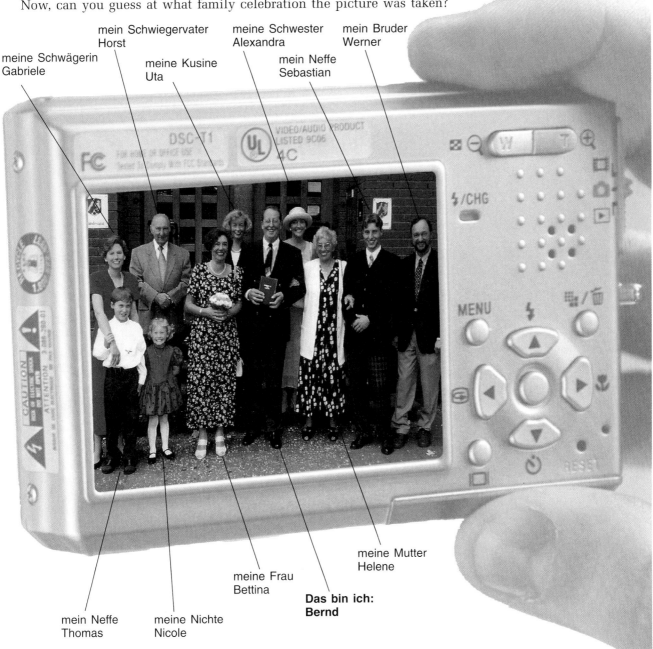

meine Schwägerin Gabriele

mein Schwiegervater Horst

meine Kusine Uta

meine Schwester Alexandra

mein Neffe Sebastian

mein Bruder Werner

mein Neffe Thomas

meine Nichte Nicole

meine Frau Bettina

Das bin ich: Bernd

meine Mutter Helene

B. Now listen as Bernd's sister, Alexandra, describes her family. As you listen, indicate whether the following statements are correct or incorrect.

	DAS STIMMT	DAS STIMMT NICHT
1. Das Foto zeigt Familie Thalhofer bei einer Geburtstagsfeier.	☐	☐
2. Familie Thalhofer wohnt in Leipzig.	☐	☐
3. Alexandra Thalhofer hat zwei Brüder.	☐	☐
4. Ihr Bruder Bernd und Bernds Frau, Bettina, sind Lehrer von Beruf.	☐	☐
5. Alexandra plant eine Reise nach Kanada.	☐	☐
6. Alexandras Bruder Werner hat zwei Kinder.	☐	☐
7. Alexandras Mutter ist nicht auf dem Foto.	☐	☐

Wörter im Kontext

A family tree **THEMA 1: Ein Familienstammbaum°**

Bernd Thalhofers Familie

¹geb. = geborene *maiden name*

Wer ist wer? How is each relative related to you?

1. der Bruder
2. der **Enkel**
3. die **Enkelin**
4. die **Geschwister** (*pl.*)
5. die **Großeltern** (*pl.*)
6. die **Großmutter (Oma)**
7. der **Großvater (Opa)**
8. die Kusine
9. der **Neffe**
10. die **Nichte**
11. der Onkel
12. der **Schwager**
13. die **Schwägerin**
14. die Schwester
15. die Tante
16. der Vetter

a. Mein ___9___: der **Sohn** meines (*of my*) Bruders oder meiner (*of my*) Schwester
b. Meine ___14___: die **Tochter** meiner Eltern
c. Meine ___10___: die Tochter meines Bruders oder meiner Schwester
d. Meine ___15___: die Schwester meines Vaters oder meiner Mutter
e. Mein ___2___: der Sohn meines Sohnes oder meiner Tochter
f. Mein ___12___: der **Mann** meiner Schwester
g. Meine ___4___: die Söhne und Töchter meiner Eltern
h. Meine ___6___: die Mutter meines Vaters oder meiner Mutter
i. Mein ___11___: der Bruder meines Vaters oder meiner Mutter
j. Mein ___1___: der Sohn meiner Eltern
k. Mein ___16___: der Sohn meines Onkels und meiner Tante
l. Meine ___3___: die Tochter meines Sohnes oder meiner Tochter
m. Meine ___13___: die **Frau** meines Bruders
n. Meine ___5___: die Eltern meiner Eltern
o. Meine ___8___: die Tochter meines Onkels und meiner Tante
p. Mein ___7___: der Vater meines Vaters oder meiner Mutter

Wer ist wer? Note: You may want to mention the French-derived variants *Cousin* and *Cousine* for *Vetter* and *Kusine* and that many Germans prefer *Cousin* for male cousins.

Alternate activity: This activity lends itself to introducing certain possessive adjectives, especially *mein, Ihr, sein,* and *ihr.* After having students work on the activity in pairs, begin by telling the class, e.g., *Mein Onkel heißt Henry,* and ask a male student *Haben Sie einen Onkel? —Ja. —Wie heißt er? —Bob.* Then turn to the rest of the class, point to the student with the uncle, and say *Sein Onkel heißt Bob.* Then do the same with a female student to present *ihr: Ihr Onkel heißt John.*

Follow-up: Have students work in pairs asking similar questions of each other in order to present *dein.*

SPRACHTIPP

As in English, to indicate that somebody is related to another person, add an **-s** to the person's name—though without an apostrophe.

Das ist Bernd **Thalhofers** Familie.
Bernds Eltern heißen Werner und Helene.

Another way to indicate relationships is with the preposition **von** (*of*).

Das ist die Familie **von** Bernd Thalhofer.
Die Eltern **von** Bernd heißen Werner und Helene.

The **von** construction is preferred if a name ends in an **-s** or **-z**.

Die Frau **von** Markus heißt Julia.
Die Eltern **von** Frau Lentz kommen aus München.

Unscramble the letters to find out which family member each item represents. The vocabulary at the top of the previous page will help you.

1. feeNf
2. eTtna
3. esKnui
4. treeVt
5. chNeti

6. klnOe
7. sewrStche
8. drerBu
9. tmßGorture
10. rVaet

Schritt 1: Ask a person in your class about his/her family.

1. Wie heißen deine Eltern?
2. Wie viele Geschwister hast du?
3. Wie heißen deine Geschwister?
4. Wo wohnt deine Familie?
5. Wie alt sind deine Geschwister?
6. ??

Schritt 2: Report back to the class about your partner's family.

BEISPIEL: Jennys Familie wohnt in Toronto. Jenny hat fünf Brüder und drei Schwestern. Ihre Brüder heißen Mark und Stephen ...

SPRACHTIPP

To indicate that someone is related only through one parent, compounds can be formed using **Stief-** (*step*) and **Halb-** (*half*). The German equivalent to English *great* is the prefix **Ur-**.

Maria ist meine **Stiefschwester.**	*Maria is my stepsister.*
Mein **Halbbruder** heißt Jens.	*My half-brother is named Jens.*
Wilhelmine ist meine **Urgroßmutter.**	*Wilhelmine is my great-grandmother.*

Schritt 1: Look closely at the family portrait on the next page and answer the questions.

1. Wie viele Generationen sind auf diesem Foto?
2. Wie heißen die Frauen mit Vornamen?
3. Wie heißen die zwei jüngsten (*youngest*) Frauen? Wie alt sind sie?
4. Wer ist die älteste (*oldest*) Frau? Wie alt ist sie?
5. Wer ist die Mutter von Susanne und Nicole?
6. Wer ist die Großmutter von Frauke?
7. Wer ist die Tochter von Pauline?

Landkinder: Tochter Susanne, 18; Großmutter Alma, 63; Tochter Nicole, 19; Urgroßmutter Pauline, 87; Mutter Frauke, 40

Schritt 2: Now fill in the missing information.

1. Susanne ist Fraukes ___Tochter___.
2. Pauline ist Susannes und Nicoles ___Urgroßmutter___ und Fraukes ___Großmutter___.
3. Alma ist Paulines ___Tochter___ und Susannes und Nicoles ___Großmutter___.
4. ___Nicole___ spielt gern Fußball. Sie ist Paulines Enkelin.
5. Alma hat zwei Enkelinnen, ___Susanne___ und ___Nicole___. Und wer ist das in der Mitte? Sie gehört (*belongs*) auch zur Familie.

Aktivität 4 Ein merkwürdiger° Stammbaum

A very special family is celebrating its birthday. What is the name of the family?

1. Welche Namen kennen Sie, welche Namen kennen Sie nicht?
2. Wer fehlt (*is missing*) in diesem Stammbaum? Ich sehe keine/keinen ___Mutter, Vater, …___.
3. Wer hat keinen Namen?   *der Großvater*
4. Das Insekt hier ist ein Käfer. Wie heißt „Käfer" auf Englisch?   *beetle*
5. Wissen Sie, wie alt der Großvater ungefähr (*roughly*) ist?
   a. über 100 Jahre
   b. ungefähr 60–70 Jahre
   c. ungefähr 10 Jahre
6. Wie heißt die „Käfer" Familie?   *Volkswagen*

peculiar

DER GROSSVATER.

DIE SCHWESTER KARMANN GHIA.   DER BRUDER KÄFER.

DER ONKEL ILTIS.   DIE TANTE GOLF.   DER NEFFE PASSAT.

DER VETTER POLO.   DIE COUSINE JETTA.   DER COUSIN SANTANA.   DER ENKELIN SCIROCCO.

Wir gratulieren der ganzen Familie.

die Monate	
Januar	Juli
Februar	August
März	September
April	Oktober
Mai	November
Juni	Dezember

Oktober

Montag	Dienstag	Mittwoch	Donnerstag	Freitag	Samstag	Sonntag
4	5	6	7	1	2	3
11	12	13	14	8	9	10
18	19	20	21	15	16	17
25	26	27	28	22	23	24
				29	30	31

Aktivität 5 Welcher Tag ist das?

Newspaper ads often abbreviate the days of the week. Can you identify which days of the week these abbreviations represent?

1. Mo _____

2. Fr _____

3. Do _____

4. So _____

5. Mi _____

6. Sa _____

7. Di _____

SPRACHTIPP

Use the following phrases to say the day or month when something takes place.

—Wann wirst du 21?
—Ich werde **am Samstag** 21.

—Wann hast du Geburtstag?
—Ich habe **im Dezember** Geburtstag.

Refer to *The Irregular Verbs* **werden** *and* **wissen**, p. 102.

Aktivität 6 Wie alt bist du?

Interview several classmates to learn their ages and birthdates.

BEISPIEL: s1: Wie alt bist du?
s2: Ich bin 23.
s1: Wann wirst du 24?
s2: Ich werde im August 24. Und du?

Aktivität 7 Eine Einladung° zum Geburtstag

invitation

Listen and take notes as Tom and Heike talk about an upcoming birthday party. Read the questions first before listening to the conversation.

1. Wer hat Geburtstag? Heike
2. Wann ist der Geburtstag? Samstag
3. Wo ist die Party? bei Heike zu Hause
4. Wer kommt sonst noch (*else*)? Gabi, Jürgen, Heikes Eltern und Geschwister
5. Kommt die Person am Telefon, oder nicht? Ja, er kommt.

Aktivität 7. Suggestion: Students should scan the questions before listening to the dialogue. Play the tape once; students answer as many questions as they can, based on one listening. Play the tape a second time and have students complete any unfinished questions.

Aktivität 8 Hin und her: Verwandtschaften°

relationships

Ask a partner questions about Bernd's family. How is each person related to Bernd?

BEISPIEL: s1: Wie ist Gisela mit Bernd verwandt?
s2: Gisela ist Bernds Tante.
s1: Wie alt ist sie denn?
s2: Sie ist 53.
s1: Wann hat sie Geburtstag?
s2: Im Februar.

Additional activity: Have students create a similar chart with real family members, keeping kinship terms but changing names, ages, and birthdays.

PERSON	VERWANDTSCHAFT	ALTER	GEBURTSTAG
Gisela	Tante	53	Februar
Alexandra	Schwester	25	März
Christoph	Schwager	36	Dezember
Andreas	Großvater	80	Juni
Sabine	Kusine	19	August

THEMA 3: Feste und Feiertage°

Geburtstagswünsche

Celebrations and holidays

Germans express birthday wishes in many ways. Here are some typical birthday wishes taken from German newspapers.

♥ **Heike**
wird heute
„21"
Herzlichen Glückwunsch

Lieber Vater und Opa!
Zu Deinem 85. Geburtstag gratulieren
Hansi −Waltraud − Angela − Torsten
Birgit − Peter − Jan und Marco

Hallo Belinda!
Viel Glück und alles Gute
zum 18.
wünschen Mutti und Papa
und der ganze Clan.
W. W. B. U. S. U. J. D. M.
S. W. P. S. W. und Chris

Ralf hat
Geburtstag!
Alles Gute!

Liebe Oma *Marie Sudhoff*
zu Deinem **80. Geburtstag** wünschen
Dir Deine Kinder, Enkel und Urenkel alles
Liebe und Gute.

Neue Wörter

wird (werden) turns, becomes
Herzlichen Glückwunsch (zum Geburtstag) Happy birthday!
gratulieren congratulate
Alles Gute! All the best!
wünschen wish

Feste und Feiertage. Suggestion: Ask students about personal announcements in the newspaper, both the local one and the student newspaper at their institution, if there is one. Brainstorm with them about the kinds of events that lead to announcements: births, deaths, retirement, graduation, anniversaries, high school reunions, and birthdays. Introduce the *Geburtstagswünsche* in **Thema 3** as examples of the kinds of birthday announcements German speakers place in the newspaper.

Answer these questions about the birthday greetings in **Thema 3**.

- Find at least two different expressions of good wishes in the ads.
- Who are the family members who are sending birthday greetings to Belinda? to Marie Sudhoff?
- Marie Sudhoff is being addressed as "**liebe Oma.**" To which family member does the term **Oma** refer? What is another word for **Oma**?
- One birthday greeting gives no name but says only "**lieber Vater und Opa.**" Is this ad directed to one or two people? What clue(s) helped you arrive at your answer? What is another word for **Opa**?

Feiertage in der Familie Thalhofer

Valentinstag ist relativ **neu** für viele Deutsche. Bernd und Alexandra **kennen** diesen Tag aus den USA. Muttertag ist für Frau Thalhofer nicht so **wichtig**, aber ihre Familie gibt ihr **oft** Blumen.

Dieses Jahr gibt es noch eine **Hochzeit** in Bernds Familie. Seine Kusine Sabine **heiratet** nämlich im September.

Die Familie **plant** ein großes **Familienfest** mit einem Abendessen in der Marxburg am Rhein. Bernds Großeltern feiern dieses Jahr ihre goldene Hochzeit, aber sie **wissen** noch nicht wo.

Bernd hat im April Geburtstag. Dieses Jahr **feiert** er mit seiner Frau Bettina bei Freunden in Berlin. Natürlich feiern sie auch bei den Eltern in Köln, und **es gibt** auch eine kleine **Party** und natürlich auch **Geschenke**.

Weihnachten hat eine lange **Tradition. Am Heiligen Abend** gibt es Geschenke und ein Familienessen. Auch am ersten Weihnachtstag (25. Dezember) feiert die Familie zusammen. Am zweiten Weihnachtstag (26. Dezember) besucht die Familie die Großeltern, Tanten und Onkel.

Silvester sind Thalhofers oft bei Freunden. **Um Mitternacht** gibt es dann oft ein kleines Feuerwerk im Garten. Manchmal bleiben sie aber auch zu Hause.

Neue Wörter

neu new
kennen know
wichtig important
die Hochzeit wedding
heiratet (heiraten) is getting married
plant (planen) is planning
das Familienfest family gathering
wissen know
feiert (feiern) celebrates
es gibt there is
das Geschenk (Geschenke, *pl.*) present
das Weihnachten Christmas
am Heiligen Abend on Christmas Eve
das Silvester New Year's Eve
um Mitternacht at midnight

To form most ordinal numbers (*first, second, third,* and so on) in German, add the suffix **-te** or **-ste** to the cardinal number. Note that the words for *first, third, seventh,* and *eighth* are exceptions to the rule.

eins	**erste**	neun	neun**te**
zwei	zwei**te**	zehn	zehn**te**
drei	**dritte**	elf	elf**te**
vier	vier**te**	zwölf	zwölf**te**
fünf	fünf**te**	dreizehn	dreizehn**te**
sechs	sechs**te**	. . .	. . .
sieben	**sieb(en)te**	zwanzig	zwanzig**ste**
acht	**achte**		

Ordinal numbers are normally used with the definite article.

Freitag ist **der erste** Oktober.

To talk about dates for special occasions, you can say:

Wann hast du Geburtstag? —**Am 18. (achtzehnten)** September.

Der erste Weihnachtstag ist **am 25. (fünfundzwanzigsten)** Dezember.

Note that ordinal numbers are written with a period: **der 4. Juli; am 4. Juli.**

Sprachtipp. Suggestion: Practice dates with ordinal numbers using the calendar at the beginning of Thema 2 or a current calendar: *Was ist Samstag? —Samstag ist (der zweite) Oktober. —Und Sonntag? —Sonntag ist (der dritte) Oktober. —Und was ist morgen? —Morgen ist _____.*

Suggestion: You may wish to point out that many German speakers give the date in numbers even in speech, e.g., *Wann hast du Geburtstag? —Am achtzehnten neunten.*

Hier klicken!

You'll find more about holidays and festivals in German-speaking countries in **Deutsch: Na klar!** on the World Wide Web at www.mhhe.com/dnk5.

KULTURTIPP

Legal holidays in German-speaking countries are largely religious holidays. The most important ones are Christmas (**Weihnachten**), New Year (**Neujahr**), and Easter (**Ostern**) and are celebrated for two days each. An important nonreligious holiday in Germany is the Day of German Unity (**Tag der deutschen Einheit**) on October 3.

There are a number of regional holidays as well. Mardi Gras (**Karneval** in the Rhineland and **Fasching** in southern Germany) is celebrated before Lent, in early spring. People get one day off work to participate in the merriment in and out of doors. Germans in northern and eastern regions do not celebrate Mardi Gras.

Germans go all out for family celebrations such as weddings and silver and golden wedding anniversaries.

Karneval in Köln

Match up the German holidays and celebrations with their English equivalents.

1. _____ Weihnachten   **a.** Mardi Gras
2. _____ Karneval   **b.** Christmas Eve
3. _____ Geburtstag   **c.** Easter
4. _____ Ostern   **d.** Labor Day
5. _____ Silvester   **e.** birthday
6. _____ Hochzeit   **f.** wedding
7. _____ der Heilige Abend   **g.** Memorial Day
8. _____ Tag der deutschen Einheit   **h.** German Unity Day
                             i. Christmas
                             j. New Year's Eve

Choose several of the following words and phrases to create birthday greetings for someone.

alles Gute   du wirst   ich gratuliere   liebe _____

herzlichen Glückwunsch   lieber _____   viel Glück

wir gratulieren   wünscht / wünschen dir   zum Geburtstag

zu deinem _____ Geburtstag   _____ wird _____

Invite someone to a party, using the expressions provided.

BEISPIEL: s1: Ich mache am Sonntag eine Party. Kommst du?
          s2: Am Sonntag? Vielen Dank. Ich komme gern. [*oder*]
              Vielen Dank. Leider kann ich nicht kommen.

OTHER EXCUSES

Es tut mir leid. / Ich bin leider nicht zu Hause. / Ich fahre nämlich nach _____. / Mein Vater / Meine Mutter usw. (*and so on*) hat nämlich auch Geburtstag.

Neue Wörter

Es tut mir leid. I'm sorry.
leider unfortunately
nämlich namely, that is to say
morgen tomorrow

SPRACHTIPP

When stating your reason for an action, use the adverb **nämlich.** Note that there is no exact equivalent of **nämlich** in English.

Ich kann nicht kommen. Ich fahre **nämlich** nach Hamburg.
I cannot come. The reason is, I am going to Hamburg.

Grammatik im Kontext

Possessive Adjectives°

Possessivartikel

Possessive adjectives (e.g., *my, your, his, our*) indicate ownership or belonging.

—Wie ist **Ihr** Name?   *What is your name?*
—**Mein** Name ist Schiller.   *My name is Schiller.*

Wie heißt **deine** Schwester?   *What's your sister's name?*

Sandra, 8 Jahre: *Meine Mutter Martina, mein Bruder Kelvin, meine Schwester Andrea, mein Vater Uli und ich beim Fahrrad fahren*

Possessive Adjectives. Suggestion: To give a contextualized introduction to possessive adjectives, point to yourself and describe your immediate family. *Mein Vater heißt _____ und meine Mutter heißt _____.* Ask a couple of students about their parents: *Wie heißen Ihre Eltern / Ihr Vater / Ihre Mutter?* Rephrase students' responses using the appropriate possessive adjective: *Seine Mutter heißt _____ und sein Vater heißt _____. Ihr Vater heißt _____* and so on.

Each possessive adjective corresponds to a personal pronoun.

SINGULAR		PLURAL	
PERSONAL PRONOUN	POSSESSIVE ADJECTIVE	PERSONAL PRONOUN	POSSESSIVE ADJECTIVE
ich	**mein** *my*	wir	**unser** *our*
du	**dein** *your (informal)*	ihr	**euer** *your (informal)*
Sie	**Ihr** *your (formal)*	Sie	**Ihr** *your (formal)*
er	**sein** *his; its*		
sie	**ihr** *her; its*	sie	**ihr** *their*
es	**sein** *its*		

Possessives—short for possessive adjectives—take the same endings as the indefinite article **ein.** They are sometimes called **ein**-words because their endings are the same as those of **ein.** Unlike **ein,** however, they also have plural forms. They agree in gender, case, and number with the nouns they modify.

The nominative and accusative forms of **mein** and **unser** illustrate the pattern for all possessives.

	SINGULAR			PLURAL
	Masculine	*Neuter*	*Feminine*	*All Genders*
Nominative	mein Freund unser Freund	mein Buch unser Buch	mein**e** Oma unser**e** Oma	mein**e** Eltern unser**e** Eltern
Accusative	mein**en** Freund unser**en** Freund	mein Buch unser Buch	mein**e** Oma unser**e** Oma	mein**e** Eltern unser**e** Eltern

Note:

- The masculine singular possessive adjective is the only one for which the accusative form differs from the nominative: **Mein   meinen, unser   unseren.**

- The formal possessive adjective **Ihr** (*your*) is capitalized, just like the formal personal pronoun **Sie** (*you*).

- The possessive adjective **euer** (*your*) drops the **e** of the stem when an ending is added: **eu̶e̶re   eure, eu̶e̶ren   euren.**

- Scan the Valentine's Day greetings taken from a German newspaper and identify all possessive adjectives.
- In each case, determine whether the possessives refer to a male or female individual or to several people. What is the gender of each name or noun?

Analyse. Suggestion: Have students create their own Valentine messages, using expressions found in the ads and possessive adjectives.

Herzliche Grüße zum Valentinstag

Liebe Beate,
ich liebe Dich

Dein Rainer

GF100037

**Für meine Lieben
Helmut und Sandra**
einen lieben Gruß und ein dickes Küsschen[1]
Eure Doris Ma   GF100081

Hallo Maus!
Nun ist es doch schon das 4. Jahr!
In Liebe Deine Katze
GE90558

**Guten Morgen,
mein Tiger**
Die Welt[2] ist wieder schön durch Dich.
Dein Stern von Rio GD81183

Lieber Andre!
Alles Liebe zum Valentinstag.
Dein Häschen
GF100036

Liebe Christina
Zum Valentinstag herzliche Grüße und alles Liebe und Gute wünscht
Dir Dein Vater
GC114748

---

[1]ein ... *a big kiss*
[2]*world*

Übung 1   Herzlichen Glückwunsch!

You will hear eight congratulatory messages taken from a radio program. Write out who receives the greetings (**der Empfänger**) and who sends them (**der Absender**). Include the possessive adjectives you hear, if any. Follow the example.

Übung 1. Note: It is a common practice on local radio stations to have a program for reading congratulatory messages. Tell students it is not necessary to write names.

	EMPFÄNGER	ABSENDER
1.	*unsere Mutter*	*deine Kinder*
2.	unser Opa	deine Enkel
3.	Uwe	deine Freundin
4.	unser Vater	deine Söhne
5.	unsere Tochter	deine Eltern
6.	Eltern	eure Kinder
7.	meine Kinder	eure Mutter
8.	Gabi	dein Tiger

Dirk und Ute machen eine Website über ihre Familie.

Schritt 1: Complete each sentence with the correct form of **unser.**

1. Hier seht ihr _____ Haus in Bonn.
2. Und das ist _____ Familie.
3. Da links ist _____ Sohn. Er heißt Dylan und ist 23 Jahre alt.
4. Und hier ist _____ Tochter. Sie heißt Lena und ist 19.
5. Und hier seht ihr _____ Hund. Er heißt Rakete.

Schritt 2: Now restate the sentences from **Schritt 1** using the correct form of **mein.**

BEISPIEL: Hier seht ihr mein Haus in Bonn.

Complete each sentence with the appropriate possessive adjective.

BEISPIEL: sie (Frau Müller): Wo ist _ihr_ Mann? Sie sucht _ihren_ Mann.

1. er (Herr Müller): Wo ist _____ Frau? Er sucht _____ Frau.
2. sie (Herr und Frau Müller): Wo sind _____ Kinder? Sie suchen _____ Kinder.
3. du: Wo ist _____ Schwester? Suchst du _____ Schwester?
4. ihr: Wo sind _____ Eltern? Ihr sucht _____ Eltern.
5. wir: Wo ist _____ Großvater? Wir suchen _____ Großvater.
6. ich: Wo ist _____ Handy? Ich suche _____ Handy schon den ganzen Tag.

everyday life

Complete the minidialogues with appropriate possessive adjectives.

1. CLAUDIA: Hier ist ____ neue Telefonnummer.

   STEFAN: Gut, und ____ neue Adresse?

   CLAUDIA: ____ neue Adresse ist Rosenbachweg 2.

2. LILO: Und dies hier ist ____ Freund.

   HELGA: Wie heißt er denn?

   LILO: ____ Name ist Max.

   HELGA: Max? Na, so was! So heißt nämlich ____ Hund.

3. HERR WEIDNER: Und was sind Sie von Beruf, Frau Rudolf?

   FRAU RUDOLF: Ich bin Automechanikerin.

   HERR WEIDNER: Und was ist ____ Mann von Beruf?

   FRAU RUDOLF: ____ Mann ist Hausmann.

   HERR WEIDNER: Hausmann?

4. FRAU SANDERS: Ach, wie niedlich! Ist das ____ Tochter?

   FRAU KARSTEN: Ja, das ist ____ Tochter.

   FRAU SANDERS: Und ist das ____ Hund?

   FRAU KARSTEN: Ja, das ist ____ Hund. Das ist der Caesar.

5. INGE: Kennst du _meinen_ Freund Klaus?

ERNST: Ich kenne Klaus nicht, aber ich kenne _seine_ Schwester.

INGE: Morgen besuchen wir _seine_ Eltern in Stuttgart.

6. KLAUS: Morgen fahren Inge und ich nach Stuttgart. Da wohnen _ihre_ (*her*) Eltern.

KURT: Wie fahrt ihr denn?

KLAUS: Wir nehmen _mein_ (*my*) Auto.

KURT: _Dein_ Auto?

KLAUS: Na, klar. Warum denn nicht?

KURT: _Dein_ Auto gehört ins Museum, nicht auf die Autobahn.

7. POLIZIST: Ist das _Ihr_ Auto?

FRAU KUNZE: Ja, leider ist das _mein_ Auto.

POLIZIST: Hier ist Parkverbot.

Übung 5 Persönliche Angaben

Schritt 1: Complete a personal profile of yourself. Add one or two items of your own choice.

_____ Name ist _____.

_____ Adresse ist _____.

_____ Telefonnummer ist _____.

_____ Familie wohnt in _____.

_____ Mutter heißt _____.

_____ Vater heißt _____.

_____ Geschwister heißen _____.

_____ Auto/Motorrad/Fahrrad ist ein _____.

_____ Geburtstag ist im _____. (z.B. Juli)

_____ Lieblingsessen (*favorite food*) ist _____.

_____ Hobby ist _____.

_____ Freund/Freundin heißt _____.

?????

Schritt 2: Exchange personal profiles with someone in your class and report about him/her to the class.

BEISPIEL: Das ist Sam Lee. Seine Telefonnummer ist 555–8762.
Sein Lieblingsessen ist Pizza. ...

Personal Pronouns in the Accusative Case°

You have already learned the personal pronouns for the nominative case. Here are the corresponding accusative forms.

SINGULAR			PLURAL		
NOMINATIVE	**ACCUSATIVE**		**NOMINATIVE**	**ACCUSATIVE**	
ich	**mich**	*me*	wir	**uns**	*us*
du	**dich**	*you (informal)*	ihr	**euch**	*you (informal)*
Sie	**Sie**	*you (formal)*	Sie	**Sie**	*you (formal)*
er	**ihn**	*him; it*			
sie	**sie**	*her; it*	sie	**sie**	*them*
es	**es**	*it*			

Note:

- The third-person singular pronouns **ihn, sie,** and **es** must agree in gender with the noun to which they refer.
- In the accusative case, **ihn** can mean *him* or *it*, and **sie** can mean *her* or *it* depending on the gender of the noun to which they refer.

—Kennst du **meinen Freund?**	*Do you know my friend?*
—Ja, ich kenne **ihn.**	*Yes, I know him.*
—Brauchst du **den Computer?**	*Do you need the computer?*
—Na klar brauche ich **ihn.**	*I absolutely do need it.*
—Hast du **meine Telefon-nummer?**	*Do you have my phone number?*
—Ich glaube, ich habe **sie.**	*I think I have it.*

Identify all personal pronouns in the ads and announcements and determine whether they are in the nominative or in the accusative case. Then provide the English meaning of each phrase.

Gourmets lieben ihn.

Mein Schatz,[1]
Ich liebe Dich.
Deine Jutta
GA140650

[1]*mein ... my dear*

Ruth Brandt,
Unsere Omi ist das Liebste,[1] was wir haben,
das wollen wir heute einmal[2] sagen:
WIR LIEBEN DICH

Deine Kinder
Deine Enkelkinder

[1]*das ... the dearest thing that* [2]*just*

Wir sind da, wo Sie uns brauchen.

SYSTEMS 93

Übung 6 Wer kennt wen?

Supply the missing direct-object personal pronouns corresponding to the nominative pronouns provided.

BEISPIEL: Ich kenne _euch_ (ihr).

1. Ich kenne ___dich___ (du).
2. Kennst du ___mich___ (ich) denn nicht?
3. Du kennst ja meine Familie. Oder kennst du ___sie___ (sie) nicht?
4. Wir kennen ___euch___ (ihr) aber schon lange.
5. Hier kommt Herr Wunderlich. Kennst du ___ihn___ (er)?
6. Herr Wunderlich kennt ___uns___ (wir).
7. Ich kenne die Stadt nicht so gut. Meine Freundin kennt ___sie___ (sie) aber sehr gut.

Übung 7 Liebst° du das? Ja oder nein?

Answer the following questions using a pronoun in your answer. The genders of unfamiliar words are provided in parentheses.

BEISPIEL: Liebst du Schweizer Käse? (der Käse) →
   Ja, ich liebe ihn.
  oder: Nein, ich liebe ihn nicht.

1. Liebst du deutsches Bier? (das Bier)
2. Liebst du den neuen BMW? (der BMW)
3. Liebst du Partys?
4. Liebst du Geld?
5. Liebst du Familienfeste?
6. Liebst du Hip-Hop-Musik? (die Musik)
7. Liebst du Jessica Simpson?
8. Liebst du Brad Pitt?

Übung 8 Im Café Kadenz

Several students are conversing at different tables at the Café Kadenz. Complete the blanks with appropriate personal pronouns in the nominative or the accusative case.

1. A: Wie findest ___du___ den Professor Klinger?
   B: Also, ich finde ___ihn___ unmöglich. ___Er___ kommt nie pünktlich. Wir warten (wait) und warten, dann kommt ___er___ endlich und hält seine Vorlesung, keine Diskussion, keine Fragen, nichts. ___Er___ ist echt langweilig.
   A: Ich verstehe ___dich___ nicht, Karin. Warum gehst du dann hin?
2. C: Machst du jetzt das Linguistik-Seminar?
   D: Ja, ich brauche ___es___ für mein Hauptfach (major).
3. E: Und wie findest du deine Mitbewohner im Wohnheim?
   F: Ich finde ___sie___ ganz prima. Da sind zwei Italienerinnen aus Venedig. ___Sie___ sind wirklich nett. Ich verstehe ___sie___ allerdings nicht immer.
4. G: Im Lumière läuft der Film „Paradies jetzt". Kennst du ___ihn___?
   H: Nein, aber die Filmkritiker finden ___ihn___ ausgezeichnet.
5. I: Da kommt endlich unser Kaffee. Wie trinkst du ___ihn___?
   J: Gewöhnlich trinke ich ___ihn___ schwarz.
6. K: Meine Eltern besuchen ___mich___ nächste Woche. Das ist immer stressig.
   L: Ja, ich verstehe ___dich___ gut.

Übung 6. Additional items: 8. Herr Wunderlich, meine Eltern kennen _____ (Sie) nicht, oder? 9. Aber Ihr Schwager kennt _____ (ich), ja? 10. Herr Wunderlich, hören Sie gern Opern von Richard Strauss? Was? Sie kennen _____ (er) nicht? 11. Seine Opern finde ich sehr schön. Kennen Sie _____ (sie) nicht? 12. Da ist das neue Restaurant Salomé. Herr Wunderlich, kennen Sie _____ (es)?

Love

Übung 7. Alternate exercise: This can also be done as a partner exercise, with students taking turns asking and answering the questions.

Additional activity: Bring in the German-language recording of the Beatles song "Sie liebt dich" ("She loves you") and give students the lyrics as a Lückentext with the accusative personal pronouns (and some of the subject pronouns) missing. Have students listen for the missing words. A second listening may be useful for catching words missed during the first listening.

Übung 8. Suggestion: Assign individual conversations to pairs of students. Have each pair act out its conversation. Also suitable as homework.

Grammatik im Kontext   **99**

With a partner, create five questions regarding student life. Then interview several people in your class.

BEISPIEL: s1: Wie findest du die Vorlesungen von Professor Ziegler?
s2: Ich finde sie ausgezeichnet. Und du?
s1: Ich finde sie zu lang.

Essen in der Mensa	ausgezeichnet
Kaffee in der Mensa	faul
Leben (*life*) an der Uni	sympathisch
Uni-Zeitung	langweilig
Studenten an der Uni	schlecht
Mitbewohner im Studentenheim	gut
Professor _____	freundlich
Film _____	interessant
Freund/Freundin	arrogant
??	??

Prepositions with the Accusative Case°

Präpositionen mit dem Akkusativ

You have already seen and used a number of German prepositions.

Ich studiere Architektur **in** Berlin.

Ich brauche eine Lampe **für** meinen Schreibtisch.

The use of prepositions, in English as well as in German, is highly idiomatic. An important difference, however, is that German prepositions require certain cases; that is, some prepositions are followed by nouns or pronouns in the accusative case, others by nouns or pronouns in other cases. In this chapter, we focus on prepositions that always require the accusative case.

Wir tun etwas **gegen** den Hunger.	*We are doing something against hunger.*
Es ist **gegen** fünf Uhr.	*It's around five o'clock.*
Herr Krause fährt **durch** die Stadt.	*Mr. Krause drives through town.*
Er braucht ein Geschenk **für** seine Tochter.	*He needs a gift for his daughter.*
Er geht **ohne** seine Frau einkaufen.	*He goes shopping without his wife.*
Die Geburtstagsfeier beginnt **um** sechs.	*The birthday party begins at six.*

Er sucht einen Parkplatz und fährt dreimal **um** den Marktplatz (**herum**).

He looks for a parking space and drives around the marketplace three times.

ACCUSATIVE PREPOSITIONS	
durch	through, across
für	for
gegen	against; around (*with time*)
ohne	without
um	at (*with time*)
um (… herum)	around (*a place*)

Note:

- When the preposition **um** is used to indicate movement around something, the word **herum** is often added after the place.

  um die Stadt (**herum**)

- Three accusative prepositions often contract with the article **das.**

  durch das → **durchs** Zimmer

  für das → **fürs** Auto

  um das → **ums** Haus

Alles fürs Auto
22 x in Bayern • 5 x in Österreich

Übung 10   Dieter braucht ein Geschenk

Choose the correct preposition.

1. Dieter braucht dringend ein Geburtstagsgeschenk __für__ (um/für) seine Freundin Sonja.

2. Leider hat Sonja schon alles, aber __ohne__ (ohne/durch) Geschenk geht es nicht.

3. Dieter gibt __um__ (für/um) sieben Uhr abends eine kleine Party __für__ (für/ohne) sie.

4. Sonja hat Partys gern, aber sie ist __gegen__ (gegen/ohne) große Partys.

5. Dieter fährt also in die Stadt. Er fährt dreimal __um__ (um/durch) den Marktplatz herum. Er sucht einen Parkplatz. Er findet nichts.

6. Er fährt und fährt __durch__ (um/durch) die Straßen.

7. Er sucht und sucht __ohne__ (für/ohne) Erfolg (*success*). Was nun?

8. Er parkt schließlich illegal. Was tut er nicht alles __für__ (ohne/für) Sonja.

9. Was macht Sonja Spaß? Kochen! Also ein Kochbuch __für__ (durch/für) Vegetarier. (Sonja ist nämlich Vegetarierin.)

10. Im Buchladen geht Dieter __um__ (für/um) den Tisch mit (*with*) Kochbüchern herum.

11. Es gibt tausend Kochbücher __für__ (für/gegen) Vegetarier. Was tun?

Uwe is having difficulty choosing birthday gifts for friends and relatives. Express your gift recommendations based on the facts provided about everyone. Include a suitable adjective in your answer, such as **perfekt, passend** (*suitable*), **praktisch, originell, nett, gut,** or **schön.**

BEISPIEL: Seine Oma geht oft in die Stadt ins Café. →
  Ich finde den Hut gut für seine Oma.

1. Seine Tante Ingrid lernt Kochen in Paris.
2. Seine Eltern reisen und fotografieren viel.
3. Sein Großvater wandert gern.
4. Sein Bruder Dirk schläft immer zu lange.
5. Seine Schwester Maria fährt nach Spanien.
6. Seine Freundin Sara trägt gern Schmuck (*jewelry*).
7. Seine Kusine Julia ist ein Fitnessfan.
8. Seine Mutter liest gern Detektivromane.
9. Sein Freund Marco ist etwas exzentrisch.

| der Wecker | das Buch | die Zehensocken | der Ring | der Hut |

| Die Fitness-DVD | zwei Wanderstöcke | der Holzlöffel | die Sonnenbrille | das Fotoalbum |

Unregelmäßige Verben

The Irregular Verbs° **werden** and **wissen**

Two common verbs that show irregularities in the present tense are **werden** (*to become*) and **wissen** (*to know*).

Heidewitzka, Herr Kapitän!
Der beste Opa der Welt wird 70!

Es gratulieren:
David
Inge
Ulf
Uwe
Sandra
Schira
Afra

Helmut
2.7. 2007

	werden	*wissen*
ich	werde	**weiß**
du	**wirst**	**weißt**
er sie es	**wird**	**weiß**
wir	werden	wissen
ihr	werdet	wisst
sie/Sie	werden	wissen

Übung 12   Kennen Sie eigentlich meine Familie?

Complete the sentences using the appropriate form of **werden.**

1. Ich __werde__ im September 16 Jahre alt.
2. Meine zwei Kusinen __werden__ am Samstag 13.
3. Mein kleiner Bruder Bernd __wird__ im November 11.
4. Meine kleine Schwester Sara __wird__ dieses Jahr 5 Jahre alt.
5. Mein Vater hat im Dezember Geburtstag. Er __wird__ 38 Jahre alt.
6. Mein Großvater fragt immer: „Wann __wirst__ du 15?" Er vergisst
   (*forgets*), dass ich schon 15 bin!

Übung 13   Eine Umfrage: Wer wird wann wie alt?

Do a class poll:

1. Wer _____ dieses Jahr _____ Jahre alt?
2. Wie viele Leute _____ dieses Jahr 19?
3. Wann _____ du 50? 100? (Ich werde in 30 Jahren 50.)
4. Wann _____ dein Freund oder deine Freundin 19, 21, 25?

Übung 13. Suggestion: Have students ask a variation of question 1 of a number of classmates and write down their answers. (*Wie alt wirst du dieses Jahr?*) Then ask the whole class the questions in the exercise. Students answer with information gathered about a classmate (e.g., *Barbara wird dieses Jahr 22; in 78 Jahren wird sie 100.*).

Wissen/Kennen. **Suggestion:** Practice *kennen* first by asking a number of simple questions that students answer simply with *nein/ja.* (*Kennen Sie ... Professor/Film/Buch/Spiel ... ?*) Then practice *wissen* with simple questions (*Wie viele Studenten studieren Deutsch?*) that allow students to answer: *Das weiß ich nicht.* Finally, add the idea of an indirect question: *Wissen Sie, wo ich wohne?* Keep questions brief to avoid complications with the end position of the verb.

Using the Verbs wissen and kennen

[1]*nobody*

The verbs **wissen** and **kennen** both mean *to know.* **Wissen** means *to know facts,* while **kennen** means *to know or be acquainted/familiar with a person or thing.*

Ich **weiß** deine Telefonnummer nicht.	*I don't know your phone number.*
Ich **kenne** Herrn Meyer nicht persönlich, aber ich **weiß,** wer er ist.	*I don't know Mr. Meyer personally, but I know who he is.*

Note:

- **Wissen** is often used with indirect questions.

Ich **weiß,** wer Goethe ist.	*I know who Goethe is.*
Ich **weiß** nicht, wo das ist.	*I don't know where that is.*

Johann Wolfgang von Goethe, 1749–1832

Übung 14 Die neue Mitbewohnerin

Wendy, an exchange student from San Diego, is new in Göttingen and lives in a dorm. Listen to Wendy's questions and check off the appropriate negative responses.

Don't know. (casual)

	WEISS ICH NICHT.°	KENNE ICH NICHT.°		WEISS ICH NICHT.	KENNE ICH NICHT.
1.	☐	☐	**5.**	☐	☐
2.	☐	☐	**6.**	☐	☐
3.	☐	☐	**7.**	☐	☐
4.	☐	☐	**8.**	☐	☐

Übung 15 Wissen oder kennen?

Complete the minidialogues with the correct form of **wissen** or **kennen**.

1. A: _____ du Goethe?

   B: Nein, aber ich _____, wer er ist.

   A: _____ du seinen Roman, „Die Leiden (_sufferings_) des jungen Werther"?

   B: Nein, den _____ ich nicht. Aber mein Professor _____ ihn bestimmt.

2. C: _____ du, welcher Film heute im Odeon läuft?

   D: Das _____ ich nicht. Aber Toni, der _____ das bestimmt. Der _____ alles.

3. E: Wo wohnt ihr eigentlich jetzt?

   F: In der Schillerstraße. _____ du die?

   E: Nein. Ich _____ aber, wo die Goethestraße ist.

4. G: _____ ihr schon, wo ihr nächstes Semester studiert?

   H: Nein, wir _____ nur, dass wir nicht hier bleiben.

5. I: Ich _____, wo eine Wohnung frei wird.

   J: Wo denn?

   I: In der Weenderstraße.

   J: Die _____ ich nicht. Wo ist die denn?

6. K: Ihr _____ doch den Peter Sudhoff?

   L: Tut mir leid, den _____ wir nicht.

inquisitive Übung 16 Ein neugieriger Mensch

Find out what your partner knows by taking turns asking each other questions.

BEISPIEL: s1: Kennst du den neuen Film von Steven Spielberg?

s2: Nein, den kenne ich nicht. Kennst du den neuen Film von Peter Jackson?

s1: Ja, den kenne ich.

Kennst du ...

das neue Buch von _____?

den neuen Film von _____?

die Mutter / den Vater von _____?

Herrn Professor _____?

Frau Professor _____?

die Rockgruppe _____?

die Stadt _____?

Weißt du ...

die Telefonnummer von _____?

die Adresse von _____?

den Vornamen von Herrn / Frau _____?

wie alt _____ ist?

wann das nächste Semester beginnt?

Sprache im Kontext

Videoclips

In these videoclips, the people interviewed are talking about their families and various celebrations. As you watch, listen to what they say and think how you would respond to the interviewer's questions.

A. Watch the interviews with Doris and Kurt Borowsky. Mark the following statements **richtig (R)** or **falsch (F)**.

1. Doris

_____ Doris ist verheiratet.

_____ Sie hat zwei Kinder.

_____ Die Kinder heißen Tina und Matthias.

_____ Die Familie feiert Weihnachten, Valentinstag und Ostern.

_____ Das Lieblingsfest von Doris ist Weihnachten.

_____ Doris hat heute Geburtstag.

2. Herr Borowsky

_____ Herr Borowsky wohnt in Berlin.

_____ Er hat eine kleine Familie.

_____ Er hat drei Enkelkinder.

_____ Er hat einen Bruder und zwei Schwestern.

_____ Er ist 67 Jahre alt.

_____ Er hat am 10. Februar Geburtstag.

B. Now listen again to the questions asked by Michael, the interviewer. Write down four questions he asks and use them to interview two other students in the class. Then report your findings about one of the students to the class.

Lesen

Zum Thema

Eine Umfrage (*survey*). Fill out the questionnaire and compare answers in class.

A. Welche Feiertage sind in Ihrer Familie wichtig?

	WICHTIG	UNWICHTIG
1. Geburtstage	☐	☐
2. Hochzeitstage	☐	☐
3. religiöse Feiertage	☐	☐
4. nationale Feiertage	☐	☐
5. Muttertag	☐	☐
6. Vatertag	☐	☐

B. Wie feiern Sie Ihren Geburtstag?

	JA	NEIN
1. Wir haben ein großes Familienfest.	☐	☐
2. Wir gehen ins Restaurant.	☐	☐
3. Familie und Freunde kaufen Geschenke für mich.	☐	☐
4. Ich mache an diesem Tag nichts Besonderes.	☐	☐
5. ??	☐	☐

A. Skim over the short texts below. Who are the respondents? What are their ages? What is the general topic?

B. Now scan the texts more closely, looking for words of the following types.

- words relating to family
- words related to places where a celebration is held
- compound nouns: locate five compound nouns in the texts, and determine their components and their English equivalents

C. The two most frequently used words in the texts are the verb **feiern** and the noun **Geburtstag**. How do they relate to the expression **"deinen großen Tag"** in the title? What is implied?

Anna, 18: Meine Zwillingsschwester[1] und ich feiern jedes Jahr zusammen[2]. Meistens machen wir eine große Party bei uns zu Hause. Unseren 18. Geburtstag haben wir bei unserer Oma im Partykeller
5   gefeiert. Dort ist mehr Platz.
  Stefan, 15: Ich gehe gerne auf Geburtstagspartys, aber ich gebe selber nicht gerne welche[3]. Deswegen feiere ich immer nur mit meinen Eltern und dem Rest der Verwandtschaft.
10 **Patrick, 19:** Seit ich 18 bin, feiere ich meinen Geburtstag nur mit meiner Freundin zusammen. Wir sind jetzt schon seit zweieinhalb Jahren ein Paar.
  Lennard, 19: Ich fahre für ein paar Tage nach Paris. Dort feiere ich dann zusammen mit meiner Brieffreundin.

15 **Uta, 42:** Ich habe am 26. März Geburtstag. Zu meinem Geburtstag lade ich meistens abends einige Freunde zu uns nach Hause ein. Ich mache dann ein Buffet. Manche Freunde bringen auch etwas zu essen mit.
  Bettina, 40: Ich feiere dieses Jahr einen runden[4] Geburtstag, meinen vierzigsten, und lade natürlich 40 Gäste ein, Freunde und Verwandte. Wir feiern in einem Restaurant in der Innenstadt. Es gibt ein klei-
20 nes Programm mit Gedichten[5] und Musik. Und es gibt auch ein Super-Essen.
  Saskia, 30: Der Geburtstag sieht gewöhnlich so bei uns aus: Das Geburtstagskind bekommt den Früh- stückstisch schön gedeckt mit Kerzen[6] und Blumen aus dem Garten. Gleich morgens kommen auch die Geschenke von der Familie auf den Tisch. Am Abend kommen immer all unsere Freunde vorbei. Zu essen gibt es ein kleines kaltes Buffet, mit etwas frischem Salat, Brot[7] und Käse. Wir tanzen auch schon
25 mal zu später Stunde.

Teilweise aus: *JUMA* 2/2004, www.juma.de, Umfrage: Kristina Dörnenburg

[1]*Zwilling- twin* [2]*together* [3]here: *any* [4]*birthday ending in 0* [5]*poems* [6]*candles* [7]*bread*

A. Now read the statements more closely and answer the following questions about them. As you work through the texts, try to guess meaning from the context as much as possible. Note which additional words you have to look up, if any, to find the information.

1. Wer feiert Geburtstag nur ganz klein und nicht mit Familie?

2. Wer feiert Geburtstag immer zusammen mit einer Schwester?

3. Wer gibt nicht gern Geburtstagspartys, geht aber selbst gerne hin?

4. Wer feiert zu Hause und wer feiert in einem Restaurant?

5. *Ein* Geburtstag ist besonders wichtig (*important*). Welcher Geburtstag ist das? Wie feiert man ihn?

B. What, if anything, did you find surprising about the way these people celebrate their birthdays? What differences, if any, are there between the way people celebrate their birthdays in your area and the way the Germans celebrate theirs?

C. Wie feiern Sie Ihren Geburtstag? Now describe briefly how you typically spend your birthday, using the texts you have just read as a model.

Zum Text. Note: It is important to do contextual guessing exercises in class. When students' guesses are off the mark, you can guide them to make better guesses by having them articulate what led them to their guess and teaching them to look for evidence to confirm their guesses. Reassure your students that we all make false assumptions about texts. The goal is to learn how to move on until they can confirm their assumptions.

KULTURTIPP

Ein runder Geburtstag ist immer ein besonders wichtiger Geburtstag. Das sind alle Geburtstage mit einer Null, zum Beispiel 20, 40 oder 50. Man feiert ihn oft groß mit Familie und Freunden in einem Lokal (*pub*). Oft gibt es ein Programm mit Reden (*speeches*), Musik und Gedichten.

Zu guter Letzt

Eine Person vorstellen

Now that you have worked with the topic of family and friends, bring a picture of your family or several friends or a magazine picture depicting your "fictional family" to class.

Zu guter Letzt. Suggestion: In preparation for **Zu guter Letzt,** with books closed ask students what kind of phrases they would use to describe a family member or close friend to someone who had not met them.

Schritt 1: Jot down phrases or sentences in German that you might want to use in describing the people in your picture. Make sure that you include names, how the people are related to you if you are describing family members, things they like to do, when they celebrate their birthdays, and so forth.

Schritt 2: Now work in groups of three. Using the items you have jotted down, describe three of the people in the picture. Your description might go something like this:

> Das ist meine Tante. Sie heißt Barbara. Sie hat am 14. April Geburtstag. Sie ist sehr aktiv. Sie kocht gern und läuft gern.

Schritt 3: Each person in the group should ask the other two members two questions about others in the picture you did not describe. Sample questions might be:

> Wer ist das? Wie heißt er/sie? Ist das deine Schwester? dein Bruder?

Schritt 4: Ein Bericht Finally, expand the information about your family or friends in a written report that might include information such as the following:

- wie groß die Familie ist und wo sie wohnt
- wann sie Geburtstag haben
- was Sie und andere Familienmitglieder (*family members*) oder Freunde gern machen (kochen, tanzen, Zeitung lesen, …)
- Lieblings … (-sport, -komponist, -musiker)
- Probleme (kein Geld, zu viel Geld, keine Hobbys, …)

Additional activity. Hand out Uwe Timm's poem "Erziehung" and read it aloud in the class. Have students guess what it is about. Have them guess the meaning of the word *Erziehung.*

Wortschatz

Der Stammbaum — Family Tree

der **Bruder**, ∹	brother
die **Eltern** (*pl.*)	parents
der **Enkel**, -	grandson
die **Enkelin**, -nen	granddaughter
die **Familie**, -n	family
die **Frau**, -en	wife
die **Geschwister** (*pl.*)	siblings
die **Großeltern** (*pl.*)	grandparents
die **Großmutter**, ∹	grandmother
der **Großvater**, ∹	grandfather
die **Kusine**, -n	(female) cousin
der **Mann**, ∹er	husband
die **Mutter**, ∹	mother
der **Neffe** (-n *masc.*), -n	nephew
die **Nichte**, -n	niece
die **Oma**, -s	grandma
der **Onkel**, -	uncle
der **Opa**, -s	grandpa
der **Schwager**, ∹	brother-in-law
die **Schwägerin**, -nen	sister-in-law
die **Schwester**, -n	sister
der **Sohn**, ∹e	son
die **Tante**, -n	aunt
die **Tochter**, ∹	daughter
der **Vater**, ∹	father
der **Vetter**, -n	(male) cousin

Die Wochentage — Days of the Week

der **Montag**	Monday
am Montag	on Monday
der **Dienstag**	Tuesday
der **Mittwoch**	Wednesday
der **Donnerstag**	Thursday
der **Freitag**	Friday
der **Samstag** / der **Sonnabend**	Saturday
der **Sonntag**	Sunday

Die Monate — Months

der **Januar***	January
im Januar	in January
der **Februar**	February
der **März**	March
der **April**	April
der **Mai**	May
der **Juni**	June
der **Juli**	July
der **August**	August
der **September**	September
der **Oktober**	October
der **November**	November
der **Dezember**	December

Feste und Feiertage — Holidays

das **Familienfest**, -e	family gathering
(der) **Fasching**	Mardi Gras (*southern Germany, Austria*)
das **Geschenk**, -e	gift, present
der **Heilige Abend**	Christmas Eve
die **Hochzeit**, -en	wedding
der **Kalender**, -	calendar
(der) **Karneval**	Mardi Gras (*Rhineland*)
der **Muttertag**	Mother's Day
das **Neujahr**	New Year's Day
(das) **Ostern**	Easter
die **Party**, -s	party
(das) **Silvester**	New Year's Eve
die **Tradition**, -en	tradition
der **Valentinstag**	Valentine's Day
das **Weihnachten**	Christmas
der **Weihnachtsbaum**, ∹e	Christmas tree

Verben — Verbs

feiern	to celebrate
geben (gibt)	to give
gratulieren	to congratulate
heiraten	to marry
kennen	to know (*be acquainted with a person or thing*)
planen	to plan
werden (wird)	to become, be
wissen (weiß)	to know (*something as a fact*)
wünschen	to wish

Adjektive und Adverbien — Adjectives and Adverbs

leider	unfortunately
morgen	tomorrow
nämlich	namely, that is to say
neu	new
verwandt mit	related to
wichtig	important

*Jänner is used in Austria.

Ordinalzahlen	Ordinal Numbers
erste	first
der erste Mai	May first
am ersten Mai	on May first
zweite	second
dritte	third
vierte	fourth
fünfte	fifth
sechste	sixth
sieb(en)te	seventh
achte	eighth
neunte	ninth
zehnte	tenth
elfte	eleventh
zwölfte	twelfth
dreizehnte	thirteenth
zwanzigste	twentieth

Possessivartikel	Possessive Adjectives
mein	my
dein	your (*informal sg.*)
sein	his; its
ihr	her; its; their
unser	our
euer	your (*informal pl.*)
Ihr	your (*formal*)

Akkusativ- präpositionen	Accusative Prepositions
durch	through
für	for
gegen	against; around (+ *time*)
ohne	without
um	at (+ *time*)
um (… herum)	around (*spatial*)

Akkusativ- pronomen	Accusative Pronouns
mich	me
dich	you (*informal sg.*)
ihn	him; it
sie	her; it; them
es	it
uns	us
euch	you (*informal pl.*)
Sie	you (*formal*)

Sonstiges	Other
Alles Gute!	All the best!
es gibt	there is, there are
Es tut mir leid.	I'm sorry.
Herzlichen Glück- wunsch zum Geburtstag!	Happy birthday!
der Hund, -e	dog
um Mitternacht	at midnight
Wann hast du Geburtstag?	When is your birthday?
Welches Datum ist heute/morgen?	What is today's/ tomorrow's date?

DAS KANN ICH NUN!

1. Wer sind die folgenden Familienmitglieder?

   a. Mein Bruder und meine Schwester sind meine _____. **b.** Meine Mutter und mein Vater sind meine _____.
   c. Familie Renner hat drei _____: einen Sohn und zwei _____.

2. Drei wichtige Feiertage sind: _____, _____, und _____.

3. Zum Geburtstag wünscht man „_____ _____ zum Geburtstag!"

4. Wann haben Sie Geburtstag? Mein Geburtstag ist _____. Dann _____ ich _____ Jahre alt.

5. Wie sagt man das auf Deutsch?

   a. Is that your car, Mrs. Singer? **b.** Do you know our parents? **c.** His brother knows that. **d.** My sister knows him.

6. Welche Präpositionen mit dem Akkusativ fehlen hier?

   a. Ich kaufe ein Geschenk _____ meinen Freund. **b.** Meine Freunde gehen heute _____ mich auf die Party bei Klaus. **c.** Meine Oma geht oft _____ den Park.

7. Nennen Sie die Wochentage mit den Buchstaben D und M am Anfang.

   a. D_____ und D_____
   b. M_____ und M_____

Erstes Zwischenspiel

Persönlichkeiten: Drei Kurzbiographien

Wolfgang Amadeus Mozart (1756–1791)

Geburtsort: Salzburg
Geburtsdatum: 27. Januar 1756
Sternzeichen: Wassermann[1]
Vater: Leopold
Mutter: Maria Anna

Wolfgang Amadeus Mozart, ca. 1783

Leopold Mozart und seine Kinder Wolfgang und „Nannerl", 1763

Geschwister: Marianne, genannt „Nannerl"
Verheiratet[2] mit: Constanze geb. Weber
Kinder: Karl und Wolfgang
Wohnort: Wien
Beruf: Kapellmeister und Komponist
Hauptwerke: Opern (z.B. „Don Giovanni", „Die Zauberflöte"); 41 Symphonien; Kirchenmusik (z.B. „Krönungsmesse"[3], „Requiem"); Konzerte und Kammermusik (z.B. „Eine kleine Nachtmusik")
Hobbys: Musik, Tanzen, Geselligkeit[4], Reisen
  Lieblingskomponist: Joseph Haydn

[1]*Aquarius* [2]*married* [3]*Coronation Mass* [4]*conviviality*

Paula Modersohn-Becker: Worpsweder Landschaft, um 1900

Paula Modersohn-Becker (1876–1909)

Paula Modersohn-Becker, Selbstbildnis

Geburtsort: Dresden
Geburtsdatum: 8. Februar 1876
Sternzeichen: Wassermann
Vater: Woldemar
Mutter: Mathilde
Geschwister: sechs; vier jüngere, zwei ältere
Verheiratet mit: Otto Modersohn
Kinder: Mathilde

Wohnort: zuletzt in Worpswede[1]
Beruf: Malerin
Hauptwerke: Landschaftsmalerei[2], Porträts, Stilleben
Hobbys: Musik, Tanzen, Kochen, Lesen, Zeichnen
Lieblingsdichter: Rainer Maria Rilke

[1]*Worpswede ist ein Künstlerdorf in der Nähe von Bremen.* [2]*landscape painting*

Albert Einstein (1879–1955)

Geburtsort: Ulm

Geburtsdatum: 14. März 1879

Sternzeichen: Fisch

Vater: Hermann

Mutter: Pauline

Geschwister: Maria („Maja")

Verheiratet mit: zuerst Mileva, dann Elsa

Kinder: Hans und Eduard

Wohnort: zuletzt in Princeton, New Jersey

Beruf: Physiker (Nobelpreis, 1921)

Hauptwerk: Relativitätstheorie

Hobbys: Musik, Geige[1] spielen, Segeln[2]

Lieblingskomponist: Mozart

Lieblingsphilosoph: Immanuel Kant

[1]*violin* [2]*sailing*

Albert Einstein als Kind, mit seiner Schwester Maja

Albert Einstein beim Segeln

Aktivität 1 Darf ich vorstellen?

Suppose you had to introduce Mozart, Einstein, or Modersohn-Becker to someone at a party. Make three statements about each that characterize who they are.

BEISPIEL: Darf ich vorstellen, das ist Herr/Frau …
   Er/Sie ist …
   Er/Sie schreibt/malt/wohnt in …

Aktivität 2 Rollenspiel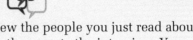

Imagine that you could interview the people you just read about. With a partner, select one of the three, then create the interview. You could begin as follows:

BEISPIEL: s1: Wo sind Sie geboren, Frau Modersohn-Becker?
   s2: In Dresden.
   s1: Sind Sie verheiratet? …

Aktivität 3 Ein Steckbrief°

Choose a well-known historical person and gather information to write a **Steckbrief** about her or him. Present the information in class without revealing who the person is. Let the members of the class guess her or his identity.

wanted poster

Mein Tag

Um wie viel Uhr beginnt die
Vorlesung hier?

In diesem Kapitel

- **Themen:** Telling time, times of the day, daily plans, movies, music, theater
- **Grammatik:** Separable-prefix verbs; modal verbs; **möchte;** the imperative; **bitte, doch, mal**
- **Kultur:** German theater
- **Lesen:** „Immer das gleiche" (Christine Wuttke)

Videoclips
Ein Tag im Leben von Jan,
Jasmin und Beatrice

Alles klar?

A. In diesem  (Brief) sehen Sie fünf  (Bilder). Die Bilder stehen für fünf Wörter oder Ausdrücke. Die Ausdrücke sind alphabetisch geordnet.

Fahrrad

Haus(e)

Herz

Sonntag

Tasse Kaffee

Lesen Sie den Brief nun mit den Wörtern.

Realia. Suggestion: Have students scan the note to determine (1) what kind of text it is and (2) what it might be about.

B. Sie hören jetzt eine telefonische Einladung. Hören Sie bitte zu und markieren Sie die richtige Information.

1. Die Einladung ist für _____.
   a. Sonntag
   b. Samstag
   c. Freitag

2. Erika und Thomas wollen _____.
   a. <u>Dirk zu Kaffee und Kuchen einladen</u>
   b. mit Dirk auf eine Party gehen
   c. mit Dirk ins Café gehen

3. Dirk soll _____ kommen.
   a. um 3 Uhr
   b. um 5 Uhr
   c. <u>um 4 Uhr</u>

Siehe *Modal Auxiliary Verbs*, S. 130.

Wörter im Kontext

Wie spät ist es?
Wie viel Uhr ist es?

Es ist eins. Es ist **ein Uhr.**
Es ist dreizehn Uhr.

Es ist zehn (Minuten) Es ist ein Uhr zehn.
nach eins. Es ist dreizehn Uhr zehn.

Es ist **Viertel nach** eins. Es ist ein Uhr fünfzehn.
Es ist dreizehn Uhr
fünfzehn.

Es ist **halb** zwei. Es ist ein Uhr dreißig.
Es ist dreizehn Uhr
dreißig.

Es ist zwanzig (Minuten) Es ist ein Uhr vierzig.
vor zwei. Es ist dreizehn Uhr
vierzig.

Es ist **Viertel vor** zwei. Es ist ein Uhr
fünfundvierzig.
Es ist dreizehn Uhr
fünfundvierzig.

Es ist zehn (Minuten) Es ist ein Uhr fünfzig.
vor zwei. Es ist dreizehn Uhr
fünfzig.

Eine **Minute** hat sechzig **Sekunden**, eine **Stunde** sechzig Minuten
und ein Tag vierundzwanzig Stunden.

Time announcements **Aktivität 1 Zeitansagen**

Markieren Sie die Uhrzeiten, die Sie hören.

1. **a.** 7.38 **b.** 17.35 **c.** 17.30
2. **a.** 3.06 **b.** 2.06 **c.** 20.16
3. **a.** 14.00 **b.** 14.15 **c.** 14.05
4. **a.** 12.25 **b.** 10.24 **c.** 11.25
5. **a.** 19.45 **b.** 9.45 **c.** 19.40
6. **a.** 13.00 **b.** 3.40 **c.** 13.40
7. **a.** 0.15 **b.** 0.05 **c.** 0.45
8. **a.** 20.05 **b.** 20.50 **c.** 21.50

In official timetables—for instance, in radio, television, movie, and theater guides—time is expressed according to the twenty-four-hour system.

1.00–12.00 Uhr	*1:00 A.M. to 12:00 noon*
13.00–24.00 Uhr	*1:00 P.M. to 12:00 midnight*

Midnight may also be referred to as **0 (null) Uhr.**

When writing time in numbers, German speakers usually separate hours and minutes with a period, instead of a colon as in English.

Analyse. Suggestion: Have students give time in both the twelve- and twenty-four-hour systems.

Realia. This cartoon appeared in *P.M.* magazine.

ANALYSE

Sehen Sie sich die Zeichnung an und beantworten Sie die Fragen.

- Wie spät ist es in New York?
- Wie spät ist es in Tokio?
- Wie spät ist es in Bombay?
- Die vierte Uhr zeigt (*shows*) die „gute alte Zeit". Warum hat der Mann wohl (*probably*) diese Uhr gern?

  a. Er hat Kuckucksuhren gern.

  b. Heute ist alles so hektisch.

  c. Die Kuckucksuhr geht langsamer als die anderen Uhren.

  d. ??

Aktivität 2   Wie viel Uhr ist es? Wie spät ist es?

BEISPIEL: Wie viel Uhr ist es? (Wie spät ist es?) →
Es ist Viertel nach sieben.

Aktivität 2. Follow-up: Have students repeat the times indicated by the clocks using 24-hour time.

1.

2.

3.

4.

5.

6.

7.

To find out at what time something takes place, ask:

Um wie viel Uhr _____?

To say at what time something takes place, use the following expressions:

um ein Uhr (1.00 Uhr)	**um ein Uhr dreißig (1.30 Uhr)**
um ein Uhr zehn (1.10 Uhr)	**um ein Uhr vierzig (1.40 Uhr)**
um ein Uhr fünfzehn (1.15 Uhr)	**um ein Uhr fünfundvierzig**
	(1.45 Uhr)

Aktivität 3 Was macht Hans-Jürgen am Wochenende?

Sehen Sie sich die Bilder an und ergänzen Sie Hans-Jürgens Pläne für das **Wochenende.**

7.20

7.05

7.45–8.30

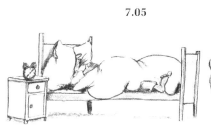  

1. Um _____ schläft Hans-Jürgen noch. Dann klingelt der Wecker.
2. Um _____ **steht** er endlich **auf.**
3. Von _____ bis _____ geht er joggen.

9.30

11.20

12.15

4. Um _____ **frühstückt** er und liest die Zeitung.
5. Um _____ **ruft** er einen Freund **an.**
6. Um _____ **trifft** er eine Freundin im Café.

Neue Wörter

das Wochenende weekend
steht ... auf (aufstehen)
  gets up
frühstückt (frühstücken)
  eats breakfast
ruft ... an (anrufen) calls
  up
trifft (treffen) meets

13.40

15.00

19.15

7. Um <u>13.40 Uhr</u> **geht** er **einkaufen.**
8. Um <u>15.00 Uhr</u> spielt Hans-Jürgen Fußball auf dem Sportplatz.
9. Um <u>19.15 Uhr</u> ist er mit Freunden im Kino.

Aktivität 4 Mein Zeitbudget

Wie viel Zeit verbringen (*spend*) Sie **gewöhnlich** mit diesen Dingen?

Schritt 1: Tragen Sie in die Tabelle ein, wie viel Zeit Sie **pro Woche** mit jeder Tätigkeit verbringen.

Neue	Wörter

**geht … einkaufen
(einkaufen gehen)** goes shopping
gewöhnlich usually
pro Woche per week

Tätigkeit	Montag bis Freitag	Wochenende	Insgesamt
Vorlesungen Labor Lesen Schreiben			
Nebenarbeit			

Essen:
    Frühstück
    Mittagessen
    Abendessen			

Einkaufen Sport Schlafen			

Zeit für mich:
    Fernsehen
    Zeitung/Bücher lesen
    Freunde besuchen
    Musik hören			

Schritt 2: Stellen Sie wenigstens 5 Fragen an einen Partner / eine Partnerin. Fragen Sie:

- Wie viel Zeit verbringst du in Vorlesungen? im Labor? mit Lesen? …
- Wie viel Zeit hast du für dich?

Schritt 3: Berichten Sie der Klasse, wie Ihr Partner / Ihre Partnerin seine/ihre Zeit verbringt.

BEISPIEL: Laura verbringt fünfzehn Stunden pro Woche mit Vorlesungen
und zehn Stunden pro Woche mit Nebenarbeit. Sie hat nicht
viel Zeit für Fernsehen aber hört oft Musik.

Hans-Jürgens Wochenplan

Hans-Jürgen **hat** viel **vor** und plant seine Zeit immer sehr genau. Dies ist sein Wochenplan für die nächsten vier Tage.

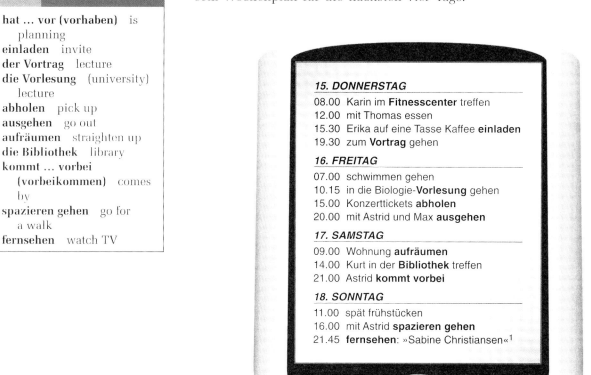

15. DONNERSTAG
08.00 Karin im **Fitnesscenter** treffen
12.00 mit Thomas essen
15.30 Erika auf eine Tasse Kaffee **einladen**
19.30 zum **Vortrag** gehen

16. FREITAG
07.00 schwimmen gehen
10.15 in die Biologie-**Vorlesung** gehen
15.00 Konzerttickets **abholen**
20.00 mit Astrid und Max **ausgehen**

17. SAMSTAG
09.00 Wohnung **aufräumen**
14.00 Kurt in der **Bibliothek** treffen
21.00 Astrid **kommt vorbei**

18. SONNTAG
11.00 spät frühstücken
16.00 mit Astrid **spazieren gehen**
21.45 **fernsehen**: »Sabine Christiansen«[1]

[1]a talk show host dealing mostly with political topics

Tageszeiten

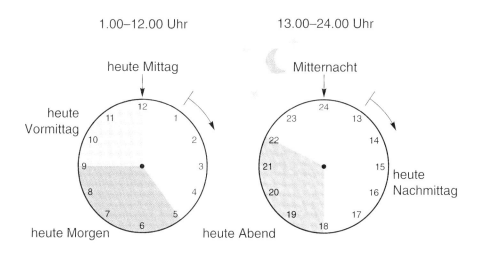

1.00–12.00 Uhr

heute Mittag
heute Vormittag
heute Morgen
heute Abend

13.00–24.00 Uhr

Mitternacht
heute Nachmittag

Further practice: Write the following on the board: _____ _möchte ich_ _____. Have the class stand up. Each student completes the sentence using words of his or her own choice. As they complete their sentences, students sit down.

Note: Point out to students that in combination with _heute_ and _morgen_ (tomorrow), the words _Morgen_ (morning), _Vormittag, Mittag,_ and _Nachmittag_ remain separate words and are capitalized, but that in combination with days of the week they form compounds.

SPRACHTIPP

To say _this morning, this evening,_ etc., combine **heute** with a period of the day such as **Morgen: heute Morgen** = _this morning._ Do the same for phrases combined with _tomorrow:_ **morgen Nachmittag** = _tomorrow afternoon;_ **heute Abend** = _this evening._

The phrase for _tomorrow morning_ is either **morgen früh** or **morgen Vormittag** (to avoid the awkward **morgen Morgen**).

The times of day can also combine with the days of the week: **Samstagabend** = _Saturday evening._ Note that these are written as one word.

A. Was **möchte** Hans-Jürgen machen – und wann? Sehen Sie sich Hans-Jürgens Wochenplan an und ergänzen Sie seine Pläne.

am Donnerstag, 15. Oktober

☐ **Heute Morgen** möchte Hans-Jürgen ins Fitnesscenter gehen.
☐ Heute **Mittag** möchte er _____ mit Thomas essen _____.
☐ **Heute Nachmittag** möchte er Erika auf eine Tasse Kaffee einladen.
☐ Heute Abend möchte er zu einem _____ Vortrag _____ gehen.

am Freitag, 16. Oktober

☐ **Morgen früh** möchte Hans-Jürgen schwimmen gehen.
☐ Morgen **Vormittag muss** er _____ in die Biologie-Vorlesung gehen _____.
☐ Morgen Nachmittag **soll** er _____ Konzerttickets abholen _____.
☐ **Morgen Abend** möchte er _____ mit Astrid und Max ausgehen _____.

am Samstag, 17. Oktober

☐ Samstagmorgen muss Hans-Jürgen die Wohnung aufräumen.
☐ Samstagnachmittag möchte er _____ Kurt in der Bibliothek treffen _____.
☐ Samstagabend _____ kommt _____ Astrid _____ vorbei _____.
☐ Samstags ist er oft bis spät in der **Nacht** bei Freunden.

am Sonntag, 18. Oktober

☐ Sonntagvormittag möchte er _____ spät frühstücken _____.
☐ Sonntagnachmittag möchte er _____ mit Astrid spazieren gehen _____.
☐ Sonntagabend möchte er _____ fernsehen _____.

B. Und Sie? Was möchten oder müssen Sie machen – und wann?

Neue Wörter

möchte would like to
der Morgen morning; tomorrow
der Mittag noon
der Nachmittag afternoon
früh early
der Vormittag morning, before noon
der Abend evening
muss (müssen) must
soll (sollen) is supposed to
die Nacht night

Siehe _Modal Auxiliary Verbs,_ S. 128.

SPRACHTIPP

When you do something on a regular basis, use the following adverbs to express the day or the time.

montags	**morgens**
dienstags	**vormittags**
mittwochs	**mittags**
donnerstags	**nachmittags**
freitags	**abends**
samstags/sonnabends	**nachts**
sonntags	

In German, general time precedes specific time.

GENERAL   SPECIFIC

Ich habe donnerstags um 13.00 Uhr Chemie.

Schritt 1: Sven und Frank sind 18 Jahre alt und gehen aufs Gymnasium (*secondary school*). Vergleichen Sie ihre Stundenpläne. Welche Kurse haben sie zusammen (*together*)?

BEISPIEL: s1: Welchen Kurs hat Frank montags um acht?
s2: Montags um acht hat Frank Informatik. Welchen Kurs hat Sven montags um acht?
s1: Montags um acht hat Sven Englisch.

Schritt 2: Sven und Frank möchten Tennis spielen. Wann ist die beste Zeit? Wann haben sie beide frei?

Zeit	Montag	Dienstag	Mittwoch	Donnerstag	Freitag	Samstag
8 – 8⁴⁵	Englisch	Informatik	Chemie	Physik	frei	Deutsch
8⁴⁵ – 9³⁰	Englisch	Informatik	Chemie	Physik	Kunst	Deutsch
9³⁵ – 10²⁰	Religion	Deutsch	Erdkunde	Deutsch	Sozialkunde	
10⁴⁰ – 11²⁵	Religion	Mathematik	Mathematik	Mathematik	Deutsch	
11³⁰ – 12¹⁵	Erdkunde	Kunst	Sozialkunde	Geschichte	Geschichte	
12¹⁵ – 13⁰⁰	Mathematik	Physik	Informatik	Englisch	Chemie	
13¹⁵ – 14⁰⁰				Sport		
14⁰⁰ – 14⁴⁵				Sport		

Svens Stundenplan

How does your schedule look?

Schritt 1: Schreiben Sie Ihren Stundenplan. Wann sind Ihre Kurse? Wann arbeiten Sie? Dann vergleichen Sie Ihren Stundenplan mit dem von zwei anderen Studenten/Studentinnen in Ihrem Kurs.

BEISPIEL: s1: Was hast du donnerstags um 10?
s2: Donnerstags um 10 habe ich _____. Und du?

Schritt 2: Wer hat Kurse mit Ihnen zusammen? Berichten (*Report*) Sie der Klasse.

Sie wollen einen Freund / eine Freundin besuchen. Sagen Sie, wann Sie vorbeikommen und wie lange Sie bleiben möchten. Benutzen Sie folgendes Sprechschema.

S1	S2
1. Bist du _____ zu Hause?	**2a.** Ja, ich bin zu Hause. **b.** Nein, ich bin leider nicht zu Hause.
3a. Kann ich dann _____ vorbeikommen? **b.** Schade. Wann kann ich denn mal vorbeikommen?	**4a.** Ja, gern. Ich sehe dich also _____. **b.** Kannst du _____ kommen?
5a. Schön. **b.** Ja, gern.	**6.** Wie lange kannst du denn bleiben?
7. _____ Stunde(n).	

THEMA 3: Kino, Musik und Theater

JAN: Ich **gehe** heute Abend **ins Theater.** Willst du mit?

ULLA: Nein, danke. Ich bin kein Theaterfan. Ich **möchte lieber ins Kino.**

JAN: So. Du bist ein Kinofan. Was für (*what kind of*) **Filme** siehst du denn gern?

ULLA: **Am liebsten** Horrorfilme und Psychothriller – die sind so **spannend.**

Was für Filme sehen Sie gern?

☐ Horrorfilme
☐ **Komödien**
☐ Psychothriller
☐ Liebesfilme

☐ **Krimis**
☐ Science-fiction-Filme
☐ Abenteuerfilme
☐ Wildwestfilme

Kino, Musik und
Theater. Suggestion:
The dialogue between
Jan and Ulla can func-
tion as a model for part-
ner work. Students can
also ask each other
about their entertainment preferences using the checklists
following the dialogue. (The *Sie-Fragen* should be rephrased as
du-Fragen; it may be useful to review the forms of the stem-
changing *sehen.*) Have students then report to the class what
their partners prefer.

Was sehen Sie gern auf der Bühne (*on stage*)?

☐ **Tragödien**
☐ Lustspiele (*comedies*)
☐ Musicals

☐ **Theaterstücke**
☐ **Opern**
☐ Tanz und **Ballett**

Was für Musik hören Sie gern?

☐ klassische Musik
☐ Heavy Metal
☐ Rockmusik
☐ Techno
☐ alternative Musik

☐ Jazz
☐ Soul
☐ Western-Musik
☐ Rap
☐ Hip-Hop

KULTURTIPP

In Deutschland gibt es in den Groß- und Kleinstädten über 400 öffentliche und private Theater. Der deutsche Staat subventioniert (*subsidizes*) die meisten von ihnen. Deshalb sind die Preise für die Theaterkarten nicht zu teuer. Viele Deutsche haben ein Theaterabonnement (*subscription*). Die deutschen Theater spielen gerne klassische Stücke, die oft modernisiert oder politisiert sind. Das macht sie aktuell und interessant.

Stadttheater Göttingen

Das Thalia in Hamburg

Aktivität 8 Zwei Einladungen

Sie hören zwei Dialoge. Wer spricht? Wohin möchten die Sprecher gehen? Warum ist es nicht möglich (*possible*)? Markieren Sie die richtige Information.

DIALOG 1	**DIALOG 2**
1. Die Sprecher sind … **a.** ein Professor und ein Student. **b.** zwei Studentinnen. **c.** eine Studentin und ein Freund.	1. Die Sprecher sind … **a.** zwei Studenten. **b.** zwei Professoren. **c.** ein Student und eine Freundin.
2. Der eine Sprecher möchte … **a.** zu Hause arbeiten. **b.** ins Kino. **c.** ins Konzert.	2. Die eine Sprecherin möchte … **a.** ins Kino. **b.** in eine Vorlesung. **c.** Karten spielen.
3. Die Sprecherin muss leider … **a.** arbeiten. **b.** in eine Vorlesung. **c.** einen Brief schreiben.	3. Der andere Sprecher … **a.** hat eine Vorlesung. **b.** hat Labor. **c.** muss in die Bibliothek.

Aktivität 9 Was machst du so am Wochenende?

Interviewen Sie Studenten/Studentinnen in der Klasse und finden Sie folgende Personen. Wer „ja" antwortet, muss unterschreiben.

BEISPIEL: s1: Gehst du tanzen, spazieren, laufen oder wandern?
　　　　　 s2: Ja, ich gehe tanzen.
　　　　　 s1: Unterschreib bitte hier.

Siehe *Separable-Prefix Verbs*, S. 124.

AM WOCHENENDE

1. _____ Wer geht tanzen, spazieren, laufen oder wandern?
2. _____ Wer steht früh auf?
3. _____ Wer steht spät auf?
4. _____ Wer räumt das Zimmer, die Wohnung, den Schreibtisch auf?
5. _____ Wer geht ins Kino, ins Theater, in die Oper, ins Konzert, zu einer Technoparty?
6. _____ Wer lädt Freunde ein?
7. _____ Wer sieht fern?
8. _____ Wer surft im Internet?

To say where you are going, use the following expressions.

Ich gehe
　{
　ins Kino.
　ins Theater.
　ins Konzert.
　in die Oper.
　in die Disko.

Aktivität 10 Was hast du vor?

Schauen Sie sich die Programme für Kino, Theater und Musik an. Sagen Sie, wohin Sie gehen wollen.

Aktivität 10. Suggestion: Write on the board or OHP a number of possible ways to accept or decline the invitation: *Ja, ich komme mit! / Super! / Prima! / Nein, das ist zu spät für mich. / Ich muss leider arbeiten.*

Vorverkauf Hardenbergstr. 6, Mo.- Fr. von 8 -16.30 Uhr

15. März, 16.00 Uhr und 20.00 Uhr sowie
2. und 3. Mai, jeweils 20.00 Uhr
4. Mai, 18.00 Uhr und 15. Juni, 18.00 Uhr

ICC BERLIN

Das Musical-Ereignis!
Endlich in deutscher Sprache!

PHANTOM DER OPER

Von Arndt Gerber u. Paul Wilhelm
nach dem Roman von G. Leroux
**Internationales Musical-Ensemble
mit Ballett, Chor und Orchester**

Karten: Kasse ICC und alle Vorverkaufsstellen

Theater in Berlin

KOMÖDIE AM KU'DAMM
47 02 10 10
19.30 Uhr **TAXI, TAXI**
Turbulenter Schwank
THEATER am KU'DAMM
Zusätzlich am Wochenende
Wilhelm heeßt er
Revue-Musical

FAME
Das Musical
im
Schiller Theater
Tickets: 030 · 31 11 31 11

THEATER	Montag, 10. 3.	Dienstag, 11. 3.
Deutsche Oper Berlin 341 02 49	20.00 Kammermusik im Foyer: **Ensemble „das neue Werk" Berlin**	17.00 Foyer: **„Klein-Siegfried"**
Berliner Kammerspiele 391 55 43	**Biedermann und die Brandstifter** von Max Frisch Freitag und Sonnabend 18.00 Uhr	

S1	S2
1. Was hast du am Samstag vor?	**2.** Ich gehe ins Kino / ins Theater / in die Oper / ? Willst du mit?
3. Was gibt es denn?	**4.** Einen Film / ein Musical / eine Oper / ? von (+ *name*).
5a. So? Wann fängt er/es/sie denn an? **b.** Ach, ich bleibe lieber zu Hause.	**6a.** _____. **b.** Schade.

Hier klicken!

Weiteres zum Thema Konzert und Theater finden Sie bei **Deutsch: Na klar!** im World-Wide-Web unter www.mhhe.com/dnk5.

Grammatik im Kontext

Separable-Prefix Verbs°

You are already familiar with sentences such as the following:

Susanne und Peter **kommen** per Fahrrad **vorbei.**	*Susanne and Peter **are coming by** on their bikes.*
Ich gehe heute tanzen. **Kommst** du **mit?**	*I am going dancing today. Will you **come along?***

German, like English, has many two-part verbs that consist of a verb and a short complement that affects the meaning of the main verb. Examples of such two-part verbs in English are *to come by, to come along, to call up, to get up.*

Wüstenrot-Rendite[1]-Programm mit 470 Euro pro anno.

Jede Million fängt klein an.[2]

[1] *yield on investment*
[2] fängt ... an: *begins*
[3] *simple*

Kommen ... vorbei, fängt ... an, rufe ... an, and **kommst ... mit** are examples of such two-part verbs in German. They are also called separable-prefix verbs. In the infinitive, the separable part of these verbs forms the verb's prefix. The prefixes are always stressed.

> **án**rufen
>
> **án**fangen
>
> vor**béi**kommen
>
> **mít**kommen

In a statement or a question, the prefix is separated from the conjugated verb and placed at the end of the sentence.

—**Kommst** du heute Abend **vorbei?**	*Are you coming by tonight?*
—Ja, aber ich **rufe** vorher **an.**	*Yes, but I'll call first.*

Here are examples of some commonly used separable-prefix verbs.

VERB	BEISPIEL
abholen (holt ... ab) to pick up	Ich **hole** dich um 6 Uhr **ab.**
anfangen (fängt ... an) to begin	Wann **fängt** die Vorlesung **an**?
anrufen (ruft ... an) to call up	Ich **rufe** dich morgen **an.**
aufhören (hört ... auf) to end, quit	Der Regen **hört** nicht **auf.**
aufräumen (räumt ... auf) to straighten up	Er **räumt** sein Zimmer **auf.**
aufstehen (steht ... auf) to get up	Er **steht** um 9 Uhr **auf.**
aufwachen (wacht ... auf) to wake up	Wann **wachst** du gewöhnlich **auf**?
einkaufen (kauft ... ein) to shop	Herr Lerche **kauft** immer morgens **ein.**
einladen (lädt ... ein) to invite	Ich **lade** dich zum Essen **ein.**
einschlafen (schläft ... ein) to fall asleep	Ich **schlafe** gewöhnlich nicht vor Mitternacht **ein.**
mitbringen (bringt ... mit) to bring along	Ich **bringe** eine Pizza **mit.**
mitkommen (kommt ... mit) to come along	**Kommst** du **mit**?
mitnehmen (nimmt ... mit) to take along	**Nimmst** du einen Regenschirm **mit**?
vorbeikommen (kommt ... vorbei) to come by	Wir **kommen** Sonntag **vorbei.**
vorhaben (hat ... vor) to plan to do	Was **hast** du heute **vor**?
zurückkommen (kommt ... zurück) to come back	Wann **kommst** du **zurück**?

Point out: The meaning of a separable prefix verb often has no apparent semantic relationship to the base verb. For example, compare: *aufhören* "to end" with *hören* "to hear."

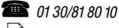

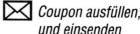

[1]*ad*
[2]*geben ... auf* place

Note:

- A separable-prefix verb shows all the same stem-vowel changes or other irregularities in the present tense as the base verb.

  Hans **schläft** immer lange.   Er **schläft** um 23 Uhr **ein.**

  Er **nimmt** den Schirm.   Er **nimmt** den Schirm **mit.**

- Separable-prefix verbs are listed in the vocabulary of this book as follows:

  auf•hören   ein•schlafen (schläft ein)   vor•haben (hat vor)

The Sentence Bracket°

Die Satzklammer

Separable-prefix verbs show a sentence structure that is characteristic for German: the conjugated verb and its complement form a bracket around the core of the sentence. The conjugated verb is the second element of the sentence, and the separable prefix is the last element.

```
                        ┌──────── SATZKLAMMER ────────┐
Ich        rufe         dich heute Abend        an.
Wann       kommst       du heute                vorbei?
Peter      geht         leider nicht            mit.
```

Another example of the sentence bracket (**Satzklammer**) can be seen in sentences with compound verbs such as **einkaufen gehen** (*to go shopping*), **tanzen gehen** (*to go dancing*), and **spazieren gehen** (*to go for a walk*).

```
                                 ┌──────── SATZKLAMMER ────────┐
Ich              gehe            morgens                    einkaufen.
Klaus und Erika  gehen           Sonntag mit Freunden       tanzen.
Daniel           geht            mit dem Hund               spazieren.
```

In the sentences above, the verb **gehen** and the infinitives **einkaufen, tanzen,** and **spazieren** form a bracket around the sentence core. You will encounter the concept of the sentence bracket in many other contexts involving verbs.

Übung 1 Daniels Tagesablauf

Daniel ist Künstler (*artist*), aber die Kunst (*art*) allein bringt nicht genug Geld ein. Sie hören jetzt eine Beschreibung von Daniels Tagesablauf. Markieren Sie alle passenden Antworten auf jede Frage.

1. Wann wacht Daniel gewöhnlich auf?
   a. sehr früh
   b. sehr spät
   c. um 5 Uhr

2. Wohnt Daniel allein oder mit jemandem zusammen?
   a. allein
   b. mit seinem Bruder
   c. mit seiner Freundin

3. Was tut Daniel für die Familie Schröder?
   a. Er geht einkaufen.
   b. Er geht mit dem Hund spazieren.
   c. Er macht Reparaturen.

4. Wann fängt Daniels Arbeit im Hotel an?
   a. um 6 Uhr
   b. um 7 Uhr
   c. um 5 Uhr

5. Wann kommt Daniel nach Hause zurück?
   a. um 12 Uhr nachts
   b. um 6 Uhr abends
   c. so gegen 3 Uhr nachmittags

6. Was macht Daniel dann zuerst?
   a. Er geht schlafen.
   b. Er geht einkaufen.
   c. Er räumt das Zimmer auf.

7. Wann fängt Daniels Leben für die Kunst an?
   a. spät nachmittags
   b. am Wochenende
   c. so gegen Mitternacht

8. Wie verbringt Daniel manchmal seinen Abend?
   a. Er sieht fern.
   b. Er lädt Freunde ein.
   c. Er ruft Freunde an.

9. Wann schläft Daniel gewöhnlich ein?
   a. um 12 Uhr nachts
   b. nicht vor 1 Uhr nachts
   c. so gegen halb eins

Übung 2 Was Daniel macht

Erzählen Sie jetzt mit Hilfe der Fragen und Antworten in **Übung 1,** was Daniel jeden Tag macht.

BEISPIEL: Daniel wacht gewöhnlich sehr früh auf.

Übung 3 Eine Verabredung°

Die folgenden Sätze sind eine Konversation zwischen Hans und Petra. Ergänzen Sie zuerst die Verben mit den fehlenden (*missing*) Präfixen. Arrangieren Sie dann die Sätze als Dialog, und üben Sie den Dialog mit einem Partner / einer Partnerin.

° A date

____4____ Um acht. Ich komme um halb acht <u>vorbei</u> und hole dich <u>ab</u>.

____2____ Ja, ich gehe ins Kino. Im Olympia läuft ein neuer Film mit Keanu Reeves. Kommst du <u>mit</u>?

____5____ Schön. Hinterher lade ich dich zu einem Bier <u>ein</u>.

____3____ Gerne. Wann fängt der Film denn <u>an</u>?

____1____ Hast du für heute Abend schon etwas <u>vor</u>?

Übung 4 Was ich so mache

Was machen Sie **immer, manchmal, selten, nie, oft, gewöhnlich?** Vergleichen Sie sich (*compare yourself*) mit den Personen in den folgenden Sätzen.

BEISPIEL: Daniel steht gewöhnlich früh auf. →
      Ich stehe nie früh auf.

1. Daniel steht gewöhnlich sehr früh auf.
2. Daniel geht nie am Wochenende einkaufen.
3. Lilo geht oft mit ihrem Hund spazieren.
4. Hans räumt selten sein Zimmer auf.
5. Lilo schläft gewöhnlich beim Fernsehen ein.
6. Daniel lädt manchmal abends Freunde ein.
7. Daniel schläft selten vor 1 Uhr nachts ein.
8. Lilo ruft ihre Eltern oft an.
9. Daniel geht selten mit Freunden aus.

Übung 5 Wie sieht dein Tag aus?

Schritt 1: Arbeiten Sie zu zweit und stellen Sie einander folgende Fragen. Formulieren Sie Ihre Antworten mit Hilfe der Ausdrücke auf der nächsten Seite. Schreiben Sie die Antworten auf.

- Was machst du gewöhnlich jeden Tag?
- Was machst du oft?
- Was machst du manchmal?
- Was machst du nie?

Übung 2. Suggestion: Do as a whole-class activity. Allow students to add as much detail as possible.

Additional Activity: Copy the audio script and white-out the prefixes of all separable-prefix verbs appearing in the text. Make copies for the entire class. This can also be done as additional homework or to reinforce new vocabulary and practice narrating a series of events.

Übung 3. Suggestion: Have students work alone to fill in the prefixes. Then have them work in pairs to rearrange the sentences and practice "making a date" in German.

Übung 4. Suggestion: Have students work in pairs, taking turns reading a statement and then commenting. Have them jot down their partner's answers. A few students will be asked to report back to the class what their partner does.

Übung 5. Suggestion: Have students scan the verbs and phrases to be used in their responses before starting the interviews.

einkaufen gehen   Zimmer aufräumen   arbeiten   spät aufwachen

nach ein Uhr einschlafen   Freunde/Eltern anrufen

mit Freunden ausgehen   vor sechs Uhr aufstehen

Freunde zu einer Party einladen   spazieren gehen

BEISPIEL: Ich stehe gewöhnlich vor sechs Uhr auf. Ich schlafe nie nach ein Uhr ein. …

Schritt 2: Geben Sie jetzt einen kurzen Bericht von etwa vier Sätzen.

BEISPIEL: Keith steht gewöhnlich vor sechs Uhr auf. Er räumt nie sein Zimmer auf. Er geht manchmal einkaufen. Jeden Tag geht er mit Freunden aus.

Modalverben

Modal Auxiliary Verbs°

Modal auxiliary verbs (for example, *must, can, may*) express an attitude toward an action.

Morgen **möchten** wir Tennis **spielen.**

Am Wochenende **wollen** wir Freunde **besuchen.**

Ich **kann** morgen **vorbeikommen.**

*Tomorrow we **would like to play** tennis.*

*On the weekend we **want to visit** friends.*

*I **can come by** tomorrow.*

Note:

- The modal auxiliary verb is the conjugated verb and is in the second position in a statement.
- Its complement—the verb that expresses the action—is in the infinitive form and stands at the end of the sentence.
- In German, sentences with modal auxiliaries and a dependent infinitive demonstrate the pattern of the sentence bracket (**Satzklammer**) that you learned earlier in this chapter.

¹novels

		SATZKLAMMER	
Morgen	**möchten**	wir Tennis	**spielen.**
Peter	**muss**	morgen leider	**arbeiten.**
Ich	**kann**	dich heute	**besuchen.**
Heute Abend	**wollen**	wir ins Kino	**gehen.**

German has the following modal verbs.

dürfen	to be allowed to, may	**Dürfen** wir hier rauchen? *May we smoke here?*
können	to be able to, can	Ich **kann** dich gut verstehen. *I can understand you well.*
mögen	to like, care for	**Mögen** Sie Bücher? *Do you like books?*
müssen	to have to, must	Er **muss** heute arbeiten. *He has to work today.*
sollen	to be supposed to, shall	Wann **sollen** wir vorbeikommen? *When are we supposed to come by?*
wollen	to want to, plan to do	**Willst** du mitgehen? *Do you want to go along?*

The Present Tense of Modals

Modals are irregular verbs. With the exception of **sollen,** they have stem-vowel changes in the singular. Note also that the first- and third-person singular forms are identical and have no personal ending.

	dürfen	können	mögen	müssen	sollen	wollen
ich	**darf**	**kann**	**mag**	**muss**	**soll**	**will**
du	darfst	kannst	magst	musst	sollst	willst
er sie } es	**darf**	**kann**	**mag**	**muss**	**soll**	**will**
wir	dürfen	können	mögen	müssen	sollen	wollen
ihr	dürft	könnt	mögt	müsst	sollt	wollt
sie	dürfen	können	mögen	müssen	sollen	wollen
Sie	dürfen	können	mögen	müssen	sollen	wollen

SIE DÜRFEN HIER NICHT PARKEN

Möchte (*would like to*), one of the most common modal verbs, is the subjunctive of **mögen**. Note that the first- and third-person singular forms are identical.

Wir **möchten** morgen Tennis
spielen.

*We would like to play tennis
tomorrow.*

möchte			
ich	**möchte**	wir	möchten
du	möchtest	ihr	möchtet
er sie es	**möchte**	sie	möchten
Sie möchten			

Note:

- The modal **mögen** is generally used without a dependent infinitive.

  Er **mag** seine Arbeit im Hotel.   *He likes his work in the hotel.*

- The infinitive in a sentence with a modal verb may be omitted when its meaning is understood.

  Ich **muss** jetzt in die Vorlesung
  (**gehen**).

  I have to go to the lecture now.

  Ich **möchte** jetzt nach Hause
  (**gehen**).

  I would like to go home now.

  Er **will** das nicht (**machen**).   *He doesn't want to do that.*

Scan the headlines and visuals.

- Identify all modal auxiliary verbs in the headlines and visual. Give the English equivalents of the sentences.

- What verbs express the action in those sentences?

- Mark the two parts of each sentence bracket.

Ich möchte mehr Informationen über Greenpeace!

So schön (spannend, aufregend) kann Fernsehen sein

Die Studenten wollen streiken

JEDER KANN AUS-
GLEITEN UND
FALLEN
MAN DARF NUR
NICHT
LIEGENBLEIBEN [1]

AUS INDIEN

[1]Jeder ... *Anyone can slip and fall;
the trick is not to stay down.*

Übung 6 . Was kann man da machen?

BEISPIEL: in der Bibliothek →
　　　　s1: Was kann man in der Bibliothek machen?
　　　　s2: Da kann man Bücher lesen!

1. im Restaurant
2. im Kino
3. im Internetcafé
4. in der Disko
5. im Kaufhaus
6. im Park
7. in der Bibliothek

a. Filme sehen
b. einkaufen
c. tanzen
d. Freunde treffen
e. Bücher lesen
f. etwas essen
g. spazieren gehen
h. am Computer arbeiten

Übung 7 Was darf man hier machen oder nicht machen?

BEISPIEL: Man darf hier nicht parken.

1.

2.

3.

4.

5.

6.

campen
schnell fahren
schwimmen
parken

spielen
rauchen (*smoke*)
von 8 bis 14 Uhr parken

Übung 8 Was möchtest du lieber° machen?

Fragen Sie einen Partner / eine Partnerin, was er/sie lieber machen möchte.

BEISPIEL: schwimmen gehen oder Tennis spielen? →
　　　　s1: Was möchtest du lieber machen: schwimmen gehen oder
　　　　　　Tennis spielen?
　　　　s2: Ich möchte lieber Tennis spielen.

1. Zeitung lesen oder im Internet surfen?
2. fernsehen oder einkaufen gehen?
3. ins Café oder ins Kino gehen?
4. deine Familie anrufen oder eine E-Mail schreiben?
5. ein Picknick machen oder spazieren gehen?
6. eine Party zu Hause machen oder ausgehen?

would you rather

Chris und Jeff wohnen im Deutschen Haus an einer amerikanischen Universität. Sie sollen so oft wie möglich deutsch miteinander sprechen. Hören Sie zu, und kreuzen Sie die richtige Information an.

	DAS STIMMT	DAS STIMMT NICHT
1. Chris muss für einen Test arbeiten.	☐	☐
2. Er redet laut (*aloud*) und stört (*disturbs*) seinen Mitbewohner Jeff.	☐	☐
3. Jeff wird jetzt böse (*annoyed*).	☐	☐
4. Chris kann nur laut lernen.	☐	☐
5. Chris geht in die Bibliothek.	☐	☐

facts

Was wissen Sie über die beiden Bewohner des Deutschen Hauses? Bilden Sie Sätze.

Chris	soll	ins Badezimmer gehen
Jeff	muss	deutsche Grammatik lernen
	kann	ein A bekommen
	will	nur laut Deutsch lernen
	möchte	Jeff nicht stören
		auch arbeiten
		jetzt auch schlafen
		nicht arbeiten
		lesen

Brigitte, Lisa und Anja haben endlich ein Dach (*roof*) über dem Kopf: eine Wohnung auf einem alten Bauernhof (*farm*). Jetzt planen sie eine Party. Setzen Sie passende Modalverben in die Lücken ein.

BRIGITTE: Also wen _____[1] (*want to*) wir denn einladen?

LISA: Die Frage ist: Wie viele Leute _____[2] (*can*) wir denn einladen? Wir haben ja nicht so viel Platz.

ANJA: Im Wohnzimmer _____[3] (*can*) bestimmt zwanzig Leute sitzen.

LISA: Und tanzen _____[4] (*can*) wir im Garten.

ANJA: Und wer _____[5] (*is supposed to*) für so viele Leute kochen?

LISA: Ich _____[6] (*want*) lieber nur ein paar Leute einladen.

ANJA: Wir sagen, jeder _____[7] (*is supposed to*) etwas zum Essen mitbringen.

BRIGITTE: Ich _____[8] (*would like to*) Kartoffelsalat mit Würstchen machen.

LISA: Gute Idee. Das ist einfach, und das _____[9] (*like*) alle.

ANJA: Tut mir leid, aber ich _____[10] (*like*) Kartoffelsalat nicht.

BRIGITTE: Ich _____[11] (*can*) auch was Italienisches machen, Pizza oder Lasagne.

LISA: Wir _____[12] (*may*) aber nicht nur Bier servieren, wir _____[13] (*have to*) auch Mineralwasser oder Cola servieren, für die Autofahrer.

Übung 12　Ein Picknick im Grünen

Übung 12. Suggestion: This exercise can be done as a written homework assignment.

Einige Mitbewohner im internationalen Studentenwohnheim planen ein Picknick. Wer bringt was mit?

BEISPIEL: Andreas will ein Frisbee mitbringen. Er soll auch Mineralwasser mitbringen.

Jürgen aus München	wollen	Brot und Käse (*cheese*)	kaufen
Stephanie aus den USA	müssen	Mineralwasser	mitbringen
Paola und Maria aus Italien	möchte sollen	Bier	machen
Nagako aus Tokio	können	ein Radio	
Michel aus Frankreich		ein Frisbee	
ich		eine Pizza	
		Kartoffelsalat	
		eine Kamera	
		einen Fußball	

Übung 13　Kommst du mit?

Übung 13. Suggestion: This activity is best done with students circulating in class. Assign several students to act as observers who jot down the different excuses they hear and report them to the class afterward.

Arbeiten Sie mit einem Partner / einer Partnerin zusammen. Laden Sie ihn/sie ein, etwas mit Ihnen zu unternehmen (*do*). Er/Sie soll die Einladung ablehnen (*decline*) und einen Grund (*reason*) dafür angeben.

BEISPIEL: S1: Ich will heute Tennis spielen. Möchtest du mitkommen?
　　　　　S2: Nein, leider kann ich nicht. Ich muss nämlich arbeiten.
oder:　S2: Ich möchte schon. Leider muss ich …

S1	S2
heute Abend ins Rockkonzert gehen	arbeiten
ins Kino gehen	meine Eltern besuchen
nach (+ *place*) fahren	zu Hause bleiben. (Mein Wagen ist kaputt.)
ins Café gehen	mein Zimmer aufräumen
Tennis spielen	Deutsch lernen
Mini-Golf spielen	eine Arbeit schreiben
zu einer Party gehen	??
tanzen gehen	
??	

The Imperative°

Der Imperativ

The Imperative. Suggestion: Introduce imperatives through Total Physical Response (TPR) techniques. Have students carry out several typical classroom actions: *Stehen Sie auf! Machen Sie die Tür auf! Gehen Sie an die Tafel! Öffnen Sie Ihr Buch!*

The imperative is the verb form used to make requests and recommendations and to give instructions, advice, or commands. You are already familiar with imperative forms used in common classroom requests.

Wiederholen Sie bitte.	*Repeat, please.*
Hören Sie zu!	*Listen!*
Sagen Sie das auf Deutsch.	*Say that in German.*
Nehmen Sie Platz!	*Be seated!*

These are examples of formal imperatives, used for anyone you would address as **Sie.** There are two additional imperative forms, used for informally addressing one or several people whom you would address individually as **du.** Imperatives in written German often end in an exclamation point, especially to emphasize a request or a command.

OVERVIEW OF IMPERATIVE FORMS			
Infinitive	*Formal*	*Informal Singular*	*Informal Plural*
kommen	**Kommen Sie** bald.	**Komm** bald.	**Kommt** bald.
fahren	**Fahren Sie** langsam!	**Fahr** langsam!	**Fahrt** langsam!
anrufen	**Rufen Sie** mich **an.**	**Ruf** mich **an.**	**Ruft** mich **an.**
sprechen	**Sprechen Sie** langsam!	**Sprich** langsam!	**Sprecht** langsam!
arbeiten	**Arbeiten Sie** jetzt!	**Arbeite** jetzt!	**Arbeitet** jetzt!
sein	**Seien Sie** freundlich.	**Sei** freundlich.	**Seid** freundlich.

Formal Imperative

The formal imperative is formed by inverting the subject **(Sie)** and the verb in the present tense.

Note:

- The formal imperative has the same word order as a yes/no question; only punctuation or intonation identifies it as an imperative.
- The imperative of the verb **sein** is irregular.

Seien Sie bitte freundlich!   *Please be friendly.*

Bitte nehmen Sie Platz

Particles and **bitte** with the Imperative

Requests or commands are often softened by adding the word **bitte** and particles such as **doch** and **mal. Bitte** can stand at the beginning, in the middle, or at the end of the sentence. The particles **doch** and **mal** follow the imperative form. They have no English equivalent.

Hören Sie **bitte** zu!	*Please listen.*
Bitte nehmen Sie Platz.	*Please have a seat.*
Kommen Sie **doch** heute vorbei.	*Why don't you come by today?*
Rufen Sie mich **mal** an.	*Give me a call (some time).* *(Why don't you give me a call some time?)*

office hour   Übung 1: In der Sprechstunde

Mary Lerner geht zum Professor in die Sprechstunde. Kreuzen Sie an, ob es um eine Frage oder eine Aufforderung (*request or command*) geht.

	FRAGE	AUFFORDERUNG		FRAGE	AUFFORDERUNG
1.	☐	☒	8.	☒	☐
2.	☐	☒	9.	☐	☒
3.	☐	☒	10.	☒	☐
4.	☒	☐	11.	☒	☐
5.	☐	☒	12.	☐	☒
6.	☒	☐	13.	☒	☐
7.	☐	☒	14.	☐	☒

Suggestion: Once students have completed the listening part and marked their answers, go over each sentence once more and illustrate the differences in intonation. Have students repeat questions and then turn them into requests or commands by changing their intonation and vice versa. In the case of questions, have students provide possible answers as well.

Informal Imperative

The singular informal imperative is used for anyone you address with **du**. It is formed for most verbs simply by dropping the **-st** ending from the present-tense **du**-form of the verb.

kommen: du **kommst** → **Komm!**

anrufen: du **rufst an** → **Ruf an!**

arbeiten: du **arbeitest** → **Arbeite!**

sprechen: du **sprichst** → **Sprich!**

nehmen: du **nimmst** → **Nimm!**

But: sein: du **bist** → **Sei!**

Verbs that show a vowel change from **a** to **ä** (or **au** to **äu**) in the present tense have no umlaut in the imperative.

du **fährst** → **Fahr!**

du **läufst** → **Lauf!**

Mach Dir ein paar schöne Stunden... geh ins **Kino**

Schreib mal wieder.
Deutsche Post AG

The plural informal imperative is used to request something from several persons whom you individually address with **du**.

Kommt doch mal zu uns.	*Why don't you come see us. (lit., Come to us.)*
Fahrt jetzt nach Hause.	*Drive home now.*
Gebt mir bitte etwas zu essen.	*Please give me something to eat.*
Seid doch ruhig!	*Be quiet!*

This imperative form is identical to the **ihr**-form of the present tense, but without the pronoun **ihr.**

GENIESS[1] **DIE KLEINE PAUSE. SAG JA ZU YES.**

Leicht wie Biscuit. Locker wie frische Torte.

[1]*enjoy*

Ergänzen Sie die Tabelle.

FORMAL	INFORMAL SING.	INFORMAL PL.
1. Kommen Sie, bitte!	Komm, bitte!	_____, bitte!
2. _____ leise, bitte!	Sprich leise, bitte!	_____ leise, bitte!
3. Laden Sie uns bitte ein.	_____ uns bitte _____.	_____ uns bitte _____.
4. _____ doch ruhig!	Sei doch ruhig!	_____ doch ruhig!
5. Fahren Sie langsam!	_____ langsam!	Fahrt langsam!
6. Rufen Sie mich mal an.	_____ mich mal _____.	Ruft mich mal an.
7. _____ das Buch mit.	_____ das Buch mit.	Nehmt das Buch mit.
8. Machen Sie schnell!	Mach schnell!	_____ schnell!
9. Hören Sie doch auf!	_____ doch _____!	_____ doch _____!

*We students say **du** to each other.*

Stellen Sie sich vor, Sie sind neu im Studentenwohnheim und reden alle Ihre Mitbewohner zuerst mit **Sie** an. Jetzt müssen Sie **du** benutzen, denn alle Studenten duzen einander. Setzen Sie die Imperativsätze in die **du**-Form.

BEISPIEL: Bitte, kommen Sie herein.   Bitte, komm herein.

1. Bitte, sprechen Sie etwas langsamer.
2. Hören Sie bitte zu.
3. Arbeiten Sie nicht so viel!
4. Fahren Sie doch am Wochenende mit mir nach Heidelberg.
5. Bleiben Sie doch noch ein bisschen.
6. Besuchen Sie mich mal.
7. Rufen Sie mich morgen um 10 Uhr an!
8. Gehen Sie doch ins Kino mit.
9. Kommen Sie doch morgen vorbei.
10. Nehmen Sie die Zeitung mit.
11. Sehen Sie mal, hier ist ein Foto von meiner Familie.
12. Seien Sie bitte ruhig!

Sie möchten Ihren Freunden sagen, was sie alles tun sollen. Machen Sie aus den Fragen Imperativsätze. Benutzen Sie dabei auch **doch, mal** oder **bitte**.

BEISPIEL: Kommt ihr heute Abend vorbei?
         Kommt bitte heute Abend vorbei!

1. Ladet ihr mich ein?
2. Ruft ihr mich morgen an?
3. Holt ihr mich ab?
4. Sprecht ihr immer deutsch?
5. Hört ihr zu?
6. Geht ihr mit?
7. Kommt ihr morgen vorbei?
8. Seid ihr morgen pünktlich?

Übung 18 Situationen im Alltag

Ergänzen Sie die passende Form des Imperativs von **sein.**

1. Ich muss Sie warnen: Autofahren in Deutschland ist ein Abenteuer.
   <u>Seien Sie</u> bitte vorsichtig!

2. Sie gehen mit zwei Freunden ins Konzert. Diese Freunde sind nie
   pünktlich und das irritiert Sie. Sie sagen zu ihnen: „<u>Seid</u> aber bitte
   pünktlich!"

3. Ihr Mitbewohner / Ihre Mitbewohnerin im Studentenwohnheim ist
   sehr unordentlich. Sie erwarten Ihre Eltern zu Besuch und bitten
   ihn/sie: „<u>Sei</u> so nett und räum deine Sachen auf!"

4. Drei Mitbewohner im Studentenwohnheim spielen um drei Uhr
   morgens immer noch laute Musik. Sie klopfen irritiert gegen die
   Wand und rufen: „Zum Donnerwetter, <u>seid</u> endlich ruhig!"

5. Frau Kümmel zu Frau Honig: „<u>Seien Sie</u> bitte so nett und kommen Sie
   morgen vorbei!"

Übung 18. Point Out: The phrase *Sei so gut/nett und …* and its variations are used in polite conversation in connection with a request. Have students add the appropriate forms of *Sei / Seid / Seien Sie so gut/nett* to *Ruf mich morgen an! Komm morgen vorbei! Öffnen Sie bitte das Fenster! Geht jetzt! Mach die Tür zu!*

Sprache im Kontext

Videoclips

A. Wie sind die Tagesroutinen von Jan und Beatrice? Was machen
sie morgens und abends? Schauen Sie sich die Interviews mit
Jan und Beatrice an und ergänzen Sie die Tabelle.

	JAN	BEATRICE
MORGENS	*7 Uhr – aufstehen*	
ABENDS		
		0–1 Uhr – ins Bett gehen

Videoclips. Suggestion: As a closed-book warm-up activity, ask students, *Was machen Studenten von morgens bis abends? Wann machen viele Studenten diese Sachen?* This can be done as a whole class activity, having them brainstorm orally, or alternately, as a free-association activity on the board. For the latter variation, write *morgens, nachmittags,* and *abends* on the board, and have students come to the board and write down what kinds of things students have to do on a daily basis. This will prepare them for the video segments of Jan and Beatrice taking about their daily routines.

Sprache im Kontext **137**

B. Schauen Sie sich das Interview mit Jasmin an und ergänzen Sie die Informationen.

1. Jasmin _____ um 8 Uhr.
2. Um _____ oder _____ Uhr kommt sie von der Arbeit nach Hause.
3. Sie geht ungefähr um 22 Uhr ins _____.
4. Am Wochenende _____ sie lange, macht Sport oder geht _____.
5. Sie geht gern _____ _____.

C. Und Sie? Machen Sie eine Tabelle für Ihre eigene (*own*) Tagesroutine. Erzählen Sie dann einem Partner / einer Partnerin, wie Ihr typischer Tag aussieht.

Lesen

Das folgende Lesestück beschreibt die tägliche Routine und die Freuden (*joys*) des Alltags.

Zum Thema

Immer das Gleiche (*the same thing*)?

A. Ergänzen Sie die Tabelle. Wie sieht Ihr Alltag aus? Und Ihr Wochenende?

MEIN ALLTAG		MEIN WOCHENENDE	
Uhrzeit	*Aktivität*	*Uhrzeit*	*Aktivität*
	aufstehen		
	ins Bett gehen		

B. Machen Sie etwas Besonderes (*something special*) am Wochenende? Berichten Sie mit Hilfe der Tabelle.

BEISPIEL: Gewöhnlich stehe ich um 7 Uhr auf. Aber am Wochenende schlafe ich lange.

Auf den ersten Blick

Überfliegen Sie (*skim*) den Text auf der nächsten Seite, „Immer das gleiche." Suchen Sie Wörter, die in die folgenden Kategorien passen: **Schule, zu Hause** und **unterwegs** (*on the road*).

BEISPIEL: SCHULE: lernen …
       ZU HAUSE: die kleineren Geschwister …
       UNTERWEGS: die vielen Menschen …

von Christine Wuttke

Jeden Tag das gleiche.
Ich geh' in die Schule,
lern was – oder auch nicht.
Sehe immer die vielen Menschen,
5 die unterwegs sind,
entweder mit der Straßenbahn[1]
oder zu Fuß
oder auch mit dem Auto.
Und ich fahr lächelnd[2] an den
10 Autoschlangen[3] vorbei.
Auch wenn[4] man als Radfahrer
Mühe[5] hat, vorwärtszukommen,
ist man doch oft schneller.
In der Schule sind es dann überall
15 dieselben Erzählungen[6] der Lehrer:
Ihr lernt für euch, nicht für mich.
Und was sonst noch so typisch ist.
In den Arbeiten frage ich mich,
was das Klima[7] ist, was der Transformator ist,
20 oder was ist der Satz aus der Wassermusik.
Und ich kann mal wieder nur abgucken[8].
Endlich wieder zu Hause,
haben die kleineren Geschwister sogar
mal das Fernsehen abgestellt[9] und spielen
25 im Kinderzimmer.
Dann geh' ich zum Klavierunterricht[10],
zu Freunden oder in die Stadt,
und zähle die Werbeplakate[11]
an den Schaufenstern.
30 Abends im Bett denke ich dann,
wie „friedlich"[12] der Tag doch wieder war.
Immer das gleiche.

Oder ist es nicht jeden Tag was Besonderes[13],
was man erlebt[14]?
35 Aber doch das gleiche?
Sehe ich nicht jeden Tag andere Leute
auf den Straßen?
Reden die Lehrer nicht doch immer
was anderes?
40 Schreiben sie nicht jedesmal andere Arbeiten,
in denen[15] man auch mal was weiß?
Aber es ist jeden Tag das gleiche.

Immer das Gleiche? Physik-Vorlesung an der Uni Potsdam

---

[1]*street car* [2]*smiling* [3]*lines of cars* [4]*Auch ... Even if* [5]*difficulty* [6]*stories* [7]*climate*
[8]*to copy from someone/cheat* [9]*haben ... abgestellt turned off* [10]*piano lesson*
[11]*advertising posters* [12]*peaceful* [13]*was ... something special* [14]*experiences*
[15]*which*

As you read a text, you may be tempted to look up most of the words you do not know. Before reaching for the dictionary, however, try to guess the meaning of words from the context. If you find you really must use a dictionary, consider the following:

- Many compound words are not listed in dictionaries. To discover their meaning, look up the components and determine the meaning of the compound from the definitions of its components.

- Some forms found in texts differ from those listed in dictionaries. For example, nouns and pronouns are listed in the nominative singular; verbs are listed under their infinitive forms.

- Some words have multiple meanings. Read through all possible meanings and choose the correct meaning of the word based on its use in the text.

For practice in using a dictionary, do the following exercise:

- Can you figure out what **Autoschlange** means by looking up its components?

- Under which entry would you find **jeden?** And what about the phrase **ich fahr ... vorbei?**

- How many different meanings can you find for the word **Satz?** Which of those meanings most closely fits the context of the word as it is used in the poem **Immer das gleiche?**

- Underline all words in the text that you do not understand. Choose five and look them up. In what form do they appear in the dictionary? How many meanings are given? Which meaning best fits the context?

Zum Text

A. Lesen Sie den Text und beantworten Sie die Fragen.

1. Ist die Autorin Schülerin, Universitätsstudentin oder Lehrerin? Woher wissen Sie das?

2. Wie alt ist sie wohl?

3. Wo lebt die Autorin? In einer Stadt oder auf dem Land? Wie beweist (*shows*) der Text das?

4. Wie groß ist ihre Familie?

B. In most of the text the author uses declarative sentences stating what she does every day. In the last verse she uses words such as **aber** and **oder** and asks herself whether each day really is the same. What does she say about each day that might make it different, even if she still has the same routine?

Zu guter Letzt

ein Besuch

Your cousin Stacy, who is learning German in high school, wants to come to visit you on campus because she will be applying to colleges next year. She will arrive on Thursday. You want to impress her with your German as well as show her around for a couple of days.

Schritt 1: So that you can get an overview of your time, jot down your usual Thursday-through-Sunday activities in the grid on the next page. Be sure to indicate the exact times at which you have things going on.

Zeit	Donnerstag	Freitag	Samstag	Sonntag
Vormittag				
Nachmittag				
Abend				

Schritt 2: Now write down six activities that you would like to do with your cousin while she is here, and put them into the schedule, too. They might include items such as:

- ins Restaurant gehen
- ins Kino gehen
- die Universität besichtigen (*tour*)
- Stacy in den Deutschkurs mitbringen

Schritt 3: Write your cousin an e-mail to tell her what you are planning for the two of you and when you will be doing those things.

Schritt 4: Working in pairs, describe to your partner what you are planning to do with your cousin. Ask at least three questions about your partner's plans.

Wortschatz

Tage und Tageszeiten
Days and Times of Day

der **Morgen**	morning
der **Vormittag**	morning, before noon
der **Mittag**	noon
der **Nachmittag**	afternoon
der **Abend**	evening
die **Nacht**	night
heute Morgen	this morning
heute Nachmittag	this afternoon
morgen früh	tomorrow morning
morgen Abend	tomorrow evening
morgens	in the morning, mornings
vormittags	before noon
mittags	at noon
nachmittags	in the afternoon, afternoons
abends	in the evening, evenings
nachts	at night, nights
montags	Mondays, on Monday(s)
dienstags	Tuesdays, on Tuesday(s)
mittwochs	Wednesdays, on Wednesday(s)
donnerstags	Thursdays, on Thursday(s)
freitags	Fridays, on Friday(s)
samstags; sonnabends	Saturdays, on Saturday(s)
sonntags	Sundays, on Sunday(s)

Unterhaltung / Entertainment

das **Ballett**, -e	ballet
die **Disko**, -s	disco; dance club
in die Disko gehen	to go clubbing
das **Fernsehen**	watching television
der **Film**, -e	film
das **Kino**, -s	cinema, (movie) theater
ins Kino gehen	to go to the movies
die **Komödie**, -n	comedy
das **Konzert**, -e	concert
ins Konzert gehen	to go to a concert
der **Krimi**, -s	crime, detective, mystery film or book
die **Oper**, -n	opera
in die Oper gehen	to go to the opera
das **Theater**, -	(stage) theater
ins Theater gehen	to go to the theater
das **Theaterstück**, -e	play (stage) drama
die **Tragödie**, -n	tragedy

Verben mit trennbaren Präfixen / Verbs with Separable Prefixes

ab•holen	to pick up (*from a place*)
an•fangen (fängt an)	to begin
an•rufen	to call up
auf•hören (mit)	to stop (*doing something*)
auf•räumen	to clean up, straighten up
auf•stehen	to get up; to stand up
auf•wachen	to wake up
aus•gehen	to go out
ein•kaufen (gehen)	to (go) shop(ping)
ein•laden (lädt ein)	to invite
ein•schlafen (schläft ein)	to fall asleep
fern•sehen (sieht fern)	to watch television
mit•kommen	to come along
mit•nehmen (nimmt mit)	to take along
vorbei•kommen	to come by
vor•haben (hat vor)	to plan (*to do*)
zu•hören	to listen
zurück•kommen	to return, come back

Modalverben / Modal Verbs

dürfen (darf)	to be permitted to; may
können (kann)	to be able to; can
mögen (mag)	to care for; to like
möchte	would like to
müssen (muss)	to have to; must
sollen	to be supposed to; ought, should
wollen (will)	to want to; to plan to

Uhrzeiten / Time

die **Minute**, -n	minute
die **Sekunde**, -n	second
die **Stunde**, -n	hour
Um wie viel Uhr?	At what time?
Wie spät ist es? / Wie viel Uhr ist es?	What time is it?
Es ist eins. / Es ist ein Uhr.	It's one o'clock.
halb: halb zwei	half: half past one, one-thirty
nach: fünf nach zwei	after: five after two
um: um zwei	at: at two
Viertel: Es ist Viertel nach/vor zwei.	quarter: It's a quarter after/to two.
vor: fünf vor zwei	to, of: five to/of two

Sonstiges / Other

frühstücken	to eat breakfast
spazieren gehen	to go for a walk
Ich gehe spazieren.	I'm going for a walk.
treffen (trifft)	to meet
die **Bibliothek**, -en	library
das **Fitnesscenter**, -	gym
der **Plan**, ̈e	plan
die **Tasse**, -n	cup
eine Tasse Kaffee	a cup of coffee
die **Vorlesung**, -en	(university) lecture
der **Vortrag**, ̈e	lecture
die **Woche**, -n	week
pro Woche	per week
das **Wochenende**, -n	weekend
am liebsten: möchte am liebsten	would like to (do) most
doch	(*intensifying particle often used with imperatives*)
früh	early
gemütlich	cozy, cozily
gewöhnlich	usual(ly)
lieber: möchte lieber	would rather
mal	(*softening particle often used with imperatives*)
man	one, people, you, they
Hier darf man nicht parken.	You may not park here.
spannend	suspenseful, exciting
spät	late

1. Wie viel Uhr ist es? Sagen Sie die Zeit auf Deutsch:

   6.00; 9.30; 12.45; 14.07; 17.15.

2. Was machen Sie gewöhnlich zwischen 6 Uhr morgens und 18 Uhr abends? Nennen Sie drei Dinge (*things*).

3. Was möchten Sie am Wochenende machen? Nennen Sie drei Dinge.

4. Bilden Sie Sätze.

   a. ich / morgens / um 7 Uhr / aufstehen
   b. die Vorlesung / um 11 Uhr / aufhören
   c. wir / einladen / 20 Leute / zur Party
   d. was / du / vorhaben / am Wochenende / ?

5. Wie sagt man das auf Deutsch?

   a. Please drop by at 6:00 p.m. (*familiar singular*)
   b. I can't go to the movies. I have to work.
   c. Please call me on Saturday morning. (*formal*)
   d. Would you like to go to the movies tonight? (*familiar plural*)
   e. Parking is not allowed here. (*familiar singular*)

Einkaufen

Was kann man auf
dem Markt kaufen?

In diesem Kapitel

- **Themen:** Clothes, colors, types of foods, names of stores and shops
- **Grammatik:** Dative case; verbs that require dative; dative prepositions
  wo, wohin, and **woher**
- **Kultur:** Clothing sizes, shopping, prices, weights and measures
- **Lesen:** „Im Hutladen" (Karl Valentin)

Videoclips
Einkaufen: was und wo?

Alles klar?

Suggestion: Give students several minutes to skim the information in class, or else assign the text for homework. Have students formulate statements similar to the ones in the examples. Be sure to personalize the material by asking students what they need or would like to buy at a department store. Ask students what differences they notice in the goods and services offered at a department store like this and those with which they are familiar. (For example, most department stores do not sell furniture, but they do include a supermarket.)

A. Sie sehen im Bild ein Kaufhaus in Deutschland. Man kann da vieles kaufen. Wo findet man alles?

BEISPIELE: Computer findet man im vierten Stock.
Bücher findet man im Erdgeschoss.

1. Schreibwaren
2. Schuhe
3. Pullover
4. Sportartikel
5. Telefonapparate
6. Teppiche
7. Make-up
8. Brokkoli
9. DVD-Spieler
10. Parfüm
11. Fernseher
12. Kaffeetassen
13. Butter
14. Shampoo

im Erdgeschoss

im vierten Stock

im dritten Stock

im Untergeschoss

im ersten Stock

im zweiten Stock

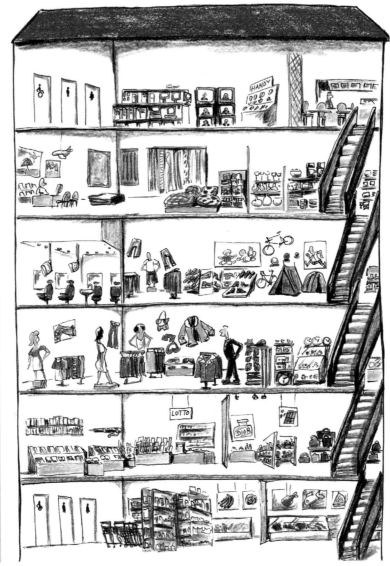

4	Computer TV/DVD/CD Center Foto/Optik Elektrogeräte Telefon/Handy Shop Kundenrestaurant Toiletten
3	Bettwäsche Gardinen Teppiche Orientteppiche Geschenkartikel Glas/Porzellan Haushaltswaren Reisebüro
2	Jeans-Wear Mode-Boutiquen Kinderkonfektion Babywäsche Schuhe Sport/Fahrräder Camping Friseursalon
1	Damenkonfektion Damenwäsche Herrenkonfektion Herrenartikel Accessoires Handschuhe Bademoden Uhren/Schmuck
E	Lederwaren Lotto/Tabak Zeitschriften Parfümerie Kosmetik/Drogerie Schreibwaren Bücher Süßigkeiten
U	Lebensmittel Toiletten

¹E = Erdgeschoss (*ground floor*)
²U = Untergeschoss (*basement*)

B. Sie hören nun vier Ansagen (*announcements*) im Kaufhaus. Markieren Sie, was die Sprecher beschreiben.

1. Kosmetik   Kameras   Fahrräder
2. Schmuck   Betten   Schuhe
3. Bücher   Kaffeemaschinen   Lederjacken
4. Jeans   Lampen   Fernseher

Wörter im Kontext

Neue Wörter

die Klamotte (Klamotten,
  pl.) duds, rags (*slang for
  clothing*)
das Hemd shirt
das Kleid dress
das Sakko sport coat
die Badehose swim trunks
der Anzug suit
die Socke (Socken, *pl.*)
  socks
der Badeanzug (woman's)
  bathing suit
der Rock skirt
der Rucksack backpack
der Schal scarf
der Hausschuh (Hausschuhe,
  pl.) slippers
der Koffer suitcase
trägt (tragen) is wearing

THEMA 1: Kleidungsstücke

A. Klamotten, Klamotten! Was sehen Sie im Schrank? Kreuzen Sie an!

Ich sehe …

- ☐ ein **Hemd**
- ☐ ein **Kleid**
- ☐ ein **Polohemd**
- ☐ ein **Sakko**
- ☐ ein **Sweatshirt**
- ☐ eine **Badehose**
- ☐ einen **Anzug**
- ☐ **Socken**
- ☐ ein **T-Shirt**
- ☐ einen **Badeanzug**
- ☐ einen **Wintermantel**
- ☐ einen **Rock**
- ☐ einen **Rucksack**
- ☐ einen **Schal**
- ☐ **Hausschuhe**
- ☐ **Jeans**
- ☐ einen **Koffer**
- ☐ einen **Pullover**

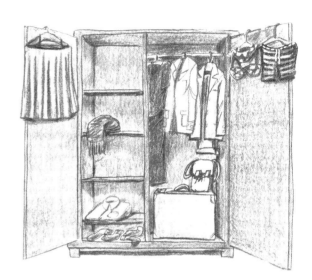

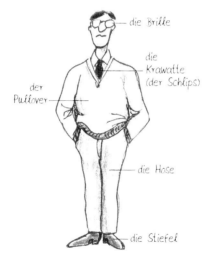

B. Wer **trägt** was?

BEISPIEL: Die Frau trägt einen Hut, einen Mantel, eine Bluse, …

C. Was haben Sie alles zu Hause in Ihrem Kleiderschrank?

BEISPIEL: Ich habe ein Sakko, 15 T-Shirts, Hemden, 5 Hosen, Socken, und
    Schuhe in meinem Kleiderschrank.

Die Koffer-Checkliste notiert Kleidungsstücke für den Urlaub (*vacation*).

- Welche Kleidungsstücke sind für den Winter? Welche sind für den Sommer?
- Welche Sachen auf dieser Liste tragen Sie besonders gern?
- Suchen Sie aus der Liste vier zusammengesetzte Wörter (*compounds*).

Bilden Sie nun Ihre eigenen Wörter.

BEISPIEL: Bade- + Hose = Badehose

Bade-
Cord-
Baumwoll-   Anzug
Trainings-   +   Mantel
Leder-   Hose
Regen-   Hemd
                 Jacke
                 Schuhe

Analyse. Point Out: *Trainings- und Jogginganzüge = Trainingsanzüge und Jogginganzüge.* The hyphen after *Trainings-* stands for the word shared with the following compound (*Anzüge*).

Koffer-Checkliste
Für den Urlaub

☐ T-Shirts   ☐ Sweatshirts
☐ Shorts   ☐ Baumwollhosen
☐ Cordhosen   ☐ Trainings- und Jogginganzüge
☐ Regenmantel   ☐ Sportschuhe
☐ Sandalen   ☐ Unterwäsche
☐ Badeanzug   ☐ Jacke
☐ Badehose   ☐ Handschuhe
☐ Blusen   ☐ Stiefel
☐ Röcke   ☐ Pullover
☐ Kleider   ☐ Mütze
☐ Hemden

Aktivität 1   Eine Reise nach Südspanien

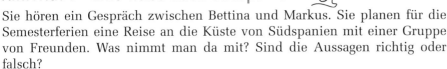

Sie hören ein Gespräch zwischen Bettina und Markus. Sie planen für die Semesterferien eine Reise an die Küste von Südspanien mit einer Gruppe von Freunden. Was nimmt man da mit? Sind die Aussagen richtig oder falsch?

	RICHTIG	FALSCH
1. Bettina und Markus nehmen einen Koffer und einen Rucksack mit.	☐	☒
2. Markus nimmt Shorts, ein paar T-Shirts und Jeans mit.	☐	☒
3. Bettina braucht unbedingt einen neuen Badeanzug.	☒	☐
4. Markus empfiehlt ihr, sie soll einen Bikini in Spanien kaufen.	☐	☒
5. Markus hat einen besonderen Gürtel für sein Geld.	☒	☐
6. Bettina steckt ihr Geld in die Schuhe.	☒	☐

Aktivität 2   Was tragen Sie gewöhnlich?

Sagen Sie, was Sie in den folgenden Situationen tragen.

BEISPIEL: Ich trage gewöhnlich Jeans und ein T-Shirt zur Uni. Zur Arbeit trage ich ein Sporthemd, eine Hose und ein Sakko.

zur Arbeit	einen Anzug
zur Uni	einen Badeanzug
im Winter	ein Kleid
im Urlaub auf Hawaii	ein Abendkleid
zu Hause	einen Wintermantel
auf einer Fete	Jeans
zu einer Hochzeit	ein T-Shirt
??	??

Aktivität 2. Alternate activity: This activity can also be converted into a *Partnerarbeit.* Have students choose 2–3 situations and tell their partners what they wear in such circumstances, then have them report what their partners wear and when. As a follow-up activity, ask students, *Und heute? Was tragen Sie heute?* You may wish to elicit full-sentence answers.

Wörter im Kontext   **147**

The impersonal expression **es gibt** means *there is* or *there are*. It can also be used to say where you can get something. The object of **es gibt** is always in the accusative case.

Schicke Blusen
Wo?
bei
Gisie
Papendiek 29

Es gibt in dieser Stadt einen Markt.	*There is a market in this town. (It exists.)*
Wo gibt es schicke Blusen?	*Where can you get stylish blouses?*

Use the preposition **bei** and the name of the place to say where you can get something.

Blusen gibt es **bei** Gisie.	*You can get blouses at Gisie's (shop).*

clothing

Was brauchen Sie, und wo gibt es das? Was kostet das?

BEISPIEL: s1: Ich brauche dringend ein Hemd. Wo gibt es hier Hemden?
s2: Hemden gibt es bei Strauss.
s1: Weißt du, wie viel ein Hemd da kostet?
s2: Es gibt Hemden für 24,90 Euro.

Stiefel	Schuhe
Hose	Gürtel
Bluse	Krawatte

Strauss
INNOVATION

ARIANE 14,90 €

Graceland 14,90 €

THE
SHOP

DEICHMANN

Aktivität 4 Koffer packen!°

Let's pack our bags!

Spielen Sie in Gruppen von vier bis fünf Personen. So spielt man es:

BEISPIEL: S1: Ich packe fünf Bikinis in meinen Koffer.
S2: Ich packe fünf Bikinis und Sportschuhe in meinen Koffer.
S3: Ich packe fünf Bikinis, Sportschuhe und Ledersandalen in meinen Koffer.

Wer etwas vergisst (*forgets*) oder falsch sagt, scheidet aus (*drops out*).

THEMA 2: Beim Einkaufen im Kaufhaus

Bernd Thalhofer geht einkaufen, denn er braucht ein paar neue Hemden.

VERKÄUFER: Bitte schön. Kann ich Ihnen **helfen?**

BERND: Ich brauche ein paar neue Sporthemden.

VERKÄUFER: Welche **Größe** brauchen Sie?

BERND: Größe 42.

VERKÄUFER: Und welche **Farbe?**

BERND: Grün oder blau.

VERKÄUFER: **Wie gefällt Ihnen** dieses **gestreifte** Hemd in Marineblau? Sehr dezent (*tasteful*) und **modisch.**

BERND: Ich finde, **die Farbe steht mir** nicht. Haben Sie das in Hellblau?

VERKÄUFER: Ja, hier ist ein Hemd in Hellblau.

BERND: Ist das aus Baumwolle oder Synthetik?

VERKÄUFER: Das ist 100 Prozent Baumwolle. Möchten Sie es **anprobieren?**

BERND: Nein, das ist nicht **nötig.** Größe 42 **passt** mir bestimmt. Wie viel kostet dieses Hemd?

VERKÄUFER: 40 Euro.

BERND: Gut. Ich nehme drei Hemden.

VERKÄUFER: **Alle** in Hellblau?

BERND: Nein, geben Sie mir bitte zwei in Blau und ein Hemd in Weiß.

VERKÄUFER: **Das macht zusammen** 120 Euro. Bitte **zahlen** Sie vorne an der **Kasse!**

BERND: Danke schön.

VERKÄUFER: Bitte sehr.

Point Out: After the preposition in, colors are capitalized, e.g., ein Hemd in Hellblau.

	kariert
	gestreift

Beim Einkaufen im Kaufhaus. Suggestion: Begin by looking at the picture. What is happening? Where can you buy a shirt? Introduce new words using pictures, mime, and classroom situations. After students have heard the dialogue and then read it, assign pairs to role-play it.

Neue	Wörter

helfen help
die Größe size
die Farbe color
Wie gefällt Ihnen ...? How do you like . . . ?
modisch fashionable
Die Farbe steht mir. The color looks good on me.
anprobieren try on
nötig necessary
passt (passen) fits
das macht zusammen all together
zahlen pay
die Kasse cashier, checkout
empfiehlt (empfehlen) recommends
glaubt (glauben) believes
zeigt (zeigen) shows
schenkt (schenken) is giving
dankt (danken) thanks

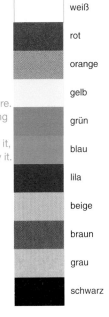

weiß
rot
orange
gelb
grün
blau
lila
beige
braun
grau
schwarz

- Was passiert im Kaufhaus? Stimmt das oder stimmt das nicht?

	DAS STIMMT	DAS STIMMT NICHT
1. Bernd braucht ein paar Sporthemden.	☒	☐
2. Er trägt Größe 42.	☒	☐
3. Der Verkäufer **empfiehlt** Bernd ein Hemd in Marineblau.	☒	☐
4. Bernd **glaubt,** Marineblau steht ihm sehr gut.	☐	☒
5. Der Verkäufer **zeigt** Bernd ein Hemd aus Baumwolle.	☒	☐
6. Bernd **schenkt** seinem Onkel die Hemden.	☐	☒
7. Bernd **dankt** dem Verkäufer.	☒	☐

Ergänzen Sie die fehlenden Informationen aus dem Dialog im Thema 2.

1. Der Kunde braucht _____.
2. Der Verkäufer möchte _____ und _____ wissen.
3. Der Kunde braucht _____ 42.
4. Größe 42 _____ ihm.
5. Das Hemd in Marineblau _____ ihm nicht.
6. Das Hemd ist aus _____ _____.
7. Der Kunde _____ 120 Euro für drei Hemden.

KULTURTIPP

Size designations in Europe vary greatly from those in North America. Shown below are approximate correlations between U.S. and German sizes.

Für Damen: Kleider, Mäntel, Jacken, Blusen

in USA	6	8	10	12	14	16
in Deutschland	34	36	38	40	42	44

Kleine Preise auch für große
Größen! Tolle Angebote,[1] wie
z. B. sportliche Pullover in modischen Dessins

Für Herren: Mäntel, Anzüge, Sakkos

in USA	36	38	40	42	44
in Deutschland	46	48	50	52	54

Herrenhemden

in USA	14	14½	15	15½	16	16½
in Deutschland	36	37	38	39	40	42

[1]Tolle ... *great deals*

Schuhgrößen für Damen

in USA	5½	6½	7½	8½	9½	10½	11½	12½
in Deutschland	36	37	38/39	39/40	41	42	43/44	44/45

Schuhgrößen für Herren

in USA	6½	7½	8½	9½	10½	11½	12½	13½
in Deutschland	39/40	41	42	43/44	44/45	46	47	48/49

In many stores you will also find the sizes S, M, L, and XL (small, medium, large, and extra-large) for clothing. In addition, shoes are sometimes labeled with American sizes.

Was brauchen die Leute? In welcher Größe und in welcher Farbe? Ergänzen Sie die Tabelle.

	WAS?	IN WELCHER GRÖSSE?	IN WELCHER FARBE?
Dialog 1			
Dialog 2			
Dialog 3			
Dialog 4			

To talk about how clothing fits, how it looks, and whether you like it, you can use the following expressions.

Gefällt Ihnen dieses Hemd?	*Do you like this shirt?*
Ja, es **gefällt mir.**	*Yes, I like it.*
Größe 42 **passt ihr** bestimmt.	*Size 42 will fit her for sure.*
Das Hemd **steht dir** gut.	*The shirt looks good on you.*

Hier klicken!

Weiteres zum Thema Einkaufen finden Sie bei **Deutsch: Na klar!** im World-Wide-Web unter www.mhhe.com/dnk5.

MUT ZUR HERRENMODE!

WORMLAND HERRENMODE

Aktivität 7 Wer trägt was?

Finden Sie folgende Personen und bilden Sie Fragen. Wer **ja** sagt muss rechts unterschreiben (*sign*).

BEISPIEL: Wer trägt gern Rot?
Frage: Trägst du gern Rot?

FRAGE	UNTERSCHRIFT
1. Wessen (*Whose*) Lieblingsfarbe ist Lila?	_____
2. Wem steht Blau sehr gut?	_____
3. Wem steht Grün nicht gut?	_____
4. Wer trägt gern bunte (*colorful*) Sachen?	_____
5. Wer trägt gern gestreifte oder karierte Sachen?	_____
6. Wer trägt Größe 39 in Hemden oder Größe 10 in Blusen?	_____
7. Wer braucht die Schuhgröße 42?	_____

Aktivität 8 Wer ist das?

Beschreiben Sie, was und welche Farben jemand in Ihrem Deutschkurs trägt. Sagen Sie den Namen der Person nicht. Die anderen im Kurs müssen erraten (*guess*), wer das ist.

BEISPIEL: Diese Person trägt eine Bluse. Die Bluse ist rotweiß gestreift. Sie trägt auch Jeans; die sind blau. Und ihre Schuhe sind, hm, lila. Wer ist das? —Das ist Winona.

Aktivität 8. Suggestion: The day before you plan on doing this activity, tell students to come to class the next day wearing something unusual.

Aktivität 9. Follow-up: Have pairs of students volunteer to perform their dialogues for the class.

Aktivität 9 Ein Gespräch

Schritt 1: Arbeiten Sie mit einem Partner / einer Partnerin. Benutzen Sie die Wörter und Ausdrücke im Kasten und schreiben Sie zusammen ein Gespräch zwischen einem Verkäufer / einer Verkäuferin und einem Kunden / einer Kundin. Was für Kleidung möchten Sie kaufen? Wie beginnt das Gespräch?

(welche) Farbe (welche) Größe Ich möchte gern _____. Was kostet _____ ?
_____ Euro preiswert passt mir (nicht) ist mir zu groß
Bitte sehr. ist mir zu klein ist mir zu teuer Wie gefällt Ihnen _____ ? anprobieren
Ich brauche _____. steht mir (nicht)
Das macht zusammen _____. Ich nehme _____. Danke schön.

Schritt 2: Spielen Sie jetzt das Gespräch mit dem Partner / der Partnerin.

SPRACHTIPP

The dative case is used with adjectives, sometimes in conjunction with the adverb **zu** (*too*).

300 Euro für dieses Kleid? Das ist **mir zu teuer.**

300 euros for this dress? *That's too expensive (for me).*

Siehe *Verbs with a Dative Object Only,* S. 162.

A. Geben Sie die englischen Bedeutungen für die folgenden Wörter. Fragen Sie andere Studentinnen / Studenten im Kurs, wenn Sie Wörter nicht kennen.

der Apfel	die Gurke	das Salz
der Aufschnitt	das Hähnchen	der Schinken
die Banane	der Joghurt	das Schnitzel
das Bier	die Karotte	das Schweinefleisch
der Blumenkohl	die Kartoffel	der Tee
der Brokkoli	der Käse	das Toilettenpapier
das Brot	der Keks	die Tomate
das Brötchen	der Kuchen	die Traube
die Butter	die Milch	der Truthahn
das Ei	das Müsli	das Wasser
das Eis	der Pfeffer	die Wurst
die Erdbeere	die Rasiercreme	die Zahnpasta
frisch	das Rindfleisch	zart
gefroren	der Saft	der Zucker

B. Nennen Sie drei **Lebensmittel** oder Produkte für jede Kategorie:

OBST	GEMÜSE	FLEISCH	GETRÄNKE
_____	_____	_____	_____
_____	_____	_____	_____
_____	_____	_____	_____

C. Mini-Umfrage: Interviewen Sie drei Studentinnen/Studenten. Was essen sie **jeden** Tag zum **Frühstück**? Zum **Mittagessen**? Zum **Abendessen**?

Aktivität 10   Kleine Läden

Was kauft man wo? Sagen Sie, wo man diese Dinge kaufen kann.

BEISPIEL: Brötchen kauft man in der Bäckerei.

am Obst- und Gemüsestand	im Bioladen	in der Bäckerei
in der Drogerie	in der Konditorei	in der Metzgerei

1. Brötchen
2. Trauben
3. Rindfleisch
4. Zahnpasta
5. Schinken
6. Blumenkohl
7. Vollkornbrot
8. Bio-Milch
9. Apfelstrudel

Neue Wörter

die Lebensmittel (*pl.*) groceries
das Obst fruit
das Gemüse vegetables
das Fleisch meat
das Getränk (Getränke, *pl.***)** drink
jeden each, every
das Frühstück breakfast
das Mittagessen lunch
das Abendessen dinner
die Metzgerei meat market
die Bäckerei bakery
die Konditorei pastry shop
der Laden store
die Drogerie toiletries and sundries store
die Apotheke pharmacy
der Bioladen natural foods store

C. Note: Point out the differences between traditional American meals and traditional German meals.

Note: You may want to point out to students that *jeder* is a *der*-word like *dieser* and *welcher*, which they learned in **Kapitel 2.**

Sprachtipp. Point Out: The American pound is 454 grams, whereas the metric pound is 500 grams. One liter is slightly more than a quart. One U.S. gallon = 3.78 liters. Normally prices are written with a comma separating *Euro* and *Cents*.

Suggestion: Practice the metric system and reading prices by asking students how much the items in the ads in *Thema 3* cost in various quantities.

Sie hören drei Dialoge: in einer Bäckerei, auf dem Markt und in einer Metzgerei. Kreuzen Sie das richtige Geschäft an. Ergänzen Sie die Tabelle.

	MARKT	BÄCKEREI	METZGEREI	WAS?	PREIS?
Dialog 1					
Dialog 2					
Dialog 3					

In der Metzgerei kauft man Fleisch.

The following words will help you organize your writing and help you put statements in order of occurrence.

zuerst first

deshalb therefore

dann then

zuletzt finally

Using these connectors will enable you to narrate effectively in German. Remember that if you begin your sentence with one of these connectors, your verb will immediately follow it.

Aktivität 12 Einkaufstag für Jutta

Jutta muss einkaufen. Sie gibt nämlich eine Party. Schreiben Sie einen Text zu jedem Bild. Benutzen Sie Elemente aus beiden Spalten (*columns*) unten.

So beginnt die Geschichte:

Jutta gibt am Wochenende eine Party. Deshalb geht sie heute einkaufen ...

Dort kauft sie ...	Obst und Gemüse – alles ganz frisch.
Zuletzt geht sie ...	Brot, Brötchen und Käsekuchen.
Zuerst geht sie ...	und geht nach Hause.
Da gibt es ...	zur Bäckerei.
Dann geht sie ...	zum Lebensmittelgeschäft.
Jutta braucht auch ...	zur Metzgerei.
Deshalb geht sie auch ...	Würstchen zum Grillen.
Jetzt hat sie alles ...	Kaffee, Zucker, Milch und Käse.
In der Bäckerei kauft sie ...	auf den Markt.
Auf dem Markt kauft sie ...	Blumenkohl und Kartoffeln.
	Äpfel, Bananen und Trauben – alles ganz frisch.

Aktivität 12. Suggestion: Have students work in pairs. They should first scan the pictures to see where Jutta is going. Review the meaning of vocabulary: *zuerst, zuletzt, deshalb, jetzt*. Students match up sentence halves and then match sentences and pictures. Call on pairs to supply a description for each picture, thereby creating a *Bildgeschichte*.

Follow-up: Have students supply a description for each picture without referring to a written text.

1.

2.

3.

4.

5.

Stellen Sie sich vor, Sie haben nur 10 Euro für Essen und Trinken übrig und müssen damit ein ganzes Wochenende auskommen. Wählen Sie Waren aus den Anzeigen (*ads*) aus. Vergleichen Sie (*compare*) Ihre Listen im Plenum.

BEISPIEL: Wir kaufen ein Kastenweißbrot für €1,59; Schinkenaufschnitt für €1,79; zwei Joghurtbecher für €0,78; zwei Suppen für €0,98; 1 Kilo Tomaten für €1,95; und Eiscreme für €2,69.

Gouda jung Holländischer Schnittkäse 48 % Fett i.Tr. oder **Milram Butterkäse Deutscher Schnittkäse** 45 % Fett i.Tr. und weitere Sorten, je 100 g — **0,39**

Aoste „luftig fein" Geflügel - oder **Schinkenaufschnitt** versch. Sorten, jede 80-g-SB-Packung — **1,79** Grundpreis: 100 g = 2,24

Kastenweissbrot jeder 750-g-Laib — **1,59** Grundpreis: 1000 g = 2,12

Knorr Suppenliebe 4 Teller Suppen versch. Sorten, jeder Beutel — **0,49**

Müller Knusperjoghurt 3,8 % Fett oder **Schlemmerjoghurt** 5 % Fett, versch. Sorten, jeder 175/150-g-Becher — **0,39** Grundpreis: 175 g = 100 g = 0,22 150 g = 100 g = 0,26

Schöller Mövenpick Eiscreme versch. Sorten, jede 1000-ml-Packung — **2,69** Eis der Woche

NeuKauf

Unser Metzgermeister empfiehlt:

vm vinzenzmurr

1a Rinderrouladen 100 g — **€-,70**

Delik. Kalbsleberwurst extra i. Fettdarm, DLG-präm. 100 g — **€-,65**

Aus den Obst- und Gemüsegärten der Welt

Spanische **Navel-Orangen** HKL II — 3 kg **€1,95**

Spanische **Satsumas** HKL II — 1 kg **€-,79**

Italienische **Kiwi** — Stück **€-,25**

Spanische **Tomaten** HKL. I — 1 kg **€1,95**

Griechische **Gurken** HKL. I — 350-450-g-Stück **€-,50**

Holländischer **Kopfsalat** HKL. I — Stück **€-,50**

Schritt 1: Planen Sie mit anderen Studenten eine Party am Wochenende. Was wollen Sie anbieten (*serve*)? Wählen Sie Getränke oder Speisen aus jeder Gruppe aus und bestimmen (*determine*) Sie die Zeit.

Zeit	heute Abend, am Wochenende, am Samstag, ???
zum Essen	Würstchen, Steaks, Hamburger, Kartoffelsalat, Kartoffelchips, Pommes frites, Salat, Gemüse, ???
zum Nachtisch	Eis, Pudding, frische Erdbeeren, Käsekuchen, ???
zum Trinken	Mineralwasser (Sprudel), Bier, Wein, ???

Schritt 2: Sprechen Sie über Ihre Pläne mit zwei oder drei anderen Studentinnen/Studenten im Kurs. Folgen Sie dem Modell.

S1	S2
1. Wollen wir ____ ____ grillen?	**2.** Gut. Machen wir ____ mit ____.
3. Und was servieren wir zum Nachtisch?	**4.** Warum nicht ____ oder ____? Was sollen wir dazu trinken?
5. ____ und ____ natürlich!	**6a.** Na, gut. **b.** Also, ____ schmeckt doch nicht dazu. Ich schlage vor (*suggest*), wir trinken ____.

Grammatik im Kontext

The Dative Case°

Der Dativ

As you have learned, the nominative case is the case of the subject; the accusative case is used for direct objects and with a number of prepositions. These cases are signaled by special endings of articles and possessive adjectives, as well as by different forms for personal pronouns.

NOMINATIVE   ACCUSATIVE

Subject   *Direct Object*

Wer   braucht   einen Rucksack?

Uwe   braucht   einen Rucksack.

Subject   *Prepositional Object*

Der Rucksack   ist   für ihn.

Like the nominative and accusative cases, the dative has special forms for pronouns and endings for articles and possessive adjectives. In previous chapters, you learned two common expressions that use dative pronouns.

Lesen macht **mir** Spaß.	*I like to read.* (lit.: *Reading is fun for me.*)
Wie geht es **dir?**	*How are you?* (lit.: *How is it going for you?*)

The dative case serves several distinct functions. It is used primarily:

■ for indirect objects (indicating the person to/for whom something is done); it answers the question **wem** (whom? to/for whom?).

Wem zeigt der Verkäufer einen Rucksack?	*To whom is the salesperson showing a backpack?*
Der Verkäufer zeigt **der Studentin** einen Rucksack.	*The salesperson is showing the student a backpack.*

Note: Students may need a little help with *wen* versus *wem*. Use examples involving questions and answers. *Wen* is looking for the accusative object: *Wen lädt Markus ein? Markus lädt seinen Freund ein. Wem* is looking for the dative object: *Wem leiht Markus 100 Euro? Markus leiht seinem Freund 100 Euro.*

- with certain verbs, such as **gefallen**.

Der Rucksack **gefällt ihm**.
He likes the backpack. (lit.: The backpack pleases him.)

- with specific prepositions, such as **mit** and **zu**.

Der Kunde geht **mit dem** Rucksack **zur** Kasse.
The customer goes to the cash register with the backpack.

- in certain expressions, such as **Spaß machen**.

Wandern **macht ihm Spaß**.
He likes to hike. (lit.: Hiking is fun for him.)

Personal Pronouns in the Dative

The following chart shows the personal pronouns in the dative case.

SINGULAR		PLURAL	
NOMINATIVE	DATIVE	NOMINATIVE	DATIVE
ich	**mir** *to/for me*	wir	**uns** *to/for us*
du	**dir** *to/for you (informal)*	ihr	**euch** *to/for you (informal)*
Sie	**Ihnen** *to/for you (formal)*	Sie	**Ihnen** *to/for you (formal)*
er	**ihm** *to/for him; to/for it*		
sie	**ihr** *to/for her; to/for it*	sie	**ihnen** *to/for them*
es	**ihm** *to/for it*		

Scan the following ads.

- Find the dative object pronouns. What are the verbs that require the dative to be used?

- What is the nominative form of each of the dative pronouns?

Sicher nicht. Schenken Sie dem Mann nicht weiter <u>Ihr</u> Geld.

DA SCHAUT JEMAND AUF IHR GELD!
WOLLEN SIE ES IHM GEBEN?

Wir wünschen unseren Gästen ein gesundes Neues Jahr.

Ab Januar möchten wir Ihnen unsere neue Speiseauswahl anbieten.[1]

Restaurant Haus Kuckuck

Horst und Christine Schmidt

Liebe Mutti,

Zum Geburtstag wünschen wir dir alles, alles Gute

Vati und die ganze Bande[2]

Wenn Sie uns schreiben wollen ...

[1]möchten ... *we would like to offer you our new menu*

[2]die ... *the whole gang*

Übung 1 Wem macht das Spaß?

Wie sagt man das anders? Setzen Sie Personalpronomen im Dativ in die Lücken.

BEISPIEL: Ich gehe gern einkaufen. Einkaufen gehen macht _mir_ Spaß.

1. Ich fotografiere gern. Fotografieren macht __mir__ Spaß.

2. Mein Bruder Alex isst gern. Essen macht __ihm__ Spaß.

3. Mein Freund und ich, wir tanzen gern. Tanzen macht __uns__ Spaß.

4. Die Studenten gehen gern in die Disko. In die Disko gehen macht __ihnen__ Spaß.

5. Ich surfe gern im Internet. Im Internet surfen macht __mir__ Spaß.

6. Meine Schwester telefoniert gern. Telefonieren macht __ihr__ Spaß.

7. Esst ihr gern Apfelstrudel frisch vom Bäcker? Apfelstrudel essen macht __euch__ bestimmt Spaß.

8. Wir gehen gern einkaufen. Einkaufen gehen macht __uns__ Spaß.

9. Was machst du gern? Was macht __dir__ Spaß?

Übung 2 Das macht mir Spaß.

Schritt 1: Was macht dir Spaß? Was macht dir keinen Spaß? Arbeiten Sie mit einer Partnerin / einem Partner.

BEISPIEL: s1: Was macht dir Spaß?
　　　　　s2: Fotografieren macht mir Spaß.
　　　　　s1: Und was macht dir keinen Spaß?
　　　　　s2: Einkaufen gehen macht mir keinen Spaß.

Schritt 2: Berichten Sie nun im Plenum über Ihre Partnerin / Ihren Partner.

BEISPIEL: Fotografieren macht Bob Spaß. Einkaufen gehen macht ihm keinen Spaß.

Übung 3 Hallo, wie geht's?

Ergänzen Sie die fehlenden Personalpronomen im Dativ.

1. A: Hallo, Brigitte, wie geht es __dir__?

   B: Danke, es geht __mir__ gut.

   A: Und wie geht's deinem Freund?

   B: Ach, es geht __ihm__ nicht besonders gut. Er hat viel Stress.

2. C: Hallo, Petra und Christoph. Na, wie geht es __euch__ denn?

   D: Danke, es geht __uns__ gut.

   C: Und was machen die Kinder?

   D: Ach, es geht __ihnen__ immer gut.

3. E: Guten Tag, Herr Professor Distelmeier.

   F: Guten Tag, Herr Liederlich. Wie geht es __Ihnen__?

   E: Es geht __mir__ schlecht. Ich habe zu viel Arbeit.

4. G: Tag, Frau Brinkmann. Wie geht es __Ihnen__?

   H: Danke, es geht __mir__ gut. Und __Ihnen__?

   G: Danke, auch gut. Und wie geht es Ihrer Mutter?

   H: Ach, es geht __ihr__ nicht besonders. Sie schläft so schlecht.

Articles and Possessive Adjectives in the Dative

The following chart shows the dative endings for definite and indefinite articles, possessive adjectives, and **der**-words. Note that the masculine and neuter endings are identical.

MASCULINE	NEUTER	FEMININE	PLURAL
dem (k)ein**em** } Mann mein**em** dies**em** **dem** Kunden	dem (k)ein**em** } Kind mein**em** dies**em**	der (k)ein**er** } Frau mein**er** dies**er**	den kein**en** } Männern mein**en** } Frauen dies**en** } Kindern **den** } Kunden

Geben Sie Ihrem Haar einen modischen Kick...

Note:

- Nouns in the dative singular do not normally take an ending, except for the special masculine nouns that take an **-n** or **-en** in the accusative as well **(Kapitel 2)**.

Nominative	Accusative	Dative
der Kunde	den Kunde**n**	dem Kunde**n**
der Student	den Student**en**	dem Student**en**

- In the dative plural, all nouns add **-n** to the plural ending, unless the plural already ends in **-n.** Exception: Those nouns whose plural ends in **-s** do not add **-n.**

	Plural	Dative Plural
	die Männer	den Männer**n**
	die Frauen	den Frauen
but:	die Autos	den Autos
	die Handys	den Handys

The Dative Case for Indirect Objects

As in English, many German verbs take both a direct object and an indirect object. The direct object, in the accusative, will usually be a thing; the indirect object, in the dative, will normally be a person.

		DATIVE indirect object	ACCUSATIVE direct object
Michael	kauft	**seiner Freundin**	einen Ring.
Der Verkäufer	zeigt	**ihm**	vier Ringe.

Following are some of the verbs that can take two objects in German:

empfehlen (empfiehlt)	to recommend
geben (gibt)	to give
glauben	to believe
leihen	to lend, borrow
schenken	to give as a gift
zeigen	to show

Note: German does not distinguish between "lend" and "borrow." Both English verbs are rendered into German by *leihen*. Thus, *Ich leihe dir Geld.* I'll lend you some money. *Ich leihe mir Geld.* I'm borrowing some money (for myself). Other common verbs that can take two objects include **kaufen, sagen, schicken, schreiben,** and **wünschen.**

Position of Dative and Accusative Objects

Ich schenke **meinem Bruder** ein **Handy** zum Geburtstag.	*I'm giving my brother a cell phone for his birthday.*
Ich gebe **es** **meinem Bruder**.	*I'm giving it (the cell phone) to my brother.*
Wann gibst du **es** **ihm**?	*When are you giving it to him?*

Note:

- The dative object precedes the accusative object when the accusative object is a noun.

- The dative object follows the accusative object when the direct object (accusative) is a personal pronoun.

Übung 4 Situationen im Alltag

Sie hören fünf Dialoge. Kreuzen Sie für jeden Dialog den Satz an, der zu dem Thema passt.

1. Hans braucht unbedingt etwas Geld.
   ☒ Sein Freund kann ihm nichts leihen.
   ☐ Sein Freund gibt ihm einen Scheck.
2. Zwei Studentinnen brauchen Hilfe.
   ☐ Ein Freund gibt ihnen etwas Geld.
   ☒ Ein Herr zeigt ihnen den Weg zum Café.
3. Helmut hat Geburtstag.
   ☒ Marianne schreibt ihm eine Karte.
   ☐ Marianne schenkt ihm eine CD.
4. Eine Studentin erzählt einem Studenten über ihren Tagesablauf.
   ☒ Sie empfiehlt ihm Yoga.
   ☐ Sie hat keine Zeit für Yoga.
5. Achim sagt, er lebt nur von Brot und Wasser.
   ☐ Er hat kein Geld.
   ☒ Man kann ihm nicht alles glauben, was er sagt.

Übung 4. Suggestion: Have students listen to each minidialogue in succession. Expand the questions about each situation. Incorporate the dative verbs in as many questions as possible. Ask students to summarize each dialogue orally.

Übung 5 Wortsalat!

Bilden Sie Sätze.

BEISPIEL: meinem Freund / macht / keinen Spaß / Telefonieren →
Telefonieren macht meinem Freund keinen Spaß.

1. einen Wecker / die Mutter / zum Geburtstag / ihrem Sohn / kauft
2. gibt / ihm / sie / wann / ihn / ?
3. den Studenten / zeigt / der Professor / eine Landkarte von Deutschland
4. dem Kunden / die Verkäuferin / einen preiswerten Computer / empfiehlt

Übung 5: Some of these sentences allow more than one correct sequence of constituents. You might want to accept some of the stylistic variants. For example, in addition to the canonical word order *Telefonieren macht meinem Freund keinen Spaß.* One might just as easily hear *Meinem Freund macht Telefonieren keinen Spaß.* If students ask, you might choose to explain that there is a subtle difference in focus. In general, when something is emphasized as new information it tends to come later in the sentence.

5. du / das Handy / zum Geburtstag / gibst / wem / ?

6. kauft / einen Ring / der Kunde / seiner Freundin

7. seiner Freundin / schenkt / zum Valentinstag / er / diesen Ring

Horst hat eine große Familie und viele Freunde. Wem schenkt Horst was?

BEISPIEL: Sein Onkel hört gern klassische Musik.
  a. Er schenkt seinem Onkel eine CD.
  b. Er schenkt ihm eine CD.

1. Seine Oma reist oft nach Hawaii.

2. Sein Bruder ist sportlich sehr aktiv.

3. Sein Vetter Klaus findet Fische interessant.

4. Seine Schwester Heike telefoniert pausenlos.

5. Seine Freundin Ute wandert gern.

6. Seine Tante Adelgunde liebt exzentrische Mode.

7. Sein Vater hat schon alles.

8. Seine Mutter trinkt morgens, mittags und abends Kaffee.

9. Seine Eltern planen eine Reise nach Spanien.

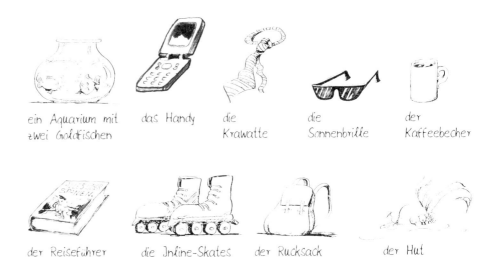

ein Aquarium mit zwei Goldfischen   das Handy   die Krawatte   die Sonnenbrille   der Kaffeebecher

der Reiseführer   die Inline-Skates   der Rucksack   der Hut

Verbs with a Dative Object Only

A number of common German verbs always take an object in the dative case. Note that these dative objects usually refer to people.

danken	Ich **danke** dir für die Karte.	*I thank you for the card.*
gefallen	Wie **gefällt** Ihnen dieses Hemd?*	*How do you like this shirt?**
gehören	Der Mercedes **gehört** meinem Bruder.	*The Mercedes belongs to my brother.*
helfen	Der Verkäufer **hilft** dem Kunden.	*The salesperson is helping the customer.*

*Lit.: *How does this shirt please you?*

passen	Größe 48 **passt** mir bestimmt.	*Size 48 will surely fit me.*
stehen	Das Kleid **steht** dir gut.	*The dress looks good on you.*

A number of frequently used idiomatic expressions also require dative objects.

Wie geht es **dir?**	*How are you?*
Das tut **mir** leid.	*I'm sorry.*
Das ist **mir** egal.	*I don't care.*

Note: With changes to the German spelling reform in the year 2006, *leidtun* is now considered a single word.

Verbs that take only a dative object are indicated in the vocabulary lists of this book as follows: (+ *dat.*)

Übung 7 Ein schwieriger° Kunde

difficult

Ergänzen Sie den Dialog mit passenden Verben und Pronomen im Dativ. Suchen Sie passende Verben aus der folgenden Liste:

Übung 7. Suggestion: Review the meanings of the verbs first. Then let students work in pairs to complete the dialogue. Have several pairs role-play the completed dialogue for the class.

Answers: 1. *Ihnen* 2. *helfen* 3. *mir* 4. *empfehlen* 5. *Zeigen* 6. *mir* 7. *passt* 8. *ihr* 9. *steht* 10. *ihr* 11. *gefällt* 12. *Ihnen* 13. *gefällt* 14. *mir* 15. *gefällt* 16. *ihr* 17. *ist* 18. *mir* 19. *(zu) teuer* 20. *Ihnen* 21. *zeigen* 22. *mir* 23. *zeigen* 24. *mir* 25. *leid* 26. *danke* 27. *Ihnen*

danken	**helfen**	**stehen**
empfehlen	**leidtun**	**(zu) teuer sein**
gefallen	**passen**	**zeigen**

VERKÄUFER: Kann ich _____¹ _____²? (*help you*)

KUNDE: Ja. Ich brauche ein Geschenk für meine Freundin. Können Sie _____³ vielleicht etwas _____⁴? (*recommend to me*)

VERKÄUFER: Eine Bluse vielleicht?

KUNDE: _____⁵ Sie _____⁶ bitte eine Bluse in Größe 50. (*Show me*)

VERKÄUFER: Größe 50? Ist das nicht zu groß?

KUNDE: Ich glaube, Größe 50 _____⁷ _____⁸ bestimmt. (*fits her*)

VERKÄUFER: Hier habe ich eine elegante Seidenbluse. In Schwarz.

KUNDE: Nein, Schwarz _____⁹ _____¹⁰ nicht. (*look good on her*)

VERKÄUFER: Wie _____¹¹ _____¹² diese Bluse in Lila? (*do you like*)

KUNDE: Schrecklich. Diese Farbe _____¹³ _____¹⁴ überhaupt nicht. (*I like*)

VERKÄUFER: Hier habe ich ein Modell aus Paris für 825 Euro. Ich garantiere, diese Bluse _____¹⁵ _____¹⁶ bestimmt. (*she will like*)

KUNDE: Sie machen wohl Spaß. Das _____¹⁷ _____¹⁸ _____.¹⁹ (*is too expensive for me*)

VERKÄUFER: Kann ich _____²⁰ etwas anderes _____²¹? (*show you*)

KUNDE: Können Sie _____²² vielleicht ein T-Shirt _____²³? (*show me*)

VERKÄUFER: Ja, natürlich. Hier habe ich ein ganz …

KUNDE: Oh, je. Es ist schon halb sechs. Es tut _____²⁴ _____.²⁵ (*I'm sorry.*) Ich muss sofort gehen. Ich _____²⁶ _____²⁷ für Ihre Hilfe. (*thank you*) Auf Wiedersehen.

Schritt 1: Wem gehört das?

BEISPIEL: s1: Wem gehört der große Hut?
s2: Der gehört dem Fotomodell Jutta.

die karierte Hose   der große Hut   das komische Hemd   die langen Stiefel

Jutta
(das Fotomodell)

Michael
(ihr Freund)

Mark
(ihr Bruder)

Sabine
(ihre Schwester)

Schritt 2: Wie gefällt dir das? Führen Sie ein Gespräch.

BEISPIEL: s1: Wie gefällt dir der große Hut?
s2: Der Hut gefällt mir. Er steht ihr gut!

der große Hut	gefallen/gefällt		gut
das komische Hemd	passen/passt	ihm	nicht gut
die karierte Hose	sind/ist	ihr	zu eng
die langen Stiefel	stehen/steht	mir	zu groß
			zu kurz
			zu lang

Prepositions with the Dative Case

Prepositions that require the dative case of nouns and pronouns include:

aus	from, out of	Richard kommt gerade **aus** dem Haus.
		Alexandra kommt **aus** Jena.
	(made) of	Das Hemd ist **aus** Polyester.
bei	near	Die Bäckerei ist **beim** Marktplatz.
	at (the place of)	Schicke Blusen gibt es **bei** Gisie.
	for, at (a company)	Manfred arbeitet **bei** VW.
	with	Sybille wohnt **bei** ihrer Großmutter.
mit	with	Herr Schweiger geht **mit** seiner Frau einkaufen.
		Katja wohnt **mit** ihrer Freundin Beate zusammen.
	by (means of)	Wir fahren **mit** dem Bus.
nach	to	Der Bus fährt **nach** Frankfurt.
		Ich fahre jetzt **nach** Hause.
	after	**Nach** dem Essen gehen wir einkaufen.

seit	since	**Seit** gestern haben wir schönes Wetter.
	for (time)	**Seit** einem Monat kauft sie nur noch Bio-Brot.
von	from	Das Brot ist frisch **vom** Bäcker.
		Frank kommt gerade **vom** Markt.
	by (origin)	Dieses Buch ist **von** Peter Handke.
zu	to	Wir gehen heute **zum** Supermarkt.
		Dirk muss schon um fünf Uhr **zur** Arbeit.
	at	Er ist jetzt wieder **zu** Hause.
	for	**Zum** Frühstück gibt es Müsli.

Point out: zu is also used to indicate going to someone else's place of residence: Ich gehe zu Susi = "I'm going to Susi's."

Note:

- **Nach Hause** and **zu Hause** are set expressions. **Nach Hause** is used to say that someone is *going* home, while **zu Hause** means someone is *at* home.

- The following contractions are common:

bei dem → **beim**	Jürgen kauft sein Brot nur **beim** Bäcker.
von dem → **vom**	Er kommt gerade **vom** Markt.
zu dem → **zum**	Er muss jetzt noch **zum** Bäcker.
zu der → **zur**	Dann geht er **zur** Bank.

Übung 9 Ein typischer Tag

Sie hören eine Beschreibung von Maxis Tagesablauf. Was stimmt? Was stimmt nicht? Geben Sie die richtige Information an.

	DAS STIMMT	DAS STIMMT NICHT
1. Maxi wohnt seit einem Monat in Göttingen.	☒	☐
2. Maxi wohnt allein in einer Wohnung.	☐	☒
3. Sie kann zu Fuß zur Universität gehen.	☒	☐
4. Maxi kommt gerade aus der Bibliothek.	☐	☒
5. Dann geht sie in die Mensa.	☐	☒
6. Maxi und Inge gehen zum Supermarkt.	☒	☐
7. Beim Bäcker kaufen sie ein Brot.	☐	☒
8. Maxi muss noch zur Bank.	☒	☐

Vom Korn zum Brot[1]

Mühlenbäckerei
BORGMANN
Mühlenstraße 11 · Kranenburg
Inh. Ralf Borgmann
Telefon 0 28 26 / 2 65

[1]*Vom ... From grain to bread*

Information

Übung 10 Auskunft° geben

Ergänzen Sie die fehlenden Präpositionen.

1. Sag mal, wo gibt es hier denn schicke Blusen? —<u>Bei</u> Gisie.
2. Die Bluse steht dir gut. Ist sie <u>aus</u> Polyester?
3. Ist diese Bluse neu? —Ja, sie ist ein Geschenk <u>von</u> meiner Mutter.
4. Das Brot schmeckt ausgezeichnet. Woher hast du es? —Es ist <u>von</u> der Bäckerei.
5. Gehst du zu Fuß zum Supermarkt? —Nein, ich fahre <u>mit</u> dem Wagen.
6. Bitte, komm nach dem Einkaufen sofort <u>nach</u> Hause.
7. Ich plane schon <u>seit</u> drei Monaten eine Grillparty.
8. Wollen wir die Party <u>bei</u> dir oder <u>bei</u> mir <u>zu</u> Hause machen?

aus	bei	mit	nach
seit	von	zu	

Setzen Sie die fehlenden Präpositionen, Artikel und Endungen ein.

1. Michael wohnt _____ sein_ Bruder zusammen in einer alten Villa in Berlin.

2. Er geht schon _____ 6 Uhr _____ _____ Haus.

3. Er fährt _____ sein_ Motorrad _____ Arbeit.

4. Er arbeitet _____ Hotel Zentral.

5. Er arbeitet da schon _____ ein_ Jahr. Die Arbeit gefällt ihm sehr.

6. Er arbeitet _____ Leute_ _____ vielen Länder_ zusammen, z. B. _____ Jugoslawien, Spanien, Afghanistan und Amerika.

7. Abends _____ _____ Arbeit trifft er oft ein paar Freunde.

8. Dann geht er _____ sein_ Freunde_ in eine Kneipe.

9. Michael kocht gern. _____ Frühstück gibt es oft so etwas wie Rührei _____ Zwiebeln und Zucchini.

10. Das ist ein Rezept _____ Mexiko.

11. Er hat das Rezept _____ sein_ Freundin Marlene.

Arbeiten Sie mit einem Partner / einer Partnerin zusammen. Stellen Sie Fragen.

BEISPIEL: s1: Seit wann wohnst du hier?
           s2: Seit drei Semestern.

1. Deutsch lernen
2. Auto fahren können
3. den Professor / die Professorin kennen

4. hier wohnen
5. an dieser Uni studieren
6. ??

Interrogativpronomen

Interrogative Pronouns° *wo, wohin,* and *woher*

The interrogative pronouns **wo** and **wohin** both mean *where*. **Wo** is used to ask where someone or something is located, **wohin** to ask about the direction in which someone or something is moving. **Woher** is used to ask where someone or something comes from.

Wo bist du denn jetzt?	Zu Hause.
Wo wohnst du?	In Berlin.
Wo kauft Maxi ihr Brot?	Beim Bäcker.
Wohin gehst du? (**Wo** gehst du **hin**?)	Zur Bibliothek.
Wohin fährst du? (**Wo** fährst du **hin**?)	Nach Deutschland.
Woher kommen die Orangen? (**Wo** kommen die Orangen **her**?)	Aus Spanien.
Woher hast du die gute Wurst? (**Wo** hast du die gute Wurst **her**?)	Vom Metzger.

Note that the words **wohin** and **woher** are frequently split (**wo ... hin, wo ... her**), especially in conversation.

Übung 13 Wo, wohin, woher?

Bilden Sie die Fragen zu den Antworten.

BEISPIEL: Ich muss heute noch <u>zur Bank</u>. →
Wohin musst du heute noch? [*oder*]
Wo musst du heute noch hin?

1. Brötchen gibt es <u>beim Bäcker</u>.
2. Mark muss heute noch <u>zur Metzgerei</u>.
3. Sein Freund kommt gerade <u>vom Bioladen</u>.
4. Wir gehen später <u>zum Supermarkt</u>.
5. Antje ist heute <u>zu Hause</u>.
6. Die Leute kommen gerade <u>aus dem Kino</u>.
7. Sie gehen jetzt alle <u>nach Hause</u>.
8. Die Studentinnen trinken einen Kaffee <u>im Café Kadenz</u>.

Sprache im Kontext

Videoclips

A. Schauen Sie sich das Interview mit Sara an. Lesen Sie die Fragen und streichen (*cross out*) Sie die Antwort durch, die nicht stimmt.

BEISPIEL: Was trägt Sara jetzt? [Jacke, ~~Hut~~, Bluse]

1. Welche Blusengröße hat Sara? [38, 83]
2. Welche Schuhgröße hat sie? [51, 41]
3. Was nimmt Sara mit in Urlaub? [Jeans, Bikini, kurze Hosen]
4. Was trägt sie zu Hause? [Pyjama, Shorts, Kleider]
5. Sara kauft Lebensmittel. Was für Gemüse kauft sie? [Gurke, Karotten, grüne Bohnen]
6. Was für Obst kauft sie? [Äpfel, Erdbeeren, Orangen]
7. Sara muss auch Kosmetik kaufen. Was muss sie kaufen? [Zahnpasta, Shampoo, Toilettenpapier]

B. Schauen Sie sich das Interview mit Harald an und beantworten Sie die Fragen.

1. Was für eine Hemdengröße hat Harald?
2. Was für eine Schuhgröße hat er?
3. Was trägt er im Sommerurlaub?
4. Was trägt er zur Arbeit?
5. Was für Lebensmittel kauft er?

C. Schauen Sie sich das Interview mit Jasmin an. Was für Getränke kauft sie?

D. Jasmin nennt auch ein Rezept für Auberginen. Wie bereitet (*prepare*) sie sie vor?

Lesen

Zum Thema

A. Wo kaufen Sie ein? Kreuzen Sie an, wo Sie oft, manchmal oder nie einkaufen.

	OFT	MANCHMAL	NIE
auf dem Flohmarkt (*flea market*)	☐	☐	☐
auf dem Markt	☐	☐	☐
im Supermarkt	☐	☐	☐
in der Drogerie	☐	☐	☐
in einer Boutique	☐	☐	☐
in einem Einkaufszentrum	☐	☐	☐
aus einem Versandkatalog	☐	☐	☐
im Internet	☐	☐	☐

B. Schauen Sie sich die Liste in **A** an. Sagen Sie, was man dort kaufen kann.

Auf den ersten Blick

Lesen Sie den Titel und überfliegen (*scan*) Sie die ersten paar Zeilen des Textes.

1. Was für ein Text ist dies?

    a. ein Artikel aus einer Zeitung

    b. ein Dialog

    c. eine Werbung für einen Hutladen

2. Suchen Sie im Text zusammengesetzte Wörter mit **Hut** oder **Hüte.** Versuchen Sie zu erraten (*guess*), was diese Wörter bedeuten, z. B. **Filzhüte** = **Filz** + **Hüte**; **Filz** = *felt*; **Hüte** = Plural von **Hut.**

3. Überfliegen Sie die ersten vier Zeilen. Was ist Ihre Meinung zu den Aussagen a–c, unten? Wo sehen Sie einen Beweis (*evidence*) für Ihre Meinung?

    a. Die Verkäuferin und der Kunde führen ein ganz normales Gespräch in einem Hutladen.

    b. Die Verkäuferin stellt ganz normale Fragen.

    c. Der Kunde ist schwierig.

von Karl Valentin

VERKÄUFERIN:	Guten Tag. Sie wünschen?	
KARL VALENTIN:	Einen Hut.	
K. V.:	Was soll das für ein Hut sein?	
K. V.:	Einer zum Aufsetzen°.	zum … for putting on

VERKÄUFERIN: Guten Tag. Sie wünschen?

KARL VALENTIN: Einen Hut.

VERKÄUFERIN: Was soll das für ein Hut sein?

K. V.: Einer zum Aufsetzen°.   *zum … for putting on*

5 VERKÄUFERIN: Ja, anziehen können Sie niemals einen Hut, den muß man immer aufsetzen.

K. V.: Nein, immer nicht – in der Kirche° zum Beispiel kann ich den Hut nicht aufsetzen.   *church*

VERKÄUFERIN: In der Kirche nicht – aber Sie gehen doch nicht immer
10 in die Kirche.

K. V.: Nein, nur da und hie.

VERKÄUFERIN: Sie meinen nur hie und da°!   *hie … now and then*

K. V.: Ja, ich will einen Hut zum Auf- und Absetzen°.   *to take off (a hat)*

VERKÄUFERIN: Jeden Hut können Sie auf- und absetzen! Wollen Sie
15 einen weichen° oder einen steifen° Hut?   *soft / firm, stiff*

K. V.: Nein – einen grauen.

VERKÄUFERIN: Ich meine, was für eine Fasson°?   *shape*

K. V.: Eine farblose° Fasson.   *colorless*

VERKÄUFERIN: Sie meinen, eine schicke Fasson – wir haben allerlei
20 schicke Fassonen in allen Farben.

K. V.: In allen Farben? – Dann hellgelb!

VERKÄUFERIN: Aber hellgelbe Hüte gibt es nur im Karneval – einen hellgelben Herrenhut können Sie doch nicht tragen.

K. V.: Ich will ihn ja nicht tragen, sondern aufsetzen.

25 VERKÄUFERIN: Mit einem hellgelben Hut werden Sie ja ausgelacht°.   *ridiculed*

K. V.: Aber Strohhüte sind doch hellgelb.

VERKÄUFERIN: Ach, Sie wollen einen Strohhut?

K. V.: Nein, ein Strohhut ist mir zu feuergefährlich°!   *flammable*

VERKÄUFERIN: Asbesthüte° gibt es leider noch nicht! – Schöne
30 weiche Filzhüte hätten wir.   *asbestos hats*

K. V.: Die weichen Filzhüte haben den Nachteil°, daß man sie nicht hört, wenn sie einem vom Kopf auf den Boden fallen°.   *disadvantage*   *auf … fall to the ground*

VERKÄUFERIN: Na, dann müssen Sie sich eben einen Stahlhelm
35 kaufen, den hört man fallen.

K. V.: Als Zivilist darf ich keinen Stahlhelm tragen.

VERKÄUFERIN: Nun müssen Sie sich aber bald entschließen°, was Sie für einen Hut wollen.   *sich … decide*

K. V.: Einen neuen Hut!

40 VERKÄUFERIN: Ja, wir haben nur neue.

K. V.: Ich will ja einen neuen.

VERKÄUFERIN: Ja, aber was für einen?

K. V.: Einen Herrenhut!

VERKÄUFERIN: Damenhüte führen wir nicht!

45 K. V.: Ich will auch keinen Damenhut!

VERKÄUFERIN: Sie sind sehr schwer zu bedienen°, ich zeige Ihnen einmal mehrere Hüte!   *schwer … difficult to serve*

K. V.: Was heißt mehrere, ich will doch nur einen. Ich habe ja auch nur einen Kopf°.   *head*

...

der Zylinder

der Strohhut

der Filzhut

der Stahlhelm

der Damenhut

Lesen Sie den Dialog mit verteilten Rollen im Kurs vor.

1. Was will der Kunde eigentlich? Wo sagt er genau, was er will?

2. Finden Sie Beispiele im Text, wo und wie der Kunde die Verkäuferin irritiert. Wie reagiert die Verkäuferin?

3. Humor in einer fremden Sprache ist oft schwer zu verstehen. Karl Valentin war ein beliebter Humorist. Finden Sie diesen Dialog komisch oder humorvoll? Wenn ja, was macht ihn komisch?

4. Sie lesen hier nur einen Auszug aus dem Dialog. Glauben Sie, dass der Kunde schließlich einen Hut kauft? Was würden Sie als Verkäufer/Verkäuferin mit diesem Kunden machen?

Zu guter Letzt

Wie geben Studentinnen und Studenten in Ihrer Klasse ihr Geld aus?

Schritt 1: Füllen Sie zuerst den Fragebogen (*questionnaire*) unten selbst aus.

Schritt 2: Interviewen Sie jetzt drei Studenten/Studentinnen und notieren Sie dabei Namen, Alter und Hauptfach (*major*). Benutzen Sie den Fragebogen (*questionnaire*) und notieren Sie die Antworten.

FRAGEBOGEN

1. Gehen Sie gern einkaufen? Warum (nicht)?

2. Wofür geben Sie das meiste Geld aus?

☐ Miete   ☐ Studiengebühren
☐ Auto   ☐ Essen im Restaurant
☐ Kleidung   ☐ Lebensmittel
☐ Unterhaltung   ☐ etwas anderes

3. Was kaufen Sie und wie oft kaufen Sie es?

WAS?		WIE OFT?
☐ Kaffee/Bier	jeden Tag	
☐ Bücher	einmal	in der Woche
☐ Kleidung	zweimal	im Monat
☐ CDs, DVDs	dreimal	im Jahr
☐ Lebensmittel	alle fünf Jahre	
☐ ein Auto	???	
☐ Möbel		

Schritt 3: Für welche anderen Dinge, die nicht auf dieser Liste stehen, geben Studenten/Studentinnen ihr Geld aus? Notieren Sie sie.

Schritt 4: Was haben Sie herausgefunden? Fassen Sie die Informationen über eine Person, die Sie interviewt haben, schriftlich (*in writing*) zusammen und geben Sie der Person dieses Profil.

Wortschatz

Lebensmittel — Groceries, Food

der **Apfel**, ∵	apple
der **Aufschnitt**	cold cuts
die **Banane**, -n	banana
das **Bier**, -e	beer
der **Blumenkohl**	cauliflower
der **Brokkoli**	broccoli
das **Brot**, -e	(loaf of) bread
das **Brötchen**, -	roll
die **Butter**	butter
das **Ei**, -er	egg
das **Eis**	ice cream; ice
die **Erdbeere**, -n	strawberry
das **Fleisch**	meat
das **Gemüse**	vegetables
das **Getränk**, -e	drink
die **Gurke**, -n	cucumber
das **Hähnchen**	chicken
der **Joghurt**	yogurt
die **Karotte**, -n	carrot
die **Kartoffel**, -n	potato
der **Käse**	cheese
der **Keks**, -e	cookie
der **Kuchen**, -	cake
die **Milch**	milk
das **Müsli**, -	granola; cereal
das **Obst**	fruit
der **Pfeffer**	pepper
das **Rindfleisch**	beef
der **Saft**, ∵e	juice
das **Salz**	salt
der **Schinken**, -	ham
das **Schnitzel**, -	cutlet
das **Schweinefleisch**	pork
der **Tee**	tea
die **Tomate**, -n	tomato
die **Traube**, -n	grape
der **Truthahn**, ∵e	turkey
das **Wasser**	water
die **Wurst**, ∵e	sausage
der **Zucker**	sugar

Geschäfte — Stores, Shops

die **Apotheke**, -n	pharmacy
die **Bäckerei**, -en	bakery
die **Drogerie**, -n	toiletries and sundries store
die **Konditorei**, -en	pastry shop

der **Laden**, ∵	store
der **Bioladen**, ∵	natural foods store
der **Getränkeladen**, ∵	beverage store
der **Markt**, ∵e	(open-air) market, marketplace
die **Metzgerei**, -en	butcher shop
der **Obst- und Gemüsestand**, ∵e	fruit and vegetable stand
der **Supermarkt**, ∵e	supermarket

Kleidungsstücke — Articles of Clothing

der **Anzug**, ∵e	suit
der **Badeanzug**, ∵e	bathing suit
die **Bluse**, -n	blouse
der **Gürtel**, -	belt
das **Hemd**, -en	shirt
die **Hose**, -n	pants, trousers
die **Badehose**, -n	swim trunk
der **Hut**, ∵e	hat
die **Jacke**, -n	jacket
die **Jeans** (*pl.*)	jeans
die **Klamotte**, -n	duds, rags (*slang for clothing*)
das **Kleid**, -er	dress
die **Krawatte**, -n	necktie
der **Mantel**, ∵	coat
die **Mütze**, -n	cap
der **Pullover**, -	pullover sweater
der **Rock**, ∵e	skirt
das **Sakko**, -s	sport coat
der **Schal**, -s	scarf
der **Schlips**, -e	necktie
der **Schuh**, -e	shoe
der **Hausschuh**, -e	slipper
der **Tennisschuh**, -e	tennis shoe
die **Socke**, -n	sock
der **Stiefel**, -	boot
der **Strumpf**, ∵e	stocking; sock
das **T-Shirt**, -s	T-shirt

Sonstige Substantive — Other Nouns

das **Abendessen**	evening meal
die **Brille**, -n	(pair of) eyeglasses
die **Farbe**, -n	color
das **Frühstück**	breakfast

die **Größe**, -n	size
die **Kasse**, -n	cash register; check-out, cashier
der **Koffer**, -	suitcase
das **Medikament**, -e	medicine
das **Mittagessen**	midday meal; lunch
die **Rasiercreme**, -s	shaving cream
der **Rucksack**, ⸚e	backpack
die **Tasche**, -n	handbag, purse
das **Toilettenpapier**	toilet paper
die **Zahnpasta**	toothpaste

Farben — Colors

beige	beige
blau	blue
braun	brown
gelb	yellow
grau	gray
grün	green
lila	purple
orange	orange
rot	red
schwarz	black
weiß	white

Verben — Verbs

an•probieren	to try on
danken (+ *dat.*)	to thank
empfehlen (empfiehlt)	to recommend
gefallen (gefällt) (+ *dat.*)	to be pleasing
Wie gefällt Ihnen ...?	How do you like . . . ?
gehören (+ *dat.*)	to belong to (*a person*)
glauben	to believe
helfen (hilft) (+ *dat.*)	to help
leihen	to lend; borrow
passen (+ *dat.*)	to fit
schenken	to give (*as a gift*)
schmecken (+ *dat.*)	to taste (good)
stehen (+ *dat.*)	to look good (*on a person*)
Die Farbe steht mir.	The color looks good on me.
tragen (trägt)	to wear; carry
zahlen	to pay
zeigen	to show

Sonstige Adjektive und Adverbien — Other Adjectives and Adverbs

frisch	fresh(ly)
gefroren	frozen
gestreift	striped
kariert	plaid
modisch	fashionable, fashionably
nötig	necessary
zart	tender

Dativpronomen — Dative Pronouns

mir	(to/for) me
dir	(to/for) you (*informal sg.*)
ihm	(to/for) him/it
ihr	(to/for) her/it
uns	(to/for) us
euch	(to/for) you (*informal pl.*)
ihnen	(to/for) them
Ihnen	(to/for) you (*formal*)

Dativpräpositionen — Dative Prepositions

aus	from; out of, (made) of
bei	at; near; with
mit	with; by means of
nach	after; to
seit	since; for (+ *time*)
von	of; from; by
zu	to; at; for

Sonstiges — Other

alle	all; every
das macht zusammen	all together, that comes to
egal: Das ist mir egal.	I don't care.
jeder	each, every
nach Hause	(to) home
wem?	(to/for) whom?
wohin?	(to) where?
zu Hause	at home

1. Welche Kleidungsstücke tragen Sie jeden Tag?

2. Nennen Sie fünf Farben! Beginnen Sie mit Ihrer Lieblingsfarbe!

3. Sie reisen nach Hawaii. Was nehmen Sie im Koffer mit?

4. Was essen Sie jeden Tag? Was ist Ihr Lieblingsessen? Was trinken Sie jeden Tag?

5. Welche Frage passt?

a. _____? —Die Jacke gefällt mir gut.
b. _____? —Ja, bitte, zeigen Sie mir Tennisschuhe, Größe 42.
c. _____? —Dieser Pullover ist zu klein.
d. _____? —Ich schenke es (das T-Shirt) meinem Bruder.

6. Wo kauft man das?

a. ein Sporthemd   **b.** Obst und Gemüse
c. Würstchen zum Grillen   **d.** Brot und Brötchen   **e.** Kaffee, Milch und Käse

7. Ergänzen Sie: **wo, woher,** oder **wohin!**

a. _____ fährst du zum Einkaufen?   **b.** _____ kommen diese Orangen?   **c.** _____ kauft man frisches Obst und Gemüse am besten?

8. Mit wem machen Sie das gern?

a. einkaufen gehen   **b.** auf Partys gehen
c. essen gehen

Wir gehen aus

KAPITEL
6

Guten Appetit!

In diesem Kapitel

- **Themen:** Places to eat and drink, ordering in a restaurant
- **Grammatik:** Two-way prepositions; describing location; describing placement; expressing time with prepositions; simple past tense of **sein, haben,** and modal verbs
- **Kultur:** Regional food specialties, menus, sharing tables in restaurants, paying the bill
- **Lesen:** „Die Soße" (Ekkehard Müller)

Videoclips
Bedienung, bitte

174

Alles klar?

¹frei ... *free delivery*

A. „Pizzeria AS" ist ein Restaurant in Bonn.

- Schauen Sie sich die Karten in der Werbung für Pizza AS an. Was bedeutet der Name „AS"?
- Pizzeria AS ist nicht nur ein Pizzarestaurant. Was für internationales Essen bekommt man da?
- An welchen Tagen hat das Restaurant Tagesangebote?
- Welches Tagesangebot interessiert Sie besonders?
- Wie viel Geld muss man mindestens ausgeben, wenn man etwas frei Haus bestellt?
- Was bekommt man, wenn man mehr als 23 Euro für Essen ausgibt?

B. Doris hat die Uni gewechselt und studiert jetzt in Berlin. Sie ist beim Info-Büro des Astas an der FU. Hören Sie jetzt ihr Gespräch mit der Asta-Referentin (*adviser*) und ordnen Sie die Charakterisierungen dem richtigen Restaurant zu.

RESTAURANT	CHARAKTERISIERUNG	
1. _____ Brazil	**a.** gemütlich	**e.** österreichische Küche
2. _____ Kartoffelkeller	**b.** in der Oranienburger Straße	**f.** rappelvoll (*coll.* crowded)
3. _____ Kellerrestaurant	**c.** macht viel Spaß	**g.** Rezepte von Helene Weigel
4. _____ Ristorante Italiano	**d.** nicht so teuer	**h.** vegetarisch

Alles klar?　**175**

Wörter im Kontext

THEMA 1: Lokale

a.

Restaurant „Schublade"

Inhaber	Stefan Höller
	Hauptstraße 17
	53804 Much, Zentrum
Telefon	0 22 45 – 44 11
Öffnungszeiten	Di - So ab 18.00 Uhr
Ruhetag	Mo
Plätze unten/oben	100/40

Spezialitäten:
Frische Salate, Steaks.
Auf Vorbestellung:
„Heufresser Menue"
Brennnesselsuppe –
Schweinefilet in Heu
gegart mit Bratkartoffeln –
Salatteller – Apfelspalten
in Karamell mit Vanilleeis
+ Sahne

ÜBER 100 GERICHTE
ZUM GENIESSEN & MITNEHMEN!
SPEZIAL-MENÜS FÜR NUR 5.- €

Side
CAFÉ ▪ BISTRO ▪ RESTAURANT
INTERNET & GAMES

VORBESTELLUNG UNTER:
☎08621/ 20 15

DURCHGEHEND WARME KÜCHE

Hauptstr. 60, Altenmarkt a. d. Alz
Montag - Sonntag 11.30 - 23.30

Inhaber: Evren Esat

b.

Griechisches
Restaurant

Tändlergasse 4

Tägl. geöffnet von 11.30 - bis 14.30 u. 17.00 - 24.00 Uhr
Dienstag von 17.00 - 24.00 Uhr

c.

Siehe *Expressing Time
with Prepositions*,
S. 193.

Pizzeria Ristorante
Da Bizi
WARME KÜCHE VON 11—23 UHR
(Sonntag geschlossen)
1030 WIEN, FASANG 7   78 91 37
(PIZZA auch zum Mitnehmen)

d.

Gasthaus ... in den »Ochsen« zum Wohlfühlen!

Original schwäbische Spezialitäten
Zünftige Hausmacher-Vesper
Pils- und Hefeweizen-Biere vom Faß
Gepflegte heimische Weine
Gartenwirtschaft
Nebenzimmer ca. 40 Personen
- Montag Ruhetag -

»Zum Ochsen«

Karl-Heinz Oetinger

Bottwartalstraße 2
71672 Marbach

www.ochsen-marbach.de
info@ochsen-marbach.de
Telefon: 07144-54 30
Fax: 07144-1 44 03

e.

Kaiser von China
China Restaurant

● In der Kaiserpassage 18 / Eingang Wesselstraße
   53113 Bonn · Telefon (02 28) 65 88 30

● **Restaurant Hong Kong**
   Brasserufer 1 · 53111 Bonn · Tel. (02 28) 65 17 06

● **Restaurant Hongdi / Siegburg**
   mit schönem Biergarten am Mühlenbach · Auf der Kälke 1-3,
   beim Kreishaus · 53721 Siegburg · Tel. (0 22 41) 5 69 94

HONGDi

f.

SURYA
INDISCHES RESTAURANT

Genießen Sie in indischer
Atmosphäre unsere Spezialitäten.
Huhn, Lamm, vegetarische
Speisen zu kleinen Preisen.

Grolmanstraße 22 · 10623 Berlin-Charlbg.
(am Savignyplatz)
☎ 312 91 23 - täglich 12.00 - 1.00 Uhr

g.

Wo gibt es das?

Schauen Sie sich die Anzeigen im **Thema 1** an. In welches Lokal können Leute gehen, die

- gern griechisch essen?
- gern im Biergarten sitzen?
- gern Bier vom Fass trinken?
- etwas zum Mitnehmen möchten?

- Vegetarier sind?
- gern schwäbische Spezialitäten essen?
- gern Wein trinken?
- nicht viel Geld haben?

Und Sie? In welches Lokal möchten Sie gehen? Warum?

KULTURTIPP

German has many different words for places where one can eat or drink something.

das **Café**	café serving mainly desserts—**Kaffee und Kuchen**—but also offering a limited menu
der **Gasthof /** das **Gasthaus**	small inn with pub or restaurant
die **Gaststätte**	full-service restaurant
der **Imbiss**	fast-food stand; snack counter
die **Kneipe**	small, simple pub or bar; typical place where students gather (**Studentenkneipe**)
das **Lokal**	general word for an establishment that serves food and drinks
das **Restaurant**	generic word for *restaurant*
das **Wirtshaus**	pub serving mainly alcoholic beverages and some food

Often the word **Stube** or **Stüberl** will appear as a part of the name, as in **Altstadtstüberl** or **Mühlenstube**. **Stube** is an older word for *room* and suggests a cozy atmosphere.

Ein Café in Hamburg

Ein Gasthof in Bad Suderode

Ein Imbiss in Berlin

Eine Kneipe in Berlin

To suggest to a friend that you do something together, you can use the expression **Lass uns (doch) ... :**

Lass uns doch ins Restaurant gehen!   *Let's go to a restaurant!*
Lass uns türkisch essen!   *Let's eat Turkish food!*

Sie haben Hunger. Der Magen knurrt schon. In kleinen Gruppen, besprechen Sie, wie Sie essen möchten. Wozu entscheiden Sie sich?

s1: Lass uns essen. Sag mir, wie?
s2: Lass uns vegetarisch essen.
s3: Nein, lass uns ... essen.

Knurr! Knuurr!

Lass uns essen. Sag mir, wie:

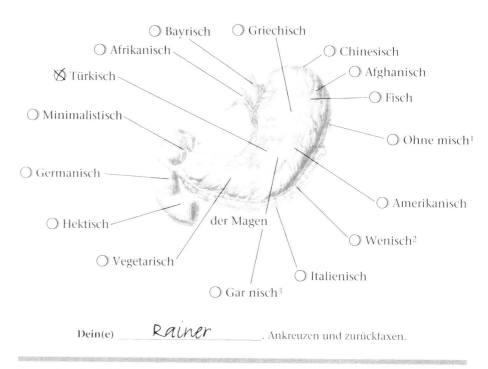

○ Bayrisch   ○ Griechisch
○ Afrikanisch   ○ Chinesisch
⊗ Türkisch   ○ Afghanisch
   ○ Fisch
○ Minimalistisch
   ○ Ohne misch[1]
○ Germanisch
   ○ Amerikanisch
○ Hektisch   ○ Wenisch[2]
der Magen
○ Vegetarisch   ○ Italienisch
○ Gar nisch[3]

Dein(e) ____*Rainer*____ . Ankreuzen und zurückfaxen.

[1]mich [2]wenig [3]nichts

Wo gibt es das?

Schauen Sie sich die Anzeigen im **Thema 1** an. In welches Lokal können Leute gehen, die

- gern griechisch essen?
- gern im Biergarten sitzen?
- gern Bier vom Fass trinken?
- etwas zum Mitnehmen möchten?

- Vegetarier sind?
- gern schwäbische Spezialitäten essen?
- gern Wein trinken?
- nicht viel Geld haben?

Und Sie? In welches Lokal möchten Sie gehen? Warum?

KULTURTIPP

German has many different words for places where one can eat or drink something.

das **Café**	café serving mainly desserts—**Kaffee und Kuchen**—but also offering a limited menu
der **Gasthof** / das **Gasthaus**	small inn with pub or restaurant
die **Gaststätte**	full-service restaurant
der **Imbiss**	fast-food stand; snack counter
die **Kneipe**	small, simple pub or bar; typical place where students gather (**Studentenkneipe**)
das **Lokal**	general word for an establishment that serves food and drinks
das **Restaurant**	generic word for *restaurant*
das **Wirtshaus**	pub serving mainly alcoholic beverages and some food

Often the word **Stube** or **Stüberl** will appear as a part of the name, as in **Altstadtstüberl** or **Mühlenstube**. **Stube** is an older word for *room* and suggests a cozy atmosphere.

Ein Café in Hamburg

Ein Gasthof in Bad Suderode

Ein Imbiss in Berlin

Eine Kneipe in Berlin

Sprachtipp. Point Out: *Lass* is the informal imperative form of *lassen*. Ask students what the *ihr*- and *Sie*-forms are.

To suggest to a friend that you do something together, you can use the expression **Lass uns (doch) ...** :

Lass uns doch ins Restaurant gehen!	*Let's go to a restaurant!*
Lass uns türkisch essen!	*Let's eat Turkish food!*

Aktivität ı   Lass uns essen!

Sie haben Hunger. Der Magen knurrt schon. In kleinen Gruppen, besprechen Sie, wie Sie essen möchten. Wozu entscheiden Sie sich?

s1: Lass uns essen. Sag mir, wie?

s2: Lass uns vegetarisch essen.

s3: Nein, lass uns ... essen.

Aktivität 1. Realia: *Der Magen knurrt* translates "*My stomach is growling.*" Use the "*Knurr! Knuurr!*" realia, a faxable invitation and response form, to practice *Lass uns ...* in preparation for **Aktivität 1**. One student proposes, *Lass uns essen. Sag mir, wie.* Another student responds, *Lass uns vegetarisch essen.* Several expressions (*Ohne misch = ohne mich; Wenisch = wenig; Gar nisch = gar nicht*); are deliberately misspelled in order to rhyme with words like *Griechisch, Hektisch,* and *Fisch.* After students have made their statements, ask: *Was isst man, wenn man italienisch, amerikanisch usw. isst?*

Knurr! Knuurr!

Lass uns essen. Sag mir, wie:

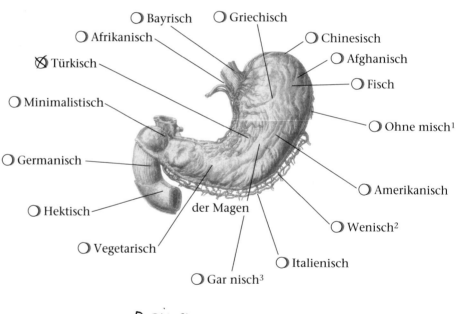

○ Bayrisch   ○ Griechisch

○ Afrikanisch   ○ Chinesisch

⊗ Türkisch   ○ Afghanisch

○ Fisch

○ Minimalistisch

○ Ohne misch[1]

○ Germanisch

○ Amerikanisch

○ Hektisch   der Magen   ○ Wenisch[2]

○ Vegetarisch

○ Italienisch

○ Gar nisch[3]

Dein(e) _____ *Rainer* _____. Ankreuzen und zurückfaxen.

[1]mich   [2]wenig   [3]nichts

Aktivität 2 Umfrage

Beantworten Sie die Fragen.

1. Gehen Sie oft aus essen? Wie oft? Einmal die Woche, einmal im Monat?
2. Essen Sie gern griechisch, chinesisch, italienisch … ?
3. Wie heißt Ihr Lieblingsrestaurant? Welche Spezialitäten gibt es dort?
4. Wann hat Ihr Lieblingsrestaurant Ruhetag? Oder ist es an allen Tagen der Woche geöffnet?
5. Was trinken Sie normalerweise, wenn Sie ausgehen?
6. Gibt es Cafés in Ihrer Stadt? Was kann man dort essen und trinken?

Aktivität 3 Ich habe Hunger. Ich habe Durst.

Wo gibt es was zu essen und zu trinken in Ihrer Stadt?

VORSCHLÄGE (*RECOMMENDATIONS*) FÜR ESSEN UND TRINKEN:

Pizza, Bier (vom Fass), griechische Küche, indische Spezialitäten (z.B. Lamm), internationale Küche (z.B. chinesische oder italienische Spezialitäten), ein Eis, eine Tasse Kaffee.

S1	S2
1. Ich habe Hunger. Ich habe Durst.	**2.** Magst du _____? Isst du gern _____? Möchtest du _____?
3. Ja. Wo kann man das bekommen?	**4.** Im _____.
5. Wann ist es geöffnet? Ist es heute geöffnet?	**6a.** Ich weiß es nicht genau. **b.** Täglich von _____ bis _____.

Das Wirtshaus Gatow in Berlin serviert traditionelle deutsche Küche.

Aktivität 2. Suggestion: 1. Have students answer the questions at home. 2. Have students work in small groups to answer these questions. Ensure that they change the questions from the *Sie*-form to the *du*-form. In each case, follow up with a class discussion of students' preferences.

Aktivität 3. Suggestion: You could use ads from restaurants from a different city. These need not necessarily be from Europe. If you have a German-language paper in your area, use that.

THEMA 2: Die Speisekarte, bitte!

Bad Oeynhausen
Herforder Str. 52
Tel. (05731) 3565
Fax (05731) 3536

Minden
Königswall 1-3
Tel. (0571) 21368
Fax (0571) 850581

Kleine Vorspeisen

Frittierte, frische Champignons................... 3,10
mit Kräuterquark und kleinem Salatbuquette

Kartoffelspieß................... 3,10
Kartoffeln, Speck, Zwiebeln, Paprika
mit Knoblauchcreme und Kräuterquark

Riesen Salatteller

Kleiner gemischter Salat................... 3,20
Großer gemischter Salatteller................... 6,60
mit Schinkenstreifen, Ei und Kräutercroutons

Salat "Korsika"................... 7,50
mit Schinken, Ei, Schafskäse, Zwiebeln und Oliven

Hausgemachte Reibekuchen[3]

mit geräuchertem Lachs................... 8,40
und Senf-Dill-Sauce

mit Apfelmus................... 4,60

Vegetarisches, gesund und lecker...

Gemüse-Pilz-Pfanne................... 7,20
mit Schupfnudeln[4] und Kräutern

Gebratene[5] Schupfnudeln................... 7,30
mit Zwiebeln, Lauch und Kräuterquark

Kartoffel-Käse-Rösti................... 7,20
mit Tomaten, Basilikum und Mozzarella

Vom Grill und aus der Pfanne

Kartoffelhauspfanne "Die Knolle"................... 13,10
mit 2 Schweinemedaillons, Schweinerückensteak,
Speckbohnen, frischen Champignons,
Sauce Bérnaise und Bratkartoffeln

"Schwaben Pfanne"................... 13,50
3 Schweinemedaillons mit Champignons à la
Creme, Sauce Hollandaise, Schupfnudeln
und Brokkoli, überbacken mit Käse

hausgemachtes Gulasch................... 12,40
vom Rind und vom Schwein, frische Paprika,
frische Champignons, Zwiebeln, Apfelrotkohl und
Kartoffelklöße

Grillteller "Die Knolle"................... 14,60
mit Rinderfilet, Schweinerückensteak,
Putenmedaillon, Grillspeck, Nackensteak, frischen
Champignons und Zwiebeln, dazu Kräuterbutter,
würzige Sauce und Pommes

Geflügel[6]

"Geflügelpfanne" Knolle................... 13,40
3 Putenmedaillons, frische Champignons, feines
Gemüse mit Sauce Bérnaise und Bratkartoffeln

kleinere Portion................... 10,10

Geflügel-Grillteller................... 13,60
2 Putenmedaillons, 1 Hähnchenbrustfilet,
Pfeffersauce, Bratkartoffeln und gemischter Salat

kleinere Portion................... 10,20

Lieblingsgerichte vom "Alten Fritz" überbacken mit Käse

"Schöne Gärtnerin"................... 8,70
Kartoffelauflauf mit Brokkoli, Blumenkohl,
Schinken und Käsesauce

Kartoffelauflauf "Hühnerdieb"................... 9,40
mit Hähnchenfleisch, Champignons, Brokkoli,
Mais und Käsesauce

Kartoffelauflauf "Indisch"................... 9,40
mit Geflügelstreifen, Currysauce, Mais, Tomaten,
und Porree

Kartoffel-Beziehungskisten

frische Bratkartoffeln aus der Pfanne mit ...

drei gebratenen Landeiern................... 5,10
und Gewürzgurke

Nürnberger Pfanne................... 7,50
6 Nürnberger, Sauerkraut und Bratkartoffeln

Matjesfilet mit Hausfrauensauce................... 9,70

Seemannspfännchen................... 7,50
Champignons, Shrimps, Schnittlauch und
Spiegelei

Nachtisch

Sylter Rote Grütze................... 2,40
mit Vanillesauce

Warmer Apfelstrudel................... 2,90
auf Vanillesauce

Schokoeisbecher................... 2,90
mit Eierlikör und Schlagcreme

Getränke

Pilsener................... 0,21 1,90
Apfelsaft, Orangensaft................... 0,21 1,90
Sprudel, Cola, Fanta............... 0,21 2,20

[1]*spud*   [2]*cozy*   [3]*potato pancakes*   [4]*small potato dumplings*   [5]*fried*   [6]*fowl*

A. Suchen Sie die Wörter unten auf der Speisekarte im **Thema 2**. Können Sie vom Kontext erraten (*guess*), wie die Wörter auf Englisch heißen?

1. _m_ das **Apfelmus**
2. _e_ die **Bohne**
3. _n_ das **Gericht**
4. _k_ der **Grill**
5. _i_ der **Mais**
6. _h_ die **Olive**
7. _l_ die **Paprika**
8. _a_ die **Pfanne**
9. _b_ die **Pommes (frites)** (*pl.*)
10. _o_ der **Salat**
11. _d_ das **Sauerkraut**
12. _f_ der **Speck**
13. _c_ das **Spiegelei**
14. _j_ der **Teller**
15. _g_ die **Zwiebel**

a. pan
b. French fries
c. fried egg
d. sauerkraut
e. bean
f. bacon
g. onion
h. olive
i. corn
j. plate
k. grill, barbecue
l. bell pepper
m. applesauce
n. dish (*a prepared item of food*)
o. salad

Die Speisekarte, bitte! The new vocabulary in this matching activity is presented without glossing in order to motivate students to practice the skill of guessing from context.

Suggestion: Have students work in pairs. First have them find each of the fifteen words somewhere on the menu on the previous page. Then have them do the matching with the English. Encourage and remind them to use context and their knowledge of cognates as much as possible. Only as a last resort should they look words up.

Die Speisekarte, bitte! Gänge. Some of the vocabulary shown here for different meal courses appears in the menu while some does not. The **Neue Wörter** box provides glossing for all but the obvious cognates.

Suggestion: Divide the class into groups and have them work on the categorization activity. Point out the **Neue Wörter** box as an aid. Follow up with a discussion, asking one or more from each group to give the solution and explain why that particular item does not belong. *Was gehört nicht in die Kategorie Vorspeise: Brezeln oder Schweinebraten?*
Schweinebraten gehört nicht in die Kategorie. Warum? Schweinebraten ist ein Hauptgericht.

B. Eine Mahlzeit (*meal*) besteht oft aus mehreren Gängen (*courses*): **Vorspeise, Hauptgericht, Beilage** und **Nachspeise (Nachtisch)**. Dazu gibt es Getränke. Welche Speise gehört nicht in die Kategorie? Streichen Sie aus, was nicht dazu gehört.

1. Vorspeise: **Suppe, ~~Schweinebraten~~**
2. Hauptgericht: **Auflauf, Leberkäs, ~~Senf~~, Weißwurst**
3. Beilage: **Nudeln, Bratkartoffeln, ~~Schnitzel~~, Reis**
4. Nachtisch: **Apfelstrudel, ~~Brezeln~~, Eisbecher**
5. Getränke: **Sprudel, Wein, ~~Sahne~~, Pilsener**

ANALYSE

Spaß mit der Speisekarte. Schauen Sie sich die Speisekarte auf der vorigen Seite noch mal an und beantworten Sie die folgenden Fragen.

- Das Restaurant „Knolle" ist ein Kartoffelrestaurant. Was kann man bestellen, wenn man Kartoffeln *nicht* mag? [Nur die Champignons (unter Vorspeisen), die Salate und die Nachtische haben keine Kartoffeln.]
- Finden Sie **Kartoffelauflauf „Indisch"** auf der Speisekarte. Was ist an (*about*) diesem Auflauf indisch? [Currysauce]
- Bei welchen anderen Speisen finden Sie geographische Namen? [Salat, „Korsika", „Schwaben Pfanne", Sylter Rote Grütze (von der Insel Sylt). Man könnte auch Sauce Hollandaise (von Holland) und sogar Pilsener (von der tschechischen Stadt Pilsen) erwähnen.]

Neue	Wörter

die Vorspeise appetizer
das Hauptgericht main dish
die Beilage side dish
die Nachspeise dessert
der Nachtisch dessert
die Suppe soup
der Schweinebraten pork roast
der Auflauf casserole
der Leberkäs Bavarian style meatloaf
der Senf mustard
die Weißwurst white sausage
die Bratkartoffeln (*pl.*) fried potatoes
die Brezel pretzel
der Eisbecher dish of ice cream
der Sprudel carbonated mineral water
die Sahne cream
das Pilsener Pilsner beer

Every area has its own regional specialties, while some dishes are available almost anywhere. Bavarian favorites include **Schweinshaxen** (pig's feet), **Spanferkel** (suckling pig), **Leberkäs** (a type of meatloaf), and **Weißwurst** (a type of veal sausage).

North German dishes include **Matjeshering** (salted young herring) and **Hamburger Labskaus,** a sailor's casserole made of cured meat, pickled herring, and various other ingredients topped with a fried egg. In the Southwest and parts of Switzerland one commonly finds **Spätzle** or **Spätzli,** egg noodles generally served with butter and cheese. The Westphalians are known for their **Pumpernickel** bread, the Thuringians for their **Thüringer Bratwurst,** and the Viennese for the **Wiener Schnitzel,** a breaded, pan-fried veal cutlet. Meat is frequently pork (**Schweinefleisch**). Beef (**Rindfleisch**) is also found on menus but is generally more expensive. Many restaurants have lighter fare such as chicken breast (**Hähnchen**) and turkey (**Truthahn** or **Pute**). Favorite dessert items include **Rote Grütze,** a compote made from crushed strawberries, currants, and cherries, and—in Bavaria—**Kaiserschmarren,** a sweet crepelike omelet.

Be prepared to get a bottle of **Sprudel** (*mineral water*) if you request water in a restaurant, and don't expect to get a lot of ice with it. It is not customary to serve a guest tap water, whether in a restaurant or a private home.

Weißwurst mit Sauerkraut

Matjeshering auf Gemüse

Rote Grütze

Aktivität 4 So viele Speisen!

Welche Speise oder welches Wort ist das?

1. B e l a t f r a n k f o r t   <u>Bratkartoffeln</u>
2. S t a l a   <u>Salat</u>
3. S c k e p   <u>Speck</u>
4. S t u r e u k a r a   <u>Sauerkraut</u>
5. N e l d u   <u>Nudel</u>
6. V e p r e s o s i   <u>Vorspeise</u>
7. Z e b w e i l   <u>Zwiebel</u>
8. H h h e n ä c n   <u>Hähnchen</u>
9. P e n a n f   <u>Pfanne</u>
10. H i g e t u t p a c h r   <u>Hauptgericht</u>
11. A l u f u f a   <u>Auflauf</u>

Aktivität 5 Was bestellen° Norbert und Dagmar? *are ordering*

Hören Sie zu und ergänzen Sie die Tabelle.

	NORBERT	DAGMAR
Vorspeise	Suppe	*Champignons*
Hauptgericht	Hähnchen	Weißwurst
Beilage	*Reis*	Sauerkraut
Getränk	Pilsener	Pilsener

Hier klicken!

Weiteres zum Thema Restaurant und Gerichte finden Sie bei **Deutsch: Na klar!** im World-Wide-Web unter www.mhhe.com/dnk5.

Aktivität 6 Was sollen wir bestellen?

Schauen Sie sich die Speisekarte auf Seite 180 an und besprechen Sie zu zweit oder zu dritt, was Sie bestellen möchten. Pro Person können Sie nur 20 Euro ausgeben.

BEISPIEL: Ich nehme Kartoffelspieß als Vorspeise. Als Hauptgericht nehme ich Matjesfilet mit Hausfrauensauce. Und als Nachspeise nehme ich rote Grütze.

Notieren Sie Ihre Bestellung:

Vorspeise:	€ 3,10	Vorspeise:
Hauptgericht:	€ 9,70	Hauptgericht:
Nachspeise:	€ 2,40	Nachspeise:
Summe:	€ 15,20	Summe:

Aktivität 6. Suggestion: First have students scan the menu given earlier, or one that you have brought in. Have them jot down what they would order without spending more than 20 euros. Then ask them to tell each other what they would like and how much it would cost. Have students report back to the class on what others have ordered. Challenge them to come up with the most interesting meal for the least amount of money.

Aktivität 7 Im Restaurant

Bilden Sie kleine Gruppen. Eine Person spielt den Ober oder die Kellnerin und nimmt die Bestellungen der Gäste an.

S1	S2
OBER/KELLNERIN	GAST
1. Bitte schön. Was darf's sein?	**2.** Ich möchte gern _____.
3. Und zu trinken?	**4.** Bringen Sie mir bitte _____.
5. Sonst noch was? (*Anything else?*)	**6a.** Ja, _____. **b.** Nein, das ist alles.

Aktivität 7. Suggestion: Group students in fours. Have them choose one to be the server. They could use their food selections from the previous activity, so that they concentrate on their language rather than choosing the food. Discuss the **Kulturtipp** below about addressing the server in a restaurant.

Im Restaurant. Suggestion: You may need to point out certain clues to the students. For example, in A the woman is handing the waiter some money. The man in B has nothing but flowers on the table. The man standing in F is pointing to the chair in front of him. Have students act out the mini-dialogues after they have matched them with the pictures.

KULTURTIPP

When you are in a restaurant and want to get the server's attention, it is polite to say **bitte schön.** Young people often call out **hallo,** but this is very informal. In more formal restaurants, you may hear people call **Herr Ober** if the server is male. Use the generic term **Bedienung (bitte)** to call for a server.

In all but the most exclusive restaurants in German-speaking countries, it is acceptable for people to ask to share a table if it is very crowded. Simply ask: **Ist hier noch frei?** The answer might be: **Ja, hier ist noch frei.** Or: **Nein, hier ist besetzt.**

THEMA 3: Im Restaurant

Welches Bild passt zu welchem Mini-Dialog?

a.

b.

c.

d.

e.

f.

Neue Wörter

der Ober waiter
die Speisekarte menu
bestellen order
Was bekommen Sie? What will you have?
war (sein) was
hatte (haben) had
vielen Dank many thanks
Entschuldigen Sie. Excuse me.
Ist hier noch frei? Is this seat available?
Hier ist besetzt. This seat is taken.
da drüben over there
der Platz room, space
das Messer knife
der Löffel spoon
die Serviette napkin
die Gabel fork
ziemlich rather
voll full
hoffentlich I/we/let's hope
warten wait
mussten (müssen) had to

1. __b__ — Herr **Ober**, die **Speisekarte**, bitte!
2. __d__ — Wir möchten **bestellen**.
   — Ja, bitte, **was bekommen Sie?**
   — Ich nehme das Hähnchen.
3. __a__ — Also, das **war** viermal Schnitzel und viermal Rotwein …
   — Nein, ich **hatte** den Grillteller.
   — Ach, ja. Das macht zusammen 68,40 Euro.
   — 70,– Euro.
   — **Vielen Dank.**
4. __f__ — **Entschuldigen Sie**, bitte! **Ist hier noch frei?**
   — Nein, **hier ist besetzt**, aber **da drüben** ist **Platz**.
5. __c__ — Herr Ober, ich habe **Messer, Löffel** und **Serviette**, aber keine **Gabel**.
   — Und ich habe keine Serviette.
6. __e__ — Hier ist es aber **ziemlich voll. Hoffentlich** müssen wir nicht lange auf einen Platz **warten**.
   — Ja, wir **mussten** lange nach einem Parkplatz suchen.

Aktivität 8   Im Brauhaus Matz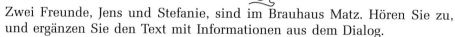

Zwei Freunde, Jens und Stefanie, sind im Brauhaus Matz. Hören Sie zu, und ergänzen Sie den Text mit Informationen aus dem Dialog.

Stefanie und Jens suchen __einen Platz__[1] in einem Restaurant. Es ist ziemlich __voll__.[2] Jens sieht zwei Leute an einem __Tisch__.[3] Da ist noch __Platz__[4] für zwei Leute. Er geht an den Tisch und fragt: „Ist __hier noch frei__[5]?" Die Antwort am ersten Tisch ist: „__Nein__.[6]" Die Antwort am zweiten Tisch ist: „__Ja__.[7]"

184   Kapitel 6 ■ Wir gehen aus

Aktivität 9 Ist hier noch frei?

Bilden Sie mehrere Gruppen. Einige Personen suchen Platz.

Ist hier noch frei?

S1	S2
1. Entschuldigen Sie. Ist hier noch frei?	**2a.** Ja, hier ist noch _____. **b.** Nein, hier ist leider _____. Aber da drüben ist noch _____.
3a. Danke schön. **b.** (*geht zu einem anderen Tisch*)	

Aktivität 9. **Suggestion:** Set up the classroom so that half the class is sitting in groups of two or three. The other half plays lone restaurant patrons, individually approaching a group and initiating a conversation.

KULTURTIPP

When adding up your restaurant bill (**Rechnung**), your server will often ask whether you want to pay separately (**getrennt**) or together (**zusammen**). When paying, you do not have to add a tip, as it is always included in your bill. The menu sometimes indicates this by stating:

Bedienungsgeld und   *Tip (service fee) and*
Mehrwertsteuer   *value-added tax*
enthalten.   *(federal sales tax)*
                           included.

It is customary to round up the figures on your bill to the next euro, but this practice is entirely up to the individual.

Aktivität 10. **Follow-up:** Put the activity and the dialogues in context by telling students about paying the bill in a German restaurant.

Aktivität 10 Wir möchten zahlen, bitte.

Was haben diese Leute bestellt? Wie viel kostet es? Kreuzen Sie an, was Sie hören.

		GETRÄNKE		ESSEN		BETRAG
Dialog 1		2 Bier	X	Knackwürste*		€10,00
		3 Cola		Weißwürste		€15,00
	X	3 Bier		Bockwürste†	X	€18,50
			X	Sauerkraut		
				Brot		

---

*a type of German frankfurter
†a type of German sausage similar to a hot dog in flavor and consistency

	GETRÄNKE	ESSEN	BETRAG
Dialog 2	2 Tassen Tee	2 Stück Käsekuchen	€6,25
	2 Tassen Kaffee	1 Stück Käsekuchen	€4,25
	1 Tasse Kaffee	1 Stück Obsttorte	€9,55
Dialog 3	2 Bier	Leberknödelsuppe*	€35,40
	5 Bier	Schweinskotelett	€39,40
	3 Bier	Brezeln	€43,40
		Weißwürste	
		Sauerkraut	

*liver dumpling soup

Grammatik im Kontext

Wechselpräpositionen

Two-Way Prepositions°

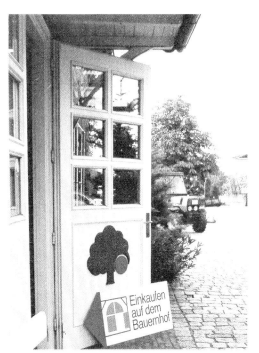

Auf dem Bauernhof kann man gut frisches Obst und Gemüse kaufen.

So far you have learned two kinds of prepositions: prepositions that are always used with the accusative case and others that are always used with the dative case.

In addition, a number of prepositions take either the dative or the accusative, depending on whether they describe a location or a direction. The most common two-way prepositions are these:

an	at, near, on
auf	on, on top of, at
hinter	behind, in back of
in	in
neben	next to
über	above, over
unter	under, beneath, below; among
vor	in front of; before
zwischen	between

Note:

- When answering the question **wo**, these prepositions take the dative case.

WO?	STATIONARY LOCATION (DATIVE)
Wo kauft man Brot?	In **der** Bäckerei.
Wo zahlt der Kunde?	An **der** Kasse.
Wo kauft man frisches Gemüse?	Auf **dem** Bauernhof.
Wo soll ich warten?	Vor **dem** Geschäft.

- When answering the question **wohin**, they take the accusative case.

WOHIN?	DIRECTION (ACCUSATIVE)
Wohin geht Frau Glättli?	In **die** Bäckerei.
Wohin geht der Kunde?	An **die** Kasse.
Wo gehst du hin?	Auf **den** Markt.
Wo geht Herr Sauer hin?	In **das** Geschäft.

- The following contractions are common:

an dem → **am**	Das Kaufhaus steht **am** Markt.
an das → **ans**	Geh doch **ans** Fenster!
in dem → **im**	Frau Kraus isst **im** Restaurant.
in das → **ins**	Nikola geht gleich **ins** Geschäft.

Ihr **Fachgeschäft**[1] für Brot und feinste Backwaren

**Derks, am Markt
Derks, am Rathaus**

CAFE DERKS BÄCKEREI KONDITOREI

[1]*specialty store*

ANALYSE

Suchen Sie in den folgenden Anzeigen alle Präpositionen mit Dativ- oder Akkusativobjekten. Ordnen Sie sie ein.

WO? (DATIV)	**WOHIN?** (AKKUSATIV)
BEISPIEL: <u>im alten Forsthaus</u>	_____

Restaurant Schubert-Stüberln

Küchenchef Franz Zimmer

hinter dem Burgtheater, vis-à-vis der Universität, beim Dreimäderlhaus

Schreyvogelgasse 4, 1010 Wien Telefon für Tischreservierung 63 71 87

Mach' Dir ein paar schöne Stunden... geh' ins Kino

Parken! Problemlos!

3.000 kostenlose Parkplätze direkt vor der Tür.

Fahren Sie in unser großes Parkhaus an der Pelkovenstraße.

PP

Kulinarische Notizen

Ein Brevier für Genießer.

Biergartenromantik im alten Forsthaus

OLYMPIA Einkaufszentrum

Hanauer Straße · Telefon 1 41 60 02

Übung 1   Am Feierabend

Was machst du gern/oft/manchmal/nie am Feierabend?

BEISPIEL: s1: Gehst du gern ins Café?

s2: Ja, ich gehe gern ins Café. [*oder*] Nein, ich gehe nicht gern ins Café.

der Biergarten	das Kino	der Sportclub
das Café	die Kneipe	die Stadt
die Disko	das Lokal	der Supermarkt
das Fitnesszentrum	das Restaurant	das Theater

Einkaufszettel

250 g Aufschnitt
Käsekuchen
150 g Emmentaler Käse
6 Brötchen
12 Würstchen zum Grillen
1 Pfund Kaffee
Schwarzbrot
2 Flaschen Sprudel
4 Tomaten
nicht vergessen:
Wörterbuch
Tennisschuhe

Übung 2   Wo gibt es das?

Mark muss heute einkaufen. Hier ist sein Einkaufszettel. Wo gibt es das?

BEISPIEL: Käsekuchen
Käsekuchen gibt es in der Konditorei.

die Bäckerei

die Buchhandlung

die Konditorei

der Markt

die Metzgerei

das Schuhgeschäft

der Supermarkt

Übung 3   Im Einkaufszentrum

Wie kommt man dahin und was kann man dort machen? Schauen Sie sich die Werbung (unten) an und beantworten Sie die Fragen.

BEISPIEL: Wie kommt man zum Einkaufszentrum Spahn?
Man kommt mit dem Bus dahin.

NÜTZLICHE WÖRTER

die Boutique

der Bus

die Buslinie

die Cafeteria

der Parkplatz

die Spielecke

das Studio

[1]*children's play corner*

1. Mit welcher Buslinie kann man dahin fahren?

2. Wo gibt es etwas zu essen?

3. Wo kann man Lampen kaufen?

4. Wo kann man parken?

5. Wo gibt es Geschenke zu kaufen?

6. Wohin kann man seine Kinder bringen?

Übung 4 Wo sollen wir nur parken?

Sie und ein Freund / eine Freundin haben heute viel vor. Sie wollen mit dem Auto in die Stadt. Wo können Sie parken?

BEISPIEL: Sie möchten ins Kino. →
        Lass uns hinter dem Kino parken.

1. Sie gehen ins Theater.
2. Sie brauchen eine Winterjacke. Sie müssen ins Kaufhaus.
3. Sie brauchen Obst und Gemüse und wollen auf den Markt.
4. Sie müssen in die Universität.
5. Sie müssen in die Apotheke.
6. Sie brauchen Würstchen zum Grillen. Sie müssen in die Metzgerei.
7. Sie möchten im Café eine Tasse Kaffee trinken.

Übung 4. Suggestion: The exercise will elicit a variety of answers. Encourage students to make counterproposals: *Lass uns hinter dem Kino parken. Nein, lass uns vor dem Kino parken.* The drawing also lends itself to describing where something is located: *Wo liegt die Apotheke?*

Describing Location

The verbs **hängen, liegen, sitzen, stecken,** and **stehen** indicate where someone or something is located.

hängen	to be (hanging)
liegen	to be (lying)
sitzen	to be (sitting)
stecken	to be (placed)
stehen	to be (standing)

When a two-way preposition is used with one of these verbs indicating location, the object of the preposition is in the dative case. Remember, the interrogative pronoun **wo** asks where someone or something is located.

Describing Location. Suggestion: These verbs can be practiced first by using simple classroom situations: *Wo liegt Jeffs Buch? (unter dem Tisch); Wo steht der Stuhl? (neben der Tür).*

Wo hängt das Bild? Es hängt **im** Wohnzimmer.	*Where is the picture hanging?* *It's hanging in the living room.*
Wo liegt die Rechnung? Sie liegt **neben der** Serviette.	*Where is the bill?* *It's next to the napkin.*
Wo sitzen die Studenten? Sie sitzen **auf einer** Bank **im** Park.	*Where are the students sitting?* *They're sitting on a bench in the park.*
Wo steckt der Schlüssel? Er steckt **in der** Tür.	*Where is the key?* *It's in the door.*
Wo steht das Motorrad? Es steht **auf dem** Parkplatz **beim** Markt.	*Where is the motorcycle?* *It's in the parking lot by the market.*

Claudia und Jürgen verbringen (*are spending*) einen Samstagnachmittag im Grünen. Beantworten Sie die Fragen zum Bild.

1. Wo liegt Jürgen?
2. Wo sitzt Claudia?
3. Wo hängt eine Spinne?
4. Wo sitzt der Hund?
5. Wo sitzt der Vogel?
6. Wo steht der Picknickkorb?
7. Wo steckt die Weinflasche?
8. Wo liegt das Buch?

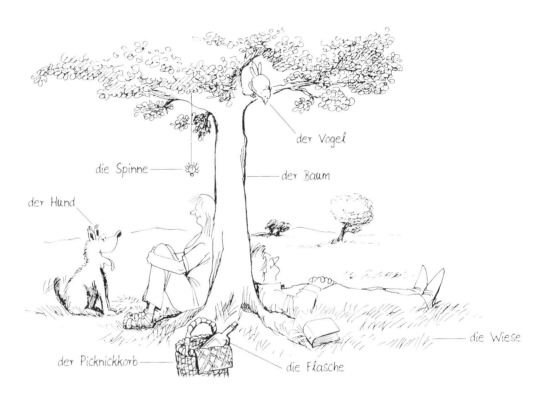

pub with a beer garden

Ergänzen Sie das passende Verb: **hängen, liegen, sitzen, stecken** oder **stehen**.

Andreas und Thomas _____[1] in einem Gartenlokal. Das Lokal heißt „Im Forsthaus". Es _____[2] sehr schön im Grünen nicht weit von Bonn. Vor dem Lokal _____[3] viele Autos. Im Biergarten _____[4] Papierlaternen. Auf dem Tisch vor Andreas und Thomas _____[5] zwei Gläser Bier. Unter dem Tisch direkt neben ihnen _____[6] ein Hund. Er gehört zu den Gästen am Nebentisch. Um den Tisch _____[7] vier Leute. Der Ober _____[8] jetzt neben Andreas. Ein Bleistift (*pencil*) _____[9] in seiner Tasche. Die Rechnung _____[10] schon auf dem Tisch.

Describing Placement

The verbs **legen, setzen,** and **stellen,** as well as **hängen** and **stecken,** can indicate where someone or something is being put or placed.

hängen	to hang, to put/place
legen	to lay, to put/place
setzen	to set, to put/place
stecken	to put/place
stellen	to stand, to put/place

When a two-way preposition is used with one of these verbs indicating placement, the object of the preposition is in the accusative case. Remember, the interrogative pronoun **wohin** asks where someone or something is being put or placed.

Wohin hängt der Mann den Mantel?	*Where is the man hanging the coat?*
Er hängt ihn **an den** Haken.	*He's hanging it on the hook.*
Wo legt der Kellner die Rechnung **hin?**	*Where is the waiter putting the bill?*
Er legt sie **auf den** Tisch.	*He's laying it on the table.*
Wohin setzt die Frau das Kind?	*Where is the woman putting the child?*
Sie setzt es **auf den** Stuhl.	*She's putting him/her on the chair.*
Wo steckt die Kellnerin das Geld **hin**?	*Where is the waitress putting the money?*
Sie steckt es **in die** Tasche.	*She's putting it in the purse.*
Wohin stellt die Kellnerin den Teller?	*Where is the waitress putting the plate?*
Sie stellt ihn **auf den** Tisch.	*She's placing it on the table.*

Describing Placement. Point out: The general rule for determining when to use *stellen* and when to use *legen* is as follows. To place an object upright use *stellen*: *Man stellt ein Glas auf den Tisch.* To place something flat or horizontal on a surface use *legen*: *Der Kellner legt die Rechnung auf den Tisch.*

Note: For a German speaker, plates are not considered flat like a piece of paper, and as such, cannot be laid upon the table. Thus one uses *stellen* to describe placing them on the table and *stehen* to describe how they rest on a table.

Die Kellnerin stellt den Teller auf den Tisch.

SPRACHTIPP

The verb **setzen** is frequently used with a personal pronoun that reflects the subject of the sentence. Used in this reflexive way, the verb means *to sit down.*

Ich setze **mich** an den Tisch.	*I sit down at the table.*
Wir setzen **uns.**	*We sit down.*

In the third-person singular and plural this reflexive pronoun is always **sich.**

Die Studenten setzen **sich** auf die Bank.	*The students sit down on the bench.*

Andreas trifft ein paar Freunde im „Nudelhaus". Ergänzen Sie die Sätze mit **hängen, legen, setzen, stecken** oder **stellen**.

1. Andreas und drei Studienfreunde _____ sich an einen Tisch beim Fenster.

2. Andreas _____ seinen Rucksack unter den Stuhl.

3. Michael _____ seinen Rucksack an seinen Stuhl.

4. Endlich kommt der Kellner und _____ die Speisekarte auf den Tisch.

5. Die vier bestellen zuerst etwas zu trinken. Der Kellner _____ vier Colas auf den Tisch.

6. Da kommt noch ein Freund, Phillip, an den Tisch zu ihnen. Andreas _____ noch einen Stuhl an den Tisch.

7. Phillip _____ sich neben Andreas.

8. Er _____ seine Bücher auf den Tisch.

9. Sein Handy _____ er in seinen Rucksack.

SPRACHTIPP

The verb **stehen** is used idiomatically to say that something has been stated (in print).

—Hier gibt es auch vegetarische Kost.   *They have vegetarian food here.*
—Wo **steht** das?   *Where does it say that?*

Übung 8 im Restaurant „Kartoffelkeller"

Ergänzen Sie die Sätze mit einem passenden Verb: **liegen, sitzen, stehen, legen, setzen** oder **stellen**.

1. Im Zentrum von Berlin _____ das Restaurant „Kartoffelkeller".

2. Im Restaurant ist es heute sehr voll. An allen Tischen _____ schon Leute und einige suchen noch Platz.

3. Ein paar Leute _____ draußen vor dem Lokal und warten, dass jemand geht.

4. Man _____ hier auch sehr gemütlich. Und die Preise sind nicht so hoch. Deshalb ist es unter Studenten populär.

5. Endlich kommt eine Kellnerin und _____ die Speisekarte auf den Tisch.

6. Auf der Speisekarte _____: „Spezialität unseres Hauses ist Kartoffelsuppe mit Brot."

7. Die Kellnerin _____ neben dem Tisch und wartet auf die Bestellung.

8. Am Nebentisch _____ einige Studenten und diskutieren laut.

9. Ein Student _____ sich an die Theke (*counter*) und bestellt ein Bier.

10. Der Kellner _____ das Bier vor ihn auf die Theke.

Übung 9 Die verlorene Theaterkarte

Michael kann seine Theaterkarte nicht finden. Wo steckt sie wohl? Eine Person denkt sich aus, wo die Karte ist. Die anderen müssen raten (*guess*), wo die Karte ist.

BEISPIEL: s1: Steckt die Theaterkarte in seiner Hosentasche?
s2: Nein.
s1: Liegt die Theaterkarte auf dem Schreibtisch?
s2: Nein. (usw.)

Übung 9. Suggestion: Have students say how Michael should clean up his room by saying where he should put things.

Expressing Time with Prepositions

The following two-way prepositions always take the dative case when expressing time:

vor drei Tagen	*three days ago*
vor dem Theater	*before the play*
in einer Stunde	*in one hour*
zwischen 5 und 7 Uhr	*between 5 and 7 o'clock*

You have learned several other prepositions expressing time—not two-way prepositions—that also take the dative case.

nach dem Theater	*after the play*
seit einem Jahr	*for a year*
von 5 bis 7 Uhr	*from 5 to 7 o'clock*

The prepositions **um** and **gegen** always take the accusative case.

bis (um) 5 Uhr	*until 5 o'clock*
(so) gegen 7 Uhr	*around 7 o'clock*

Expressing Time with Prepositions. Note: Depending on your particular class level, you may wish to elaborate further on word order with respect to time and place expressions. For example, in certain contexts, time and place elements may come before the verb: *Nach Hause komme ich erst so gegen zehn Uhr.*

Note: In German, expressions of time always precede expressions of place.

	TIME	PLACE
Wir kommen	**so gegen zehn Uhr**	nach Hause.
Ich gehe	**heute**	ins Kino.

Arbeiten Sie mit einem Partner / einer Partnerin zusammen.

BEISPIEL: S1: Was machst du nach dem Deutschkurs?
S2: Da gehe ich in die Bibliothek.

von _____ bis _____   arbeiten
zwischen _____ und _____   schlafen
so gegen _____   essen
um _____   ausgehen
vor _____   einkaufen gehen
nach _____   fernsehen
??   ??

Expressing Events in the Past

Like English, German has several tenses to express events in the past. The most common are the simple past tense (**das Imperfekt**) and the present perfect tense (**das Perfekt**).

- The present perfect tense (introduced in **Kapitel 7**) is preferred in conversation.

- The simple past tense is used primarily in writing. However, in the case of **haben, sein,** and the modals, the simple past is more common in conversation. In this chapter you will learn the simple past tense of these verbs; the simple past tense of all other verbs will be introduced in **Kapitel 10.**

The Simple Past Tense of **sein** and **haben**

	sein	**haben**
ich	war	hatte
du	warst	hattest
er, sie, es	war	hatte
wir	waren	hatten
ihr	wart	hattet
sie	waren	hatten
Sie	waren	hatten

Read the cartoon.

- What forms of the verbs **haben** and **sein** are used?
- The answer to the friend's question contains no verb or object because they are understood. What would the complete sentence be?
- How would the friend pose her questions if the speakers were adults addressing each other formally?

Du warst in Paris? Hattest du denn keine Schwierigkeiten¹ mit deinem Französisch?

Ich nicht, aber die Franzosen!

¹difficulties

Übung 11 Ausreden und Erklärungen°

Ergänzen Sie **haben** oder **sein** im Imperfekt.

1. A: Warum _____ Sie gestern und vorgestern nicht im Deutschkurs, Herr Miller?

   B: Es tut mir leid, Herr Professor, aber meine Großmutter _____ krank (*sick*).

2. C: Rolf, _____ du gestern Abend noch in der Bibliothek?

   D: Nein, die _____ geschlossen. Außerdem _____ ich keine Lust zu arbeiten. Ich _____ aber im Kino!

3. E: Warum _____ Michael und Peter nicht auf der Party bei Ulla?

   F: Sie _____ keine Zeit.

4. G: Ihr _____ doch gestern im Café Käuzchen, nicht?

   H: Nein, wir _____ im Café Kadenz. Im Käuzchen _____ es zu voll.

   G: Wie _____ es denn?

   H: Die Musik _____ gut, aber der Kaffee _____ schlecht.

Übung 12 Wo warst du denn?

Fragen Sie Ihren Partner / Ihre Partnerin!

BEISPIEL: s1: Wo warst du denn Freitagabend?
s2: Da war ich im Theater.
s1: Wie war's denn?
s2: Sehr langweilig.

WO	WIE
auf dem Sportplatz	interessant
auf einer Party	langweilig
bei Freunden	nicht besonders gut
im Kino	schön
im Restaurant	??
im Theater	
zu Hause	
??	

Excuses and explanations

Übung 11. Note: This exercise can be done individually or in pairs.

Answers: 1. A: *waren* B: *war* 2. C: *warst* D: *war, hatte, war* 3. E: *waren* F: *hatten* 4. G: *wart* H: *waren, war* G: *war* H: *war, war* 5. I: *waren* J: *hatte, war*

Additional items: 6. K: *Hattet ihr Spaß auf der Party? —L: Nein, die Musik war uns ein bisschen zu laut und Mieke hatte Kopfschmerzen* (headache). 7. M: *Mehmet, warum hattest du dein Handy gestern nicht dabei? —N: Ich weiß nicht. Vielleicht war es im Auto irgendwo.*

Übung 12. Suggestion: You may wish to reuse this activity after introducing the simple past tense of modals. Have students expand on their answers: s1: *Wo warst du denn heute Nachmittag?* s2: *Ich war im Kino.* s1: *Wie war's denn?* s2: *Nicht besonders gut. Ich konnte den Film nicht verstehen.*

The Simple Past Tense of Modals

	dürfen	**können**	**mögen**	**müssen**	**sollen**	**wollen**
ich	durfte	konnte	mochte	musste	sollte	wollte
du	durftest	konntest	mochtest	musstest	solltest	wolltest
er, sie, es	durfte	konnte	mochte	musste	sollte	wollte
wir	durften	konnten	mochten	mussten	sollten	wollten
ihr	durftet	konntet	mochtet	musstet	solltet	wolltet
sie	durften	konnten	mochten	mussten	sollten	wollten
Sie	durften	konnten	mochten	mussten	sollten	wollten

Note:

- As with **haben** and **sein,** the first- and third-person singular forms and first- and third-person plural forms of the simple past tense of modals are identical.

- Modals have no umlaut in the simple past tense.

Peter **wollte** gestern in die Disko. Ich **musste** aber zu Hause bleiben.

Peter wanted to go clubbing yesterday. But I had to stay home.

Wir **konnten** keinen Parkplatz finden.

We couldn't find a parking space.

¹*In case*

Übung 13 Ich wollte … aber ich musste …

Was wolltest du am Wochenende machen? Was musstest du machen?

A. Ergänzen Sie **wollen** im Imperfekt.

1. Ich _____ zuerst mal lange schlafen.
2. Mein Freund _____ mit mir ausgehen.
3. Bei gutem Wetter _____ wir Freunde im Park treffen.
4. Unsere Freunde _____ uns abholen.
5. _____ du am Wochenende nicht lange schlafen und dann ausgehen?

B. Ergänzen Sie **müssen** im Imperfekt.

1. Ja, aber ich _____ früh aufstehen; ich _____ nämlich arbeiten.
2. Meine Freundin _____ auch arbeiten.
3. Am Nachmittag _____ wir einkaufen gehen.
4. Meine Freunde _____ ohne mich ausgehen.

Übung 14 Kleine Probleme

Ergänzen Sie die fehlenden Modalverben im Imperfekt.

Übung 14. Answers: 1. *wollten*
2. *durfte* 3. *konnten* 4. *mussten*
5. *sollte* 6. *musste* 7. *wollten*
8. *konnten* 9. *mussten*

Gestern Abend waren wir im Theater. Wir ____[1] (wollen) in der Nähe vom Theater parken. Da ____[2] (dürfen) man aber nicht parken. Wir ____[3] (können) keinen Parkplatz auf der Straße finden. Deshalb ____[4] (müssen) wir ins Parkhaus fahren. Katrin ____[5] (sollen) vor dem Theater auf uns warten. Sie ____[6] (müssen) lange warten. Nach dem Theater ____[7] (wollen) wir noch ins Café Kadenz. Da ____[8] (können) wir keinen Platz bekommen. Wir ____[9] (müssen) also nach Hause fahren.

Übung 15 Bei mir zu Hause

Wie war das bei Ihnen zu Hause?

BEISPIEL: Als (*As a*) Kind mochte ich keinen Fisch essen.
          Mein Vater wollte abends in Ruhe die Zeitung lesen.

ich	dürfen	Fisch/Brokkoli/Salat essen
wir Kinder	können	Gemüse essen
mein Vater	mögen	am Wochenende das Auto waschen
??	müssen	jeden Tag Hausaufgaben machen
	sollen	abends in Ruhe die Zeitung lesen
	wollen	abends nicht fernsehen
		nur am Wochenende ins Kino gehen
		um zehn im Bett sein
		??

Übung 16 Hin und her: Warum nicht?

Fragen Sie Ihren Partner / Ihre Partnerin, warum die folgenden Leute nicht da waren.

BEISPIEL: s1: Warum war Andreas gestern Vormittag nicht in der Vorlesung?
          s2: Er hatte keine Lust.

PERSON	WANN	WO	WARUM
Andreas	gestern Vormittag	in der Vorlesung	keine Lust haben
Anke	Montag	zu Hause	arbeiten müssen
Frank	gestern Abend	auf der Party	keine Zeit haben
Yeliz	heute Morgen	in der Vorlesung	schlafen wollen
Mario	Samstag	im Café	kein Geld haben
Ihr Partner / Ihre Partnerin			

Sprache im Kontext

Videoclips

A. Schauen Sie sich das Interview mit dem Besitzer des Restaurants an und ergänzen Sie die Sätze.

1. Das Restaurant heißt ___.
   a. Geigenhafen
   b. Gugelhof
   c. Gartenlaube

2. Es gibt Spezialitäten vom ___, von Baden und von der Schweiz.
   a. Elsass
   b. Rheinland
   c. Mittelmeer

3. Eine Spezialität des Restaurants ist ___.
   a. Lamm provenzal
   b. Tarte flambée
   c. Steak tartare

B. Schauen Sie sich die Szene im Restaurant an, wo die Gäste Essen bestellen. Wer bestellt was?

1. ___ Michael   **a.** Putenspieß
2. ___ Claudia   **b.** Kartoffelauflauf
3. ___ Ali   **c.** Schweineschnitzel
4. ___ Sara   **d.** Tomatensuppe

C. Die Gäste sprechen über ihre Essgewohnheiten. Hören Sie zu und beantworten Sie folgende Fragen.

1. Wo isst Ali gern?
2. Was isst Claudia gern?
3. Was ist Saras Lieblingsessen?
4. Wer isst gern Falafel?
5. Was für Fastfood isst Claudia gern?

D. Und Sie? Was essen und trinken Sie gern, wenn Sie ins Restaurant gehen?

Lesen

Zum Thema

A. Beantworten Sie die folgenden Fragen, bevor Sie den Text lesen.

1. Kochen Sie gern?
2. Sind Sie ein guter Koch / eine gute Köchin?
3. Wie oft kochen Sie pro Woche?
4. Was kochen Sie am liebsten?

5. Was kochen Sie oft, wenn Sie Freunde einladen?

6. Kochen Sie lieber allein oder mit jemandem zusammen?

B. Interviewen Sie einen Studenten / eine Studentin in der Klasse und stellen Sie ihm/ihr die Fragen in **A.**

Auf den ersten Blick

Auf den ersten Blick. Suggestion: Have students do this for homework in preparation for discussion of the text.

A. Lesen Sie den Titel und die erste Zeile im Text und beantworten Sie die folgenden Fragen.

1. Was ist das Thema?

2. Was macht der Mann?
   a. Er isst.
   b. Er kocht.
   c. Er singt.

3. Mit wem spricht der Mann?
   a. mit seiner Frau
   b. mit sich selbst
   c. mit jemandem am Telefon

B. Verbinden Sie das deutsche Wort mit der englischen Bedeutung.

B. Note: Students should be able to complete this without use of a dictionary through recognition of cognates, parts of speech, and the process of elimination.

1. angebrannt	*monologue, soliloquy*
2. brennen	*splendid*
3. das Selbstgespräch	*burnt*
4. der Essig	*salty*
5. herrlich	*to burn*
6. verkochen	*sharp, spicy*
7. scharf	*to cook down*
8. sauer	*sauce*
9. salzig	*vinegar*
10. die Soße	*sour*

C. Überfliegen Sie (*scan*) jetzt den Text. Welche Lebensmittel kommen im Text *nicht* vor? Kreuzen Sie an!

☐ Salz   ☐ Essig   ☐ Paprika
☐ Zwiebeln   ☒ Tomaten   ☐ Knoblauch
☒ Wurst   ☐ Pfeffer   ☒ Karotten
☐ Wein   ☒ Kartoffeln   ☐ Oliven

D. Was für eine (*what kind of*) Soße kocht der Mann? Eine Soße für einen Schweinebraten? für ein Schnitzel vielleicht? Was meinen Sie? Begründen Sie Ihre Antwort.

DIE SOSSE

von Ekkehard Müller

Selbstgespräch eines Mannes beim Kochen:

Hoffentlich ist die Soße richtig. Hoffentlich schmeckt sie gut.
Nein. Da fehlt° noch etwas.   *is missing*
Ich muss sie noch mehr salzen.
5 Oh weh! Das war zu viel.
Was mache ich jetzt?
Ich muss sie mit Wasser verdünnen°. Oh weh. Das war auch zu viel.   *dilute*
Jetzt schmeckt sie nach gar nichts.
Macht nichts. Das Wasser wird wieder verkochen.
10 Und das Salz???

Jetzt muss ich noch Zwiebeln schneiden.
Ich hätte° sie schon vorher …   *should have*
Au, das brennt in den Augen.
So. Die Zwiebeln sind auch schon drin. Wie schmeckt sie jetzt?
15 Besser. Viel besser.
Aber es fehlt noch etwas.

Ich muss noch Wein dazugeben.
Hm. Der schmeckt aber gut.
Und noch ein Glas.
20 Ausgezeichnet!
Oh weh! Jetzt habe ich keinen Wein mehr für die Soße.
Was mache ich?
Ich nehme Essig.

Brrrrrrrrr, zu sauer!
25 Wie rette° ich die Soße?   *save*
Ich weiß es. Mit Tomatenketchup. Das schadet nie°.   *schadet … never hurts*
Hier schon.
Jetzt muss noch Pfeffer rein. Endlich scharf!
Und Paprika. Und Knoblauch°.   *garlic*
30 Schade, dass Knoblauch wie der Teufel stinkt.
Und jetzt, jetzt kommen noch Oliven in die Soße.
Ich mag Oliven.
Oliven erinnern° mich an Italien.   *remind*
Und Italien erinnert mich an Sonne.
35 Und an das Meer.
Und an Fischer.
Ah, die Sonne!
Ah, das Meer!
Ah, die Fischer!
40 Und der Duft° der Bäume im Frühling!   *fragrance*
Herrlich!
Was raucht denn hier?
Ich gehe ins Gasthaus. Die Soße ist angebrannt.

Zum Text

A. Lesen Sie den ganzen Text einmal durch und beantworten Sie dann die folgenden Fragen.

1. Mit der Soße gibt es immer wieder ein neues Problem, aber der Mann weiß immer wieder eine Lösung (*solution*). Wie löst er die folgenden Probleme?

BEISPIEL: Die Soße hat zu viel Salz. → Er verdünnt die Soße mit Wasser.

   a. Er hat keinen Wein mehr für die Soße.
   b. Die Soße ist zu sauer.
   c. Die Soße ist nicht scharf genug (*enough*).

2. Warum hat der Mann keinen Wein mehr für die Soße?

3. Warum nimmt der Mann Oliven für die Soße?

4. Immer wieder macht der Mann Kommentar wie „Oh weh!", wenn er neue Zutaten (*ingredients*) in die Soße mischt. Suchen Sie andere Kommentare im Text.

5. Was passiert mit der Soße am Ende? Warum? Wohin geht der Mann dann?

B. Ist Ihnen schon mal etwas Ähnliches (*something similar*) passiert? Was haben Sie gekocht? Erzählen Sie. Schreiben Sie einen kurzen Bericht (*report*).

Zu guter Letzt

Ihr Lieblingsrestaurant bewerten

Haben Sie ein Lieblingsrestaurant? Gemeinsam mit anderen Studenten/ Studentinnen werden Sie jetzt ein Bewertungsformular (*evaluation form*) für ein Restaurant entwickeln (*develop*), ausfüllen und darüber berichten.

Schritt 1: Machen Sie eine Liste mit Fragen über Ihr Lieblingsrestaurant, zum Beispiel: Warum essen Sie dort? Wie ist die Atmosphäre? Essen Sie oft dort? Wie oft? Mit wem? Was? Wie ist die Bedienung? Wie sind die Preise? Weitere Fragen?

Schritt 2: Arbeiten Sie in Gruppen zu dritt. Stellen Sie das Bewertungsformular zusammen. Benutzen Sie Fragen aus **Schritt 1.** Erstellen Sie mindestens 10 Fragen für Ihr Formular. Geben Sie dazu auch mögliche Antworten an, z.B.

1. Wie oft essen Sie da?
   ___-mal pro Woche
   ___-mal pro Monat
   ___-mal im Jahr

2. Wie ist die Atmosphäre?
   ☐ ruhig
   ☐ laut und lustig
   ☐ angenehm

3. …

Beantworten Sie die Fragen noch nicht!

Zum Text. Additional questions:
Der Mann meint, er braucht noch etwas für die Soße. Welche Zutaten nimmt er für die Soße? Was passiert jedes Mal? (Er nimmt mehr Salz und dann …)

Suggestion: Zum Text B can be done as a pair or group work activity. Have students interview each other, transforming the *Sie*-questions into *du*-questions. Additional questions for the interview: *Was hast du beim Kochen falsch gemacht? Hast du Zutaten vergessen? Wie hat das geschmeckt?* Have them write a follow-up short essay for homework.

Zu guter Letzt. Suggestion: As an introduction to the activity, ask students *Hatten Sie schon mal ein schlechtes Erlebnis / ein unangenehmes Abendessen in einem Restaurant? Was war das Problem?* After taking a couple of students' responses, write the phrase *Restaurantkritik* on the board to begin an associogram. Ask students, *Was kann im Restaurant ein Problem sein?* and have them come to the board.

Schritt 3: Machen Sie Fotokopien des Formulars und tauschen Sie es mit einer anderen Gruppe aus. Jede/r bekommt also ein Formular zum Ausfüllen. Füllen Sie das Formular mit Bezug auf (*with reference to*) Ihr eigenes Lieblingsrestaurant aus.

Schritt 4: Berichten Sie der Klasse über Ihr Lieblingsrestaurant. Beschreiben Sie verschiedene Aspekte des Restaurants. Die Klasse entscheidet (*decides*) Folgendes: Ist das Restaurant: **1.** exzellent, **2.** sehr gut, **3.** gut, **4.** mittelmäßig oder **5.** unterdurchschnittlich?

Wortschatz

Lokale

Eating and Drinking Establishments

der **Biergarten,** ¨	beer garden
das **Café, -s**	café
die **Gaststätte, -n**	full-service restaurant
der **Imbiss, -e**	fast-food stand
die **Kneipe, -n**	pub, bar
das **Lokal, -e**	restaurant, pub, bar
das **Restaurant, -s**	restaurant
das **Wirtshaus,** ¨er	pub

Im Restaurant

In the Restaurant

das **Apfelmus**	applesauce
der **Apfelstrudel**	apple strudel
der **Auflauf**	casserole
die **Bedienung**	service
die **Beilage, -n**	side dish
die **Bohne, -n**	bean
die **Bratkartoffeln** (*pl.*)	fried potatoes
die **Brezel, -n**	pretzel
der **Eisbecher, -**	dish of ice cream
die **Gabel, -n**	fork
das **Gericht, -e**	dish (*of prepared food*)
der **Grill**	grill, barbeque
das **Hauptgericht, -e**	main dish
der **Kellner, - / die Kellnerin, -nen**	waiter / waitress, server
die **Küche**	food, cuisine; kitchen
der **Leberkäs**	Bavarian style meatloaf
der **Löffel, -**	spoon
der **Mais**	corn
das **Messer, -**	knife
die **Nachspeise, -n**	dessert
der **Nachtisch, -e**	dessert
die **Nudel, -n**	noodle
der **Ober, -**	waiter
die **Olive, -n**	olive
die **Paprika**	bell pepper
die **Pfanne, -n**	pan

das **Pilsener, -**	Pilsner beer
der **Platz,** ¨e	place, seat
die **Pommes frites** (*pl.*)	french fries
die **Rechnung, -en**	bill
der **Reis**	rice
der **Ruhetag, -e**	*day that a business is closed*
die **Sahne**	cream; whipped cream
der **Salat, -e**	salad; lettuce
das **Sauerkraut**	sauerkraut
der **Schweinebraten, -**	pork roast
der **Senf**	mustard
die **Serviette, -n**	napkin
der **Speck**	bacon
die **Speise, -n**	dish (of prepared food)
die **Speisekarte, -n**	menu
das **Spiegelei, -er**	fried egg (sunny-side up)
der **Sprudel**	mineral water
die **Suppe, -n**	soup
der **Teller, -**	plate
die **Vorspeise, -n**	appetizer
der **Wein, -e**	wine
die **Weißwurst,** ¨e	white sausage
die **Zwiebel, -n**	onion

Verben

Verbs

bekommen	to get
Was bekommen Sie?	What will you have?
bestellen	to order
entschuldigen	to excuse
Entschuldigen Sie!	Excuse me!
hängen	to hang; to be hanging
lassen	to let
Lass uns (doch) ...	Let's ...
legen	to lay, put (*in a lying position*)
liegen	to lie; to be located
setzen	to set; to put (*in a sitting position*)
sitzen	to sit

stecken	to place, put (*inside*); to be (*inside*)	neben	next to, beside
stehen	to stand; to be located	über	over, above
stellen	to stand up; place, put (*in an upright position*)	unter	under, below, beneath; among
warten	to wait	vor	before, in front of
		zwischen	between

Adjektive und Adverbien / Adjectives and Adverbs

alkoholfrei	nonalcoholic
besetzt	occupied, taken
Hier ist besetzt.	This place is taken.
da drüben	over there
geöffnet	open
geschlossen	closed
getrennt	separate(ly)
hoffentlich	I hope
täglich	daily
vegetarisch	vegetarian
voll	full; crowded
ziemlich	somewhat, rather

Präpositionen (Temporal) / Prepositions (Temporal)

bis (um): bis (um) fünf Uhr	until: until five o'clock
(so) gegen: (so) gegen fünf Uhr	around/about: around five o'clock
in (+ *dat.*): in zwei Tagen	in: in two days
nach: nach Dienstag	after: after Tuesday
seit: seit zwei Jahren	since, for: for two years
von: von zwei bis drei Uhr	from: from two to three o'clock
vor (+ *dat.*): vor zwei Tagen	ago: two days ago
zwischen: zwischen zwei und drei Uhr	between: between two and three o'clock

Wechsel-präpositionen / Dative/Accusative Prepositions

an	at, on, to, near
auf	on, on top of, at
hinter	behind, in back of
in	in; to (*a place*)

Sonstiges / Other

Ist hier noch frei?	Is this seat available?
Vielen Dank!	Many thanks!
vom Fass	on top; draft
zum Mitnehmen	(food) to go; take-out

DAS KANN ICH NUN!

1. Nennen Sie drei andere Lokalitäten, wo man essen und trinken kann.

   a. das Restaurant   **b.** _____   **c.** _____   **d.** _____

2. Was ist Ihr Lieblingsessen? Ihr Lieblingsgetränk? Ihre Lieblingsnachspeise?

3. „Wo" oder „**wohin**"?

   a. _____ wollen wir gehen?   **b.** _____ ist noch ein Platz frei?

4. Setzen Sie passende Präpositionen und Artikel ein.

   a. _____ _____ Konzert gehen Uwe und Ute _____ _____ Kneipe.   **b.** Ihr Auto steht _____ _____ Restaurant.   **c.** Uwe setzt sich _____ _____ Tisch.   **d.** Sein Hund liegt _____ _____ Tisch.

5. Wie sagen Sie das?

   a. Ask if this seat is taken.   **b.** Ask a server to bring you the menu.   **c.** Order some mineral water and a dish of ice cream.   **d.** Let the server know that you would like to pay.

6. Ergänzen Sie **sein** oder **haben** im Imperfekt. Wo _____ du gestern? —Ich _____ in der Uni. Wir _____ eine Gastvorlesung von einem Professor aus USA.

7. Setzen Sie ein passendes Modalverb im Imperfekt ein.

   a. Ich _____ nach der Vorlesung sofort in die Mensa.   **b.** Wir _____ leider nicht mitkommen.   **c.** Wir _____ nämlich zwei Stunden in der Vorlesung bleiben.

Zweites Zwischenspiel

Begegnung mit der Kunst der Gegenwart

Was ist Kunst? Das Wort „Kunst" kommt von „können". Ein Künstler oder eine Künstlerin ist ein „Könner"; jemand, der etwas „kann", z.B. malen, zeichnen, formen, komponieren, schreiben. Was erwarten Sie als Kunstbetrachter[1] von einem Kunstwerk? Soll es z.B. „schön" sein, provozieren, zum Nachdenken anregen[2] oder die Realität darstellen[3]?

Die Beispiele moderner und zeitgenössischer[4] deutscher Kunst auf diesen Seiten zeigen Kunst im Kontext von alltäglichen Dingen und ungewöhnlichen Medien. Viele Leute bewundern[5] diese Werke, andere nennen sie Werke von „Dilettanten und hochgemuten[6] Nichtskönnern". Was meinen Sie? (Zitat: aus S. 7, Faust / de Vries. „Hunger nach Bildern")

Tisch mit Aggregat, 1958/87. Joseph Beuys

„Flaschenpost", 1990. Rolf Glasmeier

Sandzeichnung. 1975. Joseph Beuys

Aktivität 1 Kunstbewertung

A. Was halten Sie von diesen Kunstgebilden? Wie würden Sie sie charakterisieren?

BEISPIEL: Ich finde die „Flaschenpost" sehr witzig.

- ☐ aggressiv
- ☐ hässlich
- ☐ humorvoll
- ☐ komplex
- ☐ radikal
- ☐ schön
- ☐ verrückt
- ☐ kitschig
- ☐ witzig
- ☐ provozierend

- ☐ dilettantisch
- ☐ komisch
- ☐ originell
- ☐ faszinierend
- ☐ spektakulär
- ☐ kindisch
- ☐ phantasievoll
- ☐ kreativ
- ☐ tief[7]
- ☐ ??

[1]*viewer of art* [2]*incite* [3]*represent* [4]*contemporary* [5]*admire* [6]*arrogant* [7]*profound*

B. Besprechen Sie die folgender Fragen im Plenum.

1. Welches dieser Kunstwerke gefällt Ihnen besonders gut? Wenn Ihnen keins davon gefällt, warum nicht?

2. Erinnert Sie das eine oder andere dieser Kunstwerke an etwas, was Sie schon einmal, vielleicht in einem Museum, gesehen haben? Sind Ihnen die Namen der Künstler bekannt? Wenn ja, welche Namen?

3. Wer ist Ihr Lieblingskünstler / Ihre Lieblingskünstlerin?

4. Was für Kunstwerke oder Reproduktionen von Kunstwerken haben Sie in Ihrem Zimmer oder in Ihrer Wohnung?

5. Wenn Sie eins dieser Kunstwerke erwerben[1] könnten, welches würden Sie wählen, und warum?

claus bremer

Konkrete Poesie

Hier sind zwei Beispiele konkreter Poesie. Charakteristisch für sie ist der visuelle Aspekt. Das Visuelle kann z.B. ein Piktogramm sein oder eine Figur, die mit Buchstaben und Wörtern gefüllt ist. Was halten Sie von Claus Bremers und Reinhard Döhls konkreter Poesie?

reinhard döhl

Aktivität 2   Sie sind dran[2].

A. Schreiben Sie jetzt Ihr eigenes konkretes Gedicht.

B. Schreiben Sie ein Gedicht im Fünfzeilenformat:

Erste Zeile:	ein Substantiv
Zweite Zeile:	zwei Adjektive
Dritte Zeile:	drei Verben im Infinitiv
Vierte Zeile:	ein Satz, eine Frage oder ein Ausdruck
Fünfte Zeile:	Wiederholung der ersten Zeile, oder ein anderes Substantiv

„Der Leser". 1981, Georg Jiri Dokoupil

[1]*acquire*   [2]*Sie ... It's your turn.*

Freizeit und Sport

KAPITEL
7

Zwei junge Leute auf einer
Wanderung in der Schweiz

In diesem Kapitel

- **Themen:** Sports and leisure pastimes, locations, seasons, weather expressions
- **Grammatik:** Coordinating conjunctions, present perfect tense, comparative
- **Kultur:** Sports, hobbies, clubs, temperature conversion
- **Lesen:** „Vergnügungen" (Bertolt Brecht)

Videoclips
Pläne für die Freizeit

Alles klar?

A. Schauen Sie sich die Grafik an und beantworten Sie die Fragen.

Freizeitvergnügen in Deutschland. Beliebteste[1] Freizeitbeschäftigungen in %

[1]*most popular*

Mehrfachnennungen Stand 2002

| 41 | 36 | 31 | 27 | 24 | 20 | 19 | 18 | 16 | 14 | 13 | 12 |

Musik hören · Fernsehen · Tageszeitung lesen · gut essen gehen · Treffen mit Freunden · Auto fahren · Bücher lesen · Zeitschriften lesen · Rad fahren · Gartenarbeit · Ausgehen (Bar, Disco) · Sport treiben

© Globus

8592

Quelle: Verbraucheranalyse Bauer, Axel Springer Verlag

- Was ist die beliebteste Freizeitbeschäftigung der Deutschen?
- Welche Freizeitbeschäftigung haben nur 12% der Deutschen gern?
- Was ist die beliebteste Freizeitbeschäftigung in Ihrem Land?
- Welche Freizeitbeschäftigung ist in Ihrem Land nicht so beliebt?

B. Sie hören nun drei kurze Dialoge. Wie verbringen Ulrike, Wolfgang und Antje ihre Freizeit?

1. Ulrike
   a. Tanzen   **b.** sich mit Freunden treffen   **c.** Kochen   **d.** Lesen

2. Wolfgang
   a. Fußball spielen   **b.** Fernsehen   **c.** Musik hören   **d.** Rad fahren

3. Antje
   a. ins Kino gehen   **b.** Sport treiben   **c.** Musik spielen   **d.** im Internet surfen

Wörter im Kontext

THEMA 1: Sportarten

Wo macht man das? Kombinieren Sie!

BEISPIEL: Man wandert im Wald oder am Fluss.

1. Lisa turnt jeden zweiten Tag.

wandern	auf dem **Tennisplatz**
Rad fahren	im Fitnesscenter
angeln	auf dem **See**
tauchen	auf der Straße
reiten	im **Wald**
segeln	am **Fluss**
Bodybuilding machen	im **Meer**
turnen	in der **Turnhalle**
schwimmen	im **Schwimmbad**
Tennis spielen	auf der **Wiese**
	in den **Bergen**

2. Uwe und Erich machen dreimal die Woche Bodybuilding.

3. Kerstin fährt Rad.

4. Heinz angelt oft im Sommer.

5. Manfred segelt gern.

6. Renate taucht gern.

7. Eva reitet jeden Tag.

Die Karte „Naherholung" zeigt, welche Sportmöglichkeiten es in und um Göttingen gibt. Schauen Sie sich die Bildsymbole auf der Karte an. Welche Sportarten kann man hier treiben? Wo kann man das machen?

BEISPIELE: Man kann auf dem Kiessee segeln.
Man kann im Jahnstadion Fußball spielen.

im **Verein** kegeln   wandern   Golf spielen

Fußball spielen   angeln   reiten

tauchen, schwimmen   segeln   **joggen**

Tennis spielen   **Schlittschuh laufen**

Note: Point out that the various sports facilities are often combined with place names, for example, *Freibad Nikolausberg*, *Sporthalle Geismar*, and *Freibad Rosdorf*. Bowling has almost completely replaced the traditional game of ninepins, *Kegeln*.

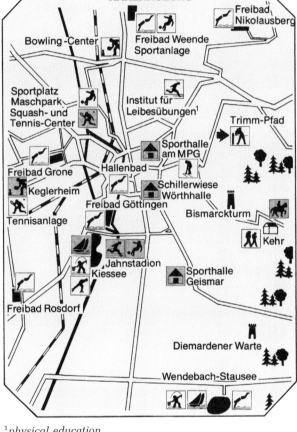

¹*physical education*

Neue Wörter

der Verein   club
das Freibad   outdoor swimming pool
der Sportplatz   athletic field
die Sporthalle   sports arena
das Hallenbad   indoor swimming pool
das Stadion   stadium
das Eisstadion   ice-skating rink

Hier klicken!

Weiteres zum Thema Freizeit und Sport finden Sie bei **Deutsch: Na klar!** im World-Wide-Web unter www.mhhe.com/dnk5.

Aktivität 1   Was braucht man für diese Sportarten?

Bilden Sie Sätze mit Elementen aus beiden Spalten (*columns*).

BEISPIEL: Zum Wandern braucht man Wanderschuhe.

zum Angeln	ein Fahrrad
zum Reiten	ein Segelboot
zum Wandern	einen Ball
zum Tauchen	eine Angelrute (*fishing pole*)
zum Fußball spielen	ein Pferd (*horse*)
zum Rad fahren	Wanderschuhe
zum Segeln	Schwimmflossen (*fins*)

To say how often you do something, use the following expressions:

jeden Tag	every day
einmal/zweimal die Woche	once/twice a week
dreimal im Monat	three times a month
einmal im Jahr	once a year

Aktivität 7 Im Gespräch über Sport

Bilden Sie kleine Gruppen und diskutieren Sie. Welche Sportarten treiben Sie gern? Wie oft?

BEISPIEL: s1: Ich jogge gern, und ich wandere auch gern.
s2: Wie oft machst du das?
s1: Ich gehe einmal im Monat wandern, aber ich jogge jeden Tag.

THEMA 2: Hobbys und andere Vergnügungen°

pleasures

Neue Wörter

Freizeit verbringen spend free time
Sport treiben play sports
die Briefmarke (Briefmarken, *pl.*) postage stamp
sammeln collect
die Spielkarte (Spielkarten, *pl.*) playing card
zeichnen draw
malen paint (pictures)
Schach spielen play chess
faulenzen do nothing, be lazy
der Brief (Briefe, *pl.*) letter
beliebt popular

Wie **verbringen** Sie Ihre **Freizeit?** Kreuzen Sie an!

- ☐ **Sport treiben**
- ☐ Musik hören
- ☐ mit Freunden ausgehen
- ☐ Motorrad fahren
- ☐ ins Museum gehen
- ☐ **Karten** spielen
- ☐ Ski fahren
- ☐ Computerspiele spielen
- ☐ **Schach spielen**
- ☐ fernsehen
- ☐ **faulenzen**
- ☐ Windsurfing gehen

- ☐ spazieren gehen
- ☐ **Briefmarken sammeln**
- ☐ **Spielkarten** sammeln
- ☐ **bloggen**
- ☐ **zeichnen**
- ☐ fotografieren
- ☐ Klavier spielen
- ☐ **malen**
- ☐ am **Wagen** arbeiten
- ☐ im Garten arbeiten
- ☐ **Briefe** schreiben
- ☐ **??**

Sie gehen oft ins Museum.

Sie bloggt.

Sie malt.

Er arbeitet am Wagen.

Sie spielen Schach.

Er faulenzt.

Vergleichen Sie Ihre Liste mit der Liste von anderen Personen im Kurs. Können Sie drei gemeinsame Dinge finden? Was ist besonders **beliebt?**

Aktivität 3   In der Freizeit

Sie hören drei junge Leute über ihre Freizeit sprechen. Kreuzen Sie an, was sie machen.

1. Nina …
   a. hört Musik. ☒
   b. geht mit Freunden aus. ☒
   c. spielt Computerspiele. ☐
   d. fotografiert. ☒
   e. zeichnet. ☐
   f. malt. ☒

2. Thomas …
   a. hat keine Freizeit. ☒
   b. träumt (*dreams*) vom Motorrad fahren. ☒
   c. fährt Ski im Traum. ☒
   d. arbeitet am Wagen. ☐
   e. bloggt. ☐

3. Annette …
   a. geht Windsurfen. ☐
   b. geht zum Flohmarkt. ☒
   c. spielt Karten. ☒
   d. sammelt Spielkarten. ☒
   e. sammelt Briefmarken. ☐
   f. surft im Internet. ☒

Aktivität 4   Wie hast du deine Freizeit verbracht?°

How did you spend your free time?

Fragen Sie einen Partner / eine Partnerin: Wie hast du in den letzten acht Tagen deine Freizeit verbracht?

BEISPIEL: Ich habe Musik gehört. Ich bin mit Freunden ausgegangen. Ich habe jeden Tag ferngesehen.

mit Freunden	bin … ausgegangen
mit einem Freund	bin … in die Disko / ins Kino gegangen
mit einer Freundin	habe … Musik gehört/gespielt
allein	habe … ferngesehen/gebloggt

Siehe *Expressing Events in the Past,* S. 217.

Aktivität 4. Suggestion: First have students scan the range of possibilities. This activity can be done with the whole group. Encourage students to link several pieces of information.

Aktivität 5   Möchtest du mitkommen?

Machen Sie eine Verabredung (*date*).

S1	S2
1. Ich gehe heute Bowling. Möchtest du mitkommen? ins Kino/Theater/Stadtbad/… in ein Rockkonzert / …	**2a.** Ja, gern, um wie viel Uhr denn? **b.** Ich kann nicht.
3a. Um _____ Uhr. Nach dem Abendessen um _____. Nach der Vorlesung um _____. **b.** Warum denn nicht?	**4a.** Wo wollen wir uns treffen (*meet*)? **b.** Ich muss arbeiten. Ich habe kein Geld / keine Zeit / …
5a. Vor dem Kino. / Vor der Bibliothek. / Im Studentenheim. / Bei mir zu Hause. / … **b.** Schade.	**6.** Gut. Ich treffe dich dann um _____.

Aktivität 6   Pläne für einen Ausflug°

excursion

Verena und Antje machen Pläne fürs Wochenende. Sie wohnen beide in Düsseldorf. Hören Sie sich den Dialog an, und markieren Sie dann die richtigen Antworten.

	DAS STIMMT	DAS STIMMT NICHT	KEINE INFORMATION
1. Verena und Antje planen einen Ausflug.	☒	☐	☐
2. Sie wollen im Neandertal wandern.	☐	☒	☐
3. Es dauert nur eine Stunde bis zum Neandertal.	☐	☒	☐
4. Der Weg führt durch den Wald.	☒	☐	☐
5. Auf dem Wege dahin wollen sie ein Picknick machen.	☐	☐	☒
6. Antje will ihren Freund Stefan einladen.	☒	☐	☐

Die Jahreszeiten

Die **Jahreszeiten**: der **Frühling**, der **Sommer**, der **Herbst**, der **Winter**.
Welches Bild passt zu welcher Jahreszeit?

1. Der Berliner Wannsee im _____.

2. Am Kornmarkt in Heidelberg im _____.

3. Der Grundlsee in Österreich im _____.

4. Das Städtchen Creuzburg im _____.

Das Wetter

DIE SONNE	DIE WOLKEN	DER REGEN	DAS GEWITTER	DER SCHNEE
Die Sonne scheint.	Es ist bewölkt.	Es regnet.	Es gibt ein Gewitter.	Es gibt Schnee.
Es ist sonnig.	Es ist kühl.	Es ist regnerisch.	Es blitzt und donnert.	Es schneit.
Es ist angenehm/ heiter/warm/heiß.		Es gibt einen Schauer.	Es ist schwül.	Es ist kalt.

A. Welche Jahreszeit ist das: Winter, Sommer, Frühling oder Herbst?

BEISPIEL: Die Blätter fallen von den Bäumen. →
Das ist Herbst.

1. Die Blätter (*leaves*) sind nicht mehr **so** grün **wie** im Sommer und **fallen** von den Bäumen. Es kann auch regnerisch werden.

2. Leute schwimmen im Freibad. An manchen Tagen ist der **Himmel wolkenlos.**

3. Es regnet viel und die Blumen blühen. Man braucht oft einen **Regenschirm.** Die Tage werden **länger als** im Winter.

4. Die Tage sind kurz. Für viele Menschen **dauert** diese Jahreszeit zu lang.

5. Es wird **kühler** als im Sommer und die Tage werden etwas **kürzer.**

6. Es ist sehr heiß und manchmal sogar schwül und unangenehm.

7. **Drinnen** ist es schön warm, **draußen** aber wirklich **kalt. Die Sonne scheint** selten. Ein starker **Wind** bläst und der Himmel ist oft **bewölkt.**

B. Welcher **Wetterbericht** passt zu welchem Bild?

1. ___f___ Im Norden beginnt es zu regnen, und morgen regnet es den ganzen Tag. Am Abend: **Regen,** eventuell auch **Hagel.**

2. ___e___ Im Moment ist es **bewölkt.** Die **Temperatur** heute Nachmittag ist nur 7 **Grad,** aber heute Abend wird es **kalt** und **windig.**

3. ___a___ In der Karibik ist es sonnig, heiter und warm. Wir haben den ganzen Tag **angenehme** Temperaturen. Morgen wird es wieder heiß.

4. ___c___ Im Süden gibt es **starke Gewitter.** Was **passiert? Es blitzt** und **donnert.**

5. ___b___ In den Bergen schneit es im Moment. Die Skifahrer sind begeistert über den Schnee.

6. ___d___ Im Rheinland gibt es heute Morgen **Nebel,** nachher einzelne **Wolken.** Auch morgen neblig und kühl.

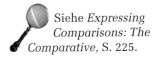
Siehe *Expressing Comparisons: The Comparative,* S. 225.

Neue Wörter	
angenehm pleasant	
heiter bright	
heiß hot	
schwül humid	
so … wie as . . . as	
der Himmel sky	
wolkenlos cloudless	
der Regenschirm umbrella	
länger (lang) longer	
als than	
dauert (deuern) lasts	
kühler (kühl) cooler	
kürzer (kurz) shorter	
drinnen inside	
draußen outside	
der Wetterbericht weather report	
der Hagel hail	
der Grad (Grad, *pl.*) degree	
windig windy	
starke (stark) strong	
das Gewitter (Gewitter, *pl.*) thunderstorm	
passiert (passieren) happens	
es blitzt there's lightning	
es donnert it's thundering	
es schneit it's snowing	
der Nebel fog	

a.

b.

c.

d.

e.

f.

Schritt 1: Lesen Sie den Text zum Wetterbericht und beantworten Sie die Fragen.

Deutschland heute: Heute bleibt es größtenteils[1] stark bewölkt oder neblig. Etwas Schnee oder Regen fällt vor allem anfangs[2] noch im Norden und auch im Osten. Später lockert sich an den Küsten die Wolkendecke durch das Hoch GERD auf[3], und die Sonne kommt öfter zum Vorschein[4]. Der Wind weht schwach bis mäßig, an den Küsten und auf den Bergen unangenehm frisch und stark böig[5] aus Nordost.

[1]*largely* [2]*early* [3]*lockert sich auf breaks up* [4]*sight* [5]*gusty*

1. Dieser Wetterbericht ist wahrscheinlich für einen Tag im _____.
   a. August
   b. Sommer
   c. Februar
   d. Mai

2. Wo gibt es heute Schnee?
   a. an den Küsten
   b. im Westen
   c. im Norden und im Osten
   d. an den Küsten und im Westen

3. An den Küsten soll es am Nachmittag _____ geben.
   a. Sonnenschein
   b. Nebel
   c. starke Gewitter
   d. Hagel

4. An der Nordküste ist die Tagestemperatur _____.
   a. 4 Grad Celsius
   b. 5 Grad Celsius
   c. 3 Grad Celsius
   d. 0 Grad Celsius

5. Der Wind weht schwach bis mäßig aus _____.
   a. Nordwest
   b. Nordost
   c. Südwest
   d. den Bergen

Schritt 2: Schauen Sie sich jetzt die Wetterkarte noch mal an, und vergleichen (*compare*) Sie das Wetter in einer Stadt mit dem Wetter in einer anderen Stadt.

BEISPIELE: In Kiel ist es sonniger als in Frankfurt.

In Nürnberg ist es genau so kalt wie in München.

Aktivität 8   Wetterberichte im Radio

Sie hören fünf kurze Wetterberichte für fünf Städte in Europa. Kreuzen Sie die richtigen Informationen an und notieren Sie die Temperaturen in Grad Celsius.

	ZÜRICH	WIEN	BERLIN	PARIS	LONDON
sonnig	☒	☐	☐	☐	☐
warm	☒	☐	☐	☒	☐
bewölkt bis heiter	☐	☐	☒	☐	☐
(stark) bewölkt	☐	☒	☐	☐	☒
Nebel	☐	☐	☐	☐	☒
Schauer	☐	☐	☒	☐	☐
Regen	☐	☐	☐	☐	☒
Wind	☐	☐	☐	☒	☐
Gewitter	☐	☒	☐	☐	☐
Grad Celsius	20–25	18	20	29	10

Aktivität 8. Suggestion: First have students scan the possibilities. Then let them hear the weather reports and fill in the information. Check students' responses by asking *Wie ist das Wetter in _____?* Students use the information on their chart in their responses.

KULTURTIPP

The Fahrenheit temperature scale is used in the United States, but the Celsius scale is used elsewhere. Swedish astronomer Anders Celsius (1701–1744) first used a scale similar to the present day Celsius scale. The German physicist Daniel Fahrenheit (1686–1736) defined the Fahrenheit unit and also invented the mercury thermometer.

To convert Celsius to Fahrenheit: divide by 5, multiply by 9, and add 32. To convert Fahrenheit into Celsius: Subtract 32, divide by 9, and multiply by 5.

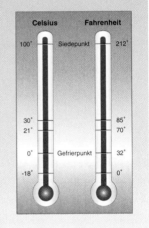

Aktivität 9   So ist das Wetter in ...

Woher kommen Sie? Wie ist das Wetter dort?

BEISPIEL: Ich komme aus San Franzisko. Dort ist das Wetter im Sommer oft kühl und neblig. Im Frühling ist es meistens sonnig. Und im Winter regnet es.

Aktivität 9. Suggestion: The activity can be done in pairs, with students jotting down what their partner says so they can report back to the whole group afterward.

Aktivität 10   Ihr Wetterbericht

Schreiben Sie einen Wetterbericht für Ihr Gebiet (*area*).

BEISPIEL: Das Wetter für Donnerstag: schwül und heiß. Temperaturen: 30–35 Grad Celsius. Das Wetter für morgen: morgens Nebel, dann sonnig, 30 Grad.

Grammatik im Kontext

koordinierende Konjunktionen

Connecting Ideas: Coordinating Conjunctions°

Coordinating conjunctions connect words, phrases, or sentences. You already know **und** and **oder.**

> Herr **und** Frau Baumann sitzen vor dem Fernseher.
> War der Film langweilig **oder** amüsant?

Other coordinating conjunctions are the following:

> **aber** but, however   **sondern** but, rather   **denn** because, for

> Erst muss ich heute arbeiten, **und** dann gehe ich Tennis spielen.
> Ich spiele gern Tennis, **aber** mein Freund spielt lieber Karten.
> Willst du mit zum Sportplatz, **oder** willst du zu Hause bleiben?
> Ich möchte zum Sportplatz, **denn** da gibt es ein Fußballspiel.
> Ich bleibe nicht zu Hause, **sondern** ich gehe zum Sportplatz.

Note:

- When used to connect sentences, coordinating conjunctions do not affect word order. Each sentence can be stated independently of the other.

Expressing a Contrast: **aber** vs. **sondern**

The conjunction **aber** is normally used for English *but* to express the juxtaposition of ideas. The adverb **zwar** is often added to the first contrasted element to accentuate the juxtaposition.

Das Spiel war kurz, **aber** spannend.	*The game was short but exciting.*
Ich spiele **zwar** gern Tennis, **aber** nicht bei dem Wetter.	*I do like playing tennis, but not in this weather.*
Der Film hat **zwar** nicht lange gedauert, **aber** er war sehr interessant.	*Admittedly the movie didn't last very long, but it was very interesting.*

If however, a negative such as **nicht** or **kein** is part of the first contrasted element *and* two mutually exclusive ideas are juxtaposed, **sondern** must be used.

Es ist **nicht** warm, **sondern** kalt draußen.	*It isn't warm but rather cold outside.*

The weather outside isn't warm and cold at the same time; therefore **warm** and **kalt** are mutually exclusive and **sondern** must be used.

Das ist **kein** Regen, **sondern** Hagel!	*That's not rain but hail!*

The precipitation in question is either rain or hail but not both; therefore **Regen** and **Hagel** are mutually exclusive and **sondern** must be used.

Übung 1 Wie ist das Wetter?

Gebraucht man hier **aber** oder **sondern?** Ergänzen Sie die Sätze.

1. Gestern war es zwar kalt, _____ sonnig.

2. Bei uns gibt es im Winter keinen Schnee, _____ nur viel Regen.

3. Im Frühling wird es hier nie heiß, _____ im Sommer wird es manchmal sehr heiß.

4. Die Sonne scheint zwar, _____ ich glaube, es gibt heute ein Gewitter.

5. Es gibt heute keinen Regen, _____ Schnee.

6. Heute ist das Wetter angenehm, _____ morgen wird es heiß.

7. Es regnet zwar nicht, _____ ich nehme doch lieber einen Regenschirm mit.

Übung 2 Freizeitpläne

Ergänzen Sie: **und, aber, oder, denn, sondern.**

Jörg _____¹ seine Freundin Karin planen einen Ausflug _____² ein Picknick. Die Frage ist: wohin _____³ wann? Heute geht es leider nicht, _____⁴ es regnet, _____⁵ morgen haben beide keine Zeit. Also müssen sie bis zum Wochenende warten. Sie wollen diesmal nicht mit dem Auto ins Grüne fahren, _____⁶ mit ihren Fahrrädern. Das dauert zwar länger, _____⁷ es macht bestimmt mehr Spaß. Sie wollen an einen See, _____⁸ da können sie schwimmen gehen. Danach wollen sie ein Picknick im Wald _____⁹ am See machen. Karin ist nicht für die öffentlichen (*public*) Picknickplätze, _____¹⁰ da sind meistens zu viele Leute, Kinder _____¹¹ Hunde, Onkel _____¹² Tanten. Jörg lädt seinen Freund Andreas ein, _____¹³ der kann leider nicht mit. Es tut ihm leid, _____¹⁴ er muss arbeiten.

Expressing Events in the Past: The Present Perfect Tense°

das Perfekt

In German, the present perfect tense is generally used to talk about past events, although a number of common verbs (**sein, haben,** and the modals) typically use the simple past tense (**Imperfekt**) in conversation. There is essentially no difference in meaning between the two tenses.

Gestern **habe** ich Fußball **gespielt.**	*I played soccer yesterday.*
Wer **hat** denn **gewonnen?**	*Who won?*
Wir **haben** fünf zu null **verloren.** Dann **sind** wir in die Kneipe **gegangen.**	*We lost five to zero. Then we went to the pub.*

Note:

■ The present perfect tense in German, as well as English, is a compound tense. It consists of two parts: the present tense of the auxiliary verb **haben** or **sein** and a past participle (**Partizip Perfekt**). (You will learn about the auxiliaries on page 221.)

■ The auxiliary verb (**haben** or **sein**) and the past participle form a sentence bracket (**Satzklammer**).

```
                  ┌──── SATZKLAMMER ────┐
Unsere Mannschaft  hat    fünf zu null      verloren.
Dann               sind   wir in die Kneipe  gegangen.
```

Uwe und Klaus reden über ihr Lieblingsthema: Fußball.

UWE: Hast du schon gehört? Bayern München hat gestern gegen Dynamo Dresden verloren. Null zu zwei!

KLAUS: Unglaublich! Hast du das in der Zeitung gelesen?

UWE: Ich habe es im Fernsehen gesehen.

KLAUS: Wie lange hat das Spiel gedauert?

UWE: Etwas über zwei Stunden. Dynamo Dresden hat sehr gut gespielt. Letzte Woche haben sie auch gegen Bremen gewonnen; eins zu null.

KLAUS: Ja, aber gegen den FC [Fußballclub] Nürnberg haben sie drei zu null verloren.

- Identify the past participles in the dialogue.
- What endings do these participles have?
- With what syllable do nearly all of the participles begin?
- What are the infinitives of these verbs?

German, like English, distinguishes between two types of verbs: so-called weak verbs (**schwache Verben**) and strong verbs (**starke Verben**). They form their past participles differently.

Weak Verbs

Ich habe **gehört**, Dynamo Dresden hat sehr gut **gespielt**.	*I heard that Dynamo Dresden played very well.*
Wir haben lange **gewartet**.	*We waited for a long time.*

Note:

- Weak verbs form the past participle by combining the verb stem with the prefix **ge-** and the ending **-(e)t**.
- The ending **-et** is used when the verb stem ends in **-t, -d,** or a consonant cluster such as **-gn-** or **-fn-**.

INFINITIVE	PREFIX	STEM	ENDING	PAST PARTICIPLE
hören	ge-	hör	-t	gehört
wandern	ge-	wander	-t	gewandert
warten	ge-	wart	-et	gewartet
regnen	ge-	regn	-et	geregnet

Weak verbs ending in **-ieren** form the past participle without adding a prefix, but they do add a final **-t.**

INFINITIVE	PAST PARTICIPLE
diskutieren	diskutiert
fotografieren	fotografiert

¹starting at

Übung 3   In meiner Kindheit

Drei Leute erzählen über ihre Hobbys als Kinder. Was hat ihnen Spaß gemacht? Was stimmt, und was wissen wir nicht?

	DAS STIMMT	KEINE INFORMATION
1. Herr Harter hat gern …		
Trompete gespielt.	☒	☐
Briefmarken gesammelt.	☒	☐
viel Fernsehen geschaut.	☐	☒
2. Frau Beitz hat gern …		
mit ihrem Hund gespielt.	☒	☐
gemalt.	☒	☐
Comic-Hefte gesammelt.	☐	☒
3. Herr Huppert hat gern …		
Bücher von Karl May gesammelt.	☒	☐
Cowboy gespielt.	☒	☐
im Schulorchester gespielt.	☐	☒
Fußball gespielt.	☒	☐

Übung 4   Haben Sie das als Kind gemacht?

Kreuzen Sie an, was Sie als Kind gern gemacht haben. Bilden Sie dann Sätze nach dem Muster.

BEISPIEL: Ich habe gern gemalt, aber ich habe nie mit Puppen gespielt.

Briefmarken sammeln	☐
Insekten sammeln	☐
Comic-Hefte sammeln	☐
__??__ sammeln	☐
mit Puppen (*dolls*) spielen	☐
ein Instrument spielen, z.B. Klavier oder Gitarre	☐
Fußball oder Baseball spielen	☐
Computerspiele spielen	☐
fernsehen	☐
malen	☐
Pop-Musik hören	☐
Hausarbeiten machen	☐
angeln	☐
im Internet surfen	☐

Realia. This is the cover of *Winnetous Erben* by Karl May, one of the last volumes in his classic *Winnetou* series. Set in the American West, May's fiction has ranked among the best-selling popular literature in Germany from the 19th century to the present day. His novels have been translated into many languages.

Übung 4. Suggestion: For variation, have students say what they liked another way: *Briefmarken sammeln hat mir Spaß gemacht*, etc.

Point Out: the expression *Spaß gemacht* requires changing the infinitives to gerunds, which are capitalized.

Übung 5. Answers: 1. *gesucht* 2. *geblitzt* 3. *gedonnert* 4. *gefragt* 5. *reserviert* 6. *gewartet* 7. *gelegt* 8. *gespielt* 9. *gelacht* 10. *geschmeckt* 11. *gekostet* 12. *geregnet*

Übung 5   Im Nudelhaus

Wie haben Inge und Claudia den Abend verbracht? Setzen Sie das Partizip Perfekt ein.

Inge und Claudia haben ein gemütliches Restaurant in der Stadt _____¹ (suchen). Draußen hat es _____² (blitzen) und _____³ (donnern), ein Gewitter! Im Nudelhaus war es sehr voll. Der Kellner hat sie _____⁴ (fragen): Haben Sie einen Tisch _____⁵ (reservieren)? Sie haben ziemlich lange auf einen Platz _____⁶ (warten). Der Kellner hat die Speisekarte auf den Tisch _____⁷ (legen). Am Nebentisch haben einige Leute Karten _____⁸ (spielen). Sie haben laut _____⁹ (lachen [*to laugh*]). Das Essen hat sehr gut _____¹⁰ (schmecken). Es hat nur 15 Euro _____¹¹ (kosten). Auf dem Weg nach Hause hat es immer noch _____¹² (regnen).

Strong Verbs

Heute Morgen **habe** ich Zeitung **gelesen**.	*This morning I read the newspaper.*
Dann **habe** ich einen Kaffee **getrunken**.	*Then I drank a cup of coffee.*

Note:

- Strong verbs form the past participle by placing the prefix **ge-** before the stem of the verb and adding the ending **-en**.
- Many strong verbs show vowel and consonant changes in the past participle.

INFINITIVE	PREFIX	STEM	ENDING	PAST PARTICIPLE
lesen	**ge-**	les	**-en**	gelesen
nehmen	**ge-**	nomm	**-en**	genommen
sitzen	**ge-**	sess	**-en**	gesessen
trinken	**ge-**	trunk	**-en**	getrunken

Following are several other familiar strong verbs and their past participles. A complete list of strong and irregular verbs is in Appendix C.

INFINITIVE	PAST PARTICIPLE	INFINITIVE	PAST PARTICIPLE
essen	gegessen	schreiben	geschrieben
finden	gefunden	sehen	gesehen
geben	gegeben	sprechen	gesprochen
helfen	geholfen	stehen	gestanden
schlafen	geschlafen	tragen	getragen

Vervollständigen Sie die Tabelle.

INFINITIV	PARTIZIP PERFEKT
1. trinken	_____
2. _____	gegessen
3. _____	gestanden
4. finden	_____
5. helfen	_____
6. _____	gesehen
7. sprechen	_____
8. _____	gegeben
9. sitzen	_____

Übung 7 Wie war's im Restaurant Nudelhaus?

Setzen Sie passende Partizipien aus der Liste in **Übung 6** ein.

1. Viele Leute haben vor dem Restaurant __gestanden__ und auf einen Platz gewartet.
2. Wir konnten zuerst keinen Platz finden. Dann haben wir endlich einen Platz __gefunden__.
3. Ich habe grüne Schinkennudeln __gegessen__, und wir haben Pilsener __getrunken__.
4. Am Tisch neben uns haben Touristen aus Brasilien __gesessen__.
5. Sie haben Portugiesisch __gesprochen__.
6. Sie konnten nur wenig Deutsch. Wir haben ihnen mit der Speisekarte __geholfen__.
7. Sie haben mir ihre Visitenkarte (*business card*) mit E-Mail-Adresse __gegeben__. Ich soll sie in Brasilien besuchen!

```
        NUDELHAUS
       ROTE STR. 13
      37073 GÖTTINGEN
      TEL: 0551/42263

    #0001        06-01-06

    RECHNUNG-#      35

    GAST/TISCH#    3

   2 HEFEWEIZEN      €4,00
   1 GRUENE SCHINKEN €5,50
   1 VOLLKORNNUDELN  €5,25

    BAR-TL    €14,75


    ES BEDIENTE SIE
            KELLNER 1
```

Realia. This bill is from a restaurant called *Nudelhaus* in Göttingen.

The Use of **haben** or **sein** as Auxiliary

Most verbs use **haben** as the auxiliary verb in the present perfect tense.

Unsere Mannschaft **hat** das Fußballspiel **gewonnen.**	*Our team won the soccer game.*
Die Fans **haben** auf den Straßen **getanzt.**	*The fans danced in the streets.*

Sein is used with verbs that indicate movement from one place to another (e.g., **gehen** and **fahren**).

Rudi **ist** zum Fußballplatz **gegangen.**	*Rudi went to the soccer field.*
Nach dem Spiel **ist** er nach Hause **gefahren.**	*After the game he went home.*

Other verbs that show motion from one place to another are **kommen (ist gekommen), laufen (ist gelaufen), fliegen (ist geflogen)** and **reiten (ist geritten).**

Sein is also used with verbs that indicate a change of condition (e.g., **werden**).

Gestern **ist** Peter 21 **geworden.**	*Yesterday Peter turned 21.*

In the previous example, the verb **werden** expresses a change in age (**ist 21 geworden**).

Other important verbs using **sein** in the present perfect tense are **sein, bleiben,** and **passieren.**

Wo **ist** Rudi gestern **gewesen?**	*Where was Rudi yesterday?*
Wir **sind** zu Hause **geblieben.**	*We stayed home.*
Unsere Mannschaft hat verloren? Wie **ist** das **passiert?**	*Our team lost? How did that happen?*

Note:

- Verbs conjugated with **sein** in the present perfect tense will be listed in the vocabulary sections as follows: **kommen, ist gekommen.**

Suggestion: Practice a number of the verbs by asking personalized questions such as *Wie alt sind Sie? Wann sind Sie (21) geworden? Wann sind Sie gestern Abend schlafen gegangen?*

Point out: *Tanzen* expresses movement, but not from one place to another; therefore, its present perfect tense is formed with *haben.*

Ergänzen Sie die Sätze mit der passenden Form von **sein** oder **haben**.

1. Ich _____ nichts gemacht. Es _____ die ganze Woche geregnet.

2. Ich _____ mit Freunden ins Kino gegangen.

3. Wir _____ einen alten Film mit Charlie Chaplin im Rialto gesehen.

4. Wir _____ zu Hause geblieben und _____ Karten gespielt.

5. Meine Eltern _____ zu Besuch gekommen. Ich hatte nämlich Geburtstag.

6. Ich _____ 21 geworden. Meine Freunde _____ mir eine große Party gemacht.

7. Mein Freund und ich _____ zum Wochenende nach London geflogen.

8. Wir _____ in die Berge gefahren und _____ an einem Fluss geangelt.

Wer hat was gemacht? Arbeiten Sie zu zweit.

BEISPIEL: s1: Was hat Dagmar gemacht?
s2: Sie ist ins Alte Land gefahren.

WER	WAS
Dagmar	
Thomas	zum Sportplatz gehen
Jürgen	
Stefanie	einen Detektivroman lesen
Susanne	
Felix und Sabine	eine Radtour machen
die Kinder	

Fremdenverkehrsverein[1]
Altes Land e. V. [2]

[1] *Tourism Office*

[2] (= eingetragener Verein) *registered association*

KULTURTIPP

In ihrer Freizeit treiben viele Deutsche gern Sport; besonders beliebt sind Fußball, Rad fahren, Schwimmen und Tennis. Andere bleiben lieber zu Hause und machen Gartenarbeit, pflegen (*take care of*) ihren Wagen, spielen mit ihren Haustieren, sammeln Briefmarken, lesen oder sehen fern. Viele Deutsche haben ein Hobby, das sie in einem Verein ausüben. In vielen Städten gibt es Gesangs- und Heimatvereine sowie (*as well as*) Vereine für Schützen (*marksmen*), Amateurfunker (*ham radio operators*) und Kegler.

Radfahrer auf der Landstraße

Mixed Verbs

On pages 218 through 220 you learned about past participle formation for weak and strong verbs. A few verbs include features of both weak and strong verbs in the past participle. They are called mixed verbs. Like weak verbs, the participles of mixed verbs end in **-t;** like most strong verbs, their verb stem undergoes a change.

INFINITIVE	PAST PARTICIPLE
bringen	gebracht
kennen	gekannt
wissen	gewusst

Past Participles of Verbs with Prefixes

Many German verbs consist of a base verb, such as **rufen** or **stellen**, and a prefix, such as **an-** or **be-,** to form verbs such as **anrufen** (*to call*) and **bestellen** (*to order*). The verb **anrufen**, as you learned in **Kapitel 4,** belongs to the group of verbs that have separable prefixes.

Ich **rufe** meinen Bruder **an.**	*I am calling my brother.*

When used in the present perfect tense, separable-prefix verbs form the past participle by inserting the **ge-** prefix between the separable prefix and the verb base. These verbs may be strong, weak, or mixed.

Ich habe meinen Bruder **angerufen.**	*I called my brother.*
Ich bin heute Morgen spät **aufgewacht.**	*I got up late this morning.*

Other examples of separable-prefix verbs and their past participles include:

INFINITIVE	PAST PARTICIPLE
aufstehen	(ist) aufgestanden
ausgeben	ausgegeben
ausgehen	(ist) ausgegangen
einkaufen	eingekauft
einladen	eingeladen
zurückkommen	(ist) zurückgekommen

Other prefixed verbs, such as **bestellen** and **verbringen**, begin with prefixes that are not separable from the base, such as **be-, emp-, ent-, er-, ge-,** and **ver-.**

Hoffentlich **gewinnen** wir das Spiel.	*I hope we win the game.*
Der Gast **bestellt** eine Pizza.	*The guest orders a pizza.*
Er **verbringt** den ganzen Abend auf dem Fußballplatz.	*He spends the entire evening at the soccer field.*

Note: If an accented separable prefix is followed by an unaccented syllable, then the **ge-** is not inserted in the past participle: *Ich probiere das Hemd an.* vs. *Ich habe das Hemd anprobiert.* **Anprobieren** is the only active vocabulary in this text that is affected by this exception. Other examples include **mitbekommen, zugehören, ausprobieren**, and the like. Since this exception to the rule affects so few relevant verbs at this level, you may choose not to bring it up unless the need arises.

A verb with an inseparable prefix forms the past participle without an additional **ge-** prefix. These verbs may be either strong, weak, or mixed.

Wir haben das Spiel **gewonnen.**	*We won the game.*
Der Gast hat eine Pizza **bestellt.**	*The guest ordered a pizza.*
Er hat den ganzen Abend auf dem Fußballplatz **verbracht.**	*He spent the entire evening at the soccer field.*

Other examples of inseparable-prefix verbs and their past participles include:

INFINITIVE	PAST PARTICIPLE
bezahlen	bezahlt
erzählen	erzählt
gefallen	gefallen
gewinnen	gewonnen
verbringen	verbracht
verlieren	verloren

Übung 10   Verbformen

Ergänzen Sie die fehlenden Verbformen.

	INFINITIV	HILFSVERB	PARTIZIP PERFEKT
1.	aufstehen	_____	aufgestanden
2.	bestellen	_____	_____
3.	einladen	hat	_____
4.	_____	ist	eingeschlafen
5.	_____	_____	gefallen
6.	_____	_____	mitgekommen
7.	_____	hat	verloren

Übung 11   Kleine Situationen

Ergänzen Sie das Partizip Perfekt.

1. Aus der Zeitung: Großer, graugetigerter Kater, rotes Halsband mit Glöckchen ____ (verlieren). Wer hat ihn ____ oder ____ (sehen, finden)? Er hört auf den Namen Charly.

2. In den letzten Tagen ist es recht kalt ____ (werden).

3. Wir haben gestern Abend noch lange über die Probleme mit dem Studium ____ (diskutieren). Ich bin erst um drei Uhr nachts ____ (einschlafen). Und dann bin ich um sechs Uhr ____ (aufstehen).

4. Wir haben für acht Uhr einen Tisch im Nudelhaus ____ (reservieren). Wir haben alle eine Pizza ____ (bestellen).

5. A: Wo hast du deinen Freund kennen ____ (lernen)?
   B: Jemand hat ihn zu einer Party ____ (einladen). Gleich am nächsten Tag hat er mich ____ (anrufen).

6. C: Wie hat es euch im Nudelhaus ____ (gefallen)?
   D: Sehr gut. Warum bist du nicht ____ (mitkommen)?
   C: Ich habe nicht ____ (wissen), wo ihr wart.

Verloren/Gefunden

Großer, graugetigerter Kater, rotes Halsband mit Glöckchen. Wer hat ihn gesehen oder gefunden? Hört auf den Namen Charly. Finderlohn.

Übung 12 Mein Wochenende

Schritt 1: Sprechen Sie mit jemand (*someone*) über Ihr Wochenende. Nennen Sie drei Aktivitäten. Folgen Sie dem Beispiel.

BEISPIEL: s1: Was hast du letztes Wochenende gemacht?
s2: Zuerst habe ich meine Freundin angerufen.
s1: Und dann?

Hier sind einige mögliche Aktivitäten:

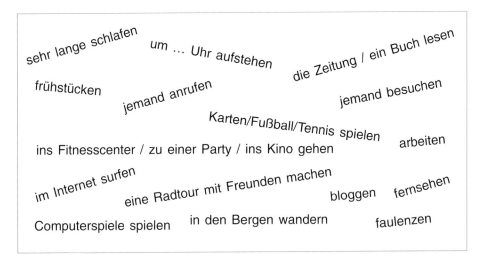

sehr lange schlafen   um ... Uhr aufstehen   die Zeitung / ein Buch lesen

frühstücken   jemand anrufen   jemand besuchen

Karten/Fußball/Tennis spielen

ins Fitnesscenter / zu einer Party / ins Kino gehen   arbeiten

im Internet surfen

eine Radtour mit Freunden machen   bloggen   fernsehen

Computerspiele spielen   in den Bergen wandern   faulenzen

Schritt 2: Berichten Sie dann im Plenum.

Expressing Comparisons: The Comparative°

der Komparativ

Adjectives and adverbs have three forms: the basic form (**die Grundform**), the comparative (**der Komparativ**), and the superlative (**der Superlativ**). In this chapter you will learn about the comparative.

Es wird **kühler**.	*It is getting cooler.*
Es regnet **öfter**.	*It rains more often.*
Die Tage werden **kürzer**.	*The days are getting shorter.*

In German, the comparative is formed by adding **-er** to the basic form of the adjective or adverb. (Remember that in German, adverbs are identical to adjectives.) Unlike English, German has only one way to form the comparative, whereas English has two:

cool → cool**er**

often → **more** often

Note:

- Most adjectives of one syllable with the vowel **a, o,** or **u** have an umlaut in the comparative.

groß → gr**ö**ßer

kurz → k**ü**rzer

oft → **ö**fter

warm → w**ä**rmer

Übung 12. Suggestion: Have students scan the list of expressions first and check those that apply to them. Ask them to add activities that are not listed and pertain to what they did, e.g., *arbeiten*. Then have student pairs create the dialogue. Ask several pairs to report to the class about their partner's weekend.

Expressing Comparisons: The Comparative. Point out: Irregular forms of comparative adjectives and adverbs, like irregular verb forms, cannot be easily predicted. As such, they must be learned.

Grammatik im Kontext   **225**

- Some adjectives that end in **-er** or **-el** drop an **e** when adding the **-er**.

teuer teurer dunkel dunkler

A small number of adjectives and adverbs have irregular forms in the comparative. Here are some common ones.

gern	lieber		hoch	höher
gut	besser		viel	mehr

Ich reite **gern**, aber ich wandere **lieber**.	*I like to ride, but I prefer hiking.*
Gestern war das Wetter **gut**, aber heute ist es noch **besser**.	*Yesterday the weather was good, but today it is even better.*
Im Sommer regnet es hier nicht **viel**, aber im Winter regnet es **mehr**.	*It doesn't rain much here in the summer, but in winter it rains more.*

The adverb **immer** is used with a comparative form to express the notion of "more and more."

Das Wetter wird **immer besser**.	*The weather is getting better and better.*
Die Tage werden **immer länger**.	*The days are getting longer and longer.*
Die Sommerabende werden **immer angenehmer**.	*The summer evenings are getting more and more pleasant.*

The conjunction **als** (*than*) can link the two parts of a comparison.

Das Wetter ist besser im Süden **als** im Norden.	*The weather is better in the South than in the North.*

The particle **noch** (*even*) intensifies a comparative.

Wandern macht mir **noch** mehr Spaß als Schwimmen.	*Hiking is even more fun than swimming.*

Freundlicher, bis 23 Grad

Es wird wieder sommerlicher. Der Himmel ist wechselnd bewölkt mit sonnigen Abschnitten. Die Temperatur steigt auf 23 Grad.

WETTER

Der Himmel ist heute meist nur leicht bewölkt, und nach Angaben der Meteorologen soll es auch trocken bleiben. Mittwoch und Donnerstag wird es noch wärmer.

23/10

1. Scan the excerpts from German weather reports and identify adjectives and adverbs in the comparative. What are the basic forms of those adjectives and adverbs?

2. The adjectives in the comparative imply a contrast to the weather elsewhere or at some other time. State this contrast by forming phrases using **als**.

Kiel 20/10

Rostock 20/12

Hamburg 21/11

Bremen 21/11

Hannover 22/11

Berlin 23/13

Magdeburg 23/12

Heute in Norddeutschland

Im Norden Deutschlands gibt es heute einen Mix aus Sonne und Wolken. An der Nordsee ist der Himmel wolkiger.

Übung 13 Wie war das Wetter?

Ergänzen Sie die Sätze mit dem Adjektiv im Komparativ.

BEISPIEL: In Berlin war es warm, aber in Hamburg war es noch ___wärmer___ .

1. Im Westen war es bewölkt, aber im Norden war es noch ___bewölkter___ .

2. Heute ist es kalt und windig, aber gestern war es noch ___kälter___ und ___windiger___ .

3. Am Meer war es sonnig, aber in den Bergen war es noch ___sonniger___ .

4. Am Nachmittag war es angenehm, aber am Abend war es noch ___angenehmer___ .

5. Zu Weihnachten hat es viel geschneit, aber an Neujahr hat es noch ___mehr___ geschneit.

6. Das Wetter in Österreich hat mir mir gut gefallen, aber in Italien hat mir das Wetter noch ___besser___ gefallen.

7. Auf dem Land gibt es oft Gewitter im Sommer, aber in den Bergen gibt es noch ___öfter___ Gewitter.

Übung 14 Vergleiche

Bilden Sie Sätze nach dem Muster.

BEISPIEL: in Berlin = 35 Grad Celsius / in Frankfurt = 25 Grad C (heiß) →
In Berlin ist es heißer als in Frankfurt.

1. in Österreich = 20 Grad C / in der Schweiz = 25 Grad C (warm)

2. in den Bergen = −2 Grad C / in der Stadt = 10 Grad C (kalt)

3. die Tage im Winter / die Tage im Sommer (kurz)

4. die Tage im Sommer / die Tage im Winter (lang)

5. das Wetter im Frühling / das Wetter im Herbst (angenehm)

6. segeln / angeln (interessant)

7. das Wetter heute / das Wetter gestern (gut)

8. die Temperatur gestern / die Temperatur heute (hoch)

9. in London / in Kairo (es regnet viel)

Übung 14. Suggestion: You may wish to allow students the flexibility of reversing the order of the constituents in #5–#8 so that the sentences can reflect personal opinion and actual local weather conditions.

Expressing Equality

An adjective or adverb combined with **so ... wie** (*as . . . as*) expresses equality. The phrase **nicht so ... wie** expresses inequality.

Das Wetter im Norden ist **so** schlecht **wie** im Süden.

The weather in the North is as bad as in the South.

Im Süden regnet es **nicht so** viel **wie** im Norden.

It doesn't rain as much in the South as in the North.

The adverb **genauso** (*just/exactly as*) can replace **so** to emphasize the point being made.

Österreich ist **genauso** schön **wie** die Schweiz.

Austria is just as beautiful as Switzerland.

Ergänzen Sie die folgenden Sätze mit **so ... wie** oder **nicht so ... wie** und einem Adjektiv aus der folgenden Liste.

> bequem, gern, groß, gut, intelligent, interessant, klein, lang, schnell, schön, teuer, viel

BEISPIEL: Wandern gefällt mir _____ Reiten.
Wandern gefällt mir _so gut wie_ Reiten.
oder Wandern gefällt mir _nicht so gut wie_ Reiten.

1. Schwimmen gefällt mir _____ Rad fahren.
2. Ein Volkswagen ist _____ ein Mercedes.
3. Ich glaube, ein BMW kann _____ ein Mercedes fahren.
4. Ich bin _____ mein Freund / meine Freundin.
5. Ich finde den Ozean _____ die Berge.
6. Während der Woche schlafe ich morgens _____ am Wochenende.
7. Ich finde Politik _____ Sport.
8. Ich esse Tofu _____ Hamburger.
9. Ich höre klassische Musik _____ Popmusik.
10. Ich finde Turnschuhe _____ Wanderschuhe.

Arbeiten Sie zu zweit und wechseln Sie einander ab (*take turns*). Folgen Sie dem Beispiel.

BEISPIEL: Ich gehe lieber _____ als _____. (ins Kino, in die Disko, ins Theater, ...)
s1: Ich gehe lieber ins Kino als ins Theater. Und du?
s2: Ich gehe genauso gern ins Theater wie ins Kino.
oder Ich gehe nicht so gern ins Kino wie ins Theater.
oder Ich gehe auch lieber ins Kino als ins Theater.

1. Ich mag _____ lieber als _____. (Fotografieren, Malen, Zeichnen, ...)
2. Ich mag _____ lieber als _____. (Musik hören, Bloggen, Fernsehen, ...)
3. Ich finde _____ schöner als _____. (klassische Musik, Rapmusik, Heavymetal, ...)
4. Ich trage _____ lieber als _____. (Sandalen, Stiefel, Turnschuhe, ...)
5. _____ gefällt mir besser als _____. (Rad fahren, Schlittschuh laufen, Inlineskaten, ...)
6. Ich finde _____ interessanter als _____. (Wien, Berlin, Zürich, ...)
7. _____ gefällt mir besser als _____. (Camping, Wandern, Segeln, ...)
8. _____ schlafe ich länger als _____. (an Wochentagen, am Wochenende, montags, ...)

Sprache im Kontext

Videoclips

A. Jan, Dennis und Beatrice sprechen über ihre Freizeit. Was machen sie nicht in der Freizeit? Streichen Sie die Aktivitäten durch, die sie *nicht* machen.

1. Jan …
verbringt seine Freizeit
  im Freien
geht ins Kino
trifft Freunde
sieht fern
macht Sport

2. Dennis …
geht ins Kino
geht ins Museum
treibt Sport
trifft Freunde

3. Beatrice …
geht ins Kino
trifft gern Freunde
macht Sport
hört Musik

Videoclips. Suggestion: As a way to review vocabulary in preparation for viewing, write the word *Freizeit* on the board and ask students, *Was kann man in der Freizeit machen?* Elicit a few responses from volunteers and write the verbs or noun-verb phrases on the board. Then invite students to come up to the board and expand the list. As a variation, write *drinnen* and *draußen* on the board so students can categorize their responses.

B. Herr Borowsky verbringt seine Freizeit ein bisschen anders. Wie verbringt er seine Freizeit?

C. Welche Sportarten treiben Jan und Dennis?

D. Wo haben diese Leute den Urlaub verbracht? Kombinieren Sie.

1. _____ Jan
2. _____ Beatrice
3. _____ Herr Borowsky
4. _____ Dennis

a. in Ägypten
b. in Wien
c. in Guatemala
d. auf den Kanarischen Inseln und in Bayern

E. Und Sie? Was machen Sie in der Freizeit? Wo haben Sie letztes Jahr Ihren Urlaub verbracht?

Lesen

Zum Thema

A. Wie viel Freizeit hat man in verschiedenen Ländern? Schauen Sie sich die Tabelle „Arbeitsfrei" an. Beantworten Sie die folgenden Fragen mit Hilfe der Tabelle.

1. Wie viele Urlaubstage haben die Deutschen im Jahr?
2. Welches Land hat mehr Urlaubstage – die Schweiz oder Österreich?
3. Wer hat mehr Freizeit – die Belgier oder die Niederländer?
4. Wie viele Urlaubstage haben die US-Amerikaner?

B. Was machen die Deutschen in ihrer Freizeit? Schauen Sie sich die Grafik auf Seite 211 an. Vergleichen Sie Ihre Freizeitbeschäftigungen mit denen der Deutschen.

- Was machen Sie gern in Ihrer Freizeit?
- Stehen Ihre Freizeitaktivitäten auf der Liste?

Zum Thema A. Suggestion: This can also be done as a pair activity. As a way of practicing comparative adjectives and adverbs, have students rephrase their answers to these questions using *mehr … als*, *nicht so … wie*, and *(genau-)so … wie*.

Sprache im Kontext **229**

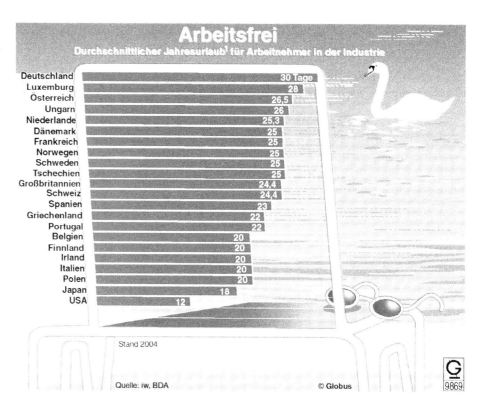

C. Machen Sie eine Liste der sechs beliebtesten Freizeitaktivitäten in Ihrer Klasse. Vergleichen Sie Ihre Klasse mit den Deutschen.

1. Was ist die beliebteste Freizeitbeschäftigung in Ihrer Klasse?

2. Was steht an zweiter Stelle (*place*) für die Klasse?

3. Steht diese Aktivität auf der Liste der Deutschen?

4. Welche Unterschiede (*differences*) und Ähnlichkeiten (*similarities*) gibt es?

A. Assoziationen: Woran denken Sie, wenn Sie _____ hören?

BEISPIEL: Schnee

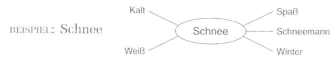

1. Reisen   **5.** Hund

2. Schwimmen   **6.** Buch

3. freundlich sein   **7.** neue Musik

4. bequeme Schuhe   **8.** Singen

B. Lesen Sie den Titel und überfliegen (*scan*) Sie den Text.

1. Was für ein Text ist das?
  a. ein Artikel aus einer Zeitung
  b. ein Gedicht (*poem*)
  c. ein Brief

2. Wie heißt der Autor? Was wissen Sie über ihn?

3. Kennen Sie andere Werke (*works*) von ihm? Wenn ja, welche?

von Bertolt Brecht

Der erste Blick[1] aus dem Fenster am Morgen
Das wiedergefundene alte Buch
Begeisterte Gesichter[2]
Schnee, der Wechsel der Jahreszeiten
5 Die Zeitung
Der Hund
Die Dialektik
Duschen, Schwimmen
Alte Musik
10 Bequeme Schuhe
Begreifen[3]
Neue Musik
Schreiben, Pflanzen
Reisen
15 Singen
Freundlich sein.

Bertolt Brecht 1898–1956

Vergnügungen. **Suggestion:** Bring in additional information about Bertolt Brecht.

---

[1]*glance*   [2]*Begeisterte … enthusiastic faces*   [3]*understanding*

Zum Text

A. Die Wörter **Duschen, Pflanzen, Reisen** können die Pluralformen sein von: **Dusche** (*shower*), **Pflanze** (*plant*), **Reise** (*trip*); oder sie können auch Verbalformen sein: **Duschen** = *taking a shower;* **Pflanzen** = *planting;* **Reisen** = *traveling.* Wie versteht Brecht diese Wörter wahrscheinlich? Als Dinge (Objekte) oder als Aktivitäten? Warum ist das wichtig?

B. Sind Brechts Vergnügungen ungewöhnlich oder ganz normal? Welche finden Sie ungewöhnlich? Warum?

C. Schreiben Sie ein Gedicht mit dem Titel „Vergnügungen". Tauschen Sie Ihr Gedicht mit dem von einem Partner / einer Partnerin aus. Lesen Sie das Gedicht Ihres Partners / Ihrer Partnerin vor.

Zu guter Letzt

Freizeitvergnügungen in der Stadt

Schreiben Sie einen Prospekt über Ihre Universitätsstadt für deutsche Touristen. Was gibt es dort alles zu unternehmen?

Schritt 1: In Gruppen zu viert schauen Sie sich **Thema 1** und **2** an und notieren Sie mindestens 10 Freizeitaktivitäten, die man in Ihrer Stadt machen kann.

BEISPIEL: wandern, segeln, …

Schritt 2: Suchen Sie Fotos aus Zeitschriften, Werbungen oder dem Internet über diese Freizeitaktivitäten und wo man diese Aktivitäten macht. Verwenden Sie sie im Prospekt. Beschreiben Sie zuerst die Plätze in je zwei bis drei Sätzen und sagen Sie, was man dort machen kann.

BEISPIEL: Nicht weit von der Uni gibt es einen Wald mit einem See. Dort kann man wandern und segeln.

Zum Text. Suggestion: Have students do activity **A** as homework after having read the text in class. Activity **B** works nicely as a short writing assignment. In addition to answering the questions given, ask students to write about where they find enjoyment in their lives: *Was sind Ihre Vergnügungen?*

Zu guter Letzt. Suggestion: Point out to students that most university websites have a page about the city in which they are located. Frequently there will be links to the local tourist bureau or chamber of commerce.

Schritt 3: Tauschen Sie Ihren Prospekt mit dem von einer anderen Gruppe aus. Die andere Gruppe soll die Orte noch weiter beschreiben und auch sagen, was man dort noch machen kann.

BEISPIEL: Der Wald heißt Huesten Woods. Viele Studenten fahren dort auch Rad.

Schritt 4: Inkorporieren Sie die Ideen der anderen Gruppe und schreiben Sie den Prospekt zu Ende.

BEISPIEL: Nicht weit von der Uni gibt es einen Wald. Er heißt Huesten Woods. Dort kann man wandern und segeln. Viele Studenten fahren dort auch Rad.

Wortschatz

Sport und Vergnügen — Sports and Leisure

angeln	to fish
bloggen	to blog
Bodybuilding machen	to do bodybuilding, weight training
der **Brief**, -e	letter
die **Briefmarke**, -n	postage stamp
faulenzen	to be lazy, lie around
die **Freizeit**	free time
der **Fußball**, ¨e	soccer; soccer ball
Fußball spielen	to play soccer
joggen	to jog
die **Karte**, -n	card
malen	to paint
Rad fahren (fährt Rad), ist Rad gefahren	to bicycle, ride a bike
reiten, ist geritten	to ride (horseback)
sammeln	to collect
Schach spielen	to play chess
Schlittschuh laufen (läuft), ist gelaufen	to ice-skate
segeln	to sail
die **Spielkarte**, -n	playing card
der **Sport**, *pl.* **Sportarten**	sports, sport
Sport treiben, getrieben	to play sports
tauchen	to dive
Tennis spielen	to play tennis
turnen	to do gymnastics
(Zeit) verbringen, verbracht	to spend (time)
der **Verein**, -e	club, association
der **Wagen**, -	car
zeichnen	to draw

Orte — Locations

der **Berg**, -e	mountain
das **Eisstadion**, *pl.* **Eisstadien**	ice-skating rink
der **Fluss**, ¨e	river
das **Freibad**, ¨er	outdoor swimming pool
das **Hallenbad**, ¨er	indoor swimming pool
das **Meer**, -e	sea, ocean
das **Schwimmbad**, ¨er	swimming pool
der **See**, -n	lake
die **Sporthalle**, -n	sports arena
der **Sportplatz**, ¨e	athletic field
das **Stadion**, *pl.* **Stadien**	stadium
der **Tennisplatz**, ¨e	tennis court
die **Turnhalle**, -n	gymnasium
der **Wald**, ¨er	forest
die **Wiese**, -n	meadow

Die Jahreszeiten — Seasons

das **Frühjahr**	spring
der **Frühling**	spring
der **Herbst**	autumn, fall
der **Sommer**	summer
der **Winter**	winter

Das Wetter — Weather

das **Gewitter**, -	thunderstorm
der **Grad**	degree(s)
35 Grad	35 degrees
der **Hagel**	hail
der **Himmel**	sky
der **Nebel**	fog
der **Regen**	rain
der **Regenschauer**, -	rain shower

der **Regenschirm, -e**	umbrella	**windig**	windy
der **Schnee**	snow	**wolkenlos**	cloudless
die **Sonne**	sun		

die **Sonne**	sun	
Die Sonne scheint.	The sun is shining.	
der **Sonnenschein**	sunshine	
die **Temperatur, -en**	temperature	
der **Wetterbericht, -e**	weather report	
der **Wind, -e**	wind	
die **Wolke, -n**	cloud	

blitzen	to flash
Es blitzt.	There's lightning.
donnern	to thunder
Es donnert.	It's thundering.
regnen	to rain
Es regnet.	It's raining.
schneien	to snow
Es schneit.	It's snowing.

angenehm	pleasant
bewölkt	overcast, cloudy
heiß	hot
heiter	fair, bright
kalt; kälter	cold; colder
kühl	cool
kurz; kürzer	short; shorter
lang; länger	long; longer
neblig	foggy
regnerisch	rainy
schwül	muggy, humid
sonnig	sunny
stark; stärker	strong; stronger
warm; wärmer	warm; warmer

Verben — Verbs

bringen, gebracht	to bring
dauern	to last; to take
fallen (fällt), ist gefallen	to fall
fliegen, ist geflogen	to fly
passieren, ist passiert	to happen
reservieren	to reserve
verlieren, verloren	to lose

Sonstiges — Other

als	than
beliebt	popular
denn	because, for
draußen	outside
dreimal	three times
drinnen	inside
einmal	once
einmal die Woche	once a week
einmal im Monat	once a month
einmal im Jahr	once a year
früher	earlier, once, used to (do, be, etc.)
genauso	just/exactly as
gestern	yesterday
jeden Tag	every day
oder	or
so … wie	as . . . as
sondern	but, rather
zweimal	twice

▼ DAS KANN ICH NUN!

1. Nennen Sie drei Sportarten. Wie oft treiben Sie Sport?

2. Setzen Sie passende Wörter ein.

   a. Zum _____ braucht man ein Segelboot.
   b. Zum Reiten braucht man ein _____.
   c. Man _____ an einem Fluss oder an einem See.

3. Nennen Sie drei Freizeitaktivitäten. Was machen Sie gern in Ihrer Freizeit?

4. Wie gut können Sie das? Verwenden Sie **besser als** oder **(nicht) so gut wie** in Ihren Antworten.

   a. Schach spielen vs. Karten spielen
   b. Fahrrad fahren vs. Schlittschuh laufen
   c. singen vs. tanzen

5. Wie heißen die vier Jahreszeiten? Beschreiben Sie sie.

6. Setzen Sie eine passende Konjunktion ein.

   a. Ist es kalt _____ warm draußen? **b.** Ich bin nicht zum Sportplatz gegangen, _____ ich bin zu Hause geblieben. **c.** Mein Freund segelt gern, _____ ich reite lieber.

7. Setzen Sie die richtige Form von **haben** oder **sein** ein.

   a. Wann _____ das passiert? **b.** Wo _____ der Mann gestanden? **c.** Wann _____ seine Frau gekommen? **d.** Wann _____ sie ihn nach Hause gebracht? **e.** Wir _____ die ganze Zeit bei ihm geblieben.

8. Wie sagt man das im Perfekt?

   a. Wir gehen aus. **b.** Er spielt Fußball. **c.** Ich weiß das leider nicht. **d.** Er bestellt eine Pizza im Restaurant. **e.** Das Wetter wird besser.

Wie man fit und gesund bleibt

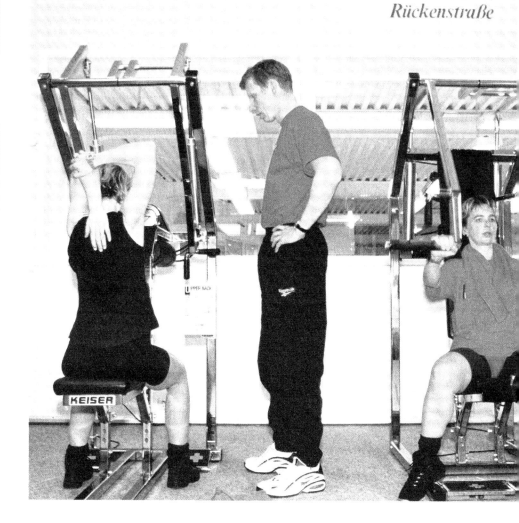

Rückenstraße

Muskeltraining im
Fitness-Studio

In diesem Kapitel

- **Themen:** Health and fitness, the human body, common illnesses and health complaints, morning activities
- **Grammatik:** Subordinating conjunctions, reflexive pronouns and verbs
- **Kultur:** Health spas in Germany, doctor visits, **Apotheken** and **Drogerien**, German breakfast
- **Lesen:** „Sage mir, was du isst …" (Monika Hillemacher)

Videoclips
Gesund leben

Alles klar?

A. Schauen Sie sich die Anzeige für Baden-Baden an, einen Kurort (*spa*) in Deutschland. Was kann man in Baden-Baden unternehmen (*do*)? Machen Sie eine Liste.

BEISPIEL:

SPORT	UNTERHALTUNG	GESUNDHEIT
schwimmen	ins Theater gehen	in die Sauna gehen

Hier klicken!

Weiteres zum Thema Kurorte finden Sie bei **Deutsch: Na klar!** im World-Wide-Web unter www.mhhe.com/dnk5.

B. Was machen diese Leute in Baden-Baden? Kreuzen Sie an.

	HERR/FRAU LOHMANN	HERR KRANZLER	FRAU DIETMOLD
Golf	☐	☒	☐
Karten spielen	☒	☐	☐
Massage	☒	☐	☒
Mini-Golf	☐	☐	☒
Sauna	☐	☒	☐
Schwimmen	☐	☒	☐
Spazierengehen	☒	☐	☐
Tanzen	☐	☐	☒
Theater	☐	☐	☒
Thermalbad	☒	☒	☒
Tischtennis	☐	☐	☒
Trinkkur	☐	☒	☒
Wandern	☐	☒	☐

There are many health spas (**Heilbäder und Kurorte**) throughout Germany, and Germans can choose to spend several weeks at a spa after an illness or when they feel stressed from their jobs. The national health-care system (**Krankenkasse**) subsidizes such a stay to a degree if rest and recuperation (**Kur und Erholung**) are prescribed by a physician. The necessity of such treatment is evaluated on a case-by-case basis. Faced with increasing health-care costs, fewer demands for **Kur und Erholung** at health spas, and the recent trends toward **Wellness,** these resorts are having to reinvent themselves. To be sure, the traditional **Kur** is still available, but at more cost to the patient. These **Kurorte** now offer additional activities such as exercise and **Wellness** programs, family excursions, and, at some, even gambling. Some resorts now offer conference facilities so that participants can combine meetings with some type of recreation. At some health spas people go on a **Trinkkur:** at prescribed intervals they drink a glass of the healthful mineral waters for which some spas are famous.

Wörter im Kontext

Neue Wörter

die Gesundheit health
tue (tun) do
versuche (versuchen) try
die Arbeit work
meistens mostly
zu Fuß on foot
der Kräutertee herbal tea
ab und zu now and then
deshalb for that reason
rauche (rauchen) smoke
d.h. = das heißt that is
wenig little
regelmäßig regularly
besonders especially
die Luft air
mich fit halten (sich fit halten) keep fit
mich beeilen (sich beeilen) hurry up
mindestens at least
mache Urlaub (Urlaub machen) go on vacation
anstrengend strenuous
die Krankenschwester nurse
achte auf (achten auf) pay attention to
die Biolebensmittel (*pl.*) organic foods
entweder ... oder either . . . or
mich entspannen (sich entspannen) relax

THEMA 1: Fit und gesund

Was machen diese Leute, um **fit** zu bleiben?

TINA: Für meine **Gesundheit tue** ich viel. Ich esse vegetarisch, **versuche** so gut es geht, den **Stress** in meinem Leben zu reduzieren. Zur **Arbeit** gehe ich **meistens zu Fuß.** Ich trinke viel **Kräutertee** und nur selten **Alkohol,** und **ab und zu** ein Glas Wein zum Essen.

WALTER: **Fitness** ist mir sehr wichtig. **Deshalb rauche** ich nie und esse gesund, **d.h. (das heißt) wenig** Fleisch und viel Gemüse. Ich treibe **regelmäßig** Sport, **besonders** an der frischen **Luft.** Ich möchte **mich fit halten.** So, und jetzt muss ich **mich beeilen.** Ich muss ins Fitnesscenter.

ANITA: **Mindestens** zweimal im Jahr **mache** ich **Urlaub,** denn meine Arbeit ist sehr **anstrengend.** Ich bin nämlich **Krankenschwester.** Ich **achte auf** meine Gesundheit und esse nur **Biolebensmittel, entweder** direkt vom Bauernhof **oder** vom Bioladen. Ich mache jede Woche Yoga. Da kann ich **mich** richtig **entspannen.**

A. Was machen Tina, Walter und Anita für ihre Gesundheit? Kombinieren Sie!

1. Stress ___g___
2. regelmäßig ___i___
3. mit Yoga ___f___
4. Kräutertee ___a___
5. gesund ___h___
6. auf die Gesundheit ___d___
7. ab und zu ___c___
8. oft Urlaub ___b___
9. nie ___e___
10. Biolebensmittel ___j___

a. trinken
b. machen
c. Alkohol trinken
d. achten
e. rauchen
f. sich entspannen
g. reduzieren
h. essen
i. Sport treiben
j. essen

B. Tina, Walter und Anita leben gesund. Wählen Sie die richtige Antwort.

1. Wie kommt Tina zur Arbeit?
   a. zu Fuß   **b.** mit dem Rad   **c.** mit dem Auto

2. Wie oft trinkt Tina ein Glas Wein?
   a. nie   **b.** ab und zu   **c.** einmal in der Woche

3. Wie viel Fleisch isst Walter?
   a. viel   **b.** wenig   **c.** keins

4. Wie oft treibt Walter Sport?
   a. einmal im Monat   **b.** regelmäßig   **c.** nie

5. Was für Lebenmittel isst Anita?
   a. Biolebensmittel   **b.** Lebensmittel vom Supermarkt

6. Wie oft macht Anita Urlaub?
   a. mindestens zweimal im Jahr   **b.** einmal im Jahr   **c.** nicht mehr als alle zwei Jahre

7. Wie entspannt sich Anita?
   a. Sie joggt.   **b.** Sie läuft Schlittschuh.   **c.** Sie macht Yoga.

Aktivität 1   Meine Fitnessroutine

Schritt 1: Was machen Sie, um fit und gesund zu bleiben? Kreuzen Sie an!

1. ☐ joggen
2. ☐ ins Fitnesscenter gehen
3. ☐ vegetarisch essen
4. ☐ meditieren
5. ☐ Urlaub machen
6. ☐ wenig Alkohol trinken
7. ☐ Stress reduzieren
8. ☐ nicht rauchen
9. ☐ mich entspannen
10. ☐ viel an die frische Luft gehen
11. ☐ viel zu Fuß gehen
12. ☐ Yoga machen
13. ☐ viel Wasser trinken
14. ☐ ??

Schritt 2: Sagen Sie nun, wie oft Sie das tun.

BEISPIEL: Ich trinke jeden Tag viel Wasser.

nie	jeden Tag
selten	mindestens/meistens einmal/zweimal die Woche
ab und zu	einmal/zweimal/dreimal im Jahr
manchmal	??
regelmäßig	

Aktivität 1. Suggestion: Assign as homework.

Follow-up: In the next class, have students move about the classroom and interview one another about their habits. Write the following guide questions on the board: *Was machst du, um fit und gesund zu bleiben? Wie oft machst du das? Warum (nicht)?*

Siehe *Reflexive Pronouns and Verbs,* S. 248.

Schritt 3: Sagen Sie nun, warum Sie das tun oder nicht tun.

BEISPIELE: Ich jogge nicht. Das ist mir zu langweilig.
Ich esse vegetarisch. Das ist gut für die Gesundheit.

macht mir (keinen) Spaß	ist zu anstrengend
ist gut/schlecht für die Gesundheit	ist (un)gesund
macht krank	reduziert Stress
kostet zu viel Geld	ist mir zu langweilig
habe keine Zeit/Lust dazu (*for that*)	??

fitness adviser

Spielen Sie ein Gespräch zwischen einem Fitnessberater und einer Klientin. Was darf man tun? Was soll man nicht tun?

BEISPIEL: s1: Darf ich Wein trinken?
s2: Ja, aber nicht zu viel. Trinken Sie lieber viel Wasser.
s1: Und wie viele Stunden soll ich pro Nacht schlafen?
s2: Mindestens sieben Stunden.

Fleisch essen	Kräutertee trinken
Vitamintabletten einnehmen	Kaffee trinken
Urlaub machen	??
Sport treiben	

body # THEMA 2: Der menschliche Körper°

Ein Telefongespräch

CHRISTOPH: Schmidt.

UTA: Hallo, Christoph? Hier ist Uta.

CHRISTOPH: Ja, grüß dich, Uta.

UTA: Nanu! Was ist denn los? Du **klingst** ja so **deprimiert**.

CHRISTOPH: Ich liege im Bett. Ich **fühle mich hundsmiserabel**.

UTA: **Was fehlt dir** denn?

CHRISTOPH: Ich habe eine **Erkältung**, vielleicht **sogar** die **Grippe**. Der Hals **tut** mir **weh**, ich kann **kaum schlucken, mir ist schlecht**. Ich habe **Fieber, Halsschmerzen, Husten** und **Schnupfen**. Ich habe auch **Kopfschmerzen** und bin so **müde** und **schlapp**. Und morgen muss ich eine Arbeit bei Professor Höhn **abgeben**.

UTA: **So ein Pech.** Warst du schon beim **Arzt?**

CHRISTOPH: Nein.

UTA: Wie lange bist du denn schon **krank**?

CHRISTOPH: Seit **fast** zwei Wochen schon.

UTA: Du bist **verrückt**! Geh doch **gleich** zum Arzt. Er kann dir sicher was* **verschreiben**.

CHRISTOPH: Aber ich kriege (*get*) wohl keinen **Termin**.

UTA: **Das macht nichts.** Geh einfach in die **Sprechstunde**.

CHRISTOPH: Na gut. Ich danke dir für den **Rat**.

UTA: **Nichts zu danken** ... Ich wünsche dir **gute Besserung**!

A. Stimmt das oder stimmt das nicht?

	DAS STIMMT	DAS STIMMT NICHT
1. Uta spricht mit Christoph am Telefon.	☒	☐
2. Christoph fühlt sich heute viel besser.	☐	☒
3. Er war gestern beim Arzt.	☐	☒
4. Uta ist deprimiert.	☐	☒
5. Uta gibt Christoph Rat.	☒	☐
6. Sie bringt Christoph zum Arzt.	☐	☒

B. Was ist los mit Christoph? Ergänzen Sie!

1. Christoph klingt _____.

2. Er fühlt sich _____.

3. Er hat eine _____.

4. Der Hals _____ ihm _____.

5. Er hat auch _____, _____, _____ und _____.

6. Christoph ist seit zwei Wochen _____.

---

*Was, as used here, is a shortened form of **etwas**. It occurs often in colloquial German.

Ein Telefongespräch. **Suggestion:** Introduce the new words before students listen to the dialogue. Then ask them to describe briefly what is wrong with Christoph and how long he has been sick. Utilize the drawing to describe Christoph's illness. Have students role-play the dialogue.

Neue Wörter

klingst (klingen) sound
deprimiert depressed
fühle mich (sich fühlen) feel
hundsmiserabel really lousy
Was fehlt dir? What's wrong with you?
die Erkältung cold
sogar even
die Grippe flu
tut weh (wehtun) hurts
kaum scarcely
schlucken swallow
mir ist schlecht I feel bad, I feel sick to my stomach
das Fieber fever
die Halsschmerzen (*pl.*) sore throat
der Husten cough
der Schnupfen runny nose, sniffles
die Kopfschmerzen (*pl.*) headache
müde tired
schlapp worn-out
abgeben drop off, give to
so ein Pech what bad luck
der Arzt doctor
krank sick
fast almost
verrückt crazy
gleich right away
verschreiben prescribe
der Termin appointment
Das macht nichts. That doesn't matter.
die Sprechstunde office hours
der Rat advice
nichts zu danken don't mention it
gute Besserung get well soon

B. Answers: 1. *deprimiert* 2. *hundsmiserabel* 3. *Erkältung* or *Grippe* 4. *tut / weh* 5. *Fieber / Halsschmerzen / Husten / Schnupfen* 6. *krank*

Erzählen Sie Christophs Geschichte. Benutzen Sie die Bilder.

1.

2.

3.

4.

5.

Sie hören eine Aerobic-Lehrerin beim Training im Aerobic-Kurs. Nummerieren Sie alle Körperteile in der Reihenfolge von 1–10, so wie Sie sie hören. Einige Wörter auf der Liste kommen nicht im Hörtext vor.

_____ Arme   _____ Füße   _____ Knie   _____ Muskeln

_____ Bauch   _____ Hals   _____ Kopf   _____ Rücken

_____ Beine   _____ Hände   _____ Ohren   _____ Schultern

_____ Finger

KULTUR...

Die Deutschen, so heißt es, sind die Arztbesuchseuropameister[1]. Niemand in Europa geht so oft und so gern zum Arzt wie die Deutschen. Elfmal pro Jahr gehen sie zum Arzt. Sechsmal tun es die Franzosen, dreimal die Schweden. 90 Prozent der Deutschen suchen mindestens einmal im Jahr einen Arzt auf. Verglichen mit den Schweizern (69 Prozent) und den Italienern (48 Prozent), steht den Deutschen die Goldmedaille zu. (Aus: *Die Zeit*)

[1]**Meister** = *champions*

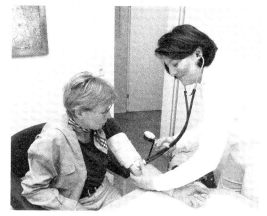

Was fehlt Ihnen?

Aktivität 5 Beschwerden°

Complaints

Was fehlt diesen Leuten? Was sollten sie dagegen tun? Markieren Sie Ihre Antworten.   **Aktivität 5. Suggestion:** Students should look over all possibilities before listening to each dialogue. After each dialogue is played, pause to let students respond.

DIALOG 1

Leni hat:	Rückenschmerzen.	eine Erkältung	Kopfschmerzen
Doris empfiehlt:	Geh zum Arzt.	Leg dich ins Bett.	Nimm Aspirin.

DIALOG 2

Doris hat:	Kopfschmerzen	Bauchschmerzen	Fieber
Leni empfiehlt:	Geh zum Arzt.	Trink Kamillentee.	Leg dich ins Bett.

DIALOG 3

Patient hat:	keine Energie	Halsschmerzen	kann nicht schlafen
Arzt empfiehlt:	mehr Schlaf	Kur im Schwarzwald	Tabletten gegen Stress

---

SPRACHTIPP

Use the following phrase to talk about how you feel:

Ich **fühle mich** nicht wohl.	*I don't feel well.*

The person with the symptoms refers to himself or herself with a pronoun in the dative case.

Mir ist schlecht.	*I feel sick to my stomach.*
Mir ist warm/kalt.	*I feel warm/cold.*

The verb **fehlen** with the dative case is frequently used to ask "What is the matter?"

Was fehlt dir/ihm denn?	*What's the matter with you/him?*

Use the verb **wehtun** with the dative case to say that something hurts.

Die Füße **tun mir/ihm/ihr weh.**	*My/His/Her feet hurt.*

Aktivität 6 Was fehlt dir denn?

Fragen Sie Ihren Partner / Ihre Partnerin: „Was fehlt dir denn?" Antworten Sie auf seine/ihre Beschwerden mit einem guten Rat.

BEISPIEL: S1: Ich fühle mich so schlapp.
S2: Geh nach Hause und leg dich ins Bett.

BESCHWERDEN	RATSCHLÄGE
Ich fühle mich so schlapp.	Nimm ein paar Aspirin.
Der Hals tut mir weh.	Geh ...
Ich habe ...	in die Sauna.
Kopfschmerzen.	nach Hause.
Rückenschmerzen.	zum Arzt.
Husten.	Leg dich ins Bett.
Schnupfen.	Nimm mal Vitamin C.
eine Erkältung.	Trink heißen Tee mit Rum.
Fieber.	??
Ich kann nicht schlafen.	
Mir ist schlecht.	

Aktivität 6. Follow-up: Each student writes a complaint on a slip of paper (no names). Slips are collected and redistributed. As slips are read by individuals, other students give advice.

EMSER PASTILLEN[1]
Naturkraft gegen Erkältung

[1]*lozenges*

a.

b.

c.

d.

e.

f.

g.

h.

A. Was bedeuten die Wörter und Ausdrücke? Kombinieren Sie!

1. _____ sich duschen   **a.** *to shave*

2. _____ sich setzen   **b.** *to stretch*

3. _____ sich kämmen   **c.** *to brush one's teeth*

4. _____ sich strecken   **d.** *to shower*

5. _____ sich das Gesicht waschen   **e.** *to sit down*

6. _____ sich rasieren   **f.** *to comb one's hair*

7. _____ sich anziehen   **g.** *to wash one's face*

8. _____ sich die Zähne putzen   **h.** *to get dressed*

B. Was machen Herr und Frau Lustig morgens? Was passt zu welchem Bild?

1. _____ Er **rasiert sich.**

2. _____ Sie **streckt sich.**

3. _____ Sie **kämmt sich.**

4. _____ Sie **putzt sich die Zähne.**

5. _____ Er **duscht sich.**

6. _____ Er **setzt sich** an den Tisch.

7. _____ Sie **wäscht sich** das **Gesicht.**

8. _____ Er **zieht sich an.**

Aktivität 7 Meine Routine am Morgen

Was machen Sie jeden Morgen? Hier sind einige Dinge, die man morgens oft macht. In welcher Reihenfolge machen Sie alles jeden Morgen? Nummerieren Sie die Aktivitäten von 1 bis 8.

_____ Ich ziehe mich an.

_____ Ich dusche mich.

_____ Ich wasche mir das Gesicht.

_____ Ich kämme mich.

_____ Ich strecke mich.

_____ Ich rasiere mich.

_____ Ich setze mich an den Frühstückstisch.

_____ Ich putze mir die Zähne.

Aktivität 7. Follow-up: Have a few students act out their morning routine. Other students have to say what each activity is.

Aktivität 8 Hin und her: Meine Routine – deine Routine

Jeder hat eine andere Routine. Was machen diese Leute und in welcher Reihenfolge? Machen Sie es auch so?

BEISPIEL: s1: Was macht Alexander morgens?
s2: Zuerst rasiert er sich und putzt sich die Zähne. Dann kämmt er sich. Danach setzt er sich an den Tisch und frühstückt.

Aktivität 8. Follow up: Ask students to report on their partners' daily routines.

WER	WAS ER/SIE MORGENS MACHT
Alexander	zuerst / sich rasieren / sich die Zähne putzen dann / sich kämmen danach / sich an den Tisch setzen / frühstücken
Elke	zuerst / sich anziehen dann / sich die Zähne putzen danach / sich kämmen
Tilo	zuerst / sich duschen / sich rasieren dann / sich an den Tisch setzen / frühstücken danach / sich die Zähne putzen
Kamal	zuerst / sich das Gesicht waschen dann / frühstücken danach / sich rasieren / sich anziehen
Sie	zuerst / ?? dann / ?? danach / ??
Ihr Partner / Ihre Partnerin	zuerst / ?? dann / ?? danach / ??

Grammatik im Kontext

unterordnende Konjunktionen

Connecting Sentences: Subordinating Conjunctions°

Subordinating conjunctions are used to connect a main clause and a dependent clause. Four frequently used subordinating conjunctions are **dass** (*that*), **ob** (*whether, if*), **weil** (*because*), and **wenn** (*whenever, if*).

Ich hoffe, **dass** du bald gesund wirst.	*I hope that you'll get well soon.*
Weißt du, **ob** Mark krank ist?	*Do you know whether Mark is ill?*
Mark bleibt zu Hause, **weil** er eine Erkältung hat.	*Mark is staying at home because he has a cold.*
Ich gehe ins Fitnesscenter, **wenn** ich Zeit habe.	*I go to the fitness center whenever I have time.*

Note:

- In dependent clauses the conjugated verb is placed at the end.
- In the case of a separable-prefix verb, the prefix is joined with the rest of the verb.
- A comma always separates the main clause from the dependent clause.

MAIN CLAUSE	DEPENDENT CLAUSE
Er bleibt zu Hause,	weil er eine Erkältung **hat.**
Ich weiß nicht,	ob er schon zum Arzt gegangen **ist.**
Er hat gesagt,	dass er zu Hause bleiben **muss.**
Ich bin sicher,	dass er **mitkommt.**

If the dependent clause precedes the main clause, the main clause begins with the conjugated verb, followed by the subject.

DEPENDENT CLAUSE	MAIN CLAUSE
Weil Mark krank war,	**musste** er zu Hause bleiben.
Wenn wir Zeit haben,	**gehen** wir am Wochenende ins Fitnesscenter.
Ob Hans Zeit hat,	**weiß** ich nicht.

Indirect Questions

An indirect question is made up of an introductory clause and a question. Interrogative pronouns function like subordinating conjunctions in indirect questions. The conjugated verb is placed at the end.

DIRECT QUESTION	INDIRECT QUESTION
Warum kauft Herr Stierli so viel Vitamin B?	Ich weiß nicht, **warum** Herr Stierli so viel Vitamin B **kauft.**
Was hat er vor?	Ich möchte wissen, **was** er **vorhat.**

A yes/no question is introduced by the conjunction **ob** in the indirect question.

Geht er zu einer Party?	Ich möchte wissen, **ob** er zu einer Party **geht.**

Übung 1 Es geht ihm hundsmiserabel.

Suchen Sie in Spalte B passende Nebensätze für die Sätze in Spalte A. Bei manchen Sätzen gibt es mehrere richtige Antworten.

A	B
1. Tobias liegt im Bett, __c__	**a.** dass er schon seit vier Tagen krank ist.
2. Inge möchte wissen, __bf__	**b.** wie es ihm geht.
3. Inge hofft (hopes), __e__	**c.** weil er die Grippe hat.
4. Er sagt ihr, __abe__	**d.** wenn er wieder gesund ist.
5. Sie fragt ihn, __bf__	**e.** dass er endlich zum Arzt geht.
6. Sie besucht ihn, __cd__	**f.** ob er schon beim Arzt war.

Übung 2 Ein großer Erfolg°

Schauen Sie sich den Cartoon „Herr Stierli" an. Beantworten Sie die Fragen, indem Sie die Konjunktion **weil** benutzen (use).

°success

1. Warum ist Herr Stierli zur Apotheke gegangen? (Er wollte Vitamin B kaufen.)

2. Warum hat er fünf Packungen Vitamin B gekauft? (Er hat mehr Energie gebraucht.)

3. Warum war Herr Stierli sehr stolz (proud)? (Er war sehr populär bei den Gästen auf der Party.)

4. Warum hat er so großen Erfolg? (Er hat so viel Vitamin B eingenommen.)

Realia. The cartoon *Herr Stierli* makes fun of society at an international party. Herr Stierli is greeted in English, German, and French (*Comment allez-vous?* = "How are you?"). The German phrase *Ich habe die Ehre* ("I am honored") is a formal way of acknowledging someone socially, especially in southern Germany and Austria.

Übung 2. Note: Explain that the expression "Vitamin B" is sometimes used figuratively as it is here: "B" stands for *Beziehungen* = connections. Thus a dose of vitamin B means you need connections. Herr Stierli, by ingesting large amounts of vitamin B, is able to make lots of connections at the party and is the most popular guest.

BEISPIEL: s1: Obst ist die beste Nahrung (*food*).
s2: Ich bezweifle, dass Obst die beste Nahrung ist.

REDEMITTEL

Essen macht Spaß

Jeder Deutsche trinkt im Leben 3.060 Liter Bier

Ich bezweifle, dass …

Ich glaube auch, dass …

Ich bin sicher, dass …

MOZART GEGEN STRESS

1. Vitamin C ist gut gegen Erkältungen.
2. Klassische Musik ist gut gegen Stress.
3. Rauchen gefährdet (*endangers*) die Gesundheit.
4. Yoga reduziert Stress.
5. Gesund ist, was gut schmeckt.
6. Hühnersuppe ist gut gegen Erkältungen.
7. Bier macht dick.
8. Vegetarisches Essen ist ideal.
9. Zu viel Zucker macht aggressiv.
10. Knoblauch (*garlic*) hilft gegen Vampire.

health-conscious Übung 4 Wie gesundheitsbewusst sind Sie?

Fragen Sie einen Partner / eine Partnerin, was er/sie für Fitness und die Gesundheit tut, und warum.

BEISPIEL: s1: Gehst du regelmäßig ins Fitnesscenter?
s2: Nein.
s1: Warum nicht?
s2: Weil ich das langweilig finde.

s1: FRAGEN	s2: ANTWORTEN
vegetarisch essen	finde das langweilig
Vitamintabletten einnehmen	kostet zu viel
zu Fuß zur Arbeit / zur Uni gehen	mag ich (nicht)
Kräutertee / Kaffee / viel Wasser trinken	reduziert Stress
rauchen	macht mir (viel/keinen) Spaß
Yoga machen	habe keine Zeit dazu
regelmäßig ins Fitnesscenter gehen	ist sehr gesund/ungesund
Biolebensmittel kaufen	
auf Kalorien achten	

KULTURTIPP

In deutschsprachigen Ländern kauft man Medikamente, sogar Aspirin, in der **Apotheke.** Vitamine, pflanzliche Heilmittel (z.B. Baldrian), Zahnpasta, Seife und Kosmetikartikel kauft man in der **Drogerie** oder auch im Supermarkt.

Medikamente gibt es in der Apotheke.

Übung 5 Das mache ich, wenn ...

Sagen Sie, wann Sie das machen.

BEISPIEL: Ich gehe zum Arzt, wenn ich krank bin.

Ich gehe zum Arzt, ...
   zum Zahnarzt, ...
   in die Sauna, ...
   in die Drogerie, ...
   in die Apotheke, ...
Ich bleibe im Bett, ...
Ich nehme viel Vitamin C ein, ...
Ich esse Hühnersuppe, ...
Ich trinke Kräutertee, ...

Ich brauche Zahnpasta.
Ich habe zu viel gegessen.
Ich brauche Aspirin.
Ich fühle mich hundsmiserabel.
Ich habe die Grippe.
Ich fühle mich schlapp.
Ich habe eine Erkältung.
Ich bin krank.
Ich habe Zahnschmerzen.
??

Übung 5. Suggestion: Review with students the difference between *wann* and *wenn*. *Wann* is used in direct and indirect questions—*Wann machen Sie das? Sagen Sie, wann Sie das machen*—whereas *wenn* is not a question word; it introduces a dependent clause.

Übung 6 Was tun Sie gewöhnlich?

Sagen Sie, was Sie in diesen Situationen machen.

BEISPIEL: Wenn ich eine Erkältung habe, trinke ich viel Kräutertee.

Wenn ich eine Erkältung habe,
Wenn ich nicht einschlafen kann,
Wenn ich gestresst bin,
Wenn ich mich schlapp fühle,
Wenn ich mich hundsmiserabel
   fühle,

im Bett bleiben
Kräutertee trinken
heiße Milch trinken
Rotwein mit Rum trinken
in die Sauna gehen
viel Vitamin C einnehmen
Hühnersuppe essen
ein Buch lesen
meditieren
Musik hören
??

Übung 6. Suggestion: Have students scan the possibilities before making four statements about themselves. Then have students work in pairs, taking turns asking questions and responding. Have them begin each question by asking, for example, *Was tust du, wenn du eine Erkältung hast?* etc. **Follow-up:** Ask the class questions like *Wer isst Hühnersuppe, wenn er/sie eine Erkältung hat?* You may want to point out that chicken soup for a cold is not a widely known folk remedy in Germany.

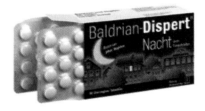

Übung 7 Ich muss es mir überlegen°.

Stefans Freunde wollen mit ihm Bungeejumping gehen. Stefan ist aber sehr skeptisch, weil er das noch nie gemacht hat. Was will er genau wissen?

BEISPIEL: Wo kann man das lernen? →
       Er will wissen, wo man das lernen kann.

Er will wissen, ...

1. Wo kann man das denn tun?
2. Wie gefährlich (*dangerous*) ist das eigentlich?
3. Warum muss es ausgerechnet Bungeejumping sein?
4. Was für Kleidung muss man dabei tragen?
5. Muss man nicht zuerst ein Training machen?
6. Wer geht sonst noch mit?
7. Wer hat diese verrückte Idee gehabt?

think it over

Reflexive Pronouns and Verbs°

When the subject and pronoun object of a sentence refer to the same person, the object is called a reflexive pronoun.

Wir informieren **uns** über Fitnesscenter.	*We're gathering information about fitness centers.*
Die Studenten informieren **sich** über die Kosten.	*The students are informing themselves about the costs.*
Informieren **Sie sich** bitte zuerst über die Kosten.	*Please get informed first about the costs.*

Note:

- The reflexive pronoun comes after the conjugated verb.
  Christoph fühlt **sich** nicht wohl.
- It follows pronoun subjects in questions and the formal imperative.
  Fühlst du **dich** nicht wohl?
  Informieren Sie **sich** zuerst!
- Reflexive pronouns are identical to personal pronouns except for the third-person forms and the formal **Sie**-forms, all of which are **sich**.

Wander-Vögel informieren sich jeden Samstag im **REISE-JOURNAL** der Rheinischen Post

REFLEXIVE PRONOUNS					
ACCUSATIVE	**DATIVE**		**ACCUSATIVE**	**DATIVE**	
mich	mir	*myself*	uns	uns	*ourselves*
dich	dir	*yourself*	euch	euch	*yourselves*
sich	sich	*yourself (formal)*	sich	sich	*yourselves (formal)*
sich	sich	*himself/herself*	sich	sich	*themselves*

Verbs with Accusative Reflexive Pronouns

German uses reflexive pronouns much more extensively than English. Some verbs are always used with an accusative reflexive pronoun, for example, **sich erkälten** (*to catch cold*). The English equivalent of many such verbs has no reflexive pronoun at all.

Er hat **sich erkältet**.	*He caught a cold.*
Wir müssen **uns beeilen**.	*We have to hurry.*

Other German verbs can be used with or without a reflexive pronoun, depending on the desired meaning. The reflexive use of such verbs is often expressed in English with a different verb altogether.

Sie **setzt** das Kind auf das Sofa.	Sie **setzt sich** auf das Sofa.
*She **puts** the child on the sofa.*	*She **sits** down on the sofa.*
Ich **lege** das Buch auf den Tisch	Ich **lege mich** ins Bett.
*I **lay** the book on the table.*	*I **lie** down on the bed.*

Infinitive: **sich setzen** (*to sit down*)	
ich setze **mich**	wir setzen **uns**
du setzt **dich**	ihr setzt **euch**
er sie es } setzt **sich**	sie setzen **sich**
Sie setzen **sich**	

Verbs that are *always* used with an accusative reflexive pronoun include the following:

sich ausruhen	to rest
sich beeilen	to hurry
sich entspannen	to relax
sich erholen	to recuperate
sich erkälten	to catch cold

Verbs that are *typically* used with an accusative reflexive pronoun include the following:

sich (hin)legen	to lie down
sich (hin)setzen	to sit down
sich informieren (über)	to inform oneself (about)
sich (wohl) fühlen	to feel (well)

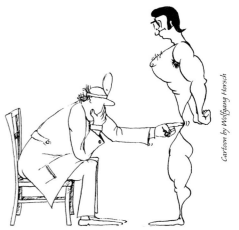

Cartoon by Wolfgang Horsch

„*Bitte entspannen Sie sich!*"

ANALYSE

Schauen Sie sich den Cartoon an.

- Lesen Sie, was Wurzel denkt, und identifizieren Sie die Sätze mit reflexiven Verben.
- Wie fühlt sich Wurzel heute?
- Fühlt er sich gewöhnlich so gut? Wie oft hat er sich schon so gefühlt?
- Warum fühlt er sich am Ende ganz deprimiert?

Analyse. Suggestion: Use the cartoon as a point of departure to ask students: *Wie fühlen Sie sich heute?*

Realia. *Wurzel* is the German name for the cartoon dog Fred Basset. **Suggestion:** Ask students, *Lesen Sie Fred Basset? Wenn nein, welche Comics lesen Sie gerne? Welche Figuren in den Comics halten sich fit? Welche sind nicht so sportlich?*

[1]unusual

[2]sign

Sie hören eine Besprechung zwischen Herrn Schneider und seinem Arzt. Markieren Sie die richtigen Antworten auf die Fragen.

1. Warum hat Herr Schneider einen Termin beim Arzt?
   a. Er hat einen chronischen Schluckauf (*hiccups*).
   b. Er hat sich beim Fitnesstraining verletzt.
   c. Er fühlt sich so schlapp.

2. Was ist die Ursache (*cause*) seines Problems?
   a. Seine Arbeit bringt viel Stress mit sich.
   b. Er sitzt den ganzen Tag am Schreibtisch.
   c. Seine Arbeit ist so langweilig.

3. Was empfiehlt ihm der Arzt?
   a. Er soll sich eine andere Arbeit suchen.
   b. Er soll sich im Schwarzwald vom Stress erholen.
   c. Er soll Sport treiben.

4. Wie reagiert Herr Schneider auf diese Vorschläge?
   a. Er ist sehr enthusiastisch.
   b. Er hat keine Zeit für eine Kur im Schwarzwald.
   c. Er interessiert sich nicht für Sport.

5. Was verschreibt ihm der Arzt?
   a. einen täglichen Spaziergang
   b. regelmäßig meditieren
   c. Vitamintabletten

6. Warum meint der Arzt, dass Herr Schneider mit seinen Nerven am Ende ist?
   a. Er hat einen Schluckauf und weiß es nicht.
   b. Er entspannt sich oft.
   c. Er redet zu viel und zu schnell.

[1]*each time*

Verbs with Reflexive Pronouns in the Accusative or Dative

A number of German verbs may be used with a reflexive pronoun in either the accusative or the dative case. They include:

sich anziehen	*to get dressed*
sich kämmen	*to comb one's hair*
sich verletzen	*to injure oneself*
sich waschen	*to wash oneself*

REFLEXIVE PRONOUN IN ACCUSATIVE	REFLEXIVE PRONOUN IN DATIVE
Ich ziehe **mich** an.	Ich ziehe **mir** die Jacke an.
I get dressed.	*I put my jacket on.*
Ich wasche **mich**.	Ich wasche **mir** die Hände.
I wash myself.	*I wash my hands.*
Du hast **dich** verletzt.	Du hast **dir** den Fuß verletzt.
You've injured yourself.	*You've injured your foot.*
Ich kämme **mich**.	Ich kämme **mir** die Haare.
I'm combing my hair.	*I'm combing my hair.*

Note:

- The reflexive pronoun functions as the indirect object in the dative case if the sentence also has a direct object in the accusative—**die Jacke, die Hände, den Fuß,** and **die Haare** in the examples above.

- For the verb **sich kämmen** the meaning is the same whether an accusative reflexive is used or a dative reflexive with the direct object **die Haare.**

- The expression **sich die Zähne putzen** is used only with the dative reflexive pronoun, to mean *to brush one's teeth.*

   Ich putze **mir** die Zähne.   *I'm brushing my teeth.*

Übung 9   Morgenroutine

Morgens geht es bei der Familie Kunze immer recht hektisch zu. Ergänzen Sie die fehlenden Reflexivpronomen.

   Herr Kunze duscht __sich__¹ zuerst. Dann rasiert er __sich__.² Seine Frau ruft: „Bitte, beeil __dich__,³ ich muss __mich__⁴ auch noch duschen."

   Cornelia, die siebzehnjährige Tochter, erklärt: „Ich glaube, ich habe __mich__⁵ erkältet. Ich fühle __mich__⁶ so schlapp. Ich lege __mich__⁷ wieder hin." Frau Kunze zu Cornelia: „Zieh __dich__⁸ bitte sofort an! Du fühlst __dich__⁹ so schlapp, weil du so spät ins Bett gegangen bist." Cornelia: „Ich ziehe __mich__¹⁰ ja schon an."

   Frau Kunze zu Thomas, dem siebenjährigen Sohn: „Es ist schon halb acht, und du musst __dich__¹¹ noch kämmen. Hast du __dich__¹² überhaupt schon gewaschen? Und hast du __dir__¹³ auch die Zähne geputzt?"

   Sabine, die zwölfjährige Tochter, duscht __sich__¹⁴ schon seit fünfzehn Minuten.

   Herr und Frau Kunze setzen __sich__¹⁵ endlich an den Frühstückstisch. Herr Kunze zu seiner Frau: „Wir müssen __uns__¹⁶ beeilen. Wo sind die Kinder?" Er ruft ungeduldig: „Könnt ihr __euch__¹⁷ nicht ein bisschen beeilen? Es ist schon acht Uhr."

   So ist es jeden Morgen: Alle müssen __sich__¹⁸ beeilen.

Übung 10   Ratschläge°

°*Advice*

Was kann man Ihnen in diesen Situationen raten?

BEISPIEL: s1: Ich habe die Grippe.
            s2: Leg dich ins Bett.
         oder Du musst dich ins Bett legen.

1. Sie haben die Grippe.
2. Sie haben sich erkältet.
3. Sie fühlen sich hundsmiserabel.
4. Sie haben den ganzen Tag in der Bibliothek verbracht.
5. Sie müssen in einer Minute an der Bushaltestelle sein.
6. Sie haben sich die große Zehe verletzt.

sich beeilen
sich gut erholen
sich ins Bett legen
sich entspannen
sich (ins Café) setzen
sich wärmer anziehen
sich ausruhen
??

Trimm Dich am Feierabend

Übung 11 Wie oft machen sie das?

Fragen Sie jemand, wie oft er/sie die folgenden Dinge macht.

BEISPIEL: sich die Zähne putzen
s1: Putzt du dir jeden Tag die Zähne?
s2: Natürlich putze ich mir jeden Tag die Zähne.

sich die Zähne putzen	nie
sich die Haare kämmen	ab und zu
sich rasieren	oft
sich die Haare waschen	jeden Tag/Morgen/Abend
sich duschen	einmal/zweimal die Woche

Expressing Reciprocity

A reflexive pronoun is used to express reciprocity.

Martina und Jörg **lieben sich.**	*Martina and Jörg love each other.*
Sie **treffen sich** im Park.	*They meet (each other) in the park.*
Sie **kennen sich** seit zwei Wochen.	*They have known each other for two weeks.*
Sie **rufen sich** oft an.	*They call each other frequently.*

Übung 12 Der neue Freund

Martina erzählt ihrer Freundin Katrin über ihren neuen Freund Jörg. Benutzen Sie die Verben unten in einem kleinen Bericht.

Hier ist der Anfang:
Wir haben uns vor zwei Wochen kennen gelernt.

1. sich kennen lernen (wo)
2. sich anrufen (wie oft)
3. sich treffen (wo, wie oft)
4. sich sehr gut verstehen
5. sich lieben

Sprache im Kontext

Videoclips

A. Im Interview erklären diese Leute, warum sie ihre Lebensmittel im Bioladen kaufen. Verbinden (*Connect*) Sie die Person mit dem Grund (*reason*).

1. Frau Simon
2. Maria
3. Peter

Der Käse aus dem Bioladen schmeckt besser als Käse aus einem Supermarkt.

Bauern gebrauchen keine Chemikalien für die Bioprodukte.

Biosäfte sind gesünder als die herkömmlichen Säfte.

B. Und Sie? Kaufen Sie auch im Bioladen ein? Warum? (Warum nicht?)

C. Welche Symptome haben diese Leute, wenn sie krank sind? Markieren Sie Oliver und/oder Maria.

OLIVER	MARIA	
☐	☐	hat oft eine Erkältung
☐	☐	hat Halsschmerzen
☐	☐	hat Fieber und Husten
☐	☐	hat Schnupfen
☐	☐	hat manchmal die Grippe

D. Welche Symptome haben Sie, wenn Sie krank sind?

E. Und was machen diese Leute, wenn sie krank sind?

1. Oliver badet heiß, schwitzt (*sweats*), ＿＿ sich ins Bett, ＿＿ viel und trinkt ＿＿.

2. Maria legt sich auf die ＿＿, trinkt Tee mit Honig und versucht, abzuschalten (*switch off*).

F. Was machen Sie, wenn Sie krank sind?

Lesen

Zum Thema

A. Wie gesund essen Sie? Was betrifft Sie? Kreuzen Sie an.

1. Gesund essen ist mir wichtig. ☐
2. Ich esse regelmäßig drei Mahlzeiten am Tag. ☐
3. Ich habe nie Zeit zum Frühstücken. ☐
4. Ich habe oft keine Zeit zum Essen oder esse sehr schnell. ☐
5. Ich esse oft vor dem Fernseher. ☐
6. Ich esse gern und oft Fastfood. ☐
7. Ich esse möglichst viele Bioprodukte. ☐
8. Ich bin Vegetarier/Vegetarierin. ☐
9. Ich möchte abnehmen (*lose weight*). ☐
10. Ich möchte zunehmen (*gain weight*). ☐
11. Ich esse sehr gesund. ☐

B. Was sind Ihre Essgewohnheiten (*eating habits*)? Füllen Sie den Fragebogen aus.

Essen Sie gesund?

Wie oft essen bzw. trinken Sie ...	täglich	mehrmals pro Woche	selten	nie
Getreideprodukte (Vollkornbrot, Weißbrot, Cerealien, Reis, Pasta usw.)	☐	☐	☐	☐
frisches Obst und Gemüse, Fruchtsaft ohne Zucker	☐	☐	☐	☐
Milchprodukte (Vollmilch, Magermilch, Quark, Joghurt, Käse usw.)	☐	☐	☐	☐
Wurst, Schinken, Speck, Aufschnitt	☐	☐	☐	☐
Fleisch (Rindfleisch, Schweinefleisch usw.)	☐	☐	☐	☐
Geflügel	☐	☐	☐	☐
Fisch, Meeresfrüchte	☐	☐	☐	☐
Butter	☐	☐	☐	☐
Süßigkeiten	☐	☐	☐	☐
Cola, Limonade	☐	☐	☐	☐
Bier, Wein, Alkohol	☐	☐	☐	☐
Kaffee, Tee	☐	☐	☐	☐

Videoclips B. Expansion: Ask students where they normally buy their groceries: *Wo kaufen Sie Ihre Lebensmittel ein? Gibt es hier in <name of town> einen Bioladen? Was kann man dort alles kaufen? Ist das teuer oder preiswert? Gibt es im normalen Supermarkt eine Bio-Abteilung? Gibt es hier einen Wochenmarkt? Was kann man dort alles kaufen? Kaufen Sie dort ein? Warum (nicht)?*

Zum Thema. Suggestion: Assign **A**, **B**, and **C** as homework. Activity **D** can be done as a group activity during the next class period to ease students into the reading topic. Give students a minute or two to work on the checklist in **E**, then ask individual students, *Was essen und trinken Sie gewöhnlich zum Frühstück? Was essen Sie und trinken Sie selten / nicht gern?*

C. Formulieren Sie nun mit Hilfe der Aussagen in **A** und dem Fragebogen etwas über Ihre Essgewohnheiten.

BEISPIEL: Gesund essen ist mir wichtig. Ich esse nicht sehr oft Fastfood. Fleisch esse ich selten, aber ich esse täglich viel Gemüse und frisches Obst.

D. Vergleichen Sie Ihre Essgewohnheiten untereinander in kleinen Gruppen. Was haben Sie erfahren? Berichten Sie dann im Plenum darüber.

BEISPIEL: Stephanie isst viel Obst und Gemüse, aber Robert isst gesünder als sie. Er isst nie Fastfood und wenig Fleisch.

Auf dem deutschen Frühstückstisch findet man traditionell Brot und Brötchen mit Butter, Marmelade, Honig und Käse, eventuell auch Aufschnitt und ein gekochtes Ei. Cerealien wie Müsli gehören auch zum Frühstück. Zum Trinken gibt es Kaffee oder Tee und Fruchtsaft.

E. Was essen und trinken Sie gewöhnlich zum Frühstück? Kreuzen Sie an.

TRINKEN		ESSEN	
Kaffee		Müsli	
Tee		Cornflakes, Cerealien	
Milch		Brot, Brötchen oder Toast	
Saft		Pfannkuchen	
Wasser		Eier	
Cola		Speck, Schinken	
_____		Obst	
		_____	

A. Schauen Sie sich den Titel, die Untertitel und die Bilder im Text **Sage mir, was du isst …** an. Was ist das Thema?

B. Schauen Sie sich die Bilder der Frühstückstypen und die Untertitel jetzt etwas genauer an. Können Sie sich mit einem dieser Typen identifizieren? Finden Sie einen besonders sympathisch?

C. Was bedeuten die fettgedruckten (*boldfaced*) Ausdrücke?

1. „Sage mir, was du frühstückst und ich sage dir, wer du bist“. **behauptet** Professor Gebert.
   a. sagt
   b. fragt
   c. wiederholt

2. Am Wochenende **lassen** Studenten **das Frühstück** besonders gerne **unter den Tisch fallen.**
   a. (Die Studenten) fallen unter den Tisch.
   b. (Die Studenten) essen kein Frühstück.
   c. Das Frühstück fällt unter den Tisch.

3. Der Müsli-Raspler **macht sich viele Gedanken über das Essen.**
   a. denkt viel über das Essen nach
   b. hat kein Interesse am Essen
   c. arbeitet beim Essen

4. Für den Müsli-Raspler sind Studium und Job eher **Nebensache.**
   a. sehr wichtig   **b.** gleich wichtig   **c.** nicht sehr wichtig

5. Der Guck-zurück-Typ **verschlingt wahllos alles,** was er im Kühlschrank findet.
   a. kontrolliert alles   **b.** isst nicht alles   **c.** isst alles

6. Der Beifahrersitz-Frühstücker **kann sich** bei der Diplomarbeit (*thesis*) **nicht festlegen.**
   a. kann (die Diplomarbeit) nicht verstehen
   b. kann sich nicht engagieren
   c. interessiert sich nicht dafür

7. Der Espresso-Mann **stürzt** seinen morgendlichen **Kaffee hinunter.**
   a. lässt den Kaffee fallen
   b. kocht den Kaffee
   c. trinkt den Kaffee sehr schnell

SAGE MIR, WAS DU ISST ...
Was Das Frühstück Über Den Charakter Verrät

von Monika Hillemacher

Haben Sie schon wieder mal keine Zeit gehabt? Typisch! Nur etwa 60 Prozent der Studenten essen morgens Frühstück. Dabei kann man Uni-Stress viel besser mit einem Frühstück im Bauch verkraften°.   cope with

Essen und trinken am Morgen kann jeder. Ernährungsexperte
5 Gerhard Jahreis: „Jeder Mensch hat seinen ganz individuellen Rhythmus. Wichtig ist nicht, wann jemand frühstückt, sondern nur, dass und was er frühstückt."

Auf den Fitness-Speiseplan gehören Milch und Milchprodukte wie Trinkmilch, Joghurt und Käse, Müsli, frisches Obst, Vollkornbrot oder
10 -brötchen und ausreichend Getränke wie Kaffee, Tee, Saft oder Wasser. Käse, Quark° und Joghurt sind wahre Kraftpakete°. Und wer oft   fresh yogurt cheese / power packs
Vollmilch, Cerealien mit Milch oder Joghurtvarianten auf dem Tisch hat, bleibt schlanker. Frische Produkte sind besser als Multivitaminsaft oder Mineralstofftabletten.
15 Am Wochenende lassen Studenten das Frühstück besonders gerne unter den Tisch fallen. Es gibt dann manchmal einen Brunch mit Freunden und Familie.

„Sage mir, was du frühstückst und ich sage dir, wer du bist", behauptet Professor Gebert von der Universität Münster: „Der Charakter bestimmt
20 das Frühstück mit." Der Psychologe und Soziologe fragt Studenten regelmäßig nach ihren Frühstücksgewohnheiten. Allerdings schaut er in erster Linie Männern auf den Teller, weil sie –
25 anders als ihre Kommilitoninnen° – „Gewohn-   fellow (female) students
heitsmenschen° und somit berechenbarer° sind."   creatures of habit / more predictable
Das Resultat sind Professor Geberts (nicht ganz ernst gemeinte) Frühstückstypenklassen.

Der **Marmeladen-Mann** ist der Schwarm°   heartthrob
30 aller Kommilitoninnen: Seine Vorliebe für Erdbeermarmelade lässt ihn auf den ersten

Der Marmeladen-Mann

Blick etwas langweilig erscheinen. Einmal erobert°,
bleibt er seiner Herzensdame jedoch genau so treu
wie seiner Lieblingsmarmelade.

35   Der **Müsli-Raspler**° startet mit frisch gepresstem
O-Saft, biologisch – logisch. Macht sich viele
Gedanken über das Essen, die Umwelt°, das Leben
im Allgemeinen, grübelt° viel über dies und das.
Studium und Job eher Nebensache. Er verliert sich
40   oft in Luftschlössern°.

Der Beifahrersitz-Frühstücker

Der **Beifahrersitz-
Frühstücker**° isst und
trinkt im Auto, in der
Bahn, im Bus, auf dem
Rad, im Laufschritt.
Diese Spezies macht vieles schnell
nebeneinander°, fühlt sich spontan.
Spätestens im Examen drohen dann
Probleme. Dieser Typ kann sich bei der
Diplomarbeit nicht festlegen. Oft schiebt
er die Prüfung hinaus°.

Der Müsli-Raspler

Der **Guck-zurück-Typ**° verschlingt wahllos
alles, was er im Kühlschrank findet. Professor
Gebert nennt ihn ein Spiegelbild° der
modernen „Spontan- und
Spaß-Gesellschaft.“ Nicht
einmal für den Kauf von
Brot und Butter haben
„solche Chaoten° einen
Plan.“ Geschweige denn°
für ihr restliches Leben.
   Der **Espresso-
Mann** stürzt seinen
morgendlichen Kaffee
hinunter. Symbol für ein
„Leben auf der
Überholspur°. Er will alles erleben°. Schnell. Sofort. Langweilig ist es nie, dazu ist sein Leben viel
zu kurz.“

Der Espresso-Mann

Der Guck-zurück-Typ

conquered

cruncher

environment

ponders

castles in the sky

multitasking breakfaster

at the same time

schiebt … hinaus *postpones*
take-my-chances type

reflection

society

scatterbrains
Geschweige … *let alone*

fast lane / experience

Quelle: Monika Hillemacher; adaptiert aus: „Sage mir, was du isst …“, UNICUM,
April 2005. Illustrationen: © Sabine Kühn, www.sabinekuehn.de.

A. Überfliegen Sie den Text bis Zeile 28 und unterstreichen Sie
Schlüsselworte (*key words*) in jedem Absatz (*paragraph*), ohne Hilfe
eines Wörterbuches. Listen Sie dann mit Hilfe der Schlüsselworte die
wichtigen Informationen in jedem Absatz auf und formulieren Sie für
jeden Absatz einen Satz, der diese Informationen zusammenfasst
(*summarizes*).

B. Lesen Sie nun die humorvollen, „nicht ganz ernst gemeinten“ (*not
entirely serious*) Beschreibungen der Frühstückstypen etwas genauer.
Welche Qualitäten sehen Sie als positiv, welche als negativ?

	POSITIV	NEGATIV
Marmeladen-Mann	_____	_____
Müsli-Raspler	_____	_____
Beifahrersitz-Frühstücker	_____	_____
Guck-zurück-Typ	_____	_____
Espresso-Mann	_____	_____

C. Warum hat Professor Gebert von der Uni in Münster in erster Linie nur Männer nach ihren Frühstücksgewohnheiten befragt?

D. Frühstückstypen in der Klasse

1. Welcher Frühstückstyp sind Sie? Schreiben Sie zwei oder drei Sätze über Ihre Frühstücksgewohnheiten und berichten Sie im Plenum.

BEISPIEL: s1: Ich bin eine Marmeladen-Frau! Ich esse jeden Tag Frühstück! Ich esse aber nur Orangenmarmelade.

s2: Freitags bin ich ein Espresso-Mann und Montags ein Beifahrersitz-Frühstücker. Dienstags, mittwochs und donnerstags schlafe ich lange und esse kein Früstück.

2. Machen Sie nun eine Liste aller Frühstückstypen in Ihrer Klasse. Welcher Typ ist besonders populär? Haben Sie noch andere Typen in der Klasse, die im Text nicht vorgekommen (*appeared*) sind?

E. Ihre Meinung Professor Gebert behauptet: „Sage mir, was du frühstückst und ich sage dir, wer du bist. Der Charakter bestimmt das Frühstück mit." Stimmt das? Arbeiten Sie zu zweit. Suchen Sie ein oder zwei Argumente für oder gegen diese Behauptung. Was spricht für diese Kategorien? Was spricht gegen diese Kategorien? (Das muss auch nicht ganz ernst gemeint sein!)

BEISPIEL: Ich bin meistens eine Marmeladen-Frau (Orangenmarmelade, bitte!), aber manchmal esse ich, was der Müsli-Raspler isst. Ich bin aber wirklich keine Chaotin! Nicht alles stimmt für alle Leute.

Zu guter Letzt

Ein idealer Fitnessplan

Machen Sie einen idealen Fitnessplan für sich.

Schritt 1: Schreiben Sie eine Liste mit Fitnessaktivitäten, die Sie während der letzten Woche gemacht haben. Analysieren Sie die Liste:

- Sind Sie viel zu Fuß gegangen?
- Haben Sie Sport getrieben?
- Haben Sie sich zu wenig entspannt?
- Was sehen Sie als positiv, was als negativ?

Schreiben Sie nun eine Liste mit allem, was Sie während der letzten Woche gegessen haben. Analysieren Sie die Liste:

- Haben Sie gesund gegessen?
- Haben Sie zu viel Fastfood gegessen?

Schritt 2: Möchten Sie mehr für Ihre Gesundheit tun? Was ist der ideale Fitnessplan für Sie? Machen Sie nun mit Hilfe der Informationen, die Sie in **Schritt 1** gesammelt haben, einen idealen Fitnessplan für sich.

BEISPIEL: MEIN IDEALER FITNESSPLAN

SPORT TREIBEN	ESSEN UND TRINKEN	SONSTIGES
dreimal die Woche joggen	mehr Gemüse essen	weniger Fernsehen
_____	_____	_____
_____	_____	_____

Weiteres zum Thema Gesundheit finden Sie bei **Deutsch: Na klar!** im World-Wide-Web unter

Schritt 3: Tauschen Sie Ihre Listen und Fitnessplan mit einem Partner / einer Partnerin aus. Lesen Sie die Fitnesspläne und machen Sie dann einander einige Vorschläge (*suggestions*). Sie können sie entweder annehmen (*accept*) oder ablehnen (*reject*).

BEISPIEL: Enspanne dich öfter und geh zu Fuß zur Uni.

Schritt 4: Revidieren (*revise*) Sie nun Ihren Fitnessplan und machen Sie eventuell Korrekturen oder Änderungen (*changes*).

Wortschatz

Körperteile — Parts of the Body

der **Arm**, -e	arm
das **Auge**, -n	eye
der **Bauch**, ⁻e	stomach, belly
das **Bein**, -e	leg
die **Brust**, ⁻e	chest; breast
der **Ell(en)bogen**, -	elbow
der **Finger**, -	finger
der **Fuß**, ⁻e	foot
das **Gesicht**, -er	face
das **Haar**, -e	hair
der **Hals**, ⁻e	throat, neck
die **Hand**, ⁻e	hand
das **Kinn**, -e	chin
das **Knie**, -	knee
der **Kopf**, ⁻e	head
der **Mund**, ⁻er	mouth
der **Muskel**, -n	muscle
die **Nase**, -n	nose
das **Ohr**, -en	ear
der **Rücken**, -	back
die **Schulter**, -n	shoulder
die **Zehe**, -n	toe

Gesundheit und Fitness — Health and Fitness

der **Alkohol**	alcohol
die **Arbeit**, -en	work; assignment; paper
der **Arzt**, ⁻e / die **Ärztin**, -nen	physician, doctor
die **Biolebensmittel** (*pl.*)	organic foods
die **Erkältung**, -en	cold
das **Fieber**	fever
die **Fitness**	fitness
die **Gesundheit**	health
die **Grippe**	flu
der **Husten**	coughing, cough
der **Krankenpfleger**, / die **Krankenschwester**, -n	nurse
der **Kräutertee**	herbal tea
die **Luft**, ⁻e	air
der **Rat**	advice
die **Schmerzen** (*pl.*)	pains
die **Halsschmerzen**	sore throat
die **Kopfschmerzen**	headache
der **Schnupfen**	nasal congestion; head cold
die **Sprechstunde**, -n	office hours
der **Stress**	stress
der **Termin**, -e	appointment

Verben — Verbs

ab•geben (gibt ab), abgegeben	to drop off, give to
achten auf (+ *acc.*)	to pay attention to
sich **an•ziehen**, angezogen	to get dressed
sich **aus•ziehen**, ausgezogen	to get undressed
sich **beeilen**	to hurry up
sich **duschen**	to shower
sich **entspannen**	to relax
sich **erholen**	to get well, recover

sich erkälten	to catch a cold
sich fit halten (hält), gehalten	to keep fit, in shape
sich (hin•)legen	to lie down
sich (hin•)setzen	to sit down
sich informieren (über)	to inform oneself (about)
sich kämmen	to comb (one's hair)
sich rasieren	to shave
rauchen	to smoke
schlucken	to swallow
sich strecken	to stretch
tun, getan	to do
sich verletzen	to injure oneself
verschreiben, verschrieben	to prescribe
versuchen	to try, attempt
sich waschen (wäscht), gewaschen	to wash oneself
weh•tun, wehgetan (+ dat.)	to hurt
Das tut mir weh.	That hurts.
sich (wohl) fühlen	to feel (well)
sich die Zähne putzen	to brush one's teeth

Adjektive und Adverbien

Adjectives and Adverbs

ab und zu	now and then, occasionally
anstrengend	tiring, strenuous
besonders	especially
deprimiert	depressed
deshalb	therefore
entweder … oder	either … or
fast	almost
fit	fit, in shape
gesund	healthy, healthful, well

gleich	immediately
hundsmiserabel (coll.)	sick as a dog
kaum	hardly, scarcely
krank	sick, ill
manchmal	sometimes
meistens	mostly
mindestens	at least
müde	tired
regelmäßig	regular(ly)
schlapp	weak, worn out
sogar	even
verrückt	crazy
wenig	little, few

Unterordnende Konjunktionen

Subordinating Conjunctions

dass	that
ob	whether
weil	because
wenn	if, when

Sonstiges

Other

d.h. (= das heißt)	that is, i.e.
Das macht nichts.	That doesn't matter.
Gute Besserung!	Get well soon!
klingen	to sound
Du klingst so deprimiert.	You sound so depressed.
Mir ist schlecht.	I'm sick to my stomach.
Nichts zu danken.	No thanks necessary; Don't mention it.
So ein Pech!	What a shame! (What bad luck!)
Urlaub machen	to go on vacation
Was fehlt Ihnen/dir?	What's the matter?
zu Fuß gehen	to go on foot, to walk

DAS KANN ICH NUN!

1. Nennen Sie sechs Körperteile mit Artikel und Plural.

2. Beschreiben Sie Ihre Morgenroutine. Bilden Sie mindestens drei Sätze mit reflexiven Verben.

3. Sie telefonieren mit einem Freund. Er klingt krank, kann kaum sprechen und hustet. Was fragen Sie ihn? Was empfehlen Sie ihm? Was wünschen Sie ihm?

4. Was machen Sie, wenn Sie eine Erkältung haben?

   Wenn ich eine Erkältung habe, …

5. Sie gehen zum Arzt, weil Sie sich hundsmiserabel fühlen. Der Arzt fragt: „Was fehlt Ihnen denn?" Was sagen Sie?

6. Was tun Sie für Fitness und Gesundheit? (Nennen Sie drei Dinge.) Wenn Sie nichts tun, sagen Sie bitte, warum Sie nichts tun.

7. Sie haben sich erkältet, aber Sie müssen unbedingt zur Arbeit. Sie reden mit einem Freund / einer Freundin über diese Situation. Was sagen Sie zu ihm/ihr?

   a. Ich weiß nicht, ob …   **b.** Ich kann heute nicht zu Hause bleiben, weil …   **c.** Ich glaube nicht, dass …

In der Stadt

Weihnachtslichter am
Kohlmarkt in Wien

In diesem Kapitel

- **Themen:** Hotel and lodging, places in the city, asking for and giving directions
- **Grammatik:** Genitive case, attributive adjectives
- **Kultur:** Services of tourist information offices, Wittenberg history
- **Lesen:** „Die Gitarre des Herrn Hatunoglu" (Heinrich Hannover)

Videoclips
Hier gefällt es mir!

Alles klar?

A. Dresden liegt im Bundesland Sachsen südlich von Berlin an der Elbe. Die Residenzstadt feierte 2006 ihr 800-jähriges Jubiläum. Es gibt viele Sehenswürdigkeiten (*tourist attractions*) in und um die Stadt. Für Jugendliche gibt es in Dresden besonders viel zu erleben.

Dresden.

Junges Dresden:
Freizeit, Unterhaltung, Szene

Dresden hat viele Facetten[1]: weltberühmte Museen und Sehenswürdigkeiten, eine romantische Elblandschaft[2], sächsische Gemütlichkeit und eine bunte Szenekultur. Ein Abend in Dresden muss nicht immer Oper, Konzert oder Theater bedeuten. Wer außerdem Lust auf einen Kneipenbummel[3] hat, kommt in der Dresdner Neustadt voll auf seine Kosten[4]. In der Hauptstraße, der Rähnitzgasse und der Königstraße gibt es Restaurants unterschiedlichster Couleur. Internationale und sächsische[5] Küche findet man auch rings um den Albertplatz. Von hier aus geht's die Alaunstraße entlang, wo sich urige[6] Szenekneipen und internationale Spezialitätenrestaurants abwechseln. Neben den individuellen Möglichkeiten der aktiven Erholung im Grünen an Dresdens Elbufern oder im Großen Garten finden Sie vielfältige[7] Angebote in den Erlebnisbädern oder den Sport- und Mehrzweckhallen. Für Skater empfiehlt sich in Dresden das Nachtskaten (von April bis Oktober): Jeden Freitag um 21 Uhr starten ca. 3000 Fans des Sports zu einer nächtlichen, 20 Kilometer langen Tour durch Dresden. Günstige Übernachtungsmöglichkeiten finden Sie in Dresdens Jugendherbergen[8] und Hostels.

---

[1]*dimensions* [2]*Elbe river landscape* [3]*pub crawl* [4]*kommt voll auf seine Kosten finds everything he/she needs* [5]*Saxon* [6]*ancient* [7]*multifaceted* [8]*youth hostels*

Suchen Sie die fehlenden Informationen im Text oben.

1. Die _____ in Dresden sind weltberühmt.
2. Wenn man Kultur erleben möchte, kann man abends in die _____, ins _____ oder ins _____ gehen. Wenn man das nicht will, kann man auch in der Dresdner Neustadt einen _____ machen.
3. Wenn man essen will, findet man _____ und _____ Küche rings um den Albertplatz in Dresden.
4. Im Grünen kann man sich an Dresdens _____ oder im _____ _____ erholen.
5. Für Skatingfans gibt es vom April bis Oktober das _____.
6. In Dresden kann man in _____ und in _____ übernachten.

Suchen Sie mehr Informationen über Dresden. Was würden Sie gern dort machen?

B. Sie machen eine Stadtführung (*guided tour*) durch Dresden. Der Fremdenführer (*tour guide*) erzählt einige Tatsachen über die Stadt. Hören Sie zu und kreuzen Sie an, was stimmt und was nicht stimmt.

Hier klicken!

Weiteres zum Thema Dresden finden Sie bei **Deutsch: Na klar!** im World-Wide-Web unter www.mhhe.com/dnk5.

	DAS STIMMT	DAS STIMMT NICHT
1. Heute leben etwa 500 000 Einwohner in Dresden.	☒	☐
2. Die erste deutsche Lokomotive kommt aus Dresden.	☒	☐
3. Bierdeckel, Kaffeefilter und Shampoo hat man in Dresden erfunden.	☐	☒
4. In Dresden hat Richard Wagner die erste deutsche Oper geschrieben.	☐	☒
5. Die Stadt bietet viel Kultur an: Musik, Museen und Theater.	☒	☐
6. Dresden ist die europäische Hauptstadt des Films.	☐	☒

Wörter im Kontext

THEMA 1: Unterkunft[0] online buchen

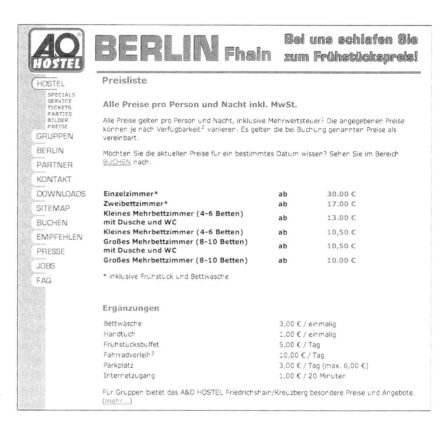

A&O HOSTEL BERLIN Fhain

Bei uns schlafen Sie zum Frühstückspreis!

Preisliste

HOSTEL
SPECIALS
SERVICE
TICKETS
PARTIES
BILDER
PREISE
GRUPPEN
BERLIN
PARTNER
KONTAKT
DOWNLOADS
SITEMAP
BUCHEN
EMPFEHLEN
PRESSE
JOBS
FAQ

Alle Preise pro Person und Nacht inkl. MwSt.

Alle Preise gelten pro Person und Nacht, inklusive Mehrwertsteuer.[1] Die angegebenen Preise können je nach Verfügbarkeit[2] variieren. Es gelten die bei Buchung genannten Preise als vereinbart.

Möchten Sie die aktuellen Preise für ein bestimmtes Datum wissen? Sehen Sie im Bereich BUCHEN nach.

Einzelzimmer*	ab	30.00 €
Zweibettzimmer*	ab	17.00 €
Kleines Mehrbettzimmer (4-6 Betten) mit Dusche und WC	ab	13.00 €
Kleines Mehrbettzimmer (4-6 Betten)	ab	10,50 €
Großes Mehrbettzimmer (8-10 Betten) mit Dusche und WC	ab	10,50 €
Großes Mehrbettzimmer (8-10 Betten)	ab	10.00 €

* inklusive Frühstück und Bettwäsche

Ergänzungen

Bettwäsche	3,00 € / einmalig
Handtuch	1,00 € / einmalig
Frühstücksbuffet	5,00 € / Tag
Fahrradverleih[3]	10,00 € / Tag
Parkplatz	3,00 € / Tag (max. 6,00 €)
Internetzugang	1,00 € / 20 Minuten

Für Gruppen bietet das A&O HOSTEL Friedrichshain/Kreuzberg besondere Preise und Angebote. (mehr...)

[1]value-added tax [2]availability [3]bicycle rental

Bad ramsach oase der erholung und entspannung

home | contact | impressum & links

Hotel & Preise
Aktuelle[1] Angebote
Restaurant
Wohlbefinden
Kuren im Ferienstil
Seminar-Oase
"Top of Ramsach" live
Stellenangebote
Aktuell
Gästebuch

Preise & Gesamt-Angebot (PDF)

Hotel & Preise

Preise 2006

Alle Zimmer ausgestattet[2] mit: Dusche/WC, Balkon, Fohn, Radio, Satelliten-TV, Direktwahltelefon, Internetanschluss (analog), Kühlschrank und Bademantel.
Lassen Sie sich verwöhnen!

Preise pro Zimmer ab 3 Nächten in CHF[3] inkl. Mehrwertsteuer:

Bergseite (Sonnseite)	1. Stock (EZ / DZ)	2. Stock (EZ / DZ)	3/4 Stock (EZ /DZ)
Vollpension	163.00 / 260.00	173.00 / 280.00	183.00 / 300.00
Halbpension	143.00 / 220.00	153.00 / 240.00	163.00 / 260.00
Zi. + Frühstück	108.00 / 150.00	118.00 / 170.00	128.00 / 190.00
Talseite[4] (Aussichtsseite)[5]	1. Stock (EZ / DZ)	2. Stock (EZ / DZ)	3/4 Stock (EZ /DZ)
Vollpension	168.00 / 270.00	178.00 / 290.00	188.00 / 310.00
Halbpension	148.00 / 230.00	158.00 / 250.00	168.00 / 270.00
Zi. + Frühstück	113.00 / 160.00	123.00 / 180.00	133.00 / 200.00

Preise pro Zimmer 1 und 2 Nächte in CHF inkl. Mehrwertsteuer:

1 und 2 Nächte	1. Stock (EZ / DZ)	2. Stock (EZ / DZ)	3/4 Stock (EZ /DZ)
Zi. + Frühstück Hotel	115.00 / 170.00	135.00 / 200.00	135.00 / 200.00

Zimmerservice: 5.00 pro Person und Mahlzeit (ausser Frühstück)

[1]current [2]furnished [3](abbreviation for Swiss francs) [4]valley side [5]view side

Bei Hotelwerbungen findet man oft folgende Bezeichnungen:

Vollpension	*all meals included*
Halbpension	*one meal besides breakfast included*
Pauschalangebot	*package offer*

Die folgenden Abkürzungen sind auch typisch:

EZ	= **das Einzelzimmer**	*single room*
DZ	= **das Doppelzimmer**	*double room*
DU	= **die Dusche**	*shower*
WC	= **die Toilette** (Engl. *water closet*)	*toilet*
inkl.	= **inklusive**	*included, including*

Unterkunft online buchen.
Suggestion: Have students work in groups. Each group chooses a type of lodging and then decides what factors are most important.

A. Was ist Ihnen wichtig, wenn Sie in einem **Hotel,** einer **Pension** oder einer **Jugendherberge übernachten** wollen? Die **Unterkunft** sollte …

☐ **in der Nähe** des **Bahnhofs** liegen.
☐ in der **Innenstadt** (im **Zentrum**) liegen.
☐ ein Restaurant im Haus haben.
☐ Kabelfernsehen oder Radio haben.
☐ in ruhiger **Lage** sein.
☐ Bad/Dusche/WC im Zimmer haben.
☐ Frühstück **im Preis enthalten.**
☐ einen **Parkplatz** in der Nähe haben.

☐ Hunde **erlauben.**
☐ Telefon im Zimmer haben.
☐ im Bad einen **Föhn** haben.
☐ preiswert sein.
☐ **günstig liegen** (z.B. im Zentrum).
☐ einen **Kühlschrank** im Zimmer haben.
☐ **Internetzugang** haben.
☐ in einer **Fußgängerzone** liegen.
☐ **Bettwäsche** haben.

B. **Daniel in Berlin.** Daniel war drei Tage in Berlin. Er wollte nicht viel Geld für ___Unterkunft___¹ (*lodging*) ausgeben, aber sie sollte ___günstig___ ___liegen___² (*be conveniently located*), am besten in der ___Innenstadt___³ (*inner city*). Er hat dort auch eine preiswerte Unterkunft in einer ___Jugendherberge___⁴ (*youth hostel*) gefunden: ein ___Einzelzimmer___⁵ (*single room*) mit WC und ___Dusche___⁶ (*shower*). ___Frühstück___⁷ (*breakfast*) und ___Bettwäsche___⁸ (*linens*) waren im Preis enthalten. Das Zimmer hatte kein Telefon und auch keinen ___Internetzugang___⁹ (*Internet access*). Dafür musste man extra bezahlen.

C. **Frau Heilmann macht Kurzurlaub.** Frau Heilmann wollte sich ein paar Tage entspannen und hat in Bad Ramsach in der Schweiz Kurzurlaub gemacht. Das Hotel war in ruhiger ___Lage___¹⁰ (*location*). Sie hatte ein ___Einzelzimmer___¹¹ (*single room*) mit Vollpension auf der Talseite des Hotels im zweiten ___Stock___¹² (*floor*). Das Zimmer war etwas teuer – es hat 178 CHF pro Nacht gekostet, aber es war sehr schön ausgestattet mit Telefon, WC, ___Dusche___¹³ (*shower*) und einem ___Kühlschrank___¹⁴ (*refrigerator*) und es hatte auch einen Balkon mit Blick auf das schöne Tal.

Neue Wörter

die Pension   bed and breakfast
die Jugendherberge   youth hostel
übernachten   to stay overnight
die Unterkunft   lodging
in der Nähe   near
der Bahnhof   train station
das Zentrum   town center
die Lage   location
im Preis enthalten   include in the price
erlauben   allow
der Föhn   hair dryer
günstig liegen   be conveniently located
der Kühlschrank   refrigerator
der Internetzugang   Internet access
die Fußgängerzone   pedestrian zone
die Bettwäsche   linens

Was stimmt? Markieren Sie die richtigen Antworten.

ERSTES TELEFONGESPRÄCH

1. Der Gast braucht ein …
   a. Einzelzimmer.
   b. Doppelzimmer.

2. Er braucht das Zimmer für …
   a. eine Nacht.
   b. mehrere (several) Nächte.

3. Das Hotel hat ein Zimmer frei …
   a. ohne Bad.
   b. mit Bad.

4. Frühstück ist im Preis …
   a. nicht enthalten.
   b. enthalten.

5. Der Gast …
   a. muss ein anderes Hotel finden.
   b. nimmt das Zimmer.

ZWEITES TELEFONGESPRÄCH

1. Das Jugendgästehaus hat …
   a. nur Doppelzimmer.
   b. nur Mehrbettzimmer.

2. Das Haus ist …
   a. ganz neu.
   b. sehr alt.

3. Die Übernachtung kostet …
   a. mehr als 20 Euro.
   b. weniger als 20 Euro.

4. Jedes Zimmer hat …
   a. WC and Dusche.
   b. fünf Betten.

5. Das Gästehaus liegt …
   a. auf dem Lande.
   b. in der Nähe der Innenstadt.

KULTURTIPP

„Tourist i" (for information) ist für viele Besucher in deutschen Städten der erste Stopp. Meist liegt er am Hauptbahnhof oder an einem anderen zentralen Ort. Hier können Touristen viel Wissenswertes über die neue Stadt erfahren. Sie können zum Beispiel Empfehlungen für Restaurants bekommen, eine Stadtrundfahrt buchen und Prospekte (brochures) von der Stadt erhalten. Hier gibt es auch eine Zimmervermittlung. Da kann der Besucher ein Zimmer in einem Hotel oder einer Pension finden.

Aktivität 2 Unterkunft in Berlin

Sie reisen mit Freunden und suchen eine Unterkunft in Berlin. Schauen Sie sich die Webseite „AO Hostel" im **Thema 1** genau an und überlegen Sie sich, in was für einem Zimmer Sie übernachten wollen. Gebrauchen Sie die folgenden Ausdrücke.

BEISPIEL: Ich schlage vor, wir übernachten in einem Mehrbettzimmer. Das ist nicht so teuer.

Ich schlage vor, …

Mir gefällt … besser.

Ich brauche … im Zimmer.

… ist mir zu teuer.

THEMA 2: Im Hotel

Teil A: *Herr Thompson **kommt** im Hotel „Mecklenheide" **an**. Zuerst muss er **sich anmelden**.*

REZEPTION: Guten Abend.

GAST: Guten Abend. Ich habe ein Zimmer für zwei Nächte bestellt.

REZEPTION: **Auf welchen Namen,** bitte?

GAST: Thompson.

REZEPTION: Ah, ja. Herr Thompson. Ein Einzelzimmer mit Bad. **Würden Sie** bitte das **Anmeldeformular ausfüllen**?

GAST: Möchten Sie auch meinen **Reisepass** sehen?

REZEPTION: Nein, das ist nicht nötig. Ihr Zimmer liegt im ersten **Stock**, Zimmer 21. Hier ist **der Schlüssel.** Der **Aufzug** ist hier **rechts.**

GAST: Danke.

REZEPTION: Wir bringen Ihr **Gepäck** aufs Zimmer. Haben Sie nur den einen Koffer?

GAST: Ja … **Übrigens,** wann gibt es morgens Frühstück?

REZEPTION: Zwischen 7 und 10 Uhr im **Frühstücksraum** hier gleich **links** im Erdgeschoss.

GAST: Danke sehr.

REZEPTION: Bitte sehr. Ich wünsche Ihnen einen **angenehmen Aufenthalt.**

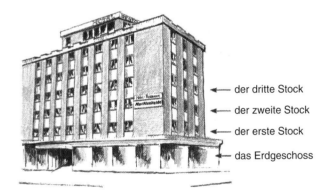

- ← der dritte Stock
- ← der zweite Stock
- ← der erste Stock
- ← das Erdgeschoss

Teil B: *Herr Thompson ruft die **Rezeption** an und **beschwert sich**, weil der Fernseher nicht **funktioniert**.*

REZEPTION: Rezeption.

THOMPSON: Guten Abend. Der Fernseher in meinem Zimmer ist **kaputt.** Es gibt kein Bild, keinen Ton, nichts.

REZEPTION: **Das tut mir leid,** Herr Thompson. Ich schicke **sofort** jemand auf Ihr Zimmer. Wenn er den **Apparat** nicht gleich **reparieren** kann, bringen wir Ihnen einen anderen.

THOMPSON: Vielen Dank. **Auf Wiederhören.**

REZEPTION: Auf Wiederhören.

Neue Wörter

Teil A

kommt … an (ankommen) arrives
zuerst first
sich anmelden register, check in
würden Sie … ausfüllen would you fill out …
das Anmeldeformular registration form
der Reisepass passport
der Schlüssel key
der Aufzug elevator
rechts to the right
das Gepäck luggage
übrigens by the way
links to the left
angenehm pleasant
der Aufenthalt stay

Teil B

die Rezeption reception desk
beschwert sich (sich beschweren) complains
kaputt broken
Das tut mir leid. I'm sorry.
sofort immediately
der Apparat TV set
reparieren repair
auf Wiederhören good-bye (*on the phone*)

Im Hotel. Note: This dialogue presents a typical situation that a visitor might encounter at a hotel. New vocabulary and expressions can be guessed from the context. **Suggestion:** Play the dialogue once, for students to get the gist. Ask a few basic questions: *Wer sind die Sprecher? Wie heißt der Gast? Wie lange möchte er bleiben?* Then ask students to scan the text once. Help them figure out the meaning of *Würden Sie bitte das Anmeldeformular ausfüllen?* by asking *Was muss ein Gast im Hotel machen, bevor er sein Zimmer bekommt?* To figure out the meaning of *im ersten Stock* and *Erdgeschoss,* refer to the drawing. *Erster Stock* corresponds to second floor; *zweiter Stock* is the third floor; *Erdgeschoss* is either the ground floor or the first floor.

Point out: *Würden Sie … ausfüllen* corresponds to the English "Would you fill out . . . ," used for polite requests.

Wörter im Kontext   **265**

Bilden Sie Sätze!

1. _c_ Ich habe ein Einzelzimmer ...
2. ___ Würden Sie bitte das Anmeldeformular ...
3. ___ Ihr Zimmer liegt ...
4. ___ Wir bringen Ihr Gepäck ...
5. ___ Ich wünsche Ihnen ...
6. ___ Der Fernseher in meinem Zimmer ...

a. ist kaputt.
b. bezahlen?
c. bestellt.
d. einen angenehmen Aufenthalt.
e. ausfüllen?
f. aufs Zimmer.
g. im ersten Stock.

Aktivität 3 Im Hotel Mecklenheide

Was passiert? Ergänzen Sie!

1. Herr Thompson bekommt ein _____ mit Bad im ersten _____.
2. Er muss das Anmeldeformular _____.
3. Seinen _____ muss er aber nicht vorzeigen.
4. Er bekommt den _____ zum Zimmer und nimmt den _____ in den ersten Stock.
5. Jemand vom Hotelpersonal bringt sein _____ aufs Zimmer.
6. Er kann zwischen 7 und 10 Uhr im Frühstücksraum im _____ frühstücken.
7. Herr Thompson _____ sich, weil der Fernseher in seinem Zimmer _____ ist.
8. Jemand vom Hotelpersonal soll den Fernseher _____.

Aktivität 4 Die Geschichte von Herrn Thompson

Sehen Sie sich die Bilder von Herrn Thompson im Hotel an. Schreiben Sie für jedes Bild einen Satz und erzählen Sie die Geschichte von Herrn Thompson.

Weiteres zum Thema Hotel und Unterkunft finden Sie bei **Deutsch: Na klar!** im World-Wide-Web unter

1.

2.

3.

4.

5.

6.

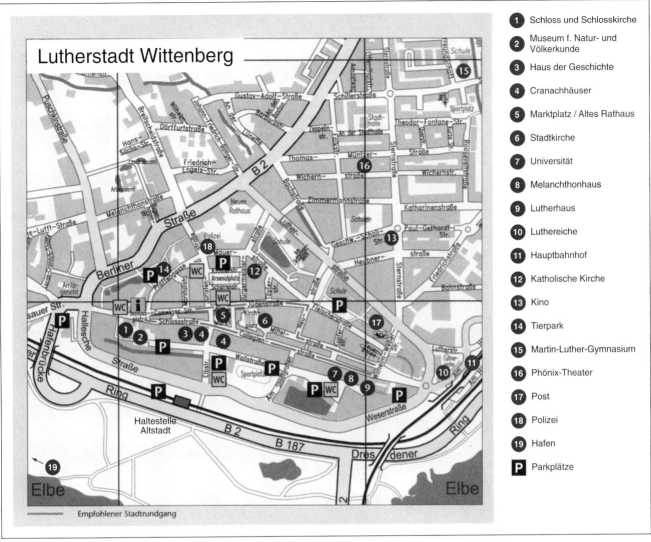

Lutherstadt Wittenberg

1 Schloss und Schlosskirche
2 Museum f. Natur- und Völkerkunde
3 Haus der Geschichte
4 Cranachhäuser
5 Marktplatz / Altes Rathaus
6 Stadtkirche
7 Universität
8 Melanchthonhaus
9 Lutherhaus
10 Luthereiche
11 Hauptbahnhof
12 Katholische Kirche
13 Kino
14 Tierpark
15 Martin-Luther-Gymnasium
16 Phönix-Theater
17 Post
18 Polizei
19 Hafen
P Parkplätze

Empfohlener Stadtrundgang

A. Verbinden Sie das deutsche Wort mit dem Englischen.

1. __j__ die **Kirche**
2. __c__ das **Museum**
3. __f__ die **Post**
4. __a__ die **Bank**
5. __e__ die **Polizei**
6. __h__ der **Hafen**
7. __d__ das **Schloss**
8. __g__ die **Haltestelle**
9. __i__ der **Tierpark**
10. __b__ das **Rathaus**

a. bank
b. city hall
c. museum
d. castle
e. police
f. post office
g. stop/station (*bus, train, etc.*)
h. harbor
i. zoo
j. church

Neue Wörter

nach dem Weg fragen   to ask for directions
Entschuldigung   excuse me
gehen Sie ... entlang (entlanggehen)   go along
biegen Sie ... ein (einbiegen)   turn
immer geradeaus   straight ahead
bis zur   as far as, up to
gegenüber vom   across from the
weit   far
ungefähr   about, approximately

*Ein **Tourist** steht in Wittenberg vor der Stadtkirche und fragt nach dem Weg.*

TOURIST: **Entschuldigung**, wie komme ich am besten zum Lutherhaus?

PASSANT: **Gehen Sie** hier die Mittelstraße **entlang**. Dann **biegen Sie** rechts in die Wilhelm-Weber Straße **ein**. Gehen Sie **immer geradeaus bis zur** Collegienstraße. Da finden Sie das Lutherhaus. Es liegt **gegenüber vom** Restaurant „Am Lutherhaus".

TOURIST: Ist es **weit** von hier?

PASSANT: Nein. **Ungefähr** 15 Minuten zu Fuß.

B.   Sie stehen am alten Markt am Rathaus und kennen Wittenberg jetzt sehr gut. Einige Touristen fragen Sie nach dem Weg.

TOURIST 1:   Wie komme ich am besten zum Haus der Geschichte?

SIE: _____ _____ *(go along)* die Elbstraße _____. Dann _____ _____ *(turn)* rechts _____. Das Haus der Geschichte ist auf der linken Seite.

TOURIST 2:   Sind das Schloss und die Schlosskirche _____ *(far)* von hier?

SIE: Nein, _____ *(about)* zehn Minuten zu Fuß. Gehen Sie die Schlossstraße _____ _____ *(straight ahead)*. Dann sehen Sie das Schloss und die Schlosskirche.

Aktivität 9   Drei Touristen

Drei Leute fragen nach dem Weg. Wohin wollen sie? Wie kommen sie dahin?

	DIALOG 1	DIALOG 2	DIALOG 3
Wohin man gehen will			
Wie man dahin kommt			

Aktivität 6 Hin und her: In einer fremden° Stadt

unfamiliar

Sie sind in einer fremden Stadt. Fragen Sie nach dem Weg. Benutzen Sie die Tabelle.

BEISPIEL: s1: Ist das Landesmuseum weit von hier?
s2: Es ist sechs Kilometer von hier, bei der Universität.
s1: Wie komme ich am besten dahin?
s2: Nehmen Sie die Buslinie 7, am Rathaus.

WOHIN?	WIE WEIT?	WO?	WIE?
Landesmuseum	6 km	bei der Universität	Buslinie 7, am Rathaus
Bahnhof	15 Minuten	im Zentrum	mit dem Taxi
Post	nicht weit	in der Nähe vom Bahnhof	zu Fuß
Schloss	15 km	außerhalb der Stadt	mit dem Auto
Opernhaus	ganz in der Nähe	rechts um die Ecke	zu Fuß, die Poststraße entlang

Aktivität 7 In Wittenberg

Schauen Sie sich den Stadtplan von Wittenberg im **Thema 3** an und fragen Sie jemand im Kurs, wie Sie am besten an einen bestimmten Ort kommen.

BEISPIEL: Sie stehen am Haus der Geschichte (Nummer 3 im Stadtplan). →
s1: Entschuldigung, wie komme ich am besten zum Markt?
s2: Geh geradeaus bis zur Elbstraße. Bieg dann links ein. Der Markt ist auf der rechten Seite gleich an der Ecke.

SIE STEHEN ...

am Haus der Geschichte
vor der katholischen Kirche
am Schloss
am Tierpark
vor der Stadtkirche
vor dem Kino
am Hauptbahnhof
vor dem alten Rathaus
am Markt

SIE WOLLEN ...

ins Kino
zum Schloss
zum alten Rathaus
zum Markt
zur Stadtkirche
zum Hauptbahnhof
in den Tierpark

REDEMITTEL

Entschuldigung, wie komme ich am besten zum/zur _____?
Wie weit ist es bis zum/zur _____?
immer geradeaus
bis zur Kreuzung/Ampel
Geh die _____-straße entlang.
Bieg links/rechts in die _____ -straße ein.
gleich an der Ecke / um die Ecke
auf der rechten/linken Seite
Es ist zehn Minuten zu Fuß.

Aktivität 7. This activity is designed for flexibility, but you may need to provide more structure. Students first agree on a starting location in the left column: *Wo sind wir jetzt?* S1 then decides where he/she wants to go and formulates the initial question.

Siehe *Attributive Adjectives*, S. 274.

Wittenberg: Ein Blick in die Geschichte

1180   erste urkundliche Erwähnung (*mention*) von Wittenberg

1502   Gründung der Wittenberger Universität

1508   Martin Luther kommt nach Wittenberg. Er wird Theologieprofessor.

1517   Luther veröffentlicht (*publishes*) seine 95 Thesen an der Tür der Schlosskirche. Die Reformation beginnt.

1537   Lucas Cranach, ein berühmter Maler der Reformation, wird Bürgermeister der Stadt.

Martin-Luther-Denkmal am Markt

1618–1648   der dreißigjährige Krieg: Wittenberg erleidet (*suffers*) Schäden.

1817   Schließung der Wittenberger Universität

Das Lutherhaus in der Collegienstraße

1883   Eröffnung des Reformationsmuseums „Lutherhaus"

1994   Die Universität wird wieder belebt (*revived*).

1996   Das Lutherhaus, das Melanchthonhaus und die Stadt- und Schlosskirche werden Teil des Weltkulturerbes (*world cultural heritage*) der UNESCO.

Quelle: www.wittenberg.de (adaptiert)

Fragen Sie nach dem Weg in Ihrer Stadt oder auf Ihrem Campus. Wählen Sie passende Fragen und Antworten aus jeder Spalte (*column*).

BEISPIEL: s1: Entschuldigung, wo ist hier die Post?
              s2: Da nehmen Sie am besten den Bus.
              s1: Wo ist die Haltestelle?
              s2: Gleich da drüben an der Kreuzung.

FRAGEN	ANTWORTEN
Wie kommt man hier zum Supermarkt / zur Bibliothek / zur Sporthalle?	immer geradeaus
	bis zur Ampel
	nächste Kreuzung rechts/links
Wie weit ist es bis ins Zentrum?	Da nehmen Sie am besten _____ (den Bus, z.B. Linie 8).
Entschuldigung, wo ist hier die Post (Bank, Mensa)?	gleich da drüben / gleich an der Ecke
Wo ist die Haltestelle? ??	fünf Minuten zu Fuß ??

Grammatik im Kontext

The Genitive Case°

The genitive case typically indicates ownership, a relationship, or the characteristics of another noun.

Der Wagen **meines Vaters** steht auf dem Parkplatz.	*My father's car is in the parking lot.*
Die Lage **des Hotels** ist günstig.	*The location of the hotel is convenient.*
Das Hotel liegt im Zentrum **der Stadt.**	*The hotel is located in the center of town.*

Der Genitiv

The Genitive Case. Suggestion: Remind students that they have used the genitive case with proper names since **Kapitel 3**, e.g., *Das ist Franks Schwester. Das ist Familie Schneiders Haus.*

Nouns in the Genitive Case. Suggestion: For quick practice of genitive forms, do a substitution exercise. *Wo liegt deine Wohnung? In der Nähe … (Universität, Bahnhof,*

SINGULAR			PLURAL
Masculine	*Neuter*	*Feminine*	*All Genders*
des eines unseres dieses } Vaters / Gastes *but:* Studenten	des eines unseres dieses } Hotels	der einer unserer dieser } Stadt	der unserer dieser } Gäste

Note:

- Most masculine and neuter nouns add **-s** in the singular genitive case.

  die Lage dieses Hotel**s**   *the location of this hotel*

- Masculine and neuter nouns of one syllable often add **-es.**

  die Unterschrift des Gast**es**   *the guest's signature*

- Masculine nouns that add **-n** or **-en** in the dative and the accusative also add **-n** or **-en** in the genitive case.

  das Gepäck des Student**en**   *the student's luggage*

- A noun in the genitive always follows the noun it modifies.

In spoken German, the genitive case is often replaced by the preposition **von** and the dative case.

  in der Nähe **vom Bahnhof**   *in the vicinity of the railroad station*

To ask for the owner of something, use the interrogative pronoun **wessen** (*whose*).

Wessen Koffer ist das?	*Whose suitcase is that?*
Wessen Unterschrift ist das?	*Whose signature is that?*

Park, Theater, Post, Einkaufszentrum, Innenstadt). Wie ist die Telefonnummer … (Freund, Freundin, Eltern, Familie, Polizei, Auskunft, Hotel, Reisebüro)?

Masculine nouns that add -n or -en. Suggestion: Review other nouns that fall into this category: *der Kunde, der Tourist, der Mensch.* For instance, *die Unterschrift des Kunden, des Touristen.*

Proper Names in the Genitive: Point Out: A genitive -s is added to names regardless of the gender of the person. If a name already ends in -s, you will see an apostrophe following the final -s to indicate that a genitive -s is implied. In modern German this is sometimes avoided by using the preposition **von** with names ending in -z or -ss (*das Haus von Familie Schmitz, der Wagen von Hans*). Genitive endings are also added to both parts of a masculine proper name: *Herrn Kramers Koffer,* but *Frau Kramers Tasche.*

Proper Names in the Genitive

Martinas Koffer	*Martina's suitcase*
Herrn Kramers Reisepass	*Mr. Kramer's passport*
Hessen: das Herz **Deutschlands**	*Hesse: the heart of Germany*

Note:

- A proper name in the genitive normally precedes the noun it modifies.
- Proper names in the genitive add **-s** without an apostrophe, in contrast to English.
- The name of a country or a region in the genitive case may precede or follow the noun it modifies.

ANALYSE

- Identify the genitive expressions in the illustrations.
- What nouns are modified by the genitive attributes?
- Give appropriate English translations of these phrases.

VERANSTALTUNGEN

Samstag. 06. August 2005

20.00 Uhr   Die Nacht der Vampire
Bergtheater Thale

August

01

Wappen der Stadt Köln

Vienna

Übung 1   Was für eine Stadt ist Wien?

Sie sind gerade in Wien. Beschreiben Sie die Stadt.

BEISPIEL: Wien ist eine Stadt der Tradition.

Wien ist eine Stadt …

die Kaffeehäuser	die Schlösser
das Theater	die Architektur
die Musik	die Kirchen
die Museen	der Walzer (*waltz*)

Übung 2   Wo ist Ihr Hotel?

Beschreiben Sie die Lage Ihres Hotels in Wien.

BEISPIEL: Unser Hotel liegt in der Nähe eines Cafés.

Unser Hotel liegt in der Nähe …

ein Park	die Ringstraße
ein Schloss	die Post
eine Bank	der Stephansdom (*St. Stephen's Cathedral*)
die Donau (*Danube*)	das Rathaus
die Universität	die U-Bahn
der Bahnhof	das Zentrum

Übung 3 Spiel mit Wörtern

In der deutschen Sprache gibt es viele zusammengesetzte (*compound*) Wörter. Oft kann man sie auseinander (*apart*) nehmen und mit Hilfe eines Genitivobjekts anders ausdrücken.

Schritt 1: Nehmen Sie zuerst die zusammengesetzten Wörter in Spalte A auseinander.

BEISPIEL: die Hotellage → die Lage des Hotels

Schritt 2: Bilden Sie dann Sätze mit Hilfe von Spalte B.

BEISPIEL: Die Lage des Hotels ist sehr günstig in der Nähe des Zentrums.

A	B
1. die Hotellage	**a.** ist nicht weit von hier entfernt.
2. der Übernachtungspreis	**b.** liegt auf dem Tisch im Hotelzimmer.
3. der Hotelmanager	**c.** ist am Wochenende geschlossen.
4. der Autoschlüssel	**d.** ist in der Tiefgarage im Hotel.
5. das Stadtzentrum	**e.** beträgt 130 Euro pro Person.
6. die Universitätsbibliothek	**f.** heißt Johannes Tiefenbach.
7. der Hotelparkplatz	**g.** ist sehr günstig in der Nähe des Zentrums.

Übung 4 Wem gehört das?

Wessen Sachen sind das? Arbeiten Sie zu zweit.

BEISPIEL: s1: Wessen Gepäck ist das?
s2: Das ist das Gepäck des Gastes.

1. das Gepäck	meine Schwester
2. der Rucksack	der Student
3. der Reisepass	der Herr auf Zimmer 33
4. die Unterschrift (*signature*)	der Gast
5. die Koffer	die Touristen
6. der Schlüssel	unsere Freunde

Prepositions with the Genitive

A number of prepositions are used with the genitive case. Here are several common ones:

außerhalb	*outside of*	außerhalb der Stadt
innerhalb	*inside of, within*	innerhalb einer Stunde
trotz	*in spite of*	trotz des Regens
während	*during*	während des Sommers
wegen	*because of*	wegen der hohen Kosten

In colloquial German, **trotz, während,** and **wegen** may also be used with the dative case.

Note: **Übung 4** also lends itself to a review of the dative with *gehören:*
— *Wessen Wagen ist das?*
— *Der gehört meiner Schwester.*
Or to practice the more colloquial version:
— *Das ist der Wagen von meiner Schwester.*

Prepositions with the Genitive.
Note: The prepositions listed here are high-frequency words. You may want to add *(an)statt* (*instead*). Note that *innerhalb* is generally used with time: *innerhalb eines Tages* (*within a day*). *Außerhalb* is always used with location.

Suggestion: Practice the preposition *wegen* individually, contrasting it with *weil*; students tend to mix up these words. Do a quick substitution exercise: *Warum studieren Sie hier? Wegen …* (*die Lage, das Wetter, der Ruf der Uni / des Colleges, der Preis, die Studenten, meine Freundin, meine Eltern, mein Vater,* etc.) Now ask students to rephrase their sentences using *weil*. Repeat the question *Warum studieren Sie hier?* Provide cues using the substitution nouns: *Der Ruf der Universität (das Wetter, die Lage,* etc.) *ist sehr gut.* Or: *Meine Freundin studiert hier; meine Eltern haben die Universität empfohlen.* Students say . . . *weil der Ruf der Universität (das Wetter, die Lage,* etc.) *gut ist,* or *weil meine Freundin hier studiert,* etc.

Setzen Sie passende Präpositionen mit dem Genitiv ein.

1. _____ unserer Reise nach Wien haben wir viel gesehen.
2. _____ der höheren Hotelpreise haben wir in einer kleinen Pension übernachtet.
3. Die Pension hat _____ der Stadt gelegen.
4. _____ der vielen Touristen war es in Wien schön.
5. _____ der vielen Besucher mussten wir lange vor der Spanischen Reitschule warten.

inquiries

Sie sind bei der Information und fragen nach dem Weg. Arbeiten Sie zu zweit.

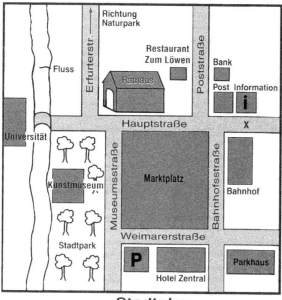

Stadtplan

FÜR DIE FRAGEN

Bitte schön, wo ist ...

Entschuldigung, wie komme ich zum/zur ...

Bitte, können Sie mir sagen, ...

FÜR DIE ANTWORTEN

in der Nähe

in der Mitte

auf der anderen Seite

innerhalb/außerhalb

(direkt) gegenüber (von)

neben

die _____-straße entlanggehen

BEISPIEL: s1: Bitte schön, wo liegt das Rathaus?
s2: Es liegt direkt gegenüber vom Marktplatz. Gehen Sie rechts die Hauptstraße entlang.

1. das Rathaus
2. das Hotel Zentral
3. ein Parkplatz
4. der Naturpark
5. das Kunstmuseum
6. die Post
7. die Universität
8. eine Bank

Attributive Adjektive

Attributive Adjectives°

You are already familiar with predicate adjectives. Predicate adjectives do not take endings.

Der Bahnhof ist **alt**.

Das Hotel ist **preiswert**.

Die Bedienung ist **freundlich**.

When adjectives precede the nouns they modify, they are called attributive. Attributive adjectives do take endings.

Der **alte** Bahnhof liegt in der Nähe des Hotels.

Das **preiswerte** Hotel liegt außerhalb der Stadt.

Die **freundliche** Bedienung hat mir gefallen.

Adjectives after a Definite Article

Whenever an adjective follows a definite article or other **der**-word, such as **dieser** or **jeder,** it takes the ending **-e** or **-en** (depending on the case and gender).*

Adjectives after a Definite Article. Suggestion: Have students look at the chart and note that in only five instances—marked by the shaded area—is the adjective ending -e, the entire nominative singular and accusative feminine and neuter

	SINGULAR			PLURAL
	Masculine	*Neuter*	*Feminine*	*All Genders*
Nom.	der große Park	das schöne Wetter	die lange Straße	die alten Häuser
Acc.	den großen Park	das schöne Wetter	die lange Straße	die alten Häuser
Dat.	dem großen Park	dem schönen Wetter	der langen Straße	den alten Häusern
Gen.	des großen Parks	des schönen Wetters	der langen Straße	der alten Häuser

SUMMARY OF ENDINGS

	SINGULAR			PLURAL
	Masculine	*Neuter*	*Feminine*	*All Genders*
Nom.	-e	-e	-e	-en
Acc.	-en	-e	-e	-en
Dat.	-en	-en	-en	-en
Gen.	-en	-en	-en	-en

singular. All the rest are -en. Since the article indicates the gender, case, and number of the noun, the adjective adds a general ending (-e or -en). **Alternate suggestion:** Another approach to learning adjective endings does not involve analysis of case but does require knowledge of gender. For singular nouns, if you see that the article is *das, die,* or masculine *der,* then the adjective ending is -e. All other adjective endings are -en.

SPRACHTIPP

When two or more attributive adjectives modify a noun, they have the same ending.

Das **kleine historische** Hotel liegt in der Altstadt.

Die **vielen alten** Häuser haben mir gefallen.

Übung 7   Was hat Ihnen in der Stadt gefallen oder nicht gefallen?

Bilden Sie Sätze mit Adjektiven. Folgen Sie dem Beispiel.

BEISPIEL: Die Menschen waren alle sehr freundlich. →
　　　　　Die freundlichen Menschen haben mir gefallen.

1. Die Häuser waren sehr alt.
2. Das Hotel war klein und gemütlich.
3. Das Frühstück im Hotel war ausgezeichnet.
4. Die Straßen waren sauber.
5. Das Bier war ausgezeichnet.
6. Der Marktplatz war klein.
7. Die Bedienung im Restaurant war leider unfreundlich.
8. Aber der Bürgermeister war sehr freundlich.

Obst aus dem Alten Land

Das familienfreundliche Museum.
Eintritt frei für Kinder bis 16 Jahre.

---

*This type of adjective ending is traditionally referred to as a *weak* adjective ending.

Bei einem Volksfest in Straubing: Die vielen netten Leute haben mir gefallen.

Setzen Sie passende Adjektive aus der Liste in die Lücken.

klein	alt	modern
groß	neu	(un)bequem

1. Das Rathaus liegt neben der ＿＿＿ Post.
2. Neben dem ＿＿＿ Rathaus ist ein Park.
3. In dem ＿＿＿ Park gibt es einen kleinen See.
4. Vor der ＿＿＿ Kirche steht eine Statue.
5. In den ＿＿＿ Hotels übernachten viele Touristen.
6. Auf dem ＿＿＿ Marktplatz kann man täglich Obst und Gemüse kaufen.
7. In dieser ＿＿＿ Stadt kann man gut leben.

Bob ist gerade von einer Reise nach Deutschland und Österreich zurückgekommen. Er hat allen etwas mitgebracht. Führen Sie kurze Gespräche mit einem Partner / einer Partnerin. Folgen Sie dem Beispiel.

BEISPIEL: seine Schwester
> s1: Was hat Bob seiner Schwester
> mitgebracht?
> s2: Er hat ihr diesen schönen
> Kalender mitgebracht.

seine Schwester

Hier sind einige Adjektive für Ihre Antworten:

schön	komisch
originell	exzentrisch
interessant	langweilig
fantastisch	nett
praktisch	billig
cool	hässlich

das 👑 Gemälde

1. seine Eltem

die Kuckucksuhr

2. seine Großmutter

der Bierkrug

3. ich

die Lederhose

4. sein Bruder

der Wanderstab

5. sein Großvater

der Hut

6. sein Profesor

Übung 10 Notizen von einem Besuch

Ergänzen Sie die Endungen.

1. Die historische̲ Stadt hat viele Sehenswürdigkeiten.
2. Das alte̲ Rathaus liegt direkt am Marktplatz.
3. Neben dem alten̲ Rathaus steht das neuen̲ Opernhaus.
4. In der Nähe des alten̲ Rathauses liegt auch der Marktplatz.
5. Morgen besuchen wir das alte̲ Rathaus.
6. Trotz des kalten̲ Wetters haben wir einen Spaziergang gemacht.
7. Der Große̲ Garten ist der Name eines Parks in Dresden.
8. Heute besuchen wir den Großen̲ Garten.
9. Unser Hotel liegt am Großen̲ Garten.
10. Die vielen̲ Touristen in Dresden kommen aus der ganzen Welt.

Adjectives after an Indefinite Article

Adjectives preceded by indefinite articles, possessives, or other **ein**-words follow the same pattern as adjectives preceded by **der**-words, except in three instances: the masculine nominative and the neuter nominative and accusative.

Heute war **ein** schön**er** Tag.	*Today was a nice day.*
Das ist **mein** neu**es** Haus.	*This is my new house.*
Ich suche **ein** preiswert**es** Hotel.	*I am looking for a reasonably priced hotel.*
Wo ist **Ihr** neu**er** Wagen?	*Where is your new car?*

	SINGULAR			PLURAL
	Masculine	*Neuter*	*Feminine*	*All Genders*
Nom.	ein groß**er** Park	ein schön**es** Haus	eine lang**e** Straße	keine neu**en** Geschäfte
Acc.	einen groß**en** Park	ein schön**es** Haus	eine lang**e** Straße	keine neu**en** Geschäfte
Dat.	einem groß**en** Park	einem schön**en** Haus	einer lang**en** Straße	keinen neu**en** Geschäften
Gen.	eines groß**en** Parks	eines schön**en** Hauses	einer lang**en** Straße	keiner neu**en** Geschäfte

SUMMARY OF ENDINGS

	SINGULAR			PLURAL
	Masculine	*Neuter*	*Feminine*	*All Genders*
Nom.	-er	-es	-e	-en
Acc.	-en	-es	-e	-en
Dat.	-en	-en	-en	-en
Gen.	-en	-en	-en	-en

Übung 11 Sehenswürdigkeiten in einer Stadt

Ergänzen Sie die Adjektive.

Hier ist …

1. ein deutsch_____ Restaurant.
2. eine bekannt_____ Universität.
3. ein alt_____ Rathaus.
4. eine modern_____ Fußgängerzone.
5. eine historisch_____ Altstadt.
6. ein groß_____ Flughafen.
7. ein berühmt_____ Kunstmuseum.
8. ein gemütlich_____ Biergarten.
9. ein historisch_____ Hotel.
10. ein groß_____, modern_____ Bahnhof.

Stellen Sie Fragen über den Heimatort eines Partners / einer Partnerin in Ihrer Klasse. Benutzen Sie die „Sehenswürdigkeiten" in **Übung 11** für Ihre Fragen. Berichten Sie dann im Plenum.

BEISPIEL: S1: Gibt es in deinem Heimatort ein deutsches Restaurant?
       S2: Nein, es gibt kein deutsches Restaurant da.
    oder Ja, es gibt ein deutsches Restaurant. Es heißt Suppenküche.

Adjectives without a Preceding Article

An attributive adjective that is not preceded by a **der-** or an **ein-**word takes an ending that signals the case, gender, and number of the noun that follows. With the exception of the genitive singular masculine and neuter, these endings are identical to those of the **der-**words.

das Obst → Wo bekommt man hier frisch**es** Obst?   *Where can you get fresh fruit?*

di**e** Brötchen → Hier gibt es jeden Tag frisch**e** Brötchen.   *You can get fresh rolls here every day.*

bei de**m** Wetter → Bei schlecht**em** Wetter bleibe ich zu Hause.   *In bad weather I stay home.*

	SINGULAR			PLURAL
	Masculine	*Neuter*	*Feminine*	*All Genders*
Nom.	schön**er** Park	gut**es** Wetter	zentral**e** Lage	alt**e** Häuser
Acc.	schön**en** Park	gut**es** Wetter	zentral**e** Lage	alt**e** Häuser
Dat.	schön**em** Park	gut**em** Wetter	zentral**er** Lage	alt**en** Häusern
Gen.	schön**en** Parks	gut**en** Wetters	zentral**er** Lage	alt**er** Häuser

SUMMARY OF ENDINGS

	SINGULAR			PLURAL
	Masculine	*Neuter*	*Feminine*	*All Genders*
Nom.	-er	-es	-e	-e
Acc.	-en	-es	-e	-e
Dat.	-em	-em	-er	-en
Gen.	-en	-en	-er	-er

Note:

- An adjective in the genitive singular masculine or neuter always takes the **-en** ending.

Circle all attributive adjectives in the illustrations. Then determine:

- the gender, case, and number of the noun.
- why a particular adjective ending is used.

[1]*furnishings* [2]*upper* [3]*lavish*

Adjectives that end in the vowel **-a** (**lila, rosa**) do not add adjective endings. They remain unchanged.

> Meine Oma hat **lila** Haare.   *My grandma has purple hair.*

Übung 13   Kurze Gespräche

Sie hören zwei kurze Gespräche. Ergänzen Sie die Adjektivendungen, so wie Sie sie hören.

DIALOG 1

GERD: Sag mal, seit wann hast du denn blau____[1] Haare?

GABI: Seit letzt____[2] Woche. Gefallen sie dir?

GERD: Na ja, ich war an deine braun____[3] Haare gewöhnt.

GABI: Ich habe ja auch blau____[4] Augen. Die blau____[5] Haare passen gut zu meinen blau____[6] Augen.

GERD: Ein merkwürdig____[7] Grund (*masc.*). Na ja, meine Oma hat lila Haare.

DIALOG 2

PASSANT: Entschuldigung, wo ist das Rathaus?

PASSANTIN: Meinen Sie das alte____⁸ oder das neue____⁹?

PASSANT: Oh, es gibt zwei? Ein altes____¹⁰ und ein neues____¹¹? Ich suche das Rathaus mit dem berühmten____¹² Glockenspiel.

PASSANTIN: Also, das ist das alte____¹³ Rathaus. Gehen Sie geradeaus, dann die zweite____¹⁴ Straße links. Das Rathaus liegt auf der rechten____¹⁵ Seite.

Das Rathaus in München am Marienplatz

Übung 14 Kleinanzeigen°: Gesucht/Gefunden

Ergänzen Sie die Lücken mit den passenden Adjektivendungen.

Classified ads

Übung 14. Answers: 1. *es, er* 2. *er, e, er* 3. *e, es, es* 4. *er, er* 5. *er, er* 6. *e, e, er*

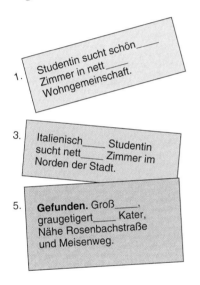

1. Studentin sucht schön____ Zimmer in nett____ Wohngemeinschaft.

2. Freundlich____ Englisch-lehrer sucht klein____ Wohnung in zentral____ Lage.

3. Italienisch____ Studentin sucht nett____ Zimmer im Norden der Stadt.

4. **Gesucht.** Klein____, schwarz____ Pudel entlaufen, Nähe Stadtpark. Hört auf den Namen Papageno. Belohnung.

5. **Gefunden.** Groß____, graugetigert____ Kater, Nähe Rosenbachstraße und Meisenweg.

6. **Gefunden.** Freundlich____, klein____ Katze, schwarz mit weiß____ Nase, Landeshauptstraße, Ecke Stadtpark.

Übung 15 Hin und her: Was gibt es hier?

Fragen Sie einen Partner / eine Partnerin nach den fehlenden Informationen.

BEISPIEL: S1: Was gibt es beim Gasthof zum Bären?
S2: Warme Küche.
S1: Was gibt es sonst noch?
S2: Bayerische Spezialitäten.

WO?	WAS?	WAS SONST NOCH?
Gasthof zum Bären	Küche / warm	Spezialitäten / bayerisch
Gasthof Adlersberg	ein Biergarten / gemütlich	liegt in Lage / idyllisch
Gasthaus Schneiderwirt	Hausmusik / originell	Gästezimmer / rustikal
Hotel Luitpold	liegt in Lage / idyllisch	Zimmer / rustikal
Restaurant Ökogarten	Gerichte / vegetarisch	Bier / alkoholfrei

Grammatik im Kontext   **281**

Adjectives Referring to Cities and Regions

Das Hotel liegt in der **Frankfurter** Innenstadt.

Wo trägt man **Tiroler** Hüte?

Wo isst man **Wiener** Schnitzel?

A city or regional name can be used attributively by adding **-er** to the name of the city or region. This is one of the rare instances where an adjective is capitalized in German. No further changes are made. One country name can also be used in this way: **die Schweiz.**

Essen Sie gern **Schweizer** Käse?

Sie sind gerade von einer Reise nach Hause gekommen. Nun müssen Sie berichten.

Was hast du da gesehen oder gemacht?

BEISPIEL: s1: Was hast du in Köln gemacht?
s2: Da habe ich den Kölner Dom besichtigt.

1. in Hamburg / den Hafen besichtigt
2. in Bremen / die Stadtmusikanten gesehen
3. in Düsseldorf / die berühmte Altstadt besucht
4. in Dortmund / Bier getrunken
5. in Berlin / eine Weiße mit Schuss getrunken [ein Spezialgetränk aus Bier und Saft]
6. in München / Weißwurst gegessen
7. in der Schweiz / Käse gekauft
8. in Wien / Walzer getanzt

Die Bremer Stadtmusikanten

Sprache im Kontext

Videoclips

A. Hotel Jurine: Interview mit Nadine Schulz. Nadine Schulz arbeitet im Hotel. Sie gibt viele Informationen über das Hotel. Was sagt sie?

1. Der Name des Hotels ist ____ ____ des Inhabers.

2. Das Hotel hat 53 ____.

3. Ein Einzelzimmer kostet zwischen ____ und ____ Euro.

4. Ein ____ kostet zwischen 80 und 140 Euro.

5. Die Zimmer haben ____, WC, ____, Telefon, ISDN-Anschluss und Modem für Computer.

B. Wie gefällt Doris und Beatrice das Hotel? Was sagen sie?

Das Hotel ist ...

C. Michael fragt Dennis nach dem Weg zum Alexanderplatz. Was sagt Dennis? Nummerieren Sie die Sätze in der richtigen Reihenfolge.

____ und dann kannst du es nicht verfehlen

____ du gehst am besten immer geradeaus

____ und dann gehst du immer geradeaus circa fünf Minuten

____ vorne an der Ampel gehst du nach links

____ Nächste gleich wieder rechts

Videoclips. Suggestion: In order to refresh vocabulary knowledge prior to viewing, review hotel-related vocabulary by asking, *Was möchte man normalerweise wissen, wenn man in einem Hotel übernachten will?* Write a couple of volunteered responses on the board, then invite other students to come to the board to write associated vocabulary on the board.

Lesen

Zum Thema

A. Vorteile (*Advantages*) **und Nachteile** (*disadvantages*) **des Stadtlebens.** Arbeiten Sie zu zweit. Machen Sie eine Liste von den Vorteilen und Nachteilen des Stadtlebens.

B. Zusammenwohnen. Interviewen Sie zwei Leute im Deutschkurs und berichten Sie danach im Plenum.

1. Was ärgert dich (*annoys you*), wenn du zu Hause bist?

2. Was machst du, wenn deine Nachbarn/Nachbarinnen zu laut sind?
a. Ich beschwere mich persönlich.
b. Ich beschwere mich beim Hausmanager.
c. Ich bin dann noch lauter als sie.

C. Was würden Sie machen?

1. Sie müssen für eine Prüfung lernen, und Ihr Mitbewohner / Ihre Mitbewohnerin spielt sehr laute Musik.

2. Sie studieren Musik (Trompete) und müssen jeden Tag üben. Ihre Nachbarn im Haus beschweren sich immer, wenn Sie spielen.

Zum Thema A. Suggestion: Have students work in pairs to make lists. Create categories *Vorteile* and *Nachteile* on the board. Ask individuals or pairs what they see as advantages and disadvantages of city living.

C. Suggestion: Divide the class into pairs and groups. Have the pairs role-play the first situation and have the larger groups do the second one. Ask for volunteers to present their role-play to the class.

A. In dem folgenden Text stehen die Verben im Imperfekt (*simple past*). Suchen Sie den Infinitiv in der zweiten Spalte.

1. _____ spielte
2. _____ gab
3. _____ stieß
4. _____ losging
5. _____ blies
6. _____ schlug
7. _____ traf
8. _____ grüßte
9. _____ einzog
10. _____ auszog
11. _____ sprach
12. _____ anfing
13. _____ störte

a. schlagen (*to hit*)
b. sprechen
c. grüßen
d. ausziehen (*to move out*)
e. einziehen (*to move in*)
f. losgehen (*to start, begin*)
g. anfangen
h. stören (*to disturb*)
i. stoßen (*to pound*)
j. spielen
k. blasen (*to blow*)
l. treffen
m. geben

B. Lesen Sie die ersten zwei Absätze (*paragraphs*). Wo findet die Geschichte statt (*takes place*)? Wie könnte die Geschichte weitergehen?

DIE GESCHICHTE VON HERRN MAIBAUM UND FRAU

von Heinrich Hannover

Frau Amanda Klimpermunter spielte oft und gern Klavier. Aber sie wohnte in einem großen Mietshaus. Und da gab es manchmal Ärger° mit den Mietern der Nachbarwohnungen. Denn die Wände und Decken des Hauses waren dünn°.

5   In der Wohnung unter Frau Klimpermunter wohnte Herr Maibaum. Wenn oben Klavier gespielt wurde, fühlte sich Herr Maibaum in seiner Ruhe gestört° und schimpfte°. Dann stieß er ein paarmal mit einem Besenstiel an die Decke. Aber Frau Klimpermunter spielte weiter. Und so schaffte sich Herr Maibaum eines Tages eine Trompete an. Und
10 immer, wenn Frau Klimpermunters Klaviermusik losging, trompetete er kräftig° dagegen.

   Das störte nun den Nachbarn des Herrn Maibaum, der sich schon über das Klavier genug geärgert hatte. Und jetzt auch noch die Trompete, das war zuviel. Ein paarmal klopfte° er mit einem Holzpantoffel gegen die
15 Wand. Aber Herr Maibaum trompetete weiter. Und so schaffte sich der Nachbar, er hieß Fromme-Weise, eine Posaune an. Und immer, wenn das Klavier und die Trompete im Haus ertönten, blies er laut wie ein Elefant auf der Posaune.

   Aber das störte nun Frau Morgenschön, die Wand an Wand mit
20 Herrn Fromme-Weise wohnte. Ein paarmal schlug sie mit dem Kochlöffel gegen die Wand, aber das kümmerte ihren Nachbarn nicht. Und so kaufte sie sich eine Flöte und düdelte° dazwischen, wenn die anderen Musikanten im Haus loslegten.

   Das störte Herrn Bollermann, der unter Frau Morgenschön wohnte.
25 Er kaufte sich ein Schlagzeug und haute, wenn die anderen herumtönten, kräftig auf die Pauke. Das gab nun alle Tage einen Höllenlärm im Haus, ein fürchterliches Durcheinander – tüdelüdelüt-bumsbums-trärä-trara-bumspeng … Wenn man sich auf der Treppe traf, grüßte keiner den

trouble

thin

disturbed / yelled, swore

powerfully, vigorously

knocked

noodled

anderen, man knallte° mit den Türen, es gab immer Krach° im Haus, *slammed / noise*
30 auch wenn keiner Musik machte.

Aber dann zog Herr Hatunoglu ins Haus ein, ein Ausländer, wie man schon am Namen merkt. Er brachte eine Gitarre mit und freute sich, daß im Haus musiziert wurde. „Da kann ich ja auch ein bißchen Gitarre spielen", sagte er. Aber obwohl man die Gitarre bei dem Lärm, den die
35 anderen Hausbewohner mit ihren Instrumenten machten, gar nicht hören konnte, waren sich plötzlich alle einig: „Die Gitarre ist zu laut." Plötzlich sprachen sie wieder miteinander.

„Finden Sie nicht auch, daß der Herr Hatunoglu mit seiner Gitarre einen unerträglichen Lärm macht?"
40 „Ja, Sie haben recht, der Mann muß raus."

Sie grüßten sich wieder auf der Treppe und hörten auf, sich gegenseitig zu nerven. Dem Herrn Hatunoglu aber machten sie das Leben schwer°. *difficult* Wenn er anfing, auf der Gitarre zu spielen, klopften sie von oben und von unten und von allen Seiten mit Besenstielen, Kochlöffeln und
45 Holzpantoffeln an Wände und Decken und riefen: „Aufhören! Ruhe im Haus!"

„Was haben die Leute bloß gegen meine Gitarre?" fragte Herr Hatunoglu. Und eines Tages zog er aus.

Kaum war Herr Hatunoglu ausgezogen, ging der Krach im Haus
50 wieder los. Sobald Frau Klimpermunter den ersten Ton auf dem Klavier gespielt hat, packen die anderen Hausbewohner ihre Instrumente aus und legen los: Tüdelüdelüt-bumsbums-trärä-trara-bumspeng ... Sie sprechen auch nicht mehr miteinander und grüßen sich nicht mehr auf der Treppe. Und sie knallen wieder mit den Türen. Aber abends, wenn
55 sie völlig entnervt ins Bett gehen, flüstern sie vor sich hin: „Was war das doch für eine schöne, ruhige Zeit, als noch der Herr Hatunoglu mit seiner Gitarre im Haus wohnte."

Zum Text

A. Wer wohnt wo? Setzen Sie die Namen der Bewohner in das Bild ein. Sehen Sie sich nun auch die Bilder auf Seite 286 an. Welches Instrument gehört zu welcher Person? Welches „Schlagzeug" gehört zu welcher Person?

Zum Text. A. Suggestion: Reproduce the house on the board or on a transparency. Have one student go to the board or the overhead projector. The rest of the class tells her or him who lives where, which instrument goes where, and who is using what to bang on the wall. **Alternate suggestion:** Have students read the text as homework and do activities **A** and **B** in preparation for the next class.

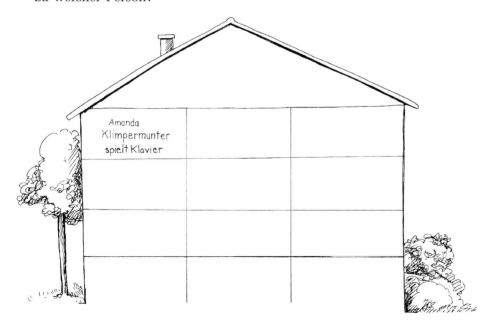

Amanda
Klimpermunter
spielt Klavier

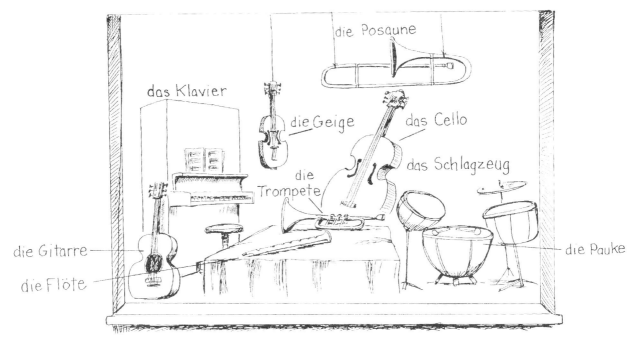

das Klavier

die Posaune

die Geige

das Cello

das Schlagzeug

die Trompete

die Gitarre

die Flöte

die Pauke

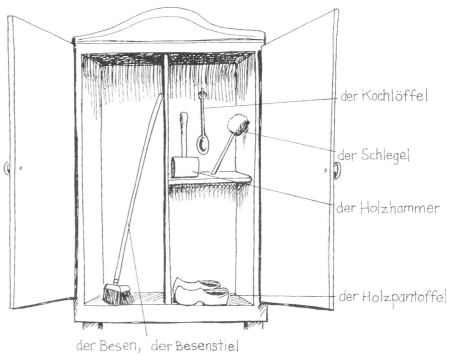

der Kochlöffel

der Schlegel

der Holzhammer

der Holzpantoffel

der Besen, der Besenstiel

B. Stimmt das? Stimmt das nicht? Oder steht das nicht im Text?

	DAS STIMMT	DAS STIMMT NICHT	DAS STEHT NICHT IM TEXT
1. Herr Hatunoglu ist unfreundlich.	☐	☐	☒
2. Nachdem Herr Hatunoglu einzieht, sprechen die Nachbarn wieder miteinander.	☒	☐	☐
3. Herr Hatunoglu spielt Gitarre und ist sehr froh, dass die anderen Bewohner so viel Musik machen.	☒	☐	☐
4. Die anderen Bewohner sagen, sie mögen Herrn Hatunoglu nicht, weil er so laut ist.	☒	☐	☐
5. Herr Hatunoglu lädt oft Freunde ein, und sie sind sehr laut.	☐	☐	☒
6. Sobald Herr Hatunoglu auszieht, werden die anderen Bewohner miteinander viel freundlicher.	☐	☒	☐

C. Die folgenden Wörter stehen im Text. Welches Wort gehört nicht in die Gruppe? Sagen Sie warum.

BEISPIEL: Holzpantoffel   Klavier   Besen →
Klavier gehört nicht dazu. Frau Klimpermunter spielt Klavier. Die Nachbarn schlagen mit dem Holzpantoffel und Besen gegen die Wand, wenn sie Musik hören.

1. sich etwas anschaffen	düdeln	trompeten
2. Nachbarn kümmern	die Tür knallen	Krach machen
3. klopfen	schlagen	flüstern
4. anschaffen	aufhören	kaufen

D. Wählen Sie eine Person aus der Geschichte „Die Gitarre des Herrn Hatunoglu". Beschweren Sie sich über die Situation im Haus aus der Perspektive dieser Person. Schreiben Sie Ihre Beschwerde (*complaint*) auf, und lesen Sie sie der Klasse vor. Die anderen müssen raten, wer Sie sind.

E. Interviewen Sie Herrn Hatunoglu und eine weitere Person im Haus. Schreiben Sie mindestens drei Fragen für jede Person auf. Arbeiten Sie in Gruppen zu viert. Zwei Studenten / Studentinnen übernehmen die Rollen. Die anderen interviewen die beiden.

Zu guter Letzt

Eine Webseite für Touristen

Entwerfen Sie eine Webseite über Ihre Heimatstadt für Touristen.

Schritt 1: Suchen Sie im Internet einen Stadtplan von Ihrer Heimatstadt oder Ihrer Universitätsstadt. Identifizieren Sie die wichtigsten Sehenswürdigkeiten, z.B. Denkmäler (*monuments*), Gebäude (*buildings*), Plätze und Parks.

Schritt 2: Schreiben Sie einen kurzen Text über fünf bis sieben der wichtigsten Sehenswürdigkeiten in der Stadt. Suchen Sie auch passende Fotos dazu.

Schritt 3: Stellen Sie nun alles zusammen und machen Sie die Webseite. Benutzen Sie die Stadt Wittenberg als Modell (www.wittenberg.de). Vergessen Sie nicht, einen kurzen historischen Überblick zu geben.

D. Suggestion: Collect the complaints and read some aloud or have a student read them. Have students guess which character in the story is complaining.

E. Suggestion: Have the interviewers in each group take notes while they interview Herr Hatunoglu and the other resident, and then write the interview up as a short text. As a follow-up, have the groups present their written interviews to the class. Then have members of other groups ask Herr Hatunoglu and the other resident of the house if the interviewers fairly represented their viewpoints: *Herr Hatunoglu, stimmt das alles, was man gesagt hat? Oder haben Sie vielleicht etwas Anderes gemeint?*

Zu guter Letzt. Suggestion: Have students create their brochures on a computer using PowerPoint. If your classroom has access to a computer and projector, have students present their brochures on the screen, while their partners tell the class what they learned. Have the class take notes during the presentation; ask them *Haben Sie auch etwas gelernt? Was?*

Schritt 4: Tauschen Sie Ihre Webseite mit einem Partner / einer Partnerin aus. Jeder muss dann drei Fragen über die Webseite vorbereiten.

Schritt 5: Stellen Sie Ihrem Partner / Ihrer Partnerin die Fragen und notieren Sie die Antworten. Berichten Sie dann der Klasse, was Sie über die Stadt gelernt haben.

Wortschatz

In der Stadt — In the City

die **Ampel**, -n	traffic light
der **Bahnhof**, ̈e	train station
die **Bank**, -en	bank
die **Fußgängerzone**, -n	pedestrian zone
der **Hafen**, ̈	harbor, port
das **Hotel**, -s	hotel
die **Innenstadt**, ̈e	downtown
die **Jugendherberge**, -n	youth hostel
die **Kirche**, -n	church
die **Kreuzung**, -en	intersection
die **Lage**, -n	location
das **Museum**, *pl.* **Museen**	museum
der **Passant** (-en *masc.*), -en / die **Passantin**, -nen	passer-by
die **Pension**, -en	bed and breakfast, small family-run hotel
die **Polizei**	police, police station
die **Post**, *pl.* **Postämter**	post office
das **Rathaus**, ̈er	city hall
das **Schloss**, ̈er	castle, palace
der **Tierpark**, -s	zoo
der **Tourist** (-en *masc.*), -en / die **Touristin**, -nen	tourist
der **Weg**, -e	way, path; road
das **Zentrum**, *pl.* **Zentren**	center (of town)

Im Hotel — At the Hotel

das **Anmeldeformular**, -e	registration form
der **Apparat**, -e	set, appliance (*such as TV, telephone, camera*)
der **Aufenthalt**, -e	stay; layover
der **Aufzug**, ̈e	elevator
die **Bettwäsche**	linens
das **Doppelzimmer**, -	room with two beds, double room
die **Dusche**, -n	shower
das **Einzelzimmer**, -	room with one bed, single room
das **Erdgeschoss**, -e	ground floor
der **Föhn**, -e	hair dryer
der **Frühstücksraum**, ̈e	breakfast room
das **Gepäck**	luggage
der **Internetzugang**	Internet access
die **Kreditkarte**, -n	credit card
der **Kühlschrank**, ̈e	refrigerator
der **Parkplatz**, ̈e	parking space; parking lot
der **Preis**, -e	price; cost
im Preis enthalten	included in the price
der **Reisepass**, ̈e	passport
die **Rezeption**	reception desk
der **Schlüssel**, -	key
der **Stock**, *pl.* **Stockwerke**	floor, story
die **Übernachtung**, -en	overnight stay
die **Unterkunft**, ̈e	accommodation
das **WC**, -s	bathroom, toilet

Nach dem Weg fragen — Asking Directions

bis: bis zum/zur	to, as far as
gegenüber von (+ *dative*)	across from
geradeaus	straight ahead (keep on going)
immer geradeaus	straight ahead
links	left
nach links	to the left
rechts	right
nach rechts	to the right
weit	far
die **Ecke**, -n	corner
an der Ecke	at the corner
die **Haltestelle**, -n	bus stop

die **Mitte**	middle, center
in der Mitte (der Stadt)	in the center (of the city)
die **Nähe**	vicinity
in der Nähe (des Bahnhofs)	near (the train station)

Verben / Verbs

ab•reisen, ist abgereist	to depart
an•kommen, ist angekommen	to arrive
sich an•melden	to check in, register
aus•füllen	to fill out
sich beschweren über (+ *acc.*)	to complain about
ein•biegen	to turn, to make a turn
entlang•gehen, ist entlanggegangen	to walk along
erlauben	to allow, permit
funktionieren	to work, function
reparieren	to repair
übernachten	to stay overnight

Adjektive und Adverbien / Adjectives and Adverbs

| **günstig** | favorable, convenient(ly) |
| **günstig liegen** | to be conveniently located |

kaputt	broken
sofort	immediately
übrigens	by the way
ungefähr	about, approximately
zuerst	first, at first

Genitivpräpositionen / Genitive Prepositions

außerhalb	outside of
innerhalb	inside of, within
trotz	in spite of
während	during, while
wegen	because of, on account of

Sonstige Ausdrücke / Other Expressions

Auf welchen Namen?	Under what name?
Auf Wiederhören!	Good-bye! (*on telephone*)
Das tut mir leid.	I'm sorry.
Entschuldigung	excuse me
jemand nach dem Weg fragen	to ask someone for directions
Wie komme ich am besten dahin?	What's the best way to get there?
Würden Sie (bitte) … ?	Would you (please) . . . ?

DAS KANN ICH NUN!

1. Sie sind beim Informationszentrum einer deutschen Stadt und suchen ein Zimmer. Nennen Sie 3–4 Dinge, die Ihnen wichtig sind.

2. Sie sind an der Rezeption eines Schweizer Hotels. Sie haben eine Reservierung. Was sagen Sie?

3. Sie sind in einer fremden Stadt und suchen das Rathaus. Fragen Sie jemand auf der Straße nach dem Weg.

4. Wie heißen diese Wörter auf Deutsch?

   a. *street crossing* **b.** *traffic light* **c.** *straight ahead*

5. Sie sind in einem Hotel in einer deutschen Stadt und erzählen einem Freund/einer Freundin etwas über das Hotel. Wie sagen Sie dies auf Deutsch?

   a. *My room is on the first floor.* **d.** *The hotel is located in the center of town near the railroad station.* **c.** *Behind the hotel is a big, beautiful park.* **d.** *In the park there is a small lake.*

6. Sie schreiben eine Postkarte aus Wien. Ergänzen Sie die Adjektivendungen.

   Wien ist eine sehr schön___ Stadt mit viel___ interessanten Museen und historisch___ Kirchen. Neben meinem Hotel liegt ein alt___ Schloss. Hinter dem alt___ Schloss liegt ein wunderschön___ Park. Gestern habe ich im Restaurant ein Wien___ Schnitzel gegessen. Zum Glück haben wir gut___ Wetter.

Drittes Zwischenspiel

Die Entwicklung der Stadt

Im Laufe der Zeit hat sich das Bild der Stadt sehr verändert[1]. Viele Städte in Deutschland, wie auch anderswo in Europa, haben aber zum Teil ihren ursprünglichen[2] Charakter aus der mittelalterlichen Zeit erhalten[3]. Sie sind stolz auf ihre Vergangenheit, die oft bis ins Mittelalter und manchmal bis in die Römerzeit zurückreicht. Köln wurde zum Beispiel im Jahre 50 gegründet, Erfurt im 9. Jahrhundert. Die Geschichte Goslars reicht in das 10. Jahrhundert zurück. Gelegentlich sind sogar noch Überreste alter Bauten und Denkmäler[4] aus frühen Zeiten zu sehen.

Aktivität 1 Mittelalterliche Städte

Wie sahen Städte im Mittelalter aus? Was gehörte zum typischen Stadtbild? Kreuzen Sie an.

- ☐ Restaurants
- ☐ Gefängnis[5]
- ☐ Burg/Schloss
- ☐ Universität
- ☐ Kirche/Dom
- ☐ Bürgerhäuser[6]
- ☐ Wachttürme[7]
- ☐ Krankenhaus
- ☐ Markt
- ☐ Geschäfte
- ☐ Parks
- ☐ Bibliothek
- ☐ Schule
- ☐ Fabrik
- ☐ Stadtmauer[8]
- ☐ Rathaus
- ☐ Museum
- ☐ Stadttor[9]

[1]changed [2]original [3]preserved [4]Bauten ... buildings and monuments [5]prison [6]patrician houses [7]watch-towers [8]city wall [9]city gate

Aktivität 2 Nürnberg damals

Schauen Sie sich jetzt die Stadtansicht von Nürnberg aus dem Jahr 1533 an. Identifizieren Sie die Hauptmerkmale der Stadt.

1. _____ Burg
2. _____ Kirche
3. _____ Brücke
4. _____ Bürgerhäuser
5. _____ Stadtmauer
6. _____ Wachtturm

- Welche(s) Gebäude[10] bildete(n) den Kern[11] einer mittelalterlichen Stadt? Warum?
- Wer wohnte in der Stadt? Wer wohnte außerhalb der Stadt?

[10]building(s) [11]center

Erfurt

Köln

Nürnberg heute

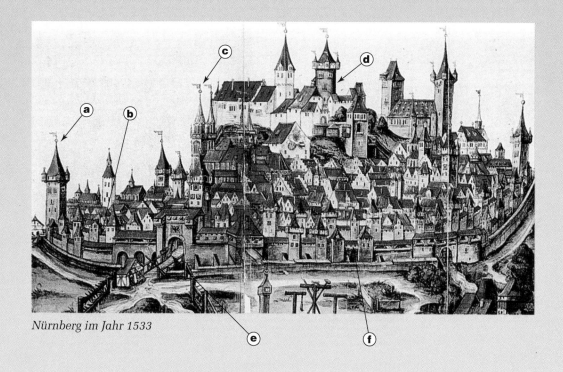

Nürnberg im Jahr 1533

Aktivität 3   Nürnberg heute

Vergleichen Sie die zwei Ansichten von Nürnberg.
Obwohl Nürnberg während des Zweiten Weltkriegs
fast völlig zerstört[1] wurde, sind noch einige
Bauten und Denkmäler aus dem Mittelalter und
der Renaissance erhalten. Wie viele der folgenden
Bauten und Denkmäler können Sie auf dem
Stadtplan finden?

1. St. Sebaldus Kirche (14. Jahrhundert)
2. St. Lorenz Kirche (13.–14. Jahrhundert)
3. das Rathaus (14. Jahrhundert)
4. die Stadtmauer (14.–15. Jahrhundert)
5. der Schöne Brunnen (1389–1396)
6. die Burg (11.–12. Jahrhundert)

Aktivität 4   Auf den Spuren[2] der Stadtentwicklung

Wählen Sie eine Stadt in Ihrem Land aus. Es
kann auch Ihre Heimatstadt sein. Beschreiben Sie
folgendes:

- Wie sah die Stadt vor 100 Jahren aus?
- Was gehörte damals zum Stadtbild?

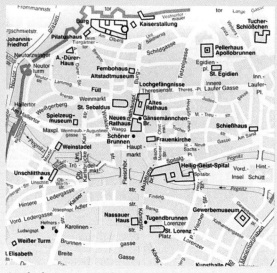

Stadtplan von Nürnberg

- Gab es einen Mittelpunkt der Stadt? Wenn ja,
  was gehörte dazu? Ein Markt, eine Kirche oder
  ein anderes Gebäude?
- Welche alten Bauten und Denkmäler sind noch
  in dieser Stadt erhalten? Welche sind
  verschwunden[3]? Warum?

[1]*destroyed*   [2]*Auf ... On the trail*   [3]*disappeared*

Auf Reisen

Alles einsteigen!

In diesem Kapitel

- **Themen:** Travel, vacations, modes of transportation, items to take on vacation
- **Grammatik:** Superlative, adjectival nouns, simple past tense, conjunction **als,** past perfect tense
- **Kultur:** German vacations, German geography, dealing with a travel agency, buying a train ticket
- **Lesen:** „The American Dream" (Bernd Maresch)

Videoclips
Wohin im Urlaub?

Alles klar?

A. Was planen Sie für Ihren nächsten Urlaub? Was interessiert Sie? Lesen Sie die folgenden Anzeigen.

- Auf welcher Reise kann man eine Fremdsprache lernen?
- Welche Reisen sind für sportliche Leute am geeignetsten (*most suited*)? Welche Sportarten kann man auf diesen Reisen machen?
- Welche Reise verbindet (*connects*) Sport und Kultur? Welche verbindet Action mit Erholung in der Natur?
- Was macht Ihnen persönlich in den Ferien Spaß: eine Fremdsprache lernen? Tennisspielen lernen? eine Kanutour machen? Mountainbiking?

Tennis, Biken, Wassersport, Marathon und vieles mehr
AKTIV URLAUB

SportScheck Reisen

Sun and Fun Sportreisen GmbH
Franz-Joseph-Str 43
D-80801 Munchen

Hammer Str. 418
48153 Münster
Telefon 0251/87188-0

RUCKSACK REISEN
Aktivurlaub, Gruppenreisen und Kanutouren

Wildwasser-Kajak

Eine faszinierende Sportart, die Action und Adrenalin mit intensiver Erholung in unverbrauchter[1] Natur verbindet. Erlernbar für jeden, der bereit ist, im Team zu agieren und Spaß zu haben. Die Reviere[2] in Frankreich, Slowenien und Österreich zählen zu den Klassikern des Wildwassersports.

[1]unspoiled   [2]preserves

SPANISCH in LATEINAMERIKA

z.B. Bolivien
2 Wo Einzelunterricht[3] 25 Std/Wo
Wochenend-Tourenprogramm
Unterkunft m. VP bei Gastfamilie
Kleinkinderbetreuung[4]

schon ab **€ 700,–**

ALR Wolfgang Retz Postfach 390 153/D
Conradstr. 16/4 Berlin 13509
Tel: (030) 805 49 30 Fax: (030) 805 15 52

[3]one-on-one instruction
[4]child care

TENNIS & KULTUR IN PRAG

€ 200,–

1 Wo inkl.: 5x2(4) Std. Tennistraining
+ HP + Kulturprogramm · Info + Buchung:
Tel. (089) 53 94 34 od. 53 64 35 · Fax 532 84 70
Tamar-Reisen·Häberlstraße 13·München 80337

B. Sie hören drei Gespräche über den Urlaub. Wo haben die Urlauber ihre Ferien verbracht? Was haben sie unternommen?

	WO		WAS
1.	**a.** an der Nordsee	**a.**	segeln
	b. an der Ostsee	**b.**	Camping
2.	**a.** Mexiko	**a.**	Spanisch lernen
	b. Bolivien	**b.**	tauchen
3.	**a.** in den Dolomiten	**a.**	Bergsteigen
	b. im Schwarzwald	**b.**	wandern

Wörter im Kontext

THEMA I: Ich möchte verreisen

Wie reisen Sie am liebsten?

mit dem Wagen   mit dem **Flugzeug**   mit dem Fahrrad

mit dem **Zug** / mit der **Bahn**   mit dem **Taxi**   mit dem Motorrad

mit dem **Schiff**   **per Autostop**   mit dem **Bus**

BEISPIEL: Ich reise am liebsten mit dem Bus.

A. Und warum? Was finden Sie ...

am interessantesten?   am langweiligsten?   am praktischsten?

am **sicher**sten?   am **gefährlich**sten?   am **laut**esten?

am **schnell**sten?   am **langsam**sten?   am bequemsten?

 Siehe *Expressing Comparisons: The Superlative,* S. 301.

B. Fragen Sie jemand, wie er oder sie **verreisen** möchte.

BEISPIEL: s1: Also Sven, du möchtest verreisen? Wohin?
s2: Nach Marokko.
s1: Wie kommst du dahin?
s2: Mit dem Schiff.
s1: Und warum?
s2: Das ist am interessantesten.

Ihre Checkliste vor der Reise – haben Sie nichts vergessen?

In den Koffer packen ...

Bekleidung
☐ Unterwäsche
☐ Regenmantel
☐ **Handschuhe**

☐ Jogginganzug
☐ Schlafanzug
☐ Schal
☐ Sportbekleidung

Schuhwerk
☐ Hausschuhe   ☐ Turnschuhe

Toilettensachen
☐ Hautcreme   ☐ Haarshampoo
☐ Zahnpasta   ☐ Zahnbürste

Für Ihre Aktivitäten im Urlaub
☐ Kamera, Filme   ☐ Stadtpläne
☐ **Reiseführer**   ☐ Landkarten

Für den Strand
☐ **Sonnenschutzmittel**   ☐ Sonnenbrille
☐ Badehose/Badeanzug

Für die Berge
☐ Wanderstock
☐ Wanderschuhe
☐ Rucksack

Das sollte im Handgepäck nicht fehlen ...
☐ Reiseapotheke
☐ Reiselektüre

Auch das muss mit - aber nicht im Koffer!
☐ **Bargeld**
☐ **Reiseschecks,** Euroschecks
   Achtung! Scheckkarte!
☐ Reisepass, **Personalausweis**
☐ **Fahrkarten**
☐ **Platzkarten**
☐ **Fahrplan**
☐ Kofferschlüssel
☐ Wohnungsschlüssel

Neue Wörter

sicher safe
schnell fast
laut loud
gefährlich dangerous
langsam slow
verreisen go on a trip
die Reise trip
vergessen forgotten
der Handschuh (Handschuhe, *pl.*) glove
der Reiseführer travel guide
der Strand beach
das Sonnenschutzmittel suntan lotion, sunscreen
das Handgepäck carry-on luggage
das Bargeld cash
der Reisescheck (Reiseschecks, *pl.*) travelers' check
der Personalausweis ID card
die Fahrkarte (Fahrkarten, *pl.*) ticket
die Platzkarte (Platzkarten, *pl.*) seat-reservation cards
der Fahrplan schedule

Aktivität 1   Alles für die Reise

Diese Wörter haben alle mit Reisen zu tun. Welches Wort in jeder Gruppe passt nicht?   *Aktivität 1. Suggestion: This can be done as a whole-class activity to begin working with the new vocabulary.* **Follow-up:** *Have students explain why the word doesn't belong.*

1. Stadtplan, Landkarte, Reiseführer, Zahnbürste
2. Badeanzug, Sportbekleidung, Stadtplan, Regenmantel
3. Bargeld, Turnschuhe, Reiseschecks, Reisepass
4. Wanderschuhe, Wanderstock, Kofferschlüssel, Rucksack

Aktivität 2   Haben Sie etwas vergessen?

Schauen Sie sich die Reise-Checkliste aus **Thema 1** an und nennen Sie zwei Dinge aus der Liste, die Sie unbedingt (*absolutely*) mitnehmen würden.

BEISPIEL: Ich möchte eine Mountainbike-Tour machen. Ich nehme Sonnenschutzmittel und eine Kamera mit.

eine Wanderreise durch Europa

eine Reise nach Hawaii

eine Safari nach Afrika

eine Reise nach _____

Exercises. Suggestion: Have students answer the questions after you have introduced the vocabulary using pictures. Follow up with a class poll to find out the favorite means of transportation and which mode of transport students associate with which adjective. Ask students, *Was sind die Vorteile und Nachteile von ... (dem Zug, dem Taxi, usw.)?*, writing the adjectives on the board. **B:** Have students work in pairs and follow the model to find out their partner's transportation preferences. Call on individual students afterward to find out what they and their classmates said.

Aktivität 2. Suggestion: This can be an individual activity or for small groups of 2–3 students. **Alternative:** Have students name three things from the *Reise-Checkliste* that they could manage without. Ask students what items they usually forget when they go someplace.

Deutsche Arbeitnehmer bekommen im Jahr durchschnittlich (*on average*) sechs Wochen bezahlten Urlaub. Das erklärt, warum der Urlaub ein so wichtiges Thema ist. Wie kann man sechs Wochen freie Zeit sinnvoll planen? Die meisten, vor allem Familien, nehmen den größten Teil des Urlaubs im Sommer, wenn die Kinder Ferien (*school holidays*) haben. Viele Deutsche machen auch im Winter Urlaub: Sie fahren in den Bergen Ski oder suchen ein wärmeres Klima im Süden.

Aktivität 5   Hin und her: Was nehmen sie mit?

Wohin fahren diese Leute im Urlaub? Was nehmen sie mit? Und warum? Ergänzen Sie die Informationen.

BEISPIEL: s1: Wohin fährt Angelika Meier in Urlaub?
s2: Sie fährt in die Türkei.
s1: Warum fährt sie in die Türkei?
s2: Weil …
s1: Was nimmt sie mit?
s2: Sie nimmt …

PERSONEN	WOHIN?	WARUM?	WAS NIMMT ER/SIE MIT?
Angelika Meier	in die Türkei	sich am Strand erholen	Buch, Sonnenbrille, Badesachen
Peter Bayer			
Roland Metz	nach Thüringen	wandern, Weimar besichtigen	Stadtpläne, Reiseführer, Wanderschuhe
Sabine Graf			

Advantages and disadvantages   **Aktivität 6   Vorteile und Nachteile**

Alles hat seine Vorteile und Nachteile. Was meinen Sie?

BEISPIELE: Mit dem Fahrrad sieht man viel, aber es ist anstrengend.
Mit dem Auto geht es schneller, aber es ist _____.

mit dem/der _____	geht es	nicht	bequem / anstrengend
Bahn (Zug)	ist es	sehr	billig / teuer
Bus	kostet es	zu	praktisch / unpraktisch
Fahrrad	sieht man		romantisch / langweilig
Flugzeug			schnell / langsam
Wagen (Auto)			sicher / gefährlich
per Autostop			viel / wenig
zu Fuß			
??			

THEMA 2: Eine Wandertour

Teil A: *Ein Gespräch im Reisebüro zwischen Claudia Siemens und Herrn Bittner, einem Angestellten im Reisebüro.*

FRAU SIEMENS: Mein Freund und ich möchten dieses Jahr mal einen Aktivurlaub machen. Wir wollen mal was anderes **erleben**. Können Sie etwas **vorschlagen**?

HERR BITTNER: Ja, gern. Wofür interessieren Sie sich denn? Es gibt so viele **Möglichkeiten**. Sind Sie sportlich **aktiv**?

FRAU SIEMENS: Nicht besonders. Manchmal spielen wir Tennis und fahren auch schon mal Rad.

HERR BITTNER: Wie wäre es mit einer Radreise durchs Elsass – oder mit einem Segelkurs an der Ostsee?

FRAU SIEMENS: Ach, ein Segelkurs ist mir zu anstrengend. Ich kann auch nicht gut schwimmen. Und eine Radreise … ich weiß nicht. Was können wir **sonst noch unternehmen**?

HERR BITTNER: Wir haben hier ein **Angebot** für eine viertägige Wandertour im Naturpark Solling-Vogler in der Nähe von Göttingen. Hier ist ein **Reiseprospekt**. Das kann ich sofort für Sie **buchen**.

FRAU SIEMENS: Hmm, klingt gut. Wo übernachtet man denn?

HERR BITTNER: Im **Zelt** natürlich.

FRAU SIEMENS: Ach, ich weiß nicht, ob mein Freund **damit einverstanden ist**. Er liebt die **Natur** zwar, aber in der Natur übernachten? Wir werden es **uns überlegen**.

Teil B: *Ein Gespräch zu Hause zwischen Claudia und ihrem Freund Manfred. Sie zeigt ihm den Reiseprospekt vom Reisebüro.*

CLAUDIA: Also, wie findest du diese Wandertour im Naturpark?

MANFRED: Hmm. Mit einer Wandertour bin ich einverstanden aber in der Natur übernachten? Das ist nicht mein **Ding**. Schauen wir mal im Internet nach. Vielleicht finden wir dort noch andere Möglichkeiten.

CLAUDIA: Ja, schau mal, hier ist etwas. Auch eine Wandertour – eine dreitägige – im Thüringer Wald.

MANFRED: Und wo **beginnt** die Tour?

CLAUDIA: Die Teilnehmer treffen sich mit einem Reiseleiter in Großbreitenbach nicht weit von Ilmenau. Von da aus fährt die Gruppe mit einem Bus zum Park. Die **Fahrt** dauert nicht lange und unterwegs sieht man viel Grünes.

MANFRED: Und wo schläft man unterwegs? Ich **hoffe** nicht im Zelt.

CLAUDIA: Nein, nicht im Zelt. In kleinen **Hütten**.

MANFRED: Hm, klingt gut. Was soll die Reise **insgesamt** kosten?

CLAUDIA: 300 Euro **pro Person**. Sollen wir das sofort buchen?

MANFRED: Mir ist es recht. Das ist günstig.

CLAUDIA: Ich werde Georg und Monika anrufen. Vielleicht wollen die beiden mitkommen. Wir machen das **zu viert**.

Neue Wörter

das Reisebüro   travel agency
erleben   experience
vorschlagen   suggest
die Möglichkeit (Möglichkeiten, *pl.*)   possibility
sonst noch   otherwise
unternehmen   undertake, do
das Angebot   offer
der Reiseprospekt   travel brochure
buchen   book
das Zelt   tent
damit einverstanden ist (sein)   will agree to that
uns überlegen (sich überlegen)   think over
das Ding   thing
die Fahrt   trip
hoffe (hoffen)   hope
die Hütte (Hütten, *pl.*)   cabin
insgesamt   altogether
zu viert   as a foursome

SPRACHTIPP

Eine Wandertour von vier Tagen ist eine **viertägige** Wandertour. Eine Fahrt von einer Woche ist eine **einwöchige** Fahrt. Ein Aufenthalt von fünf Monaten ist ein **fünfmonatiger** Aufenthalt. So macht man es:

ein-	-stündig	
zwei-	-tägig	+ Adjektivendung
drei- +	-wöchig	
…	-monatig	

In einem Reisebüro

Ergänzen Sie:

1. Im Reisebüro kann man eine Reise
   _____.

2. Das Reisebüro hat ein _____ für eine
   Wandertour.

3. Über die Reise kann man im _____
   lesen.

4. Die Tour im Naturpark Solling-Vogler dauert
   _____.

5. Manfred ist mit der Wandertour im Thüringer
   Wald _____.

6. Der Preis für die Wandertour ist _____.

7. Claudia will Georg und Monika einladen und die
   Reise _____ machen.

Claudia Siemens trifft sich mit ihren Freunden Georg und Monika im
Café und berichtet über die Internetsuche. Ergänzen Sie die Sätze mit
Informationen aus dem Gespräch im **Thema 2**.

CLAUDIA: Manfred und ich wollen eine _____¹ machen. Im
Internet haben wir etwas Interessantes gefunden – im
Thüringer Wald. Habt ihr Lust?

MONIKA: Wie lange dauert denn so eine Tour?

CLAUDIA: _____.²

MONIKA: Und wo übernachtet man?

CLAUDIA: _____.³

GEORG: Was soll das denn kosten?

CLAUDIA: _____.⁴

GEORG: Ist das nicht ein bisschen teuer?

CLAUDIA: _____.⁵

MONIKA: Du, Georg, was meinst du? Sollen wir das machen?

GEORG: Also, ich finde das ist mal was anderes.

MONIKA: Gut, dann sind wir damit _____.⁶ Wir kommen mit!

Weiteres zum Thema Reisen
finden Sie bei **Deutsch: Na
klar!** im World-Wide-Web
unter

Sie hören vier Gespräche im Reisebüro. Wie, wohin und warum wollen die
Leute in Urlaub fahren? Wie lange wollen sie dort bleiben?

PERSONEN	WIE?	WOHIN?	WARUM?	WIE LANGE?
1. Nicola Dinsing				
2. Marianne Koch und Astrid Preuß				
3. Herbert und Sabine Lucht				
4. Sebastian Thiel				

Aktivität 7 Überredungskünste°

Art of persuasion

Versuchen Sie, einen Partner / eine Partnerin zu einem Plan für einen gemeinsamen Urlaub zu überreden (*persuade*). Die Anzeigen (*ads*) in **Alles klar?** bieten mögliche Reisen.

s1	s2
1. Ich möchte dieses Jahr nach/in _____. Willst du mit?	**2.** Was kann man denn da unternehmen?
3. Man kann da zum Beispiel _____.	**4.** Ist das alles? Was sonst noch?
5. Nein, man kann auch _____.	**6.** Wo übernachtet man denn?
7. _____.	**8.** Wie viel soll das kosten?
9. _____.	**10.** Wie kommt man dahin?
11. _____.	**12a.** Ich will es mir überlegen. **b.** Ich weiß nicht, das ist mir zu _____ (teuer, langweilig usw.). **c.** Klingt gut. Ich komme mit.

Aktivität 7. **Suggestion:** Cue students in different pairs to react in different ways, e.g., to be cooperative, to be skeptical, to be uncooperative. Have various pairs role-play their conversations for the class.

THEMA 3: Eine Fahrkarte, bitte!

Eine Fahrkarte, bitte! **Note:** Tell students about the types of trains in Germany. The fastest are the high-speed ICE (*Inter-City Express*) trains, which are equivalent to the *TGV* in France. The IC (*Inter-City*) trains travel quickly and stop only in larger cities.

Wo ist das?

Wo ist das? **Answers:**
1. *Fahrkartenschalter* 2. *Gleis*
3. *Auskunft* 4. *Fahrplan* 5. *Bahnsteig*

1. Am _____ kauft man Fahrkarten für den Zug.

2. Der Zug fährt von _____ 2 ab.

3. Man bekommt Informationen über Züge bei der _____.

4. Auf dem _____ kann man lesen, wann ein Zug ankommt oder abfährt.

5. Die Leute stehen auf dem _____ und warten auf den Zug.

Reiseverbindungen

Deutsche Bahn **DB**

```
VON    Bad Harzburg                    Gültig¹ am Montag, dem 09.08.
NACH   Hamburg Hbf
ÜBER

BAHNHOF                  UHR    ZUG        BEMERKUNGEN²

Bad Harzburg         ab 10:46 E    3622
 Hannover Hbf        an 12:25
                     ab 12:43 ICE   794   Zugrestaurant
Hamburg Hbf          an 13:56
```

¹*valid* ²*notes*

Am Fahrkartenschalter im Bahnhof

hin und zurück	round-trip
einfach	one-way
zweiter Klasse	second class
umsteigen	change trains
der Anschluss	connection

Weiteres zum Thema
Bahnfahren finden Sie bei
Deutsch: Na klar! im World-
Wide-Web unter

MICHAEL: Eine Fahrkarte nach Hamburg, bitte.

ANGESTELLTER: **Hin und zurück?**

MICHAEL: Nein, **einfach, zweiter Klasse,** bitte.

ANGESTELLTER: Das macht €42. Das ist übrigens der Sparpreis für Jugendliche. Haben Sie Ihren Ausweis dabei?

MICHAEL: Ja, natürlich. Wann fährt denn der nächste Zug?

ANGESTELLTER: In dreißig Minuten. In Hannover müssen Sie dann **umsteigen.**

MICHAEL: Habe ich da gleich **Anschluss?**

ANGESTELLTER: Sie haben achtzehn Minuten Aufenthalt. Dann können Sie mit dem ICE weiter nach Hamburg fahren. Für den ICE müssen Sie allerdings noch einen Platz reservieren. Möchten Sie im Großraumwagen sitzen, oder lieber in einem Abteil?

MICHAEL: Lieber in einem Abteil. Nichtraucher, bitte. Wann komme ich in Hamburg an?

ANGESTELLTER: Um 13.56 Uhr.

MICHAEL: Danke schön.

ANGESTELLTER: Bitte sehr.

Aktivität 8 Michaels Pläne

Ergänzen Sie den Text mit Informationen aus dem Dialog.

Michael fährt mit dem _____¹ nach Hamburg. Er kauft seine Fahrkarte am Schalter im _____.² Er fährt zweiter _____.³ Der nächste Zug nach Hannover fährt in _____⁴ ab. Michael muss in Hannover _____.⁵ Dort hat er gleich _____⁶ an den ICE nach Hamburg. Für den ICE muss er einen _____⁷ reservieren.

300 Kapitel 10 ■ Auf Reisen

Aktivität 9 Am Fahrkartenschalter

Sie hören drei kurze Dialoge am Fahrkartenschalter. Setzen Sie die richtigen Informationen in die Tabelle ein.

INFORMATION	DIALOG 1	DIALOG 2	DIALOG 3
Fahrkarte nach	Hamburg	Salzburg	Bonn
1. oder 2. Klasse	1.	keine Information	keine Information
einfach oder hin und zurück	hin und zurück	hin und zurück	einfach
für wie viele Personen	zwei	fünf	eine
Platzkarten?	ja	keine Information	keine Information

Grammatik im Kontext

Expressing Comparisons: The Superlative°

Der Superlativ

In **Kapitel 7** you learned how to express comparisons using the comparative. In this chapter you will learn about the superlative form of adjectives and adverbs. The superlative indicates the highest degree of a quality or quantity.

Mit dem Zug fährt man **am bequemsten.**	*Traveling by train is the most comfortable.*
Zu Fuß ist es **am schönsten.**	*Walking is the nicest.*
Mit dem Heißluftballon sieht man **am meisten.**	*By hot air balloon you see the most.*

Zu Fuß ist es am schönsten.

Mit dem Heißluftballon sieht man am meisten.

Note:

- The superlative form of adverbs and predicate adjectives is **am ___-sten.**
- German has only one form of the superlative, in contrast to English (*most* and *-(e)st*).

bequem	**am bequemsten**	*the most comfortable*
freundlich	**am freundlichsten**	*the most friendly/the friendliest*
schnell	**am schnellsten**	*the fastest*

Note: Superlatives as attributive adjectives (those which precede a noun) will be treated in the next section.

Point Out: The superlative of *oft* (*öftest-*) is rarely used; instead, *häufigst-* (*most frequently*) is used.

Was machen Berliner am liebsten?

Urlaub.

Beratung[1] und Buchung bei uns im TUI Reisebüro.

Sie haben es sich verdient.[2] Urlaub mit der TUI.

[1]*advice* [2]*sich ... earned*

- Most adjectives of one syllable with the vowel **a**, **o**, or **u** in the stem add an umlaut in the superlative.

hoch	**am höchsten**	*highest*
lang	**am längsten**	*longest*

- Adjectives ending in **-s**, **-ß**, **-z**, or **-t** add **-esten** to the basic form.

heiß	**am heißesten**	*hottest*
kurz	**am kürzesten**	*shortest*
laut	**am lautesten**	*loudest*

- Some common irregular forms are these:

gern	**am liebsten**	*most preferred*
groß	**am größten**	*biggest, largest*
gut	**am besten**	*best*
viel	**am meisten**	*most*

Ergänzen Sie die Tabelle mit den fehlenden Formen.

	GRUNDFORM	KOMPARATIV	SUPERLATIV
1.	bequem	bequemer	am bequemsten
2.	_____	jünger	_____
3.	hoch	_____	_____
4.	_____	mehr	_____
5.	_____	lieber	_____
6.	_____	besser	_____
7.	laut	_____	_____
8.	_____	_____	am kürzesten

Schritt 1: Ergänzen Sie zuerst die Fragen mit dem Superlativ des Adjektivs oder Adverbs in Klammern.

BEISPIEL: Wo regnet es ___*am meisten*___ ? (viel)

1. Wo sind die Berge _____? (hoch)
2. Wo schmeckt das Bier _____? (gut)
3. Wo sind die Bierkrüge (*beer mugs*) _____? (groß)
4. Wo verbringen die Deutschen einen warmen Sommerabend _____? (gern)
5. Wo feiert man _____? (viel)
6. Wo singen die Deutschen _____? (laut)
7. Wo fahren die Autos _____? (schnell)
8. Wo übernachtet man _____? (günstig)

Schritt 2: Arbeiten Sie nun zu zweit und beantworten Sie abwechselnd (*taking turns*) die Fragen in **Schritt 1.** Im Kasten sind mögliche Antworten.

BEISPIEL: s1: Wo regnet es am meisten?

        s2: Ich glaube, am meisten regnet es in Norddeutschland.

---

in Österreich   in einem Biergarten   auf der Autobahn

                                  zu Hause

in einer Jugendherberge   in der Schweiz

beim Karneval in Köln   in Bayern

im Hofbräuhaus in München   in Norddeutschland

Übung 3   Hin und her: Wie war der Urlaub?

Herr Ignaz Huber aus München war drei Wochen im Urlaub in Norddeutschland. Er war zwei Tage in Hamburg, eine Woche in Cuxhaven und nicht ganz zwei Wochen auf der Insel Sylt. Stellen Sie Ihrem Partner / Ihrer Partnerin Fragen über seinen Urlaub. Benutzen Sie den Superlativ.

BEISPIEL: s1: Wo war es am wärmsten?

        s2: Am wärmsten war es in Cuxhaven.

	IN HAMBURG	IN CUXHAVEN	AUF DER INSEL SYLT
1. *Wo war es (kalt/warm)?*	20°C	25°C	15°C
2. *Wo waren die Hotels (günstig/teuer)?*	150 Euro	90 Euro mit Halbpension	200 Euro
3. *Wo hat es (viel) geregnet?*	zwei Tage	einen Tag	fünf Tage
4. *Wo war das Hotelpersonal (freundlich)?*	freundlich	sehr freundlich	unfreundlich
5. *Wo war der Strand (schön)?*	kein Strand	sehr sauber, angenehm	zu windig
6. *Wo hat das Essen (gut) geschmeckt?*	ziemlich gut	nicht besonders	ausgezeichnet

Attributive Adjectives in the Comparative

When adjectives in the comparative are used attributively, i.e. before a noun, they take adjective endings.

Ich brauche einen größer**en** Koffer.	*I need a larger suitcase.*
Sie suchen ein günstiger**es** Hotel?	*You're looking for a more reasonably priced hotel?*
Günstiger**e** Hotels findet man in kleiner**en** Städten.	*You'll find more reasonably priced hotels in smaller towns.*
Wo finde ich ein besser**es** Restaurant?	*Where do I find a better restaurant?*

Note:

■ Attributive adjectives in the comparative add appropriate adjective endings to the comparative forms:

größer	Hier ist ein größerer Koffer.
besser	Wo gibt es ein besseres Restaurant?
kleiner	Das kleinere Hotel war günstiger.

■ When used attributively, **mehr** and **weniger** (the comparatives of **viel** and **wenig**) do not take adjective endings.

Ich brauche **mehr** Geld für die Reise.	*I need more money for the trip.*
Ich habe jetzt **weniger** Zeit zum Reisen.	*I now have less time for traveling.*

Übung 4   Werners Reisevorbereitungen

Werner erzählt von seinen Reisevorbereitungen. Hören Sie zu und markieren Sie die beste Ergänzung zu jedem Satz.

1. Werner braucht …

   a. mehr Geld.   **b.** mehr Zeit.   **c.** mehr Arbeit.

2. Er braucht auch …

   a. einen kleineren Koffer.   **b.** einen größeren Koffer.
   c. zwei kleinere Koffer.

3. Er nimmt ____ mit.

   a. die kleinere Kamera   **b.** die neuere Kamera
   c. die größere Kamera

4. Dies ist Werners …

   a. längster Urlaub.   **b.** teuerster Urlaub.   **c.** kürzester Urlaub.

Übung 5   Probleme im Urlaub

Herr Ignaz Huber aus München fährt in Urlaub. Aber überall gibt es Probleme.

BEISPIEL: Sein Mietwagen ist zu klein.
          Er wünscht sich einen größeren Wagen.

1. Das Hotel ist zu teuer.

2. Das Hotelzimmer ist ungemütlich.

3. Das Bett ist zu kurz.

4. Das Bad ist zu klein.

5. Die Bedienung ist unhöflich.

6. Das Essen ist schlecht.

7. Seine Wanderschuhe sind unbequem.

8. Das Wetter ist zu heiß.

9. Der Urlaub ist zu kurz.

Attributive Adjectives in the Superlative

Arnstadt ist die **älteste** Stadt Thüringens.	*Arnstadt is the oldest city in Thuringia.*
In Thüringen gibt es die **schönsten** Rathäuser.	*The most beautiful city halls are in Thuringia.*
Das **beste** Bier gibt es in München.	*You'll find the best beer in Munich.*

Note:

■ Attributive adjectives in the superlative add **-(e)st** plus an appropriate adjective ending to the adjective.

■ A definite article usually precedes the adjective in the superlative.

Übung 6 Tatsachen° über Deutschland

Facts

Die meisten Antworten finden Sie im **Kulturtipp**.

BEISPIEL: Berlin ist die größte Stadt Deutschlands.

Die schönsten Rathäuser in Thüringen

Hessen-Thüringen

ADAC Freizeitservice

Bayern	ist	das nördlichste Bundesland
Bremen	hat	die meiste Industrie
Frankfurt	produziert	die höchsten Berge
Berlin		die älteste Universität
Heidelberg		das berühmteste Porzellan
Nordrhein-Westfalen		das kleinste Bundesland
Meißen		den größten Flughafen
Rheinland-Pfalz		die größte Stadt
Mecklenburg-Vorpommern		den meisten Wein
Schleswig-Holstein		die meisten Seen
??		??

Suggestion: Have students locate the places indicated in the Übung on a map.

Wissenswertes über Deutschland

■ Zwei Drittel allen Weins kommt aus Rheinland-Pfalz.

■ Mecklenburg-Vorpommern hat 600 Seen.

■ Nordrhein-Westfalen hat mehr Industrie als die anderen Bundesländer.

■ Die meisten Touristen und Besucher landen auf dem Frankfurter Flughafen.

■ Berlin hat über drei Millionen Einwohner.

■ Meißen produziert das berühmteste Porzellan.

■ Die größte Insel ist Rügen (926 km²).

■ Der längste Fluss ist der Rhein (865 km), der zweitlängste ist die Elbe (700 km).

■ Der höchste Berg ist die Zugspitze (2962 m), der zweithöchste ist der Watzmann (2713 m).

■ Die Universität Heidelberg existiert seit 1386.

Burg Katz am Rhein

Sie planen eine Reise nach Österreich und brauchen Information. Was möchten Sie wissen?

1. Wie heißt die _____ (schön) Stadt Österreichs?
2. Wie heißt das _____ (preiswert) Hotel in Wien?
3. Wo liegen die _____ (interessant) Sehenswürdigkeiten?
4. Welches ist das _____ (alt) Schloss?
5. In welchem Café gibt es den _____ (gut) Kaffee?
6. Wo gibt es die _____ (freundlich) Leute?
7. Wie heißt der _____ (groß) Vergnügungspark in Österreich?

Substantivierte Adjektive

Adjectival Nouns°

Adjectives can be used as nouns. As nouns, they are capitalized.

Deutsche und Amerikaner bezahlen Rechnungen oft mit Plastik.	*Germans and Americans frequently pay their bills with credit cards.*
Die meisten **Deutschen** zahlen mit Scheckkarte oder in bar.	*Most Germans pay with a debit card or cash.*
Auch die Kreditkarte ist **nichts Ungewöhnliches.**	*Even the credit card is nothing unusual.*

Note:

- An adjectival noun takes the same endings as an attributive adjective.

Ein **deutscher** Tourist hat mich nach dem Weg gefragt.	*A German tourist asked me for directions.*
Ein **Deutscher** hat mich nach dem Weg gefragt.	*A German asked me for directions.*

- The gender and number of an adjectival noun are determined by what it designates: people are masculine or feminine.

ein Deutscher = a German (*man*)	**der** Deutsche = the German (*man*)
eine Deutsche = a German (*woman*)	**die** Deutsche = the German (*woman*)
[zwei] Deutsche = [two] Germans	**die** Deutschen = the Germans

- The case of the adjectival noun depends on its function within the sentence.

Eine Deutsche hat den Zoo gesucht.	*A German (woman) was looking for the zoo.*
Ich habe **der Deutschen** den Weg gezeigt.	*I showed the German (woman) the way.*

- Abstract concepts are neuter. They are frequently preceded by words such as **etwas, nichts,** or **viel.**

Steht in der Zeitung **etwas Neues?**	*Is there anything new in the paper?*
Es gibt **nichts Neues.**	*There is nothing new.*
Er hat **viel Interessantes** von seiner Reise erzählt.	*He told a lot of interesting things about his trip.*

Übung 8   Die Urlauber sind alle aus Deutschland.

Ergänzen Sie die Sätze mit dem Wort **deutsch** als Nomen.

BEISPIEL: Die _Deutschen_ reisen gern.

1. Das Traumziel (*dream destination*) der _Deutschen_ ist Spanien.
2. Im Hotel auf Mallorca findet man nur _Deutsche_.
3. Herr Keller ist aus Deutschland. Er ist _Deutscher_.
4. Frau Keller ist auch _Deutsche_.
5. Für die _Deutschen_ sind Sonne und Meer sehr wichtig.
6. Die _Deutschen_ liegen den ganzen Tag am Strand in der Sonne.
7. Abends gehen sie mit anderen _Deutschen_ in die Diskos.
8. Am Ende des Urlaubs fliegen die _Deutschen_ von der Sonne gebräunt nach Deutschland zurück. Die Bekannten zu Hause sind alle neidisch.

¹*jealous*

Übung 9   Was erwarten diese Leute vom Urlaub?

BEISPIEL: Ich möchte im Urlaub etwas _Schönes_ (schön) erleben.

1. Herr Lüders aus Berlin will nichts _Anstrengendes_ (anstrengend). Er braucht nur gutes Wetter, Sonne und Meer.
2. Das Reisebüro Fröhlich bietet eine Reise zum Mars zum Sparpreis von nur 5 000 Euro. Das ist wirklich etwas _Tolles_ (toll)! Ich buche das sofort.
3. Ingrid und ihr Freund Horst möchten mit dem Rad durch Portugal fahren. Da sieht man viel _Interessantes_ (interessant).
4. Herr und Frau Lindemann wollen nichts _Neues_ (neu) sehen. Wie jedes Jahr fahren sie in die Alpen.
5. Marion sucht etwas _Ungewöhnliches_ (ungewöhnlich). Sie bucht einen Kochkurs in der Toskana.

Narrating Events in the Past:
The Simple Past Tense°

You recall that in conversation about events in the past, the present perfect tense is preferred except for the verbs **haben, sein,** and modal verbs. These verbs are commonly used in the simple past tense in conversation as well as in written or formal language.

The simple past tense of other verbs is generally used in German to narrate past events in writing or in formal speech. By choosing this tense, the narrator or writer generally establishes a distance from the events.

Weak Verbs°

Weak verbs form the simple past tense by adding the marker **-(e)te** to the stem.

Wir **packten** unsere Sachen in einen Rucksack.	We packed our things in a backpack.
Wir **warteten** auf den Bus.	We waited for the bus.
Die Fahrt **dauerte** drei Stunden.	The trip took three hours.
Wir **übernachteten** in einer Jugendherberge.	We stayed at a youth hostel.

reisen			
ich	reis**te**	wir	reis**ten**
du	reis**test**	ihr	reis**tet**
er sie es	reis**te**	sie	reis**ten**
Sie reis**ten**			

warten			
ich	wart**ete**	wir	wart**eten**
du	wart**etest**	ihr	wart**etet**
er sie es	wart**ete**	sie	wart**eten**
Sie wart**eten**			

Note:

- The first- and third-person singular are identical, as are the first- and third-person plural.
- Verbs with stems ending in **-t** or **-d,** as well as some verbs with a consonant + **-n** in the stem (e.g., **regnen, öffnen**), add **-ete** to the stem.
- Weak verbs with separable and inseparable prefixes have the same past tense stem as the base verb.

In Wien **besuchten** sie die Spanische Reitschule.	In Vienna they visited the Spanish Riding School.
Die Familie **reiste** letzten Donnerstag **ab.**	The family departed last Thursday.

Übung 10 Kleine Erlebnisse° im Urlaub

experiences

Ergänzen Sie die Sätze mit passenden Modalverben im Imperfekt: **dürfen, können, müssen, wollen.**

BEISPIEL: Wir _wollten_ per Autostop nach Spanien fahren.

1. Niemand _____ uns mitnehmen.
2. Wir _____ zwei Stunden an der Autobahn warten.
3. Ein Fahrer _____ uns bis nach Freiburg mitnehmen.
4. Wir _____ in der Jugendherberge übernachten, aber dort war kein Platz mehr.
5. Deshalb _____ wir im Park übernachten.
6. Im Park _____ man aber nicht übernachten. Es war verboten.
7. Wir _____ aber noch eine Übernachtung auf einem Bauernhof bekommen.

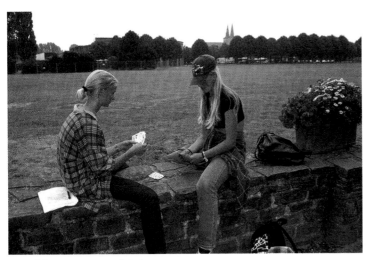

Eine kleine Pause auf Reisen

Übung 11 Eine Reise nach Spanien

Rainer hat in der Schule über seine Sommerferien geschrieben. Setzen Sie Rainers Sätze ins Imperfekt.

BEISPIEL: Wir haben eine Reise nach Spanien gemacht. →
          Wir machten eine Reise nach Spanien.

1. Schon drei Wochen vor der Reise habe ich meinen Koffer gepackt.
2. Bei unserer Abfahrt in Deutschland hat es geregnet.
3. Wir haben auf einem Campingplatz übernachtet.
4. Am Urlaubsort ist es jeden Tag regnerisch gewesen. So ein Pech!
5. Wir haben in einer kleinen Stadt gewohnt.
6. Wir haben alle Museen da besucht.
7. Die Reise hat nicht viel Spaß gemacht.
8. Das Schlimmste (*worst*): In Deutschland ist ein Traumsommer gewesen. Schade. Ohne mich.

Im Stau auf der Autobahn

Strong Verbs°

Strong verbs change their stem vowel in the simple past tense. Many verbs that are strong in English are also strong in German. You will find a comprehensive list of strong verbs in the Appendix.

Familie Stieber **fuhr** im Urlaub nach Spanien.	*The Stieber family drove to Spain on their vacation.*
Sie **standen** lange im Stau auf der Autobahn.	*They were in a traffic jam on the* Autobahn *for a long time.*
Der Urlaub **fing** nicht gut **an.**	*The vacation did not start out well.*

	fahren	**stehen**	**anfangen**	**verlieren**
ich	fuhr	stand	fing an	verlor
du	fuhr**st**	stand**est**	fing**st** an	verlor**st**
er sie es	fuhr	stand	fing an	verlor
wir	fuhr**en**	stand**en**	fing**en** an	verlor**en**
ihr	fuhr**t**	stand**et**	fing**t** an	verlor**t**
sie/Sie	fuhr**en**	stand**en**	fing**en** an	verlor**en**

Note:

- The first- and third-person singular are identical; they have no personal endings.
- A past tense stem ending in a **-d, -t,** -or **-s** adds **-est** to the **du**-form and **-et** to the **ihr**-form.
- Like weak verbs, strong verbs with separable and inseparable prefixes have the same past tense stem as the base verb.

Mixed Verbs°

Mischverben

Several verbs change their stem vowel *and* add **-te** to the changed stem in the simple past, combining aspects of both strong and weak verbs. These verbs include:

bringen → brachte   verbringen → verbrachte

denken → dachte   wissen → wusste

kennen → kannte

The simple past tense of **werden** (*to become*) is **wurde.**

Mixed Verbs. Note: You may wish to point out that the English cognates of *bringen* and *denken* are also mixed verbs: bring – brought, think – thought.

The Conjunction als

The conjunction **als** has several important functions in German. You have learned to use it in the comparison of adjectives.

Mit dem Zug fährt man bequemer **als** mit dem Bus.

Additionally, **als** can be used as a subordinating conjunction meaning *when*, referring to a one-time event in the past. Sentences with the conjunction **als** are often in the simple past tense, even in conversation.

Note: You may want to briefly review the meaning and usage of **wann** (*when* as interrogative pronoun) and **wenn** (*if, whenever*) to reinforce the use of **als** (*when*) to refer to a one-time event in the past.

Als meine Reise nach Russland begann, war es schon Winter.

When my trip to Russia began, it was already winter.

Als ich am Morgen aufwachte, fand ich mich mitten im Dorf.

When I woke up in the morning, I found myself in the middle of the village.

ANALYSE

Sonderbares° Erlebnis einer Reise

Der Baron von Münchhausen lebte im 18. Jahrhundert und hatte einige merkwürdige Abenteuer. Man nannte ihn auch den „Lügenbaron" (*"lying baron"*), weil man ihm seine Geschichten nicht glaubte. Lesen Sie die folgende Geschichte und identifizieren Sie alle Verben im Imperfekt. Machen Sie eine Liste mit den Verben und geben Sie den Infinitiv an. Welche Verben sind stark? Welche sind schwach? Sie finden die Liste mit starken Verben im Anhang (*appendix*).

Münchhausens Reise nach Russland

Meine Reise nach Russland begann im Winter. Ich reiste zu Pferde°, weil das am bequemsten war. Leider trug ich nur leichte Kleidung, und ich fror° sehr. Da sah ich einen alten Mann im Schnee. Ich gab ihm meinen Reisemantel und ritt weiter. Ich konnte leider kein Dorf° finden. Ich war müde und stieg vom Pferd ab°. Dann band° ich das Pferd an einen Baumast° im Schnee und legte mich hin. Ich schlief tief und lange. Als ich am anderen Morgen aufwachte, fand ich mich mitten in einem Dorf auf dem Kirchhof°. Mein Pferd war nicht da, aber ich konnte es über mir hören. Ich schaute in die Höhe° und sah mein Pferd am Wetterhahn des Kirchturms° hängen. Ich verstand sofort, was passiert war. Das Dorf war in der Nacht zugeschneit° gewesen. In der Sonne war der Schnee geschmolzen°. Der Baumast, an den ich mein Pferd gebunden hatte°, war in Wirklichkeit die Spitze des Kirchturms gewesen. Nun nahm ich meine Pistole und schoss° nach dem Halfter°. Mein Pferd landete ohne Schaden° neben mir. Dann reiste ich weiter.

Analyse. Suggestion: Introduce this exercise by telling about the Baron von Münchhausen. In a modern film version of his adventures, Münchhausen rides on a cannonball into the enemy camp and back to his own camp without harm. In another adventure, Münchhausen and his horse are about to drown in a river when he pulls himself and his horse up and out of the water by his own long ponytail. **Suggestion:** Preview unknown strong verbs first. Then assign the exercise for homework.

Bizarre

zu … on horseback

froze
village
stieg … got off the horse / tied
branch of a tree

churchyard (cemetery)
in … up
am … on the weather vane on top of the church tower / snowed under
melted
gebunden … had tied

shot / halter / damage

Ergänzen Sie die Verben im Imperfekt.

Ich _____¹ (beginnen) meine Reise nach Russland im Winter. Ich
_____² (reisen) zu Pferde, weil das am bequemsten _____.³ (sein)
Leider _____⁴ (frieren) ich sehr, weil ich nur leichte Kleidung
_____.⁵ (tragen) Plötzlich _____⁶ (sehen) ich einen alten Mann im
Schnee. Ich _____⁷ (geben) ihm meinen Mantel und _____⁸
(reiten) weiter. Bald _____⁹ (sein) ich müde und _____¹⁰ vom
Pferd _____.¹¹ (ab•steigen) Ich _____¹² (binden) das Pferd an
einen Baumast im Schnee. Dann _____¹³ ich mich _____¹⁴
(hin•legen) und _____ _____.¹⁵ (ein•schlafen) Als ich am
anderen Morgen _____¹⁶ (auf•wachen), _____¹⁷ (finden) ich mich
mitten in einem Dorf. Ich _____¹⁸ (wissen) zuerst nicht. wo mein
Pferd war. Ich _____¹⁹ (kennen) keinen Menschen in diesem Dorf.

Übung 13 Münchhausens Reise

Sie hören die Geschichte von Münchhausens Reise nach Russland mit
sechs Veränderungen (*changes*). Können Sie sie identifizieren?

Übung 14 Wann war das?

Sagen Sie, wie alt Sie damals waren.

BEISPIEL: den Führerschein machen
          Ich war 17 Jahre alt. als ich den Führerschein machte.

1. in den Kindergarten kommen

2. das erste Geld verdienen (*to earn*)

3. sich zum ersten Mal verlieben (*to fall in love*)

4. den Führerschein machen

5. meine Familie nach ____ umziehen (*to move*)

6. ____ (besten Freund oder beste Freundin) kennen lernen

7. meine erste Reise ins Ausland machen

8. zum ersten Mal tanzen gehen

The Past Perfect Tense°

The past perfect tense describes an event that precedes another event in the past.

Bevor wir in Urlaub fuhren, **hatten** wir alle Rechnungen **bezahlt.**

*Before we went on vacation we **had paid** all the bills.*

Nachdem wir auf Mallorca **angekommen waren,** gingen wir sofort an den Strand.

*After we **had arrived** in Mallorca, we immediately went to the beach.*

The conjunctions **bevor** and **nachdem** are commonly used to connect sentences with the simple past and past perfect tenses.

To form the past perfect, combine the simple past of **haben** (*hatte*) or **sein** (*war*) and the past participle of the main verb. Verbs using **sein** in the present perfect tense also use **sein** in the past perfect.

PRESENT PERFECT	PAST PERFECT
Ich **bin** gegangen.	Ich **war** gegangen. (*I had gone.*)
Wir **haben** bezahlt.	Wir **hatten** bezahlt. (*We had paid.*)

Übung 15   Die Fahrt hatte kaum begonnen

Ergänzen Sie die Sätze durch Verben im Plusquamperfekt.

1. Ich _____ schon früh aus dem Haus _____ (gehen), denn mein Flugzeug nach Frankfurt flog um 8 Uhr ab.

2. Ich _____ am Tag zuvor ein Taxi _____ (bestellen).

3. Am Flughafen fiel mir ein (*I remembered*), dass ich die Schlüssel in der Haustür _____ _____ (vergessen).

4. Kein Wunder, denn letzte Nacht _____ ich kaum _____ (schlafen).

5. Sobald ich am Flughafen _____ _____ (ankommen), rief ich eine Nachbarin (*neighbor*) an.

6. Der Flug nach Frankfurt war verspätet (*late*). Nachdem wir drei Stunden _____ _____ (warten), konnten wir endlich abfliegen.

Sprache im Kontext

Videoclips

A. Thomas Möllmann arbeitet im Reisebüro. Schauen Sie sich das Interview mit ihm an und ergänzen Sie die folgenden Informationen.

1. Ein Reiseziel, das im Moment „in" ist, ist _____.

2. Andere beliebte Reiseziele der Kunden sind _____ und die _____ _____.

3. Wie kommen die Kunden an den Urlaubsort? Die meisten Kunden _____.

4. Herr Möllmann hat dieses Jahr eine _____ an die _____ gemacht. Er ist mit der _____ gefahren.

5. Herr Möllmann hat vor, in ungefähr sechs Wochen nach _____ zu reisen.

6. Herr Möllmann arbeitet seit ungefähr _____ Jahren im Reisebüro.

B. Was sind beliebte Reiseziele in Ihrem Land?

C. Alex spricht über seine Urlaubspläne und über seinen Urlaub letztes Jahr. Schauen Sie sich das Interview an und machen Sie sich Notizen in der Tabelle. Benutzen Sie dann Ihre Notizen, um wenigstens 3–4 Sätze über den Urlaub von Alex zu schreiben.

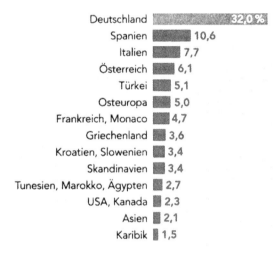

Am schönsten ist's im eigenen Land

Wo die Deutschen 2005 ihren Urlaub verbrachten

Deutschland **32,0 %**
Spanien **10,6**
Italien **7,7**
Österreich **6,1**
Türkei **5,1**
Osteuropa **5,0**
Frankreich, Monaco **4,7**
Griechenland **3,6**
Kroatien, Slowenien **3,4**
Skandinavien **3,4**
Tunesien, Marokko, Ägypten **2,7**
USA, Kanada **2,3**
Asien **2,1**
Karibik **1,5**

Datenbasis: 4000 befragte Personen ab 14 Jahren im Januar 2006.
Quelle: BAT Freizeit-Forschungsinstitut

Urlaub dieses Jahr:	
Wohin? Wie lange?	
Wie kommt er dahin?	
Wo hat er gebucht?	
Urlaub letztes Jahr:	
Wo? Wie lange? Mit wem?	
Was hat er mitgenommen?	
Was hat er erlebt?	

D. Fragen Sie drei Personen in der Klasse, wohin sie dieses Jahr in Urlaub fahren und wo sie letztes Jahr waren. Berichten Sie der Klasse darüber.

Lesen

A. Ihr letzter Urlaub. Beantworten Sie die folgenden Fragen und vergleichen Sie Ihre Antworten untereinander.

1. Wann haben Sie zum letzten Mal Urlaub gemacht?

2. Wohin sind Sie gefahren?

3. Sind Sie allein oder mit Freunden gefahren?

4. Was haben Sie dort gemacht?

5. Wie war das Wetter dort?

6. Wie lange waren Sie dort?

7. Was hat Ihnen dort (nicht) gefallen?

B. Ein Aktivurlaub. Die Werbung „Sportreisen" auf der nächsten Seite zeigt viele Möglichkeiten für einen Aktivurlaub. Schauen Sie sich die Tabelle mit einem Partner / einer Partnerin an.

- Welche Sportarten gibt es?
- Wo finden diese Aktivitäten statt *(take place)*?
- Was macht man alles da?
- Für welche Sportart muss man am fittesten sein?
- Welche Reise möchten Sie machen? Warum?

SPORTREISEN ...

Sportart	Ort	Leistungen	Reisetermin	Preis	Grad*
Rafting	Colorado/ USA	zwei Übernachtungen im Hotel, Transfer, Raftingtour, Bootsführer, alle Mahlzeiten während der Tour, Camping-ausrüstung, Anreise in Eigenregie[1]	1., 8., 15. und 22.9.	ab 800 € für 7 Tage	●●
Katamaran-segeln	Levkada/ Griechenland	Flug, Übernachtungen im Appartement, kostenlose Benutzung der Katamarane und Segelflotte,[2] Teilnahme am Unterricht[3]	1., 8., 15., 22. und 29.9.	ab 715 € pro Woche	●●●
Tauchen	Villi Varu/ Malediven	Flug ab Düsseldorf, sechs Übernachtungen mit Vollpension, Sechs-Tage-Tauchpaket à 1 Tauchgang[4] täglich und 2 Haus-riff-Tauchgänge (inkl. Boot, Flasche, Blei und Bleigurt)[5]	3., 10., 17. und 24.9.	115 € pro Woche	●
Aktiv-Camp	Berchtes-gaden/ Deutschland	Schnupperkurs[6] im Klettergarten,[7] River-Rafting auf der Saalach, Mountainbike-Tour, Bergwanderung, Paragliding-Schnupper-kurs, sechs Übernachtungen mit Frühstück, Ausrüstung,[8] Führung[9]	6.–12.9.	300 €	●
Surfen	Bonaire/ Karibik	Flug ab Amsterdam, Übernachtung im Appartement mit Selbstversorgung[10] oder im Hotel mit Frühstück, Surfboard-Miete 115 Euro pro Woche	6., 13., 20. und 27.9.	ab 1100 € pro Woche	●●
Reiten	Costa Blanca/ Spanien	Flug, acht Tage mit sieben Übernachtungen im Appartement mit Selbstversorgung, Reitprogramm, Reitführung, Unterlagen, Qualifikation: sicher in den Grundgangarten,[11] gute Kondition	9.–16.9.	ab 1050 €	●●

* Zeigt den Grad der körperlichen[12] Fitneß, die der Teilnehmer[13] mitbringen muß: ●●● = sehr gut trainiert, ●● = körperlich fit, ● = auch für Anfänger[14]

[1]Anreise ... *passage excluded*   [2]*sailing fleet*   [3]Teilnahme ... *participation in instruction*   [4]*dive*   [5]Blei ... *weight and weight belt*   [6]*sampler class*   [7]*climbing garden*   [8]*equipment*   [9]*guide*   [10]*no meals provided*   [11]sicher ... *secure in all the basic paces*   [12]*physical*   [13]*participant*   [14]*beginners*

Auf den ersten Blick

A. Schauen Sie sich den Text „The American Dream" an. Was für ein Text ist das?
1. ein Interview   2. ein Gedicht   3. ein Reisebericht

B. Überfliegen Sie das Lesestück. Der Text berichtet über:
1. die Arbeitserfahrung eines deutschen Studenten in den USA
2. eine Reise für Studenten in die USA
3. eine Beschreibung von Städten und Regionen in den USA

C. Präziser bitte! Suchen Sie diese Informationen im Text!
1. Wie lange war Bernd insgesamt in den USA?
2. Was hat er in den USA gemacht?
3. In welchen Bundesstaaten hat er gearbeitet?

von Bernd Maresch

Jobben in den USA

Just another summer of my life?! „ … aber es wird noch ein bisschen dauern, es ist gerade rush-hour in New York City", säuselt° mir die *murmurs*
freundliche amerikanische Stimme ins Ohr. Vor ein paar Minuten sind wir im JFK-Airport gelandet. Nun bin ich im Land der unbegrenzten
5 Möglichkeiten, die Vordiplomprüfungen sind vorbei, die Semesterferien liegen vor mir, und warum sollte ich diese nicht jobbenderweise° in den USA verbringen, um die Mythen dieses Landes *while working*
kennen zu lernen?

New York Times Square: Im Land der unbegrenzten Möglichkeiten

Was folgte, waren drei aufregende Monate, die ich als „American
10 Dream" bezeichne: In Manhattan arbeitete ich zusammen mit 20 jungen Leuten aus zwölf Nationen im „New York Student Center". Mit einem Drücken° im Magen starte ich zu meinem ersten Auftrag: Ich sollte eine *sinking feeling*
Gruppe von 35 Briten am JFK in Empfang nehmen° und sie über *in … to receive*
die „dos & don'ts" dieser Stadt aufklären. Es war ein seltsames Gefühl,
15 allein in einer fremden Stadt vor einer Gruppe englischsprechender Menschen zu stehen und ihnen in ihrer Muttersprache mit meinem deutsch-akzentuierten Englisch das Programm zu erklären.

Dennis Hopper in Manhatten und Bruce Willis im Central Park

New York zeigte sich von seiner weltstädtischen° Seite. Zu acht *cosmopolitan*
20 wohnten wir in einem großzügigen° Appartement, das wir in der Nähe *spacious*
von SoHo anmieteten. Die Seiten meines Tagebuchs der folgenden Wochen lesen sich wie ein Star-Report aus der Yellow-Press: Wir trafen Dennis Hopper bei Dreharbeiten° mitten auf den Straßen von *filming*
Manhattan und Bruce Willis beim Rollerbladen im Central Park. Bon
25 Jovi gab ein Spontan-Konzert am Times Square vor dem Auftritt bei David Letterman.
Nach sechs Wochen wechselte ich den Schauplatz. Arbeiten mit Rangern in einem von Utahs Nationalparks. Die pralle° Natur stand *intense*
freilich im krassen° Gegensatz zum New Yorker Großstadtleben. Unsere *stark*
30 Crew lebte selbstversorgend in „bunk houses" inmitten des Uinta National Forest. Arbeitslohn erhielten wir in Form von Unterkunft und Verpflegung°. *Unterkunft … room and board*

Jeep, Motorboot und Pferde

Wir mussten hart zupacken°: Holzzäune errichten°, Pipelines für
35 Tränken° der Waldtiere in den Boden graben und Wanderwege anlegen.
Dabei standen uns ein Jeep, ein Motorboot und Pferde zur Verfügung.
Ein Demolition-Derby, ein echtes Rodeo, Indianerkultur in Form von
alten Felsmalereien° und historische Ausgrabungen an einem alten
Schlachtfeld spiegelten die Höhepunkte im Leben einer
40 amerikanischen Kleinstadt wider.

knuckle down / Holzzäune ... build wooden fences / watering

rock paintings

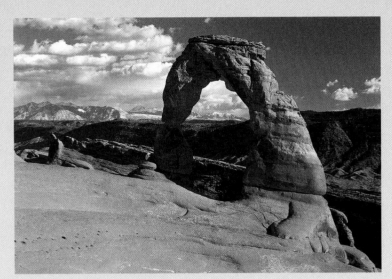

Der berühmte Arches Naturpark im Bundesstaat Utah

Nach vier Wochen in Utah führte mich der Weg nach California, wo
ich den Rest meines Aufenthaltes verbrachte. Noch in Deutschland
hatte ich Amerikaner kennen gelernt, die ich nun besuchte. Und so flog
ich nach San Francisco. Die Gastfreundschaft ging soweit, dass ich das
45 Auto benutzen konnte, was mir so manchen Ausflug auf den Highway
No. 1 und nach Napa Valley möglich machte.

Als Clou° für mein Studium konnte ich in den Bibliotheken von
Berkeley und Stanford University so manches Schnäppchen° für meine
anstehende Hausarbeit erstöbern°, wenngleich es mich nach einem
50 Besuch an einer amerikanischen Uni gar nicht mehr zum Studium nach
Hause zog.

(coll.) side benefit

find, bargain

uncover

„ ... erreichen wir in Kürze Frankfurt am Main. Wir bitten Sie, die
Gurte° anzulegen und hoffen, Sie hatten einen guten Flug und einen
angenehmen Aufenthalt." Die Stimme der Stewardess weckt mich, und
55 erst nach Beginn des Semesters an einer deutschen Hochschule wurde
mir so richtig bewusst°, dass mein „American Dream" wahr gewesen ist.

seat belts

wurde ... I truly realized

—Quelle: Bernd Maresch; adaptiert aus: "The American Dream," *UNICUM*,
April 2006

A. Beantworten Sie die folgenden Fragen über Bernds Aufenthalt in den USA.

1. Warum wollte er in die USA kommen?

2. Was war Bernds erster Auftrag in New York?

3. Welche Erlebnisse und Erfahrungen hat Bernd in seinem Tagebuch niedergeschrieben?

4. Wo hat Bernd nach seinem Aufenthalt in New York gearbeitet? Was hat er dort erlebt? Was für Arbeit hat er dort gemacht?

5. Welche amerikanischen Sehenswürdigkeiten hat Bernd in Utah gesehen?

6. Wen hat Bernd in Kalifornien besucht? Was hat er in den Bibliotheken dort gefunden?

B. Bernd hat viele Höhepunkte seines Aufenthaltes in Amerika beschrieben aber nur wenige Details gegeben. Was möchten Sie zusätzlich noch gern wissen? Formulieren Sie drei Fragen für Bernd, wo Sie ihn nach mehr Details fragen.

1. _____

2. _____

3. _____

C. Bernd benutzt drei Arten von „Englisch" in seinem Reisebericht: (1) eingedeutschte (*Germanized*) Wörter, (2) Namen auf Englisch für Sehenswürdigkeiten in Amerika und (3) andere englische Wörter.

1. Suchen Sie diese Wörter und sortieren Sie sie in drei Kategorien.

(1) EINGEDEUTSCHTE WÖRTER	**(2)** NAMEN AUF ENGLISCH	**(3)** ANDERE ENGLISCHE WÖRTER
jobben	*Napa Valley*	*American Dream*

2. Suchen Sie deutsche Wörter oder Äquivalente für die Wörter, die Sie in Kategorie 3 gefunden haben.

3. Warum benutzt Bernd wohl diese drei Kategorien von Wörtern?

D. Bernds Reisebericht kurz und bündig (*in a nutshell*). Erzählen Sie Bernds Reisebericht mit Hilfe des folgenden Rasters (*template*) nach.

1. Bernds Aufenthalt begann _____.
2. Dort arbeitete er als _____.
3. Für seinen ersten Auftrag musste er _____.
4. In New York erlebte er _____.
5. Nach seinem Aufenthalt in New York _____.
6. Dort musste er schwere Arbeit machen, z.B. _____.
7. Danach _____.
8. Dort _____.
9. Für Bernd war die Reise nach Amerika _____.

Zu guter Letzt

Ein Reisebericht

Haben Sie je eine interessante Reise gemacht? allein? mit Freunden oder mit Familie? Schreiben Sie einen Bericht darüber – so kreativ wie möglich. Wenn Sie wollen, können Sie einen fiktiven Reisebericht oder im Stil von Bernd Maresch schreiben.

Schritt 1: Beginnen Sie mit einem Zitat (*quote*), das den Ton und die Stimmung Ihres Berichts angibt, z.B. aus einem Roman, einer Geschichte oder einem Lied. Das Zitat kann auf Englisch oder auf Deutsch sein. Erklären Sie dann, warum Sie die Reise gemacht haben.

- Freunde oder Familie besuchen?
- etwas Exotisches erleben?
- ein neues Land oder eine neue Stadt kennen lernen?
- einen Ferienjob finden?
- ??

Schritt 2: Schreiben Sie über zwei oder drei spezifische, interessante Erlebnisse auf der Reise. Geben Sie möglichst viele Details. Haben Sie interessante Leute kennen gelernt oder ungewöhnliche Dinge gesehen oder erlebt? (Benutzen Sie bitte drei Adjektive in der Komparativform und drei in der Superlativform. Gebrauchen Sie auch mindestens zehn Verben im Imperfekt.)

Schritt 3: Beenden Sie Ihren Reisebericht mit einer Überraschung (*surprise*) oder einer interessanten Bemerkung (*comment*) für den Hörer oder den Leser. Seien Sie hier so kreativ wie möglich.

Schritt 4: In kleinen Gruppen zu viert lesen Sie Ihre Reiseberichte Ihren Mitstudenten und Mitstudentinnen vor. Sie sollen Ihnen Fragen über den Reisebericht stellen und raten, ob Ihre Geschichte wahr ist oder nicht.

Zu guter Letzt. Additional Activity: Have students bring in a photograph of a trip they took. Divide students into small groups and have them briefly tell about their trip. They can also play Baron von Münchhausen, bringing in any picture and telling a tall tale of a trip they took.

Zu guter Letzt. Note: You may wish to tell students that many German-language song lyrics can be found online. Additionally, many older German-language poems are available via the Projekt Gutenberg public domain database: http://gutenberg.spiegel.de

Wortschatz

Beginning with this chapter, the vocabulary section at the end of each chapter will list strong or irregular verbs with their principal parts as follows: **bringen, brachte, gebracht** or **fahren (fährt), fuhr, ist gefahren.**

Verkehrsmittel

Means of Transportation

die **Bahn, -en**	railway; train
der **Bus,** *pl.* **Busse**	bus
das **Fahrrad, -̈er**	bicycle
das **Flugzeug, -e**	airplane
das **Schiff, -e**	ship
das **Taxi, -s**	taxicab
der **Zug, -̈e**	train

Im Reisebüro

At the Travel Agency

das **Angebot, -e**	(special) offer; selection
die **Fahrkarte, -n**	ticket
die **Reise, -n**	trip
das **Reisebüro, -s**	travel agency
der **Reiseprospekt, -e**	travel brochure

Unterwegs

En Route

die **Abfahrt, -en**	departure
die **Ankunft, -̈e**	arrival
der **Anschluss, -̈e**	connection
die **Auskunft, -̈e**	information
der **Bahnsteig, -e**	(train) platform
das **Ding, -e**	thing
der **Fahrkarten-schalter, -**	ticket window
der **Fahrplan, -̈e**	schedule
die **Fahrt, -en**	trip; ride
die **Gepäckaufbe-wahrung**	baggage check
das **Gleis, -e**	track
die **Hütte, -n**	cabin
die **Möglichkeit, -en**	possibility, opportunity
die **Natur**	nature
die **Platzkarte, -n**	seat reservation card
der **Reiseführer, -**	travel guide (book)
der **Strand, -̈e**	beach

Zum Mitnehmen auf Reisen

Things to Take Along on a Trip

das **Bargeld**	cash
das **Handgepäck**	carry-on luggage
der **Handschuh, -e**	glove

die **Kamera, -s**	camera
der **Personalausweis, -e**	ID card
der **Reisescheck, -s**	traveler's check
das **Sonnenschutzmittel**	suntan lotion, sunscreen
das **Zelt, -e**	tent

Verben

Verbs

ab•fahren (fährt ab), fuhr ab, ist abgefahren	to depart, leave
beginnen, begann, begonnen	to begin, start
buchen	to book (a trip)
ein•steigen, stieg ein, ist eingestiegen	to board, get into (*a vehicle*)
erleben	to experience
hoffen (auf)	to hope (for)
packen	to pack
sich überlegen, überlegt	to think over
um•steigen, stieg um, ist umgestiegen	to transfer, change (trains)
unternehmen (unter-nimmt), unternahm, unternommen	to undertake
vergessen (vergisst), vergaß, vergessen	to forget
verreisen, ist verreist	to go on a trip
vor•schlagen (schlägt vor), schlug vor, vorgeschlagen	to suggest, propose

Adjektive und Adverbien

Adjectives and Adverbs

aktiv	active(ly)
gefährlich	dangerous(ly)
insgesamt	altogether, total
jung	young
langsam	slow(ly)
laut	loud(ly)
schnell	quick(ly), fast
sicher	safe(ly)

Sonstiges

Other

alles	everything
als (*subord. conj.*)	when
bevor (*subord. conj.*)	before

einfach	one-way (ticket); simple
einverstanden sein (mit)	to agree (with), be in agreement (with)
erster/zweiter Klasse fahren	to travel first/second class
hin und zurück	round-trip
nachdem (*subord. conj.*)	after

per Autostop reisen	to hitchhike
pro Person	per person
sonst noch	otherwise
Sonst noch etwas?	Anything else?
sportlich aktiv	active in sports
zu zweit, zu dritt, zu viert, ...	as a twosome threesome, foursome, . . .

DAS KANN ICH NUN!

1. Sagen Sie, wie Sie am liebsten reisen.

2. Sagen Sie, was Sie am liebsten im Urlaub machen.

3. Sie sind mit Freunden unterwegs in Deutschland und gehen in ein Reisebüro. Sie suchen Information über Wandertouren in den Alpen. Sagen Sie etwas über:

    a. was Sie möchten **b.** wie lange, wie viele Leute (kleine/große Gruppe) **c.** die Kosten

4. Sie stehen am Fahrkartenschalter am Kölner Hauptbahnhof. Sie wollen eine Tagesreise von Köln nach Düsseldorf machen. Was sagen Sie?

5. Sie packen Ihren Koffer für eine Reise in die Schweiz im August. Sagen Sie, was Sie mitnehmen.

6. Sie kommen von der Reise zurück und berichten in Ihrem Deutschkurs auf Deutsch:

    a. *The food tasted best in smaller restaurants.* **b.** *Staying overnight in a youth hostel was the the best deal* (**günstig**). **c.** *The most beautiful and best-known mountain is called* **das Matterhorn.**

7. Sie berichten über eine Reise. Schreiben Sie mit Hilfe der folgenden Notizen einen Bericht im Imperfekt.

    Reise in Frankfurt beginnen / in einem kleinen Hotel günstig übernachten / am nächsten Morgen mit dem Zug von Frankfurt nach Berlin fahren / am späten Nachmittag in Berlin ankommen / sehr lange auf ein Taxi warten / essen in einem gemütlichen Restaurant im Hotel

Der Start in die Zukunft

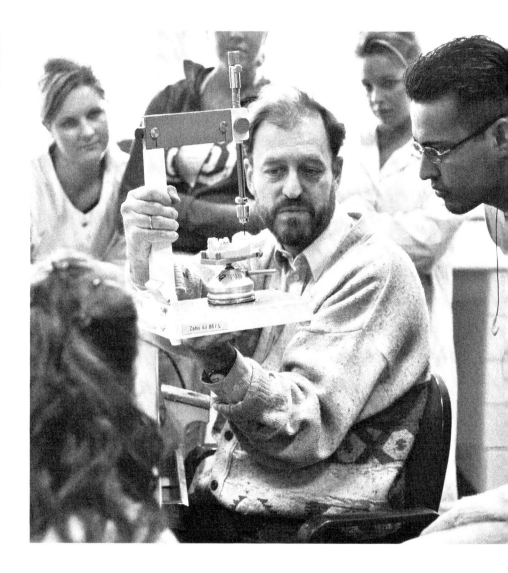

Gemeinsam lernen in einem
Lehrgang für Zahntechnik

In diesem Kapitel

- **Themen:** Career expectations, world of work, professions, job applications
- **Grammatik:** Future tense, relative clauses, **was für (ein)**, negating sentences with **nicht** and **kein**
- **Kultur:** Help-wanted ads, applying for a job, the German school system, civilian service
- **Lesen:** „Karriere beim Film"

Videoclips
Mein Beruf – mein Leben

Alles klar?

Alles klar? A. Follow-up: Ask students, *Finden Sie die Resultate der Umfrage überraschend? Warum / Warum nicht?*

A. Was wollen junge Deutsche vom Beruf? Die Informationen finden Sie im Schaubild.

Wünsche an den zukünftigen Beruf

Von je 100 Schülern nennen als sehr wichtig für ihren späteren Beruf

junge Frauen:

gesichertes[1] Einkommen	86
mit Menschen in Kontakt kommen	79
mit anderen zusammenarbeiten	78
nebenbei genug Zeit für Hobbys	75
gute Arbeits-marktchancen	73
Kenntnisse und Fähig-keiten weiterentwickeln	70
eigene geistige[3] Kräfte voll einsetzen[4] können	67
eigene Ideen verwirklichen[5]	67
neue Herausforderungen[6]	65
sich bei der Arbeit bewegen können	64

junge Männer:

gesichertes Einkommen	86
Kenntnisse und Fähig-keiten weiterentwickeln[2]	76
nebenbei genug Zeit für Hobbys	75
viel Geld verdienen	73
gute Arbeits-marktchancen	73
Karrierechancen	70
am Wochenende frei haben	64
eigene Ideen verwirklichen	62
mit anderen zusammenarbeiten	62
abwechslungsreiche Tätigkeit	58

Mehrfachnennungen
Umfrage 2003/2004

G 0038 © Globus   Quelle: BIBB

[1]*secure*   [2]Kenntnisse ... *continue to develop knowledge and skills*   [3]*intellectual*   [4]*apply*
[5]*realize*   [6]*challenges*

- Das Wichtigste für den Beruf junger Frauen und junger Männer ist
  _____.

- _____ ist wichtiger für junge Frauen als für junge Männer.

- _____ und _____ sind genau so wichtig im Beruf für junge Frauen und junger Männer.

- Welche Berufswünsche haben junge Frauen, die junge Männer nicht haben und umgekehrt (*vice versa*)? Suchen Sie fünf Unterschiede.

B. Sie hören Gabriele Sommer über ihre Berufspläne sprechen.

- Wie ist sie auf ihre Berufswahl gekommen?

- Wo studiert sie?

- Was studiert sie?

- Was hat sie in ihrem späteren Berufsleben vor?

Wörter im Kontext

wishes

expectations

THEMA 1: Meine Interessen, Wünsche° und Erwartungen°

Wie **stellen** Sie **sich** Ihr **Berufsleben vor?** Was erwarten Sie vom Beruf? Kreuzen Sie an.

Ich möchte gern:	WICHTIG	UNWICHTIG
▪ **selbständig** arbeiten	☐	☐
▪ einen sicheren **Arbeitsplatz** haben	☐	☐
▪ **mich** mit Finanzen **beschäftigen**	☐	☐
▪ **im Freien arbeiten**	☐	☐
▪ **Gelegenheit** zum Reisen haben	☐	☐
▪ **im Ausland** arbeiten	☐	☐
▪ ein gutes **Gehalt** haben (viel Geld **verdienen**)	☐	☐
▪ eine **abwechslungsreiche Tätigkeit** haben	☐	☐
▪ ohne viel Arbeit **erfolgreich** sein	☐	☐
▪ einen **Chef** / eine **Chefin** haben, der/die meine Arbeit anerkennt (*appreciates*)	☐	☐
▪ sympathische **Mitarbeiter/Mitarbeiterinnen** haben	☐	☐
▪ mit Menschen zu tun haben	☐	☐
▪ mit Computer **Technik/Elektronik** arbeiten	☐	☐
▪ eine kurze **Ausbildung**szeit haben	☐	☐
▪ Prestige/**Ansehen** haben	☐	☐
▪ im **Büro** arbeiten	☐	☐
▪ eine **verantwortliche** Position bei einer großen **Firma** haben	☐	☐
▪ einen Beruf haben, der mich **herausfordert**	☐	☐

Vergleichen Sie Ihre Antworten untereinander. Suchen Sie jemand im Kurs, mit dem Sie mehr als fünf Antworten gemeinsam haben.

Ein Schornsteinfeger arbeitet meistens im Freien.

Neue Wörter

stellen sich vor (sich vorstellen) imagine
das Berufsleben professional life
selbständig independent(ly)
der Arbeitsplatz position, workplace
mich ... beschäftigen (sich beschäftigen) occupy myself
im Freien outdoors
die Gelegenheit opportunity
im Ausland abroad
das Gehalt salary
verdienen earn
abwechslungsreich varied
die Tätigkeit position; activity
erfolgreich successful
der Chef / die Chefin manager, boss
der Mitarbeiter (Mitarbeiter, *pl.*)/die Mitarbeiterin (Mitarbeiterinnen, *pl.*) co-worker, colleague
die Technik technology
die Ausbildung training
das Ansehen prestige
das Büro office
verantwortlich responsible
die Firma firm, company
herausfordert (herausfordern) challenges

Aktivität 1 Drei junge Leute

Sie hören drei junge Leute über ihre Interessen, Wünsche und Erwartungen sprechen. Was tun sie gern oder nicht gern? Was ist ihnen wichtig oder nicht wichtig?

PERSON	WAS ER/SIE (NICHT) GERN TUT	WAS IHM/IHR (NICHT) WICHTIG IST
Tina	arbeitet gern im Freien, möchte nicht gern im Büro arbeiten	nicht wichtig: großes Ansehen und viel Geld
Markus	reist gern und möchte im Ausland arbeiten	wichtig: mit Menschen zu tun haben; abwechslungsreiche Tätigkeit
Andrea	arbeitet gern mit ihren Händen; interessiert sich für Maschinen, Computer	keine Information

Erste Adresse für Ihren Karrierestart

Kreativ? Flexibel? Verantwortlich?
Wir fordern Sie heraus! ✔WestLB

Aktivität 2 Hin und her: Wer macht was, und warum?

Ergänzen Sie die Informationen.

BEISPIEL: s1: Was macht Corinna Eichhorn?
s2: Sie ist Sozialarbeiterin.
s1: Warum macht sie das?
s2: Weil …

NAME	BERUF	WARUM?
Corinna Eichhorn	Sozialarbeiterin	Menschen helfen
Karsten Becker	Bibliothekar	sich für Bücher interessieren
Erika Lentz	Filmschauspielerin	mit Menschen zu tun haben
Alex Böhmer	Informatiker	mit Computern arbeiten

Fragen Sie einen Partner / eine Partnerin: „Was erwartest du von deinem Beruf? Was ist dir nicht so wichtig?" Verwenden Sie einige der folgenden Redemittel.

BEISPIEL: s1: Mir ist ein sicherer Arbeitsplatz wichtig.
s2: Ein sicherer Arbeitsplatz ist mir nicht so wichtig, aber ich erwarte, dass ich Gelegenheit zum Reisen habe.

REDEMITTEL	ERWARTUNGEN
Mir ist _____ (nicht) wichtig.	ein gutes Gehalt (haben)
Ich erwarte, dass _____.	viel Kontakt mit Menschen (haben)
Ich möchte gern _____.	Menschen helfen
An erster Stelle kommt _____.	Spaß an der Arbeit (haben)
_____ interessiert mich (nicht).	nette Mitarbeiter/Mitarbeiterinnen (haben)
	Gelegenheit zum Reisen (haben)
	selbständig arbeiten
	im Freien arbeiten
	im Ausland arbeiten
	Ansehen (haben)
	einen sicheren Arbeitsplatz (haben)
	kreativ arbeiten
	flexible Arbeitszeit (haben)
	??

THEMA 2: Berufe

BERUFE

Gesundheitswesen

Arzt/Ärztin
Krankenpfleger/Krankenschwester
Psychologe/Psychologin
Sozialarbeiter/Sozialarbeiterin
Tierarzt/Tierärztin
Zahnarzt/Zahnärztin

Technischer Bereich

Elektroinstallateur/Elektroinstallateurin
Ingenieur/Ingenieurin
Mechaniker/Mechanikerin
Radio- oder Fernsehtechniker/
   Radio- oder Fernsehtechnikerin

Verwaltung

Rechtsanwalt/Rechtsanwältin
Diplomat/Diplomatin
Finanzbeamter/Finanzbeamtin
Personalchef/Personalchefin

Naturwissenschaften

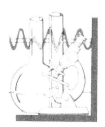

Biotechnologe/Biotechnologin
Chemiker/Chemikerin
Laborant/Laborantin
Meteorologe/Meteorologin
Physiker/Physikerin

Wirtschaft und Handel
Geschäftsmann/Geschäftsfrau
Informatiker/Informatikerin
Kaufmann/Kauffrau
Sekretär/Sekretärin

Verkehrswesen
Flugbegleiter/Flugbegleiterin
Flugingenieur/Flugingenieurin
Pilot/Pilotin
Reisebüroleiter/Reisebüroleiterin

Kommunikationswesen
Bibliothekar/Bibliothekarin
Dolmetscher/Dolmetscherin
Journalist/Journalistin
Nachrichtensprecher/Nachrichtensprecherin

Kreativer Bereich
Architekt/Architektin
Designer/Designerin
Fotograf/Fotografin
Künstler/Künstlerin
Musiker/Musikerin
Schauspieler/Schauspielerin
Zeichner/Zeichnerin

Welcher Beruf passt zu welcher Beschreibung?

BEISPIEL: Eine Architektin entwirft Häuser.

1. __c__ spielt im Film oder auf der Bühne (*stage*).
2. __f__ spielt in einem Orchester.
3. __a__ **untersucht** Patienten.
4. __g__ **entwirft** Gebäude, Häuser und Wohnungen.
5. __h__ verkauft Produkte einer Firma.
6. __b__ hat mit Computern zu tun.
7. __j__ malt Bilder.
8. __d__ arbeitet in einer Bibliothek.
9. __i__ **übersetzt** Texte mündlich (*orally*).
10. __e__ repariert Autos.

a. Arzt/Ärztin
b. Informatiker/Informatikerin
c. Schauspieler/Schauspielerin
d. Bibliothekar/Bibliothekarin
e. Automechaniker/Automechanikerin
f. Musiker/Musikerin
g. Architekt/Architektin
h. Kaufmann/Kauffrau
i. Dolmetscher/Dolmetscherin
j. Künstler/Künstlerin

Aktivität 4 Was meinen Sie?

Suchen Sie Ihre Antworten auf die folgenden Fragen in der Liste von Berufen im **Thema 2**.

1. Wer hat die gefährlichste Arbeit?
2. Welcher Beruf hat das meiste Prestige?
3. Wer hat mit Tieren zu tun?
4. Wer arbeitet meistens in einem Büro?
5. Wer verdient das meiste Geld?
6. Für welche Berufe muss man studieren?
7. Welche Arbeit bringt den meisten Stress mit sich?
8. Wer hat die längsten Arbeitsstunden?
9. Wer hat die langweiligste Arbeit?

Neue Wörter

der Zahnarzt / die Zahnärztin dentist
der Rechtsanwalt / die Rechtsanwältin lawyer, attorney
der Handel sales, trade
der Geschäftsmann / die Geschäftsfrau businessman/ businesswoman
der Informatiker / die Informatikerin computer scientist
der Kaufmann / die Kauffrau salesman/saleswoman
der Bibliothekar / die Bibliothekarin librarian
der Dolmetscher / die Dolmetscherin interpreter
der Künstler / die Künstlerin artist
der Schauspieler / die Schauspielerin actor
der Zeichner / die Zeichnerin graphic artist
untersucht (untersuchen) examines
entwirft (entwerfen) designs
übersetzt (übersetzen) translates

famous

Diese berühmten Menschen, die alle einen Beruf ausübten, hatten auch andere Interessen. Ergänzen Sie die Informationen.

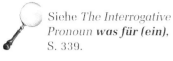

Siehe *The Interrogative Pronoun* **was für (ein)**, S. 339.

BEISPIEL: s1: Was war Martin Luther von Beruf?
s2: Er war Priester.
s1: Was für andere Interessen hatte er?
s2: Er interessierte sich für Literatur, Musik und die deutsche Sprache.

NAME	BERUF	INTERESSEN
Martin Luther		
Käthe Kollwitz	Künstlerin	Politik
Bertha von Suttner		
Rainer Werner Fassbinder	Filmregisseur	Literatur, Theater
Marlene Dietrich		
Willi Brandt	Politiker	Ski fahren, Lesen

Machen Sie eine Liste von den Kriterien, die Ihnen im Beruf wichtig sind. Benutzen Sie die Vokabeln vom **Thema 1**. Fragen Sie dann jemand im Kurs, was für einen Beruf er/sie Ihnen empfehlen würde.

BEISPIEL: s1: Ich möchte eine abwechslungsreiche Tätigkeit haben, vielleicht im Büro arbeiten und viel Kontakt mit Menschen haben. Was empfiehlst du mir?
s2: Ich empfehle dir, Kaufmann/Kauffrau zu werden.

THEMA 3: Stellenangebote und Bewerbungen

Neue Wörter

das Stellenangebot   help-wanted ad
die Zukunft   future
der Hersteller   producer, manufacturer
die Stärke (Stärken, *pl.***)**   strength
das Unternehmen   company
beschäftigen   employ
der Leiter   director
engagiert   committed
übernehmen   take over
die Beratung   advising
die Unterstützung   support
die Erfahrung (Erfahrungen, *pl.***)**   experience
die Fähigkeit (Fähigkeiten, *pl.***)**   skill, ability
die Kenntnis (Kenntnisse, *pl.***)**   knowledge
der Vorteil   advantage
die Bewerbung   application
das Personal   personnel

Ein Stellenangebot

Sehen Sie sich das Stellenangebot auf der folgenden Seite an und beantworten Sie die Fragen.

- Was für eine Person sucht die Firma?
- Was für ein Studium braucht man für diesen Job?
- Welche Qualifikationen und Eigenschaften sind der Firma wichtig?
- Wie viele Mitarbeiter und Mitarbeiterinnen hat die Firma?
- In wie vielen Ländern ist die Firma vertreten?

[1]Zeichen ... *pointing the way*   [2]*creation*   [3]*content*   [4]*service providers*   [5]*relevant*

Eine Bewerbung

Wie **bewirbt** man **sich um** eine **Stelle**? Bringen Sie folgende Schritte in eine logische Reihenfolge.

_____ einen tabellarischen **Lebenslauf** schreiben

_____ ein **Bewerbungsformular** ausfüllen

__1__ Interessen, Wünsche und Erwartungen mit Familie und Freunden besprechen

_____ **Unterlagen** (**Abiturzeugnis** oder anderen **Abschluss** und **Zeugnisse** von früheren **Arbeitgebern**) sammeln

_____ **sich auf** das **Vorstellungsgespräch vorbereiten**

_____ die Stellenangebote in der Zeitung durchlesen

_____ Informationen über verschiedene Karrieren und Berufe sammeln

_____ zum **Arbeitsamt** an der Uni gehen und mit **Berufsberatern** sprechen

Suggestion: Introduce a fictional character and describe the steps he/she went through to apply for a job.

Lesen Sie das Angebot der Firma „testo" auf Seite 329 und wählen Sie passende Wörter aus dem Kasten, um die Sätze zu ergänzen.

Eigeninitiative   Engagement   Fähigkeit   Kenntnisse   Kontakten

Teamgeist   Vorteil   Web-Master   Websites

Weiteres zum Thema Stellenanzeigen finden Sie bei **Deutsch: Na klar!** im World-Wide-Web unter

1. Die Firma „testo" sucht einen _____ für ihre _____ weltweit.
2. Drei wichtige Eigenschaften sind _____, _____ und _____.
3. Kommunikative _____ in englischer Sprache ist auch sehr wichtig.
4. Sehr gute _____ in Internettechnologien und Programmieren sind von _____.
5. Die Person, die die Stelle bekommt, wird in dem „testo" Team mit vielen internationalen _____ arbeiten.

Was stimmt? Was stimmt nicht? Korrigieren Sie die falschen Aussagen.

	DAS STIMMT	DAS STIMMT NICHT
1. Petra sucht einen Ausbildungsplatz.	☐	☐
2. Petra ist noch nicht zum Arbeitsamt gegangen.	☐	☐
3. Petra hat ein interessantes Stellenangebot in der Zeitung gefunden.	☐	☐
4. Petra hat sich um eine Ausbildungsstelle beworben.	☐	☐
5. Petra hat die Firma sofort angerufen.	☐	☐
6. Petra ist sehr enthusiastisch, weil sie die Firma gut kennt.	☐	☐
7. Die Firma verlangt, dass Bewerber Biologie studiert haben.	☐	☐

Führen Sie mit einem Partner / einer Partnerin ein Gespräch über eine Stellensuche. Sie können die Anzeigen in diesem Kapitel oder Anzeigen aus einer Zeitung oder dem Internet zur Information benutzen.

S1	S2
1. Was wirst du _____ machen? ■ nach dem Studium ■ in den Semesterferien ■ ??	**2.** Ich werde eine Stelle _____ suchen. ■ in einem Büro ■ bei einer Firma ■ in einer Fabrik ■ ??
3. Wie findet man _____?	**4.** Man muss mindestens _____ (2/3/4/5/?) Dinge machen: _____. ■ Informationen über verschiedene Berufe sammeln ■ Stellenangebote in der Zeitung / im Internet durcharbeiten ■ zur Arbeitsvermittlung an der Uni gehen ■ Freunde/Familie/Bekannte fragen ■ zum Arbeitsamt / zur Berufsberatung gehen ■ ??
5. Was braucht man für eine Bewerbung?	**6.** Man muss gewöhnlich _____.
7. Wie lange dauert es, bis _____?	**8.** ■ _____ geht schnell. ■ Manchmal dauert es _____. ■ Meistens dauert es _____ Monate.
9. Na, dann viel Glück!	**10.** Vielen Dank!

Aktivität 10. **Suggestion:** This activity can be done as homework or as an in-class *Partnerarbeit*. Either way, you may wish to review how to express dates and years in German before beginning the activity.

Aktivität 10   Ein Lebenslauf

Hier sehen Sie einen typischen tabellarischen Lebenslauf.

Schritt 1: Beantworten Sie die Fragen:

- Welche Schulen hat Birgit in Bonn besucht?
- Welche Ausbildung hat sie gemacht?
- Was ist ihr jetziger Beruf?
- Welche anderen Interessen hat Birgit?

Schritt 2: Nun erzählen Sie Birgits Lebenslauf in vollständigen Sätzen. Benutzen Sie folgendes Format.

BEISPIEL: Birgit ist am 22. Dezember 1984 in
      Bonn geboren.
      Von _____ bis _____ …
      Seit …
      Danach …

Grundschule besucht

Realschule besucht

Ausbildung als Bürokauffrau gemacht

als Reisebürokauffrau in Bonn gearbeitet

Lebenslauf

Name	Birgit Hermsen
Geburtsdatum	22. Dezember 1984
Geburtsort	Bonn
Eltern	Friedrich Hermsen Elsbeth Hermsen, geb. Marx

Ausbildungsgang

1990–1994	Grundschule: Elisabethschule, Bonn
1994–2001	Realschule, Bonn
1999–2000	Austauschschülerin in USA (Experiment in International Living) Redwood City, Kalifornien
2001	Realschulabschluss: Mittlere Reife
2001–2003	Ausbildung als Bürokauffrau, Bonn Reisebüro Wilmers
Seit 2003	Reisebürokauffrau, Bonn Reisebüro am Markt
Familienstand	ledig
Interessen	Reisen (USA, Nepal, Australien und Neuseeland) Sport (Tennis, Reiten) Lesen und Musik

Mit sechs Jahren beginnt für Kinder in Deutschland die Schule. Alle Kinder gehen zuerst vier bis sechs Jahre lang gemeinsam auf **die Grundschule.** Danach trennen sich die Wege.

Ein Teil der Schüler und Schülerinnen geht dann auf **die Hauptschule,** die nach dem neunten oder zehnten Schuljahr mit dem Hauptschulabschluss endet. Danach suchen sich die meisten Schulabgänger eine Ausbildungsstelle für einen praktischen Beruf. Zweimal die Woche müssen die „Azubis" (<u>Au</u>szu<u>bi</u>ldende oder Lehrlinge) auf **die Berufsschule** gehen. Dort lernen sie vor allem praktische Fächer, die für den künftigen Beruf wichtig sind.

Ein anderer Teil der Schüler und Schülerinnen geht von der Grundschule auf **die Realschule.** Sie endet nach dem zehnten Schuljahr mit dem **Abschluss** der **mittleren Reife.** Danach geht man auf eine **Fachschule** oder auch auf eine **Berufsschule.**

Als dritte Möglichkeit gibt es **das Gymnasium,** das als Vorbereitung auf ein Universitätsstudium dient. Das traditionelle Gymnasium umfasst neun Klassen, vom fünften bis zum dreizehnten Schuljahr. Neuerdings (*Recently*) wird die Zeit auf dem Gymnasium auf acht Jahre reduziert. Immer mehr Gymnasien gehen nur bis zum zwölften Schuljahr. Am Ende des Gymnasiums machen Schüler **das Abitur.** Ohne Abitur kann man nicht studieren.

Als Alternative für die drei verschiedenen Schultypen gibt es in Deutschland heutzutage **die Gesamtschule.** Ähnlich wie in nordamerikanischen Schulen gehen alle Schüler zur selben Schule bis zum Abschluss; daher der Name Gesamtschule.

Der erste Schultag: Der Ernst des Lebens beginnt.

Vom Kindergarten zur Universität

			Berufsqualifizierender Studienabschluß
Berufsqualifizierender Abschluß	Allgemeine Hochschulreife		**Universität/Technische Universität, Pädagogische Hochschule Fachhochschule Verwaltungsfachhochschule Kunsthochschule Gesamthochschule**
Fachschule	Abendgymnasium/ Kolleg		

	Berufsbildender Abschluß			Allgemeine Hochschulreife	
13	Mittlerer Bildungsabschluß		Fachhochschulreife	**Gymnasiale Oberstufe**	13
12	Berufsausbildung in Betrieb u. Berufsschule (Duales System)	Berufs- aufbau- Schule	Berufs- fach- Schule	Fach- ober- Schule	(Gymnasium, Berufliches Gymnasium, Fachgymnasium, Gesamtschule)	12
11					11
10	Berufsgrundbildungsjahr				10

Abschlüsse an Hauptschulen nach 9 oder 10 Jahren / Realschulabschluß

10	10. Schuljahr	—	—	—		10
9		—	—	—		9
8	Sonder- schule	**Hauptschule**	**Realschule**	**Gymnasium**	**Gesamt- schule**	8
7					—	7
6		*Orientierungs-Stufe*				6
5		*(schulformabhängig oder schulformunabhängig)*				5

4			4
3	Sonder- schule	**Grundschule**	3
2			2
1			1

Schuljahr	Sonder- kinder- garten	**Kindergarten**

Grammatik im Kontext

Future Tense°

Das Futur

You recall that in German the present tense can also refer to future action, particularly when an adverb of time is present.

Nächstes Jahr macht Sabine ein Praktikum in den USA.
Next year Sabine is going to do an internship in the USA.

Morgen schickt sie mehrere Bewerbungen ab.
Tomorrow she will send off several applications.

In German, the future tense is used most frequently to express future time when the context provides no other explicit reference to the future.

Eines Tages **werde** ich Erfolg **haben.**
Someday I will be successful.

Millionen **werden** meine Bücher **kaufen.**
Millions will buy my books.

Wir **werden** mal **sehen.**
We shall see (if that's the case).

kaufen			
ich	werde kaufen	wir	werden kaufen
du	wirst kaufen	ihr	werdet kaufen
er sie es	wird kaufen	sie	werden kaufen
Sie werden kaufen			

Note:

- The future tense is formed with the auxiliary verb **werden** and the infinitive of the main verb.
- The auxiliary **werden** and the infinitive at the end of the sentence form a sentence bracket (**Satzklammer**).

Eines Tages **werden** Millionen meine Bücher **kaufen.**

Some day, millions will buy my books.

Ich **werde** in einer großen Villa **wohnen.**

I will live in a large villa.

Note: You may wish to ask students what other verb forms they have learned follow the sentence bracket pattern (e.g., modal verbs). You may also wish to review *werden* as a nonauxiliary verb, e.g., *Es wird kalt, ich werde 21.*

Was ist Ihr Wunschtraum? Was werden Sie eines Tages sein? Wo werden Sie wohnen?

BEISPIEL: Ich werde Millionär sein.
Ich werde in einem Schloss wohnen.

Was möchtest du werden?

WAS?	WO?
Akrobat/Akrobatin beim Zirkus	auf dem Mars
Präsident/Präsidentin von …	in einem Schloss
Astronaut/Astronautin	in einer Grashütte auf Tahiti
Fußballspieler/Fußballspielerin	in einer netten kleinen Villa
Milliardär/Milliardärin	in einem Wohnwagen
berühmte/r Schauspieler/ Schauspielerin	im Weißen Haus
berühmte/r Sänger/Sängerin	in einer Kommune
??	in einer großen Villa
	??

Lesen Sie den Cartoon „Poesie" (*Poetry*).

Poesie von Erich Rauschenbach

- Identify the verbs in each sentence. Which verbs clearly refer to the present?
- How does the poet express his wishful thinking?
- For each sentence expressing the poet's hopes for the future, state the unspoken reality of his present life.

BEISPIEL: Er hat keinen Erfolg mit seinen Gedichten.

[1]*poems*
[2]Erfolg … *be successful*
[3]in den … *praise me to the skies*
[4]*famous*
[5]*afterward*
[6]mache … *continue*
[7]wie … *as before*
[8]ausgewählte … *select readership*

Expressing Probability

The future tense is also used in German to express probability, often with the adverb **wohl** or **wahrscheinlich** (*probably*).

Consider the following hypothetical scenario concerning the unsuccessful poet of the cartoon "*Poesie.*"

> Zehn Jahre später: Der Dichter, Anselmus Himmelblau, fährt jetzt einen tollen BMW mit Autotelefon und Navi (GPS) und wohnt in einer Villa in Spanien. Auf seiner Luxusjacht in Monte Carlo trifft sich die Prominenz der ganzen Welt ...

What is probably true about Anselmus?

Er **wird wohl** endlich Erfolg haben.	*He is probably finally successful.*
Millionen **werden** jetzt **wahrscheinlich** seine Bücher **kaufen.**	*Millions are probably buying his books now.*
Er **wird wohl** sehr reich **sein.**	*He is probably very rich.*

Übung 2 Wahrscheinlich

Führen Sie ein Gespräch. Reden Sie mit mindestens zwei Leuten. Jemand hat gerade eine Million Dollar in der Lotterie gewonnen. Was wird er/sie wahrscheinlich mit dem Geld machen?

BEISPIEL: s1: Meine Mutter hat eine Million Dollar gewonnen.
s2: Was wird sie mit dem Geld machen?
s1: Sie wird sich wahrscheinlich einen tollen Ferrari kaufen.

WER?	WAS?
Mutter	das Geld auf die Bank bringen
Vater	(sich) einen tollen Ferrari kaufen
Eltern	nach Florida ziehen
Freundin	(sich) ein Schloss in Frankreich kaufen
Freund	vielen Leuten helfen
ich	(sich) ein tolles Motorrad kaufen
??	auf eine Insel in der Karibik ziehen
	eine Weltreise machen
	??

Describing People or Things: Relative Clauses°

Relativsätze

A relative clause provides additional information about a person or an object named in the main clause.

> XYZ Company is looking for bright and energetic trainees *who are interested in a career in communications technology.*

> XYZ Company is looking for trainees *whose background includes a degree in computer science.*

> XYZ Company is looking for trainees *for whom the sky is the limit.*

Expressing Probability. Point out: The use of *wohl* and *wahrscheinlich* with the future tense tends to refer to present probability, athough it may also refer to *future* probability.

Übung 2. Follow-up: Find out what students will do with their lottery winnings.

The Relative Pronoun°

In German, a relative clause is always introduced by a relative pronoun. The forms of the relative pronoun are identical to those of the definite article, except in the genitive singular and the genitive and dative plural.

	SINGULAR			**PLURAL**
	Masculine	*Neuter*	*Feminine*	*All Genders*
Nominative	der	das	die	die
Accusative	den	das	die	die
Dative	dem	dem	der	**denen**
Genitive	**dessen**	**dessen**	**deren**	**deren**

NOMINATIVE SUBJECT

Ich wünsche mir einen Job, **der** Spaß macht.

*I want a job **that** is fun.*

ACCUSATIVE OBJECT

Wie heißt der junge Mann, **den** du gestern kennen gelernt hast?

*What is the name of the young man (**whom**) you met yesterday?*

DATIVE OBJECT

Sind Sie einer von den Menschen, **denen** ein sicherer Arbeitsplatz wichtig ist?

*Are you one of those people **to whom** a secure position is important?*

GENITIVE OBJECT

Wir sind eine Firma, **deren** Produkte weltbekannt sind.

*We are a company **whose** products are known worldwide.*

PREPOSITIONAL OBJECT

Informatikerin ist ein Beruf, **für den** ich mich interessiere.

*Being a computer scientist is an occupation **in which** I am interested.*

Note:

- Relative pronouns correspond in gender and number to their antecedent—that is, to the noun to which they refer.
- The case of the relative pronoun is determined by its function within the relative clause. It can be the subject, an object, or a prepositional object.
- The conjugated verb is placed at the end of the relative clause.
- A relative clause in German is always set off from the rest of the sentence by a comma.
- The relative pronoun must always be expressed in German; it cannot be omitted as it sometimes can in English.

Der Personalchef, **den** ich kürzlich kennen lernte, ...

The personnel director I met recently . . . (The personnel director whom I met recently . . .)

Die Berufsberaterin, **mit der** ich sprach, ...

The career adviser I spoke with . . . (The career adviser with whom I spoke . . .)

denen Ihr Radius zu eng ist...'

Malte Fischer
Beratung
und Management
für Unternehmen
Schlebenweg 2
D-51610 Overath
Tel 0 2206/2231

Ich will einen Job, der zu mir passt.

Wir suchen einen qualifizierten

Mitarbeiter

der mindestens ein Jahr Erfahrung mit Airlines vorweisen kann.

Wir suchen noch Hausfrauen, Rentner, Studenten oder Berufstätige, die es frühmorgens in ihren Betten nicht mehr aushalten.

Lesen Sie, was Leute lesen, **die Karriere** machen wollen.

- Identify the main clause and the relative clause(s) in each of the four ads.
- About whom or what do the relative clauses provide information?
- Where is the conjugated verb placed in each relative clause?

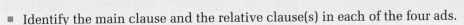

Übung 3   Attribute

Ergänzen Sie die Relativpronomen. Wie heißen die Sätze auf Englisch?

A. Nominativ

1. Gabriele ist eine Frau, _____ selbständig arbeiten möchte.
2. Nicholas ist ein Mann, _____ selbständig arbeiten möchte.
3. Das sind junge Leute, _____ selbständig arbeiten möchten.
4. Dies ist eine Firma, _____ junge Leute mit Verkaufstalent sucht.
5. ABC ist ein Unternehmen, _____ Azubis sucht.

B. Akkusativ

1. Wie heißt der Arzt, _____ du gestern kennen gelernt hast?
2. Wie heißt die Ärztin, _____ du gestern kennen gelernt hast?
3. Wie heißt der Schauspieler, _____ du gern kennen lernen möchtest?
4. Wie heißen die Musiker, _____ du gern hören möchtest?
5. Wie heißt das Buch, _____ du zum Geburtstag bekommen hast?

C. Dativ

1. Wir suchen eine Studentin, _____ Reisen Spaß macht.
2. Wir suchen einen Studenten, _____ Auto fahren Spaß macht.
3. Wir suchen Leute, _____ Technik Spaß macht.
4. Er ist ein Mensch, _____ Prestige sehr wichtig ist.
5. Plus ist eine Firma, _____ motivierte Manager wichtig sind.

D. Genitiv

1. Dies ist eine Firma, _____ Produkte überall bekannt sind.
2. Dies ist ein Unternehmen, _____ Produkte überall bekannt sind.
3. Das sind Schulen, _____ Schüler eine gute Ausbildung bekommen.

Übung 3. Answers: A. 1. *die* 2. *der* 3. *die* 4. *die* 5. *das* B. 1. *den* 2. *die* 3. *den* 4. *die* 5. *das* C. 1. *der* 2. *dem* 3. *denen* 4. *dem* 5. *der* D. 1. *deren* 2. *dessen* 3. *deren*

Grammatik im Kontext   **337**

Schritt 1: Kreuzen Sie drei Dinge an, die auf Sie zutreffen (*apply*).

Ich bin ein Mensch, … der Gruppenarbeit nicht mag. ☐
                     der gut zuhören kann. ☐
                     dem man vertrauen (*trust*) kann. ☐
                     dem Lernen Spaß macht. ☐
                     den alle Leute mögen. ☐
                     dem kreative Arbeit gefällt. ☐
                     der gut organisieren kann. ☐
                     der am liebsten für sich allein ist. ☐
                     der weiß, was er will. ☐

Schritt 2: Arbeiten Sie nun zu viert und machen Sie eine Liste mit den Qualitäten, die in Ihrer Gruppe vorkommen (*are found*).

BEISPIELE: Es gibt drei Leute, die Gruppenarbeit nicht mögen.
          Es gibt einen Studenten, dem kreative Arbeit gefällt.
          Es gibt eine Studentin, die gut organisieren kann.

Die folgenden Sätze sind aus Stellenangeboten in deutschen Zeitungen. Setzen Sie die passenden Relativpronomen ein.

1. Unsere Firma sucht Abiturienten, _____ Kreativität und Flexibilität besitzen.

2. Wenn Sie eine junge Dame sind, _____ sich für technische Berufe interessiert, schicken Sie uns Ihre Bewerbung.

3. Wir suchen einen Auszubildenden (Azubi), _____ das Bäckerhandwerk lernen möchte.

4. Elektroniker ist ein Beruf, für _____ sich viele junge Leute interessieren.

5. Wir sind eine Firma, mit _____ Sie über Ihre Zukunft reden sollten.

6. Ist Ihnen die Umwelt, in _____ Sie leben, wichtig? Dann werden Sie doch Umwelt-Techniker, ein Beruf für engagierte Menschen, _____ unsere Umwelt wichtig ist.

7. Wir suchen junge Leute, _____ ein gesundes Selbstbewusstsein (*self-confidence*) haben.

8. Wir suchen junge Leute, _____ einen sicheren Arbeitsplatz suchen und _____ bei der Post Karriere machen wollen.

Herr Grimmig, Briefträger von Beruf, hat – wie Sie sehen – mal wieder einen schlechten Tag. Schauen Sie sich zuerst die zwei Bilder an.

Schritt 1: Lesen Sie die folgenden Tatsachen (*facts*).

- Fritz, der Hund, hasst Briefträger. Er hat den Briefträger, Herrn Grimmig, ins Bein gebissen.
- Fritz ist Nikos Hund.
- Herr Sauer ist Nikos Vater. Er ist sehr böse und irritiert.
- Frau Kluge, die Nachbarin, hat alles genau gesehen.
- Herr Grimmig, der Briefträger, hat die Polizei geholt.
- Der Polizist, Herr Gründlich, schreibt alles genau auf.

NÜTZLICHE WÖRTER	
hassen	*to hate*
beißen, gebissen	*to bite*
böse	*angry*
holen	*to fetch, get*
auf•schreiben, aufgeschrieben	*to write down*

Schritt 2: Sagen Sie nun mit Hilfe der Tatsachen etwas über diese Situation.

BEISPIEL: Fritz ist der Hund. Er hasst Briefträger. →
Fritz ist der Hund, der Briefträger hasst.

1. Fritz ist der Hund, …
2. Niko ist …,
3. Herr Grimmig ist …,
4. Frau Kluge ist …,
5. Herr Sauer ist …,
6. Herr Gründlich ist …,

The Interrogative Pronoun° was für (ein)

Das Interrogativpronomen

NOMINATIVE

Was für ein Beruf ist das? *What kind of a profession is that?*

Was für eine Firma ist das? *What kind of a firm is that?*

ACCUSATIVE

Was für einen Chef hast du? *What kind of a boss do you have?*

Was für eine Chefin hast du? *What kind of a boss do you have?*

Was für Arbeit machst du dort? *What kind of work do you do there?*

DATIVE

In **was für einer** Firma arbeitest du?	*What kind of a firm do you work for?*
Mit **was für einem** Kollegen arbeitest du?	*What kind of a colleague do you work with?*
Mit **was für** Kollegen arbeitest du?	*What kind of colleagues do you work with?*

Note:

- The interrogative pronoun **was für (ein)** is always followed by a noun.

- The case of the noun that follows **was für (ein)** depends on its function in the sentence. **Für** does not function as a preposition and, therefore, does not determine the case of the noun.

- The expression is always **was für** (without **ein**) when the noun is plural.

Hören Sie zu und markieren Sie die richtige(n) Antwort(en).

1. Der eine Sprecher …

   a. liest ein Buch.   **b.** sieht fern.   **c.** schreibt ein Buch.

2. *Das literarische Oktett* ist …

   a. ein Gedicht.   **b.** der Titel eines Buches.   **c.** der Titel einer Erzählung.   **d.** der Name eines Klubs.

3. Die Autoren sind …

   a. fünf Studentinnen.   **b.** acht Studenten.   **c.** acht Hausfrauen.

4. Im Buch stehen …

   a. nur Geschichten.   **b.** nur Gedichte.
   c. hauptsächlich (*mainly*) Geschichten und ein paar Gedichte.

5. Die Themen, über die die Autoren schreiben, beziehen sich auf …

   a. Politik.   **b.** Sex.   **c.** Liebe.   **d.** Deutschland.

6. Der Leser des Buches findet das Buch …

   a. merkwürdig.   **b.** originell.   **c.** dumm.   **d.** provozierend.

Fragen Sie!

BEISPIEL: s1: Was für Filme siehst du am liebsten?
         s2: Am liebsten sehe ich Dokumentarfilme.

1. Was für Filme siehst du am liebsten? (z.B. Abenteuerfilme, Dokumentarfilme, Liebesfilme, Horrorfilme)

2. Was für einen Wagen fährst du?

3. Was für Musik hörst du gern?

4. Was für Kleidung trägst du am liebsten?

5. Was für Getränke trinkst du am liebsten?

6. Was für einen Job hast du? (z.B. interessant, langweilig, …)

7. In was für einer Stadt möchtest du gern leben? (z.B. Kleinstadt, Großstadt, in überhaupt keiner Stadt)

8. Was für eine Stadt ist _____? (z.B. New York, Toronto, …)

Negating Sentences

Summary: The Position of **nicht**

You recall that **nicht** is used in negation when the negative article **kein** cannot be used. The position of **nicht** varies according to the structure of the sentence.

When **nicht** negates a specific sentence element, it precedes this sentence element.

Ich komme **nicht heute,** sondern morgen.

Wir haben **nicht viel Geld.**

When **nicht** negates an entire statement, it generally stands at the end of the sentence.

Petra kommt morgen leider **nicht.**

Sie gibt mir das Buch **nicht.**

However, **nicht** precedes:

- *predicate adjectives*   Petras Bewerbungsbrief ist **nicht lang.**
- *predicate nouns*   Das ist **nicht Petras Brief.**
- *verbal complements at the end of the sentence*
  - a. *separable prefixes*   Sie schickt den Brief **nicht ab.**
  - b. *past participles*   Sie hat sich **nicht beworben.**
  - c. *infinitives*   Sie will sich **nicht bewerben.**
- *prepositional phrases*   Sie hat sich **nicht um die Stelle** beworben.

Übung 9   Schwierige° Zeiten

difficult

Beantworten Sie alle Fragen negativ mit **nicht.**

BEISPIEL: Hat Hans die Prüfung bestanden (*passed*)? →
          Nein, er hat die Prüfung nicht bestanden.

1. Hat er sich um die Stelle bei der Zeitung beworben?
2. Kennt er den Personalchef der Zeitung?
3. Hat er seine Bewerbung zur Post gebracht?
4. Hat der Personalchef ihn gestern angerufen?
5. Hat der Personalchef ihn zum Gespräch eingeladen?
6. War der Personalchef sehr beeindruckt von (*impressed by*) Hans?
7. Hat Hans die Stelle bekommen?
8. War er traurig?
9. Wird er sich noch einmal bewerben?

Negation: **noch nicht / noch kein(e); nicht mehr / kein(e) … mehr**

To respond negatively to a question that includes the adverb **schon** (*already, yet*), use either **noch nicht** (*not yet*), **noch kein** (*no . . . yet*), or **noch nie** (*never yet*) in your answer.

Geht Ute **schon** zur Schule?   Nein, sie geht **noch nicht** zur Schule.

Hat Dieter **schon** eine Stelle?   Nein, er hat **noch keine** Stelle.

To respond negatively to a question that includes the adverb **noch** or **immer noch** (*still*), use either **nicht mehr** (*no longer*) or **kein ... mehr** (*no . . . any longer*) in your answer.

Ist Sabine **immer noch** arbeitslos?   Nein, sie ist **nicht mehr** arbeitslos.

Hat Dieter **noch** Arbeit?   Nein, er hat **keine** Arbeit **mehr**.

Arbeiten Sie zu zweit und stellen Sie Fragen.

BEISPIEL: s1: Weißt du schon, was du mal werden willst?
           s2: Nein, das weiß ich noch nicht.

1. Weißt du schon, wo du arbeiten möchtest?
2. Ist dein Bruder / deine Schwester schon mit der Ausbildung fertig?
3. Hast du schon eine Stelle für den Sommer?
4. Hast du heute schon die Zeitung gelesen?
5. Hast du dich schon um eine Stelle beworben?
6. Hast du den Personalchef der Firma schon angerufen?
7. Hast du schon ein Angebot von der Firma bekommen?

Beantworten Sie die Fragen mit **ja** und dann mit **nein.** Arbeiten Sie zu dritt und wechseln Sie sich ab.

BEISPIEL: s1: Studiert Barbara noch?
           s2: Ja, sie studiert immer noch.
           s3: Nein, sie studiert nicht mehr.

1. Wohnt Barbara noch in Heidelberg?
2. Arbeitet Andreas immer noch als Reiseführer?
3. Hat Anna noch Arbeit?
4. Hat Klaus noch ein Motorrad?
5. Macht Astrid die Arbeit als Journalistin noch Spaß?
6. Spricht sie immer noch so enthusiastisch über ihre Arbeit?

Sprache im Kontext

Videoclips

A. Schauen Sie sich die Interviews mit Oliver, Jasmin und Alex an. Wie sind sie zu ihrem Beruf gekommen? Ergänzen Sie die Sätze.

1. Oliver ist selbständig, er ist _____. Er hat eine _____ in neuen Medien wie Fernsehen und Computeranimation gemacht. An seinem Beruf gefällt ihm die _____. Sein Beruf ist aber sehr _____.

2. Jasmin ist _____ bei der Deutschen Bank. Wie hat sie ihre Stelle bekommen? Sie hat die _____ in der Zeitung gelesen und hat sich _____. Sie hat ihren _____ mit Passfoto an die Bank geschickt und hat ein _____ erhalten.

3. Alex ist _____ von Beruf. Wie hat er seine Stelle bekommen? Von einer Freundin hat er erfahren, dass eine _____ frei war. Er hat sich _____. Er arbeitet seit _____ Jahren in diesem Beruf.

B. Was für Schulen haben Peter und Jasmin besucht? Kreuzen Sie an.

	PETER	JASMIN
Grundschule	☐	☐
Gesamtschule	☐	☐
Gymnasium	☐	☐
Realoberschule	☐	☐
Universität	☐	☐

C. Was wollten Oliver, Jasmin und Alex als Kinder werden? Und Sie? Was wollten Sie als Kind werden?

D. Was werden Peter, Jasmin und Alex in zwanzig Jahren tun?

E. Und Sie? Was werden Sie in zwanzig Jahren tun?

Lesen

Zum Thema

Was sind Berufe, von denen junge Leute manchmal träumen? Zu dritt, listen Sie drei Traumberufe. Nennen Sie für jeden Beruf einen Grund (*reason*), warum viele junge Leute sich dafür interessieren. Machen Sie dann eine Umfrage (*survey*) in der Klasse. Was sind Traumberufe für die meisten Leute? Warum?

Auf den ersten Blick

A. Schauen Sie sich den Titel „Karriere beim Film" und alle Bilder (S. 344–346) an. Lesen Sie die ersten drei Zeilen (*lines*). Welche Informationen erwarten Sie von diesen Texten?

B. Überfliegen Sie beide Texte kurz und suchen Sie Informationen über Franka Potente und Daniel Brühl.

	FRANKA POTENTE	DANIEL BRÜHL
Geburtsort		_____
Alter	_____	_____
Familie	_____	_____
Anfang der Karriere	_____	_____

C. Raten im Kontext. Was bedeuten die folgenden Sätze?

1. Die Schauspielschülerin wurde in einer Münchner Kneipe von einer Filmagentin angesprochen.

   a. Die Schauspielschülerin lernte in einer Münchner Kneipe eine Filmagentin kennen.

   b. Die Schauspielschülerin spielte in einem Film in einer Münchner Kneipe.

   c. Die Filmagentin hatte sich mit der Schauspielschülerin in einer Münchner Kneipe verabredet.

2. 1996 brach Franka Potente die Ausbildung ab.

   a. Franka ging weiter zur Schauspielschule.

   b. Sie ging nicht mehr zur Schauspielschule.

   c. Sie fing eine Ausbildung als Schauspielerin an.

3. Sie bekam viele Angebote.

   a. Viele Leute wollten sie in ihren Filmen haben.

   b. Sie nahm viele Rollen nicht an.

   c. Sie spielte in sehr wenigen Filmen.

4. Daniel Brühl gilt als das neue deutsche Schauspielwunder.

   a. Es ist ein Wunder, dass Daniel Brühl Schauspieler geworden ist.

   b. Daniel Brühl findet neue deutsche Filme wunderbar.

   c. Daniel Brühl ist der neue, große deutsche Filmstar.

5. Daniel folgte dem Rat seines Vaters und machte zunächst sein Abitur.

   a. Er handelte gegen den Rat seines Vaters und machte kein Abitur.

   b. Es hat getan, was sein Vater ihm empfohlen hat.

   c. Er brach die Schule ab gegen den Rat seines Vaters.

6. 2002 erhielt Daniel Brühl den Bayrischen Filmpreis als bester Nachwuchsdarsteller.

   a. Daniel Brühl bekam einen Preis als bester bayrischer Filmschauspielschüler.

   b. Daniel Brühl bekam einen Preis als bester Schauspieler in ganz Deutschland.

   c. Daniel Brühl bekam einen Preis als bester Schauspieler der neuen Generation von Filmschauspielern.

Spätestens seit *Lola rennt!* und *Good Bye, Lenin!* ist deutsches Kino wieder international erfolgreich. Mit den jungen Filmen sind auch neue Gesichter auf die Leinwand° gekommen. JUMA stellt zwei von ihnen vor.   *silver screen*

Franka Potente

Franka ist die Tochter eines Lehrers. Als 19-jährige
5 Abiturientin zog sie nach München und besuchte eine Schauspielschule. Ihre Karriere begann in einer Münchner Kneipe. Dort wurde die Schauspielschülerin von einer Filmagentin angesprochen. Als Ferienjob bekam sie eine Rolle
10 in der Komödie *Nach fünf im Urwald* (Bayrischer Filmpreis 1996). 1996 brach sie die Ausbildung ab und hatte danach viele Angebote, meistens schlechte. Doch mit dem Kinostart von Tom Tykwers *Lola rennt* im Jahre 1998 wurde Franka Potente überall bekannt. Die Geschichte: Lola
15 und Manni sind Anfang 20 und ein Liebespaar. Manni jobbt als Geld-kurier° und verliert 100 000 Mark, die seinem Chef gehören. Manni ruft   *money courier* Lola an. Die hat eine Idee – und rennt los.

Franka Potente
Geburtstag: 22.7.1974

Der Film Lola rennt *mit Franka Potente hatte auch außerhalb Deutschlands Erfolg.*

1998 sah man Franka auch in Doris Dörries Tragikomödie *Bin ich schön?* neben Iris Berben, Senta Berger, Joachim Król und Uwe
20 Ochsenknecht. 1999 folgte ihr erster Thriller *Anatomie* 2000 drehte sie mit Johnny Depp das Drama *Blow.* Weitere Filme mit Franka Potente; *Coming In; Rennlauf* (beide 1997); *Downhill City* (1998); *Schlaraffenland; Südsee, eigene Insel* (beide 1999); *Der Krieger und die Kaiserin* (2000); *Die Bourne Identität* (2002) mit Matt Damon; *Blueprint;*
25 *Anatomie 1* (beide 2003); *Die Bourne Verschwörung* und *Creep* (beide 2004).

Daniel Brühl

Seit dem großen Erfolg der Komödie *Good bye,*
Lenin! gilt Daniel Brühl als das neue deutsche
Schauspielwunder. Daniel wurde in Barcelona
30 geboren und ist in Köln aufgewachsen. Sein
Onkel war Hörspielregisseur° beim Radio. Er
besorgte ihm im Alter von acht Jahren einen
Job hinter dem Mikrofon. Bereits kurze Zeit
später synchronisierte Daniel Spielfilme
35 und versuchte sich im Schultheater als
Schauspieler. Im Alter von 16 Jahren stand er
zum ersten Mal vor der Kamera und übernahm in Roland Suso Richters
TV-Film *Svens Geheimnis°* eine Rolle.
    Daniel Brühl folgte dem Rat seines Vaters und machte trotz erster
40 Erfolge zunächst sein Abitur. Während seines Zivildienstes° arbeitete er
wieder fürs Fernsehen. Eine Schauspielschule hat er nie besucht.
    Sein Debüt auf der Kinoleinwand° feierte Daniel Brühl mit knapp 20
Jahren in dem Film *Schlaraffenland.* Im Jahre 2000 war er in der
Erfolgskomödie *Schule* zu sehen. Darin spielte er einen Schüler in der
45 Zeit vor dem Abitur. 2002 erhielt er für die Darstellung eines
Schizophrenen in *Das weiße Rauschen* den Bayerischen Filmpreis als
bester Nachwuchsdarsteller. Für seine Leistung in der melancholischen
Liebesgeschichte *Nichts bereuen* bekam er den Deutschen Filmpreis.

Daniel Brühl
Geburtstag: 16. Juni 1978

director of radio plays

secret

community service

movie screen

Kann man die DDR weiterleben lassen? Daniel Brühl
versucht es in dem Film Good bye, Lenin!

Mit dem Erfolg von *Good bye, Lenin!* wurde Daniel Brühl auch
50 international bekannt. In dieser Komödie spielte er einen jungen
Ostberliner, dessen Mutter während der Öffnung der Mauer im Koma
liegt. Der Sohn will die treue DDR-Bürgerin° nach ihrem Aufwachen
vor einem Schock bewahren. Darum lässt er die DDR in ihrer
Umgebung weiterleben. Der Film war ein riesiger Erfolg und brachte
55 allen Beteiligten zahlreiche Preise ein. Daniel Brühl selbst wurde beim
Deutschen und beim Europäischen Filmpreis als bester Darsteller
ausgezeichnet.

Im Jahre 2004 war er in dem Drama *Was nützt die Liebe in Gedanken*
zu sehen. In *Die fetten Jahre sind vorbei* spielte er eine Hauptrolle. Der
60 Film von Hans Weingartner erhielt 2004 den Preis der deutschen
Filmkritik in der Kategorie bester Spielfilm.

Aus: *JUMA* 4/2005, www.juma.de.

citizen of the GDR (Deutsche
Demokratische Republik = German
Democratic Republic)

Zum Text

A. Lesen Sie die Kurzbiografien von Franka Potente und Daniel Brühl
nun etwas genauer.

1. Wie begann Franka Potentes Karriere?

2. Wie wissen wir, dass sie nicht über Nacht berühmt wurde?

3. Was für eine Rolle hat Franka Potente berühmt gemacht? Um welches
Problem geht es in diesem Film?

4. Daniel Brühls Karriere hat mehrere Stationen (*stages*) durchlaufen.
Was erfahren wir über den Anfang seiner Karriere?

5. Welche Beweise stehen im Text, dass Daniel Brühl ein sehr
talentierter Schauspieler ist?

6. Welche Rolle hat ihn international berühmt gemacht?

B. Stellen Sie sich vor: Die beiden Schauspieler kommen zu Besuch.
Welche Fragen möchten Sie den beiden stellen? Was möchten Sie
gern über sie wissen?

In Deutschland ist ein Jahr Militärdienst Pflicht (*required*) für deutsche Männer. Im Allgemeinen geht der junge Deutsche mit 18 Jahren oder direkt nach der Ausbildung zum Militär. Viele sind Kriegsdienstverweigerer (*conscientious objectors*) und machen stattdessen Zivildienst. Das bedeutet, dass sie während dieser Zeit in einem Krankenhaus, Altenheim oder einem anderen sozialen oder auch ökologischen Bereich arbeiten. Oft helfen die sogenannten „Zivis" älteren Menschen zu Hause oder auch im Pflegeheim. So helfen sie z.B. morgens beim Anziehen, besorgen Mahlzeiten und helfen in der Wohnung.

Zu guter Letzt

Zu guter Letzt. Suggestion: Have students prepare Schritt 1 and 2 before coming to class.

Berufswünsche

Was sind Ihre eigenen Berufswünsche? Wie sehen Sie Ihren zukünftigen Beruf? Machen Sie eine Umfrage in der Klasse und analysieren Sie die Ergebnisse.

Schritt 1: Was würden (*would*) Sie über Ihre eigenen Berufswünsche sagen? Schreiben Sie drei Möglichkeiten für jede der vier Kategorien.

BEISPIEL: Das würde mir gefallen. →
- im Labor experimentieren
- alten Leuten helfen
- Baupläne entwerfen

1. Das würde mir gefallen.

   _____

2. Dort würde ich gern arbeiten.

   _____

3. Das würde ich gern machen.

   _____

4. Für eine gute Stelle würde ich …

   _____

Schritt 2: Machen Sie aus jeder Kategorie eine Frage.

1. _Was würde Ihnen am Beruf gefallen?_
2. _____
3. _____
4. _____

Schritt 3: Interviewen Sie fünf Studenten/Studentinnen in der Klasse. Stellen Sie ihnen die vier Fragen und schreiben Sie die Antworten auf.

Schritt 4: Arbeiten Sie in Gruppen und stellen Sie eine Liste von allen Antworten auf die vier Fragen zusammen.

Schritt 5: Analysieren Sie die Antworten. Gibt es Ähnlichkeiten in den Antworten der Studenten/Studentinnen?

Wortschatz

Arbeitswelt	**World of Work**
das **Ansehen**	prestige
der **Arbeitsplatz, ⸚e**	workplace; position
die **Ausbildung**	(career) training
das **Ausland** *(no pl.)*	foreign countries
im **Ausland**	abroad
das **Berufsleben**	professional life
das **Büro, -s**	office
der **Chef, -s** / die	manager, boss, head
Chefin, -nen	
das **Einkommen**	income
die **Entwicklung, -en**	development
der **Erfolg, -e**	success
Erfolg haben	to be successful
die **Firma,** *pl.* **Firmen**	firm, company
das **Gehalt, ⸚er**	salary
die **Gelegenheit, -en**	opportunity
das **Leben** *(no pl.)*	life
der **Mitarbeiter, -** / die	co-worker, colleague;
Mitarbeiterin, -nen	employee
die **Tätigkeit, -en**	activity; position
die **Technik, -en**	technique; technology

Berufe	**Professions**
der **Bibliothekar, -e** /	librarian
die **Bibliothekarin,**	
-nen	
der **Dolmetscher, -** / die	interpreter
Dolmetscherin, -nen	
der **Geschäftsmann,** *pl.*	businessman/
Geschäftsleute / die	businesswoman
Geschäftsfrau, -en	
der **Handel**	sales, trade
der **Informatiker, -** / die	computer scientist
Informatikerin, -nen	
der **Kaufmann,** *pl.*	salesman/saleswoman
Kaufleute / die	
Kauffrau, -en	
der **Künstler, -** / die	artist
Künstlerin, -nen	
der **Mechaniker, -** / die	mechanic
Mechanikerin, -nen	
der **Psychologe (-n**	psychologist
masc.)**, -n** / die	
Psychologin, -nen	
der **Rechtsanwalt, ⸚e** / die	lawyer, attorney
Rechtsanwältin, -nen	

der **Schauspieler, -** / die	actor
Schauspielerin, -nen	
der **Zahnarzt, ⸚e** / die	dentist
Zahnärztin, -nen	
der **Zeichner, -** / die	graphic artist
Zeichnerin, -nen	

Stellensuche	**Job Search**
das **Abitur, -e**	*examination at the end*
	of Gymnasium
der **Abschluss, ⸚e**	completion; degree
der **Arbeitgeber, -** / die	employer
Arbeitgeberin, -nen	
das **Arbeitsamt, ⸚er**	employment office
die **Beratung**	advising
der **Berufsberater, -** / die	employment counselor
Berufsberaterin, -nen	
die **Bewerbung, -en**	application
das **Bewerbungs-**	application form
formular, -e	
die **Erfahrung, -en**	experience
die **Fähigkeit, -en**	ability, skill
die **Grundschule, -n**	primary school
das **Gymnasium,** *pl.*	secondary school
Gymnasien	
der **Hersteller,-**	manufacturer, producer
die **Kenntnis, -se**	knowledge
der **Kontakt, -e**	contact
der **Lebenslauf**	résumé
der **Leiter, -** / die	director
Leiterin, -nen	
das **Personal**	personnel
die **Stärke, -n**	strength
die **Stelle, -n**	position, job
das **Stellenangebot, -e**	job offer;
	help-wanted ad
die **Unterlagen** *(pl.)*	documentation, papers
das **Unternehmen, -**	company, enterprise
die **Unterstützung**	support
das **Vorstellungs-**	job interview
gespräch, -e	
der **Vorteil, -e**	advantage
die **Website, -s**	website
das **Zeugnis, -se**	report card; transcript;
	recommendation
	(from a former
	employer)
die **Zukunft**	future

Verben	Verbs
sich beschäftigen (mit)	to occupy oneself (with)
besitzen, besaß, besessen	to own, possess
sich bewerben (um) (bewirbt), bewarb, beworben	to apply (for)
entwerfen (entwirft), entwarf, entworfen	to design
heraus•fordern	to challenge
her•stellen	to produce, manufacture
sich interessieren für (+ acc.)	to be interested in
nach•denken (über + acc.), dachte nach, nachgedacht	to think (about)
übernehmen (übernimmt), übernahm, übernommen	to take over
übersetzen, übersetzt	to translate
untersuchen, untersucht	to examine
verdienen	to earn; to deserve
sich vor•bereiten (auf + acc.)	to prepare (for)
sich (dat.) vor•stellen	to imagine
sich (acc.) vor•stellen	to introduce

Adjektive und Adverbien / Adjectives and Adverbs

abwechslungsreich	varied, diverse
engagiert	committed
erfolgreich	successful(ly)
selbständig	independent(ly)
verantwortlich	responsible
wahrscheinlich	probably
wohl	probably

Sonstiges / Other

im Freien	outdoors
was für (ein)	what kind of (a)

DAS KANN ICH NUN!

1. Beschreiben Sie in drei Sätzen, was Ihnen für Ihren zukünftigen Beruf wichtig ist.

2. Welche Berufe sind gemeint?

   a. Man arbeitet auf der Bühne. **b.** Man untersucht Patienten. **c.** Man repariert Autos. **d.** Man entwirft Gebäude und Häuser. **e.** Man verkauft Produkte einer Firma.

3. Wenn man sich um eine Stelle bewirbt, muss man oft einen tabellarischen _____ schreiben. Sehr wichtig für eine erfolgreiche Bewerbung sind die _____ von früheren Arbeitgebern.

4. In Deutschland gibt es mehrere Schultypen. Nennen Sie drei.

5. Wenn ein Deutscher / eine Deutsche studieren will, muss er / sie am Ende des Gymnasiums _____ machen.

6. Wie sagt man das auf Deutsch? Benutzen Sie **werden.**

   a. *Someday I will be rich and famous.*
   b. *My brother is going to be a pilot.*
   c. *Niels is probably at home now.*

7. Ergänzen Sie die Sätze mit Relativpronomen.

   a. Ich bin ein Mensch, _____ weiß, was er will. **b.** Meine Mutter ist eine Frau, _____ man vertrauen kann. **c.** Niko ist der Junge, _____ Hund den Briefträger gebissen hat.

8. Wie heißen die Fragen? Wie heißen die Antworten?

   a. _____ ? —Das ist ein BMW Sportkabriolett. **b.** _____ ? —Ich habe sehr nette Kollegen. **c.** _____ ? —Er hat noch nicht von der Firma gehört. **d.** Hast du noch Arbeit? —Nein, _____ . **e.** Studierst du immer noch? —Nein, _____ .

Haus und Haushalt

Das neue Haus und
seine Bewohner

In diesem Kapitel

- **Themen:** Money matters, housing, the home, renting, household appliances
- **Grammatik:** Verbs with fixed prepositions, **da-** and **wo-**compounds, subjunctive II, **würde**
- **Kultur:** The Swiss franc, BAföG, paying for college, store hours
- **Lesen:** „Fahrkarte bitte" (Helga M. Novak)

Videoclips
Beatrice, Dennis und Jan
sprechen über ihre Finanzen

Alles klar?

Alles klar? A. Answers: *Vorsorge fürs Alter; Wohneigentum, Konsum, Anschaffungen; Ausbildung; Notgroschen*

A. Die Deutschen sparen aus verschiedenen Gründen. Die Grafik zeigt, wofür sie sparen.

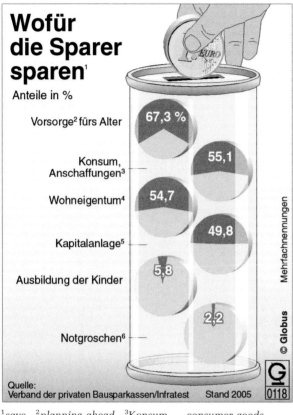

Wofür die Sparer sparen[1]

Anteile in %

Vorsorge[2] fürs Alter — **67,3 %**

Konsum, Anschaffungen[3] — **55,1**

Wohneigentum[4] — **54,7**

Kapitalanlage[5] — **49,8**

Ausbildung der Kinder — **5,8**

Notgroschen[6] — **2,2**

Mehrfachnennungen

© Globus

Quelle:
Verband der privaten Bausparkassen/Infratest   Stand 2005

0118

[1]*save* [2]*planning ahead* [3]Konsum ... *consumer goods, major purchases* [4]*home ownership* [5]*investments* [6]der Notgroschen *emergency fund for a rainy day*

- Die Deutschen sparen am meisten für _____.
- Mehr als die Hälfte der Deutschen sparen für _____ und _____.
- Weniger als 6% der Deutschen sparen für die _____ der Kinder.
- Am wenigsten sparen die Deutschen für einen _____.

B. „Was bedeutet euch Geld?" Diese Frage haben wir Jens, Lucia und Elke gestellt. Hören Sie ihre Antworten. Schreiben Sie J (Jens), L (Lucia) oder E (Elke) neben die zutreffenden Aussagen.

B. Suggestion: Ask students, *Welche Idee finden Sie gut? Was würden Sie mit viel Geld machen?*

1. __E__ lange Urlaub machen und dann wieder arbeiten
2. __L__ Armen (*poor people*) helfen
3. __J__ Geld für medizinische Forschung spenden (*donate*)
4. __L__ ein eigenes Geschäft aufmachen
5. __J__ ein neues Auto oder eine neue Wohnung kaufen
6. __E__ investieren
7. __L__ weiter studieren – vielleicht im Ausland
8. __E__ Geld für Welthungerorganisationen spenden

Wörter im Kontext

Neue Wörter

geben ... aus (ausgeben)
 spend
durchschnittlich on
 average
die Ausgabe (Ausgaben, *pl.*)
 expense

Siehe *Asking
Questions:*
wo-*Compounds*, S. 364.

THEMA 1: Finanzen der Studenten

A. Wie **geben** Studenten in der Schweiz ihr Geld **aus**? Schauen Sie sich das Schaubild an.

- Wie viel Geld brauchen Studenten in der Schweiz **durchschnittlich** pro Monat?

- Wofür geben sie das meiste Geld aus? das wenigste Geld?

- Welche **Ausgaben** sind mit „Kommunikation" gemeint?

- Das Budget ist nur für Studenten, die nicht bei den Eltern wohnen. Wofür würden Studenten, die bei den Eltern wohnen, wahrscheinlich weniger Geld ausgeben?

Das Budget der Studierenden
in der Schweiz

Durchschnittliche Ausgaben der Studierenden, die ausserhalb des Elternhauses wohnen:
1 900 Franken pro Monat
davon in % für

Unterkunft	31 %
Nahrung¹ und Kleidung	23
Studium	
Freizeit	
Gesundheit	9
Transport	6
Kommunikation	5
Sonstiges	5

Quelle: BfS Stand 2005 © Globus 047S

¹*food*

KULTURTIPP

Die Schweiz ist eines der Länder, die kein Mitglied der Europäischen Union (EU) sind und deswegen ihr eigenes Geld beibehalten haben. In der Schweiz zahlt man mit dem Schweizer Franken (CHF). Der Franken ist in 100 Rappen unterteilt.

B. Wie leben deutsche Studenten? Antworten Sie mit Informationen aus der Grafik rechts.

- Wie viel Geld braucht der deutsche „Normalstudent" **monatlich** für Essen? für Kleidung? für die Gesundheit?
- Wofür geben deutsche Studenten das meiste Geld aus?
- Wofür geben sie das wenigste Geld aus?
- Was gehört alles in die Rubrik „Lernmittel"?

C. Ihr monatliches Budget:

- Wofür geben Sie monatlich Geld aus und durchschnittlich ungefähr wie viel?
- Wofür geben Sie das meiste Geld aus? das wenigste?
- Wofür geben Sie nur ab und zu oder gar kein Geld aus?

D. Prozent Ihrer monatlichen Ausgaben:

_____ Miete

_____ **Nebenkosten** im **Haushalt** (**Strom, Heizung,** eigenes Telefon, Handy, Wasser)

_____ Auto (**Benzin, Reparaturen**)

_____ Fahrtkosten (öffentliche Verkehrsmittel, z.B. Bus, Flugzeug, Fahrten nach Hause)

_____ **Ernährung** (Essen, Trinken, Mensa, Restaurants)

_____ **Studiengebühren** (pro Semester, pro Quartal)

_____ Lernmittel (Bücher, **Hefte, Bleistifte, Kugelschreiber, Papier, Computerdisketten,** Sonstiges)

_____ Freizeit (Kino, Theater, Partys, Hobbys)

_____ **sparen** (**Sparkonto,** Sparschwein)

_____ **Versicherungen,** Arztkosten, Medikamente

_____ INSGESAMT (*total*)

- Haben Sie genügend (*enough*) **Einnahmen**? Haben Sie am Ende des Monats etwas Geld **übrig,** oder sind Sie **pleite**? Müssen Sie sich manchmal Geld von Freunden oder Ihrer Familie leihen? **Unterstützen** Ihre Eltern Sie finanziell? Sind Sie **sparsam**? Müssen Sie nebenbei **jobben**?
- **Vergleichen** Sie Ihre monatlichen Ausgaben mit denen eines Mitstudenten / einer Mitstudentin. Wer hat höhere monatliche Ausgaben?

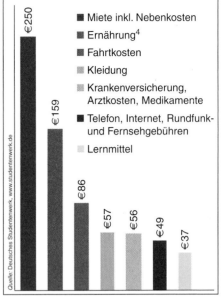

Monatliche Ausgaben der Studierenden in Deutschland

Bezugsgruppe[1] "Normalstudent", arith. Mittel[2] ausgewählte Ausgabenpositionen[3] (2003)

- ■ Miete inkl. Nebenkosten
- ■ Ernährung[4]
- ■ Fahrtkosten
- ▨ Kleidung
- ▨ Krankenversicherung, Arztkosten, Medikamente
- ■ Telefon, Internet, Rundfunk- und Fernsehgebühren
- ▨ Lernmittel

€250 · €159 · €86 · €57 · €56 · €49 · €37

Quelle: Deutsches Studentenwerk, www.studentenwerk.de

[1]*reference group* [2]*arith. ... arithmetic mean (= average)* [3]*ausgewählte ... selected expenditures* [4]*food*

KULTURTIPP

Wie finanziert man das Studium in Deutschland?

- Eltern: Nach dem Gesetz (*law*) müssen Eltern für die Ausbildung ihrer Kinder zahlen, und zwar bis zum Abschluss einer Berufsausbildung, oder für Abiturient/innen bis zum Abschluss eines Studiums.
- Stipendien oder Darlehen (*loans*): Das **BAföG** (= Bundesausbildungsförderungsgesetz) ist ein deutsches Gesetz, das die staatliche Unterstützung von Schüler/innen und Student/innen regelt. BAföG besteht aus Darlehen und Zuschüssen (*grants*).
- Jobben: Studierende können während des Studiums nebenbei jobben.

Neue Wörter

Nebenkosten (*pl.*) utilities
der Strom electricity
die Heizung heat
das Benzin gasoline
die Ernährung food
Studiengebühren (*pl.*) tuition
das Heft (Hefte, *pl.*) notebook
der Bleistift (Bleistifte, *pl.*) pencil
der Kugelschreiber (Kugelschreiber, *pl.*) ballpoint pen
sparen to save
das Sparkonto savings account
die Versicherung (Versicherungen, *pl.*) insurance
Einnahmen (*pl.*) income
übrig left over
pleite broke
unterstützen support
sparsam thrifty
jobben work (at a temporary job)
vergleichen compare

Schauen Sie sich Ihr monatliches Budget im **Thema 1** an. Vergleichen Sie jetzt Ihre Ausgaben mit den Ausgaben eines Partners / einer Partnerin und berichten Sie darüber. Gebrauchen Sie folgende Redemittel.

Ich gebe das meiste Geld für _____ aus.

Das wenigste Geld gebe ich für _____ aus.

Ich gebe nur ab und zu oder gar kein Geld für _____ aus.

Für _____ und _____ gebe ich mehr/weniger Geld aus als mein Partner / meine Partnerin.

Lesen Sie oder hören Sie sich den Dialog an, und ergänzen Sie die Sätze unten.

ANDREA: Sag mal, könntest du mir einen Gefallen (*favor*) tun?

STEFAN: Was denn?

ANDREA: Würdest du mir bis Ende der Woche 50 Euro leihen? Ich bin total pleite.

STEFAN: Fünfzig Euro? Das ist viel Geld.

ANDREA: Ich musste 100 Euro für Bücher ausgeben. Und jetzt habe ich keinen Cent mehr übrig. Ich warte auf Geld von meinen Eltern.

STEFAN: Hm, ich würde es dir gern leihen. Aber 50 Euro habe ich selber nicht mehr. Ich kann dir höchstens 20 Euro leihen.

ANDREA: Ich zahle es dir bis Ende des Monats bestimmt zurück.

STEFAN: Eben hast du gesagt, bis Ende der Woche.

ANDREA: Ja, ja. Das Geld von meinen Eltern kann jeden Tag kommen.

STEFAN: Na gut. Hier ist ein Zwanziger.

ANDREA: Vielen Dank.

Siehe *The Subjunctive,* S. 364.

Andrea hat kein _____[1] mehr; sie ist total _____.[2] Sie möchte sich von Stefan _____.[3] Sie hat nämlich ihr ganzes Geld für _____[4] ausgegeben. Deshalb hat sie jetzt nichts mehr für Essen und Trinken _____.[5] Stefan kann ihr aber _____[6] leihen. Andrea hofft, dass sie Stefan das Geld bis _____[7] zurückzahlen kann. Sie wartet auf _____.[8]

Vergleichen Sie die Ausgaben der drei Studenten auf der nächsten Seite und beantworten Sie die Fragen.

1. Wie viel Geld geben Marion, Wolfgang und Claudia insgesamt monatlich aus?

2. Wofür geben sie das meiste Geld aus?

3. Wer bezahlt die höchste Miete? Wo ist die Miete billiger?

4. Warum bezahlt Marion weniger als die zwei anderen fürs Telefon?

5. Wer hat die höchsten Kosten für Bücher und Arbeitsmittel?

6. Was ist – außer Miete – günstig, wenn man im Studentenwohnheim wohnt?

7. Wer unterstützt die drei Studenten finanziell?

8. Warum hat Marion keine Ausgaben für Verkehrsmittel?

9. Wer lebt am sparsamsten?

	MARION	WOLFGANG	CLAUDIA
Studienfach	Übersetzer (*translator*)/ Dolmetscher	Medizin	Romanistik/Politik
Studiengebühren pro Semester	keine	keine	500 Euro
Unterhalt (support)	Eltern	BAföG	jobben
Miete	200 Euro (1 Zi, Studenten- wohnheim)	300 Euro (1 Zi, Küche, Bad außerhalb)	400 Euro (1 Zi, Küche, Bad)
Verkehrsmittel	keine (alles mit dem Fahrrad erreichbar)	60 Euro	50 Euro
Lebensmittel und Mensa	200 Euro	250 Euro	200 Euro
Bücher/Arbeitsmittel	30 Euro	70 Euro	40 Euro
Telefon, Handy, Internet	20 Euro (kein Internet)	60 Euro (eigenes Telefon)	80 Euro
Freizeit	70 Euro	80 Euro	100 Euro
Fahrt nach Hause	20 Euro (Mitfahrgelegenheit) 40 Euro (mit der Bahn)	—	20 Euro
sonstiges	40 Euro	35 Euro	40 Euro

Aktivität 4 Einnahmen und Ausgaben

Vier Studenten sprechen über ihre monatlichen Einnahmen und Ausgaben. Kreuzen Sie das Zutreffende (*the items that apply*) an. Notieren Sie unter „Ausgaben", wie viel die Studenten für ihre Miete ausgeben.

	STEFANIE	GERT	SUSANNE	MARTIN
1. Einnahmen von:				
a. Job während des Semesters	☐	☐	☒	☒
b. Job während der Semesterferien	☒	☒	☐	☒
c. Eltern	☒	☐	☒	☒
d. Stipendium/BAföG	☐	☒	☐	☐
2. Ausgaben für:				
a. Zimmer (privat)	____	€150	____	____
b. Studentenwohnheim	€100	____	____	____
c. eigene Wohnung	____	____	____	€200
d. Wohngemeinschaft	____	____	€150	____

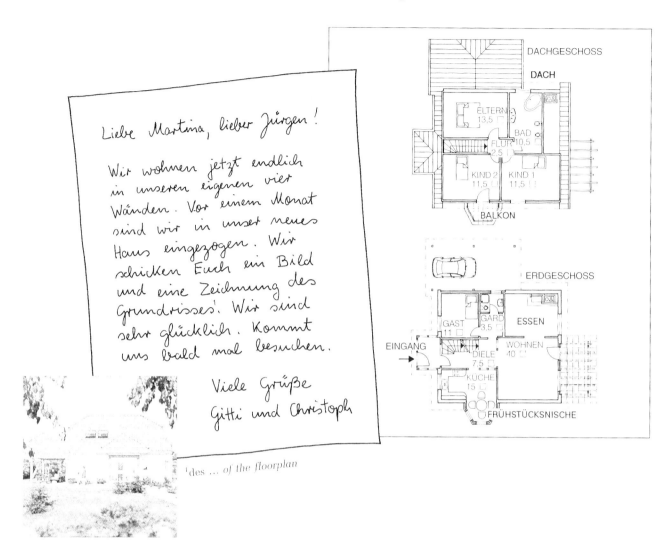

Liebe Martina, lieber Jürgen!

Wir wohnen jetzt endlich in unseren eigenen vier Wänden. Vor einem Monat sind wir in unser neues Haus eingezogen. Wir schicken Euch ein Bild und eine Zeichnung des Grundrisses¹. Wir sind sehr glücklich. Kommt uns bald mal besuchen.

Viele Grüße
Gitti und Christoph

¹des ... *of the floorplan*

Schauen Sie sich die **Zeichnung** von Gittis und Christophs neuem Haus an. Ergänzen Sie dann die folgenden Sätze durch ein passendes Wort aus der Liste:

Bad	Esszimmer	Schlafzimmer
Dachgeschoss	**Frühstücksnische**	Terrasse
Diele	**Gästezimmer**	**Treppe**
Erdgeschoss	Küche	Wohnzimmer

1. Das Haus hat zwei Stockwerke: ein _____ und ein _____.
2. Vom **Eingang** kommt man zuerst in die _____.
3. Links neben der Diele ist eine **Garderobe** und ein _____.
4. Von der Diele geht man rechts in die _____ und eine kleine _____.
5. **Unten** liegen noch zwei Zimmer: ein _____ und ein _____.
6. Das Wohnzimmer führt auf die _____ und in den Garten.
7. In der Diele führt eine _____ nach **oben** ins Dachgeschoss.
8. Im Dachgeschoss sind drei _____ und ein _____.

eigen own
eingezogen (einziehen)
    moved in
die Zeichnung drawing
bald soon
das Dachgeschoss attic, top
    floor
der Eingang entrance
die Garderobe closet
die Diele entry, foyer
die Treppe staircase
unten below, downstairs
oben above; upstairs

Aktivität 5   Die ideale Wohnung

Drei Leute (Frau Heine, Herr Zumwald und Thomas) berichten, was für eine Wohnung sie suchen, und was ihnen in der Wohnung wichtig oder unwichtig ist. Stellen Sie zuerst fest, wer welchen Wohnungstyp sucht. Dann notieren Sie in der Tabelle, was jedem wichtig (w) oder unwichtig (u) ist.

Aktivität 5. Follow-up: Have students work in small groups to find out what would be important to them in an apartment. You may wish to add additional vocabulary on the board such as *die Klimaanlage* and *die Spülmaschine*.

Wer sucht:

ein älteres Haus außerhalb der Stadt?   <u>Herr Zumwald</u>

eine Neubauwohnung in der Innenstadt?   <u>Frau Heine</u>

eine gemütliche Altbauwohnung in der Stadt?   <u>Thomas</u>

WICHTIG/UNWICHTIG	FRAU HEINE	HERR ZUMWALD	THOMAS
Lage	w	w	w
Zentralheizung	w	w	w
Balkon	w		
Garage	u		u
Garten		w	
Teppichboden (carpeting)		u	u
Waschmaschine			w

Aktivität 6   Hin und her: Eine neue Wohnung

Diese Leute haben entweder eine neue Wohnung oder ein neues Haus gekauft. Wer hat was gekauft? Wie viele Stockwerke gibt es? Wie groß ist das Wohnzimmer? Wie viele WCs oder Badezimmer gibt es?

Aktivität 6. Suggestion: Make sure students go beyond the model in asking questions: *Wie groß ist das Wohnzimmer? Hat die Wohnung ein Bad oder mehr als ein Bad?*

BEISPIEL: s1: Was für eine Wohnung hat Bettina Neuendorf gekauft?
s2: Eine Eigentumswohnung.
s1: Wie viele Stockwerke hat die Wohnung?
s2: Eins.
s1: Und wie viele Schlafzimmer? ...

PERSON	TYP	STOCKWERKE	SCHLAFZIMMER	WOHNZIMMER	WC/BAD
Bettina Neuendorf	Eigentumswohnung	eins	eins, aber auch ein kleines Gästezimmer	mit Esszimmer kombiniert 30 Quadratmeter	eins
Uwe und Marion Baumgärtner	Haus	zwei	drei: Elternschlafzimmer, Kinderschlafzimmer, Gästezimmer	sehr groß mit Balkon 37 Quadratmeter	zwei Badezimmer: eins im Dachgeschoss und eins im Erdgeschoss
Sven Kersten	Eigentumswohnung	zwei	zwei, eins als Gästezimmer benutzt	mit Esszimmer zusammen 35 Quadratmeter, Balkon vom Wohnzimmer	zwei, ein WC und ein Bad
Carola Schubärth	Haus	eins	zwei: ein Schlafzimmer ist Arbeitszimmer	klein 25 Quadratmeter	ein Bad

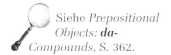 Siehe *Prepositional Objects: **da-** Compounds*, S. 362.

Aktivität 7 Der Grundriss

Schritt 1: Sie sehen hier unten einen Grundriss. Identifizieren Sie, wo das Wohnzimmer, das Esszimmer, die Küche, das Schlafzimmer und andere Räume sind. Beschreiben Sie dann, wo die Zimmer liegen.

Zuerst kommt man in _____.

Rechts von _____ ist _____.

Von der _____ führt eine Tür ins _____.

Links neben der _____ ist ein _____ und daneben ein _____.

Vom Wohnzimmer geht man auf _____.

Schritt 2: Zeichnen Sie nun den Grundriss Ihrer Wohnung / Ihres Hauses. (Wenn Sie in einem Studentenheim wohnen, zeichnen Sie eine Phantasiewohnung.) Geben Sie jemandem die Zeichnung und beschreiben Sie ihm/ihr, wo die Zimmer liegen. Ihr Partner / Ihre Partnerin setzt die Zimmernamen in den Grundriss. Schauen Sie sich dann die Zeichnung an, um zu sehen, ob alles richtig identifiziert ist.

Beginnen Sie so: Zuerst kommt man in _____.

Unsere Eigentumswohnungen: **Ideal– für das Leben zu zweit.**

THEMA 3: Unser Zuhause

Mieten und Vermieten

Neue Wörter

mieten to rent (from someone)
vermieten to rent out (to someone)
die Umgebung vicinity

[1]*auf ... in the country*
[2]*Gö = Göttingen university town in north central Germany*
[3]*community* [4]*since*
[5]*lead*

1.

**Land-WG sucht
Mitbewohner(in)!**

Wir, Bruno (26) und Britta (21), Hund
und Katze, vermieten eine ganze
obere Etage in einem älteren
Bauernhaus 1 1/2 Zimmer, ca 38 qm[1].
Benutzbar[2] sind Küche, Bad, großer
Garten. Die Miete beträgt monatlich
€300,— plus €30,— Nebenkosten. 20
km von Göttingen. Ab 1. Juni.

2.

Mieter gesucht für große, helle 3
Zimmer in Neubau, ab 1. August, ca.
70 qm. Balkon, eingerichtete Küche
(Spülmaschine, Kühlschrank,
Mikrowellenherd), Waschraum mit
Waschmaschine, Zentralheizung,
Teppichboden, Bad und WC, Garage.
Zu Fuß ca. 15 Minuten von der
Universität, 5 vom Bahnhof, 10
Minuten vom Zentrum.Tiere nicht
erwünscht. Miete €400,— Nebenkosten
€60,—.

[1]qm = Quadratmeter *square meters* [2]*available for use*

A. Lesen Sie zuerst das Mietgesuch (*rental flyer*). Wer sucht was und wo?

B. Lesen Sie dann die zwei Mietangebote (*rental ads*). Welches Angebot empfehlen Sie Brigitte und Matthias?

1. Ich finde Angebot Nummer _____ ideal für Brigitte und Matthias, denn es gibt dort _____.

2. Ich empfehle Brigitte und Matthias Angebot Nummer _____, denn _____. Es gibt jedoch ein Problem: _____

B. Suggestion: Have students write their own *Mietangebot* or *Mitbewohner(in) gesucht* ads.

Geräte im Haushalt

C. Zum modernen Haushalt gehören immer mehr Elektrogeräte.

- Welche von diesen **Geräten** haben Sie in Ihrem Arbeitszimmer oder Schlafzimmer? Kreuzen Sie an.

- Welche sind für Sie **unbedingt notwendig**?

- Welche sind **nützlich** aber nicht absolut notwendig?

- **Auf** welche könnten Sie **verzichten**?

Elektrogeräte . . .

...im Arbeitszimmer		...im Schlafzimmer
Telefon	Lautsprecher-Boxen (2-4 Dosen)	Telefon
Anrufbeantworter[1]	Kopierer	Fernsehgerät
Telefax-Gerät	Rechen-maschine[2]	Videogerät
Fernsehgerät	Computer	Radio
Videogerät	Drucker[3]	Radiowecker
Radio	Uhr	Alarmanlage
CD-Player	Aquarium (3-5 Dosen)	Staubsauger
DVD-Spieler	Staubsauger	Fernsehgerät

[1]*answering machine* [2]*calculator* [3]*printer*

D. Was passt zusammen?

1. __c__ Damit macht man den Teppichboden sauber.
2. __g__ Dieses Gerät wäscht die Wäsche.
3. __b__ Man kann damit das Essen schnell zubereiten.
4. __d__ Damit trocknet man die Wäsche.
5. __f__ Dieses Gerät spült das **schmutzige** Geschirr.
6. __a__ Das ist ein Haus auf dem Land.
7. __e__ Das ist ein modernes Haus.
8. __h__ Ein anderes Wort für „Region".

a. das **Bauernhaus**
b. der **Mikrowellenherd**
c. der **Staubsauger**
d. der **Wäschetrockner**
e. der **Neubau**
f. die **Spülmaschine**
g. die **Waschmaschine**
h. die **Umgebung**

Frau Krenz hat eine große, helle Dreizimmerwohnung zu vermieten. Die Anzeige stand in der Zeitung. Herr Brunner hat auf die Anzeige hin angerufen. Er weiß, wie groß die Wohnung ist und wie hoch die Miete ist. Was möchte er noch von der Vermieterin wissen? Kreuzen Sie alles Zutreffende an.

1. Herr Brunner möchte wissen,
   - ☐ ob die Heizung in den Nebenkosten einbegriffen ist.
   - ☐ ob die Küche einen Mikrowellenherd hat.
   - ☐ wie er vom Haus in die Innenstadt kommt.
   - ☐ wo die Wohnung liegt.
   - ☐ ob es einen Aufzug gibt.
   - ☐ wo man parken kann.
   - ☐ ob Hund und Katze willkommen sind.

2. Frau Krenz möchte von Herrn Brunner wissen,
   - ☐ wie viele Kinder er hat.
   - ☐ ob er verheiratet ist.
   - ☐ ob er Arbeit hat.
   - ☐ wann er vorbeikommen kann.
   - ☐ wann er einziehen möchte.

Sie interessieren sich für ein Mietangebot, das Sie in der Zeitung gesehen haben und rufen deshalb den Vermieter / die Vermieterin an. Benutzen Sie die Konversationstipps.

<table>
<tr><td>

S1
VERMIETER/VERMIETERIN

</td><td>

S2
ANRUFER/ANRUFERIN

</td></tr>
</table>

1. State your last name.	2. Greet the person, state your last name, and ask whether the apartment is still available.
3. Say it is still available.	4. Ask how much the rent is.
5. State a price.	6. Ask whether this price includes all household bills.
7. State that everything is included (**inklusive**) except the heat.	8. Tell the landlord/landlady that you have a cat or dog.
9. Say that it's all right.	10. Find out where the apartment is located.
11. Give the address and location. Suggest to the caller a time when he/she can come to see it.	12. Say that the time is suitable.
13. Say good-bye.	14. Say good-bye.

Weiteres zum Thema
Wohnungsangebote finden
Sie bei **Deutsch: Na klar!** im
World-Wide-Web unter

Grammatik im Kontext

Verbs with Fixed Prepositions

Many German verbs require the use of fixed prepositions; these verb-preposition combinations are usually different from their English equivalents.

Ich **interessiere mich für** schnelle Autos.

I'm interested in fast cars.

Wir **warten auf** den Bus.

We are waiting for the bus.

Die Studenten **ärgern sich über** die hohen Studienkosten.

The students are annoyed about the high cost of tuition.

Verbs with Fixed Prepositions. **Suggestion:** Ask students for any other verbs with special prepositions that they might remember. Stress the importance of the correct use of prepositions in idiomatic speech.

The following verbs take fixed prepositions:

Angst haben vor (+ *dat.*) — *to be afraid of*

sich ärgern über (+ *acc.*) — *to be annoyed about*

sich beschäftigen mit — *to occupy oneself with*

sich bewerben um — *to apply for*

bitten um — *to ask for; to request*

denken an (+ *acc.*) — *to think of*

sich freuen auf (+ *acc.*) — *to look forward to*

sich freuen über (+ *acc.*) — *to be happy about*

sich interessieren für — *to be interested in*

nach•denken über (+ *acc.*) — *to think about*

verzichten auf (+ *acc.*) — *to do without*

sich vor•bereiten auf (+ *acc.*) — *to prepare for*

warten auf (+ *acc.*) — *to wait for*

Point out: The fixed two-way prepositions here all take accusative except for *Angst haben vor.* An easy way for students to remember the case is that accusative is generally used for figurative speech, whereas dative is used for literal speech. Compare, for example, *Ich warte auf dem Bahnsteig* (the speaker is literally on the platform) with *Ich warte auf meinen Bruder* (the speaker is not literally on his brother).

Übung 1   So ist das Studentenleben

Was passt zusammen?

Übung 1. Answers: 1. d 2. g 3. f 4. b 5. a 6. h 7. c 8. e

1. Die Studenten warten …
2. Sie haben Angst …
3. Der Professor ärgert sich …
4. Die Studenten freuen sich …
5. Der Professor beschäftigt sich …
6. Die Studenten bitten …
7. Sie interessieren sich …
8. Sie bewerben sich …

a. mit seiner Forschung (*research*) im Labor.

b. auf das Ende des Semesters.

c. für die Arbeit im Labor.

d. auf den Professor.

e. um ein Praktikum.

f. über die Studenten.

g. vor der Prüfung (*exam*).

h. um mehr Zeit für die Semesterarbeit.

Prepositional Objects: **da**-Compounds°

In German, a personal pronoun following a preposition generally refers to a person or another living being.

| Der Student wartet auf **die Professorin.** | *The student is waiting for the professor.* |
| Er wartet schon lange **auf sie.** | *He has been waiting for her for a long time.* |

When the object of a preposition refers to a thing or an idea, this is represented by a **da**-compound consisting of the adverb **da** and a preposition.

Wer ist **für eine Erhöhung der Studiengebühren?**	*Who is for a tuition increase?*
Nicht viele Leute sind **dafür.**	*Not many people are for it.*
Die Studenten sind **dagegen.**	*The students are against it.*

Note:

- **Da-** becomes **dar-** when the preposition begins with a vowel.

| Marion wartet auf Geld von ihrem Vater. | *Marion is waiting for money from her father.* |
| Sie wartet schon eine Woche **darauf.** | *She has been waiting for it for a week.* |

- **Da-/Dar-** can combine with most accusative, dative, and two-way prepositions.

- The preposition **ohne** does not form a **da**-compound; it is always used with an accusative pronoun.

| Christian hat **einen neuen Porsche.** | *Christian owns a new Porsche.* |
| **Ohne ihn** kann er nicht leben. | *He can't live without it.* |

- Identify all **da**-compounds in the following text.
- What nouns do these **da**-compounds refer to?
- Restate all **da**-compounds as prepositional objects using the nouns to which they refer.

BEISPIEL: dafür → Sabines Zimmer → für Sabines Zimmer

Sabines Zimmer im Studentenwohnheim

Sie zahlt nur 150 Euro im Monat dafür. Links an der Wand ist ein Waschbecken. Darüber hängt ein Spiegel. Daneben hängt ein Haken mit einem Handtuch. Rechts an der Wand steht ein Schreibtisch. Darauf liegen viele Bücher und Papiere. Hinten an der Wand steht ein Bett. Darunter stehen Sabines Schuhe und rechts daneben steht ein kleines Bücherregal. Dahinter ist ein Fenster. Davor steht ein Vogelkäfig. Sabines Kanarienvogel, Caruso, wohnt darin und singt pausenlos.

The adverbs **dahin** ([*going*] *there*) and **daher** ([*coming*] *from there*) are commonly used with verbs of motion.

Review: Go over **wo … hin** in conjunction with **da … hin** to emphasize the customary splitting of these pronouns in conversational German.

Wann fliegt Martina **nach Spanien**?   —Sie fliegt morgen **dahin.**

Ich war heute **auf der Bank.**   —Ich komme gerade **daher.**

In informal spoken German, **dahin** is often abbreviated to **hin.**

Hans muss noch zur Bank.   Er geht später **hin.**

In conversational German, **da** may be placed at the beginning of a sentence and **hin** at the end.

Gehst du oft ins Museum?   **Da** gehe ich nur selten **hin.**

Übung 2 Gemeinsames und Kontraste

Sabine und ihr Freund Jürgen haben einiges, aber nicht alles gemein (*in common*).

BEISPIEL: Sie interessiert sich für klassische Musik. →
     Er interessiert sich nicht *dafür*.

1. Jürgen gibt viel Geld für sein Auto aus.
   Sabine gibt nichts _____ aus.
2. Er spricht nicht über seine Finanzen.
   Sie spricht oft _____.
3. Er hat nur wenig Geld für Essen und Trinken übrig.
   Sie hat auch wenig _____ übrig.
4. Sie freut sich immer über kleine Geschenke.
   Er freut sich auch _____.
5. Sie denkt immer an alle Geburtstage.
   Er denkt nie _____.
6. Er kommt immer pünktlich zur Vorlesung.
   Sie kommt nie pünktlich _____.
7. Er ärgert sich über die laute Musik im Wohnheim.
   Sie ärgert sich überhaupt nicht _____.
8. Sie freut sich auf das Ende des Studiums.
   Er freut sich auch _____.

Übung 2. Answers: 1. *dafür* 2. *darüber* 3. *dafür* 4. *darüber* 5. *daran* 6. *dahin* 7. *darüber* 8. *darauf*

No. 6. Note: Remind students that verbs of motion take a special *da*-compound.

Übung 3 Beschreibungen und Situationen

Setzen Sie passende Pronominaladverbien in die Lücken ein.

1. In meinem Zimmer steht ein Sofa. *Daneben* steht eine Stehlampe. _____ steht ein kleiner Tisch. _____ liegen tausend Dinge.
2. —Wir wollen heute ins Kino.
   —Wann geht ihr _____?
3. Im Sommer fahre ich nach Rom. Ich freue mich schon _____.
4. Letztes Jahr hat Robert in Göttingen studiert und viel Spaß gehabt.
   Er denkt noch oft _____.
5. Gestern kam endlich ein Brief von Jürgen. Melanie hat sich sehr _____ gefreut. Sie hat lange _____ gewartet.
6. Morgen hat Thomas eine große Prüfung (*test*). Er hat keine Angst _____. Aber er muss schon um acht Uhr da sein. Er ärgert sich _____, weil er nämlich so früh noch nicht denken kann.

Übung 3. Answers: 1. *daneben* or *darunter* or *davor* or *dahinter; darauf* or *darunter* 2. *dahin* 3. *darauf* 4. *daran* 5. *darüber; darauf* 6. *davor; darüber*

Grammatik im Kontext   **363**

Stellen Sie einander Fragen in kleinen Gruppen oder im Plenum.

BEISPIEL: Wie viele Leute haben Angst vor Prüfungen?
Sechs Leute haben Angst davor.

1. Wie viele Leute interessieren sich für Politik? für Sport? für Yoga?
2. Wer hat Angst vor Prüfungen?
3. Wer denkt (oft, nie, manchmal) an das Leben nach dem Studium?
4. Wie viele Leute sind für oder gegen eine nationale Krankenversicherung? Wer soll dafür zahlen: Arbeitgeber? Arbeitnehmer? der Staat?
5. Wer freut sich auf das Ende des Studiums? auf eine Reise im Sommer?
6. Wer ärgert sich über die hohen Preise für Bücher?

Asking Questions: **wo**-Compounds°

Pronominaladverbien mit **wo**

There are two ways to formulate questions with prepositions when asking about things or ideas. One way is to use a preposition with the interrogative pronoun **was.**

Für was interessiert er sich?	*What is he interested in?*
An was denkst du?	*What are you thinking of?*
Auf was warten Sie?	*What are you waiting for?*

Another way is to combine **wo-** with a preposition to form a **wo-**compound. **Wo-** becomes **wor-** when the preposition begins with a vowel.

Wofür interessiert er sich?	*What is he interested in?*
Woran denkst du?	*What are you thinking of?*
Worauf warten Sie?	*What are you waiting for?*

Formulieren Sie zuerst Fragen. Arbeiten Sie dann zu zweit und beantworten Sie die Fragen abwechselnd (*taking turns*).

Wofür …	freust du dich?
Womit …	denkst du oft?
Woran …	gibst du viel Geld aus?
Worauf …	interessierst du dich?
Worüber …	wartest du?
Wovor …	hast du Angst?
	ärgerst du dich?
	beschäftigst du dich am liebsten?

The Subjunctive°

Der Konjunktiv

The most important function of the subjunctive mood is to express polite requests and convey wishful thinking, conjectures, and conditions that are contrary to fact. You are already familiar with one frequently used subjunctive form: **möchte.**

Expressing Requests Politely

Ich **möchte** gern bezahlen.	*I would like to pay.*
Ich **hätte** gern eine Tasse Kaffee.	*I would like a cup of coffee.*
Könntest du mir einen Gefallen tun?	*Could you do me a favor?*
Würdest du mir 50 Euro leihen?	*Would you lend me 50 Euro?*
Dürfte ich mal Ihren Pass sehen?	*May I see your passport?*

The forms **möchte, hätte, könntest, würdest,** and **dürfte** are subjunctive forms of the verbs **mögen, haben, können, werden,** and **dürfen.** They are frequently used in polite requests.

Forms of the Present Subjunctive II°

Konjunktiv II Präsens

haben	sein	können	mögen	werden	wissen
ich hätte	wäre	könnte	möchte	würde	wüsste
du hättest	wär(e)st	könntest	möchtest	würdest	wüsstest
er sie es } hätte	wäre	könnte	möchte	würde	wüsste
wir hätten	wären	könnten	möchten	würden	wüssten
ihr hättet	wär(e)t	könntet	möchtet	würdet	wüsstet
sie hätten	wären	könnten	möchten	würden	wüssten
Sie hätten	wären	könnten	möchten	würden	wüssten

Present Subjunctive of Weak Verbs. Point Out: In English, "would" plus an infinitive is most often used to express nonreality, whereas German has a choice between two forms: 1. the subjunctive based on the simple past tense form, or 2. **würde** plus an infinitive. There is no difference in meaning between the two forms. More and more, the **würde** plus infinitive construction is replacing the subjunctive based on the simple past tense.

The Present Subjunctive II is based on the simple past forms. Some verbs with an **-a-, -o-,** or **-u-** in the simple past form require an umlaut to be added to the vowel.

The forms of the subjunctive described here are known as Subjunctive II because they are derived from the simple past tense, the second principal part of the verb.

Note:

- Modals with an umlaut in the infinitive retain this umlaut in the subjunctive.

INFINITIVE	SIMPLE PAST	PRES. SUBJ.		INFINITIVE	SIMPLE PAST	PRES. SUBJ.
können →	konnte →	**könnte**	*but:*	sollen →	sollte →	**sollte**
mögen →	mochte →	**möchte**				

- Strong and irregular weak verbs with an **-a-, -o-,** or **-u-** in the simple past form add an umlaut to the vowel.

sein →	war →	**wäre**		werden →	wurde →	**würde**
haben →	hatte →	**hätte**		wissen →	wusste →	**wüsste**
geben →	gab →	**gäbe**				

- Weak verbs remain unchanged.

kaufen →	kaufte →	**kaufte**
wünschen →	wünschte →	**wünschte**

ICH? DEN GARTEN UMGRABEN?[1] ICH WÜSSTE GAR NICHT WONACH ICH SUCHEN SOLLTE...?

[1]*dig up*   *Uli Stein 2006, www.miceandmoreusa.com*

Übung 6   Im Café: Was hätten Sie gern?

BEISPIEL: Ich *hätte gern* ein Stück Käsekuchen.

1. Wir _____ einen Platz am Fenster.
2. Ich _____ einen Espresso.
3. Kerstin _____ einen Eiskaffee.
4. Herr und Frau Haese _____ einen Platz in der Nichtraucherecke.
5. Wir _____ zwei Eisbecher mit Vanilleeis und Sahne.
6. _____ ihr _____ einen Platz draußen?

Übung 7   Wünsche im Restaurant

Formulieren Sie die Wünsche und Fragen sehr höflich.

BEISPIEL: Ich will ein Bier.
       Ich hätte gern ein Bier.
 [oder] Ich möchte gern ein Bier.

1. Wir wollen die Speisekarte.
2. Ich will eine Tasse Kaffee.
3. Mein Freund will ein Bier.
4. Und was wollen Sie?
5. Willst du ein Stück Kuchen?
6. Wollen Sie sonst noch etwas?
7. Wir wollen die Rechnung.

The Use of **würde** with an Infinitive

In spoken German, one of the most commonly used forms of the subjunctive is **würde** plus infinitive. Like English *would,* the **würde** form can be used with almost any infinitive to express polite requests or wishes, or to give advice.

Würdest du mir **helfen?**	*Would you help me?*
Ich **würde** gerne **mitkommen.**	*I would like to come along.*

Note:

- Verbs that are generally not used with **würde** include **sein, haben, wissen,** and the modals.

Wenn die Studienkosten nur nicht so hoch **wären.**	*If only the cost of studying weren't so high.*
Wenn ich nur **wüsste,** wo meine Schlüssel sind.	*If I only knew where my keys were.*

Übung 8 Etwas höflicher, bitte!

Drücken Sie die folgenden Wünsche höflicher aus.

BEISPIEL: Leih mir bitte 50 Euro. →
　　　　　Würdest du mir bitte 50 Euro leihen?
[*oder*] Könntest du mir bitte 50 Euro leihen?

1. Tu mir bitte einen Gefallen.
2. Tut mir bitte einen Gefallen.
3. Leih mir bitte 100 Euro bis zum Monatsende.
4. Wechseln Sie mir bitte 200 Euro.
5. Geben Sie mir auch etwas Kleingeld.
6. Hilf mir bitte!
7. Helft mir bitte!
8. Unterschreiben Sie die Reiseschecks, bitte.
9. Zeigen Sie mir bitte Ihren Pass.

Übung 8. Note: Because subjunctive forms to express politeness are commonly used in German, use this exercise to elicit as many variations of individual sentences from students as possible.

Suggestion: One student requests something of another, using an imperative. The other in turn says *Etwas höflicher bitte: Würdest du bitte ...,* etc. You may want to review the imperative quickly before doing this activity.

Suggestion: Have students make up additional requests in the imperative. Ask individual students to rephrase the requests more politely.

Übung 9 Wie würden Sie darauf reagieren?

BEISPIEL: Sie haben eine Reise nach Österreich gewonnen. →
　　　　　Das wäre toll.

1. Sie sollen mit Freunden Bungeejumping gehen.
2. Ein Freund / Eine Freundin hat eine Million Dollar gewonnen.
3. Sie haben ein Praktikum bei einer deutschen Firma bekommen.
4. Sie sind im Supermarkt und haben Geld und Kreditkarte zu Hause gelassen.
5. Sie haben Ihre Autoschlüssel verloren.
6. Ihre Freunde machen ohne Sie eine Reise in die Karibik.
7. Sie haben eine Reise nach Las Vegas gewonnen.

Das wäre toll.

Das wäre nichts für mich.

Ich wäre sehr ärgerlich darüber.

Ich hätte Angst davor.

Ich wäre neidisch (*envious*).

Ich würde mich darüber freuen.

Übung 9. Suggestion: This exercise is also suitable for pair work. One student reads the first hypothetical situation and the other responds. Students should then switch roles for the next situation, and so on. Follow-up by asking a few students how they would respond to the situations listed. Ask if other students have different reactions to the situations, *Hat jemand eine andere Meinung dazu?*

Expressing Wishes and Hypothetical Situations

Wishes introduced with **wenn** require the subjunctive. The particles **doch**, **nur**, and **doch nur** are frequently added to conversational **wenn**-clauses for emphasis.

Wenn ich **doch** mehr Geld **hätte**.	*If only I had more money.*
Wenn ich **doch nur** mehr sparen **könnte**.	*If only I could save more money.*
Wenn Benzin nicht so teuer **wäre**.	*If only gasoline weren't so expensive.*
Wenn ich **nur wüsste**, wo meine Autoschlüssel sind.	*If I only knew where my car keys were.*
Wenn Stefan **doch** nicht so viel Geld für seinen Wagen **ausgeben würde**.	*If only Stefan didn't spend so much money on his car.*

Note:

- The conjugated verb in the **wenn**-clause stands at the end of the clause.

Ich wünschte and **ich wollte** (*I wish*) are fixed expressions in the subjunctive when expressing a wish that is counter to reality. They are always followed by a verb in the subjunctive or **würde** + infinitive.

Ich wollte, die Geschäfte in Deutschland **wären** länger geöffnet.	*I wish (that) the stores in Germany were open longer.*
Frau Schiff **wünschte**, sie **könnte** auch sonntags einkaufen.	*Ms. Schiff wishes she could go shopping on Sundays, too.*

The expression **an deiner Stelle** (*if I were you / in your place*) is always used with a verb in the subjunctive. The possessive adjective changes depending on the person in question.

An deiner Stelle würde ich alles bar bezahlen.	*If I were you, I would pay cash for everything.*
An seiner Stelle würde ich nicht mit Kreditkarte bezahlen.	*If I were in his place, I would not pay with a credit card.*

KUL...

In Deutschland gibt es das sogenannte Ladenschlussgesetz (*law regulating store hours*). Die einzelnen (*individual*) Bundesländer regeln die Öffnungszeiten. In den meisten Ländern dürfen die Geschäfte montags bis samstags rund um die Uhr öffnen, wenn sie wollen. In einigen Ländern müssen sie spätestens um 22.00 Uhr schließen. In kleineren Städten und auf dem Land jedoch schließen viele Geschäfte besonders am Samstag schon vor 18.00 Uhr.

Am Sonntag und an Feiertagen bleibt praktisch alles geschlossen. Es gibt aber einige Ausnahmen, Bäckereien, Konditoreien und Blumengeschäfte dürfen für einige Stunden verkaufen. Apotheken sowie Geschäfte an Bahnhöfen und Flughäfen dürfen auch sonntags geöffnet sein.

Der Laden ist geschlossen!

Übung 10   Was sind die Tatsachen hier?

Folgen Sie dem Beispiel.

BEISPIEL: Ich wünschte, ich könnte dir Geld leihen. →
Ich habe aber kein Geld. Ich kann dir nichts leihen.

1. Ich wünschte, ich hätte keine Kreditkarte. Dann hätte ich keine Schulden.
2. Ich wollte, die Kosten für das Studium wären nicht so hoch.
3. Ich wünschte, ich könnte genug Geld für eine Weltreise sparen.
4. Klaus wünschte, er würde nicht so viel Geld für Telefonieren ausgeben.
5. Wir wünschten, wir könnten eine preiswerte Wohnung in München finden.
6. Ich wollte, ich hätte mehr Zeit für Sport.
7. Mein Freund wollte, er könnte sich einen BMW kaufen.
8. Ich wünschte, das Semester wäre zu Ende.
9. Die Studenten wünschten, sie müssten nicht so schwer arbeiten.

Übung 11   Wenn doch nur ...

Was wünscht Helga sich?

BEISPIEL: Helgas Katze ist weg. →
Wenn die Katze doch nur wieder da wäre!

1. Helga kann ihre Autoschlüssel nicht finden.
2. Sie weiß nicht, wo die Schlüssel sind.
3. Ihre Zimmerkollegin kommt sehr spät nach Hause.
4. Sie ist ganz allein.
5. Sie kann nicht zu Hause bleiben.
6. Sie muss um drei zu einer Vorlesung gehen.

Wenn sie doch nur wüsste ...

Übung 12   Wer wünscht sich was?

Drücken Sie aus, was sich diese Leute wünschen. Benutzen Sie dabei Konjunktivformen.

BEISPIEL: Gerhard hat nie Zeit. Was wünscht er sich? →
Er wünschte sich, er hätte mehr Zeit.
[*oder*] Wenn er doch mehr Zeit hätte!

1. Frau Schmidt fährt viel zu schnell auf der Autobahn. Was wünscht sich Herr Schmidt?
2. Herr Schmidt kann nicht gut Auto fahren. Was wünscht sich Frau Schmidt?
3. Es gibt nichts Interessantes im Fernsehen. Was wünsche ich mir?
4. Max ist total pleite. Was wünscht er sich?
5. Die Gäste bleiben viel zu lange, es ist schon nach Mitternacht. Was wünscht sich der Gastgeber?
6. Morgen fliegt mein Freund nach Tahiti. Ich muss leider zu Hause bleiben. Was wünsche ich mir?

7. Alex und Tanja besuchen Berlin, aber sie können leider kein Deutsch sprechen. Was wünschen sie sich?

8. Petra kann keine Wohnung finden. Was wünscht sie sich?

9. Die Kosten für Bücher sind zu hoch. Was wünschen die Studenten sich?

Beschreiben Sie zuerst die Situation auf jedem Bild. Suchen Sie einen passenden Ausdruck aus der Liste. Überlegen Sie sich dann, was Sie an seiner oder ihrer Stelle tun würden.

BEISPIEL: An ihrer Stelle würde ich weggehen.

1.   2.   3.

1. weggehen; „Guten Tag" sagen; freundlich sein; nichts sagen; böse (*angry*) sein; nicht mit ihm reden; ??

2. eine Reparaturwerkstatt anrufen; sich ins Auto setzen und warten, bis der Regen aufhört; Hilfe anbieten (*offer*); um Hilfe bitten; zu Fuß weitergehen; den Reifen wechseln (*change the tire*); ??

3. nicht länger warten; allein ins Kino gehen; ungeduldig (*impatient*) sein; bei … anrufen; ??

Talking about Contrary-to-Fact Conditions

Compare the following sentences:

Wenn ich Geld **brauche, gehe** ich zur Bank.

When I need money, I go to the bank.

Wenn ich Geld **hätte, würde** ich mir einen neuen Wagen **kaufen.**

If I had money, I would buy a new car.

The first example states a condition of fact. The second example states a condition that is contrary to fact. The implication is that the speaker does not have enough money to buy a new car. In such cases, the subjunctive II is used.

Die Schnecke in diesem Cartoon singt ein bekanntes deutsches Volkslied (*folk song*).

- Circle the verbs that express the snail's wishful thinking. Note that these verb forms differ from those you have learned: they have no **-e** ending. What could be the reason for this?

- State the three things the snail wishes to be, to have, or to do. (Note that the suffix **-lein,** when added to a noun, makes a diminutive of this noun.)

    der Vogel (*bird*) → das Vöglein

    der Flügel (*wing*) → das Flüglein

    Sie möchte …

- Was sind die Tatsachen (*facts*) ihres Lebens?

    **Eine Schnecke ist kein Vöglein; sie hat …
    und …**

- Interessiert sich die zweite Schnecke für die Sängerin? Was würden Sie als Beweise (*evidence*) dafür anführen?

Analyse: Play or sing this well-known folk tune, which describes the longing of a young lover who is separated from his/her beloved. A rock and roll version of the song exists on the soudtrack to Katja von Garnier's 1997 film *Bandits*. Point out that the text uses a form of the subjunctive of the strong verb *fliegen (flög[e])* that is less common in contemporary German but is still used and found in writing.

Unglückliche Verhältnisse[1]

[1]Unglückliche … *Unhappy conditions*

[2]*little bird*

[3]*little wings*

[4]Diese … *This lame snail gets on my nerves.*

Übung 14   Was würden Sie machen, wenn … ?

Sagen Sie, was Sie machen würden, wenn alles anders wäre.

BEISPIEL: Wenn ich Talent hätte, würde ich Opernsängerin werden.

Wenn ich Zeit hätte,
    Geld
    Talent
    mehr Freizeit
    Präsident/Präsidentin
      wäre,
    ??

ein berühmter / eine berühmte
   __??__ (z.B. Sänger/Sängerin)
  werden.

interessante Leute kennen
  lernen.

öfter ins Kino gehen.

eine Insel im Pazifik kaufen.

jeden Tag die Zeitung lesen.

??

Übung 14. Follow-up: Half the class writes *wenn*-clauses, the other half result-clauses only. Call on students to combine clauses; the attempt might produce some odd and amusing combinations!

Übung 15 Rat geben

Stellen Sie sich vor, ein Freund / eine Freundin hat ein Problem. Was raten Sie?

BEISPIEL: s1: Ich bin total pleite. Was soll ich nur machen?
s2: Du solltest dir eine Arbeit suchen.
|oder| Ich würde mir eine Arbeit suchen.

PROBLEM	RAT
habe Zahnschmerzen	Arbeit suchen
kann nicht schlafen	Geld von jemand leihen
esse zu viele Süßigkeiten	sofort zum Zahnarzt gehen
bin immer müde und schlapp	keine Süßigkeiten mehr kaufen
habe kein Geld	Vitamintabletten einnehmen
??	nicht so spät schlafen gehen
	??

The Past Subjunctive II°

Der Konjunktiv II der Vergangenheit

The Past Subjunctive II is used to express wishes and conjectures concerning events in the past.

Wenn ich in der Lotterie **gewonnen hätte, wäre** ich überglücklich **gewesen.**

If I had won the lottery, I would have been ecstatic.

The conjecture (*If I had . . .*) speculates about an event in the past: The speaker did not win the lottery. Both English and German require the past subjunctive in this case.

The past subjunctive II forms are derived from the past perfect tense. Use the subjunctive II form **hätte** or **wäre** plus the past participle of the main verb.

INFINITIVE	PAST PERFECT	PAST SUBJUNCTIVE II
kaufen	ich hatte gekauft	ich hätte gekauft
sein	ich war gewesen	ich wäre gewesen

Ich wünschte, ich **hätte** den neuen Porsche nicht **gekauft.**

I wish I had not bought the new Porsche.

Ein gebrauchter Wagen **wäre** billiger **gewesen.**

A used car would have been cheaper.

Note:

- Use **hätte** or **wäre** according to the same rules that determine the use of **haben** or **sein** in the perfect tense (see **Kapitel 7**).

Ich **habe** die Miete **bezahlt.**

Lars **hätte** die Miete nicht **bezahlt.**

Er **ist** in die Stadt **gefahren.**

Ich **wäre** nicht in die Stadt **gefahren.**

A clause stating a hypothetical situation usually begins with the conjunction **wenn.** As in English, the conjunction can be omitted, in which case the conjugated verb is placed at the beginning.

Wenn wir das nur gewusst hätten!

If we had only known that!

Hätten wir das nur gewusst!

Had we only known that!

ANALYSE

Schauen Sie sich den Cartoon an.

- Find the verb forms in the past subjunctive and give their infinitives.
- What is the woman speculating about?
- What stereotype does the cartoon allude to? Formulate a conclusion to the hypothesis **"Wenn ich als Blondine geboren wär(e) …"**
- What is the reality of her life?

Analyse. Suggestion: Have students first describe the cartoon in German. Ask *Finden Sie diese Situation typisch? Komisch?*

EWIGE FRAGEN

Immer wieder frag ich mich, wie mein Leben geworden wär wenn ich als Blondine geboren wär…

Wie ist das passiert? Sie sehen hier Andreas' Ausgaben für eine Woche. Schauen Sie sich die Liste an. Wofür hat er Ihrer Meinung nach (*in your opinion*) zu viel Geld ausgegeben? Machen Sie ein paar Vorschläge (*suggestions*), was Sie anders gemacht hätten.

	AUSGABEN
Geburtstagsgeschenk, Buch und Blumen für Freundin	€ 65,00
drei Sporthemden	120,00
Karte für „Phantom der Oper"	80,00
zweimal im Kino	22,00
Briefmarken	6,50
zweimal mit Freunden in der Kneipe	25,00
Bücher für Biologie und Computerwissenschaften (*computer science*)	125,00
Benzin fürs Auto	90,00
Zigaretten	48,00
dreimal zum Essen ausgegangen	59,00
Spende für Amnesty International	25,00
Telefon	120,00

REDEMITTEL

An seiner Stelle hätte ich nicht so viel für … ausgegeben.

Das wäre wirklich nicht nötig gewesen.

Braucht er wirklich … ? Ich hätte …

Zweimal … ? Einmal wäre genug (*enough*) gewesen.

Sprache im Kontext

Videoclips

A. Beatrice, Dennis und Jan sprechen über Geld und ihre monatlichen Ausgaben.

1. Alle drei beantworten diese Frage anders: „Was würdest du tun, wenn du eine Million Euro gewinnen würdest?". Was sagt Beatrice? Was sagt Dennis? Und Jan?

2. Wenn Sie eine Million in der Lotterie gewinnen würden, würden Sie dasselbe wie die drei machen oder etwas ganz anderes? Was?

B. Ergänzen Sie die Informationen in der Tabelle. Wenn es keine Information gibt, schreiben Sie „keine Information".

Wie viel Geld gibt er/sie aus für …	BEATRICE	DENNIS	JAN
Miete?	_____	_____	_____
Telefon?	_____	_____	_____
Lebensmittel?	_____	_____	_____
Sonstiges?	_____	_____	_____
Woher bekommt er/sie sein/ihr Geld?	_____	_____	_____

C. Schauen Sie sich alle drei Interviews noch einmal an. Wen beschreiben diese Sätze? Schreiben Sie **B** für Beatrice, **D** für Dennis und **J** für Jan.

1. _____ kann nicht sehr gut mit Geld umgehen.
2. _____ will in der Zukunft Lehrer werden und kleine Kinder unterrichten.
3. _____ wohnt mit einer Freundin zusammen und teilt die Kosten.
4. _____ wohnt allein in einer Wohnung mit Kochnische.
5. _____ macht ein Magisterstudium in Kulturwissenschaften und studiert noch Politik dazu.
6. _____ lebt relativ sparsam.

Lesen

Zum Thema

Fragen zum Thema Geld. Beantworten Sie die folgenden Fragen erst selber, und interviewen Sie dann einige Personen im Kurs.

1. Haben Sie als Kind Taschengeld erhalten? Wie viel? Wie oft und wann?
2. Was war Ihr erster bezahlter Job? Was haben Sie mit dem Geld gemacht?
3. Können Sie gut sparen, oder geben Sie Ihr Geld impulsiv aus?

Auf den ersten Blick

A. Überlegen Sie sich, was Sie in den folgenden Situationen machen würden.

1. Sie sind im Restaurant und gerade mit dem Essen fertig. Da bemerken Sie, dass Sie weder Geld noch Kreditkarten bei sich haben. Was würden Sie machen?
2. Sie fahren durch Europa. Gewöhnlich übernachten Sie in Jugendherbergen, aber an einem Ort gibt es nur Hotels. Dafür haben Sie aber nicht genug Geld. Was würden Sie machen?

B. Lesen Sie die ersten zehn Zeilen der Geschichte „Fahrkarte bitte", und beantworten Sie die folgenden Fragen.

1. Wer sind die Hauptpersonen?
2. Wo findet die Geschichte statt? („Kiel" allein genügt nicht [*is not sufficient*] als Antwort.)
3. Zu welcher Tageszeit beginnt die Erzählung?
4. Was ist das Hauptproblem oder der Konflikt?

Auf den ersten Blick. Suggestions: A. Have students discuss the hypothetical situations in small groups or pairs. B. Have students work in pairs to answer the pre-reading questions. Ask them to come up with a hypothesis about how the story will likely end. While reading the story for homework, they should write down how the story does or does not conform to their predictions.

von Helga M. Novak

Kiel sieht neu aus. Es ist dunkel. Ich gehe zum Hafen. Mein Schiff ist
nicht da. Es fährt morgen. Es kommt morgen vormittag an und fährt um
dreizehn Uhr wieder ab. Ich sehe ein Hotel. Im Eingang steht ein junger
Mann. Er trägt einen weinroten Rollkragenpullover°.   *turtleneck sweater*

5 Ich sage, haben Sie ein Einzelzimmer?
Er sagt, ja.
Ich sage, ich habe nur eine Handtasche bei mir, mein ganzes Gepäck ist
auf dem Bahnhof in Schließfächern°.   *lockers*
Er sagt, Zimmer einundvierzig. Wollen Sie gleich bezahlen? Ich sage, ach

10 nein, ich bezahle morgen.
Ich schlafe gut. Ich wache auf. Es regnet in Strömen°. Ich gehe hinunter.   *Es ... It's pouring.*
Der junge Mann hat eine geschwollene Lippe.
Ich sage, darf ich mal telefonieren?
Er sagt, naja.

15 Ich rufe an.
Ich sage, du, ja, hier bin ich, heute noch, um eins, ja, ich komme gleich,
doch ich muß, ich habe kein Geld, mein Hotel, ach fein, ich gebe es dir
zurück, sofort, schön.
Der junge Mann steht neben mir. Er hat zugehört.

20 Ich sage, jetzt hole ich Geld. Dann bezahle ich.
Er sagt, zuerst bezahlen.
Ich sage, ich habe kein Geld, meine Freundin.
Er sagt, das kann ich mir nicht leisten.
Ich sage, aber ich muß nachher weiter.

25 Er sagt, da könnte ja jeder kommen°.   *da ... anyone could say that*
Ich sage, meine Freundin kann nicht aus dem Geschäft weg.
Er lacht.
Ich sage, ich bin gleich wieder da.
Er sagt, so sehen Sie aus°.   *idiom: so ... I bet you are (sarcastic)*

30 Ich sage, lassen Sie mich doch gehen. Was haben Sie denn von mir?
Er sagt, ich will Sie ja gar nicht.
Ich sage, manch einer wäre froh°.   *manch ... many a man would be glad*
Er sagt, den zeigen° Sie mir mal.   *show*
Ich sage, Sie kennen mich noch nicht.

35 Er sagt, abwarten und Tee trinken°.   *idiom: abwarten ... let's wait and see*
Es kommen neue Gäste.
Er sagt, gehen Sie solange° in die Gaststube.   *for the time being*
Er kommt nach.
Ich sage, mein Schiff geht um eins.

40 Er sagt, zeigen Sie mir bitte Ihre Fahrkarte.
Er verschließt° sie in einer Kassette°.   *locks / box*
Ich sitze in der Gaststube und schreibe einen Brief.
Liebe Charlotte, seit einer Woche bin ich im „Weißen Ahornblatt"
Serviererin. Nähe Hafen. Wenn Du hier vorbeikommst, sieh doch zu

45 mir herein. Sonst geht
es mir glänzend. Deine Maria.

Zum Text

A. Beantworten Sie die folgenden Fragen.

1. Wer erzählt die Geschichte, ein Mann oder eine Frau? Welchen Beweis (*evidence*) können Sie dafür bringen?

2. Suchen Sie nach Wörtern und Äußerungen, die weitere Informationen über die Hauptpersonen geben. Was können Sie aus diesen Details schließen (*conclude*)? Es steht z.B. im Text, dass der junge Mann „eine geschwollene Lippe" hat.

3. Wann erfahren die Leser, dass eine der Hauptpersonen ein großes Problem hat? Wie würden Sie in dieser Situation handeln (*act*)? Welche Rolle spielt die Fahrkarte?

4. Sie hören nur eine Seite des Telefongesprächs. Was könnte die Person am anderen Ende sagen?

5. Lesen Sie die Geschichte ein zweites Mal. Glauben Sie dieser Frau? Wenn nicht, was für Beweise haben Sie, dass sie lügt (*is lying*)?

6. Die Geschichte endet mit einem Brief. Was sagt uns der Brief über die Erzählerin? Ist Charlotte eventuell (*possibly*) dieselbe Person, mit der die Erzählerin am Telefon gesprochen hat? Welchen Beweis haben Sie dafür oder dagegen?

B. Ein Monat ist vergangen. Was ist aus der Frau geworden? Schreiben Sie eine Fortsetzung (*continuation*) der Geschichte. Was macht die Frau jetzt? Ist sie noch in Kiel? Ist sie abgereist? Hat sie Geld? Ist sie glücklich?

Zu guter Letzt

Vom Lesestück zum Theaterstück

Die Kurzgeschichte „Fahrkarte bitte" von Helga M. Novak ist zum großen Teil in Form eines Dialogs geschrieben. Aus der Geschichte kann man ein interessantes Theaterstück machen. Erstellen Sie einen Bühnentext (*stage text*) und spielen Sie das Stück der Klasse vor.

Schritt 1: Schreiben Sie alle direkten Reden in Form eines Bühnentextes um:

- Schreiben Sie die „Ich sage"-Sätze als Marias Reden neu:

BEISPIEL: Ich sage, ich habe nur eine Handtasche bei mir, mein ganzes Gepäck ist auf dem Bahnhof in Schließfächern. →
  MARIA: „Ich habe nur eine Handtasche bei mir, mein ganzes Gepäck ist auf dem Bahnhof in Schließfächern."

- Schreiben Sie die „Er sagt"-Sätze als Reden des jungen Mannes:

BEISPIEL: Er sagt, zuerst bezahlen. →
  JUNGER MANN: „Zuerst bezahlen."
  oder JUNGER MANN: „Bezahlen Sie zuerst."

- Gewisse Sätze können von einem Erzähler / einer Erzählerin gesagt werden:

BEISPIEL: Ich schlafe gut. Ich wache auf. Es regnet in Strömen. →
  ERZÄHLER(IN): „Sie schläft gut. Sie wacht auf. Es regnet in Strömen."

- Wenn Sie wollen, können Sie zusätzlich Text dazu schreiben. Zum Beispiel könnte der junge Mann Maria fragen, wie viele Tage sie bleiben möchte.

Zum Text A. Suggestion: Have students do these questions as homework after they have finished reading the story at home.

Additional comprehension questions: *1. Was will die Erzählerin im Hotel? 2. Was hat sie nicht dabei (on her person)? 3. Mit wem telefoniert sie? 4. Warum kann sie das Hotel nicht verlassen? 5. Warum arbeitet die Frau jetzt als Serviererin im „Weißen Ahornblatt"?*

B. Suggestion: Assign this as an in-class activity the day after students have read the text at home. Students can do this in groups and perform the continuation or read their stories aloud to the rest of the class.

Additional Activity: Assign students the task of playing Charlotte and answering Maria's letter.

Zu guter Letzt. Suggestion: Have students work in groups of 3 to 5, depending on class size and talents. One person might be assigned to prepare props or sketch the stage set, while the director and actors practice the lines. Students need not necessarily memorize all the lines. They might use notes, cue cards, and/or take turns playing roles.

Zu guter Letzt. Alternate Suggestion: If your department has access to video or DV cameras, have students film their productions outside of class.

Schritt 2: Schreiben Sie nun einige Bühnenanweisungen (*stage directions*) in den Text. Wo findet die Handlung statt? Was sieht man auf der Bühne? Wie sehen die Hauptpersonen aus? Was für Requisiten (*props*) werden gebraucht, z.B. Handtasche, Telefon? Die Erzählung gibt Ihnen Auskunft, aber Sie können auch eigene Ideen entwickeln.

Schritt 3: Eine Skizze (*sketch*) zum Bühnenbild (*stage set*) gibt die Atmosphäre und den Ton eines Theaterstücks an. Sie zeigt, wie die Szenen aussehen und was die Personen machen. Zeichnen Sie ein oder mehrere Bilder zu den Szenen. Sie können auch Fotos oder Poster benutzen.

Schritt 4: Bestimmen Sie nun:

- wer den Erzähler / die Erzählerin spielt
- wer die junge Frau Maria spielt
- wer den jungen Mann spielt
- wer der Regisseur / die Regisseurin ist

Schritt 5: Üben Sie die Rollen und spielen Sie das Theaterstück anschließend der Klasse vor.

Wortschatz

Geldangelegen-heiten — Money Matters

die **Ausgabe, -n**	expense
das **Benzin**	gasoline
der **Bleistift, -e**	pencil
die **Computerdiskette, -n**	computer diskette
die **Einnahmen** (*pl.*)	income
die **Ernährung**	food, nutrition
der **Haushalt, -e**	household
das **Heft, -e**	notebook
die **Heizung**	heat, heating system
der **Kugelschreiber, -**	ballpoint pen
der **Müll**	trash, garbage
die **Nebenkosten**	utilities; extra costs
das **Papier, -e**	paper
die **Reparatur, -en**	repair
das **Sparkonto,** *pl.* **Sparkonten**	savings account
der **Strom**	electricity
die **Studiengebühren** (*pl.*)	tuition, fees
die **Versicherung, -en**	insurance

Das Haus — The House

das **Bauernhaus, ⸚er**	farmhouse
das **Dach, ⸚er**	roof
das **Dachgeschoss, -e**	top floor, attic
die **Diele, -n**	front hall
der **Eingang, ⸚e**	entrance
die **Etage, -n**	floor, story
der **Flur, -e**	hallway
die **Frühstücksnische, -n**	breakfast nook
die **Garderobe, -n**	wardrobe; closet
das **Gästezimmer, -**	guest room
das **Gerät, -e**	appliance, device
der **Mikrowellenherd, -e**	microwave oven
der **Neubau, -ten**	modern building
die **Spülmaschine, -n**	dishwasher
der **Staubsauger**	vacuum cleaner
der **Teppichboden, ⸚**	wall-to-wall carpeting
die **Treppe, -n**	staircase
die **Umgebung, -en**	area, neighborhood, vicinity
die **Waschmaschine, -n**	washing machine
der **Wäschetrockner, -n**	clothes dryer

Verben — Verbs

sich ärgern über (+ *acc.*)	to be annoyed about
aus•geben (gibt aus), gab aus, ausgegeben	to spend (*money*)
bauen	to build
bitten um, bat, gebeten	to ask for, request
denken an (+ *acc.*), **dachte, gedacht**	to think about, of
ein•richten	to furnish, equip
ein•ziehen in (+ *acc.*), **zog ein, ist eingezogen**	to move in

sich freuen auf (+ *acc.*)	to look forward to	**nützlich**	useful
sich freuen über (+ *acc.*)	to be glad about	**oben**	above; upstairs
jobben	to work (*at a temporary job*)	**nach oben**	above; upstairs (*directional*)
mieten	to rent (*from someone*)	**pleite**	broke, out of money
sparen	to save	**schmutzig**	dirty
unterstützen, unterstützt	to support	**sparsam**	thrifty
vergleichen, verglich, verglichen	to compare	**spätestens**	at the latest
		übrig	left over
vermieten	to rent out (*to someone*)	**unbedingt**	absolutely, by all means
verzichten auf (+ *acc.*)	to do without	**unten**	below; downstairs
		nach unten	below; downstairs (*directional*)

Adjektive und Adverbien

Adjectives and Adverbs

ab	from, as of
ab 1. Juni (ab erstem Juni)	as of June 1st
bald	soon
deswegen	because of that
durchschnittlich	on average
eigen	own
ganz	complete(ly), total(ly), entire(ly)
monatlich	monthly
notwendig	necessary

Sonstiges

Other

an deiner Stelle	if I were you, (if I were) in your place
die **Angst, ⸚e**	fear
Angst haben vor (+ *dat.*)	to be afraid of
der **Gruß, ⸚e**	greeting
viele Grüße	best wishes
die **Katze, -n**	cat
das **Tier, -e**	animal
die **Zeichnung, -en**	drawing

DAS KANN ICH NUN!

1. Machen Sie eine Liste mit den fünf größten Ausgaben, die Sie monatlich haben.

2. Beschreiben Sie das Haus, in dem Sie wohnen, das Haus Ihrer Eltern oder das Haus von Freunden. Wie viele Zimmer gibt es? Was für Zimmer? Wo liegen sie? Was für Geräte gibt es?

3. Beschreiben Sie Ihr Zimmer oder Ihr Klassenzimmer. Benutzen Sie dabei Wörter wie: **daneben, dazwischen, darauf, darunter,** usw.

4. Formulieren Sie passende Fragen zu folgenden Antworten. (Use a **wo**-compound.)

    a. ____? —Das Kind hat Angst vor Gewitter. **b.** ____? —Die Studenten beschäftigen sich mit Politik. **c.** ____? —Wir warten auf die Post.

5. Wie sagt man dies sehr höflich auf Deutsch?

    a. *You are at a restaurant and would like a table by the window.* (*two ways*) **b.** *You would like to see the menu.* **c.** *You would like to pay by credit card.*

6. Sie haben viele Wünsche. Wie drückt man sie auf Deutsch aus?

    a. *You wish you had more time and money.* **b.** *You wish you could stay home today.* **c.** *You are asking someone, very politely, to help you.*

7. Schreiben Sie die Sätze zu Ende.

    a. Wenn ich das Geld für eine Reise hätte, ____. **b.** Wenn ich gewusst hätte, dass es ein Gewitter gibt, ____. **c.** Du hast eine Erkältung? An deiner Stelle ____.

Viertes Zwischenspiel

Deutsche Einwanderung[1] nach Nordamerika

Laut US-Census aus dem Jahre 2000 gibt es ca. 43 Millionen Amerikaner deutscher Abstammung[2] in den USA. Die ersten Deutschen kamen schon 1608 nach Jamestown in Virginia. Die Menschen verließen ihre Heimat hauptsächlich aus drei Gründen: aus religiösen, politischen oder wirtschaftlichen Motiven.

Im Jahre 1683 wanderten zum Beispiel achtzehn Familien aus Krefeld mit Franz Daniel Pastorius (1651–1719) nach Pennsylvanien aus, wo sie die erste deutsche Siedlung[3], Germantown, gründeten. Die Beziehung zwischen Krefeld und Germantown wird bis heute aktiv gepflegt.

Die Vorfahren der Amischen wurden in Europa wegen ihrer Religion verfolgt[4] und getötet. (Der Name „Amisch" kommt von dem Begründer der Sekte, dem Prediger Jakob Amman.) Noch heute leben viele Amische in den USA und Kanada. Die größten Siedlungen findet man in Ohio, Pennsylvanien und Indiana. Viele Amische sind dreisprachig: zu Hause sprechen sie ihren deutschen Dialekt und in der Kirche sprechen sie Hochdeutsch. Außerhalb der Gemeinschaft sprechen sie Englisch.

Im Jahre 1848 gab es in den deutschen Staaten eine demokratische Revolution. Deutschland existierte noch nicht als vereinigte Nation. Die Revolution scheiterte[5] allerdings und viele der Revolutionäre mussten flüchten[6]. Einer dieser revolutionären Generation war Carl Schurz (1829–1906), der später in der amerikanischen Regierung eine prominente Rolle spielte.

In den 30er Jahren des 20. Jahrhunderts flohen viele prominente deutsche und österreichische, jüdische sowie nicht-jüdische Intellektuelle vor politischer und rassistischer Verfolgung durch die Hitler-Diktatur nach Nordamerika, unter anderem Albert Einstein, Thomas Mann, Paul Tillich und Billy Wilder.

Im 19. Jahrhundert gab es eine steigende Massenemigration Deutscher aus wirtschaftlichen Gründen. Sie wollten der Armut[7] entfliehen und suchten im Land der „unbegrenzten[8] Möglichkeiten" einen Neuanfang. So verließ Johann Jakob Astor 1784 seine Heimat in Walldorf bei Heidelberg. Mit 25 Dollar in der Tasche landete er

Amische in Lancaster County, Pennsylvanien

in New York. Er brachte es zu einem Vermögen[9] im Immobilienhandel[10] und Pelzhandel[11].

Im Alter von nur 14 Jahren wanderte Levi Strauss (1829–1902) im Jahre 1847 von Bayern in die USA aus. 1853 kam er nach Kalifornien, wo er den Goldgräbern[12] stabile Hosen aus einem Material mit dem französichen Namen „serge de Nîmes" verkaufte. Danach wurde das Material „Denim" benannt.

Levi Strauss

[1] *immigration* [2] *heritage* [3] *settlement* [4] *persecuted* [5] *failed* [6] *flee* [7] *poverty* [8] *unlimited* [9] *fortune* [10] *real estate* [11] *fur trade* [12] *gold-diggers*

Chronologie: A useful web source on German immigration is "The German Americans: An Ethnic Experience," found on the Indiana University website at www.ulib.iupui.edu/KADE/adams/toc.html.

Chronologie deutscher Einwanderung nach Amerika

1608 Deutsche Glasmacher kommen nach Jamestown in Virginia.

1683 Mennoniten und Quäker gründen Germantown, Pennsylvanien.

1709 Massenauswanderung aus der Pfalz beginnt.

1732 Erste deutschsprachige Zeitung in Nordamerika, *Die Philadelphische Zeitung*, erscheint.

1741 Die Herrnhuter Brüdergemeinde (*Moravian Brethren*) siedelt im Bundesstaat Pennsylvanien an.

1743 Christoph Sauer druckt die erste deutsche Bibel in Amerika.

1750 Die erste große Welle deutscher Einwanderer kommen nach Neuschottland.

1777 Deutsche spielen eine große Rolle im amerikanischen Revolutionskrieg.

1845 Deutsche gründen Neu Braunfels in Texas.

1850–60 Fast 1.000.000 Deutsche kommen nach Amerika.

1880–90 1.500.000 Deutsche wandern nach Amerika aus, davon 250.000 allein im Jahr 1882.

1894 Es gibt mehr als 800 deutschsprachige Zeitungen und Zeitschriften in Amerika.

1917 Erster Weltkrieg: antideutsche Hysterie bricht aus; die deutsche Sprache wird verboten.

1933 Hitler kommt an die Macht; jüdische Intellektuelle und Künstler verlassen Deutschland.

1950 Über 120.000 Deutsche kommen nach Amerika.

Quelle: Adams, Willi Paul: *The German Americans: An Ethnic Experience* (1993).

Aktivität 1 Fragen zur Einwanderung

1. Warum kamen Deutsche nach Nordamerika?

2. Wie viele Amerikaner waren im Jahre 2000 deutscher Abstammung?

3. Wo leben die meisten Amischen heute?

4. Was für eine Sprache sprechen die Amischen?

5. Warum musste Carl Schurz sein Land verlassen?

6. Welche politischen Ereignisse verursachten (*caused*) die deutsche Auswanderung (*emigration*) im 19. und 20. Jahrhundert?

7. Welcher deutscher Einwanderer wurde durch Immobilienhandel reich? Welcher wurde durch seine Jeans-Hosen bekannt?

8. In welchem Bundesstaat ließen sich (*settled*) viele frühe deutsche Einwanderer nieder?

Aktivität 2 Menschen und Momente

Es gibt viele wichtige Personen und Momente in der Geschichte der deutschen Einwanderung nach Nordamerika. Treiben Sie etwas Forschung und suchen Sie Informationen zu den folgenden Namen. Warum sind sie von Bedeutung?

1. Nikolaus de Meyer

2. Barbara Heck

3. Hessische Truppen

4. Joseph Heister

5. J. A. Sutter

6. *Illinois Staatsanzeiger*

7. Frederick Pabst

8. Mary McCauley

Barbara Heck

Aktivität 3 Mini-Forschungsprojekte

1. Schreiben Sie eine Kurzbiographie eines Einwanderers / einer Einwanderin mit Bildern als Posterpräsentation.

2. Erforschen Sie die deutschen Wurzeln (*roots*) Ihrer Stadt oder Ihrer Region und schreiben Sie einen Bericht darüber.

3. Berichten Sie über eines der folgenden Themen:

   a. eine deutschsprachige Zeitung in den USA/Kanada

   b. Nordamerikanische Firmen, die von Deutsch-Amerikanern gegründet wurden

4. Erstellen Sie eine Grafik über deutsche Einwanderung nach Nordamerika bzw. in die USA oder nach Kanada.

Medien und Technik

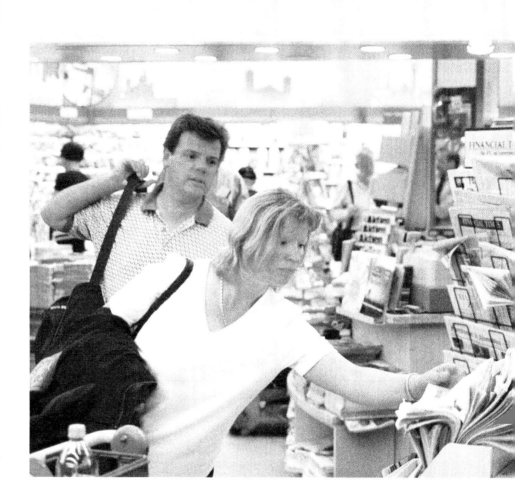

Gibt's was Neues in der
Zeitung?

In diesem Kapitel

- **Themen:** Television, newspapers, and other media; technology, computers
- **Grammatik:** Infinitive clauses with **zu**, verbs **brauchen** and **scheinen**, infinitive clauses with **um … zu** and **ohne … zu**, indirect discourse
- **Kultur:** Radio and television, inventions
- **Lesen:** „Gute Freunde im Netz" (Kerstin Kohlenberg)

Videoclips
In der Zeitung steht …

Alles klar?

A. Hier sehen Sie verschiedene deutschsprachige Zeitungen.

- Finden Sie drei Zeitungen, die deutsche Städtenamen tragen.
- Welche Zeitung ist für das Rheinland?
- Welche Zeitung erscheint wöchentlich (*weekly*)?
- Zwei Zeitungen sind sehr bunt (*colorful*) und bringen sensationelle Nachrichten. Wie heißen sie?

Alles klar? Suggestion:
Personalization questions: *Lesen Sie Zeitung? Welche? Lesen Sie (auch/lieber) die Nachrichten im Internet? Auf welcher Website? Gibt es an unserer Uni/an unserem College eine Studentenzeitung? Lesen Sie diese Zeitung?*

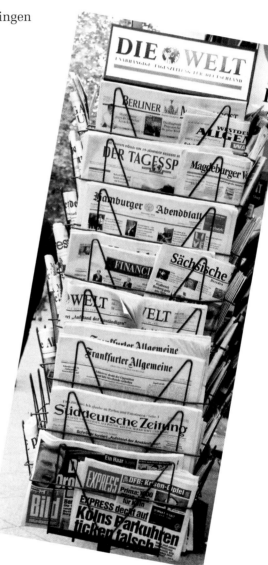

B. Sie hören vier kurze Berichte aus dem Radio. Welche Schlagzeile passt zu welchem Bericht? Schreiben Sie die passende Zahl (1–4) vor die Schlagzeile.

  3   Kluges (*smart*) Köpfchen vorm Mittagessen

  4   Spender (*donor*) der Woche

  2   Unbekanntes Dorf im Iran entdeckt

  1   Autodieb (*car thief*) auf Surfbrett gefangen

Wörter im Kontext

Was gibt's im Fernsehen?

THOMAS: Was gibt's denn heute Abend im Fernsehen?

BARBARA: Nach den **Nachrichten** um 19 Uhr kommt im zweiten **Programm** ein Krimi, „Die Rosenheim-Cops".

THOMAS: Ein Krimi, nein danke! Das ist nichts für mich. **Das ist mir zu blöd.** Was gibt's denn bei RTL?

BARBARA: Eine Seifenoper, „Gute Zeiten, schlechte Zeiten" und eine Quiz-Show, „Wer wird Millionär?".

THOMAS: Auch **nichts Gescheites.**

BARBARA: Was für eine **Sendung** möchtest du denn sehen?

THOMAS: Na, vielleicht Sport … oder einen **Dokumentarfilm.** Ich kann **mich** noch nicht **entschließen.**

Neue Wörter

die Nachrichten (*pl.*)   news
das Programm   program, channel
Das ist mir zu blöd.   I think that's really stupid.
nichts Gescheites   nothing decent
die Sendung   TV program
mich … entschließen (sich entschließen)   decide
der Bericht   report
der Spielfilm   movie, feature film
ansehen   watch
Such dir was aus! (sich etwas aussuchen)   Choose something!
Wie wäre es mit … ?   How about . . . ?
Na und?   So what?
auf jeden Fall   in any case
Wovon handelt sie? (handeln von)   What's it about?

RTL

18.00	**Guten Abend RTL**	3-923
	Oder Regionalprogramme	
18.30	**Exclusiv** Starmagazin	28-010
18.45	**RTL aktuell**	450-126
	Anschließend: **19.03 Uhr Wetter**	
19.05	**Explosiv** Mit Markus Lanz	567-381
19.40	**Gute Zeiten,**	
	schlechte Zeiten	8-381-720
	Deutschland 2006 (3460)	

SERIE

Wollen Freunde sein: Franzi (Jasmin Weber) und Philip (Jörn Schlönvoigt) Durch eine auffallend heftige Reaktion gegenüber Schüttler lenkt Paula ihren Freund John auf die richtige Fährte. In einer Aussprache versuchen Franzi und Philip ihr Verhältnis zueinander zu klären, so daß einem freundschaftlichen Miteinander künftig nichts im Wege steht. Doch bei der Theaterprobe sieht die Sache dann wieder ganz anders aus.

20.15 Wer wird Millionär? 114-297

Moderation: Günther Jauch

QUIZSHOW

Die Web-Mutti ist die Beste: Jauch sucht bei Problemen im Haushalt weltweit weibliche Hilfe

Es geschah an einem Montag im März, da schnellte die Anzahl der Zugriffe auf eine Internetseite explosionsartig in die Höhe. Was außer Sex, Geld und Tierbabys besitzt solche Anziehungskraft? Ganz einfach: Hausmittel gegen „Stinkeschuhe" und Rotweinflecken. Für die Aufregung war allein Quizmaster Günther Jauch verantwortlich. Der hatte - ganz Hausfrauen versteht sich - im Plausch mit einer Kandidatin vor einem Millionenpublikum für die Ratgeberseite www.frag-mutti.de bekennende Werbung gemacht. Fans wird es gefreut haben, wieder etwas über den kauzigen Medienstar erfahren - und von ihm gelernt zu haben.

WEITERE SPIELFILME

11.30 NDR — Rache ist süß ⑤ⓦ
KOMÖDIE Starreporter Jeff soll für seinen rachsüchtigen Boss einen dunklen Fleck auf der weißen Weste einer attraktiven Richterin finden… Nette Unterhaltung. SV 5-187-268
USA 1941 D Walter Pidgeon, Rosalind Russell, Edward Arnold R Norman Taurog 80 Min. →12.50 ➡

20.15 PRO 7 — Borderline – Unter Mordverdacht
NEU: THRILLER Gefängnispsychologin Lila wird verdächtigt nach einem Sorgerechtsstreit um die beiden Kinder, ihren Ex-Mann und dessen Freundin ermordet zu haben. Sie glaubt, den wahren Täter aus ihrem Umfeld zu kennen… Spannend. SV 83-341
USA 2002 D Gina Gershon, Sean Patrick Flanery, Eddie Driscoll R Evelyn Purcell 105/87 Min. →22.00 ↗

21.45 BR — Bella Martha
LIEBESKOMÖDIE Martha kann gut kochen, aber vom Genießen versteht sie nichts. Ein temperamentvoller Italiener und ein kleines Mädchen tauen das Herz der verschlossenen Köchin auf… Garniert mit feinem Humor. SV 7-202-744
Dtl./Ital. 2001 D Martina Gedeck, Sergio Castellitto B+R Sandra Nettelbeck 100 Min. →23.25 ↗

22.05 MDR — Tatort: Das Phantom
TV-KRIMI Schenk erkennt, daß er vor Jahren einen Unschuldigen hinter Gitter gebracht hat. Bevor er den Fehler wieder gutmachen kann, bricht der junge Mann aus und tötet einen Polizisten… Melancholische Story. SV 3-728-812
Dtl. 2003 D Klaus J. Behrendt, Dietmar Bär, Roman Knizka R Kaspar Heidelbach 90 Min. →23.35 ↗

23.20 SWR — Virus im Paradies (1)
TV-THRILLER Der Tod eines bretonischen Hühnerzüchters alarmiert Ärzte und Politiker. Die Hühner werden getötet, es beginnt die Jagd auf das Virus… 2. Teil: am Mi. SV 9-844-687
Frkr./Schw./Island/Belg. 2003 D Richard Bohringer R Oliver Langlois 90 Min. →0.50 ↗

0.45 DAS VIERTE — Cocktail für eine Leiche ⑤ⓦ
THRILLER Um ihrem Professor zu beweisen, daß ein perfekter Mord möglich ist, töten zwei Studenten einen Kommilitonen und geben am Tatort eine Party… Von nur einem Kamerastandpunkt aus gedrehter Klassiker. SV 41-952-850
USA 1948 D James Stewart, Farley Granger, John Dall R Alfred Hitchcock FSK 12 90/76 Min. →2.15 ↗

SYMBOLE: ⬆ Großartig ↗ Gelungen
↗ Annehmbar ⬇ Schwach

BARBARA: Um 20.15 Uhr gibt es ein Fußballspiel … und später um 22.40 Uhr kommt ein **Bericht** über die Arbeitslage in Deutschland. Aber keine Dokumentarfilme. Ich möchte mir mal einen guten **Spielfilm ansehen.**

THOMAS: Du hast ja das Programm für heute Abend. **Such dir was aus!**

BARBARA: **Wie wäre es mit** „Cocktail für eine Leiche" von Hitchcock?

THOMAS: So ein alter Schinken (*old hat*).

BARBARA: **Na und?** Das ist **auf jeden Fall** ein guter, alter Klassiker. Ach, nein, Moment, der kommt erst um 0.45 Uhr.

THOMAS: Lass mal sehen … Um 22.05 Uhr läuft im MDR „Tatort: Das Phantom."

BARBARA: Das ist mir auch zu spät.

THOMAS: Wie wäre es mit einer Liebeskomödie, „Bella Martha" um 21.45 Uhr?

BARBARA: Klingt gut. **Wovon handelt** sie denn?

Ergänzen Sie die folgenden Sätze. Die Informationen finden Sie im Gespräch zwischen Barbara und Thomas.

1. Die „Rosenheim-Cops" läuft im zweiten ___Programm___.
2. Thomas möchte vielleicht Sport oder einen ___Dokumentarfilm___ sehen.
3. Barbara möchte gern einen ___Spielfilm___ sehen.
4. Thomas meint, Serien wie „Gute Zeiten, schlechte Zeiten" sind nichts ___Gescheites___.
5. Um 22.40 kommt im Zweiten Programm ein ___Bericht___ über die Arbeitslage in Deutschland.
6. Barbara fragt Thomas, wovon der Film „Bella Martha" ___handelt___.

Was steht in der Zeitung?

Neue Wörter

die Zeitschrift magazine
die Schlagzeile headline
das Inland at home,
   domestic, national
Aktuelles current events
die Wirtschaft economy
die Börse stock market
das Forschen research

Hier sind einige typische Rubriken (*sections*) aus der Zeitung, bzw. der **Zeitschrift**.

A. Welche Rubriken …

- lesen Sie immer? nie? manchmal?
- finden Sie am interessantesten?

B. Finden Sie nun eine passende **Schlagzeile** für die Rubriken.

RUBRIKEN

Lokalnachrichten	**Aktuelles**	Sport
Inland	**Wirtschaft** und **Börse**	Reisen
Ausland	Arbeit und Karriere	**Horoskop**
Politik	Wissen und **Forschen**	Kultur

SCHLAGZEILEN

Ein Drittel der Lebensmittel enthält gentechnisch modifizierte Organismen

Niedersachsens Justizminister kritisiert Kanzlerin

Atomstreit mit Iran

Macht Ihr Beruf noch Spaß?

15 Kinder bei Busunfall schwer verletzt

Delfine[1] erkennen sich am Namen

Börse reagiert mit Absturz

Wird der Rhein sauberer?

Was sagen uns die Sterne?

USA gehen gegen Cyberkriminalität vor

Fußball-Weltmeisterschaft: 12 Städte, 32 Mannschaften, 64 Spiele

OUTSOURCING: DIE ARBEIT WANDERT AUS

Bayreuther Festspiele am 25. Juli eröffnet

[1]*dolphins*

Suchen Sie im Fernsehprogramm auf der nächsten Seite eine Sendung, die zu jeder der folgenden Kategorien passt.

BEISPIEL: Spielfilm
   Um 0.20 Uhr kommt der Spielfilm „Kansas" im ersten Programm.

1. Nachrichten
2. Komödie (*f.*)
3. Talk-Show (*f.*)
4. Krimi (*m.*)
5. Reportage (*f.*)
6. Dokumentarfilm
7. Sportsendung

 **① DAS ERSTE**	**ZDF**	**RTL**	**SAT.1**	**⁊ PRO SIEBEN**

① DAS ERSTE

20.15 Schmunzelkrimiserie

Adelheid und Eugen finden ein aufschlußreiches Video: **Adelheid und ihre Mörder**

5.30 Morgenmagazin 98-487-688 **9.05** Ein Haus in der Toskana. Familienserie 2-727-441 **10.03** Brisant. Boulevardmagazin 302-279-441 **10.40** Himmel auf Erden ■ Lustspiel, A 1935 4-587-422 **12.00** Tagesschau 65-880 **12.15** ARD-Buffet 6-892-354 **13.00** ARD-Mittagsmagazin 78-170 **14.00** Tagesschau 79-489 **14.15** In aller Freundschaft. Arztserie ▨ 57-083

15.00 Fliege 52-118
16.00 Tagesschau ▨ 84-373
16.15 Abenteuer Wildnis
Tierdoku. Grizzlys – Riesenbären in Amerika 3-070-809
17.00 Tagesschau ▨ 35-083
17.15 Brisant
Boulevardmagazin 690-809
17.50 Verbotene Liebe 43-083
18.20 Marienhof 95-422
18.50 Plötzlich erwachsen!
Familienserie, D 2001/05
„Geplatze Träume" 16-915
19.20 Das Quiz mit Jörg Pilawa 494-977
19.55 Börse 4-314-286

20.00 Tagesschau ▨ 33-441
20.15 Adelheid und ihre Mörder ▢▨ 9-567-460
Schmunzelkrimiserie, D '03
„Botschaft aus dem Grab":
Als ein Verleger sein Testament zu Gunsten eines Tierschutzvereins ändert, gibt es Tote
21.05 In aller Freundschaft
Arztserie ▨
„Geschwisterliebe" 2-775-199
21.55 Plusminus 3-788-460
Wirtschaftsmagazin, moderiert von Jörg Boecker
22.30 Tagesthemen 731
23.00 Frau Thomas Mann
Porträt, D 2005 87-880
0.00 Nachtmagazin 95-774
0.20 Kansas 2-305-126
Thriller, USA 1988
Regie: David Stevens. Auf Tramptour verstrickt Ex-Knacki Doyle (Matt Dillon) seine Zufallsbekanntschaft Wade (Andrew McCarthy) in einen Banküberfall...
2.05 Tagesschau 25-457-887
2.10 Fliege 2-534-316
3.10 ARD-Ratgeber: Reise
New York – Sightseeing für Filmfreaks (Wh.) 2-381-403
3.40 Weltreisen 4-898-316
Alaska (Wh.)

ZDF

1.05 TV-Thriller

Anwalt Gavin (Tom Berenger) trifft auf blondes Gift (Heidi Schanz). **Body-Language**

5.05 hallo Deutschland 4-984-731 **5.30** Morgenmagazin 15-953-970 **9.05** Volle Kanne 4-756-147 **10.30** Leichtathletik-WM live. Wettbewerbe der Männer: Zehnkampf (1.Tag mit 100 m-Lauf und Weitsprung); Qualifikationen: Speerwurf; Stabhochsprung sowie 200 m und 400 m Vorläufe 86-993-828 **14.00** heute 60-731 **14.15** Wunderbare Welt ▢ 55-625

15.00 heute – Sport 65-903
15.15 Frauenarzt Dr. Markus Merthin 6-050-712
16.00 heute – in Europa 82-915
16.15 Bianca 3-061-151
17.15 hallo Deutschland
Boulevardmagazin 516-712
17.35 Leichtathletik: WM
Live. Männer: Hochsprung im Zehnkampf; Frauen: Diskuswurf-Finale; 100-m-Hürden-Vorläufe 3-319-248
19.00 heute ▨ 90-712
19.25 Leichtathletik: WM
Live. Finals: 3000-m-Hindernis (M), 800 m (F) 6-823-373

20.15 Familie Hitler ▢▨
TEXT Im Schatten des Diktators 630-151
(VPS 20.14) 409-575-489
21.00 Frontal 21 45-083
Politmagazin mit Theo Koll
21.45 heute-journal 104-977
22.15 37°: Teure Liebe 743-880
TEXT Gesellschaftsreportage, D 2005. Frauen in der Schuldenfalle. Über bürgschaftsgeschädigte Frauen
22.45 Wo steht Deutsch-
TEXT **land? (3)** 6-428-712
Wahl 2005. Ernstfall für die Bundeswehr
23.15 Die Affäre 6-750-373
TEXT **Semmeling (1)** ▢
TV-Familiensaga, D/A 2002
Regie: Dieter Wedel
Mit Fritz Lichtenhahn, Antje Hagen und Stefan Kurt
Die letzte Küche
(2. Teil am 11. August)
0.45 heute nacht 5-967-403
Nachrichtenmagazin
1.05 Body Language –
Verführung in der Nacht
TV-Thriller, USA 1995 ▨
Regie: George Case
Mit Tom Berenger, Nancy Travis, Heidi Schanz 7-094-584
2.45 37°: Teure Liebe
Reportage (Wh.) 7-908-652

RTL

20.15 Krimiserie

Horatio (l.) und Bernstein vom **CSI: Miami** stehen fassungslos vor der aufgehängten Leiche

5.10 EXTRA (Wh.) 7-596-625 **6.00** Punkt 6 61-828 **7.00** Unter uns 4-489 **7.30** GZSZ 8-169-083 **8.05** RTL-Shop 5-158-688 **9.00** Punkt 9 5-199 **9.30** Mein Baby 8-286 **10.00** Dr. Stefan Frank 73-462 **11.00** Einsatz in 4 Wänden 5-335 **11.30** Unsere Klinik 8-422 **12.00** Punkt 12 85-460 **13.00** Die Oliver Geissen Show. Daily Talk 61-880 **14.00** Das Strafgericht 72-996

15.00 Das Familiengericht
Gerichtsshow 45-828
16.00 Das Jugendgericht
Gerichtsshow 49-644
17.00 Einsatz in 4 Wänden
Mit Tine Wittler 3-557
17.30 Unter uns 6-644
Daily Soap, D 2005
18.00 Guten Abend RTL 7-373
18.30 EXCLUSIV – Das Star-Magazin 51-422
18.45 RTL Aktuell 986-557
19.10 Explosiv – Das Magazin
Boulevardmagazin 496-335
19.40 Gute Zeiten, schlechte Zeiten Daily Soap 7-294-267

20.15 CSI: Miami ▨▨ 143-606
Krimiserie, USA 2002
„Der Tote am Baum":
Professor Metzger, zu dessen Forschungsfeld Gewalt und Folter gehören, wird grausam verstümmelt aufgefunden...
21.15 Im Namen des Gesetzes 8-691-828
Polizeiserie, D 2002
„Das zweite Gesicht"
22.15 Monk 4-718-538
Krimiserie, USA 2002
„Mr. Monk im Flugzeug":
Als Monk in einem Flieger einen Mörder zu erkennen glaubt, vergisst er seine panische Flugangst
23.10 Law & Order 8-141-002
Krimiserie, USA 2002
„Im Namen der Liebe"
0.00 RTL-Nachtjournal 8-045
Nachrichtenmagazin
0.30 Golden Girls 2-452-300
Comedy, USA 1988
„Das aufregende Leben der Sophia Petrillo"
1.00 Susan 2-533-229
Comedyserie, USA 1999
1.30 Das Familiengericht
Gerichtsshow 5-406-942
2.20 Die Oliver Geissen Show (Wh.) 6-470-478

SAT.1

20.15 TV-Komödie

Ein ganzer Kerl für Mama:
Scheidungsanwältin und Supermacho kommen sich näher

5.10 blitz 4-476-977 **5.30** Frühstücksfernsehen 16-715-083 **9.00** HSE24 99-199 **10.00** Lenßen & Partner 4-118 **10.30** Verliebt in Berlin. Telenovela 9-809 **11.00** Stefanie – Eine Frau startet durch 66-847 **12.00** Vera am Mittag 37-335 **13.00** Britt – Der Talk um Eins. Profi-Hure – „Warum gibst du dich für sowas her?" 46-083 **14.00** Zwei bei Kallwass 57-199

15.00 Richterin Barbara Salesch 13-731
16.00 Richter Alexander Hold 24-847
17.00 Niedrig und Kuhnt – Kommissare ermitteln
Ermittler Soap 5-422
17.30 17:30 Live 5-809
18.00 Lenßen & Partner 6-538
Ermittler-Soap
18.30 SAT.1 News 44-644
18.50 blitz 9-713-199
19.15 Verliebt in Berlin
Telenovela, D 2005 796-847
19.45 K 11 – Kommissare im Einsatz 328-460

20.15 Ein ganzer Kerl für Mama 2-733-977
TV-Komödie, D 2002
Regie: Zoltan Spirandelli
„Du bist eine frustrierte, streitsüchtige Zicke!" Paul Wackernagel (Jörg Schüttauf) hat rasch ein Urteil über jene Frau gefällt, die sein Ferienhaus besetzt. Der Autor von Ratgebern wie „Keine Mark für die Ex" hat einen gültigen Mietvertrag und pocht auf sein Wohnrecht. So wie Tanja (Nina Kronjäger) auf das ihre: Die Villa wurde ihr als Ersatz angeboten, weil das eigentlich geplante Urlaubsdomizil ausgebrannt ist
22.15 alphateam – 5-351-354
Die Lebensretter im OP
Krankenhausserie, D 2005
„Kaltes Land": Das Personal muss sich mit Skinheads und niederträchtigen Zuhältern rumschlagen. Danach:
„Falsche Liebe" ('99)
0.15 Sat.1 News 26-768
0.45 Quiz Night 5-573-010
2.05 HSE24 8-603-381
3.05 Richterin Barbara Salesch 1-652-720
3.55 Richter Hold 1-677-039

⁊ PRO SIEBEN

19.25 Wissensmagazin

Aiman Abdallah erklärt bei **Galileo** anschaulich Tageserеignisse und Zeitphänomene

5.25 Do It Yourself – S.O.S. 9-121-625 **5.55** taff (Wh.) 2-950-625 **6.50** Galileo 56-392-793 **7.25** Scrubs – Die Anfänger 4-456-002 **7.50** ClipMix 5-448-460 **8.50** Eure letzte Chance 9-906-557 **10.00** talk talk talk 91-557 **11.00** S.O.S. Style & Home 64-489 **12.00** AVENZIO – Schöner leben! 35-977 **13.00** SAM 44-625 **14.00** Das Geständnis – Heute sage ich alles 48-441

15.00 Freunde – Das Leben geht weiter! 11-373
16.00 Eure letzte Chance
Ratgeber-Show 22-489
17.00 taff 70-369
18.00 Die Simpsons 7-880
Zeichentrickserie, USA '93
„Am Kap der Angst"
18.30 Futurama 14-489
Zeichentrickserie, USA '02
„Der letzte Trekki"
18.55 Scrubs – Die Anfänger
Comedyserie, USA '02 74-441
„Mein Ticket nach Reno"
19.25 Galileo 626-199
Windkraftwerk

20.00 Newstime 18-644
20.15 Sex and the City 303-151
Comedyserie, USA 1999
„Mädchen gegen Frauen":
Die Freundinnen machen Urlaub auf Long Island und müssen sehr bald feststellen, dass sie sehr unterschiedliche Auffassungen von Entspannung haben
20.45 Friends 968-002
Comedyserie, USA 2004
„Was mein ist, ist nicht dein": Joeys Date mit Sarah verläuft anders als geplant
21.15 Desperate Housewives
Satireserie, USA 2004
„Schlachtfelder": Gabrielle schleppt ihre ehemals spielsüchtige Schwiegermutter zum Zocken 5-566-557
22.20 Sarah & Marc in Love – Die Hochzeit des Jahres
Doku-Soap 9-667-625
23.10 BIZZ 145-373
Unter dem Motto: „BIZZ motzt auf" findet „das große Tuning-Event" statt
23.55 „taff" Spezial 3-397-712
Das Familienhotel – Hinter den Kulissen des „Schwarzen Adlers" in Innsbruck (4+5)
1.00 Sex and the... 1-415-132

▣ Zweikanalton ▣▣ Dolby-Surround ■ schwarzweiß ▢ Breitbild ▨ Untertitel für Hörgeschädigte (OmU) Original mit Untertiteln TEXT siehe Spielfilm- und TV-Auswahl

Lange Zeit gab es in Deutschland nur drei Programme. Die ARD (Arbeitsgemeinschaft der Rundfunkanstalten Deutschlands) – auch „Erstes Programm" genannt – und das ZDF (Zweites Deutsches Fernsehen) senden auch heute noch das erste und zweite Programm. Das „Dritte Programm" besteht aus regionalen Sendern aus ganz Deutschland. In diesen drei Programmen werden die meisten Sendungen nicht durch Werbung unterbrochen. Alle Werbespots werden blockweise zu einem bestimmten Zeitpunkt gezeigt. Jeder Haushalt muss für Radio und Fernsehen eine Gebühr, die sogenannte Rundfunkgebühr, bezahlen. Man zahlt die Gebühr an die GEZ (Gebühreneinzugszentrale).

    Heutzutage gibt es in deutschsprachigen Ländern eine Vielfalt an Fernsehprogrammen. Kabelfernsehen und Satellitenprogramme, z.B. PRO 7, NBC Super-Channel und CNN, sind sehr beliebt und zeigen viele Sendungen im amerikanischen Stil. Kabelfernsehen muss man abonnieren. Für Sender wie Premiere (sogenannte Pay TV) muss man weitere Gebühren bezahlen.

Ich bin noch nicht bei der GEZ angemeldet
Ich bin schon angemeldet unter der Nr.

WDR N1/97121

Name/Vorname   Geburtsdatum

Straße/Hausnummer

Postleitzahl   Ort

Ich melde an   Radio   Fernsehgerät   ab

Ich zahle   jährlich im Voraus zum 1. Januar   vierteljährlich im Voraus zum 1. Januar, April, Juli, Oktober

         halbjährlich im Voraus zum 1. Januar, Juli   in der Mitte eines Dreimonatszeitraumes jeweils zum 15.

Ich zahle   per Überweisung/mit Zahlschein   Lastschrift (s.u.)

Kontonummer   Bankleitzahl

Bank/Sparkasse   Kontoinhaber

Datum   Unterschrift

Bitte informieren Sie die GEZ, wenn Sie umziehen oder einen Umzug planen. Formulare zur Änderungsmeldung liegen bei Banken und Sparkassen aus. Auch telefonisch, per Fax oder im Internet können Sie (unter Angabe Ihrer Teilnehmer Nummer) Ihre Anschrift korrigieren lassen. Bitte melden Sie sich nicht ab und unter neuer Anschrift wieder an. www.gez.de

GEZ Service-Hotline 0180 501 65 65 · Faxline 0180 582 10 10 (12 Cent/Min) · www.gez.de

Antwort

GEZ

50656 Köln

Übrigens: Für Radio und TV zahlen Sie nur 53 Cent am Tag

Weiteres zum Thema Medien finden Sie bei **Deutsch: Na klar!** im World-Wide-Web unter

Wie informieren sich diese Personen? Was lesen sie zur Unterhaltung? Stellen Sie Fragen an Ihren Partner / Ihre Partnerin.

BEISPIEL: s1: Was sieht Martin gern im Fernsehen? Was liest er oft?
          s2: Er _____.

PERSON	FERNSEHSHOWS	ZEITUNGEN UND ZEITSCHRIFTEN
Martin	Talk-Shows und Dokumentarfilme	die Zeit
Stephanie		
Patrick	Quizsendungen wie „Der Preis ist heiß", die Nachrichten	die Frankfurter Allgemeine und Stern
Kristin		
Mein Partner / Meine Partnerin		

Aktivität 3 Das sehe ich gern!

Was mögen Sie im Fernsehen? Warum? Was finden Sie nicht besonders gut im Fernsehen? Geben Sie Beispiele.

BEISPIEL: Ich mag Serien, zum Beispiel „Tatort". Die finde ich spannend. Aber Quizsendungen finde ich schrecklich langweilig.

Krimis	gewöhnlich	aktuell
Nachrichten	immer	interessant
Dokumentarfilme	meistens	komisch
Quizsendungen	schrecklich	langweilig
Talk-Shows	sehr	schlecht
Seifenopern		spannend
Sport		unterhaltsam
Serien		
Musik		
Komödien		
Musicals		
Dramen		

Aktivität 4 Eine Sendung auswählen

Besprechen Sie mit einem Partner / einer Partnerin, was Sie heute Abend sehen möchten. Wählen Sie eine Sendung aus dem Fernsehprogramm in **Aktivität 1** aus.

Aktivität 4. Suggestion: You may also wish to do this activity using today's actual TV listings in a German-speaking country. (Search for *Fernsehprogramm*.) If your classroom has a projector and computer, have the listing displayed in a web browser on the screen; otherwise, print out the listings and display them on the OHP (or make copies for students).

S1	S2
1. Was gibt es heute Abend im Fernsehen?	**2.** Um _____ gibt es _____.
3. Was ist denn das?	**4a.** Das ist eine Sendung über _____. **b.** Keine Ahnung, klingt aber interessant.
5. Wer spielt mit?	**6.** Hier steht _____.
7. Wie lange dauert das?	**8a.** _____ Stunden/Minuten **b.** Von _____ Uhr bis _____ Uhr.
9. Was gibt es sonst noch?	**10a.** Magst du _____ ? **b.** Wie wäre es mit _____ ?
11a. Ja, das finde ich _____. **b.** Nein, ich sehe lieber _____. **c.** Ich lese heute Abend lieber.	**12.** Na gut.

Neue Wörter

der Kabelanschluss cable
TV connection
der Anrufbeantworter
answering machine
die Sat-Empfangsanlage
satellite receiver
erfunden (erfinden)
invented
die Erfindung (Erfindungen,
pl.) invention
der Drucker printer
speichern store, save
empfangen receive
hinterlassen leave (behind)
drucken print
aufnehmen record

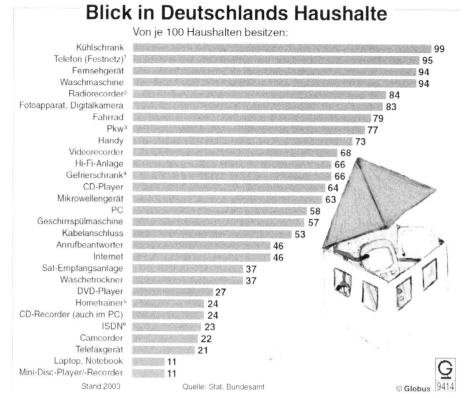

Blick in Deutschlands Haushalte

Von je 100 Haushalten besitzen:

Kühlschrank	99
Telefon (Festnetz)[1]	95
Fernsehgerät	94
Waschmaschine	94
Radiorecorder[2]	84
Fotoapparat, Digitalkamera	83
Fahrrad	79
Pkw[3]	77
Handy	73
Videorecorder	68
Hi-Fi-Anlage	66
Gefrierschrank[4]	66
CD-Player	64
Mikrowellengerät	63
PC	58
Geschirrspülmaschine	57
Kabelanschluss	53
Anrufbeantworter	46
Internet	46
Sat-Empfangsanlage	37
Wäschetrockner	37
DVD-Player	27
Hometrainer[5]	24
CD-Recorder (auch im PC)	24
ISDN[6]	23
Camcorder	22
Telefaxgerät	21
Laptop, Notebook	11
Mini-Disc-Player/-Recorder	11

Stand 2003   Quelle: Stat. Bundesamt   © Globus 9414

[1]*conventional fixed-line network* [2]*boom box* [3]= Personenkraftwagen *automobile* [4]*freezer*
[5]*home exercise equipment* [6][*type of communications link: here:*] *high-speed Internet*

A. Schauen Sie sich das Schaubild an und beantworten Sie die Fragen.

- Wie viel Prozent der Haushalte haben einen Fernseher? einen Pkw? eine **Digitalkamera**? einen PC? **Internet**? ein **Notebook**?

- Haben Deutsche öfter **Kabelanschluss** oder eine **Sat-Empfangsanlage**?

- Welche Geräte im Schaubild hat man in den letzten dreißig Jahren **erfunden**? Was sind **Erfindungen** der letzten fünfzig Jahre?

- Welche von diesen Geräten besitzen Sie?

B. Wozu benutzt man die folgenden Geräte? Verbinden Sie die Satzteile. Für manche Geräte sind mehrere Anworten möglich!

BEISPIEL: Man benutzt eine Digitalkamera, um Fotos zu machen.

Man benutzt …

Siehe *Infinitive Clauses with* **um … zu** *and* **ohne … zu**. S. 395.

1. eine Digitalkamera
2. einen PC / einen Heimcomputer
3. einen Kabelanschluss / eine Sat-Empfangsanlage
4. ein **(Tele-)Faxgerät**
5. einen Laptop / ein Notebook
6. einen Mini-Disc-Player / einen MP3-Player
7. einen **Anrufbeantworter**
8. einen **Drucker**
9. einen **Camcorder**

a. um unterwegs am Computer zu arbeiten
b. um Musik digital zu **speichern** und abzuspielen
c. um mehr Programme im Fernsehen zu **empfangen**
d. um **Dokumente** über das Telefonnetz zu schicken
e. um telefonische Nachrichten zu **hinterlassen**
f. um **Dokumente** und Bilder zu **drucken**
g. um **E-Mails** zu schicken
h. um Videos **aufzunehmen**
i. um Fotos zu machen

Aktivität 5   Am Computer

Die Sprache der modernen Technologie kommt zum großen Teil aus dem Englischen. Die moderne Computertechnologie verwendet auch viele Symbole.

Aktivität 5. **Note:** Be aware that these computer icons are by no means universal, but merely widespread: *Einige Computer verwenden andere Symbole. Diese sind nur Beispiele.* The purpose of the activity is to practice some of the new vocabulary.

Schritt 1: Verbinden Sie Symbole mit ihren üblichen (*conventional*) Bedeutungen.

1. ____ ⊠
2. ____ 🖫
3. ____ 🗑
4. ____ ☞
5. ____ 🔊
6. ____ ▶▶
7. ____ ✂
8. ____ 🖨

a. Audio/Video vorspulen (*fast forward*)
b. das Dokument drucken
c. das Dokument speichern
d. den Text ausschneiden (*cut*)
e. das Dokument löschen (*delete*)
f. eine E-Mail lesen
g. Hier kann man etwas hören.
h. Hier kann man klicken

Schritt 2: Suchen Sie passende Verben zu den Substantiven. (Manchmal ist mehr als eine Antwort richtig.)

BEISPIEL: Am Computer kann man E-Mails bekommen.

Am Computer kann man ...

1. E-Mails ____.
2. Softwareprogramme ____.
3. ein Thema oder ein Wort ____.
4. eine Zeitung im Internet ____.
5. über viele Themen ____.
6. Dokumente ____.

bloggen   herunterladen/downloaden
googeln   lesen   schicken
speichern
bekommen   kaufen   schreiben

ANALYSE

Schauen Sie sich das Schaubild an und beantworten Sie dann die folgenden Fragen.

- Welche Firma hatte 2004 die meisten Patentanmeldungen in Deutschland?
- Welche Firma auf dieser Liste hatte die wenigsten?
- Aus welchen Ländern sind diese Firmen?
- Nennen Sie mindestens zwei Erfindungen aus Ihrem Land.

Analyse. Note: Students may be interested in knowing that the MP3 audio format was developed by a team led by Karlheinz Brandenburg and others at the German *Fraunhofer-Gesellschaft* in 1989.

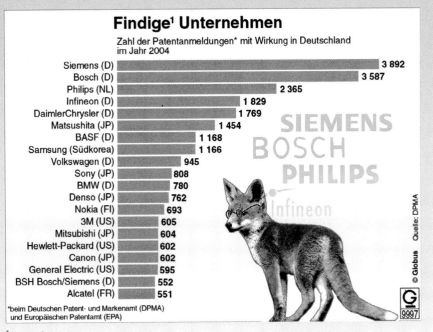

Findige[1] Unternehmen

Zahl der Patentanmeldungen* mit Wirkung in Deutschland im Jahr 2004

Siemens (D)	3 892
Bosch (D)	3 587
Philips (NL)	2 365
Infineon (D)	1 829
DaimlerChrysler (D)	1 769
Matsushita (JP)	1 454
BASF (D)	1 168
Samsung (Südkorea)	1 166
Volkswagen (D)	945
Sony (JP)	808
BMW (D)	780
Denso (JP)	762
Nokia (FI)	693
3M (US)	605
Mitsubishi (JP)	604
Hewlett-Packard (US)	602
Canon (JP)	602
General Electric (US)	595
BSH Bosch/Siemens (D)	552
Alcatel (FR)	551

*beim Deutschen Patent- und Markenamt (DPMA) und Europäischen Patentamt (EPA)

© Globus   Quelle: DPMA

9997

[1]*inventive*

Wie erfinderisch sind Sie? Beschreiben Sie eine nützliche Erfindung.

BEISPIEL: Medizin

Ein Hustenbonbon, das wie Schokolade schmeckt.

BEREICHE

1. Medizin
2. Technik
3. Verkehr
4. Haushalt
5. Tiere
6. Stadtplanung
7. Umwelt
8. Häuser

Sie möchten erfahren, wer was und wann erfunden hat. Arbeiten Sie zu zweit.

BEISPIELE: s1: Wer hat _____ erfunden?
s2: _____.
s1: Wann hat er/sie es erfunden?
s2: (Im Jahre) _____.

[oder:] s1: Was hat _____ erfunden?
s2: Er/Sie hat _____ erfunden.
s1: In welchem Jahr?
s2: (Im Jahre) _____.

ERFINDER	ERFINDUNG	JAHR
	der Buchdruck mit beweglichen Lettern (*movable type*)	
	das Alkoholthermometer	
Karl von Drais	das Fahrrad (Draisine)	1817
Herta Heuwer		
Gottlieb Daimler	das Motorrad	1885
Rudolf Diesel	der Dieselmotor	1893
Wilhelm Conrad Röntgen		
Melitta Bentz	der Kaffeefilter	1908

Grammatik im Kontext

Infinitive Clauses with zu°

Der Infinitivsatz

Infinitive clauses may be complements of verbs, nouns, or adjectives. When used this way, the infinitive is always preceded by **zu.**

Familie Baier **hat vor,** einen neuen Computer **zu kaufen.**	*The Baier family is planning to buy a new computer.*
Es macht mir **Spaß,** E-Mail aus der ganzen Welt **zu bekommen.**	*I enjoy receiving e-mail from all over the world.*
Es ist **leicht,** einen Brief per E-Mail **zu schicken.**	*It is easy to send a letter via e-mail.*

Note:

- The infinitive with **zu** is always the last element of the sentence.
- With separable-prefix verbs, **zu** is placed between the prefix and the main verb.

Ich habe versucht, dich gestern **anzurufen.**	*I tried to call you yesterday.*
Du hast versprochen **vorbeizukommen.**	*You promised to come by.*

- A comma generally sets off an infinitive clause that includes more than just the infinitive with **zu.** No comma is used otherwise.

Übung I   Felix

Felix studiert Medien an der Hochschule für Technik in Dresden. Er ist ein Erstsemester und es gibt viel Neues für ihn. Bilden Sie Sätze.

BEISPIEL: er hat vor: einen neuen Computer kaufen →
            Er hat vor, einen neuen Computer zu kaufen.

1. er findet es nicht leicht: ein Zimmer in einer WG finden
2. er hat versprochen: seine Familie regelmäßig anrufen
3. es macht ihm Spaß: jeden Mittwoch zum Kickboxen gehen
4. er hat keine Zeit: jeden Abend ausgehen
5. er hat sich entschlossen: etwas Geld mit Jobben verdienen
6. er versucht: im Inter-Treff Club andere Studenten kennen lernen
7. er findet es interessant: in Dresden studieren

Hoffentlich sieht Sie ein Professor bei der Lektüre!

Macht sich nicht schlecht, eine der renommiertesten Zeitungen der Welt zu lesen. Abos mit 40% Rabatt über Tel. 0130 81 58 98.

Neue Zürcher Zeitung

Dem Gesamtbild zuliebe.

Übung 1. Additional items: 8. er hat keine Lust: den ganzen Tag am Computer arbeiten 9. er versucht: nicht den ganzen Abend im Internet surfen

Drücken Sie Ihre Meinung aus.

BEISPIEL: Es macht mir Spaß, Seifenopern anzusehen.

Ich habe keine Zeit	stundenlang am Computer sitzen
Es macht mir (keinen) Spaß	im Internet surfen
Ich finde es langweilig	Computerspiele/Videospiele spielen
wichtig	Kriegsfilme/Sportsendungen im Fernsehen ansehen
schwierig	eine Fremdsprache lernen
interessant	über Politik diskutieren
spannend	per E-Mail korrespondieren
schwer	mein Horoskop in der Zeitung lesen
	jeden Tag die Zeitung lesen
	Nachrichten im Fernsehen ansehen
	Radio hören
	einen guten Job finden
	studieren und nebenbei jobben

Schauen Sie sich Cornelias Kalender an. Was hat sie vor? Was darf sie nicht vergessen?

BEISPIEL: Sie hat vor, Sonntag mit Klaus ins Kino zu gehen.
Sie darf nicht vergessen, Montag …

Sonntag	19.30 mit Klaus ins Kino gehen
Montag	nicht vergessen: Videogerät zur Reparatur bringen Reise nach Spanien buchen
Dienstag	nicht vergessen: Radio und Fernsehen anmelden 14.30 Prof. Hauser: Seminararbeit besprechen
Mittwoch	Job für den Sommer suchen
Donnerstag	nicht vergessen: Mutter anrufen, Geburtstag!
Freitag	Seminararbeit fertig schreiben 20.00 Vera treffen: Café Kadenz
Samstag	14.00 mit Klaus Tennis spielen 20.30 „Casablanca" im Fernsehen ansehen

resolutions

Schritt 1: Sie haben vor, in Zukunft alles besser zu machen. Was haben Sie sich versprochen? Was haben Sie vor? Überlegen Sie sich zwei gute Vorsätze.

BEISPIELE: Ich habe vor, weniger Geld für CDs auszugeben.
Ich habe mir versprochen, meine Eltern regelmäßig anzurufen.

Schritt 2: Vergleichen Sie Ihre Vorsätze mit den Vorsätzen eines Partners / einer Partnerin. Haben Sie gemeinsame Vorsätze? Wenn ja, welche? Was sind die häufigsten guten Vorsätze Ihrer Kursmitglieder?

The Verbs brauchen and scheinen

The verbs **brauchen** (*to need*) and **scheinen** (*to seem*) are often used with a dependent infinitive preceded by **zu. Brauchen** is used instead of the modal **müssen** when the sentence has a negative meaning.

Heute muss ich arbeiten, aber morgen **brauche** ich **nicht zu arbeiten.**

Today I have to work, but tomorrow I don't have to work.

Ich **brauche keinen** neuen Computer **zu kaufen,** der alte ist noch gut genug.

I don't have to buy a new computer; the old one is still good enough.

Das Faxgerät **scheint** kaputt **zu sein.**

The fax machine seems to be broken.

Übung 5   Nichts scheint zu funktionieren

Was scheint hier los zu sein? Folgen Sie dem Beispiel.

BEISPIEL: Das Telefon klingelt nicht. (Es ist kaputt.) →
　　　　　Es scheint kaputt zu sein.

1. Der Computer funktioniert mal wieder nicht. (Er ist kaputt.)
2. Hast du meine Nachricht nicht bekommen? Ich habe eine Nachricht auf deinem Anrufbeantworter hinterlassen. (Er funktioniert nicht.)
3. Meine Kamera funktioniert nicht. (Sie braucht eine neue Batterie.)
4. Bei Firma Bär meldet sich niemand am Apparat. (Niemand ist im Büro.)
5. Drei von meinen Kollegen sind heute nicht zur Arbeit gekommen. (Sie sind alle krank.)

Übung 6   Nein, heute nicht

Fragen Sie einen Partner / eine Partnerin: Was musst du heute noch machen? Folgen Sie dem Beispiel.

BEISPIEL: s1: Musst du heute arbeiten?
　　　　　s2: Nein, heute brauche ich nicht zu arbeiten.
　　　　　s2: Musst du heute zur Uni gehen? usw.

1. im Labor arbeiten
2. Hausaufgaben machen
3. in die Vorlesung gehen
4. den Computer benutzen
5. ein Fax schicken
6. Rechnungen bezahlen
7. zum Arzt gehen
8. kochen
9. früh ins Bett gehen

Infinitive Clauses with **um ... zu and ohne ... zu**

German uses many different ways to explain the reasons for an action. You have already learned a number of them. Compare the following sentences.

Warum spart Stefan?

1. Stefan spart **für einen neuen Computer.**　　← Prepositional phrase

2. Stefan will einen neuen Computer kaufen. **Deswegen** muss er jetzt sparen.　　← Adverb: **deswegen** = *therefore*

Brauchen and *scheinen.* **Note:** These verbs are similar to modal verbs, except of course that the dependent infinitive is preceded by *zu.* Students need to actively master only the present tense and be able to recognize other tenses in reading.

Point Out: Even though *brauchen ... zu* is used instead of *müssen* when a sentence contains *nicht* or *kein, müssen* can be used in a sentence with a negative whenever *müssen* is stressed (*Ich **muss** nicht arbeiten; aber ich will*). Make sure you point out the meaning "to not have to."

Point Out: Remind students that the English equivalent of "must not" is expressed with *dürfen* + *nicht: Das darfst du nicht machen!* **Note:** In colloquial German it is quite common to omit the *zu* with *brauchen: Du brauchst nicht kommen.* Such usage is not considered standard.

Übung 5. Additional items:
6. *Warum kann ich Melanie nicht erreichen? (Ihr Handy ist aus.)* 7. *Ich kann diese MP3-Dateien nicht auf meinen iPod speichern. (Die Festplatte ist voll.)*

3. Stefan spart. Er will **nämlich** einen Computer kaufen.

4. Stefan spart, **denn** er will einen Computer kaufen.

5. Stefan spart, **weil** er einen Computer kaufen möchte.

Adverb: **nämlich** [*no English equivalent*]

Coordinating conjunction: **denn** = *because*

Subordinating conjunction: **weil** = *because*

Yet another way to explain one's reasons for an action is with an infinitive clause with **um ... zu.**

Stefan spart, **um** einen neuen Computer **zu kaufen.**

Manche Leute leben, **um zu arbeiten.**

Ich arbeite schwer, **um** mich auf das Examen **vorzubereiten.**

Stefan is saving money in order to buy a new computer.

Some people live in order to work.

I am working hard to prepare for the exam.

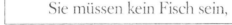
Sie müssen kein Fisch sein,   um Meerwasser[1] trinken zu können.

[1]*sea water*

reasons

Geben Sie die Gründe an. Benutzen Sie dabei **um ... zu, weil, nämlich, denn** oder **deswegen.**

BEISPIEL: Ich muss sparen. Ich möchte mir einen Plasmamonitor kaufen.
Ich muss sparen, um mir einen Plasmamonitor zu kaufen.
[*oder:*] Ich will mir einen Plasmamonitor kaufen. Deswegen muss ich sparen.

1. Barbara macht den Fernseher an. Sie will die Nachrichten sehen.

2. Thomas setzt sich in den Sessel. Er will die Tageszeitung lesen.

3. Barbara schaut sich das Filmprogramm an. Sie sucht sich einen Spielfilm aus.

4. Thomas programmiert den digitalen Videorecorder. Er möchte die Fußballweltmeisterschaft im Fernsehen aufnehmen.

5. Stephanie füllt ein Formular aus. Sie meldet ihr Radio und ihren Fernseher an.

6. Oliver überfliegt nur die Schlagzeilen in der Zeitung. Er will Zeit sparen.

7. Andreas hört sich die Tagesschau an. Er informiert sich.

To express that you do one thing without doing another, use **ohne ... zu.**

Hubers wollen ein Haus bauen, **ohne** große Schulden **zu machen.**

The Hubers want to build a house without going heavily into debt.

Er ist an mir vorbeigegangen, **ohne** mich **zu erkennen.**

He went past me without recognizing me.

Übung 8 Man sollte daran denken.

Kombinieren Sie mit **ohne ... zu.**

BEISPIEL: Oliver kauft einen Computer über das Internet. Er sieht ihn vorher nicht. →
Oliver kauft einen Computer über das Internet, ohne ihn vorher zu sehen.

1. Erika kauft eine Digitalkamera. Sie fragt nicht nach dem Preis.
2. Der Radfahrer fährt um die Ecke. Er sieht die Kinder auf der Straße nicht.
3. Jemand hat eine Nachricht auf meinem Anrufbeantworter hinterlassen. Er nennt seinen Namen nicht.
4. Herr Wunderlich hat eine Wohnung gemietet. Er fragt nicht nach den Nebenkosten.
5. Patrick ist heute Morgen zur Arbeit gegangen. Er frühstückt nicht.
6. Silvia sitzt wie hypnotisiert am Computer. Sie hört das Telefon nicht.
7. Meine Freunde kommen oft vorbei. Sie rufen vorher nicht an.

Indirect Discourse°

Die indirekte Rede

When you report what another person has said, you can quote that person verbatim, using direct discourse. In writing, this is indicated by the use of quotation marks. Note that in German, opening quotation marks are placed just below the line.

DIRECT DISCOURSE

Der Autofahrer behauptete: „Ich habe den Radfahrer nicht gesehen."

The automobile driver claimed, "I did not see the bicyclist."

Another way of reporting what someone said uses indirect discourse—a style commonly found in newspapers. In this case, German often uses subjunctive verb forms, especially the indirect discourse subjunctive, also called Subjunctive I.

INDIRECT DISCOURSE

Der Autofahrer behauptete, er **habe** den Radfahrer nicht **gesehen.**

The driver claimed he did not see the bicyclist.

In using the indirect discourse subjunctive, a speaker or writer signals that the information reported does not necessarily reflect the speaker's own knowledge or views. The indirect discourse subjunctive establishes distance between the reporter and the topic. This is useful when people want to be objective or neutral.

Indirect Discourse. Note: The grammar introduces only a limited number of forms and verbs for active knowledge because the indirect discourse subjunctive is used less and less in spoken German. It is still quite common in writing, however, especially in newspapers.

Suggestion: Review the more common forms of the Subjunctive II. These are also used for indirect discourse whenever there is no special indirect discourse form available.

Subjunctive I: Present Tense°

The present tense of the indirect discourse subjunctive, Subjunctive I, is derived from the stem of the infinitive. Only the verb **sein** has a complete set of forms that are used in modern German. For all other verbs, Subjunctive I forms are limited to the third-person singular plus a few verbs in the first-person singular.

Forms Commonly Used in Subjunctive I						
Infinitive	sein	haben	wissen	tun	werden	können
ich	sei	—	wisse	—	—	könne
du	sei(e)st	—	—	—	—	—
er/sie/es	sei	habe	wisse	tue	werde	könne
wir	seien	—	—	—	—	—
ihr	sei(e)t	—	—	—	—	—
sie/Sie	seien	—	—	—	—	—

Note:

- All verbs add -**e** to the infinitive stem to form the third-person singular except for **sein.**

- The verb **wissen** and all modals add -**e** to the infinitive stem to form the first-person singular.

If indirect discourse requires the use of any other verb forms, then Subjunctive II is used as an alternate for Subjunctive I. In spoken or informal German, it is quite common to use exclusively Subjunctive II or **würde** + infinitive for all indirect discourse. In the following examples, the forms in parentheses are more informal.

Der Student sagte, er **sei (wäre)** krank und **habe (hätte)** keine Zeit.	*The student said he is sick and has no time.*
Es **tue (täte)** ihm leid, dass er nicht zur Vorlesung kommen **könne (könnte).**	*He is sorry that he cannot come to the lecture.*
Er **gebe** seine Hausarbeit morgen **ab. (würde ... abgeben)**	*He will turn in his homework tomorrow.*
Die Wähler meinten, sie **wüssten** nicht, wem man glauben **könne (könnte).**	*The voters said they don't know whom to believe (lit. whom one can believe).*
Politiker behaupten, sie **würden** immer die Wahrheit **sagen.**	*Politicians claim they always tell the truth.*

Note:

- Weak verbs such as **sagen** use **würde** + infinitive in indirect discourse, except for the third-person singular.

Der Präsident behauptet, er **sage** nur die Wahrheit. (**würde ... sagen**)	*The president claims he's stating only the truth.*

Lesen Sie die folgenden Texte und markieren Sie alle Verben in indirekter Rede. Was sind die Infinitive der Verben? Wie würden Sie diese Sätze auf English ausdrücken?

Im Fernsehen hat man berichtet, das Land sei in einer großen Krise. Niemand wisse, wie es enden soll. Niemand habe eine Lösung.[1]

Technikstress: Telefonieren, Fernsehen, Internet surfen; der moderne Mensch sei zwar immer bestens informiert, aber manchmal ziemlich gestresst von zu viel Technik.

Ein Kriminologe und Jugendforscher schreibt, der durchschnittliche männliche Schüler bringe es auf 5 Stunden Medienkonsum am Tage. Das sei ein krankes Leben. Je mehr Zeit Kinder am Fernseher und Computer verbrächten, desto[3] schlechter seien sie in der Schule. In einigen Computerspielen könne man eine Erklärung für die erhöhte Gewaltbereitschaft finden.

[1]*solution* [2]*to close down* [3]je mehr ... desto schlechter *the more . . . the worse*

Übung 9   Was man über Fernsehen gesagt hat

Ergänzen Sie die Sätze mit dem Konjunktiv I von **sein**.

1. Herr Schwarz hat gesagt, ohne Fernsehen ___sei___ sein Leben schöner.
2. Frau Schwarz meinte, für Kinder ___seien___ Programme wie „Die Sendung mit der Maus" etwas Besonderes.
3. Man hat mir gesagt, ohne Fernsehen ___sei___ ich nicht gut informiert. So ein Quatsch.
4. Die Frau von der Marktforschung fragte, warum wir nicht am Fernsehen interessiert ___seien___.
5. Man hat mir berichtet, dass du jetzt ganz ohne Fernseher ___seiest___.
6. Frau Schmidt meinte, ohne ihre tägliche Telenovela ___sei___ sie nicht glücklich.
7. Familie Schulte hat gesagt, die Sportprogramme ___seien___ immer ausgezeichnet.

Übung 10   Das stand in der Zeitung

Berichten Sie in indirekter Rede, was Sie in der Zeitung gelesen haben.

BEISPIEL: Der Mensch denkt am schnellsten vor dem Mittagessen. →
    In der Zeitung stand, der Mensch denke am schnellsten vor dem Mittagessen.

1. Man soll also schwierige Probleme zwischen 11 and 12 Uhr lösen.
2. Die Sinne (*senses*) funktionieren dagegen besser abends.
3. Das Abendessen schmeckt deshalb besser als das Frühstück.
4. Wir sind deshalb abends für Theater, Musik und auch für die Liebe am empfänglichsten (*most receptive*).
5. Für den Sport ist der Spätnachmittag ideal.
6. Man wird spätnachmittags nicht so schnell müde.

Sie hören drei Dialoge. Machen Sie sich zuerst Notizen. Erzählen Sie dann mit Hilfe Ihrer Notizen, was das Problem ist und was für Ausreden (*excuses*) die Personen in den Dialogen haben.

BEISPIEL: Peter hat gesagt, er könne nicht mit ins Kino ...

SPRECHER/IN	PROBLEM	AUSREDE
1. *Peter*		
2. *Jens*		
3. *Ursula*		

Subjunctive I: Past Tense

To express the past tense in indirect discourse, use the Subjunctive I of the auxiliary verb **sein** or **haben** and the past participle of the main verb.

Die Autofahrerin behauptete, der Motorradfahrer **sei** bei Rot **gefahren.**

The driver claimed the motorcyclist ran a red light.

Sie **habe** ihn nicht rechtzeitig **gesehen.**

She did not see him in time.

Note:

- Whether to use **sein** or **haben** depends on the main verb. The choice is identical to which auxiliary the verb would use in the perfect tenses.

Er **ist** gefahren.   Er **sei** gefahren.

Sie **hat** gesehen.   Sie **habe** gesehen.

- With **haben**, only the third-person singular Subjunctive I, **habe**, is used; Subjunctive II is used for the remaining forms.

Der Motorradfahrer berichtete, seine Bremsen **hätten** nicht funktioniert.

The motorcyclist reported that his brakes weren't functioning.

- In informal German, Subjunctive II is increasingly used for all forms in past-tense indirect discourse.

The following table shows examples of the more commonly used third-person forms.

INDIRECT DISCOURSE PAST TENSE: FORMS COMMONLY USED		
INFINITIVE	THIRD-PERSON SINGULAR	THIRD-PERSON PLURAL
sein werden fahren haben wissen tun	er, sie, es { sei/wäre gewesen sei/wäre geworden sei/wäre gefahren habe/hätte gehabt habe/hätte gewusst habe/hätte getan	sie { seien/wären gewesen seien/wären geworden seien/wären gefahren hätten gehabt hätten gewusst hätten getan

Übung 12   Ungewöhnliches° aus den Nachrichten

Unusual happenings

Schreiben Sie die folgenden Sätze in indirekter Rede der Vergangenheit um. Benutzen Sie dabei Konjunktiv I oder Konjunktiv II.

Heute habe ich im Radio gehört:

1. Im Südwesten Irans hat man ein unbekanntes Dorf entdeckt.

2. Ein Mann im Gorillakostüm hat in den Straßen von Dallas 50-Dollar-Scheine an Fußgänger verteilt (*distributed*).

3. Im Jahre 1875 haben die Leute noch 65 Stunden pro Woche gearbeitet. Heutzutage arbeiten die meisten nur noch 39 Stunden pro Woche im Durchschnitt.

4. Bei einer Verkehrskontrolle in Cocoa Beach ist ein Autodieb ins Meer gesprungen. Er ist immer weiter raus geschwommen. Ein Polizist in voller Uniform hat sich auf ein Surfbrett geschwungen und hat den Dieb nach zehn Minuten eingeholt.

5. Gestern ist auf einem Spielplatz in Russland ein UFO gelandet. Die Leute, die aus dem UFO gestiegen sind, sind sehr freundlich gewesen. Nach kurzer Zeit sind sie wieder abgeflogen.

Übung 13   Sensationelles aus der Presse

Lesen Sie zuerst die zwei kurze Berichte aus einer Zeitung und unterstreichen Sie die Verben in indirekter Rede. Wiederholen Sie dann die Sätze als Bericht in direkter Rede.

A. In der Zeitung stand, gestern Abend sei bei einer Geburtstagsfeier in einem Restaurant ein Geburtstagskuchen explodiert. Der Kellner habe zu viel Cognac über den Kuchen gegossen. Die Gäste und der Kellner seien, Gott sei Dank, unverletzt gewesen.

B. In einem Kölner Kiosk habe ein Mann seine Zigaretten mit einem 600-Euro-Schein bezahlt. Der Verkäufer habe geglaubt, es handele sich um einen neuen, noch nicht bekannten Schein. Er habe dem „Kunden" über 500 Euro Wechselgeld zurückgegeben. Erst ein Bekannter des Verkäufers habe die blaue Banknote als Fälschung erkannt und habe die Polizei gerufen. Der Mann mit den Zigaretten sei spurlos verschwunden.

Sprache im Kontext

Videoclips

Jasmin, Peter und Maria sprechen über ihre Lese- und Fernsehgewohnheiten.

A. Schauen Sie sich die Interviews mit Jasmin und Maria an und füllen Sie die Tabelle aus. Wenn die Person keine Information zu dem Thema gibt, schreiben Sie „keine Information."

	PETER	JASMIN	MARIA
Welche Zeitung liest du?			
Was liest du zuerst?			
Welchen Teil liest du ganz genau?			
Was überfliegst du?			
Was siehst du im Fernsehen?			
Welche Filme siehst du gern im Kino?			

B. Schauen Sie sich das Interview mit Peter an und beantworten Sie die Fragen.

1. Welche Tageszeitungen liest er?
2. Peter vergleicht drei verschiedene Zeitungen, den *Tagesspiegel*, die *Welt* und die *Süddeutsche Zeitung*. Wie beschreibt er jede Zeitung?
    a. den *Tagesspiegel*: _____.
    b. die *Welt*: _____.
    c. die *Süddeutsche Zeitung*: _____.
3. Welche Zeitung liest er nie? Warum?
4. Was liest Peter ganz genau? Was überfliegt er?

C. Ein Interview. Benutzen Sie die Tabelle in **Teil A**, um zwei andere Personen zu interviewen. Machen Sie Notizen zu jedem Interview und berichten Sie der Klasse darüber.

Lesen

A. Wie wichtig sind die folgenden Sachen in Ihrem Leben? Kreuzen Sie zuerst an, was sehr wichtig und was nicht so wichtig ist. Geben Sie an, wie viele Stunden pro Woche Sie damit verbringen. Ordnen Sie sie dann in eine Reihenfolge (1–6) ein: 1 = das wichtigste.

	SEHR WICHTIG	NICHT SO WICHTIG	STUNDEN PRO WOCHE	REIHENFOLGE
Fernsehen	☐	☐	——	——
Radio hören	☐	☐	——	——
Zeitung lesen	☐	☐	——	——
am Computer arbeiten	☐	☐	——	——
im Internet surfen	☐	☐	——	——
Bücher lesen	☐	☐	——	——
Videos, Filme sehen	☐	☐	——	——
Musik hören	☐	☐	——	——

B. Was liegt an erster Stelle unter Ihren Klassenmitgliedern? Wie viel Zeit verbringen sie damit?

C. Womit beschäftigen Sie sich, wenn Sie am Computer sitzen? Kreuzen Sie alles an, was Sie machen.

☐ bloggen
☐ chatten
☐ Filme/Fotos herunterladen
☐ forschen, Information für Kurse und Referate sammeln
☐ Fotos bearbeiten
☐ Hausaufgaben machen
☐ im Internet surfen
☐ Instant-Messaging betreiben
☐ mailen
☐ Musik hören und herunterladen
☐ Nachrichten lesen
☐ Sonstiges: _____

D. Berichten Sie kurz über die drei wichtigsten Dinge, die Sie am Computer machen.

Auf den ersten Blick

A. Schauen Sie sich den Titel des Lesetexts an und lesen Sie die zwei ersten Sätze. Was erwarten Sie von diesem Text?

☐ Informationen über die Freunde junger Deutscher
☐ einen Bericht über den negativen Einfluss von Computer und Fernsehen
☐ Informationen über die Rolle vom Computer im Leben junger Deutscher

B. Überfliegen Sie den Artikel und suchen Sie im Text Wörter, die etwas mit Computer und Internet zu tun haben. Machen Sie eine Liste. Woher stammt das Vokabular zum größten Teil?

C. Was passt zusammen?

1. Man schaltet _____.
2. Man klickt _____.
3. Man checkt _____.
4. Man lädt _____.
5. Man googelt _____.
6. Man bearbeitet _____.
7. Man surft _____.

auf den Internet-Button   den Computer an

die E-Mail

einen Namen   im Internet

Fotos am Computer   Musik herunter

von Kerstin Kohlenberg

Wer heute 17 ist, kennt ein Leben ohne Internet
nicht. Für die meisten ist der Computer
wichtiger als Fernsehen.

     Seit einigen Wochen sind die Ferien vorbei.
5 Mel geht wieder zur Schule. Sie kommt aus der
Schule nach Hause, schmeißt den Rucksack
auf den Sessel in ihrem Zimmer, zieht die
Turnschuhe aus und schaltet den Computer im
Wohnzimmer an. Sie ist allein in der Wohnung.
10 Heute gehört ihr der Familiencomputer ganz
allein.

Eine junge Deutsche am Computer

     Sie geht in die Küche, macht sich ein Stück
Pizza warm und trägt es zurück zum Computer.
Ihr tägliches Ritual beginnt. Mel klickt auf den
15 Internet-Button, schaltet den MSN-Messenger
an, ein Programm, das ihr sagt, dass Lisa online ist und der Rest ihrer
Freunde noch offline. Sie checkt ihre E-Mail bei Hotmail – nur ein
Kettenbrief°, den sie weiterschickt – sie checkt ihre E-Mail bei Yahoo –   *chain letter*
ihre Mutter aus Paris. Dann betritt° sie ihr Leben: Skyblog.com. Das   *enters*
20 tägliche Ritual geht weiter. Mel surft, guckt sich die Top 40 Lieder an,
und wenn ihr ein neues Lied gefällt, dann lädt sie es herunter. Musik
und ihre Freunde, das ist es, was Mel interessiert. Dass sie gestern
Spinoza° gegoogelt hat, liegt daran, dass sie über ihn ein Referat° in der   *Baruch Spinoza (philospher) / report*
Schule halten muss.
25   Ihre Internet-Seite berichtet über Mel: Sie ist 17 Jahre alt, hat viele
Freunde, und fährt oft nach Paris. Ihre Mutter lebt nämlich jetzt wieder
in Paris. Die Eltern sind geschieden. Mel lebt mit ihrem Vater und ihrem Bruder in Berlin. Mel hat vier Freundinnen und auch einen Freund
und geht auf ein französisches Gymnasium in Berlin. Mel hat zu Hause
30 eine Flatrate, für rund 30 Euro im Monat kann sie ständig° online sein.   *constantly*
    Valentin geht mit Mel in eine Klassenstufe am französischen
Gymnasium. Er besitzt einen eigenen Computer – ein Geschenk von
seinem Vater zum 17. Geburtstag – und einen eigenen Internet-Zugang.
Valentin sitzt jetzt auf einem Schreibtischstuhl am Computer. Der
35 Bildschirmschoner auf seinem Computerdisplay zeigt Fotos seiner
Freunde. An den Wänden seines Zimmers sind Poster von Musikern
und Breakdancern, und auch Graffiti.
    In Valentins Zimmer sieht man zuerst den Computer (Apple), einen
Fernseher, Videorecorder, DVD Spieler, ein Handy, einen Walkman,
40 einen Discman, einen MP3-Player, Mini-Disc-Player, Plattenspieler,
Mischpult° und eine Digitalkamera. Valentin benutzt den Computer   *mixer*
hauptsächlich zum Surfen und Mailen, für die Schule, zum
Herunterladen von Filmen und Musik und um seine Fotos und Musik
zu bearbeiten. Valentin ist nebenbei DJ.
45   Mels und Valentins Generation ist mit dem Computer aufgewachsen.
Der war vor ein paar Jahren noch vor allem ein Spielzeug der Jungen.
Doch inzwischen ist er auch für Mädchen wie Mel ein wichtiger Teil
des Lebens. Von den Jugendlichen in Deutschland zwischen 12 und 19
haben so gut wie alle, nämlich 96 Prozent, mindestens einen Computer
50 zu Hause. 85 Prozent haben Internet-Zugang, ein Drittel surft vom
eigenen Zimmer aus. Mehr als die Hälfte dieser Internet-Nutzer ist über
10 Stunden pro Woche online. Eine Stuttgarter-Studie berichtet, dass

für Mädchen der Computer noch hinter Fernsehen, Radio und Büchern
rangiert. Für Jungen dagegen ist der Computer der wichtigste
55 Zeitvertreib°.

Was an Valentin, Mel und ihren Freunden auffällt°, ist ihre fehlende°
Angst vor Menschen. Die Sicherheit, mit der sie auf Fremde° zugehen,
die Offenheit°, mit der sie von ihren Leben erzählen, wirken überraschend
erwachsen. Wie Kinder, die in einem Hotel aufgewachsen sind und
60 jeden Tag mit anderen Leuten am Speisetisch gesessen und geredet
haben. Und die darüber nicht vergessen haben, dass das eigentliche
Leben außerhalb des Hotels stattfindet.

Adaptiert aus: Kerstin Kohlenberg, *Die Zeit,* Nr. 41, 6 Oktober 2005, S. 68

pastime

is striking / lack of

strangers

candor

Zum Text

A. Lesen Sie nun den Text genauer und suchen Sie Information über die
beiden Hauptpersonen: Mel und Valentin. Was erfahren wir über die
folgenden Themen?

Zum Text. Additional questions:
1. Was für Musik gefällt Mel? Und
ihrem Freund Valentin? 2. Was für
Hobbys hat Valentin? 3. Wie viele
deutsche Jugendlichen besitzen
einen Computer zu Hause?
4. Wie viele haben ihren eigenen
Internet-Zugang im Schlafzimmer?

	MELS	VALENTINS
Familie	_____	_____
Freunde	_____	_____
Schule	_____	_____
Interessen	_____	_____

B. Die Rolle des Computers

1. Was erfahren wir über die jungen Deutschen und die Rolle des
Computers in ihrem Leben?

2. Gibt es einen Unterschied zwischen Jungen und Mädchen?

3. Glauben Sie, dass es einen Unterschied zwischen jungen US-
Amerikanern/Kanadiern und jungen Deutschen im Gebrauch des
Computers gibt?

C. Im letzten Abschnitt des Artikels sagt die Autorin des Artikels, was
ihr bei diesen jungen Berlinern aufgefallen ist:

- die fehlende Angst vor Menschen
- die Sicherheit, mit der sie auf Fremde zugehen
- die Offenheit, mit der sie von ihren Leben erzählen
- sie wirken überraschend erwachsen

1. Sehen Sie diese Qualitäten als etwas Positives oder haben sie auch
eine negative Seite?

2. Können Sie sich damit identifizieren?

D. Die Autorin schließt mit einem Vergleich (*comparison*). Mit wem
vergleicht sie die junge Generation, die mit dem Computer
aufgewachsen ist? Finden Sie diesen Vergleich passend (*fitting*)?

Zu guter Letzt

Sind Sie kreativ und erfinderisch? Benutzen Sie Ihr Talent, um eine neue Erfindung auf den Markt zu bringen.

Schritt 1: In Gruppen zu dritt überlegen Sie sich eine Kategorie für die Erfindung, z.B. Kommunikation, Auto/Transport, Computertechnologie oder Haushalt. Was ist der Zweck (*purpose*) der Erfindung?

Schritt 2: Jede Gruppe arbeitet nun die Einzelheiten (*details*) ihrer Erfindung aus. Wie sieht sie aus? Wie funktioniert sie? Welche Materialien braucht man, um die Erfindung zu bauen?

Schritt 3: Zeichnen Sie die Erfindung als Poster. Die Zeichnung muss etwas detailliert sein, braucht aber nicht total akkurat zu sein.

Schritt 4: Präsentieren Sie der Klasse die Erfindung. Beschreiben Sie Ihre Erfindung mit Hilfe der Zeichnung.

Schritt 5: Die Klasse entscheidet durch Applaus, welche Gruppe die beste Erfindung hat.

Wortschatz

Im Fernsehen — On Television

der **Bericht**, -e	report
der **Dokumentarfilm**, -e	documentary (film)
das **Programm**, -e	station, TV channel; program
die **Sendung**, -en	TV or radio program
der **Spielfilm**, -e	feature film, movie
die **Unterhaltung**	entertainment
zur Unterhaltung	for entertainment

Die Presse — The Press

das **Abo(nnement)**, -s	subscription
die **Börse**, -n	stock market
das **Horoskop**, -e	horoscope
das **Inland**	at home, domestic, national
im Inland und Ausland	at home and abroad
die **Nachrichten** (*pl.*)	news
die **Lokalnachrichten**	local news
die **Politik**	politics
die **Schlagzeile**, -n	headline
die **Wirtschaft**	economy
die **Zeitschrift**, -en	magazine; periodical

Technik — Technology

der **Anrufbeantworter**, -	answering machine
der **Camcorder**, -	camcorder
die **Digitalkamera**, -s	digital camera
das **Dokument**, -e	document
der **Drucker**, -	printer
die **E-Mail**, -s	e-mail
die **Erfindung**, -en	invention
das **Faxgerät**, -e	fax machine
das **Internet**	Internet
der **Kabelanschluss**, ⸚e	cable TV connection
das **Notebook**, -s	notebook computer
die **Sat-Empfangsanlage**, -n	satellite receiver

Verben — Verbs

abonnieren	to subscribe
sich (*dat.*) **etwas an•schauen**	to watch, look at
sich (*dat.*) **etwas an•sehen** (sieht an), sah an, angesehen	to look at, watch
auf•nehmen (nimmt auf), nahm auf, aufgenommen	to record (e.g., on video)

sich (et)was aus•suchen	to select, find, choose something
behaupten	to claim, assert
berichten	to report, narrate
drucken	to print
empfangen (empfängt), empfing, empfangen	to receive
sich entschließen, entschloss, entschlossen	to decide
erfinden, erfand, erfunden	to invent
forschen	to do research
handeln (von)	to deal with, be about
Wovon handelt es?	What's it about?
hinter lassen (hinterlässt), hinterließ, hinterlassen	to leave (behind) (e.g., a message)
sich melden	to answer (phone)
Niemand meldet sich.	No one is answering.
scheinen, schien, geschienen	to seem, appear
speichern	to save, store
überfliegen, überflog, überflogen	to skim (a text), read quickly
sich unterhalten (unterhält), unterhielt, unterhalten	to entertain (oneself); to converse

Adjektive und Adverbien

Adjectives and Adverbs

aktuell	current, topical
Aktuelles	current events
blöd	stupid
gescheit	intelligent, bright; sensible, decent
nichts Gescheites	nothing decent
unterhaltsam	entertaining

Ausdrücke

Expressions

auf jeden Fall	in any case
Das ist mir zu blöd.	I think that's really stupid.
Na und?	So what?
Wie wäre es mit … ?	How about . . . ?

DAS KANN ICH NUN!

1. Sie reden mit Freunden über Fernsehen und Zeitung. Füllen Sie die Lücken mit einem passenden Ausdruck aus dem Kasten.

> ansehen Dokumentarfilm Fernsehen
>
> gibt es handelt Nachrichten
>
> Schlagzeilen such aus wäre es

    a. Na, was _____ denn heute Abend im _____? **b.** Um 20.00 Uhr kommen die _____. **c.** Wie _____ mit einem _____ über die Sahara? **d.** Ich möchte mir lieber einen guten Spielfilm _____. **e.** Na gut, _____ dir was _____. **f.** Wovon _____ der Film übrigens? **g.** Die _____ in der *Bild* Zeitung zeigen immer nur Sensationelles.

2. Was sehen Sie gerne im Fernsehen? Wofür interessieren Sie sich nicht?

3. Nennen Sie zwei deutschsprachige Zeitungen (aus Deutschland, Österreich oder der Schweiz). Was lesen Sie gewöhnlich in der Zeitung? Was nie?

4. Nennen Sie drei technologische Geräte und erklären Sie, wozu sie nützlich sind.

5. Schreiben Sie die folgenden Sätze zu Ende.

    a. Ich habe heute vor, _____. (*to go to the movies*) **b.** Kai hat versucht, _____. (*to call me yesterday*) **c.** Er hat während des Semesters gejobbt, _____. (*in order to pay his rent*) **d.** Er hat das Buch gelesen, _____. (*without understanding it*)

6. Berichten Sie folgende Information in indirekter Rede.

    a. Der Junge sagte: „Ich habe das Comic-Heft nicht genommen." **b.** Er sagte: „Das Geld dafür ist in meiner Tasche." **c.** Inge behauptet: „Ich sehe nicht gern Seifenopern im Fernsehen." **d.** Der Reporter fragte: „Worum handelt es sich?" **e.** In der Zeitung steht: „Immer mehr Berliner wandern aus. Sie suchen bessere Arbeit und wärmeres Klima." **f.** Der Reporter berichtet: „Der Autofahrer ist bei Rot gefahren und hat den Radfahrer nicht gesehen."

Die öffentliche Meinung

Junge Deutsche protestieren
gegen die neuen Studien-
gebühren an der Universität.

In diesem Kapitel

- **Themen:** Global problems, public opinion, environment, discussion strategies
- **Grammatik:** Passive voice, the present participle
- **Kultur:** The environment, speed limits in Europe, recycling
- **Lesen:** „Was in der Zeitung steht" (Reinhard Mai)

Videoclips
Globale Probleme

Alles klar?

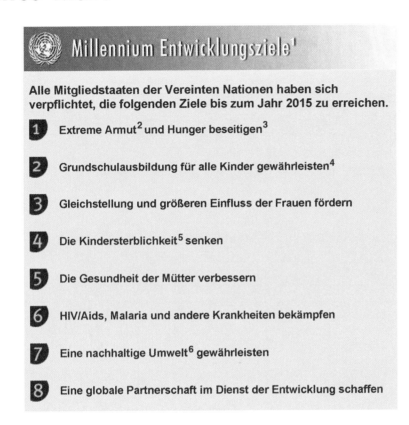

Millennium Entwicklungsziele[1]

Alle Mitgliedstaaten der Vereinten Nationen haben sich verpflichtet, die folgenden Ziele bis zum Jahr 2015 zu erreichen.

1. Extreme Armut[2] und Hunger beseitigen[3]
2. Grundschulausbildung für alle Kinder gewährleisten[4]
3. Gleichstellung und größeren Einfluss der Frauen fördern
4. Die Kindersterblichkeit[5] senken
5. Die Gesundheit der Mütter verbessern
6. HIV/Aids, Malaria und andere Krankheiten bekämpfen
7. Eine nachhaltige Umwelt[6] gewährleisten
8. Eine globale Partnerschaft im Dienst der Entwicklung schaffen

[1]*development goals* [2]*poverty* [3]*eliminate* [4]*ensure* [5]*child mortality* [6]*nachhaltige ... sustainable environment*

Alles klar? A. Suggestion: In order to activate students' background knowledge, ask *Was wissen Sie über die UNO?* and write *UNO = die Vereinten Nationen* on the board or OHP. *Was für Probleme will die UNO lösen?*

Alles klar? A: If students are interested in more information on the United Nations Millennium Development Project, you can refer them to the website at www.unmillenniumproject.org. The statistics are derived from data published by the United Nations Regional Information Center for Western Europe on their website at www.runiceurope.org.

A. Deutschland ist seit 1973 Mitglied der Vereinten Nationen (UNO). Diese Organisation sucht Lösungen (*solutions*) für globale Probleme. Im Jahr 2000 stellte die UNO acht Entwicklungsziele vor. Schauen Sie sich die acht Entwicklungsziele an. Lesen Sie dann die folgenden Probleme. Welches Ziel richtet sich auf welches Problem?

a. __5__ Jeden Tag sterben (*die*) irgendwo auf der Welt 1.400 Frauen während der Schwangerschaft (*pregnancy*) oder bei der Entbindung (*giving birth*).

b. __4__ Mehr als 6 Millionen Kinder sterben jedes Jahr an vermeidbaren (*avoidable*) Ursachen (*causes*).

c. __6__ Jeden Tag sterben 6.000 Menschen an HIV/Aids.

d. __1__ Alle 3,6 Sekunden verhungert (*dies of starvation*) ein Mensch irgendwo auf der Welt.

e. __3__ 584 Millionen Frauen auf der Welt können nicht lesen und schreiben.

f. __2__ 114 Millionen Kinder besuchen keine Grundschule.

g. __8__ Viele Entwicklungsländer haben finanzielle Probleme und brauchen internationale Hilfe.

h. __7__ Mehr als eine Milliarde Menschen haben keinen Zugang zu sauberem Trinkwasser.

B. Sie hören jetzt eine Beschreibung von vier verschiedenen Seminaren über Probleme in der Welt. Welche Themen behandeln diese Seminare? Schreiben Sie die entsprechende Nummer vor jedes Thema.

__2__ Kriminalität/Gewalt   __4__ Menschenrechte

__3__ Umweltverschmutzung   __1__ Medizin/Umwelt

Wörter im Kontext

Neue Wörter

die Welt world

sich Sorgen machen um worry about

die Krankheit (Krankheiten, *pl.*) disease, illness

die Arbeitslosigkeit unemployment

die Armut poverty

die Ausländerfeindlichkeit hatred of foreigners

die Drogensucht drug addiction

die Gewalttätigkeit violence

die Erwärmung warming

die Regierung government

der Krieg war

die Obdachlosigkeit homelessness

die Umweltverschmutzung environmental pollution

die Verletzung violation

das Menschenrecht (Menschenrechte, *pl.*) human right

möglich possible

die Lösung (Lösungen, *pl.*) solution

lösen solve

der Fortschritt (Fortschritte, *pl.*) progress

teilnehmen (an) participate (in)

die Forschung research

entwickeln develop

vermindern lessen

verbieten forbid

die Gefahr (Gefahren, *pl.*) danger

verbreiten spread

erziehen raise

das Gefängnis (Gefängnisse, *pl.*) prison

einführen introduce

Obdachlose homeless persons

der Lärm noise

fördern promote

schaffen create

umschulen retrain

wählen elect

THEMA 1: Globale Probleme

A. Was sind Ihrer Meinung nach die drei größten Probleme in der **Welt**, in Ihrem Staat und in Ihrer Heimatstadt? Wor**um machen** Sie **sich Sorgen**?

	WELT	STAAT	STADT
Aids und andere sexuell übertragbare **Krankheiten**	☐	☐	☐
Arbeitslosigkeit	☐	☐	☐
Armut	☐	☐	☐
Ausländerfeindlichkeit	☐	☐	☐
Drogensucht	☐	☐	☐
Gewalttätigkeit	☐	☐	☐
globale Erwärmung	☐	☐	☐
Hunger	☐	☐	☐
Korruption in der **Regierung**	☐	☐	☐
Krieg	☐	☐	☐
Obdachlosigkeit	☐	☐	☐
Rassismus	☐	☐	☐
Rechtsextremismus	☐	☐	☐
Terrorismus	☐	☐	☐
Umweltverschmutzung	☐	☐	☐
Verletzung der Menschenrechte	☐	☐	☐
??	☐	☐	☐

B. Mögliche Lösungen. Wie kann man diese Probleme **lösen**? Wie können **Fortschritte** gemacht werden? Suchen Sie aus der folgenden Liste passende Ausdrücke (*expressions*), um Ihre Meinung auszudrücken.

BEISPIEL: In meiner Heimatstadt ist Obdachlosigkeit ein großes Problem. Man sollte mehr Sozialbauwohnungen bauen.

- **an Demonstrationen teilnehmen**
- mehr Fußgängerzonen einrichten
- mehr Geld für **Forschung** ausgeben
- Alternativenergie **entwickeln**
- Giftstoffe (*toxics*) **vermindern** oder **verbieten**
- Hilfsorganisationen mit Geld unterstützen
- Informationen über die **Gefahren** von Alkohol und **Drogen verbreiten**
- Kinder besser **erziehen**
- mehr **Gefängnisse** bauen
- Recyclingprogramme **einführen**
- Safer Sex praktizieren
- Sozialbauwohnungen für **Obdachlose** bauen
- Stressfaktoren (z.B. **Lärm**) reduzieren
- Umschulungsprogramme **fördern**
- Arbeitsplätze **schaffen** und Arbeiter **umschulen**
- verantwortungsbewusste **Politiker/Politikerinnen wählen**

- **sich** politisch **engagieren**
- **öffentliche Verkehrsmittel** fördern
- Umwelt **schützen**
- Luftverschmutzung **streng** kontrollieren
- **??**

Die Kunst der Diskussion

DISKUSSIONSREDEMITTEL

Suggestion: Focus on the expressions used to express an opinion. Use them in other contexts, e.g., *Ich bin der Meinung, man sollte mehr Recycling-programme beginnen.* Then go back to B above and have students do the exercise again incorporating these expressions.

Achten Sie auf die Redemittel in der folgenden Diskussion:

ich bin der Meinung	I am of the opinion
So ein Unsinn!	Such nonsense!
ich halte ... für ...	I think . . . is/are . . .
ich stimme (dir/Alexandra) zu	I agree (with you/Alexandra)
(ich bin) dafür	(I am) for that
(ich bin) dagegen	(I am) against that
meiner Meinung nach	in my opinion

Neue Wörter

öffentlich public
**das Verkehrsmittel
(Verkehrsmittel** *pl.*)
means of transportation
streng strictly
meint (meinen) think
behandeln deal with
betrifft (betreffen) affects
im Grunde genommen
basically
der Umweltschutz
environmental protection
das Windrad wind power
generator
der Bürger citizen
übertrieben exaggerated
vertraut familiar
außerdem besides
stimmen ab (abstimmen)
take a vote
unterbrechen interrupt

Fünf Studenten und Studentinnen sollen in Team-Arbeit einen Vortrag über ein globales oder lokales Problem für ihr Hauptseminar in Soziologie vorbereiten. Sie sitzen im Uni-Café und diskutieren.

CHRISTIAN: Also, was **meint** ihr? Sollen wir ein globales Thema wie Terrorismus **behandeln**?

CORNELIA: Aktuell ist es schon, aber ich würde lieber ein Problem behandeln, das uns hier in Deutschland täglich **betrifft,** z.B. Arbeitslosigkeit oder Umweltverschmutzung.

ERMAN: ... oder auch Ausländerfeindlichkeit.

NIELS: **Im Grunde genommen** sind ja all diese Probleme global.

ALEXANDRA: **Ich bin der Meinung, Umweltschutz** ist besonders wichtig, gerade jetzt, wo wir mehr alternative Energie produzieren müssen.

NIELS: Ja, Solarenergie und Windenergie. Könnt ihr euch das vorstellen: hinter jedem Haus ein **Windrad** im Garten? (*Gelächter*) Es gibt sogar schon **Bürgerinitiativen,** die das fördern.

CORNELIA: **So ein Unsinn!** Ich **halte** das **für übertrieben.**

ERMAN: Das ist deine Meinung, nicht unbedingt meine.

CORNELIA: Also, ich **stimme** Alexandra **zu,** Umweltschutz ist relevant und allen irgendwie **vertraut.** Es betrifft uns alle. Und **außerdem** gibt es viel darüber zu sagen.

CHRISTIAN: **Stimmen** wir **ab:** Wer ist **dafür** und wer **dagegen?**

ALLE ANDEREN: Dafür.

CHRISTIAN: Nun gut. Ich mache auch mit. Wie sollen wir das Thema behandeln?

ERMAN: Jeder soll sich einen Aspekt des Themas aussuchen. Ich würde z.B. gern mehr über alternative Energie erfahren.

CORNELIA: Und ich möchte mich mit Bürgerinitiativen zum Umweltschutz beschäftigen.

Windräder erzeugen saubere Energie

CHRISTIAN: Neulich habe ich von einer Bürgerinitiative gelesen, die gegen Handys in Bussen und Bahn demonstriert. **Meiner Meinung nach** ist das auch Umweltschutz.

ALEXANDRA: Also, ich schlage vor, wir machen jetzt gleich einen konkreten Plan, wer welchen Aspekt des Themas behandelt.

NIELS: Tut mir leid, dass ich **unterbrechen** muss. Ich muss jetzt leider weg. Ich habe eine Vorlesung. Wann treffen wir uns wieder?

ALEXANDRA: Ich schicke dir eine Mail mit allen Informationen.

ALLE: Tschüss.

Ergänzen Sie die folgenden Sätze mit Informationen aus dem Dialog oben.

1. Cornelia möchte ein Thema ____, das sie in Deutschland täglich ____.

2. Alexandra ist der ____, dass ____ besonders wichtig ist. Cornelia ____ ihr zu.

3. Cornelia hält die Bürgerinitiativen für Windenergie für ____.

4. Niels muss ____, denn er hat eine Vorlesung.

Stellen Sie Ihrem Partner / Ihrer Partnerin Fragen zu den folgenden Problemen, um herauszufinden, welche möglichen Lösungen es gibt.

BEISPIEL: s1: Was kann man gegen Krieg tun?
s2: Man kann an Antikriegsdemonstrationen teilnehmen.

PROBLEME	MÖGLICHE LÖSUNGEN
Krieg	an Antikriegsdemonstrationen teilnehmen
Inflation	
Drogensucht	Informationen über die Gefahren von Drogen verbreiten
Umweltverschmutzung	
Verletzung der Menschenrechte	Organisationen wie Amnesty International unterstützen
Obdachlosigkeit	
Arbeitslosigkeit	Arbeiter umschulen

Vier Leute sprechen über Probleme in ihrer Stadt und wie man sie lösen könnte. Setzen Sie die passende Nummer (1–4) vor das Problem, über das der Sprecher / die Sprecherin redet, und markieren Sie auch die Lösung, die er/sie vorschlägt.

SPRECHER	PROBLEM	LÖSUNG	
____	Atomkraft (*nuclear power*)	**a.** Solarenergie	**b.** Windenergie
____	Giftstoffe in Nahrungsmitteln	**a.** strenge Staatskontrolle	**b.** weniger Gemüse essen
____	Verkehr	**a.** Tempolimit	**b.** Wagen am Stadtrand parken
____	Lärm	**a.** weniger Flugzeuge	**b.** Autos verbieten

Aktivität 3 Um welche Probleme geht es hier?

Buttons, Aufkleber (*stickers*) und Poster sind beliebte Formen, die Meinung zu äußern (*express*).

Schritt 1: Schauen Sie sich die Buttons und Poster an und stellen Sie fest, wofür oder wogegen sie sind. Schreiben Sie dann die passenden Zahlen in die Liste.

a. __7__ gegen Energieverschwendung

b. __9__ gegen Armut

c. __10__ gegen Autoabgase
(*emissions*)

d. __12__ gegen Welthunger

e. __2__ für den Tierschutz

f. __4__ gegen Rauchen

g. __6__ gegen Obdachlosigkeit

h. __8__ gegen Krieg

i. __5__ für höhere Gehälter

j. __11__ gegen Pestizide in
Nahrungsmitteln

k. __1__ gegen Kernenergie

l. __3__ für sauberes
Trinkwasser

Aktivität 3. Realia: The pictures of buttons were found on a calendar distributed by the Goethe Institut. Note: Some of the posters can be interpreted in more than one way, and you will want to be flexible with the answers. While #9 is the only poster with word *Armut* on it, #6 and #12 can easily be explained as ultimately caused by poverty as well. You may wish to involve the class in discussion of underlying problems. *Warum haben viele Menschen auf der Welt nicht genug zu essen? Warum sind viele obdachlos? —Sie haben nicht genug Geld, sie leben in Armut.* and so forth.

Schritt 2: Wählen Sie ein Problem aus **Thema 1** und entwerfen Sie einen Button, einen Aufkleber oder ein Poster.

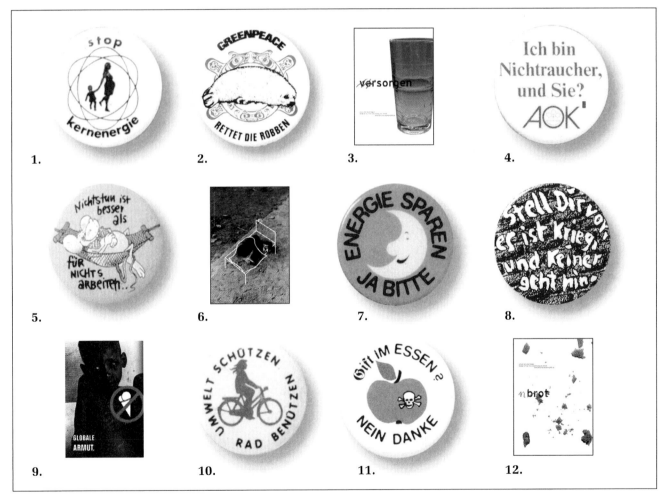

Nr. 3, 6, 9, 12: Die Plakate sind Motive des Wettbewerbs „Farbe bekennen. Gegen globale Armut" des deutschen Bundesministeriums für wirtschaftliche Zusammenarbeit und Entwicklung (BMZ) zum Aktionsprogramm 2015. Weitere Informationen erhalten Sie unter www.ap2015.de.

In Vierergruppen, äußern Sie sich zu einigen Problemen im **Thema 1.** Benutzen Sie dabei die Redemittel im **Thema 1.** Jemand nennt das Gesprächsthema; die anderen sagen ihre Meinung.

BEISPIEL: s1: Verkehrsbelästigung (*traffic disturbances*)
s2: Ich bin der Meinung, man sollte Autos in der Innenstadt verbieten.
s3: Meiner Meinung nach sollte man mehr Fußgängerzonen haben.
s4: Ich finde es schade, dass Leute immer ihren Wagen benutzen. Sie sollten öfter zu Fuß gehen.

THEMA 2: Umwelt

Was kann man für die Umwelt tun?

Die Zeitschrift „Natur" fragte ihre Leser, „Bei welchen dieser Punkte auf der Liste glauben Sie, dass Sie mehr für die Umwelt tun könnten?" Hier sind die Antworten.

Keine Wegwerfflaschen oder Getränkedosen kaufen	35
Beim Einkauf auf Artikel mit umweltfreundlicher Verpackung achten	29
Öffentliche Verkehrsmittel dem Auto vorziehen	29
Aluminium getrennt vom Hausmüll sammeln	26
Beim Einkauf keine Plastiktüten verwenden	25
Weniger Strom verbrauchen	24
Alte Arzneimittel in der Apotheke abgeben	24
Energiesparende Haushaltsgeräte anschaffen	22
Heizwärme sparen, die Wohnung besser isolieren	21
Alte Batterien bei den Sammelstellen abgeben	20
Sonderabfälle[1] (z.B. Altöl) zur Deponie[2] bringen	18
Organische Abfälle kompostieren	16
Alte Kleider in die Sammlung geben	15
Auto mit Katalysator fahren	14
Altpapier in die Sammlung geben	13
Glas zum Container bringen	12
Nichts davon	18

[1]*special types of garbage* [2]*garbage dump*

Was tun Sie persönlich für die Umwelt?

Neue Wörter

**die Wegwerfflasche
(Wegwerfflaschen,** *pl.*)
nonrecyclable bottle
**die Getränkedose
(Getränkedosen,** *pl.*)
beverage can
**mit umweltfreundlicher
Verpackung** with
environmentally friendly
packaging
vorziehen (+ *dat.*) give
preference to . . . (over . . .)
die Plastiktüte (Plastiktüten,
pl.) plastic bag
verwenden use, apply
verbrauchen use; consume
**das Arzneimittel
(Arzneimittel,** *pl.*)
medication
anschaffen buy, acquire
isolieren insulate; isolate
**die Sammelstelle
(Sammelstellen,** *pl.*)
recycling center
der Abfall (Abfälle, *pl.*)
waste

In allen Ländern Europas außer in der Bundesrepublik gibt es eine Höchstgeschwindigkeit auf der Autobahn. In Deutschland ist die Richtgeschwindigkeit (*suggested speed*) 130 km pro Stunde auf der Autobahn. Natürlich gibt es streckenweise (*for certain stretches*) Geschwindigkeitsbegrenzungen, zum Beispiel an Baustellen. Über der Autobahn sind manchmal Kameras angebracht, die einen Wagen, der zu schnell fährt, filmen. Man bekommt dann einen Strafzettel (*ticket*) mit dem Bild des Wagens und dem Nummernschild ins Haus geschickt. Niemand kann dann sagen: Das war jemand anders.

Kulturtipp. **Note:** The cameras use infrared light to take pictures after dark, so it is not safe to speed at any time.

Aktivität 5 Langsamer, bitte!

Sie hören zuerst ein Gespräch zwischen Andreas, einem deutschen Autofahrer, und Jennifer, seinem Gast aus den USA. Hören Sie zuerst den Dialog, und lesen Sie die Sätze unten. Bringen Sie dann die Sätze in die richtige Reihenfolge.

   _3_   Bei uns ist die Höchstgeschwindigkeit (*speed limit*) 110 km pro Stunde.

   _6_   Wahrscheinlich eine Baustelle (*construction zone*) in der Nähe.

   _7_   Also doch ein Tempolimit. Gott sei Dank. Bei 100 km pro Stunde fühle ich mich direkt wie zu Hause.

   _2_   Keine Angst. Der Wagen schafft das spielend.

   _4_   Dann kann man gleich zu Fuß gehen.

   _5_   Schau mal. Dort ist ein Schild. Höchstgeschwindigkeit 100 km pro Stunde.

   _1_   Fliegen wir eigentlich oder fahren wir?

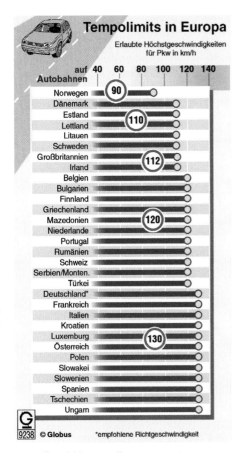

Tempolimits in Europa

Erlaubte Höchstgeschwindigkeiten für Pkw in km/h

© Globus 9238   *empfohlene Richtgeschwindigkeit

Hier klicken!

Weiteres zum Thema Umwelt finden Sie bei **Deutsch: Na klar!** im World-Wide-Web unter www.mhhe.com/dnk5.

Viele Menschen leben heutzutage viel umweltbewusster als früher. Sie sind daran interessiert, wie man die Umwelt schützen kann und wie man selbst mithelfen kann, umweltfreundlicher zu leben. Dieses Umweltbewusstsein zeigt sich auch in der modernen Sprache. So gebraucht man oft **alt** als Präfix, wenn man von Dingen spricht, die zur Deponie, zu Sammelstellen oder zur Wiederverwertung gebracht werden; z.B. **Altbatterien, Altöl, Altpapier, Altglas** und **Altkleidung.** Das Altglas wird nach Farben sortiert: **Braunglas, Grünglas** und **Weißglas.**

Wie gut kennen Sie Ihre Umwelt? Beantworten Sie die Fragen und vergleichen Sie dann Ihre Antworten mit denen eines Partners / einer Partnerin.

1. Was ist am sparsamsten im Energieverbrauch?
   - **a.** das Motorrad
   - **b.** das Auto
   - **c.** das Fahrrad
   - **d.** die Bahn

2. In welchem Jahr und wo wurden erstmals Mülleimer (*garbage cans*) benutzt?
   - **a.** 1213 in Rom
   - **b.** 1473 in Amsterdam
   - **c.** 1621 in Hamburg
   - **d.** 1872 in Chicago

3. Wann und wo wurde die Konservendose erfunden?
   - **a.** 1746 in Norwegen
   - **b.** 1810 in England
   - **c.** 1899 in Deutschland
   - **d.** 1902 in der Schweiz

4. Wie viel Wasser verbrauchen Deutsche pro Person im Durchschnitt am Tag?
   - **a.** 14 Liter
   - **b.** 130 Liter
   - **c.** 295 Liter
   - **d.** 320 Liter

Siehe *The Passive Voice*, S. 417.

5. In welchem Land wird 69% des Stroms aus Wasserkraft gewonnen?
   - **a.** in den Niederlanden
   - **b.** in Deutschland
   - **c.** in der Schweiz
   - **d.** in Österreich

Seit über dreißig Jahren wächst das Umweltbewusstsein der Deutschen. Daher werden Berufe im Umweltbereich immer beliebter. Hier sind drei neue Berufe.

Beate Lehmkuhl, 41, ist Fachärztin für Umweltmedizin in Hamburg. Sie studierte Humanmedizin in Freiburg. „Ich beschäftige mich hauptsächlich mit Schadstoffen und ihrer Wirkung auf den Menschen. Diese Schadstoffe sind in Boden, Wasser, Luft, Lebensmitteln und in Dingen, die wir jeden Tag benutzen."

Dr. Ralph Hantschel, 34, zählt zu den ersten Studienabgängern der Geoökologie: „Die Ausbildung in Bayreuth war intensiv und gut." Heute sucht er Wege zu einer umweltverträglichen Landwirtschaft und ist beim Forschungszentrum für Umwelt und Gesundheit (GSF) tätig.

Siegfried Müller vom Amt für Abfallwirtschaft der Stadt München: „Es macht Spaß. Aber die Verwaltungswege erscheinen mir mitunter zu lang." Der 32jährige studierte Physik. Er arbeitet in der Entsorgungsplanung.

- Dr. Beate Lehmkuhl. Fachärztin für Umweltmedizin. Was hat sie studiert? Wo arbeitet sie jetzt?
- Dr. Ralph Hantschel. Geoökologe. Wo hat er studiert? Wo arbeitet er jetzt?
- Siegfried Müller. Entsorger (*waste management engineer*). Was hat er studiert? Wo arbeitet er jetzt?

Gibt es diese oder ähnliche (*similar*) Berufe in Ihrem Land? Wer befasst sich mit dem Folgenden? Schreiben Sie **F** (für Facharzt/Fachärztin), **G** (für Geoökologe/Geoökologin) oder **E** (für Entsorger/Entsorgerin).

1. _____ Altöl, Altbatterien und ihre Wirkung (*effect*) auf die Umwelt

2. _____ Kontrolle der Verpackungsflut (*glut of packaging*)

3. _____ Messung des sauren Regens

4. _____ organische Abfälle und Kompost

5. _____ Bakterien oder Gift in Lebensmitteln

6. _____ Verschmutzung der Seen, Flüsse

7. _____ Einfluss auf den Menschen durch Schadstoffe (*toxins*)

Grammatik im Kontext

The Passive Voice°

Das Passiv

So far you have learned to express sentences in German in the active voice. In the active voice, the subject of a sentence performs the action expressed by the verb. In the passive voice, the subject is acted on by an agent, the person or thing performing the action. This agent is not always named, because it is either understood, unimportant, or unknown. Compare the following sentences.

The Passive Voice. Note: It is important for students to learn to recognize a passive voice sentence in reading; however, active mastery—integrating passive voice sentences freely in conversation—should not be expected at this level. Students should merely be able to produce simple sentences in the passive voice. **Point out:** Teachers frequently tell students in English composition classes to avoid passive voice in their writing. Passive voice is much more common in German.

ACTIVE VOICE

Viele Leute lesen täglich eine Zeitung.	*Many people read a newspaper daily.*
Welche Zeitung lesen die Deutschen am meisten?	*Which paper do Germans read the most?*

PASSIVE VOICE

In Deutschland werden viele Zeitungen verkauft.	*Many newspapers are sold in Germany.*
Welche Zeitung wird am meisten gelesen?	*Which newspaper is read the most?*

The active voice emphasizes the subject that carries out an activity; in the passive voice the emphasis shifts to the activity itself. For this reason, the passive voice tends to be more impersonal. It is commonly used in newspapers, scientific writing, and descriptions of procedures and activities.

Formation of the Passive Voice

The passive voice is formed with the auxiliary verb **werden** and the past participle of the main verb. (English uses *to be* and the past participle.) Although it can be used in all personal forms, the passive occurs most frequently in the third-person singular or plural. Following are the commonly used tenses of the passive.

Formation of the Passive Voice. Suggestion: Review the conjugation of *werden*. To practice the passive with all personal forms, use *ich werde gefragt* or *ich werde eingeladen*.

PRESENT

Die Zeitung **wird verkauft.**	*The newspaper is (being) sold.*
Die Zeitungen **werden verkauft.**	*The newspapers are (being) sold.*

SIMPLE PAST

Die Zeitung **wurde verkauft.**	*The newspaper was (being) sold.*
Die Zeitungen **wurden verkauft.**	*The newspapers were (being) sold.*

PRESENT PERFECT

Die Zeitung **ist verkauft worden.**	*The newspaper has been sold.*
Die Zeitungen **sind verkauft worden.**	*The newspapers have been sold.*

Die Zeitung **war verkauft worden**.	*The newspaper had been sold.*
Die Zeitungen **waren verkauft worden**.	*The newspapers had been sold.*

Note:

- In the perfect tenses of the passive, the past participle **geworden** is shortened to **worden**.
- The presence of **worden** in any sentence is a clear signal that the sentence is in the passive voice.

You now know three ways in which the verb **werden** can function.

1. **werden** as independent verb (*to become*)
2. **werden** + infinitive (future tense)
3. **werden** + past participle (passive voice)

Read the headlines and captions and determine . . .

■ how the verb **werden** is used in each case (independent verb, future tense, passive)

■ the position of the past participle in

  a. a main clause in the passive voice

  b. a dependent clause in the passive voice

Muß unser Dorf so häßlich werden?

In jeder Minute werden 21 Hektar[1] Regenwald vernichtet[2]

Schon in wenigen Jahren wird es die „Grünen Lungen[3] der Erde" nicht mehr geben

GREENPEACE

Wie konnten Sie es zulassen[4], daß unsere Erde[5] in so kurzer Zeit vergiftet[6] wurde?

Du meinst, Fleisch essen und Umweltschutz vertragen sich?

Denk mal genau nach!

Wenn dir wirklich was an diesem Planeten liegt, werde Vegetarier!

[1]Hektar = 2.47 acres [2]destroyed [3]lungs [4]allow [5]earth [6]poisoned

Expressing the Agent

As already noted, the agent causing the action in a passive voice sentence is often not stated. However, when it is stated, the agent is expressed with the preposition **von** (+ *dat.*).

In einer Stunde werden 1,5 Millionen Briefe **von Deutschen** geschrieben.

*In one hour 1.5 million letters are written **by Germans**.*

When the action is caused by an impersonal force, the preposition **durch** (+ *acc.*) is used.

Die Ozonschicht wird **durch Luftverschmutzung** zerstört.

*The ozone layer is being destroyed **by air pollution**.*

Sentences in the passive voice that state the agent can also be expressed in the active voice. There is no difference in meaning, only in emphasis.

PASSIVE: In einer Stunde werden **1,5 Millionen Briefe** **von Deutschen** geschrieben.

SUBJECT   PREPOSITIONAL OBJECT (AGENT)

ACTIVE: **Die Deutschen** schreiben in einer Stunde **1,5 Millionen Briefe.**

SUBJECT (AGENT)   DIRECT OBJECT

Note that the subject in the passive voice sentence becomes the direct object in the active voice sentence, and the subject in the active voice sentence becomes the prepositional object (**von**) in the passive voice sentence.

Übung 1   Was passiert alles in 60 Minuten in Deutschland?

Schritt 1: Bilden Sie Sätze im Passiv Präsens.

BEISPIEL: 1,5 Millionen Briefe werden geschrieben.

1. 1,5 Millionen Briefe	exportiert
2. mehr als eine Million Liter Bier	geboren
3. weniger als 80 Kinder	gegessen
4. 434 Autos	gekauft
5. 639 Fernsehgeräte	geschrieben
6. über eine Million Zeitungen	getrunken
7. 57 Menschen / in Unfällen auf der Straße	produziert
8. 786 Tonnen Brot	verletzt

Schritt 2: Drücken Sie die Sätze aus **Schritt 1** im Passiv Perfekt aus.

BEISPIEL: In einer Stunde sind weniger als 80 Kinder geboren worden.

Übung 2   Wer handelt hier?

Ergänzen Sie die folgenden Sätze im Passiv mit **von** order **durch**.

1. In den 80er Jahren ist das Ozonloch __von__ Wissenschaftlern entdeckt worden.
2. Die Umwelt wird __durch__ Luftverschmutzung zerstört.
3. Die Aktion „Saubere Luft" wird __von__ vielen Bürgern unterstützt.
4. Bei der Initiative „Gegen Atomkraft" sind einige Studenten __von__ der Polizei verhaftet (*arrested*) worden.

Übung 1. Note: By and large, these are actual statistics from the year 2006 taken from a variety of sources. **Answers:** 1. *1,5 Millionen Briefe werden geschrieben.* 2. *Mehr als eine Million Liter Bier werden getrunken.* 3. *Weniger als 80 Kinder werden geboren.* 4. *434 Autos werden exportiert.* 5. *639 Fernsehgeräte werden produziert.* 6. *Über eine Million Zeitungen werden gekauft.* 7. *57 Menschen werden in Unfällen auf der Straße verletzt.* 8. *786 Tonnen Brot werden gegessen.*

5. Die Bürgerinitiative „Kein Handy in Bus und Bahn" ist _____ Zeitung und Fernsehen verbreitet worden.

6. Manche Leute glauben, in Bus und Bahn werden Sitznachbarn von Handytelefonierern _____ Strahlen belastet (*contaminated by radiation*). Deswegen soll es verboten werden.

Übung 3 In der Schweiz

Ergänzen Sie die folgenden Sätze mit Verben im Passiv Präsenz.

1. In der Schweiz _____ vier Sprachen _____: deutsch, französisch, italienisch und rätoromanisch. (sprechen)

2. In 17 Kantonen _____ Deutsch _____. (sprechen)

3. Jährlich _____ rund drei Milliarden Franken für Umweltschutz _____. (ausgeben)

4. 237 Liter Wasser _____ per Person pro Tag _____. (verbrauchen)

5. Im Durchschnitt _____ mehr Kaffee von den Schweizern als von den Deutschen _____. (trinken)

6. Die Bahn _____ zweimal so oft von den Schweizern _____ wie von den Deutschen. (benutzen)

Übung 4 Achtung, Uhren umstellen!

Lesen Sie folgende Nachricht über die Sommerzeit (*daylight saving time*).

1. Identifizieren Sie alle Sätze im Passiv.

2. Was sind die Tatsachen?

    a. Die Uhren ...   **c.** Die Sommerzeit ...

    b. Die Nacht ...   **d.** Das Ziel (*goal*) ...

NÜTZLICHE WÖRTER

die Uhr umstellen *to change the clock*

die Uhr vorstellen *to set the clock ahead*

verkürzen *to shorten*

einführen *to introduce*

erreichen *to reach*

Achtung, Uhren umstellen: Die Sommerzeit beginnt

BM/dpa Hamburg, 26. März

Der Osterhase[1] bringt in diesem Jahr auch die Sommerzeit: In der Nacht zum Sonntag um 2 Uhr werden die Uhren auf 3 Uhr vorgestellt; die Nacht wird um eine Stunde verkürzt. Die Sommerzeit endet am 24. September – traditionsgemäß wieder eine Sonntag-Nacht.

    Die Sommerzeit war in der Bundesrepublik Deutschland – nach 30 Jahren Unterbrechung[2] – erstmals 1980 wieder eingeführt worden. Das eigentliche[3] Ziel, Energie einzusparen, wurde jedoch nicht erreicht. Dafür genießen[4] viele ihre Freizeit an den langen hellen Abenden.

In der Nacht zum Sonntag...

...Uhr 1 Stunde vorstellen

[1]*Easter Bunny*   [2]*interruption*   [3]*real*   [4]*enjoy*

Expressing a General Activity

Sometimes a sentence in the passive voice expresses a general activity without stating a subject at all. In such cases, the "impersonal" **es** is generally understood to be the subject, and therefore the conjugated verb always appears in the third-person singular. This grammatical feature has no equivalent in English.

Hier wird gerudert.	*People are rowing here.*
Im Fernsehen wird viel über Terrorismus gesprochen.	*There's a lot of talk about terrorism on television.*
Hier wird Deutsch gesprochen.	*German (is) spoken here.*

Eins – und eins – und eins . . .

Hier wird mächtig gerudert! **Jochen** sitzt zwischen **Peter** und **Stefan, Armin** sitzt zwischen **Martin** und **Thomas**. Vorn in einem Boot sitzt **Peter**, während **Martin** hinten sitzt. **Kalli** und **Stefan** rudern nicht in demselben Boot. Wer ist wer?

Lösung: 1. Stefan, 2. Jochen, 3. Peter, 4. Martin, 5. Armin, 6. Thomas, 7. Kalli

Realia. Suggestion: Give students several minutes to figure out who sits where.

Übung 5 Was ist hier los?

Beschreiben Sie, was die Leute auf diesen Bildern machen. Gebrauchen Sie die Verben:

debattieren	feiern	reden
demonstrieren	lachen	tanzen
diskutieren	Musik machen	trinken
essen		

BEISPIEL: Bild 1: Da wird gefeiert und …

Übung 5. Follow-up: Ask students, *Was wird im Deutschkurs gemacht? —Hier wird gelernt. Hier wird Deutsch gesprochen. Hier werden Fragen beantwortet.* and so forth.

1.

2.

3.

Grammatik im Kontext   **421**

In zwei Städten, Altstadt und Neustadt, wird für eine bessere Umwelt gesorgt.

BEISPIEL: s1: Was ist zuerst in Altstadt gemacht worden?
s2: Zuerst sind Autos aus der Innenstadt verbannt worden. Und in Neustadt?
s1: Zuerst sind naturnahe Gärten angelegt worden.

	ALTSTADT	NEUSTADT
zuerst		naturnahe Gärten anlegen
dann		Kinderspielplätze verbessern
danach		Park im Zentrum säubern
schließlich		keine Wegwerfartikel in Geschäften verkaufen
zuletzt		nach Alternativenergie suchen

KULTURTIPP

In einigen Orten Deutschlands können alte Medikamente in die Apotheke zurückgebracht werden, damit sie nicht in den Abfall geworfen werden und als Giftstoffe die Umwelt gefährden. Andere potentiell gefährliche Substanzen wie alte Batterien und Farben werden von "Umweltbussen" abgeholt.

The Passive with Modal Verbs

Modal verbs used with a passive infinitive convey something that should, must, or can be done. Only the present tense, the simple past tense, and the present subjunctive of modals are commonly used in the passive.

Die Umwelt **muss geschützt werden.**	*The environment must be protected.*
Die Natur **darf** nicht **zerstört werden.**	*Nature must not be destroyed.*
Recyclingprogramme **sollten gefördert werden.**	*Recycling programs ought to be promoted.*
Alte Medikamente **konnten** in die Apotheke **zurückgebracht werden.**	*Old medications could be returned to the pharmacy.*

Note:

- The passive infinitive consists of the past participle of the main verb and **werden**:

ACTIVE INFINITIVE	PASSIVE INFINITIVE
schützen *to protect*	geschützt werden *to be protected*
zerstören *to destroy*	zerstört werden *to be destroyed*
fördern *to promote*	gefördert werden *to be promoted*
zurückbringen *to return*	zurückgebracht werden *to be returned*

Schützt Flüsse und Auen

Diese Lebensräume vieler wildlebender Tier- und Pflanzenarten dürfen nicht weiter zerstört werden!

Spendenkonto: 1703-203, Postgiroamt Hamburg, oder werden Sie Mitglied im Bund der aktiven Naturschützer.

Übung 7   Aus Liebe zur Umwelt

Was kann und muss gemacht werden? Folgen Sie dem Beispiel.

BEISPIEL: die Umwelt schonen / müssen →
Die Umwelt muss geschont werden.

1. alle Menschen über Umweltschutz informieren / müssen
2. mehr Energie sparen / sollen
3. Recyclingprogramme fördern / sollen
4. Altglas sammeln / können
5. Wälder und Flüsse schützen / müssen
6. Alternativenergie entwickeln / müssen
7. Luftverschmutzung vermindern / müssen
8. globale Erwärmung verhindern / können
9. Abfälle wie Plastiktüten und Einwegflaschen vermeiden / müssen
10. Altbatterien nicht in den Müll werfen / dürfen
11. Wegwerfprodukte (wie z.B. Einmal-Rasierer, Einmal-Fotoapparate) nicht kaufen / sollen
12. Verpackungen (wie die Mehrweg-Eierbox) wieder ins Geschäft bringen / können

Aus Liebe zur Umwelt
Mehrweg-Eierbox
Bring'sie wieder mit

10x frische Eier, selbst ausgewählt
1x aktiv Umwelt geschont

Übung 8   Was ist das Problem?

Was soll, kann oder darf damit (nicht) gemacht werden?

BEISPIEL: Digitaluhren können nicht repariert werden.

1. Billiguhren (Digitaluhren)
2. Einmal-Fotoapparate
3. alte Batterien
4. Einwegflaschen
5. alte Medikamente
6. Giftstoffe

a. vom Umweltbus abholen
b. in fast alle Apotheken zurückbringen
c. nur für einen Film gebrauchen
d. nicht in den Müll werfen
e. nicht wieder füllen
f. nicht reparieren

Übung 8. **Suggestion:** Go over both columns to make sure students understand the vocabulary. **Point out:** Many German *Apotheken* accept expired drugs from customers and dispose of them properly, so that the drugs do not end up in landfills or lakes, eventually contaminating ground water, water supplies, or the oceans. *Umweltbusse* are used by municipal waste management agencies to collect *Problemstoffe* such as paint remover, used oil, chemicals, paint, car batteries, and alkaline and/or rechargeable batteries. Students can find more examples of recycling and waste collection on the Web by searching on the keyword *Entsorgung*.

Grammatik im Kontext   **423**

Use of **man** as an Alternative to the Passive

Generally, the passive voice is used whenever the agent of an action is unknown. One alternative to the passive is to use the pronoun **man** in the active voice.

PASSIVE VOICE	ACTIVE-VOICE ALTERNATIVE
Die Gefahr ist nicht erkannt worden.	**Man hat** die Gefahr nicht **erkannt.**
The danger was not recognized.	*People (One) did not recognize the danger.*
Die Zerstörung der Altstadt muss verhindert werden.	**Man muss** die Zerstörung der Altstadt **verhindern.**
The destruction of the old city must be prevented.	*People (One) must prevent the destruction of the old city.*

Übung 9 Was kann man für die Umwelt tun?

Bilden Sie neue Sätze mit **man.**

BEISPIEL: Wegwerfprodukte sollen vermieden werden.
Man soll Wegwerfprodukte vermeiden.

1. Die Umwelt darf nicht weiter zerstört werden.
2. Altpapier und Glas sollten zum Recycling gebracht werden.
3. In Göttingen ist Geld für den Umweltschutz gesammelt worden.
4. Mehr Recycling-Container sind aufgestellt worden.
5. Chemikalien im Haushalt sollen vermieden werden.
6. Batterien sollen nicht in den Hausmüll geworfen werden.
7. Der Wald muss besonders geschützt werden.

Übung 10 Lebensqualität

Was kann man tun, um die Lebensqualität zu verbessern? Bilden Sie zwei Sätze je mit **man** und Passiv.

BEISPIEL: alte Zeitungen
Man kann alte Zeitungen zum Recycling bringen.
Alte Zeitungen können zum Recycling gebracht werden.

alte Zeitungen	bauen
Plastiktüten	fördern
Windenergie	vermeiden
Kinderspielplätze	sammeln
Altpapier	schützen
öffentliche Verkehrsmittel	benutzen
Wälder	zum Recycling bringen

Das Partizip Präsens

The Present Participle°

The present participle (ending in *-ing* in English) is used in a more limited way in German than it is in English. In German it functions primarily as an adjective or an adverb. As an attributive adjective (preceding a noun), the participle takes appropriate adjective endings. The present participle of a German verb is formed by adding **-d** to the infinitive.

INFINITIVE	PRESENT PARTICIPLE
kommen	kommend (*coming*)
steigen	steigend (*climbing, increasing*)

PRESENT PARTICIPLE AS ATTRIBUTIVE ADJECTIVE

im **kommenden** Sommer	*in the coming (next) summer*
die **steigende** Arbeitslosigkeit	*increasing unemployment*

PRESENT PARTICIPLE AS ADVERB

Jennifer spricht **fließend** Deutsch.	*Jennifer speaks German fluently.*

Übung 11 In der Zeitung

Worüber liest man fast täglich? Ergänzen Sie die Sätze mit einem Partizip Präsens.

Man liest oft über …

1. ___wachsende___ Obdachlosigkeit. (wachsen)
2. die ___steigenden___ Preise. (steigen)
3. ___demonstrierende___ Studenten. (demonstrieren)
4. ___wachsende___ Arbeitslosigkeit. (wachsen)
5. die ___steigende___ Luftverschmutzung. (steigen)
6. die ___streikenden___ Arbeiter. (streiken)
7. die ___hungernden___ Menschen. (hungern)

Sprache im Kontext

Videoclips

A. Claudia, Harald und Wiebke sprechen über die Probleme in der Welt.

1. Was sind für sie die drei größten Probleme heute?
2. Und für Sie? Was sind für Sie die drei größten Probleme heute in der Welt?

B. Harald spricht über ein ganz spezifisches Problem in Berlin. Erklären Sie das Problem.

C. Wiebke spricht über Aids und was dagegen gemacht wird. Was sagt sie? Ergänzen Sie ihre Worte.

„Ich verfolge in der Zeitung ab und zu die Entwicklung von Aids. Ich sehe, dass es in Afrika sehr stark _____ hat, dass auch die _____ Versorgung für Aids noch nicht das _____, was es bringen könnte. Man arbeitet an Wirkstoffen und _____, aber die Versorgung zum Beispiel für _____ Leute in Afrika oder für Leute in den Ostblockländern ist nicht so gut. Und Medikamente sind auch nicht so verfügbar, wie man sich das _____.“

D. Was tun Claudia und Wiebke für die Umwelt? Schauen Sie sich die Interviews an und schreiben Sie vor jede Aussage entweder **C** für Claudia oder **W** für Wiebke.

_____ sammelt Zeitungen

_____ benutzt öffentliche Verkehrsmittel oder Fahrrad

_____ bringt leere Flaschen zurück

_____ benutzt Stoffbeutel statt Plastikbeutel

_____ lässt das Wasser beim Zähneputzen nicht laufen

_____ badet und duscht weniger und wäscht sich mehr, denn es ist gesünder für die Haut

_____ gebraucht so wenig Strom wie möglich

E. Und Sie? Was machen Sie für die Umwelt?

Lesen

Zum Thema

Die Skandalpresse. In den meisten Ländern gibt es Zeitschriften, die von den jüngsten Sensationen und Skandalen berichten. Auch im Fernsehen wird oft von sensationellen und skandalösen Ereignissen (_events_) berichtet, die aber oft erfunden sind.

Machen Sie eine Umfrage im Kurs.

1. Wie heißen die Zeitungen und Zeitschriften, die sich auf Sensationen und Skandale spezialisieren?

2. Wer liest sie regelmäßig? Welche? Warum?

Auf den ersten Blick

Lesen Sie den Text, eine Ballade von Reinhard Mai, kurz durch.

1. Wovon handelt diese Ballade?

2. Wer sind die Hauptfiguren?

3. Wo spielt sich das Ereignis ab?

von Reinhard Mai

Wie jeden Morgen war er pünktlich dran, seine
Kollegen sahen ihn fragend an, „Sag' mal,
hast du noch nicht gesehen, was in der
Zeitung steht?"
5 Er schloß die Türe hinter sich,
hängte Hut und Mantel in den Schrank fein säuberlich°,   _neatly_
setzte sich, „da wollen wir erst mal sehen,
was in der Zeitung steht."

Und da stand es fett auf Seite zwei
10 „Finanzskandal", sein Bild dabei
und die Schlagzeile „Wie lang das wohl so weitergeht?"
Er las den Text,
und ihm war sofort klar,
eine Verwechslung°, nein, da war kein Wort von wahr,   *mistake, mix-up*
15 aber wie kann so etwas verlogen° sein,   *fabricated*
was in der Zeitung steht?

Er starrte auf das Blatt°,   *paper*
das vor ihm lag,
es traf ihn wie ein heimtückischer° Schlag°,   *malicious / blow*
20 wie ist das möglich, daß so etwas in der Zeitung steht?
Das Zimmer ringsherum begann sich zu drehen°,   *sich … to turn*
die Zeilen konnte er nur noch verschwommen° sehen.   *as blurred*
Wie wehrt man sich° nur gegen das,   *wehrt … does one defend oneself*
was in der Zeitung steht?

25 Die Kollegen sagten, „stell dich einfach stur"°,   *stell … be stolid*
er taumelte° zu seinem Chef über den Flur,   *staggered*
„aber selbstverständlich,
daß jeder hier zu Ihnen steht,
ich glaube, das Beste ist, Sie spannen erst mal aus,
30 ein paar Tage Urlaub, bleiben Sie zu Haus,
Sie wissen ja, die Leute glauben gleich alles,
nur weil es in der Zeitung steht."

Er holte Hut und Mantel, wankte° aus dem Raum,   *swayed*
nein, das war wirklich kalt, das war kein böser Traum,
35 wer denkt sich sowas aus, wie das,
was in der Zeitung steht?
Er rief den Fahrstuhl°, stieg ein und gleich wieder aus,   *elevator*
nein, er ging doch wohl besser durch das Treppenhaus°.   *stairwell*
Da würde ihn keiner sehen, der wüßte,
40 was in der Zeitung steht.
Er würde durch die Tiefgarage gehen, er war zu Fuß.
Der Pförtner° würde ihn nicht sehen,   *custodian*
der wußte immer ganz genau,
was in der Zeitung steht.
45 Er stolperte° die Wagenauffahrt° rauf,   *stumbled / driveway*
sah den Rücken des Pförtners,
das Tor war auf,
das klebt wie Pech° an dir,   *klebt wie … sticks like tar*
das wirst du nie mehr los°,   *wirst … you will never get rid of*
50 was in der Zeitung steht,
was in der Zeitung steht,
was in der Zeitung steht,
was in der Zeitung steht.

Er eilte° zur U-Bahnstation,   *hurried*
55 jetzt wüßten es die Nachbarn schon,
jetzt war es im ganzen Ort herum,
was in der Zeitung steht.
Solange die Kinder in der Schule waren,
solange würden sie es vielleicht nicht erfahren°,   *find out*
60 aber irgendwer hat ihnen längst erzählt,
was in der Zeitung steht.

Er wich den Leuten auf dem Bahnsteig aus°,   *wich ... aus avoided*
ihm schien, die Blicke, alle richteten sich nur auf ihn,
der Mann im Kiosk da, der wußte Wort für Wort,
65   was in der Zeitung steht.
Wie eine Welle° war es, die über ihm zusammenschlug°,   *wave / crashed down*
wie die Erlösung° kam der Vorortszug°,   *deliverance / suburban train*
du wirst nie mehr ganz frei, das hängt dir ewig an,
was in der Zeitung steht.

70   „Was wollen Sie eigentlich?" fragte der Redakteur°,   *editor*
„Verantwortung°, Mann, wenn ich das schon hör',   *responsibility*
die Leute müssen halt nicht gleich alles glauben,
nur weil es in der Zeitung steht."
„Na, schön, so eine Verwechslung kann schon mal passieren,
75   da kannst du noch so sorgfältig° recherchieren°.   *carefully / research*
Mann, was glauben Sie, was Tag für Tag für ein Unfug°   *nonsense*
in der Zeitung steht?"

„Ja", sagte der Chef vom Dienst, „das ist wirklich zu dumm,
aber ehrlich°, man bringt sich doch nicht gleich um°,   *honestly / bringt ... one doesn't kill oneself*
80   nur weil mal aus Versehen°   *aus ... by mistake*
was in der Zeitung steht."
Die Gegendarstellung° erschien am Abend schon,   *retraction, corrected version*
fünf Zeilen mit dem Bedauern° der Redaktion,   *regret*
aber Hand aufs Herz, wer liest, was so klein
85   in der Zeitung steht?

Zum Text

A. Lesen Sie die folgenden Sätze, und setzen Sie sie in die richtige Reihenfolge.

_____ Er eilte zur U-Bahnstation, um nach Hause zu fahren.

_____ Es war ganz klein gedruckt.

_____ Der Chef vom Dienst fand, dass sein Selbstmord (*suicide*) übertrieben war.

_____ Kein Wort war wahr. Es war eine Verwechslung.

_____ Er verließ das Gebäude durch die Parkgarage, um die Leute zu vermeiden.

1 Ein Mann ging ins Büro zur Arbeit und las zuerst die Zeitung.

_____ Er sah sein Bild neben der Schlagzeile „Finanzskandal" in der Zeitung.

_____ Er ging zu seinen Kollegen und zu seinem Chef.

_____ Er warf sich vor den Zug.

_____ In der Zeitung stand später, dass der Bericht ein Irrtum (*mistake*) war.

_____ Sein Chef schickte ihn nach Hause.

_____ Der Redakteur der Zeitung meinte, dass er keine Verantwortung trage.

B. Beantworten Sie die folgenden Fragen.

1. Wie reagieren die Personen in der Ballade auf die falsche Information in der Zeitung?

2. Wie steht der Liedermacher zu der Presse?

3. „Was in der Zeitung steht" ist eine Ballade. Was ist charakteristisch für eine Ballade? Was macht diesen Text zu einer Ballade?

C. Was finden Sie über die deutschsprachigen Länder in den Nachrichten und Zeitungen? Suchen Sie sich mehrere Zeitungen oder Zeitschriften aus. Schauen Sie nach, was in den letzten zwei Monaten über die deutschsprachigen Länder berichtet wurde. Welche Themen über die deutschsprachigen Länder kommen vor? Warum sind diese Themen wichtig? Wählen Sie ein Thema und geben Sie einen kurzen Bericht in der Klasse.

D. Schreiben Sie einen kurzen Artikel über die Fakten in der Ballade von Reinhard Mai. Nehmen Sie dazu Stellung. Benutzen Sie dabei die indirekte Rede.

Zu guter Letzt

Diskussion im Plenum

Diskutieren Sie im Plenum einen Vorschlag zur Lösung eines globalen oder lokalen Problems.

Schritt 1: Das Thema. Wählen Sie ein Thema oder Problem aus der Liste mit globalen Problemen auf S. 410 oder ein aktuelles Thema an Ihrer Universität oder in Ihrer Stadt.

BEISPIELE: Armut
Verkehr in der Innenstadt
Umweltverschmutzung

Schritt 2: Die Lösung. Formulieren Sie eine mögliche Lösung des Problems. Sie brauchen nicht unbedingt alle mit dieser Lösung einverstanden zu sein.

BEISPIEL: Umweltverschmutzung → Die Benzinsteuern sollen drastisch erhöht werden.

Schritt 3: Dafür oder dagegen? Entscheiden Sie sich, ob Sie dafür oder dagegen sind. Schreiben Sie drei Argumente, um Ihre Meinung auszudrücken.

Schritt 4: Redemittel. Wie führen Sie Ihre Argumente ein? Wählen Sie mindestens drei Redemittel aus der Liste auf S. 411, um Ihre Argumente einzuleiten.

Schritt 5: Die Klasse wählt eine/n Diskussionsmoderator/in, um die Diskussion zu leiten. Zwei Klassenmitglieder führen Protokoll (*take notes*).

Schritt 6: Diskutieren Sie über die vorgeschlagene Lösung im Plenum. Hier sind einige Redemittel, die dem/der Moderator/in behilflich sein können.

Wir sind hier, um das Thema _____ zu besprechen.	*We are here to discuss the topic _____.*
Wer möchte etwas dazu sagen?	*Who would like to say something about that?*
Einer nach dem anderen bitte!	*Please take turns!*
Wir müssen die Diskussion jetzt zu Ende führen.	*We have to bring the discussion to a close now.*

Schritt 7: Jeder bekommt eine Kopie des Protokolls, um damit eine Zusammenfassung der Diskussion zu schreiben.

Wortschatz

Weltweite Probleme	World Problems
die **Arbeitslosigkeit**	unemployment
die **Armut**	poverty
die **Ausländer-feindlichkeit**	xenophobia, hatred directed toward foreigners
die **Drogensucht**	drug addiction
die **Gewalttätigkeit, -en**	(act of) violence
der **Hunger**	hunger, famine
die **Korruption**	corruption
die **Krankheit, -en**	illness, disease, ailment
der **Krieg, -e**	war
das **Menschenrecht, -e**	human right (*usu. plural*)
der/die **Obdachlose** (*decl. adj.*)	homeless (person)
die **Obdachlosigkeit**	homelessness
der **Rassismus**	racism
der **Rechtsextremismus**	right-wing extremism
der **Terrorismus**	terrorism
die **Umwelt-verschmutzung**	environmental pollution
die **Verletzung, -en**	injury, violation
die **Welt**	world, earth

Umwelt	Environment
der **Abfall, -̈e**	waste, garbage, trash, litter
die **Dose, -n**	(tin or aluminum) can; jar
die **Erwärmung**	warming
die **Flasche, -n**	bottle
die **Wegwerfflasche, -n**	nonrecyclable bottle
die **Getränkedose, -n**	beverage can
der **Lärm**	noise
die **Plastiktüte, -n**	plastic bag
die **Sammelstelle, -n**	recycling center
der **Umweltschutz**	environmental protection
das **Verkehrsmittel, -**	vehicle, means of transportation
die **Verpackung, -en**	packaging, wrapping
das **Windrad, -̈er**	wind power generator

Sonstige Substantive	Other Nouns
das **Arzneimittel, -**	medication
der **Ausländer, -** / die **Ausländerin, -nen**	foreigner

der **Bürger, -** / die **Bürgerin, -nen**	citizen
die **Demonstration, -en**	demonstration
die **Droge, -n**	drug; medicine
die **Forschung, -en**	research
der **Fortschritt, -e**	progress
Fortschritte machen	to make progress
die **Gefahr, -en**	danger
das **Gefängnis, -se**	prison, jail
die **Lösung, -en**	solution
die **Meinung, -en**	opinion
ich bin der Meinung …	I'm of the opinion . . .
meiner Meinung nach …	in my opinion . . .
der **Politiker, -** / die **Politikerin, -nen**	politician
die **Regierung, -en**	government
die **Steuer, -n**	tax

Verben	Verbs
ab•stimmen	to take a vote
sich etwas an•schaffen	to purchase or acquire something
behandeln	to deal with
betreffen (betrifft), betraf, betroffen	to affect
ein•führen	to introduce
sich engagieren	to get involved
entwickeln	to develop
erziehen, erzog, erzogen	to raise, bring up
fördern	to promote
halten für (hält), hielt, gehalten	to consider, think
isolieren	to isolate; to insulate
lösen	to solve
sich Sorgen machen um (etwas)	to worry about (something)
meinen	to think, be of the opinion
schaffen, schuf, geschaffen	to create
schützen	to protect
teil•nehmen an (+ *dat.*) (nimmt teil), nahm teil, teilgenommen	to participate (in)
(sich) trennen	to separate
um•schulen	to retrain

unterbrechen (unterbricht), unterbrach, unterbrochen	to interrupt	sauber	clean
		streng	strict(ly)
		übertrieben	exaggerated
verbieten, verbot, verboten	to prohibit, forbid	umweltfreundlich	environmentally friendly
		vertraut	familiar

Andere Ausdrücke / Other Expressions

verbrauchen	to consume	außerdem	besides, in addition
verbreiten	to spread, disseminate	Ich bin dafür.	I'm in favor of it.
vermeiden, vermied, vermieden	to avoid	Ich bin dagegen.	I'm against it.
		im Grunde genommen	basically
vermindern	to decrease, lessen	So ein Unsinn!	Nonsense!
verwenden	to use, apply		
vor•ziehen, zog vor, vorgezogen	to prefer		
wählen	to vote, elect; to choose		

Adjektive und Adverbien / Adjectives and Adverbs

global	global
möglich	possible, possibly
öffentlich	public

DAS KANN ICH NUN!

1. Nennen Sie fünf globale Probleme.

2. Welche Verben assoziieren Sie mit den Substantiven? (Mehrere Antworten sind möglich.)

   a. an Demonstrationen _____ entwickeln
   b. die Umwelt _____ einführen
   c. Plastiktüten _____ schützen
   d. Obdachlosigkeit _____ fördern
   e. Fußgängerzonen _____ vermindern
   f. Recylingprogramme _____ verbieten
   g. Umweltschutz _____ teilnehmen
   h. Alternativenergie _____ einrichten

3. Nennen Sie zwei oder drei Sachen, die man in Ihrer Stadt tut oder die Sie persönlich machen, um die Umweltz zu schützen.

4. Sie diskutieren mit einem Bekannten über globale Klimaerwärmung. Wie sagt man folgende Ausdrücke auf Deutsch?

   a. *In my opinion . . .*   b. *I think it is exaggerated . . .*   c. *I agree with you that . . .*   d. *I am against that.*

5. Bilden Sie nun vier Sätze mit den Ausdrücken aus Übung **4**, in denen Sie etwas über globale Erwärmung aussagen.

6. Drücken Sie die folgenden Sätze im Passiv aus.

   a. Man muss die Umwelt schützen.   b. Kann man globale Klimaerwärmung verhindern?   c. Man darf Altbatterien nicht in den Abfall werfen.

7. Ergänzen Sie die folgenden Sätze im Passiv.

   a. In Deutschland _____ viele Zeitungen gelesen.   b. Letztes Jahr _____ Millionen Digitalkameras gekauft _____.   c. In der Schweiz _____ in 17 Kantonen Deutsch gesprochen.   d. Handytelefonieren in Bus and Bahn soll verboten _____.   e. Mozart _____ in Salzburg geboren.

8. Ergänzen Sie die fehlenden Partizipial-adjektive.

   a. Im kommen_____ Sommer mache ich ein Praktikum im Umweltschutz.   b. Die steigen_____ Klimaerwärmung ist ein globales Problem.   c. Die Studenten demonstrierten wegen wachsen_____ Arbeitslosigkeit nach dem Studium.

Gestern und heute

ÜBERGANG

Die Skulptur "Berlin" mit Blick auf die Kaiser Wilhelm-Gedächtniskirche im Zentrum Berlins

In diesem Kapitel

- Short history of modern Germany, remembrances of war and survival, Berlin—the capital, European Union, looking to the future

Videoclips
Berlin: Damals und heute

Kleine Chronik deutscher Geschichte

Kleine Chronik. Suggestion: If it is available, show the film *Triumph des Willens* by filmmaker Leni Riefenstahl, which documents Hitler's effect on the German people, as shown in the annual ritual of the *Parteitag* in Nürnberg. A more recent film, Oliver *armed forces* Hirschbiegel's 2004 Oscar-nominated *Downfall (Der Untergang)*, depicts the last days of Adolf Hitler and those around him as Berlin comes under siege by Allied troops in 1945.

1. September 1939	Der Zweite Weltkrieg beginnt mit der Invasion Polens durch deutsche Truppen.
9. Mai 1945	Um null Uhr eins endet der Zweite Weltkrieg in Europa offiziell mit der Kapitulation der Deutschen Wehrmacht°. Durch diesen Krieg verloren insgesamt 55 Millionen Menschen ihr Leben.

Das zerbombte Reichstagsgebäude, Berlin 1945

Trümmerfrauen bei der Arbeit

Suggestion: Assign the *Kleine Chronik* reading as homework. Discuss and elaborate on dates and events the following day, bringing in additional pictures and slides.

5. Juni 1945	Die vier Alliierten (die Vereinigten Staaten, die Sowjetunion, Großbritannien und Frankreich) übernehmen die oberste Regierungsgewalt in Deutschland. Deutschland wird in vier Besatzungszonen° aufgeteilt. Berlin, die ehemalige Hauptstadt, wird separat in vier Besatzungszonen aufgeteilt.
5. Juni 1947	Der Marshallplan wird für Deutschland die Grundlage° für das kommende Wirtschaftswunder°.

occupation zones

foundation
economic miracle

Menschenschlangen stehen 1946 nach Lebensmitteln an.

Die „Luftbrücke": Ein „Rosinenbomber" kurz vor der Landung in Berlin

20. Juni 1948	Es gibt neues Geld: die Deutsche Mark. Jeder Bürger der Westzonen und West-Berlins bekommt zu Anfang 40 Mark.
24. Juni 1948	Beginn der Berliner Blockade. Die Sowjetunion blockiert alle Wege nach West-Berlin außer den Luftwegen. Elf Monate lang werden die Berliner durch die „Luftbrücke" versorgt.
23. Mai 1949	Gründung der Bundesrepublik Deutschland (BRD).

7. Oktober 1949	Gründung der Deutschen Demokratischen Republik (DDR).
17. Juni 1953	Volksaufstand° in Ost-Berlin und der DDR gegen das kommunistische Regime.
13. August 1961	Bau der Mauer° in Berlin.
26. Juni 1963	Besuch Präsident John F. Kennedys in Berlin. Seine Erklärung der Solidarität mit Berlinern endet mit den oft zitierten Worten: „Ich bin ein Berliner."
9. November 1989	Die Grenzen zwischen der DDR und der BRD werden geöffnet.
3. Oktober 1990	Tag der offiziellen deutschen Einigung. Fünf neue Bundesländer (Brandenburg, Mecklenburg-Vorpommern, Sachsen, Sachsen-Anhalt und Thüringen) treten der Bundesrepublik bei.°
20. Juni 1991	Der deutsche Bundestag wählt Berlin zum Regierungssitz° des vereinigten Deutschlands.
1. Januar 1993	Der Vertrag über die Europäische Union tritt in Kraft.°
8. September 1994	Offizieller Abschied der Besatzungstruppen von Berlin.
19. April 1999	Der Bundestag tagt zum ersten Mal im neuen Reichstagsgebäude in Berlin.
1. Januar 2002	Der Euro ersetzt die Deutsche Mark als Währung im täglichen Gebrauch.
2003–2004	Die Bundesrepublik wird zwei Jahre lang Mitglied des UNO-Sicherheitsrates.
22. November 2005	Deutschland bekommt seine erste Bundeskanzlerin, Angela Merkel, eine ehemalige Bürgerin der DDR.

popular uprising

wall

treten ... bei join

seat of government

tritt ... Kraft comes into force

Suggestion: If you have access to a multi-region DVD player, you might want to show Sönke Wortmann's 2003 film *Das Wunder von Bern*, which depicts the 1954 West German World Cup victory, as well as post-war reconstruction and the issues raised by German soldiers returning from Soviet war captivity to their families.

Suggestion: Another topic-appropriate film is Wolfgang Becker's *Good Bye Lenin!*, about which students read in **Kapitel 11**.

KULTURTIPP

Die Kaiser-Wilhelm-Gedächtniskirche liegt am Kudamm (Kurfürstendamm), dem großen Einkaufsboulevard Berlins. Die Kirche lag am Ende des Zweiten Weltkriegs in Trümmern (*ruins*). Man baute eine neue, moderne Kirche auf, ließ aber die schwarze Ruine des Turms als Mahnmal (*memorial*) an die dunklen Jahre des Krieges stehen.

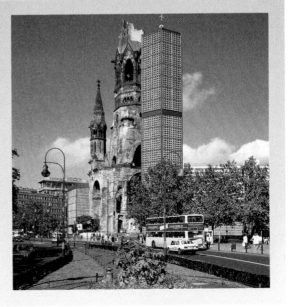

Die Kaiser-Wilhelm-Gedächtniskirche in Berlin

Ordnen Sie zuerst die Daten und die Satzteile einander zu. Welches Bild passt zu welchem Satz?

a. Am 9. Mai 1945

b. Am 13. August 1961

c. Am 9. November 1989

d. Am 19. April 1999

—— wurde die Grenze zwischen Ost- und West-Berlin durch den Bau der Mauer geschlossen. BILD ——.

—— feierte ganz Deutschland die Öffnung der Grenze zwischen Ost- und West-Berlin und zwischen der DDR und der BRD. BILD ——.

—— tagte der Bundestag zum ersten Mal im neuen Reichstagsgebäude. BILD ——.

—— als der Zweite Weltkrieg in Europa endete, lag ganz Deutschland in Trümmern. BILD ——.

1.

2.

3.

4.

Aktivität 2 Faktum oder nicht?

Aktivität 2. Suggestion: This also works well as a pair activity.

Stimmt das oder stimmt es nicht? Korrigieren Sie die falschen Aussagen.

	DAS STIMMT	DAS STIMMT NICHT
1. Der Zweite Weltkrieg begann mit der Invasion der Sowjetunion durch deutsche Truppen im September 1939.	☐	☒
2. Der Zweite Weltkrieg kostete 55 Millionen Menschen das Leben.	☒	☐
3. Deutschland wurde nach dem Zweiten Weltkrieg in vier Besatzungszonen geteilt.	☒	☐
4. Berlin gehörte ganz zur russischen Besatzungszone.	☐	☒
5. Die BRD und die DDR wurden 1945 gegründet.	☐	☒
6. Der Marshallplan spielte eine wichtige Rolle beim Wiederaufbau Europas.	☒	☐
7. Im Juni 1948 blockierte die Sowjetunion alle Transportwege nach Berlin.	☐	☒
8. Im Jahre 1990 wurden die DDR und die BRD vereinigt.	☒	☐
9. Im Jahre 1992 trat der Vertrag über die Europäische Union in Kraft.	☐	☒
10. 2005 wurde Angela Merkel, ehemalige Bürgerin der DDR, die erste Bundeskanzlerin Deutschlands.	☐	☒

Aktivität 3 Ein kleines Quiz

Bilden Sie mehrere Gruppen. Machen Sie mit Hilfe der kleinen Chronik deutscher Geschichte ein Quiz. Das Format bleibt jeder Gruppe überlassen. Es könnte z.B. in Form einer Quizshow sein: Wer bin ich?; es könnte eine Serie von Fragen sein, die Sie gemeinsam entwickeln; oder es könnte ein Wortratespiel sein. Die anderen im Kurs übernehmen die Rolle der Teilnehmer (*participants*).

Aktivität 3. Suggestion: Assign the creation of the quiz to each group for homework. Brainstorm some ideas with students, and do the quiz in class the next day.

Große Freude nach der Öffnung der Grenzen: Eine Westberlinerin begrüßt eine DDR-Bürgerin.

Das neue Regierungsviertel in Berlin

Das moderne Sony Center am Potsdamer Platz

Berlin: Hauptstadt im Wandel

Im Juni 1991 wählte der deutsche Bundestag die Stadt Berlin zum offiziellen Regierungssitz. Mit etwa 3,4 Millionen Einwohnern ist Berlin die größte Stadt des vereinigten Deutschlands und dazu ein eigenständiger Staat der Bundesrepublik.

Von der Mauer, die von 1961 bis 1989 West-Berlin von Ost-Berlin trennte, ist kaum eine Spur geblieben. Stattdessen sieht man überall moderne Bürohäuser, Einkaufszentren und Wohnhäuser, sowohl wie renovierte und neue Regierungsgebäude. Das Stadtbild Berlin hat sich sehr verändert, vor allem am Potsdamer Platz und im früheren östlichen Teil. Die Stadt Berlin ist stolz auf ihre Rolle als Metropole.

Contributions # Beiträge° zur deutschen Geschichte

Wie berührt (*touches*) Geschichte unser Leben? In diesem Teil des Kapitels erleben Sie Geschichte, indem Sie persönliche Dokumente, Auszüge aus einer Autobiographie und Briefe lesen. Diese persönlichen Dokumente bringen uns historische Ereignisse auf ungewöhnliche Weise näher.

Der folgende Text, ein kurzer Ausschnitt aus der Autobiographie der Zigeunerin (*Gypsy*) Ceja Stojka, *Wir leben im Verborgenen: Erinnerungen einer Rom-Zigeunerin*, ist im Jahre 1989 erschienen. Ceja Stojka wurde 1933 in einem Gasthaus in der Steiermark in Österreich geboren. Während des Dritten Reiches wurde sie als Zigeunerin – sie gehörte zu der Rom Gruppe – aus rassistischen Gründen verfolgt (*persecuted*). Sie kam zusammen mit ihrer Mutter und ihren Schwestern in die Konzentrationslager Auschwitz und Ravensbrück.

Überfliegen Sie den ersten Abschnitt des Textes. Welche der folgenden Namen und Wörter stehen im Text?

- ☐ Auschwitz
- ☐ Hitler
- ☐ experimentieren
- ☐ nach Hause gehen
- ☐ Berlin
- ☐ SS-Soldaten
- ☐ sterilisieren
- ☐ Ravensbrück
- ☐ SS-Frauen
- ☐ Konzentrationslager

KULTURTIPP

Die Aufseherinnen (*female guards*) in den Konzentrationslagern wurden automatisch zu Mitgliedern der SS. Daher die Bezeichnung SS-Frauen, die Ceja Stojka benutzt.

Für „arische" Frauen waren Verhütungsmittel (*birth control*), Abtreibungen (*abortions*) und Sterilisation gegen das Gesetz; aber für andere Frauen, die nicht der Norm entsprachen, gab es Zwangssterilisation (*forced sterilization*). In den Konzentrationslagern wurden Zwangssterilisationen an vielen Frauen vorgenommen, um mit neuen Methoden der Sterilisation zu experimentieren.

Kulturtipp. Note: The *SS (Schutzstaffel)* was created by Hitler in 1925 as a military organization within his party and was totally loyal to him. It became the most feared party organization during the Nazi years.

Realia. This is a campaign poster for Adolf Hitler: "Rettet die deutsche Familie. Wählt Adolf Hitler."

WIR LEBEN IM VERBORGENEN

von Ceja Stojka

Ja, es war nicht einfach in diesem Frauenlager Ravensbrück. Die SS-Frauen waren schlechter als jeder Satan. Eines Tages kamen zwei von ihnen und sagten zu uns: „Hört alle gut zu, was wir euch sagen. Es ist ein Schreiben aus Berlin gekommen und das sagt, alle Frauen und
5 Kinder, die sich sterilisieren lassen, können bald nach Hause gehen." Und weiter sagten sie: „Na, ihr braucht ja keine Kinder mehr, also kommt morgen und unterschreibt°, daß ihr freiwillig dazu bereit seid. — *sign* Der Oberarzt wird euch diesen Eingriff° machen. In ein paar Tagen — *operation* könnt ihr dann das Lager verlassen." (Das war alles eine Lüge°. Ja, — *lie*
10 es war eine Lüge, denn wir standen alle schon auf der Liste.)

Die SS-Frauen wurden immer böser. So verging° ein Tag um den — *passed* anderen. Täglich warf man Frauen in den Bunker, und sie kamen nicht mehr zurück. So ging es wochenlang.

Die Tage wurden nun schon länger und manchesmal war es nicht
15 mehr so kalt. Ich, Mama, Kathi, Chiwe mit Burli und Rupa mußten in die Waschküche. Wir machten dort unsere Arbeit und als wir zurückkamen, sahen wir, wie zwei Häftlinge° einen Bretterwagen° vor unsere — *inmates / wooden wagon* Baracke zogen. Viele Frauen waren darauf, wie Schweine lagen sie übereinander. Ganz oben lag unsere kleine liebe Resi. Sie waren
20 sterilisiert worden, alle hatten große Schmerzen, sie konnten nicht einmal ein einziges Wort sagen. Die kleine Resi starb° gleich, auch die anderen — *died*

kamen nicht mehr durch. Alle waren tot. Die SS-Frauen sagten dann zu
uns: „Ihr braucht keine Angst zu haben, der Oberarzt hat ein neues
Gerät bekommen, das alte hatte einen Kurzschluß°, also ein Versehen°."   *short circuit / accident*

25 Wir wußten ganz genau, daß sie uns nur besänftigen° wollten, aber wir   *quiet*
wußten auch, daß wir ihnen nicht entkommen°. Eines Tages kamen   *escape*
Binz und Rabl und holten Mama, Kathi und mich ab. Sie sprachen
nicht viel und sagten nur: „Marsch, Marsch". Wir gingen sehr schnell.
In diesem Moment war uns alles egal. Wir kamen zu einem richtigen

30 Haus. Es ging stockaufwärts. Die SS-Frauen machten im Vorraum dem
Oberarzt ihre Meldung°. Nun warteten wir. Mama zeigte uns mit ihren   *report*
blauen Augen, daß wir mutig° sein sollten, sprechen durften wir ja   *brave*
nicht. Die Zeit verging und es geschah nichts. Plötzlich kam der
Oberarzt und sagte: „Heute ist nichts mehr, wir haben leider keinen

35 Strom." Er schaute uns mit großen Augen an und machte seine Tür zu.
Zwei SS-Frauen brachten uns wieder in das Lager zurück. Unterwegs
sahen wir eine Baracke. Drinnen waren viele Frauen mit Schreibma-
schinen. Das war die Schreibstube. Nun waren wir wieder in unserer
Baracke. Alle fragten, was geschehen war, und alle Frauen weinten

40 vor Freude.
       Mama sagte: „*O swundo Dell gamel awer wariso de gerel amenza.*"
(Der liebe Gott hat was anderes mit uns vor.)

A. Wie wurden Ceja und ihre Familie durch die Rassenpolitik der Nazis
betroffen?

B. Welche Erfahrungen beschreibt die Autorin?

1. Die SS-Frauen versprachen den Häftlingen, wenn sie sich freiwillig
sterilisieren lassen, …

   a. bekommen sie besseres Essen.

   b. brauchen sie eine Woche nicht zu arbeiten.

   c. werden sie bald freigelassen.

2. Der Sterilisationsprozess im Lager war …

   a. freiwillig.

   b. ein medizinisches Experiment.

   c. eine Gesundheitsmaßnahme (*health precaution*).

3. Die Autorin erinnert sich daran, dass sie im Konzentrationslager …

   a. zur Schule ging.

   b. in der Waschküche arbeitete.

   c. auf der Schreibstube arbeitete.

4. Die ersten Frauen, die sterilisiert wurden …

   a. starben an den Folgen der Sterilisation.

   b. kamen nie in die Baracken zurück.

   c. durften nach Hause gehen.

5. Die Autorin wurde nicht sterilisiert, weil …

   a. der Oberarzt Mitleid (*sympathy*) mit ihr hatte.

   b. man sie in der Waschküche brauchte.

   c. es keine Elektrizität gab.

Auf den ersten Blick 2

Im Frühjahr 1947 reiste der ehemalige Präsident Herbert Hoover nach Deutschland und Österreich, um die katastrophale Ernährungssituation zu untersuchen (*investigate*). Das Resultat war die Hoover-Speisung für Schulkinder in beiden Ländern. Kinder schickten Hoover Hunderte von Briefen, um ihm für seine Hilfe zu danken. Sie lesen hier zwei dieser Briefe, die jetzt in den Archiven des Hoover Instituts in Stanford, Kalifornien, gesammelt sind.

Überfliegen Sie die zwei Briefe kurz.

A. Wer hat die Briefe geschrieben? (Namen und ungefähres Alter)

B. Aus welchem Jahr stammen die Briefe?

C. Wie reden (*address*) die Kinder Herbert Hoover an? Wie enden ihre Briefe?

DANK
FÜR ALLE SPENDEN
AUS AMERIKA!
DIE DANKBAREN
KINDER AUS
WIEN.

BRIEFE AN HERBERT HOOVER

THE HERBERT HOOVER ARCHIVES

Eckernförde, den 26.3.47.
Lieber Onkel Hoover!
Ich habe Dich neulich im Kino gesehen und da Du so lieb und gut aussiehst, will ich Dir heute schreiben. Wir sind aus Oberschlesien hierher gekommen und haben dort unsre schönen Sachen lassen müssen.

Giebt es in Aberika schon Puppen mit langen Haaren zu kaufen? Wir sind so oft allein, weil unsre Mutti nach Brot anstehen muß. Werden bei euch alle Leute satt? Nun willst Du uns ja hier helfen in Deutschland. Viele Grüße, von Heike Leopold.

Margot Fränkel

Bayreuth, den 28.9.1947.

Sehr geehrter Herr Hoover!

Wir freuten uns sehr, als uns ver-
kündet[1] wurde, daß alle die Auslands
speisen bekommen. Denn es wurde
durch Wägen und Messen festgestellt,[2]
daß viele unterernährt[3] sind. Wir
sind schon immer auf die Minute
gespannt,[4] wenn es läutet[5] und wir
unser Essen bekommen. Heute gibt
es Teigwaren[6] mit Obsttunke.[7] Wenn
manchmal ein Rest übrig bleibt,
freuen wir uns am meisten, wenn
wir es bekommen. Es gibt jetzt schon
2½ Wochen Essen. Am meisten aber
freuen wir uns, wenn es am Ende
der Wochen Eiscrempaste gibt. Als es
das erstemal die Auslandsspeisen gab,

bekamen wir am Ende der Woche
eine Tafel Schokolade. Wir mußten
sie gleich anbeißen,[8] damit wir nicht
Schwarzhandel treiben.[9] Jeder geht jetzt
gerne in die Schule.
Ich danke Ihnen nochmals dafür,
für die guten Gaben.[10]
Mit dankbarem Gruß
eine ergebene Schülerin
Margot Fränkel

[1]announced [2]es ... it was found by weighing and measuring [3]malnourished [4]eager [5]the bell rings [6]noodles [7]fruit syrup [8]bite into it [9]Schwarzhandel ... deal on the black market [10]gifts

1. Was erfahren wir über die Folgen (*consequences*) des Krieges für die Kinder?

2. Welche Probleme erwähnen die Kinder? Wer schreibt davon, dass

- die meisten Kinder unterernährt sind?
- die Kinder wissen, wie man Schwarzhandel treibt?
- die Familie aus ihrer Heimat geflüchtet (*fled*) ist?
- sie oft allein ist, weil die Mutter nach Brot anstehen muss?

KULTURTIPP

Der Weg nach Europa

Nach dem Zweiten Weltkrieg beschlossen einige europäische Länder, internationale Konflikte in Zukunft durch Zusammenarbeit und Gemeinschaft zu lösen anstatt durch Gewalt. Dies begann mit der wirtschaftlichen Zusammenarbeit von sechs Staaten, die 1957 die Europäische Wirtschaftsgemeinschaft (EWG) gründeten. Die Europäische Union (EU) wurde dann 1993 durch den Maastrichter Vertrag gegründet. Dieser Vertrag bahnte den Weg zur weiteren europäischen Integration.

Die Mitgliedstaaten planten in vielen Bereichen zusammenzuarbeiten, z.B. in Sicherheitspolitik, Justiz und Wirtschaft. Eine gemeinsame Währung, der Euro, wurde am 1. Januar 1999 eingeführt. Allerdings begannen die Länder erst am 1. Januar 2002, den Euro im täglichen Gebrauch zu benutzen.

Belgien, Dänemark, Deutschland, Frankreich, Griechenland, Großbritannien, Irland, Italien, Luxemburg, die Niederlande, Portugal und Spanien waren die ersten Länder der EU. Finnland, Österreich und Schweden wurden 1995 Mitgliedstaaten. Im Jahr 2004 traten noch mehr Länder der EU bei: Estland, Lettland, Litauen, Malta, Polen, die Slowakei, Slowenien, die Tschechische Republik, Ungarn und Zypern.

Wie sieht die Zukunft der EU aus? Wie viele andere Länder wollen der EU noch beitreten? Wird die Integration der europäischen Länder erfolgreich sein? Das sind Fragen, die die Zukunft beantworten wird.

Europa Europa

Suchen Sie die Informationen im Text und beantworten Sie die Fragen:

1. Warum wurde die EU gegründet?
2. Welcher Vertrag signalisierte die Gründung der EU?
3. Wann wurde der Euro im täglichen Gebrauch in den Ländern der EU eingeführt?

Kulturtipp. Follow-up: Have students research the practical results of European integration in citizens' lives. What does being a European citizen mean for young Germans and Austrians in terms of travel, job opportunities, residence, and voting rights?

Zu guter Letzt

Die Welt im Jahre 2050

Wie wird die Welt im Jahre 2050 aussehen? Wie wird sich Ihr Leben ändern?

Schritt 1: Was sind Ihre Hoffnungen für die Zunkuft? Ihre Erwartungen, Phantasien und auch Ihre Ängste? Zwei Studenten/Studentinnen sammeln die Ideen aller Kursmitglieder und schreiben sie an die Tafel oder auf eine Folie (*transparency*).

Schritt 2: Arbeiten Sie zu dritt, um Ihre Vorstellung von der Welt im Jahre 2050 zu präsentieren. Wählen Sie aus den Erwartungen, Phantasien und eventuell auch Ängsten Ihrer Mitstudenten/Mitstudentinnen ein Thema und machen Sie Ihre Vorstellung so kreativ wie möglich, z.B. mit Bildern, Postern oder als PowerPoint Präsentation.

Schritt 3: Präsentieren Sie Ihre Ideen der Klasse. Die anderen machen sich Notizen und stellen drei Fragen.

Schritt 4: Wie wird die Welt im Jahre 2050 persönlich auf Sie wirken? Schreiben Sie einen Aufsatz mit dem Titel: „1. Januar 2050 – Ein Tag in meinem Leben".

Sprache im Kontext

Videoclips

 Video

Hören Sie das Interview mit Herrn Borowsky und schauen Sie sich gleichzeitig die Bilder an. Er spricht über die Kriegszeit, Berlin in Trümmern, den Bau der Mauer, den Fall der Mauer und die Wiedervereinigung.

A. Die Kriegszeit. Beantworten Sie die Fragen.

1. Wann ist Herr Borowsky geboren?

2. Wann musste er Soldat werden?

3. In welchen Ländern war er stationiert?

4. Wann ist er dann zurückgekommen?

B. Berlin in Trümmern. Schauen Sie sich diesen Teil noch einmal an und ergänzen Sie diese kurze Zusammenfassung.

Herr Borowsky kannte Berlin, wie es in _____ lag. 1943 war das meiste _____. Durch die Endkämpfe war noch mehr _____. Er war erschüttert aber darauf _____. Er hat Arbeit in seinem erlernten Beruf als _____ bekommen. Damals gab es die _____ von Westberlin und es gab wenig _____ und die _____ haben nicht gearbeitet. Daher ist er zur _____ gegangen und war _____ Jahre Polizeibeamter.

C. Als die Mauer gebaut wurde. Warum war Herr Borowsky von dem Bau der Mauer nicht so betroffen?

D. Als die Mauer fiel. Bringen Sie die Aussagen von Herrn Borowsky in die richtige chronologische Reihenfolge.

1. _____ Er sagte seiner Frau, „Du, die Mauer ist auf."

2. _____ Er ist mit der U-Bahn in den Osten gefahren. An der Grenze waren die Volkspolizisten überfreundlich und sehr behilflich.

3. _____ Er war zu Hause und hat alles im Fernsehen verfolgt.

4. _____ Herr Borowsky hat gesehen, wie viele vom Osten in den Westen mit ihren Trabbis gefahren sind.

E. Die Wiedervereinigung und Berlin. Beantworten Sie die Fragen.

1. Wie beantwortet Herr Borowsky die Frage des Interviewers: „Glauben Sie, dass Ost und West gut wieder zusammengefunden haben?"

2. Was für ein Gefühl hat Herr Borowsky, wenn er heute durch Berlin geht?

Appendix A: Hin und her, Part 2

Einführung

Aktivität 13 Hin und her°: Wie ist die Postleitzahl?

back and forth

This is the first of many activities in which you will exchange information with a partner. Take turns asking each other for the postal codes missing from your charts.

BEISPIEL: s1: Wie ist die Postleitzahl von Bitburg?
s2: D-54634. Wie ist die Postleitzahl von Salzburg?
s1: A-5020.

D-54634	Bitburg
A-5020	Salzburg
CH-3800	Interlaken
D-94315	Straubing
D-06217	Merseburg
D-21614	Buxtehude
FL-9490	Vaduz
D-99817	Eisenach

Kapitel 2

BEISPIEL 3 Wie und wie oft machen Sie das gern?

Find out what the following people like to do or don't like to do by asking your partner.

BEISPIEL: s1: Was macht Denise gern?
 s2: Sie reist gern. Was macht Thomas nicht gern?
 s1: Er fährt nicht gern Auto.

	GERN	NICHT GERN
Thomas		
Denise	reisen	kochen
Niko		
Anja	laufen	Bier trinken
Sie		
Ihr Partner / Ihre Partnerin		

Kapitel 3

relationships

Ask a partner questions about Bernd's family. How is each person related to Bernd?

BEISPIEL: s1: Wie ist Gisela mit Bernd verwandt?
 s2: Gisela ist Bernds Tante.
 s1: Wie alt ist sie denn?
 s2: Sie ist 53.
 s1: Wann hat sie Geburtstag?
 s2: Im Februar.

PERSON	VERWANDTSCHAFT	ALTER	GEBURTSTAG
Gisela	Tante	53	Februar
Alexandra			
Christoph	Schwager	36	Dezember
Andreas			
Sabine	Kusine	19	August

Kapitel 4

Aktivität 5 Hin und her: Zwei Stundenpläne

Schritt 1: Sven und Frank sind 18 Jahre alt und gehen aufs Gymnasium (*secondary school*). Vergleichen Sie ihre Stundenpläne. Welche Kurse haben sie zusammen (*together*)?

BEISPIEL: s1: Welchen Kurs hat Frank montags um acht?
          s2: Montags um acht hat Frank Informatik. Welchen Kurs hat Sven montags um acht?
          s1: Montags um acht hat Sven Englisch.

Schritt 2: Sven und Frank möchten Tennis spielen. Wann ist die beste Zeit? Wann haben sie beide frei?

Zeit	Montag	Dienstag	Mittwoch	Donnerstag	Freitag	Samstag
8 – 8⁴⁵	Informatik	Physik	Kunst	Englisch	frei	Deutsch
8⁴⁵ – 9³⁰	Informatik	Physik	Kunst	Englisch	frei	Deutsch
9³⁵ – 10²⁰	Religion	Deutsch	Mathematik	Geschichte	Sozialkunde	
10⁴⁰ – 11²⁵	Religion	Mathematik	Deutsch	Mathematik	Deutsch	
11³⁰ – 12¹⁵	Erdkunde	frei	Sozialkunde	Erdkunde	Geschichte	
12¹⁵ – 13⁰⁰	Mathematik	Englisch	Physik	Informatik	frei	
13¹⁵ – 14⁰⁰			Sport			
14⁰⁰ – 14⁴⁵			Sport			

Franks Stundenplan

Kapitel 6

Fragen Sie Ihren Partner / Ihre Partnerin, warum die folgenden Leute nicht
da waren.

BEISPIEL: s1: Warum war Andreas gestern Vormittag nicht in der Vorlesung?
s2: Er hatte keine Lust.

PERSON	WANN	WO	WARUM
Andreas	gestern Vormittag	in der Vorlesung	keine Lust haben
Anke			arbeiten müssen
Frank	gestern Abend	auf der Party	
Yeliz			schlafen wollen
Mario	Samstag	im Café	
Ihr Partner / Ihre Partnerin			

Kapitel 7

Wer hat was gemacht? Arbeiten Sie zu zweit.

BEISPIEL: s1: Was hat Dagmar gemacht?
s2: Sie ist ins Alte Land gefahren.

WER	WAS
Dagmar	ins Alte Land fahren
Thomas	
Jürgen	zu Hause bleiben
Stefanie	
Susanne	bis 11 Uhr schlafen
Felix und Sabine	
die Kinder	Schlittschuh laufen

Kapitel 8

Aktivität 8 Hin und her: Meine Routine – deine Routine

Jeder hat eine andere Routine. Was machen diese Leute und in welcher Reihenfolge? Machen Sie es auch so?

BEISPIEL: s1: Was macht Alexander morgens?
      s2: Zuerst rasiert er sich und putzt sich die Zähne. Dann kämmt er sich. Danach setzt er sich an den Tisch und frühstückt.

WER	WAS ER/SIE MORGENS MACHT
Alexander	zuerst / sich rasieren / sich die Zähne putzen dann / sich kämmen danach / sich an den Tisch setzen / frühstücken
Elke	zuerst / sich anziehen dann / sich die Zähne putzen danach / sich kämmen
Tilo	zuerst / sich duschen / sich rasieren dann / sich an den Tisch setzen / frühstücken danach / sich die Zähne putzen
Kamal	zuerst / sich das Gesicht waschen dann / frühstücken danach / sich rasieren / sich anziehen
Sie	zuerst / ? dann / ? danach / ?
Ihr Partner / *Ihre Partnerin*	zuerst / ? dann / ? danach / ?

unfamiliar

Sie sind in einer fremden Stadt. Fragen Sie nach dem Weg. Benutzen Sie die Tabelle unten.

BEISPIEL: s1: Ist das Landesmuseum weit von hier?
s2: Es ist sechs Kilometer von hier, bei der Universität.
s1: Wie komme ich am besten dahin?
s2: Nehmen Sie die Buslinie 7, am Rathaus.

WOHIN?	WIE WEIT?	WO?	WIE?
Landesmuseum	6 km	bei der Universität	Buslinie 7, am Rathaus
Bahnhof			
Post	nicht weit	in der Nähe vom Bahnhof	zu Fuß
Schloss			
Opernhaus	ganz in der Nähe	rechts um die Ecke	zu Fuß, die Poststraße entlang

Fragen Sie einen Partner / eine Partnerin nach den fehlenden Informationen.

BEISPIEL: s1: Was gibt es beim Gasthof zum Bären?
s2: Warme Küche.
s1: Was gibt es sonst noch?
s2: Bayerische Spezialitäten.

WO?	WAS?	WAS SONST NOCH?
Gasthof zum Bären	Küche / warm	Spezialitäten / bayerisch
Gasthof Adlersberg		
Gasthaus Schneiderwirt	Hausmusik / originell	Gästezimmer / rustikal
Hotel Luitpold		
Restaurant Ökogarten	Gerichte / vegetarisch	Bier / alkoholfrei

Kapitel 10

Aktivität 3 Hin und her: Was nehmen sie mit?

Wohin fahren diese Leute im Urlaub? Was nehmen sie mit? Und warum?
Ergänzen Sie die Informationen.

BEISPIEL: s1: Wohin fährt Angelika Meier in Urlaub?
  s2: Sie fährt in die Türkei.
  s1: Warum fährt sie in die Türkei?
  s2: Weil ...
  s1: Was nimmt sie mit?
  s2: Sie nimmt ...

PERSONEN	WOHIN?	WARUM?	WAS NIMMT ER/SIE MIT?
Angelika Meier	in die Türkei	sich am Strand erholen	Buch, Sonnenbrille, Badesachen
Peter Bayer	auf die Insel Rügen	Windsurfen gehen	Sonnenschutzmittel, Badehose
Roland Metz	nach Thüringen	wandern, Weimar besichtigen	Stadtpläne, Reiseführer, Wanderschuhe
Sabine Graf	nach Griechenland	eine Studienreise machen	Reiseführer, Wörterbuch, Kamera

Übung 3 Hin und her: Wie war der Urlaub?

Herr Ignaz Huber aus München war drei Wochen im Urlaub in Norddeutschland. Er war zwei Tage in Hamburg, eine Woche in Cuxhaven und nicht ganz zwei Wochen auf der Insel Sylt. Stellen Sie Ihrem Partner / Ihrer Partnerin Fragen über seinen Urlaub. Benutzen Sie den Superlativ.

BEISPIEL: s1: Wo war es am wärmsten?
  s2: Am wärmsten war es in Cuxhaven.

	IN HAMBURG	IN CUXHAVEN	AUF DER INSEL SYLT
1. *Wo war es (kalt/warm)?*	20°C	25°C	15°C
2. *Wo waren die Hotelpreise (günstig/teuer)?*	150 Euro	90 Euro mit Halbpension	200 Euro
3. *Wo hat es (viel) geregnet?*	zwei Tage	einen Tag	fünf Tage
4. *Wo war das Hotelpersonal (freundlich)?*	freundlich	sehr freundlich	unfreundlich
5. *Wo war der Strand (schön)?*	kein Strand	sehr sauber, angenehm	zu windig
6. *Wo hat das Essen (gut) geschmeckt?*	ziemlich gut	nicht besonders	ausgezeichnet

Aktivität 2 Hin und her: Wer macht was, und warum?

Ergänzen Sie die Informationen.

BEISPIEL: s1: Was macht Corinna Eichhorn?
s2: Sie ist Sozialarbeiterin.
s1: Warum macht sie das?
s2: Weil ...

NAME	BERUF	WARUM?
Corinna Eichhorn	Sozialarbeiterin	Menschen helfen
Karsten Becker	Bibliothekar	sich für Bücher interessieren
Erika Lentz		
Alex Böhmer	Informatiker	mit Computern arbeiten

famous

Aktivität 3 Hin und her: Berühmte Personen

Diese berühmten Menschen, die alle einen Beruf ausübten, hatten auch andere Interessen. Ergänzen Sie die Informationen.

BEISPIEL: s1: Was war Martin Luther von Beruf?
s2: Er war Priester.
s1: Was für andere Interessen hatte er?
s2: Er interessierte sich für Literatur, Musik und die deutsche Sprache.

NAME	BERUF	INTERESSEN
Martin Luther	Priester	Literatur, Musik, die deutsche Sprache
Käthe Kollwitz		
Bertha von Suttner	Schriftstellerin	die europäische Friedensbewegung (*peace movement*)
Rainer Werner Fassbinder		
Marlene Dietrich	Schauspielerin	Ski fahren
Willi Brandt		

Kapitel 12

Aktivität 6 Hin und her: Eine neue Wohnung

Diese Leute haben entweder eine neue Wohnung oder ein neues Haus gekauft. Wer hat was gekauft? Wie viele Stockwerke gibt es? Wie groß ist das Wohnzimmer? Wie viele WCs oder Badezimmer gibt es?

BEISPIEL: s1: Was für eine Wohnung hat Bettina Neuendorf gekauft?
s2: Eine Eigentumswohnung.
s1: Wie viele Stockwerke hat die Wohnung?
s2: Eins.
s1: Und wie viele Schlafzimmer? ...

PERSON	TYP	STOCKWERKE	SCHLAFZIMMER	WOHNZIMMER	WC/BAD
Bettina Neuendorf	Eigentums-wohnung	eins	eins, aber auch ein kleines Gästezimmer	mit Esszimmer kombiniert 30 Quadratmeter	eins
Uwe und Marion Baumgärtner	Haus	zwei	drei: Elternschlaf-zimmer, Kinder-schlafzimmer, Gästezimmer	sehr groß mit Balkon 37 Quadratmeter	zwei Badezim-mer: eins im Dachgeschoss und eins im Erdgeschoss
Sven Kersten	Eigentums-wohnung	zwei	zwei, eins als Gästezimmer benutzt	mit Esszimmer zusammen 35 Quadratmeter, Balkon vom Wohnzimmer	zwei, ein WC und ein Bad
Carola Schubärth	Haus	eins	zwei: ein Schlaf-zimmer ist Arbeitszimmer	klein 25 Quadratmeter	ein Bad

Wie informieren sich diese Personen? Was lesen sie zur Unterhaltung? Stellen Sie Fragen an Ihren Partner / Ihre Partnerin.

BEISPIEL: s1: Was sieht Martin gern im Fernsehen? Was liest er oft?
s2: Er _____.

PERSON	FERNSEHSHOWS	ZEITUNGEN UND ZEITSCHRIFTEN
Martin	Talkshows und Dokumentarfilme	*die Zeit*
Stephanie	klassische Spielfilme und Komödien	*der Spiegel*
Patrick		
Kristin	Sportsendungen, Krimi-Serien wie „Die Rosenheim-Cops"	die *Süddeutsche Zeitung* und *Brigitte*
Mein Partner / Meine Partnerin		

Sie möchten erfahren, wer was und wann erfunden hat. Arbeiten Sie zu zweit.

BEISPIELE: s1: Wer hat _____ erfunden?
s2: _____.
s1: Wann hat er / sie es erfunden?
s2: (Im Jahre) _____.
[oder:] s1: Was hat _____ erfunden?
s2: Er / Sie hat _____ erfunden.
s1: In welchem Jahr?
s2: (Im Jahre) _____.

PERSON	ERFINDUNG	DATUM
Johannes Gutenberg	der Buchdruck mit beweglichen Lettern (*movable type*)	um 1450
Daniel Gabriel Fahrenheit	das Alkoholthermometer	1709
	das Fahrrad (Draisine)	
Herta Heuwer	Currywurst	1949
Gottlieb Daimler		
	der Dieselmotor	
Wilhelm Conrad Röntgen	Röntgenstrahlen (*X rays*)	1895
Melitta Bentz		1908

Kapitel 14

Aktivität 1 Hin und her: Probleme und Lösungen

Stellen Sie Ihrem Partner / Ihrer Partnerin Fragen zu den folgenden Problemen, um herauszufinden, welche möglichen Lösungen es gibt.

BEISPIEL: s1: Was kann man gegen Krieg tun?
s2: Man kann an Antikriegsdemonstrationen teilnehmen.

PROBLEME	MÖGLICHE LÖSUNGEN
Krieg	an Antikriegsdemonstrationen teilnehmen
Inflation	die Ausgaben der Regierung kontrollieren
Drogensucht	Informationen über die Gefahren von Drogen verbreiten
Umweltverschmutzung	alternative Energiequellen (*energy sources*) entwickeln
Verletzung der Menschenrechte	Organisationen wie Amnesty International unterstützen
Obdachlosigkeit	neue Wohnungen bauen
Arbeitslosigkeit	Arbeiter umschulen

Übung 6 Hin und her: Zwei umweltbewusste Städte

In zwei Städten, Altstadt und Neustadt, wird für eine bessere Umwelt gesorgt.

BEISPIEL: s1: Was ist zuerst in Altstadt gemacht worden?
s2: Zuerst sind Autos aus der Innenstadt verbannt worden. Und in Neustadt?
s1: Zuerst sind naturnahe Gärten angelegt worden.

	ALTSTADT	NEUSTADT
zuerst	Autos aus der Innenstadt verbannen	naturnahe Gärten anlegen
dann	neue Siedlungen am Stadtrand bauen	Kinderspielplätze verbessern
danach	Bürger über Umweltschutz informieren	Park im Zentrum säubern
schließlich	neue, moderne Busse kaufen	keine Wegwerfartikel in Geschäften verkaufen
zuletzt	ein großes Umweltfest in der Innenstadt feiern	nach Alternativenergie suchen

Appendix B

Studienfächer

Anthropologie	anthropology
Architektur	architecture
Astronomie	astronomy
Bauingenieurwesen	structural engineering
Betriebswirtschaftslehre	business administration
Bibliothekswissenschaft	library science
Biochemie	biochemistry
Biologie	biology
Chemie	chemistry
Elektrotechnik	electrical engineering
Ernährungswissenschaft	nutritional science
Forstwissenschaft	forestry
Geographie/Erdkunde	geography
Geologie	geology
Geophysik	geophysics
Germanistik	German Studies
Geschichte/Geschichtswissenschaft	history
Informatik	computer science
Journalistik/Publizistik	journalism
Kerntechnik/Reaktortechnik	nuclear engineering
Kunstgeschichte	art history
Maschinenbau	mechanical engineering
Mathematik	mathematics
Medizin	medicine
Musik	music
Pädagogik	education
Pharmakologie/Pharmazie	pharmacology
Philosophie	philosophy
Physik	physics
Politikwissenschaft	political science
Psychologie	psychology
Rechtswissenschaft/Jura	law
Sport	physical education
Sprachwissenschaft/Linguistik	linguistics
Städtebau/Stadtplanung	urban planning
Statistik	statistics
Theaterwissenschaft	dramatic arts
Theologie	theology
Tiermedizin	veterinary science
Volkswirtschaftslehre	economics
Zahnmedizin	dentistry

Appendix C

Grammar Tables

1. Personal Pronouns

	SINGULAR					PLURAL		
Nominative	ich	du / Sie	er	sie	es	wir	ihr / Sie	sie
Accusative	mich	dich / Sie	ihn	sie	es	uns	euch / Sie	sie
Dative	mir	dir / Ihnen	ihm	ihr	ihm	uns	euch / Ihnen	ihnen

2. Definite Articles

	SINGULAR			PLURAL
	Masculine	*Neuter*	*Feminine*	*All genders*
Nominative	der	das	die	die
Accusative	den	das	die	die
Dative	dem	dem	der	den
Genitive	des	des	der	der

Words declined like the definite article: **jeder, dieser, welcher**

3. Indefinite Articles and the Negative Article kein

	SINGULAR			PLURAL
	Masculine	*Neuter*	*Feminine*	*All genders*
Nominative	(k)ein	(k)ein	(k)eine	keine
Accusative	(k)einen	(k)ein	(k)eine	keine
Dative	(k)einem	(k)einem	(k)einer	keinen
Genitive	(k)eines	(k)eines	(k)einer	keiner

Words declined like the indefinite article: all possessive adjectives (**mein, dein, sein, ihr, unser, euer, Ihr**)

4. Relative and Demonstrative Pronouns

	SINGULAR			PLURAL
	Masculine	*Neuter*	*Feminine*	*All genders*
Nominative	der	das	die	die
Accusative	den	das	die	die
Dative	dem	dem	der	denen
Genitive	dessen	dessen	deren	deren

5. Principal Parts of Strong and Mixed Verbs

The following is a list of the most important strong and mixed verbs that are used in this book. Included in this list are the modal auxiliaries. Since the principal parts of compound verbs follow the forms of the base verb, compound verbs are generally not included, except for a few high-frequency compound verbs whose base verb is not commonly used. Thus you will find **anfangen** and **einladen** listed, but not **zurückkommen** or **ausgehen**.

INFINITIVE	(3RD PERS. SG. PRESENT)	SIMPLE PAST	PAST PARTICIPLE	MEANING
anbieten		bot an	angeboten	*to offer*
anfangen	(fängt an)	fing an	angefangen	*to begin*
backen		backte	gebacken	*to bake*
beginnen		begann	begonnen	*to begin*
begreifen		begriff	begriffen	*to comprehend*
beißen		biss	gebissen	*to bite*
bitten		bat	gebeten	*to ask, beg*
bleiben		blieb	(ist) geblieben	*to stay*
bringen		brachte	gebracht	*to bring*
denken		dachte	gedacht	*to think*
dürfen	(darf)	durfte	gedurft	*to be allowed to*
einladen	(lädt ein)	lud ein	eingeladen	*to invite*
empfehlen	(empfiehlt)	empfahl	empfohlen	*to recommend*
entscheiden		entschied	entschieden	*to decide*
essen	(isst)	aß	gegessen	*to eat*
fahren	(fährt)	fuhr	(ist) gefahren	*to drive*
fallen	(fällt)	fiel	(ist) gefallen	*to fall*
finden		fand	gefunden	*to find*
fliegen		flog	(ist) geflogen	*to fly*
geben	(gibt)	gab	gegeben	*to give*
gefallen	(gefällt)	gefiel	gefallen	*to like; to please*
gehen		ging	(ist) gegangen	*to go*
genießen		genoss	genossen	*to enjoy*
geschehen	(geschieht)	geschah	(ist) geschehen	*to happen*
gewinnen		gewann	gewonnen	*to win*

INFINITIVE	(3RD PERS. SG. PRESENT)	SIMPLE PAST	PAST PARTICIPLE	MEANING
haben	(hat)	hatte	gehabt	*to have*
halten	(hält)	hielt	gehalten	*to hold; to stop*
hängen		hing	gehangen	*to hang*
heißen		hieß	geheißen	*to be called*
helfen	(hilft)	half	geholfen	*to help*
kennen		kannte	gekannt	*to know*
kommen		kam	(ist) gekommen	*to come*
können	(kann)	konnte	gekonnt	*can; to be able to*
lassen	(lässt)	ließ	gelassen	*to let; to allow (to)*
laufen	(läuft)	lief	(ist) gelaufen	*to run*
leihen		lieh	geliehen	*to lend; to borrow*
lesen	(liest)	las	gelesen	*to read*
liegen		lag	gelegen	*to lie*
mögen	(mag)	mochte	gemocht	*to like (to)*
müssen	(muss)	musste	gemusst	*must; to have to*
nehmen	(nimmt)	nahm	genommen	*to take*
nennen		nannte	genannt	*to name*
raten	(rät)	riet	geraten	*to advise*
reiten		ritt	(ist) geritten	*to ride*
scheinen		schien	geschienen	*to seem; to shine*
schlafen	(schläft)	schlief	geschlafen	*to sleep*
schließen		schloss	geschlossen	*to close*
schreiben		schrieb	geschrieben	*to write*
schwimmen		schwamm	(ist) geschwommen	*to swim*
sehen	(sieht)	sah	gesehen	*to see*
sein	(ist)	war	(ist) gewesen	*to be*
singen		sang	gesungen	*to sing*
sitzen		saß	gesessen	*to sit*
sollen	(soll)	sollte	gesollt	*should, ought to; to be supposed to*
sprechen	(spricht)	sprach	gesprochen	*to speak*
stehen		stand	gestanden	*to stand*
steigen		stieg	ist gestiegen	*to rise; to climb*
sterben	(stirbt)	starb	(ist) gestorben	*to die*
tragen	(trägt)	trug	getragen	*to carry; to wear*
treffen	(trifft)	traf	getroffen	*to meet*
trinken		trank	getrunken	*to drink*
tun		tat	getan	*to do*
umsteigen		stieg um	(ist) umgestiegen	*to change; to transfer*
vergessen	(vergisst)	vergaß	vergessen	*to forget*
vergleichen		verglich	verglichen	*to compare*
verlieren		verlor	verloren	*to lose*
wachsen	(wächst)	wuchs	(ist) gewachsen	*to grow*
waschen	(wäscht)	wusch	gewaschen	*to wash*
werden	(wird)	wurde	(ist) geworden	*to become*
wissen	(weiß)	wusste	gewusst	*to know*
wollen	(will)	wollte	gewollt	*to want (to)*
ziehen		zog	(ist/hat) gezogen	*to move; to pull*

6. Conjugation of Verbs

In the charts that follow, the pronoun **Sie** (*you*) is listed with the third-person plural **sie** (*they*).

Present Tense

Auxiliary Verbs

	sein	**haben**	**werden**
ich	bin	habe	werde
du	bist	hast	wirst
er/sie/es	ist	hat	wird
wir	sind	haben	werden
ihr	seid	habt	werdet
sie/Sie	sind	haben	werden

Regular Verbs, Verbs with Vowel Changes, Irregular Verbs

	REGULAR		**VOWEL CHANGE**		**IRREGULAR**
	fragen	**finden**	**geben**	**fahren**	**wissen**
ich	frage	finde	gebe	fahre	weiß
du	fragst	findest	gibst	fährst	weißt
er/sie/es	fragt	findet	gibt	fährt	weiß
wir	fragen	finden	geben	fahren	wissen
ihr	fragt	findet	gebt	fahrt	wisst
sie/Sie	fragen	finden	geben	fahren	wissen

Simple Past Tense

Auxiliary Verbs

	sein	**haben**	**werden**
ich	war	hatte	wurde
du	warst	hattest	wurdest
er/sie/es	war	hatte	wurde
wir	waren	hatten	wurden
ihr	wart	hattet	wurdet
sie/Sie	waren	hatten	wurden

	WEAK	STRONG		MIXED
	fragen	**geben**	**fahren**	**wissen**
ich	fragte	gab	fuhr	wusste
du	fragtest	gabst	fuhrst	wusstest
er/sie/es	fragte	gab	fuhr	wusste
wir	fragten	gaben	fuhren	wussten
ihr	fragtet	gabt	fuhrt	wusstet
sie/Sie	fragten	gaben	fuhren	wussten

Present Perfect Tense

	sein	**haben**	**geben**	**fahren**
ich	bin	habe	habe	bin
du	bist	hast	hast	bist
er/sie/es	ist	hat	hat	ist
wir	sind ⎱ gewesen	haben ⎱ gehabt	haben ⎱ gegeben	sind ⎱ gefahren
ihr	seid	habt	habt	seid
sie/Sie	sind	haben	haben	sind

Past Perfect Tense

	sein	**haben**	**geben**	**fahren**
ich	war	hatte	hatte	war
du	warst	hattest	hattest	warst
er/sie/es	war	hatte	hatte	war
wir	waren ⎱ gewesen	hatten ⎱ gehabt	hatten ⎱ gegeben	waren ⎱ gefahren
ihr	wart	hattet	hattet	wart
sie/Sie	waren	hatten	hatten	waren

Future Tense

	geben
ich	werde
du	wirst
er/sie/es	wird ⎱ geben
wir	werden
ihr	werdet
sie/Sie	werden

Subjunctive

Present Tense: Subjunctive I (Indirect Discourse Subjunctive)

	sein	haben	werden	fahren	wissen
ich	sei	—	—	—	wisse
du	sei(e)st	habest	—	—	—
er/sie/es	sei	habe	werde	fahre	wisse
wir	seien	—	—	—	—
ihr	sei(e)t	habet	—	—	—
sie/Sie	seien	—	—	—	—

For those forms left blank in the chart above, the subjunctive II forms are preferred in indirect discourse.

Present Tense: Subjunctive II

	fragen	sein	haben	werden	fahren	wissen
ich	fragte	wäre	hätte	würde	führe	wüsste
du	fragtest	wär(e)st	hättest	würdest	führ(e)st	wüsstest
er/sie/es	fragte	wäre	hätte	würde	führe	wüsste
wir	fragten	wären	hätten	würden	führen	wüssten
ihr	fragtet	wär(e)t	hättet	würdet	führ(e)t	wüsstet
sie/Sie	fragten	wären	hätten	würden	führen	wüssten

Past Tense: Subjunctive I (Indirect Discourse)

	fahren	wissen
ich	sei	—
du	sei(e)st	habest
er/sie/es	sei } gefahren	habe } gewusst
wir	seien	—
ihr	sei(e)t	habet
sie/Sie	sei(e)n	—

Past Tense: Subjunctive II

	sein	geben	fahren
ich	wäre	hätte	wäre
du	wär(e)st	hättest	wär(e)st
er/sie/es	wäre } gewesen	hätte } gegeben	wäre } gefahren
wir	wären	hätten	wären
ihr	wär(e)t	hättet	wär(e)t
sie/Sie	wären	hätten	wären

Passive Voice

	einladen		
	Present	*Simple Past*	*Present Perfect*
ich	werde	wurde	bin
du	wirst	wurdest	bist
er/sie/es	wird	wurde	ist
wir	werden } eingeladen	wurden } eingeladen	sind } eingeladen worden
ihr	werdet	wurdet	seid
sie/Sie	werden	wurden	sind

Imperative

	sein	geben	fahren	arbeiten
Familiar Singular	sei	gib	fahr	arbeite
Familiar Plural	seid	gebt	fahrt	arbeitet
Formal	seien Sie	geben Sie	fahren Sie	arbeiten Sie

Appendix D

Alternate Spelling and Capitalization

As a result of the recent German spelling reform, some words now have an alternate, old spelling along with a new one. In some realia and literature selections, you may see alternate spellings. The vocabulary lists at the end of each chapter in this text present the new spelling. Listed here are words appearing in the end of chapter vocabulary lists that are affected by the spelling reform, along with their traditional alternate spellings. This list is not a complete list of words affected by the spelling reform.

NEW	ALTERNATE
Abschluss (ːe)	Abschluß (Abschlüsse)
Anschluss (ːe)	Anschluß (Anschlüsse)
auf Deutsch	auf deutsch
Dachgeschoss (-e)	Dachgeschoß (Dachgeschosse)
dass	daß
Erdgeschoss (-e)	Erdgeschoß (Erdgeschosse)
essen (isst), aß, gegessen	essen (ißt), aß, gegessen
Esszimmer (-)	Eßzimmer (-)
Fass (ːer)	Faß (Fässer)
Fitness	Fitneß
Fluss (ːe)	Fluß (Flüsse)
heute Abend / ... Mittag / ... Morgen / ... Nachmittag / ... Vormittag	heute abend /... mittag / ... morgen / ... nachmittag / ... vormittag
Imbiss (-e)	Imbiß (Imbisse)
kennen lernen, kennen gelernt	kennenlernen, kennengelernt
lassen (lässt), ließ, gelassen Lass uns doch ...	lassen (läßt), ließ, gelassen Laß uns doch ...
leidtun, leidgetan	Leid tun, Leid getan
morgen Abend / ... Mittag / ... Nachmittag / ... Vormittag	morgen abend / ... mittag / ... nachmittag / ... vormittag
müssen (muss), musste, gemusst	müssen (muß), mußte, gemußt
passen (passt), gepasst	passen (paßt), gepaßt
Rad fahren (fährt Rad), fuhr Rad, ist Rad gefahren	radfahren (fährt Rad), fuhr Rad, ist radgefahren
Reisepass (ːe)	Reisepaß (Reisepässe)
Samstagabend / -mittag / -morgen / -nachmittag / -vormittag	Samstag abend / ... mittag / ... morgen / ... nachmittag / ... vormittag
Schloss (ːer)	Schloß (Schlösser)
spazieren gehen (geht spazieren), ging spazieren, ist spazieren gegangen	spazierengehen (geht spazieren), ging spazieren, ist spazierengegangen
Stress	Streß
vergessen (vergisst), vergaß, vergessen	vergessen (vergißt), vergaß, vergessen
wie viel	wieviel

Vocabulary

German–English

This vocabulary contains the German words as used in various contexts in this text, with the following exceptions: (1) compound words whose meaning can be easily guessed from their component parts; (2) most identical or very close cognates that are not part of the active vocabulary. (Frequently used cognates are, however, included so students can verify their gender.)

Active vocabulary in the end-of-chapter **Wortschatz** lists is indicated by the number of the chapter in which it first appears. The letter E refers to the introductory chapter, **Einführung.**

The following abbreviations are used:

acc.	accusative	*indef. pron.*	indefinite pronoun
adj.	adjective	*inform.*	informal
adv.	adverb	**-(e)n** *masc.*	masculine noun ending in
coll.	colloquial		**-n** or **-en** in all cases but
coord. conj.	coordinating conjunction		the nominative singular
dat.	dative	*pl.*	plural
decl. adj.	declined adjective	*sg.*	singular
form.	formal	*subord. conj.*	subordinating conjunction
gen.	genitive		

A

ab (+ *dat.*) from; as of (12); **ab 1. Juni (ab erstem Juni)** as of June 1st (12)

ab und zu now and then, occasionally (8)

abblitzen (blitzt ab) to be rebuffed

abbrechen (bricht ab), brach ab, abgebrochen to break off, cut short

der Abend (-e) evening (4); **am Abend** in the evening, at night; **gestern Abend** last night; **guten Abend** good evening (E); **der Heilige Abend** Christmas Eve (3); **heute Abend** this evening (1); **jeden Abend** every evening; **morgen Abend** tomorrow evening (4)

das Abendessen (-) evening meal (5); dinner, supper; **zum Abendessen** for dinner, supper

das Abendkleid (-er) evening gown

abends in the evening, evenings (4)

das Abenteuer (-) adventure

der Abenteuerfilm (-e) adventure film

aber (*coord. conj.*) but (1); however

abfahren (fährt ab), fuhr ab, ist abgefahren to depart, leave (10)

die Abfahrt (-en) departure (10)

der Abfall (-̈e) waste, garbage, trash, litter (14)

die Abfallwirtschaft waste management

abfliegen (fliegt ab), flog ab, ist abgeflogen to depart, leave (by plane)

abgeben (gibt ab), gab ab, abgegeben to drop off, turn in (8)

abgucken (guckt ab) to copy (someone else's work)

abhängig dependent

abholen (holt ab) to pick up (*from a place*) (4)

das Abitur (-e) *examination at the end of Gymnasium* (11)

der Abiturient (-en *masc.*) **(-en)** / **die Abiturientin (-nen)** *graduate of the Gymnasium, person who has passed the Abitur*

die Abkürzung (-en) abbreviation

ablehnen (lehnt ab) to decline

ableiten (leitet ab) to derive

ablenken (lenkt ab) to distract

abnehmen (nimmt ab), nahm ab, abgenommen to lose weight

das Abo(nnement) (-s) subscription (13)

abonnieren to subscribe (13)

die Abrechnung (-en) final account

abreisen (reist ab), ist abgereist to depart, leave (on a trip) (9)

der Absatz (-̈e) paragraph

abschalten (schaltet ab) to shut down, turn off

abschicken (schickt ab) to send off, mail

der Abschied (-e) farewell

der Abschluss (-̈e) completion; degree (11)

der Abschnitt (-e) section; phase

der Absender (-) sender

absetzen (setzt ab) to take off

absolut absolute(ly)

sich abspielen (spielt ab) to take place, proceed

die Abstammung origin, heritage

absteigen (steigt ab), stieg ab, ist abgestiegen to dismount, get off

abstellen (stellt ab) to turn off

abstimmen (stimmt ab) to take a vote (14)

die Abstimmung vote; coordination

der Absturz (-̈e) fall; crash

das Abteil (-e) compartment

die Abteilung abortion

abwarten (wartet ab) to wait; **abwarten und Tee trinken** wait and see

abwechseln (wechselt ab) to alternate, take turns

abwechslungsreich varied, diverse (11)

das Accessoire (-s) accessory

ach oh; **Ach so!** I see!

acht eight (E)

achte eighth (3)

achten auf (+ *acc.*) to pay attention to, watch (8)

die Achtung attention

achtzehn eighteen (E)

achtzehnte eighteenth

achtzig eighty (E)

der ADAC = Allgemeiner Deutscher Automobilclub *German automobile club*

das Adjektiv (-e) adjective

die Adjektivendung (-en) adjective ending

der Adler, - eagle

das Adrenalin adrenaline

die Adresse (-n) address (E)

das Adverb (-ien) adverb

das Aerobic aerobics

afghanisch Afghan

(das) Afghanistan Afghanistan

(das) Afrika Africa

afrikanisch African

(die) AG = Aktiengesellschaft corporation

der Agent (-en *masc.***) (-en) / die Agentin (-nen)** agent

das Aggregat (-e) set; setting

aggressiv aggressive

agieren to play one's part

(das) Ägypten Egypt

ah ah; **Ah so!** I see! I get it!

ähnlich similar(ly)

die Ähnlichkeit (-en) similarity

die Ahnung: Keine Ahnung! (I have) no idea!

das Ahornblatt (-̈er) maple leaf

das Aids AIDS

akkurat precise(ly), exact(ly)

der Akkusativ accusative case

das Akkusativobjekt (-e) accusative object

die Akkusativpräposition (-en) preposition governing the accusative case

das Akkusativpronomen (-) pronoun in the accusative case

der Akrobat (-en *masc.***) (-en) / die Akrobatin (-nen)** acrobat

die Aktion (-en) (political) action

aktiv active(ly) (10); **sportlich aktiv** active in sports (10)

die Aktivität (-en) activity

aktuell current, topical (13); **Aktuelles** current events (13)

akzentuieren to accentuate; **deutschakzentuiert** German-accented

die Alarmanlage (-n) alarm system

alarmieren to alarm

der Alkohol alcohol (8)

alkoholfrei nonalcoholic (6)

all all; **vor allem** above all

alle (*pl.*) all; every (5); **alle zwei Jahre** every two years; **aller** of all

die Allee, -n avenue

allein(e) alone

allerdings however; to be sure

allerlei all kinds of; **Leipziger Allerlei** *Leipzig-style mixed vegetables*

alles everything (10); **Alles Gute!** All the best! (3); **Alles klar.** I get it., Everything is clear. (E); **das ist alles** that is all

allgemein general; **im Allgemeinen** in general

die Alliierten (*pl.*) the Allies, the Allied Forces

der Alltag everyday routine; workday

alltäglich everyday, ordinary

die Alpen (*pl.*) the Alps

alphabetisch alphabetical(ly)

als (*subord. conj.*) as; when (10); than (7); **als Kind** as a child

also thus, therefore; so; well

alt (älter, ältest-) old (1); **Alt-** used

die Altbatterie (-n) used-up battery

die Altbauwohnung (-en) apartment in a pre-World-War-II building

das Altenheim (-e) old people's home

das Alter (-) age

alternativ alternative(ly)

das Altglas used glass

die Altkleidung used clothing

das Altöl used oil

das Altpapier used paper

die Altstadt (-̈e) old part of town

das Aluminium aluminum

am = an dem: am ersten Mai on May first (3); **am Montag** on Monday (3); **möchte am liebsten** would like to (do) most (4)

der Amateurfunker (-) / die Amateurfunkerin (-nen) amateur radio operator

(das) Amerika America

der Amerikaner (-) / die Amerikanerin (-nen) American (*person*) (1)

amerikanisch American

die Amischen (*pl.*) Amish (*people*)

die Ampel (-n) traffic light (9)

das Amt (-̈er) bureau, agency

amüsant amusing, entertaining

an (+ *acc./dat.*) at; near; on; onto; to (6); **an deiner Stelle** if I were you, (if I were) in your place (12); **an der Ecke** at the corner (9)

der Analphabet (-en *masc.***) (-en)** illiterate person

die Analyse (-n) analysis

analysieren to analyze

die Anatomie (-n) anatomy

anbeißen (beißt an), biss an, angebissen to take a bite (out of)

anbieten (bietet an), bot an, angeboten to offer

anbrennen (brennt an), brannte an, angebrannt to burn

anbringen (bringt an), brachte an, angebracht to put up, install

ander- different, other; **am anderen Morgen** the next morning; **der/die/das andere** (*decl. adj.*) the other one, different one; **(et)was anderes** something else

(sich) ändern to change

anders different(ly), in another way; **jemand anders** somebody else

anderswo elsewhere, somewhere/ anywhere else

die Änderung (-en) change

anerkennen, erkannte an, anerkannt to recognize, acknowledge

der Anfang (-̈e) beginning, start; **am Anfang** in the beginning

anfangen (fängt an), fing an, angefangen to begin, start (4)

der Anfänger (-) / die Anfängerin (-nen) beginner

anfordern (fordert an) to request, order

anführen (führt an) to lead; to give, quote

die Angabe (-n) statement, information; **persönliche Angaben** personal information

angeben (gibt an), gab an, angegeben to state, declare, give

das Angebot (-e) (special) offer; selection (10)

die Angelegenheit (-en) matter, issue, affair

angeln to fish (7)

die Angelrute (-n) fishing rod

angenehm pleasant(ly) (7)

der/die Angestellte (*decl. adj.*) employee

die Anglistik (study of) English language and literature

die Angst (-̈e) fear (12); **Angst haben (vor** + *dat.*) to be afraid (of) (12); **keine Angst** don't be afraid

angucken (guckt an) (*coll.*) to look at; **sich** (*dat.*) **etwas angucken** (*coll.*) to look at something

der Anhang (-̈e) appendix; attachment

sich anhören (hört an) to listen to

der Ankauf purchase; **An- und Verkauf** buying and selling

ankommen (kommt an), kam an, ist angekommen to arrive (9)

ankreuzen (kreuzt an) to mark; to check off

die Ankunft (-̈e) arrival (10)

anlegen (legt an) to put on; to put down, lay out

das Anmeldeformular (-e) registration form (9)

(sich) anmelden (meldet an) to check in, register (9)

anmieten (mietet an) to rent

annehmbar acceptable

annehmen (nimmt an), nahm an, angenommen to accept, take

anno: pro anno per year, annual(ly)

anprobieren (probiert an), anprobiert to try on (5)

anreden (redet an) to address

anregen (regt an) to prompt, stimulate

die Anreise (-n) journey to a place; arrival

der Anruf (-e) (telephone) call

der Anrufbeantworter (-) answering machine (13)

anrufen (ruft an), rief an, angerufen to call up (on the phone) (4); **sich anrufen** to call one another

der Anrufer (-) / die Anruferin (-nen) caller

ans = an das

die Ansage (-n) announcement

der Ansager (-) / die Ansagerin (-nen) announcer

(sich) etwas anschaffen (schafft an) to purchase something, acquire something (14)

die Anschaffung (-en) purchase, acquisition

anschalten (schaltet an) to turn on

anschauen (schaut an) to look at; **sich** (*dat.*) **etwas anschauen** to look at, watch (13)

der Anschlagzettel (-) notice, bulletin

anschließend afterward

der Anschluss (-̈e) connection (10)

die Anschrift (-en) address

ansehen (sieht an), sah an, angesehen to watch; **sich** (*dat.*) **etwas ansehen** to watch, look at (13)

das Ansehen prestige (11)

die Ansicht (-en) view

ansprechen (spricht an), sprach an, angesprochen to talk to

(an)statt (+ *gen.***)** instead of

anstehen (nach + *dat.***) (steht an), stand an, angestanden** to stand in line (for)

anstehend upcoming, waiting to be done

anstrengend tiring, strenuous (8)

der Anteil (-e) share

die Antikriegsdemonstration (-en) anti-war demonstration

das Antiquariat secondhand bookshop; **modernes Antiquariat** *shop or department selling remaindered books*

der Antrag (⸚e) application, request

die Antwort (-en) answer

antworten (auf + *acc.***)** to answer (to)

die Anzahl amount; number

die Anzeige (-n) (newspaper) advertisement

die Anzeigenannahme (-n) classified ad department

anziehen (zieht an), zog an, angezogen to put on; **sich anziehen** to get dressed (8)

die Anziehungskraft (⸚e) force of attraction; allure

der Anzug (⸚e) suit (5)

der Apfel (⸚) apple (5)

das Apfelmus applesauce (6)

der Apfelrotkohl *dish containing apples and red cabbage*

der Apfelstrudel (-) apple strudel, apple pastry (6)

die Apotheke (-n) pharmacy (5)

der Apparat (-e) set, appliance (*such as TV or telephone*) (9); **sich am Apparat melden** to answer the telephone

das Appartement (-s) one-room apartment

der Applaus (-e) applause

die Aprikose (-n) apricot

(der) April April (3)

das Aquarium (Aquarien) aquarium

das Äquivalent (-e) equivalent

(das) Arabien Arabia

die Arbeit (-en) work; job; assignment; paper (8)

arbeiten to work (1)

der Arbeiter (-) / die Arbeiterin (-nen) worker, laborer

der Arbeitgeber (-) / die Arbeitgeberin (-nen) employer (11)

der Arbeitnehmer (-) / die Arbeitnehmerin (-nen) employee

das Arbeitsamt (⸚er) employment office (11)

die Arbeitserfahrung (-en) work experience

arbeitsfrei off from work

die Arbeitsgemeinschaft (-en) work group, team

die Arbeitslage (-n) employment situation

der Arbeitslohn (⸚e) wage(s)

arbeitslos unemployed

die Arbeitslosigkeit unemployment (14)

der Arbeitsmarkt job market

das Arbeitsmittel (-) material(s); tool

der Arbeitsplatz (⸚e) workplace; position (11)

die Arbeitsstunde (-n) working hour

die Arbeitssuche (-n) job search

die Arbeitsvermittlung (-en) employment agency

die Arbeitszeit (-en) working hours

das Arbeitszimmer (-) workroom, study (2)

der Architekt (-en *masc.***) (-en) / die Architektin (-nen)** architect

die Architektur (-en) architecture

das Archiv (-e) archive

die ARD = Arbeitsgemeinschaft der Rundfunkanstalten Deutschlands (*German radio and television network*)

die Arena (Arenen) arena

(das) Argentinien Argentina

der Ärger annoyance, trouble

ärgerlich annoyed, angry; annoying, vexing

ärgern to annoy; **sich ärgern (über +** *acc.***)** to be annoyed (about) (12)

das Argument (-e) argument

arisch Aryan

arith. = arithmetisch arithmetical(ly)

arm poor

der Arm (-e) arm (8)

die Armee (-n) armed forces

die Armen (*pl.*) poor people

die Armut poverty (14)

arrangieren to arrange

arrogant arrogant(ly)

die Art (-en) kind, type; manner

der Artikel (-) article; item

das Arzneimittel (-) medication (14)

der Arzt (⸚e) / die Ärztin (-nen) physician, doctor (8)

die Arztkosten (*pl.*) medical costs

der Asbesthut (⸚e) asbestos hat

der Aspekt (-e) aspect

das Aspirin aspirin

die Assoziation (-en) association

assoziieren to associate

der AStA = Allgemeiner Studentenausschuss students' union

der Astronaut (-en *masc.***) (-en) / die Astronautin (-nen)** astronaut

die Atmosphäre (-n) atmosphere

die Atomkraft nuclear power

der Atomstreit nuclear conflict

attraktiv attractive(ly)

ätzend corrosive; caustic

au ouch

die Aubergine (-n) eggplant

auch also, too (1); **ich auch** me too

die Aue (-n) meadow

auf (+ *acc./dat.***)** on, upon; on top of; at (6); onto; to; **auf Deutsch** in German (E); **auf jeden Fall** in any case (13); **auf welchen Namen?** under what name? (9); **auf Wiederhören** good-bye (*on the phone*) (9); **auf Wiedersehen** good-bye (E)

der Aufenthalt (-e) stay; layover (9)

auffallen (fällt auf), fiel auf, ist aufgefallen to stand out, be conspicuous

auffallend conspicuous(ly)

die Aufforderung (-en) request

die Aufgabe (-n) task; exercise

aufgeben (gibt auf), gab auf, aufgegeben to give up; to hand in

aufhören (mit + *dat.***) (hört auf)** to end, quit, stop (doing something) (4)

aufklären (über + *acc.***) (klärt auf)** to inform (about)

der Aufkleber (-) sticker

der Auflauf (⸚e) casserole (6)

auflisten (listet auf) to list

(sich) auflockern (lockert auf) to loosen up

aufmachen (macht auf) to open

aufnehmen (nimmt auf), nahm auf, aufgenommen to record (*on tape, video, etc.*) (13)

aufräumen (räumt auf) to clean up, straighten up (*a room*) (4)

aufregend exciting

die Aufregung (-en) excitement

aufs = auf das

der Aufsatz (⸚e) essay

der Aufschnitt cold cuts (5)

aufschreiben (schreibt auf), schrieb auf, aufgeschrieben to write down

der Aufseher (-) / die Aufseherin (-nen) guard, overseer

aufsetzen (setzt auf) to put on

der Aufstand (⸚e) rebellion, uprising

aufstehen (steht auf), stand auf, ist aufgestanden to get up; to stand up (4)

auftauen (taut auf) to thaw (out)

aufteilen (teilt auf) to divide

der Auftrag (⸚e) task, assignment

der Auftritt (-e) appearance (*on stage*)

aufwachen (wacht auf), ist aufgewacht to wake up (4)

aufwachsen (wächst auf), wuchs auf, ist aufgewachsen to grow up

aufweisen (weist auf), wies auf, aufgewiesen to demonstrate, show

der Aufzug (⸚e) elevator (9)

das Auge (-n) eye (8)

der Augenarzt (⸚e) / die Augenärztin (-nen) eye doctor, optometrist

die Augenfarbe (-n) eye color

(der) August August (3)

aus (+ *dat.***)** from; out of; (made) of (5); **aus Baumwolle** made of cotton; **Ich komme aus …** I'm from . . . (E)

ausarbeiten (arbeitet aus) to work out, develop

ausbauen (baut aus) to convert (*a room or building*)

die Ausbildung (-en) (career) training (11)

der Ausbildungsgang (⸚e) training course

der Ausbildungsplatz (⸚e) training position

die Ausbildungsstelle (-n) training position

die Ausbildungszeit (-en) training period

ausbrechen (bricht aus), brach aus, ausgebrochen to break out

der Ausdruck (⸚e) expression

ausdrücken (drückt aus) to express

auseinandernehmen (nimmt auseinander), nahm auseinander, auseinandergenommen to take apart

der Ausflug (¨e) excursion

die Ausflugsfahrt (-en) excursion (*by car, bus, etc.*)

ausfüllen (füllt aus) to fill out (9)

die Ausgabe (-n) expense (12)

ausgeben (gibt aus), gab aus, ausgegeben to spend (*money*) (12)

ausgehen (geht aus), ging aus, ist ausgegangen to go out (4)

ausgerechnet of all things

ausgesucht chosen, choice, select

ausgezeichnet excellent (E)

ausgleiten (gleitet aus), glitt aus, ist ausgeglitten to slip and fall

die Ausgrabung (-en) excavation

aushalten (hält aus), hielt aus, ausgehalten to endure

auskommen (kommt aus), kam aus, ist ausgekommen to make ends meet, get by with (*money*)

die Auskunft (¨e) information (10)

auslachen (lacht aus) to laugh at

das Ausland (*sg. only*) foreign countries (11); im Ausland abroad (11)

der Ausländer (-) / die Ausländerin (-nen) foreigner (14)

die Ausländerfeindlichkeit xenophobia, hatred toward foreigners (14)

die Auslandsspeise (-n) foreign food

die Ausnahme (-n) exception

ausprobieren (probiert aus), ausprobiert to try out

die Ausrede (-n) excuse

ausreichend sufficient(ly), enough

sich ausruhen (ruht aus) to rest

die Ausrüstung (-en) equipment

die Aussage (-n) statement

ausscheiden (scheidet aus), schied aus, ist ausgeschieden to be eliminated

ausschneiden (schneidet aus), schnitt aus, ausgeschnitten to cut out

der Ausschnitt (-e) excerpt

aussehen (sieht aus), sah aus, ausgesehen to look, appear

außer (+ *dat.*) except for, besides

äußer- outer

außerdem besides, in addition (14)

außerhalb (+ *gen.*) outside of (9)

(sich) äußern to express (oneself); die Meinung äußern to voice an opinion

die Äußerung (-en) statement

die Aussicht (-en) view, prospect

die Aussichtsseite (-n) side with a view

ausspannen (spannt aus) to rest, relax, take a break

die Aussprache (-n) pronunciation; discussion, talk

ausstatten (stattet aus) to equip, furnish

ausstellen (stellt aus) to put out; to display, exhibit

ausstreichen (streicht aus), strich aus, ausgestrichen to cross out, strike through

sich (*dat.*) (et)was aussuchen (sucht aus) to select, find, choose something (13)

austauschen (tauscht aus) to trade, exchange

der Austauschschüler (-) / die Austauschschülerin (-nen) exchange student (*high school*)

(das) Australien Australia

ausüben (übt aus) to practice, exercise, do

auswählen (wählt aus) to choose, select

auswandern (wandert aus), ist ausgewandert to emigrate

ausweichen (+ *dat.*) (weicht aus), wich aus, ist ausgewichen to get out of the way of, make way for

der Ausweis (-e) ID card

ausziehen (zieht aus), zog aus, ist ausgezogen to move out; sich (*acc.*) ausziehen to get undressed (8); sich (*dat.*) etwas ausziehen to take something off (*clothing etc.*)

der/die Auszubildende (*decl. adj.*) trainee, apprentice

der Auszug (¨e) excerpt, extract

das Auto (-s) car, auto (2)

die Autoabgase (*pl.*) exhaust fumes

die Autobahn (-en) highway

der Autodieb (-e) car thief

der Autofahrer (-) / die Autofahrerin (-nen) (automobile) driver

automatisch automatic(ally)

der Automechaniker (-) / die Automechanikerin (-nen) car mechanic

das Automobil (-e) automobile, car

der Autor (-en) / die Autorin (-nen) author

die Autoschlange (-n) long line of cars

Autostop: per Autostop reisen to hitch-hike (10)

das Autotelefon (-e) car telephone

der/die Azubi (-s) = der/die Auszubildende

B

die Babywäsche baby clothes

der Bäcker (-) / die Bäckerin (-nen) baker

die Bäckerei (-en) bakery (5)

das Bäckerhandwerk bakery trade

die Backwaren (*pl.*) baked goods

das Bad (¨er) bath; bathroom (2); spa

der Badeanzug (¨e) bathing suit (5)

die Badehose (-n) bathing trunks

der Bademantel (¨) bathrobe

die Bademoden (*pl.*) beachwear

baden to bathe

die Badesachen (*pl.*) beach accessories

das Badezimmer (-) bathroom (2)

das BAföG = Bundesausbildungsförderungsgesetz government financial aid for students

die Bahn (-en) train; railway (10); mit der Bahn by train; die U-Bahn (-en) subway

bahnen: den Weg bahnen to pave the way

der Bahnhof (¨e) train station (9)

der Bahnsteig (-e) (train) platform (10)

die Bakterie (-n) bacterium

bald soon (12); möglichst bald as soon as possible

der Baldrian (-e) valerian

der Balkon (-e) balcony (2)

der Ball (¨e) ball

die Ballade (-n) ballad

das Ballett (-e) ballet (4)

die Banane (-n) banana (5)

die Bande (-n) gang, mob

die Bank (¨e) bench

die Bank (-en) bank (*financial institution*) (9)

die Bankkauffrau (-en) (female) bank administrator

der Bankkaufmann (Bankkaufleute) (male) bank administrator

die Banknote (-n) banknote

bar in cash

die Bar (-s) bar

der Bär (-en *masc.*) (-en) bear

die Baracke (-n) hut, shack

die Barfrau (-en) barmaid

das Bargeld cash (10)

der Baron (-e) / die Baronin (-nen) baron / baroness

der Baseball baseball

Baseler (*adj.*) of/from Basel (Switzerland)

das Basilikum basil

die Basis (Basen) basis

die Batterie (-n) battery

der Bau (Bauten) building; construction

der Bauch (¨e) belly, abdomen, stomach (8)

der Bauchredner (-) / die Bauchrednerin (-nen) ventriloquist

die Bauchschmerzen (*pl.*) bellyache, stomachache

bauen to build (12)

der Bauer (-n *masc.*) (-n) / die Bäuerin (-nen) farmer

das Bauernhaus (¨er) farmhouse (12)

der Bauernhof (¨e) farm

der Baum (¨e) tree

der Baumast (¨e) tree branch, bough

die Baumwolle cotton

der Bauplan (¨e) building plan

die Baustelle (-n) building site

bayerisch (*adj.*) Bavarian

(das) Bayern Bavaria

Bayreuther (*adj.*) of/from Bayreuth (*a town in Bavaria*)

bayrisch (*adj.*) Bavarian

der Beamte (*decl. adj.*) / die Beamtin (-nen) agent; government employee

beantworten to answer

bearbeiten to work on, deal with

das Bedauern regret

bedeuten to mean, signify; Was bedeutet . . . ? What does . . . mean? (E)

die Bedeutung (-en) meaning, significance

bedienen to serve

die Bedienung service (6)

das Bedienungsgeld service charge

sich beeilen to hurry (up) (8)

beeindrucken to impress

beenden to complete, finish, end

sich befassen mit (+ *dat.*) to occupy oneself with

befehlen (befiehlt), befahl, befohlen to order, command

das Befinden health, well-being

befragen to question

beginnen, begann, begonnen to begin, start (10)

die Begegnung (-en) meeting, encounter

begeistert enthusiastic(ally)

begreifen, begriff, begriffen to understand, comprehend

der Begründer (-) / die Begründerin (-nen) founder

begrüßen to greet, welcome

die Begrüßung (-en) greeting

behandeln to treat, deal with (14)

behaupten to claim, assert (13)

die Behauptung (-en) claim, assertion

behilflich helpful

bei (+ *dat.*) at; near; with (5); at the place of

beibehalten (behält bei), behielt bei, beibehalten to keep, retain

beide (*pl.*) both

der Beifahrer (-) / die Beifahrerin (-nen) (front-seat) passenger

der Beifahrersitz (-e) passenger seat

beifügen (fügt bei) to add; to enclose

beige beige (5)

die Beilage (-n) side dish (6)

beim = bei dem

das Bein (-e) leg (8)

das Beispiel (-e) example; **zum Beispiel** for example

beißen, biss, gebissen to bite

der Beitrag (-̈e) contribution

beitreten (+ *dat.*) **(tritt bei), trat bei, ist beigetreten** to join

bekämpfen to combat, fight against

bekannt acquainted, known; well-known; **bekannt werden** to get acquainted

der/die Bekannte (*decl. adj.*) acquaintance

bekennen, bekannte, bekannt to admit, confess

die Bekleidung clothing, attire

bekommen, bekam, bekommen to receive, get (6); **Was bekommen Sie?** What will you have? (6)

belasten to burden

beleben to animate, liven up

(das) Belgien Belgium (E)

der Belgier (-) / die Belgierin (-nen) Belgian (*person*)

beliebt popular (7)

die Belohnung (-en) reward

bemerken to observe, notice

die Bemerkung (-en) remark, comment

benutzbar usable

benutzen to use

der Benutzerausweis (-e) user ID

die Benutzung use

das Benzin gasoline (12)

die Benzinsteuer (-n) gasoline tax

bequem comfortable, comfortably (2)

die Beratung (-en) advising (11); consultation

berechenbar predictable

der Bereich (-e) area, field

bereit sein to be ready, be willing

bereits already

bereuen to regret

der Berg (-e) mountain (7)

die Bergseite (-n) side facing the mountain(s)

das Bergsteigen mountain climbing

die Bergwanderung (-en) hike in the mountains

der Bericht (-e) report (13)

berichten to report, narrate (13)

Berliner (*adj.*) of/from Berlin; **der Berliner Pfannkuchen (-)** jelly doughnut

der Berliner (-) / die Berlinerin (-nen) person from Berlin

der Beruf (-e) profession, occupation (1); **Was sind Sie von Beruf?** What do you do for a living? (1)

beruflich professional(ly), on business

die Berufsaufbauschule (-n) *(night) school toward a vocational college degree*

die Berufsausbildung vocational training

der Berufsberater (-) / die Berufsberaterin (-nen) employment counselor (11)

die Berufsberatung job counseling, vocational guidance

berufsbildender Abschluss trade school degree

die Berufsfachschule (-n) vocational college

das Berufsgrundbildungsjahr (-e) year of basic vocational training

das Berufsleben professional life, working life (11)

der Berufsplan (-̈e) career plan

berufsqualifizierend providing qualifications for a profession

die Berufsschule (-n) vocational school

der/die Berufstätige (*decl. adj.*) working person

die Berufswahl (-en) career choice

berühmt famous

berühren to touch; to affect

besänftigen to appease, placate

die Besatzungstruppen (*pl.*) occupation troops

die Besatzungszone (-n) occupied zone

beschäftigen to employ (11); **sich beschäftigen mit** (+ *dat.*) to occupy oneself with (11)

beschließen, beschloss, beschlossen to decide

beschreiben, beschrieb, beschrieben to describe

die Beschreibung (-en) description

die Beschwerde (-n) complaint

sich beschweren (über + *acc.*) to complain (about) (9)

beseitigen to remove, get rid of

der Besen (-) broom

der Besenstiel (-e) broomstick

besetzen to occupy; **besetzt** occupied, taken (6); **Hier ist besetzt.** This place is taken. (6)

besichtigen to view, see

besitzen, besaß, besessen to own, possess (11)

der Besitzer (-) / die Besitzerin (-nen) owner

besonder- special, particular; **etwas/nichts Besonderes** something/nothing special

besonders especially, particularly (8); **nicht besonders gut** not especially well (E)

besorgen to purchase, procure, get

besprechen (bespricht), besprach, besprochen to discuss, talk about

die Besprechung (-en) discussion; conference

besser better

die Besserung: Gute Besserung! Get well soon! (8)

best- best; **am besten** (the) best; **Wie komme ich am besten dahin?** What's the best way to get there? (9)

beständig continous(ly)

bestehen, bestand, bestanden to pass (an exam); **bestehen aus** (+ *dat.*) to consist of

bestellen to order (6); to reserve

der Bestellservice order service

die Bestellung (-en) order; reservation

bestens excellently, to the highest level

bestimmen to determine, decide

bestimmt (*adj.*) particular, certain; (*adv.*) no doubt; definitely (1)

der Besuch (-e) visit; visitors; **zu Besuch kommen** to come for a visit

besuchen to visit (1)

der Besucher (-) / die Besucherin (-nen) visitor, guest

der/die Beteiligte (*decl. adj.*) person involved

betragen (beträgt), betrug, betragen to amount to, come to; **die Miete beträgt …** the rent comes to . . .

betreffen (betrifft), betraf, betroffen to concern; to affect (14)

betreiben, betrieb, betrieben to drive; to run

der Betrieb (-e) business, firm; operation

die Betriebswirtschaft business management

das Bett (-en) bed (2)

die Bettwäsche linens (9)

bevor (*subord. conj.*) before (10)

bewahren vor (+ *dat.*) to protect from

(sich) bewegen to move, move about

beweglich movable

der Beweis (-e) proof, evidence

beweisen, bewies, bewiesen to prove

sich bewerben (um + *acc.*) **(bewirbt), bewarb, beworben** to apply (for) (11)

der Bewerber (-) / die Bewerberin (-nen) applicant

die Bewerbung (-en) application (11)

das Bewerbungsformular (-e) application form (11)

bewerten to evaluate

die Bewertung (-en) evaluation, assessment

bewirken to cause, bring about

der Bewohner (-) / die Bewohnerin (-nen) resident, tenant

bewölkt cloudy, overcast (7)

bewundern to admire

bewusst conscious, aware

bezahlen to pay

bezeichnen als to call, describe as

die Bezeichnung (-en) label, term

sich beziehen auf (+ acc.), bezog, bezogen to refer to

die Beziehung (-en) relationship; affair

die Beziehungskiste (-n) (coll.) difficult relationship

der Bezug: mit Bezug auf (+ acc.) with reference to

die Bezugsgruppe (-n) reference group

bezweifeln to doubt

bezwingen, bezwang, bezwungen to conquer

die Bibliothek (-en) library (4)

der Bibliothekar (-e) / die Bibliothekarin (-nen) librarian (11)

der Bielefelder (-) / die Bielefelderin (-nen) person from Bielefeld (town in northern Germany)

das Bier (-e) beer (5)

der Bierdeckel (-) beer coaster

der Biergarten (-̈) beer garden (restaurant) (6)

der Bierkeller (-) type of restaurant where beer is served

der Bierkrug (-̈e) beer stein, beer mug

bieten, bot, geboten to offer, present

das Biken (motor)biking

der Bikini (-s) bikini, two-piece bathing suit

das Bild (-er) picture

bilden to form

der Bildschirmschoner (-) screen saver

das Bildsymbol (-e) pictogram

der Bildungsabschluss (-̈e) educational diploma

die Bildungswissenschaft (-en) science/field of education

das Billard (-e) billiards

billig inexpensive(ly), cheap(ly) (2)

die Billiguhr (-en) cheap watch

bin am; Ich bin ... I am . . . (E)

binden, band, gebunden to tie (up)

die Biographie (-n) biography

die Biokost organic food

der Bioladen (-̈) natural foods store (5)

das Biolebensmittel (-) organic food (8)

die Biologie biology

biologisch biological(ly)

der Biotechnologe (-n masc.) (-n) / die Biotechnologin (-nen) biotechnician

bis (+ acc.) until (6); to, up to; bis (um) fünf Uhr until five o'clock (6); bis zum/zur (+ dat.) to, as far as (9); von zwei bis drei Uhr from two to three o'clock (6)

bisher so far, up to now

bisherig previous

ein bisschen a little (bit); somewhat

bissig biting; cutting, caustic

bist are (2nd person inform. sg.): du bist you are

das Bistro (-s) bistro

bitte please; you're welcome (E); bitte schön you're welcome; please; bitte sehr you're welcome; please; Wie bitte? Pardon? What did you say? (E); Würden Sie bitte ... ? Would you please . . . ? (9)

bitten, bat, gebeten to ask; bitten um (+ acc.) to ask for, request (12)

blasen (bläst), blies, geblasen to blow

das Blatt (-̈er) leaf; sheet (of paper)

blau blue (5); in Blau in blue

blauweiß blue and white

das Blei (-e) lead

bleiben, blieb, ist geblieben to stay, remain (1)

der Bleigurt (-e) lead belt

der Bleistift (-e) pencil (12)

der Blick (-e) look, glance; view;

blitzen to flash (7); Es blitzt. There's lightning. (7)

die Blockade (-n) blockade

blockieren to block; to blockade

blockweise in blocks

blöd stupid (13); Das ist mir zu blöd. I think that's really stupid. (13)

bloggen to blog, keep an online journal (7)

die Blondine (-n) blonde woman

bloß merely; only

blühen to blossom

die Blume (-n) flower

das Blumengeschäft (-e) flower shop

der Blumenkohl cauliflower (5)

die Bluse (-n) blouse (5)

die Blusengröße (-n) blouse size

der BMW (-s) (Bayerische Motoren Werke) BMW automobile

die Bockwurst (-̈e) type of German sausage

der Boden (-̈) floor of a room; ground

das Bodybuilding bodybuilding; Bodybuilding machen to do bodybuilding, do weight training (7)

das Bogenschießen archery

die Bohne (-n) bean (6); grüne Bohne green bean, string bean

böig gusty; squally

(das) Bolivien Bolivia

das Boot (-e) boat

der Bootsführer (-) / die Bootsführerin (-nen) boat guide

die Börse (-n) stock exchange (13)

böse angry, mad; angrily; mean; bad

(das) Bosnien Bosnia

der Boss (-e) (coll.) boss

die Boutique (-n) boutique, trendy shop

das Bowling bowling

die Box (-en) stereo speaker

der Brandstifter (-) arsonist

(das) Brasilien Brazil

braten (brät), briet, gebraten to fry; to roast

die Bratkartoffeln (pl.) fried potatoes (6)

die Bratwurst (-̈e) type of German sausage

brauchen to need (2)

das Brauhaus (-̈er) brewery

braun brown (5)

bräunen to tan

das Braunglas brown glass

die BRD = Bundesrepublik Deutschland

das Breakdancen break dancing

brechen (bricht), brach, gebrochen to break

Bremer (adj.) of/from Bremen: die Bremer Stadtmusikanten the Bremen Town Musicians

die Bremse (-n) brake

brennen, brannte, gebrannt to burn

bretonisch (adj.) Breton

das Brett (-er) board; das Schwarze Brett bulletin board

der Bretterwagen (-) wagon/truck for hauling lumber

das Brevier (-e) breviary

die Brezel (-n) pretzel (6)

der Brief (-e) letter (7)

der Brieffreund (-e) / die Brieffreundin (-nen) pen pal

die Briefmarke (-n) postage stamp (7)

der Briefträger (-) / die Briefträgerin (-nen) mail carrier

die Brille (-n) (pair of) eyeglasses (5)

bringen, brachte, gebracht to bring (7)

der Brite (-n masc.) (-n) / die Britin (-nen) Briton, British person

britisch (adj.) British

der Brokkoli broccoli (5)

die Broschüre (-n) brochure, pamphlet

das Brot (-e) (loaf of) bread (5)

das Brötchen (-) bread roll (5)

die Brücke (-n) bridge

der Bruder (-̈) brother (3)

der Brunch (-[e]s) brunch

der Brunnen (-) spring, well; fountain

die Brust (-̈e) breast; chest (8)

das Buch (-̈er) book (3)

der Buchdruck letterpress printing

buchen to book (a trip) (10)

das Bücherregal (-e) bookcase, bookshelf (2)

die Büchertasche (-n) bookbag

die Buchhandlung (-en) bookshop

der Buchstabe (-n masc.) (-n) letter (of the alphabet)

buchstabieren to spell

die Buchung (-en) booking, reservation

das Budget (-s) budget

das Büffet (-s) buffet

die Bühne (-n) stage

die Bühnenanweisung (-en) stage direction

das Bühnenbild (-er) stage decoration

der Bühnentext (-e) script (for a stage play)

das Bundesausbildungsförderungsgesetz (BAföG) government financial aid for students

die Bundesbank (-en) federal bank

der Bundeskanzler (-) / die Bundeskanzlerin (-nen) (German or Austrian) chancellor

das Bundesland (-̈er) German state

die Bundesliga federal division, federal league

das Bundesministerium (Bundesministerien) federal ministry

die Bundesrepublik federal republic: die Bundesrepublik Deutschland (BRD) Federal Republic of Germany

der Bundesstaat (-en) federal state; state (of the USA)

der Bundestag federal German parliament

das Bundestagsgebäude federal German parliament building

bündig concise, succinct

das Bungeejumping bungee jumping

der Bunker (-) bunker

bunt colorful

die Burg (-en) fortress, castle

der Bürger (-) / die Bürgerin (-nen) citizen (14)

das Bürgerhaus (¨er) (bourgeois) town house

die Bürgerinitiative (-n) citizens' group; grassroots movement

der Bürgermeister (-) / die Bürgermeisterin (-nen) mayor

das Büro (-s) office (11)

das Bürohaus (¨er) office building

die Bürokauffrau (-en) (female) office administrator

der Bürokaufmann (¨er) (male) office administrator

der Bus (-se) bus (10)

die Bushaltestelle (-n) bus stop

die Buslinie (-n) bus line

der Busunfall (¨e) bus accident

die Butter butter (5)

der Button (-s) button

bzw. = beziehungsweise respectively; or

C

ca. = circa, zirka approximately, about

das Café (-s) café (6)

die Cafeteria (Cafeterien) cafeteria

der Camcorder (-) camcorder, handheld video camera (13)

das Camp (-s) camp

campen to camp

das Camping camping

die Campingausrüstung camping equipment

der Campingplatz (¨e) campground

der Campus (-) (school) campus

der Cappuccino (-s) cappuccino

der Cartoon (-s) cartoon

das Casino (-s) casino

das Cassettendeck (-s) cassette deck, tape deck

die CD (-s) CD, compact disc

der CD-Spieler (-) CD player (2)

das Cello (-s) cello

Celsius centigrade

der Cent (-[s]) cent

die Cerealien (pl.) cereal

CH (= Confoederatio Helvetica) official name of Switzerland

der Champignon (-s) mushroom

die Chance (-n) chance; opportunity

der Chaot (-en masc.**) (-en)** scatterbrain; anarchist

chaotisch chaotic

der Charakter (-e) character, personality

charakterisieren to characterize

die Charakterisierung (-en) characterization

charakteristisch characteristic

chatten to chat (online)

die Checkliste (-n) checklist

checken to check

der Chef (-s) / die Chefin (-nen) manager, boss, head (11)

die Chemie chemistry

die Chemieprüfung (-en) chemistry test

die Chemikalie (-n) chemical

der Chemiker (-) / die Chemikerin (-nen) chemist

chemisch chemical

CHF = der Schweizer Franken Swiss Franc

(das) China China

chinesisch (adj.) Chinese

der Chor (¨e) choir, chorus

die Chronik (-en) chronicle

chronisch chronic(ally)

chronologisch chronological(ly)

circa = zirka approximately, about

der Clou (-s) (coll.) main point, highlight

der Clown (-s) / die Clownin (-nen) clown

der Club = der Klub

der Cocktail (-s) cocktail

der Cognac (-s) cognac

die Cola (-s) cola

das Comicheft (-e) comic book

der Computer (-) computer (2)

der Computeranschluss (¨e) computer connection (2)

die Computerdiskette (-n) computer diskette (12)

das Computerspiel (-e) computer game; **Computerspiele spielen** to play computer games (1)

die Computertechnik computer technology

die Computertechnologie (-n) computer technology

die Computerwissenschaft (-en) computer science

der Container (-) recycling bin

die Cornflakes (pl.) cornflakes

der Couchtisch (-e) coffee table (2)

die Couleur (-s) shade, persuasion; sort

der Coupon (-s) coupon

der Cousin (-s) male cousin

die Cousine (-n) = Kusine female cousin

der Cowboy (-s) cowboy

die Crew (-s) crew, team

die Currywurst (¨e) sausage served with curry powder and ketchup

die Cyberkriminalität cybercrime

D

da there (2); here; (subord. conj.) since; **da drüben** over there (6); **hie und da** here and there

dabei with that; in that context

dabeihaben (hat dabei) to have with one

das Dach (¨er) roof (12)

das Dachgeschoss (-e) top floor, attic (12)

die Dachwohnung (-en) attic apartment

dafür for that; **Ich bin dafür.** I'm in favor of it. (14)

dagegen against that; on the other hand; **Ich bin dagegen.** I'm against it. (14)

daher from there; for that reason, therefore

dahin there (to that place); **Wie komme ich am besten dahin?** What's the best way to get there? (9)

dahinter behind that

damals formerly; at that time, (back) then

die Dame (-n) lady; **meine Damen und Herren** ladies and gentlemen

der Damenhut (¨e) ladies' hat

die Damenkonfektion (-en) ladies' wear

der Damenschuh (-e) ladies' shoe

die Damenwäsche lingerie, ladies' undergarments

damit with that; (subord. conj.) so that

danach after that; afterward

daneben next to that

(das) Dänemark Denmark (E)

der Dank thanks; **Gott sei Dank** thank God; **Vielen Dank!** Many thanks! (6)

dankbar grateful, thankful

danke thanks (E); **danke, gut** fine, thanks (E); **danke schön** thank you very much (E); **danke sehr** thanks a lot (1); **nein danke** no, thank you

danken (+ dat.) to thank (5); **Nichts zu danken.** No thanks necessary; Don't mention it. (8)

dann then

daran on that; at that; to that; **es liegt daran, dass ...** it is because . . .

darauf on that; for that; to that

darin in that; in there

das Darlehen (-) loan

darstellen (stellt dar) to portray, depict

der Darsteller (-) / die Darstellerin (-nen) actor/actress

die Darstellung (-en) portrayal

darüber above that; about that

darum therefore

darunter under that; among them

das that, this; **Das ist ...** This is . . . (E); the

dass (subord, conj.) that (8)

dasselbe the same

die Datei (-en) data file

die Daten (pl.) data

der Dativ dative case

das Dativobjekt (-e) dative object

die Dativpräposition (-en) preposition governing the dative case

das Dativpronomen (-) pronoun in the dative case

das Datum (Daten) date; **Welches Datum ist heute/morgen?** What is today's/tomorrow's date? (3)

dauerhaft durable

dauern to last; to take (time) (7)

davon of that; about that; of them

davor before that; in front of that

dazu to that; for that; in addition to that

dazugeben (gibt dazu), gab dazu, dazugegeben to add

dazugehören (gehört dazu) to belong to that/them

dazwischen between them; during that

die DDR = Deutsche Demokratische Republik German Democratic Republic

debattieren to debate

das Debüt (-s) debut

die Decke (-n) ceiling; blanket, cover

decken to cover; **den Tisch decken** to set the table

dein your (*inform. sg.*) (3)

die Delikatesse (-n) delicacy

demokratisch democratic(ally)

die Demonstration (-en) demonstration, rally (14)

demonstrieren to demonstrate

denken, dachte, gedacht to think; **denken an** (+ *acc.*) to think about/of (12)

das Denkmal (ẹer) monument

denn (*coord. conj.*) for, because (7); then; (*particle used in questions to express interest*); **Was ist denn los?** What's the matter? (2)

die Deponie (-n) garbage dump

deprimiert depressed (8)

der, die, das the; that one; who, which

derselbe the same

deshalb therefore, for that reason (8)

der Designer (-) / die Designerin (-nen) designer

das Dessin (-s) design, pattern

desto: je ... desto ... the . . . the . . .

deswegen because of that (12)

das Detail (-s) detail

detailliert detailed

der Detektiv (-e) / die Detektivin (-nen) (private) detective

der Detektivroman (-e) detective novel

deutsch (*adj.*) German; **deutsch-akzentuiert** German-accented

(das) Deutsch German (language) (1); **auf Deutsch** in German (E)

der/die Deutsche (*decl. adj.*) German (person)

die Deutsche Demokratische Republik (DDR) German Democratic Republic (GDR)

die Deutsche Mark (DM) (-) German mark

der Deutschkurs (-e) German course

(das) Deutschland Germany (E); **die Bundesrepublik Deutschland (BRD)** Federal Republic of Germany (FRG)

der Deutschlehrer (-) / die Deutschlehrerin (-nen) German teacher

deutschsprachig German-speaking

deutschstämmig of German heritage

der Deutschunterricht German class

(der) Dezember December (3)

dezent discreet(ly), unostentatious(ly)

der DFB-Pokal DFB Cup (*championship trophy of the* **Deutscher Fußball-Bund**)

d.h. = das heißt that is, i.e. (8)

der Dialekt (-e) dialect

die Dialektik dialectics

der Dialog (-e) dialogue

dich you (*inform. sg. acc.*) (3); **grüß dich** hello, hi (*among friends and family*) (E)

der Dichter (-) / die Dichterin (-nen) poet

dichtmachen (macht dicht) (*coll.*) to close, shut (down)

dick fat; **dick machen** to be fattening

die the

der Dieb (-e) / die Diebin (-nen) thief

die Diele (-n) front hall (12)

dienen to serve, be in service

der Dienst (-e) service; duty

(der) Dienstag Tuesday (3)

dienstags Tuesdays, on Tuesday(s) (4)

das Dienstjubiläum (Dienstjubiläen) anniversary of service

der Dienstleister (-) / die Dienstleisterin (-nen) worker

dieselbe the same

der Dieselmotor (-en) diesel engine

dieser, diese, dies(es) this (2)

diesmal this time

digital digital(ly)

die Digitalkamera (-s) digital camera (13)

die Digitaluhr (-en) digital watch

die Diktatur (-en) dictatorship

das Dilemma (-s) dilemma

der Dilettant (-en *masc.*) **(-en) / die Dilettantin (-nen)** dilettante

dilettantisch amateurish(ly)

der Dill dill (*herb*)

das Ding (-e) thing, object (10)

die Diplomarbeit (-en) dissertation (*for an academic degree*)

der Diplomat (-en *masc.*) **(-en) / die Diplomatin (-nen)** diplomat

dir (to/for) you (*inform. sg. dat.*) (5); **Was fehlt dir?** What's the matter? (8); **Wie geht's dir?** How are you? (*inform.*) (E)

direkt direct(ly); (*coll.*) really

das Direktwahltelefon (-e) direct-dial telephone

der Dirigent (-en *masc.*) **(-en) / die Dirigentin (-nen)** (orchestra) conductor

der Discman (-s) Discman, portable CD player

die Disko (-s) disco, dance club (4); **in die Disko gehen** to go to a disco, go clubbing (4)

die Diskussion (-en) discussion

diskutieren über (+ *acc.*) to discuss (1); to debate

die D-Mark = die Deutsche Mark

doch still, nevertheless; (*intensifying particle used with imperatives*) (4)

das Dokument (-e) document (13)

der Dokumentarfilm (-e) documentary film (13)

der Dollar (-[s]) dollar

der Dollarschein (-e) dollar bill

der Dolmetscher (-) / die Dolmetscherin (-nen) interpreter (11)

die Dolomiten (*pl.*) the Dolomites

der Dom (-e) cathedral

die Donau Danube (*river*)

donnern to thunder (7); **Es donnert.** It's thundering. (7)

(der) Donnerstag Thursday (3)

donnerstags Thursdays, on Thursday(s) (4)

das Donnerwetter: (zum) Donnerwetter! (*exclamation of anger or annoyance*)

das Doppelzimmer (-) double room, room with two beds (9)

das Dorf (ẹer) village

der Dorfkrug (ẹe) village inn, village pub

dort there

die Dose (-n) (tin or aluminum) can; jar (14); box

downloaden (downloadet), downgeloadet to download

dpa = Deutsche Presse-Agentur German Press Agency

Dr. = Doktor doctor

der Draht (ẹe) wire; thread

die Draisine (-n) dandy-horse (*predecessor of the bicycle*)

das Drama (Dramen) drama

dran = daran; dran sein to have (one's) turn

drastisch drastic(ally)

draußen outside (7)

die Dreharbeiten (*pl.*) shooting of a film

(sich) drehen to turn, spin; **einen Film drehen** to shoot a film

drei three (E)

dreihundert three hundred (E)

dreimal three times (7)

dreisprachig trilingual

dreißig thirty (E)

dreißigjährig: der Dreißigjährige Krieg the Thirty Years' War

dreitägig lasting three days

dreitausend three thousand (E)

dreizehn thirteen (E)

dreizehnte thirteenth (3)

die Dreizimmerwohnung (-en) three-room apartment

Dresdner (*adj.*) of/from Dresden (*city in eastern Germany*)

drin = darin (*coll.*) inside

dringend urgent(ly) (2)

drinnen inside (7)

dritt: zu dritt as a threesome (10)

dritte third (3)

ein Drittel a third

die Droge (-n) drug; medicine (14)

die Drogensucht drug addiction (14)

die Drogerie (-n) drugstore (*toiletries and sundries*) (5)

drohen to threaten

drüben, da drüben over there (6); on the other side

drucken to print (13)

das Drücken pressure

der Drucker (-) printer (13)

drum = darum (*coll.*) therefore

der Dschungel (-) jungle

du you (*inform. sg.*) (1)

dual (*adj.*) dual

dudeln to toot

der Duft (ẹe) aroma, fragrance

dumm dumb, stupid

die Dummheit (-en) stupidity

dunkel dark (2)

dunkelblau dark blue

dünn thin; slender, skinny

durch (+ *acc.*) through (3); by, by means of

durcharbeiten (arbeitet durch) to work through

das Durcheinander confusion; commotion

durchkommen (kommt durch), kam durch, ist durchgekommen to come through, get through

durchlaufen (läuft durch), lief durch, ist durchgelaufen to run through, go through

durchlesen (liest durch), las durch, durchgelesen to read through

durchs = durch das

der Durchschnitt (-e) average; **im Durchschnitt** on average

durchschnittlich on average (12)

durchstreichen (streicht durch), strich durch, durchgestrichen to cross out, strike through

dürfen (darf), durfte, gedurft to be permitted to; may (4); **Hier darf man nicht parken.** You may not park here. (4); **Was darf's sein?** What will you have?

der Durst thirst; **Durst haben** to be thirsty (2)

die Dusche (-n) shower, shower bath (9)

(sich) duschen to take a shower (8)

duzen to address with **du** (*informally*)

die DVD (-s) DVD

der DVD-Spieler (-) DVD player (2)

dynamisch dynamic(ally)

E

eben just; simply

die Ebene (-n) plain; plane, level

echt genuine(ly); (*coll.*) really (1)

die Ecke (-n) corner (9); **an der Ecke** at the corner (9)

egal: Das ist mir egal. I don't care. (5)

ehemalig former

eher rather, sooner

die Ehre (-n) honor

ehrlich honest

das Ei (-er) egg (5)

die Eierbox (-en) egg carton

der Eierlikör egg liqueur

eigen own (12)

die Eigeninitiative (-n) one's own initiative

die Eigenregie one's own control

die Eigenschaft (-en) characteristic; trait

eigenständig independent(ly)

eigentlich actual(ly), real(ly)

die Eigentumswohnung (-en) condominium

eilen to hurry

ein, eine a(n); one; **Es ist eins. / Es ist ein Uhr.** It's one o'clock. (4); **was für ein …** what kind of a . . . (11)

einander one another, each other

einbegriffen included

einbiegen (biegt ein), bog ein, ist eingebogen to turn, make a turn (9)

einbringen (bringt ein), brachte ein, eingebracht to bring in, yield

einer, eine, eines one (of several)

einfach simple, simply; one-way (*ticket*) (10)

einfallen (fällt ein), fiel ein, ist eingefallen: etwas fällt mir ein something occurs to me

der Einfluss (⁻e) influence

einführen (führt ein) to introduce (14)

die Einführung (-en) introduction

der Eingang (⁻e) entrance, entryway (12)

eingedeutscht Germanized

der Eingriff (-e) small (surgical) operation

einheimisch native; local

die Einheit (-en) unity; unit

einholen (holt ein) to catch up with

einhundert one hundred (E)

einig united; in agreement

einige (*pl.*) several, some

einiges several things

die Einigung (-en) unification

der Einkauf (⁻e) purchase

einkaufen (kauft ein) to shop (4); **einkaufen gehen** to go shopping (4)

der Einkaufsboulevard (-s) street for shopping

der Einkaufstag (-e) day for shopping

das Einkaufszentrum (Einkaufszentren) shopping center

der Einkaufszettel (-) shopping list

das Einkommen income (11)

einladen (lädt ein), lud ein, eingeladen to invite (4)

die Einladung (-en) invitation

einleiten (leitet ein) to introduce

die Einleitung (-en) introduction

einmal once (7); **einmal die Woche** once a week (7); **einmal im Monat/ Jahr** once a month/year (7)

der Einmal-Fotoapparat (-e) disposable camera

einmalig unique

der Einmalrasierer (-) disposable razor

die Einnahmen (*pl.*) income (12)

einnehmen (nimmt ein), nahm ein, eingenommen to take (*medicine*)

einordnen (ordnet ein) to put in order; to classify, categorize

einrichten (richtet ein) to furnish, equip (12)

die Einrichtung (-en) furnishings

eins (*numeral*) one (E); **Es ist eins.** It's one (o'clock). (4)

einschlafen (schläft ein), schlief ein, ist eingeschlafen to fall asleep (4)

einschlägig specialist, relevant

einsenden, sandte ein, eingesandt to send in

einsetzen (setzt ein) to insert

der Einsetzer (-) / die Einsetzerin (-nen) risk taker

einsparen (spart ein) to save, conserve

einsteigen (steigt ein), stieg ein, ist eingestiegen to board, get into (*a vehicle*) (10)

eintausend one thousand (E)

die Eintracht harmony

eintragen (trägt ein), trug ein, eingetragen to register; **eingetragener Verein (e.V.)** registered organization

einverstanden sein (mit + *dat.*) to agree (with), be in agreement (with) (10)

der Einwanderer (-) / die Einwanderin (-nen) immigrant

einwandern (wandert ein), ist eingewandert to immigrate

die Einwanderung (-en) immigration

die Einwanderungsbehörde (-n) department of immigration

die Einwegflasche (-n) nonreturnable bottle

einwöchig lasting one week

der Einwohner (-) / die Einwohnerin (-nen) resident, inhabitant

das Einwohnermeldeamt (⁻er) *government office for registration of residents*

die Einzelheit (-en) detail, particular

einzeln individual; scattered

der Einzelunterricht (-e) one-on-one teaching

das Einzelzimmer (-) single room, room with one bed (9)

einziehen in (+ *acc.*) (zieht ein), zog ein, ist eingezogen to move in(to) (12)

einzig only, sole; **nicht ein einziges Wort** not a single word

das Eis ice cream; ice (5)

der Eisbecher (-) dish of ice cream (6)

die Eiscreme ice cream

die Eiscrempaste ice cream paste

der Eiskaffee (-s) iced coffee (mixed with ice cream and topped with whipped cream)

der Eissalat (-e) iceberg lettuce

das Eisstadion (Eisstadien) ice-skating rink (7)

die Elbe Elbe (River)

die Elblandschaft (-en) landscape of the Elbe River region

das Elbufer (-) bank of the Elbe

der Elefant (-en *masc.*) (-en) elephant

elegant elegant(ly)

die Elektrizität electricity

das Elektrogerät (-e) electrical appliance

der Elektroinstallateur (-e) / die Elektroinstallateurin (-nen) electrician

die Elektronik electronics

der Elektroniker (-) / die Elektronikerin (-nen) electronics engineer

elektronisch electronic(ally)

das Element (-e) element

elf eleven (E)

elfmal eleven times

das Elfmeterschießen penalty kick

elfte eleventh (3)

der Ell(en)bogen (-) elbow (8)

(das) Elsass Alsace

die Eltern (*pl.*) parents (3)

das Elternschlafzimmer (-) parents' bedroom

die E-Mail (-s) e-mail (13)

der Emmentaler Käse Emmental cheese

der Empfang (⁻e) reception

empfangen (empfängt), empfing, empfangen to receive (13)

der Empfänger (-) / die Empfängerin (-nen) recipient

empfänglich receptive, susceptible

die Empfangsanlage (-n) receiver

empfehlen (empfiehlt), empfahl, empfohlen to recommend (5)

die Empfehlung (-en) recommendation

Emser (*adj.*) of/from Bad Ems (*town in western Germany*) das Ende (-n) end; am Ende at the end, in the end; Ende April at the end of April; zu Ende to completion

enden to end

der Endkampf (¨e) final battle; final (game)

endlich finally, at last

die Endung (-en) ending

die Energie (-n) energy

die Energiequelle (-n) source of energy

energiesparend energy-saving

die Energiesparlampe (-n) energy-saving lamp

der Energieverbrauch energy consumption

die Energieverschwendung waste of energy

eng narrow, tight

das Engagement involvement

sich engagieren (für + acc.) to get involved (with), become committed (to) (14)

engagiert committed (11)

(das) England England

(das) Englisch English (language); auf Englisch in English

englisch (adj.) English

englischsprechend English-speaking

der Enkel (-) grandson (3)

die Enkelin (-nen) granddaughter (3)

das Enkelkind (-er) grandchild

das Ensemble (-s) ensemble

die Entbindung (-en) birth, delivery of a child

entdecken to discover

entfernt von (+ dat.) away from

entfliehen (+ dat.), entfloh, ist entflohen to escape

enthalten (enthält), enthielt, enthalten to contain, include; im Preis enthalten included in the price (9)

enthusiastisch enthusiastic(ally)

entlanggehen (geht entlang), ging entlang, ist entlanggegangen to go along, walk along (9)

entlaufen (entläuft), entlief, ist entlaufen to run away

entnervt unnerved

(sich) entscheiden, entschied, entschieden to decide

sich entschließen, entschloss, entschlossen to decide (13)

entschuldigen to excuse (6); Entschuldigen Sie! Excuse me! (6)

die Entschuldigung (-en) apology, excuse; Entschuldigung. Excuse me. (9)

der Entsorger (-) / die Entsorgerin (-nen) (toxic) waste disposal worker

die Entsorgungsplanung waste disposal planning

sich entspannen to relax, take a rest (8)

entsprechen (+ dat.) (entspricht), entsprach, entsprochen to correspond to

entsprechend corresponding

entweder … oder either … or (8)

entwerfen (entwirft), entwarf, entworfen to design, draw up (11)

entwickeln to develop (14)

die Entwicklung (-en) development (11)

das Entwicklungsland (¨er) developing country

das Entwicklungsziel (-e) developmental goal

entzündlich flammable

er he; it (1)

die Erdbeere (-n) strawberry (5)

die Erdbeermarmelade (-n) strawberry jam

die Erde Earth

das Erdgeschoss (-e) ground floor (9)

die Erdkunde geography

das Ereignis (-se) event

erfahren (erfährt), erfuhr, erfahren to find out, learn; to experience

die Erfahrung (-en) experience (11)

erfinden, erfand, erfunden to invent (13)

der Erfinder (-) / die Erfinderin (-nen) inventor

erfinderisch inventive

die Erfindung (-en) invention (13)

der Erfolg (-e) success (11); Erfolg haben to be successful (11)

erfolgreich successful(ly) (11)

die Erfolgskomödie (-n) hit comedy

erfragen to inquire, ask for; to ascertain

das Erfrischungstuch (¨er) towelette

erfüllen to fulfill

ergänzen to complete; to add to

die Ergänzung (-en) completion; addition

ergeben (adj.) devoted

das Ergebnis (-se) result

erhalten (erhält), erhielt, erhalten to get, receive

erhöhen to raise, increase

die Erhöhung (-en) raising, increase

sich erholen to get well, recover (8)

die Erholung rest and recuperation

erinnern an (+ acc.) to remind of; sich erinnern an (+ acc.) to remember

die Erinnerung (-en) memory; remembrance

sich erkälten to catch a cold (8)

die Erkältung (-en) cold (8)

erkennen, erkannte, erkannt to recognize

erklären to explain

die Erklärung (-en) explanation

sich erkundigen to seek information, inquire

die Erkundigung (-en) inquiry

erlauben to allow, permit (9)

erleben to experience (10)

das Erlebnis (-se) experience, event

erleiden, erlitt, erlitten to suffer

erlernbar learnable

erlernen to learn

die Erlösung (-en) redemption, salvation

ermorden to murder

die Ernährung food; nutrition (12)

ernst serious(ly) (1)

der Ernst seriousness

erobern to conquer

eröffnen to open

die Eröffnung (-en) opening

erraten (errät), erriet, erraten to guess

erreichbar reachable

erreichen to reach

errichten to build, put up

erscheinen, erschien, ist erschienen to appear

erschießen, erschoss, erschossen to shoot dead

erschüttern to shake

ersetzen to replace

erst only, not until

erste first (3); ab erstem Juni as of June 1st (12); am ersten Mai on May first (3); der erste Mai May first (3); der erste Stock second floor; erster Klasse fahren to travel first class (10); zum ersten Mal for the first time

erstellen to build; to draw up

die Erstellung construction; drawing up

erstmals (adv.) for the first time

erstöbern to browse

erstrahlen, ist erstrahlt to shine

das Erstsemester (-) first-semester student; freshman

ertönen, ist ertönt to sound, ring out

erwachsen (adj.) grown-up

erwähnen to mention

die Erwähnung (-en) mention

die Erwärmung warming, increase in temperature (14)

erwarten to expect; to wait for

die Erwartung (-en) expectation

erwerben (erwirbt), erwarb, erworben to acquire, buy

erwünscht desired; desirable

erzählen to tell, narrate

der Erzähler (-) / die Erzählerin (-nen) narrator

die Erzählung (-en) story; narration

erziehen, erzog, erzogen to raise, bring up (14)

es it (1, 3); es gibt … (+ acc.) there is/are … (3); Es ist eins. / Es ist ein Uhr. It's one o'clock. (4); Es regnet. It's raining. (7) Es tut mir leid. I'm sorry; Wie geht es dir? / Wie geht's dir? How are you? (inform.) (E); Wie geht es Ihnen? How are you? (form.) (E); Wie wäre es mit … ? How about … ? (13)

der Espresso (-s) espresso (coffee)

essen (isst), aß, gegessen to eat (1)

das Essen (-) food; meal; eating (1); Essen und Trinken food and drinks; zum Essen for dinner

der Essig vinegar

der Esstisch (-e) dining room table

das Esszimmer (-) dining room (2)

(das) Estland Estonia

die Etage (-n) floor, story (12)

etwa approximately, about

etwas something; (adv.) somewhat, a little (2); etwas anderes something different; etwas Neues something new; Hast du etwas Geld? Do you have some money?; Sonst noch etwas? Anything else? (10)

die EU (= die Europäische Union) European Union

euch you (inform. pl. acc.) (3); (to/for) you (inform. pl. dat.) (5)

euer, eure your (*inform. pl.*) (3)
der Euro (-[s]) euro (*monetary unit*) (2)
der Euro-Schein (-e) euro banknote, bill
(das) Europa Europe
europäisch (*adj.*) European; **die Europäische Union (EU)** European Union
der Euroscheck (-s) *type of personal check used in Europe*
die Eurostats (*pl.*) European statistics
e.V. = eingetragener Verein registered organization
eventuell possible; possibly, perhaps
ewig eternal(ly); constant(ly)
das Examen (-) examination
die Ex-Frau (-en) ex-wife
existieren to exist
exklusiv exclusive(ly)
der Ex-Mann (¨er) ex-husband
exotisch exotic(ally)
das Experiment (-e) experiment
experimentieren to experiment
der Experte (-n *masc.*) **(-n) / die Expertin (-nen)** expert
explodieren to explode
explosionsartig like an explosion
explosiv explosive(ly)
exportieren to export
extern external(ly)
extra extra
extrem extreme(ly)
exzellent excellent(ly)
exzentrisch excentric(ally) (1)

F

die Fabrik (-en) factory
die Facette (-n) facet
das Fach (¨er) subject, field of study
der Facharzt (¨e) / die Fachärztin (-nen) specialist (*physician*)
das Fachgeschäft (-e) specialty store
das Fachgymnasium (Fachgymnasien) technical high school
die Fachhochschule (-n) technical college
die Fachhochschulreife technical college degree
die Fachoberschule (-n) trade school
die Fachschule (-n) technical school
die Fähigkeit (-en) ability, skill (11)
fahren (fährt), fuhr, ist gefahren to drive, ride; **erster/zweiter Klasse fahren** to travel first/second class (10); **Fahrrad/Rad fahren** to ride a bicycle (1, 7); **Ski fahren** to ski
die Fahrkarte (-n) ticket (*for train or bus*) (10)
der Fahrkartenschalter (-) ticket window (10)
der Fahrplan (¨e) (train or bus) schedule (10)
das Fahrrad (¨er) bicycle (10); **Fahrrad fahren** to ride a bicycle (1)
der Fahrradverleih (-e) bicycle rental company
der Fahrstuhl (¨e) elevator
die Fahrt (-en) trip; ride (10)
die Fährte (*pl.*) trail, tracks
die Fahrtkosten (*pl.*) traveling expenses
der Faktor (-en) factor

das Faktum (Fakten) fact
der Fall (¨e) case; **auf jeden Fall** in any case (13)
fallen (fällt), fiel, ist gefallen to fall (7)
falls (*subord. conj.*) if; in case
falsch false(ly), wrong(ly), incorrect(ly)
die Fälschung (-en) fake, counterfeit
die Familie (-n) family (3)
das Familienessen (-) family meal
das Familienfest (-e) family celebration (3)
das Familienmitglied (-er) family member
der Familienname (-n *masc.*) **(-n)** family name, last name
der Familienstand marital status
der Fan (-s) fan, enthusiast
fangen (fängt), fing, gefangen to catch
die Fantasie (-n) fantasy
fantastisch fantastic(ally) (1)
die Farbe (-n) color (5)
farblos colorless
(der) Fasching Mardi Gras (*southern Germany and Austria*) (3)
das Fass (¨er) barrel, vat; **vom Fass** on tap, draft (6)
die Fasson (-s) style
fast almost (8)
faszinierend fascinating
faul lazy, lazily (1)
faulenzen to be lazy, lie around (7)
das Fax (-e) fax
das Faxgerät (-e) fax machine (13)
die FAZ (= Frankfurter Allgemeine Zeitung) *major German newspaper*
der FC = Fußballclub
(der) Februar February (3)
fehlen to be missing; to lack; to need; **Was fehlt Ihnen/dir?** What's the matter? (8)
fehlend missing
der Fehler (-) mistake, error
der Feierabend (-e) end of the workday; **am Feierabend** after work
feiern to celebrate (3)
der Feiertag (-e) holiday
fein fine, delicate; all right; **fein säuberlich** nice(ly) and neat(ly)
die Felsmalerei (-en) rock painting
das Fenster (-) window (2)
die Fensterbank (¨e) windowsill
die Ferien (*pl.*) vacation
der Ferienjob (-s) job during the vacation
der Ferientraum (¨e) dream vacation
das Fernglas (¨er) binoculars
fernsehen (sieht fern), sah fern, ferngesehen to watch television (4)
das Fernsehen television; watching television (4); **im Fernsehen** on television
der Fernseher (-) TV set (2)
die Fernsehgebühr (-en) television license fee
das Fernsehgerät (-e) television set
das Fernsehprogramm (-e) TV program, TV schedule
die Fernsehshow (-s) TV show
der Ferrari Ferrari (automobile)
fertig finished, done; ready
das Fest (-e) festival; party, feast
sich festlegen (legt fest) to commit oneself

das Festnetz (-e) conventional fixed-line network
das Festspiel (-e) festival production
feststellen (stellt fest) to establish
die Fete (-n) (*coll.*) party
fett fat; greasy; **fett gedruckt** printed in boldface
feucht damp
das Feuer (-) fire
feuergefährlich flammable
die Feuerwehr (-en) fire department
das Feuerwerk (-e) fireworks
das Fieber fever (8)
fiktiv fictitious
die Filiale (-n) branch office
das Filet (-s) filet
der Film (-e) film, movie (4)
filmen to film
die Filmkritik film criticism
der Filmkritiker (-) / die Filmkritikerin (-nen) movie critic
der Filmpreis (-e) film prize
das Filmprogramm (-e) movie program
der Filmschauspieler (-) / die Filmschauspielerin (-nen) movie actor/actress
der Filmstar (-s) movie star
der Filter (-) filter
der Filz felt (*material*)
der Filzhut (¨e) felt hat
der Finanzbeamte (*decl. adj.*) / die Finanzbeamtin (-nen) tax official
die Finanzen (*pl.*) finance(s)
finanziell financial(ly)
finanzieren to finance
der Finanzskandal (-e) financial scandal
finden, fand, gefunden to find; to think (1); **Ich finde ...** I think . . . ; **Wie findest du ... ?** How do you like . . . ? What do you think of . . . ? (1)
der Finderlohn (¨e) finder's reward
findig resourceful
der Finger (-) finger (8)
(das) Finnland Finland
die Firma (Firmen) firm, company (11)
der Fisch (-e) fish
der Fischer (-) / die Fischerin (-nen) fisherman/fisherwoman
fit fit, in shape (8); **sich fit halten (hält), hielt, gehalten** to keep fit, stay in shape (8)
die Fitness fitness (8)
die Fitnessaktivität (-en) fitness activity
der Fitnessberater (-) / die Fitnessberaterin (-nen) fitness consultant, personal trainer
das Fitnesscenter (-) fitness center; gym (4)
der Fitnessplan (¨e) fitness plan
die Fitnessroutine (-n) fitness routine
das Fitnessstudio (-s) fitness studio
das Fitnesszentrum (Fitnesszentren) fitness center; gym
die Flasche (-n) bottle (14)
die Flaschenpost (-en) message in a bottle
die Flatrate flat rate
der Fleck (-e) *also* **der Flecken (-)** stain, spot

das Fleisch meat (5)

fleißig industrious(ly), diligent(ly), hardworking (1)

flexibel flexible, flexibly

die Flexibilität flexibility

fliegen, flog, ist geflogen to fly (7)

fliehen, floh, ist geflohen to flee

fließend fluent(ly)

der Flitzer (-) (*coll.*) sporty car

der Flohmarkt (-̈e) flea market

die Flöte (-n) flute

flüchten, ist geflüchtet to flee

der Flug (-̈e) flight

der Flugbegleiter (-) / die Flugbegleiterin (-nen) flight attendant

der Flügel (-) wing

der Flughafen (-̈) airport

das Flüglein (-) little wing

das Flugzeug (-e) airplane (10)

der Flur (-e) hallway (12): **für den ganzen Flur** for the whole floor

der Fluss (-̈e) river (7)

flüstern to whisper

der Föhn (-e) hair dryer (9)

die Folge (-n) consequence, result

folgen (+ *dat.*), **ist gefolgt** to follow; **folgend** following

die Folie (-n) foil; sheet; film

fordern to demand

fördern to promote (14)

die Form (-en) form, shape

das Format (-e) format

das Formular (-e) form (*paper to be filled out*)

formulieren to formulate

forschen to do research (13)

der Forscher (-) / die Forscherin (-nen) researcher

die Forschung (-en) research (14)

das Forsthaus (-̈er) forester's house

der Fortschritt (-e) progress (14): **Fortschritte machen** to make progress (14)

die Fortsetzung (-en) continuation

(die) Fortuna Fortune: **Glücksrad Fortuna** *Wheel of Fortune* (quiz show)

das Foto (-s) photograph (2)

das Fotoalbum (Fotoalben) photo album

der Fotoapparat (-e) camera

der Fotograf (-en *masc.*) **(-en) / die Fotografin (-nen)** photographer

fotografieren to photograph

das Fotografieren taking photographs

die Fotokopie (-n) photocopy

das Fotomodell (-e) photo model

das Foyer (-s) foyer

die Frage (-n) question: **eine Frage stellen** to ask a question; **Ich habe eine Frage.** I have a question. (E)

der Fragebogen (-) questionnaire

fragen to ask (2); **fragen nach** (+ *dat.*) to ask about; **nach dem Weg fragen** to ask for directions (9)

der (Schweizer) Franken (-) (Swiss) franc

Frankfurter (*adj.*) of/from Frankfurt

(das) Frankreich France (E)

der Franzose (-n *masc.*) **(-n) / die Französin (-nen)** French person

französisch (*adj.*) French

(das) Französisch French (language)

(die) Frau (-en) Mrs., Ms.; woman (E); wife (3)

frei free(ly) (2); vacant, available, unoccupied; **Ist hier noch frei?** Is this seat available? (6)

das Freibad (-̈er) outdoor swimming pool (7)

Freien: im Freien outdoors (11)

freihaben (hat frei), hatte frei, freigehabt (*coll.*) to have free, have off

die Freiheit (-en) freedom

freilassen (lässt frei), ließ frei, freigelassen to set free, release

freilich admittedly; of course

(der) Freitag Friday (3)

freitags Fridays, on Friday(s) (4)

freiwillig voluntary, voluntarily

die Freizeit free time (7)

die Freizeitaktivität (-en) leisure activity

die Freizeitbeschäftigung (-en) leisure activity

die Freizeitpläne (*pl.*) plans for leisure time

fremd strange; unknown; foreign

der/die Fremde (*decl. adj.*) stranger

der Fremdenführer (-) / die Fremdenführerin (-nen) tour guide

der Fremdenverkehrsverein (-e) tourist association

die Fremdsprache (-n) foreign language

die Freude (-n) joy: **vor Freude** with joy

freuen to please; **sich freuen auf** (+ *acc.*) to look forward to (12); **sich freuen über** (+ *acc.*) to be glad about (12); **Freut mich.** Pleased to meet you. (E)

der Freund (-e) / die Freundin (-nen) friend (1); boyfriend/girlfriend

freundlich friendly (1)

freundschaftlich friendly

der Friede (-n *masc.*) (*also* **der Frieden**) peace

die Friedensbewegung (-en) peace movement

friedlich peaceful(ly)

frieren, fror, gefroren to freeze

das Frisbee (-s) Frisbee

frisch fresh(ly) (5)

frittieren to deep-fry

froh glad, happy

fröhlich cheerful(ly)

frönen (+ *dat.*) to indulge in

der Frosch (-̈e) frog

die Frucht (-̈e) fruit

früh early (4): **morgen früh** tomorrow morning (4)

früher earlier; once; used to (*do, be, etc.*) (7)

das Frühjahr (-e) spring (*season*) (7)

der Frühling (-e) spring (*season*) (7)

frühmorgens early in the morning

das Frühstück (-e) breakfast (5): **zum Frühstück** for breakfast

frühstücken to eat breakfast (4)

die Frühstücksnische (-n) breakfast nook (12)

der Frühstücksraum (-̈e) breakfast room (9)

der Frühstückstisch (-e) breakfast table

die FU = Freie Universität (Berlin) Free University (of Berlin)

(sich) fühlen to feel (8): **sich wohl fühlen** to feel well (8)

führen to lead, guide, conduct; to carry (*merchandise*); **führend** leading; **ein Gespräch führen** to have a conversation; **Protokoll führen** to make a transcript, keep the minutes

der Führerschein (-e) driver's license

die Führung (-en) management; guide, lead; tour

füllen to fill; to fill in

fünf five (E)

fünfmonatig lasting five months

fünfte fifth (3)

fünfzehn fifteen (E)

das Fünfzeilenformat (-e) five-line format

fünfzig fifty (E)

funktionieren to work, function (9)

für (+ *acc.*) for (3); **was für (ein)** what kind of (a) (11)

fürchterlich horrible, horribly

fürs = für das

der Fuß (-̈e) foot (8): **zu Fuß gehen, ging, ist gegangen** to walk, go on foot (8)

der Fußball (-̈e) soccer; soccer ball (7); **Fußball spielen** to play soccer (7)

der Fußballplatz (-̈e) soccer field

der Fußballspieler (-) / die Fußballspielerin (-nen) soccer player

der Fußballtrainer (-) / die Fußballtrainerin (-nen) soccer coach

die Fußballweltmeisterschaft (-en) world soccer championship, World Cup

der Fußgänger (-) / die Fußgängerin (-nen) pedestrian

die Fußgängerzone (-n) pedestrian zone (9)

G

die Gabe (-n) gift

die Gabel (-n) fork (6)

der Gang (-̈e) course (*of a meal*)

ganz complete(ly), total(ly), entire(ly) (12); quite, very, really (1): **ganz gut** quite good; **ganz toll** really great

gar even; **gar kein(e)** not any; **gar nicht** not at all; **gar nichts** nothing at all

die Garage (-n) garage (2)

garantieren to guarantee

die Garderobe (-n) wardrobe; closet (12)

die Gardine (-n) curtain, drapes

garnieren to garnish

der Garten (-̈) garden; yard (2)

die Gartenarbeit (-en) gardening; yard work

die Gartenlaube (-n) garden house

das Gartenlokal (-e) garden restaurant

der Gärtner (-) / die Gärtnerin (-nen) gardener

die Gasse (-n) lane, narrow street

der Gast (-̈e) guest

das Gästehaus (-̈er) guesthouse

das Gästezimmer (-) guest room (12)

die Gastfamilie (-n) host family

gastfreundlich hospitable

die Gastfreundschaft hospitality
der Gastgeber (-) / die Gastgeberin (-nen) host/hostess
das Gasthaus (¨er) restaurant; inn
der Gasthof (¨e) hotel; restaurant; inn
die Gastronomie gastronomy
die Gaststätte (-n) full-service restaurant (6)
die Gaststube (-n) (hotel) dining room, lounge
der Gastwirt (-e) / die Gastwirtin (-nen) restaurant owner; restaurant manager
geb. = **geboren(e)**
das Gebäck (-e) baked goods; cakes and pastries
das Gebäude (-) building
geben (gibt), gab, gegeben to give (3); to put; **es gibt** there is/are (3); **eine Party geben** to have a party, throw a party; **Rat geben** to advise
geboren born; **geboren werden** to be born; **geborene** née (*maiden name*); **ich bin geboren** I was born (1)
der Gebrauch use
gebrauchen to use
gebraucht used
die Gebühr (-en) fee
das Geburtsdatum (Geburtsdaten) date of birth
der Geburtsort (-e) birthplace (1)
der Geburtstag (-e) birthday, date of birth (1); **Herzlichen Glückwunsch zum Geburtstag!** Happy birthday! (3); **Wann hast du Geburtstag?** When is your birthday? (3)
die Geburtstagsfeier (-n) birthday celebration
die Gedächtniskirche *famous church in Berlin*
der Gedanke (-n *masc.***) (-n)** thought; **sich über etwas** (*acc.*) **Gedanken machen** to think about something, to ponder something
das Gedicht (-e) poem
geehrt: sehr geehrter/geehrte (+ *proper name*) *formal letter address form*
geeignet suitable, appropriate
die Gefahr (-en) danger (14)
gefährden to endanger
gefährlich dangerous(ly) (10)
gefallen (+ *dat.*) **(gefällt), gefiel, gefallen** to be pleasing (5); **Wie gefällt Ihnen … ?** How do you like … ? (5)
der Gefallen (-) favor; **einen Gefallen tun** to do a favor
das Gefängnis (-se) prison, jail (14)
das Geflügel poultry
der Gefrierpunkt (-e) freezing point
der Gefrierschrank (¨e) (upright) freezer
gefroren frozen (5)
das Gefühl (-e) feeling; emotion
gegen (+ *acc.*) against; around, about (+ *time*) (3, 6); **(so) gegen fünf Uhr** around five o'clock (6)
die Gegend (-en) area, region
die Gegendarstellung (-en) opposing view
der Gegensatz (¨e) contrast
gegenseitig mutual(ly); reciprocal(ly)
das Gegenteil (-e) opposite

gegenüber von (+ *dat.*) across from (9)
gegenwärtig present(ly), current(ly)
das Gehalt (¨er) salary (11)
das Geheimnis (-se) secret
gehen, ging, ist gegangen to go (1); **einkaufen gehen** to go shopping (4); **Geht's gut?** Are you doing well? (E); **Na, wie geht's?** How are you? (*casual*) (E); **spazieren gehen** to go for a walk (4); **Wie geht es Ihnen?** How are you? (*form.*) (E); **Wie geht's (dir)?** How are you? (*inform.*) (E); **zu Fuß gehen** to walk, go on foot (8)
gehoben upper; elevated
gehören (+ *dat.*) to belong to (*a person*) (5); **gehören zu** (+ *dat.*) to be a part of
die Geige (-n) violin
geistig mental, intellectual
das Gelächter (-) laughter
gelb yellow (5)
das Geld money (2)
der Geldkurier (-e) money courier
gelegen situated, located; **zentral gelegen** centrally located (2)
die Gelegenheit (-en) opportunity (11); occasion
gelegentlich occasional(ly)
gelten (+ *dat.*) **(gilt), galt, gegolten** to be valid; **gelten als** to be considered as
gelungen inspired; priceless
das Gemälde (-) painting
gemein common; **gemein haben** to have in common
die Gemeinde (-n) community
gemeinsam common; in common; together
die Gemeinschaft (-en) community
gemischt mixed
das Gemüse vegetable(s) (5)
der Gemüsestand (¨e) vegetable stand
gemütlich cozy, cozily (4); comfortable, comfortably; leisurely
die Gemütlichkeit comfort; informality
genau exact(ly) (2); meticulous(ly)
genauso just/exactly as (7); **genauso … wie** just/exactly as … as
die Generation (-en) generation
das Genie (-s) genius
genießen, genoss, genossen to enjoy, savor, relish
der Genießer (-) / die Genießerin (-nen) connoisseur
der Genitiv (-e) genitive case
das Genitivobjekt (-e) genitive object
die Genitivpräposition (-en) preposition governing the genitive case
gentechnisch modifizert genetically modified
genug enough, sufficient(ly)
genügen to suffice
genügend enough, sufficient(ly)
geöffnet open (6)
die Geographie geography
geographisch geographical(ly)
der Geoökologe (-n *masc.***) (-n) / die Geoökologin (-nen)** geo-ecologist
die Geoökologie geo-ecology
das Gepäck luggage (9)

die Gepäckaufbewahrung baggage check (10)
gerade just, exactly (2); straight
geradeaus straight ahead (9); **immer geradeaus** (keep on going) straight ahead (9)
das Gerät (-e) appliance, device (12)
geräuchert smoked
das Gericht (-e) dish (*of prepared food*) (6)
germanisch Germanic, Teutonic
die Germanistik German studies
gern(e) (lieber, liebst-) gladly (2); **gern** (+ *verb*) to like to (*do something*) (2); **gern haben** to like (*a person or thing*) (2); **ich hätte gern** I would like to have
das Gesamtbild (-er) overall view, big picture
die Gesamthochschule (-n) *combined scientific and pedagogical university*
die Gesamtschule (-n) German secondary school (*grades 6 to 12*)
der Gesangsverein (-e) choral society
das Geschäft (-e) store, shop; business
die Geschäftsfrau (-en) businesswoman (11)
die Geschäftsleute (*pl.*) businesspeople
der Geschäftsmann (Geschäftsleute) businessman (11)
geschehen (geschieht), geschah, ist geschehen to happen
gescheit intelligent, bright; sensible, decent (13); **nichts Gescheites** nothing decent (13)
das Geschenk (-e) present, gift (3)
die Geschichte (-n) story; history
das Geschirr dishes
die Geschirrspülmaschine (-n) dishwasher
geschlossen closed (6)
der Geschmack (¨e) taste
geschützt protected
geschweige denn … let alone . . .
die Geschwindigkeit (-en) speed
die Geschwindigkeitsbegrenzung (-en) speed limit
die Geschwister (*pl.*) brothers and sisters, siblings (3)
geschwollen swollen
die Geselligkeit good company
die Gesellschaft (-en) society
das Gesetz (-e) law
das Gesicht (-er) face (8)
gespannt eager(ly), expectant(ly)
das Gespräch (-e) conversation
gestern yesterday (7); **gestern Abend** yesterday evening; **gestern Vormittag** yesterday morning
gestreift striped (5)
gestresst (*adj.*) under stress
gesund healthy, healthful; well (8)
die Gesundheit health (8)
gesundheitsbewusst health-conscious(ly)
gesundheitsschädlich unhealthy, unhealthily
das Gesundheitswesen health-care system
das Getränk (-e) beverage, drink (5)
die Getränkedose (-n) beverage can (14)
der Getränkeladen (¨) beverage store (5)
das Getreide (-) cereal, grain

getrennt separate(ly) (6)

gewährleisten to guarantee, ensure

die Gewalt violence, force; power, dominion

die Gewaltbereitschaft readiness for violence

die Gewalttätigkeit (-en) (act of) violence (14)

das Gewicht (-e) weight

gewinnen, gewann, gewonnen to win

gewiss certain(ly)

das Gewitter (-) thunderstorm (7)

die Gewohnheit (-en) habit

der Gewohnheitsmensch (-en *masc.***) (-en)** creature of habit

gewöhnlich usual(ly) (4)

gewöhnt an (+ *acc.*) accustomed to

die Gewürzgurke (-n) pickle, pickled gherkin

gießen, goss, gegossen to pour

das Gift (-e) poison

giftfrei nontoxic

der Giftstoff (-e) toxic substance

die Gitarre (-n) guitar

das Gitter (-) bars; **hinter Gitter(n)** (*coll.*) behind bars

glänzend shiny; excellent(ly)

das Glas (Ëer) glass

glauben to believe (5); **Ich glaube dir nicht.** I don't believe you.

gleich right away, immediately (8); same; **gleich da drüben** right over there

gleichfalls likewise (E)

die Gleichstellung equality, equal rights

gleichzeitig simultaneous(ly)

das Gleis (-e) track (10); platform

global global(ly) (14)

die Globalisierung globalization

der Globus (Globen) globe

das Glöckchen (-) little bell

das Glockenspiel (-e) chimes, glockenspiel

das Glück fortune, luck; happiness; **Viel Glück!** Good luck! (1)

glücklich happy, happily

das Glücksrad (Ëer) wheel of fortune

der Glückwunsch (Ëe) congratulations; **Herzlichen Glückwunsch zum Geburtstag!** Happy birthday! (3)

die Glühbirne (-n) lightbulb

die Glühlampe (-n) lightbulb

GmbH = Gesellschaft mit beschränkter Haftung corporation

das Gold gold

golden golden

der Goldgräber (-) gold digger

die Goldmedaille (-n) gold medal

(das) Golf golf

googeln to Google, use the Google search engine

der Gott (Ëer) God; god; **Gott sei Dank** thank God; **grüß Gott** hello (*in southern Germany and Austria*)

der Gourmet (-s) gourmet

Gr. = Größe

graben (gräbt), grub, gegraben to dig

der Grad (-e) degree (7); **35 Grad** 35 degrees (7)

die Graffiti (*pl.*) graffiti

die Grafik (-en) drawing

das Gramm (-e) gram

die Grammatik (-en) grammar; grammar book

grandios magnificent(ly)

das Gras (Ëer) grass

gratulieren (+ *dat.*) to congratulate (3); **Ich gratuliere!** Congratulations!

grau gray (5)

graugetigert with gray stripes

die Grenze (-n) border, boundary

(das) Griechenland Greece

griechisch (*adj.*) Greek

der Grill (-s) grill, barbeque (6)

grillen to grill, barbeque

der Grillteller (-) grill platter

die Grippe flu (8)

groß big, large (2); tall (1); great

großartig magnificent(ly)

(das) Großbritannien Great Britain

die Größe (-n) size (5); height

die Großeltern (*pl.*) grandparents (3)

die Großmutter (Ë) grandmother (3)

der Großraumwagen (-) rail car without compartments

die Großstadt (Ëe) big city, metropolis

größtenteils for the most part

der Großvater (Ë) grandfather (3)

großzügig generous(ly)

grün green (5)

der Grund (Ëe) reason; ground; **im Grunde genommen** basically (14)

gründen to found, establish

die Grundform (-en) basic form

die Grundgangart (-en) basic pace

die Grundlage (-n) basis, foundation

der Grundlsee *lake in Austria*

der Grundriss (-e) outline; layout; blueprint

die Grundschule (-n) primary school (11)

die Gründung (-en) founding, establishment

das Grüne (*decl. adj.*) green, greenery; **im Grünen** in the country; **ins Grüne fahren** to drive out to the country

die Gruppe (-n) group

der Gruß (Ëe) greeting (12); **herzliche Grüße** kind regards; **viele Grüße** best wishes (12)

(sich) grüßen to say hello (to one another); **grüß dich** hello, hi (*among friends and family*) (E); **grüß Gott** hello (*in southern Germany and Austria*)

die Grütze: rote Grütze *dessert made of red berries*

(das) Guatemala Guatemala

gucken (*coll.*) to look

das Gulasch (-e) goulash

gültig valid

günstig convenient(ly); favorable, favorably (9); reasonable (in price); **günstig liegen** to be conveniently located (9)

die Gurke (-n) cucumber (5)

der Gurt (-e) strap; seatbelt

der Gürtel (-) belt (5)

gut (besser, best-) good, well (1); **Alles Gute!** All the best! (3); **danke, gut** fine, thanks (E); **Er tanzt gut.** He dances well. (1); **Es geht mir gut.** I am fine; **Geht's gut?** Are you doing well? (E); **Gute Besserung!** Get well soon! (8); **gute Nacht** good night (E); **guten Abend** good evening (E); **guten Morgen** good morning (E); **guten Tag** hello, good day (E); **Mach's gut.** Take care, so long. (*inform.*) (E); **nicht besonders gut** not particularly well (E); **sehr gut** very well; fine; good (E); **zu guter Letzt** in the end, at long last

gutmachen (macht gut) to make good

gymnasial pertaining to secondary school

der Gymnasiast (-en *masc.***) (-en) / die Gymnasiastin (-nen)** secondary school student

das Gymnasium (Gymnasien) secondary school (*leading to university*) (11)

H

das Haar (-e) hair (8)

haben (hat), hatte, gehabt to have (2); **Angst haben (vor** + *dat.***)** to be afraid (of) (12); **Durst haben** to be thirsty (2); **Erfolg haben** to be successful (11); **gern haben** to like (*a person or thing*) (2); **Hunger haben** to be hungry (2); **Ich habe eine Frage.** I have a question. (E) **Ich hätte gern . . .** I would like to have . . . ; **Lust haben** to feel like (*doing something*) (2); **Recht haben** to be correct (2); **Wann hast du Geburtstag?** When is your birthday? (3); **Zeit haben** to have time (2)

der Hackbraten (-) meatloaf

der Hafen (Ë) harbor, port (9)

der Häftling (-e) prisoner

der Hagel hail (7)

das Hähnchen (-) chicken (5)

der Haken (-) hook

halb half (4); **halb zwei** half past one, one-thirty (4)

das Halbfinale semifinal

die Halbpension *accommodation with two meals per day included*

die Hälfte (-n) half

der Halfter (-) halter

das Hallenbad (Ëer) indoor swimming pool (7)

hallo hello (*among friends and family*) (E)

der Hals (Ëe) neck; throat (8)

das Halsband (Ëer) (animal) collar

die Halsschmerzen (*pl.*) sore throat (8)

halt (*particle*) just

halten (hält), hielt, gehalten to hold, keep; to stop; **sich fit halten** to keep fit, stay in shape (8); **halten für** (+ *acc.*) to hold; to consider, think (14); **halten von** (+ *dat.*) to think of; **ein Referat halten** to give a paper; **eine Vorlesung halten** to deliver a lecture

die Haltestelle (-n) (bus or streetcar) stop (9)

die Haltung (-en) posture, stance; attitude

Hamburger (*adj.*) of/from Hamburg

der Hamburger (-) hamburger

Hamelner (*adj.*) of/from Hamelin

der **Hamster (-)** hamster
die **Hand (¨e)** hand (8)
der **Handel** sales, trade (11)
handeln to act; **sich handeln um** (+ *acc.*) to be about; **handeln von** (+ *dat.*) to deal with, be about (13); **Wovon handelt es?** What's it about? (13)
das **Handgepäck** carry-on luggage (10)
die **Handlung (-en)** plot, action
der **Handschuh (-e)** glove (10)
die **Handtasche (-n)** handbag
das **Handtuch (¨er)** towel
das **Handy (-s)** cell phone (2)
hängen, hängte, gehängt to hang (up), put up (6)
hängen, hing, gehangen to hang, be hanging (6)
hart hard; severe(ly)
das **Häschen (-)** bunny, little rabbit (*term of endearment*)
hassen to hate
hässlich ugly (2)
der **Hauch (-e)** breath; wind; whiff
hauen, haute, gehauen to beat
häufig frequent(ly), often
Haupt- main, major, central (*used in compound words*)
das **Hauptfach (¨er)** major subject
die **Hauptfigur (-en)** main character, protagonist
das **Hauptgericht (-e)** main dish, entrée (6)
hauptsächlich mainly, mostly
die **Hauptschule (-n)** junior high school (*grades 5–9/10*)
das **Hauptseminar (-e)** advanced seminar
die **Hauptstadt (¨e)** capital (city)
die **Hauptstraße (-n)** main street
das **Haus (¨er)** house (2); **nach Haus(e) gehen** to go home (5); **zu Haus(e)** at home (5)
die **Hausarbeit (-en)** housework; homework
die **Hausaufgabe (-n)** homework
der **Hausbewohner (-) / die Hausbewohnerin (-nen)** tenant
die **Hausfrau (-en)** homemaker, housewife
die **Hausfrauensauce (-n)** homemade sauce
hausgemacht homemade
der **Haushalt (-e)** household (12)
die **Haushaltswaren** (*pl.*) household utensils
der **Hausmanager (-) / die Hausmanagerin (-nen)** building manager
der **Hausmann (¨er)** house husband, stay-at-home husband
das **Hausmittel (-)** household remedy
die **Hausmusik** music performed at home
die **Hausnummer (-n)** street address (number) (E)
der **Hausschuh (-e)** slipper (5)
das **Haustier (-e)** pet
die **Haustür (-en)** front door
die **Haut (¨e)** skin
die **Hautcreme (-s)** skin cream
Hbf. = Hauptbahnhof main train station
heben, hob, gehoben to lift
das **Hefeweizen** *unfiltered wheat beer*

das **Heft (-e)** notebook (12); **das Comic-Heft (-e)** comic book
heftig heavy, heavily; violent(ly)
heikel awkward, delicate
das **Heilbad (¨er)** spa
der **Heilige Abend** Christmas Eve (3); **am Heiligen Abend** on Christmas Eve
das **Heilmittel (-)** remedy
die **Heimat (-en)** homeland, hometown
der **Heimatverein (-e)** local history society
der **Heimcomputer** home computer
heimtückisch treacherous
heiraten to marry, get married (3)
heiß hot (7)
heißen, hieß, geheißen to be called, be named (1); **das heißt (d.h.)** that is, i.e. (8); **Ich heiße …** My name is . . . (E); **Wie heißen Sie?** What's your name? (*form.*) (E); **Wie heißt … ?** What's the name of . . . ? (E); **Wie heißt du?** What's your name? (*inform.*) (E)
der **Heißluftballon (-s)** hot air balloon
heiter pleasant, fair, bright (7)
die **Heizung (-en)** heating (12)
die **Heizwärme** warmth from a heater
das **Hektar (-e)** hectare (= 2.471 acres)
hektisch hectic(ally)
helfen (+ *dat.*) **(hilft), half, geholfen** to help (5)
hell light, bright(ly) (2)
hellblau light blue
hellgelb light yellow
das **Hemd (-en)** shirt (5)
her this way; here; **hin und her** back and forth
herausfinden (findet heraus), fand heraus, herausgefunden to find out
herausfordern (fordert heraus) to challenge (11)
die **Herausforderung (-en)** challenge
der **Herbst (-e)** autumn, fall (7)
hereinkommen (kommt herein), kam herein, ist hereingekommen to come inside
hereinsehen (sieht herein), sah herein, hereingesehen to look in (on somebody)
herhaben (hat her), hatte her, hergehabt (*coll.*): **Wo hast du die gute Wurst her?** Where did you get the good sausage?
herkommen (kommt her), kam her, ist hergekommen to come here; to come from
herkömmlich conventional, traditional
der **Herr (-n** *masc.*) **(-en)** Mr.; gentleman (E); **meine Damen und Herren** ladies and gentlemen
der **Herrenartikel (-)** men's accessory
die **Herrenkonfektion** men's ready-to-wear clothing
herrlich wonderful(ly), magnificent(ly)
herstellen (stellt her) to produce, manufacture (11)
der **Hersteller (-)** producer, manufacturer (11)
herum: um … herum around (*a place*)
herumfahren (um + *acc.*) **(fährt herum), fuhr herum, ist herumgefahren** to drive around

herumtönen (tönt herum) to resound
herunter down
herunterladen (lädt herunter), lud herunter, heruntergeladen to download
das **Herz (**gen. **-ens,** dat. **-en) (-en)** heart
die **Herzensdame (-n)** woman in one's heart
herzlich cordial(ly); **herzlich willkommen** welcome (E); **Herzlichen Glückwunsch zum Geburtstag!** Happy birthday! (3)
(das) Hessen Hesse (*a German state*)
heute today (1); **heute Abend** this evening (1); **heute Morgen** this morning (4); **heute Nachmittag** this afternoon (4); **heute Nacht** last night; tonight **Welches Datum ist heute?** What is today's date? (3)
heutzutage nowadays
hi (*coll.*) hi (E)
hie und da here and there
hier here (1); **Ist hier noch frei?** Is this seat available? (6)
hierher (to) here, hither
die **Hi-Fi-Anlage (-n)** hi-fi system
die **Hilfe** help, assistance; **um Hilfe bitten** to ask for help
die **Hilfsorganisation (-en)** aid organization
das **Hilfsverb (-en)** helping verb, auxiliary verb
der **Himmel (-)** sky (7); heaven
hin (to) there, thither; **hin und her** back and forth; **hin und zurück** round-trip (10); **vor sich hin** to oneself
hinaufgehen (geht hinauf), ging hinauf, ist hinaufgegangen to go up
hinausschieben (schiebt hinaus), schob hinaus, hinausgeschoben to put off, postpone
hinfahren (fährt hin), fuhr hin, ist hingefahren to go there, drive there, ride there
hingehen (geht hin), ging hin, ist hingegangen to go there
hinlegen (legt hin) to lay down; **sich hinlegen** to lie down (8)
sich hinsetzen (setzt hin) to sit down (8)
hinstecken (steckt hin) to stick (in), put (in)
hinten in the back
hinter (+ *acc./dat.*) behind, in back of (6)
hinterher afterward
hinterlassen (hinterlässt), hinterließ, hinterlassen to leave behind; leave (*e.g., a message*) (13)
hinuntergehen (geht hinunter), ging hinunter, ist hinuntergegangen to go down
hinunterstürzen (stürzt hinunter) to throw down; to gulp down
der **Hinweis (-e)** tip, clue
historisch historical(ly)
der **Hit (-s)** hit
das **HIV (= humanes Immundefizienzvirus)** HIV
hm (*interjection*) hmm
das **Hobby (-s)** hobby (1)

hoch (hoh-) (höher, höchst-) high(ly) (2); tall

hochgemut cheerful(ly)

die Hochschule (-n) university, college

der Hochschullehrer (-) / die Hochschullehrerin (-nen) university instructor (1)

die Hochschulreife college qualification

die Höchstgeschwindigkeit (-en) maximum speed, speed limit

die Hochzeit (-en) wedding (3)

der Hof (⸚e) farm; court

das Hofbräuhaus famous beer hall in Munich

hoffen (auf + acc.) to hope (for) (10)

hoffentlich hopefully; I/we/let's hope (6)

die Hoffnung (-en) hope

höflich polite(ly)

die Höhe (-n) height; in die Höhe upward

der Höhepunkt (-e) climax, peak; highlight

holen to get, fetch

(das) Holland Holland

holländisch (adj.) Dutch

der Höllenlärm hellish noise

das Holz wood

der Holzhammer (-) (wooden) mallet

der Holzpantoffel (-n) wooden shoe, clog

der Holzzaun (⸚e) wooden fence

der Hometrainer (-) home exercise equipment

der Honig honey

die Honigmelone (-n) honeydew melon

hören to hear, listen to (1)

das Horoskop (-e) horoscope (13)

das Hörspiel (-e) radio play

der Hörtext (-e) listening text

die Hose (-n) (pair of) pants, trousers (5)

das Hotel (-s) hotel (9)

das Hotelpersonal hotel personnel

das Huhn (⸚er) chicken

der Humor (-e) humor, sense of humor

der Humorist (-en masc.) (-en) / die Humoristin (-nen) humorist; comedian

humorvoll full of humor, humorous(ly)

der Hund (-e) dog (3) / die Hündin (-nen) female dog

hundert one hundred (E)

hundsmiserabel (coll.) sick as a dog (8)

der Hunger hunger; famine (14) Hunger haben to be hungry (2)

husten to cough

der Husten (-) cough, coughing (8)

das Hustenbonbon (-s) cough drop

der Hut (⸚e) hat (5)

die Hütte (-n) hut, cabin (10)

hypnotisieren to hypnotize

I

der ICE (= Intercityexpresszug) intercity express train

ich I (1); ich auch me too (1); ich bin ... geboren I was born . . . (1)

ideal ideal(ly)

die Idee (-n) idea

identifizieren to identify

die Identität (-en) identity

das Idyll (-e) idyllic setting

idyllisch idyllic(ally)

ihm (to/for) him/it (dat.) (5)

ihn him; it (acc.) (3)

Ihnen (to/for) you (dat., form.): Was fehlt Ihnen? What's the matter? (8); Wie gefällt Ihnen ... ? How do you like . . . ? (5); Wie geht es Ihnen? How are you? (form.) (E)

ihnen (to/for) them (dat.) (5)

Ihr your (form.) (3)

ihr you (inform. pl.) (1); her, its; their (3); (to/for) her/it (dat.) (5)

illegal illegal(ly)

im = in dem; im Freien outdoors (11); im Grunde genommen basically (14); im Januar in January (3); im Kaufhaus at the department store

der Imbiss (-e) fast-food stand (6)

immer always (1); immer geradeaus (keep on going) straight ahead (9) immer noch still

die Immobilien (pl.) real estate

der Imperativ (-e) imperative verb form

der Imperativsatz (⸚e) imperative clause

das Imperfekt (-e) imperfect tense, simple past

impulsiv impulsive(ly)

in (+ acc./dat.) in/into; inside; to (a place) (6); in der Mitte (der Stadt) in the center (of the city) (9); in der Nähe (des Bahnhofs) near (the train station) (9); in die Disko gehen to go to a disco, go clubbing (4); in die Oper gehen to go to the opera (4); in zwei Tagen in two days (6)

incl. = inkl.

indem (subord. conj.) while, as

der Indianer (-) / die Indianerin (-nen) American Indian (person)

indirekt indirect(ly)

indisch (adj.) Indian, of/from/pertaining to India

individuell individual(ly)

die Industrie (-n) industry

der Infinitiv (-e) infinitive verb form

die Inflation (-en) inflation

das Info (-s) (coll.) info(rmation)

die Informatik computer science

der Informatiker (-) / die Informatikerin (-nen) computer scientist (11)

die Information (-en) information

(sich) informieren (über + acc.) to inform (oneself) (about) (8)

der Ingenieur (-e) / die Ingenieurin (-nen) engineer

Inh. = Inhaber(in)

der Inhaber (-) / die Inhaberin (-nen) proprietor

der Inhalt (-e) content(s)

die Initiative (-n) initiative

inkl. = inklusive

inklusive inclusive; included

das Inland (sg. only) home country (13); im Inland und Ausland at home and abroad (13)

das Inlineskaten inline skating

inmitten (+ gen.) in the midst of

die Innenstadt (⸚e) downtown, city center (9)

innerhalb (+ gen.) within, inside of (9)

ins = in das; ins Kino gehen to go to the movies (4); ins Theater gehen to go to the theater (4)

das Insekt (-en) insect

die Insel (-n) island

insgesamt altogether, in total (10)

das Institut (-e) institute

das Instrument (-e) instrument

die Integration (-en) integration

intelligent intelligent(ly)

intensiv intense(ly); intensive(ly)

die Interaktion (-en) interaction

interessant interesting (1); nichts Interessantes nothing interesting

das Interesse (-n) interest (1)

der Interessensträger (-) / die Interessensträgerin (-nen) stakeholder

interessieren to interest; sich interessieren für (+ acc.) to be interested in (11)

interessiert (an + dat.) interested (in)

intern internal(ly)

international international(ly)

das Internet Internet (13)

die Internetsuche (-n) Internet search

der Internetzugang Internet access (9)

das Interrogativpronomen (-) interrogative pronoun

der Inter-Treff-Club (-s) club for meeting one another

das Interview (-s) interview

interviewen to interview

der Interviewer (-) / die Interviewerin (-nen) interviewer

investieren to invest

inzwischen in the meantime, meanwhile

der Iran Iran

irgendwer (coll.) somebody

irgendwie somehow

irgendwo somewhere

(das) Irland Ireland

irritieren to irritate

der Irrtum (⸚er) error

das Isartal Isar Valley

isolieren to isolate; to insulate (14)

(das) Israel Israel

ist is: Das ist ... This is . . . (E)

(das) Italien Italy (E)

der Italiener (-) / die Italienerin (-nen) Italian (person)

italienisch (adj.) Italian

(das) Italienisch Italian (language)

J

ja yes (E); of course

die Jacke (-n) jacket (5)

die Jagd (-en) hunt

der Jagdpächter (-) / die Jagdpächterin (-nen) game tenant

der Jäger (-) / die Jägerin (-nen) hunter

das Jahr (-e) year (1): dieses Jahr this year; einmal im Jahr once a year (7); im Jahr(e) ... in the year . . . ; jedes Jahr every year; letztes Jahr last year; mit 10 Jahren at age 10; nächstes Jahr next year (1); **die 90er Jahre** the nineties; **seit zwei Jahren** for two years (6)

die Jahreszeit (-en) season

das Jahrhundert (-e) century

-jährig: 12-jährig (*adj.*) twelve-year(-old), twelve years old; **der/die 12-Jährige** (*decl. adj.*) twelve-year-old (person)

jährlich annual(ly)

(das) Jamaika Jamaica

(der) Jänner January (*Austrian*)

(der) Januar January (3); **im Januar** in January (3)

der Jazz jazz

je ever; every, each **je** (+ *comparative*) ... **desto** (+ *comparative*) ... the ... the ...; **je nachdem** depending on

je (*interjection*): **oh je** oh dear

die Jeans (*pl.*) jeans (5)

jeder, jede, jedes each, every (5); everybody; **auf jeden Fall** in any case (13); **jeden Abend** every evening; **jeden Morgen** every morning; **jeden Tag** every day (7); **jedes Jahr** every year

jedesmal every time

jedoch however, but

der Jeep (-s) jeep

jemand somebody, someone

Jenaer (*adj.*) of/from Jena (*a town in central Germany*)

jetzig current, present

jetzt now (1)

jeweils each time, in each case

der Job (-s) (temporary) job

jobben to work (at a temporary job) (12)

jobbenderweise with respect to working at a temporary job

die Jobbörse (-n) job-finding agency

joggen to jog (7)

der Joghurt yogurt (5)

der Joghurtbecher (-) carton of yogurt

das Journal (-e) journal

der Journalist (-en *masc.*) **(-en) / die Journalistin (-nen)** journalist (1)

das Jubiläum (Jubiläen) anniversary

die Jugend youth; young people

das Jugendgästehaus (¨er) (type of) youth hostel

die Jugendherberge (-n) youth hostel (9)

der/die Jugendliche (*decl. adj.*) young person; teenager

(das) Jugoslawien Yugoslavia

(der) Juli July (3)

jung young (10)

der Junge (-n *masc.*) **(-n)** boy (2)

(der) Juni June (3)

(die) Jura (*pl.*) law (*as a subject of study*)

die Justiz justice

K

das Kabel (-) cable

der Kabelanschluss (¨e) cable TV connection (13)

der Käfer (-) beetle (*also Volkswagen Beetle*)

der Kaffee (-s) coffee

der Kaffeebecher (-) coffee cup

die Kaffeemaschine (-n) coffeemaker

der Käfig (-e) cage

(das) Kairo Cairo

der Kaiser (-) / die Kaiserin (-nen) emperor/empress

der Kaiserschmarren *broken-up pancake sprinkled with powdered sugar and raisins*

der Kajak (-s) kayak

die Kalbsleberwurst (¨e) veal liver sausage

der Kalender (-) calendar (3)

(das) Kalifornien California

die Kalorie (-n) calorie

kalt (kälter, kältest-) cold (7)

die Kamera (-s) camera (10)

der Kamerastandpunkt (-e) camera's point of view

der Kamillentee chamomile tea

der Kamin (-e) fireplace, hearth

(sich) kämmen to comb (one's hair) (8)

die Kammermusik chamber music

das Kammerspiel (-e) chamber drama

(das) Kanada Canada

der Kanadier (-) / die Kanadierin (-nen) Canadian (person)

der Kanarienvogel (¨) canary

die Kanarischen Inseln (*pl.*) Canary Islands

der Kandidat (-en *masc.*) **(-en) / die Kandidatin (-nen)** candidate

der Kanton (-e) canton (*division of Switzerland*)

die Kanu (-s) canoe

der Kanzler (-) / die Kanzlerin (-nen) chancellor

der Kapellmeister (-) / die Kapellmeisterin (-nen) bandleader; conductor

die Kapitalanlage (-n) investment of capital

der Kapitän (-e) captain

das Kapitel (-) chapter

die Kapitulation (-en) capitulation

kaputt broken (9)

die Karibik the Caribbean

kariert checkered, plaid (5)

Karlsruher (*adj.*) of/from Karlsruhe (*city in southwestern Germany*)

(der) Karneval Mardi Gras (*Rhineland*) (3)

die Karotte (-n) carrot (5)

die Karriere (-n) career; **Karriere machen** to be successful in a career

die Karte (-n) card (7); ticket; chart; map; **Karten spielen** to play cards (1)

die Kartoffel (-n) potato (5)

die Kartoffelchips (*pl.*) potato chips

der Kartoffelkloß (¨e) potato dumpling

das Kartoffelpüree mashed potatoes

der Kartoffelspieß (-e) *potatoes (and other ingredients) roasted on a spit*

der Käse (-) cheese (5)

das Käsesortiment (-e) range of cheeses

die Kasse (-n) cash register; check-out (5); **vorne an der Kasse** up front at the cash register

die Kassette (-n) cash box; cassette (tape)

der Kasten (¨) box

das Kastenweißbrot (-e) *white bread baked in a square loaf pan*

der Katalysator (-en) catalytic converter

der Katamaran (-e) catamaran

katastrophal catastrophic(ally)

die Kategorie (-n) category

der Kater (-) tomcat, male cat

katholisch Catholic

die Katze (-n) cat (12)

der Kauf (¨e) purchase; buying, purchasing

kaufen to buy (2)

die Kauffrau (-en) saleswoman (11)

das Kaufhaus (¨er) department store (2); **im Kaufhaus** at the department store

die Kaufleute (*pl.*) salespeople (11)

der Kaufmann (Kaufleute) salesman (11)

kaum hardly, scarcely (8)

kauzig (*coll.*) odd, weird

der Kaviar (-e) caviar

das KDW (= Kaufhaus des Westens) *large department store in Berlin*

kegeln to bowl

der Kegler (-) / die Keglerin (-nen) bowler

kein, keine no, none, not any (2); **kein(e) ... mehr** no more ... ; **noch kein(e)** no ... yet

der Keks (-e) cookie (5)

der Keller (-) cellar, basement

der Kellner (-) / die Kellnerin (-nen) waiter, waitress; server (6)

kennen, kannte, gekannt to know, be acquainted with (*person or thing*) (3); **kennen lernen (lernt kennen)** to meet, get to know

die Kenntnis (-se) knowledge (11)

der Kern (-e) core; nucleus

die Kernenergie nuclear energy

die Kerze (-n) candle

der Ketchup (-s) ketchup

der Kettenbrief (-e) chain letter

der Kick (-s) kick

das Kickboxen kickboxing

das Kilo (-s) = Kilogramm (-e) kilogram

der Kilometer (-) kilometer

das Kind (-er) child; **als Kind** as a child

der Kindergarten (¨) nursery school, preschool

die Kinderkonfektion (-en) children's wear

die Kindersterblichkeit child mortality

die Kindheit childhood

kindisch childish(ly)

das Kinn (-e) chin (8)

das Kino (-s) cinema, (movie) theater (4); **ins Kino gehen** to go to the movies (4)

die Kinoleinwand (¨e) movie screen

der Kiosk (-e) kiosk

die Kirche (-n) church (9)

der Kirchhof (¨e) churchyard; graveyard, cemetery

kitschig kitschy

die Kiwi (-s) kiwi (fruit)

die Klammer (-) parenthesis

die Klamotte (-n) duds, rags (*slang for clothes*)

klar clear; of course; **Alles klar.** Everything is clear. I get it. (E); **na klar** absolutely (E); but of course, you bet

klären to clarify

die Klasse (-n) class; classroom;
    erster/zweiter Klasse fahren (fährt),
    fuhr, ist gefahren to travel first/second
    class (10)
der Klassiker (-) classic
klassisch classic; classical(ly)
das Klavier (-e) piano
kleben to stick, adhere
das Kleid (-er) dress (5)
die Kleider (pl.) clothes
der Kleiderschrank (=e) wardrobe; clothes
    closet (2)
die Kleidung clothing, clothes
klein small, little (2)
die Kleinanzeige (-n) classified ad
das Kleingeld (small) change
die Kleinkinderbetreuung child care
die Kleinstadt (=e) small city, town
der Klettergarten (=) climbing garden
klettern, ist geklettert to climb
klicken to click
der Klient (-en masc.) (-en) / die Klientin
    (-nen) client
das Klima climate
klingeln to ring
klingen, klang, geklungen to sound (8);
    Du klingst so deprimiert. You sound
    so depressed. (8)
die Klinik (-en) hospital; clinic
klopfen to knock
der Klub (-s) club
klug smart, intelligent(ly)
km = Kilometer
die Knackwurst (=e) type of German
    sausage
knallen to slam, bang
knapp just about, barely
die Kneipe (-n) pub, bar (6)
der Kneipenbummel (-) pub-crawl,
    bar-hopping
das Knie (-) knee (8)
der Knoblauch garlic
die Knolle (-n) tuber
knurren to growl
die Kobra (-s) cobra
der Koch (=e) / die Köchin (-nen)
    cook, chef
kochen to cook (1); to boil; gekochtes Ei
    boiled egg
die Kochnische (-n) kitchen nook
der Kochschinken (-) boiled ham
der Koffer (-) suitcase (5)
das Kolleg (-s) lecture
der Kollege (-n masc.) (-n) / die Kollegin
    (-nen) colleague, co-worker
(das) Köln Cologne (city in western
    Germany)
Kölner (adj.) of/from Cologne
das Koma (-s) coma
kombinieren to combine
der Komfort (-s) comfort
komisch funny, funnily; strange(ly)
kommen, kam, ist gekommen to come (1);
    Ich komme aus … I'm from . . . (E); Wie
    komme ich am besten dahin? What's
    the best way to get there? (9); Woher
    kommen Sie? (form.) / Woher kommst
    du? (inform.) Where are you from? (E)

der Kommentar (-e) commentary
der Kommilitone (-n masc.) (-n) / die
    Kommilitonin (-nen) fellow student
der Kommissar (-e) detective inspector;
    commissioner
die Kommode (-n) dresser (2)
die Kommune (-n) commune
die Kommunikation (-en) communication
das Kommunikationswesen
    communications
kommunikativ communicative(ly)
kommunistisch communist
die Komödie (-n) comedy (4)
der Komparativ (-e) comparative
die Komparativform (-en) comparative
    form (of adjective)
komplett complete(ly)
komplex complex
kompliziert complicated (1)
komponieren to compose
der Komponist (-en masc.) (-en) / die
    Komponistin (-nen) composer
das Kompositum (Komposita) compound
    word
der Kompost (-e) compost
kompostieren to compost
die Kondition (-en) condition
die Konditorei (-en) pastry shop (5)
die Konferenz (-en) conference
der Konflikt (-e) conflict
der Kongress (-e) congress, convention
der König (-e) / die Königin (-nen)
    king/queen
die Konjunktion (-en) conjunction
der Konjunktiv (-e) subjunctive
die Konjunktivform (-en) subjunctive
    form (of verb)
konkret concrete(ly)
können (kann), konnte, gekonnt to be
    able to; can (4); to know how to
der Könner (-) / die Könnerin (-nen) one
    who can, expert
konservativ conservative(ly) (1)
die Konservendose (-n) can
der Konstrukteur (-e) / die
    Konstrukteurin (-nen) technical
    designer
der Konsum consumption
der Kontakt (-e) contact (11)
der Kontext (-e) context
kontinuierlich continuous(ly)
der Kontrast (-e) contrast
die Kontrolle (-n) control
kontrollieren to control
die Konversation (-en) conversation
das Konzentrationslager (-) concentration
    camp
der Konzern (-e) concern, group of
    companies
das Konzert (-e) concert (4); ins Konzert
    gehen to go to a concert (4)
die Koordination (-en) coordination
der Kopf (=e) head (8)
das Köpfchen (-): kluges Köpfchen clever
    little person
der Kopfsalat (-e) lettuce
die Kopfschmerzen (pl.) headache (8)
die Kopie (-n) copy

der Kopierer (-) copying machine
(das) Korea Korea
(das) Korfu Corfu
das Korn (=er) grain, kernel
der Körper (-) body
körperlich physical(ly)
der Körperteil (-e) body part (8)
die Korrektur (-en) correction, revision
korrespondieren to correspond
korrigieren to correct
die Korruption (-en) corruption (14)
(das) Korsika Corsica
die Kosmetik cosmetics
die Kost food
kosten to cost (2)
die Kosten (pl.) cost, expense
kostenlos free of charge
das Kostüm (-e) costume; fancy dress
der Krach loud noise
die Kraft (=e) power, strength; in Kraft
    treten (tritt), trat, ist getreten to come
    to power
kräftig strong(ly), powerful(ly)
krank sick, ill (8)
das Krankenhaus (=er) hospital
der Krankenpfleger (-) / die
    Krankenschwester (-n) nurse (8)
die Krankenversicherung (-en) health
    insurance
die Krankheit (-en) illness, disease,
    ailment (14)
krass blatant(ly), crass(ly)
das Kraut (=er) herb
die Kräuterbutter herb butter
der Kräutertee herbal tea (8)
die Krawatte (-n) necktie (5)
kreativ creative(ly)
die Kreativität creativity
die Kreditkarte (-n) credit card (9)
die Kreuzung (-en) intersection (9)
das Kreuzworträtsel (-) crossword puzzle;
    Kreuzworträtsel machen to do
    crossword puzzles (1)
der Krieg (-e) war (14)
kriegen (coll.) to get, receive
der Krieger (-) / die Kriegerin (-nen)
    warrior
der Kriegsdienstverweigerer (-)
    conscientious objector
der Krimi (-s) crime/detective/mystery
    story, film, or TV show (4)
die Kriminalität criminality
der Kriminologe (-n masc.) (-n) / die
    Kriminologin (-nen) criminologist
die Krimiserie (-n) detective series
die Krise (-n) crisis
das Kriterium (Kriterien) criterion
der Kritiker (-) / die Kritikerin (-nen)
    critic
kritisch critical(ly)
kritisieren to criticize
die Krönungsmesse (-n) coronation mass
(das) Kuba Cuba
die Küche (-n) kitchen (2); cuisine,
    food (6)
der Kuchen (-) cake (5)
der Kuckuck (-e) cuckoo
die Kuckucksuhr (-en) cuckoo clock

der Ku'damm = Kurfürstendamm *famous shopping street in Berlin*

der Kugelschreiber (-) ballpoint pen (12)

kühl cool(ly) (7)

der Kühlschrank (¨e) refrigerator (9)

kulinarisch culinary

die Kultur (-en) culture

der Kulturtipp (-s) cultural tip

die Kulturwissenschaften (*pl.*) cultural sciences, arts and humanities

kümmern to concern

der Kunde (-n *masc.*) **(-n) / die Kundin (-nen)** customer (2)

künftig future; in the future

die Kunst (¨e) art

der Kunstbetrachter (-) / die Kunstbetrachterin (-nen) art viewer

das Kunstgebilde (-) art object

die Kunsthalle (-n) art museum, exhibition hall

der Künstler (-) / die Künstlerin (-nen) artist (11)

das Kunstwerk (-e) work of art

die Kur (-en) health cure, treatment (at a spa)

der Kurfürstendamm *famous shopping street in Berlin*

der Kurort (-e) health spa, resort

der Kurs (-e) course

kurz (kürzer, kürzest-) short, brief(ly), for a short time (7)

die Kürze: in Kürze soon, shortly

die Kurzgeschichte (-n) short story

kürzlich recently

der Kurzschluss (¨e) short circuit

die Kusine (-n) female cousin (3)

das Küsschen (-): ein dickes Küsschen a big kiss

die Küste (-n) coast

L

das Labor (-s) laboratory

der Laborant (-en *masc.*) **(-en) / die Laborantin (-nen)** laboratory technician

das Labskaus *type of beef stew eaten with a fried egg*

lächeln to smile

das Lächeln smile

lachen to laugh

der Lachs (-e) salmon

laden (lädt), lud, geladen to load

der Laden (¨) store, shop (5)

das Ladenschlussgesetz (-e) law regulating store-closing times

die Lage (-n) location (9); situation

das Lager (-) camp

lala: so lala (*coll.*) OK, so-so (E)

das Lamm (¨er) lamb

die Lampe (-n) lamp (2)

das Land (¨er) country; nation, land; **auf dem Land(e)** in the countryside

das Landei (-er) farm egg

landen, hat/ist gelandet to land

die Landkarte (-n) map

das Landkind (-er) rural person

die Landschaft (-en) landscape, scenery

die Landung (-en) landing

die Landwirtschaft agriculture

lang (länger, längst-) long (7)

lange long (*temporal*); **wie lange** (for) how long

langsam slow(ly) (10); **Langsamer, bitte.** Slower, please. (E)

längst (*adv.*) long since, a long time ago

langweilig boring (1)

der Laptop (-s) laptop (computer)

der Lärm noise (14)

das Laserspektakel (-) laser show, laser spectacle

lassen (lässt), ließ, gelassen to leave (behind); to let (6); to have something done; **Lass uns (doch) . . .** Let's . . . (6)

(das) Lateinamerika Latin America

der Lauch (-e) leek

der Lauf (¨e) course; **im Laufe der Zeit** over the course of time

laufen (läuft), lief, ist gelaufen to run, jog (2); to walk; **der Film läuft im . . .** the film is playing at . . . ; **Schlittschuh laufen** to ice skate (7)

der Laufschritt (-e): im Laufschritt at a running pace

laut loud(ly) (10); according to

läuten: es läutet the bell is ringing

die Lautsprecherbox (-en) (stereo) speaker

leben to live

das Leben life (11)

der Lebenslauf (¨e) résumé (11); **tabellarischer Lebenslauf** résumé in outline form

das Lebensmittel (-) food, groceries

das Lebensmittelgeschäft (-e) grocery store

der Lebensraum (¨e) habitat

der Leberkäs *Bavarian-style meatloaf* (6)

der Lebkuchen (-) gingerbread

lecker tasty, delicious

das Leder (-) leather

die Lederhose (-n) leather pants (*mostly worn in southern Germany*)

die Lederwaren (*pl.*) leather goods

ledig unmarried, single

leer empty

legen to lay, put (*in a lying position*) (6); **sich legen** to lie down (8)

der Lehrer (-) / die Lehrerin (-nen) teacher (E)

der Lehrling (-e) apprentice, trainee

die Leibesübungen (*pl.*) physical education

die Leiche (-n) corpse

leicht easy, easily; light(ly)

das Leid sorrow, grief

leidtun (+*dat.*) **(tut leid), tat leid, leidgetan** (*impersonal*) to be sorry **Das tut mir leid.** I'm sorry. (9)

leider unfortunately (3)

leihen, lieh, geliehen to lend; to borrow (5)

Leipziger (*adj.*) of/from Leipzig

leise quiet(ly); softly

sich (*dat.*) **etwas leisten** to afford something

die Leistung (-en) accomplishment

leiten to lead

der Leiter (-) / die Leiterin (-nen) leader, director (11)

die Lektüre (-n) reading (material)

lernen to learn; to study (1); **kennen lernen (lernt kennen)** to meet, get to know

die Lernmittel (*pl.*) school supplies

das Leseexemplar (-e) copy of a book

lesen (liest), las, gelesen to read (1, 2)

der Leser (-) / die Leserin (-nen) reader

die Leserschaft readers, readership

das Lesestück (-e) reading selection

die Letter (-n) piece of type (used in printing)

(das) Lettland Latvia

letzt- last; **letzte Nacht** last night; **letzte Woche** last week; **letztes Jahr** last year; **zum letzten Mal** for the last time

Letzt: zu guter Letzt in the end

leuchten to shine, glow

die Leute (*pl.*) people (2)

liberal liberal(ly)

lieb kind; dear **alles Liebe** all my love (*at end of letter*)

die Liebe (-n) love

lieben to love

lieber (+ *verb*) rather, preferably; **möchte lieber** would rather (4)

das Liebespaar (-e) couple, pair of lovers

der Liebling (-e) darling; **Lieblings-** favorite (*first component of compound nouns*)

am liebsten (+ *verb*) the best, the most; **möchte am liebsten** would like to (do) most (4)

(das) Liechtenstein Liechtenstein (E)

das Lied (-er) song

der Liedermacher (-) / die Liedermacherin (-nen) (folk) songwriter

liegen, lag, gelegen to lie; to be located (6); **es liegt daran, dass . . .** it is because . . . ; **günstig liegen** to be conveniently located (9)

liegen bleiben (bleibt liegen), blieb liegen, ist liegen geblieben to stay down

lila purple, violet (5)

die Limonade (-n) lemonade; any flavored soda, soft drink

die Linguistik linguistics

die Linie (-n) line; **in erster Linie** first and foremost

link- left, left-hand; **auf der linken Seite** on the left side

links (on the) left (9); **nach links** to the left (9)

Linzer (*adj.*) of/from Linz (*city in Austria*)

die Lippe (-n) lip

die Liste (-n) list

(das) Litauen Lithuania

der Liter (-) liter

literarisch literary

die Literatur (-en) literature

locker loose(ly); relaxed

sich lockern to relax, loosen

der Löffel (-) spoon (6)

logisch logical(ly)

lokal local(ly)

das Lokal (-e) restaurant, pub, bar (6)

die Lokalität (-en) locality

die Lokalnachrichten (pl.) local news (13)

die Lokomotive (-n) locomotive

los loose; off; **Was ist denn los?** What's the matter? (2)

lösbar solvable

löschen to delete

lösen to solve (14)

losgehen (geht los), ging los, ist losgegangen to start

loslegen (legt los) (coll.) to start, let rip

losrennen (rennt los), rannte los, ist losgerannt to run off

die Lösung (-en) solution (14)

loswerden (wird los), wurde los, ist losgeworden (coll.) to get rid of

losziehen (zieht los), zog los, losgezogen (coll.) to take off, leave

die Lotterie (-n) lottery

das Lotto (-s) lottery

die Lücke (-n) gap, space, blank

das Lückendiktat (-e) fill-in-the-blank dictation

die Luft (̈e) air (8)

die Luftbrücke "air bridge," Berlin airlift (1948–49)

das Luftschloss (̈er) castle in the air, pipe dream

die Luftverschmutzung air pollution

der Luftweg (-e) air route

die Lüge (-n) lie, falsehood

der Lügebaron lying baron (Münchhausen)

lügen, log, gelogen to lie, tell a falsehood

die Lunge (-n) lung

die Lupe (-n) magnifying glass

Lust haben to feel like (doing something) (2)

lustig cheerful(ly); fun-loving (1); funny, funnily

das Lustspiel (-e) comedy

(das) Luxemburg Luxembourg (E)

die Luxusjacht (-en) luxury yacht

(das) Luzern Lucerne (in Switzerland)

M

der Maastrichter Vertrag the Maastricht Treaty (which formed the European Union)

machen to make; to do (1): **Das macht nichts.** That doesn't matter. (8): **Das macht Spaß.** That's fun. (1): **das macht zusammen ...** all together, that comes to ... (5) **Fortschritte machen** to make progress (14): **Kreuzworträtsel machen** to do crossword puzzles (1): **Mach schnell!** Hurry up!: **Mach's gut.** Take care, so long (inform.) (E): **ein Praktikum machen** to do an internship (1): **sich Sorgen machen um** (+ acc.) to worry about (14): **Urlaub machen** to go on vacation (8): **Was machst du gern?** What do you like to do?

mächtig powerful(ly)

das Mädchen (-) girl

der Magen (̈) stomach

die Magermilch skim milk

das Magisterstudium study toward a master's degree

die Mahlzeit (-en) meal

das Mahnmal (̈er) memorial

(der) Mai May (3); **der erste Mai** May first (3): **am ersten Mai** on May first (3)

die Mail (-s) e-mail

mailen to e-mail

der Main Main (river, tributary of the Rhine)

der Mais corn, maize (6)

mal = einmal once; just; (softening particle used with imperatives) (4); **-mal** time(s): **ich möchte lieber mal** I would rather: **noch mal** again, once again; **sag mal** tell me (1): **schau mal** look

die Malaria malaria

die Malediven (pl.) the Maldives

malen to paint (7)

der Maler (-) / die Malerin (-nen) painter

(das) Mallorca Majorca

(das) Malta Malta

die Mama (-s) mom, mommy

man (indef. pron.) one; you; they; people (4): **Hier darf man nicht parken.** You may not park here. (4): **Wie sagt man ... auf Deutsch?** How do you say . . . in German? (E)

das Management (-s) management

der Manager (-) / die Managerin (-nen) manager

mancher, manche, manches some; **manch ein(e)** many a; **manches Mal** many a time

manchmal sometimes (8)

der Mann (̈er) man (1); husband (3)

männlich masculine, male

die Mannschaft (-en) team

der Mantel (̈) (over)coat (5)

das Marathon (-s) marathon

das Märchen (-) fairy tale

marineblau navy blue

die Mark (-) mark (former German currency): **die D-Mark (Deutsche Mark)** German mark

das Marketing marketing

markieren to mark

der Markt (̈e) (open-air) market, marketplace (5): **auf dem Markt** at the market

der Marktplatz (̈e) market square

die Marmelade (-n) jam

(das) Marokko Morocco

der Mars Mars

marschieren to march; **marsch!** march!

der Marshallplan Marshall Plan (American recovery program for Europe after World War II)

(der) März March (3)

die Masche (-n) (coll.) trick

die Maschine (-n) machine

der Maschinenbau mechanical engineering

die Massage (-n) massage

mäßig moderate(ly)

die Maßnahme (-n) measure, action

das Material (-ien) material

die Mathematik mathematics

die Matheprüfung (-en) math test

das Matjesfilet (-s) herring filet

der Matjeshering (-e) young, slightly salted herring

das Matterhorn (mountain in the Swiss Alps)

die Mauer (-n) wall

die Maus (̈e) mouse (also as term of endearment)

maximal maximum

der MDR = Mitteldeutscher Rundfunk broadcasting company in Germany

der Mechaniker (-) / die Mechanikerin (-nen) mechanic (11)

(das) Mecklenburg-Vorpommern one of the German states

die Medien (pl.) media

die Medienwissenschaft (-en) media science

das Medikament (-e) medicine, medication (5)

die Meditation (-en) meditation

meditieren to meditate

die Medizin (field of) medicine

medizinisch medical(ly)

das Meer (-e) sea; ocean (7): **am Meer** at the seaside

die Meeresfrüchte (pl.) seafood

mehr more: **immer mehr** more and more; **kein(e) ... mehr** no more; **nicht mehr** not anymore; **nie mehr** never again

das Mehrbettzimmer (-) room with several beds

mehrere (pl.) several

die Mehrfachnennungen (pl.) multiple mentions

mehrmals often, several times, on several occasions

die Mehrweg-Eierbox (-en) recyclable egg carton

die Mehrwertsteuer (-n) value-added tax: national sales tax

die Mehrzweckhalle (-n) multipurpose hall

mein my (3)

meinen to mean; to think, be of the opinion (14): **Was meinen Sie?** (form.) / **Was meinst du?** (inform.) What do you think?

die Meinung (-en) opinion (14): **ich bin der Meinung ...** I'm of the opinion . . . (14): **meiner Meinung nach ...** in my opinion . . . (14)

meist mostly

meist- most: **am meisten** (the) most

meistens mostly (8)

der Meister (-) / die Meisterin (-nen) master; champion

melancholisch melancholic(ally)

die Melange (-n) blend; coffee with milk

sich melden to answer (phone) (13): **Niemand meldet sich.** No one is answering. (13)

die Meldung (-en) message, announcement

das Memo (-s) memo

die Mensa (-s) student cafeteria (1)

der Mensch (-en masc.) (-en) human being, person (2)

das Menschenrecht (-e) human right (*usually pl.*) (14)

die Menschenschlange (-n) (long) line of people

menschlich human

der Mercedes (-) Mercedes (*automobile*)

merken to notice, observe

das Merkmal (-e) feature, characteristic

merkwürdig strange(ly); remarkable, remarkably

messen (misst), maß, gemessen to measure

das Messer (-) knife (6)

das Messgerät (-e) measuring device

die Messung (-en) measurement

der Meteorologe (-n *masc.*) (-n) / die Meteorologin (-nen) meteorologist

der/das Meter (-) meter

die Methode (-n) method

die Metropole (-n) metropolis, large city

der Metzger (-) / die Metzgerin (-nen) butcher

die Metzgerei (-en) butcher shop (5)

(das) Mexiko Mexico

mich me (*acc.*) (3); **Freut mich.** Pleased to meet you. (E)

das Mietangebot (-e) rental offer

die Miete (-n) rent (2)

mieten to rent (*from someone*) (12)

der Mieter (-) / die Mieterin (-nen) renter

das Mietgesuch (-e) rental request

das Mietshaus (¨er) apartment building

der Mietwagen (-) rental car

das Mikrofon (-e) microphone

das Mikrowellengerät (-e) microwave oven

der Mikrowellenherd (-e) microwave oven (12)

die Milch milk (5)

das Militär armed forces, military

das Millennium (Millennien) millennium

der Milliardär (-e) / die Milliardärin (-nen) billionaire

die Milliarde (-n) billion (1,000,000,000)

der Milliliter (-) milliliter, one thousandth of a liter

die Million (-en) million

der Millionär (-e) / die Millionärin (-nen) millionaire

das Millionenpublikum audience of millions

die Mindestbestellung (-en) minimum order

mindestens at least (8)

die Mineralstofftablette (-n) mineral salt tablet

das Mineralwasser mineral water

der Minidialog (-e) mini-dialogue

das Minigolf miniature golf (game)

minimalistisch minimalistic(ally)

der Minister (-) / die Ministerin (-nen) (government) minister

die Minute (-n) minute (4)

mir (to/for) me (*dat.*) (5); **Das ist mir zu blöd.** I think that's really stupid. (13); **Mir ist schlecht.** I'm sick to my stomach (8)

mischen to mix

das Mischpult (-e) mixing desk, mixing console

die Mischung (-en) mixture

mit (+ *dat.*) with; by means of (5); **Wie wäre es mit … ?** How about . . . ? (13); **Willst du mit?** (*coll.*) Do you want to come along?

der Mitarbeiter (-) / die Mitarbeiterin (-nen) co-worker, colleague; employee (11)

mitbekommen (bekommt mit), bekam mit, mitbekommen to get to take along; to notice

mitbestimmen (bestimmt mit) to have an influence on

der Mitbewohner (-) / die Mitbewohnerin (-nen) roommate (2)

mitbringen (bringt mit), brachte mit, mitgebracht to bring along

miteinander together, with one another

die Mitfahrgelegenheit (-en) ride-sharing opportunity

mitgehen (geht mit), ging mit, ist mitgegangen to come along, go along

das Mitglied (-er) member

mithelfen (hilft mit), half mit, mitgeholfen to help, lend a hand

mitkommen (kommt mit), kam mit, ist mitgekommen to come along (4)

das Mitleid compassion, pity

mitmachen (macht mit) to join in

mitnehmen (nimmt mit), nahm mit, mitgenommen to take along (4); **zum Mitnehmen** (food) to go; take-out (6)

mitspielen (spielt mit) to play along

der Mitstudent (-en *masc.*) (-en) / die Mitstudentin (-nen) fellow student

der Mittag (-e) noon (4); **heute Mittag** today at noon

das Mittagessen (-) midday meal; lunch (5)

mittags at noon (4)

die Mitte (-n) middle, center (9); **in der Mitte (der Stadt)** in the center (of the city) (9)

das Mittel (-) means, method

das Mittelalter Middle Ages

mittelalterlich medieval

die Mittelklasse (-n) middle class

mittelmäßig mediocre, indifferent(ly)

der Mittelpunkt (-e) center

mittelständisch middle-class

der Mittelwesten Midwest (USA)

mitten in the midst; **mitten im Dorf** in the middle of the village

die Mitternacht midnight; **um Mitternacht** at midnight (3)

mittler- middle; **die mittlere Reife** high school diploma (*not sufficient for university studies*)

(der) Mittwoch Wednesday (3)

mittwochs Wednesdays, on Wednesday(s) (4)

mitunten sometimes

die Mitwohnzentrale (-n) shared housing agency

der Mix (-e) mix

ml = Milliliter

die Möbel (*pl.*) furniture (2)

möbliert furnished (2)

möchte would like to (4); **ich möchte (gern)** I would like; **möchte am liebsten** would like to (do) most (4); **möchte lieber** would rather (4)

das Modalverb (-en) modal verb

die Mode (-n) fashion

das Modell (-e) example, model

der/das Modem (-s) modem

die Moderation (-en) presentation; presenter, moderator

der Moderator (-en) / die Moderatorin (-nen) presenter, moderator

modern modern, in a modern manner

modernisieren to modernize

modifizieren to modify

modisch fashionable, fashionably (5)

mögen (mag), mochte, gemocht to care for; to like (4); **ich möchte (gern)** I would like; **Wo mag das sein?** Where can that be?

möglich possible, possibly (14)

die Möglichkeit (-en) possibility, opportunity (10)

möglichst as . . . as possible

die Möhre (-n) carrot

der Moment (-e) moment; **im Moment** at the moment; **Moment (mal)** just a moment

der Monat (-e) month; **einmal im Monat** once a month (7)

-monatig lasting . . . months

monatlich monthly (12)

die Mongolei Mongolia

(der) Montag Monday (3); **am Montag** on Monday (3)

montags Mondays, on Monday(s) (4)

der Mord (-e) murder

der Mörder (-) / die Mörderin (-nen) murderer

der Mordverdacht suspicion of murder

morgen tomorrow (3); **morgen Abend** tomorrow evening (4); **morgen früh** tomorrow morning (4); **morgen Nachmittag** tomorrow afternoon; **morgen Vormittag** tomorrow morning; **Welches Datum ist morgen?** What is tomorrow's date? (3)

der Morgen (-) morning (4); **am Morgen** in the morning; **(guten) Morgen** good morning (E); **heute Morgen** this morning (4); **jeden Morgen** every morning

morgendlich (*adj.*) morning

die Morgenpost (-en) morning mail

die Morgenroutine (-n) morning routine

morgens in the morning, mornings (4)

das Motel (-s) motel

das Motiv (-e) motive; motif

motivieren to motivate

der Motor (-en) motor, engine

das Motorrad (¨er) motorcycle (2); **Motorrad fahren** to ride a motorcycle

das Mountainbike (-s) mountain bike

das Mountainbiking mountain biking

der Mozzarella mozzarella (cheese)

müde tired (8)

die Mühe (-n) trouble

die Mühle (-n) mill

der Müll trash, garbage (12)

der Mülleimer (-) garbage can

der Multivitaminsaft (ẗe) multivitamin juice

(das) München Munich

Münchner (adj.) of/from Munich

der Mund (ẗer) mouth (8)

mündlich oral(ly), verbal(ly)

das Museum (Museen) museum (9)

das Musical (-s) musical

die Musik music (1)

der Musikant (-en masc.) (-en) / die Musikantin (-nen) musician, music maker

der Musiker (-) / die Musikerin (-nen) (professional) musician

der Musikfreund (-e) / die Musikfreundin (-nen) music lover

musizieren to make music, play an instrument

der Muskel (-n) muscle (8)

das Müsli (-) granola; cereal (5)

müssen (muss), musste, gemusst to have to; must (4)

das Muster (-) pattern, model, example; nach dem Muster according to the example

mutig brave(ly)

die Mutter (ẗ) mother (3)

die Muttersprache (-n) mother tongue, native language

der Muttertag Mother's Day (3)

die Mutti (-s) mommy, mom

die Mütze (-n) cap (5)

Mwst. = Mehrwertsteuer

der Mythos (Mythen) myth

N

na well; so; na ja oh well; na klar absolutely (E); but of course; you bet; Na und? So what? (13); Na, wie geht's? How are you? (casual) (E)

nach (+ dat.) after (4, 6); to (place name) (5); according to; Es ist Viertel nach zwei. It's a quarter after two. (4); fünf nach zwei five after two (4); meiner Meinung nach . . . in my opinion . . . (14); nach dem Befinden fragen to ask about someone's well-being; nach dem Weg fragen to ask for directions (9); nach Dienstag after Tuesday (6); nach links/rechts to the left/right (9); nach Hause (to) home (5); nach oben above, upstairs (directional) (12); nach unten below, downstairs (directional) (12)

der Nachbar (-n masc.) (-n) / die Nachbarin (-nen) neighbor

nachdem (subord. conj.) after (10); je nachdem it all depends

nachdenken (über + acc.) (denkt nach), dachte nach, nachgedacht to think (about), ponder (over) (11)

nachhaltig lasting; for a long time

nachher afterward

nachkommen (kommt nach), kam nach, ist nachgekommen to come later, follow

der Nachmittag (-e) afternoon (4); am Nachmittag in the afternoon; heute Nachmittag this afternoon (4); morgen Nachmittag tomorrow afternoon

nachmittags in the afternoon, afternoons (4)

der Nachname (gen. -ns, acc./dat. -n) (-n) family name, surname (1)

die Nachricht (-en) message; die Nachrichten (pl.) news (13)

der Nachrichtensprecher (-) / die Nachrichtensprecherin (-nen) news anchor

nachschauen (schaut nach) to check, look up

die Nachspeise (-n) dessert (6)

nächst- next, following; closest, nearest; am nächsten Tag on the next day; nächstes Jahr next year

die Nacht (ẗe) night (4); gute Nacht good night (E); letzte Nacht last night; über Nacht overnight

der Nachteil (-e) disadvantage

der Nachtisch (-e) dessert (6)

nächtlich nocturnal, during the night

nachts at night, nights (4)

der Nachttisch (-e) nightstand (2)

der Nachwuchsdarsteller (-) / die Nachwuchsdarstellerin (-nen) up-and-coming actor/actress

das Nackensteak (-s) neck steak

nah (näher, nächst-) close by, near

die Nähe vicinity (9); in der Nähe (des Bahnhofs) near (the train station) (9)

die Naherholung (-en) vacationing nearby

die Nahrung nutrition; food

das Nahrungsmittel (-) food

der Name (gen. -ns, acc./dat. -n) (-n) name (1); auf den Namen . . . hören to answer to the name . . . ; Auf welchen Namen? Under what name? (9); Mein Name ist . . . My name is . . . (E); Wie ist Ihr/dein Name? What is your name? (form./inform.) (E)

nämlich namely, that is to say (3)

nanu now what

die Nase (-n) nose (8)

die Nation (-en) nation; die Vereinten Nationen United Nations

national national(ly)

die Natur (-en) nature (10)

das Naturbett (-en) natural bed

die Naturkraft (ẗe) natural energy

die Naturkunde nature study

natürlich natural(ly); of course (1)

naturnah close to nature

die Naturwissenschaft (-en) natural science

das Navi (-s) navigation system

der Nazi (-s) (abbreviation for) member of the German National Socialist Party

'ne = eine

das Neandertal valley near Düsseldorf

der Nebel fog (7)

neben (+ acc./dat.) next to, beside (6)

die Nebenarbeit (-en) side job

nebenbei on the side

nebeneinander next to each other

die Nebenkosten (pl.) utilities; extra costs (12)

die Nebensache (-n) something of secondary importance

der Nebentisch (-e) adjacent table

neblig foggy (7)

der Neffe (-n masc.) (-n) nephew (3)

negativ negative(ly)

nehmen (nimmt), nahm, genommen to take (2); im Grunde genommen basically (14); Platz nehmen to take a seat; zu etwas (dat.) Stellung nehmen to take a stand on something

neidisch envious(ly)

nein no (E)

nennen, nannte, genannt to name, call

(das) Nepal Nepal

der Nerv (-en) nerve

nerven (coll.) to irritate, get on one's nerves

nervös nervous(ly)

nett nice(ly) (1); pleasant(ly)

das Netz (-e) net; network

neu new(ly) (3); nichts Neues nothing new

neuartig new kind of

der Neubau (Neubauten) modern building (12)

neuerdings recently

neugierig curious, nosy, inquisitive(ly)

das Neujahr New Year's Day (3)

neulich recently, the other day

neun nine (E)

neunte ninth (3)

neunzehn nineteen (E)

neunzig ninety (E)

(das) Neuseeland New Zealand

die Neustadt (ẗe) new part of town

nicht not (1); Das weiß ich nicht. I don't know. (E); Ich verstehe das nicht. I don't understand. (E); nicht besonders gut not particularly well (E); nicht mehr no longer; noch nicht not yet; nicht wahr? isn't that so?

die Nichte (-n) niece (3)

der Nichtraucher (-) / die Nichtraucherin (-nen) nonsmoker (2)

nichts nothing (2); Das macht nichts. That doesn't matter. (8); gar nichts nothing at all; nichts Gescheites nothing decent (13); nichts Neues nothing new; Nichts zu danken. No thanks necessary; Don't mention it. (8)

der Nichtskönner (-) incompetent person

das Nichtstun inactivity, doing nothing

nie never (1); nie mehr never again

die Niederlande (pl.) the Netherlands (E)

der Niederländer (-) / die Niederländerin (-nen) Dutch person

sich niederlassen (lässt nieder), ließ nieder, niedergelassen to settle down

(das) Niedersachsen Lower Saxony (German state)

niederschlagen (schlägt nieder), schlug nieder, niedergeschlagen to strike down

niederschreiben (schreibt nieder), schrieb nieder, niedergeschrieben to write down

niedlich sweet(ly), cute(ly)
niedrig low (2)
niemals never
niemand nobody; **Niemand meldet sich.** No one is answering. (13)
das Niveau (-s) level; standard
der Nobelpreis (-e) Nobel prize
noch still; yet (2); **Ist hier noch frei?** Is this seat available? (6); **noch (ein)mal** once more; **noch mehr** even more; **noch nicht** not yet; **Sonst noch (et)was?** Anything else? (10)
nochmals again, once again
das Nomen (-) noun
der Nominativ (-e) nominative case
nordamerikanisch (*adj.*) North American
(das) Norddeutschland northern Germany
der Norden north; **im Norden** in the north
nördlich (**von** + *dat.*) north (of)
Nordost (*without article*) northeast
(das) Nordrhein-Westfalen North Rhine-Westphalia (*German state*)
die Nordsee North Sea
Nordwest (*without article*) northwest
die Norm (-en) norm
normal normal(ly)
normalerweise normally, usually
der Normalstudent (-en *masc.*) **(-en) / die Normalstudentin (-nen)** average student
(das) Norwegen Norway
das Notebook (-s) notebook computer (13)
der Notgroschen (-) savings for a rainy day
notieren to write down
nötig necessary (5); urgent(ly)
die Notiz (-en) note; **sich Notizen machen** to take notes
notwendig necessary, necessarily (12)
(der) November November (3)
die Nudel (-n) noodle (6)
null zero (E)
nummerieren to number
die Nummer (-n) number
das Nummernschild (-er) license plate
nun now
nur only (2); **nicht nur** not only
(das) Nürnberg Nuremberg
Nürnberger (*adj.*) of/from Nuremberg
der Nutzer (-) / die Nutzerin (-nen) user
nützen to be of use
nützlich useful(ly) (12)

O

die Oase (-n) oasis
ob (*subord. conj.*) if, whether (or not) (8)
der/die Obdachlose (*decl. adj.*) homeless person (14)
die Obdachlosigkeit homelessness (14)
oben at the top; above; upstairs (12); **nach oben** above, upstairs (*directional*) (12)
ober upper
der Ober (-) waiter (6)
der Oberarzt (-̈e) / die Oberärztin (-nen) chief physician
(das) Oberschlesien Upper Silesia
die Oberschule (-n) secondary school
die Oberstufe (-n) upper level

das Objekt (-e) object
das Obst fruit (5)
die Obsttunke (-n) fruit sauce
der Obst- und Gemüsestand (-̈e) fruit and vegetable stand (5)
obwohl (*subord. conj.*) although, even though
oder (*coord. conj.*) or (7); **entweder … oder** either . . . or (8)
offen open
die Offenheit openness, candor
öffentlich public(ly) (14); **öffentliche Verkehrsmittel** (*pl.*) means of public transportation
offiziell official(ly)
der Offizier (-e) / die Offizierin (-nen) officer
öffnen to open
die Öffnung (-en) opening
oft often (1)
oh oh; **oh je!** oh, dear!
ohne (+ *acc.*) without (3)
das Ohr (-en) ear (8)
der Ökogarten (-̈) organic garden
die Ökologie ecology
ökologisch ecological(ly)
das Oktett (-e) octet
(der) Oktober October (3)
die Olive (-n) olive (6)
die Oma (-s) (*coll.*) grandma (3)
die Omi (-s) (*coll.*) granny
der Onkel (-) uncle (3)
der Opa (-s) (*coll.*) grandpa (3)
die Oper (-n) opera (4); **in die Oper gehen** to go to the opera (4)
die Optik optics
optimal optimal(ly)
orange (*adj.*) orange (color) (5)
die Orange (-n) orange
die Orangenmarmelade (-n) orange marmelade
das Orchester (-) orchester
die Ordinalzahl (-en) ordinal number
die Ordnung order
die Organisation (-en) organization
organisch organic(ally)
organisieren to organize
der Organismus (Organismen) organism
die Orientierungsstufe (-n) orientation level (*in German school system*)
der Orientteppich (-e) oriental rug
originell original, in an original fashion; inventive(ly), unique(ly)
der Ort (-e) place; locality; location
Ost (*without article*) east
(das) Ostberlin East Berlin
der Ostberliner (-) / die Ostberlinerin (-nen) person from East Berlin
das Ostblockland (-̈er) country in the Eastern Bloc
der Osten east; **im Osten** in the east
der Osterhase (-n *masc.*) **(-n)** Easter bunny
(das) Ostern Easter (3)
(das) Österreich Austria (E)
österreichisch (*adj.*) Austrian
östlich (**von** + *dat.*) east (of)
die Ostsee Baltic Sea
das Outsourcing outsourcing

oxydieren to oxidize
der Ozean (-e) ocean
das Ozonloch (-̈er) hole in the ozone layer
die Ozonschicht (-en) ozone layer

P

das Paar (-e) pair
ein paar a few, a couple of; **ein paar Mal** a couple of times
packen to pack (10)
die Packung (-en) package; box
die Pädagogik pedagogy
pädagogisch pedagogical(ly)
das Paket (-e) package, packet
der Papa (-s) dad, daddy
das Papier (-e) paper (12)
die Papierlaterne (-n) paper lantern
die Paprika bell pepper (6)
das Paradies (-e) paradise
das Paragliding paragliding
das Parfüm (-s) perfume
die Parfümerie (-n) perfumery
der Park (-s) park
parken to park; **Hier darf man nicht parken.** You may not park here. (4)
der Parkplatz (-̈e) parking space; parking lot (9)
das Parkverbot: hier ist Parkverbot no parking here
die Partei (-en) (political) party
die Partie (-n) game, round
das Partizip (-ien) participle; **das Partizip Perfekt** past participle; **das Partizip Präsens** present participle
das Partizipialadjektiv (-e) participial adjective
der Partner (-) / die Partnerin (-nen) partner
die Partnerschaft (-en) partnership
die Party (-s) party (3); **eine Party geben** to throw a party, have a party
der Pass (-̈e) passport; pass
der Passant (-en *masc.*) **(-en) / die Passantin (-nen)** passerby (9)
passen (+ *dat.*) to match; to fit (5); **passen zu** (+ *dat.*) to be suitable for
passend fitting, suitable
das Passfoto (-s) passport photo
passieren, ist passiert to happen (7)
das Passiv (-e) passive voice (of the verb)
die Pasta pasta
die Pastille (-n) pastille
die Patentanmeldung (-en) patent application
der Patient (-en *masc.*) **(-en) / die Patientin (-nen)** patient
die Pauke (-n) kettle drum
das Pauschalangebot (-e) package tour offer
die Pause (-n) pause, break
pausenlos continuous(ly), without interruption
der Pazifik Pacific Ocean
der PC = Personalcomputer (-) personal computer
das Pech pitch; bad luck; **So ein Pech!** What a shame! What bad luck! (8)
der Pelz (-e) fur

die Pension (-en) small family-run hotel; bed and breakfast (9)

per via; by way of; per Autostop reisen to hitchhike (10)

perfekt perfect

das Perfekt present perfect tense; das Partizip Perfekt past participle

die Person (-en) person; pro Person per person (10)

das Personal personnel, staff (11)

der Personalausweis (-e) (personal) ID card (10)

das Personalpronomen (-) personal pronoun

der Personenkraftwagen (Pkw) (-) automobile, car

persönlich personal(ly)

die Persönlichkeit (-en) personality

die Perspektive (-n) perspective

das Pestizid (-e) pesticide

der Pfad (-e) path; der Trimm-Pfad (-e) parcourse, jogging path

die Pfanne (-n) pan (6)

der Pfannkuchen (-) pancake; der Berliner Pfannkuchen (-) jelly doughnut

der Pfeffer pepper (5)

der Pfennig (-e) penny (former German monetary unit)

das Pferd (-e) horse

das Pferderennen (-) horse race

das Pfifferling chanterelle mushroom

pfiffig clever(ly); stylish(ly)

die Pflanze (-n) plant

pflanzen to plant

pflanzlich (adj.) plant, vegetable

das Pflegeheim (-e) nursing home

pflegen to look after, care for; maintain

die Pflicht (-en) duty

der Pförtner (-) / die Pförtnerin (-nen) porter, doorkeeper

das Pfund (-e) pound; 500 grams

phantasievoll imaginative(ly)

das Phantom (-e) phantom

die Philharmonie (-n) philharmonic (orchestra)

die Philosophie philosophy

die Physik physics

der Physiker (-) / die Physikerin (-nen) physicist

das Picknick (-s) picnic

der Picknickkorb (-̈e) picnic basket

der Pilot (-en masc.) (-en) / die Pilotin (-nen) pilot

(das) Pilsen Plzeň (town in the Czech Republic)

das Pilsener (-) Pilsner beer (6)

der Pilz (-e) mushroom

die Pipeline (-s) pipeline

die Pistole (-n) pistol, revolver

die Pizza (-s) pizza

die Pizzeria (-s) pizzeria

der Pkw = Personenkraftwagen

der Plan (-̈e) plan (4)

planen to plan (3)

das Plasmamonitor (-en) plasma screen

das Plastik plastic

der Plastikbeutel (-) plastic bag

die Plastiktüte (-n) plastic bag (14)

der Plattenspieler (-) record player

der Platz (-̈e) place; seat (6); room, space; plaza, square; Platz nehmen to take a seat

die Platzkarte (-n) place card, seat reservation card (10)

der Plausch (-e) chat

pleite (coll.) broke, out of money (12)

das Plenum; im Plenum all together

plötzlich sudden(ly); unexpected(ly)

die Pluralform (-en) plural form

plus plus

das Plusquamperfekt (-e) past perfect tense, pluperfect tense

die Poesie poetry

der Pokal (-e) trophy, cup

das Pokalfinale (-) cup final(s)

(das) Polen Poland (E)

die Politik politics (13)

der Politiker (-) / die Politikerin (-nen) politician (14)

politisch political(ly)

politisieren to politicize

die Politologie political science

die Polizei police; police station (9)

der Polizist (-en masc.) (-en) / die Polizistin (-nen) police officer

der Polyester polyester

die Pommes (frites) (pl.) French fries (6)

die Popmusik pop music

populär popular(ly)

der Porree (-s) leek

der Porsche (-) Porsche (automobile)

die Portion (-en) portion; helping, serving

das Porträt (-s) portrait

(das) Portugal Portugal

(das) Portugiesisch Portuguese (language)

das Porzellan porcelain, china

die Posaune (-n) trombone

die Position (-en) position

positiv positive(ly)

das Possessivadjektiv (-e) possessive adjective

die Post mail; postal system; (pl. Postämter) post office (9)

das Postamt (-̈er) post office (9)

das Poster (-) poster (2)

das Postfach (-̈er) post office box

die Postleitzahl (-en) postal code (E)

potentiell potential(ly)

das Präfix (-e) prefix

(das) Prag Prague

das Praktikum (Praktika) internship (1); ein Praktikum machen to do an internship (1)

praktisch practical(ly) (1)

praktizieren to practice

prall full(y); intense(ly)

die Präposition (-en) preposition

das Präsens (Präsentia) present tense; das Partizip Präsens present participle

präsentieren to present

die Präsentierung (-en) presentation

der Präsident (-en masc.) (-en) / die Präsidentin (-nen) president

das Präteritum (Präterita) preterit tense, simple past tense

präzis precise(ly)

der Prediger (-) / die Predigerin (-nen) preacher

der Preis (-e) price, cost (9); prize; im Preis enthalten included in the price (9)

preiswert inexpensive(ly), bargain (2); recht preiswert quite inexpensive, reasonable (2)

die Presse press (newspapers, etc.)

pressen to press, squeeze

das Prestige prestige

der Priester (-) / die Priesterin (-nen) priest

prima great, super (E)

der Prinz (-en masc.) (-en) / die Prinzessin (-nen) prince/princess

das Prinzip (-ien) principle; im Prinzip in principle

privat private(ly)

pro per; pro Person per person (10); pro Woche per week (4)

die Probe (-n) rehearsal

das Problem (-e) problem (2); ein Problem lösen to solve a problem

problemlos without any problem

das Produkt (-e) product

produzieren to produce

der Professor (-en) / die Professorin (-nen) professor (1)

das Profil (-e) profile

das Programm (-e) program; TV station, channel (13); im ersten Programm on channel 1

programmieren to program

die Programmierkenntnis (-se) knowledge of programming

progressiv progressive(ly)

das Projekt (-e) project

promenieren to promenade

die Prominenz prominent people, socialites

das Pronomen (-) pronoun

das Pronominaladverb (Pronominaladverbien) pronominal adverb

der Prospekt (-e) brochure

das Protokoll (-e) transcript, minutes; Protokoll führen to make a transcript, take the minutes

provozieren to provoke

provozierend provocative(ly)

das Prozent (-e) percent

der Prozess (-e) process; legal case

die Prüfung (-en) test, exam

PS = Postskript postscript

der Psychologe (-n masc.) (-n) / die Psychologin (-nen) psychologist (11)

die Psychologie psychology

der Psychothriller (-) psycho-thriller (movie, etc.)

der Pudding (-e) pudding

der Pudel (-) poodle

der Pulli (-s) (coll.) sweater, pullover

der Pullover (-) pullover sweater (5)

der Pumpernickel pumpernickel (bread)

der Punkt (-e) point

pünktlich punctual(ly), on time

die Puppe (-n) doll

die **Pute (-n)** turkey (hen)
das **Putenmedaillon (-s)** turkey medallion, small slice of turkey
der **Putenspieß (-e)** turkey kebab, turkey on a skewer
putzen to polish, clean; **sich** (*dat.*) **die Zähne putzen** to brush one's teeth (8)
der **Pyjama (-s)** pajamas

Q

qm = Quadratmeter
der/das **Quadratmeter (-)** square meter
die **Qualifikation (-en)** qualification
qualifizieren to qualify
die **Qualität (-en)** quality
der **Quark** curd cheese (*German-style yogurt cheese*)
das **Quartal (-e)** (academic) quarter
der **Quatsch** (*coll.*) nonsense; **So ein Quatsch!** Nonsense!
die **Quelle (-n)** source
das **Quiz (-)** quiz
der **Quizmaster (-)** quizmaster, host of a quiz show
die **Quizsendung (-en)** quiz show
die **Quizshow (-s)** quiz show

R

der **Rabatt (-e)** discount
rachsüchtig vengeful(ly)
das **Rad (¨er)** wheel; bicycle; **Rad fahren (fährt Rad), fuhr Rad, ist Rad gefahren** to bicycle, ride a bike (7)
der **Radfahrer (-) / die Radfahrerin (-nen)** bicyclist
radikal radical(ly)
das **Radio (-s)** radio (2); **im Radio** on the radio
der **Radiorecorder (-)** boom box
der **Radiowecker (-)** clock radio
der **Radius (Radien)** radius
das **Rafting** rafting
die **Rakete (-n)** rocket
der **Rand (¨er)** edge, border
die **Rapmusik** rap music
rappelvoll (*coll.*) crazily full
der **Rappen (-)** (Swiss) centime
rar rare, scarce
die **Rasiercreme (-s)** shaving cream (5)
sich rasieren to shave (8)
die **Rassenpolitik** politics of race
der **Rassismus** racism (14)
rassistisch (*adj.*) racist
die **Rast (-en)** rest
der **Raster (-)** grid
der **Rat** advice (8); **Rat geben** to give advice
raten (rät), riet, geraten to guess; to advise
das **Ratespiel (-e)** guessing game
die **Ratgeberseite (-n)** advice page
das **Rathaus (¨er)** city hall (9)
(das) Rätoromanisch Rhaeto-Romance (language)
der **Ratschlag (¨e)** piece of advice
der **Rattenfänger (-)** ratcatcher; **der Rattenfänger von Hameln** the Pied Piper of Hamelin
rauchen to smoke (8)

räuchern to smoke (*meat*)
rauf = herauf: raufstolpern (stolpert rauf), ist raufgestolpert (*coll.*) to stumble up
der **Raum (¨e)** room; space
raus = heraus (*adv.*) out
das **Rauschen** rush, roar; **das weiße Rauschen** white noise
reagieren to react
die **Reaktion (-en)** reaction
das **Reaktionsvermögen (-)** ability to react
die **Realität (-en)** reality
die **Realoberschule (-n)** *secondary school with a curriculum emphasizing mathematics and science*
die **Realschule (-n)** *secondary school with a commercially oriented curriculum*
das **Rebland (¨er)** wine country
die **Rechenmaschine (-n)** calculator
recherchieren to research, investigate
die **Rechnung (-en)** bill (6)
recht quite, rather (2); **recht preiswert** quite inexpensive, reasonable (2)
recht- right, right-hand; **auf der rechten Seite** on the right-hand side
das **Recht (-e)** right; law; **Recht haben** to be correct (2)
rechts (on the) right (9); **nach rechts** to the right (9)
der **Rechtsanwalt (¨e) / die Rechtsanwältin (-nen)** attorney, lawyer (11)
der **Rechtsextremismus** right-wing extremism (14)
rechtzeitig in time, on time
das **Recycling** recycling
der **Redakteur (-e) / die Redakteurin (-nen)** chief editor
die **Redaktion (-en)** editorial staff
die **Rede (-n)** speech; **indirekte Rede** indirect discourse
das **Redemittel (-)** speaking resources
reden to talk (about)
reduzieren to reduce
das **Referat (-e)** paper, report; **ein Referat halten (hält), hielt, gehalten** to give a paper/report
der **Referent (-en** *masc.***) (-en) / die Referentin (-nen)** speaker; advisor, expert
reflexiv reflexive(ly)
das **Reflexivpronomen (-)** reflexive pronoun
die **Reformation** Reformation
das **Regal (-e)** shelf (2)
regelmäßig regular(ly) (8)
regeln to regulate, control
der **Regen** rain (7)
der **Regenschauer (-)** rain shower (7)
der **Regenschirm (-e)** umbrella (7)
die **Regierung (-en)** government (14); administration
die **Regierungsgewalt (-en)** governmental power
der **Regierungssitz (-e)** seat of government
das **Regime (-)** regime
die **Region (-en)** region
regional regional(ly)

der **Regisseur (-e) / die Regisseurin (-nen)** (film) director
regnen to rain (7); **Es regnet.** It's raining. (7)
regnerisch rainy (7)
der **Reibekuchen (-)** *pancake made of grated potatoes*
reich rich(ly)
das **Reich (-e)** empire, realm; **das Dritte Reich** the Third Reich, Nazi Germany (1933–1945)
reichhaltig extensive; abundant
das **Reichstagsgebäude** *German Parliament Building*
die **Reife: mittlere Reife** *diploma attained at the end of the **Realschule***
der **Reifen (-)** tire
die **Reihenfolge (-n)** sequence, order
rein = herein (*adv.*) in
der **Reis** rice (6)
die **Reise (-n)** trip, journey (10)
die **Reiseapotheke (-n)** portable first-aid kit
der **Reisebericht (-e)** travel report, travelogue
das **Reisebüro (-s)** travel agency (10)
die **Reisecheckliste (-n)** travel checklist
der **Reiseführer (-)** travel guide (book) (10)
das **Reisejournal (-e)** travel journal
der **Reiseleiter (-) / die Reiseleiterin (-nen)** tour guide
die **Reiselektüre** vacation reading material
reisen, ist gereist to travel (1); **per Autostop reisen** to hitchhike (10)
das **Reisen** traveling
der **Reisepass (¨e)** passport (9)
der **Reiseprospekt (-e)** travel brochure (10)
der **Reisescheck (-s)** traveler's check (10)
der **Reisetermin (-e)** date of travel
die **Reiseverbindung (-en)** travel connection
reiten, ritt, ist geritten to ride (on horseback) (7)
die **Reitführung** riding instruction
die **Reitschule (-n)** riding school
relativ relative(ly)
die **Relativitätstheorie** theory of relativity
das **Relativpronomen (-)** relative pronoun
relevant relevant
die **Religion (-en)** religion
religiös religious(ly)
die **Renaissance** Renaissance (period)
die **Rendite (-n)** yield on an investment
rennen, rannte, ist gerannt to run, race
renommiert renowned
renovieren to renovate
der **Rentner (-) / die Rentnerin (-nen)** retiree
die **Reparatur (-en)** repair (12)
die **Reparaturwerkstatt (¨e)** repair shop
reparieren to repair (9)
der **Report (-e)** report
die **Reportage (-n)** report
der **Reporter (-) / die Reporterin (-nen)** reporter
die **Reproduktion (-en)** reproduction
die **Republik (-en)** republic
das **Requiem (-s)** requiem
das **Requisit (-en)** prop

reservieren to book, reserve (7)

die Reservierung (-en) reservation

die Residenzstadt (¨e) royal capital

der Rest (-e) remainder

das Restaurant (-s) restaurant (6)

restlich remaining

das Resultat (-e) result

retten to save, rescue

die Rettungsleitstelle (-n) control room for rescue operations

revidieren to revise

das Revier (-e) province, region; preserve

das Rezept (-e) recipe; prescription

die Rezeption reception desk (9)

der Rhein Rhine (River)

rheinisch Rhenish, of the Rhine River

(die) Rheinland-Pfalz Rhineland-Palatinate (*German state*)

der Rhythmus (Rhythmen) rhythm

sich richten auf (+ *acc.*) to be directed at

die Richtgeschwindigkeit (-en) recommended maximum speed

richtig correct(ly), right(ly)

die Richtigkeit correctness, accuracy

die Richtung (-en) direction

der Riese (-n *masc.*) **(-n)** giant

riesig enormous, gigantic

das Riff (-e) reef

das Rind (-er) cow, bull, head of cattle

das Rinderfilet (-s) beef filet

die Rinderroulade (-n) beef roulade

das Rindfleisch beef (5)

der Ring (-e) ring

rings: rings um (+ *acc.*) all around

ringsherum all around

ringsum all around

der Risotto (-s) risotto

das Ritual (-e) ritual

die Robbe (-n) seal

der Rock (¨e) skirt (5)

das Rodeo (-s) rodeo

die Rolle (-n) role

das Rollenspiel (-e) role-play

das Rollerbladen rollerblading

der Rollkragenpullover (-) turtleneck sweater

(das) Rom Rome

der Rom (-a) non-German Romany (gypsy)

der Roman (-e) novel

die Romanistik (study of) Romance languages and literatures

romantisch romantic(ally) (1)

die Römerzeit Roman era

die Röntgenstrahlen (*pl.*) X-rays

der Rosinenbomber (-) raisin bomber (*supply plane in the Berlin Airlift*)

die Rösti (Swiss) thinly sliced fried potatoes

rot red (5); **rote Grütze** *dessert made of red berries*

der Rotwein (-e) red wine

rotweiß red and white

die Routine (-n) routine

RTL *radio and television broadcasting company based in Luxembourg*

die Rubrik (-en) category, section; column

der Rücken (-) back (8)

die Rückenschmerzen (*pl.*) backache

der Rucksack (¨e) backpack (5)

die Rückseite (-n) back, back side

rudern, ist gerudert to row

rufen, rief, gerufen to call (out), shout

die Ruhe quiet; calm(ness); rest; **in Ruhe** in peace and quiet

der Ruhetag (-e) *day that a business is closed* (6)

ruhig quiet(ly) (1); calm(ly)

das Rührei (-er) scrambled egg

die Ruine (-n) ruin

der Rum (-s) rum

(das) Rumänien Romania

rund round; around; **rund um** (+ *acc.*) all around

die Rundfahrt (-en) (circular) tour

der Rundfunk radio; broadcasting

die Rundfunkanstalt (-en) broadcasting corporation; radio station

die Rundschau (-en) panorama

rundum all around

russisch (*adj.*) Russian

(das) Russland Russia

rustikal rustic

S

die Sache (-n) thing, object; matter

die Sachertorte (-n) *type of rich chocolate torte from Vienna*

(das) Sachsen Saxony (*German state*)

(das) Sachsen-Anhalt Saxony-Anhalt (*German state*)

sächsisch (*adj.*) Saxon

die Safari (-s) safari

der Safer Sex safe sex

der Saft (¨e) juice (5)

sagen to say, tell (1); **sag mal** tell me (1); **Wie sagt man ... auf Deutsch?** How do you say . . . in German? (E)

die Sahara Sahara (Desert)

die Sahne cream; whipped cream (6)

das Sakko (-s) man's jacket, sport coat (5)

der Salat (-e) salad; lettuce (6)

das Salz salt (5)

salzen, salzte, gesalzen to salt

salzig salty

sammeln to collect (7); to gather **sich sammeln** to gather, come together

die Sammelstelle (-n) recycling center (14)

die Sammlung (-en) collection

(der) Samstag Saturday (3)

samstags Saturdays, on Saturday(s) (4)

der Sand (-e) sand

die Sandale (-n) sandal

der Sänger (-) / die Sängerin (-nen) singer

der Satan (-e) Satan, devil

die Sat-Empfangsanlage (-n) satellite receiver (13)

satt full, having had enough to eat

der Satz (¨e) sentence

die Satzklammer (-n) sentence frame

der Satzteil (-e) part of a sentence, clause

sauber clean(ly) (14)

säuberlich neat(ly)

säubern to clean (up)

die Sauce = die Soße

sauer sour; **saurer Regen** acid rain

das Sauerkraut sauerkraut, pickled cabbage (6)

die Sauna (-s) sauna

säuseln to murmur

(das) Schach chess; **Schach spielen** to play chess (7)

schade too bad

schaden to harm

der Schaden (¨) damage, injury

der Schadstoff (-e) harmful substance

schaffen, schuf, geschaffen to create (14)

schaffen, schaffte, geschafft to manage to do; **sich schaffen** to busy oneself

der Schafskäse sheep's milk cheese

der Schal (-s) scarf (5)

die Schallplatte (-n) (phonograph) record

schalten to switch

der Schalter (-) counter; window

scharf sharp; spicy

der Schatz (¨e) treasure; **mein Schatz** my darling

das Schaubild (-er) diagram

schauen (auf + *acc.*) to look (at/to); **Fernsehen schauen** to watch TV; **Schau mal!** Look!

der Schauer (-) (rain) shower

das Schaufenster (-) store window

der Schauplatz (¨e) scene

der Schauspieler (-) / die Schauspielerin (-nen) actor/actress (11)

der Scheck (-s) check

scheiden, schied, geschieden to separate

der Schein (-e) banknote, bill, piece of paper money; **der Dollar-Schein** dollar bill; **der Euro-Schein** euro note/bill

scheinen, schien, geschienen to shine; to seem, appear (13); **Die Sonne scheint.** The sun is shining. (7)

scheitern, ist gescheitert to fail

schenken to give (as a gift) (5)

die Scheu shyness

schick stylish(ly)

schicken to send (1); **SMS schicken** to send text messages

schießen, schoss, geschossen to shoot

das Schiff (-e) ship (10)

das Schild (-er) sign, road sign

schildern to describe, portray

schimpfen to scold; to grumble, curse

der Schinken (-) ham (5)

der Schirm (-e) umbrella

der/die Schizophrene (*decl. adj.*) schizophrenic (person)

das Schlachtfeld (-er) battlefield

der Schlaf sleep

schlafen (schläft), schlief, geschlafen to sleep (2)

der Schlafsack (¨e) sleeping bag

das Schlafzimmer (-) bedroom (2)

der Schlag (¨e) blow, punch, slap; whipped cream

die Schlagcreme whipped cream

schlagen (schlägt), schlug, geschlagen to beat, strike

schlagkräftig powerful(ly)

die Schlagzeile (-n) headline (13)

das Schlagzeug (-e) (set of) drums; percussion instruments

schlank slender

schlapp weak, worn out (8)

das Schlaraffenland fool's paradise

schlecht bad(ly), poor(ly) (E); **Mir ist schlecht.** I feel bad; I'm sick to my stomach. (8)

der Schlegel (-) mallet

(das) Schleswig-Holstein one of the German states

schließen, schloss, geschlossen to close; **schließen (aus** + *dat.*) to conclude (from)

das Schließfach (ö̈er) locker

schließlich finally, in the end

die Schließung (-en) closing

schlimm bad

der Schlips (-e) necktie (5)

schlittern, ist geschlittert to slip, slide

der Schlittschuh (-e) ice skate; **Schlittschuh laufen (läuft), lief, ist gelaufen** to ice skate (7)

das Schloss (ö̈er) castle, palace (9)

der Schluckauf hiccup(s)

schlucken to swallow (8)

der Schlüssel (-) key (9)

schmecken (+ *dat.*) to taste (good) (5); **schmecken nach (+** *dat.*) to taste of

schmeißen, schmiss, geschmissen to hurl, fling

schmelzen (schmilzt), schmolz, geschmolzen to melt

der Schmerz (-en) pain (8)

der Schmuck jewelry

schmutzig dirty (12)

das Schnäppchen (-) (*coll.*) bargain

die Schnecke (-n) snail

der Schnee snow (7)

der Schneefall (ö̈e) snowfall

schneiden, schnitt, geschnitten to cut

schneien to snow (7); **Es schneit.** It's snowing. (7)

schnell fast, quick(ly) (10); **Machen Sie schnell!** (*form.*) / **Mach schnell!** (*inform.*) Hurry up!

schnellen, ist geschnellt to shoot (upward)

der Schnittlauch chives

das Schnitzel (-) cutlet; **das Wiener Schnitzel** breaded veal cutlet

der Schnupfen nasal congestion; head cold (8)

der Schnupperkurs (-e) introductory course

der Schock (-s) shock

der Schokoeisbecher (-) dish of chocolate ice cream

die Schokolade (-n) chocolate

schon already (2); yet

schön nice(ly), beautiful(ly) (2); **bitte schön** please; you're welcome; **danke schön** thank you very much (E)

schonen to protect

der Schornsteinfeger (-) / die Schornsteinfegerin (-nen) chimney sweep

(das) Schottland Scotland

der Schrank (ö̈e) cupboard; closet; wardrobe

schrecklich horrible, horribly

schreiben, schrieb, geschrieben to write (2); **Wie schreibt man ... ?** How do you write . . . ? (E)

die Schreibmaschine (-n) typewriter

der Schreibtisch (-e) desk (2)

die Schreibwaren (*pl.*) stationery goods

der Schriftsteller (-) / die Schriftstellerin (-nen) writer, author

der Schritt (-e) step

die Schublade (-n) drawer

der Schuh (-e) shoe (5)

das Schuhwerk footwear

der Schulabgänger (-) / die Schulabgängerin (-nen) school graduate

die Schuld guilt

die Schulden (*pl.*) debts; **Schulden machen** to go into debt

die Schule (-n) school; **in die Schule gehen, ging, ist gegangen** to go to school; **zur Schule gehen, ging, ist gegangen** to go to school

der Schüler (-) / die Schülerin (-nen) pupil, student in primary or secondary school

die Schulter (-n) shoulder (8)

die Schupfnudeln (*pl.*) potato noodles

der Schuss (ö̈e) shot; **eine (Berliner) Weiße mit Schuss** light, fizzy beer served with raspberry syrup

schützen to protect (14)

(das) Schwaben Swabia (*region in southwestern Germany*)

schwäbisch (*adj.*) Swabian

schwach weak(ly); gentle, gently

der Schwager (ö̈) / die Schwägerin (-nen) brother-in-law (3) / sister-in-law (3)

die Schwangerschaft (-en) pregnancy

der Schwank (ö̈e) comic tale, farce

der Schwarm (ö̈e) swarm; heartthrob, idol

schwarz black (5); **das Schwarze Brett** bulletin board

schwarzhaarig dark-haired

der Schwarzhandel black market

der Schwarzwald Black Forest

(das) Schweden Sweden

das Schwein (-e) pig

der Schweinebraten (-) pork roast (6)

das Schweinefleisch pork (5)

das Schweinemedaillon (-s) pork medallion, small slice of pork

die Schweinshaxe (-n) pork knuckle

das Schweinskotelett (-s) pork cutlet

die Schweiz Switzerland (E); **aus der Schweiz** from Switzerland; **in die Schweiz** to Switzerland

Schweizer (*adj.*) of/from Switzerland; **der Schweizer Franken (-)** Swiss franc

der Schweizer (-) / die Schweizerin (-nen) Swiss person

schwer heavy, heavily; difficult, with difficulty

die Schwester (-n) sister (3)

die Schwiegermutter (ö̈) mother-in-law

der Schwiegervater (ö̈) father-in-law

schwierig difficult, with difficulty

das Schwimmbad (ö̈er) swimming pool (7)

schwimmen, schwamm, ist geschwommen to swim (2)

die Schwimmflosse (-n) flipper

sich schwingen, schwang, geschwungen to swing oneself, jump

schwitzen to sweat

schwül muggy, humid (7)

der Schwung: voll Schwung full of zest

sechs six (E)

sechsmal six times

sechste sixth (3)

sechzehn sixteen (E)

sechzig sixty (E)

der See (-n) lake (7)

die See (-n) sea, ocean

das Seemannspfännchen (-) *fried seafood dish*

die Segelflotte (-n) fleet of sailboats

segeln to sail (7)

sehen (sieht), sah, gesehen to see (2)

die Sehenswürdigkeit (-en) (tourist) attraction

sehr very (1); very much; **bitte sehr** you're welcome; **danke sehr** thanks a lot (1); **sehr gut** very well; fine; good (E)

seid (you [*inform. pl.*]) are

die Seidenbluse (-n) silk blouse

die Seife (-n) soap

das Seil (-e) rope; cable

sein (ist), war, gewesen to be (1)

sein his, its (3)

seit (+ *dat.*) since; (+ *time*) for (5, 6); (*subord. conj.*) since; **seit zwei Jahren** for two years (6)

die Seite (-n) side; page; **die Internet-Seite (-n)** web page

der Sekretär (-e) / die Sekretärin (-nen) secretary

die Sekte (-n) sect

die Sekunde (-n) second (4)

selb- (*adj.*) same

selber self (my-, your-, him-, her-, *etc.*)

selbst self (my-, your-, him-, her-, *etc.*)

selbständig independent(ly) (11)

das Selbstbewusstsein self-confidence

das Selbstbildnis (-se) self-portrait

das Selbstgespräch (-e) conversation with oneself

der Selbstmord (-e) suicide

selbstversorgend self-sufficient

die Selbstversorgung self-sufficiency

selbstverständlich natural(ly), of course

selten rare(ly) (2), seldom

seltsam strange(ly)

das Semester (-) semester (1)

das Seminar (-e) seminar

senden, sandte, gesandt to send

senden, sendete, gesendet to broadcast

der Sender (-) broadcaster

die Sendung (-en) broadcast, TV or radio program (13)

der Senf mustard (6)

senken to sink, drop

die Sensation (-en) sensation

sensationell sensational(ly)

sensitiv sensitive

separat separate(ly)

(der) September September (3)

die Serie (-n) series; **die Krimi-Serie (-n)** detective series

der Service service; service department

servieren to serve

der Servierer (-) / die Serviererin (-nen) server

die Serviette (-n) napkin (6)

der Sessel (-) armchair (2)

setzen to set; to put (*in a sitting position*) (6); **sich setzen** to sit down (8)

der Sex sex; **der Safer Sex** safer sex

sexuell sexual(ly)

das Shampoo (-s) shampoo

der Sheriff (-s) sheriff

die Show (-s) show

der Shrimp (-s) shrimp

sich oneself, yourself (*form.*), himself, herself, itself, themselves

sicher safe(ly) (10); sure(ly), certain(ly)

die Sicherheit security, safety

die Sicherheitspolitik security policy; politics of security

der Sicherheitsrat (¨e) security council

sichern to make secure

Sie you (*form. sg./pl.*) (1, 3)

sie she; it; they (1); her; it; them (*acc.*) (3)

sieben seven (E)

sieb(en)te seventh (3)

siebenjährig seven-year-(old), seven years old

siebzehn seventeen (E)

siebzehnjährig seventeen-year-(old), seventeen years old

siebzig seventy (E)

der Siedepunkt (-e) boiling point

die Siedlung (-en) settlement; housing development

signalisieren to signal, indicate

der Silbershop (-s) silver shop

(das) Silvester New Year's Eve (3)

sind (we/they/you [*form.*]) are

singen, sang, gesungen to sing

der Sinn (-e) sense

sinnvoll sensible, sensibly

die Sitte (-n) custom, tradition

die Situation (-en) situation

sitzen, saß, gesessen to sit, be (sitting) (6)

der Sitznachbar (-n *masc.*) (-n) / die Sitznachbarin (-nen) person seated nearby

(das) Sizilien Sicily

der Skandal (-e) scandal

skandalös scandalous(ly)

der Skater (-) / die Skaterin (-nen) skater

das Skeetschießen skeet shooting

skeptisch skeptical(ly)

Ski fahren (fährt), fuhr, ist gefahren to ski

der Skifahrer (-) / die Skifahrerin (-nen) skier

die Skizze (-n) sketch

die Slowakei Slovakia (E)

(das) Slowenien Slovenia (E)

SMS schicken to send text messages

so so (2); like that; **so ein(e)** such a; **So ein Pech!** What a shame! What bad luck! (8); **So ein Unsinn!** Nonsense! (14); **(so) gegen fünf Uhr** around five o'clock (6); **so lala** (*coll.*) OK, so-so (E); **so was**

something like that; **so weit** so far; **so ... wie** as . . . as (7)

sobald (*subord. conj.*) as soon as

die Socke (-n) sock (5)

das Sofa (-s) sofa (2)

sofort immediately (9)

die Software (-s) (piece of) software

sofür for that

sogar even (8)

sogenannt so-called

der Sohn (¨e) son (3)

solange (*subord. conj.*) as long as

die Solarenergie solar energy

solch such

der Soldat (-en *masc.*) (-en) / die Soldatin (-nen) soldier

die Solidarität solidarity

der Solist (-en *masc.*) (-en) / die Solistin (-nen) soloist

sollen (soll), sollte, gesollt to be supposed to; shall; ought to; should (4); to be said to be

somit with that, thus

der Sommer (-) summer (7)

sommerlich summer(y)

die Sommerzeit (-en) daylight savings time

der Sonderabfall (¨e) toxic waste

die Sonderaktion (-en) special (sales) offer

sonderbar strange(ly)

der Sonderkindergarten (¨) special preschool

sondern (*coord. conj.*) but, rather (7)

die Sonderschule (-n) special school

(der) Sonnabend Saturday (3)

sonnabends Saturdays, on Saturday(s) (4)

die Sonne (-n) sun (7); **Die Sonne scheint.** The sun is shining. (7)

die Sonnenbrille (-n) (pair of) sunglasses

der Sonnenschein sunshine (7)

das Sonnenschutzmittel (-) suntan lotion, sunscreen (10)

sonnig sunny (7)

(der) Sonntag Sunday (3)

sonntags Sundays, on Sunday(s) (4)

sonst otherwise; else; other than that (10); **Sonst noch (et)was?** Anything else? (10)

sonstig other, additional

Sonstiges other items, miscellaneous

die Sorge (-n) worry; **sich Sorgen machen um** (+ *acc.*) to worry about (14)

sorgen für (+ *acc.*) to take care of, look after

der Sorgerechtsstreit (-e) custody battle

sorgfältig careful(ly)

die Sorte (-n) kind, sort

sortieren to sort

die Soße (-n) sauce; gravy

sowie as well as

die Sowjetunion Soviet Union

sowohl (als/wie) as well (as)

sozial social(ly)

der Sozialarbeiter (-) / die Sozialarbeiterin (-nen) social worker

die Sozialbauwohnung (-en) low-income apartment

die Sozialkunde social studies

der Soziologe (-n *masc.*) (-n) / die Soziologin (-nen) sociologist

die Soziologie sociology

die Spalte (-n) (printed) column

das Spanferkel (-) roasted suckling pig

(das) Spanien Spain

(das) Spanisch Spanish (language)

spannend exciting(ly), suspenseful(ly) (4)

sparen to save, conserve (12)

der Sparer (-) / die Sparerin (-nen) saver

der Spargel (-) asparagus

die Spargelzeit (-en) asparagus season

das Sparkonto (Sparkonten) savings account (12)

der Sparpreis (-e) discount price

sparsam thrifty, economical(ly) (12)

das Sparschwein (-e) piggy bank

der Spaß (¨e) fun (1); **Das macht Spaß.** That's fun. (1); **Spaß haben** to have fun; **Viel Spaß!** Have fun! (1)

spät late (4); **Wie spät ist es?** What time is it? (4)

spätestens at the latest (12)

die Spätzle, Spätzli (*pl.*) *a kind of noodles*

spazieren gehen (geht spazieren), ging spazieren, ist spazieren gegangen to go for a walk (4)

der Spaziergang (¨e) walk, stroll

der Speck bacon (6)

die Speckbohnen (*pl.*) beans with bacon

speichern to store, save (13)

die Speise (-n) food; dish (of prepared food) (6)

die Speisekarte (-n) menu (6)

der Speiseplan (¨e) menu, diet

die Speisung (-en) feeding, supplying

spektakulär spectacular(ly)

die Spende (-n) donation, contribution

spenden to donate, contribute

der Spender (-) / die Spenderin (-nen) donor, contributor

das Spezial (-s) special

spezialisieren to specialize

die Spezialität (-en) specialty

die Spezies (-) species

spezifisch specific(ally)

der Spiegel (-) mirror

das Spiegelbild (-er) reflection

das Spiegelei (-er) fried egg (sunny-side up) (6)

spiegeln to reflect

das Spiel (-e) game; play

spielen to play (1); **Computerspiele spielen** to play computer games (1); **Fußball spielen** to play soccer (7); **Karten spielen** to play cards (1); **Schach spielen** to play chess (7); **Tennis spielen** to play tennis (7)

spielend (*adv.*) without effort, easily

der Spieler (-) / die Spielerin (-nen) player; **der CD-Spieler (-)** CD player

der Spielfilm (-e) feature film, movie (13)

die Spielkarte (-n) playing card (7)

der Spielplatz (¨e) playground

das Spielzeug (-e) toy

die Spinne (-n) spider

spitze (*coll.*) marvelous(ly)

die Spitze (-n) tip; (pointed) top

spontan spontaneous(ly)

der Sport (*pl.* **Sportarten**) sports, sport (7); **Sport treiben, trieb, getrieben** to play sports (7)

die Sportanlage (-n) sports field

die Sporthalle (-n) gymnasium, sports arena (7)

das Sportkabriolett (-s) sports convertible

sportlich athletic(ally) (1); **sportlich aktiv** active in sports (10)

der Sportplatz (ˣe) athletic field (7)

die Sporttasche (-n) athletic bag

der Spot (-s) advertising spot, commercial

die Sprache (-n) language

das Sprachinstitut (-e) institute for language

der Sprachkurs (-e) language course

der Sprachtipp (-s) language tip

der Sprachurlaub (-e) language-learning vacation

sprechen (spricht), sprach, gesprochen to speak (2)

der Sprecher (-) / die Sprecherin (-nen) speaker

das Sprechschema (-s) conversational pattern

die Sprechstunde (-n) office hour (8)

der Springbrunnen (-) fountain

springen, sprang, ist gesprungen to jump

der Sprudel (-) mineral water (6)

spülen to wash, rinse; **das Geschirr spülen** to wash the dishes

die Spülmaschine (-n) dishwasher (12)

die Spur (-en) track, trail; trace

spurlos without a trace

das Squash squash (game)

die SS = Schutzstaffel *elite organization within the Nazi party*

der Staat (-en) state, nation

staatlich governmental(ly), of/by the state

die Staatsangehörigkeit (-en) nationality

das Stadion (Stadien) stadium (7)

die Stadt (ˣe) town; city (E)

die Stadtansicht (-en) view of a town

das Stadtbad (ˣer) municipal bath/pool

das Stadtbild (ˣer) townscape; cityscape

das Städtchen (-) little town

die Stadtentwicklung (-en) urban development

der Stadtplan (ˣe) city street map

die Stadtplanung urban planning

der Stadtrat (ˣe) city council

der Stahlhelm (-e) steel helmet

der Stammbaum (ˣe) family tree

stammen aus (+ *dat.*) to come from, originate in

der Standard (-s) standard

ständig constant(ly); permanent(ly)

stark (stärker, stärkst-) strong(ly) (7); heavy, heavily

die Stärke (-n) strength (11)

das Starmagazin *German entertainment magazine*

starren (auf + *acc.***)** to stare (at)

der Start (-s) start

starten to start

die Station (-en) station

stationieren to station

statt (+ *gen.*) instead of

stattdessen instead (of that)

stattfinden (findet statt), fand statt, stattgefunden to take place

die Statue (-n) statue

der Stau (-s) traffic jam

der Staubsauger (-) vacuum cleaner (12)

das Steak (-s) steak

der Steckbrief (-e) personal details; wanted poster

stecken to place, put (*inside*); to be (*inside*) (6)

stehen, stand, gestanden to stand; to be located (6); (+ *dat.*) to look good (on a person) (5); **Die Farbe steht mir.** The color looks good on me. (5)

die Stehlampe (-n) floor lamp

die Steiermark Styria (*one of the Austrian states*)

steif stiff(ly)

steigen, stieg, ist gestiegen to climb, go up, rise

steigend increasing

die Stelle (-n) place, position; job (11) **an deiner Stelle** if I were you, (if I were) in your place (12)

stellen to stand up, place, put (*in a standing position*) (6); **eine Frage stellen** to ask a question; **sich stellen** to place oneself

das Stellenangebot (-e) job offer; help-wanted ad (11)

die Stellensuche (-n) job search

die Stellung (-en) position; **Stellung nehmen zu** (+ *dat.*) to state one's opinion on

der Stephansdom St. Stephen's Cathedral

sterben (an + *dat.***) (stirbt), starb, ist gestorben** to die (of)

die Stereoanlage (-n) stereo (system) (2)

die Sterilisation (-en) sterilization

sterilisieren to sterilize

der Stern (-e) star

das Sternzeichen (-) star sign, sign of the zodiac

die Steuer (-n) tax (14)

der Steward (-s) / die Stewardess (-en) steward/stewardess, flight attendant

das Stichwort (ˣer) key word, cue

der Stiefbruder (ˣ) stepbrother

der Stiefel (-) boot (5)

die Stiefschwester (-n) stepsister

der Stil (-e) style

das Stillleben (-) still life

die Stimme (-n) voice

stimmen to be correct; **(das) stimmt** that is correct

die Stimmung (-en) mood

stinken, stank, gestunken to stink

das Stipendium (Stipendien) scholarship, stipend

der Stock (*pl.* **Stockwerke**) floor, story (9); **im ersten Stock** on the second floor

stockaufwärts up to the next floor

das Stockwerk (-e) floor, story

der Stoffbeutel (-) fabric bag

der Stollen (-) (type of) fruit cake

stolpern, ist gestolpert to stumble

stolz proud(ly)

der Storch (ˣe) stork

stören to bother, disturb

stoßen (stößt), stieß, gestoßen to push

der Strafzettel (-) (parking/speeding) ticket

der Strahl (-en) ray, beam

der Strand (ˣe) beach (10)

die Straße (-n) street (E)

die Straßenbahn (-en) streetcar

die Strategie (-n) strategy

sich strecken to stretch (8)

streckenweise in places, at times

der Streifen (-) strip; band

streiken to go on strike

streng strict(ly) (14)

der Stress (-e) stress (8)

stressig stressful (1)

der Strohhut (ˣe) straw hat

der Strom (ˣe) stream; (electrical) current, electricity (12); **Es regnet in Strömen.** It is pouring rain.

der Strumpf (ˣe) stocking; sock (5)

die Stube (-n) room

das Stüberl (-) (*Austrian, Bavarian*) small room

das Stück (-e) piece; (theater) play

der Student (-en *masc.***) (-en) / die Studentin (-nen)** (university) student (1)

die Studentenbude (-n) (*coll.*) student's room

das Studentenheim (-e) dormitory

das Studentenwerk (-e) student service organization

das Studentenwohnheim (-e) dormitory (2)

die Studie (-n) study

der Studienabgänger (-) graduate

das Studienfach (ˣer) academic subject

die Studiengebühren (*pl.*) fees, tuition (12)

studieren to study (1); to major in

der/die Studierende (*decl. adj.*) student

das Studio (-s) studio

das Studium (Studien) study, course of studies

die Stufe (-n) step; level

der Stuhl (ˣe) chair (2)

die Stunde (-n) hour (4)

stundenlang for hours

der Stundenplan (ˣe) hourly class schedule

-stündig lasting . . . hours

stur obstinate(ly)

Stuttgarter (*adj.*) of/from Stuttgart

das Substantiv (-e) noun

die Substanz (-en) substance

subventionieren to subsidize

die Suche (-n) search

suchen to search, look for (2); **nach etwas** (*dat.*) **suchen** to look for something (14)

süddeutsch (*adj.*) southern German

(das) Süddeutschland southern Germany

der Süden south; **im Süden** in the south

südlich (von + *dat.***)** south (of)

(das) Südspanien southern Spain

Südwest (*without article*) southwest

der Südwesten southwest; **im Südwesten** in the southwest

die **Summe** (-n) sum, total
super (*coll.*) super
der **Superlativ** (-e) superlative
die **Superlativform** (-en) superlative form (of an adjective)
der **Supermarkt** (¨e) supermarket (5)
die **Suppe** (-n) soup (6)
surfen to surf (1): **im Internet surfen** to surf the Internet
das **Surfboard** (-s) surfboard
das **Surfbrett** (-er) surfboard
das **Sushi** sushi
süß sweet(ly)
die **Süßigkeiten** (*pl.*) sweets
das **Sweatshirt** (-s) sweatshirt
(das) **Sylt** *German island in the North Sea*
Sylter (*adj.*) of/from Sylt
das **Symbol** (-e) symbol
sympathisch likable, pleasant, nice (1)
die **Symphonie** (-n) symphony
symphonisch symphonic(ally)
das **Symptom** (-e) symptom
synchronisieren to dub (*film*)
das **Synthetik** synthetic material
das **System** (-e) system
die **Szene** (-n) scene
die **Szenekneipe** (-n) trendy bar
die **Szenekultur** (-en) trendy culture

T

der **Tabak** (-e) tobacco
tabellarisch tabular, in tabular/outline form
die **Tabelle** (-n) table, chart
die **Tablette** (-n) tablet, pill
die **Tafel** (-n) (chalk)board: **eine Tafel Schokolade** a bar of chocolate
der **Tag** (-e) day (2): **eines Tages** one day: **(guten) Tag** hello, good day (E): **in zwei Tagen** in two days (6): **jeden Tag** every day (7): **vor zwei Tagen** two days ago
das **Tagebuch** (¨er) diary
tagen to meet, convene
der **Tagesablauf** (¨e) daily routine
das **Tagesangebot** (-e) daily special
der **Tagesspiegel** "daily mirror" (*German newspaper*)
die **Tagestemperatur** (-en) temperature during the day
die **Tageszeit** (-en) time of day
die **Tageszeitung** (-en) daily newspaper
-tägig lasting ... days
täglich daily (6)
die **Tagung** (-en) convention, meeting
das **Tal** (¨er) valley
das **Talent** (-e) talent
talentiert talented
der **Tango** (-s) tango
die **Tante** (-n) aunt (3)
der **Tanz** (¨e) dance
tanzen to dance (1): **Er tanzt gut.** He dances well. (1)
die **Tasche** (-n) handbag, purse (5); pocket
das **Taschengeld** (monetary) allowance
die **Tasse** (-n) cup (4): **eine Tasse Kaffee** a cup of coffee (4)
der **Täter** (-) / die **Täterin** (-nen) culprit
tätig active, working

die **Tätigkeit** (-en) activity: position (11)
der **Tatort** (-e) scene of the crime
die **Tatsache** (-n) fact
tatsächlich actual(ly): in fact
tauchen to dive (7)
der **Tauchgang** (¨e) dive
tauglich suitable: usable
taumeln, ist getaumelt to stagger
tauschen to exchange
tausend one thousand (E)
das **Taxi** (-s) taxicab (10)
das **Team** (-s) team
der **Teamgeist** team spirit
die **Technik** technique: technology (11): technical engineering
der **Techniker** (-) / die **Technikerin** (-nen) technician
der **Technikstress** (-e) technological stress
technisch technical(ly); mechanical(ly)
das/der **Techno** techno (music)
die **Technologie** (-n) technology
der **Tee** tea (5)
die **Teigwaren** (*pl.*) pasta
der/das **Teil** (-e) part: share
teilen to divide; to share; **sich** (*dat.*) **etwas teilen (mit** + *dat.*) to share something (with)
die **Teilnahme** (-n) participation
teilnehmen (an + *dat.*) **(nimmt teil), nahm teil, teilgenommen** to participate (in) (14)
der **Teilnehmer** (-) / die **Teilnehmerin** (-nen) participant
das **Telefaxgerät** (-e) fax machine
das **Telefon** (-e) telephone (2)
telefonieren to telephone, talk on the phone (1)
telefonisch by telephone
die **Telefonnummer** (-n) telephone number (E): **Wie ist deine/Ihre Telefonnummer?** What is your telephone number? (*inform./form.*) (E)
das **Telegramm** (-e) telegram
die **Telekom** = **Deutsche Telekom AG** (*German telecommunications corporation*)
die **Telenovela** (-s) type of soap opera
das **Telephon** (-e) = das **Telefon** (-e)
das **Telex** telex
der **Teller** (-) plate (6)
temperamentvoll spirited, lively
die **Temperatur** (-en) temperature (7)
das **Tempolimit** (-s) speed limit
temporal temporal
(das) **Tennis** tennis: **Tennis spielen** to play tennis (7)
die **Tennisanlage** (-n) tennis court
der **Tennisplatz** (¨e) tennis court (7)
der **Tennisschuh** (-e) tennis shoe (5)
der **Teppich** (-e) rug, carpet (2)
der **Teppichboden** (-) wall-to-wall carpeting (12)
der **Termin** (-e) appointment (8)
die **Terrasse** (-n) terrace, patio (2)
der **Terrorismus** terrorism (14)
der **Test** (-s) test
teuer expensive(ly) (2)
der **Teufel** (-) devil

der **Text** (-e) text
das **Theater** (-) theater (4): **ins Theater gehen** to go to the theater (4)
das **Theaterstück** (-e) play, (stage) drama (4)
die **Theke** (-n) bar, counter
das **Thema** (**Themen**) theme: topic
die **Theologie** theology
das **Thermalbad** (¨er) thermal bath
der **Thermalbrunnen** (-) thermal spring
die **Thermalkur** (-en) thermal cure
die **These** (-n) thesis
(das) **Thüringen** Thuringia (*German state*)
Thüringer (*adj.*) Thuringian
der **Tick** (-s) tic
das **Ticket** (-s) ticket
tief deep(ly)
die **Tiefgarage** (-n) underground garage
das **Tier** (-e) animal (12)
der **Tierarzt** (¨e) / die **Tierärztin** (-nen) veterinarian
das **Tierbaby** (-s) baby animal
der **Tierpark** (-s) zoo (9)
der **Tierschutz** animal protection
der **Tiger** (-) tiger
der **Tipp** (-s) tip, hint
der **Tiroler Hut** (¨e) Tyrolean hat
der **Tisch** (-e) table (2)
der **Titel** (-) title
der **Toast** (-e) toast
die **Tochter** (¨) daughter (3)
das **Tochterunternehmen** (-) subsidiary company
der **Tod** (-e) death
der **Tofu** tofu
die **Toilette** (-n) toilet
das **Toilettenpapier** toilet paper (5)
die **Toilettensachen** (*pl.*) toiletries
(das) **Tokio** Tokyo
tolerant tolerant(ly)
toll! (*coll.*) super! (1): **ganz toll!** super! great! (1)
die **Tomate** (-n) tomato (5)
der **Ton** (¨e) tone: (musical) note
die **Tonne** (-n) ton: barrel
das **Tor** (-e) gate
die **Torte** (-n) torte, pie, cake
die **Toskana** Tuscany
tot dead
total total(ly)
töten to kill
die **Tour** (-en) tour: trip
der **Tourist** (-en *masc.*) (-en) / die **Touristin** (-nen) tourist (9)
der **Trabbi** (-s) (*coll.*) Trabant (*automobile made in the former GDR*)
die **Tradition** (-en) tradition (3)
traditionell traditional(ly)
traditionsgemäß traditionally
tragbar portable
tragen (trägt), trug, getragen to wear: to carry (5): **die Verantwortung tragen** to be responsible
die **Tragikomödie** (-n) tragicomedy
die **Tragödie** (-n) tragedy (4)
trainieren to train; to practice
das **Training** training: practice
der **Trainingsanzug** (¨e) jogging suit
die **Tränke** (-n) watering hole

der Transfer (-s) transfer
der Transformator (-en) transformer
der Transport (-e) transportation
der Transportweg (-e) transport road
die Traube (-n) grape (5)
der Traum (ÿe) dream
träumen (von + *dat.***)** to dream (of)
traurig sad(ly)
treffen (trifft), traf, getroffen to hit; to meet (4); **sich treffen mit** (+ *dat.*) to meet with
treiben, trieb, getrieben to drive; **Schwarzhandel treiben** to trade on the black market; **Sport treiben** to play sports (7)
das Treibhaus (ÿer) greenhouse
der Treibhauseffekt greenhouse effect
der Trend (-s) trend
trennbar separable
(sich) trennen to separate (14)
die Trennung (-en) separation
die Treppe (-n) staircase (12)
das Treppenhaus (ÿer) stairwell
treten (tritt), trat, ist getreten to step; **in Kraft treten** to go into effect
treu loyal(ly) (1); faithful(ly)
der Trimm-Pfad (-e) jogging path
trinken, trank, getrunken to drink (2)
die Trinkkur (-en) mineral water drinking cure
die Trinkmilch low-fat pasteurized milk
das Trinkwasser drinking water
der Triumph (-e) triumph
trocken dry
trocknen to dry
die Trompete (-n) trumpet
der Tropenwald (ÿer) tropical forest
die Trophäe (-n) trophy
trotz (+ *gen.*) in spite of (9)
die Trümmer (*pl.*) rubble, ruins
die Trümmerfrau (-en) *woman who cleared away rubble after World War II*
die Truppen (*pl.*) troops
der Truthahn (ÿe) turkey (5)
das T-Shirt (-s) T-shirt (5)
(das) Tschechien Czech Republic (E)
tschechisch (*adj.*) Czech
tschüss so long, bye (*inform.*) E
tun (tut), tat, getan to do (8)
die Tür (-en) door (2)
der Türke (-n *masc.***) (-n) / die Türkin (-nen)** Turk, Turkish person
die Türkei Turkey
türkisch (*adj.*) Turkish
der Turm (ÿe) tower; steeple
turnen to do gymnastics (7)
das Turnen gymnastics
die Turnhalle (-n) gymnasium (7)
der Turnschuh (-e) gym shoe, sneaker
der Typ (-en) type, sort
der Typ (-en *masc.***) (-en)** (*coll.*) guy
typisch typical(ly)

U

über (+ *acc./dat.*) over, above (6); about
überall everywhere
überbacken: mit Käse überbacken topped with cheese and baked

der Überblick (-e) overview
übereinander on top of one another
überfliegen, überflog, überflogen to skim (*a text*), read quickly (13)
überfreundlich super-friendly
überglücklich super-happy, overjoyed
übergroß huge; plus-sized
überhaupt at all; **überhaupt nicht** not at all
die Überholspur (-en) passing lane
überlassen (überlässt), überließ, überlassen to leave up to; **Das bleibt dir überlassen.** That's up to you.
überleben to survive
sich (*dat.*) **etwas überlegen** to consider something, think something over (10)
übernachten to stay overnight (9)
die Übernachtung (-en) overnight stay (9)
übernehmen (übernimmt), übernahm, übernommen to take over (11)
überraschen to surprise; **überraschend** surprising(ly)
die Überraschung (-en) surprise
überreden to persuade
die Überredungskunst (ÿe) persuasiveness, ability to persuade
der Überrest (-e) remnant; ruin
übersetzen to translate (11)
der Übersetzer (-) / die Übersetzerin (-nen) translator
übertragbar transferable, communicable
übertreiben, übertrieb, übertrieben to exaggerate; **übertrieben** exaggerated (14)
üblich usual
übrig left over, remaining (12)
übrigens by the way (9)
die Übung (-en) exercise
das Ufo (-s) UFO (flying saucer)
die Uhr (-en) clock (2); watch; o'clock; **bis (um) fünf Uhr** until five o'clock (6); **Es ist ein Uhr.** It's one o'clock. (4); **(so) gegen fünf Uhr** around five o'clock (6); **um ein Uhr** at one o'clock; **Um wie viel Uhr?** At what time? (4); **von zwei bis drei Uhr** from two to three o'clock (6); **Wie viel Uhr ist es?** What time is it? (4); **zwischen zwei und drei Uhr** between two and three o'clock (6)
die Uhrzeit (-en) time of day
um (+ *acc.*) at (+ *time*) (3, 4); around; circa; **bis (um) fünf Uhr** until five o'clock (6); **sich Sorgen machen um** to worry about (14); **um ein Uhr** at one o'clock; **um ... herum** around (*spatial*) (3); **um Mitternacht** at midnight (3); **Um wie viel Uhr?** At what time? (4); **um ... zu** in order to; **um zwei** at two (o'clock) (4)
sich umbringen (bringt um), brachte um, umgebracht to commit suicide
umfassen to contain, include
das Umfeld (-er) milieu, surroundings
die Umfrage (-n) poll, survey
die Umgebung (-en) area, neighborhood, vicinity (12)
umgehen mit (+ *dat.*)**, ging um, ist umgegangen** to handle, deal with
umgekehrt the other way around

der Umlaut (-e) *changed vowel sound represented by* **ä, ö,** *or* **ü**
umschulen (schult um) to retrain (14)
die Umschulung (-en) retraining
umsteigen (steigt um), stieg um, ist umgestiegen to transfer, change (trains) (10)
umstellen (stellt um) to reset
die Umwelt environment
umweltbewusst environmentally conscious
das Umweltbewusstsein environmental consciousness
das Umweltbundesamt federal department of the environment
der Umweltbus (-se) ecological bus
umweltfreundlich environmentally friendly (14)
der Umweltschutz environmental protection (14)
die Umweltverschmutzung environmental pollution (14)
umweltverträglich environmentally safe
umziehen (zieht um), zog um, ist umgezogen to move (residence)
unabhängig independent(ly)
unangenehm unpleasant(ly)
unbedingt absolutely, by all means (12)
unbegrenzt unlimited
unbekannt unknown
unbequem uncomfortable, uncomfortably
und (*coord. conj.*) and (E); **Na und?** So what? (13)
unerträglich unbearable, unbearably
die UNESCO UNESCO (United Nations Educational, Scientific and Cultural Organization)
unfair unfair(ly)
der Unfall (ÿe) accident, mishap
unfreundlich unfriendly (1)
der Unfug nonsense
(das) Ungarn Hungary (E)
ungeduldig impatient(ly)
ungefähr approximately, about (9)
ungemütlich uncomfortable, uncomfortably
ungesund unhealthy, unhealthily
ungewöhnlich unusual(ly)
unglaublich unbelievable, unbelievably
unglücklich unhappy, unhappily
unhöflich impolite(ly)
die Uni (-s) (*coll.*) = **Universität**
die Uniform (-en) uniform
uninteressant uninteresting
die Union (-en) union; **die Europäische Union** European Union
die Universität (-en) university (1); college
unkonventionell unconventional(ly)
unmittelbar direct(ly), immediate(ly)
unmöbliert unfurnished (2)
unmöglich impossible, impossibly
die UNO UN (United Nations)
unordentlich disorderly
unpraktisch impractical (1)
uns us (*acc.*) (3); (to/for) us (*dat.*) (5)
unschuldig innocent(ly)
unser our (3)

der Unsinn nonsense; **So ein Unsinn!** (Such) nonsense! (14)

unsympathisch unlikable (1)

unten below; downstairs (12); **nach unten** below; downstairs (*directional*) (12)

unter (+ *acc./dat.*) under, below, beneath; among (6)

unterbrechen (unterbricht), unterbrach, unterbrochen to interrupt (14)

die **Unterbrechung (-en)** interruption

unterdurchschnittlich below average

untereinander amongst ourselves/ yourselves/themselves

unterernährt malnourished

das **Untergeschoss (-e)** basement

sich unterhalten (unterhält), unterhielt, unterhalten to entertain (oneself); to converse (13)

unterhaltsam entertaining (13)

die **Unterhaltung** entertainment (13); **zur Unterhaltung** for entertainment (13)

die **Unterkunft (-̈e)** accommodation (9)

die **Unterlagen** (*pl.*) documentation, papers (11)

unternehmen (unternimmt), unternahm, unternommen to undertake (10)

das **Unternehmen (-)** business, company, enterprise (11)

die **Unternehmenskommunikation (-en)** business communication

unterordnend: unterordnende Konjunktion (-en) subordinating conjunction

der **Unterricht (-e)** instruction, lesson

unterrichten to teach

der **Unterschied (-e)** difference

unterschiedlich different

unterschreiben, unterschrieb, unterschrieben to sign

die **Unterschrift (-en)** signature

unterstreichen, unterstrich, unterstrichen to underline

unterstützen to support (12)

die **Unterstützung** support (11)

untersuchen to examine (11)

unterteilen to divide, subdivide

der **Untertitel (-)** subtitle

die **Unterwäsche** underwear

unterwegs on the way, en route

untrennbar inseparable

unverbraucht unused; untouched

unverletzt unharmed, uninjured

unwichtig unimportant

der **Urenkel (-) / die Urenkelin (-nen)** great-grandson/great-granddaughter

die **Urgroßmutter (-̈)** great-grandmother

der **Urgroßvater (-̈)** great-grandfather

urig natural; cozy

urkundlich documentary, in a document

der **Urlaub (-e)** vacation; **Urlaub machen** to go on vacation (8)

der **Urlauber (-) / die Urlauberin (-nen)** person on vacation

der **Urlaubsort (-e)** vacation resort

die **Ursache (-n)** cause

ursprünglich original(ly)

der **Urwald (-̈er)** primeval forest

die **USA** (*pl.*) United States; **aus den USA** from the United States

der **US-Amerikaner (-) / die US-Amerikanerin (-nen)** American, person from the USA

usw. = **und so weiter** and so on

V

der **Valentinstag** Valentine's Day (3)

der **Vampir (-e)** vampire

das **Vanilleeis** vanilla ice cream

variieren to vary

der **Vater (-̈)** father (3)

väterlicherseits on the father's side

der **Vatertag (-e)** Father's Day

der **Vati (-s)** dad, daddy

der **Vegetarier (-) / die Vegetarierin (-nen)** vegetarian (*person*)

vegetarisch vegetarian (6)

(das) Venedig Venice (Italy)

sich verabreden mit (+ *dat.*) to arrange to meet with

die **Verabredung (-en)** appointment; date

verabschieden to say goodbye to

verändern to change

die **Veränderung (-en)** change

die **Veranstaltung (-en)** event

verantworten to take responsibility for

verantwortlich responsible (11)

die **Verantwortung (-en)** responsibility

verantwortungsbewusst responsible, conscious of responsibility

verarbeiten to process

das **Verb (-en)** verb

die **Verbalform (-en)** verbal form

verbannen to ban; to banish

verbessern to correct; to improve

die **Verbform (-en)** verb form

verbieten, verbot, verboten to prohibit, forbid (14)

verbinden, verband, verbunden to connect

verborgen: im Verborgenen leben to live in isolation

der **Verbrauch** consumption

verbrauchen to use; to consume (14)

der **Verbraucher (-)** consumer

das **Verbrechen (-)** crime

verbreiten to spread, disseminate (14)

verbringen, verbrachte, verbracht to spend (*time*) (7)

verdächtigen to suspect

verdienen to earn; to deserve (11); **sich** (*dat.*) **etwas verdient haben** to have deserved something

verdünnen to dilute

der **Verein (-e)** club, association (7)

vereinbaren to agree; to arrange

vereinen to unite; **die Vereinten Nationen** (*pl.*) United Nations

vereinigen to unite; **die Vereinigten Staaten** (*pl.*) United States

verfehlen to miss

verfolgen to follow, pursue; to persecute

die **Verfolgung (-en)** persecution

verfügbar available

die **Verfügbarkeit** availability

die **Verfügung: zur Verfügung stehen, stand, gestanden** to be available, to be at one's disposal

die **Vergangenheit** past

vergehen, verging, ist vergangen to pass; **ein Monat ist vergangen** a month has passed

vergessen (vergisst), vergaß, vergessen to forget (10)

vergiften to poison

der **Vergleich (-e)** comparison

vergleichen, verglich, verglichen to compare (12)

das **Vergnügen (-)** pleasure; leisure

die **Vergnügung (-en)** amusement, entertainment

verhaften to arrest

das **Verhältnis (-se)** relationship

verheiratet married

verhindern to prevent

verhungern, ist verhungert to die of starvation

das **Verhütungsmittel (-)** contraceptive

der **Verkauf (-̈e)** sale

verkaufen to sell

der **Verkäufer (-) / die Verkäuferin (-nen)** salesperson (2)

der **Verkehr** traffic

die **Verkehrsbelästigung (-en)** traffic disturbance

die **Verkehrskontrolle (-n)** vehicle checkpoint

das **Verkehrsmittel (-)** vehicle, means of transportation (14)

das **Verkehrsmuseum (Verkehrsmuseen)** transportation museum

das **Verkehrswesen (-)** transportation system

verkochen, ist verkocht to boil away

verkraften to handle, cope with

verkünden to announce

verkürzen to shorten

der **Verlag (-e)** publishing house

verlagern to move, transfer

verlangen to demand

die **Verlängerung (-en)** lengthening; prolongation

verlassen (verlässt), verließ, verlassen to leave

(sich) verletzen to injure (oneself) (8)

die **Verletzung (-en)** injury; violation (14)

sich verlieben (in + *acc.*) to fall in love (with)

verlieren, verlor, verloren to lose (7)

der/die **Verlobte** (*decl. adj.*) fiancé/ fiancée

verlocken to tempt, entice

verlogen: verlogen sein to be full of lies

vermeidbar avoidable

vermeiden, vermied, vermieden to avoid (14)

vermieten to rent out (*to someone*) (12); **zu vermieten** for rent

der **Vermieter (-) / die Vermieterin (-nen)** landlord/landlady

vermindern to decrease, lessen (14)

das **Vermögen (-)** fortune; wealth

vernichten to destroy

veröffentlichen to publish

die Verpackung (-en) packaging, wrapping (14)

die Verpackungsflut (-en) excess use of packaging

die Verpflegung (-en) food; **Unterkunft und Verpflegung** room and board

sich verpflichten to commit oneself

verraten (verrät), verriet, verraten to betray, give away

verreisen, ist verreist to go on a trip (10)

verrückt crazy, crazily (8)

der Versandkatalog (-e) mail-order catalogue

verschieden different

verschließen, verschloss, verschlossen to close; to lock

verschlingen, verschlang, verschlungen to devour

verschlossen taciturn; reserved

die Verschmutzung (-en) pollution

verschreiben, verschrieb, verschrieben to prescribe (8)

verschwinden, verschwand, ist verschwunden to disappear

verschwommen blurred

die Verschwörung (-en) conspiracy

das Versehen (-) oversight

die Versicherung (-en) insurance (12)

versorgen to supply

die Versorgung (-en) supplying

verspätet delayed, late

versprechen (verspricht), versprach, versprochen to promise

versprühen to spray

verstehen, verstand, verstanden to understand; **Ich verstehe das nicht.** I don't understand. (E)

versuchen to try, attempt (8)

verteilen to distribute

der Vertrag (-̈e) contract; treaty

vertrauen (+ dat.) to trust

vertraut familiar (14)

vertreten (vertritt), vertrat, vertreten to represent

vervollständigen to complete

die Verwaltung (-en) administration

die Verwaltungsfachhochschule (-n) *college that provides training for higher-level civil service positions*

der Verwaltungsweg (-e) administrative route

verwandt mit (+ dat.) related to (3)

die Verwandtschaft (-en) relationship

die Verwechslung (-en) confusion, mistake, mix-up

verwenden to utilize, use, apply (14)

verwirklichen to make real

verwöhnen to spoil, pamper

das Verzeichnis (-se) list, directory, schedule

verzichten auf (+ acc.) to do without (12)

der Vetter (-n) male cousin (3)

das Video (-s) video; videotape (2)

das Videogerät (-e) video recorder (VCR)

der Videorecorder (-) video recorder (VCR) (2)

viel (mehr, meist-) a lot, much (1, 2); **Um wie viel Uhr?** At what time? (4); **Viel Glück!** Good luck! (1); **Viel Spaß!** Have fun! (1); **Vielen Dank!** Many thanks! (6); **wie viel** how much; **Wie viel Uhr ist es?** What time is it? (4)

viele (pl.) many (2); **viele Grüße** best wishes (12); **wie viele** how many

die Vielfalt diversity

vielfältig many and diverse

vielleicht maybe, perhaps (1)

vier four (E)

die Vierergruppe (-n) group of four

viermal four times

viert: zu viert as a foursome (10)

viertägig four-day, lasting four days

vierte fourth (3)

das Viertel (-) quarter (4); **Es ist Viertel nach/vor zwei.** It's a quarter after/to two. (4)

vierzehn fourteen (E)

vierzig forty (E)

die Villa (Villen) villa

das Virus (Viren) virus

vis-à-vis (+ dat.) across from

die Visitenkarte (-n) business card

das Vitamin (-e) vitamin

der Vogel (-̈) bird

das Vög(e)lein (-) little bird

die Vokabeln (pl.) vocabulary

das Vokabular (-e) vocabulary

das Volk (-̈er) people; nation

die Völkerkunde ethnology

der Volksaufstand (-̈e) people's revolt

das Volksfest (-e) public festival; fair

das Volkslied (-er) folk song

der Volkspolizist (-en masc.) (-en) / die Volkspolizistin (-nen) officer of the People's Police (GDR)

der Volkswagen (-) Volkswagen (*automobile*)

die Volkswirtschaft economics

voll full; crowded (6); **voller Leben** full of life

die Vollendung (-en) completion

völlig total(ly), complete(ly)

das Vollkornbrot (-e) whole-grain bread

die Vollkornnudeln (pl.) whole-grain pasta

die Vollmilch whole milk

die Vollpension accommodation with three meals per day included

vollständig complete(ly)

vom = von dem; vom Fass on tap; draft (6)

von (+ dat.) of; from; by (5, 6); out of; **gegenüber von** across from (9); **von zwei bis drei Uhr** from two to three o'clock (6); **weit (weg) von** far away from (2)

vor (+ acc./dat.) before; in front of; ago (6); (+ *time*) to, of (4) **Es ist Viertel vor zwei.** It's a quarter to two. (4); **fünf vor zwei** five to/of two (4); **vor allem** above all; **vor zwei Tagen** two days ago (6)

vorbei past, gone, over

vorbeifahren (fährt vorbei), fuhr vorbei, ist vorbeigefahren to drive past

vorbeigehen (geht vorbei), ging vorbei, ist vorbeigegangen to pass by

vorbeikommen (kommt vorbei), kam vorbei, ist vorbeigekommen to drop in, come by (4)

(sich) vorbereiten (auf + acc.) (bereitet vor) to prepare (oneself) (for) (11)

die Vorbereitung (-en) preparation

die Vorderseite (-n) front side

der Vorfahr (-en masc.) (-en) / die Vorfahrin (-nen) ancestor, predecessor

vorgehen (geht vor), ging vor, ist vorgegangen to happen, go on

vorgestern the day before yesterday

vorhaben (hat vor) to plan (*to do*) (4)

vorher before that; before

vorig previous, last

vorkommen (kommt vor), kam vor, ist vorgekommen to occur

vorlesen (liest vor), las vor, vorgelesen to read aloud

die Vorlesung (-en) (university) lecture (4)

die Vorliebe (-n) preference; particular fondness

vorm = vor dem

der Vormittag (-e) morning, before noon (4); **gestern Vormittag** yesterday morning; **heute Vormittag** this morning; **morgen Vormittag** tomorrow morning

vormittags before noon (4)

der Vorname (gen. -ns, acc./dat. -n) (-n) first name, given name (1)

vorne in front

vornehmen (nimmt vor), nahm vor, vorgenommen to plan; to carry out

der Vorort (-e) suburb

der Vorortszug (-̈e) commuter train

der Vorraum (-̈e) front hall

der Vorsatz (-̈e) intention, resolution

der Vorschein: zum Vorschein kommen to appear, come to light

der Vorschlag (-̈e) suggestion

vorschlagen (schlägt vor), schlug vor, vorgeschlagen to suggest, propose (10)

die Vorsicht care, caution

vorsichtig careful(ly), cautious(ly)

die Vorsorge precautions, provisions

die Vorspeise (-n) appetizer (6)

vorspielen (spielt vor): das Stück der Klasse vorspielen to perform the piece in front of the class

vorspulen (spult vor) to fast forward

vorstellen (stellt vor) to set forward (*clock*); to introduce; **sich (acc.) vorstellen** to introduce oneself (11); **sich (dat.) etwas vorstellen** to imagine something (11)

die Vorstellung (-en) idea, concept; introduction

das Vorstellungsgespräch (-e) job interview (11)

der Vorteil (-e) advantage (11)

der Vortrag (-̈e) lecture (4)

der Vorverkauf (-̈e) advance sale

vorwärts kommen (kommt vorwärts), kam vorwärts, ist vorwärts gekommen to get ahead

vorweisen (weist vor), wies vor, vorgewiesen to show, present
vorzeigen (zeigt vor) to show
vorziehen (zieht vor), zog vor, vorgezogen to prefer (14)
der VW (-s) = Volkswagen

W

wachsen (wächst), wuchs, ist gewachsen to grow
der Wachtturm (¨e) watchtower
der Wagen (-) car (7)
die Wagenauffahrt (-en) driveway
wählen to choose; to vote, elect (14)
der Wähler (-) / die Wählerin (-nen) voter
wahllos indiscriminate(ly)
wahr true; real, genuine
während (+ gen.) during (9); (subord. conj.) while, whereas
die Wahrheit (-en) truth
wahrscheinlich probable, probably (11)
die Währung (-en) currency
der Wald (¨er) forest (7)
der Walkman (-s) Walkman (portable cassette player)
der Walzer (-) waltz
die Wand (¨e) wall (2); die vier Wände one's own home
der Wandel change; im Wandel in transition
wandern, ist gewandert to hike (1)
der Wanderschuh (-e) hiking shoe
der Wanderstab (¨e) hiking staff
der Wanderstock (¨e) hiking staff
der Wandervogel (¨) enthusiastic hiker
der Wanderweg (-e) hiking trail
wanken, ist gewankt to stagger, sway
wann when (1); seit wann since when; Wann hast du Geburtstag? When is your birthday? (3)
der Wannsee lake in Berlin
wäre: Wie wäre es mit ... ? How about . . . ? (13)
warm (wärmer, wärmst-) warm(ly) (7); heated
warnen to warn
die Warte (-n) vantage point, lookout
warten (auf + acc.) to wait (for) (6)
warum why (2)
was what (1); something (colloquial form of etwas); na, so was something like that; Was bedeutet ... ? What does . . . mean? (E); Was fehlt dir/Ihnen? What's the matter? (8); was für (ein) what kind of (a) (11); Was ist denn los? What's the matter? (2); Was sind Sie von Beruf? What do you do for a living? (1)
das Waschbecken (-) sink
die Wäsche laundry
(sich) waschen (wäscht), wusch, gewaschen to wash (oneself) (8)
der Wäschetrockner (-) clothes dryer (12)
die Waschküche (-n) laundry room
die Waschmaschine (-n) washing machine (12)
das Wasser water (5)
der Wassermann Aquarius (sign of the Zodiac)

das Watt (-) watt
die Wattstunde (-n) watts per hour
das WC (-s) toilet; bathroom (9)
das Web (World Wide) Web
die Webseite (-n) webpage
die Website (-s) website (11)
der Wechsel (-) change, alternation
das Wechselgeld change (money)
wechseln to change, exchange; wechselnd bewölkt with variable cloudiness
die Wechselpräposition (-en) two-way preposition, preposition governing either accusative or dative case
wecken to wake
der Wecker (-) alarm clock (2)
weder ... noch neither . . . nor
weg away, off; weit weg von (+ dat.) far away from
der Weg (-e) path, trail, way; road (9); nach dem Weg fragen to ask for directions (9)
wegen (+ gen.) because of, on account of (9)
weggehen (geht weg), ging weg, ist weggegangen to leave, go away
der Wegwerfartikel (-) disposable item
die Wegwerfflasche (-n) nonrecyclable bottle (14)
weh: oh weh alas
wehen to blow
sich wehren (gegen) to defend oneself (against)
die Wehrmacht armed forces (especially the German army during World War II)
wehtun (+ dat.) (tut weh), tat weh, wehgetan to hurt (8); Das tut mir weh. That hurts. (8)
weiblich feminine, female
weich soft
das Weihnachten Christmas (3)
der Weihnachtsbaum (¨e) Christmas tree (3)
der Weihnachtstag (-e): der erste Weihnachtstag Christmas Day; der zweite Weihnachtstag the day after Christmas, Boxing Day
weil (subord. conj.) because (8)
der Wein (-e) wine (6)
weinen to cry
weinrot wine-red
die Weintraube (-n) (wine) grape
die Weise (-n) manner, way
weiß white (5)
die (Berliner) Weiße: eine Weiße mit Schuss light, fizzy beer served with raspberry syrup
das Weißglas colorless glass
die Weißwurst (¨e) white sausage (made from veal) (6)
weit far (9); weit (weg) von (+ dat.) far (away) from
weiter further, farther
weiterentwickeln (entwickelt weiter) to continue to develop
weiterfahren (fährt weiter), fuhr weiter, ist weitergefahren to ride on, continue to ride
weitergehen (geht weiter), ging weiter, ist weitergegangen to go on, continue to go

weiterleben (lebt weiter) to go on living
weitermachen (macht weiter) to carry on, continue
weiterreisen (reiste weiter), ist weitergereist to continue to travel
weiterreiten, ritt weiter, ist weitergeritten to ride on, continue to ride (on horseback)
weiterschicken (schickt weiter) to forward, send on
weiterspielen (spielt weiter) to play on, continue to play
das Weizenbier (-e) wheat beer
welcher, welche, welches which (2); Auf welchen Namen? Under what name? (9); Welches Datum ist heute/morgen? What is today's/tomorrow's date? (3)
die Welle (-n) wave
die Welt (-en) world, earth (14)
weltbekannt world-famous
weltberühmt world-famous
der Weltkrieg (-e) world war
das Weltkulturerbe world cultural heritage
die Weltmeisterschaft (-en) world championship
weltstädtisch cosmopolitan
weltweit worldwide
wem (to/for) whom (dat.) (5)
wen whom (acc.)
wenig little (8); zu wenig too little
wenige (pl.) few, a few (8)
wenn (subord. conj.) if; when (8); whenever
wenngleich (subord. conj.) even though, although
wer who (1)
das Werbeplakat (-e) advertising poster
der Werbespot (-s) commercial
die Werbung (-en) advertisement, commercial
werden (wird), wurde, geworden to become (3); (+ infinitive) future tense; (+ past participle) passive voice; Würden Sie bitte ... ? Would you please . . . ? (9)
werfen (wirft), warf, geworfen to throw
das Werk (-e) work, opus
werten to judge, assess, rate
wessen whose
West (without article) west
(das) Westberlin West Berlin
der Westberliner (-) / die Westberlinerin (-nen) person from West Berlin
die Weste (-n) vest
der Westen west; im Westen in the west
die Western-Musik country-western music
(das) Westfalen Westphalia (region of Germany)
westfälisch (adj.) Westphalian
die Westzone (-n) western zone (the occupation zone that later became the Federal Republic of Germany)
das Wetter weather
der Wetterbericht (-e) weather report (7)
der Wetterhahn (¨e) weathercock
die WG = Wohngemeinschaft (2)
wichtig important(ly) (3)
widerspiegeln (spiegelt wider) to reflect

wie how (1); as; **so … wie** as … as (7); **Um wie viel Uhr?** At what time? (4); **Wie bitte?** Pardon? What did you say? (E); **Wie findest du … ?** How do you like … ? What do you think of … ? (1); **Wie geht es Ihnen?** How are you (*form.*) (E); **Wie geht's (dir)?** How are you? (*inform.*) (E); **Wie heißen Sie? / Wie heißt du?** What's your name? (*form./inform.*) (E); **Wie heißt die Stadt?** What is the name of the town/city? (E); **Wie ist Ihr/dein Name?** What's your name? (*form./inform.*) (E); **Wie komme ich am besten dahin?** What's the best way to get there? (9); **Wie sagt man … auf Deutsch?** How do you say … in German? (E); **Wie spät ist es? / Wie viel Uhr ist es?** What time is it? (4); **wie viel** how much; **wie viele** how many; **Wie wäre es mit … ?** How about … ? (13)

wieder again (2); back; **schon wieder** yet again (*emphatic*)

der Wiederaufbau reconstruction

wiederholen to repeat; to review

die Wiederholung (-en) review; **zur Wiederholung** as a review

das Wiederhören: (auf) Wiederhören good-bye (*on the phone*) (9)

das Wiedersehen: (auf) Wiedersehen good-bye (E)

die Wiedervereinigung (-en) reunification

die Wiederverwertung recycling

wiegen, wog, gewogen to weigh

(das) Wien Vienna

Wiener (*adj.*) of/from Vienna; **das Wiener Schnitzel** breaded veal cutlet; **das Wiener Würstchen (-)** wiener, frankfurter

die Wiese (-n) meadow (7)

wieso why

das Wildgehege (-) game preserve

wildlebend wild, free

das Wildwasser white water

der Wildwestfilm (-e) Western (*movie*)

willkommen (*adj.*) welcome; **herzlich willkommen** welcome (E)

der Wind (-e) wind (7)

die Windenergie wind energy

windig windy (7)

das Windrad (¨er) wind power generator (14)

das Windsurfen / das Windsurfing windsurfing

der Winter (-) winter (7)

wir we (1)

wirken (auf + *acc.*) to have an effect (on)

wirklich real(ly) (1)

die Wirklichkeit (-en) reality

der Wirkstoff (-e) active agent

die Wirkung (-en) effect

die Wirtschaft (-en) economy (13)

wirtschaftlich economic(ally)

das Wirtschaftswunder (-) economic miracle

das Wirtshaus (¨er) pub (6)

wissen (weiß), wusste, gewusst to know (*something as a fact*) (3); **Das weiß ich nicht.** I don't know. (E)

die Wissenschaft (-en) science

der Wissenschaftler (-) / die Wissenschaftlerin (-nen) scientist, scholar

wissenswert worth knowing

Wittenberger (*adj.*) of/from Wittenberg

witzig amusing(ly)

wo where (1)

die Woche (-n) week (4); **einmal die Woche** once a week (7); **pro Woche** per week (4)

das Wochenende (-n) weekend (4); **am Wochenende** on the weekend

wochenlang for weeks

der Wochenplan (¨e) weekly schedule

der Wochentag (-e) day of the week

-wöchig lasting … weeks

wofür for what; why

wogegen against what

woher from where (1); **Woher kommen Sie?** (*form.*) / **Woher kommst du?** (*inform.*) Where are you from? (E)

wohin (to) where (5); **Wohin gehst du?** Where are you going?

wohl well; probably (11); **sich wohl fühlen** to feel well (8)

das Wohlbefinden well-being

das Wohneigentum residential property

wohnen to reside, live (1)

die Wohngemeinschaft (-en) (WG) shared housing (2)

das Wohnheim (-e) dormitory

der Wohnort (-e) place of residence (1)

die Wohnung (-en) apartment (2)

der Wohnwagen (-) camper, trailer

das Wohnzimmer (-) living room (2)

die Wolke (-n) cloud (7)

die Wolkendecke cloud cover

wolkenlos cloudless (7)

wolkig cloudy

wollen (will), wollte, gewollt to want to; to plan to (4)

womit with what

woran on what; about what

worauf on what; for what

Worpsweder (*adj.*) of/from Worpswede

das Wort (¨er) word; **Worte** (*pl.*) words (*in connected speech*)

das Wörterbuch (¨er) dictionary

das Wortratespiel (-e) word-guessing game

der Wortschatz vocabulary

worüber about what

worum about what; around what

wovon of what; **Wovon handelt es?** What's it about? (13)

wovor before what; in front of what; of what

wozu for what; why

das Wunder (-) wonder, miracle; **kein Wunder** no wonder

wunderbar wonderful(ly)

der Wunsch (¨e) wish

wünschen to wish (3)

der Wunschtraum (¨e) wishful dream

die Wurst (¨e) sausage (5)

das Würstchen (-) small sausage; hot dog

die Wurzel (-n) root

würzig tasty; spicy

der Wüstenstamm (¨e) desert tribe

X

das Xylophon (-e) xylophone

Y

der/das Yoga yoga

Z

die Zahl (-en) number; amount

zahlen to pay (5)

zählen to count; **zählen zu** (+ *dat.*) to be one of, belong to

das Zahlenlotto (-s) number lottery

zahlreich numerous

die Zahlung (-en) payment

der Zahn (¨e) tooth **sich** (*dat.*) **die Zähne putzen** to brush one's teeth (8)

der Zahnarzt (¨e) / die Zahnärztin (-nen) dentist (11)

die Zahnpasta (Zahnpasten) toothpaste (5)

die Zahnschmerzen (*pl.*) toothache

zart tender(ly) (5)

die Zauberflöte *Magic Flute*

(das) ZDF = Zweites Deutsches Fernsehen (*German television network*)

die Zehe (-n) toe (8)

zehn ten (E)

zehnte tenth (3)

das Zeichen (-) sign

zeichnen to draw, sketch (7)

der Zeichner (-) / die Zeichnerin (-nen) graphic artist (11)

die Zeichnung (-en) drawing (12)

zeigen to show (5)

die Zeile (-n) line (*of text*)

die Zeit (-en) time (2); **Zeit haben** to have time (2); **Zeit verbringen, verbrachte, verbracht** to spend time (7)

die Zeitansage (-n) time recording

zeitgenössisch contemporary

der Zeitpunkt (-e) moment, point in time

die Zeitschrift (-en) magazine; periodical (13)

die Zeitung (-en) newspaper (1)

der Zeitvertreib (-e) pastime

das Zelt (-e) tent (10)

der Zentimeter (-) centimeter

zentral central(ly); **zentral gelegen** centrally located (2)

das Zentrum (Zentren) center (of town) (9); **im Zentrum** in the center of town

zerbomben to destroy by bombing

zerschlagen (*adj.*) worn-out, tired out

zerstören to destroy

die Zerstörung (-en) destruction

zeugen to testify

das Zeugnis (-se) report card; transcript; recommendation (from a former employer)

ziehen, zog, gezogen to pull, drag; **ziehen, zog, ist gezogen** to move; to go on

das Ziel (-e) goal, target; destination

ziemlich somewhat, rather (6)

zieren to decorate

die Zigarette (-n) cigarette
der Zigeuner (-) / die Zigeunerin (-nen) gypsy;
das Zimmer (-) room (2)
die Zimmerbestellung (-en) room reservation
der Zimmerkollege (-n *masc.*) (-n) / die Zimmerkollegin (-nen) roommate
die Zimmerpflanze (-n) houseplant (2)
die Zimmervermittlung (-en) room rental agency
zirka approximately, about
der Zirkus (-se) circus
das Zitat (-e) quotation
zitieren to quote
der Zivi (-s) (*coll.*) *person who does Zivildienst*
der Zivildienst community service (*as an alternative to military conscription*)
der Zivilist (-en *masc.*) (-en) / die Zivilistin (-nen) civilian
der Zoo (-s) zoo
zu (+ *dat.*) to; at; for (5); (+ *infinitive*) to; (*adv.*) too; **ab und zu** now and then, occasionally (8); **bis zu** until; to, as far as (9); **Das ist mir zu blöd.** I think that's really stupid. (13); **ohne ... zu** without doing; **um ... zu** in order to; **zu Fuß gehen, ging, ist gegangen** to walk, go on foot (8); **zu Hause** at home (5); **zu zweit** in pairs; as a couple, as a twosome (10)
zubereiten (bereitet zu) to prepare
die Zucchini (*pl.*) zucchini
der Züchter (-) / die Züchterin (-nen) breeder, grower
der Zucker sugar (5)
zueinander to one another
zuerst first, at first (9)
zufrieden content, satisfied
der Zug (⸚e) train (10)
der Zugang (⸚e) access
zugehen auf (+ *acc.*) (geht zu), ging zu, ist zugegangen to approach
zugehören (+ *dat.*) (gehört zu) to belong to
der Zugriff (-e) grasp
die Zugspitze *name of the highest mountain in Germany*
das Zuhause home
zuhören (hört zu) to listen (4)
zukriegen (kriegt zu) (*coll.*) to get shut
die Zukunft future (11)

zukünftig in the future
zulassen (lässt zu), ließ zu, zugelassen to allow, permit
zuletzt last(ly), finally
zuliebe (+ *dat.*) for the sake of
zum = zu dem; zum Mitnehmen (food) to go; take-out (6)
zumachen (macht zu) to close
zunächst first, at first; for the time being
zünftig proper(ly)
zupacken (packt zu) to work hard, pitch in
zur = zu der
Zürcher (*adj.*) of/from Zurich
(das) Zürich Zurich
zurück back; hin und zurück round-trip (10)
zurückbringen (bringt zurück), brachte zurück, zurückgebracht to bring back
zurückfaxen (faxt zurück) to fax back
zurückgeben (gibt zurück), gab zurück, zurückgegeben to give back
zurückhaltend reserved, restrained
zurückkommen (kommt zurück), kam zurück, ist zurückgekommen to return, come back (4)
zurückliegen (liegt zurück), lag zurück, zurückgelegen to lie behind, be in the past
zurückreichen (reicht zurück) to reach back, extend back
zurückrufen (ruft zurück), rief zurück, zurückgerufen to call back
zurückzahlen (zahlt zurück) to pay back
zusammen together; das macht zusammen ... all together, that comes to ... (5)
die Zusammenarbeit teamwork; cooperative effort
zusammenarbeiten (arbeitet zusammen) to work together, collaborate
zusammenfassen (fasst zusammen) to summarize
die Zusammenfassung (-en) summary
sich zusammenfinden (findet zusammen), fand zusammen, zusammengefunden to get together
zusammenpassen (passt zusammen) to match, go together
zusammenschlagen über (+ *dat.*) (schlägt zusammen), schlug zusammen, ist zusammengeschlagen to engulf

zusammensetzen (setzt zusammen) to put together; zusammengesetztes Wort compound word
zusammenstellen (stellt zusammen) to put together
zusammenwohnen (wohnt zusammen) to live together, cohabitate
zusätzlich additional(ly)
zuschneien (schneit zu), ist zugeschneit to snow in
der Zuschuss (⸚e) contribution; grant
zustimmen (+ *dat.*) (stimmt zu) to agree with
die Zutat (-en) ingredient
zutreffen auf (+ *acc.*) (trifft zu), traf zu, zugetroffen to apply to
die Zuversicht confidence
zu viel too much
zuvor before
zuweilen now and again
die Zwangssterilisation (-en) forced sterilization
zwanzig twenty (E)
der Zwanziger (-) twenty-euro/mark/dollar bill
zwanzigste twentieth (3)
zwar admittedly; und zwar that is to say
der Zweck (-e) purpose
zwei two (E)
das Zweibettzimmer (-) double room, room with two beds
zweieinhalb two and a half
zweihundert two hundred (E)
zweimal twice (7)
zweit: zu zweit in pairs; as a couple, as a twosome (10)
zweitausend two thousand (E)
zweite second (3); zweiter Klasse fahren to travel second class (10)
zweithöchst- second highest
zweitlängst- second longest
die Zwiebel (-n) onion (6)
der Zwilling (-e) twin
zwischen (+ *acc./dat.*) between (6); zwischen zwei und drei Uhr between two and three o'clock (6)
das Zwischenspiel (-e) interlude
zwölf twelve (E)
zwölfjährig twelve-year-(old), twelve years old
zwölfte twelfth (3)
(das) Zypern Cyprus

English–German

This list contains all the words from the end-of-chapter vocabulary sections.

A

a ein, eine

ability die Fähigkeit (-en) (11)

able: to be able to können (kann), konnte, gekonnt (4)

about über (+ *acc.*); gegen (+ *time*) (6); ungefähr (9); **to be about** handeln von (+ *dat.*) (13); **How about . . . ?** Wie wäre es mit … ? (13); **What's it about?** Wovon handelt es? (13)

above über (+ *acc./dat.*) (6); (*adv.*) oben; (*directional*) nach oben (12)

abroad im Ausland (11); **at home and abroad** im Inland und Ausland (13)

absolutely na klar (E); unbedingt (12)

access: Internet access der Internetzugang (9)

accommodation die Unterkunft (¨e) (9)

account: on account of wegen (+ *gen.*) (9); **savings account** das Sparkonto (Sparkonten) (12)

to acquire something sich (*dat.*) etwas anschaffen (schafft an) (14)

across from gegenüber von (+ *dat.*) (9)

act of violence die Gewalttätigkeit (-en) (14)

active(ly) aktiv (10); **active in sports** sportlich aktiv (10)

activity die Tätigkeit (-en) (11)

actor/actress der Schauspieler (-) / die Schauspielerin (-nen) (11)

ad: help-wanted ad das Stellenangebot (-e) (11)

addiction: drug addiction die Drogensucht (14)

addition: in addition außerdem (14)

address die Adresse (-n) (E); **street address** die Hausnummer (-n) (E)

advantage der Vorteil (-e) (11)

advice der Rat (8)

advising die Beratung (11)

to affect betreffen (betrifft), betraf, betroffen (14)

afraid: to be afraid of Angst haben vor (+ *dat.*) (12)

after nach (+ *dat.*) (4, 5, 6); (*subord. conj.*) nachdem (10); **after Tuesday** nach Dienstag (6); **five after two** fünf nach zwei (4); **It's a quarter after two.** Es ist Viertel nach zwei. (4)

afternoon der Nachmittag (-e) (4); **afternoons, in the afternoon** nachmittags (4); **this afternoon** heute Nachmittag (4)

again wieder (2)

against gegen (+ *acc.*) (3); **I'm against it.** Ich bin dagegen. (14)

agency: travel agency das Reisebüro (-s) (10)

ago vor (+ *dat.*) (6); **two days ago** vor zwei Tagen (6)

to agree (with), be in agreement (with) einverstanden sein (mit + *dat.*) (10)

ahead: straight ahead geradeaus (9)

ailment die Krankheit (-en) (14)

air die Luft (¨e) (8)

airplane das Flugzeug (-e) (10)

alarm clock der Wecker (-) (2)

alcohol der Alkohol (8)

all alle (5); **All the best!** Alles Gute! (3); **all together, that comes to** das macht zusammen (5); **by all means** unbedingt (12)

to allow erlauben (9)

almost fast (8)

along: to come along mitkommen (kommt mit), kam mit, ist mitgekommen (4); **to take along** mitnehmen (nimmt mit), nahm mit, mitgenommen (4); **to walk along** entlanggehen (geht entlang), ging entlang, ist entlanggegangen (9)

already schon (2)

also auch (1)

altogether insgesamt (10)

aluminum can die Dose (-n) (14)

always immer (1)

am bin; **I am** Ich bin (E)

American der Amerikaner (-) / die Amerikanerin (-nen) (1)

among unter (+ *acc./dat.*) (6)

an ein, eine

and (*coord. conj.*) und (E)

animal das Tier (-e) (12)

annoyed: to be annoyed about sich ärgern über (+ *acc.*) (12)

to answer (*phone*) sich melden (13); **No one is answering.** Niemand meldet sich. (13)

answering machine der Anrufbeantworter (-) (13)

any: in any case auf jeden Fall (13); **not any** kein (2)

anything: Anything else? Sonst noch etwas? (10)

apartment die Wohnung (-en) (2)

to appear scheinen, schien, geschienen (13)

appetizer die Vorspeise (-n) (6)

apple der Apfel (¨) (5); **apple strudel** der Apfelstrudel (-) (6)

applesauce das Apfelmus (6)

appliance das Gerät (-e) (12); (*TV, telephone, camera, etc.*) der Apparat (-e) (9)

application die Bewerbung (-en) (11); **application form** das Bewerbungsformular (-e) (11)

to apply verwenden (14); **to apply (for)** sich bewerben (um + *acc.*) (bewirbt), bewarb, beworben (11)

appointment der Termin (-e) (8)

approximately ungefähr (9)

April (der) April (3)

are (*you sg. inform.*) bist; (*you pl. inform.*) seid; (*you sg./pl. form.; we; they*) sind; **Are you doing well?** Geht's gut? (E); **there are** es gibt (3)

area die Umgebung (-en) (12)

arena: sports arena die Sporthalle (-n) (7)

arm der Arm (-e) (8)

armchair der Sessel (-) (2)

around (*spatial*) um… herum (3); gegen (+ *time*) (3, 6); **around five o'clock** (so) gegen fünf Uhr (6); **to lie around** faulenzen (7)

arrival die Ankunft (¨e) (10)

to arrive ankommen (kommt an), kam an, ist angekommen (9)

article of clothing das Kleidungsstück (-e) (5)

artist der Künstler (-) / die Künstlerin (-nen) (11); **graphic artist** der Zeichner (-) / die Zeichnerin (-nen) (11)

as: as . . . as so … wie (7); **as a twosome/threesome/foursome** zu zweit/dritt/viert (10); **as far as** biz zum/zur (9); **as of** ab (+ *dat.*) (12); **as of June 1st** ab 1. Juni (ab erstem Juni) (12)

to ask fragen (2); **to ask for** bitten um (+ *acc.*), bat, gebeten (12); **to ask someone for directions** jemanden nach dem Weg fragen (9)

asleep: to fall asleep einschlafen (schläft ein), schlief ein, ist eingeschlafen (4)

to assert behaupten (13)

assignment die Arbeit (-en) (8)

association der Verein (-e) (7)

at (+ *time*) um (+ *acc.*) (3, 4); bei (+ *dat.*) (5); zu (+ *dat.*) (5); an (+ *acc./dat.*) (6); auf (+ *acc./dat.*) (6); **at first** zuerst (9); **at home** zu Hause (5); **at home and abroad** im Inland und Ausland (13); **at least** mindestens (8); **at midnight** um Mitternacht (3); **at night** nachts (4); **at noon** mittags (4); **at the corner** an der Ecke (9); **at the latest** spätestens (12); **at two** um zwei (4); **At what time?** Um wie viel Uhr? (4)

athletic sportlich (1); **athletic field** der Sportplatz (¨e) (7)

to **attempt** versuchen (8)

attention: to pay attention to achten auf (+ *acc.*) (8)

attic das Dachgeschoss (-e) (12)

attorney der Rechtsanwalt (¨e) / die Rechtsanwältin (-nen) (11)

August (der) August (3)

aunt die Tante (-n) (3)

Austria (das) Österreich (E)

autumn der Herbst (-e) (7)

available: Is this seat available? Ist hier noch frei? (6)

average: on average durchschnittlich (12)

to avoid vermeiden, vermied, vermieden (14)

away: far away from . . . weit weg von … (2)

B

back der Rücken (-) (8); **in back of** hinter (+ *acc./dat.*) (6); **to come back** zurückkommen (kommt zurück), kam zurück, ist zurückgekommen (4)

backpack der Rucksack (¨e) (5)

bacon der Speck (6)

bad(ly) schlecht (E); **What bad luck!** So ein Pech! (8)

bag: plastic bag die Plastiktüte (-n) (14)

baggage check die Gepäckaufbewahrung (10)

bakery die Bäckerei (-en) (5)

balcony der Balkon (-e) (2)

ball: soccer ball der Fußball (¨e) (7)

ballet das Ballett (-e) (4)

ballpoint pen der Kugelschreiber (-) (12)

banana die Banane (-n) (5)

bank die Bank (-en) (9)

bar die Kneipe (-n) (6); das Lokal (-e) (6)

(a) bargain preiswert (2)

basically im Grunde genommen (14)

bathing suit der Badeanzug (¨e) (5)

bathroom das Bad (¨er) (2); das Badezimmer (-) (2); das WC (-s) (9)

to be sein (ist), war, ist gewesen (1); (+ *past participle*) werden (wird), wurde, ist geworden (3)

to be able to können (kann), konnte, gekonnt (4)

to be about handeln von (+ *dat.*) (13)

to be afraid of Angst haben vor (+ *dat.*) (12)

to be annoyed about sich ärgern über (+ *acc.*) (12)

to be called heißen, hieß, geheißen (1)

to be correct Recht haben (hat Recht) (2)

to be glad about sich freuen über (+ *acc.*) (12)

to be hanging hängen, hing, gehangen (6)

to be hungry Hunger haben (hat Hunger) (2)

to be inside stecken (6)

to be interested in sich interessieren für (+ *acc.*) (11)

to be lazy faulenzen (7)

to be located liegen, lag, gelegen (6); stehen, stand, gestanden (6)

to be named heißen, hieß, geheißen (1)

to be of the opinion meinen (14)

to be permitted to dürfen (darf), durfte, gedurft (4)

to be pleasing to gefallen (+ *dat.*) (gefällt), gefiel, gefallen (5)

to be successful Erfolg haben (11)

to be supposed to sollen (soll), sollte, gesollt (4)

to be thirsty Durst haben (hat Durst) (2)

beach der Strand (¨e) (10)

bean die Bohne (-n) (6)

beautiful(ly) schön (2)

because (*coord. conj.*) denn (7); (*subord. conj.*) weil (8); **because of** wegen (+ *gen.*) (9); **because of that** deswegen (12)

to become werden (wird), wurde, ist geworden (3)

bed das Bett (-en) (2); **bed and breakfast** die Pension (-en) (9); **room with one bed** das Einzelzimmer (-) (9); **room with two beds** das Doppelzimmer (-) (9)

bedroom das Schlafzimmer (-) (2)

beef das Rindfleisch (5)

beer das Bier (-e) (5); **beer garden** der Biergarten (¨) (6); **Pilsner beer** das Pilsener (-) (6)

before vor (+ *acc./dat.*) (6); (*subord. conj.*) bevor (10); **before noon** der Vormittag (-e) (4); (*adv.*) vormittags (4)

to begin anfangen (fängt an), fing an, angefangen (4); beginnen, begann, begonnen (10)

behind hinter (+ *acc./dat.*) (6)

beige beige (5)

Belgium (das) Belgien (E)

to believe glauben (5)

bell pepper die Paprika (6)

belly der Bauch (¨e) (8)

to belong to (*a person*) gehören (+ *dat.*) (5)

below unter (+ *acc./dat.*) (6); (*adv.*) unten; (*directional*) nach unten (12)

belt der Gürtel (-) (5)

beneath unter (+ *acc./dat.*) (6)

beside neben (+ *acc./dat.*) (6)

besides außerdem (14)

best best-; **All the best!** Alles Gute! (3); **best wishes** viele Grüße (12); **What's the best way to get there?** Wie komme ich am besten dahin? (9)

better besser

between zwischen (+ *acc./dat.*) (6); **between two and three o'clock** zwischen zwei und drei Uhr (6)

beverage: beverage can die Getränkedose (-n) (14); **beverage store** der Getränkeladen (¨) (5)

bicycle das Fahrrad (¨er) (10); **to bicycle, ride a bicycle** Fahrrad/Rad fahren (fährt), fuhr, ist gefahren (1, 7)

big groß (2)

bill die Rechnung (-en) (6)

birth: date of birth der Geburtstag (-e) (1)

birthday der Geburtstag (-e) (1); **Happy birthday!** Herzlichen Glückwunsch zum Geburtstag! (3); **When is your birthday?** Wann hast du Geburtstag? (3)

birthplace der Geburtsort (-e) (1)

black schwarz (5)

to blog bloggen (7)

blouse die Bluse (-n) (5)

blue blau (5)

to board (*a vehicle*) einsteigen (steigt ein), stieg ein, ist eingestiegen (10)

body: part of the body der Körperteil (-e) (8)

bodybuilding: to do bodybuilding Bodybuilding machen (7)

book das Buch (¨er) (1)

to book (*a trip*) buchen (10)

bookcase, bookshelf das Bücherregal (-e) (2)

boot der Stiefel (-) (5)

boring langweilig (1)

born: I was born ich bin geboren (1)

to borrow leihen, lieh, geliehen (5)

boss der Chef (-s) / die Chefin (-nen) (11)

bottle die Flasche (-n) (14); **nonrecyclable bottle** die Wegwerfflasche (-n) (14)

boy der Junge (-n *masc.*) (-n) (2)

bread das Brot (-e) (5)

breakfast das Frühstück (-e) (5); **bed and breakfast** die Pension (-en) (9); **breakfast nook** die Frühstücksnische (-n) (12); **breakfast room** der Frühstücksraum (¨e) (9); **to eat breakfast** frühstücken (4)

breast die Brust (¨e) (8)

bright(ly) hell (2); (*weather*) heiter (7); (*intelligent*) gescheit (13)

to bring bringen, brachte, gebracht (7); **to bring up** (*raise children*) erziehen, erzog, erzogen (14)

broccoli der Brokkoli (5)

brochure: travel brochure der Reiseprospekt (-e) (10)

broke (*coll.*) pleite (12)

broken kaputt (9)

brother der Bruder (¨) (3)

brother-in-law der Schwager (¨) (3)

brown braun (5)

to brush one's teeth sich die Zähne putzen (8)

to build bauen (12)

building: modern building der Neubau (-ten) (12)

bus der Bus (-se) (10); **bus stop** die Haltestelle (-n) (9)

business: day that a business is closed der Ruhetag (-e) (6)

businessman der Geschäftsmann (*pl.* Geschäftsleute) (11)

businesswoman die Geschäftsfrau (-en) (11)

but (*coord. conj.*) aber (1); **but rather** (*coord. conj.*) sondern (7)

butcher shop die Metzgerei (-en) (5)

butter die Butter (5)

to buy kaufen (2)

by von (+ *dat.*) (5); **by all means** unbedingt (12); **by means of** mit (+ *dat.*) (5); **by the way** übrigens (9); **to come by** vorbeikommen (kommt vorbei), kam vorbei, ist vorbeigekommen (4)

bye tschüss (*inform.*) (E)

C

cabin die Hütte (-n) (10)

cable TV connection der Kabelanschluss (¨e) (13)

café das Café (-s) (6)

cafeteria: student cafeteria die Mensa (-s) (1)

cake der Kuchen (-) (5)

calendar der Kalender (-) (3)

to call (up) anrufen, rief an, angerufen (4)

called: to be called heißen, hieß, geheißen (1)

camcorder der Camcorder (-) (13)

camera die Kamera (-s) (10); **digital camera** die Digitalkamera (-s) (13)

can (*tin or aluminum*) die Dose (-n) (14); **beverage can** die Getränkedose (-n) (14)

can, to be able to können (kann), konnte, gekonnt (4)

cap die Mütze (-n) (5)

car das Auto (-s) (2); der Wagen (-) (7)

card die Karte (-n) (7); **credit card** die Kreditkarte (-n) (9); **ID card** der Personalausweis (-e) (10); **playing card** die Spielkarte (-n) (7); **report card** das Zeugnis (-se) (11); **seat reservation card** die Platzkarte (-n) (10); **to play cards** Karten spielen (1)

care: I don't care. Das ist mir egal. (5); **Take care.** Mach's gut. (*inform.*) (E)

to care for mögen (mag), mochte, gemocht (4)

career training die Ausbildung (11)

carpet der Teppich (-e) (2)

carpeting (wall-to-wall) der Teppichboden (:) (12)

carrot die Karotte (-n) (5)

to carry tragen (trägt), trug, getragen (5)

carry-on luggage das Handgepäck (10)

case: in any case auf jeden Fall (13)

cash das Bargeld (10); **cash register** die Kasse (-n) (5)

cashier die Kasse (-n) (5)

casserole der Auflauf (:e) (6)

castle das Schloss (:er) (9)

cat die Katze (-n) (12)

to catch a cold sich erkälten (8)

cauliflower der Blumenkohl (5)

CD player der CD-Spieler (-) (2)

to celebrate feiern (3)

cell phone das Handy (-s) (2)

center die Mitte (9); **center (of town)** das Zentrum (Zentren) (9); **in the center (of the city)** in der Mitte (der Stadt) (9); **recycling center** die Sammelstelle (-n) (14)

centrally located zentral gelegen (2)

cereal das Müsli (-) (5)

chair der Stuhl (:e) (2)

to challenge herausfordern (fordert heraus) (11)

to change (*trains*) umsteigen (steigt um), stieg um, ist umgestiegen (10)

channel (*TV*) das Programm (-e) (13)

cheap(ly) billig (2)

check der Scheck (-s); **baggage check** die Gepäckaufbewahrung (10); **traveler's check** der Reisescheck (-s) (10)

to check in (*hotel*) sich anmelden (meldet an) (9)

check-out die Kasse (-n) (5)

cheerful lustig (1)

cheese der Käse (5)

chess: to play chess Schach spielen (7)

chest die Brust (:e) (8)

chicken das Hähnchen (-) (5)

chin das Kinn (-e) (8)

to choose wählen (14); **to choose something** sich (*dat.*) etwas aussuchen (sucht aus) (13)

Christmas das Weihnachten (3); **Christmas Eve** der Heilige Abend (3); **Christmas tree** der Weihnachtsbaum (:e) (3)

church die Kirche (-n) (9)

cinema das Kino (-s) (4)

citizen der Bürger (-) / die Bürgerin (-nen) (14)

city die Stadt (:e) (E); **city hall** das Rathaus (:er) (9); **in the center of the city** in der Mitte der Stadt (9)

to claim behaupten (13)

class: to travel first/second class erster/zweiter Klasse fahren (fährt), fuhr, ist gefahren (10)

clean sauber (14)

to clean up aufräumen (räumt auf) (4)

cleaner: vacuum cleaner der Staubsauger (-) (12)

clear: Everything is clear. Alles klar. (E)

clock die Uhr (-en) (2); **alarm clock** der Wecker (-) (2); **It's one o'clock** Es ist eins. / Es ist ein Uhr. (4)

closed geschlossen (6); **day that a business is closed** der Ruhetag (-e) (6)

closet die Garderobe (-n) (12); **clothes closet** der Kleiderschrank (:e) (2)

clothes dryer der Wäschetrockner (-) (12)

clothing: article of clothing das Kleidungsstück (-e) (5)

cloud die Wolke (-n) (7)

cloudless wolkenlos (7)

cloudy bewölkt (7)

club der Verein (-e) (7)

clubbing: to go clubbing in die Disko gehen, ging, ist gegangen (4)

coat der Mantel (:) (5); **sport coat** das Sakko (-s) (5)

code: postal code die Postleitzahl (-en) (E)

coffee der Kaffee; **coffee table** der Couchtisch (-e) (2); **a cup of coffee** eine Tasse Kaffee (4)

cold (*adj.*) kalt (kälter, kältest-) (7)

cold die Erkältung (-en) (8); **head cold** der Schnupfen (8); **to catch a cold** sich erkälten (8)

cold cuts der Aufschnitt (5)

colleague der Mitarbeiter (-) / die Mitarbeiterin (-nen) (11)

to collect sammeln (7)

color die Farbe (-n) (5)

to comb (one's hair) sich kämmen (8)

to come kommen, kam, ist gekommen (1); **to come along** mitkommen (kommt mit), kam mit, ist mitgekommen (4); **to come back** zurückkommen (kommt zurück), kam zurück, ist zurückgekommen (4); **to come by** vorbeikommen (kommt vorbei), kam vorbei, ist vorbeigekommen (4); **that comes to** das macht zusammen (5)

comedy die Komödie (-n) (4)

comfortable, comfortably bequem (2)

committed engagiert (11)

company die Firma (Firmen) (11); das Unternehmen (-) (11)

to compare vergleichen, verglich, verglichen (12)

to complain about sich beschweren über (+ *acc.*) (9)

complete(ly) ganz (12)

completion (*of training or school*) der Abschluss (:e) (11)

complicated kompliziert (1)

computer der Computer (-) (2); **computer connection** der Computeranschluss (:e) (2); **computer diskette** die Computerdiskette (-n) (12); **computer scientist** der Informatiker (-) / die Informatikerin (-nen) (11); **notebook computer** das Notebook (-s) (13); **to play computer games** Computerspiele spielen (1)

concert das Konzert (-e) (4); **to go to a concert** ins Konzert gehen (4)

congestion: nasal congestion der Schnupfen (8)

to congratulate gratulieren (+ *dat.*) (3)

connection der Anschluss (10); **cable TV connection** der Kabelanschluss (:e) (13); **computer connection** der Computeranschluss (:e) (2)

conservative konservativ (1)

to consider halten (für + *acc.*) (hält), hielt, gehalten (14)

to consume verbrauchen (14)

contact der Kontakt (-e) (11)

convenient(ly) günstig (9); **to be conveniently located** günstig liegen, lag, gelegen (9)

to converse sich unterhalten (unterhält), unterhielt, unterhalten (13)

to cook kochen (1)

cookie der Keks (-e) (5)

cool kühl (7)

corn der Mais (6)

corner die Ecke (-n) (9); **at the corner** an der Ecke (9)

correct: to be correct Recht haben (hat Recht) (2)

corruption die Korruption (14)

cost der Preis (-e) (9); **extra costs** die Nebenkosten (*pl.*) (12)

to cost kosten (2)

cough, coughing der Husten (8)

counselor: employment counselor der Berufsberater (-) / die Berufsberaterin (-nen) (11)

country das Land (:er); **foreign countries** das Ausland (*sg. only*) (11); **home country** das Inland (*sg. only*) (13)

course: of course natürlich (1)

court: tennis court der Tennisplatz (:e) (7)

cousin (*female*) die Kusine (-n) (3); (*male*) der Vetter (-n) (3)

co-worker der Mitarbeiter (-) / die Mitarbeiterin (-nen) (11)

cozy, cozily gemütlich (4)

crazy verrückt (8)

cream die Sahne (6); **dish of ice cream** der Eisbecher (-) (6); **ice cream** das Eis (5); **shaving cream** die Rasiercreme (-s) (5); **whipped cream** die Sahne (6)

to create schaffen, schuf, geschaffen (14)

credit card die Kreditkarte (-n) (9)

crime film or book der Krimi (-s) (4)

crossword: to do crossword puzzles Kreuzworträtsel machen (1)

crowded voll (6)

cucumber die Gurke (-n) (5)

cuisine die Küche (6)

cup die Tasse (-n) (4); **a cup of coffee** eine Tasse Kaffee (4)

current aktuell (13); **current events** Aktuelles (13)

customer der Kunde (-n *masc.*) (-n) / die Kundin (-nen) (2)

cutlet das Schnitzel (-) (5)

Czech Republic Tschechien (E)

D

daily täglich (6)

to dance tanzen (1); **He dances well.** Er tanzt gut. (1)

dance club die Disko (4)

danger die Gefahr (-en) (14)

dangerous(ly) gefährlich (10)

dark dunkel (2)

date das Datum (Daten); **date of birth** der Geburtstag (-e) (1); **What is today's/tomorrow's date?** Welches Datum ist heute/morgen? (3)

daughter die Tochter (-) (3)

day der Tag (-e) (2); **day of the week** der Wochentag (-e) (3); **day that a business is closed** der Ruhetag (-e) (6); **every day** jeden Tag (7); **good day** (guten) Tag (E); **in two days** in zwei Tagen (6); **time of day** die Tageszeit (-en) (4); **two days ago** vor zwei Tagen (6)

to deal with (*be about*) handeln von (+ *dat.*) (13); (*treat, take care of*) behandeln (14)

December (der) Dezember (3)

decent gescheit (13); **nothing decent** nichts Gescheites (13)

to decide sich entschließen, entschloss, entschlossen (13)

to decrease vermindern (14)

definitely bestimmt (1)

degree (*school*) der Abschluss (-e) (11); (*temperature*) der Grad (-e) (7); **35 degrees** 35 Grad (7)

demonstration die Demonstration (-en) (14)

Denmark (das) Dänemark (E)

dentist der Zahnarzt (-e) / die Zahnärztin (-nen) (11)

to depart abreisen (reist ab), ist abgereist (9); abfahren (fährt ab), fuhr ab, ist abgefahren (10)

department store das Kaufhaus (-er) (2)

departure die Abfahrt (-en) (10)

depressed deprimiert (8); **You sound so depressed.** Du klingst so deprimiert. (8)

to deserve verdienen (11)

to design entwerfen (entwirft), entwarf, entworfen (11)

desk der Schreibtisch (-e) (2); **reception desk** die Rezeption (9)

dessert die Nachspeise (-n) (6); der Nachtisch (-e) (6)

detective film or book der Krimi (-s) (4)

to develop entwickeln (14)

development die Entwicklung (-en) (11)

device das Gerät (-e) (12)

digital camera die Digitalkamera (-s) (13)

diligent fleißig (1)

dining room das Esszimmer (-) (2)

directions: to ask someone for directions jemanden nach dem Weg fragen (9)

director der Leiter (-) / die Leiterin (-nen) (11)

dirty schmutzig (12)

disco die Disko (-s) (4); **to go to a disco** in die Disko gehen (4)

to discuss diskutieren (1)

disease die Krankheit (-en) (14)

dish (*of prepared food*) das Gericht (-e) (6); die Speise (-n) (6); **dish of ice cream** der Eisbecher (-) (6); **main dish** das Hauptgericht (-e) (6); **side dish** die Beilage (-n) (6)

dishwasher die Spülmaschine (-n) (12)

diskette: computer diskette die Computerdiskette (-n) (12)

to disseminate verbreiten (14)

to dive tauchen (7)

diverse abwechslungsreich (11)

to do machen (1); tun (tut), tat, getan (8); **to do an internship** ein Praktikum machen (1); **to do body-building** Bodybuilding machen (7); **to do crossword puzzles** Kreuzworträtsel machen (1); **to do gymnastics** turnen (7); **to do research** forschen (13); **to do weight training** Bodybuilding machen (7); **to do without** verzichten auf (+ *acc.*) (12); **Are you doing well?** Geht's gut? (E); **What do you do for a living?** Was sind Sie von Beruf? (1)

doctor der Arzt (-e) / die Ärztin (-nen) (8)

document das Dokument (-e) (13)

documentary (film) der Dokumentarfilm (-e) (13)

documentation die Unterlagen (*pl.*) (11)

dog der Hund (-e) (3); **sick as a dog** (*coll.*) hundsmiserabel (8)

door die Tür (-en) (2)

dormitory das Studentenwohnheim (-e) (2)

double room das Doppelzimmer (-) (9)

doubt: no doubt bestimmt (1)

down: to lie down sich (hin)legen (legt hin) (8); **to sit down** sich (hin)setzen (setzt hin) (8)

downstairs unten; (*directional*) nach unten (12)

downtown die Innenstadt (-e) (9)

draft vom Fass (6)

drama (*stage*) das Theaterstück (-e) (4)

to draw zeichnen (7)

drawing die Zeichnung (-en) (12)

dress das Kleid (-er) (5)

dressed: to get dressed sich anziehen (zieht an), zog an, angezogen (8)

dresser die Kommode (-n) (2)

drink das Getränk (-e) (5)

to drink trinken, trank, getrunken (2)

to drive fahren (fährt), fuhr, ist gefahren (1)

to drop off abgeben (gibt ab), gab ab, abgegeben (8)

drug die Droge (-n) (14); **drug addiction** die Drogensucht (14)

drugstore (*toiletries and sundries*) die Drogerie (-n) (5)

dryer: clothes dryer der Wäschetrockner (-) (12); **hair dryer** der Föhn (-e) (9)

during während (+ *gen.*) (9)

DVD player der DVD-Spieler (-) (2)

E

each jeder, jede, jedes (5)

ear das Ohr (-en) (8)

early früh (4); **earlier** früher (7)

to earn verdienen (11)

earth die Welt (14)

Easter (das) Ostern (3)

to eat essen (isst), aß, gegessen (1); **to eat breakfast** frühstücken (4)

eating das Essen (1)

eccentric exzentrisch (1)

economy die Wirtschaft (13)

egg das Ei (-er) (5); **fried egg** das Spiegelei (-er) (6)

eight acht (E)

eighteen achtzehn (E)

eighth achte (3)

eighty achtzig (E)

either . . . or entweder … oder (8)

elbow der Ell(en)bogen (-) (8)

to elect wählen (14)

electricity der Strom (12)

elevator der Aufzug (-e) (9)

eleven elf (E)

eleventh elfte (3)

else: Anything else? Sonst noch etwas? (10)

e-mail die E-Mail (-s) (13)

to employ beschäftigen (11)

employee der Mitarbeiter (-) / die Mitarbeiterin (-nen) (11)

employer der Arbeitgeber (-) / die Arbeitgeberin (-nen) (11)

employment: employment counselor der Berufsberater (-) / die Berufsberaterin (-nen) (11); **employment office** das Arbeitsamt (-er) (11)

enterprise das Unternehmen (-) (11)

to entertain oneself sich unterhalten (unterhält), unterhielt, unterhalten (13)

entertaining unterhaltsam (13)

entertainment die Unterhaltung (13); **for entertainment** zur Unterhaltung (13)

entire(ly) ganz (12)

entrance der Eingang (-e) (12)

enivironment die Umwelt (14)

environmental: environmental pollution die Umweltverschmutzung (14); **environmental protection** der Umweltschutz (14); **environmentally friendly** umweltfreundlich (14)

to equip einrichten (richtet ein) (12)

especially besonders (8)

euro das Euro (-[s]) (2)

even sogar (8)

evening der Abend (-e) (4); **evening meal** das Abendessen (-) (5); **good evening** guten Abend (E); **in the evening, evenings** abends (4); **this evening** heute Abend (1); **tomorrow evening** morgen Abend (4)

event: current events Aktuelles (13)

every alle (5); jeder, jede, jedes (5); **every day** jeden Tag (7)

everything alles (10); **Everything is clear.** Alles klar. (E)

exact(ly) genau (2); **exactly** gerade (2); **exactly as . . . as** genauso … wie (7)

exaggerated übertrieben (14)

examination (*at the end of Gymnasium*) das Abitur (-e) (11)

to examine untersuchen, untersucht (11)

excellent ausgezeichnet (E)

exciting spannend (4)

to excuse entschuldigen (6); **Excuse me!** Entschuldigen Sie! (6), Entschuldigung! (9)

expense die Ausgabe (-n) (12)

expensive(ly) teuer (2)

experience die Erfahrung (-en) (11)

to experience erleben (10)

extra costs die Nebenkosten (*pl.*) (12)

extremism: right-wing extremism der Rechtsextremismus (14)

eye das Auge (-n) (8)

eyeglasses die Brille (-n) (5)

F

face das Gesicht (-er) (8)

fair (*weather*) heiter (7)

fall (*autumn*) der Herbst (-e) (7)

to fall fallen (fällt), fiel, ist gefallen (7); **to fall asleep** einschlafen (schläft ein), schlief ein, ist eingeschlafen (4)

familiar vertraut (14)

family die Familie (-n) (3); **family gathering** das Familienfest (-e) (3); **family name** der Nachname (*gen.* -ns, *acc./dat.* -n) (-n) (1); **family tree** der Stammbaum (¨e) (3); **small family-run hotel** die Pension (-en) (9)

famine der Hunger (14)

fantastic fantastisch (1)

far weit (9); **as far as** bis zum/zur (9); **far (away) from . . .** weit (weg) von … (2)

farmhouse das Bauernhaus (¨er) (12)

fashionable, fashionably modisch (5)

fast schnell (10)

fast-food stand der Imbiss (-e) (6)

father der Vater (¨) (3)

favor: I'm in favor of it. Ich bin dafür. (14)

favorable günstig (9)

fax machine das Faxgerät (-e) (13)

fear die Angst (¨e) (12)

feature film der Spielfilm (-e) (13)

February (der) Februar (3)

to feel (well) sich (wohl) fühlen (8); **to feel like** (*doing something*) Lust haben (hat Lust) (2)

fees (*tuition*) die Studiengebühren (*pl.*) (12)

female cousin die Kusine (-n) (3)

fever das Fieber (8)

few wenig (8)

field: athletic field der Sportplatz (¨e) (7)

fifteen fünfzehn (E)

fifth fünfte (3)

fifty fünfzig (E)

to fill out ausfüllen (füllt aus) (9)

film der Film (-e) (4); **feature film** der Spielfilm (-e) (13)

to find finden, fand, gefunden (1); **to find something** sich (*dat.*) etwas aussuchen (sucht aus) (13)

fine sehr gut (E); **fine, thanks** danke, gut (E)

finger der Finger (-) (8)

firm die Firma (Firmen) (11)

first erste (3); (*at first*) zuerst (9); **first name** der Vorname (*gen.* -ns, *acc./dat.* -n) (-n) (1); **May first** der erste Mai (3); **on May first** am ersten Mai (3)

to fish angeln (7)

fit (*adj.*) fit (8); **to keep fit** sich fit halten (hält), hielt, gehalten (8)

to fit passen (+ *dat.*) (5)

fitness die Fitness (8)

five fünf (E)

to flash blitzen (7)

floor der Stock (*pl.* Stockwerke) (9); die Etage (-n) (12); **ground floor** das Erdgeschoss (-e) (9); **top floor** das Dachgeschoss (-e) (12)

flu die Grippe (8)

to fly fliegen, flog, ist geflogen (7)

fog der Nebel (7)

foggy neblig (7)

food das Essen (-) (1); die Küche (6); die Ernährung (12); **food to go** zum Mitnehmen (6); **natural foods store** der Bioladen (¨) (5); **organic foods** die Biolebensmittel (*pl.*) (8)

foot der Fuß (¨e) (8); **to go on foot** zu Fuß gehen, ging, ist gegangen (8)

for für (+ *acc.*) (3); (+ *time*) seit (+ *dat.*) (5, 6); zu (+ *dat.*) (5); (*coord. conj.*) denn (7); **for two years** seit zwei Jahren (6)

to forbid verbieten, verbot, verboten (14)

foreign countries das Ausland (*sg. only*) (11)

foreigner der Ausländer (-) / die Ausländerin (-nen) (14); **hatred directed toward foreigners** die Ausländerfeindlichkeit (14)

forest der Wald (¨er) (7)

to forget vergessen (vergisst), vergaß, vergessen (10)

fork die Gabel (-n) (6)

form das Formular (-e); **application form** das Bewerbungsformular (-e) (11); **registration form** das Anmeldeformular (-e) (9)

forward: to look forward to sich freuen auf (+ *acc.*) (12)

four vier (E)

foursome: as a foursome zu viert (10)

fourteen vierzehn (E)

fourth vierte (3)

France (das) Frankreich (E)

free(ly) frei (2)

free time die Freizeit (7)

French fries die Pommes frites (*pl.*) (6)

fresh(ly) frisch (5)

Friday (der) Freitag (3); **Fridays, on Friday(s)** freitags (4)

fried: fried egg das Spiegelei (-er) (6); **fried potatoes** die Bratkartoffeln (*pl.*) (6)

friend der Freund (-e) / die Freundin (-nen) (1)

friendly freundlich (1); **environmentally friendly** umweltfreundlich (14)

fries: French fries die Pommes frites (*pl.*) (6)

from aus (+ *dat.*) (5); von (+ *dat.*) (5, 6); ab (+ *dat.*) (12); **across from** gegenüber von (+ *dat.*) (9); **far (away) from . . .** weit (weg) von … (2); **from two to three o'clock** von zwei bis drei Uhr (6); **from where** woher (1); **I'm from . . .** Ich komme aus … (E); **Where are you from?** Woher kommen Sie? (*form.*) / Woher kommst du? (*inform.*) (E)

front: front hall die Diele (-n) (12); **in front of** vor (+ *acc./dat.*) (6)

frozen gefroren (5)

fruit das Obst (5); **fruit and vegetable stand** der Obst- und Gemüsestand (¨e) (5)

full voll (6)

full-service restaurant die Gaststätte (-n) (6)

fun der Spaß (¨e) (1); **have fun!** viel Spaß! (1); **That's fun.** Das macht Spaß. (1)

to function funktionieren (9)

fun-loving lustig (1)

to furnish einrichten (richtet ein) (12)

furnished möbliert (2)

furniture die Möbel (*pl.*) (2)

future die Zukunft (11)

G

game das Spiel (-e); **to play computer games** Computerspiele spielen (1)

garage die Garage (-n) (2)

garbage der Müll (12); der Abfall (¨e) (14)

garden der Garten (¨) (2); **beer garden** der Biergarten (¨) (6)

gasoline das Benzin (12)

gathering: family gathering das Familienfest (-e) (3)

generator: wind power generator das Windrad (¨er) (14)

gentleman der Herr (-n *masc.*) (-en) (E)

German deutsch; (*language*) (das) Deutsch (1); **How do you say . . . in German?** Wie sagt man … auf Deutsch? (E)

Germany (das) Deutschland (E)

to get (*receive*) bekommen, bekam, bekommen (6); **What's the best way to get there?** Wie komme ich am besten dahin? (9)

to get dressed sich anziehen (zieht an), zog an, angezogen (8)

to get into (*a vehicle*) einsteigen (steigt ein), stieg ein, ist eingestiegen (10)

to get involved sich engagieren (14)

to get undressed sich ausziehen (zieht aus). zog aus. ausgezogen (8)

to get up aufstehen (steht auf). stand auf. ist aufgestanden (4)

to get well sich erholen (8); **Get well soon!** Gute Besserung! (8)

gift das Geschenk (-e) (3)

to give geben (gibt). gab. gegeben (3); (*as a gift*) schenken (5); (*drop off. turn in*) abgeben (gibt ab). gab ab. abgegeben (8)

given name der Vorname (*gen. -ns. acc./dat. -n*) (1)

glad: to be glad about sich freuen über (+ *acc.*) (12)

gladly gern (2)

glasses (eyeglasses) die Brille (-n) (5)

global global (14)

glove der Handschuh (-e) (10)

to go gehen. ging. ist gegangen (1); **(food) to go** zum Mitnehmen (6); **to go clubbing** in die Disko gehen (4); **to go for a walk** spazieren gehen (geht spazieren) (4); **to go on a trip** verreisen. ist verreist (10); **to go on foot** zu Fuß gehen (8); **to go on vacation** Urlaub machen (8); **to go out** ausgehen (geht aus). ging aus. ist ausgegangen (4); **to go shopping** einkaufen gehen (geht einkaufen) (4); **to go to a concert** ins Konzert gehen (4); **to go to a disco** in die Disko gehen (4); **to go to the movies** ins Kino gehen (4); **to go to the opera** in die Oper gehen (4); **to go to the theater** ins Theater gehen (4)

good sehr gut (E); gut (1); **good day** (guten) Tag (E); **good evening** guten Abend (E); **good luck!** viel Glück! (1); **good morning** (guten) Morgen (E); **good night** gute Nacht (E); **to look good** (*on a person*) stehen (+ *dat.*). stand. gestanden (5); **to taste good** schmecken (+ *dat.*) (5)

good-bye (auf) Wiedersehen (E); (*on telephone*) auf Wiederhören! (9)

government die Regierung (-en) (14)

granddaughter die Enkelin (-nen) (3)

grandfather der Großvater (-) (3)

grandma die Oma (-s) (3)

grandmother die Großmutter (-) (3)

grandpa der Opa (-s) (3)

grandparents die Großeltern (*pl.*) (3)

grandson der Enkel (-) (3)

granola das Müsli (-) (5)

grape die Traube (-n) (5)

graphic artist der Zeichner (-) / die Zeichnerin (-nen) (11)

gray grau (5)

great prima (E); **great!** ganz toll! (1)

green grün (5)

greeting der Gruß (-e) (12)

grill der Grill (-s) (6)

ground floor das Erdgeschoss (-e) (9)

guest room das Gästezimmer (-) (12)

guide: travel guide (book) der Reiseführer (-) (10)

gym das Fitnesscenter (-) (4)

gymnasium die Turnhalle (-n) (7)

gymnastics: to do gymnastics turnen (7)

H

hail der Hagel (7)

hair das Haar (-e) (8); **hair dryer** der Föhn (-e) (9)

half halb (4); **half past one** halb zwei (4)

hall: city hall das Rathaus (-er) (9); **front hall** die Diele (-n) (12)

hallway der Flur (-e) (12)

ham der Schinken (-) (5)

hand die Hand (-e) (8)

handbag die Tasche (-n) (5)

to hang (*something*) hängen (6); **to hang, be hanging** hängen. hing. gehangen (6)

to happen passieren. ist passiert (7)

happy glücklich; **Happy birthday!** Herzlichen Glückwunsch zum Geburtstag! (3)

harbor der Hafen (-) (9)

hardly kaum (8)

hardworking fleißig (1)

hat der Hut (-e) (5)

hatred directed toward foreigners die Ausländerfeindlichkeit (14)

to have haben (hat). hatte. gehabt (2); **have fun!** viel Spaß! (1); **to have time** Zeit haben (hat Zeit) (2); **to have to** müssen (muss). musste. gemusst (4); **I have a question.** Ich habe eine Frage. (E); **What will you have?** Was bekommen Sie? (6)

he er (1)

head der Kopf (-e) (8); (*boss*) der Chef (-s) / die Chefin (-nen) (11); **head cold** der Schnupfen (-) (8)

headache die Kopfschmerzen (*pl.*) (8)

headline die Schlagzeile (-n) (13)

health die Gesundheit (8)

healthful, healthy gesund (8)

to hear hören (1)

heat, heating system die Heizung (12)

hello grüß dich (*inform.*) (E); (guten) Tag (E); hallo (*among friends and family*) (E)

to help helfen (+ *dat.*) (hilft). half. geholfen (5)

help-wanted ad das Stellenangebot (-e) (11)

her ihr (3); sie (*acc.*) (3); **(to/for) her** ihr (*dat.*) (5)

herbal tea der Kräutertee (8)

here hier (1)

hi grüß dich (*inform.*) (E); hi (E)

high(ly) hoch (hoh-) (2)

to hike wandern. ist gewandert (1)

him ihn (*acc.*) (3); **(to/for) him** ihm (*dat.*) (5)

his sein (3)

to hitchhike per Autostop reisen. ist gereist (10)

hobby das Hobby (-s) (1)

to hold halten (hält). hielt. gehalten (14)

home (to home) nach Hause (5); **at home** zu Hause (5); **at home and abroad** im Inland und Ausland (13); **home country** das Inland (*sg. only*) (13)

homeless person der/die Obdachlose (*decl. adj.*) (14)

homelessness die Obdachlosigkeit (14)

to hope (for) hoffen (auf + *acc.*) (10); **I hope** hoffentlich (6)

horoscope das Horoskop (-e) (13)

horseback: to ride on horseback reiten. ritt. ist geritten (7)

hostel: youth hostel die Jugendherberge (-n) (9)

hot heiß (7)

hotel das Hotel (-s) (9); **small family-run hotel** die Pension (-en) (9)

hour die Stunde (-n) (4); **office hour** die Sprechstunde (-n) (8)

house das Haus (-er) (2)

household der Haushalt (-e) (12)

houseplant die Zimmerpflanze (-n) (2)

housing: shared housing die Wohngemeinschaft (-en) / die WG (-s) (2)

how wie (1); **How about . . . ?** Wie wäre es mit … ? (13); **How are you?** Na. wie geht's? (*casual*) / Wie geht's (dir)? (*inform.*) / Wie geht es Ihnen? (*form.*) (E); **How do you like . . . ?** Wie findest du … ? (1); Wie gefällt Ihnen … ? (5); **How do you say . . . in German?** Wie sagt man … auf Deutsch? (E); **How do you write . . . ?** Wie schreibt man … ? (E)

human (being) der Mensch (-en *masc.*) (-en) (2); **human right** das Menschenrecht (-e) (14)

humid schwül (7)

hundred (ein)hundert (E)

Hungary Ungarn (E)

hunger der Hunger (14)

hungry: to be hungry Hunger haben (hat Hunger) (2)

to hurry up sich beeilen (8)

to hurt wehtun (+ *dat.*) (tut weh). tat weh. wehgetan (8); **That hurts.** Das tut mir weh. (8)

husband der Mann (-er) (3)

I

I ich (1); **I am** Ich bin… (E); **I don't care** Das ist mir egal. (5); **I don't know.** Das weiß ich nicht. (E); **I'm from . . .** Ich komme aus … (E); **I think that's really stupid!** Das ist mir zu blöd. (13); **I was born** ich bin geboren (1)

ice, ice cream das Eis (5); **dish of ice cream** der Eisbecher (-) (6)

to ice skate Schlittschuh laufen (läuft Schlittschuh). lief Schlittschuh. ist Schlittschuh gelaufen (7)

ice-skating rink das Eisstadion (Eisstadien) (7)

ID card der Personalausweis (-e) (10)

i.e. d.h. (= das heißt) (8)

if (*subord. conj.*) wenn (8); **if I were you** an deiner Stelle (12)

ill krank (8)

illness die Krankheit (-en) (14)

to imagine sich (*dat.*) vorstellen (stellt vor) (11)

immediately gleich (8). sofort (9)

important wichtig (3)

impractical unpraktisch (1)

in in (+ *acc./dat.*) (6); **in addition** außerdem (14); **in any case** auf jeden Fall (13); **in back of** hinter (+ *acc./dat.*) (6); **in front of** vor

(+ acc./dat.) (6); **in January** im Januar (3); **in shape** fit (8); **in spite of** trotz (+ gen.) (9); **in the afternoon** nachmittags (4); **in the evening** abends (4); **in the morning** morgens (4); **in two days** in zwei Tagen (6); **to keep in shape** sich fit halten (hält), hielt, gehalten (8)
included in the price im Preis enthalten (9)
income das Einkommen (11); die Einnahmen (12)
independent(ly) selbständig (11)
indoor swimming pool das Hallenbad (¨er) (7)
inexpensive(ly) billig (2); preiswert (2); **quite inexpensive** recht preiswert (2)
to inform oneself (about) sich informieren (über + acc.) (8)
information die Auskunft (¨e) (10)
to injure oneself sich verletzen (8)
injury die Verletzung (-en) (14)
inside drinnen (7); **inside of** innerhalb (+ gen.) (9)
instructor: university instructor der Hochschullehrer (-) / die Hochschullehrerin (-nen) (1)
to insulate isolieren (14)
insurance die Versicherung (-en) (12)
intelligent gescheit (13)
interest das Interesse (-n) (1)
interested: to be interested in sich interessieren für (+ acc.) (11)
interesting interessant (1)
Internet das Internet (13); **Internet access** der Internetzugang (9)
internship das Praktikum (Praktika) (1); **to do an internship** ein Praktikum machen (1)
interpreter der Dolmetscher (-) / die Dolmetscherin (-nen) (11)
to interrupt unterbrechen (unterbricht), unterbrach, unterbrochen (14)
intersection die Kreuzung (-en) (9)
interview das Interview (-s); **job interview** das Vorstellungsgespräch (-e) (11)
to introduce einführen (führt ein) (14); **to introduce oneself** sich (acc.) vorstellen (stellt vor) (11)
to invent erfinden, erfand, erfunden (13)
invention die Erfindung (-en) (13)
to invite einladen (lädt ein), lud ein, eingeladen (4)
involved: to get involved sich engagieren (14)
is ist; **that is** d.h. (= das heißt) (8); **there is** es gibt (3); **This is . . .** Das ist … (E); **What is . . . ?** Wie ist … ? (E)
to isolate isolieren (14)
it es, er, sie (1); es, ihn, sie (acc.) (3); **(to/for) it** ihm, ihr (dat.) (5); **It's one o'clock** Es ist eins. / Es ist ein Uhr. (4)
Italy (das) Italien (E)
its sein, ihr (3)

J

jacket die Jacke (-n) (5)
jail das Gefängnis (-se) (14)
January (der) Januar (3); **in January** im Januar (3)

jar die Dose (-n) (14)
jeans die Jeans (5)
job die Stelle (-n) (11); **job interview** das Vorstellungsgespräch (-e) (11); **job offer** das Stellenangebot (-e) (11)
to jog joggen (7); laufen (läuft), lief, ist gelaufen (2)
journalist der Journalist (-en masc.) (-en) / die Journalistin (-nen) (1)
juice der Saft (¨e) (5)
July (der) Juli (3)
June (der) Juni (3)
just gerade (2); **just as . . . as** genauso … wie (7)

K

to keep fit, in shape sich fit halten (hält), hielt, gehalten (8)
to keep on going straight ahead immer geradeaus (9)
key der Schlüssel (-) (9)
kind: what kind of (a) was für (ein) (11)
kitchen die Küche (-n) (2, 6)
knee das Knie (-) (8)
knife das Messer (-) (6)
to know (be acquainted with) kennen, kannte, gekannt (3); **to know** (something as a fact) wissen (weiß), wusste, gewusst (3); **I don't know.** Das weiß ich nicht. (E)
knowledge die Kenntnis (-se) (11)

L

lake der See (-n) (7)
lamp die Lampe (-n) (2)
large groß (2)
to last dauern (7)
late spät (4); **at the latest** spätestens (12)
lawyer der Rechtsanwalt (¨e) / die Rechtsanwältin (-nen) (11)
to lay legen (6)
layover der Aufenthalt (-e) (9)
lazy faul (1); **to be lazy** faulenzen (7)
to learn lernen (1)
least: at least mindestens (8)
to leave (depart) abfahren (fährt ab), fuhr ab, ist abgefahren (10); (e.g., a message) hinterlassen (hinterlässt), hinterließ, hinterlassen (13)
lecture der Vortrag (¨e) (4); **university lecture** die Vorlesung (-en) (4)
left links (9); **to the left** nach links (9)
left over übrig (12)
leg das Bein (-e) (8)
to lend leihen, lieh, geliehen (5)
to lessen vermindern (14)
to let lassen (lässt), ließ, gelassen (6); **Let's . . .** Lass uns (doch) … (6)
letter der Brief (-e) (7)
lettuce der Salat (-e) (6)
librarian der Bibliothekar (-e) / die Bibliothekarin (-nen) (11)
library die Bibliothek (-en) (4)
to lie, be lying down liegen, lag, gelegen (6); **to lie around** faulenzen (7); **to lie down** sich (hin)legen (legt hin) (8)
Liechtenstein (das) Liechtenstein (E)
life das Leben (11); **professional life** das Berufsleben (11)

light (adj.) hell (2)
light: traffic light die Ampel (-n) (9)
lightning: There's lightning. Es blitzt. (7)
likable sympathisch (1)
to like mögen (mag), mochte, gemocht (4); **to like** (a person or thing) gern (hat gern) (2); **to like** (to do something) gern (+ verb) (2); **to feel like** (doing something) Lust haben (hat Lust) (2); **How do you like . . . ?** Wie findest du … ? (1); Wie gefällt Ihnen … ? (5); **would like to** möchte (4); **would like to (do) most** möchte am liebsten (4)
likewise gleichfalls (E)
linens die Bettwäsche (9)
to listen hören (1); zuhören (hört zu) (4)
litter der Abfall (¨e) (14)
little wenig (8); **a little** (adv.) etwas (2)
to live wohnen (1)
living: What do you do for a living? Was sind Sie von Beruf? (1)
living room das Wohnzimmer (-) (2)
loaf of bread das Brot (-e) (5)
local news die Lokalnachrichten (pl.) (13)
located: to be located liegen, lag, gelegen (6); stehen, stand, gestanden (6); **centrally located** zentral gelegen (2); **to be conveniently located** günstig liegen, lag, gelegen (9)
location die Lage (-n) (9)
long lang (länger, längst-) (7); **So long.** Mach's gut. (inform.) (E); tschüss (inform.) (E)
to look at something sich (dat.) etwas anschauen (schaut an) (13); sich (dat.) etwas ansehen (sieht an), sah an, angesehen (13)
to look for suchen (2)
to look forward to sich freuen auf (+ acc.) (12)
to look good (on a person) stehen (+ dat.), stand, gestanden (5)
to lose verlieren, verlor, verloren (7)
lot: a lot viel (1); **thanks a lot** danke sehr (1)
lot: parking lot der Parkplatz (¨e) (9)
lotion: suntan lotion das Sonnenschutzmittel (10)
loud(ly) laut (10)
low niedrig (2)
loyal treu (1)
luck: good luck! viel Glück! (1); **What bad luck!** So ein Pech! (8)
luggage das Gepäck (9); **carry-on luggage** das Handgepäck (10)
lunch das Mittagessen (-) (5)
Luxembourg (das) Luxemburg (E)

M

machine die Maschine (-n); **answering machine** der Anrufbeantworter (-) (13); **fax machine** das Faxgerät (-e) (13); **washing machine** die Waschmaschine (-n) (12)
made of aus (+ dat.) (5)
magazine die Zeitschrift (-en) (13)
main dish das Hauptgericht (-e) (6)

to make machen (1); to make a turn einbiegen (biegt ein), bog ein, ist eingebogen (9); to make progress Fortschritte machen (14)

male cousin der Vetter (-n) (3)

man der Mann (-er) (1)

manager der Chef (-s) / die Chefin (-nen) (11)

to manufacture herstellen (stellt her) (11)

manufacturer der Hersteller (-) (11)

many viele (2); Many thanks! Vielen Dank! (6)

March (der) März (3)

Mardi Gras (der) Fasching (*southern Germany, Austria*) (3); (der) Karneval (*Rhineland*) (3)

market, marketplace der Markt (-e) (5); stock market die Börse (-n) (13)

to marry heiraten (3)

to matter: That doesn't matter. Das macht nichts. (8); What's the matter? Was ist denn los? (2); Was fehlt Ihnen/dir? (8)

May (der) Mai (3); May first der erste Mai (3); on May first am ersten Mai (3)

may, to be permitted to dürfen (darf), durfte, gedurft (4); You may not park here. Hier darf man nicht parken. (4)

maybe vielleicht (1)

me mich (*acc.*) (3); (to/for) me mir (*dat.*) (5); me too ich auch (1)

meadow die Wiese (-n) (7)

meal: evening meal das Abendessen (-) (5); midday meal das Mittagessen (-) (5)

to mean: What does . . . mean? Was bedeutet ... ? (E)

means: by all means unbedingt (12); by means of mit (+ *dat.*) (5); means of transportation das Verkehrsmittel (-) (14)

meat das Fleisch (5)

meatloaf: Bavarian-style meatlofe der Leberkäs (6)

mechanic der Mechaniker (-) / die Mechanikerin (-nen) (11)

medication das Arzneimittel (-) (14)

medicine das Medikament (-e) (5); die Droge (-n) (14)

to meet treffen (trifft), traf, getroffen (4); Pleased to meet you. Freut mich. (E)

to mention: Don't mention it. Nichts zu danken. (8)

menu die Speisekarte (-n) (6)

microwave oven der Mikrowellenherd (-e) (12)

midday meal das Mittagessen (-) (5)

middle die Mitte (9)

midnight: at midnight um Mitternacht (3)

milk die Milch (5)

mineral water der Sprudel (6)

minute die Minute (-n) (4)

modern building der Neubau (-ten) (12)

Monday (der) Montag (3); Mondays, on Monday(s) montags (4); on Monday am Montag (3)

money das Geld (2); out of money (*coll.*) pleite (12)

month der Monat (-e) (3); once a month einmal im Monat (7)

monthly monatlich (12)

morning der Morgen (-) (4); der Vormittag (-e) (4); good morning (guten) Morgen (E); in the morning, mornings morgens (4); this morning heute Morgen (4); tomorrow morning morgen früh (4)

most: would like to (do) most möchte am liebsten (4)

mostly meistens (8)

mother die Mutter (-) (3)

Mother's Day der Muttertag (3)

motorcycle das Motorrad (-er) (2)

mountain der Berg (-e) (7)

mouth der Mund (-er) (8)

to move in einziehen in (+ *acc.*), zog ein, ist eingezogen (12)

movie der Spielfilm (-e) (13); movie theater das Kino (-s) (4); to go to the movies ins Kino gehen (4)

Mr. Herr (E)

Mrs., Ms. Frau (E)

much viel (1, 2); thank you very much danke schön (E)

muggy schwül (7)

muscle der Muskel (-n) (8)

museum das Museum (Museen) (9)

music die Musik (1)

must, to have to müssen (muss), musste, gemusst (4)

mustard der Senf (6)

my mein (3); My name is . . . Ich heiße ... (E); Mein Name ist... (E)

mystery film or book der Krimi (-s) (4)

N

name der Name (*gen.* -ns, *acc./dat.* -n) (-n) (1); family name der Nachname (*gen.* -ns, *acc./dat.* -n) (-n) (1); first name, given name der Vorname (*gen.* -ns, *acc./dat.* -n) (-n) (1); My name is . . . Ich heiße ... (E); Mein Name ist ... (E); Under what name? Auf welchen Namen? (9); What is the name of . . . ? Wie heißt ... ? (E); What's your name? Wie heißen Sie? (*form.*) / Wie heißt du? (*inform.*) (E); Wie ist Ihr Name? (*form.*) / Wie ist dein Name? (E)

named: to be named heißen, hieß, geheißen (1)

namely nämlich (3)

napkin die Serviette (-n) (6)

to narrate berichten (13)

nasal congestion der Schnupfen (8)

natural(ly) natürlich (1); natural foods store der Bioladen (-) (5)

nature die Natur (10)

near bei (+ *dat.*) (5); near (the train station) in der Nähe (des Bahnhofs) (9)

necessary nötig (5); notwendig (12); No thanks necessary. Nichts zu danken. (8)

neck der Hals (-e) (8)

necktie die Krawatte (-n) (5); der Schlips (-e) (5)

to need brauchen (2)

neighborhood die Umgebung (-en) (12)

nephew der Neffe (-n *masc.*) (-n) (3)

Netherlands die Niederlande (*pl.*) (E)

never nie (1)

new neu (3)

New Year's Day das Neujahr (3)

New Year's Eve (das) Silvester (3)

news die Nachrichten (*pl.*) (13); local news die Lokalnachrichten (*pl.*) (13)

newspaper die Zeitung (-en) (1)

next nächst-; next to neben (+ *acc./ dat.*) (6); next year nächstes Jahr (1)

nice(ly) nett (1); schön (2)

niece die Nichte (-n) (3)

night die Nacht (-e) (4); at night, nights nachts (4); good night gute Nacht (E)

nightstand der Nachttisch (-e) (2)

nine neun (E)

nineteen neunzehn (E)

ninety neunzig (E)

ninth neunte (3)

no nein (E); no (not any) kein (2); no doubt bestimmt (1); No one is answering. Niemand meldet sich. (13); No thanks necessary. Nichts zu danken. (8)

noise der Lärm (14)

nonalcoholic alkoholfrei (6)

none kein (2)

nonrecyclable bottle die Wegwerfflasche (-n) (14)

nonsense: Nonsense! So ein Unsinn! (14)

nonsmoker der Nichtraucher (-) / die Nichtraucherin (-nen) (2)

noodle die Nudel (-n) (6)

nook: breakfast nook die Frühstücksnische (-n) (12)

noon der Mittag (-e) (4); at noon mittags (4); before noon der Vormittag (-e) (4); (*adv.*) vormittags (4)

nose die Nase (-n) (8)

not nicht (1); not any kein (2); not particularly well nicht besonders gut (E)

notebook das Heft (-e) (12); notebook computer das Notebook (-s) (13)

nothing nichts (2); nothing decent nichts Gescheites (13)

November (der) November (3)

now jetzt (1); now and then ab und zu (8)

number die Nummer (-n); telephone number die Telefonnummer (-n) (E)

nurse der Krankenpfleger (-) / die Krankenschwester (-n) (8)

nutrition die Ernährung (12)

O

occasionally ab und zu (8)

occupation der Beruf (-e) (1)

occupied besetzt (6)

to occupy oneself (with) sich beschäftigen (mit + *dat.*) (11)

ocean das Meer (-e) (7)

o'clock: It's one o'clock Es ist eins. / Es ist ein Uhr. (4)

October (der) Oktober (3)

of von (+ *dat.*) (5); five of/to two fünf vor zwei (4); made of aus (+ *dat.*) of course natürlich (1); (5); out of aus (+ *dat.*) (5)

offer das Angebot (-e) (10); job offer das Stellenangebot (-e) (11)

office das Büro (-s) (11); **employment office** das Arbeitsamt (¨er) (11); **office hour** die Sprechstunde (-n) (8); **post office** die Post (*pl.* Postämter) (9)

often oft (1)

OK so lala (E)

old alt (älter, ältest-) (1)

olive die Olive (-n) (6)

on an (+ *acc./dat.*) (6); auf (+ *acc./dat.*) (6); **on account of** wegen (+ *gen.*) (9); **on average** durchschnittlich (12); **on May first** am ersten Mai (3); **on Monday** am Montag (3); **on Monday(s)** montags (4); **on tap** vom Fass (6); **on top of** auf (+ *acc./dat.*) (6)

once einmal (7); früher (7); **once a month/year** einmal im Monat/Jahr (7); **once a week** einmal die Woche (7)

one eins (E); (*indef, pron.*) man (4); **half past one, one-thirty** halb zwei (4); **It's one o'clock** Es ist eins. / Es ist ein Uhr. (4)

one-way (ticket) einfach (10)

onion die Zwiebel (-n) (6)

only nur (2)

open geöffnet (6)

open-air market der Markt (¨e) (5)

opera die Oper (-n) (4); **to go to the opera** in die Oper gehen (4)

opinion die Meinung (-en) (14); **to be of the opinion** meinen (14); **I'm of the opinion . . .** ich bin der Meinung … (14); **in my opinion . . .** meiner Meinung nach … (14)

opportunity die Möglichkeit (-en) (10); die Gelegenheit (-en) (11)

or (*coord. conj.*) oder (7); **either . . . or** entweder … oder (8)

orange (*adj.*) orange (5)

to order bestellen (6)

organic foods die Biolebensmittel (*pl.*) (8)

otherwise sonst, sonst noch (10)

ought to sollen (soll), sollte, gesollt (4)

our unser (3)

out of aus (+ *dat.*) (5); **out of money** (*coll.*) pleite (12)

outdoor swimming pool das Freibad (¨er) (7)

outdoors im Freien (11)

outside draußen (7); **outside of** außerhalb (+ *gen.*) (9)

oven: microwave oven der Mikrowellenherd (-e) (12)

over über (+ *acc./dat.*) (6); **over there** da drüben (6); **left over** übrig (12)

overcast bewölkt (7)

overnight stay die Übernachtung (-en) (9); **to stay overnight** übernachten (9)

own (*adj.*) eigen (12)

to own besitzen, besaß, besessen (11)

P

to pack packen (10)

packaging die Verpackung (-en) (14)

pains die Schmerzen (*pl.*) (8)

to paint malen (7)

pair of eyeglasses die Brille (-n) (5)

palace das Schloss (¨er) (9)

pan die Pfanne (-n) (6)

pants die Hose (-n) (5)

paper das Papier (-e) (12); (*report*) die Arbeit (-en) (8); **papers** (*documents*) die Unterlagen (*pl.*) (11); **toilet paper** das Toilettenpapier (5)

Pardon? Wie bitte? (E)

parents die Eltern (*pl.*) (3)

to park parken; **You may not park here.** Hier darf man nicht parken. (4)

parking lot, parking space der Parkplatz (¨e) (9)

part der/das Teil (-e); **part of the body** der Körperteil (-e) (8)

to participate (in) teilnehmen (an + *dat.*) (nimmt teil), nahm teil, teilgenommen (14)

particularly besonders; **not particularly well** nicht besonders gut (E)

party die Party (-s) (3)

passer-by der Passant (-en *masc.*) (-en) / die Passantin (-nen) (9)

passport der Reisepass (¨e) (9)

past: half past one halb zwei (4)

pastry shop die Konditorei (-en) (5)

path der Weg (-e) (9)

patio die Terrasse (-n) (2)

to pay zahlen (5); **to pay attention to** achten auf (+ *acc.*) (8)

pedestrian zone die Fußgängerzone (-n) (9)

pen: ballpoint pen der Kugelschreiber (-) (12)

pencil der Bleistift (-e) (12)

people die Leute (*pl.*) (2); (*indef. pron.*) man (4)

pepper der Pfeffer (5); **bell pepper** die Paprika (6)

per pro; **per person** pro Person (10); **per week** pro Woche (4)

perhaps vielleicht (1)

periodical die Zeitschrift (-en) (13)

to permit erlauben (9)

permitted: to be permitted to dürfen (darf), durfte, gedurft (4)

person der Mensch (-en *masc.*) (-en) (2); **per person** pro Person (10)

personnel das Personal (11)

pharmacy die Apotheke (-n) (5)

phone das Telefon (-e) (2); **cell phone** das Handy (-s) (2); **to talk on the phone** telefonieren (1)

photograph das Foto (-s) (2)

physician der Arzt (¨e) / die Ärztin (-nen) (8)

to pick up (*from a place*) abholen (holt ab) (4)

Pilsner beer das Pilsener (-) (6)

place der Platz (¨e) (6); **place of residence** der Wohnort (-e) (1); **(if I were) in your place** an deiner Stelle (12); **This place is taken.** Hier ist besetzt. (6)

to place (*in a standing position*) stellen (6); **to place inside** stecken (6)

plaid kariert (5)

plan der Plan (¨e) (4)

to plan planen (3); **to plan** (*to do*) vorhaben (hat vor), hatte vor, vorgehabt (4); **to plan to** wollen (will), wollte, gewollt (4)

plastic bag die Plastiktüte (-n) (14)

plate der Teller (-) (6)

platform (*train*) der Bahnsteig (-e) (10)

play (*theater*) das Theaterstück (-e) (4)

to play spielen (1); **to play cards** Karten spielen (1); **to play chess** Schach spielen (7); **to play computer games** Computerspiele spielen (1); **to play soccer** Fußball spielen (7); **to play sports** Sport treiben, trieb, getrieben (7); **to play tennis** Tennis spielen (7)

player: CD player der CD-Spieler (-) (2); **DVD player** der DVD-Spieler (-) (2)

playing card die Spielkarte (-n) (7)

pleasant angenehm (7)

please bitte (E); **Slower, please.** Langsamer, bitte. (E); **Would you please . . . ?** Würden Sie bitte … ? (9)

pleased: Pleased to meet you. Freut mich. (E)

pleasing: to be pleasing to gefallen (+ *dat.*) (gefällt), gefiel, gefallen (5)

Poland (das) Polen (E)

police, police station die Polizei (9)

politician der Politiker (-) / die Politikerin (-nen) (14)

politics die Politik (13)

pollution: environmental pollution die Umweltverschmutzung (14)

pool: swimming pool das Schwimmbad (¨er) (7); **indoor swimming pool** das Hallenbad (¨er) (7); **outdoor swimming pool** das Freibad (¨er) (7)

poor(ly) schlecht (E)

popular beliebt (7)

pork das Schweinefleisch (5); **pork roast** der Schweinebraten (-) (6)

port der Hafen (¨) (9)

position der Arbeitsplatz (¨e) (11); die Stelle (-n) (11); die Tätigkeit (-en) (11)

to possess besitzen, besaß, besessen (11)

possibility die Möglichkeit (-en) (10)

possible, possibly möglich (14)

post office die Post (*pl.* Postämter) (9)

postage stamp die Briefmarke (-n) (7)

postal code die Postleitzahl (-en) (E)

poster das Poster (-) (2)

potato die Kartoffel (-n) (5); **fried potatoes** die Bratkartoffeln (*pl.*) (6)

poverty die Armut (14)

practical praktisch (1)

to prefer vorziehen (zieht vor), zog vor, vorgezogen (14)

to prepare (for) sich vorbereiten (auf + *acc.*) (bereitet vor) (11)

to prescribe verschreiben, verschrieb, verschrieben (8)

present das Geschenk (-e) (3)

prestige das Ansehen (11)

pretzel die Brezel (-n) (6)

price der Preis (-e) (9); **included in the price** im Preis enthalten (9)

primary school die Grundschule (-n) (11)

to print drucken (13)

printer der Drucker (-) (13)

prison das Gefängnis (-se) (14)

probably wahrscheinlich (11); wohl (11)

problem das Problem (-e) (2)

to produce herstellen (stellt her) (11)

producer der Hersteller (-) (11)

profession der Beruf (-e) (1)

professional life das Berufsleben (11)

professor der Professor (-en) / die Professorin (-nen) (1)

program das Programm (-e) (13); **TV or radio program** die Sendung (-en) (13)

progress der Fortschritt (-e) (14); **to make progress** Fortschritte machen (14)

to prohibit verbieten, verbot, verboten (14)

to promote fördern (14)

to propose vorschlagen (schlägt vor), schlug vor, vorgeschlagen (10)

to protect schützen (14); **environmental protection** der Umweltschutz (14)

psychologist der Psychologe (-n *masc.*) (-n) / die Psychologin (-nen) (11)

pub die Kneipe (-n) (6); das Lokal (-e) (6); das Wirtshaus (¨er) (6)

public öffentlich (14)

pullover sweater der Pullover (-) (5)

to purchase something sich (*dat.*) etwas anschaffen (schafft an) (14)

purple lila (5)

purse die Tasche (-n) (5)

to put (*in a lying position*) legen (6); (*in a sitting position*) setzen (6); (*inside*) stecken (6); (*in a standing position*) stellen (6)

puzzle: to do crossword puzzles Kreuzworträtsel machen (1)

Q

quarter das Viertel (-) (4); **It's a quarter after/to two.** Es ist Viertel nach/vor zwei. (4)

question die Frage (-n); **I have a question.** Ich habe eine Frage. (E)

quick(ly) schnell (10); **to read quickly** überfliegen, überflog, überflogen (13)

quiet ruhig (1)

quite ganz (1); recht (2); **quite inexpensive** recht preiswert (2)

R

racism der Rassismus (14)

radio das Radio (-s) (2); **radio program** die Sendung (-en) (13)

railway die Bahn (-en) (10)

rain der Regen (7)

to rain regnen (7); **It's raining.** Es regnet. (7)

rain shower der Regenschauer (-) (7)

rainy regnerisch (7)

to raise erziehen, erzog, erzogen (14)

rare(ly) selten (2)

rather recht (2); ziemlich (6); (*coord. conj.*) sondern (7); **would rather** möchte lieber (4)

to read lesen (liest), las, gelesen (1, 2); **to read quickly** überfliegen, überflog, überflogen (13)

really echt (*coll.*) (1); ganz (1); wirklich (1)

reasonable (*in price*) preiswert (2)

to receive empfangen (empfängt), empfing, empfangen (13)

receiver: satellite receiver die Sat-Empfangsanlage (-n) (13)

reception desk die Rezeption (9)

to recommend empfehlen (empfiehlt), empfahl, empfohlen (5)

recommendation (*from a former employer*) das Zeugnis (-se) (11)

to record (*e.g., on video*) aufnehmen (nimmt auf), nahm auf, aufgenommen (13)

recorder: video recorder der Videorecorder (-) (2)

to recover sich erholen (8)

recycling center die Sammelstelle (-n) (14)

red rot (5)

refrigerator der Kühlschrank (¨e) (9)

register: cash register die Kasse (-n) (5)

to register sich anmelden (meldet an) (9)

registration form das Anmeldeformular (-e) (9)

regular(ly) regelmäßig (8)

related to verwandt mit (3)

to relax sich entspannen (8)

to remain bleiben, blieb, ist geblieben (1)

rent die Miete (-n) (2)

to rent (*from someone*) mieten (12); **to rent out** (*to someone*) vermieten (12)

repair die Reparatur (-en) (12)

to repair reparieren (9)

report der Bericht (-e) (13); **report card** das Zeugnis (-se) (11); **weather report** der Wetterbericht (-e) (7)

to report berichten (13)

to request bitten um (+ *acc.*), bat, gebeten (12)

research die Forschung (-en) (14)

research: to do research forschen (13)

reservation: seat reservation card die Platzkarte (-n) (10)

to reserve reservieren (7)

to reside wohnen (1)

residence: place of residence der Wohnort (-e) (1)

responsible verantwortlich (11)

restaurant das Restaurant (-s) (6); das Lokal (-e) (6); **full-service restaurant** die Gaststätte (-n) (6)

résumé der Lebenslauf (¨e) (11)

to retrain umschulen (schult um) (14)

to return zurückkommen (kommt zurück), kam zurück, ist zurückgekommen (4)

rice der Reis (6)

ride die Fahrt (-en) (10)

to ride fahren (fährt), fuhr, ist gefahren (1); **to ride a bike** Fahrrad/Rad fahren (fährt Fahrrad/Rad) (1, 7); **to ride on horseback** reiten, ritt, ist geritten (7)

right rechts (9); **to the right** nach rechts (9)

right das Recht (-e); **human right** das Menschenrecht (-e) (14)

right-wing extremism der Rechtsextremismus (14)

rink: ice-skating rink das Eisstadion (Eisstadien) (7)

river der Fluss (¨e) (7)

road der Weg (-e) (9)

roast: pork roast der Schweinebraten (-) (6)

roll das Brötchen (-) (5)

romantic romantisch (1)

roof das Dach (¨er) (12)

room das Zimmer (-) (2); **breakfast room** der Frühstücksraum (¨e) (9); **dining room** das Esszimmer (-) (2); **guest room** das Gästezimmer (-) (12); **living room** das Wohnzimmer (-) (2); **room with one bed** das Einzelzimmer (-) (9); **room with two beds** das Doppelzimmer (-) (9)

roommate der Mitbewohner (-) / die Mitbewohnerin (-nen) (2)

round-trip hin und zurück (10)

rug der Teppich (-e) (2)

to run laufen (läuft), lief, ist gelaufen (2)

S

safe(ly) sicher (10)

to sail segeln (7)

salad der Salat (-e) (6)

salary das Gehalt (¨er) (11)

sales der Handel (11)

salesman der Kaufmann (*pl.* Kaufleute) (11)

salesperson der Verkäufer (-) / die Verkäuferin (-nen) (2)

saleswoman die Kauffrau (-en) (11)

salt das Salz (5)

satellite receiver die Sat-Empfangsanlage (-n) (13)

Saturday (der) Samstag (3); (der) Sonnabend (3); **Saturdays, on Saturday(s)** samstags (4); sonnabends (4)

sauerkraut das Sauerkraut (6)

sausage die Wurst (¨e) (5); **white sausage** die Weißwurst (¨e) (6)

to save (*conserve*) sparen (12); (*store*) speichern (13)

savings account das Sparkonto (Sparkonten) (12)

to say sagen (1); **How do you say . . . in German?** Wie sagt man ... auf Deutsch? (E); **that is to say** nämlich (3); **What did you say?** Wie bitte? (E)

scarcely kaum (8)

scarf der Schal (-s) (5)

schedule der Fahrplan (¨e) (10)

school die Schule (-n); **primary school** die Grundschule (-n) (11); **secondary school** das Gymnasium (Gymnasien) (11)

scientist: computer scientist der Informatiker (-) / die Informatikerin (-nen) (11)

sea das Meer (-e) (7)

season die Jahreszeit (-en) (7)

seat der Platz (¨e) (6); **Is this seat available?** Ist hier noch frei? (6); **seat reservation card** die Platzkarte (-n) (10)

second (*adj.*) zweite (3)

second die Sekunde (-n) (4)

secondary school das Gymnasium (Gymnasien) (11)

to see sehen (sieht), sah, gesehen (2)

to seem scheinen, schien, geschienen (13)

to select something sich (*dat.*) etwas aussuchen (sucht aus) (13)

selection das Angebot (-e) (10)

semester das Semester (-) (1)

to send schicken (1)

sensible gescheit (13)

to separate (sich) trennen (14)

separate(ly) getrennt (6)

September (der) September (3)

serious ernst (1)

server der Kellner (-) / die Kellnerin (-nen) (6)

service die Bedienung (6)

set (*TV, telephone, camera, etc.*) der Apparat (-e) (9)

to set setzen (6)

seven sieben (E)

seventeen siebzehn (E)

seventh sieb(en)te (3)

seventy siebzig (E)

shame: What a shame! So ein Pech! (8)

shape: in shape fit (8); **to keep in shape** sich fit halten (hält), hielt, gehalten (8)

shared housing die Wohngemeinschaft (-en) / die WG (-s) (2)

to shave sich rasieren (8)

shaving cream die Rasiercreme (-s) (5)

she sie (1)

shelf das Regal (-e) (2)

to shine scheinen, schien, geschienen; **The sun is shining.** Die Sonne scheint. (7)

ship das Schiff (-e) (10)

shirt das Hemd (-en) (5); **T-shirt** das T-Shirt (-s) (5)

shoe der Schuh (-e) (5); **tennis shoe** der Tennisschuh (-e) (5)

shop das Geschäft (-e) (5); **butcher shop** die Metzgerei (-en) (5); **pastry shop** die Konditorei (-en) (5)

to shop einkaufen (kauft ein) (4)

shopping: to go shopping einkaufen gehen (geht einkaufen), ging einkaufen, ist einkaufen gegangen (4)

short kurz (kürzer, kürzest-) (7)

should, to be supposed to sollen (soll), sollte, gesollt (4)

shoulder die Schulter (-n) (8)

to show zeigen (5)

shower die Dusche (-n) (9); **rain shower** der Regenschauer (-) (7)

to shower sich duschen (8)

siblings die Geschwister (*pl.*) (3)

sick krank (8); **sick as a dog** (*coll.*) hundsmiserabel (8); **I'm sick to my stomach.** Mir ist schlecht. (8)

side dish die Beilage (-n) (6)

simple einfach (10)

since seit (+ *dat.*) (5, 6)

single room das Einzelzimmer (-) (9)

sister die Schwester (-n) (3)

sister-in-law die Schwägerin (-nen) (3)

to sit sitzen, saß, gesessen (6); **to sit down** sich (hin)setzen (setzt hin) (8)

six sechs (E)

sixteen sechzehn (E)

sixth sechste (3)

sixty sechzig (E)

size die Größe (-n) (5)

to skate: to ice skate Schlittschuh laufen (läuft Schlittschuh), lief Schlittschuh, ist Schlittschuh gelaufen (7)

skill die Fähigkeit (-en) (11)

to skim (a text) überfliegen, überflog, überflogen (13)

skirt der Rock (¨-e) (5)

sky der Himmel (7)

to sleep schlafen (schläft), schlief, geschlafen (2)

slipper der Hausschuh (-e) (5)

Slovakia die Slowakei (E)

Slovenia (das) Slowenien (E)

slow(ly) langsam (10); **Slower, please.** Langsamer, bitte. (E)

small klein (2)

to smoke rauchen (8)

snow der Schnee (7)

to snow schneien (7); **It's snowing.** Es schneit. (7)

so so (2); **So long.** Mach's gut. (*inform.*) (E); tschüss (*inform.*) (E); **So what?** Na und? (13)

soccer, soccer ball der Fußball (¨-e) (7); **to play soccer** Fußball spielen (7)

sock die Socke (-n) (5); der Strumpf (¨-e) (5)

sofa das Sofa (-s) (2)

solution die Lösung (-en) (14)

to solve lösen (14)

something etwas (2)

sometimes manchmal (8)

somewhat etwas (2); ziemlich (6)

son der Sohn (¨-e) (3)

soon bald (12); **Get well soon!** Gute Besserung! (8)

sore throat die Halsschmerzen (*pl.*) (8)

sorry: I'm sorry. Das tut mir leid. (9)

to sound klingen, klang, geklungen (8); **You sound so depressed.** Du klingst so deprimiert. (8)

soup die Suppe (-n) (6)

space: parking space der Parkplatz (¨-e) (9)

to speak sprechen (spricht), sprach, gesprochen (2)

special offer das Angebot (-e) (10)

to spend (*money*) ausgeben (gibt aus), gab aus, ausgegeben (12); (*time*) verbringen, verbrachte, verbracht (7)

spite: in spite of trotz (+ *gen.*) (9)

spoon der Löffel (-) (6)

sport, sports der Sport (*pl.* Sportarten) (7); **active in sports** sportlich aktiv (10); **to play sports** Sport treiben, trieb, getrieben (7); **sport coat** der/das Sakko (-s) (5); **sports arena** die Sporthalle (-n) (7)

to spread verbreiten (14)

spring (*season*) das Frühjahr (-e), der Frühling (-e) (7)

stadium das Stadion (Stadien) (7)

staircase die Treppe (-n) (12)

stamp: postage stamp die Briefmarke (-n) (7)

stand der Stand (¨-e); **fast-food stand** der Imbiss (-e) (6); **fruit and vegetable stand** der Obst- und Gemüsestand (¨-e) (5)

to stand stehen, stand, gestanden (6); **to stand up** (*get up*) aufstehen (steht auf), stand auf, ist aufgestanden (4); **to stand up** (*put in a standing position*) stellen (6)

to start beginnen, begann, begonnen (10)

station (*TV or radio*) das Programm (-e) (13); **police station** die Polizei (9); **train station** der Bahnhof (¨-e) (9)

stay der Aufenthalt (-e) (9); **overnight stay** die Übernachtung (-en) (9)

to stay bleiben, blieb, ist geblieben (1); **to stay overnight** übernachten (9)

stereo die Stereoanlage (-n) (2)

still (*yet*) noch (2)

stock market die Börse (-n) (13)

stocking der Strumpf (¨-e) (5)

stomach der Bauch (¨-e) (8); **I'm sick to my stomach.** Mir ist schlecht. (8)

stop: bus stop die Haltestelle (-n) (9)

to stop (*doing something*) aufhören (mit + *dat.*) (hört auf) (4)

store das Geschäft (-e) (5); der Laden (¨-) (5); **beverage store** der Getränkeladen (¨-) (5); **department store** das Kaufhaus (¨-er) (2); **natural foods store** der Bioladen (¨-) (5); **toiletries and sundries store** die Drogerie (-n) (5)

to store speichern (13)

story (*level*) der Stock (*pl.* Stockwerke) (9); die Etage (-n) (12)

straight ahead geradeaus (9)

to straighten up aufräumen (räumt auf) (4)

strawberry die Erdbeere (-n) (5)

street die Straße (-n) (E); **street address** die Hausnummer (-n) (E)

strength die Stärke (-n) (11)

strenuous anstrengend (8)

stress der Stress (8)

stressful stressig (1)

to stretch sich strecken (8)

strict(ly) streng (14)

striped gestreift (7)

strong stark (stärker, stärkst-) (7)

strudel: apple strudel der Apfelstrudel (-) (6)

student der Student (-en *masc.*) (-en) / die Studentin (-nen) (1); **student cafeteria** die Mensa (-s) (1)

study (*room*) das Arbeitszimmer (-) (2)

to study (*at university*) studieren (1); (*for an exam*) lernen (1)

stupid blöd (13); **I think that's really stupid.** Das ist mir zu blöd. (13)

to subscribe abonnieren (13)

subscription das Abo(nnement) (-s) (13)

success der Erfolg (-e) (11)

successful(ly) erfolgreich (11); **to be successful** Erfolg haben (11)

sugar der Zucker (5)

to suggest vorschlagen (schlägt vor), schlug vor, vorgeschlagen (10)

suit der Anzug (¨-e) (5); **bathing suit** der Badeanzug (¨-e) (5)

suitcase der Koffer (-) (5)

summer der Sommer (-) (7)

sun die Sonne (7); **The sun is shining.** Die Sonne scheint. (7)

Sunday (der) Sonntag (3); **Sundays, on Sunday(s)** sonntags (4)

sunny sonnig (7)

sunscreen das Sonnenschutzmittel (10)

sunshine der Sonnenschein (7)

suntan lotion das Sonnenschutzmittel (10)

super prima (E); **super!** (*coll.*) (ganz) toll! (1)

supermarket der Supermarkt (¨e) (5)

support die Unterstützung (11)

to support unterstützen, unterstützt (12)

supposed: **to be supposed to** sollen (soll), sollte, gesollt (4)

to surf surfen (1)

surname der Nachname (*gen.* -ns, *acc./dat.* -n) (-n) (1)

suspenseful spannend (4)

to swallow schlucken (8)

sweater: **pullover sweater** der Pullover (-) (5)

to swim schwimmen, schwamm, ist geschwommen (2)

swimming pool das Schwimmbad (¨er) (7); **indoor swimming pool** das Hallenbad (¨er) (7); **outdoor swimming pool** das Freibad (¨er) (7)

Switzerland die Schweiz (E)

T

table der Tisch (-e) (2)

table: **coffee table** der Couchtisch (-e) (2)

to take nehmen (nimmt), nahm, genommen (2); **to take** (*time*) dauern (7); **to take a vote** abstimmen (stimmt ab) (14); **to take along** mitnehmen (nimmt mit), nahm mit, mitgenommen (4); **Take care.** Mach's gut. (*inform.*) (E); **to take over** übernehmen (übernimmt), übernahm, übernommen (11); **take-out** zum Mitnehmen (6)

taken besetzt (6); **This place is taken.** Hier ist besetzt. (6)

to talk on the phone telefonieren (1)

tall groß (1)

tap: **on tap** vom Fass (6)

to taste (good) schmecken (+ *dat.*) (5)

tax die Steuer (-n) (14)

taxicab das Taxi (-s) (10)

tea der Tee (5); **herbal tea** der Kräutertee (8)

teacher der Lehrer (-) / die Lehrerin (-nen) (E)

technique die Technik (-en) (11)

technology die Technik (-en) (11)

telephone das Telefon (-e) (2); **telephone number** die Telefonnummer (-n) (E); **to talk on the telephone** telefonieren (1)

television (set) der Fernseher (-) (2); **to watch television** fernsehen (sieht fern), sah fern, ferngesehen (4); **watching television** das Fernsehen (4)

to tell sagen (1); **tell me** sag mal (1)

temperature die Temperatur (-en) (7)

ten zehn (E)

tender zart (5)

tennis das Tennis; **tennis court** der Tennisplatz (¨e) (7); **tennis shoe** der Tennisschuh (-e) (5); **to play tennis** Tennis spielen (7)

tent das Zelt (-e) (10)

tenth zehnte (3)

terrace die Terrasse (-n) (2)

terrorism der Terrorismus (14)

than als (3)

to thank danken (+ *dat.*) (5); **thank you very much** danke schön (E)

thanks danke (E); **thanks a lot** danke sehr (1); **fine, thanks** danke, gut (E); **Many thanks!** Vielen Dank! (6); **No thanks necessary.** Nichts zu danken. (8)

that das; (*subord. conj.*) dass (8); **that comes to** das macht zusammen (5); **That doesn't matter.** Das macht nichts. (8); **that is** d.h. (= das heißt) (8); **that is to say** nämlich (3); **That's fun.** Das macht Spaß. (1)

the der, die, das

theater das Theater (-) (4); **to go to the theater** ins Theater gehen (4); **movie theater** das Kino (-s) (4)

their ihr (3)

them sie (*acc.*) (3); **(to/for) them** ihnen (*dat.*) (5)

then: **now and then** ab und zu (8)

there da (2); **there is/are** es gibt (3); **over there** da drüben (6); **What's the best way to get there?** Wie komme ich am besten dahin? (9)

therefore deshalb (8)

they sie (1); (*indef. pron.*) man (4)

thing das Ding (-e) (10)

to think (about/of) denken (an + *acc.*), dachte, gedacht (12); **to think (about)** nachdenken (über + *acc.*) (denkt nach), dachte nach, nachgedacht (11); **to think** (*be of the opinion*) meinen (14); **to think** (*consider*) halten (für + *acc.*) (hält), hielt, gehalten (14); **to think over** sich überlegen, überlegt (10); **I think that's really stupid.** Das ist mir zu blöd. (13); **What do you think of . . . ?** Wie findest du ... ? (1)

third dritte (3)

thirsty: **to be thirsty** Durst haben (hat Durst) (2)

thirteen dreizehn (E)

thirteenth dreizehnte (3)

thirty dreißig (E)

this dieser, diese, dies(es) (2); **this afternoon** heute Nachmittag (4); **this evening** heute Abend (1); **This is . . .** Das ist ... (E); **this morning** heute Morgen (4)

thousand (ein)tausend (E)

three drei (E); **three times** dreimal (7)

threesome: **as a threesome** zu dritt (10)

thrifty sparsam (12)

throat der Hals (¨e) (8); **sore throat** die Halsschmerzen (*pl.*) (8)

through durch (+ *acc.*) (3)

to thunder donnern (7); **It's thundering.** Es donnert. (7)

thunderstorm das Gewitter (-) (7)

Thursday (der) Donnerstag (3); **Thursdays, on Thursday(s)** donnerstags (4)

ticket (*bus or train*) die Fahrkarte (-n) (10); **ticket window** der Fahrkartenschalter (-) (10)

time die Zeit (-en) (2); **At what time?** Um wie viel Uhr? (4); **to have time** Zeit haben (hat Zeit) (2); **to spend time** Zeit verbringen, verbrachte, verbracht (7); **three times** dreimal (7); **time of day** die Tageszeit (-en) (4); **What time is it?** Wie spät ist es? / Wie viel Uhr ist es? (4)

tin can die Dose (-n) (14)

tired müde (8)

tiring anstrengend (8)

to nach (+ *dat.*) (5); zu (+ *dat.*) (5); (*a place*) in (+ *acc.*) (6); **five to two** fünf vor zwei (4); **It's a quarter to two.** Es ist Viertel vor zwei. (4); **to (as far as)** bis zum/zur (9); **(to) home** nach Hause (5); **to the left/right** nach links/rechts (9); **to where** wohin (5)

today heute (1); **What is today's date?** Welches Datum ist heute? (3)

toe die Zehe (-n) (8)

together zusammen; **all together, that comes to** das macht zusammen (5)

toilet das WC (-s) (9); **toilet paper** das Toilettenpapier (5)

toiletries and sundries store die Drogerie (-n) (5)

tomato die Tomate (-n) (5)

tomorrow morgen (3); **tomorrow evening** morgen Abend (4); **tomorrow morning** morgen früh (4); **What is tomorrow's date?** Welches Datum ist morgen? (3)

too (*also*) auch; **me too** ich auch (1)

tooth der Zahn (¨e); **to brush one's teeth** sich die Zähne putzen (8)

toothpaste die Zahnpasta (Zahnpasten) (5)

top: **on top of** auf (+ *acc./dat.*) (6); **top floor** das Dachgeschoss (-e) (12)

topical aktuell (13)

total insgesamt (10); **total(ly)** ganz (12)

tourist der Tourist (-en *masc.*) (-en) / die Touristin (-nen) (9)

town die Stadt (¨e) (E); **center of town** das Zentrum (Zentren) (9)

track das Gleis (-e) (10)

trade der Handel (11)

tradition die Tradition (-en) (3)

traffic light die Ampel (-n) (9)

tragedy die Tragödie (-n) (4)

train der Zug (¨e) (10); (*railway*) die Bahn (-en) (10); **train platform** der Bahnsteig (-e) (10); **train station** der Bahnhof (¨e) (9)

training die Ausbildung (11); **to do weight training** Bodybuilding machen (7)

transcript das Zeugnis (-se) (11)

to transfer (*trains*) umsteigen (steigt um), stieg um, ist umgestiegen (10)

to translate übersetzen, übersetzt (11)

transportation: **means of transportation** das Verkehrsmittel (-) (14)

trash der Müll (12); der Abfall (¨e) (14)

travel: travel agency das Reisebüro (-s) (10); **travel brochure** der Reiseprospekt (-e) (10); **travel guide (book)** der Reiseführer (-) (10)

to travel reisen, ist gereist (1); **to travel first/second class** erster/zweiter Klasse fahren (fährt), fuhr, ist gefahren (10)

traveler's check der Reisescheck (-s) (10)

tree der Baum (¨-e); **Christmas tree** der Weihnachtsbaum (¨-e) (3); **family tree** der Stammbaum (¨-e) (3)

trip die Fahrt (-en) (10); die Reise (-n) (10); **to go on a trip** verreisen, ist verreist (10)

trousers die Hose (-n) (5)

to try versuchen (8); **to try on** anprobieren (probiert an) (5)

T-shirt das T-Shirt (-s) (5)

Tuesday (der) Dienstag (3); **Tuesdays, on Tuesday(s)** dienstags (4)

tuition die Studiengebühren (pl.) (12)

turkey der Truthahn (¨-e) (5)

to turn einbiegen (biegt ein), bog ein, ist eingebogen (9)

TV das Fernsehen; **cable TV connection** der Kabelanschluss (¨-e) (13); **TV channel** das Programm (-e) (13); **TV program** die Sendung (-en) (13); **TV set** der Fernseher (-) (2)

twelfth zwölfte (3)

twelve zwölf (E)

twentieth zwanzigste (3)

twenty zwanzig (E)

twice zweimal (7)

two zwei (E)

twosome: as a twosome zu zweit (10)

U

ugly hässlich (2)

umbrella der Regenschirm (-e) (7)

uncle der Onkel (-) (3)

under unter (+ acc./dat.) (6); **Under what name?** Auf welchen Namen? (9)

to understand verstehen, verstand, verstanden; **I don't understand.** Ich verstehe das nicht. (E)

to undertake unternehmen (unternimmt), unternahm, unternommen (1)

undressed: to get undressed sich ausziehen (zieht aus), zog aus, ausgezogen (8)

unemployment die Arbeitslosigkeit (14)

unfortunately leider (3)

unfriendly unfreundlich (1)

unfurnished unmöbliert (2)

university die Universität (-en) (1); **university instructor** der Hochschullehrer (-) / die Hochschullehrerin (-nen) (1); **university lecture** die Vorlesung (-en) (4)

unlikable unsympathisch (1)

until bis (um) (+ acc.) (6); **until five o'clock** bis (um) fünf Uhr (6)

upstairs oben; (directional) nach oben (12)

urgent(ly) dringend (2)

us uns (acc.) (3); **(to/for) us** uns (dat.) (5)

to use verwenden (14)

used to (do, be, etc.) früher (7)

useful nützlich (12)

usual(ly) gewöhnlich (4)

utilities die Nebenkosten (pl.) (12)

V

vacation: to go on vacation Urlaub machen (8)

vacuum cleaner der Staubsauger (-) (12)

Valentine's Day der Valentinstag (3)

varied abwechslungsreich (11)

VCR der Videorecorder (-) (2)

vegetable das Gemüse (5); **fruit and vegetable stand** der Obst- und Gemüsestand (¨-e) (5)

vegetarian vegetarisch (6)

vehicle das Verkehrsmittel (-) (14)

very ganz (1); sehr (1); **thank you very much** danke schön (E); **very well** sehr gut (E)

vicinity die Nähe (9); die Umgebung (-en) (12)

video(tape) das Video (-s) (2); **video recorder** der Videorecorder (-) (2)

violation die Verletzung (-en) (14)

violence die Gewalttätigkeit (14)

to visit besuchen (1)

vote: to take a vote abstimmen (stimmt ab) (14)

to vote wählen (14)

W

to wait warten (6)

waiter der Kellner (-) (6); der Ober (-) (6)

waitress die Kellnerin (-nen) (6)

to wake up aufwachen (wacht auf) (4)

to walk zu Fuß gehen, ging, ist gegangen (8); **to go for a walk** spazieren gehen (geht spazieren), ging spazieren, ist spazieren gegangen (4); **to walk along** entlanggehen (geht entlang), ging entlang, ist entlanggegangen (9)

wall die Wand (¨-e) (2)

wall-to-wall carpeting der Teppichboden (¨-) (12)

to want to wollen (will), wollte, gewollt (4)

war der Krieg (-e) (14)

wardrobe die Garderobe (-n) (12)

warm warm (wärmer, wärmst-) (7)

warming die Erwärmung (14)

to wash (oneself) sich waschen (wäscht), wusch, gewaschen (8)

washing machine die Waschmaschine (-n) (12)

waste der Abfall (¨-e) (14)

to watch something sich (dat.) etwas anschauen (schaut an) (13); sich (dat.) etwas ansehen (sieht an), sah an, angesehen; **to watch television** fernsehen (sieht fern), sah fern, ferngesehen (4); **watching television** das Fernsehen (4)

water das Wasser (5); **mineral water** der Sprudel (6)

way der Weg (-e) (9); **by the way** übrigens (9); **What's the best way to get there?** Wie komme ich am besten dahin? (9)

we wir (1)

weak schlapp (8)

to wear tragen (trägt), trug, getragen (5)

weather das Wetter (7); **weather report** der Wetterbericht (-e) (7)

website die Website (-s) (11)

wedding die Hochzeit (-en) (3)

Wednesday (der) Mittwoch (3); **Wednesdays, on Wednesday(s)** mittwochs (4)

week die Woche (-n) (4); **day of the week** der Wochentag (-e) (3); **once a week** einmal die Woche (7); **per week** pro Woche (4)

weekend das Wochenende (-n) (4)

weight training: to do weight training Bodybuilding machen (7)

welcome herzlich willkommen (E); **you're welcome** bitte (E)

well gut (1); (healthy) gesund (8); **Are you doing well?** Geht's gut? (E); **to feel well** sich wohl fühlen (8); **to get well** sich erholen (8) **Get well soon!** Gute Besserung! (8); **He dances well.** Er tanzt gut. (1); **not particularly well** nicht besonders gut (E); **very well** sehr gut (E)

were: if I were you an deiner Stelle (12)

what was (1); **At what time?** Um wie viel Uhr? (4); **So what?** Na und? (13); **Under what name?** Auf welchen Namen? (9); **What a shame! What bad luck!** So ein Pech! (8); **What did you say?** Wie bitte? (E); **What do you do for a living?** Was sind Sie von Beruf? (1); **What do you think of . . . ?** Wie findest du . . . ? (1); **What does . . . mean?** Was bedeutet . . . ? (E); **What is . . . ?** Wie ist . . . ? (E); **What is the name of . . . ?** Wie heißt . . . ? (E); **What is today's/tomorrow's date?** Welches Datum ist heute/morgen? (3); **what kind of (a)** was für (ein) (11); **What's it about?** Wovon handelt es? (13); **What's the best way to get there?** Wie komme ich am besten dahin? (9); **What's the matter?** Was ist denn los? (2); Was fehlt Ihnen/dir? (8); **What's your name?** Wie heißen Sie? (form.) / Wie heißt du? (inform.) (E); Wie ist Ihr Name? (form.) / Wie ist dein Name? (E); **What time is it?** Wie spät ist es? / Wie viel Uhr ist es? (4); **What will you have?** Was bekommen Sie? (6)

when (adv.) wann (1); (subord. conj.) wenn (8); (subord. conj.) als (10); **When is your birthday?** Wann hast du Geburtstag? (3)

where wo (1); **(to) where** wohin (5); **from where** woher (1); **Where are you from?** Woher kommen Sie? (form.) / Woher kommst du? (inform.) (E)

whether (subord. conj.) ob (8)

which welcher, welche, welches (2)

while (subord. conj.) während (9)

whipped cream die Sahne (6)

white weiß (5); **white sausage** die Weißwurst (¨-e) (6)

who wer (1)

whom wen (*acc.*); **(to/for) whom** wem (*dat.*) (5)

why warum (2)

wife die Frau (-en) (3)

wind der Wind (-e) (7); **wind power generator** das Windrad (¨er) (14)

window das Fenster (-) (2); **ticket window** der Fahrkartenschalter (-) (10)

windy windig (7)

wine der Wein (-e) (6)

winter der Winter (-) (7)

wish: best wishes viele Grüße (12)

to wish wünschen (3)

with mit (+ *dat.*) (5); bei (+ *dat.*) (5)

within innerhalb (+ *gen.*) (9)

without ohne (+ *acc.*) (3); **to do without** verzichten auf (+ *acc.*) (12)

woman die Frau (-en) (E)

work die Arbeit (-en) (8)

to work arbeiten (1); (*at a temporary job*) jobben (12); (*function*) funktionieren (9)

workplace der Arbeitsplatz (¨e) (11)

workroom das Arbeitszimmer (-) (2)

world die Welt (14)

worn out schlapp (8)

to worry about sich Sorgen machen um (+ *acc.*) (14)

would: would like to möchte (4); **would like to (do) most** möchte am liebsten (4); **would rather** möchte lieber (4); **Would you please . . . ?** Würden Sie bitte ... ? (9)

wrapping die Verpackung (-en) (14)

to write schreiben, schrieb, geschrieben (2); **How do you write . . . ?** Wie schreibt man ... ? (E)

X

xenophobia die Ausländerfeindlichkeit (14)

Y

yard der Garten (¨) (2)

year das Jahr (-e) (1); **for two years** seit zwei Jahren (6); **next year** nächstes Jahr (1); **once a year** einmal im Jahr (7)

yellow gelb (5)

yes ja (E)

yesterday gestern (7)

yet noch (2)

yogurt der Joghurt (5)

you du (*inform. sg.*), ihr (*inform. pl.*), Sie (*form. sg./pl.*) (1); dich (*inform. sg. acc.*), euch (*inform. pl. acc.*), Sie (*form. sg./pl. acc.*) (3); dir (*inform. sg. dat.*), euch (*inform. pl. dat.*), Ihnen (*form. sg./pl. dat.*) (5); (*indef. pron.*) man (4); **You may not park here.** Hier darf man nicht parken. (4); **you're welcome** bitte (E)

young jung (jünger, jüngst-) (10)

your dein (*inform. sg.*), euer (*inform. pl.*), Ihr (*form. sg./pl.*) (3)

youth hostel die Jugendherberge (-n) (9)

Z

zero null (E)

zone: pedestrian zone die Fußgängerzone (-n) (9)

zoo der Tierpark (-s) (9)

Index

The index is followed by a list of major topics. **Kulturtipp** categories are listed under the heading **Culture;** vocabulary items are grouped by category under **Vocabulary;** reading titles are listed under **Readings;** and Video subjects are listed under **Videoclips.** References to reading strategies are listed in the index under *reading strategies.*

Note: KT = **Kulturtipp;** *ST =* **Sprachtipp.**

A

aber vs. **sondern,** 216
academic subjects, 29
accusative case
    of definite articles, 57 *ST,* 65 (*chart*)
    of demonstrative pronouns, 74
    of der-words, 67 (*chart*)
    direct object in, 67
    es gibt with, 148 *ST*
    of indefinite articles, 68 (*chart*)
    of interrogative pronouns, 69
    of negative article **kein,** 68 (*chart*)
    of nouns, 64–65
    of personal pronouns, 98 (*chart*)
    of possessive adjectives, 100–101,
        186–187
    prepositions requiring, 97, 186–187, 194
    of reflexive pronouns, 249–250
    of relative pronouns, 336
    of weak masculine nouns, 65
    word order of, 64, 161
active voice, 417
address, forms of, 5–6
    du vs. **Sie,** 3 *KT*
    Herr, Frau, 3
addresses, 10–11
adjectival nouns, 306–307 (*chart*)
adjective endings, 55 *ST,* 274, 306–307.
        See also attributive adjectives
adjectives
    ending in **–a,** 280 *ST*
    attributive, 274, 275 *ST,* 303–304, 305
    comparative form, 225–226, 303–306
    after definite article, 275 (*chart*)
    demonstrative, 165
    after indefinite article, 278 (*chart*)
    possessive, 93–94 (*charts*), 271
    possessive, with dative case, 157
    without preceding article, 279 (*chart*)
    present participles used as, 424–425
    referring to city names, 282
    superlative form, 305
    three forms of, 225
    used as nouns, 306–307
adverbs
    comparative form, 225–226
    dahin, 362
    gern, 59 *ST,* 226
    immer, with comparative, 226
    nämlich, 92 *ST*
    nicht, 341

present participles used as,
        424–425
    superlative form, 301–302
    of time, 119 *ST*
agent
    in passive sentences, 419
    passive without (using **es**), 421
alle, 165
alphabet, German, 4–5
als
    with comparative form, 226
    as subordinating conjunction, 311
alternatives to passive
    with impersonal **es,** 421
    with **man,** 424
an-, 223
antecedent
    personal pronouns agreeing with, 34
    relative pronouns referring to, 336
arbeiten vs. **lernen/studieren,** 27 *ST*
articles. *See* definite articles;
        indefinite articles; **kein**
attributive adjectives
    city names used as, 282
    comparative form, 303–304
    endings of, 55 *ST,* 274
    present participles used as, 424–425
    superlative form, 305
aus, 164
auxiliary verbs, 217, 221, A16 (*chart*). *See*
        also **haben;** modal auxiliary verbs;
        sein; werden

B

be-, 223
bei, 146 *ST,* 164
besser, 226
Beuys, Joseph, 204
bitte, used with imperative, 134
brauchen, with dependent infinitive plus
        zu, 395
Brecht, Bertolt, 231
Bremer, Claus, 205

C

capitalization, A20
    of adjectival nouns, 306
    of adjectives referring to cities and
        regions, 282
    of nouns, 32
    of pronouns, 34
    of **Sie,** 3, 34

cardinal numbers, 91 *ST*
case. *See* accusative case; dative case;
        genitive case; nominative case
Celsius scale, 215
city names, attributive adjectives
        referring to, 282
clauses
    dependent clauses, 244
    infinitive clauses, 395
    main clauses, 244
    relative clauses, 335–336
clock, 114, 115 *ST,* 116 *ST,* 118, 119 *ST*
cognates, 14
commands. *See* imperative
comparative form, 225–226. *See also*
        superlative form
compound nouns, 33
compounds
    da-, 362
    noun, 33
    wo-, 166, 364
conjugation, verb, A16–A19 (*chart*)
conjunctions
    coordinating, 216
    subordinating, 244 (*chart*)
contractions of prepositions and
        articles, 165
contrary-to-fact conditions, 370. *See also*
        subjunctive mood
conversational phrases, standard, 13, 14,
        26, 27 *ST*
coordinating conjunctions, 216
counting, 8–9
country abbreviations, 11

D

da-compounds, 362
daher, 362
dahin, 362
dann, 154 *ST*
dates, 88 *ST*
dative case, 157–166
    adjectives with, 151 *ST*
    contractions of prepositions in, 165
    of definite and indefinite articles,
        160 (*chart*), A13 (*chart*)
    of der-words, 160 (*chart*)
    and indirect objects, 160–161
    of nouns, 157–158
    of personal pronouns, 158 (*chart*)
    of possessive adjectives, 160 (*chart*)

Credits

Photos Page 1 © Ulrike Welsch; 2 (top) © JOKER/Ausserhofer/ullstein bild/The Granger Collection, New York; 2 (bottom) © Paul Vozdic/Getty Images; 3 © Ulrike Welsch; 20 © Grabowsky/ullstein bild/The Granger Collection, New York; 21 © Yavuz Arslan/Peter Arnold, Inc.; 22 (top left) © Kevin Galvin; 22 (right) © Ulrike Welsch; 22 (bottom left) © Owen Franken/Stock Boston; 30 © Beryl Goldberg; 50 © Ullstein bild/The Granger Collection, New York; 60 (left) © Photofusion Picture Library/Alamy; 60 (right) © Robert Harding Picture Library Ltd/Alamy; 66 © Benja Weller/Das Fotoarchiv; 82 © Sylent Press/ullstein bild/The Granger Collection, New York; 83 (camera) © Bartomeu Amengual/Age Fotostock; 83 (inset) © Wolfgang Kaehler; 87 © Koelb Stern; 90 (top) © Schmied-HELGA LADE FOTOAGENTUR/Peter Arnold, Inc.; 90 (bottom) © BAV-HELGA LADE FOTOAGENTUR/Peter Arnold, Inc.; 91 © McGraw-Hill, Inc; 103 © Archive Fur Kunst und Geschichte, Berlin; 106 © Monica Clyde; 107 © Wodicka/ullstein bild/The Granger Collection, New York; 101 (all) © Archive Fur Kunst und Geschichte, Berlin; 111 (top) © Bilderdienst Suddeutscher Verlag, Munchen; 111 (bottom) © Archive Fur Kunst und Geschichte, Berlin;112 © Peter Hirth/Peter Arnold, Inc.; 121 (left) © Zefa/Damm/Corbis; 121 (right) © Visum/ullstein bild/The Granger Collection, New York; 135 © Monica Clyde; 139 © Eckel/ullstein bild/The Granger Collection, New York; 144, 154, 167 Courtesy of Monica Clyde; 174 © oterhauser/CARO/ullstein bild/The Granger Collection, New York; 177 (top left) © Mahns Techau/ullstein bild/The Granger Collection , New York; 177 (top right) © Fishman/ullstein bild/The Granger Collection, New York; 177 (bottom left) © Ilona Studre/ullstein bild/The Granger Collection, New York; 177 (bottom right) © Lengemann/ullstein bild/The Granger Collection, New York; 179 © Chybiak/ullstein bild/The Granger Collection, New York; 182 (left) © Brinckmann/ullstein bild/The Granger Collection, New York; 182 (middle) © Kujath/ullstein bild/The Granger Collection, New York; 182 (right) © Springer-Pics/ullstein bild/The Granger Collection, New York; 191 Courtesy of Monica Clyde; 204 (top left) © 1995 Artists Rights Society, NY/Bild Kunst, Bonn © AKG London; 204 (middle) © 1995 Artists Rights Society, NY/Bild Kunst, Bonn; 204 (bottom left) © 1995 Artists Rights Society, NY/Bild Kunst, Bonn © AKG London; 205 "Der Leser" by Jiri Georg Dokoupil. Reproduced with permission. 206 © Ric Ergenbright; 212 (top left) © Julie Marcotte/Stock Boston; 212 (top right) © Reichmann; 212 (bottom left) © Fridmar Damn/eStock; 212 (bottom right) © David Ulmer/Stock Boston; 218 © Ulrike Welsch/PhotoEdit; 222 © CARO/Riedmiller/ ullstein bild/The Granger Collection, New York; 231 © Topham/The Image Works; 234 © Oberhäuser/CARO/ullstein bild/The Granger Collection, New York; 236 (top) © Michael P. Gadomski/Photo Researchers; 236 (middle) © Teich/Caroullstein bild/The Granger Collection, New York; 236 (bottom) © Photodisc; 240 © Wodicka/ullstein bild/The Granger Collection, New York; 246 © Ulrike Welsch; 254 © MEDIUM / ullstein bild / The Granger Collection, New York; 260 © Bob Krist/CORBIS; 264 © Keith/ullstein bild/The Granger Collection, New York; 270 (left) Lutherstadt Wittenberg; 270 (right) © Lange/ullstein bild/The Granger Collection, New York; 276 © Monica Clyde; 281 © Shaun Egan/Getty; 282 © Jochen Kallhardt/BlueBox; 290 (both) © Helga Lade/Peter Arnold; 209 (bottom right) © Hartmann/ullstein bild/The Granger Collection, New York; 292 © Theissen/ullstein bild/The Granger Collection, New York; 296 © Werner Otto/AGE Fotostock; 298 © Thomas Rosenthal/ullstein bild/The Granger Collection, New York; 305 © Merlen/The Granger Collection, New York; 309 © Ulrike Welsch/PhotoEdit; 310 © Visum/The Image Works; 316 © Pixtal/age fotostock; 317 © Digital Vision; 322 © Visum/Plus 49/The Image Works; 331 © David Young-Wolff/PhotoEdit, Inc.; 332 © Helga Lade/Peter Arnold; 344 © Scherf/ullstein bild/The Granger Collection, New York; 345 (top) © KPA Honorar & Belege/ullstein bild/The Granger Collection, New York; 345 (bottom) © Stephane Masson/Corbis; 346 © KPA Honorar & Belege/ullstein bild/The Granger Collection, New York; 350 © Visum/Plus 49/The Image Works; 352 (bottom) © Jüschke/ullstein bild/The Granger Collection, New York; 368 © Neuhauser/ullstein bild/The Granger Collection, New York; 382 © CARO Fotoagentur/A. Bastian; 383 (left) © Wodicka/ullstein bild/The Granger Collection, New York; 383 (right) © Joko/ullstein bild/The Granger Collection , New York; 394 © Wodicka/ullstein bild/The Granger Collection, New York; 400 © KPA/ullstein bild/The Granger Collection, New York; 404 © Froese/ullstein bild/The Granger Collection, New York; 408 © Helga Lade/Peter Arnold, Inc.; 411 © Royalty Free/Corbis; 415 (bottom) © David Frazier/The Image Works; 416 (left) © BananaStock/Alamy; 432 © Paul Thompson/ImageState/Heritage Image Partnership; 433 (left) © Topham/The Image Works; 433 (right) © UPI/Bettmann Archive; 434 (top) © Keystone Press/The Image Works; 434 (bottom) © Bettmann Archive; 435 © Dallas and John Heaton/Stock Boston; 436 (top left) © ReutersNewmedia Inc./CORBIS; 436 (top right) © UPI Bettmann Archive; 436 (bottom right) © Topham/The Image Works; 437 © Michael Schwarz/The Image Works; 438 (top) © Rufus F. Folkks/Corbis; 438 (bottom): © Walter Bibikow/AGE; 443 © Kaiser/Caro/ullstein bild/The Granger Collection, New York.

Realia Page 5 (bottom right) © Eva Heller, from *Vielleicht sind wir eben zu verschieden;* 6 (elephant cartoon) Michel & Co.; 8 (top left) *Funk Uhr;* 9 © *Berliner Morgenpost;* 10 Gebecke Buchandlung & Antiquariat, Quedlinburg; 11 Volkswagen AG; 37 (top left) Courtesy of Universität Leipzig, Uni-Journal 4/25, photo Randy Kühn; (top right) Photo: PR;

(bottom right) Volksbanken Raiffeisenbanken; *39* Henniger/Saxacon Verlag; *40, 41* From *Huhnstage von Peter Gaymann,* © Fakelträger Verlag 1984; *42* Courtesy of Leipzig Tourist Service e.V./Grafik: Simons & Schreiber WA GmbH; *52 Pro Fertighaus,* Fachschriften-Verlag GmbH & Co. KG; *59* © Goldmann Verlag; *68* Reprinted with permission of Werner Buchi/*Brückenbauer;* *72* Reprinted with permission of Wolfgang Horsch; *87* Courtesy of DSM-Heerlen; *93 Känguru: Stadtmagazin für Familien in Köln;* *100* Reprinted with permission of Deutsche Welthungerhilfe; *115 P.M./*Hurzlmeier; *120* Reprinted with permission of Langenscheidt-Verlag, Berlin and Munich; *123* (top left) ICC Berlin; (middle left & middle right) Reprinted with permission of Thilo Beu; *128* © Droemer Knauer Verlag, Munich; *129* Reprinted with permission of Christine Sielung, Düsseldorf; *130* Beate Heinen, Kunstverlag, D 56653 Maria Laach, Nr. 2705; *148* (bottom left) Strauss Innovation GmbH, www.strauss-innovation.de; (bottom right) Heinrich Deichmann Schuhe GmbH, http:shop.deichmann.com; *165* (top right) Courtesy of Der Tagesspiegel, Berlin; *176* Side Café Bistro Restaurant, Haupstr., Altenmarkt d. a. Alz; Gausthaus Zum Ocksen," Marbach; *178* Deutsche Telekom; *180* Adapted from die Knolle, Bad Oeynhausen and Minden. © 2006 by www.pagewerbung.de, Bad Oeynhausen, Germany; *195* Detlef Kersten/Cartoon-Caricature-Contor, Munich; *205* (lower left) "Der Leser" by Georg Jiři Dokoupil; (upper right) Illustration by Claus Bremer from *Konkrete Poesie* (Ditzingen: Philipp Reclam Jun. Verlag, 1976); (middle right) Illustration: !Postkarte 1965! by Reinhard Döhl from *Konkrete Poesie* (Ditzingen: Philipp Reclam Jun. Verlag, 1976); *209* Jugendamt und Sport- und Bäderamt, Göttingen; *214* Courtesy of SPIEGEL ONLINE and Weathernews Deutschland GmbH; *219* Book cover: *Winnetou I* by Karl May. Courtesy of KARL-MAY-VERLAG; *222* Reprinted with permission of Fremdenverkehrsverein Altes Land e.V., D 21635 Jork; *245* Cartoon by René Fehr,"Brückenbauer," Zurich; *247* Courtesy of SOLVAY Arzneimittel GmbH; *248 Reinisch Post,* Düsseldorf; *249* (middle right) Cartoon used by permission of Wolfgang Horsch; (bottom) WURZEL by Alex Graham/Solo Syndication, London; *250* Reprinted with permission of Uli Stein; *261* Courtesy of Dresden—Werbung und Tourismus; *262* (top) Courtesy of A&O Hostel Friedrichschain GmbH; (botton) Hotel Bad-Ramasch Läufelfingen, Switzerland; *267* Stadtplan Wittenberg auf Lutherstadt Wittenberg: Weltgeschichte erleben; *293* (top right) Courtesy of sun + fun group, sun + fun sportfeisen GmbH, Munich; (middle left) Courtesy of Rucksack Reisen, http://www.rucksack-reisen.de; *305* ADAC Hessen-Thüringen, Schumannstrasse 4-6, Thüringen D 60325; *306* Courtesy of Vogelpark WAlsrode GmbH, Walsrode; *307* Wolfgang Hersch; *314* Courtesy of STERN; *315 Sports—Die Sportzeitschrift,* Jahr-Verlag GmbH; *325* WestLB; *326–327* From *Berufswahl—Trips, Trends, Tests,* Commerzbank, Frankfurt am Main; *329* Courtesy of TESTO AG; *332 Tatsachen über Deutschland* © Societäts-Verlag, Frankfurt; *334* Erich Rauschenbach, Cartoon-Caricature-Cartoon, Munich; *337* (top right) Handelsblatt GmbH, Düsseldorf; *353* Courtesy of Deutsches Studentenwerk, Berlin; *356 Pro Fertighaus,* Fachschriften-Verlag GmbH & Co. KG; *366* © Uli Stein 2006, www.miceandmoreusa.com; *371* © *Eva Heller. From Vielleicht sind wir eben zu verschieden;* *372* Reprinted with permission of Wolfgang Horsch; *373* © *Eva Heller. From Vielleicht sind wir eben zu verschieden;* *384, 385* © HÖRZU/ASV AG; *387* STERN/TV-Beilage v. 4.8.05 and Picture Press; *389* © HÖRZU/ASV AG; *393 Neue Zürcher Zeitung;* *396* © Du Pont de Nemours GmbH; *399* Detlev Kersten © Lappan Verlag; *409* UNRIC, United Nations Milennium Project; *413* (nos. 3, 6, 9, 12) Courtesy of GTZ Sektorvorhaben Aktionsprogramm 2015,www.ap20015.de; *414 Natur,* Ringier Verlag; *416* (middle and right) *Natur,* Ringier Verlag; Photos: Thomas Lomberg, Munich; *418* (left) Reprinted with permission of Greenpeace Germany; (middle) Courtesy of PETA, Germany www.PETA.de; *420* Index Funk/*Berliner Morgenpost;* *421* (top) © ALI Press Agency; *439, 441, 442* Herbert Hoover Collection, Memorabilia, Hoover Institution Archives.

Readings *46* "Dialog" by Nasrin Siege from *Text dagegen,* Silvia Bartholl (Hrsg.), 1993 Beltz Verlag, Weinheim und Basel Programm Beltz & Gelberg, Weinheim; *106* Excerpts from „Wie feierst du deinen großen Tag?" by Kristina Dörnenburg, *JUMA* 2/2004, www.juma.de; *139* Christine Wuttke, "Immer das gleiche" © Christine Wuttke; *169* Karl Valentin, "Im Hutladen" from *Gesammelte Werke in einem Band* © Piper Verlag GmbH, Munich, 1985; *199* Ekkhard Müller, "Die Sosse" © Gebühr; *231* Bertolt Brecht, "Vergnügungen" from *Gesammelte Werke* by Bertolt Brecht © Surhkamp Verlag, Frankfurt am Main, 1967; *255–256* Text: Monica Hillemacher, adapted from "Sage mir, was du isst . . ." UNICUM, APRIL 2005. Used by permission of Monika Hillemacher; Illustrations: © Sabine Kühn, www.sabinekuehn.de; *284* "Die Gitarre des Herrn Hatunoglu" by Heinrich Hannover from *Als der Clown die Grippe hatte.* Copyright © 1992 by Rowohlt Taschenbuch Verlag GmbH, Reinbek bei Hamburg; *316* From "The American Dream" by Bernd Maresch, *UNICUM* April 2006. Used courtesy of Bernd Maresch; *344* From *JUIMA* 4/2005, www.juma.de http://www.juma.de; *376* "Fahrkarte bitte" by Helga M. Novak from *Palisaden* © 1980 Luchterhand Literaturverlag; *404* Adapted excerpts from „Gute Freudeim Netz" by Kerstin Kohlenberg, *DIE ZEIT,* No. 41/2005; *426* Was in der Zeitung steht" by Reinhard Mai, *Alle meine Lieder,* Maikäfer Musik Verlagsgesellschaft, Berlin; *439* From *Wir leben im Verborgenen* by Ceja Stojka, reprinted with permission of Picus Verlag.

About the Authors

Robert Di Donato is Professor of German and Chair of the Department of German, Russian, and East Asian Languages with Hebrew and Arabic at Miami University in Oxford, Ohio. He received his Ph.D. from The Ohio State University. He is the chief academic and series developer of **Fokus Deutsch,** a telecourse with accompanying texts and materials for teaching and learning German, and coauthor of **The Big Yellow Book of German Verbs.** He has also edited two volumes for the Central States Conference, written articles about language methodology, and has given numerous keynote speeches, workshops, and presentations – both in the United States and abroad – on teaching methods and teacher education. He has won a number of awards for his work in language education, including the Florence Steiner Award for Leadership in Foreign Language Education.

Monica D. Clyde is a native of Düsseldorf. She received her Ph.D. in German literature from the University of California at Berkeley. She has taught German language and literature at Mills College, Cañada College, the Defense Language Institute, and the College of San Mateo. She was Director of Faculty Development and Scholarship at Saint Mary's College of California until her retirement in 2003. She coauthored **Texte und Kontexte** and was a contributor to **Mosaik: Deutsche Kultur und Literatur,** Third Edition, both intermediate college-level German textbooks.

Jacqueline Vansant received her Ph.D. from the University of Texas at Austin. She has taught at Hamilton College and Miami University in Oxford, Ohio, and currently teaches at the University of Michigan-Dearborn, where she also heads the German section of the Department of Humanities. Her particular interest in language pedagogy lies in reading and reading strategies. She has written widely on contemporary Austrian literature and culture, served as coeditor of *Modern Austrian Literature* from 2000–05, and is presently working on a book entitled *Austria: Made in Hollywood.*

Listening Comprehension Scripts

Einführung

Hallo! Guten Tag! Herzlich willkommen!

(See textbook pages 2–3.)

Aktivität 9 Wie geht's?

Dialog 1
URSEL: 'n Abend, Thomas.
THOMAS: 'n Abend, Ursel.
URSEL: Na, wie geht's?
THOMAS: Ach, nicht besonders gut. Und dir?
URSEL: Danke, gut.

Dialog 2
FRAU ENGELHARDT: Grüß Gott, Herr Kümmerli.
HERR KÜMMERLI: Grüß Gott, Frau Engelhardt.
FRAU ENGELHARDT: Wie geht es Ihnen?
HERR KÜMMERLI: Danke, gut. Und wie geht es Ihnen?
FRAU ENGELHARDT: Danke, auch gut.
HERR KÜMMERLI: Na, dann, auf Wiedersehen.
FRAU ENGELHARDT: Auf Wiedersehen, Herr Kümmerli.

Dialog 3
NINA: Grüß dich, Dieter.
DIETER: Nina. Wie geht's?
NINA: Ach, es geht nicht besonders gut und nicht besonders schlecht. Und dir?
DIETER: Ausgezeichnet.
NINA: Na, dann mach's gut!
DIETER: Tschüss.

Aktivität 11 Wichtige Telefonnummern

Polizei	1 10
Kinoprogramme	1 15 11
Küchenrezepte	11 67
Sportnachrichten	11 63
Konzerte	1 15 17
Feuerwehr/Rettungsleitstelle	1 12
Wetter	38 53
Zahlenlotto	11 62
Zeit	19 94

Aktivität 12 Die Adresse und Telefonnummer, bitte!

1. A: Wie ist die Adresse von Professor Hauser, bitte?
   B: Moment mal. Gartenstraße 19.
   A: Und die Postleitzahl?
   B: 82067 Ebenhausen/Isartal.
   A: Und wie ist die Telefonnummer?
   B: 41 34 76.
   A: Vielen Dank.
   B: Bitte schön.
2. A: Bitte schön, die Adresse von Margas Fitnessstudio?
   B: Bautzner Straße 15.

A: Wissen Sie übrigens die Postleitzahl?
B: Jawohl. 01093 Dresden.
A: Und die Telefonnummer?
B: Die Telefonnummer ist 20 86 73.
A: Danke sehr. Wiederhören!
B: Wiederhören!
3. A: Könnten Sie mir bitte die Adresse von Autohaus Becker sagen?
   B: Freilich. Das wäre Landstuhler Straße 54.
   A: Haben Sie die Postleitzahl?
   B: Ja. Die ist 66482 Zweibrücken-Ixheim.
   A: Und die Telefonnummer?
   B: 1 88 42.
   A: Vielen Dank. Wiederhören!
   B: Wiederhören!

Aktivität 16 Sie verstehen schon etwas Deutsch!

1. Der neue Renault Clio: Komfort, Sicherheit und Technik. Das europäische Auto des Jahres.
2. Im Neuen Theater Hamburg spielt heute Abend um 20.00 Uhr „Das Phantom der Oper" von Andrew Lloyd Webber.
3. Turin, Italien, Olympische Spiele. Die Deutschen gewinnen 11 Goldmedaillen.
4. Café-Restaurant Schönberger sucht einen Koch oder eine Köchin mit klassischer Ausbildung.
5. Bei Kinderfreude haben wir Freude an Kindern. Unsere Kinderkrippe ist kinderfreundlich, sauber, modern und sicher.

Kapitel 1

Alles klar?

B. 1. Grüß Gott. Mein Name ist Nikolaus Euba. Ich bin Student und komme aus München.
   2. Guten Tag. Mein Name ist Marco Berger. Ich bin Journalist und komme aus Köln.
   3. Guten Tag. Ich heiße Andrea Rubik. Ich bin Sportlehrerin. Ich komme aus Wien.
   4. Mein Name ist Marion Hintze. Ich bin Architektin und komme aus Leipzig.
   5. Guten Tag. Ich heiße Zafir Brückner. Ich bin Physiker und komme aus Zürich.

Wörter im Kontext

Aktivität 1 Interessante Personen

1. a. Haralds Nachname ist Lohmann.
   b. Er ist Journalist.
   c. Er kommt aus Deutschland.
   d. Er wohnt in Regensburg.
   e. Seine Adresse ist Bahnhofstraße 20.
   f. Er ist 1,82 groß.

2. **a.** Die Frau heißt Daniela Lercher.
   b. Sie wohnt in Salzburg.
   c. Sie kommt aus Österreich.
   d. Sie ist Studentin.
   e. Sie ist 1,75 groß.
3. **a.** Herr Rütli ist Architekt von Beruf.
   b. Er heißt Anton mit Vornamen.
   c. Er kommt aus Luzern in der Schweiz.
   d. Seine Adresse ist Kirchplatz 76.
   e. Er ist 1,74 groß.

BEAMTER: Ihr Name, bitte?
JULIE: Julie Harrison.
BEAMTER: Buchstabieren Sie das bitte.
JULIE: Vorname: J-u-l-i-e Nachname: H-a-r-r-i-s-o-n
BEAMTER: Beruf?
JULIE: Studentin.
BEAMTER: Und woher kommen Sie?
JULIE: Aus den USA, Cincinnati.
BEAMTER: Ihr Pass, bitte.
JULIE: Hier, bitte.
BEAMTER: Ihre Adresse hier in Berlin?
JULIE: Brandenburger Straße 37.
BEAMTER: Geburtstag?
JULIE: Vierter April 1987.
BEAMTER: Danke, jetzt brauche ich nur noch Ihre Unterschrift.

(See textbook page 25.)

(See textbook page 26.)

1. A: Wie heißt du?
   B: Ich heiße Dieter.
2. A: Woher kommen Sie?
   B: Ich studiere hier.
3. A: Was machen Sie hier?
   B: Wir besuchen Freunde.
4. A: Wie heißen Sie?
   B: Mein Name ist Lentz.
5. A: Hallo. Grüß dich, Helmut!
   B: Auf Wiedersehen.
6. A: Woher kommst du?
   B: Aus Berlin.
7. A: Wie finden Sie Berlin?
   B: Ich komme aus den USA.
8. A: Wo ist denn das?
   B: Das ist in den USA.
9. A: Auf Wiedersehen, Frau Keller.
   B: Guten Tag!
10. A: Was studieren Sie?
    B: Englisch.

Grammatik im Kontext

Übung 1 Was hören Sie?

1. Wie bitte, wie ist der Name?
2. Die Frau kommt aus Amerika.
3. Wie heißt das Land?
4. Wie ist die Adresse von McDonald's?
5. Woher kommt der Student?
6. Die Studentin lernt Deutsch in Erfurt.
7. Was macht das Mädchen in Berlin?
8. Wo wohnt der Professor?

Schritt 1. Karin Renner kommt ursprünglich aus Dresden. Familie Renner wohnt immer noch da. Jetzt wohnt Karin aber in Göttingen. Sie studiert da nämlich Informatik. Sie ist sehr gut in Mathematik. Karin wohnt in einem Studentenwohnheim am Rosenbachweg. Das Wohnheim ist sehr groß und modern, aber auch unpersönlich. Karin arbeitet viel für ihre Kurse.

Sie ist auch sportlich sehr aktiv. Sie geht regelmäßig schwimmen. Sie geht auch oft ins Café. Sie findet das Café Kadenz besonders nett. Sie trifft da oft ein paar Freunde, und dann diskutieren sie über ihre Kurse, die Arbeit, die Politik und natürlich die Professoren.

Kapitel 2

Alles klar?

B. 1. INGRID: Was suchst du in der Zeitung?
   KIRSTEN: Eine Wohnung. Ich brauche eine Dreizimmerwohnung.
   INGRID: Warum so groß?
   KIRSTEN: Für mich und Angelika.
2. GERD: Suchst du eine neue Wohnung?
   JOCHEN: Ja. Die alte ist zu klein. Ich suche eine Zweizimmerwohnung mit Küche und Bad.
3. GABI: Suchst du im Moment ein Zimmer?
   ANJA: Ja. Bei einer Familie.
   GABI: Ein Appartement ist besser. Es ist privater.

Wörter im Kontext

(See textbook page 52.)

1. Fotodesignerin, 22, sucht preiswertes Zimmer in junger Wohngemeinschaft, zum ersten Juli.
2. Freundlicher Schauspieler aus Hamburg sucht Zimmer in Wohngemeinschaft vom ersten Mai bis ersten August in München.
3. Architekturstudentin, 25, sucht zum ersten oder fünfzehnten Mai ruhiges Zimmer bis 200 Euro inklusive, in Wohngemeinschaft.

4. Freundlicher, junger 37-jähriger Englischlehrer sucht ein Zimmer in Wohngemeinschaft, um mit euch Deutsch zu sprechen und es besser zu lernen.
5. Musiker, 24, sucht Zimmer oder Raum in Wohngemeinschaft zum ersten Juni oder etwas früher. Zahle bis 250 Euro inklusive.

Aktivität 5   Ulla hat jetzt endlich ein Zimmer.

KARIN: Tag, Ulla. Wie geht's dir denn?

ULLA: Tag, Karin. Es geht mir prima. Ich habe jetzt endlich ein Zimmer.

KARIN: Wo denn?

ULLA: Schillerstraße 13.

KARIN: Toll, zentral gelegen. Ist das Zimmer möbliert?

ULLA: Ja. Es hat ein Bett, einen Schreibtisch, einen Stuhl, einen Tisch und einen Sessel. Ich brauche nur noch eine Lampe für den Schreibtisch und ein Bücherregal.

KARIN: Wie hoch ist die Miete?

ULLA: Nur 125 Euro.

KARIN: Hast du Telefon?

ULLA: Nein, noch nicht.

Aktivität 7   Ein Gespräch im Kaufhaus

VERKÄUFER: Bitte sehr?

ULLA: Ich suche eine Lampe für meinen Schreibtisch.

VERKÄUFER: Hier haben wir Lampen.

ULLA: Was kostet die Lampe hier?

VERKÄUFER: 200 Euro. Die ist aus Italien.

ULLA: Die ist sehr schön, aber zu teuer.

VERKÄUFER: Hier ist eine Lampe für 25 Euro, sehr preiswert und modern. Ein Sonderangebot.

ULLA: Gut, die nehme ich. Und wo finde ich hier Bücherregale?

VERKÄUFER: Tut mir leid. Wir führen keine Bücherregale.

Grammatik im Kontext

Übung 7   Neu in Göttingen

STEFAN: Hallo, Birgit. Komm bitte rein.

BIRGIT: Tag Stefan. Also das ist deine neue Wohnung. Du hast wirklich Glück. Ich suche nämlich immer noch eine Wohnung.

STEFAN: Komm, ich zeige dir die Wohnung erst mal. Hier ist das Wohnzimmer mit Kochnische. Und hier ist das Bad.

BIRGIT: Na, das Zimmer ist ja ein bisschen klein. Wo schläfst du denn?

STEFAN: Ich brauche noch ein paar Möbel, ein Bett zum Beispiel. Im Moment schlafe ich auf dem Boden im Schlafsack.

BIRGIT: Kauf doch so ein japanisches Futon-Bett. Das ist ganz praktisch. Tagsüber ist es eine Couch, und dann kannst du es ausziehen, und es ist ein Bett.

STEFAN: Gute Idee. Bitte, setz dich doch. Leider habe ich nur einen Stuhl im Moment.

BIRGIT: Nein, danke, ich sitze gern auf dem Boden.

STEFAN: Morgen kaufe ich einen Schreibtisch und ein Bücherregal. Möchtest du einen Kaffee?

BIRGIT: Gern. Komm, ich helfe.

STEFAN: Ach, da fällt mir gerade ein: Ich habe Kaffee, aber ich brauche noch eine Kaffeemaschine. Gehen wir doch ins Café. Kennst du das Café Kadenz? Das ist mein Lieblingscafé.

BIRGIT: Na, gut.

Übung 12   Immer diese Ausreden!

1. KALLE: Grüß dich, Reinhard! Heute Abend spielt ein toller Film im Kino. Kommst du mit?

   REINHARD: Tut mir leid, es geht wirklich nicht. Ich habe nur noch einen Euro.

2. ALEXANDRA: Morgen gehen wir in die Disko. Kommst du mit, Erika?

   ERIKA: In die Disko? Wer geht denn sonst noch mit?

   ALEXANDRA: Nur Peter und ich. Helmut kommt doch sicher mit, nicht?

   ERIKA: Helmut ist nicht da. Und allein habe ich keine Lust.

3. FRAU WEISS: Frau Becker, haben Sie jetzt Zeit für eine Tasse Kaffee?

   FRAU BECKER: Tut mir wirklich leid, aber ich trinke keinen Kaffee. Kaffee trinken macht mich zu nervös.

4. FRANK: Hallo, Jens! Servus, Ulla! Kommt ihr heute Abend zur Party? Wir haben Pizza und Bier.

   JENS: Hmmm, wir möchten gerne, aber wir müssen leider morgen unsere Examen schreiben. Ich habe noch viel Arbeit und brauche die Zeit heute Abend zum Lernen.

5. LYDIA: Peter, hast du Lust, mit ins Museum zu gehen?

   PETER: Ins Museum? Heute? Ach, ich bin kein Museumsfan. Ins Museum gehen macht mir überhaupt keinen Spaß. Ich bin eher Fußballfan.

Kapitel 3

Alles klar?

B. Hallo, ich bin Alexandra Thalhofer aus Köln. Auf dem Foto seht ihr meine Familie vor dem Standesamt in Köln. Mein Bruder Bernd hat geheiratet. Bernd und seine Frau, Bettina, sind beide Lehrer an einem Gymnasium. Bernd unterrichtet Mathematik und Physik und Bettina ist Deutschlehrerin. Die beiden reisen gern und machen ihre Hochzeitsreise nach Kanada.

Ich habe noch einen Bruder, Werner. Er steht ganz rechts auf dem Bild. Er ist vierzig Jahre alt, ist verheiratet und hat zwei Kinder, einen Jungen und ein Mädchen. Seine Frau, Antje, ist nicht auf dem Bild. Meine Mutter steht vorne neben Bernd.

Wörter im Kontext

Aktivität 7   Eine Einladung zum Geburtstag

TOM: Tom McKay.

HEIKE: Hallo, Tom? Hier ist Heike.

TOM: Tag, Heike.

HEIKE: Du, Tom, ich mache eine kleine Party zu Hause. Ich habe nämlich Geburtstag. Ich möchte dich einladen.

TOM: Vielen Dank für die Einladung. Ich komme gern. Wann ist die Party denn?

HEIKE: Am Samstag.

TOM: Schön. Wer kommt sonst noch?

HEIKE: Du kennst doch die Gabi? Die kommt auch. Und vielleicht Jürgen. Sonst sind nur meine Eltern und Geschwister da.

TOM: Also gut, bis Samstag dann.

HEIKE: Mach's gut. Tschüss.

Grammatik im Kontext

Übung ... Herzlich ...

Guten Morgen, liebe Hörerinnen und Hörer. Willkommen zu unserem Programm: Von Haus zu Haus. Unsere Hörer senden Glückwünsche zum Geburtstag. Außerdem ist heute ein ganz besonderer Tag: Valentinstag.

1. Unsere liebe Mutter. Frau Sibille Heinemann aus Krefeld. ist heute achtzig. Herzlichen Glückwunsch senden dir deine Kinder.
2. Unser Opa, der beste Opa der Welt, wird heute sechzig. Es gratulieren deine Enkel Kai, Inge, Uwe, Sandra und Claudia aus Würzburg.
3. Hallo, Uwe! Endlich ist es so weit. Du bist achtzehn. Alles Gute wünscht dir deine Freundin Elke.
4. Hurra, unser Vater wird heute vierzig Jahre. Er ist der Beste. Wir wünschen dir noch viele schöne Jahre. Alles Liebe zum Geburtstag, deine Söhne Helmut, Friedrich und Klaus-Daniel.
5. Unsere Tochter Hannelore wird heute einundzwanzig. Wir wünschen dir alles Liebe und Gute, deine Eltern.
6. Liebe Eltern, zum Valentinstag liebe Grüße aus Dresden. eure Kinder Wolfgang und Martina.
7. Für meine Kinder Steffi und Sebastian in Weimar alles Liebe, viel Spaß und alles Gute zum Valentinstag, eure Mutter.
8. Liebe Gabi, zum Valentinstag alles Liebe und Gute, dein Tiger.

1. Wann beginnt das Semester?
2. Kennst du das Buch von Professor Seufert?
3. Wo ist die Unibibliothek?
4. Ist das Theater hier gut?
5. Wie sind die anderen Mitbewohner hier im Wohnheim?
6. Ist das Wetter hier immer so schlecht?
7. Kennst du den Professor Kreuzer?
8. Weißt du, wo das Sportzentrum ist?

Kapitel 4

B. DIRK: Hier Dirk Krekel. Ich bin im Moment nicht zu Hause. Hinterlassen Sie bitte eine kurze Nachricht. Warten Sie bitte auf den Pfeifton.

ERIKA: Hallo, Dirk! Hier ist Erika. Hast du Samstagnachmittag schon etwas vor? Thomas und ich machen nämlich eine kleine Fete bei uns zu Hause. Um vier gibt's Kaffee und Kuchen. Hast du Zeit? Ruf uns bitte zurück!

Wörter im Kontext

1. Die Zeit ist 17 Uhr 35.
2. Die Zeit ist 3 Uhr 6.
3. Die Zeit ist 14 Uhr 15.
4. Die Zeit ist 11 Uhr 25.
5. Die Zeit ist 19 Uhr 45.
6. Die Zeit ist 13 Uhr 40.
7. Die Zeit ist 0 Uhr 15.
8. Die Zeit ist 21 Uhr 50.

Thema 3: Kino, Musik und Theater

(See textbook page 121.)

Aktivität 8: Zwei Einladungen

Dialog 1

PETER: Möchtest du heute Abend ins Kino?

KARLA: Leider kann ich nicht. Ich habe nämlich am Montag eine Klausur.

PETER: Eine Klausur?

KARLA: Ja, in Physik. Ich muss noch dafür arbeiten.

PETER: Na, dann wünsche ich dir viel Glück.

KARLA: Danke, ich kann es brauchen.

Dialog 2

GABI: Hallo, Hans. Hast du heute Abend Zeit? Im Olympia läuft ein toller Film, „Good Bye, Lenin!".

HANS: Ich möchte schon mitgehen. Wann fängt er denn an?

GABI: Um 17 Uhr.

HANS: Das ist mir zu früh. Ich habe nämlich noch eine Vorlesung bis fünf.

GABI: So spät am Freitag noch?

HANS: Ja, leider.

Grammatik im Kontext

Ich wache morgens schon früh auf und stehe um fünf Uhr auf. Ich wohne zusammen mit meinem Bruder Mark in einer alten Villa in Berlin. Wir haben ein Zimmer unter dem Dach. Das kostet uns nichts. Wir beide sind nämlich so etwas wie Hausmänner für die Familie Schröder: Wir gehen für sie einkaufen, reparieren Sachen und arbeiten im Garten.

Ich habe zwei Tagesabläufe: einen für das Geld und einen für die Kunst. An drei Tagen arbeite ich im Hotel als Junge für alles. Um sieben fängt die Arbeit an. Im Hotel arbeiten Leute aus Afghanistan, Italien und Amerika. Ich arbeite gern da. So gegen drei Uhr nachmittags komme ich nach Hause zurück. Dann schlafe ich erst mal ein bis zwei Stunden. Da habe ich die Illusion, mein Tag fängt noch einmal neu an. Dann fängt nämlich mein Leben für die Kunst an. Meistens habe ich ein Projekt vor. Ich mache Skulpturen aus Metall und Plastik. Abends rufe ich manchmal ein paar Freunde an. Die kommen dann vorbei, und dann reden wir und trinken Bier bis Mitternacht. Vor ein Uhr nachts schlafe ich nie ein. Ich brauche auch nicht viel Schlaf.

CHRIS: Ich will schlafen.
Du willst schlafen.
Er will schlafen.
Wir wollen schla...

JEFF: Chris, was machst du da?

CHRIS: Ich lerne deutsche Grammatik.

JEFF: Das kann ich hören.

CHRIS: Morgen haben wir einen Test über Modalverben. Ich muss unbedingt ein A bekommen.

JEFF: Musst du das denn so laut machen? Kannst du das nicht leise machen?

CHRIS: Ich kann leider nur laut Deutsch lernen.

JEFF: Ich muss aber auch arbeiten, und ich höre nur immer „Ich will schlafen". Du hypnotisierst mich. Jetzt will ich auch schon schlafen.

CHRIS: Also gut, ich gehe ins Badezimmer. Da kannst du mich nicht hören. Ich will dich nicht stören.

Übung 14   In der Sprechstunde

1. PROFESSOR: Guten Tag, Frau Lerner. Bitte, kommen Sie herein!
2. PROFESSOR: Bitte, nehmen Sie Platz!
3. MARY: Herr Professor, erklären Sie mir bitte, was dieser Satz heißt.
4. PROFESSOR: Verstehen Sie das nicht?
5. MARY: Sprechen Sie etwas langsamer, bitte!
6. PROFESSOR: Gehen Sie regelmäßig jede Woche ins Sprachlabor?
7. PROFESSOR: Warten Sie einen Moment, bitte.
8. STUDENT: Hallo, Herr Professor Schwermut, kommen Sie heute Abend zu unserm Filmabend im Deutschklub?
9. PROFESSOR: Rufen Sie mich bitte später wieder an. Ich habe im Moment keine Zeit.
10. PROFESSOR: Haben Sie ein Wörterbuch zu Hause, Frau Lerner?
11. PROFESSOR: Lesen Sie jeden Tag eine Stunde Deutsch?
12. PROFESSOR: Kommen Sie nächste Woche wieder vorbei.
13. MARY: Haben Sie nächsten Mittwoch Zeit?
14. PROFESSOR: Vergessen Sie Ihre Bücher nicht! Also dann, auf Wiedersehen.
    MARY: Auf Wiedersehen.

Kapitel 5

Alles klar?

B.
1. Heute im vierten Stock. Preiswerte Kameras. Nur 150 Euro.
2. Modische italienische Herrenschuhe im zweiten Stock. Aus Leder von hoher Qualität. Nur 85 Euro.
3. In unserer Elektroabteilung im dritten Stock bieten wir Krups Kaffeemaschinen. Heute Sonderpreis 29 Euro 50.
4. Zu Hause haben Sie bestimmt Platz für einen neuen Fernseher. Heute im Sonderangebot für 595 Euro. Im vierten Stock.

Wörter im Kontext

Aktivität 1   Eine Reise nach Südspanien

BETTINA: Ich weiß nicht, was ich mitnehmen soll.
MARKUS: Ich nehme nur einen Rucksack mit. Da passt sowieso nicht viel rein.
BETTINA: Ich nehme auch nur einen Rucksack mit. Sind Jeans und T-Shirts genug?
MARKUS: Ich nehme nur Shorts und ein paar T-Shirts mit. Jeans sind mir zu warm. Es ist nämlich unglaublich heiß da im Sommer. Ach ja, und Sandalen natürlich.
BETTINA: Ich nehme Tennisschuhe mit, zwei Paar … Ich brauche unbedingt einen neuen Badeanzug. Mein Badeanzug ist bestimmt schon fünf Jahre alt.
MARKUS: Also in Südspanien am Strand … das kann ich dir sagen, da brauchst du gar keinen Badeanzug!
BETTINA: (laughs) Also nein, … das ist nichts für mich … Und was machst du mit deinem Geld?
MARKUS: Ich habe einen besonderen Gürtel für mein Geld. Da ist es ganz sicher.
BETTINA: Ich stecke mein Geld immer in die Schuhe.
MARKUS: In die Schuhe?
BETTINA: Ja, in die Schuhe im Rucksack. Mein zweites Paar Tennisschuhe.

MARKUS: Ach so, ich kann mir auch nicht vorstellen, dass du mit Geld im Schuh durch Südspanien läufst.
BETTINA: Also, mach's gut. Tschüss!
MARKUS: Servus, Bettina.

Thema 2:   Beim Einkaufen im Kaufhaus

(*See textbook page 149.*)

Aktivität 6   Gespräche im Geschäft

Dialog 1
VERKÄUFER: Bitte schön, kann ich Ihnen helfen?
KUNDE: Ich brauche ein Paar Schuhe.
VERKÄUFER: Welche Größe bitte?
KUNDE: Größe 44.
VERKÄUFER: Und welche Farbe?
KUNDE: Schwarz bitte.

Dialog 2
VERKÄUFERIN: Guten Tag. Kann ich Ihnen helfen?
KUNDIN: Ich brauche eine Hose.
VERKÄUFERIN: Welche Größe, bitte?
KUNDIN: Ich glaube Größe 38. Aber ich bin nicht sicher.
VERKÄUFERIN: Und welche Farbe soll es sein?
KUNDIN: Haben Sie etwas in Blauweiß gestreift?

Dialog 3
VERKÄUFERIN: Guten Tag, kann ich Ihnen helfen?
KUNDE: Ja, ich suche ein Geschenk für meine Freundin. Eine Bluse vielleicht.
VERKÄUFERIN: Und welche Größe hat Ihre Freundin?
KUNDE: Hmm, ich weiß nicht, sie ist ziemlich klein. Ich glaube ungefähr Größe 44.
VERKÄUFERIN: Das ist aber ziemlich groß. Sie sagen, sie ist ziemlich klein?
KUNDE: Ja.
VERKÄUFERIN: Ich empfehle Ihnen Größe 38.
KUNDE: Vielen Dank. Also, Größe 38.
VERKÄUFERIN: Und welche Farbe?
KUNDE: Rot.

Dialog 4
VERKÄUFER: Bitte schön. Kann ich Ihnen helfen?
KUNDE: Ich suche einen Wintermantel.
VERKÄUFER: Und welche Größe brauchen Sie?
KUNDE: Größe 44.
VERKÄUFER: Und welche Farbe?
KUNDE: Haben Sie was in Dunkelblau?
VERKÄUFER: Ja, da bin ich ganz sicher.

Aktivität 11   Wo? Was? Wie viel?

Dialog 1
VERKÄUFERIN: Bitte schön. Was darf's sein?
KUNDE: Ich möchte gern ein Dutzend Würstchen.
VERKÄUFERIN: Sonst noch etwas?
KUNDE: Ja, ein Pfund Aufschnitt.
VERKÄUFERIN: Und sonst noch etwas?
KUNDE: Nein, danke. Das ist alles.
VERKÄUFERIN: Das macht zusammen 8 Euro 50.

Dialog 2
VERKÄUFERIN: Guten Morgen, Frau Linder.
KUNDIN: Guten Morgen. Haben Sie frische Brötchen?
VERKÄUFERIN: Ja, natürlich. Ganz frisch von heute Morgen. Wie viele möchten Sie?
KUNDIN: Sechs Brötchen, bitte, und noch ein Schwarzbrot.

VERKÄUFERIN: Sonst noch etwas?

KUNDIN: Nein, danke.

VERKÄUFERIN: Das macht zusammen 3 Euro 20.

Dialog 3

VERKÄUFERIN: Bitte schön?

KUNDIN: Haben Sie frische Tomaten?

VERKÄUFERIN: Ja, Tomaten haben wir, ganz frisch aus Holland.

KUNDIN: Wie viel kosten die denn?

VERKÄUFERIN: 5 Euro das Kilo.

KUNDIN: Das ist aber teuer. Was haben Sie denn an Obst?

VERKÄUFERIN: Erdbeeren sind sehr preiswert. Nur 1 Euro 70 für 500 Gramm.

KUNDIN: Na, dann nehme ich ein Pfund Erdbeeren und ungefähr ein Pfund Tomaten.

VERKÄUFERIN: Das macht zusammen 4 Euro 20.

Grammatik im Kontext

Dialog 1

HANS: Du, Werner, ich brauche unbedingt etwas Geld. Kannst du mir ein paar Euro leihen bis morgen? Meine Mutter hat nämlich Geburtstag, und ich möchte ihr unbedingt ein paar Blumen schicken.

WERNER: Es tut mir Leid, Hans, aber ich habe selber kein Geld. Schreib ihr doch einen Brief.

Dialog 2

STUDENTIN: Können Sie uns bitte sagen, wo das Café Kadenz ist?

PASSANT: Natürlich. Kommen Sie. Ich zeige es Ihnen. Es liegt in der Berliner Straße.

Dialog 3

MARIANNE: Helmut hat morgen Geburtstag. Was soll ich ihm bloß schenken? Er hat ja alles.

UTE: Schenk ihm doch eine CD.

MARIANNE: Ich glaube, ich schreibe ihm nur eine Karte.

Dialog 4

STUDENTIN: Ich stehe jeden Morgen um fünf Uhr auf und mache Yoga.

STUDENT: Und das soll ich dir glauben? Wieso kommst du denn dann immer zu spät in die Vorlesung?

STUDENTIN: Doch, ich mache das schon lange. Ich kann es dir nur empfehlen.

Dialog 5

STUDENT: Achim sagt, er lebt nur von Wasser und Brot.

STUDENTIN: Du musst ihm nicht alles glauben, was er sagt. Er geht doch fast jeden Abend aus.

Maxi wohnt seit einem Monat in Göttingen. Sie studiert da Geschichte. Sie wohnt mit drei anderen Studentinnen zusammen in einer Wohnung. Sie wohnen nicht zu weit von der Universität. Sie können zu Fuß gehen.

Maxi kommt gerade mit ihrer Freundin Inge aus dem Café Kadenz. Jetzt muss sie noch schnell einkaufen. Inge geht gleich mit. Sie braucht auch einiges. Zuerst gehen sie zum Supermarkt. Da kaufen sie aber nur ein paar Bananen. Dann kaufen sie frische Brötchen beim Bäcker direkt um die Ecke. Ach, da ist der neue Laden mit den tollen CDs! Die beiden möchten ja gerne mal schnell hineinschauen, aber es wird

spät, und Maxi muss noch zur Bank. Sie gehen schnell durch die Fußgängerzone zur Bank. Maxi muss etwas Geld von der Bank holen. Es ist inzwischen fünf Uhr, und die Bank ist zu. Gott sei Dank kann sie mit der Bankkarte am Geldautomaten Geld bekommen.

Kapitel 6

B. DORIS: So. Jetzt wo ich das Problem mit dem BAföG gelöst habe, hätte ich gern eine weitere Information.

REFERENTIN: Gern. Wie kann ich dir weiter helfen?

DORIS: Meine Eltern kommen am Wochenende zu Besuch, und ich möchte mit ihnen im Restaurant essen. Ich bin ja neu hier in Berlin und kenne mich nicht so gut aus.

REFERENTIN: Du hast Glück. Wir haben gerade einen Kneipenführer zusammengestellt. Aber Berlin ist eine riesige Stadt. Wo seid ihr dann am Wochenende?

DORIS: Wohl in Mitte oder Prenzlauer Berg.

REFERENTIN: Wenn einer von euch vegetarisch isst, dann kann ich den Kartoffelkeller im Nikolaiviertel empfehlen. Außer Kartoffeln gibt es verschiedene Salate, und man sitzt dort sehr gemütlich.

DORIS: Ich habe von einem Restaurant im Brecht Haus gehört. Warst du schon mal dort? Meine Eltern interessieren sich für Brecht.

REFERENTIN: Nein, aber Freunde von mir waren dort. Es heißt einfach „Kellerrestaurant“ und serviert österreichische Küche. Einige Gerichte sollen nach Rezepten von Helene Weigel, Brechts Frau, sein.

DORIS: Kennst du ein gutes italienisches Restaurant?

REFERENTIN: Ja. Da geht ihr am besten in die Oranienburger Straße. So weit ich weiß, heißt das Restaurant einfach „Ristorante Italiano“. Dort kann man eine sehr gute Pizza bekommen, und es ist nicht so teuer. Mir fällt auch ein neues Restaurant in der Gormannstraße ein. Es heißt „Brazil“ und bietet brasilianische Spezialitäten, vor allem Fleischgerichte – sehr beliebt unter Studenten und jungen Leuten. Es ist immer rappelvoll und für deine Eltern vielleicht ein wenig laut, aber es macht viel Spaß, dort zu essen.

DORIS: Vielen Dank. Berlin hat wirklich viele tolle Lokale. Tschüss.

REFERENTIN: Tschüss.

Wörter im Kontext

NORBERT: Was möchtest du essen?

DAGMAR: Ich nehme Weißwurst mit Sauerkraut.

NORBERT: Nimmst du eine Vorspeise?

DAGMAR: Ich nehme Champignons. Und du?

NORBERT: Ich nehme Suppe. Hmm. Und dann Hähnchen mit Reis. Und was willst du trinken?

DAGMAR: Ich nehme ein Pilsener.

NORBERT: Ich auch. Herr Ober, wir möchten bestellen.

STEFANIE: Hier ist es aber ziemlich voll. Hoffentlich finden wir noch Platz.

JENS: Da drüben ist noch etwas frei. Da sitzen nur zwei Leute am Tisch. Ich gehe mal dahin und frage.

JENS: Entschuldigen Sie bitte! Ist hier noch frei?

HERR AM TISCH: Nein, hier ist besetzt.

JENS: Entschuldigen Sie. Ist hier noch frei?

DAME AM TISCH: Ja, hier ist noch frei. Bitte sehr.

JENS: Danke schön.

Aktivität 10 Wir möchten zahlen, bitte.

Dialog 1

HERR X: Bedienung, ich möchte zahlen.

KELLNERIN: Jawohl. Drei Bier, zwei Knackwürste und Sauerkraut. Und hatten Sie auch Brot?

HERR X: Nein.

KELLNERIN: Das macht zusammen 18 Euro 50.

Dialog 2

FRAU X: Herr Ober, wir möchten zahlen.

OBER: Zwei Tassen Kaffee, ein Stück Käsekuchen und ein Stück Obsttorte. Das macht zusammen 9 Euro 55.

Dialog 3

HERR Y: Bedienung, wir möchten zahlen.

KELLNERIN: Zusammen oder getrennt?

HERR Y: Zusammen, bitte.

KELLNERIN: Dreimal Leberknödelsuppe, zweimal Schweins-kotelett mit Salat und einmal zwei Münchner Weißwürste.

HERR Y: Und fünf Brezeln.

KELLNERIN: Ja, und fünf Bier und eine Portion Emmentaler Käse. Das macht zusammen 39 Euro 40.

Kapitel 7

Alles klar?

B. 1. X: Was machst du so in deiner Freizeit?

ULRIKE: Ich lese sehr sehr viel und ich tanze.

X: Wo tanzt du denn? In der Disko?

ULRIKE: Nein, nein, ich gehe einmal die Woche zum Ballettunterricht.

X: Ach so.

2. X: Und wie verbringst du deine Freizeit?

WOLFGANG: Na, mit Fernsehen.

X: Und sonst nichts?

WOLFGANG: Ab und zu spiele ich Fußball mit ein paar Freunden. Fußball spielen macht mir Spaß.

3. X: Sag mal, Antje, was machst du so in deiner Freizeit?

ANTJE: Freizeit, kenn' ich nicht. Ich studiere und habe eine Nebenbeschäftigung. Da bleibt mir keine Freizeit.

X: Na, hör mal, das gibt's doch wohl nicht.

ANTJE: Na ja, gelegentlich gehe ich mal ins Kino. Ach ja, und ich habe übrigens einen neuen Computer. Da surfe ich schon mal im Internet. Das macht mir Spaß.

Wörter im Kontext

Aktivität 3 In der Freizeit

1. NINA: Ich bin Kunststudentin und verbringe meine Zeit hauptsächlich mit Malen, auch meine Freizeit! Malen

ist für mich Leben. In letzter Zeit habe ich aber ein neues Hobby für die Freizeit: Fotografieren. Ich habe nämlich eine Digitalkamera zum Geburtstag bekommen. Das macht mir auch Spaß. Malen und fotografieren, das mache ich also in meiner Freizeit. Dann höre ich aber auch gern mal Musik, brasilianische Musik, die finde ich besonders toll, die hat wirklich Rhythmus. Ja, und dann gehe ich natürlich auch mal mit Freunden aus, tanzen oder einfach gemütlich ins Café oder in eine Kneipe. Hier ist ja immer was los mit den vielen Studenten in der Stadt.

2. THOMAS: Ich arbeite den ganzen Tag von morgens bis abends fürs Studium. Ich mache jetzt Staatsexamen und habe keine Freizeit. Aber ich träume von der Freizeit! Also, ich träume, ich schwinge mich auf meine neue Harley-Davidson und brause wie ein Easy Rider die Autobahn runter und überhole alle die dicken Mercedes und BMWs. Motorrad fahren, das ist was ich in der Freizeit mache! Im Winter fahre ich dann zum Ski fahren, nach Österreich. Ja, das ist mein Traum von der Freizeit. So, und jetzt muss ich zur Uni.

3. ANNETTE: In meiner Freizeit gehe ich gewöhnlich zum Flohmarkt in unserer Stadt. Ich sammle nämlich alte Spielkarten und so was kann man gut auf dem Flohmarkt finden. Und dann gehe ich auch ins Internet in meiner Freizeit. Da habe ich eine Gruppe gefunden. Die machen Auktionen für Spielkarten im Internet. Also, das ist super. Ich habe Spielkarten aus Indien, aus Deutschland, Amerika und Russland, und England. Natürlich spiele ich auch gern Karten in meiner Freizeit, Bridge und Rommé, mit Freunden. Das macht auch Spaß. Ja, das ist alles. Wer hat schon viel Freizeit?

Aktivität 6 Pläne für einen Ausflug

VERENA: Sag mal, wie wäre es mit einem Ausflug am Wochenende?

ANTJE: Prima Idee! Ich brauche unbedingt Abwechslung. Die Arbeit geht mir im Moment auf die Nerven. Was schlägst du denn vor?

VERENA: Warst du schon mal im Neandertal?

ANTJE: Nein, noch nie. Wie weit ist das von hier?

VERENA: Nicht zu weit. Wir können mit dem Rad dahin. Man kann bequem in zwei Stunden da sein. Der Weg führt fast nur durch den Wald.

ANTJE: Soll ich Stefan auch einladen?

VERENA: Schön. Wenn er Lust hat.

ANTJE: Ich weiß, dass er gern mitkommt. Hoffentlich bleibt das Wetter schön.

Aktivität 8 Wetterberichte im Radio

Der Wetterbericht aus Zürich: Sonnig und warm. Temperaturen zwischen 20 und 25 Grad.

Und aus Wien: Bewölkt. Vor allem in der zweiten Tageshälfte Neigung zu Gewittern. Höchsttemperaturen um 18 Grad.

Und nun unser Wetterbericht für Berlin: Morgens noch Schauer, dann nachmittags bewölkt bis heiter. Tagestemperaturen bis zu 20 Grad.

Der Wetterbericht aus Paris: Schön mit leichtem Wind aus Südwest. Tagestemperatur: 29 Grad.

Und aus London: Morgens Nebel, später stark bewölkt und Regen. Tagestemperaturen nicht über 10 Grad.

Grammatik im Kontext

1. HERR HARTER: Was hat mir als Kind Spaß gemacht? Also, ich habe immer viel gesammelt, zum Beispiel Briefmarken, tote Insekten, Bilder mit Fußballspielern. Und dann habe ich Trompete gespielt. Ich habe dann in der Schule in unserer Band gespielt. Das hat mir immer viel Spaß gemacht.

2. FRAU BEITZ: Ich mochte Tiere immer gern, und als Kind hatte ich einen Hund. Das war der Charly. Ich habe mit meinem Hund gespielt. Ich war auch gern im Zoo und habe die Tiere gefüttert. Ja, das hat mir Spaß gemacht. Und ich habe auch gerne gemalt und gezeichnet.

3. HERR HUPPERT: Als Junge habe ich leidenschaftlich gern Cowboy gespielt. Meine Eltern haben mir immer Bücher von Karl May zum Geburtstag geschenkt. Ich bin immer noch ein großer Karl-May-Fan, und ich fahre manchmal nach Bad Segeberg zu den Karl-May-Spielen. Ich habe alle Bücher von Karl May gesammelt. Ich war auch in einem Fußballverein und habe Fußball gespielt. Das hat wirklich Spaß gemacht.

Kapitel 8

B. HERR LOHMANN: Jeden Tag gehen wir ins Thermalbad. Danach bekommen wir auch eine Massage. In die Sauna gehen wir nie. Mittags essen wir gern vegetarisch. Nachmittags spielen wir manchmal Karten mit einigen anderen Kurgästen. Und natürlich gehen wir viel spazieren.

HERR KRANZLER: Ich bin allein hier. Meine Familie wohnt in Mainz. Ich spiele viel Golf, gehe auch gern wandern und schwimmen. Danach gehe ich immer in die Sauna und ins Thermalbad. Und dann mache ich eine Trinkkur. Da trinke ich jede Stunde ein Glas Wasser.

FRAU DIETMOLD: Ja, ich mache auch eine Trinkkur, und dann gehe ich ins Thermalbad und bekomme Massagen. Tischtennis macht mir viel Spaß. Ich gehe hier abends oft ins Theater. Ich spiele auch Mini-Golf, und dann tanze ich gern.

Wörter im Kontext

(See textbook page 236.)

(See textbook page 239.)

AEROBIC-LEHRERIN: Strecken Sie die Arme nach oben. Langsam den Rücken nach vorne beugen. Die Knie gerade halten. Mit den Fingern bis an die Füße reichen. Langsam wieder hoch kommen.

Drehen Sie den Kopf erst nach rechts, dann nach links, dann langsam rollen. Das ist gut für den Hals. Jetzt die Schultern bis an die Ohren hoch ziehen und langsam wieder fallen lassen. So und jetzt geht's etwas flotter. Fünf Minuten auf der Stelle laufen. Eins, zwei, eins, zwei, eins, zwei!

MANN: Morgen tun mir bestimmt alle Muskeln weh.

Dialog 1

LENE: Ich fühle mich hundsmiserabel.
DORIS: Was fehlt dir denn?
LENE: Ich hab' 'ne Erkältung. Ich muss immer husten, habe Kopfschmerzen, und ich kann mich auf nichts konzentrieren.
DORIS: Du siehst auch wirklich müde aus. Geh doch nach Hause, und leg dich ins Bett. Gute Besserung!
LENE: Danke.

Dialog 2

DORIS: Na, geht's dir wieder besser?
LENE: Ja, ich habe mich ein paar Tage zu Hause ausgeruht. Jetzt bin ich wieder fit.
DORIS: Ich fühle mich heute überhaupt nicht gut. Ich glaube, ich werde auch krank.
LENE: Na, hoffentlich nicht. Was ist denn los?
DORIS: Also, es ist mein Bauch. Ich habe irgendetwas gegessen.
LENE: Geh lieber gleich zum Arzt. Übrigens, trink viel Kamillentee. Der ist gut gegen Bauchschmerzen.

Dialog 3

ARZT: Was fehlt Ihnen denn?
PATIENT: Ach, Herr Doktor. Ich habe überhaupt keine Energie, fühle mich immer schlapp. Und nachts kann ich nicht schlafen. Ich bin immer nervös. Ich kann mich nicht konzentrieren.
ARZT: Hmm. Wie lange haben Sie diese Symptome schon?
PATIENT: Schon seit Monaten.
ARZT: Sie brauchen Urlaub. Sie haben zu viel Stress in Ihrem Leben. Ich empfehle Ihnen eine Kur im Schwarzwald. Ich schreibe Ihnen auch ein Rezept für Schlaftabletten.

Grammatik im Kontext

HERR SCHNEIDER: Guten Tag, Herr Doktor.
ARZT: Guten Tag, Herr Schneider. Bitte, setzen Sie sich. Was fehlt Ihnen denn?
HERR SCHNEIDER: Ich fühle mich so schlapp, ich kann mich überhaupt nicht konzentrieren.
ARZT: Seit wann fühlen Sie sich schon so schlapp?
HERR SCHNEIDER: Schon seit Wochen.
ARZT: Müssen Sie sich bei der Arbeit zu sehr anstrengen?
HERR SCHNEIDER: Ja, leider ist meine Arbeit mit sehr viel Stress verbunden. Ich bin Vertreter für eine Firma und bin ständig unterwegs. Termine mit Kunden. Staus auf der Autobahn. Ich habe einfach keine Zeit, mich mal zu entspannen.
ARZT: Sie müssen sich aber einfach entspannen. Der ständige Stress ist sehr schlecht für Ihre Gesundheit. Ich empfehle Ihnen eine Kur im Schwarzwald. Da können Sie sich vom Stress erholen.
HERR SCHNEIDER: Ja, das sagt meine Frau auch. Ich habe leider keine Zeit, in Urlaub zu fahren.
ARZT: Interessieren Sie sich für Sport? Etwas Aerobic kann Ihnen nicht schaden.
HERR SCHNEIDER: Leider interessiere ich mich nicht für Sport. Aerobic ist mir zu anstrengend.
ARZT: Nun, dann verschreibe ich Ihnen ein paar Vitamintabletten. Nehmen Sie abends und morgens 125 Stück. Und kommen Sie in vier Wochen wieder. – Übrigens, seit wann haben Sie diesen Schluckauf schon?
HERR SCHNEIDER: Schluckauf? Welchen Schluckauf?
ARZT: Herr Schneider, ich muss Ihnen dringend raten, sofort auf Kur zu gehen. Sie brauchen dringend Entspannung. Sie sind mit Ihren Nerven am Ende!

Kapitel 9

Alles klar?

B. Jedes Jahr kommen rund vier Millionen Touristen in die sächsische Hauptstadt Dresden. Heute leben in der Stadt etwa 500 000 Einwohner. Dresden ist für viele Sachen bekannt. Zum Beispiel, die erste deutsche Lokomotive kommt aus Dresden. Und hier hat man Bierdeckel, Kaffeefilter und Zahnpasta entwickelt! Dresden ist aber auch eine Stadt der Musik. Heinrich Schütz hat hier die erste deutsche Oper geschrieben. Und später hat der Komponist Richard Wagner viele Jahre in Dresden verbracht. Zwei seiner Opern, „Tannhäuser" und „Der fliegende Holländer", wurden hier uraufgeführt. Den Dresdener Besucher erwartet ein großes kulturelles Angebot: Musik, Museen und Theater. Dresden gilt auch als die europäische Hauptstadt des Dixieland. Der alte Zoologische Garten in Dresden ist einer der ältesten deutschen Tiergärten – gebaut im Jahr 1861.

Wörter im Kontext

Aktivität 1   Zwei telefonische Zimmerbestellungen

Erstes Telefongespräch
REZEPTION: Hotel Mecklenheide, guten Tag.
HERR DEGENER: Guten Tag. Haben Sie noch ein Zimmer frei?
REZEPTION: Brauchen Sie ein Einzelzimmer oder ein Doppelzimmer?
HERR DEGENER: Ich hätte gern ein Doppelzimmer mit Bad für drei Nächte.
REZEPTION: Wir haben noch ein Doppelzimmer frei, aber leider ohne Bad.
HERR DEGENER: Hmmm. Na gut. Und was kostet das Zimmer?
REZEPTION: 50 Euro, mit Frühstück.
HERR DEGENER: Also gut. Ich nehme es. Übrigens, ich habe einen Hund, einen Pudel. Ich hoffe, Sie haben nichts dagegen.
REZEPTION: Oh, es tut mir schrecklich leid, aber Hunde sind leider nicht erlaubt.
HERR DEGENER: Na, dann muss ich es eben woanders versuchen. Auf Wiederhören.
REZEPTION: Auf Wiederhören.

Zweites Telefongespräch
FRAU BETZ: Jugendgästehaus am Stadtgraben.
GABRIELE: Ich möchte ein Zimmer für August bestellen. Haben Sie noch ein Einzelzimmer?
FRAU BETZ: Wir haben überhaupt keine Einzelzimmer. Unsere Schlafräume haben jeweils zehn Betten.
GABRIELE: Hmm, zehn Betten?
FRAU BETZ: Ja, aber die Räume sind sehr gemütlich. Unser Haus ist fast 800 Jahre alt. Es liegt ganz in der Nähe der Innenstadt.
GABRIELE: Gibt es auch Bad und Dusche und WC im Haus?
FRAU BETZ: Aber natürlich. Jedes Zimmer hat einen Waschraum mit Dusche und Toilette.
GABRIELE: Eine Dusche für zehn Leute? Hm. Und was kostet die Übernachtung?
FRAU BETZ: 15 Euro pro Übernachtung, mit Frühstück.
GABRIELE: Na, das ist ja sehr günstig. Bitte reservieren Sie mir ein Bett für vier Nächte vom ersten August an.
FRAU BETZ: Gut, geht in Ordnung. Und wie ist Ihr Name?
GABRIELE: Holzschuh, Gabriele.

Thema 2:   Im Hotel

(*See textbook page 265.*)

Thema 3:   Nach dem Weg fragen

(*See textbook page 268.*)

Aktivität 5   Drei Touristen

Dialog 1
JULIA: Entschuldigung, wie kommt man hier zum Markt?
KATRIN: Gehen Sie immer geradeaus bis zur Ampel, dann links.

Dialog 2
ULRICH: Bitte, können Sie mir sagen, wo das Hotel Continental ist?
GISELA: Gehen Sie zwei Straßen geradeaus, dann rechts.

Dialog 3
PETER: Entschuldigung, wo ist hier eine Post?
SEPP: Tut mir leid. Ich bin Tourist und kenne die Stadt auch nicht.

Grammatik im Kontext

Übung 13   Kurze Gespräche

Dialog 1
GERD: Sag mal, seit wann hast du denn blaue Haare?
GABI: Seit letzter Woche. Gefallen sie dir?
GERD: Na ja, ich war an deine braunen Haare gewöhnt.
GABI: Ich habe ja auch blaue Augen. Die blauen Haare passen gut zu meinen blauen Augen.
GERD: Ein merkwürdiger Grund. Na ja, meine Oma hat lila Haare.

Dialog 2
PASSANT: Entschuldigung, wo ist das Rathaus?
PASSANTIN: Meinen Sie das alte oder das neue?
PASSANT: Oh, es gibt zwei? Ein altes und ein neues? Ich suche das Rathaus mit dem berühmten Glockenspiel.
PASSANTIN: Also, das ist das alte Rathaus. Gehen Sie geradeaus, dann die zweite Straße links. Das Rathaus liegt auf der rechten Seite.

Kapitel 10

Alles klar?

B. **Dialog 1**
TONI: Wo wart ihr denn im Urlaub?
ELKE: An der Ostsee. In Warnemünde. Es war einfach herrlich! Strand, Wind und Meer!
TONI: Habt ihr dort viel unternommen?
ELKE: Wir wollten unbedingt segeln lernen – und das haben wir auch getan. Karl ist ein begeisterter Segler. Nächstes Jahr will er wieder dahin.

Dialog 2
UTE: Wo hast du denn dieses Jahr Urlaub gemacht?
BERND: In Südamerika, in Bolivien.
UTE: In Bolivien? Wie war es denn?

BERND: Fantastisch. Ich wollte ja immer schon mein
   Spanisch verbessern. Da habe ich mich zu einem
   Sprachurlaub in Bolivien entschlossen.
UTE: Hast du im Hotel gewohnt?
BERND: Nein. Ich hatte Glück. Ich habe eine Privatunterkunft
   bei einer Familie gefunden. Die waren alle unheimlich
   nett. Wir haben natürlich nur Spanisch gesprochen.
   Wir haben auch gemeinsam was unternommen. So habe
   ich viel gesehen und erlebt. Ich kann das nur empfehlen.
   So, ich muss jetzt gehen. Also, hasta mañana.
UTE: Tschüss.

Dialog 3
HANS: Einen Aktivurlaub habt ihr gemacht? Wieso?
JENS: Ganz einfach. Wir wollten mal was anderes machen.
   Da haben wir uns für einen Aktivurlaub entschieden –
   Wandern und Bergsteigen in den Dolomiten. Am
   aufregendsten war das Bergsteigen. Das war ein Erlebnis.
   Es hat mir unheimlich viel Spaß gemacht.

Wörter im Kontext

Thema 2:   Eine Wandertour

(See textbook page 297.)

Dialog 1
NICOLA: Ja, guten Tag. Ich möchte bitte Information über
   italienische Sprachkurse für Reisende.
ANGESTELLTE: Was halten Sie von Sizilien?
NICOLA: Das wäre nicht schlecht. Sizilien soll traumhaft schön
   sein.
ANGESTELLTE: Sehen Sie, hier im Reiseprospekt: „Italienisch für
   Anfänger" – vier Wochen lang in der Nähe von Palermo. Sie
   fliegen von hier aus direkt nach Palermo.
NICOLA: Das klingt fantastisch. Aber ich möchte natürlich nicht
   nur arbeiten, sondern auch etwas von der Gegend sehen.
ANGESTELLTE: Der Unterricht findet am Morgen statt, die
   Nachmittage und Wochenenden stehen Ihnen zur freien
   Verfügung.

Dialog 2
ANGESTELLTER: Guten Tag. Kann ich Ihnen helfen?
MARIANNE: Wir suchen Urlaubstipps für einen Alternativurlaub.
   Wir interessieren uns nämlich für Meditation. Können Sie
   etwas vorschlagen?
ANGESTELLTER: Es gibt ein paar interessante Möglichkeiten. Hier
   ist zum Beispiel ein Angebot auf der griechischen Insel
   Korfu – eine Woche Meditationsurlaub mit Workshops.
ASTRID: Hm, Korfu und Meditation? Na, was meinst du,
   Marianne?
MARIANNE: Ich weiß noch nicht. Ich will es mir überlegen.

Dialog 3
ANGESTELLTE: Grüß Gott, kann ich Ihnen helfen?
SABINE: Wir haben vor, Urlaub in Alaska zu machen. Haben Sie
   Reiseprospekte über Alaska?
ANGESTELLTE: Natürlich. Alaska ist ein sehr beliebtes Ziel. Natur,
   spektakuläre Berge, Gletscher, Eisbären, um nur ein paar
   Sehenswürdigkeiten zu nennen. Wie lange wollen Sie
   insgesamt bleiben?
HERBERT: Zwei bis drei Wochen.

ANGESTELLTE: Hier ist ein Angebot für eine vierzehntägige Reise.
   Sie fliegen zuerst nach Anchorage. Von dort aus kommen Sie
   mit Bus und Schiff weiter.
SABINE: Haben Sie gesagt Eisbären? Davor habe ich aber Angst.
ANGESTELLTE: Keine Sorge! Das war nur im Spaß gemeint. Sie
   sehen sie höchstens aus der Ferne, wenn überhaupt.

Dialog 4
SEBASTIAN: Guten Tag. Ich möchte bitte Information über eine
   Studienreise nach Israel. Haben Sie einen Reiseprospekt?
ANGESTELLTER: Ich kann Ihnen den Studiosus-Prospekt geben.
SEBASTIAN: Ich interessiere mich sehr für die Kulturstätten in
   Israel.
ANGESTELLTER: Wie wäre es mit diesem Angebot: Felsendom,
   Ölberg, Klagemauer, Schwimmen im Toten Meer und
   Aufenthalt im Kibbuz.
SEBASTIAN: Das klingt ja alles sehr interessant.
ANGESTELLTER: Wie viel Zeit haben Sie?
SEBASTIAN: Drei Wochen. Können Sie die Reise noch heute
   buchen?
ANGESTELLTER: Selbstverständlich.
SEBASTIAN: Danke schön.
ANGESTELLTER: Bitte sehr.

Thema 3:   Am Fahrkartenschalter im
           Bahnhof

(See textbook page 300.)

Aktivität 9   Am Fahrkartenschalter

Dialog 1
HERR BOLL: Zwei Fahrkarten nach Hamburg, hin und zurück,
   erster Klasse.
HERR STEIN: Zweimal, hin und zurück. Das macht 200 Euro.
HERR BOLL: Hat der Zug einen Speisewagen?
HERR STEIN: Ja.
HERR BOLL: Ich möchte auch Platzkarten.
HERR STEIN: Raucher oder Nichtraucher?
HERR BOLL: Nichtraucher.

Dialog 2
HERR FRANK: Ich möchte gern fünf Fahrkarten, hin und zurück,
   nach Salzburg.
FRAU BETZ: Alles Erwachsene?
HERR FRANK: Nein, zwei Erwachsene und drei Kinder.
FRAU BETZ: Kinder fahren zum halben Preis.
HERR FRANK: Gibt es ein Restaurant im Zug?
FRAU BETZ: Ja.

Dialog 3
FRAU SACHS: Einmal einfache Fahrt nach Bonn.
FRAU BETZ: Das macht 40 Euro.
FRAU SACHS: Und wann fährt der nächste Zug?
FRAU BETZ: In fünf Minuten fährt ein Zug nach Bonn.
FRAU SACHS: Danke, da muss ich mich aber beeilen.

Grammatik im Kontext

Übung 4   Werners Reisevorbereitungen

SEBASTIAN: Sag mal, Werner. Hast du eigentlich schon gepackt?
WERNER: Ach wo. Ich hatte einfach noch keine Zeit. Ich musste
   bis um sieben Uhr arbeiten.
SEBASTIAN: Wann fährt denn dein Zug?

WERNER: Morgen um vierzehn Uhr fünfzig. Übrigens, kannst du mir einen Koffer leihen? Mein alter ist zu klein.

SEBASTIAN: Hast du schon alles für die Reise?

WERNER: Fast alles. Ich brauche noch Film für meine Kamera.

SEBASTIAN: Welche nimmst du mit?

WERNER: Die kleine. Sie nimmt nicht so viel Platz wie die Videokamera. Ich kann sie praktisch in meine Hosentasche stecken.

SEBASTIAN: Wie lange bleibst du weg?

WERNER: Insgesamt sechs Wochen.

SEBASTIAN: So eine lange Reise?

WERNER: Ja, so lange habe ich noch nie Urlaub gemacht.

Übung 13   Münchhausens Reise

Münchhausens Reise nach Russland begann im Winter. Er reiste mit Pferd und Wagen, weil das am bequemsten war. Leider trug er nur leichte Kleidung, und er fror sehr. Da sah Münchhausen eine alte Frau im Schnee. Er gab ihr etwas zu essen und ritt weiter. Er konnte leider kein Gasthaus finden. Er war müde und stieg vom Pferd ab. Dann band er das Pferd an einen Baumast im Schnee und legte sich hin. Er schlief tief und lange. Als Münchhausen am Morgen aufwachte, fand er sich mitten auf dem Marktplatz eines Dorfes. Wo aber war sein Pferd? Er konnte es über sich hören. Er schaute in die Höhe und sah sein Pferd vom Dach des Rathauses hängen. Was war passiert? Das Dorf war in der Nacht zugeschneit gewesen. In der Sonne war der Schnee geschmolzen. Der Baumast, an den Münchhausen sein Pferd gebunden hatte, war in Wirklichkeit die Spitze des Rathauses gewesen. Nun nahm er seine Pistole und schoss nach dem Halfter des Pferdes. Das Pferd landete ohne Schaden direkt neben Münchhausen. Dann reiste er weiter.

Kapitel 11

Alles klar?

B. INTERVIEWER: Frau Sommer, wie sind Sie darauf gekommen, Tierärztin zu werden?

GABRIELE: Schon als Kind habe ich mich sehr für Tiere interessiert. Ich bin zu Hause mit Hunden, Katzen, drei Kanarienvögeln und sogar einem Pferd aufgewachsen. Meine Familie wohnte damals nämlich am Rande der Lüneburger Heide und da hatten wir Kinder immer ein Reitpferd. In der Schule war ich in naturwissenschaftlichen Fächern immer am besten. Ich hatte Glück, denn ich habe nach dem Abitur sofort einen Studienplatz in Erlangen bekommen. In Tiermedizin bekommt man schon eher einen Studienplatz. Ich bin jetzt im letzten Studienjahr. Mein Traum ist eine eigene Praxis in einer Kleinstadt, aber das wird noch lange dauern.

Wörter im Kontext

Aktivität 1   Drei junge Leute

INTERVIEWERIN: Tina, was möchtest du beruflich tun?

TINA: Eigentlich möchte ich gerne im Freien arbeiten, als so etwas wie Landschaftsarchitektin oder als Gärtnerin. Ich habe keine Lust, Büroarbeit zu machen. Großes Ansehen zu haben oder viel Geld zu verdienen – das ist mir nicht wichtig.

INTERVIEWERIN: Und du, Markus? Was würde dich am meisten beruflich interessieren?

MARKUS: Am liebsten würde ich in meinem Beruf viel reisen und vielleicht sogar im Ausland arbeiten. Meine Tätigkeit soll abwechslungsreich sein. Mit Menschen zu tun haben – das gefällt mir.

INTERVIEWERIN: Und du, Andrea? Wofür interessierst du dich beruflich?

ANDREA: Ich arbeite gerne mit meinen Händen und interessiere mich für technische Sachen – wie zum Beispiel Maschinen. Computer interessieren mich auch – ich würde gern mit Computern arbeiten.

Aktivität 8   Ein Gespräch unter Freunden

GÜNTHER: Wie steht's denn mit deiner Suche nach einem Ausbildungsplatz? Hast du schon was gefunden?

PETRA: Ich habe noch nichts Definitives. Gestern war ich mal wieder beim Arbeitsamt.

GÜNTHER: Na, da kannst du lange warten, bevor die was für dich finden.

PETRA: Man kann nie wissen. Vor ein paar Tagen stand eine Anzeige in der Zeitung für Ausbildungsstellen für Laboranten.

GÜNTHER: Bei welcher Firma?

PETRA: Alpha Pharma. Die suchen Bewerber.

GÜNTHER: Muss man Abitur haben?

PETRA: Für die Ausbildung als Biologielaborantin braucht man Abitur. Aber für die Ausbildung zur Chemielaborantin braucht man nur Realschulabschluss.

GÜNTHER: Ist ja super. Hast du dich schon beworben?

PETRA: Ja, ich habe gleich meine Unterlagen eingeschickt, das Übliche: Lebenslauf, Foto und Zeugnisse.

GÜNTHER: Hast du schon mal angerufen?

PETRA: Nein, noch nicht. Wenn die Firma einen will, muss man noch einen Test machen.

GÜNTHER: Weißt du irgendetwas über die Firma?

PETRA: Nur, was in der Anzeige stand. Ich muss erst mal abwarten und sehen, ob sie mich zum Test einladen.

Grammatik im Kontext

Übung 7   Ein unkonventioneller Klub

SVEN: Was liest du denn da?

ANJA: Ein Buch.

SVEN: Na, das kann ich auch sehen! Was für ein Buch ist das denn?

ANJA: Es heißt *Das literarische Oktett*.

SVEN: Was für ein merkwürdiger Titel ist das denn?

ANJA: Das ist ein Buch, das acht Studenten geschrieben haben. Sie haben einen Klub der Dichter gegründet. Der Klub nennt sich auch „das literarische Oktett".

SVEN: Was für Gedichte schreiben sie denn? Komplizierte Gedichte, die kein Mensch verstehen kann?

ANJA: Nein, sie schreiben hauptsächlich kleine, freche Geschichten. Aber es gibt auch ein paar Gedichte im Buch.

SVEN: Über was für Themen schreiben die denn?

ANJA: Na, für was für Themen interessieren sich Studenten schon? Sex, Liebe, Studentenalltag, Essen, Trinken, und so weiter. Es ist alles recht provozierend, aber auch originell und unkonventionell.

SVEN: Ich möchte es auch mal lesen.

ANJA: Gut, wenn ich fertig bin, gebe ich es dir.

B. INTERVIEWER: Jens, was bedeutet dir Geld?

JENS: Geld bedeutet für mich zwei Dinge: etwas für andere damit tun, aber auch etwas für mich selbst tun. Ich habe nicht viel, denn ich bin Student, aber wenn ich genug Geld hätte, würde ich einen Teil davon für medizinische Forschung spenden. Ich bin aber auch ein bisschen Egoist und würde mir vielleicht einen neuen Wagen oder eine neue Wohnung kaufen.

INTERVIEWER: Welche Bedeutung hat Geld für dich, Lucia?

LUCIA: Ja, ich meine auch, mit Geld muss man anderen Menschen helfen, besonders den Armen. Wenn ich Geld nur für mich ausgeben würde, würde ich wahrscheinlich weiter studieren – vielleicht im Ausland. Ich musste mein Studium unterbrechen, weil ich im Moment kein Geld habe. Später aber möchte ich vielleicht mein eigenes Geschäft aufmachen.

INTERVIEWER: Und für dich, Elke?

ELKE: Wenn ich viel Geld hätte, würde ich es bestimmt investieren. Ich würde einen langen Urlaub machen, aber dann würde ich wieder arbeiten. Wichtig für mich sind die Welthungerorganisationen – denen würde ich soviel Geld wie möglich geben.

Wörter im Kontext

Aktivität 2 Spielen wir Lotto!

ANDREA: Sag mal, könntest du mir einen Gefallen tun?

STEFAN: Was denn?

ANDREA: Würdest du mir bis Ende der Woche 50 Euro leihen? Ich bin total pleite.

STEFAN: Fünfzig Euro? Das ist viel Geld.

ANDREA: Ich musste 100 Euro für Bücher ausgeben. Und jetzt habe ich keinen Cent mehr übrig. Ich warte auf Geld von meinen Eltern.

STEFAN: Hm, ich würde es dir gern leihen. Aber 50 Euro habe ich selber nicht mehr. Ich kann dir höchstens 20 Euro leihen.

ANDREA: Ich zahle es dir bis Ende des Monats bestimmt zurück.

STEFAN: Eben hast du gesagt, bis Ende der Woche.

ANDREA: Ja, ja. Das Geld von meinen Eltern kann jeden Tag kommen.

STEFAN: Na gut. Hier ist ein Zwanziger.

ANDREA: Vielen Dank.

Aktivität 4 Einnahmen und Ausgaben

Dialog 1

INTERVIEWER: Woher bekommst du monatlich Geld, Stefanie?

STEFANIE: Hauptsächlich von meinen Eltern, aber während der Semesterferien arbeite ich und verdiene mir etwas Geld zum Studium.

INTERVIEWER: Als was arbeitest du denn?

STEFANIE: Gewöhnlich als Kellnerin. Während des Semesters habe ich aber keine Zeit zum Jobben.

INTERVIEWER: Und wo wohnst du?

STEFANIE: Ich habe Glück. Ich habe nämlich ein Zimmer im Studentenwohnheim. Da kostet die Miete nur 100 Euro im Monat.

Dialog 2

INTERVIEWER: Woher bekommst du monatlich Geld, Gert?

GERT: Ich bekomme BAföG. Und in den Semesterferien arbeite ich dann. Letztes Jahr habe ich bei der Post als Briefträger gearbeitet.

INTERVIEWER: Und wo wohnst du?

GERT: Ich wohne privat bei Bekannten von meinen Eltern. Ich habe da ein Zimmer.

INTERVIEWER: Und was musst du dafür bezahlen?

GERT: Es ist sehr günstig. Nur 150 Euro pro Monat. Das Haus liegt allerdings etwas außerhalb. Ich muss jeden Tag mit der U-Bahn zur Uni fahren.

Dialog 3

INTERVIEWER: Und wie finanzierst du dein Studium, Susanne?

SUSANNE: Meine Eltern unterstützen mich. Aber ich arbeite auch während des Semesters nebenbei.

INTERVIEWER: Was machst du denn?

SUSANNE: Ich gebe Englischunterricht. Ich habe drei Schüler.

INTERVIEWER: Und wo wohnst du?

SUSANNE: Ich wohne mit drei anderen Studentinnen in einer Wohngemeinschaft. Wir teilen uns die Miete für eine Vierzimmerwohnung. Jeder bezahlt 150 Euro im Monat.

Dialog 4

INTERVIEWER: Und nun zu Martin. Woher bekommst du Geld fürs Studium?

MARTIN: Ich bekomme Geld von meinen Eltern, aber es ist nicht genug. Ich muss also nebenbei arbeiten, auch während des Semesters und in den Semesterferien.

INTERVIEWER: Und wo wohnst du?

MARTIN: Seit letztem Jahr wohne ich in der Studentenstadt. Da habe ich eine kleine Wohnung. Die kostet nur 200 Euro.

Aktivität 5 Die ideale Wohnung

Dialog 1

INTERVIEWER: Frau Heine, Sie suchen eine Wohnung. Wie stellen Sie sich Ihre ideale Wohnung vor?

FRAU HEINE: Die Wohnung muss in der Innenstadt liegen. Ich arbeite nämlich dort. Ich möchte gern einen Neubau mit Zentralheizung. Ich bin gern an der frischen Luft. Deswegen muss meine Wohnung einen Balkon haben. Ich habe keinen Wagen. Eine Garage brauche ich deshalb nicht.

Dialog 2

INTERVIEWER: Ich spreche jetzt mit Herrn und Frau Zumwald aus Hannover. Herr und Frau Zumwald, was für eine Wohnung wäre für Sie und Ihre Kinder ideal?

HERR ZUMWALD: Wir suchen ein komfortables Haus außerhalb der Stadt. Wir brauchen einen großen Garten für unsere zwei Kinder und unseren Hund. Wir möchten gern ein älteres Haus, weil Altbauten oft gemütlicher sind. Allerdings muss das Haus Zentralheizung haben. Unwichtig ist uns, ob das Haus Teppichboden hat.

Dialog 3

INTERVIEWER: Meine Herren, Sie studieren hier an der Uni?

THOMAS: Ja. Meine zwei Freunde hier und ich suchen eine komfortable Altbauwohnung in der Innenstadt. Die Mietkosten dürfen natürlich nicht zu hoch sein. Wir haben alle Fahrräder. Deswegen ist eine Garage nicht so wichtig. Eine Waschmaschine im Haus ist wichtig, aber ein Teppichboden in der Wohnung interessiert uns überhaupt nicht. Aber ohne Zentralheizung möchten wir nicht sein. Die ist sehr wichtig.